CONTEMPORARY

THE IRWIN SERIES IN MARKETING

Consulting Editor
Gilbert A. Churchill, Jr.
University of Wisconsin, Madison

CONTEMPORARY

Advertising

Third Edition

Courtland L. Bovée
William F. Arens

1989

IRWIN

Homewood, Illinois 60430

Sponsoring editor: Elizabeth J. Schilling
Developmental editors: Kathryn D. Wickham and Ann M. Granacki
Project editor: Jean Roberts
Production manager: Irene H. Sotiroff
Text and cover design: Image House, Inc. Stuart D. Paterson
Part opening photos: Dean Photographic, Inc. S. C. Dean
Calligraphy: Mary Malone
Cover airbrush art: Edward W. Lawler, Jr.
Compositor: York Graphic Services
Typeface: 10/12 ITC Garamond Light
Printer: Von Hoffman Press

Library of Congress Cataloging-in-Publication Data

Bovée, Courtland L.
    Contemporary advertising/Courtland L. Bovée, William F. Arens.
—3rd ed.
p. cm.
    Includes index.
    ISBN 0-256-06519-5
    1. Advertising.   I. Arens, William F.   II. Title.
HF5821.B62 1989
659.1—dc19   88–10302

Printed in the United States of America
 2 3 4 5 6 7 8 9 0 VH 5 4 3 2 1 0 9

To Doris Hill
With deep appreciation
—C.L.B.

To Olivia
Con todo mi cariño
—W.F.A.

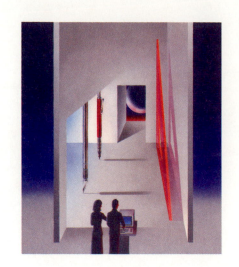

PREFACE

British novelist Norman Douglas may have captured the essence of advertising's worldwide significance when he remarked, "You can tell the ideals of a nation by its advertisements." Indeed, while the advertising business was viewed as a particularly American institution in the first half of this century, that is certainly no longer the case. Today, everyone living and working in the modern world is under the influence of advertising. Thus, the study of advertising has taken on new importance, not only for students of business or journalism—who may one day be practitioners—but also for students of sociology, psychology, political science, economics, history, language, art, or the sciences, all of whom will continue to be consumers of advertising.

There are six major reasons why students profit from studying advertising. It can help them to:

Understand the impact of advertising on the American economy and on the economies of foreign nations.

Comprehend advertising's role in fashioning society and, conversely, society's impact on advertising.

See how advertising fits within the broader disciplines of business and marketing.

Learn how advertising relates to journalism and the field of communications.

Appreciate the artistic creativity and technical expertise required in advertising.

Discover what advertising people do and how they do it, and the career opportunities the field offers.

Our mission in the previous editions of *Contemporary Advertising* was to present advertising as it is actually practiced. Our purpose remains the same. We believe advertising should be taught as it really is—as a business, as a marketing tool, as a creative process, and as a hybrid discipline that employs elements of the various arts and sciences—in a manner and style relevant to today's student.

AIDS FOR THE STUDENT

This text is intended to put flesh on the bones of academic theory. To capture and hold student interest, the opening story of each chapter describes an actual situation that illustrates a basic concept in the study of advertising. This opening example is then used throughout the chapter to demonstrate how textbook concepts are applied in real-life situations.

Because active participation enhances learning, "Advertising Laboratories" are incorporated into every chapter. These unique sidebars to the world of advertising introduce students to a controversial or interesting topic and then involve them through questions that stimulate critical thinking. Another feature found to be valuable by instructors and students alike is the many checklists, which aid in organizing thinking and facilitate decision making. A third boxed feature found in all the chapters is "People in Advertising"—profiles of individuals who have achieved success in the field of advertising and who offer useful suggestions based on their experience.

Each of the 19 chapters is heavily illustrated with current, award-winning advertisements and campaigns. All the major media are represented—print, electronic, outdoor—in a balanced manner. Furthermore, we have included local as well as national ads, and business-to-business as well as consumer ads. In addition to the individual print ads and actual frames from TV commercials, most in full color, the book contains several portfolios of outstanding creative work. In-depth captions tell the stories behind many of the ads and explain how the ads demonstrate the concepts discussed in the text.

The text is also heavily illustrated with diagrams, charts, graphs, and tables that encapsulate useful information about the advertising industry, media, and production.

Each chapter concludes with a summary and questions for review and discussion. Both pedagogical aids are designed to help students review chapter content and assimilate what they have learned. Throughout the text, key ideas and terms are highlighted with italic type and are defined when introduced. Definitions of all these terms are collected in the extensive glossary at the end of the book.

CHANGES FOR THIS EDITION

Our goal is to personally involve students with practical experiences and simultaneously give them a solid understanding of advertising's role in marketing management. In pursuit of this objective, we have made a number of significant modifications and improvements in this edition of *Contemporary Advertising*.

The most noticeable difference between this edition and the second edition is that there is now one less chapter. We have dropped the topic of political advertising, and we have combined coverage of noncommercial advertising with corporate advertising and public relations.

Throughout the book, we have updated statistics and strengthened documentation and footnoting. More real-world examples have been added throughout the text. Many of the chapter openers, Ad Labs, Checklists, and People in Advertising profiles have been updated, expanded, or replaced with more recent examples. Among the profiles new to this edition, for example, are those of Hal Riney, Ruth Ziff, Thomas J. Burrell, Herb Schmertz, and Jerry Della Femina.

Other highlights of this revision include:

Chapter 1: "The Evolution of Advertising." This chapter remains an overview of the advertising field, its history, and its social and economic importance. The sections dealing with the functions of advertising have been revised to clarify not only the uses of advertising but also its effects. The definition of demarketing has been expanded to include its use today by some companies as a sophisticated marketing tactic. The segment on the history of advertising has been compiled to show how advertising evolves to reflect the world in which we live. Finally, the discussion of the economic impact of advertising has been expanded with greater emphasis on its effect on competition and on the value of products. This last section has been reorganized and edited for clarity, enabling us to more effectively introduce the concept of the perceptual value of products.

Chapter 2: "The Social and Legal Aspects of Advertising." Arguments defending advertising have been strengthened, and discussions of regulation by the states and by the media have been expanded. The section on the FDA has been completely revised and updated. A new section has been added on the role of the courts, covering such topics as advertising's protection by the First Amendment, the right to privacy, and comparative advertising. Ad Labs on two important topics have been added: advertising to children, and the controversy over issue advertising.

Chapter 3: "The Advertising Business." The chapter has been shortened to present just the advertisers and the ad agencies. The discussion of media and suppliers has been moved to the unit on media, and material has been added on the change in Procter & Gamble's structure, the advertiser-agency relationship, and the impact of the megamerger trend.

Chapter 4: "Advertising and the Marketing Mix." The topic of market types and the section on locating and measuring the market have been expanded, and material has been added on the issue of market demand.

Chapter 5: "Consumer Behavior and Market Segmentation." Material on perception, consumer habits, social class, culture, and segmenting business markets has been expanded and clarified. The example of Leon Levine's Family Dollar Stores has been used to introduce the concept of market segmentation. Throughout, an up-to-date discussion of VALS has been incorporated into the text rather than being relegated to a box.

Chapter 6: "Marketing and Advertising Research." The chapter has been updated with new material on J. C. Penney, an expanded discussion of the observation research method, and a more concise exposition of the various testing methods.

Chapter 7: "Marketing and Advertising Planning." A new opening example of Paul Fireman and Reebok is woven throughout the chapter. The treatment of advertising strategy and the creative mix has been reorganized and expanded, while the section on methods for allocating advertising dollars has been made more concise.

Chapter 8: "Creative Copywriting." A new section on creativity and concept development precedes discussion of copy objectives. The discussion on naming products has been revised. A new Ad Lab focuses on the eye versus the ear.

Chapter 9: "Creative Art Direction." We have clarified the role of graphics in communicating the advertising concept and have introduced new terminology and illustrations to aid in this clarification.

Chapter 10: "Creative Production: Print Media." Among concepts added are electronic retouching, computer pagination systems, and desktop publishing. A new Creative Department demonstrates the electronic methods used on Lipton Soup Classics.

Chapter 11: "Creative Production: Electronic Media." A new section examines how the concept for a commercial is developed and basic mechanics of script development. The California Raisin campaign is used to discuss stop-motion techniques, and the latest Coors Light campaign is used to demonstrate special effects.

Chapter 12: "Media Planning and Selection." The introduction has been expanded with a discussion of the complexity of media planning today. Sample media objectives have been provided, and a new section on the role of computers in media planning has been added.

Chapter 13: "Print Media." Some of the controversy in the field has been brought out through discussions of the newspaper national/local rate differential, negotiation for ad space, and criticisms of the Audit Bureau of Circulation. The latest SAUs are provided.

Chapter 14: "Electronic Media." The chapter has been extensively revised, with a new section added on cable TV, updates on trends in broadcast TV and radio, and such current developments as zipping and zapping, 15-second spots, people meters, and the rise of syndication. A new chapter opener focuses on the Bartles & Jaymes TV campaign, while the section on radio is now introduced with an examination of Spam's effective and successful use of radio.

Chapter 15: "Direct Mail and Outdoor Media." Material has been added or expanded on telemarketing, mailing list databases, spectaculars, and variations in transit/outdoor (such as mobile billboards).

Chapter 16: "Sales Promotion and Supplementary Media." A promotional campaign for Cap'n Crunch is used to draw readers into the topic. Many subjects have been expanded, including trade deals, FSIs, P-O-P, rebates/refunds, specialty advertising, and directories/yellow pages. The increased emphasis on pull strategies is examined.

Chapter 17: "Local Advertising." Many new examples have been added, including Bullock's in Los Angeles and Office Furniture Warehouse in Chicago. A discussion of media mix has been added, as has the concept of total market coverage (TMC). Among expanded topics are co-op advertising and directory advertising.

Chapter 18: "Corporate Advertising, Public Relations, and Noncommercial Advertising." This chapter was created by combining material from two previous chapters ("Corporate Advertising and Public Relations" and "Noncommercial and Political Advertising"), with the topic of political advertising being dropped. New trends in corporate advertising are examined. The section on public relations activities has been condensed, although the portion on news releases has been revised and expanded. The billion-dollar media campaign of the Partnership for a Drug-Free America is introduced as an example of noncommercial advertising.

Chapter 19: "International Advertising." China is presented as an example of the problems of international advertising. Discussion of the global debate has been expanded, and numerous examples have been added.

Appendix. New to this edition are three appendixes. Appendix A provides a sample outline for a marketing plan, while Appendix B presents a sample advertising plan outline. Appendix C gives pointers on how to look for a job in advertising, outlines the types of careers that are available, and lists resources for information on the advertising industry and career planning.

Glossary. The glossary has been extensively revised and expanded.

In addition to text changes, the book itself has been totally redesigned, and all the diagrams, graphs, charts, and tables are new or revised. Almost all the ads are new in this edition, chosen to reflect the actual state of advertising today. And the ads and their captions have been tied in more strongly to the text they accompany.

SUPPLEMENTARY MATERIALS

While the text itself is a complete introduction to the field of advertising, it is accompanied by a number of valuable supplemental materials designed to assist the instructor.

Instructor's Manual

The manual offers a wealth of suggestions for classroom lectures and discussions. It includes answers to all discussion questions, course and subject outlines, and a comprehensive testing program to facilitate the administration of examinations.

Testing Systems

An extensive bank of objective test questions carefully designed to provide a fair, structured program of evaluation is available in several formats:

Irwin Computerized Test Generator System—a convenient and flexible question retrieval device for mainframe systems, providing an extensive bank of questions to use as is or with additional questions of your own.

COMPUTEST—a microcomputer testing system that provides convenient and flexible retrieval from an extensive bank of questions to use as is or with additional questions of your own.

COMPUGRADE—a microcomputer gradebook that stores and prints all grades by name or ID number. Capable of weighting and averaging grades.

Teletest—a toll-free phone-in service to request customized exams prepared for classroom use.

TextPLUS™ Case Studies

To illustrate how the principles discussed in the text have actually been applied in business, the book is supplemented by special TextPLUS Case Study Programs produced by Meridian Educational Systems, Inc., exclusively for *Contemporary Advertising*.

Each TextPLUS Program is associated with one of the chapters in the text and is designed to help the instructor teach real-world decision making. The integrated system of TextPLUS materials includes: an in-depth, illustrated, eight-page Case Study booklet that may be copied and used for supplemental reading; a TextPLUS Instructor's Guide with lecture outline, suggested projects and workshops, sample tests, and answers to all discussion questions; and a 12- to 15-minute video interview with the key people at the company and/or agency responsible for the work being studied.

Offered at no charge to adopters of *Contemporary Advertising,* three TextPLUS Programs are currently available: Sunkist Growers, Inc., for Chapter 7; Coors Light, Chapter 11; and Great American First Savings Bank, Chapter 17.

USES FOR THIS TEXT

Contemporary Advertising was originally intended for the undergraduate student in business or journalism schools. Because of its approach, depth of coverage, and marketing management emphasis, it has also been found appropriate for university extension courses and courses on advertising management. The wealth of award-winning advertisements also makes it a resource guide to the best work in the field for students in art and graphic design courses as well as for professionals in the field.

Many of the stories, materials, and techniques included in this text come from our own personal experiences as a college professor and as a full-time marketing and advertising executive. Others come from the experiences of professional friends and colleagues. We hope that this book will be a valuable resource guide, not only in the study of advertising but later on in practice. In all cases, we hope that through reading this text students will experience the feel and the humanness of the advertising world, whether they intend to become professionals in the business, to work with practitioners, or simply to become more sophisticated consumers.

ACKNOWLEDGMENTS

We are deeply indebted to many individuals in advertising and related fields for their personal encouragement and professional assistance. These include, but are certainly not limited to: Klaus Schmidt and Alistair Gillett at Young & Rubicam; Kathy Taylor at Saatchi & Saatchi DFS Compton; Susan Irwin at McCann Erickson; Sid Stein at J. C. Penney; Charles Meding, Ted Regan, Brad Lynch, and Agi Clark at N. W. Ayer; Marsie Wallach at Sedelmaier Film Productions; Larry Jones, Steve Moses, Nicoletta Poloynis, Larry Corby, Larry McIntosh, and Bob Simon at Foote, Cone & Belding; Russ Hanlin and Ray Cole at Sunkist Growers, Inc.; Mike Hudson at Weyerhaeuser Credit Union; Holly Smith and John Gillis at Reebok; and Al Ries at Trout & Ries.

Thanks, also, to Gerry Wilson and Nancy Coleman at the Union-Tribune Publishing Company; Sid Bernstein, Rance Crain, and the entire staff at *Advertising Age;* John O'Toole at the American Association of Advertising Agencies; Gordon Luce, Jan Strode, and Bill Haynor at Great American First Savings Bank; Phil Franklin and Bob Cerasoli of Franklin and Associates; Swede Johnson, Gary Naifeh, June Smith, Mark Reiss, Mike Wood, and Colleen Plummer at Adolph Coors Company; Jay Chiat and Steve Doctrow at Chiat/Day; Earl Cavanah at Scali, McCabe, Sloves; and Gerry Rubin at Rubin Postaer.

Special thanks to Jackie Estrada, whose sound advice and remarkable talents were invaluable. Recognition and thanks also to Roy Simon; John V. Thill; Rebecca Smith; Jane Pogeler; Christopher Klein; Marie Painter; Gene Rupe; John S. Jackson; Robert P. Irwin; Courtney and Shirlee Bovée; Kevin, Lynelle, and Ryan Coates; Gary Bovée; Marilyn Bovée; Ivan L. Jones; Eve Lill; Michele Nelson; and Gerald Ashley.

In addition, we are appreciative of the support, encouragement, and assistance of Roger Tilton, Tom Michael, Littleton Waller, John Davies, John Kaesman, Linda German, Bev Oster, Mike Sims, Mark McCormack, Jack Whidden, Doris Lee McCoy, and Don and Deborah McQuiston. Special gratitude to Tony Alessandra, Gary Burke, Al Goodyear, E. L. Deckinger, Elizabeth Marzoni, Mike Green, Jack Savidge, Rob Settle, Pam Alreck, Atsuo Mihara, Doug Shearer, Homer Torrey, Don and Ann Ritchey, John and Ruth Arens, and—for their unbelievable tolerance—Olivia, William, and Christian Arens. For very special assistance when needed most, a big thank you to Colleen Madigan and Stanley L. Urlaub.

We also feel that it's important to recognize and thank the American Academy of Advertising, an organization whose publications and meetings provide a valuable forum for the exchange of ideas and for professional growth.

We are deeply grateful to the reviewers whose ideas and critical insights were invaluable in the preparation of this edition. They include: Julianne Hastings, NW Ayer Inc.; Don Sedik, William Rainey Harper Community College; Susan Irwin, Dancer Fitzgerald Sample; William Lesch, Illinois State University; Paul Wyatt Jackson, Ferris State College; Glen Gelderloos, Grand Rapids Junior College; Thomas Hitzelberger, Southern Oregon University; Wayne Lockwood, Broome Community College; Helena Czepiec, California State University at Hayward; Shay Sayre, San Jose State University; John P. Thurin, Markmakers; John C. Sutherland, University of Florida, Gainesville; Keith Adler, Michigan State University; and David Stringer, De Anza College.

To all of you, thank you.

Courtland L. Bovée
William F. Arens

CONTENTS

PART I

ADVERTISING PERSPECTIVES 2

1

THE EVOLUTION OF ADVERTISING 4

Advertising Defined 4
Functions and Effects of Advertising 7
    Advertising's Role in Marketing 8   Advertising as
    Communication 9   The Educational Effect of Advertising 10
    Advertising's Effect on Commerce and the Economy 10
    Advertising's Function in Society 11

Classifications of Advertising 12
    Classification by Target Audience 12   Classification by Geographic
    Area Covered 14   Classification by Medium 16   Classification by
    Function or Purpose 17

Evolution of Modern Advertising 19
    Impact of Printing and Photography 20   Early U.S. Advertising 21
    The First Advertising Agencies 22   Advertising Enters the 20th
    Century 22   Rise of Broadcast Advertising 23   Postwar
    Advertising 24   Advertising Today 27

The Economic Impact of Advertising 27
    The Billiard-Ball Principle 27   Microeconomic Impact of
    Advertising 29   Macroeconomic View of Advertising 34
    Economic Impact of Advertising in Perspective 41

Ad Lab 1-A: It Had to Be Good to Get Where It Is! 6
People in Advertising: John O'Toole 20
Coca-Cola Illustrates the History of Modern Advertising 30

2

THE SOCIAL AND LEGAL ASPECTS OF ADVERTISING 44

Social Criticisms of Advertising 45
    Advertising Debases Our Language 46   Advertising Makes Us Too
    Materialistic 47   Advertising Manipulates Us into Buying Things We
    Don't Need 47   Advertising Is Excessive 49   Advertising Is
    Offensive or in Bad Taste 49   Advertising Perpetuates
    Stereotypes 51   Advertising Is Deceptive 53   Defense of
    Advertising 54

Government Regulation of Advertising 55
    Regulation by the Federal Government 55   Regulation by State
    Government 66   Regulation by Local Government 67

Nongovernmental Regulation 67
    Self-Regulation by Advertisers 67   *The Role of the Better Business
Bureau* 68   *Regulation by the Media* 69   *Self-Regulation by the
Advertising Profession* 72   *National Advertising Review Council* 73
Regulation by Consumer Groups 75

Ad Lab-2-A: You, the Jury: Judge the Guilt or Innocence of These Ads 50
Ad Lab 2-B: Unfair and Deceptive Practices in Advertising 53
People in Advertising: Robert J. Posch, Jr. 54
Ad Lab 2-C: Advertising to Children: What You Can and Cannot Do 68
Ad Lab 2-D: The Issue of Issue Ads 71

3

THE ADVERTISING BUSINESS 78

The Companies That Advertise 80
What Company Advertising Departments Do 81
    Tasks Common to All Advertisers 81   *How Large Advertisers
Work* 82   *How Small Advertisers Work* 87

The In-House Agency 89
The Advertising Agencies 90
    The Role of the Advertising Agency 90   *Types of Agencies* 92
What Do Agency People Do? 97   *How Are Agencies
Organized?* 102   *How Do Agencies Make Money?* 103   *How Do
Agencies Get Clients?* 107

The Client-Agency Relationship 109
    Stages in the Client-Agency Relationship 109   *Factors Affecting the
Client-Agency Relationship* 111

Ad Lab 3-A: How Big Is the Agency Business? 91
Ad Lab 3-B: Megamergers Make Agency Supergroups 93
People in Advertising: Larry R. Jones 94
Checklist for Agency Review 110
Checklist for Ways to Be a Better Client 112

PART II

MARKETING AND ADVERTISING PLANS AND STRATEGIES 114

4

ADVERTISING AND THE MARKETING MIX 116

What Is Marketing? 116
    Evolution of the Marketing Concept 117   *The Task of Marketing
and Advertising* 118

What Is a Market? 119

The Majority Fallacy 120   *Types of Markets* 121   *Locating, Measuring, and Selecting the Market* 123

The Marketing Mix 126
   Advertising and the Product Element 127   *Advertising and the Price Element* 135   *Advertising and the Place Element* 139   *Advertising and the Promotion Element* 142   *The Marketing Mix in Perspective* 144

Ad Lab 4-A: Marketing Mac: Apple Computer's Counterattack against IBM 120

People in Advertising: Al Ries and Jack Trout 124

Ad Lab 4-B: Marketing Mac: Who Is the Target Market? 126

Checklist of Product Classifications 129

Ad Lab 4-C: Marketing Mac: Understanding the Product 136

Ad Lab 4-D: Marketing Mac: Price and Distribution Strategies 141

Ad Lab 4-E: Marketing Mac: Deciding on Promotion 144

5

CONSUMER BEHAVIOR AND MARKET SEGMENTATION 146

Consumer Behavior: The Directional Force in Advertising 146
The Complexity of Consumer Buying Decisions 148
   Personal Influences on Consumer Behavior: The Importance of Your Inner Self 149   *Environmental Influences on Consumer Behavior: The Importance of What's Around You* 158   *Integrating the Components of Consumer Behavior* 163

Market Segmentation 163
   Segmenting Consumer Markets 164   *Segmenting Business Markets* 173

Ad Lab 5-A: Using Needs to Stimulate Motivation 152

Ad Lab 5-B: Subliminal Manipulation: Fact or Fantasy? 153

People in Advertising: Jay Chiat 160

Ad Lab 5-C: How Understanding Consumer Behavior Helps Create Effective Advertising 164

Ad Lab 5-D: The Decision Matrix: Can You Predict Consumer Behavior? 165

6

MARKETING AND ADVERTISING RESEARCH: INPUTS TO THE PLANNING PROCESS 178

The Need for Research in Marketing and Advertising 179
   Marketing Research 180   *Advertising Research* 181

Basic Steps in the Research Procedure 182
    Problem Definition and Research Objectives 182 *Exploratory Research* 184 *Performing Primary Research* 188 *Interpreting the Findings* 197

Applying Research to Marketing and Advertising Strategy 198
    Developing Marketing Strategy 198 *Developing Advertising Strategy* 199 *Concept Testing* 201 *Testing and Evaluation of Advertising* 202

Ad Lab 6-A: Market Research versus Marketing Research: Xerox Knew the Difference 181

Ad Lab 6-B: Using Marketing Research for New-Product Development 185

People in Advertising: Ruth Ziff 188

Ad Lab 6-C: How Reliable Is Sampling? 193

Checklist for Developing an Effective Questionnaire 195

Checklist of Methods for Pretesting Advertisements 206

Checklist of Methods for Posttesting Advertisements 208

7

MARKETING AND ADVERTISING PLANNING 214

The Marketing Plan 215
    What Is a Marketing Plan? 215 *Effect of the Marketing Plan on Advertising* 218 *Elements of the Marketing Plan* 220

The Advertising Plan 227
    Review of the Marketing Plan 227 *Setting Advertising Objectives* 227 *Advertising Strategy and the Creative Mix* 233

Allocating Funds for Advertising 240
    An Investment in Future Sales 240 *Methods of Allocating Funds* 242 *The Bottom Line* 246

Ad Lab 7-A: The 1980s: An Era of Marketing Warfare 216

Checklist for Situation Analysis 221

People in Advertising: Thomas J. Burrell 230

Checklist for Developing Advertising Objectives 234

Ad Lab 7-B: Creative Use of the Creative Mix 238

Ad Lab 7-C: How Economists View the Effect of Advertising on Sales 241

Checklist of Ways to Set Advertising Budgets 243

PART III

ADVERTISING CREATIVITY 248

8

CREATIVE COPYWRITING 250

Copywriting and Advertising Strategy 251
  Building the Message Strategy 253   *Developing the Big Idea* 257

Objectives of Good Copy 258
  Attention 259   *Interest* 260   *Credibility* 260   *Desire* 260
  Action 261

Understanding the Copywriter's Terminology 261
  Headlines 261   *Subheads* 264   *Body Copy* 264   *Boxes and
  Panels* 273   *Slogans* 274   *Seals, Logotypes, and Signatures* 274

Common Pitfalls in Writing Copy 275
Creating Names for Products 278

People in Advertising: Hal Patrick Riney 252

Checklist of Product Marketing Facts for Copywriters 254

Ad Lab 8-A: The Eye versus the Ear 265

Checklist for Writing Effective Copy 267

Copywriter's Portfolio 270

Ad Lab 8-B: Writing Readable Advertising Copy: A Self-Test 275

9

CREATIVE ART DIRECTION 280

What Is Art? 281
Role of the Advertising Artist 282
  Art Directors 282   *Graphic Designers* 282   *Illustrators* 282
  Production Artists 283

Creating the Advertisement 284
  Laying Out the Ad 286   *The Use of Layouts* 286   *Steps in
  Advertising Layout* 288   *Which Kind of Layout Design Works
  Best?* 291

The Advertising Visual 292
  Purpose of the Visual 292   *Visualizing Techniques* 294   *Choosing
  the Visual* 297

Packaging Design 298
  Packaging 299   *Packaging Specialists* 304   *When Should a
  Package Be Changed?* 304

People in Advertising: George H. Lois 284

Ad Lab 9-A: Which Ad Would You Select? 288

Checklist of Design Principles 292

Checklist of Chief Focus for Visuals 297

Ad Lab 9-B: The Psychological Impact of Color 299

Art Director's Portfolio 300

Ad Lab 9-C: Bringing Up Betty 306

10

CREATIVE PRODUCTION: PRINT MEDIA 308

The Production Process 309

Planning Print Production 310

Typography 312

Classes of Type 313   Type Groups 313   Type Families 315   Type Structure and Measurement 315   Type Selection 317   Type Specification and Copy Casting 320

Typesetting Methods

Strike-On Composition 322   Photocomposition 322   The Typesetting Process 323

The Printing Process 324

Preparing Materials for the Press 324   Methods of Printing 325 Printing in Color 328   Preparing Materials for Publications 335 Selecting Papers for Printing 335

Ad Lab 10-A: How to Use Type as the Major Graphic Design Element 318

Ad Lab 10-B: The Most Unforgettable Characters You Will Ever Meet 319

People in Advertising: Klaus F. Schmidt 320

Creative Department: From Concept through Production of a Magazine Advertisement 330

11

CREATIVE PRODUCTION: ELECTRONIC MEDIA 338

Creating Commercials for Television 339

Developing the Concept for the Commercial 339   Types of Television Commercials 343

Production Techniques 347

Animation Techniques 348   Live Action 351   Special Effects 351

The Production Process 351

Preproduction 353   Production 354   Postproduction 355   Film versus Tape 355   Costs 356

Producing Radio Commercials 356
   Writing Radio Copy 364   *Types of Radio Commercials* 365

The Radio Production Process 367

Checklist for Creating Effective TV Commercials 342

People in Advertising: Joe Sedelmaier 346

Creative Department: From Concept through Production of a Television
Commercial 358

Checklist for Creating Effective Radio Commercials 364

Ad Lab 11-A: Creative Ways to Sell on Radio 366

PART IV

ADVERTISING MEDIA 370

12

MEDIA PLANNING AND SELECTION 372

Media Planning: An Overview 373

The Role of Media in the Marketing Framework 375
   Marketing Objectives and Strategy 375   *Advertising Strategy* 376

Defining Media Objectives 376
   Audience Objectives 378   *Distribution Objectives* 379

Developing a Media Strategy 382
   Geographic Scope 383   *Nature of the Medium and the
Message* 385   *Consumer Purchase Patterns* 388   *Mechanical
Considerations* 389   *Competitive Strategy and Budget
Considerations* 391   *Stating the Media Strategy* 391

Media Selection and Scheduling 391
   Considerations in Selecting Individual Media 392   *Scheduling
Criteria* 402   *The Use of Computers in Media Selection and
Scheduling* 404

Ad Lab 12-A: Media Selection: As the Creative Person Sees It 386

Ad Lab 12-B: Off-the-Wall Media That Pull Customers off the Fence 395

People in Advertising: Mark S. Oken 398

13

PRINT MEDIA 408

Using Newspapers in the Creative Mix 408
   Advantages of Newspapers 408   *Some Drawbacks to
Newspapers* 411   *Who Uses Newspapers?* 411   *How Newspapers
Are Categorized* 412   *Types of Newspaper Advertising* 415

How to Buy Newspaper Space 419
   Reading Rate Cards 421   *Co-op Insertions* 424   *Insertion Orders
   and Tear Sheets* 424

Using Magazines in the Creative Mix 424
   Advantages of Magazines 425   *Some Drawbacks to Magazines* 430
   Special Possibilities with Magazines 432   *How Magazines Are
   Categorized* 434

How to Buy Magazine Space 437
   Understanding Magazine Circulation 437   *Reading Rate
   Cards* 438

Sources of Print Media Information 441

People in Advertising: Rance Crain 420
Portfolio of Award-Winning Magazine Advertisements 426
Checklist of What Works Best in Print 431
Ad Lab 13-A: Innovations in Magazine Advertising 433

14

ELECTRONIC MEDIA 444

Using Broadcast Television in the Creative Mix 445
   Advantages of Broadcast Television 445   *Drawbacks of Broadcast
   Television* 447

Overview of the Broadcast Television Medium 451
   Audience Trends 451   *Growth of Television Advertising* 451   *Types
   of Broadcast Advertising* 452

Television Audience Measurement 455
   Rating Services: "The Book" 456   *Television Markets* 457
   Dayparts 457   *Audience Measures* 459   *Gross Rating Points* 460

Buying Television Time 460
   Requesting Avails 460   *Selecting Programs for Buys* 461
   Negotiating Prices and Contracts 461

Using Cable Television in the Creative Mix 462
   Advantages of Cable 462   *Drawbacks of Cable* 464   *Overview of
   the Cable Medium* 465   *Buying Cable Time* 467   *Other Forms of
   Television* 467

Using Radio in the Creative Mix 468
   Advantages of Radio 468   *Drawbacks to Radio* 472

Overview of the Radio Medium 474
   Who Uses Radio? 474   *Radio Programming and Audiences* 475

Buying Radio Time 477
   Types of Radio Advertising 477   *Radio Terminology* 479
   Preparing a Radio Schedule 482

Checklist of What Works Best in Television 448

People in Advertising: Jerry Della Femina 454

Ad Lab 14-A: Where Do Those Infamous TV Ratings Come From? 458

Checklist of What Works Best in Radio 473

Ad Lab 14-B: The Reports That Make or Break Radio Stations 480

15

DIRECT MAIL AND OUTDOOR MEDIA 484

Direct Mail Advertising 484
  Direct Mail versus Direct Marketing 485   *Growth of Direct Mail* 487

Using Direct Mail in the Creative Mix 488
  Advantages of Direct Mail 489   *Drawbacks to Direct Mail* 492
  Types of Direct Mail 495

Buying Direct Mail 498
  Direct-Mail Lists 499   *Production and Handling* 500
  Distribution 501

Outdoor Advertising 501
  Advantages of Outdoor Advertising 502   *Drawbacks to Outdoor Advertising* 506   *Standardization of the Outdoor Advertising Business* 507   *Types of Outdoor Structures* 511

Transit Advertising 514
  Types of Transit Advertising 515   *Advantages of Transit Advertising* 516   *Drawbacks to Transit Advertising* 517   *Buying Transit Advertising* 518

Ad Lab 15-A: College Grad Gets Job through Mail 489

Checklist of What Works Best in Direct Mail 493

People in Advertising: Don Hauptman 496

Checklist of What Works Best in Outdoor 506

Portfolio of Outdoor Advertising: A 20th-Century Art Form 508

Ad Lab 15-B: How to Use Color in Outdoor Advertising 513

16

SALES PROMOTION AND SUPPLEMENTARY MEDIA 522

Role of Sales Promotion 522
Sales Promotion: The Sales Accelerator 524
Push Strategy Techniques 525
  Trade Deals 526   *Display Allowances* 527   *Dealer Premiums and Contests* 527   *Cooperative Advertising and Advertising Materials* 527   *Push Money* 528   *Collateral Material* 529
  Company Conventions and Dealer Meetings 529

Pull Strategy Techniques 530
    *Sampling 530   Cents-Off Promotions and Refunds/
    Rebates 532   Coupons 532   Combination Offers 533
    Premiums 534   Contests and Sweepstakes 535   Point-of-Purchase
    (P-O-P) Advertising 537*

Supplementary Media 539
    *Specialty Advertising 539   Trade Shows and Exhibits 540
    Directories and Yellow Pages 541*

People in Advertising: William A. Robinson 528
Ad Lab 16-A: The 10 Commandments of Creative Promotion 531
Ad Lab 16-B: Smell: Powerful Armament in the Retailer's Arsenal 538

PART V

SPECIAL TYPES OF ADVERTISING 544

 17

LOCAL ADVERTISING 546

Local Advertising: Where the Action Is 546
    Types of Local Advertising 548   Objectives of Local Advertising 548

Planning the Advertising Effort 549
    *Analyzing the Local Market and Competition 551   Conducting
    Adequate Research 551   Determining Objectives and Strategy 555
    Establishing the Budget 557   Planning Media Strategy 562*

Creating the Local Advertisement 569
    Creating the Message 571   Seeking Creative Assistance 574

Checklist of Local Advertising Objectives 550
People in Advertising: Jane Trahey 552
Ad Lab 17-A: Mistakes Commonly Made by Local Advertisers 557
Checklist for Setting Local Advertising Budgets 561
Checklist for Creating Local Advertising 572
Ad Lab 17-B: The Co-op Battleground 578

18

CORPORATE ADVERTISING, PUBLIC RELATIONS, AND NONCOMMERCIAL ADVERTISING 580

The Role of Public Relations 580
    *Advertising versus Public Relations 582   Advertising versus Public
    Relations Practitioners 582*

Corporate Advertising 583
   Public Relations Advertising 583   *Corporate/Institutional*
   Advertising 584   *Corporate Identity Advertising* 594   *Recruitment*
   Advertising 595

Public Relations Activities and Tools 595
   Public Relations Activities 598   *Public Relations Tools* 601

Noncommercial Advertising 606
   Objectives of Noncommercial Advertising 608   *Types of*
   Noncommercial Advertising 608   *The Advertising Council* 611

Ad Lab 18-A: David Ogilvy Talks about Corporate Advertising 586
Portfolio of Corporate Advertising 588
People in Advertising: Herb Schmertz 598
Checklist for Writing News Releases 603

19

INTERNATIONAL ADVERTISING 614

Growth and Status of International Advertising 616
Managing International Advertising 616
   Foreign Marketing Structures 618   *Agency Selection* 621

Creative Strategies in International Advertising 624
   Market Considerations 625   *Media Considerations* 630   *Message*
   Considerations 634

Ad Lab 19-A: Advertising in the Soviet Union 617
People in Advertising: Keith Reinhard 624
Checklist for International Media Planning 632

APPENDIX A: MARKETING PLAN OUTLINE 642

APPENDIX B: ADVERTISING PLAN OUTLINE 648

APPENDIX C: CAREER PLANNING IN ADVERTISING 652

ENDNOTES E–1

CREDITS AND ACKNOWLEDGMENTS C

GLOSSARY G–1

INDEX I–1

CONTEMPORARY

Advertising

Part I

Advertising Perspectives

Perception and Reality

1

THE EVOLUTION
OF ADVERTISING

A century ago in Atlanta, Georgia, there lived a pharmacist named John S. Pemberton. He was not particularly successful financially, but Dr. Pemberton was destined to develop something that would later become the most popular consumer packaged product in the world. In fact, it would revolutionize the beverage industry and write a new chapter in the history of marketing and advertising.

As legend goes, Dr. Pemberton, while working over a three-legged pot in his backyard in 1886, produced a sweet-tasting brown syrup from the juices of certain plants and nuts. Mixed with soda fountain water, the syrup produced a remarkable, sparkling taste. On May 8, 1886, Pemberton's new elixir was placed on sale as a soda fountain drink for 5 cents a glass at Jacobs' Pharmacy in downtown Atlanta (see Figure 1–1). It was an immediate success. On May 29, a newspaper ad in the *Atlanta Journal* invited Atlantans to try "the new and popular soda fountain drink." The ad also proclaimed that Coca-Cola, as Pemberton called it, was "Delicious and Refreshing," a theme that continues today.

Following is a list of possible advertising slogans and headlines for Coca-Cola. Test your knowledge of advertising by trying to determine which ones were actually used by the Coca-Cola Company:

> The drink of quality.
> The great national temperance beverage.
> Whenever you see an arrow, think of Coca-Cola.
> Thirst knows no season.
> Around the corner from anywhere.
> The pause that refreshes.
> Universal symbol of the American way of life.
> Midsummer magic.
> Enjoy Coca-Cola.

In fact, all nine slogans have been used by Coca-Cola. For the company's complete list of slogans, campaigns, and themes spanning more than 100 years, see Ad Lab 1-A. The list chronicles not only the history of the world's most successful product but also the history of modern advertising itself.

ADVERTISING DEFINED

What is advertising? According to McCann Erickson, Inc., the advertising agency that develops Coca-Cola's national campaigns, advertising is "truth well told." This philosophy is echoed by Coke's management:

> [Coke's advertising] should be a pleasurable experience, refreshing to watch and pleasant to listen to. It should reflect quality by being quality. And it should make you say, "I wish I'd been there. I wish I had been drinking Coke with these people."[1]

That's what advertising is to Coca-Cola. But can the same be said for other products and services in the marketplace today? How do we define the advertising we see for those commodities?

Albert Lasker, who has been called the father of modern advertising, said that advertising is "salesmanship in print." That may well be. But he gave us that definition long before the advent of radio and television and at a time when the nature and scope of advertising were considerably different from what they are now.

Today, we all have strong concepts of what advertising is, and we also tend to have very strong opinions and prejudices about it. Definitions of advertising are many and varied. It may be defined as a communication process, a marketing process, an economic and social process, a public relations process, or an information and persuasion process, depending on the point of view.

We shall discuss some of these views shortly, but first let's determine a working definition of advertising as it is presented in this text:

> *Advertising* is the nonpersonal communication of information, usually paid for and usually persuasive in nature, about products, services, or ideas by identified sponsors through various media.

Let's take this definition apart and analyze its components. Advertising is directed to groups of people and is therefore *nonpersonal*. The groups, for example, might be teenagers who enjoy rock music or older adults who attend cultural events. But in either case, advertising to these groups is not personal or face-to-face communication.

In direct-mail advertising, an attempt is often made to personalize the message by inserting the receiver's name one or more times in the letter. But direct mail is still nonpersonal; a computer inserted the name. And the signature on the direct-mail advertisement is produced electronically.

Most advertising is *paid for* by sponsors. General Motors, K mart, Coca-Cola, and the local record shop pay money to the media to carry the advertisements we read, hear, and see. But some advertisements are not paid for by their sponsors. The American Red Cross, United Way, and American Cancer Society are only three of hundreds of organizations whose messages are customarily presented by the media at no charge as a public service.

A company usually sponsors advertising in order to convince people that its product will benefit them. Most advertising is intended to be *persuasive*—to win converts to a product, service, or idea. Some advertisements, though, such as legal announcements, are intended merely to inform, not to persuade.

FIGURE   1–1

Coca-Cola was first served at Jacobs' Pharmacy in Atlanta in 1886. Little did they know at that time that it would become the world's leading consumer packaged good.

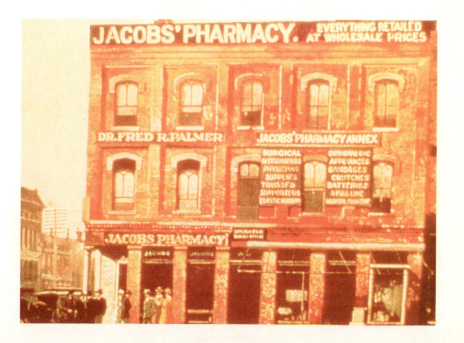

In addition to promoting tangible *products* such as soap and soft drinks, advertising is also used extensively to help sell the *services* of bankers, beauticians, and bike shops. And increasingly, advertising is being used to sell a wide variety of *ideas*—economic, political, religious, and social.

For a message to be considered an advertisement, the sponsor must be *identified*. Naturally, the sponsor usually wants to be identified—or else why advertise? However, one of the distinguishing characteristics between advertising and *public relations* is that certain public relations activities like *publicity* are normally not openly sponsored. This subject will be explored further in Chapter 18.

Advertising reaches us through various *media*. In addition to the traditional mass media—radio, television, newspapers, magazines, and billboards—advertising makes use of other means such as direct mail, shopping carts, blimps, and videocassettes.

Now, with this working definition in mind, let's consider some of the important functions and effects of advertising.

AD LAB 1-A   It Had to Be Good to Get Where It Is!

1886 Drink Coca-Cola.	1932 Thirst come, thirst served.
1904 Delicious and refreshing.	1933 Bounce back to normal.
1904 Coca-Cola . . . satisfies.	1933 Don't wear a tired, thirsty face.
1905 Coca-Cola revives and sustains.	1935 Coca-Cola . . . the pause that brings friends together.
1905 Wherever you go . . . you'll find Coca-Cola.	
1906 The drink of quality.	1937 America's favorite moment.
1906 The great national temperance beverage.	1938 The best friend thirst ever had.
1907 Coca-Cola is full of vim, vigor and go—is a snappy drink.	1938 Thirst asks nothing more.
	1939 Coca-Cola goes along.
1908 Get the genuine.	1939 Coca-Cola has the taste thirst goes for.
1909 Whenever you see an arrow, think of Coca-Cola.	1939 Whoever you are, whatever you do, wherever you may be, when you think of refreshment, think of ice-cold Coca-Cola.
1911 Enjoy a glass of liquid laughter.	
1917 Three million a day.	
1920 Coca-Cola . . . good things from 9 climes poured into a single glass.	1940 Within easy reach of your thirst.
	1940 America's year-round answer to thirst.
1922 Thirst knows no season.	1941 Work refreshed.
1923 Enjoy thirst.	1941 Coca-Cola belongs . . .
1925 It has the charm of purity.	1942 The only thing like Coca-Cola is Coca-Cola itself.
1925 With a drink so good . . . 'tis folly to be thirsty.	1942 Coca-Cola has that extra something.
1925 Six million a day.	1942 The best is always the better buy.
1926 Coca-Cola is the shortest distance between thirst and refreshment.	1942 It's the real thing.
	1943 Universal symbol of the American way of life . . . Coca-Cola.
1927 It had to be good to get where it is.	
1927 Around the corner from anywhere.	1943 With a taste all its own.
1927 At the little red sign.	1945 The happy symbol of a friendly way of life.
1928 Coca-Cola . . . a pure drink of natural flavors.	1945 Why grow thirsty?
1929 The best served drink in the world.	1946 The world's friendliest club . . . admission 5¢.
1929 The pause that refreshes.	1946 Yes.
1932 Ice-cold sunshine.	1947 Coca-Cola . . . continuous quality.

FUNCTIONS AND EFFECTS OF ADVERTISING

As soon as Dr. Pemberton had developed his new drink, he and his partner, Frank M. Robinson, came up with a name for it (see Figure 1–2). They also decided to write the name in a unique way, using the flowing Spencerian script of the day. Later, the name and script were trademarked with the U.S. Patent Office to ensure their sole usage by the Coca-Cola Company in its advertising and packaging. This demonstrates perhaps one of the most basic functions, purposes, or uses of advertising—*to identify products and differentiate them from others.*

No sooner had they named the product than they ran an ad to tell people about it and where they could get it. Within a year, as more soda fountains began to sell the product, handpainted oilcloth signs with "Coca-Cola" began to appear, attached to store awnings. Then the word *Drink* was added to inform passersby that the product was a soda fountain beverage. Here we see another basic function, or use, of advertising—*to communicate information about the product, its features, and its location of sale.*

1947	Continuous quality is quality you trust.
1947	The quality of Coca-Cola is a friendly quality you can always trust.
1948	Where there's Coke there's hospitality.
1949	Coca-Cola . . . along the highway to anywhere.
1950	Thirst, too, seeks quality.
1951	For home and hospitality.
1951	You taste its quality.
1952	What you want is a Coke.
1952	Coke follows thirst everywhere.
1953	Drive safely . . . Drive refreshed.
1953	Midsummer magic.
1955	Bright and bracing as sunshine.
1956	Coca-Cola . . . makes good things taste better.
1956	The friendliest drink on earth.
1956	Gives a bright little lift.
1956	Coca-Cola puts you at your sparkling best.
1957	Sign of good taste.
1958	The cold, crisp taste of Coke.
1959	Cheerful life of Coke.
1959	Relax refreshed with ice-cold Coca-Cola.
1959	Be really refreshed.
1959	The cold, crisp taste that so deeply satisfies.
1961	Coca-Cola refreshes you best.
1963	The big bold taste that's always just right.
1963	Things go better with Coke.
1963	Go better refreshed.
1964	Coca-Cola gives that special zing . . . refreshes best.
1965	Enjoy Coca-Cola.
1965	For extra fun—take more than one! Take an extra carton of Coke!
1966	Coca-Cola has the taste you never get tired of.
1968	Tells your thirst to go fly a kite.
1968	Wave after wave—drink after drink.
1968	For twice the convenience, bring home two cartons of Coke.
1968	It's twice time.
1970	It's the real thing.
1971	I'd like to buy the world a Coke.
1972	Coke . . . goes with the good times.
1975	Look up America, see what we've got.
1976	Coke adds life . . .
1980	Have a Coke and a smile.
1982	Coke is it.
1985	We've got a taste for you (Coca-Cola).
1985	America's real choice (Coca-Cola Classic).
1986	Red, white and you (Coca-Cola Classic).
1986	Catch the wave (Coca-Cola).
1987	You can't beat the feeling!

Laboratory Applications

1. Which slogans would no longer be appropriate?
2. What new slogan might Coca-Cola use to reflect the 1990s?

FIGURE   1-2

In 1886, John Pemberton (top), the creator of Coca-Cola, went into business with F. M. Robinson (bottom) to market the new product. They sold the rights two years later.

In 1888, the rights to Coca-Cola were bought for $2,300 by Asa G. Candler. Pemberton was in ill health and died in August of that year. Unfortunately, he never saw the success his product would eventually achieve.

Candler was a promoter and a firm believer in advertising. He printed and distributed thousands of coupons offering a complimentary glass of Coca-Cola (see Figure 1-3). As more and more people saw the advertisements and received free coupons, they tried the product and then tried it again. That's another reason for advertising: *to induce consumers to try new products and to suggest reuse.*

After more people tried the soft drink, liked it, and requested it, more pharmacies bought the product to sell to their customers. *Stimulating the distribution of a product* is yet another function of advertising.

Up to that time, Coca-Cola had been sold only at soda fountains. One of the many purposes of advertising, though, is *to increase product usage.* In 1899, the first bottling plant opened in Chattanooga, Tennessee. The second opened the following year in Atlanta. Now people could buy bottles of Coke to take with them and enjoy at home. In 30 years, these first two bottling plants increased to 1,000 with 95 percent of them locally owned and operated.

As with anything popular, however, imitators immediately appeared, and the battle against these competitors has been continuous from the beginning. Another major purpose or function of advertising is *to build brand preference and loyalty,* and Candler's use of an ongoing, consistent promotional campaign helped accomplish this.

In 1916, the famous Coca-Cola bottle with its distinctive contour design was introduced. This helped identify Coke and differentiate it from competitors to such an extent that the bottle was registered as a trademark by the U.S. Patent Office. At the same time, the bottle enhanced the company's other promotional efforts and also assured the public of the standardized quality of Coke with every purchase (see Figure 1-4).

From this brief history of the beginnings of the Coca-Cola Company, we can see that advertising may perform a variety of functions for any business with a product or service to sell and that its effects may be dramatic on that organization. At the same time, though, advertising also has an effect on individuals, on consumers as a group, and on society as a whole. Generally, all these various functions and effects can be grouped into five categories: marketing, communication, education, economic, and social. We shall discuss each of these briefly.

Advertising's Role in Marketing

To achieve profits (or other objectives), companies manufacture and sell products and services that compete in the marketplace. To increase their sales or profits, companies identify groups of prospective customers called *target markets* and then develop *marketing strategies* in order to appeal to them. The marketing strategy is determined by the particular way companies mix, blend, and employ various marketing options. This *marketing mix* includes a variety of elements generally known as the *four Ps* and categorized under the headings of *product, price, place,* and *promotion.* Each of these elements will be discussed more fully in Chapter 4.

Advertising falls in the promotion category and is part of the promotional mix along with personal selling, sales promotion, and public

FIGURE   1–3

Coupons encouraged people to try the new soft drink in its early years. This is an example of one used in the 1890s.

relations—all of which may be used to sell or win acceptance of the company's products, services, or ideas.

In order to lower the cost of sales, advertising uses the media to communicate the sales message to a large group of people known as the *target audience*. Through advertising, the cost of reaching a thousand people in the target audience is usually far less than the cost of reaching one prospect through personal selling.

For example, consider how much it would cost to have a sales rep make a personal sales call on every football fan who watches the Super Bowl on television in order to sell each a bottle of Coke. It would be unbelievably expensive. The McGraw-Hill Laboratory reports that the average face-to-face sales call now costs a company well over $220.[2] If we multiply that by the more than 100 million people who watch the Super Bowl, the cost is mind-boggling (over $22 billion). However, you could buy a 30-second television commercial during the Super Bowl and tell those same 100 million people about Coca-Cola for only $650,000. That's a lot less. In fact, through advertising, you would be able to talk to a thousand of those prospects for only $6.50—about 4 percent of what it costs to talk to *one* prospect through personal selling.

Thus, in terms of the marketing function, the overall effect of advertising is to lower the cost of sales.

Advertising as Communication

All forms of advertising communicate some message to a group of people. As a communication process, advertising had its beginnings in ancient civilizations. Most historians believe the outdoor signs carved in clay, wood, or stone and used by ancient Greek and Roman merchants were the first form of advertising. At this time, the persuasive aspect of advertising was absent; it was pure communication. Since most of the population was

FIGURE   1–4

Putting Coca-Cola in a bottle greatly widened its distribution. Bottles evolved over the years from the straight Hutchinson style used in 1899, and they have enjoyed decades of public acceptance. Management had great fear when it was suggested that it add sizes larger than the traditional 6-ounce container. Today, however, Coke is available in a wide variety of sizes.

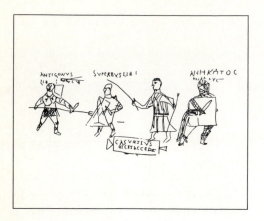

FIGURE   1–5

From a wall in Pompeii, this inscription promoting a contest of gladiators represents one of the earliest forms of advertising.

unable to read, the signs often symbolized the goods for sale, such as a boot for a shoemaker's shop (see Figure 1–5).

As early artisans took pride in their work, they placed special, personal marks on the goods they produced such as cutlery, cloth, and pottery. These *trademarks* enabled buyers to identify the work of a particular artisan, just as trademarks do today, thus assuring consumers they were getting the goods they wanted.

Today, the simple communication of information is still an important function of advertising. In fact, in terms of time costs—the time required to collect data relevant to the selection of goods—the informational value of advertising is significant to most consumers.[3] Some advertising, therefore, is used primarily for the communication of basic information. Examples include the ads in telephone directories, newspaper classified ads, and the legal notices published by various organizations and government bodies.

The Educational Effect of Advertising

People learn from advertising. They learn about the products available to them, and they learn how they can better their lives:

> Advertising, as an educator, speeds the adoption of the new and untried and, in so doing, accelerates technological advances in industry and hastens the realization of a fuller life for all. It helps reduce accidents and waste of natural resources and contributes to building a better understanding and appreciation of American ideologies.[4]

But advertising must be more than educational to be successful. It must also be persuasive to move people to action, whether that action is the purchase of a different brand of breakfast cereal or regular attendance at church. This persuasiveness usually has little in common with the impartiality of education.

Advertising's Effect on Commerce and the Economy

We shall discuss some of the far-reaching economic aspects of advertising later in this chapter. For now, though, it is important to realize that by making people aware of products, services, and ideas, advertising promotes sales and thereby commerce. As a buyer's guide, it provides consumers with news of new products or prices, and it gives industrial buyers important information about new equipment and technology. By informing many people at once about available products and services, advertising greatly reduces the cost of distribution and eases the task of personal selling. This leads to lower costs and higher profits, which can be invested in more capital equipment and jobs.

The freedom to advertise enables competitors to enter the marketplace. This encourages the improvement of existing products and the development of new, improved models. These actions translate into increased productivity, higher quality, and the disappearance of products that don't measure up. Thus, as advertising invites people to try new products, it accelerates the success of good products and the failure of unacceptable products.

Advertising's Function in Society

Advertising, as a tool of the mass-marketing system, is one of the major forces that has helped improve the standard of living in this country and around the world. By publicizing the material, social, and cultural opportunities of a free enterprise, consumer society, advertising has encouraged increased productivity by both management and labor.

By giving consumers an attractive picture of the products available to them, advertising motivates them to buy. For example, advertising has created a personality for each automobile make and model on the market.

Advertising also serves social needs. The media, for example, all receive their primary income from advertising. This facilitates freedom of the press because they are not dependent on government for support.

In addition, various advertising organizations also foster growth and understanding of important social causes through public-service advertising. The Red Cross, Community Chest, United Way, and other noncommercial organizations, for instance, receive continuous financial support and volunteer assistance because of the power of advertising (see Figure 1–6).

FIGURE   1–6

Stevie Wonder may be blind, but even he can see that it's stupid to drive with a drunk. The Fallon McElligott advertising agency in Minneapolis was retained by the non-profit Reader's Digest Foundation to create this noncommercial advertisement supporting sober driving. This is typical of the millions of dollars' worth of advertising created and placed as a public service every year by the advertising industry.

Finally, advertising has had both positive and negative effects on society that have led to important social and legal changes. But, as we shall see in Chapter 2, advertising itself has been greatly affected by the very laws it has been instrumental in creating.

CLASSIFICATIONS OF ADVERTISING

The word *advertising* is often preceded by an adjective that indicates the kind of advertising being discussed. To understand what advertising is, it is helpful to classify it—and thereby learn some basic terminology.

Classification by Target Audience

Advertising is always aimed at a particular segment of the population. When you see ads that don't appeal to you, sometimes it is because the ad is aimed at a group of people to which you do not belong. For example, a television commercial for a new laundry detergent might offer little relevance to a teenager. Similarly, a homemaker with three small children may have very little interest in an advertisement for denture cream. The *target audience* is generally defined as that group of individuals to whom the advertising message is directed.

There are many classifications of target audiences. The two major ones, though, are consumers and businesses.

Consumer Advertising

Most of the ads we see in the mass media—television, radio, newspapers, and magazines—are consumer advertisements. They are sponsored by the manufacturer of the product or the dealer who sells the product. They are usually directed at people who will buy the product for their own personal use or at those people who will buy the product for someone else's use. For example, a magazine advertisement for Coca-Cola may be aimed at both the purchaser and the user, who may or may not be the same person. A television commercial for dog food, however, is aimed at the purchaser, not the user, of the product. Both examples, though, would still be referred to as consumer advertisements.

Business Advertising

People who buy or specify products for use in business make up the target audience for business advertising. Business advertising is often said to be invisible because, unless you are actively involved in some business, you are not likely to see it.

The majority of advertising you see as a consumer appears in mass-consumer media. Business advertising, on the other hand, tends to be concentrated in specialized business publications or professional journals, in direct-mail pieces mailed to business establishments, or in trade shows held for specific areas of business. Until recently, business advertising was rarely seen in the mass media.

Business advertising comes in four distinct types: industrial, trade, professional, and agricultural.

Industrial advertising is aimed at individuals in business who buy or influence the purchase of *industrial goods*. Industrial goods include those products and services used in the manufacture of other goods (plants, machinery, equipment, and so forth) or become a physical part of another product (raw materials, semimanufactured goods, components, and so on). Industrial goods also include goods used to conduct business and do not become part of another product, like capital goods (office machines, computers, desks, operating supplies) and business services for which the user contracts (see Figure 1–7).

Advertising for such products as computer mainframes and software systems in such magazines as *Iron Age, Electronics,* and *Business Week* would be referred to as industrial advertising. In recent years, however, we have begun to see some of these products advertised in mass-consumer media like radio and television, although the target audience is still businesspeople who are purchasers or users of industrial goods.

Manufacturers use *trade advertising*—the advertising of goods and services to middlemen—to stimulate wholesalers and retailers to buy goods for resale to their customers. An example of trade advertising is an ad promoting Coca-Cola to food store managers in a trade publication like *Progressive Grocer.* Some items advertised to the trade, such as office equipment, store fixtures, or specialized business services, might be bought for use in the middleman's own business. The major objective of trade advertising, though, is to obtain greater distribution of the product being sold. That may be accomplished by developing more sales outlets or by selling more products to existing sales outlets (see Figure 1–8).

Individuals who are normally licensed and operate under a code of ethics or professional set of standards—such as teachers, accountants, doctors, dentists, architects, engineers, and lawyers—are called *professionals,*

Figure   1–8

Advertising by manufacturers that is directed to wholesalers and retailers is called trade advertising. It is usually designed to promote wider distribution, and thereby increase sales, of the manufacturer's product. Here, Stanley Hardware uses tongue-in-cheek humor to suggest to hardware retailers that their customers will be pleased by the strength of Stanley hinges.

and advertising aimed at them is called *professional advertising.* Often the publications used for professional advertising are the official organs of professional societies such as the *Archives of Ophthalmology,* published by the American Medical Association, or the *Music Educators Journal,* published by the Music Educators National Conference.

Professional advertising has three objectives: (1) to convince professional people to buy items, equipment, and supplies by brand name for use in their work; (2) to encourage professionals to recommend or prescribe a specific product or service to their clients or patients; and (3) to persuade the person to use the product personally.

Farming is still America's largest single industry. Farmers are consumers, of course; but they are businesspeople, too, and as such they make up the audience for *farm (or agricultural) advertising.* Farm advertising is aimed at: (1) establishing awareness of particular brands of agricultural goods, (2) building dealer acceptance of advertised products, and (3) creating preference for products by showing the farmer how the products will increase efficiency, reduce risks, and widen profit margins. Publications such as *California Farmer* and *American Vegetable Grower* serve these markets.

Classification by Geographic Area Covered

A neighborhood dress shop would most likely advertise in the local area near the store. On the other hand, many American products are advertised not only in the United States but in foreign countries from Africa to Asia.

The four classifications of advertising based on geography are: international, national, regional, and local.

International Advertising

Travel to Europe and you might see advertisements for Crest in Norwegian. Go to Russia and you'll find the virtues of Pepsi-Cola extolled. Visit Brazil and watch an ad for Levi's on television (in Portuguese). International advertising is advertising directed at foreign markets, and as a field of study, it has grown so fast and become so important we have devoted an entire chapter (Chapter 19) to the subject (see Figure 1–9).

National Advertising

Advertising aimed at customers in several regions of the country is called *national advertising,* and its sponsors are called *national advertisers.* The majority of advertising we see on prime-time network television is national advertising (see Figure 1–10).

Regional Advertising

Many products are sold in only one area or region of the country. The region might cover several states but not the entire nation. Publications

Entre na dimensão Pierre Cardin.
Um universo de moda muito exclusivo.

PIERRE CARDIN

FIGURE   1–9

In South America, advertisers must be able to use Spanish, of course. But Portuguese is extremely important for the marketer wanting any share of the dynamic Brazilian business. In this Pierre Cardin ad created in Rio, avant-garde surrealism abounds: "Enter the Pierre Cardin dimension. A most exclusive universe of fashion."

FIGURE   1–10

Burger King is perennially one of the nation's largest national advertisers and targets a variety of customer groups via TV, radio, magazine, and newspaper advertising.

ANNCR: Due to the nature of this Burger King commercial, viewers are advised to watch at their own risk.

SINGER: *Ohh, that hot and sizzling bacon.*

ANNCR: The Bacon Double Cheeseburger is for mature audiences only.

SINGER: *Two juicy, flame broiled burgers, melted cheese* . . .

ANNCR: This is your last warning.

CHORUS: *Aren't You Hungry? Aren't You Hungry? Aren't You Hungry for Burger King Now?*

ANNCR: The Bacon Double Cheeseburger has been rated PD. Perfectly delicious . . .

such as *The Wall Street Journal* and *Time* sell space on either a national or a regional basis. Thus, an airline that operates in only one part of the nation can purchase space in a regional edition of certain publications or buy television time on a regional rather than national network basis.

Local Advertising

Many advertisers such as department stores, automobile dealers, and restaurants use *local advertising* because their customers come from only one city or local trading area. Local advertising is often called *retail advertising* simply because most of it is paid for by retailers. Remember, however, that not all retail advertising is local. Increasingly, retailers such as Sears Roebuck and K mart advertise beyond the local areas where their stores are located.

Whereas national and regional advertisements usually explain the merits and special features of a product, most local advertising tells consumers where to buy it. National and regional automobile commercials explain the durability, gas mileage, design, and other product qualities. Local advertising by automobile dealers emphasizes price, friendly salespeople, and other reasons to visit the particular dealership.

Classification by Medium

Advertising can be classified on the basis of the *medium* used to transmit the message. An advertising medium is any paid means used to present an advertisement to its target audience. It does not, therefore, include "word-of-mouth" advertising. The principal *media* (plural of medium) used in advertising are newspapers, magazines, radio, television, direct mail, and out-of-home media such as outdoor signs and billboards and transit ads (on buses or trucks). Thus, there is newspaper advertising, magazine advertising, and so on.

Classification by Function or Purpose

Another way to classify advertising is on the basis of the sponsor's general objectives. Some advertising, for example, is designed to promote a particular product, while other advertisements seek other purposes.

Product versus Nonproduct Advertising

Product advertising is intended to promote products and services. Nonproduct advertising is designed to sell ideas. When Phillips Petroleum places an advertisement for its gasoline, it is a product ad. Ads placed by companies that offer insurance services are also product advertisements. It should be pointed out here, by the way, that in this text the term *product* refers to both products and services.

On the other hand, if Phillips Petroleum tells about its ability to drill for oil without disturbing or polluting the environment, the advertisement is promoting the company's mission or philosophy rather than a particular product. This form of advertising is called *corporate, nonproduct,* or *institutional* advertising (see Figure 1–11). Corporate advertising can have

FIGURE   1–11

Great American First Savings Bank, in San Diego, California, used outdoor, transit, and TV advertising to wage an intensive public service campaign against high school truancy. While this may be considered a form of corporate advertising, its motive is obviously not commercial but rather community service.

La toute nouvelle façon de déguster les délicieux légumes Del Monte:

Buvez-les.

This ad for Del Monte, prepared by McCann-Erickson/Canada, seeks a direct action on the part of the reader. By clipping the coupon, the reader can receive an immediate discount on the price of Del Monte's product.

various objectives. Sometimes referred to as "image" advertising, it can be used in an effort to counter public criticism. In other instances, it is designed to promote noncontroversial causes such as support for the arts or charities. This subject will be the focus of Chapter 18.

Commercial versus Noncommercial Advertising

A *commercial* advertisement promotes goods, services, or ideas for a business with the expectation of making a profit. A *noncommercial* advertisement is sponsored by or for a charitable institution, civic group, or religious or political organization. Many noncommercial advertisements seek money and are placed in the hope of raising funds. Others hope to change consumer behavior ("Buckle up for safety"). Chapter 18 will also discuss noncommercial advertising.

Direct-Action versus Indirect-Action Advertising

Some advertisements are intended to bring about immediate action on the part of the reader. Mail-order advertisements, for example, fall into the category of *direct-action* advertising. Likewise, some newspaper and magazine advertisements include a coupon for the reader to use to request catalogs or additional information. These ads are seeking an immediate, direct action from the reader (see Figure 1–12).

Advertisements that attempt to build the image of a product or familiarity with the name and package are seeking an indirect action. Their objective is often to influence readers to select a specific brand the next time they are in the market for that product.

Most advertisements on television and radio are indirect action. Some, however, are a mixture of the two. It is not uncommon to see a 60-second

Figure 1–13	Leaders in national advertising in the 1890s
Adams Tutti Frutti Gum	Heinz's Baked Beans
American Express Traveler's Cheques	Hires' Root Beer
Armour Beef Extract	Ivory Soap
Baker's Cocoa	Kodak
Beeman's Pepsin Gum	Lipton's Teas
Cook's Tours	Dr. Lyon's Toothpowder
Cuticura Soap	Mennen's Talcum Powder
Edison Mimeograph	Munsing Underwear
Elgin Watches	Oneita Knitted Goods
Edison Phonograph	Postum Cereal
Ferry's Seeds	Prudential Insurance Co.
Franco American Soup	Quaker Oats

| | Figure | 1–14 | The leading advertisers by rank, 1986 (millions of dollars) | | | |

Rank	Company	Advertising	Rank	Company	Advertising
1	Procter & Gamble Co.	$1,435.5	15	J. C. Penney Co.	$496.2
2	Philip Morris Inc.	1,364.5	16	Pillsbury Co.	494.9
3	Sears Roebuck & Co.	1,004.7	17	Ralston Purina Co.	478.0
4	R. J. R. Nabisco	935.0	18	American Telephone & Telegraph	439.9
5	General Motors Corp.	839.0	19	Kraft Inc.	438.0
6	Ford Motor Co.	648.5	20	Chrysler Corp.	426.0
7	Anheuser-Busch Cos.	643.5	21	Johnson & Johnson	410.7
8	McDonald's Corp.	592.0	22	American Home Products Corp.	395.7
9	K mart Corp.	590.4	23	Kellogg Co.	374.0
10	PepsiCo Inc.	581.3	24	Coca-Cola Co.	370.4
11	General Mills	551.6	25	General Electric Co.	354.3
12	Warner-Lambert Co.	548.7			
13	BCI Holdings	535.9			
14	Unilever U.S.	517.7			

television commercial that devotes the first 50 seconds to image building and the last 10 seconds to a local phone number for further information.

Experienced advertisers, though, exercise caution in their use of direct-action devices. The more they are used, the more they tend to detract from the image-building qualities of an advertisement. And that can adversely affect the advertiser's long-term marketing objectives.

EVOLUTION OF MODERN ADVERTISING

As the world's industrial output has grown, so has the use of advertising. In the United States, it is now a significant industry in relation to the total U.S. economy. In 1986, it made up 2.3 percent of the gross national product and represented a total expenditure of $85 billion (see Figures 1–13 and 1–14).[5] The media that received the most advertising expenditures (from high to low) were: newspapers, television, direct mail, radio, magazines, and outdoor. How did this industry grow to be so large?

Throughout history, the purpose of advertising—to inform and persuade—has not changed. While advertising as we know it is a modern, evolutionary process, it actually dates back many centuries. We have already seen how advertising as a communication function was born thousands of years ago. At that time, ancient civilizations had only hand tools to produce goods. Therefore, since goods weren't produced in great quantity, the use of advertising to stimulate mass purchases of merchandise was not necessary. Also, no mass media were available for advertisers to promote their wares.

Impact of Printing and Photography

Perhaps the most important event that ushered in the era of modern advertising was the invention of movable type by Johann Gutenberg in 1440. His invention made possible new advertising media and the first forms of mass advertising, including printed posters, handbills, and newspaper advertisements. In London, in about 1472, the first printed advertisement in English, tacked on church doors, announced a prayer book for sale. The first newspaper advertisement, which appeared on the back of a London newspaper in 1650, offered a reward for the return of 12 stolen horses. Later, ads appeared for coffee, chocolate, tea, real estate, and medicines as well as "personal ads." The advertising was directed to a limited number of people who were customers of coffeehouses where the newspapers were read.

Another major technological breakthrough was the invention of photography in the early 1800s. Before this time, products in printed advertisements could be illustrated only by drawings. Photography added credibility and a whole new world of creativity to advertising because it allowed products, people, and places to be shown as they are, rather than as visualized by an artist.

PEOPLE IN ADVERTISING

John O'Toole

Executive Vice President
American Association of
Advertising Agencies
Retired Chairman
Foote, Cone & Belding
Communications, Inc.

John O'Toole, born in Chicago in 1929, began his writing career at 15 when his first poem was published. He went on to obtain his B.S. degree in journalism at Northwestern University and then served a tour of active duty in the Marines. After his discharge he interviewed with Foote, Cone & Belding (FCB) first, and he stayed there until his retirement. He started as a copywriter under the guidance of the legendary Fairfax Cone, one of the agency's partners. He was promoted to creative director and then rose through the ranks to become president and chief creative officer.

In 1981, he was elected chairman of the board of Foote, Cone & Belding Communications, Inc. This corporate entity comprises 62 full-service advertising operations in 32 countries (5 of them in the United States) plus the offices of subsidiaries engaged in public relations, recruitment advertising, direct response, directory advertising, sales promotion, and financial and pharmaceutical advertising. He has since retired from Foote, Cone & Belding Communications, Inc., to become executive vice president of the American Association of Advertising Agencies.

Early U.S. Advertising

The first newspaper advertisements in the American colonies appeared in the *Boston Newsletter* in 1704. Later, Benjamin Franklin made advertisements more readable by using large headlines and by surrounding the advertisements with considerable white space. He is credited with being the first American to use illustrations in advertisements.

The Industrial Revolution in the United States started in the early 1800s. For the first time, manufacturers were able to mass-produce goods with uniform quality. In order to mass-produce, however, they needed mass consumption, which required vast numbers of people to purchase their products. They could no longer be content to sell only in their local area. Manufacturers soon realized the tremendous value of advertising as an aid in selling to the exciting frontier markets in the West as well as the growing industrial markets in the East.

In July 1844, the first magazine advertising appeared in the *Southern Messenger,* a publication edited for a short time by Edgar Allan Poe. Magazines were the first medium used by manufacturers to reach the mass market and to stimulate mass consumption. Magazines made national advertising possible and thereby the sale of products nationwide.

In a recent interview, portions of which were quoted in advertisements for *The Wall Street Journal,* O'Toole shared the following insights on advertising:

If I want to write to individual consumers, then I must know how they think, and live, and buy. So I believe it's essential to go beyond the statistics of public opinion, to look at what's happening in the real world. There's a new spirit of individualism, people seeking to satisfy their own goals, serve their ambitions, feed their individual appetites, find lifestyles to suit their needs. Small wonder there's such distrust of advertising that treats people as a homogeneous mass. Today's great advertising speaks to individual needs—to the strong drive to be yourself.

Also, there's an enormous amount of advertising and communication fighting for attention. So visibility is difficult to achieve. Yet, you must gain the eyes of the people you want to reach, or you haven't a chance of winning their minds. But making an ad visible means running risks. If an ad is provocative, interesting, intriguing, it's apt to create some adverse comments. Consider the alternative: advertising so bland there's no bite.

O'Toole is deeply dedicated to his trade. He has been chairman of the American Association of Advertising Agencies and of the National Advertising Review Council. He has served as a director of The Advertising Council and as an original member of the National Advertising Review Board. His book, *The Trouble with Advertising,* was published in 1981, and his articles on advertising have appeared in *The Atlantic, Columbia Journalism Review,* and other magazines.

Currently, in his position with the American Association of Advertising Agencies, O'Toole works as an advocate and a lobbyist for the advertising industry with government officials throughout the country, legislators in Washington, and the media. As such, he is in a position to counsel our nation's leaders on pending legislation and national policy pertaining to business in general and the advertising industry in particular.

The First Advertising Agencies

Historians consider Volney B. Palmer, who started business in Philadelphia in 1841, to be the earliest advertising agent in the United States. He contracted with newspapers for large volumes of advertising space at discount rates and then resold this space to advertisers at a higher rate. The advertisers usually prepared the advertisements themselves. In 1890, N. W. Ayer & Son, another Philadelphia advertising organization, offered its services to advertisers. This company was the first advertising agency to operate as agencies do today—planning, creating, and executing complete advertising campaigns for clients in return for a commission paid by the media or for fees received from advertisers.

Other developments during the 19th century directly affected the growth of advertising. The population was growing rapidly, thus providing an increasingly large market for manufacturers. At the same time, the number of people who could read increased substantially. The literacy rate was up to 90 percent by the late 1800s. This large reading public provided an audience that could understand advertising messages.

The development of a nationwide railroad transportation system quickly moved the United States into a period of spectacular growth. In 1896, the federal government inaugurated rural free delivery (RFD). Direct-mail advertising and mail-order selling flourished with mass production. Manufacturers had an ever-increasing variety of products for their catalogs. And they had a means of delivering their advertising (via newspapers and magazines) and their goods to the public.

The invention of important communications devices, including the telegraph, telephone, and typewriter as well as the phonograph and motion pictures, further enabled people to communicate as never before. In short, the country was growing, and with that growth, the national marketing system evolved, enhanced and propelled by advertising.

Advertising Enters the 20th Century

In 1800, the United States was agricultural, but it ended the century as a great industrial nation. During the first two decades of the 1900s, advertising underwent an era of reexamination. Unsubstantiated advertising claims, which caused widespread resentment, resulted in a consumer revolt. The focal point of the attack was the advertising for patent medicines and health devices. Regulation came from within the advertising industry and from the government (see Figure 1–15).

In the 1920s, after World War I, the "era of salesmanship" arrived, and advertising truly became "salesmanship in print." Testimonial advertising by movie stars became popular, and full-color printing was employed lavishly by magazine advertisers (see Figure 1–16).

On October 29, 1929, the stock market crashed, the Great Depression began, and advertising expenditures were drastically reduced. However, perhaps due to desperation, false and misleading advertising continued to thrive. Several best-selling books exposed advertising as an unscrupulous exploiter of consumers, giving root to the consumer movement and resulting in further government regulation.

Due to the sales resistance of consumers and the budget-cutting attitude of management during the depression, advertising turned to research to

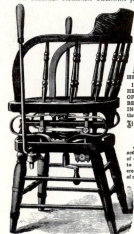

FIGURE   1–15

Advertisements for health gimmicks and patent medicines in weekly newspapers in the 1880s were typical of the era. They exemplified the attitude of manufacturers at that time known by the Latin expression *caveat emptor* ("Let the buyer beware"). The result was the first consumer movement in this country leading to regulatory legislation (see Chapter 2).

FIGURE   1–16

If you ever wondered where the name "Palmolive" (of Colgate-Palmolive) came from, here's the answer. A 1922 Palmolive shampoo ad says results come from "palm and olive oils, the softening, soothing cleansers discovered three thousand years ago in ancient Egypt." The company had not yet merged into Colgate-Palmolive.

regain its credibility and effectiveness. Daniel Starch, A. C. Nielsen, and George Gallup founded research organizations to delve into the attitudes and preferences of consumers. By providing information to advertisers on public opinion, the performance of advertising messages, and the sales of advertised products through food stores and drugstores, they gave birth to a new phenomenon—the research industry.

Rise of Broadcast Advertising

A powerful new advertising medium, radio, started on November 2, 1920, in Pittsburgh, Pennsylvania, and rapidly became the primary means of mass communication. World and national news could now arrive direct from the scene; and a whole new world of family entertainment—music, drama, sports—now became possible. Suddenly, radio enabled national advertisers to reach the large, captive audiences that were tuned in to popular programs. In fact, the first radio shows were produced by the advertisers that sponsored them.

The greatest expansion of any medium, though, occurred after the first television program was broadcast in 1941. Following World War II, the use of television advertising grew rapidly. In 1955, color TV was born. Today, television has become the second largest advertising medium (after newspapers) in terms of total dollars spent by advertisers.

Postwar Advertising

Since World War II, the growth of both advertising and the money spent on it has been phenomenal. Postwar prosperity brought a boom of war babies eager to consume the products of the nation's manufacturers. As the war economy changed to a peacetime economy, the manufacturers of war equipment reverted to producing consumer products, offering through advertising greater luxury, style, and convenience.

The late 1940s and early 1950s were marked by a consumer society vigorously chasing itself up the social ladder by buying more products to keep up with the Joneses. Ads of the era stressed product features that implied social acceptance, style, luxury, and success. Rosser Reeves of the Ted Bates advertising agency introduced the idea that every advertisement must point out the product's USP—*unique selling proposition*—those features that differentiated it from competitive products. But soon there were so many imitation USPs that consumers couldn't take any more. Ford Motor Company discovered this to its regret when consumers failed to accept another new, medium-priced, chromium-filled, "keep-up-with-the-Joneses" car model—the Edsel—despite massive advertising expenditures (see Figure 1–17).

The transition to the image era of the 1960s, then, was perhaps a natural evolution. During this period, the emphasis in advertising shifted from product features to product image, or personality. Cadillac became the

FIGURE 1–17

Ford Motor Company told us hopefully that the Edsel was here to stay. They were wrong. To the tune of $350 million, it was perhaps the largest single product marketing disaster in U.S. history.

image of luxury and the bourgeois symbol of success surpassed only by the aristocratic snootiness of Rolls Royce. The Marlboro man created a macho image for male smokers, and Marlboro suddenly soared to the top of the sales charts where it has stayed for over 25 years—this in spite of having once been pink-tipped and promoted as a "lady's" cigarette (see Figure 1–18).

The Positioning Era

In the early 1970s, Jack Trout and Al Ries wrote that just as the "me-too" (imitative) products of the 1950s killed the product era, the "me-too" images of the 1960s killed the image era.[6]

The 1970s saw a new kind of advertising strategy, where the competitor's strengths became as important as the advertiser's. This was called the *positioning era,* and Trout and Ries were its greatest advocates. Acknowledging the importance of product features and image, they insisted that what was really important was how the product ranked against the competition in the consumer's mind.

The most famous ads of the positioning era were Volkswagen ("Think small") (see Figure 1–19), Avis ("We're only No. 2"), and 7UP ("The uncola"). But many other manufacturers tried it with great success. Trout and Ries also pointed to product disappointments of the period and suggested that poor positioning was the reason.

FIGURE   1–18

Until 1954 Marlboro had been a pink-tipped "women's" cigarette with sales to a restricted market. The ad claim had been "Mild as May," and the name Marlboro was written in delicate script. The restaged product included a flip-top box and a series of ads featuring rugged men, each with a tattoo on the back of his hand. Eventually the campaign settled on the now famous cowboy theme.

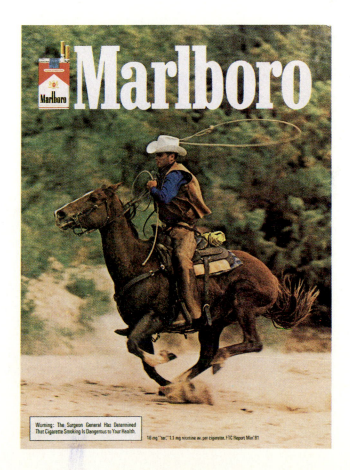

FIGURE 1–19

Jack Trout and Al Ries called this "probably the most famous ad of the 60s." In their view it helped usher in the positioning era of the 70s. By opting for the "small" position, Volkswagen assumed a leadership rank that took many years and millions of competitors' dollars to overcome.

The "Me" Decade

Trout and Ries did not address the consumer movement, which received its greatest impetus from the disillusioning setbacks of the Vietnam War, the Watergate scandals, and the sudden shortage of vital natural resources. These issues fostered cynicism and distrust of the establishment and everything traditional, giving rise to a new twist in moral consciousness. On the one hand, individual irresponsibility and self-indulgence were defended in the name of personal self-fulfillment. On the other hand, the concept of corporate self-fulfillment was attacked in the name of social accountability. This all led to another evolution in the style and the subjects of advertising.

By the mid-1980s, Americans had already witnessed an avalanche of ads—especially in the toiletry and cosmetics industries—aimed at the "me" generation that played off the self-fulfillment climate ("L'Oreal. Because I'm worth it.").[7] At the same time, the nation's largest industrial concerns were spending millions of dollars on corporate advertising to extol their social consciousness and good citizenship for cleaning up after themselves and otherwise protecting the environment.

Likewise, following the energy shortages, a new marketing tactic called *demarketing* appeared as producers of energy and energy-consuming goods used marketing and advertising techniques to actually *slow* the demand for their products. In time, demarketing became a strategic tool for certain noncommercial, issue advertisers (Figure 1–20) as well as for

FIGURE   1–20

The American Lung Association has waged a demarketing campaign against cigarette smoking for years. In this commercial prepared by Ketchum Advertising/Los Angeles, a young woman is seen lying on a bed, futilely trying to light a cigarette. Each match, though, is mysteriously blown out. Then, when she stands, we see that she is pregnant. An off-camera voice says: "Maybe someone's trying to tell you something."

some financial institutions who used it as a way to segment prospective customers. By actively discouraging patronage from some customers, the banks could concentrate on those that appeared most profitable.[8]

Advertising Today

This brief history shows us how advertising evolves to reflect the world in which we live. As a tool of marketing, advertising has come a long way from the simple sign on the bootmaker's shop. Today, it is a powerful, persuasive device that not only announces the availability and location of products and services but even defines the quality and value of those products and the personality of the people who buy them.

As advances in technology are constantly changing our lives, so are the actions and attitudes of special-interest groups—from big business to big labor, from progrowth advocates to environmentalists, from big religion to big cults. While some of these groups may fight progress all the way, they also all use the tools of this progress to effect their aims. One of these tools, today and in the days ahead, will be advertising—in revolutionary new media yet to be conceived.

THE ECONOMIC IMPACT OF ADVERTISING

Earlier in this chapter, we mentioned that one of the major functions of advertising is an economic one. As we pointed out, by making people aware of new products and services or reminding people to repurchase the products they like, advertising promotes sales and thus commerce.

The Billiard-Ball Principle

The economic effect of advertising can be likened to the opening "break" shot in pool or billiards. The moment a company begins to advertise, a chain reaction of economic events takes place. Usually the extent of this chain reaction is very difficult to measure; but as in billiards, its scope is certainly related to the force of the shot. And because it inevitably occurs at the same time as a host of other economic events, even the direction of the chain reaction is often in dispute (see Figure 1–21).

For example, consider these questions about the effect of advertising: Does advertising promote competition or discourage it? Does advertising raise or lower prices? What is the effect of advertising on the total demand for a product category? Does advertising widen consumer choice or narrow it? How does advertising influence the business cycle? These are just

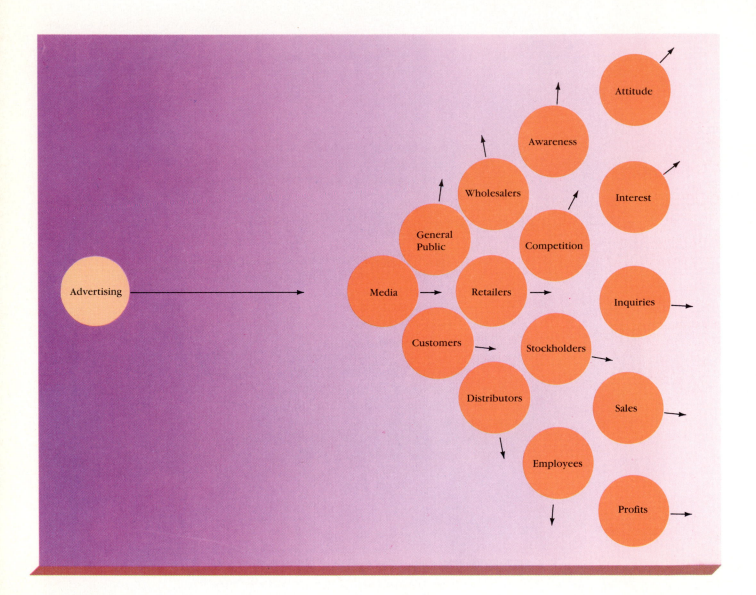

FIGURE   1–21

The billiard-ball principle describes the chain reaction of economic events that takes place the moment a company begins to advertise. As in billiards, the magnitude of these events depends, to a great extent, on the force of the initial impact.

some of the many questions frequently asked (and seldom answered) that relate to the chain of economic events caused by the effective use of advertising.

To gain a deeper insight into the overall economic impact of advertising, a discussion of these questions is appropriate.

Microeconomic Impact of Advertising

What happened when Dr. Pemberton ran that first advertisement for his new soft drink back in 1886? Perhaps by focusing on this tiny, seemingly insignificant event, we can understand some broader concepts about the economic impact of advertising.

Impact on the Product and Medium

First, there was an impact on the product itself. Some people became aware of something new at Jacobs' Pharmacy, and they may have decided to try the new drink the next time they were there. Others forgot about the ad, but when told at the pharmacy about the new drink, said, "Oh, yes, I've heard of that." Competitive stores may have been interested in selling the new drink: "What does Jacobs' have that we don't have?" In all cases, the initial impact on the product was sales, or at least an improved market attitude, as a result of the advertisement that was designed to gain additional sales.

There is also an economic impact on the medium that carries the advertisement—in this case the newspaper. Pemberton may have spent only $10 on his advertisement, but that was $10 the *Atlanta Journal* did not have before. That $10, mixed with the thousands of dollars from other advertisers, paid for the salaries of the journalists employed by the paper as well as the newspaper's rent, utilities, and overhead that month.

Impact on the Company

The second step in the chain reaction is the impact on the company that advertises the product. Pemberton was able to sell shares of stock in his company because investors were able to see sales occurring. As he advertised more and sold more, the company's stock became more valuable. At the same time, by advertising the availability of this new product, Jacobs' Pharmacy was able to attract new customers. This may have translated into increased sales of other products in the store, increased salaries for employees, and increased profits for the company.

Impact on Competitors

Other soft drink companies, seeing the advertisement for Coca-Cola, may have felt threatened by this newcomer. Their reaction might have been to lower their prices, to change their product, to advertise more, or to do nothing and just watch. In reality, as Coca-Cola achieved more and more success, imitators did appear on the scene. This spurred Coca-Cola to concentrate on standardizing the quality of its product and to use more advertising aimed at creating *brand loyalty,* as many of the slogans illustrated earlier in Ad Lab 1-A show.

Coca-Cola Illustrates the History of Modern Advertising

A. Coca-Cola was already in wide distribution "at all (soda) fountains" before the Ford name became a household word. In those days, only the wealthy could afford an automobile, and it was still considered quite avant-garde. Thus, it was an attractive and interesting association for Coke illustrated in this 1905 advertisement.

B. With the "charm of purity," a single Coke, one of 6,000,000 per day, was served by a white-uniformed bellhop in this classic 1925 advertisement.

C. Coca-Cola discovered the benefits of merchandising very early. This 1934 tray with pictures of famous movie stars Maureen O'Sullivan and Johnny Weismuller (Tarzan) proved to be appealing to their fans.

D. While many ads of the 1930s showcased movie stars, later advertising, such as this 1943 ad, reflected life during wartime. Coke followed the troops with a total of 64 bottling plants shipped abroad during the war and set up as close as possible to combat areas in North Africa, Europe, and the Pacific. An order from Coca-Cola's president gave the assurance that "every man in uniform gets a bottle of Coke for 5¢ wherever he is and whatever it costs the company."

E. As Coca-Cola spread around the world, ads and news coverage in major American magazines continued to echo the themes of refreshment and availability. The *Time* magazine cover that appeared in the 1950s describes Coke as the world's "friend."

G. When the new Coke formula was introduced in 1985, so many consumers were vocal in their opposition to the change that Coca-Cola reintroduced its original drink as Coca-Cola Classic. The introductory campaign played off the familiar and popular slogan, "It's the Real Thing" by promoting "The Real Choice" to consumers.

H. Patriotic themes and modern American lifestyles typified Coca-Cola ads in the mid-80s.

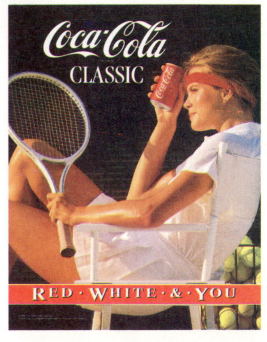

F. "I'd like to teach the world to sing in perfect harmony. I'd like to buy the world a Coke and keep it company." A product such as Coca-Cola rarely changes; society, though, is constantly changing. Consequently, the advertising must change to reflect current lifestyles. An indication of Coke's success as the world's number one consumer product was the flashing sign at Times Square that greeted the Apollo astronauts returning from their moonflight: "Welcome Back to Earth, Home of Coca-Cola."

I. Max Headroom, the first computerized celebrity presenter, was a
popular symbol of New Coke for
several years.

J. Coke classic was supported by two
advertising ideas in 1987: one, that
Coca-Cola is (and always has been)
a part of your life; and two, that you
can't beat the feeling—which related both to the product and to the
lifestyle associated with the product.

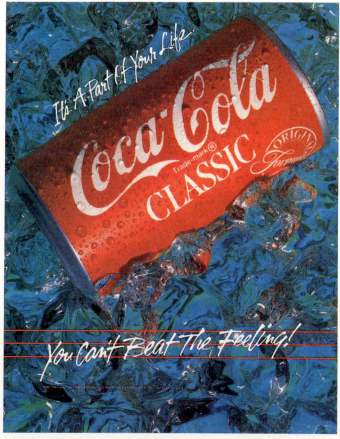

Impact on Customers

As competitors are influenced, so is the community of consumers at whom the advertising is aimed. Before the advent of Coca-Cola, people were limited in their choice to whatever soft drinks were currently available. The moment Coke was advertised, though, Pemberton created wider consumer choice. Then, as imitators appeared and advertising offered consumers *selection alternatives,* they had an even greater choice.

Impact on the Business Community

Finally, advertising has an impact on the general business environment and on the business cycle. For example, in a recent annual report, the Coca-Cola Company specifically pointed out the effect building a new bottling plant has on the local business environment in some less-developed countries:

> Setting up a bottling plant means virtually creating a system of local suppliers—putting into business everything from construction firms to build the plant to truck service garages to glass manufacturing plants. Mechanics and salesmen must be trained, and in many cases local craftsmen must be recruited to set up plants to make cases for bottles.
>
> A glass plant set in motion to produce bottles for Coca-Cola may also eventually produce bottles for milk, medicine, and many other products that make contributions to the local economy.

Macroeconomic View of Advertising

Looking at the economic impact of advertising by one firm as we have just done gives us some simple answers to the complex questions raised earlier. But how realistic are these answers in the larger world of national and international economics?

Importance of Mass Distribution

Most economists seem to believe that mass production has been the great stimulus to the success of our free enterprise system, giving it credit for making tremendous selection alternatives available to American consumers, for maintaining low prices for most consumer goods, and for making possible the highest standard of living in the world.

However, the success of mass production is entirely dependent on having an efficient system of mass distribution. It requires a formidable network of warehouses, transportation facilities, wholesalers, distributors, dealers, packing plants, advertising media, salespeople, clerks, and stores to deliver the low-priced, mass-produced goods from the manufacturer to the consumer. This mass-distribution system, which includes promotional activities like advertising, has drawn a certain degree of criticism from consumer groups, legislators, and economists. The dirty words so often spoken—*middlemen's profits*—convey the implication of overpriced goods. Of course, the most conspicuous activity in the mass-distribution system is advertising, and that visibility alone contributes to advertising's role as a target of criticism.

While most people concede that advertising helps the individual firm, they disagree greatly about the benefits of advertising to the economy as a whole. The questions raised earlier, therefore, should be discussed from a macroeconomic point of view.

Effect of Advertising on Competition

The complaint is often heard that small companies, or newcomers to an industry, can't possibly compete with the immense advertising budgets of big business. The belief seems to be that advertising restricts competition. Let's look at two specific cases for example: beer and automobiles.

It has often been said that small beer companies have been driven out of business by the big breweries with their enormous advertising expenditures. Is this true?

The fact is, the number of breweries has indeed been declining for more than a generation. And beer is one of the most highly advertised products. Thus, it may be that intense competition does indeed tend to reduce the number of businesses in an industry, and those that remain must compete vigorously for consumer dollars. However, it also may be that the firms eliminated through competition were those that served the consumer least effectively.

No advertiser is large enough to completely dominate the whole country geographically. Regional brands of beer outsell national brands in many areas. Local oil companies, likewise, compete very successfully with national oil companies on the local level (see Figure 1–22). And nonadvertised store brands of food compete with nationally advertised brands on the very same shelves.

In industries characterized by heavy advertising expenditures, though, it is certainly true that advertising may act as one of the barriers to market entry by new competitors. In fact, in some markets those brands that were the original pioneers probably enjoy the protection of very high barriers. But studies have indicated that this is because of consumer perception, not

costs.[9] Furthermore, the necessity for a new company to spend heavily on plants and machinery is also a barrier to entry and usually a far more significant one than marketing costs. This is certainly borne out by the automobile industry.

For many years, it was said that a new manufacturer could never compete in the United States because the big four American automakers, with their mighty advertising campaigns, had a monopolistic stranglehold on the American market. Today there are only three major auto manufacturers in the United States, but the number of automobiles successfully marketed here by foreign manufacturers has steadily increased since 1950. The barrier to entry, therefore, has obviously *not* been marketing costs but rather manufacturing costs.

Certain well-known Keynesian economists, such as Galbraith and Samuelson, have held that advertising creates industrial concentration. They point out that those companies which dominate particular industries invariably have the largest advertising budgets. But this, of course, raises the chicken-or-the-egg question. Which came first?

Studies conducted by Aaker and Myers to discover this relationship of advertising expenditures to industrial concentration concluded, "There is a positive relationship, but it is weaker than might be expected."[10] Overly simplistic statements that attribute unreasonable power to advertising fail to acknowledge the importance of other, usually more significant influences such as product quality, price, convenience, and customer satisfaction. Hershey Foods' chocolate bars, for instance, achieved and maintained market dominance for many years before spending any money on advertising (see Figure 1–23). Interestingly, while Hershey only began advertis-

FIGURE   1–23

A holiday season magazine ad for HERSHEY'S KISSES Chocolates grabs the reader's attention and focuses it directly on the product and its colorful foil wrapping. What more needs to be said? Hershey Foods realized great success over the years in spite of the fact that the company didn't start advertising until 1969.

ing its products in 1969, today it consistently ranks in the top 100 advertisers nationally.[11]

Businesses compete in many ways—for employees, plant and warehouse locations, materials, customers, and so on. Competition also occurs not only between companies in the same industry but between companies in different industries. An auto manufacturer is obviously competing with other automakers for consumer patronage. But the firm is also competing for the consumer's discretionary dollar with boats, air travel, new homes, and other products. As the number and variety of products increase, interindustry competition also increases.

The most obvious and most public form of competition is advertising. But does intensely competitive advertising actually result in increased or decreased competition? As we have seen, this is a tangled question with no simple answer. The fact is that heavy advertising may encourage competition in some cases and discourage it in others.

Effect of Advertising on the Value of Products

Why do most people prefer Coca-Cola to some other cola? Similarly, why do more women prefer Estée Lauder to some other unadvertised, inexpensive perfume? Is it because the advertised products are better products? Possibly. But certainly not necessarily.

Advertising can add perceptual value to a product in the consumer's mind. For example, what do you think most people would prefer to buy: an unadvertised brand of denim pants or Levi's?

Dr. Ernest Dichter, a psychologist known as the father of motivational research, has supported the view that the *image* of a product, which is produced partially by advertising and promotion, *is an inherent feature of the product itself.*[12] Further studies have concluded that while advertising may say nothing directly about the quality of a product, the positive image conveyed by advertising may denote quality, make the product more desirable to the consumer, and thereby add value to the product.[13] It is for this reason that even though most aspirin is the same, people pay more for Bayer than for an unadvertised house brand (as in Figure 1–24).

This fact was borne out in a landmark court case between the Federal Trade Commission (FTC) and the Borden Company in the 1960s. The FTC accused Borden of selling milk of "physically identical and equal quality" at different prices. The Borden Company justified the price differences by pointing out that it sold the higher-priced milk under a nationally branded label and the rest under private labels. In 1967, the U.S. Circuit Court of

FIGURE   1–24

As prices have climbed steadily upward, many consumers have switched to unadvertised house brands to save money. Many others, though, prefer the convenience and confidence of buying nationally advertised brands. One of the benefits of our system is this freedom of choice.

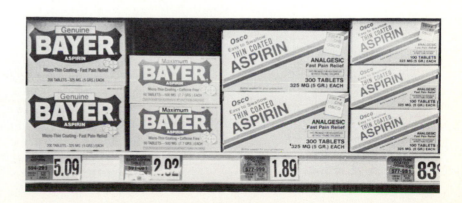

Appeals issued a decision saying, in effect, that the price differential represented *the added value that had been given to the branded product through extensive advertising and promotion.*[14]

Advertising can also create utility value by showing consumers new uses for products. Arm & Hammer Baking Soda has done this effectively. Television commercials demonstrating its air-purifying qualities in refrigerators and its water-purifying qualities in swimming pools have added a new dimension to an old product.

One advantage of the free market system is that consumers can choose the values they want in the products they buy. If price is important, for example, they can buy an inexpensive economy car. If image and luxury are more important, they can buy a fancy sedan or a racy sports car. Many of our wants are emotional, social, or psychological rather than functional. Advertising allows people in a free society the opportunity to satisfy those wants.

Effect of Advertising on Prices

If advertising adds value to products, then it follows that advertising also adds costs. Right? And if companies stopped all that expensive advertising, then products would cost less. Right? Wrong.

There is no question that in some cases advertised products cost more than unadvertised products. However, the opposite is probably true in just as many cases. For example, Timex watches, which are heavily advertised, cost less than most less-advertised brands.

For years, Tylenol was not advertised. As an over-the-counter pain reliever, it was sold as an aspirin substitute for people who could not tolerate the side effects of aspirin. It sold for $2.85 per 100 tablets. Datril was then introduced and advertised as having an identical formula with identical results. It sold for $1.85 per 100 tablets. Tylenol immediately dropped its price and began to advertise. Thereafter, the two engaged in heavy, competitive promotion, and prices continued to fall.

In recent years, the Federal Trade Commission and the Supreme Court have ruled that because advertising has the competitive effect of keeping prices down, professional people such as attorneys and accountants must be allowed to advertise.

Any broad, sweeping statements about the positive or negative effect of advertising on prices are likely to be too simplistic. Nevertheless, some important points can be made about the relationship between advertising and prices:

1. As one of the many costs of doing business, advertising is indeed paid for by the consumer who buys the product. The amount spent on advertising, though, is usually very small compared with total sales. Nevertheless, it may increase the cost of some products.
2. As pointed out earlier, advertising is just one element of the mass-distribution system. This system enables many manufacturers to engage in mass production. The long, uninterrupted runs used in mass production lower the unit cost of products. These economies of scale can then be passed on to consumers in the form of lower prices. In this indirect way, advertising may be credited with lowering prices.
3. Many industries, like agriculture, utilities, and oil, have been so heavily regulated by the government that advertising has had no effect on their prices whatsoever. In recent years, the government has been deregulat-

ing certain industries in an effort to return free market pressures on prices. In these cases, advertising does affect price—often downward, sometimes upward.

4. Our economic system is complex and dynamic with a whole dictionary full of different market structures operating at the same time. These include pure competition, pure monopoly, monopolistic competition, monopsony, discriminating monopoly, bilateral monopoly, and oligopoly. Marketing and advertising practices differ widely from one market structure to another. So the impact of advertising on prices also varies.

5. Price competition is perhaps most evident in retailing. However, even though prices are featured in many advertisements, there is less price competition than most people realize. Price is only one basis for competition. In retailing, store location, service, size of selection, reputation, clientele, and store image are also very important. In manufacturing, companies attempt to market products that are different from those of competing firms. As a result, the main subject of competition and advertising is *product differentiation*—"Why our product is superior"—not price. In price competition, advertising forces prices down; in nonprice competition, advertising tends to hold prices up.

Effect of Advertising on Consumer Demand

Critics of advertising sometimes accuse marketers of using their massive advertising expenditures to foist unwanted products on the public—of creating consumer demand where none existed before. The question of what effect advertising has on total consumer demand is extremely complex. Both economists and advertising professionals have puzzled over this relationship. Numerous studies show general agreement that promotional activity has some effect on aggregate consumption but no agreement as to the extent. More significant, though, is the effect of many other social and economic forces, including technological advances, education of the general populace, increases in population and per capita income, and revolutionary changes in lifestyle. These forces have a dynamic impact on the demand for different products.

For example, the demand for automobiles, mopeds, televisions, instant foods, and pocket calculators has expanded at a tremendous rate, thanks in part to advertising but especially to favorable market conditions. At the same time, advertising has done little to slow the decline in popularity of such items as men's and women's hats, train travel, fur coats, and home permanents.

We might conclude, therefore, that advertising can help to get new products off the ground by stimulating total consumer demand for the product class. But in declining markets, advertising can only hope to slow the rate of decline. We can also conclude that in growing markets, advertisers generally compete for shares of that growth. In declining markets, they compete for each other's shares.

Effect of Advertising on Consumer Choice

If the greatest area of competition is product differentiation, then logically, manufacturers are always looking for ways to make their products different, or at least make them seem different, in order to appeal to a greater number of consumers. For example, look at the long list of automobile models, sizes, colors, and features available to attract the most discriminating buyers. Similarly, grocery shelves may carry 15 to 20 different brands of breakfast cereals—something for everybody (see Figure 1–25).

The freedom to advertise gives manufacturers an incentive to create new brands and improve old ones. When one brand reaches a point of market dominance, smaller brands may disappear for a short time. But inevitably, the moment a better product comes along and is advertised skillfully, the tables suddenly turn and the dominant brand rapidly loses to the new, better product. What Walter Taplin pointed out many years ago still holds true today: the consumer is the master, and "the producer and advertiser is the slave."[15]

Effect of Advertising on the Business Cycle

The relationship between advertising and the gross national product (GNP) has also been a subject of debate for many years. Friends of advertising point with pride to this century's growth in GNP, disposable income (DI), and personal consumption expenditures (PCE). They boast that advertising has been the primary cause of all these blessings.[16] Critical economists, on the other hand, have traditionally tended to see advertising as a wasteful expenditure with little relationship to the overall business cycle.[17]

Both sides make very strong points and back up their claims with numerous studies. The problem with most of these studies, though, is that with so many uncontrollable social and economic factors constantly pushing and pulling on the economic system, studying the effects of one small element like advertising is nearly impossible. The results are invariably questionable.

The most positive study to date was conducted by Charles Y. Yang and published in 1964. He concluded that an increase in advertising expenditures of 1 percent over the rate of increase in the gross national product

FIGURE   1–25

The competition for consumer dollars is fierce in the $5.2 billion ready-to-eat cereal business. The freedom to advertise has brought a wide diversity in consumer choices to the grocery store shelves.

can produce an increase in consumption of .1 percent. Subsequent increases in investment and income are then generated, finally resulting in $16 of increased income generated by each $1 of increased advertising expenditure.[18]

This, of course, assumes increases in GNP. What about when GNP decreases? And if what he says is true, why would GNP ever decrease if all we have to do is spend more advertising dollars? Again we're left with the chicken-and-egg syndrome.

Historically, when business cycles dip, worried executives cut advertising expenditures. That may help immediate short-term profits, but numerous studies have proved that businesses that cut their advertising expenses least during a recession fare better after the recession.[19] No study, though, has ever shown that if everybody just kept advertising, the recessionary cycle would be turned around.

We must conclude, therefore, that when business cycles are up, advertising contributes to the increase. When business cycles are down, advertising may act as a stabilizing force, but up to now, the extent has been impossible to measure.

Economic Impact of Advertising in Perspective

To individual businesses like Coca-Cola, Procter & Gamble, Sears Roebuck, the local car dealer, and the little appliance store on the corner, advertising pays more in results than it costs. If advertising did not pay, businesses and other institutions would not use it, and the various news and entertainment media, which depend on advertising for financial support, would all go out of business.

For the consumer, advertising costs less than most people believe. The various media that carry the advertisements we see are amazingly efficient. The cost of a bottle of Coke includes about a penny for advertising. And the $8,000 price tag on a new car includes an advertising cost of less than $100.

To the economy as a whole, the importance of advertising may best be demonstrated by the *abundance principle.* This states that in an economy that produces more goods and services than can be consumed, advertising serves two important purposes: (1) it keeps consumers informed of their selection alternatives and (2) it allows companies to compete more effectively for consumer dollars.

The American economy produces an enormous selection for consumers. More than 10,000 different items are on the average supermarket shelf. Each of the three American automobile manufacturers markets dozens of models. Clothing and shelter alternatives are seemingly endless. In short, the American economy is characterized by many suppliers competing for the consumer dollar. This competition generally tends to produce more and better products at similar or lower prices.

As a competitive tool, advertising has stimulated this phenomenon. Moreover, because American consumers have more income to spend after their physical needs are satisfied, advertising also stimulates the innovation and sale of new products to satisfy consumers' social and psychological needs.

However, no amount of advertising can achieve long-term acceptance for products that do not meet consumer approval. Less than a dozen of the 50 best-known automobile brands developed in this century are still with us despite major advertising expenditures. Only 2 of the nation's 10 largest

FIGURE   1–26

Studebaker was an old, reliable company that had originally achieved success building top-of-the-line prairie schooners in the 19th century. In spite of spending millions of dollars to advertise Studebaker as "the postwar leader in motor car style," however, that company as well as many others from the 1940s and 50s is no longer with us.

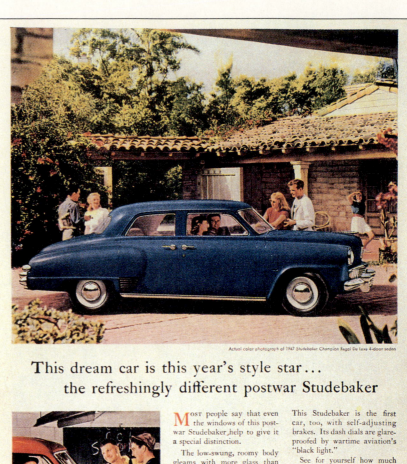

industrial firms in 1900 remain in the top 10 today despite massive advertising (see Figure 1–26).

As advertising has stimulated a healthy economy, it has also stimulated a financially healthy consumer who is more informed, better educated, and more demanding. One of the loudest demands of consumers has been for accountability by manufacturers in their advertising, thus leading to an unprecedented level of social and legal regulation, the subject of our next chapter.

Summary

Advertising is defined as the nonpersonal communication of information usually paid for and usually persuasive in nature, about products, services, or ideas by identified sponsors through various media.

As a marketing tool, advertising serves several functions:

1. To identify products and differentiate them.
2. To communicate information about the product.
3. To induce the trial of new products by new users and to suggest repurchasing by existing users.
4. To stimulate a product's distribution.
5. To increase product use.
6. To build brand preference and loyalty.

Aside from marketing, advertising may also serve several other functions: communication, education, economic, and social.

There are many different types of advertising. It may be classified by target audience (e.g., consumer, industrial), by geography (e.g., local, international), by medium (e.g., radio, television), or by its function or purpose (e.g., product advertising, noncommercial advertising, and direct-action advertising).

Advertising began in early times when most people could not read or write. The post–World War II era has been marked by the growth of television advertising, intense marketing competition, and increased attempts to differentiate products through positioning strategies or other techniques.

The economic impact of advertising can be likened to the opening shot in billiards—a chain reaction that affects the company that advertises as well as its competitors, customers, and the business community.

On a broader scale, advertising is often considered the trigger on America's mass-distribution system that enables manufacturers to produce the products Americans want in high volume, at low prices, with standardized quality. Disagreement exists, however, about whether advertising encourages or discourages competition, adds value to products, makes products more or less expensive, affects total consumer demand, and narrows or widens consumer choice, and whether it has any real effect on national business cycles.

While controversy surrounds most of these economic issues, the importance of advertising can best be understood by accepting the abundance principle. This states that in an economy that produces more goods and services than can be consumed, advertising keeps consumers informed of their selection alternatives and helps companies compete more effectively.

Questions for Review and Discussion

1. How does the advertising for the American Cancer Society compare with the standard definition of advertising?
2. What examples can you give to demonstrate the primary functions of advertising today?
3. Is an advertisement for an office computer industrial advertising, trade advertising, or professional advertising?
4. What is the difference between the media used for local and for regional advertising?
5. How did the railroad affect the growth of advertising?
6. What examples can you think of (or conceive of) in which companies or organizations use a demarketing strategy?
7. As a consumer, are you more likely to save money by buying at a store that doesn't spend a lot of money on advertising? Explain.
8. In what ways can advertising increase a product's value?
9. How would you explain the overall effect of advertising on consumer choice?
10. How would the advertising for a new shopping center affect the local economy in your area? Are retailers in your area advertising more or less because of present economic conditions?

2

The Social and Legal Aspects of Advertising

On a flight from New York to Chicago, John O'Toole, then chairman of Foote, Cone & Belding advertising agency, sat next to a woman who inquired what he did for a living. When he responded that he was in advertising, she stated somewhat scornfully, "I think advertising is destroying our language."

O'Toole debated whether to launch into his "case for national advertising as a preserver of clear, concise, colorful, and correct English." He refrained from that. Nor did this well-known poet tell her that advertising is "a portal for introducing new constructions and expressions into a constantly evolving language to enrich and renew it." He felt the flight would be far too short for such a long dissertation.

As he reported in a memo to his agency, he decided simply to cite an institution that, in his thinking, has done a far more thorough job of debasing language than advertising.

Regular readers of these memos will assume that I took out after the federal government, or Harvard Business School, or that perennial favorite, the legal profession. Not so.

I didn't have to look beyond the vehicle we were in to find a first-class miscreant: the airline industry.

I showed her this paragraph I had just read in the in-flight magazine.

"TWA is required by the federal government to ensure compliance with the regulations concerning smoking on board its flights. For the comfort and safety of all, we earnestly solicit each passenger's cooperation in strictly observing these rules. Persistent disregard could result in the offending passenger's disembarkation."

What I think they're saying, amidst all the passive and conditional gobbledygook (I like that one, too), is this:

"The government makes us enforce the no-smoking rules. Please obey them or we'll have to throw you off the plane."

Now being thrown off a plane, presumably in flight, is a disquieting prospect. So perhaps they deliberately obscured the thought with gratuitous verbiage to soften its impact. Whatever the motive, comprehension is the victim.

Pompous as it sounds, *disembarkation* is a more accurate word to describe getting off an airplane than the one they normally use: *deplaning*. "We will be deplaning tonight," says the stewardess, "through the forward exit." I have an image of passengers standing at the forward exit picking tiny planes off their persons and dropping them out into the darkness. We are not deplaning. Actually the plane is depeopling. But what's wrong with just "getting off"? Then there's the matter of redundancy in airline talk. "For your own personal safety and convenience," for example. Or, "Be sure your seat backs and tray tables are returned to their original upright positions."

Compare that kind of language, which is the airline itself speaking, to the precision of advertising speaking for the airline: "Fly the friendly skies." "You're going to like us." "Doing what we do best."

Anyone who concludes advertising is the offender deserves to be disembarked.[1]

John O'Toole, currently executive vice president of the American Association of Advertising Agencies (see "People in Advertising," Chapter 1), happens to be one of the most articulate "defenders of the faith" in advertising. However, the advertising industry has had to deal with a growing number of equally articulate critics who condemn it for a wide variety of sins far worse than the simple misuse of the English language. These attacks have led to a stream of actions on the part of consumer groups, business, and governmental bodies to regulate what advertisers say and do in their advertising.

In this chapter, we will address the major social criticisms of advertising. Then we shall examine the methods that have been used by government, business, the advertising industry, and consumer groups to regulate advertising in an effort to remedy advertising abuses that have led to many of the criticisms.

SOCIAL CRITICISMS OF ADVERTISING

Advertising is the most visible activity of business. What a company may have been doing privately for many years suddenly becomes public the moment it starts to advertise. By inviting people to try their products, companies also invite public criticism and attack if their products do not live up to the promised benefits. Defenders of advertising say it is therefore safer to buy advertised than unadvertised products. Because makers of advertised items are putting their company name and reputation on the line, they will try harder to fulfill their claims and promises (see Figure 2–1).

Advertising is widely criticized not only for the role it plays in selling products but also for the way it influences our society. As a selling tool, advertising is attacked for its excesses. Some critics charge that, at its worst, advertising is downright untruthful, and at best, it presents only positive information about products. Others charge that advertising manipulates people psychologically to buy things they can't afford by promising greater sex appeal or improved social status. Still others attack advertising for being offensive, in bad taste, or simply too excessive.

To adequately detail all the pros and cons of the charges against advertising would require volumes. However, it is important for the beginning advertising student to understand the essence of these attacks and the impact they have on advertising. Let's therefore examine some of the more common criticisms as they are usually expressed.

FIGURE   2–1

Advertising helps build a reputation for a product. Advertisers realize that if they don't fulfill advertising claims, they will damage their product's good name.

Advertising Debases Our Language

The very reasons John O'Toole likes advertising are the reasons defenders of traditional English usage don't like it. They feel advertising copy is too breezy, too informal, too casual, and therefore improper (see Figure 2–2). Advertising, they believe, has destroyed the dignity of the language.

Grammar rules and especially punctuation rules are commonly broken by advertising copywriters, and this truly infuriates the critics. R. J. Reynolds Tobacco Co. introduced the line "Winston tastes good like a cigarette should." The academic community created such a flap that the advertiser followed up with another commercial filmed on the steps of a university. When the student in the commercial voiced the famous slogan, another

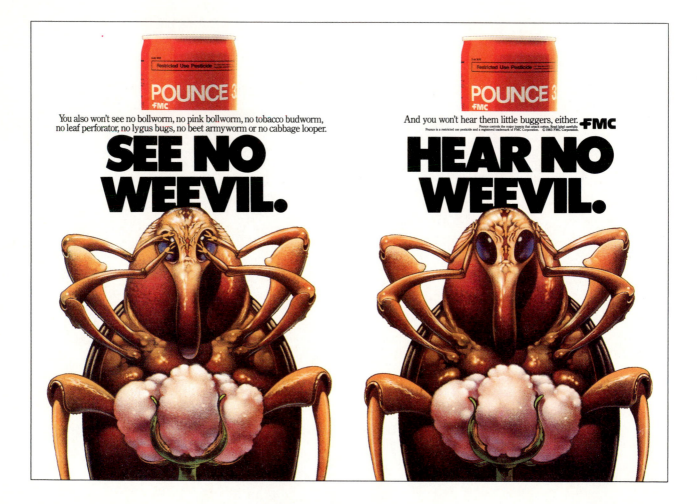

FIGURE   2–2

The misuse of the English language in the body copy of this ad might appall grammarians and might be used to bolster critics' assertions that advertising debases our language. Critics might also call the copywriter to task for stereotyping the audience (farmers). Nevertheless, this cleverly written ad won numerous awards from the advertising industry.

student in cap and gown quickly corrected her, saying: "Winston tastes good *as* a cigarette should." This temporarily quieted the critics, but the company continued to use the "like a cigarette should" slogan for many years.

The fact is, to do its job, advertising must speak to people. It must be understandable and readable. Advertising research shows that people respond better to a down-to-earth, conversational tone than to a more dignified, formal tone. Therefore, good copywriters develop a style that is descriptive, colorful, and even picturesque as well as warm, human, and personal. Because of the need for brevity, they try to use words that are simple, lively, and full of personality and to use punctuation to build a conversational tone rather than to construct purely grammatical sentences.

However, not all copywriters are good copywriters, and literary license is a feeble excuse for what is sometimes just plain bad English.

Advertising Makes Us Too Materialistic

Critics claim advertising adversely affects our value system because it suggests that the means to a happier life is the acquisition of more things instead of spiritual or intellectual enlightenment. Advertising, they say, encourages people to buy more automobiles, more clothing, and more appliances than they need, all with the promise of greater status, greater social acceptance, and greater sex appeal. For example, they point to the fact that millions of Americans own 20 or more pairs of shoes, several TV sets, and often more than one vehicle.

Frankly, all of us have needs and desires beyond the basics of food, clothing, and shelter. One benefit of a free society is that we can choose the degree to which we wish to indulge our desires, needs, and fantasies. Some people prefer a simpler life without an elegant house, fancy cars, and trips abroad, while others enjoy the material pleasures of a modern, technological society. There are advertising sponsors at both ends of that spectrum. Food companies offer natural products as well as convenience packaged goods. Shoe companies offer simple sandals as well as formal footwear.

Defenders of advertising also point out that material comfort is necessary before a person can devote time to higher cultural and spiritual values. Therefore, they say, the stress on material things doesn't rule out spiritual and cultural values. In fact, they believe it may create a greater opportunity for attaining such values since the satisfaction of a person's higher desires is more likely when that person's lower, more basic desires have been met.[2] They also like to point out that through its support of the media, advertising has brought literature, opera, drama, and symphonies to millions who would never have seen them otherwise.

Advertising Manipulates Us into Buying Things We Don't Need

One of the oft-heard criticisms of advertising is that it forces people to buy things they don't need by playing on their emotions. Underlying this criticism is a belief that the persuasive techniques of advertising are so powerful that consumers are helpless to defend themselves.

DESPITE WHAT SOME PEOPLE THINK, ADVERTISING CAN'T MAKE YOU BUY SOMETHING YOU DON'T NEED.

Some people would have you believe that you are putty in the hands of every advertiser in the country.

They think that when advertising is put under your nose, your mind turns to oatmeal.

It's mass hypnosis. Subliminal seduction. Brain washing. Mind control. It's advertising.

And you are a pushover for it.

It explains why your kitchen cupboard is full of food you never eat.

Why your garage is full of cars you never drive.

Why your house is full of books you don't read, TV's you don't watch, beds you don't use, and clothes you don't wear.

You don't have a choice. You are forced to buy.

That's why this message is a cleverly disguised advertisement to get you to buy land in the tropics.

Got you again, didn't we? Send in your money.

ADVERTISING
ANOTHER WORD FOR FREEDOM OF CHOICE.
American Association of Advertising Agencies

FIGURE 2–3

The American Association of Advertising Agencies has produced a series of well-thought-out ads that answer the major criticisms leveled at advertising. This ad uses a bit of sarcasm coupled with a striking visual to succinctly make its point.

The fact is, however, that no matter how much advertisers try to convince us that using their product will make us sexier or healthier or more successful, they can't *make* us buy the product if we don't want it (see Figure 2–3). No matter how many ads we see for disposable diapers, we aren't going to buy any if we don't have a baby. And even if an advertisement succeeds in convincing us to buy a product once ("This frozen pizza looked really great on TV"), it can't get us to buy the product again if we don't like it ("Ugh! This tastes like cardboard!").

Those who accuse advertising of manipulating consumers in effect have very little respect for people's decision-making abilities, assuming as they do that people are unable to resist advertising's hypnotic messages. But if advertising has such power to persuade, why is it that so many more products fail than succeed in the marketplace, and why have some products been highly successful with minimal or no advertising? (Hershey's candy comes to mind.)

As sociologist Michael Shudson points out in his book *Advertising, the Uneasy Persuasion,* the powers of advertising have been greatly exaggerated.[3] For one thing, people simply don't pay that much attention to ads. And when they do pay attention, they may not recall what product went with which ad (quick—which product is the "heartbeat of America"?). For another thing, most Americans are highly skeptical of advertising. As we shall see in a few pages, the public's main criticism of advertising is its lack of credibility. In one survey consumers reported their buying decisions were primarily influenced by company or product image and by word-of-mouth recommendations; only about 20 percent indicated that advertising directly played the major role in their choices.[4]

Another aspect of the manipulation argument is that advertising *creates* needs. Are underarm deodorants really necessary to life, or has advertising created an artificial need by making us feel anxious about "offending" body odors? Shudson suggests, "Any new consumer product that does not disappear quickly is probably related to deep social currents." In other words, products that sell are meeting some kind of existing need in people; they are not creating that need. The fact that critics of deodorants do not see a "need" for such products does not mean that users of the products don't perceive such a need. Do you *need* a VCR? Do you *need* frozen orange juice? Do you *need* ballpoint pens? These are all items you could live without but would probably buy anyway, even if they were not advertised. The role of advertising, then, is to help you make a decision about *which* VCR, frozen orange juice concentrate, or ballpoint pen brand to purchase.

Robert Samuelson, writing in *Newsweek* magazine, makes the case for the "sovereignty of the consumer."[5] He argues that rather than corporate America controlling consumer buying habits through advertising, it is, in fact, the other way around: consumers control the marketplace through their choices of how to spend their discretionary income. He points out that the most vital consumer choices "are often those involving broad economic, technological, and sociological changes beyond corporate control." For example, the microwave oven is today's best-selling consumer appliance not because it has been heavily advertised but because it fills an important need in the lives of two-income families.

In short, marketers have found that the only logical way to advertise and sell their products is to meet genuine needs and wants rather than to try to "invent" needs to go with otherwise useless products.

Advertising Is Excessive

One of the most common complaints about advertising is simply that there is too much of it. Consumer organizations protest "billboard blight" on the nation's highways. Local politicians criticize sign pollution in their communities. Advertisements reach us in cars, elevators, parking lots, hotel lobbies, and subways and in our homes on radio and television, in newspapers, and through the mail. According to most experts the average American is exposed to over 500 commercial messages a day. Some give even higher figures. According to the advertising critics, we are awash in a sea of commercials that make life less pleasant than it might otherwise be.

There is no doubt that we live in an overcommunicated society. With so many products from which we can choose (over 10,000 in the average supermarket), companies must often shout to be heard, and advertising is their megaphone.

Advertising professionals themselves are concerned about this. In an effort to control the ad proliferation and make their advertisements more effective, most media impose voluntary restrictions on advertising volume. This, of course, limits the supply of space and time and contributes to the rising cost of media ads.

Consumers' tolerance of advertising in the print media seems to be greater than in the broadcast media. Readers can simply turn the pages and ignore the advertising if they so desire. Broadcast media tend to be more intrusive and therefore receive greater criticism.

However, because mass distribution supports our free enterprise system, advertising volume is here to stay. And most Americans seem to accept this as the price they have to pay for free television, freedom of the press, and their high standard of living.

Advertising Is Offensive or in Bad Taste

Many people find advertising offensive to their religious convictions, morality, or political perspective. Others find the use of advertising techniques that emphasize sex, violence, or body functions to be in bad taste. (See Ad Lab 2-A.)

Taste is highly subjective. What is good taste to some is bad taste to others. And tastes change. What is considered offensive today may not be offensive in the future. People were outraged when the first advertisement for underarm deodorant was published in the *Ladies Home Journal,* but today, no one questions such an advertisement. Some people find liquor ads offensive, while others find them entertaining or informative.

Up until 1987, ads for birth control products were virtually absent from television, but fears about AIDS finally led cable and local TV stations to begin carrying carefully designed commercials for condoms. The ads had to meet certain restrictions specified by the stations, but the standards of taste for condom ads varied from station to station.[6] Some of the first ads to be accepted did not even mention the word *condom*. The AIDS scare has also led many print media, including *USA Today* and *The New York Times,* to reverse their policy against carrying condom advertising. However, the three major networks are still unwilling to accept condom ads—although numerous network affiliates have chosen to air them.

In the not-so-distant past, nude figures were rarely seen in print advertisements. Today, it is often featured in ads for grooming and personal hygiene products. Where nudity is relevant to the product being advertised, people are less likely to regard it as obscene or offensive.[7]

Often the products themselves are not offensive, but the way they are advertised may be open to criticism. Advertising frequently emphasizes the sensational aspects of a product, particularly a book or motion picture. Shock value may be used to gain attention, especially by inexperienced copywriters. However, this sensationalism is often a reflection of the tastes and interests of the American people. If the advertisements don't attract the people they seek, the advertising campaign will falter and die. The audience, therefore, has the ultimate veto authority by ignoring offensive material.

AD LAB 2-A   You, the Jury: Judge the Guilt or Innocence of These Ads

Laboratory Application

All these ads were submitted by readers to *Advertising Age* as candidates for "ads we can do without." Now it's your turn to judge. Which ones would you judge guilty of being offensive or in bad taste? Why?

FIGURE 2–4

Advertisers have realized that members of racial and ethnic groups
represent significant markets for
their products and services and thus
have developed ads aimed specifically at those markets.

It is unrealistic to assume that advertising, particularly mass advertising,
will ever be free of this criticism. But reputable advertisers try to be aware
of what the public considers to be tasteful advertising.

Advertising Perpetuates Stereotypes

Advertising has often been criticized for portraying members of racial and
ethnic groups in stereotypical ways and for perpetuating stereotypical sex
roles. However, advertisers have become increasingly sensitive to their
treatment of minorities and women, not only because they want to avoid
the bad publicity that results when watchdog groups protest their ads but
also because they do not want to alienate entire segments of their market.

Blacks, Hispanics, Italians, Chinese, Native Americans, and other members of minority groups are now being portrayed favorably in ads, not only
because of organized pressure but because it's just good business—these
groups represent sizable target markets for products. In fact, some advertisers have created campaigns designed to appeal to specific minority
groups (see Figure 2–4). In addition, new advertising agencies staffed with
minority personnel are succeeding in reaching minority markets.

The image of women in advertising has changed significantly in the past
few years. Feminists protested in the past that the great majority of ads

portrayed women either as homemakers and mothers who were constantly seeking advice and help from men or as sex objects whose role was to be dominated by men and to fulfill men's desires. Today, it is getting harder and harder to find ads that show women in the traditional housewife/mother role. Rather, women are being portrayed as corporate managers, doctors, lawyers, and even construction workers. In home settings, husbands are shown as having equal responsibility for such household tasks as cooking, cleaning, and taking care of the kids.[8]

This changing portrayal of women in advertising has not come about simply because advertisers did not want to antagonize feminists. Rather, it has occurred in response to changes in the marketplace. More than 50 percent of all women work outside the home, and more than 10 million of them are in professional and managerial careers. That is a sizable market of upwardly mobile consumers that many advertisers are attempting to reach (see Figure 2–5). In fact, as one advertising analyst put it, "The income of baby-boomer women is not going to diminish. Advertisers would be foolish to treat this as a fad."[9]

One aspect of advertising that still has feminists angry is the portrayal of women as "sex objects." Sex sells, and advertising has been making use of sex for decades. In print media in particular, sexually oriented ads have become more and more explicit. As one ad agency executive put it, "What's amazing is what you can get away with now. And over the next five years there will be even greater use of blatant sex in advertising because it's become part of our culture."[10] Many feminists do not object to the use of sex per se. In fact, Gloria Steinem, after accepting a steamy ad for Calvin

FIGURE   2–5

An increasing number of ads, like this one for Northwestern Bell, are featuring busy career women as opposed to the traditional housewife/mother. This change may be as much in response to market forces (working women are constituting a larger and larger target market) as to feminist pressures.

(SFX: MUSIC UP, AMBIENT NOISE, SHUFFLING PAPERS, ETC.) WOMAN (TO HERSELF): Well . . . it's been a long and productive day. Oh listen, Jerry, thanks an awful lot for the suggestion. We'll get back to this again next week, OK?

FEMALE VO ON PHONE INTERCOM: Mrs. Harrison, there's a phone call for you. It's your daughter.

WOMAN: I'll take it in my office, Pat.

SINGER VO: Drift away, drift away . . . How the time disappears . . . Just the blink of an eye and the days turn into years . . .

SINGER VO: Drift away, drift away . . . How the time drifts away . . .

DAUGHTER VO ON PHONE: I need some advice again, Mom.

WOMAN (AD LIB UNDER): Don't pressure yourself so much, honey. You just have to try to relax and get through it.

Klein's Obsession perfume to run in *Ms.* magazine, said, "Sexuality and nudity are a part of life, and if it's appropriate it's fine."[11] The feminist complaint has to do with ads that present women in demeaning ways or that imply violence toward or exploitation of women.

Advertising Is Deceptive

Perhaps the greatest criticism of advertising is that it attempts to deceive the public. Deception in advertising has also received the greatest regulatory scrutiny, as we shall see in the next section.

Critics define deceptiveness not only as false and misleading statements but also as any false impression conveyed, whether intentional or unintentional. Advertising deception can take a number of forms, and many of these are highly controversial with no hard-and-fast rules. Common practices considered deceptive include those listed in Ad Lab 2-B.

AD LAB 2-B   Unfair and Deceptive Practices in Advertising

The courts have held that these acts constitute unfair or deceptive trade practices and are therefore illegal.

False promises

Making an advertising promise that cannot be kept, such as "restores youth" or "prevents cancer."

Incomplete description

Stating some, but not all, of the contents of a product, such as advertising a "solid oak" desk without mentioning that only the top is solid oak and that the rest is made of hardwoods with an oak veneer.

Misleading comparisons

Making meaningless comparisons, such as "as good as a diamond," if the claim cannot be verified.

Bait-and-switch offers

Advertising an item at an unusually low price to bring people into the store and then "switching" them to a higher priced model than the one advertised by stating that the advertised product is "out of stock" or "poorly made."

Visual distortions

Making a product look larger than it really is—for example, a TV commercial for a "giant steak" dinner special showing the steak on a miniature plate that makes it appear extra large. Or showing a "deluxe" model that is not the same as the one offered at a "sale" price.

False testimonials

Implying that a product has the endorsement of a celebrity or an authority who is not a bona fide user of the product.

False comparisons

Demonstrating one product as superior to another without giving the "inferior" item a chance or by comparing it with the least competitive product available, such as comparing the road performance of a steel-belted radial tire with that of an average "economy" tire.

Partial disclosures

Stating what a product can do but not what it cannot do, such as claiming that an electrically powered automobile will go "60 miles per hour—without gasoline" and not mentioning that it needs an eight-hour battery recharge every 100 miles.

Small-print qualifications

Making a statement in large print ("Any new suit in stock— $50 off!") only to qualify or retract it in smaller type elsewhere in the ad ("With the purchase of a suit at the regular price").

Laboratory Application

What examples have you seen of deception?

Advertising must have the confidence of consumers if it is to be effective. Continued deception is self-defeating because, in time, it causes consumers to turn against a product. Furthermore, there is little evidence that deceptive advertising actually helps sales anyway.

Advertising puts the advertiser on record for all who care to look. Because of greater scrutiny by consumers and the government, it is in the advertiser's own interest to avoid trouble by being honest.

Defense of Advertising

Advertising professionals acknowledge that over the years advertising has often been used irresponsibly. But they like to use the analogy of a high-powered automobile: If a drunk is at the wheel, there's going to be a lot of damage. The problem, though, is not the car but the drunk at the wheel.

In other words, they admit that advertising has been and is sometimes still misused. But they believe the abuse that has been heaped on advertising as a marketing tool and as a social influencer is no longer justified and is so excessive as to make all advertising appear bad. In support, they point out that of all the advertising reviewed by the Federal Trade Commission in a typical year, 97 percent is found to be satisfactory. Moreover, they say, advertising benefits society in a number of ways. Economically, it encourages the development of new and better products, it gives consumers a wider variety of choices, it helps keep prices down, and it encourages

PEOPLE IN ADVERTISING

Robert J. Posch, Jr.

Associate Counsel
Doubleday & Company, Inc.

Robert J. Posch, Jr., is associate counsel of Doubleday & Company, Inc., where he is responsible for a variety of legal areas, including compliance with governmental regulation of printed material.

His background in both law and marketing brings a unique perspective to this role. Posch received his degree in law from Hofstra University, then went on to obtain his M.B.A. there and was elected to the National Honor Societies of Business and Marketing.

He has served in the legal department of Doubleday & Company for the past 10 years.

Posch believes that federal regulations governing advertising serve to protect both consumers and marketers. "The Federal Trade Commission," he explains, "seeks through these regulations to promote two objectives—to provide useful, truthful information to consumers and to maintain effective competition in the marketplace.

"One way the FTC does this," notes Posch, "is by enforcing minimal standards of advertising compliance. It will act against deceptive ads that influence consumers' buying decisions when such ads would harm either the consumer or the advertiser's competitor—and when it feels such action would be in the public interest."

competition. It also subsidizes the media, supports freedom of the press, and provides a means for the dissemination of public information about health and social issues as well as about products and services.

Nevertheless, the sins of the past still haunt advertising today. What was once an unchecked, free-swinging business activity is now a closely scrutinized and heavily regulated profession. The excesses with which advertising has been rightfully or wrongfully charged have created layer upon layer of laws, regulations, and regulatory bodies. These are used by consumer groups, government, special-interest groups, and even other advertisers to review, check, control, and change advertising.

GOVERNMENT REGULATION OF ADVERTISING

The strictest advertising controls are imposed by federal and state laws and by judicial interpretations of those laws. Enforcement is the task of various government agencies that must determine the scope and application of these laws and then act accordingly.

Regulation by the Federal Government

Among the major federal regulators of advertising are the Federal Trade Commission, the Federal Communications Commission, the Food and Drug Administration, the Patent and Trademark Office, and the Library of

How does the FTC determine whether an ad might be harmful to consumers? By reviewing it, says Posch, against these seven important standards:

1. Who is the audience? Ads directed at vulnerable groups, such as children, receive closer scrutiny from the FTC.
2. The FTC views an advertisement in its entirety. The total net impression is what counts.
3. Literal truth will not save an ad if it is misleading when read in its entire context. The advertiser must avoid deception by the use of half-truths or by failing to disclose material facts.
4. An ad may be found to be false and deceptive if any one of two possible meanings is false.
5. Statements of subjective opinion, or puffery, may be actionable by the FTC if they give the impression of being factual or relate to material terms.
6. If an ad contains a mock-up that does not accurately represent the specific product or service it is selling, the ad may be found to be deceptive.
7. The advertiser has a continuing obligation to substantiate all material claims made in the ad, such as test results, price claims, and user endorsements.

Another way the FTC seeks to promote truth in advertising, says Posch, is by encouraging broader consumer information. "Since 1971," he notes, "it has actively encouraged truthful ads which make direct comparisons with competing products. Without the prodding of the FTC, ads probably would still be featuring 'comparisons,' mostly with Brand X."

Posch has written three legal guidebooks for marketers: *The Direct Marketer's Legal Advisor, What Every Manager Needs to Know about Marketing and the Law,* and *Marketing and the Law.*

His other writings include "Legal Outlook," a column in *Direct Marketing,* and articles in marketing publications such as the *Journal of Marketing* and *Fund Raising.* He is also a frequent speaker on law at colleges and trade associations.

Congress (see Figure 2–6). The jurisdiction of these agencies is often overlapping, which can make the advertiser's efforts to comply with regulations even more difficult.

Federal Trade Commission

The Federal Trade Commission (FTC) is the major regulator of national advertising used to promote products sold in interstate commerce. Its efforts are largely directed toward consumer protection by policing the marketing done through the media. This includes monitoring advertising for deception and unfairness. What exactly constitutes deception and unfairness is a matter of some controversy, however.

Defining Deception Although the FTC was established in 1914, it did not acquire the power to pursue deceptive advertisers until passage of the

FIGURE   2–6   Federal regulators of advertising

Agency	Function	Agency	Function
Federal Trade Commission	Regulates all commerce between the states. Formed in 1914, the FTC is the leading federal regulatory agency for advertising practices and is the subject of the greatest criticism by the advertising profession.	Alcohol and Tobacco Tax Division	Has almost absolute authority over liquor advertising through its powers to suspend, revoke, or deny renewal of manufacturing and sales permits for distillers, vintners, and brewers found to be in violation of regulations.
Federal Communications Commission	Formed by the Communications Act of 1934, has jurisdiction over the radio, television, telephone, and telegraph industries. It maintains indirect control over advertising through its authority to license or revoke the license of all broadcast stations.	Office of Consumer Affairs	Is the chief consumer protection department in the federal government. Established in 1971, the OCA coordinates, maintains, and publicizes information on all federal activities in the field of consumer protection. Publications produced and circulated by the OCA include consumer education guidelines, monthly newsletters, and a consumer services column that is released to some 4,500 weekly newspapers.
Food and Drug Administration	Has authority over the advertising, labeling, packaging, and branding of all packaged goods and therapeutic devices. It requires full disclosure labels, regulates the use of descriptive words on packages, and has jurisdiction over the packaging of poisonous or otherwise hazardous products.	U.S. Postal Service	Has authority to halt mail delivery to any firm or person guilty of misusing the mails. The U.S. Postal Service maintains control over false and deceptive advertising, pornography, lottery offers, and guarantees which deceive or defraud.
Patent and Trademark Office	Regulates registration of patents and trademarks. It enforces the Trade-Mark Act of 1947.	Department of Agriculture	Closely monitors the distribution of misbranded or unregistered commercial poisons. The Department of Agriculture (USDA) works with the FTC to enforce regulations governing certain products.
Library of Congress	Registers and protects all copyrighted material including advertisements, music, books, booklets, computer software, and other creative material.		

Wheeler-Lea Amendment to the FTC Act in 1938. Once it acquired this power, it interpreted "deceptive" as referring to advertising that had "the tendency or capacity to mislead substantial numbers of consumers in a material way." Under this definition, the FTC did not have to prove actual deception—it needed only establish that an ad had a "capacity" for deception.

In 1983, the FTC issued what has become a controversial policy statement regarding its definition of deception. In that statement, the FTC defined as deceptive any ad in which "there is a misrepresentation, omission, or other practice that is likely to mislead the consumer acting reasonably in the circumstances, to the consumer's detriment."

This revised definition has been interpreted by many as putting a greater onus on the FTC to prove that deception has actually taken place. Furthermore, the requirement that a deceptive act be "to the consumer's detriment" means that more than just deception must be proved; the FTC

Agency	Function	Agency	Function
	The USDA Grain Division has regulatory authority over false and deceptive advertising for seeds and grain products. The Grain Division is also empowered to initiate action against violators.	Consumer Product Safety Commission	Was established in 1972 to develop and enforce standards for potentially hazardous consumer products. It derives its power from four acts: the Flammable Fabrics Act of 1954, the Federal Hazardous Substances Act of 1960, the Children Protection Act of 1966, and the Standard for the Flammability of Children's Sleepwear of 1972. It has jurisdiction over the placement of warning statements in advertisements and other promotional materials for products covered under these acts. Its authority extends to household products, toys, and hazardous substances that cause accidental poisoning. The Consumer Product Safety Commission actively investigates product advertising and labeling violations brought to its attention by consumers and consumer protection groups. Continued violations by product makers are grounds for prosecution and punitive action by the Attorney General.
Civil Aeronautics Board	Regulates air traffic and advertising of all air carriers engaged in interstate commerce.		
Securities and Exchange Commission	Was established in 1934 and has jurisdiction over all advertising of stocks, bonds, and other securities sold via interstate commerce. The SEC requires that public offerings of such issues contain full disclosure of all pertinent information on the company and the securities offered so that the prospective investor can make an informed buying decision. This disclosure must mention any negative elements that may affect the investment.		
Department of Justice	Normally does not initiate legal action against persons or firms charged with violating the federal laws governing advertising. Instead, the Department of Justice enforces these laws and represents the federal government in the prosecution of cases referred to it by other federal agencies.		

must show that consumer decisions were actually influenced in a material way. Finally, the reference to a "reasonable" consumer implies that the ad's effects on unthinking or ignorant consumers are not a main consideration—a major change from the previous definition of deception.

The FTC chairman who drafted the new definition, James C. Miller III, believed it would help the commission determine which cases are worth pursuing and would prevent it from having to deal with trivial cases. Critics of the new definition are worried, however, that it will now be harder and costlier to win deceptive advertising cases.[12] They fear that under the new rules advertisers will feel freer to engage in deceptive practices because they perceive the FTC as being more lax in enforcing its powers.

Court cases interpreting the new FTC definition have not helped matters. In a 1985 case, the 10th Circuit Court of Appeals refused to apply the new standard because it had not been "formally adopted," but in a 1986 case, the 9th Circuit Court of Appeals declared the FTC standard as binding on advertisers.[13] It will take a few years to see what actual effect the revised definition will have on the FTC's actions and effectiveness.

Defining Unfairness The FTC also has the authority to prosecute those who engage in "unfair" advertising. Again, however, what constitutes unfairness is a matter of controversy. According to FTC policy, unfairness exists when a consumer is "unjustifiably injured" or when there has been a "violation of public policy" (such as of other government statutes). Among practices that might be judged unfair are significant omissions of important information. In its 1984 case against International Harvester, for example, the commission found that the company's failure to warn of a safety problem was not deception but did constitute an unfair practice.[14] Advertising organizations have argued that the word *unfair* is vague and "can mean whatever any given individual's value judgment may assign to it."[15] As a consequence, they have lobbied in Congress to have the FTC's power to prosecute on unfairness grounds eliminated entirely. However, Congress has not been receptive to this proposal.

Substantiating Claims One of the things the FTC looks at closely in determining whether an ad is deceptive or unfair is whether the advertiser is able to substantiate the claims made about a product. In particular, the FTC monitors ads that cite survey findings, scientific studies, and the like and may ask to see substantiation of this cited research. Up until 1980, when Miller took over the FTC chairmanship, the commission had required that advertisers have *prior* substantiation of all claims, and this rule was supported by the courts. However, Miller questioned the need for prior substantiation in all cases and suggested that after-the-fact substantiation might be allowable in some cases. In 1984, the commission issued a new policy statement on substantiation, but the changes from the previous policy were minimal. Thus, advertisers are still expected to have supporting data in hand before running an ad, although the new policy does allow for postclaim evidence in some instances.[16] The other significant change is that the FTC will no longer solicit substantiation from advertisers other than those it is actively investigating for deceptive practices.

The FTC also closely scrutinizes ads that contain endorsements or testimonials (see Figure 2–7). Endorsement of a product by an "expert" must be based on actual use by the expert. If an ad implies that the endorser has superior qualifications for making the judgment stated, the endorser's qualifications must bear this out. An endorser or celebrity who offers a testimonial for a product also becomes responsible for any deception in the claims that person makes. Take the landmark case of Pat Boone's endorsement of Acne-Statin. He said, "With four daughters, we've tried the leading acne medication at our house, and nothing ever seemed to work until our girls met a Beverly Hills doctor and got some real help through a product called Acne-Statin." The FTC discovered that Boone had not investigated the claims he pronounced in the ad, that not all of Boone's daughters had used the product, and that none of them had had more than even a mild acne problem anyway. The upshot of the case was the FTC's conclusion that endorsers, like the companies that place the ads, must verify the claims before they go on the air or into print with them. In other words,

Martin Scorsese is challenging. Like his pictures. *Mean Streets. Alice Doesn't Live Here Anymore. Raging Bull. The Last Waltz. The King of Comedy.*

As a kid, he gobbled up films like popcorn. As an adult, he makes films, collects films, and leads the movement to preserve films.

Preservation. "The idea is to raise the consciousness of the studios, to make them realize that with the advent of cable, they had to start preserving their stuff. Even the stuff they think is no good. You can't make a value judgement. The old pictures that you think are no good, very often are 10 years later the most influential.

Classics like 'Psycho' and 'The Searchers' were panned in their own time. I found out that something like 20 years of Johnny Carson were erased because they needed the space.

The goal is to save everything."

Television. "I have TV on all the time, in every room. I have a library, American directors, obscure films, maybe 4,000 titles. It appears that my own films may have more of life on home video than in the theater. This means that composition, lighting, size of people in the frame will be affected, as will the choice of black and white or color, mono or stereo sound.

You have to be sure what you want to say will have as full an impact on the small screen as on the big screen."

The cinematic visions of filmmakers like Martin Scorsese challenge the manufacturer to offer video equipment capable of capturing the totality of their art in all its subtlety and nuance. Mitsubishi accepts that challenge.

For a detailed look at Mitsubishi telecommunication equipment for the home, send for our brochure, Mitsubishi: The Thinking Inside.

Martin Scorsese On Television.

▲ MITSUBISHI

Mitsubishi Electric Sales America, Inc., 5757 Plaza Drive, Cypress, CA 90630-0007

Television featured
Mitsubishi CK-3501 R.

FIGURE   2–7

Many advertisers use celebrities to promote their products. Any statements attributed to these celebrities in endorsement of the product are subject to FTC scrutiny for possible deception. Note that in this ad, film director Martin Scorsese is quoted extensively but makes no statements about the product itself. Yet the ad succeeds in associating a famous personality concerned about quality TV reproduction with the client's own televisions.

endorsers are not allowed to say anything the advertiser wouldn't be allowed to say.[17]

Making Affirmative Disclosures The FTC has also expanded its emphasis on affirmative disclosure, which means that advertisers must disclose not only the positive qualities of their products but also the negative ones, such as limitations or deficiencies. Examples of affirmative disclosure include EPA mileage ratings for automobiles, pesticide warnings, and statements that soft drinks containing saccharin may be hazardous to one's health.

Investigating Claims How does the FTC decide which advertisers to go after? Complaints against advertisements usually come from consumers, competitors, and the FTC's own monitors, which are actively engaged in examining ads in various media. Determination of whether a particular complaint will be investigated is made by the Bureau of Consumer Protection. Cases chosen for investigation are pursued by staff attorneys. The FTC has broad powers to investigate suspected violators and to demand information from companies being investigated. Following the investigation, the staff attorney makes recommendations for any action to be taken. If the commission determines that deception or unfairness has been used, the usual action is to issue a cease-and-desist order, prohibiting further use of the objectionable advertising. In the majority of cases, a consent decree is then signed by the advertiser, who agrees, without admitting guilt, to halt the advertising and to not indulge in the practice again. The small percentage of cases not resolved this way are submitted for adjudication. Advertisers judged to be deceptive or unfair in their advertising practices are subject to a civil penalty of up to $10,000 per incident.

The FTC may also require corrective advertising, in which a portion of the company's advertising for a period of time must be devoted to explaining that the previous advertising was inaccurate or misleading. The initial case that established the FTC's authority to order corrective advertising involved a Profile bread advertisement. The ad claimed that each slice contained fewer calories than slices of other brands. However, the ad did not mention that slices of Profile were thinner than those of other brands. The company was ordered to devote 25 percent of its advertising for one year to correct this misleading statement. In another case, Ocean Spray Cranberry Juice used the words "high-energy food" to describe its product. The FTC charged that the words were misleading because, technically, high-energy food means calories, a fact not recognized by many consumers. The company was required to spend 25 percent of its advertising for one year to explain the meaning of "high-energy food" and to confess that it means calories. For many years Warner-Lambert advertised Listerine as a cold and sore-throat remedy based on tests they had conducted. The FTC proved the tests were invalid. Not only was Listerine required to stop making such claims, but in a landmark case, it was called on by the court to run $10.2 million of advertising stating, "Listerine will not help prevent colds or sore throats or lessen their severity."

To prevent problems, the FTC is readily available to review advertising before it runs and to render "advance clearance" to the advertiser in an advisory opinion. The FTC also establishes advertising standards for the protection of consumers. To promote compliance with these standards, the FTC supplies advertisers, agencies, and the media with ongoing information about the regulations governing advertising in its *Industry Guides* and *Trade Regulation Rules.*

Federal Communications Commission

The seven-member Federal Communications Commission (FCC), established as a result of the Communications Act of 1934, has jurisdiction over the radio, television, telephone, and telegraph industries. Through its authority to license broadcasting stations and to remove a license or deny license renewal, the FCC has indirect control over broadcast advertising. This authority derives from the right of public domain over the airwaves and the mandate of broadcasting stations to operate in the public interest. The FCC stringently controls the airing of obscenity and profanity, and it has restricted both advertising content and what products may be advertised on radio and television. Even before Congress banned cigarette advertising on television and radio (per the Public Health Cigarette Smoking Act of 1970), the FCC required stations to run commercials about the harmful effects of smoking.

The FCC has now dropped many of its rules and regulations for both radio and television stations, having decided that marketplace forces can do an adequate job of controlling broadcast media. For example, the FCC no longer limits the amount of time that can be devoted to commercials and has dropped minimum requirements for local programs and news/public affairs programs. And stations no longer have to maintain detailed program and commercial logs. However, stations still keep records of commercial broadcasts so advertisers can be assured of value received for the advertising time they purchased.

Food and Drug Administration

A unit of the Department of Health and Human Services, the Food and Drug Administration (FDA) has authority over the labeling, packaging, and branding of packaged foods and therapeutic devices and has limited authority over nutritional claims made in food advertising (see Figure 2–8). It requires manufacturers to disclose all the ingredients on product labels, in all product advertising featured in stores, and in all accompanying or separately distributed product literature. The label must accurately state the weight or volume of the contents. Labels on therapeutic devices must give clear instructions for use. The FDA is authorized to require warning and caution statements on packages of poisonous or otherwise hazardous products. It regulates "cents off" and other promotional statements on package labels. The FDA also has jurisdiction over the use of accurate words (such as *giant* or *family*) to describe package sizes.

In recent years, the FDA has been keeping a particularly close eye on food ads that make health claims. Dairy industry ads that suggest milk will help prevent osteoporosis, cereal ads that claim their high-fiber product will help guard against cancer, and margarine commercials that proclaim the value of their product in reducing the risk of heart attack have been of particular concern. The FDA is worried that such ads don't tell the whole story and that consumers will make inappropriate assumptions about the health values of foods. Consumers may believe, for example, that simply eating certain foods will prevent diseases such as cancer and heart disease when, in fact, the foods at best only help deter these ailments. Although the FDA has not acted against such ads, it has issued voluntary guidelines for advertisers who make nutritional and health claims. These guidelines suggest that food manufacturers who promote the benefits of their product within a total well-balanced diet are on safe ground.[18]

FIGURE   2–8

The Food and Drug Administration scrutinizes food ads that make nutritional claims. If this ad had claimed that butter has fewer calories than margarine, the California Milk Advisory Board would have had to do some explaining to the FDA.

Patent and Trademark Office

A *trademark,* according to the Lanham Trade-Mark Act (1947), is "any word, name, symbol, or device or any combination thereof adopted and used by a manufacturer or merchant to identify his goods and distinguish them from those manufactured or sold by others." Ownership may be designated in advertising or on a label, package, or letterhead by the word *Registered,* the symbol ®, or the symbol ™. If a trademark is used illegally by another, the trademark owner can complain by notifying the violator in writing. If the illegal use continues, the trademark owner can ask the courts to order the violator to refrain from further infringement.

Ownership of a trademark can be lost for many reasons. Probably the most bitter and spectacular method of losing a trademark comes in court decisions that declare the trademark "generic," which means the term has come into common use and is now the dictionary name for the product. Advertising's very success may sometimes prove to be its failure. This is precisely what has happened to famous brand names like thermos, escalator, and cellophane. They have become so thoroughly identified with a useful article or common function that the public uses them as the generic name. When a trademark ceases to indicate that the product derives from one particular source, exclusive legal rights to it are in jeopardy. Other examples of lost trademarks include shredded wheat, yo-yo, cube steak, and trampoline.

Owners of most trademarks take particular care to prevent them from becoming generic. They always see that the trademark is distinguished from surrounding words and always followed by the generic name of the product (Band-Aid Brand Adhesive Bandages, Scotch brand tape, Kleenex tissues, Jell-O brand gelatin).[19] They never refer to the trademark in the plural. It is not three Xeroxes but three Xerox copies (see Figure 2–9).

Some useful trademark terminology is presented in Figure 2–10.

Library of Congress

All copyrighted material, including advertising, is registered and protected by the Library of Congress. A copyright issued to an advertiser grants the exclusive right to print, publish, or reproduce the protected ad for a period of time equal to the life span of the copyright owner plus 50 additional years. An advertisement can be copyrighted only if it contains original copy or illustrations. Slogans, short phrases, and familiar symbols and designs cannot be copyrighted. Although a copyright prevents a whole advertisement from being legally used by another, it does not prevent others from using the general concept or idea of the ad or from paraphrasing the copy and expressing it in another way.

The use of any original creative written, musical, illustrative, or other material by an outside source in an advertisement without the express written consent of its creator is an infringement of copyright that may constitute grounds for legal action. For this reason, advertisers and agencies obtain permission before they use creative material from any outside source.

Copyright is indicated in an advertisement by the word *Copyright,* the abbreviation *Copr.,* or the copyright symbol © near the name of the advertiser. An advertisement that has foreign or international copyright protection usually contains the year of copyright as well. These copyright marks

FIGURE   2–9

Xerox Corporation has conducted an active campaign to remind the public that the name Xerox is a registered trademark in an effort to keep the word from becoming generic.

are also used to denote protection in other forms of print advertising, including booklets, sales brochures, and catalogs.

The Courts

The courts became involved in a number of advertising issues in the 1980s. Chief among these issues were First Amendment protection of "commercial speech," the right of professionals such as lawyers and doctors to advertise, advertising infringements on the right to privacy, and lawsuits over comparative advertising.

Historically, the Supreme Court has distinguished between "speech" and "commercial speech" (defined as speech that promotes a commercial transaction), but in the last decade or so it has made a series of decisions suggesting that truthful commercial speech is entitled to full protection under the First Amendment.[20] In the summer of 1986, however, the Court made a ruling that many interpret as a setback to the First Amendment rights of commercial speech. The case in question involved advertising of gambling in Puerto Rico. Although gambling is legal there, a law prohibits casinos from advertising to the island residents; ads must be designed

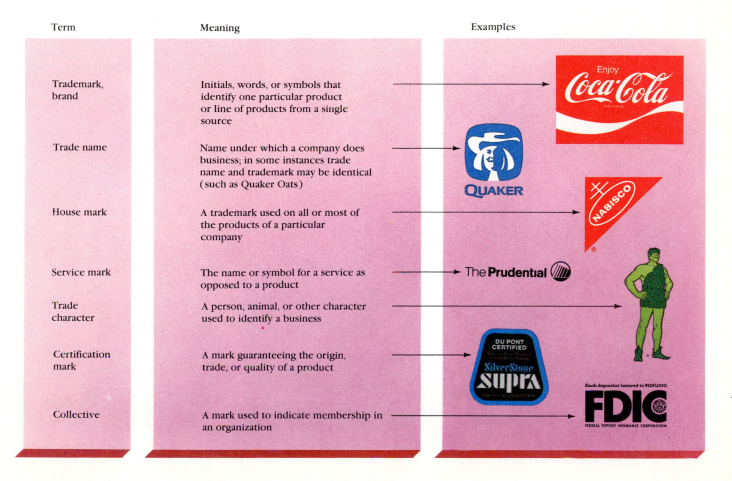

Term	Meaning	Examples
Trademark, brand	Initials, words, or symbols that identify one particular product or line of products from a single source	
Trade name	Name under which a company does business; in some instances trade name and trademark may be identical (such as Quaker Oats)	
House mark	A trademark used on all or most of the products of a particular company	
Service mark	The name or symbol for a service as opposed to a product	
Trade character	A person, animal, or other character used to identify a business	
Certification mark	A mark guaranteeing the origin, trade, or quality of a product	
Collective	A mark used to indicate membership in an organization	

FIGURE   2–10

Trademark terminology.

solely to attract tourists. Responding to a challenge of the law by one of the casino owners, the U.S. Supreme Court upheld the Puerto Rican legislature's power to ban the advertising, ruling that even truthful ads for goods and services may be restricted by the state to protect the "health, safety, and welfare" of its citizens.

What has the advertising industry upset are the implications of the decision for the advertising of other products that a government might deem harmful, particularly tobacco and alcohol. Justice William Rehnquist, in writing the majority decision, declared that it is up to state and federal legislatures, not the courts, to decide how best to regulate legal but potentially harmful businesses such as gambling, liquor, and tobacco.[21] It didn't take long after the Court decision for antismoking activists to begin lobbying for legislation that would ban cigarette ads in many states. Current FTC Chairman Daniel Oliver has come out in opposition to such bans, saying they represent "an attack on consumer sovereignty itself."[22]

Other significant Supreme Court decisions in the last decade or so have opened the way for advertising by professionals who were previously forbidden to advertise by state law or by professional associations. The landmark decision came in 1977 when the Court declared state bar association bans on members' advertising to be in violation of the First Amendment. Since that time, some 15 percent of the country's lawyers have tried advertising, and of those, more than 80 percent have been pleased enough with the results to continue the practice.[23] (See Figure 2–11.) As a result, the American Bar Association has issued guidelines for advertising by attorneys to help guard against deceptive and misleading legal ads.

In 1982, the Supreme Court upheld an FTC order allowing physicians and dentists to advertise, and since that time, advertising by medical and dental organizations has exploded, with ad expenditures for medical and

FIGURE   2–11

Before 1977, you couldn't have seen ads like this on TV because state bar associations banned advertising by lawyers. Now lawyers spend an esti-mated $60 million a year on TV ad time alone. Joel Hyatt, with 185 legal clinics in 22 states, spends about $5 million a year on TV advertising.

JOEL HYATT: A lot of accident claims never get a fair hearing because many people think you have to be rich to have a lawyer. But it costs you plenty to settle your own claim and you don't have to. At Hyatt Legal Services we took the fear out of legal fees. Before you sign something you don't understand, come in and talk to one of our lawyers. We'll help you fight for what you're entitled to. I'm Joel Hyatt and you have my word on it. We took the fear out of legal fees across the country and in your neighborhood.

FIGURE 2–12

Medical and dental organizations, from individual practitioners to clinics and hospitals, have become major advertisers in print, broadcast, and outdoor media since restrictions on this type of advertising were lifted in 1982.

Starting March 2, We're Lowering The Cost Of Mammograms To $50. Just Think What You Could Save.

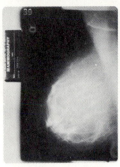

Considering 250 women in Rhode Island will die of breast cancer this year, a mammogram could save your life.

Which is why we urge you to take advantage of our special, low-cost

mammography screenings available only during March and April.

A mammogram is a safe, low-dosage x-ray that can detect breast cancer three to five years before

you can feel a lump.

To qualify, you must be over 40 years old with no symptoms of breast disease and must not have had a mammogram in at least two years.

All screenings will be done at the Ambulatory Patient Center at Rhode Island Hospital from 3:30 p.m. to 8:00 p.m. Special parking will be provided.

And if you can't afford the $50, don't worry. Nobody is going to be denied an important opportunity like this.

To register, call 277-4881 Monday through Friday, 9 a.m. to 4 p.m., starting February 17th.

And call soon. Because when it comes to detecting breast cancer, you can never be too early.

Rhode Island Hospital
Providence, Rhode Island

dental services reaching more than $62 million in 1984 alone[24] (see Figure 2–12). More recently, individual physicians and dentists have begun to use advertising, and their ads are becoming more visible.

Another issue recently addressed by the courts has been the violation of an individual's right to privacy. Most advertisers realize it is illegal to use a person's likeness in an ad without getting the individual's permission, but it has now also been ruled that using a "look-alike" of a famous person can violate that person's rights. The case that led to this decision involved an ad for Christian Dior that depicted a fictional wedding attended by a number of well-known celebrities. One of the celebrity wedding guests appeared to be Jacqueline Kennedy Onassis but was, in fact, a woman named Barbara Reynolds who worked professionally as a Jackie Onassis look-alike. Ms. Onassis sued on the grounds that the use of the look-alike without her permission constituted a violation of her right to privacy. The New York court agreed that the ad did indeed violate the state's law against the use of a person's "name, portrait, or picture" without the person's consent.[25] Other court cases have determined that the right of privacy continues after death. Thus, individuals who attempt to capitalize on a dead celebrity's name or likeness without obtaining permission from the person's estate are now likely to run afoul of the law in many states.

A final area in which the courts are seeing a lot of cases is comparative advertising. Comparative ads are those that claim superiority to competitors in some aspect: this paper towel is more absorbent than that paper towel; this analgesic provides more pain reliever than that one; this cold remedy is longer lasting than the others (see Figure 2–13). Because the FTC has been actively encouraging comparative advertising, it has not made a point of pursuing advertisers who may be getting a little carried away in their claims. However, competitors who are unhappy with the

American Express: The Disadvantages of Membership—No. 3 in a series.

MEMBERS ARE FINDING IT'S A SMALL WORLD AFTER ALL.

For years, American Express has been telling its members that their card is accepted the world over. Unfortunately, their world just doesn't measure up to Visa's.

Acceptance In The Visa World Is Three Times As Great.

The Visa card is accepted at three times as many places around the world as American Express, with over 5 million shops, hotels and restaurants in over 160 countries where you can use it.

Cash In Five Times As Many Places As Their World.

There are also nearly 200,000 bank branches around the world where you can get emergency cash with just your Visa card. And that's five times more places worldwide than if you just have an American Express card.

So whether it's a pair of silver earrings that catch your eye in Paris, or you need cash to catch a cab crosstown, the Visa card makes it simple.

If these facts have made you a little skeptical about the privileges of membership, join the club. Or better yet, don't.

It's Everywhere You Want To Be.

FIGURE   2–13

With encouragement by the FTC to "name names," comparative ads have flourished in the last few years. Although we often associate comparative advertising with headache remedies, laundry detergents, and breakfast cereals, financial services have entered the comparative fray as well. Here Visa turns the tables on American Express's "The Privileges of Membership" campaign with its own "Disadvantages of Membership" series.

treatment their products are getting in comparative ads have found recourse for civil action under the Lanham Act, which states that "any person who believes that he is or is likely to be damaged by the use of [a] false description or representation" of goods or services can sue an advertiser. Thus, in 1984, a federal district court judge ruled that ads run by a company called Jartran contained "false, misleading, deceptive, and incomplete statements of fact" about its rival, U-Haul, and ordered Jartran to stop running the ads and to pay U-Haul $40 million in damages.[26]

For a comparative ad to be legally defensible, it must truthfully compare its own product with the competitor's in terms of some objectively measurable characteristic. When it comes to documenting these comparative claims, however, some litigants have succeeded only in confusing or annoying the judges handling their case. This happened when Procter & Gamble and Chesebrough Pond's sued each other for false advertising, each alleging that the other's ads for hand lotion made false claims of superiority. After hearing more than seven days of "scientific" testimony, the judge commented that much of it had been "incomprehensible," adding, "The parties are sparring to obtain commercial advantage over what is at most a cosmetological distinction." He concluded that both parties should probably remove ad claims that their product is the most effective available.[27] Despite the fact that several suits litigated under the Lanham Act have resulted in a loss to both parties, competitors continue to resort to this civil means of sparring with one another.

Regulation by State Government

Much media advertising falls into the category of interstate commerce and is, therefore, regulated by federal agencies. Intrastate advertising, however, including local newspaper, radio, and television advertising, is under the jurisdiction of state laws and enforcement agencies. A great deal of state legislation governs advertising, and it is often based on the "truth-in-advertising" model statute developed by *Printer's Ink,* the pioneer trade paper of the industry, which is no longer published. The statute holds that any maker of an advertisement found to contain "untrue, deceptive, or misleading" material shall be guilty of a misdemeanor. Today 46 states—with the exception of Arkansas, Delaware, Mississippi, and New Mexico—enforce laws patterned after this statute to control fraudulent and deceptive advertising.

All states also have what have been referred to as "little FTC acts," or consumer protection acts, which govern unfair and deceptive business practices. Under such acts, states themselves can investigate and prosecute cases, and individual consumers can bring civil suits against businesses.

Because the current FTC is perceived by many as going after only the most blatant cases of advertising deception and focusing on small, offbeat companies (of 13 cases brought by the FTC in 1984, only 3 did not involve products that were fakes),[28] many state attorneys general are bringing cases against national advertisers whose ads appear in their state. For instance, the New York State Attorney General's office has succeeded in altering several national media campaigns by bringing complaints against the advertisements in that state. Through the state's efforts, the Beef Industry Council changed its "Beef Gives Strength" campaign (the Attorney General's office considered the ads deceptive because eating beef alone cannot increase strength and endurance), and Campbell Soup Co. stopped using the phrase "health insurance" in ads for low-sodium soups.[29] These national advertisers concluded it was not worth their while to have a separate ad campaign for just one state, which is why state actions can lead to changes in national campaigns.

Advertisers also need to be aware of unique state regulations governing what can and cannot be advertised and what can be depicted in ads. Some states prohibit certain types of wine and liquor advertising, for example, and most states restrict the use of federal and state flags in advertising.

Regulation by Local Government

Many cities and counties, usually through consumer protection agencies, enforce laws regulating local advertising practices. These agencies function chiefly to protect local consumers against unfair and misleading practices by area merchants.

NONGOVERNMENTAL REGULATION

A substantial amount of voluntary self-regulation has been achieved by the nation's advertisers in recent years. This reflects their desire for acceptance and growth in a competitive marketplace where consumer confidence is essential. Most large advertisers maintain careful systems of advertising review and gather strong data to substantiate their claims. In addition, regulatory mechanisms have been instituted by industries, trade groups, business organizations, the media, and even the advertising profession itself.

Self-Regulation by Advertisers

Most large advertisers reflect a sense of social responsibility in their advertising. Falstaff Brewing Company, for example, specifically avoids implying that beer will give people "a lift." It also rejects any appeals to adolescents and children as well as any references to sex. Most large corporations have set up review systems for ensuring that ads meet their own standards as well as industry, media, and legal requirements.

In addition, many industries maintain their own advertising codes, which reflect an agreement by companies in the same industry to abide by certain advertising standards and practices. The codes establish a basis for complaints, whereby a member may ask the executive board of the association to review existing competitive conditions in terms of the advertising code to which all members have subscribed.

Some industry codes reflect a high degree of social conscience. The code of the national distilling industry prohibits liquor advertising on television and radio, outdoor advertising near a military or naval base, and advertising in any publication that bears a Sunday dateline. The Wine Institute code prohibits references to athletes, appeals to children, and inferences that wine is associated with religion.

Codes like these are only as effective as the powers of enforcement vested in individual trade associations. Since enforcement may conflict with antitrust laws that prohibit interference with open competition, trade associations usually exert peer pressure on member companies that violate their codes rather than resorting to hearings or penalties.

The Role of the Better Business Bureau

Several business-monitoring organizations provide effective controls over advertising practices, particularly at the local level. The largest of these organizations is the Better Business Bureau. Established in 1916, the Better Business Bureau (BBB) has national and local offices funded by dues from over 100,000 member companies. It operates to protect consumers against fraudulent and deceptive advertising and sales practices. These bureaus, composed of advertisers, agency and media representatives, and laypeople, monitor advertising in their communities. They receive and investigate complaints from consumers and other advertisers. Violators are contacted and asked to revise their advertising. In many cases, this is sufficient. The BBB also maintains files on violators, which are open to the public. Records of violators who do not comply are sent to appropriate government agencies for further action. The BBB often works with local law enforcement agencies to prosecute advertisers guilty of fraud and misrep-

AD LAB 2-C   Advertising to Children: What You Can and Cannot Do

Many people are concerned about the effects advertising has on children. Television advertising for toys and breakfast cereals, in particular, has come under fire from watchdog groups.

The TV networks themselves have established highly restrictive guidelines for children's advertising, and all ads submitted for Saturday morning programs undergo close scrutiny by network censors. Many advertisers complain that network regulations are so precise that no room is left for creativity in ads. For example, only 10 seconds of a toy ad may contain animation and other special effects, and the last 5 seconds must display all toys shown earlier in the ad and disclose whether they are sold separately and whether batteries are included.

Advertising to children is also policed by the Council of Better Business Bureaus. The council's staff monitors commercials on network children's shows and checks ads in children's comics and magazines against the following guidelines:

1. Advertisers should always take into account the level of knowledge, sophistication, and maturity of the audience to which their message is primarily directed. Younger children have a limited capability for evaluating the credibility of what they watch. Advertisers, therefore,

have a special responsibility to protect children from their own susceptibilities.

2. Realizing that children are imaginative and that make-believe play constitutes an important part of the growing-up process, advertisers should exercise care not to exploit that imaginative quality of children. Unreasonable expectations of product quality or performance should not be stimulated either directly or indirectly by advertising.

3. Recognizing that advertising may play an important part in educating the child, information should be communicated in a truthful and accurate manner with full recognition by the advertiser that the child may learn practices from advertising that can affect his or her health and well-being.

4. Advertisers are urged to capitalize on the potential of advertising to influence social behavior and to develop advertising that, wherever possible, addresses itself to social standards generally regarded as positive and beneficial, such as friendship, kindness, honesty, justice, generosity, and respect for others.

5. Although many influences affect a child's personal and social development, it remains the prime responsibility of the parents to provide guidance for children. Advertisers should contribute to this parent-child relationship in a constructive manner.

resentation. Each year the BBB investigates thousands of advertisements for possible violations of truth and accuracy.

The Council of Better Business Bureaus, Inc., is the parent organization of the Better Business Bureau and part of the National Advertising Review Council. One of its functions is helping new industries develop standards for ethical and responsible advertising. It also provides ongoing information about advertising regulations and recent court and administrative rulings that affect advertising. In 1983, the National Advertising Division of the Council of Better Business Bureaus published guidelines for advertising to children, a particularly sensitive area (see Ad Lab 2-C).

Regulation by the Media

Almost all media maintain some form of advertising review and reserve the right to reject any material they regard as objectionable, even if it is not deceptive.

VO: Get ready for a toothpaste that tastes so great, kids will rush to brush. New Crest for Kids, with a flavor that is so different, some kids call it berrylicious. No matter what they call it they'll rush to brush. And while they're enjoying the flavor they'll be fighting cavities too. New Crest for Kids. It tastes so great they'll rush to brush.

Laboratory Application

Should advertising to children be banned? Why or why not?

National magazines monitor all advertising, particularly those by new advertisers and for new products. While newer publications that are eager to sell space may not be so vigilant, some established magazines, including *Time* and *Newsweek,* are highly scrupulous. *Good Housekeeping* tests every product before accepting advertising for it. If the tests do not substantiate the claims made, the ad is rejected. Products that are accepted, however, may feature the *Good Housekeeping* "Seal of Approval" on their labels and in advertising. If any such product is later found to be defective, *Good Housekeeping* promises to refund the money paid for it. A similar product seal and warranty are offered by *Parents Magazine. The New Yorker* will not accept discount retail store advertising or advertisements for feminine hygiene products or self-medication products. *Reader's Digest* will not accept tobacco advertising.

Newspapers also monitor and review advertising. Larger newspapers have clearance staffs that read every ad submitted, while most smaller newspapers rely on the advertising manager, sales personnel, or proofreaders to check ad copy. The general advertising policies set forth in *Newspaper Rates and Data* (Standard Rate and Data Service) include such restrictions as "No objectionable medical, personal, matrimonial, clairvoyant, or palmistry advertising accepted; no stock promotion or financial advertising, other than those securities of known value, will be accepted." Another rule prohibits the publication of any advertisement that simulates reading matter that cannot be readily recognized as advertising unless such an ad features the word *advertisement* or *advt.*

In addition, most papers have their own codes of acceptability governing advertising. These codes can range from 1 page for small local papers to more than 50 pages for large dailies such as the *Los Angeles Times.* Some of these codes are quite specific in what they will and will not allow. For example, the *Detroit Free Press* will not accept classified ads containing such words as *affair, discreet,* or *swinger.* The *Kansas City Star and Times* requires advertisers who claim "the lowest price in town" to include in the ad a promise to meet or beat any lower price readers find elsewhere within 30 days.[30]

One of the problems newspaper advertisers face is that there is little uniformity to these codes. A survey conducted by the *Los Angeles Times* found, for example, that ads for handguns are totally prohibited by the *Boston Globe,* are accepted by the *Chicago Tribune* only if the guns are antique, and are permitted in the *Orlando Sentinel* as long as the guns are not automatic.[31] Some newspapers ban tobacco ads, while others do not; papers in many southern states prohibit liquor ads, and they also tend to be the most strict when it comes to sexually related ads, such as those for X-rated movies. Newspapers do revise their policies from time to time, however, as occurred recently when many large papers reversed their policy on the acceptability of condom advertising.

By far the strictest review of advertising is conducted by the television networks. Advertisers are required to submit all commercials intended for a network or affiliated station to the broadcast standards department of the network. Estimates are that as many as half of all commercials (in storyboard form) are returned to the advertisers with suggestions for changes or greater substantiation of claims.[32] Some ads are totally rejected for violating network policies, as is discussed in Ad Lab 2-D.

Although the policies of the three major networks are all based on the original National Association of Broadcasters Television Code (which was suspended by the NAB in 1983 following court invalidation of part of the

AD LAB 2-D   The Issue of Issue Ads

The TV commercial depicts a dilapidated courtroom 30 years from now. Testifying in front of a teenage prosecutor and a jury of other youngsters, an old man tries to explain why nothing was done decades before to protect them from the ravages of deficit spending: "It was all going to work out somehow, but no one was willing to make the sacrifices." When the young prosecutor says, "In 1986, the national debt had reached $2 trillion. Didn't that frighten you?" The old man shrugs helplessly. "Are you ever going to forgive us?"

This commercial, produced by W. R. Grace & Co., was rejected by all three networks. The networks claimed the ad violated their policies against carrying "issue" advertising that advocates a particular point of view. Part of their concern stemmed from the Fairness Doctrine, which requires giving equal time to opposing points of view. But the networks also have a policy of rejecting advocacy ads if they feel that such ads allow those with the most money to have their opinions heard. The Supreme Court ruled in 1973 that networks can reject paid editorial messages without violating the Communications Act or the First Amendment.

The Grace case has prompted some commentators to point out, however, that the networks may have gotten too paranoid in their attempts to determine what might or might not be "controversial." The Grace commercial was accepted and aired by cable networks and independent stations as well as by some network affiliates. At one point in the controversy over the network rejection of the ad, 122 independent TV stations banded together and aired the commercial as a public-service announcement, free of charge. CBS eventually accepted the ad after Grace made one minor change in it, and ABC subsequently said it would accept the ad if it were resubmitted. NBC, however, stood by its evaluation of the commercial as "controversial" and refused to air it.

Corporations that wish to place issue ads on network television argue that the airwaves belong to the public and that it is a violation of their First Amendment rights for the networks not to carry their ads.

The networks defend their position by citing the 1973 Supreme Court decision and by pointing out that they are fulfilling their obligations to free speech and public service through their news and public affairs programming.

Laboratory Applications

1. Do you think networks should alter their policy on corporate issue advertising? In what way?
2. The FCC has repealed the Fairness Doctrine, but Congress is currently considering legislation that would make the doctrine law. Are you in favor of such legislation? Why or why not?

OLD MAN: I've already told you, it was all going to work out somehow. There was even talk of an amendment. But no one was willing to make the sacrifices. I'm afraid you're much too young to understand.

BOY: Maybe so. But I'm afraid the numbers speak for themselves. By 1986, for example, the national debt

had reached 2 trillion dollars. Didn't that frighten you?

ANNCR VO: No one really knows what another generation of unchecked federal deficits will bring.

OLD MAN: This frightens me.

BOY: No more questions.

OLD MAN: I have a question. Are you ever going to forgive us?

ANNCR VO: But we know this much. You can change the future. You have to. At W. R. Grace, we want all of us to stay one step ahead of a changing world.

code for violating the Sherman Antitrust Act), the policies vary enough from each other that preparing commercials acceptable to all can be a real headache. Cable networks and local stations tend to be much less stringent in their requirements, as demonstrated by their acceptance of condom ads.

Self-Regulation by the Advertising Profession

Most advertising agencies monitor their own practices. In addition, professional advertising associations oversee the activities of their agency members to prevent any problems that may trigger government intervention. Advertising publications actively report issues and actions before the courts in an effort to educate agencies and advertisers about possible legal infractions.

Advertising Agencies

Although information about a product or service is supplied to the agency by the advertiser, it is the agency's responsibility to research and verify all product claims and comparative product data before using them in advertising. The media may require such documentation before accepting the advertising, and substantiation also may be needed if government or consumer agencies challenge the claims. Agencies can be held legally liable for fraudulent or misleading advertising claims. For these reasons, most major advertising agencies have legal counsel and regularly submit their advertisements for review. If any aspects of the advertising are challenged, the advertiser is asked to again review the advertising and either confirm it is true or replace unverified material.

Advertising Associations

The American Association of Advertising Agencies (AAAA) and two other national organizations—the Association of National Advertisers and the American Advertising Federation—are actively engaged in monitoring industrywide advertising practices.

The AAAA, an association of advertising agencies throughout the United States, controls agency practices by denying membership to any agency judged unethical. The AAAA *Standards of Practice* and *Creative Code* set forth advertising principles for member agencies.

The American Advertising Federation (AAF) is also a nationwide association of advertising people. The AAF helped to establish the FTC, and its early "vigilance" committees were the forerunners of the Better Business Bureaus. The AAF "Advertising Principles of American Business," adopted in 1984, defines standards for truthful and responsible advertising. Since most local advertising clubs belong to the AAF, this organization has been instrumental in influencing agencies and advertisers to abide by these principles.

The Association of National Advertisers (ANA) is composed of 400 major manufacturing and service companies that are clients of member agencies of the AAAA. These companies, which are pledged to uphold the ANA code of advertising ethics, work with the ANA through a joint Committee for Improvement of Advertising Content.

Advertising Publications

Magazines and newspapers that serve the advertising industry maintain close watch over advertising practices. *Advertising Age,* the industry's leading trade publication, continually champions the cause of more ethical and responsible advertising.

National Advertising Review Council

In 1971, the National Advertising Review Council (NARC) was established by the Council of Better Business Bureaus, Inc., in conjunction with the American Association of Advertising Agencies, the American Advertising Federation, and the Association of National Advertisers. Its primary purpose is to promote and enforce standards of truth, accuracy, taste, morality, and social responsibility in advertising. Composed of members drawn from the leadership of these four organizations, NARC is regarded as the most comprehensive and effective regulatory mechanism in the advertising industry. Indeed, a U.S. district court judge noted in a 1985 case that the "speed, informality, and modest cost" as well as expertise of the self-regulatory organization gives it special advantages over the court system in resolving advertising disputes.[33]

Under NARC's direction, two regulatory divisions were established: the National Advertising Division (NAD) of the Council of Better Business Bureaus, an investigative body, and the National Advertising Review Board (NARB), an appeals board for NAD decisions. The NAD monitors advertising industry practices. It reviews complaints received from consumers and consumer groups, brand competitors, local Better Business Bureaus, NAD monitors, and others about objectionable advertisements. These complaints chiefly concern false or misleading advertising claims and ads that depart from taste, morality, or social responsibility (see Figure 2–14). The NAD does not reveal the identity of the challenger except with permission. When a complaint is found to be valid, the NAD contacts the advertiser's chief executive officer specifying the claims to be substantiated. The advertiser is also asked to furnish examples of all current national advertising containing similar claims in print or on radio or television. The advertiser is then asked to name its advertising agency, and a copy of the initial inquiry is sent to the agency's chief executive officer. No investigation is conducted if the claims in question are withdrawn prior to receipt of the NAD's first inquiry or if they are the subject of litigation by a government agency. Once the investigation is concluded and the NAD is satisfied that the advertising claims are supported, it will close its file and advise the advertiser and the challenger. If the NAD finds substantiation to be inadequate, it will request modification or discontinuance of the claims.

If the NAD and an advertiser reach an impasse in their discussions, either party has the right to review by a panel from the National Advertising Review Board. The NARB consists of a chairperson and 50 volunteer members: 30 national advertisers, 10 agency representatives, and 10 laypeople from the public sector. A five-member panel, composed of three advertisers, one agency representative, and one layperson, is then selected from this board to review the case. The panel's decision is binding on the NAD. If an NARB panel finds against an advertiser and the advertiser refuses to modify or discontinue the advertising in accordance with the

FIGURE   2–14

The NARB uses advertising to encourage consumers to report ads they think are misleading, untruthful, or deceptive.

panel decision, NARB will refer the matter to an appropriate governmental authority and indicate the fact in its public record (see Figure 2–15). In all its years of operation, no advertiser who participated in the complete process of an NAD investigation and NARB appeal has declined to abide by the panel decision.[34] In fact, very few cases have made it to the NARB. Of 103 NAD investigations conducted in 1985, 31 ad claims were substantiated, 70

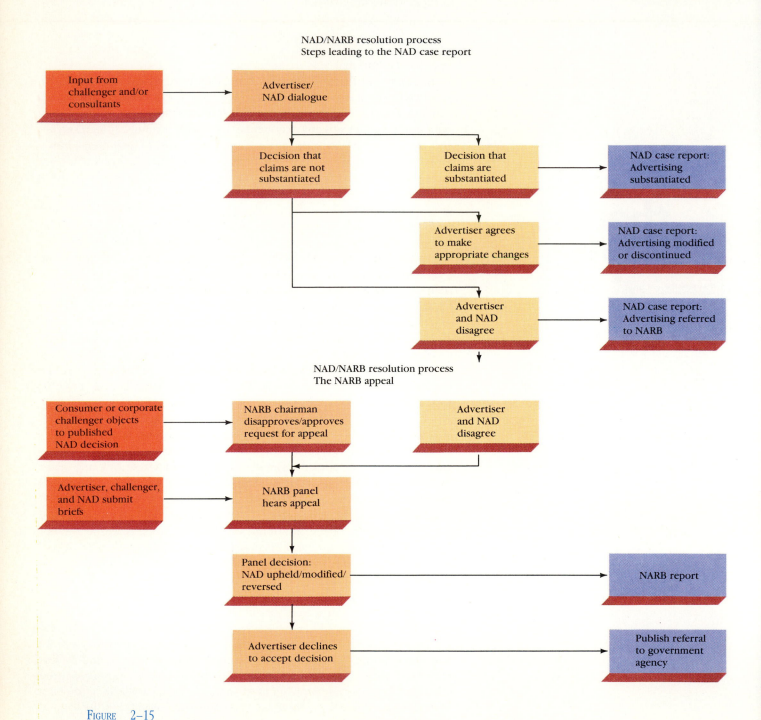

FIGURE   2–15

Flowchart of the NAD/NARB review process.

ads were modified or discontinued, and only 2 decisions were disputed and referred to the NARB for resolution.[35]

The NAD/NARB system is not without its critics. Although investigations and actions tend to be reasonably swift, the staff is small and the number of cases investigated is only about 100 per year. Many consumers are unaware of the fact that they can file complaints with the NAD, and the details of all cases under investigation are kept confidential until the findings are announced. Furthermore, the organization lacks clout in that it can only request changes in ads, not order them. However, because media may accept or reject advertising on the basis of NAD findings, they do have significant ramifications.

Both the NARB and the NAD issue monthly reports to help establish practicable standards for the advertising industry. The NARB also sponsors advisory panels to study such specialized topics as comparative advertising and women in advertising. The NAD is available to evaluate and render decisions about proposed advertising campaigns prior to their completion and placement in the media.

Regulation by Consumer Groups

The greatest recent growth among the regulatory forces governing advertising has been that of consumer protection organizations. Starting in the 1960s, the consumer movement began to play an increasingly active role in fighting fraudulent and deceptive advertising. Consumers demanded not only that products perform as advertised but also that more product information be provided so people can compare and make better buying decisions. The impact of the consumer movement and its growing pressure for more stringent advertising regulation soon gave rise to a new word: *consumerism,* or social action designed to dramatize the rights of the buying public. Since then, one fact has become clear to both advertisers and agencies: The American consumer has the power to influence advertising practices.

The growing consumer movement has caused advertisers and agencies to pay more attention to product claims, especially those related to energy use (such as the estimated miles per gallon of a new auto) and the nutritional value of processed foods (such as sugar-coated breakfast cereals). Consumerism has fostered the growth of consumer advocate groups and regulatory agencies. It has also promoted more consumer research by advertisers, agencies, and the media in an effort to learn what consumers want—and how to provide it. Many advertisers agree that the creation of customer relations departments and investment in public goodwill ultimately will pay off in improved consumer relations and sales.

Consumer Information Networks

Several large organizations serve as mass-communication networks for the exchange of consumer information, enabling consumers to express their views on advertising and marketing infractions. These organizations include the Consumer Federation of America (CFA), the National Council of Senior Citizens, and the National Consumer League. They have the following functions: (1) to serve as a central clearinghouse for the exchange and dissemination of information among its members; (2) to aid in the development of state, regional, and local consumer organizations; and (3) to work with and provide services to national, regional, county, and municipal consumer groups.

Consumer interests also are served by several private, nonprofit testing organizations such as Consumers Union, Consumers' Research, and Underwriters Laboratories.

Consumer Advocates

Consumer advocate groups focus on issues that involve advertising and advertisers. These groups act on complaints received from consumers as well as on those that grow out of their own research. Their normal procedures are: (1) to investigate the complaint; (2) if warranted, to contact the advertiser and ask that the objectionable advertisement or practice be halted; (3) if the advertiser does not comply, to release publicity or criticism about the offense to the media; (4) to submit complaints with substantiating evidence to appropriate government agencies for further action; and (5) in some instances, to file a lawsuit and seek to obtain from the courts a cease-and-desist order or a fine or other penalty against the violator.

Summary

As advertising has proliferated in the media, the criticism of advertising has also intensified. Detractors say advertising debases our language, makes us too materialistic, and manipulates us into buying products we do not need. Furthermore, they say, advertising is not only excessive but also offensive or in bad taste and even deceptive.

Defenders of advertising admit that advertising has been and sometimes still is misused. However, they point out that the abuse heaped on advertising is often unjustified and excessive and that advertisers have been responsive to criticism by making efforts to avoid stereotypes, to control the proliferation of ads, and to make ads more informative and entertaining. Advertisers realize that the best way to sell their products is to appeal to genuine consumer needs and to be honest in their claims.

One result of past abuses by advertisers is the current large body of laws and regulations governing advertising. Regulation comes in several forms: regulation by local, state, and federal government agencies; self-regulation by advertisers and business organizations; regulation by the advertising profession and the media; and regulation by consumer protection organizations.

The FTC is the major federal regulator of advertising. Its recent definitions of what constitutes "deceptive" and "unfair" advertising have been controversial. In determining whether ads are deceptive or unfair, the FTC looks for substantiation of claims that are made and scrutinizes endorsements and testimonials for any signs of deception. After investigating a complaint, the FTC may issue a cease-and-desist order or it may order corrective advertising.

The FCC has jurisdiction over the radio and television industries, but deregulation has severely limited the amount of control the FCC has over advertising in these media. The FDA keeps an eye on advertising for food and drugs in addition to regulating product labels and packaging. The Patent and Trademark Office governs ownership of trademarks, trade names, house marks, and similar distinctive features of companies and brands. The Library of Congress registers and protects all copyrighted materials.

The federal courts have been involved in several advertising issues, including First Amendment protection of "commercial speech," the right of professionals such as lawyers and doctors to advertise, infringements of advertising on the right to privacy, and lawsuits over comparative advertising.

State and local governments also have consumer protection laws that regulate aspects of advertising.

Nongovernmental forms of advertising regulation include self-regulation on the part of advertisers themselves, standards and guidelines offered by industries, monitoring on the part of the Council of Better Business Bureaus, print media and broadcasting codes and policies, and regulation within the advertising industry.

The most effective body for self-regulation has been the National Advertising Division (NAD) of the Council of Better Business Bureaus. It investigates complaints received from consumers, brand competitors, or local Better Business Bureaus and suggests corrective measures. Advertisers that refuse to comply are referred to the National Advertising Review Board (NARB), which may uphold, modify, or reverse the NAD's findings.

Finally, consumer organizations and consumer advocates exert some control over advertising by investigating and filing complaints against advertisers and by providing information to consumers.

Questions for Review and Discussion

1. Is advertising's responsibility to lead or to reflect society? Explain.
2. Do you believe advertising tends to create monopolies? How?
3. Why have feminists been so upset about advertising? Is their displeasure reasonable?
4. What is the relationship between the FTC and the advertising industry? Do you feel the FTC has overstepped its authority? Explain. Can you cite recent examples of FTC action against advertisers?
5. Compare the new and old FTC definitions of "deception." Which do you consider to be preferable? Why?
6. If you were to help the FDA draft guidelines for health claims in food ads, what items would you include?
7. In what way is "commercial speech" different from free speech? Should this distinction be maintained, or should advertising be given the same First Amendment protection as other types of speech?
8. What effect, if any, does physician advertising have on the practice of medicine?
9. It is estimated that 35 percent of current advertising is comparative. What is the value of comparative advertising? What are the drawbacks?
10. What is the importance of the NAD/NARB system to consumers and advertisers?

3

THE ADVERTISING
BUSINESS

rank Perdue was being interviewed for an article in *Esquire* magazine. "I could say I planned all this," he said, "but I was just back there with my father and a couple of other guys working my ass off every day. I wasn't even sure for a long time that I even liked the chicken business. But my advantage is that I grew up having to know my business in every detail. I dug cesspools, made coops, and cleaned them out. I know I'm not very smart, at least from the point of view of pure IQ, and that gave me one prime ingredient of success—fear. I mean a man should have enough fear so that he's always second-guessing himself."

He pulled out a wrinkled clipping from his wallet. The words were Alexander Hamilton's: "Men give me credit for some genius. All the genius I have lies in this. When I have a subject in hand, I study it profoundly. Day and night it is before me. I explore it in all its bearings. My mind becomes pervaded with it. Then the effort I have made is what people are pleased to call the fruit of genius. It is the fruit of labor and thought."

Chickens are not a very glamorous business. And Frank Perdue didn't know anything about advertising. But when Madison Avenue learned that this chicken farmer from the Delmarva Peninsula (located between the Chesapeake Bay on the west and the Atlantic Ocean on the east) was ready to take a big plunge into advertising, everybody scrambled for the account. So many people were fawning all over Perdue that it made him uncomfortable. He pulled back for a while.

To make sure that nobody put him in that position again, Perdue immersed himself in advertising day and night. He devoured great volumes on the subject, and he can still drop quotes by people like David Ogilvy and Rosser Reeves the way other people cite the Bible or Shakespeare. He haunted an advertising institute, studying all the pamphlets and textbooks. He called up advertising journalists and radio and TV station managers in New York, systematically trying to pick brains. Almost nobody knew him, but many helped simply because they were impressed by his industrious curiosity.

By the time he was ready to be courted again by Madison Avenue, Perdue was an expert. Altogether, he interviewed almost 50 agencies. Eventually, he narrowed his list down to a championship flight of nine. Then he really went on the offensive—grilling, double-checking, interviewing. He called one very prominent agency and asked their representatives to have lunch with him in the Oak Room of the Plaza Hotel. The whole top executive force trooped over to the Plaza, licking their chops, convinced Perdue was going to tell them he had selected their agency for his chickens. Instead, as soon as they settled at the table, Perdue informed them they hadn't even made his final list, but he would appreciate it if they would rank the nine agencies that were still left in the running. Stunned and flabbergasted, the agency boys dived into another round of martinis and patiently did as he requested.

The losers were really the lucky ones. When Perdue called up Ed McCabe, the copy chief at Scali, McCabe, Sloves, for about the 800th time in a week, McCabe finally blew his cork. "You know, Frank," he said, "I'm not even sure that we want your account anymore because you're such a pain in the ass." McCabe recalls, "You know all he said to that? He just said, 'Yeah, I know I'm a pain in the ass, and now that we've got that settled, here's what I want to ask you this time.'"

Sometime later, Perdue picked McCabe's agency. One of the first commercials they shot, in a campaign built around Perdue himself (another idea he never cottoned to), won an award for excellence. Ed McCabe won more honors than any other copywriter in the nation that year because of his work on the Perdue campaign. Therefore, Frank Perdue became the biggest chicken man in the nation's biggest city and a celebrity to boot (see Figure 3–1).

The rest is history. Perdue's sales doubled every two years. Throughout the 1980s, as fast-food and convenience restaurants specializing in chicken proliferated, Perdue became a major supplier to them.[1] By 1987, with 11,000 employees, his company was selling over 450 million birds a year and realizing revenues of over $850 million.[2] That makes Perdue Farms one of the top 50 private companies in the United States. But after appearing in over 70 commercials and spending untold millions of dollars to promote his birds, Frank Perdue may be as much in the advertising business as in the chicken business.

"I could write a book about advertising," he says matter-of-factly.[3]

The advertising business is composed of two primary groups of organizations. First are the companies that advertise—the *advertisers*—which, like Perdue Farms, advertise themselves and their products or services. Assisting them are the *advertising agencies,* which plan, create, and prepare advertising campaigns and materials for the advertisers. In addition to these two groups are the *media,* which sell *time,* in the case of electronic media, and *space,* in the case of print media, to carry the advertiser's message to the target audience. And finally, there is another group known as the *suppliers.* These include the photographers, illustrators, printers, video production houses, and many others who assist both advertisers and agencies in the preparation of advertising materials.

Our purpose in this chapter is to examine the two primary groups—advertisers and agencies—to understand who they are, what they do, and

FIGURE   3–1

The Perdue campaign has been revolutionary in the business since it demonstrated that fresh meat could be branded and sold like packaged products. A large supermarket chain put Perdue side by side against a house brand selling for 6 cents a pound less. Incredibly, 40 percent of the customers chose Perdue at the premium price.

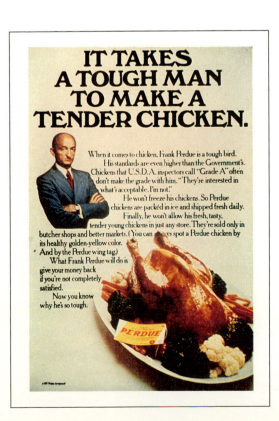

how they work together to create effective advertising. In subsequent chapters, we will deal with both the media and the suppliers of advertising in order to grasp the full breadth and complexity of the advertising business and also to learn about the career opportunities in the field (a topic covered most fully in Appendix C).

THE COMPANIES THAT ADVERTISE

Virtually every successful business uses advertising, and the majority of people who work in advertising are employed by such businesses. Advertisers may range in size from small retail stores to multinational firms, or from small industrial concerns to large service organizations. All these companies have an advertising department—of some size—even if it is just one person who shares the advertising responsibility with other job functions.

Most of us probably think of advertising people as the copywriters and art directors who work for the advertising agencies. But in reality, the people who work for the agency's clients—the companies that advertise—are, like Frank Perdue, also very much involved in the advertising business.

The importance of the advertising person in the company may vary depending on several factors: the size of the company, the type of industry in which the company operates, the size of the advertising program, the role of advertising in the company's marketing mix, and most of all, the degree of top management involvement in the advertising function.

Company presidents and other top executives, who are usually very interested in how their advertising represents the company, are often directly involved in advertising decisions. Sales and marketing personnel, of

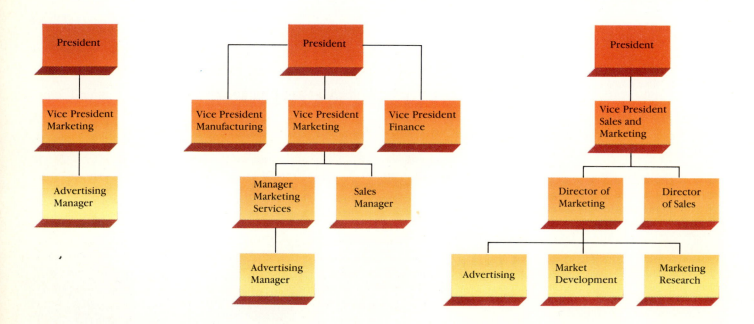

FIGURE   3–2

How advertising is positioned in company structure.

course, have a direct relationship to advertising. They frequently provide input to the creative process, assist in deciding which advertising agency to use, and help evaluate proposed advertising programs.

Large companies may have a separate advertising department employing from one to several hundred people and headed by an advertising manager who reports to a marketing director or marketing services manager (see Figure 3–2).

Product people such as engineers and designers are often asked to make recommendations about product features or to help advertising by providing information about competitive products. Similarly, administrative people in accounting or purchasing are frequently asked to consider the impact of advertising programs on the company's financial status or to help determine appropriate budgets for the next campaign.

Even clerical people can get involved in the advertising process by virtue of their position within the organization and their knowledge of company activities. It is not uncommon, in fact, for secretaries in small firms to be promoted to the position of administrative assistant and then, eventually, to manager of a department like advertising.

Just about everybody who works for a company that advertises thinks that the organization's advertising represents him or her in some way and therefore has some feeling about it. As a result, the more we can learn about advertising, how it works, and why it is prepared the way it is, the more help we can offer the companies that employ us.

WHAT COMPANY ADVERTISING DEPARTMENTS DO

The ways advertising departments function are as varied as the companies that operate them. Many companies perform all their advertising activities themselves, whereas others hire outside advertising agencies or suppliers to help them. Regardless of the way responsibilities are divided, there are certain things all advertisers must do.

Tasks Common to All Advertisers

Every advertiser, large or small, must have an understanding of and some expertise in communications to perform the basic functions necessary to a successful advertising program. These functions include administration, planning, budgeting, and coordination with other company departments and with outside advertising services. We shall discuss each of these functions briefly.

Administration

Organizing and staffing the advertising department, supervising and controlling the department's activities, and selecting the advertising agencies to be used are normal administrative functions. An advertising manager (or committee in some companies) is also responsible for recommending specific advertising programs based on the company's marketing plans and budgets. It is imperative, therefore, that the advertising manager have a thorough understanding of all the major factors influencing the company's marketing activities. Advertising managers should establish an efficient procedure for handling inquiries, analyzing competitive advertising, and evaluating their own ads.

Planning

It is occasionally necessary to draw up formal advertising proposals for the approval of management, but in between those times the planning process should still be ongoing. Planning is a constant and never-ending process of defining and redefining goals and objectives, developing strategies, scheduling advertisements, and evaluating advertising results. The way marketing and advertising plans are developed will be discussed in greater detail in Chapter 7.

Budgeting

The advertising budget is usually determined annually or semiannually (see Chapter 7). The advertising manager's task is to formulate the budget and sell it to top management, which always has the last word on how much will actually be allocated to advertising functions. It is the advertising department's responsibility to see that the budget is followed and not squandered before each of the advertising tasks has been performed (see Figure 3–3).

Coordination with Other Departments

The activities of business are usually divided into three broad functional areas: production, finance, and marketing. Advertising, like sales, is a marketing activity. The advertising manager, therefore, must coordinate the department's activities with other marketing functions. The advertising department must also coordinate its work with those departments involved in production and finance.

For example, both the sales and advertising departments sometimes find out and communicate to the production department what product and packaging features may improve customer satisfaction.

The accounting department may be consulted for records on overhead, ad production, and media costs. Controlling costs is a joint responsibility of both the accounting and the advertising departments. Similarly, the legal department can help protect the company from trademark and copyright infringement and also keep it from inadvertently violating truth-in-advertising laws.

Coordination with Outside Advertising Services

The advertising department is the liaison between the firm and any outside advertising services it employs. These may include advertising agencies, the media, or advertising suppliers. It has the responsibility of screening and analyzing the various services available, making recommendations to management, and (usually) deciding which outside services to use. The advertising manager is then responsible for supervising and evaluating the work performed.

How Large Advertisers Work

Just as the size and the function of the advertising department depend on a variety of factors, so does the way in which the department is organized and managed. No two firms, product lines, or markets are exactly alike.

Therefore, the method of organization depends on the unique circumstances of each company. The two basic management structures that large companies use are *centralized* and *decentralized* organizations.

Centralized Organization

What do Wheaties, Betty Crocker, Red Lobster restaurants, and Foot Joy golf shoes have in common? For one thing, they are just a few of the many products owned and marketed by General Mills, Inc., of Minneapolis,

Space and time costs in regular media	Catalogs for consumers	Premium handling charges
Advertising consultants	Classified telephone directories	House-to-house sample distribution
Ad-pretesting services	Space in irregular publications	Packaging charges for premium promotions
Institutional advertising	Advertising aids for salespeople	Cost of merchandise for tie-in promotions
Industry directory listings	Financial advertising	Product tags
Readership or audience research	Dealer help literature	Showrooms
Media costs for consumer contests, premium and sampling promotions	Contributions to industry ad funds	Testing new labels and packages
Ad department travel and entertainment expenses	Direct mail to dealers and jobbers	Package design and artwork
Ad department salaries	Office supplies	Cost of non-self-liquidating premiums
Advertising association dues	Point-of-sale materials	Consumer education programs
Local cooperative advertising	Window display installation costs	Product publicity
Direct mail to consumers	Charges for services performed by other departments	Factory signs
Subscriptions to periodicals and services for ad department	Catalogs for dealers	House organs for salespeople
Storage of advertising materials	Test-marketing programs	Signs on company-owned vehicles
	Sample requests generated by advertising	Instruction enclosures
	Costs of exhibits except personnel	Press clipping services
	Ad department share of overhead	Market research (outside produced)
	House organs for customers and dealers	Samples of middlemen
	Cost of cash value or sampling coupons	Recruitment advertising
	Cost of contest entry blanks	Price sheets
	Cross-advertising enclosures	Public relations consultants
	Contest judging and handling fees	Coupon redemption costs
	Depreciation of ad department equipment	Corporate publicity
	Mobile exhibits	Market research (company produced)
	Employee fringe benefits	Exhibit personnel
	Catalogs for salespeople	Gifts of company products
	Packaging consultants	Cost of deal merchandise
	Consumer contest awards	Share of corporate salaries
		Cost of guarantee refunds
		Share of legal expenses
		Cost of detail or missionary people
		Sponsoring recreational activities
		Product research
		House organs for employees
		Entertaining customers and prospects
		Scholarships
		Plant tours
		Annual reports
		Outright charity donations

FIGURE   3–3

The black, white, and gray list identifies those budget items that should be charged to the advertising budget (white), items that are debatable (gray), and items that should not be charged (black).

Minnesota. One of the 25 largest national advertisers, General Mills operates a vast advertising and marketing services department with 330 employees and a $320 million advertising budget.[4]

Located at corporate headquarters in Minneapolis, Marketing Services (as the department is called) is really many departments within a department. As a centralized advertising department, it is responsible for administering, planning, budgeting, and coordinating the promotion of more than 50 different brands. In the process, it supervises 26 outside advertising agencies and operates its own in-house agency for new or smaller brands.

Organized around functional specialties (e.g., market research, media, graphics, copy), Marketing Services consults with General Mills's brand managers and consolidates many of their expenditures for maximum efficiency. The Media Department, for example, is involved daily in all media plans and dollar allocations with the various marketing divisions. The Production and Art Services Department handles the package design for all brands as well as the graphic requirements of the company's in-house agency. In addition, Betty Crocker Kitchens provides promotional services for the various marketing programs associated with Betty Crocker products.

The result is a highly effective series of mostly unrelated advertising programs for a wide variety of products and brands, all directed from one central spot. While this structure may sometimes make it more difficult for management to provide a general overview of marketing strategies and execution, it does give General Mills great efficiency in its advertising programs and provides the company with appreciable savings.

The centralized organization, like the one at General Mills, is the most common type of advertising department because of the several advantages this structure offers. For example, communication flows more easily in the organization. The need for a large staff of advertising specialists is reduced. Lower-level personnel do not need to be exceptionally skilled or experi-

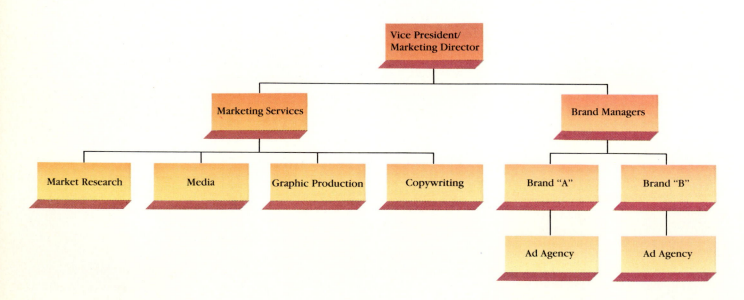

FIGURE   3–4

Centralized department.

enced because the firm's top management can take part in advertising decision making. And unlike the case with decentralized organizations, maintaining continuity in the company's various communications programs is more feasible—at a substantial cost savings.

As shown in Figure 3–4, the advertising manager in the large centralized department typically reports to a marketing vice president, and the department is usually organized in one of five ways:

1. By product or brand.
2. By subfunction of advertising (such as sales promotion, print production, TV/radio buying, and outdoor advertising).
3. By end user (consumer products, industrial products).
4. By media (radio, television, newspapers, and so forth).
5. By geography (western advertising, eastern advertising).

The way these large centralized departments work depends primarily on the attitude of management, the firm's marketing needs, and the nature of the company's customers and products.

Decentralized Organization

As companies become larger, take on new brands or products, acquire subsidiaries, and establish divisions in several parts of the country (or several countries), a centralized advertising department often becomes highly impractical. A company may then begin to decentralize its advertising and establish departments assigned to the various divisions, subsidiaries, products, countries, regions, brands, or other categories that most suit the firm's needs. The final authority for each division's advertising, then, rests with the general manager of the particular division.

Commonly referred to as the nation's number-one marketing practitioner, Procter & Gamble in Cincinnati, Ohio, is a 150-year-old, $17 billion company that manufactures and sells over 200 different consumer products.[5] These include many brands that are the leaders in their fields: Tide, Ivory soap, Crest toothpaste, Pampers diapers, Duncan Hines cake mixes, Crisco shortening, and Charmin paper products, just to mention a few (see Figure 3–5).

Procter & Gamble has eight consumer product divisions, five industrial product divisions, and four international divisions. Historically, each division has been set up almost like a separate company, each with its own research and development department, manufacturing plant, advertising department, sales force, and finance and accounting staff. Likewise, every brand within each division has a brand manager, two assistant brand managers, and one or two staff assistants. The whole purpose of this system is to assure that each brand has the single-minded drive and personal commitment from the managers it needs to succeed.[6]

Each brand manager of P&G has his or her own advertising agency, which develops and creates the brand's media advertising. To coordinate sales promotion and merchandising programs, the manager has the help of the division's advertising department and the support of the corporate advertising department's media and research supervisors for statistical information and guidance. The brand manager reports to an associate advertising manager who oversees three or four brand groups. The associate advertising manager reports to the division's advertising manager, who, in turn, is responsible to the division's general manager.[7]

For new recruits from college, P&G's brand manager development

FIGURE   3–5

This example of Procter & Gamble advertising is a classic that has won the approval of the professional advertising community.

program has been legendary as the Marine Corps of marketing. Apprentice brand managers live with and learn the statistics of their brand's performance against competitors. They are assigned to work on store displays. They develop sales projections for their brand, help plan advertising budgets, and coordinate with other sections of the division's advertising department: media, copy, art and packaging, sampling and couponing, and legal. They learn how market research helps determine the packages, scents, sizes, and colors people want; how product research improves the brand in response to competition; and how the division's sales force tries to muscle more shelf space for the brand in the supermarket.

While this decentralized brand manager system has been the most sacred of sacred cows at P&G for many years, it has recently come under attack for a variety of ills—primarily that it is no longer capable of satisfying the needs of a rapidly changing marketplace, that it is too product-oriented rather than market-oriented.[8] The result is that P&G has reviewed

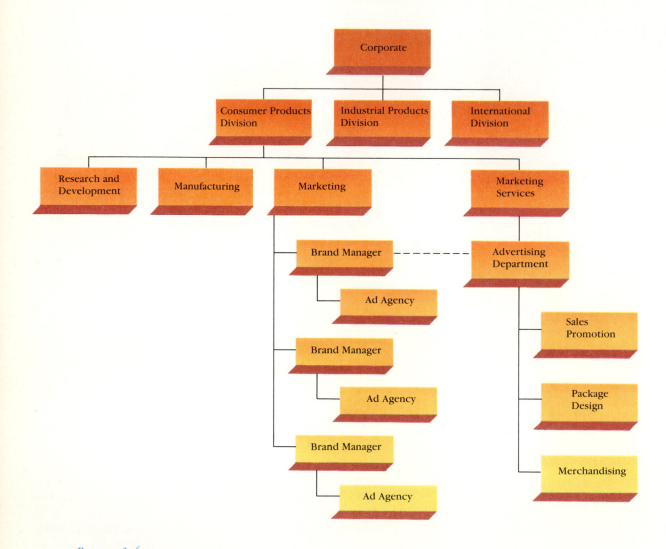

FIGURE   3–6

Decentralized department.

the system and grafted onto it new executive titles such as "category" brand managers, "future" brand managers (for products planned for the future), and regional marketing managers. While competition between brand managers has traditionally typified the system, the company is now developing teams that include manufacturing, sales, and research managers who all work together for the common good of the company.[9] While the system is still decentralized, many activities are becoming more centralized for reasons of economy, efficiency, and control. For example, the function of buying advertising space and time from the media— traditionally performed by agencies—is now performed by the company internally.[10]

For large multidivision companies, decentralized advertising offers a number of advantages. For instance, it more easily conforms to the specific problems and needs of the division. Flexibility is increased, allowing quicker and easier adjustments in campaigns and media schedules. New approaches and creative ideas are introduced more easily. And the results of each division's advertising may be measured independently of the others. In effect, each division is its own marketing department, and the advertising manager reports to each division head (see Figure 3–6).

However, individual department heads sometimes tend to be more concerned with their budgets, problems, and promotions than with determining what will benefit the firm as a whole. The potential power of repetitive advertising is often diminished because there is no uniformity in the advertising among divisions. Rivalry between brand managers may become fierce and may further deteriorate into secrecy and jealousy. It is virtually impossible to standardize styles, themes, or approaches. In fact, after one multidivision company decentralized, it had difficulty just getting the product brand managers to use the same logo in their various advertisements and brochures.

In summary, both centralized and decentralized advertising departments have their advantages. What works successfully in one market, though, may not work in the next. There are no constants in determining which form or organization is best. And no organizational structure is purely one form or the other. They are, in fact, all different and individually designed to fit the needs of each particular company.

How Small Advertisers Work

A small retailer—say, a hardware, clothing, or electronics store—might have just one person in charge of advertising. That person would be responsible for performing all the basic tasks discussed earlier—the administrative, planning, budgeting, and coordinating functions. But what else might be done? In many cases, that same person might also lay out the newspaper ads, write the advertising copy, and select the media to be used. However, unless that person were also a commercial artist or graphic designer, it is unlikely he or she would physically create the actual advertisements, setting type and doing the mechanical pasteup of materials (see Chapter 10).

On the other hand, a larger chain of stores might have a complete advertising department staffed and equipped to perform a range of activities internally. These may include *advertising production, media placement,* and *marketing support services.* We'll discuss each of these briefly.

FIGURE   3–7

Small advertiser.

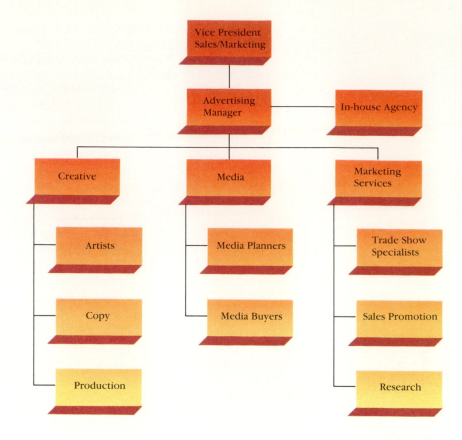

Advertising Production

If a firm does not use an advertising agency, the advertising department may be responsible for creating and producing all advertising materials. This means writing the ads, designing the way they will look on the page or on TV, ordering type, arranging for photos or illustrations or broadcast talent, then assembling all the parts into a usable advertisement or commercial. The department would then need its own staff of artists, copywriters, and production specialists to produce this work, and the department's head would likely report to the company's sales or marketing manager (see Figure 3–7).

Media Placement

The people who work in company advertising departments often perform the media function, too. This means analyzing and evaluating available media vehicles according to coverage, cost, services to advertisers, and editorial content. The department, then, would also develop media schedules according to the available budget, purchase space and broadcast airtime, and finally, verify performance.

Other Marketing Support Services

Often an advertising agency is retained to prepare media advertising, while the company's advertising department performs other marketing support services such as the production of sales materials and displays for distribution to managers, salespeople, dealers, and distributors.

Some advertisers produce their own product photography, technical films, trade-show exhibits, and direct-mail campaigns, as well as performing a variety of other functions. The degree of responsibility depends on the company.

THE IN-HOUSE AGENCY

Some companies, in an effort to save money and centralize their advertising activities, have set up their own *in-house agencies* wholly owned by the company. Many large firms, including Bristol-Myers, Procter & Gamble, and General Foods, have turned to in-house media buying to monitor and control soaring media costs.[11]

The full-service house agency is a total-capability advertising department, set up and staffed to do all the work of an independent full-service agency. All aspects of advertising creativity, production, and media placement are performed in-house. Being fully self-contained, it is able to develop and accomplish almost every type of advertising, publicity, and sales promotion required by the company.

Advertisers set up their own agencies for several reasons. Usually they hope to save money by cutting overhead expenses and keeping the 15 percent commission the agency usually gets for placing ads in the media. Moreover, with a house agency the company is not charged the standard markup on printing or art production, which ranges from 17.65 to 25 percent when such items are purchased through an outside agency.

Advertisers likewise feel they can receive more attention from their agency if the company is its only client. House agencies tend to have a greater depth of understanding of the company's products and markets, and they can usually respond better to pressure deadlines because they can focus their full resources on the project. Although outside agencies may be able to produce just as quickly, they often have to hire free-lance help, thereby incurring potentially large overtime charges.

Finally, many companies feel their management has better control of and involvement in the advertising when it is done in-house by company people—especially when the organization is a "single-business" company whose products and services are similar[12] (see Figure 3–8).

In spite of these advantages, many full-service house agencies do not succeed. While attempting to save as much of the independent agency's commission as possible, some companies sacrifice considerably more than they gain.

First, while the in-house agency offers greater flexibility, it is often at the expense of the creativity offered by autonomous agencies.[13] Large, independent agencies provide experience, versatility, and a diversity of talent. In-house agencies, on the other hand, typically find it quite difficult to attract the best creative talent. In part, this may be because of the slower wage-raise policy in some corporations. But more important, creative people generally fear getting trapped in what they perceive to be a "stagnant" environment lacking the incentive, vitality, and stiff competition of the agency world.

Perhaps even worse than the loss of creativity is the loss of objectivity that the independent agency normally brings to the client. Advertising suffers when it becomes excessively company-oriented rather than consumer-oriented. By overly reflecting the internal politics, policies, and views of corporate management, it rapidly becomes stiff and self-serving. The result, all too often, is work that is simply boring.

FIGURE   3–8

Every year the in-house advertising agency for Bloomingdale's department store produces a variety of top-quality, award-winning advertisements that keep the company on the cutting edge of retail advertising creativity.

For years, advertisers and agencies have squabbled over the pros and cons of in-house advertising agencies. Independent agencies resent the intrusion of house agencies and harbor a degree of bitterness toward the media that allow these intruders to collect the commissions they feel should be reserved for "real" agencies. It's unlikely this argument will be settled in the near future.

THE ADVERTISING AGENCIES

Why would a shrewd businessman like Frank Perdue, who spends millions of dollars a year advertising his chickens, want to hire an advertising agency? Couldn't he afford to hire his own people and then save money by doing his advertising in-house? And how does Scali, McCabe, Sloves get such a multimillion-dollar advertising account? Do all the agency's accounts have to be that big for an agency to make money? How do smaller agencies make money?

These and many other questions are logical ones for the beginning student of advertising. A discussion of the agency side of the advertising business can shed some light on these issues and give a clearer understanding of the important role agencies play. We will first discuss what an advertising agency is and why so many advertisers use one.

The Role of the Advertising Agency

An *advertising agency* is an independent organization of creative people and businesspeople who specialize in the development and preparation of advertising plans, advertisements, and other promotional tools. The agency also arranges or contracts for the purchase of advertising space and time in the various media. It does all this on behalf of different advertisers, or sellers, who are referred to as its *clients,* in an effort to find customers for their goods and services.[14]

This definition gives us some good clues as to why so many advertisers hire advertising agencies. The first thing the definition points out is that agencies are *independent*. That means they are not owned by the advertiser, the media, or the suppliers. This independence allows them to bring an outside, objective viewpoint to the advertiser's business. Their daily exposure to a broad spectrum of marketing situations and problems is what gives agencies the savvy, skill, and competence to serve the needs of their various clients. For some clients, those needs can be immense. Ad Lab 3-A provides an overview of the extent of the ad agency business in the United States.

The agency employs a combination of creative people and businesspeople who are specialists in applying the complex art and science of advertising to business problems. They include writers, artists, market and media analysts, researchers, and specialists of all sorts who apply their skills and talents to help make their clients successful. They have day-to-day contact with outside specialists and suppliers who illustrate advertisements, take photographs, set type, retouch art, shoot commercials, and record sound—all the steps required to produce quality work. They are able to stay abreast of the latest advances in technology, the most recent changes in prices, and the most current production problems.

By arranging and contracting for the purchase of broadcast time and magazine or newspaper space, the agency provides yet another service to the client. For one thing, it saves the client money. Most media allow the agency to keep 15 percent of the gross amount of money placed in their medium. This *agency commission* reduces the amount of money the advertiser would otherwise have to pay the agency for its services. For its commission, the agency is expected to maintain an expertise in the various media available to the advertiser. This is no small task.

Finally, agencies work for a variety of different sellers to find customers for their goods and services. Agencies work for their clients, not for the media and/or the suppliers. Their moral, ethical, financial, and sometimes even legal obligation is to their clients—to find them the best prices, give

AD LAB 3-A　　　　　How Big Is the Agency Business?

Although New York, Los Angeles, and Chicago are the three leading advertising centers in the United States, few cities with at least 100,000 people are without an advertising agency. Indeed, many small cities and towns support one or more agencies. Of 9,995 agencies, however, only 275, or 2.75 percent, have gross incomes of $5 million or more. These agencies represent approximately $34 billion in domestic billing—that is, the amount of client money the agency spends on media and equivalent activities. Interestingly, the top 10 agencies (which account for approximately one-tenth of 1 percent of all agencies) handle 27 percent of the total volume of business (see table).

An estimated 105,319 people are employed by United States–based advertising agencies today. Most agencies, however, have a low "body count" compared with that of other professions. When an agency staff is well balanced in skills and versatility, only five or six people can easily handle $1 million in annual billing. In agencies that bill $20 million or more per year, this ratio is usually even lower.

Basic information about advertising agencies in the United States can be found in the *Standard Directory of Advertising Agencies.* Known as the "Red Book" because of its cover color, this guide to the industry lists the names and addresses of most of the nation's agencies by state. It names the associations to which they belong, if any, and the media associations that recognize them for credit purposes. It also lists each agency's annual billings by media classification, the names and titles of its executives, and the names of its current accounts.

A related volume, the *Standard Directory of Advertisers,* lists the names of thousands of U.S. companies that advertise and the names and titles of their executives. Also cited are the names of their advertising agencies, their total annual advertising budget, and the principal media they use.

Top 10 U.S. agencies in U.S. income ($ millions)

Rank	Agency	Gross income 1987	Billings Rank	Billings 1987
1	Young & Rubicam	$735	(1)	$4,906
2	Saatchi & Saatchi Advertising	694	(2)	4,609
3	BBDO Worldwide	537	(3)	3,664
4	Ogilvy & Mather Worldwide	529	(4)	3,663
5	McCann-Erickson Worldwide	513	(5)	3,418
6	Backer Spielvogel Bates Worldwide	499	(6)	3,330
7	J. Walter Thompson Co.	483	(7)	3,222
8	Lintas: Worldwide	418	(8)	2,787
9	D'Arcy Masius Benton & Bowles	371	(10)	2,494
10	Leo Burnett Co.	369	(12)	2,462

United States-based agencies are ranked by worldwide gross income and billings. DDB Needham Worldwide is ranked ninth by billings.

Laboratory Application

From your library, obtain a copy of the agency "Red Book." Are agencies in your town listed? If so, how many? If not, what is the town nearest you that has agency listings? How many?

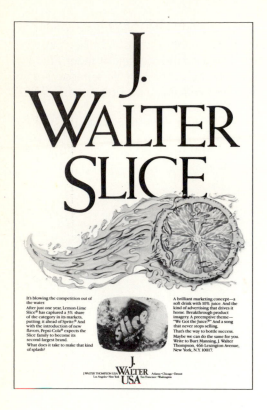

It's blowing the competition out of the water.
After just one year, Lemon-Lime Slice® has captured a 5% share of the category in its markets, putting it ahead of Sprite® And with the introduction of new flavors, Pepsi-Cola® expects the Slice family to become its second-largest brand.
What does it take to make that kind of splash?

A brilliant marketing concept—a soft drink with 10% juice. And the kind of advertising that drives it home. Breakthrough product imagery. A preemptive theme—"We Got the Juice®" And a song that never stops selling. That's the way to bottle success. Maybe we can do the same for you. Write to Burt Manning, J. Walter Thompson, 666 Lexington Avenue, New York, N.Y. 10017.

J. WALTER THOMPSON USA
Los Angeles • New York   Atlanta • Chicago • Detroit   San Francisco • Washington

FIGURE 3–9

Agencies typically advertise their current clients' successes in an effort to win new clients. In this self-promotion ad, J. Walter Thompson points to the splash it made introducing Slice, the new lemon-lime drink from Pepsi-Cola. "That's the way to bottle success," says the agency.

them the best-quality work, and help them grow and prosper. For much the same reason that a well-run business seeks professional help from an attorney, accountant, banker, or management specialist, advertisers use agencies because they are usually equipped to create more effective advertising—and select more effective media—than the advertisers can do themselves. Today, almost all sizable advertisers rely on an advertising agency for expert, objective counsel and unique creative skills[15] (see Figure 3–9).

Notwithstanding these facts, many agency switches are still made every year. Moreover, some advertisers determine that it is in their best interest to work without an agency. Why is this so, if the agencies have all that independence, skill, expertise, and talent we just discussed?

First, there is the obvious problem of personality conflicts and lack of communication that sometimes enters every human relationship. Second, not every agency possesses as much independence, skill, expertise, or talent as it should. In fact, some advertisers outgrow their agencies and need the additional services offered by larger firms. Further, while an agency may produce outstanding results for one type of client, it may be totally incapable of grasping the problem or devising an appropriate solution for another type. Finally, some agencies lack the backbone to remain truly independent. Some clients—and this is very common—fail to see the expertise being offered and try to force their agencies to give them safe, but unexciting, advertising. In the constant effort to please the client, the agency may yield too often to this pressure. The common excuse for this is simply, "It's the client's money."

The corollary to this problem is agency arrogance. Some agencies simply refuse to listen to the client and, instead, try to impose inappropriate creative solutions. In any of these cases, the advertising work invariably suffers, the results received by the advertiser are less than desired, and either the agency or the client becomes restless and desires a change.

A recent phenomenon has also contributed to agency switching. During the 1980s, the agency business has undergone the same merger-mania experienced in other industries. As the big agencies have gobbled up one another, conflicts have arisen over the handling of competitive accounts. When Saatchi & Saatchi bought the Ted Bates agency, for example, it became the world's largest advertising agency, but it immediately lost Bates's Colgate-Palmolive account because of the conflict with Saatchi & Saatchi's client Procter & Gamble.[16] (See Ad Lab 3-B.)

The fact is, the advertising business has always been characterized by tension between the advertisers and their agencies. The advertiser is the employer—the client who pays the bill. The agency works at the pleasure of the client; it is employed for the sole purpose of benefiting the client's business; and its services can be terminated at any time. This tension may be healthy at times, contributing to better effort and outstanding work on the agency's part. But if the relationship is mishandled or abused, it can also result in a very unhappy marriage.

Types of Agencies

Advertising agencies are normally classified by two criteria: (1) the range of services they offer and (2) the type of business they handle. Agency services, for example, may be described as *full-service* or *à la carte*. And the type of business may generally be categorized as either *consumer* or *industrial.* While there are many possible subdivisions within each of these groups, we will discuss these four major categories briefly.

Full-Service Agencies

The modern *full-service advertising agency* is staffed to serve its clients in all areas of communication and promotion. Its services are essentially grouped in two categories—advertising and nonadvertising.

Advertising services include planning, creating, and producing advertisements as well as performing research and media selection services. Nonadvertising functions may run the gamut from packaging to public

AD LAB 3-B   Megamergers Make Agency Supergroups

Historians will record the 1980s as the decade of merger-mania as America's largest corporations gobbled one another up to make the big still bigger and the small proportionately smaller still. The advertising agency business was not immune to this peculiar virus. And in fact, according to some sources, the agencies caught this disease from their corporate clients—as a result of either trying to emulate them or keep up in size.

Some of the agencies infected by this contagion included Bozell & Jacobs, Kenyon & Eckhardt, Doyle Dane Bernbach, BBDO, Needham Harper Worldwide, Young & Rubicam, Dancer Fitzgerald Sample, and many others. But the biggest empire builder of all was London-based Saatchi & Saatchi PLC, which rapidly became the world's largest agency by acquiring, in succession, Compton Advertising, Dancer Fitzgerald Sample, and the giant Ted Bates Worldwide. In addition, the Saatchi brothers, Charles and Maurice, also bought up a host of other firms in related communications fields, including the major research firms of Yankelovich, Skelly and White and Clancy Shulman.

All this shuffling of the agency decks resulted in the establishment of several advertising supergroups with gross billings in the billions of dollars. However, it also resulted in a period of unprecedented turmoil due to the inevitable conflicts of client loyalties, confusion of employees, and misunderstanding of management direction. With the Ted Bates merger, for example, Colgate-Palmolive withdrew its $100 million account from Bates since Saatchi handled Colgate's prime competitor, Procter & Gamble. Further defections from the agency after the merger quickly climbed to a total of $300 million. This, no doubt, caused other potential mergerers to pause and consider the potential jeopardy, but the trend still continued.

Fortune magazine reported that with this consolidation of the industry, new consideration had to be given to how agencies operate, how to handle the issue of competing clients within one agency, and how to foster creativity in a large organizational structure. As Colgate's Chairman Reuben Mark said, "The most important thing when you work with an agency is to get truly great creative [work]. I fail to see how these mergers are going to improve the creative [product]."

This view was echoed by James Tappan at General Foods, who said they did not believe that agency mega-mergers represent the client's best interest.

Agency spokespeople, on the other hand, defended the merger trend saying that as clients go global with their products and their marketing, the major agencies have to do the same thing in order to adequately serve their clients' interests. According to Robert Bloom of the Bloom Companies, the effect of a merger on an agency is based not on the size of the merged company but rather on the intimacy of the client relationship. That relationship, though, may be difficult to maintain in an institutional environment.

Laboratory Applications

1. Do you think the consternation of major advertisers over the agency mergers was warranted? Why or why not?
2. What effect might the megamerger trend have on smaller or medium-sized agencies? Why?

relations and producing sales promotion materials, annual reports, trade-show exhibits, and sales training materials.[17]

The two basic types of full-service agencies include the general consumer agency and the business or industrial agency.

General Consumer Agencies A *general agency* is one that is willing to represent the widest variety of accounts. In practice, however, it concentrates on *consumer* accounts—that is, companies that make goods purchased chiefly by consumers. Soaps, cereals, automobiles, pet foods, and toiletries are examples. Most of the advertising produced by the general agency is placed in consumer media—television, radio, billboards, newspapers, and magazines—which are commissionable to the agency. As a result, the general agency has traditionally obtained most of its income from media commissions.

PEOPLE IN ADVERTISING

Larry R. Jones

Senior Vice President/Group Management Director
Foote, Cone & Belding

As a group management director, Larry Jones is responsible for overseeing and managing all the agency's work for a group of clients, such as Denny's Restaurants and Sunkist Growers, Inc., at Foote, Cone & Belding's offices in Los Angeles, California. He is a line officer in the agency's ranks, working his way up in the organization, dealing with client needs and problems on a day-to-day basis. At the same time, he also sits on Foote, Cone's Executive Committee and Operations Committee, and he has served as president of the Management Advisory Board.

But Jones was not always in the advertising business. An honors graduate from San Diego State University, he began his business career in sales as a marketing representative for IBM. He spent four years learning about customers, their needs, IBM products, competitive products, how to sell, and how to handle frustration. He finally left because he felt the products he had to offer were not always the best for his customers' needs, yet they were the only products he had to sell.

One of the main reasons he went into the advertising business was "because I knew we could make a product based on customer needs, and I could play a key role in developing that product."

Larry first joined the account management program at Grey Advertising, which had one of the few training programs in Los Angeles, and he felt lucky to join them and learn from the ground floor up. After eight months of working in every department in the agency, he was promoted to assistant account executive on the Honda motorcycle account. His career as an advertising man had begun.

Over the next seven years, Larry worked on Honda, on various power products, on Bank of America, and on Taco

General agencies may include the international superagencies and the other large New York firms we frequently hear about (Saatchi & Saatchi, Young & Rubicam, Ogilvy & Mather, Foote, Cone & Belding, N. W. Ayer, to name just a few), (see Figure 3–10). However, they may also include the thousands of smaller *entrepreneurial* agencies that inhabit every major city in the United States and Canada (Rubin/Postaer, Los Angeles; Ruhr/Paragon, Minneapolis; Goodis-Wolf, Toronto; The Martin Agency, Richmond; and so on).

While profit margins in the entrepreneurial agencies are often slim, their service is often more responsive to the smaller clients they serve, and the quality of their work is frequently startling in its creativity.[18] Moreover, some entrepreneurial agencies have carved out a niche for themselves by serving the needs of particular market segments. These include, for example, the many ethnic-specialty agencies now proliferating in the country

---

Bell. During this time, he learned that a successful account management person has to combine many skills as he or she is called upon to act as the agency's representative to the client and the client's representative to the agency.

When he left Grey, it was to join Foote, Cone & Belding as a vice president/management director on the Denny's Restaurant account, and he since has been promoted to senior vice president/group management director.

"While the responsibilities change as you move up in agency management," says Jones, "the basic ingredients for good account management work remain the same."

He offers several rules for success as an account manager in the advertising business:

Know Your Business Know every part of the agency business. The creative product is a result of many agency functions and disciplines, and to be a great account manager you must know research, media, production, and even billing and paying.

Know Your Client's Business While you will never know it as well as your client, a thorough understanding of your client's business will be the basis for selling better work and developing a stronger client-agency relationship.

Be Curious Don't ignore anything. Question, probe, and dig deep to understand about your client's products, customers, and goals. The insights you discover and bring to the agency will help provide the basis for outstanding creative work. Omit information and you eliminate opportunity.

Listen This is a business of ideas and feeling. Often people—both clients and agency folks—don't articulate exactly what they mean. You must listen carefully—very carefully—not just to hear what they are saying but to hear what they mean.

Have a Point of View You represent the agency. Be sure you bring a point of view about the agency's work to your client. A yes-man insults the client's intelligence and misrepresents the agency.

Understand the Creative Process This is not a linear process. Ideas rarely come out fully formed, and they must be encouraged, nurtured, and grown. Creative people and account people think differently. Neither style is right or wrong. But when combined, the result can be outstanding work. So don't stifle the creative person's ideas or feelings.

Build Teams Great creative work is a product of all functions in an agency. The account manager must blend those teams efficiently to get great advertising. Acknowledge the contributions your team members make.

Be Enthusiastic You set the tone for the energy that goes into the work for your client. Your enthusiasm will make a difference; it's contagious.

Be Sure It's Still Fun The advertising business is a great deal of fun; but to some people it can be crazy. If you are not having fun, get out. It must not be right for you.

You can really fly
once you know where you're going.

We believe the sharpest advertising strategies provide the greatest creative freedom. Only when you know exactly where you're going can the imagination soar free, without fear or formulas.
YOUNG & RUBICAM INC.

FIGURE   3–10

Young & Rubicam Inc., the largest American advertising agency, uses beautiful imagery to illustrate a basic truth about advertising . . . and life.

(e.g., Bermudez Associates, Los Angeles; Castor Spanish International, New York; Burrell Advertising, Chicago; and Sosa & Associates, San Antonio).

Industrial Agencies An *industrial agency* represents client companies that make goods to be sold to other businesses. Computer hardware and software, smelting furnaces, locomotives, and radium counters are examples of such goods. Business and industrial advertising is a very important aspect of the profession requiring highly developed technical knowledge as well as the ability to translate this knowledge into precise and persuasive communication (see Figure 3–11).

Most industrial advertising is placed in trade magazines and other business publications. These media are commissionable, but since their circulation is smaller, their rates are far lower than those of consumer media. The result is that the commissions are usually not large enough to cover the cost of the agency's services, so industrial agencies frequently charge the client an additional service fee. While this can be expensive, especially for small advertisers, the failure to obtain an industrial agency's expertise may carry an even higher price tag in terms of lost marketing opportunities.[19]

Business and industrial agencies may be large, international firms like HCM/New York, which handles such major industrial corporations as Ashland Chemical, IBM, and United Technologies; or they may be smaller firms experienced in such specialties as recruitment advertising (help wanted), health and medicine, or electronics.

À la Carte Services

In recent years, as the trend toward specialization has grown, there have been a number of offshoots from the agency business. Among these are the small agency-type groups called *creative boutiques* and specialty businesses such as *media-buying services*.

Creative Boutiques Some talented specialists like art directors, designers, and copywriters have set up their own creative services called *creative boutiques*. Working for advertisers and occasionally subcontracting to advertising agencies, their mission is to develop exciting creative concepts and to produce fresh, distinctive advertising messages.

Because advertising effectiveness depends largely on originality in concept, design, and writing, advertisers tend to value this quality highly. However, the creative services of the boutique are usually provided without the marketing and sales direction that full-service agencies offer. This factor tends to limit the boutique to the role of a creative supplier.

For small advertisers, though, the creativity, responsiveness, and economy of the creative boutique are often worth these trade-offs. Moreover, creative boutiques are ubiquitous—good ones can be found in almost every metropolitan area.

Media-Buying Services Just as some copywriters and art directors have set up creative boutiques, some experienced media specialists have set up organizations that purchase and package radio and television time. The largest of these is Western International Media, Los Angeles, which places over $300 million worth of media advertising annually. Such companies owe their success, in part, to the fact that radio and TV time is "perishable"; that is, a 60-second radio spot at 8 P.M. cannot be sold after that hour has arrived. For that reason, radio and television stations try to presell as much advertising time as possible and discount their rates to anyone who buys a large amount of time. Therefore, the media-buying service can negotiate a special discount rate with radio and TV stations. It then sells this time to advertising agencies or advertisers.

As part of their service, media-buying firms provide their customers (both clients and agencies) with a detailed analysis of the media buy. Once the media package is sold, the buying service orders the spots on each of the stations involved, verifies performance, sees to it that stations "make good" for any spots missed, and even pays the media bills.

The method of compensation used by media-buying services varies. Some receive a set fee. Others operate on an incentive basis, receiving a prescribed percentage of the money they save the client.

What Do Agency People Do?

The American Association of Advertising Agencies (AAAA) is the national organization of the advertising agency business. Its standards for membership are very high, and it has endeavored to be the most responsible speaker for the advertising industry. Its almost 400 members, representing the largest and oldest agencies in the business, place almost 80 percent of all advertising handled by agencies in the United States.

In its *Standards of Practice,* the AAAA explains that the purpose of an agency is to interpret to an advertiser's audience the advantages of a product or service. How does it do this? First, the agency conducts a study of the client's product or service in order to determine its strengths and weaknesses. Next, it analyzes the present and potential market for the product.

FIGURE   3–11

The van Bronkhorst Group, Inc., an industrial agency in California's Silicon Valley, seeks creative people who have the ability to develop a diversity of collateral sales material besides just ads. At the same time, they promote their rapid growth and high profitability to entice ambitious new employees.

Then, using its knowledge of the channels of distribution and sales and of all the available media, the agency formulates a plan for carrying the advertiser's message to consumers, wholesalers, dealers, or contractors.

Finally comes the execution of the plan. That includes the writing and designing of advertisements, the contracting of space and time with the media, the proper production of ads and commercials and the forwarding of these to the media, the verifying of media insertions, and the billing for services and media used.

The agency also cooperates with the client's marketing staff to enhance the effect of advertising through package design, sales research and training, and production of sales literature and displays.[20]

To understand more fully the various functions just outlined, let us look at all the agency people involved in the case of Perdue Chickens presented earlier in this chapter. While Scali, McCabe, Sloves was the agency Frank Perdue selected to handle his account, it was not one of New York's largest agencies. In fact, at the time, it was one of the smaller shops, but it had piled up an impressive record of award-winning advertising with several other accounts such as Volvo and Dictaphone (see Figure 3–12). As a full-service agency, Scali, McCabe, Sloves provides all the services suggested by the AAAA service standards.

Research

Sam Scali, the agency's creative director, has said, "We can't create on intuition. Give artists all the information they need to do a job—because advertising is based on information."[21] Before any advertising is created, therefore, research must be undertaken to study the uses and advantages

FIGURE   3–12

Many advertisers and agencies claim that award-winning advertising doesn't sell. Scali, McCabe, Sloves answers with the facts of Volvo's growth, Perdue's sales success, and testimonials from Dictaphone, all of whom had many award-winning ads. As they say, it's possible to do both.

of the product or service, to analyze the present and potential customers, and to determine what will influence them to buy. In Chapters 5 and 6, we will discuss some of the many types of research conducted by agencies to discover this information.

Planning

The planning process actually begins before research and continues afterward. In the case of Perdue, Sam Scali, Ed McCabe, and Alan Pesky, the director of account services, were responsible for initiating this process with the client to determine his marketing and advertising objectives. They then met with the agency's market analysts, media planners, and other creative people to determine the appropriate advertising strategy. The results of research were considered, and the evaluation of the agency's planning team was then distilled into a detailed marketing and advertising plan. After the client approves this plan, it becomes the blueprint for the agency's creative and media program. (See Chapter 7.)

Creative Services

Most advertising relies heavily on *copy*—the words that make up the headline and message of the ad. People like Ed McCabe who create these words are called *copywriters*. Their work requires skill since they must be able to condense all that can be said about a product or service into just those points that are salient and pertinent to a given advertisement. Thus, what copywriters don't say is just as important as what they do say (see Chapter 8). Copywriters usually work closely with the agency artists and production staff.

The agency art department is composed of art directors, like Sam Scali, and graphic designers whose primary job is to *lay out* advertising—that is, to illustrate in sketches how the various components of an ad will fit together. When their assignment is to conceive a television commercial, the artists lay it out in a comic-strip series of sequential frames called a *storyboard*.

Most large agencies have their own art departments (see Figure 3–13). Others prefer to purchase art services from independent studios or outside free-lance designers (see Chapter 9).

Print and Broadcast Production

After the advertisement is designed and written and the client has approved it, it goes into production. This is the responsibility of the agency's print production manager or broadcast producers and directors (see Chapters 10 and 11).

For print advertising, the production department buys type, photographs, illustrations, and other components needed for the finished art. Production personnel then work with photoplatemakers, color separators, and other graphic arts suppliers to obtain the materials needed for the media.

If the ad is a broadcast commercial, the broadcast production personnel take the approved script or the storyboard and set about producing the finished product. Working with actors, camerapeople, and other production specialists, they produce the commercial on tape (for radio) or on film or videotape (for television).

WANTED: ART DIRECTOR FOR A SLIMEBUCKET ACCOUNT.

Oh sure, we have the typical complement of glitzy high technology and packaged goods accounts and junkets to the coast to overproduce TV spots. And of course, the Art Director we hire will work on many of them.

But he or she will also work on one of the nation's largest manufacturers of sanitary equipment. That's right, slimebuckets. We're talking trash here. And this A.D. will have his or her pretty head in trash for a few days every month. Sound exciting? We think so.

The Art Director we want is an excellent conceptual thinker. He or she brings at least 3 years of agency experience—and a closetful of awards for print and television advertising.

We offer a terrific compensation package. So if you'd like to explore the possibility of working for a slimebucket agency, call Mark Travers, Executive Creative Director.

KERLICK, SWITZER & JOHNSON ADVERTISING, INC.
727 North First Street • St. Louis, Missouri 63102

(314) 241-4656

FIGURE   3–13

Kerlick, Switzer & Johnson Advertising, Inc., a high-tech agency in St. Louis, uses humor to attract creative talent. This type of approach is very common in the business and often produces outstanding results. Creative people want to work for agencies and on accounts that are interesting, challenging, and fun.

Traffic

One of the greatest sins in the advertising agency business is to miss a deadline; and the whole business revolves around deadlines. If Scali, McCabe, Sloves intends to run an ad in a monthly trade magazine read by Perdue's grocers and they miss the deadline, they will have to wait another whole month for that ad to appear. That does not please clients.

The job of the agency traffic department, therefore, is to make sure the work flow is smooth and efficient. It coordinates all the phases of production and checks to see that everything is completed on time and that all ads and commercials are received by the media before the deadline.

As the keystone position in the agency, the traffic department is often the first position for entry-level college graduates and is an excellent place to learn the operations of an agency.

Media

When Frank Perdue started advertising, the agency recommended subway posters as an initial medium for three reasons: it required only a small budget, the art could be used again in butcher-shop windows, and the message would be read by working mothers and lower- to middle-income groups. Later, as the campaign developed and more money became available, other more expensive media were considered and used.

The job of the media director is to match the profile of the desired target market with the profiles of the audiences of a wide range of media. The media are then evaluated according to efficiency and cost, and the media director recommends the best medium or media combination to use (see Chapter 12).

For the client, unbiased and authenticated media information is one of the most valuable services an agency can offer.

Account Management

Scali, McCabe, Sloves's account management team is an essential part of the agency's organization. *Account executives (AEs)* are virtually in business for themselves. They are the liaison between the agency and the client. Responsible on the one hand for mustering all the agency's services for the benefit of the client and on the other hand for representing the agency's point of view to the client, the account executive is often caught in the middle. AEs, therefore, must be tough, tactful, diplomatic, creative, communicative, persuasive, knowledgeable, sensitive, honest, and courageous—all at once. And they must be on time for meetings.[22]

Scali, McCabe, Sloves and other large agencies have many account executives who report to *management (or account) supervisors,* who, in turn, report to the agency's director of account services.

New Business

To survive, agencies must grow. The best creative people always want to work for the "hot shops," the ones that are growing. Growth requires a steady flow of new business. Often this comes from new products developed by existing clients. In other cases, clients seek out agencies whose work they are familiar with. Scali, McCabe, Sloves receives 15 to 20 calls per week, for example, because they are well known for the work they have done on Perdue, Volvo, Maxell recording tape, and Nikon cameras, to mention just a few.

Most agencies keep a constant eye open for new business and have either "new-business representatives" or agency principals assigned to target prospective clients and sell the agency's services (see Figure 3–14).

Administration

It has been said that agencies are as much in the bookkeeping business as the advertising business. Scali, McCabe, Sloves, for example, receives invoices every day from radio and TV stations, magazines, newspapers, billboard companies, transit companies, type houses, platemakers, free-lance artists and illustrators, talent agencies, photographers, television production companies, sound studios, music producers, printers, and so on. These bills are totaled by the accounting department on periodic invoices to the clients. Client payments are received and recorded, and the accounting department has to pay all these outside suppliers.

Dealing with variations in media commissions, agency markups, errors in invoices, cash discounts, and the complex flow of large amounts of cash

FIGURE 3–14

A regional agency in Minneapolis, Martin/Williams, suggests that clients come there not for the weather but for their outstanding creative work. Interestingly enough, Minneapolis has indeed become one of the major advertising centers in the country.

for dozens of clients requires a highly competent accounting staff. At the same time, the staff must monitor the agency's income and expenses and keep management informed of the company's financial status.

Additional Services

What has just been described might be considered basic to the advertising agency business. Many agencies, however, provide a variety of other services and employ specialists to perform these tasks. Scali, McCabe, Sloves, for instance, has a highly regarded sales promotion department that is used by most of the firm's clients to produce dealer ads, window posters, point-of-purchase displays, dealer contest materials, and sales material.

Other agencies maintain public relations specialists, direct-marketing specialists, home economics experts, package designers, or economists depending on the nature and needs of their clients.

How Are Agencies Organized?

How an advertising agency organizes its functions, operations, and personnel may vary greatly according to its size, the types of accounts it serves, and whether it is local, regional, national, or international.

In small agencies (annual billings less than $15 million–$20 million), daily business operations are usually supervised by the owner or president, who may be in charge of new business development as well (see Figure 3–15). Client contact is generally handled by account executives and account supervisors. The account executive may also produce creative concepts for the clients and even write copy. Artwork may be produced by an inside art director or purchased from an independent studio or freelance designer. Most small agencies have a production and traffic department or an employee who fulfills these functions. They also may have a media buyer, but in very small agencies the account executives also purchase media time and space for their accounts.

FIGURE   3–15

Typical structure of a small advertising agency.

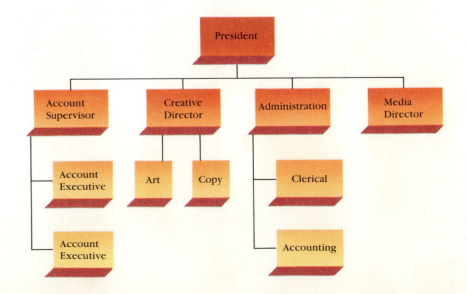

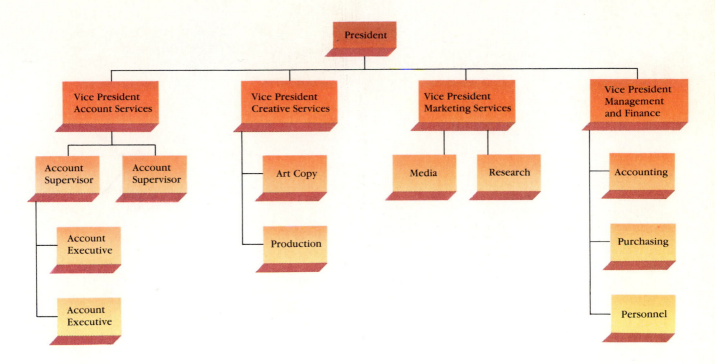

FIGURE   3–16

Departmental system.

In medium and large agencies, organization is generally more formal and is usually structured according to the departmental system or the group system.

In the *departmental system,* each of the agency's varied functions—account services, creative services, marketing services, and administration—is set up as a separate department (see Figure 3–16). Each department is called on as needed to perform its specialty. The account executive handles the client contact, the creative department writes the ad and lays it out, marketing services selects media, and so forth.

As agencies get larger, though, they tend to use the *group system* in which the agency is divided into a number of "little" agencies or groups. Each group, which is headed by an account supervisor, is composed of account executives, copywriters, art directors, a media director, and any other specialists needed (see Figure 3–17). The group may be assigned to serve only one account—if the account is large—or, as in many cases, three or four clients. A very large agency may have dozens or more groups. It may even have separate production and traffic units to serve each one.

Each of these systems has its advantages. The organization that best enables the agency to provide its services effectively, efficiently, and profitably is the one that should be implemented.

How Do Agencies Make Money?

Like any other business, an advertising agency must make a fair profit on the services it renders. Lately, though, realizing this profit has become more and more difficult. Numerous forces have caused agencies to rethink their compensation policies. Some of these forces have included the

FIGURE 3–17

Group system.

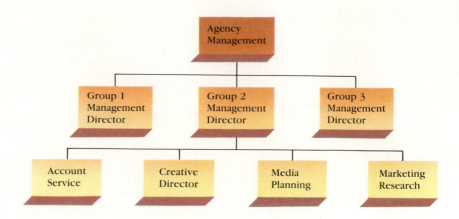

megamerger trend, the reduction of traditional media advertising budgets, shifts in promotional emphasis from media advertising to sales promotion vehicles, increases in production costs, and the fragmentation of media vehicles, to name just a few. Moreover, inasmuch as the amount of agency service typically varies from client to client, agencies have been forced to develop a variety of compensation methods to arrive at an equitable financial arrangement. Basically, agencies make money from three sources: (1) media commissions, (2) markups on outside purchases, and (3) fees or retainers. We will discuss each of these briefly.

Media Commissions

Agencies save the media considerable expense in sales and collections. So, historically, the major media have allowed recognized agencies to retain a 15 percent commission on any space or time they purchase for their clients. (For outdoor advertising the commission is usually 16⅔ percent.) The way this system works is simple. Assume you are an advertiser and plan to spend $100 on a magazine ad for your company. Working with you, your agency arranges to buy the space from the magazine, places the order for you, and delivers the ad to the magazine. When the ad appears, the magazine bills the agency $100. The agency then bills you $100. You pay the agency this gross amount, and the agency remits the money to the magazine *less* its 15 percent commission, as follows:

$$\$100 - (100 \times 0.15) = \$85$$

If you spent $1 million, the agency's commission would be $150,000, and it would remit $850,000 to the media. For large accounts (those billing more than $5 million annually), the agency normally provides its creative services, media services, and accounting and account management services for this fee. For smaller accounts, though, the commission is usually not enough to cover the cost of all these services, so additional compensation is required.

Many media also allow a 2 percent discount for prompt payment of their invoices (normally within 10 days). Agencies usually pass this savings on to their clients in the form of a bill reduction. In the advertising business, when the media rep quotes rates to the agency, he or she describes this prompt payment policy by simply saying, "The cost of the ad is $10,000, less 15 and 2."

Markups

To create a magazine ad, the agency normally has to buy type, photography, illustrations, and a variety of other services or materials from outside suppliers. These suppliers do not normally allow the agency a commission, so the agency buys these services and adds a markup to the client's bill.

Traditionally, advertising agencies have added a 17.65 percent markup to outside purchases. The reason for this figure goes back to the tradition of the 15 percent commission. When you add 17.65 percent to an invoice, the amount added becomes 15 percent of the new total, as follows:

$$\$85 \times 17.65\% = \$15$$
$$\$85 + \$15 = \$100$$
$$\$15 = 15\% \times \$100$$

Thus, the agency ends up with 15 percent of the total bill, which is the traditional agency commission. Some media, especially local media, do not allow for an agency commission. Local newspapers, for example, may allow a commission on the higher, national rates they charge national advertisers but not on the lower rates charged to local advertisers. Therefore, advertising agencies that use these media frequently use the markup formula to receive their commission. In this case, when your agency places an advertisement costing $1,000, the agency will bill you $1,176.50. The agency keeps the $176.50 markup and remits the $1,000 to the medium.

In recent years, many agencies found that 17.65 percent is not a sufficient markup to cover the cost of services they perform in dealing with outside suppliers. This is especially true on smaller accounts where the sums spent are minor. As a result, some agencies increased their markups to as much as 20 to 25 percent. While this has helped, the squeeze on agency profits still increases every year and has forced many agencies to move to a fee system in place of, or in addition to, commissions and markups.

Fees

Assume you are a very small advertising agency (fewer than 10 employees) with several local advertising clients. Perhaps your largest advertiser spends only $20,000 per month in commissionable media, yet you spend a lot of time servicing the account, providing in-depth media plans, staging in-store promotions, supervising press interviews, and developing posters and displays for windows and counters. Obviously, the $3,000 per month you receive from the media commissions does not cover the amount of work you, your secretary, art director, copywriter, and media person have to devote to this client. Nor does the $100 to $200 extra you pick up in markups offset the tremendous amount of time required plus the cost of your office overhead (see Figure 3–18). You need to charge your client an additional fee for your work to cover all of these costs. How do you determine a reasonable amount?

Agencies that serve their clients on a fee basis frequently use one of two pricing methods. The first is a *fee-commission* combination. With this method, the agency establishes a fixed monthly fee for all its services to the

FIGURE   3–18   Survey of percentages of costs and profits for 242 agencies

Rent, light, and depreciation	7.22%
Taxes (other than U.S. income)	4.11
Other operating expenses	16.89
Total payroll	61.02
Payments into retirement plans	2.32
Insurance for employee benefit	1.71
Total expenses	93.27
Profit before U.S. income tax for all agencies	6.73
U.S. income taxes	1.64

client. If, during a given month, the agency earns any media commissions for time or space purchased for the client, it retains these commissions in addition to the fee.

The second method is a *straight fee* arrangement. This is frequently used for accounts in which the services needed produce no commission income. Examples of this might be research for public relations, brochures, or annual reports. Straight fee arrangements are also used for accounts in which any media commissions received are credited to the client against the fee. The straight fee is frequently called a *retainer* and is similar to the retainers paid to attorneys or accountants for their legal and financial services.

The retainer system is based on a cost plus fixed fees formula. It assures the agency it will receive a fair profit. Under this system, the agency estimates the amount of staff time the client's work will require, determines the cost of that personnel, multiplies by a factor of 2.5 to 3.5 for overhead and another factor (for example, .5) for profit, and that total becomes the fee charged (see Figure 3–19).

Using the data shown in Figure 3–19, you might offer to handle your client's account for a total monthly retainer of $3,000 and to credit any media commissions you might earn against that fee. Or you might decide that a retainer will have to be charged in addition to any commissions that your agency might earn since most of the time you spend will be for noncommissionable work in the areas of public relations and sales promotion.

In either case, it will be up to you to convince your client of the value of your services and to negotiate a compensation arrangement that will be fair for both.

While the traditional commission system is still the predominant form of agency compensation, there is now a trend toward modification of that system. A survey by the Association of National Advertisers found that the large consumer goods advertisers are more likely to use the commission or commission-variation system while the smaller business-to-business advertisers are more likely to use fees.[23]

FIGURE 3-19		How to compute a monthly retainer			
Employee	Monthly salary	Hourly rate*	Billable rate†	Est. hours/ month	Total
1	$1,000	$ 7.69	$23.00	× 10	$ 230
2	2,000	15.38	46.00	× 20	940
3	2,500	19.23	58.00	× 15	870
4	1,750	13.46	40.00	× 20	800
					$2,840

*Assuming approximately 130 hours a month.
†Using 3 as total factor.

FIGURE 3-20

"Big is not necessarily better" is the proclamation in this humorous ad for Justamere Agency. While the principals of this small New Jersey firm point with pride to their work at larger shops, they hope to attract those clients who want the enthusiasm, drive, and personal service that are the hallmarks of small agencies.

How Do Agencies Get Clients?

To succeed, advertising agencies must have clients. But where do those clients come from? What can an agency do when it has a staff of artists, copywriters, account executives, media people, secretaries, and bookkeepers but not enough billing to pay the salaries?

An advertising agency, like any other business, has a product or a service to sell. Clients come to an advertising agency, therefore, in much the same way as they come to an attorney, a doctor, a hairdresser, or a clothier: by referral, through advertising, because they were solicited, or because of reputation (see Figure 3–20).

Referrals

Most good advertising agencies get their clients by referral. The president of one company asks the president of another company who does those great ads, and the next week the agency gets a call. If an agency feels a prospective client may pose a conflict of interest with an existing client, it will refer the new client to another agency.

In the case of local advertisers, representatives of the media frequently refer clients to an agency with whom they have a working relationship. It's important, therefore, for agencies to maintain good relationships with their existing clients, with the media, and with other agencies, and it is common practice for them to put the word out when they are looking for new business.

Solicitations for New Business

An agency may decide to openly solicit new business by (1) advertising, (2) writing solicitation letters, (3) making "cold" calls on prospective clients, or (4) following up leads from sources within the business. Few agencies advertise their services. Considering the business they are in, one survey turned up some amusing answers as to why agencies don't advertise. Among the most common responses were:

> "Advertising is not very effective."
> "We have never been able to agree on an advertising theme."
> "We have never budgeted for advertising."[24]

Most major agencies get their new clients by referral—from existing clients, from friends, or simply because of their reputation. Other lesser-known agencies, though, must take a more aggressive approach, seeking new business through direct solicitation or any other means available.

The important task of soliciting new business usually falls to one of the agency's principals, since the rest of the staff is normally assigned to the work of existing clients. Once a new business prospect has been found, however, staffers may be called in to help prepare the presentation.

Public Relations

Agencies frequently find that their best source of business is simply their good reputation. Although a good reputation normally takes a long time to develop, most agencies participate in activities that help raise their profile in the business community. Some work on charitable committees; others assist local politicians; and some are active in the arts, education, religion, or social circles. Some give seminars; others write articles in magazines; and many others become active in advertising clubs or other professional organizations. All these activities contribute to getting the agency known and respected in the community.

Presentations

Once an advertiser becomes interested in an agency, the agency may be asked to make a presentation. This may mean anything from a simple discussion of the agency's philosophy, experience, personnel, and track record to a full-blown audiovisual show complete with slides, films, sample commercials, or even proposed campaigns. In the profession, the latter is commonly, and somewhat disdainfully, referred to as a "dog and pony show."

Some advertisers ask or imply that they want the agency to make a *speculative presentation,* meaning they want to see what the agency would do for them before they hire them. Most reputable agencies resist giving "spec" presentations because they generally consider it unethical and unprofessional, not to mention expensive. Smaller agencies think it gives larger agencies an unfair advantage. And large agencies do not like to invest money in presentations that allow clients to pick their brains for free. Likewise, many advertisers do not appreciate their agencies "wasting" the time and talent they are paying for on presentations to other clients.

Most agencies try to build their nonspeculative presentations around the work they have performed for other advertisers. In this way, they can demonstrate their versatility, philosophy, expertise, and depth of understanding of the marketplace and the client's business.

A simple fact, often overlooked, is that the presentation process allows the agency and the advertiser to get to know each other and find out if they like one another. Advertising is a very human business, and the advertiser-agency relationship is a peculiar kind of marriage. But as in any marriage, there must be mutual friendship, trust, and communication.

THE CLIENT-AGENCY RELATIONSHIP

What determines the success of a company's advertising program? Obviously, there are many factors. Numerous studies conducted on this question, though, have turned up one consistent determinant—the relationship between the advertiser and its agency.[25] Indeed, it is clear that if an advertiser's relationship with its creative source is less than satisfactory, then that creativity will logically suffer. Therefore, it is important to understand the factors that affect this very unique and special relationship between agency and client in order to improve it. First, though, we should discuss the relationship itself and the various phases through which every agency-client partnership must pass.

Stages in the Client-Agency Relationship

Just as people have life cycles, so do relationships. In the advertising business, the life cycle of the agency-client relationship includes four very definite stages: prerelationship, development, maintenance, and termination.[26] Each of these stages has unique characteristics that ultimately affect the longevity of the partnership. One cynic has rephrased this by saying that in the agency business, every day after you are hired you are one day closer to being fired. And as discussed earlier, the number of agency switches every year would seem to confirm this point of view.

The *prerelationship* phase includes all the time before an agency and client officially get together to do business. They may never have heard of one another, or they may know each other only by reputation or through social contact. Whatever the case, this will naturally affect the perception each has of the other. It is during this time that those all-important first impressions are gained. If the agency meets the prospective client, makes a good impression, and is invited to "pitch" the account, then they may have the opportunity to get to know each other a little and begin working together. Through the presentation, though, the agency's effort will invariably be to maintain the best impression it possibly can. After all, the advertising agency is selling, and the client is buying. (For guidelines that clients can use in choosing an agency see the Checklist for Agency Review.)

Once the agency has been appointed, the *development* phase begins. This is commonly referred to as the honeymoon period, as both the agency and the client are at the peak of their optimism, and they are most anxious to quickly develop a mutually profitable mechanism for working together. Expectations are at their highest, and both sides are most forgiving.

However, this is also when reality first sets in. During this stage, the rules of the relationship are established—either directly or nonverbally. The respective roles get set very quickly; the true personalities of all the players are discovered; the first work of the agency is created; and the agency's work product and work process are awaited with great expectation and then judged very thoroughly by the client. This is also when the agency discovers how well the client pays its bills, how receptive the client is to new ideas, and how the client's various personalities are to work with. The first problems in the relationship occur during the development phase. If they are successfully handled, then the maintenance phase may begin soon afterward.

Maintenance is just that. It is the day-to-day working relationship that, when successful, may go on for many years. Sunkist, for example, has had

Checklist for Agency Review

Rate each agency on a scale from 1 (strongly negative) to 10 (strongly positive).

General Information

☐ Agency size compatible with our needs.

☐ Strength of agency's management.

☐ Stability of agency's financial position.

☐ Compatibility with type of clients agency handles.

☐ Range of services agency is able to offer.

☐ Cost of agency services; billing policies.

Marketing Information

☐ Agency's ability to offer marketing counsel.

☐ Agency's understanding of the markets we serve.

☐ Agency's experience dealing in our market.

☐ Agency's success record; case histories.

Creative Abilities

☐ Well-thought-out creativity; relevance to strategy.

☐ Agency's art strength.

☐ Agency's copy strength.

☐ Overall creative quality.

☐ Effectiveness compared to work of competitors.

Production

☐ Faithfulness to creative concept and execution.

☐ Diligence to schedules and budgets.

☐ Agency's ability to control outside services.

Media

☐ Existence and soundness of media research.

☐ Effective and efficient media strategy.

☐ Ability to achieve objectives within budget.

☐ Strength at negotiating and executing schedules.

☐ Attitude toward periodic review of plan and budget.

Personality

☐ Agency's overall personality, philosophy, or position.

☐ Compatibility with client staff and management.

☐ Willingness to assign top people to account.

Additional Considerations or Comments

_____

_____

_____

_____

_____

the same advertising agency—Foote, Cone & Belding—for over 80 years. Unfortunately, though, the average client-agency relationship lasts only three or four years. During the maintenance stage, all the problems come up sooner or later, and each player's testiness is eventually observed. Whether it is a dispute over billing, a difference of opinion about strategy or execution, or a disagreement over responsibility for an expensive printing error, problems are normal occurrences, and how they are resolved is the true test.

At some point, an irreconcilable difference may occur, and the relationship must be terminated. It may simply be that one or the other decides it is time to move on. The way the termination itself is handled will affect both sides for a long time and is an important factor in determining the possibility of the two ever getting back together (see Figure 3–21).

Factors Affecting the Client-Agency Relationship

Naturally, many forces influence this marriage. They may best be grouped in the following four categories: chemistry, communication, conduct, and changes. We shall discuss each of these four Cs briefly.

Chemistry

The most important critical factor is the personal chemistry between the client's employees and the agency's staff.[27] Good chemistry can create opportunities between the two and can overcome most problems. Poor chemistry will create problems where none exist and will ruin a potentially good campaign. Agencies are usually very conscious of this and, therefore, make efforts to "wine and dine" their clients in hopes of improving this chemistry. While many clients take advantage of this, the smart clients also try to improve the chemistry with their agencies.

Communication

Poor communication, a problem often cited by both agencies and advertisers, can lead to misunderstandings of objectives, strategies, or tactics. It makes the work process inefficient and eventually hurts the work product. It should go without saying that constant and open communication is the key to the understanding and mutual respect essential to a good relationship.[28] Yet it seems that this is a most difficult thing to achieve due to poor systems or poor discipline or poor attitudes on both sides.

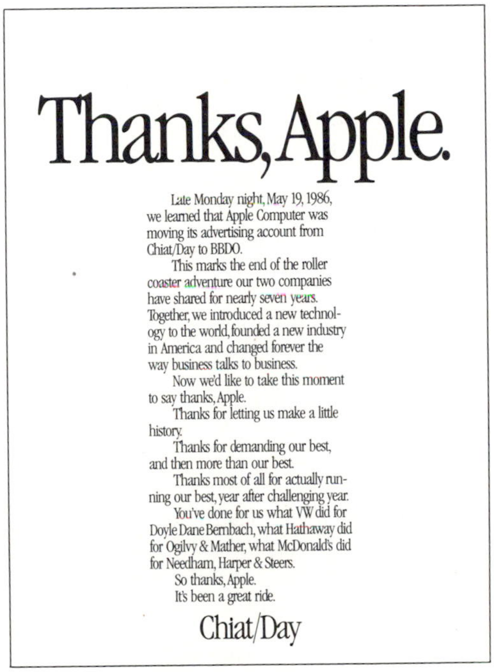

Conduct

Dissatisfaction with agency performance is perhaps the most commonly cited reason for agency switches.[29] *Conduct* includes what everyone in the relationship does—both the work process and the work product. Does the client give timely, accurate information to the agency? Does the agency understand the client's problem and market and offer realistic alternatives to the client? Does the work measure up to the client's subjective idea of good advertising? Does the client appreciate good work when it's presented? Are bills paid promptly without nitpicking, or is billing always a problem? Does the client give the agency any freedom? Does the agency ever exercise any leadership? And does the agency bring work in on time and on budget? (For more on how clients hold up their end of the relationship, see the Checklist for Ways to Be a Better Client.)

Changes

In every relationship, changes take place. Some of them may be damaging to the agency-client partnership. The client's market position may change as new competitors come on the scene and do a better job. Client policy may change, or new management personnel, who may want their own team of players, may arrive. Agencies may lose some of their creative staff to other agencies. Or with the megamerger wave, client conflicts may arise when one agency buys another that handles competing accounts. While changes cannot be avoided, the way they are handled will determine the future of the relationship.

Thanks, Apple.

Late Monday night, May 19, 1986, we learned that Apple Computer was moving its advertising account from Chiat/Day to BBDO.

This marks the end of the roller coaster adventure our two companies have shared for nearly seven years. Together, we introduced a new technology to the world, founded a new industry in America and changed forever the way business talks to business.

Now we'd like to take this moment to say thanks, Apple.

Thanks for letting us make a little history.

Thanks for demanding our best, and then more than our best.

Thanks most of all for actually running our best, year after challenging year.

You've done for us what VW did for Doyle Dane Bernbach, what Hathaway did for Ogilvy & Mather, what McDonald's did for Needham, Harper & Steers.

So thanks, Apple.

It's been a great ride.

Chiat/Day

FIGURE   3-21

When it lost the Apple Computer account, Chiat/Day gave the advertising profession a lesson in "class" with its public thank you letter to the client. Over the years it had produced an array of brilliant, highly creative—and sometimes even controversial—advertisements that had been instrumental in Apple's success.

Checklist for Ways to Be a Better Client

☐ Look for the big idea. Concentrate first on positioning and brand personality. Too many products have neither. Do not allow a *single* advertisement—no matter how brilliant—to change your positioning or your brand personality.

☐ Learn the fine art of conducting a creative meeting. Deal with the important issues first. Strategy. Consumer benefit. Reason why.

☐ Cultivate honesty. Tell your agency the truth. Make sure your advertising tells the truth and *implies* the truth as well.

☐ Be enthusiastic. When you like the advertising, let the creative people know you like it. Applause is their staff of life.

☐ Be frank when you *don't like the advertising*. Copywriters won't hate you for turning down an idea if you give them a *reason*.

☐ Be human. Try to react like a person, not a corporation. Be human enough to laugh at a funny advertisement, even if it is off-strategy.

☐ Be willing to admit you aren't sure. Don't let your agency press you by asking for the order *immediately* after a new copy presentation. You may need time to absorb what they've been thinking about for a long while.

☐ Insist on creative discipline. Professionals don't bridle at discipline. A strategy helps creative people zero in on a target.

☐ Keep the creative people involved in your business. Successful copywriters want to know the latest market shares just as much as you do. Tell them what's happening, good *and* bad.

☐ Don't insulate your top people from the creative people. Agency creative people want to receive objectives directly—not filtered through layers. Good work is done in an atmosphere of involvement, not insulation.

☐ Make the agency feel responsible. Be a leader, not a nitpicker. *Tell them what you think is wrong, not how to fix it.*

☐ Don't be afraid to ask for great advertising. Let your agency know you have confidence in them to deliver more than just "good solid advertising." Aiming for greatness involves trying new directions—and some risks.

☐ Set objectives. If you expect action and results, you must know where you want to go. So set objectives for your advertising and your business.

☐ Switch people, not agencies. If there are problems, ask for new people to work on your account. A different copywriter or account executive on your business may provide a fresh approach, without depriving the business of necessary continuity.

☐ Be sure the agency makes a profit on your account. Clients who demand more service than the income can cover are shortsighted. In a good relationship, the agency grows as the client grows.

☐ Avoid insularity. Don't isolate yourself with the same people. Force yourself to go beyond the comfortable world of your own lifestyle.

☐ Care about being a client. Creative people do their best work on accounts they like, for clients they like to work with. *Good clients.* That doesn't mean *easy* clients. That's why good clients wind up with the best writers and the best account executives.

☐ Suggest work sessions. Set up informal give-and-take discussions where copywriters can air rough ideas and you can talk about your objectives. These sessions are especially helpful just before the agency starts a complex assignment.

Summary

The advertising a company uses affects virtually every person in the organization. The advertising department is responsible for planning, administration, budgeting, and coordination with other departments or outside advertising services.

The way a company's advertising department is organized depends on many variables. The two basic structures are the centralized and the decentralized department, and there are advantages and disadvantages to both. The centralized organization is the most typical and may be structured by product, by subfunction of advertising, by end user, or by geography. Decentralized departments are typical of large far-flung organizations that have numerous divisions, subsidiaries, products, countries, regions, or brands that need to be served.

Some advertising departments take responsibility for ad production, media placement, and other marketing support services. Some firms have even developed in-house advertising agencies in hopes of saving money by keeping the normal agency commissions for themselves. However, they have sometimes saved money but lost objectivity and creativity.

Advertising agencies are independent organizations of creative people and businesspeople who specialize in the development and preparation of advertising plans, advertisements, and other promotional tools on behalf of clients.

Agencies may be classified by the range of services they offer and the types of business they handle. The two basic types of agencies are the full-service agencies and the agencies that offer à la carte services. The latter include creative boutiques and media-buying services. Further, agencies may specialize in either consumer or industrial accounts.

The people who work in agencies may be involved in research, planning, creative services, traffic, media, account management, new business administration, or a host of other activities.

Agencies may also be organized around functional specialties or by groups who work as teams on various accounts.

To make money, agencies may charge fees or retainers, receive commissions from the media, or mark up outside purchases made on behalf of their clients. Most agencies get their clients through referral, advertising, public relations, or personal solicitation.

The client-agency relationship goes through a number of stages. Numerous factors affect the relationship, including chemistry, communication, conduct, and changes.

Questions for Review and Discussion

1. If a company has an advertising agency, does it still need an advertising manager? Why?
2. What are the advantages and disadvantages of an in-house advertising agency for a small retail chain?
3. In what ways can a full-service advertising agency help a manufacturer of industrial goods?
4. What do you think are the most important points for an advertiser to consider in selecting an agency?
5. Do you think an advertiser should change agencies on a regular basis? Why or why not?
6. Where do you think the most highly paid people in advertising work—with the advertisers, the agencies, or the media and suppliers? Why?
7. What is the best way to compensate an advertising agency? Explain.
8. What does media proliferation mean, and how will it affect the future of advertising?
9. How do the various media functions interrelate with advertising?
10. What methods can an advertiser or advertising agency use to locate suppliers and evaluate their services?

Part II

Marketing and Advertising Plans and Strategies

friends, foes, and War

4

ADVERTISING AND THE MARKETING MIX

 hile studying for his master's degree in mechanical engineering at Princeton University, Lido Anthony Iacocca began his automotive career as a student engineer at the Ford Motor Company.

Less than four decades later, as the new chairman who had been brought in to rescue the ailing Chrysler Corporation, he accomplished one of the most astonishing feats of "engineering" (and marketing) in the history of American business. For that feat, the editors of *Advertising Age* named Lee Iacocca "Adman of the Year."

For several years, Chrysler had teetered on the edge of collapse. Short of cash, saddled with huge overhead and inefficient plants, and overstocked with unwanted products, the company had to go begging to the U.S. government for a complicated $1.2 billion bailout loan guarantee program.

Nay-sayers abounded. Many people were against the bailout program, and experts everywhere predicted the government guarantee would only prolong the agony by delaying the company's inevitable bankruptcy. And then, the very next year, Chrysler hit its low point, recording a $1.7 billion loss—the largest single-year loss in U.S. history.

Iacocca persevered.

Less than three years later, the company paid back the total $1.2 billion loan and recorded record profits. In fact, the company made more money in the first three months of that year than in any previous year in Chrysler's history—$706 million.

Suddenly, Chrysler was once again a viable contender in its field. As *Advertising Age* reported, it had an array of trend-setting products in its stable (with more on the drawing board), a significantly more efficient operation, and a chief executive who broke new ground as a powerful advertising spokesman for his product—and, in fact, for American-made goods generally[1] (see Figure 4–1).

His mystique as a spokesperson was so extraordinary that car dealers soon began using pictures of Iacocca in ads for their local dealerships—even though they sold non-Chrysler brands.[2]

How did he do it? Was Chrysler's sudden good fortune really due to its chairman's advertising skill?

To Iacocca, who naturally is very much guided by his engineering background, the product is king. To him, the job of turning Chrysler around was a very difficult product task as well as a quality and productivity task.

Veteran marketing and advertising people see it differently, though. To them, what was accomplished at Chrysler smacks of marketing acumen of the first degree.

In this case, they're both right.

WHAT IS MARKETING?

In every business organization, countless projects and functions have to be performed on a daily basis. Management typically classifies these diverse activities into three broad functional divisions: production, finance, and marketing. Students majoring in business will study many subjects that relate to one or all of these areas. For instance, courses in accounting relate to the finance area. Courses in purchasing, quality control, or manufacturing relate to the production division. And advertising is one of the specialty courses within the domain of marketing.

Marketing also includes a host of other disciplines such as marketing

FIGURE   4-1

After Lee Iacocca turned Chrysler around, appeared in America's living rooms as Chrysler's spokesman, and penned his autobiography, his familiarity and popularity soared. Some even touted him as a presidential candidate.

research, product transportation and distribution, inventory control, and sales training and management, to mention a few. All of these subjects also have a relationship to and an impact on the advertising a firm employs. In today's world, to be an effective specialist in advertising, a person also needs a solid understanding of the marketing framework within which advertising operates. The purpose of this chapter, therefore—and, in fact, this whole unit—is to define and outline the whole subject of marketing in order to clarify advertising's proper role in the marketing function.

Evolution of the Marketing Concept

Unfortunately, *marketing* may be one of the most misunderstood terms in business. In the past, it was defined as those various business activities concerned with directing the flow of goods and services from the company that makes them to the people who use them. However, this definition tended to emphasize the activities of distribution and transportation. Today, the field of marketing has evolved to include many other equally important activities.

A century ago, when there were relatively few products for many consumers, the main concern of business was merely to provide more merchandise to satisfy the demand. During this *production-oriented period,* the concept of marketing was indeed focused on the transportation and distribution of these goods.

With the introduction of mass-production techniques, though, the consumer was soon deluged with products, and the focus of marketing changed to selling. This *sales-oriented period* was marked by extravagant advertising claims and a business attitude expressed by the Latin phrase *caveat emptor* ("let the buyer beware") as companies tried to foist their goods on a generally unsophisticated public.

Eventually, as manufacturers learned that no amount of high-pressure selling or slick advertising could move any more of their unwanted goods, sales declined and inventories went unsold. Many businesses folded, and others incurred substantial losses. Marketing had to change again.

In the last half-century, business has found it more profitable to try to determine in advance what customers want and then to make products that will satisfy those desires.[3] This has been called the *marketing-oriented period.* Unfortunately, some companies still operate under the sales-oriented concept or even the production-oriented concept. But they are constantly courting failure, and they risk experiencing situations similar to Chrysler's.

According to Iacocca, Chrysler's problems were due in large part to the company's own disgraceful mismanagement. And marketing was one area where the mistakes seemed to be continuous. All too often the company had been building the wrong cars for the wrong people. Chrysler buyers traditionally tended to be older, more conservative, blue-collar workers who were less likely to buy cars with high-profit optional equipment and who were most likely to be hurt in an economic downturn. Even to this group, though, Chrysler's products were often disappointing, and yet the company never succeeded in attracting another one. In short, when new cars were designed, the company failed to assess the needs and wants of the car-buying public. Thus, as the company's president admitted, fully half the people buying a new automobile never even considered a Chrysler product. This was not good marketing.

The usual objective of business is to make a profit, and profits are normally achieved through economic exchanges of the firm's goods and services for things of perceived equal value from its customers. As we shall see later in this chapter, the firm's products may be purely functional or they may offer more symbolic values.[4] The job of marketing, though, is to help the firm achieve its profit objective by facilitating the *perceived equal-value exchange*. This is best accomplished by providing customers with products or services that meet their utilitarian or symbolic objectives, in places that are convenient, and at prices they can afford.

As we shall see in Chapter 18, nonbusiness organizations, which are not usually driven by a profit motive, may have other noneconomic objectives. However, they, too, may operate under this marketing concept as they endeavor to satisfy the needs of their constituents through the services they develop.[5]

Ideally, companies steered by the marketing concept are more concerned with shaping products and marketing systems to meet their customers' needs than with forcing consumers to buy whatever the manufacturer wants to produce. As a result, they are intensely interested in the consumer's point of view, and they allow that point of view to dictate many company activities.

The Task of Marketing and Advertising

For firms operating under this concept, then, the task of marketing is to manage the *marketing-exchange cycle*. This responsibility is divided into three areas: (1) to discover, locate, and measure the functional and symbolic needs, attitudes, and desires of prospective customers; (2) to interpret this information for management so that services and products may be improved and new ones developed; and (3) to devise and implement a system that makes the product available, to inform prospective customers about the product's need-satisfying capabilities, and finally, to execute the exchange (see Figure 4–2).

Where does advertising fit into this responsibility? Advertising is primarily concerned with marketing's duty to *inform;* it is also concerned with *persuading* and *reminding* customers to believe in and buy the product. Sometimes, it may even be directly involved in making the exchange. But in all cases, the effectiveness of the firm's advertising is greatly dependent on the adequate performance of the company's diverse marketing activities.

Chrysler showed that a company can spend millions and millions of dollars on advertising every year and still fail. Before advertising can work, the product must be what the consumer wants. The price must be acceptable. There must be a place where consumers can buy the product conveniently. And there must be people ready and able to sell the product to the consumer and coordinate all these other activities adequately and successfully. As we shall see in the Ad Labs for this chapter, Apple Computer Co. has also demonstrated an interesting blend of these same principles with the introduction of its Macintosh computer. (See Ad Lab 4-A.)

To more fully understand the importance of these activities, we will briefly examine what a market is and how markets are located, measured, and selected. Then we will discuss the elements of the marketing mix—product, price, place, and promotion—which are referred to as the *four Ps* and which are used to achieve the company's marketing objectives.[6] As we

FIGURE   4–2

The marketing exchange cycle. The tasks of marketing management under the marketing concept are: (step 1) locating and measuring the demand for products; (step 2) interpreting this demand for management, which then develops products to satisfy the need; and (step 3) developing and implementing a plan that makes the products available and informs consumers about the products' capabilities. Marketing, therefore, begins and ends with the consumer.

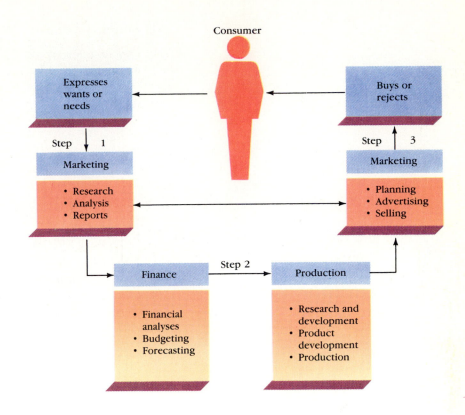

shall see, the way a company decides to coordinate these elements has a profound effect on the advertising it uses.

First, though, let's be sure we understand what a market is and where it can be found.

WHAT IS A MARKET?

At an advertising seminar for the Savings Institutions Marketing Society of America, delegates were shown a number of different advertisements from savings institutions around the country. The savings officers in the audience were to grade each of the ads on a scale of 1 to 10. One of the ads presented was an amusing example of tongue-in-cheek humor by Clearwater Federal Savings and Loan Association, a $450 million savings institution in Florida.

A millionaire was pictured standing in the hallway of his mansion before a large, ornately framed painting. The headline on the ad read: "I keep the family jewels in the safe behind the portrait of my first wife. I keep my money at Clearwater Federal." This was followed by a column of light, humorous copy, which told how rich the man was, how security conscious he was, and how much he liked all the free services at Clearwater Federal that helped keep his money safe from his *second wife's* shopping sprees. The ad was signed: "Clearwater Federal. Where those who've made it keep it" (see Figure 4–3).

Most savings and loan executives who viewed the ad gave it a very low rating. They said they didn't like it because it wouldn't appeal to everybody, only to the very rich.

The Majority Fallacy

Their reaction is a typical example of the *majority fallacy*—a common misconception that to be successful a product or service must appeal to everybody or at least to the majority of people. Sophisticated marketing and advertising people know this is just not true. Often several products or services compete for the same customers, and therefore each is able to attract only a fraction of the market. A new competitive product might do

AD LAB 4-A   Marketing Mac: Apple Computer's Counterattack against IBM

The Macintosh is Apple Computer's latest weapon in the computer war being waged against the industry kingpin, IBM. The IBM Personal Computer caused Apple to lose its dominant share of all its markets—home, business, educational, and scientific. "Apple can't outsell or outservice IBM," says E. Floyd Kvamme, Apple's executive vice president for marketing and sales. "So we are out to establish and maintain a technological leadership position." And the company feels it has done that with Macintosh.

The Macintosh is an intriguing machine. Weighing less than 17 pounds, the Macintosh takes up only 10 × 10 inches of desk space. Information and documents on the display screen can be shown simultaneously in "windows," or boxes, and can be moved, expanded, or shrunk by means of a "mouse," a small hand-held pointing device. And on-the-screen "paper" can be shuffled, documents revised or discarded, and charts drawn, all with a few simple commands executed with the mouse. The Macintosh relies heavily on symbols and pictures on the screen to help people conquer computer phobia. It cost more than $100 million to develop. Apple spent another $20 million for a highly automated factory to build only the Macintosh.

Apple has a national sales team to penetrate the corporate market, but most of its sales come from retail dealers. The dealers are essential because no person is going to buy a computer without first reading about it, asking friends about it, and especially talking to a dealer about it. Apple feels that the Mac's best prospects will be small businesses and college students.

The advertising messages IBM and Apple are using to sell their personal computers are alike in one way. Both stress ease of use in order to allay buyers' fears about computers. Nevertheless, there is a big difference in the way Apple and IBM want to be seen as companies. IBM emphasizes dependability and trades on its name recognition value. As an IBM spokesperson explains it, "The PC product line has the excellent quality and service that are the hallmarks of IBM."

Apple, on the other hand, takes pride in being unique. "We want to be known as the innovators," says John Scully, Apple's president. "Apple is a gathering place for very bright people who have the opportunity and the resources to create significantly different products than what might be turned out in a larger, more structured environment."

Conventional wisdom maintains that computer buyers care less about achievement than about such factors as compatibility and customer support, prime virtues of IBM. In the volatile computer business, however, history has shown that significant technical achievements can attract customers away from the most deeply entrenched standards. Only time will tell whether Apple's Macintosh will provide yet another example of dubious conventional wisdom.

Laboratory Application

From your reading of the text so far and your knowledge of the Macintosh, what marketplace need or needs do you think the Macintosh was aimed at satisfying?

FIGURE   4–3

Clearwater Federal targeted a very profitable market segment in this tongue-in-cheek ad. Wealthy people can afford to laugh at themselves, and the not-so-wealthy can enjoy the joke, too. Unfortunately, most savings executives viewing this ad failed to understand its sophisticated humor and marketing strategy, fearing it would not appeal to everybody. This is called the majority fallacy.

considerably better if it is specifically aimed at just one group of customers (like wealthy people) rather than at the majority of customers.

What is a market then? In its simplest terms, a market is people. But a market rarely includes everybody. In fact, by definition, a market includes one or more groups of potential customers who share a common interest, need, or desire, who are able to use the product or service offered to some advantage, and who are able to afford the purchase price.

Types of Markets

Clearwater Federal actually did a good job of selecting a very profitable market segment (that is, wealthy people and those who like symbols of wealth) and catering to it. This group, though, represented just one narrow subset of the total consumer market. Other companies might select broader segments of the consumer market or other market categories altogether. There are five broad classifications of markets to which companies advertise and sell:

1. *Consumer markets* are composed of people who buy products and services for their own personal use. Both Chrysler and Clearwater Federal, for example, aim at the consumer market but at different groups within that market. Typical consumer groups might include single women, upscale young families, children, older retired people, joggers,

skiers, concertgoers, or people who live in a certain part of town. In Chapter 5, "Consumer Behavior and Market Segmentation," we shall discuss some of the many ways to categorize consumer groups.

2. *Reseller markets* are individuals or companies that buy products for the purpose of reselling them, like retail stores, wholesalers, and car dealers. Chrysler, for example, has to aim a portion of its marketing activities at a reseller market—its dealers. Likewise, a food manufacturer first needs to convince food wholesalers and then retail grocers to carry its brands, or they will never be sold to consumers. The same is true for a sporting goods manufacturer. The reseller market, therefore, is extremely important to most companies even though we, as consumers, may be completely unaware of any marketing or advertising activities aimed at that market.

3. *Industrial markets* are individuals or companies (like manufacturing companies) that buy products needed for the production of other products or services. Plant equipment and machinery manufacturers aim at industrial markets. But so do telephone companies, office suppliers, and computer companies (see Figure 4–4). In fact, auto manufacturers also aim at the industrial market to sell the many cars and trucks used in business. As we shall see in Chapter 5, industrial markets are categorized by many factors, such as their industry segment or geographical location or size.

4. *Government markets* are governmental bodies that buy products for the successful coordination of municipal, state, federal, or other governmental activities. Think of all the vehicles used by the Post Office, the weapons bought by police and the military services, the desks, computers, and even pencils used by the IRS. Every city, county, state, and

FIGURE 4–4

To promote its VisionLab II computer-imaging process, Comtal/3M employs an unusual analogy in this ad aimed at high-tech industrial markets. The Indian brave's quest for power, vision, and understanding involved the ritual utilization of colorful paints. The ad implies that true color computer imaging from Comtal/3M is the modern equivalent of scouting the frontier.

federal office represents part of the vast government market; and some firms have been immensely successful selling only to the government market.

5. *International markets* are any of the previously mentioned markets that are located in foreign countries. Every country has consumers, resellers, industries, and governments. Targeting those groups across national boundaries, though, presents interesting problems as we shall discuss in Chapter 19, "International Advertising."

Locating, Measuring, and Selecting the Market

Now that we understand what a market is, let's look briefly at the process companies go through to select a market. The whole purpose of marketing and advertising is to find the right people and get them together with the right products. The advertisements we see every day are usually intended to appeal to a particular group of people who belong to or are associated with the market the company selects. The more it understands about that market, therefore, the better chance of success the company will have.

Market Research

To locate the most desirable targets for their marketing activities, companies try to learn as much as they can about the total market and its various subgroups. To do so, they use a variety of *marketing research* techniques to systematically gather, record, and analyze data about the size, composition, and structure of markets for their goods and services. Their first effort is to measure the size of the total market for the particular product category. Then they try to estimate the size and profitability of various segments within that market. In the case of Clearwater Federal, for example, they might have attempted to measure:

1. The total market for savings and loans and banks in Clearwater Federal's local area.
2. The size of the "wealthy-people" segment in that community.
3. The size of the segment with "wealthy attitudes."
4. The size of other potential segments (e.g., retired people or middle-aged business executives).

Next the company tries to measure the share of the market it might attract if it aimed (1) at the whole market or (2) at a specific market segment. Historically, the advantage of specializing in one segment is that the firm can achieve deeper penetration into a segment. If that segment is large enough, then it offers the potential for a greater share of the market and a stronger, more entrenched marketing position.[7]

Various research methods are used to measure the size of market segments depending on the type of market being considered. Some of these methods will be more completely described in Chapter 6, "Marketing and Advertising Research."

Market Segmentation

After the completion of adequate market research, the selection of market segments may commence. Markets for products may be selected according to a variety of classifications based on shared characteristics of customers.

By aggregating (clustering together) these customers into fairly homogeneous segments, the company can determine which groups are potentially the most profitable markets. It can then select one or more groups as a *target market*—that segment to which a company wishes to appeal and for which it designs products and aims all of its marketing activities.[8]

This strategy of discovering meaningful subgroups within major markets and developing products for them is called *market segmentation* and

PEOPLE IN ADVERTISING

Al Ries and Jack Trout

Chairman of the Board and President
Trout & Ries, Inc.

Al Ries and Jack Trout are widely known for developing the "positioning" approach to advertising. Their agency, Trout & Ries, Inc., is a New York City firm noted for its strategic approach to advertising and marketing. The agency has created corporate and marketing strategies for many of America's major corporations, including Xerox, Digital Equipment, Monsanto, Merck, and Burger King.

Positioning has received widespread attention in business, consumer, and advertising publications. Articles have brought Trout and Ries more than 150,000 reprint requests and scores of speaking invitations. Their book *Positioning, the Battle for Your Mind,* from which the following is quoted, has become an industry text. As a result, *positioning* has become the buzzword of advertising and marketing people not only in this country but around the world.

What Is Positioning?

Positioning is a simple principle that can best be demonstrated by asking yourself some simple questions. Who was the first person to fly solo across the North Atlantic? Don't think it couldn't be Charles Lindbergh, because it was. Now who was the second person to fly solo across the North Atlantic? Not so easy to answer, is it? Who was the first person to walk on the moon? Neil Armstrong, right? Now who was the second? The first person, the first company to occupy the position in the prospect's mind is going to be awfully hard to dislodge: IBM in computers, Hertz in rent-a-cars, Coke in cola.

The Mind: A Memory Bank

Like a memory bank, the mind has a slot or position for each bit of information it has chosen to retain. In its operation, the mind is a lot like a computer. But there is one important difference. A computer has to accept what is put into it, whereas the mind does not. In fact, quite the opposite. As a defense mechanism against the volume of today's communications, the mind screens and rejects much of the information offered it. In general, the mind accepts only new information that matches its prior knowledge or experience. It filters out everything else.

For example, when a viewer sees a television commer-

will be more fully discussed in Chapter 5, "Consumer Behavior and Market Segmentation."

For now, let's simply look at the segment selected by Clearwater Federal. It was composed of those individuals who were either wealthy or achieving wealth or who liked to affiliate with the wealthy and who were interested in security and high interest on their investments. A federally insured savings account that pays high interest, comes complete with many

cial that says, "NCR means computers," he doesn't accept it. IBM means computers; NCR means National Cash Register. The computer "position" in the minds of most people is filled by a company called IBM (International Business Machines Corp.). For a competitive computer manufacturer to obtain a favorable position in the prospect's mind, it must relate its company to IBM's position.

To cope with advertising's complexity, people have learned to rank products and brands. Perhaps this can best be visualized by imagining a series of ladders in the mind. On each step is a brand name, and each different ladder represents a different product category. For advertisers to increase their brand preference, they must move up the ladder.

This is difficult, especially if the new category is not positioned against an old one. The mind has no room for the new and different unless they are related to the old. Therefore, it you have a truly new product, it's often better to tell the prospect what the product is not, rather than what it is.

The first automobile, for example, was called a "horseless" carriage, a name that positioned the concept against the existing mode of transportation. Words like *offtrack betting, lead-free gasoline,* and *tubeless tires* are examples of how new concepts can best be positioned against the old ones.

Number-One Strategy

Successful marketing strategy usually consists of keeping your eyes open to possibilities and then striking before the product ladder is firmly fixed. The marketing leader is usually the one who moves the ladder into the mind with his or her brand nailed to the one and only rung.

Once there, what can a company do to keep its top-dog position? As long as a company owns the position, there's no point in running ads that scream "We're No. 1." It is much better to enhance the product category in prospects' minds. Notice the current IBM campaign that ignores competition and sells the value of computers—all computers, not just the company's types.

Number-Two Strategy

Most companies are in the number two, three, four, or even worse category. What then? Hope springs eternal in the human breast. Nine times out of 10, the also-ran sets out to attack the leader. The result is disaster.

In the communication jungle, the only hope is to be selective, to concentrate on narrow targets, and to practice segmentation. For example, Anheuser-Busch found an opening for a high-priced beer and filled it with Michelob. Advertisers must assess the competitors. They must locate weak points in their positions and then launch marketing attacks against them. Savin developed small, inexpensive copiers and took advantage of a weakness in the Xerox product line.

Simply stated, the first rule of positioning is this: You can't compete head-on with a company that has a strong, established position. You can go around, under, or over, but never head-to-head. The leader owns the high ground, the top position in the prospect's mind, the top rung of the product ladder.

In positioning, the name of a company or product is important. Allegheny Airlines was regarded as "small" and "regional" in consumers' minds until it changed its name to USAir. Similarly, if your corporate name is inappropriate for a new product you plan to market, create a new corporate name—and a new position. Singer Company put its name on business machines and lost $371 million. They committed the ultimate positioning mistake by trying to transfer a brand name to a different product sold to a different market.

Importance of Objectivity

To be successful in positioning, advertising and marketing people must be brutally frank. They must try to eliminate all ego from the decision-making process; it only clouds the issue. One critical aspect of positioning is objectively evaluating products and how they are viewed by customers and prospects. Successful companies get their information from the marketplace. That is where the program has to succeed, not in the product manager's office.

AD LAB 4-B   Marketing Mac: Who Is the Target Market?

Review the Macintosh story in Ad Lab 4-A and relate that information to what you read in the text about locating and measuring the market for products.

Laboratory Applications

1. Is the Macintosh intended to appeal to all computer buyers or just particular groups? What groups?
2. Why do you suppose the Macintosh was aimed at the particular target groups you just identified? Explain your reasoning.

specially designed free services, and is located at an institution frequented by the upper classes is likely to be an attractive offer to these people.

Target Marketing

Once the company selects a market segment as its target market, the planning of other marketing activities is greatly simplified. Special services catering to that segment may be designed; the pricing of services may be determined; the number and location of stores, dealers, or branches needed will become apparent; and the most suitable type of advertising can be prepared. Everything can be aimed at appealing to that target market. (See Chapter 7, "Marketing and Advertising Planning.")

If the wealthy-people segment of the market had not appeared large enough to be profitable, Clearwater Federal would have had to select a different target market, and consequently, the company's other marketing and advertising activities would have been altered, too. Now in the case of Apple Computers, consider how it selected the target market for the Macintosh. (See Ad Lab 4-B.)

THE MARKETING MIX

Advertising, as the communications device in marketing, is just one of the many marketing tools used to help create the *perceived equal-value exchange* between the company and its target market. And the importance of advertising's role varies from business to business, depending on the nature of the business and the other marketing activities it employs.

As we mentioned earlier, every company has the option of adding, subtracting, or changing four elements in its marketing program to achieve its desired marketing mix—the four Ps: product, price, place, and promotion.

Consider two vastly different examples. First, a certified public accountant wishes to increase the size of his or her small, private practice. Some marketing-related communications might be business cards, a sign on the door, formal announcements, a listing or an ad in the Yellow Pages, and direct-mail reminders to clients that they should come in prior to tax time. Overall, though, professional ethics have traditionally barred or limited most CPAs from the use of extensive promotion. So media advertising may play little or no part in the accountant's business. Of greater importance are the CPA's auditing and accounting skills, experience, the cost of services, the location of the office, the size of the staff, and the professional manner in which clients are handled.

On the other hand, Charles Atlas has marketed his body-building course and equipment for more than half a century through mail-order advertisements in magazines read by boys and young men. In that time, the company has made many millions of dollars in sales. Furthermore, the entire effort has been made through advertising, without the use of a single salesperson. In fact, Charles Roman, who created the series of ads first used in 1929, continued using basically the same ads for the next 50 years (see Figure 4–5).

From these two examples, we can see that advertising plays vastly different roles in the marketing of various items. These differences are the result of company decisions about the appropriate mix of marketing activities used to promote its products or services.

The remainder of this chapter will focus further on the relationship of each of these four Ps to the advertising a company may use.

Advertising and the Product Element

While the target market is the most important consideration in the development of a marketing mix, the most important element of that mix is almost invariably the particular product or service being offered and the numerous values associated with it. For that reason, companies employ various means to make their products unique—to distinguish them from the products of their competitors. One of these may be the way the product is advertised.

Consider the ads for the Honda Civic and the Dodge Daytona in Figure 4–6. We see not only two very different styles of advertising but also two different ways of distinguishing products from one another. Look at the Honda ad first. What is the advertised uniqueness of the Honda? What features does the car have that make it stand out? How are those features important to the consumer? How would you answer the same questions for the Daytona ad? Is it trying to sell something more than the functional transportation delivered by the car? What?

What we learn from these two examples provides a clue to the answer to one of the most basic marketing questions: What is a product?

What Is a Product?

When you buy an automobile, what are you really buying? Is it the massive, tangible configuration of steel, plastic, rubber, and chrome you see? Is it the product's functional use (in this case, transportation) that it will deliver? Is it the economy of better gas mileage you will realize? Or on the other hand, is the product really the excitement created by the sleek, racy

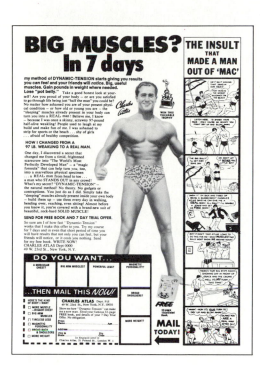

FIGURE   4–5

From this classic ad campaign came the famous question: "Do friends kick sand in your face?" Also came the classic concept of the "97-pound weakling." The basic ad remained virtually unchanged for 50 years, which reminds us of another famous line: "Stick with a winner."

Honda promotes the functional practicality of its Honda Civic model, while Dodge accentuates the Daytona's symbolic values of excitement, power, and sex appeal. These product concepts are obviously intended to satisfy the needs of two very different target markets.

design of the car, the sense of speed you experience, and the self-esteem and confidence you have as people look at you admiringly in your gleaming, sexy machine? What is this product you are buying?

Today's marketers know that a product may be any or all of these things. A product represents a *bundle of values*—that is, an array of various benefits, attributes, or satisfactions that are valuable according to the individual consumer's particular needs and desires. In the case of the automobile, the satisfactions the consumer receives, known as the *benefits,* may be simply functional, such as transportation, better gas mileage, or larger size. Or the satisfactions may be more intangible—socially, psychologically, or emotionally symbolic—such as beauty, self-esteem, pride, luxury, and sex appeal. By definition, therefore, *a product is a bundle of utilitarian and symbolic values designed to satisfy functional, social, psychological, economic, and other consumer needs.*

One of the keys to marketing success is to find an unsatisfied need and a unique way to satisfy it. While that may seem obvious, in today's product-glutted world it may not be so simple.[9] The first step in developing new products or services for specific markets should be to determine both the functional and symbolic needs and desires of that market—often a difficult task. Once accomplished, though, new products and services can be developed as complete *product concepts* with corresponding bundles of functional and symbolic satisfactions in mind. The product concept can be carried over into the way the product is designed, named, classified, packaged, labeled, displayed, and advertised.

Consider the names Volkswagen, Subaru, Chrysler, and Ford. Are these functional names, or do they have some emotional or psychological connotations? Now consider these names: Jaguar, Mustang, El Dorado. Do these names imply functional benefits or symbolic satisfactions?

Even the way a company classifies its product is important in defining the product concept and its marketing mix. There are many ways in which products may be classified. They may be grouped by markets—that is, by who buys them. They may be classified by how fast they are used up or by how tangible they are. They may be grouped according to the purchasing habits of the people who buy them. Or they may be classified according to some physical description. (See the Checklist of Product Classifications.)

 ## Checklist of Product Classifications

By Market

☐ Consumer goods. Products and services we use in our daily lives (food, clothing, furniture, automobiles).

☐ Industrial goods. Products used by companies for the purpose of producing other products (raw materials, agricultural commodities, machinery, tools, equipment).

By Rate of Consumption and Tangibility

☐ Durable goods. Tangible products that are long lasting and infrequently replaced (cars, trucks, refrigerators, furniture).

☐ Nondurable goods. Tangible products that may be consumed in one or a few uses and usually need to be replaced at regular intervals (food, soap, gasoline, oil).

☐ Services. Activities, benefits, or satisfactions offered for sale (travel, haircuts, legal and medical services, massages).

By Purchasing Habits

☐ Convenience goods. Purchases made frequently with a minimum of effort (cigarettes, food, newspapers).

☐ Shopping goods. Infrequently purchased items for which greater time is spent comparing price, quality, style, warranty (furniture, cars, clothing, tires).

☐ Specialty goods. Products with such unique characteristics that consumers will make special efforts to purchase them even if they're more expensive (fancy photographic equipment, special women's fashions, stereo components).

By Product Description

☐ Package goods. Cereals, hair tonics, and so forth.

☐ Hard goods. Furniture, appliances.

☐ Soft goods. Clothing, bedding.

☐ Services. Nontangible products.

Product Differentiation

Henry Ford is reputed to have said, "They can have any color they want as long as it's black." Marketers have since come to realize that if they don't offer customers what they want, the competition will. Therefore, the concept of *product differentiation*—creating differences in products in order to gain competitive advantage by appealing to a variety of consumer tastes—has long been a basic marketing strategy and was a predecessor to the strategy of market segmentation. The differences between products may be perceptible, imperceptible, or induced.

Perceptible Differences When differences between products are visibly apparent to the consumer they are called *perceptible differences*. For example, a red automobile is visibly different from a black one and may appeal to more people without increasing the manufacturing cost. Similarly, refrigerators are designed with right- and left-hand doors, single doors, and double doors and in different colors.

Imperceptible Differences Even though they may certainly exist, *imperceptible differences* are not readily apparent. Some cigarette brands may look pretty much alike from the outside, but once people buy a certain pack and open it, they may discover a different shaped filter or a different color of paper. Once they light up, they may experience a difference in taste (menthol, for example). The same is true with chewing gum (sugarless) and many food products (caffeine-free colas). The differences may be imperceptible, or hidden, at first, but they do exist, and they may greatly affect the desirability of the product.

Induced Differences For many products, such as aspirin, gasoline, packaged foods, liquor, financial services, and certain major brands of cigarettes, *induced differences* may be created by advertising or other promotional devices. One of the most successful product introductions in recent years was L'eggs hosiery. The product itself was not differentiated other than through unique branding, packaging, distribution, merchandising, and advertising—all of which added new *perceived value* to a product that was not new functionally. Similarly, banks, brokerage houses, and insurance companies traditionally use advertising and promotion to differentiate themselves because the services and financial products they offer are virtually identical.[10] In fact, it is this ability to create the perception of differences in functionally similar products and services that has made the strategy of product differentiation so very popular and the effective use of branding, advertising, and packaging so important (see Figure 4–7).

Product Packaging

In the average supermarket, more than 10,000 items compete for customer attention and dollars. It is the package that often determines the outcome of this competition. Because of the emphasis on self-service, packaging is increasingly important not only in grocery stores but in drugstores, variety stores, and other retail establishments as well. The package quickly displays the *brand*—the name that identifies the product and its source—to current users and endeavors to convince nonusers to try its contents for the first time.

The five functions of packaging are: (1) containment and protection,

It's got sweet and juicy written all over it.

FIGURE   4–7

Good oranges are good oranges. But by putting the brand name on its best fruit and advertising consistently for 80 years, Sunkist has created the perception that its product is better than the nonbranded orange. This is a juicy example of an induced difference.

(2) identification, (3) convenience, (4) consumer appeal, and (5) economy. Since these functions may have a profound effect on the marketing of a product, we should discuss each of them briefly.

Containment and Protection The basic purpose of any package is to hold and protect the product. Packages must keep the products fresh and protect their contents from shipping damage, water vapor (frozen foods), grease, infestation, and odors. Consumers don't want contaminated food, leaky packages, cut fingers, or tampering by criminals. Protection requirements are established by both the government and trade associations.

Identification Packaging has become so important as an identification device that companies such as Heinz and Coca-Cola have adhered to the same basic bottle and label designs for years. Why? Because it is the unique combination of the trade name, trademark, or trade character with the package that quickly identifies the product's brand. Branding makes the consumer's job easier by quickly assuring him or her of a consistent standard of quality. This adds value to the product for both the consumer and the manufacturer.

Since shoppers seldom wear their reading glasses, they like high visibility and clear legibility in packaging. Type must be easy to read, and color combinations should provide high contrast.

Convenience Packages must be able to survive storage and reshipment, and they must be easy to stack and display. This is why there are so few pyramid-shaped bottles. The retailer also looks for a full range of sizes to fit the customer's needs.

Consumers, likewise, want packages that can be stored and opened easily. A package designed to fit on the shelf of a refrigerator will differ from one stored in a medicine cabinet or on a laundry-room shelf. Products for a dressing table should be packaged so they don't spill or tip over easily. Shampoo bottles should be easy to grip.

Convenience cannot interfere with protection. Cellophane wrappings permit easy inspection, but they may not always protect well. Spouts make pouring much easier, but they may limit the strength of the package.

Consumer Appeal The product's market success may depend on how well the package appeals to the consumer. Appeal is the result of many factors—size, color, material, and shape. Consumer appeal can even be enhanced by easy-to-read package instructions.

A choice of sizes will satisfy the different needs and budgets of a variety of customers. On the other hand, the retailer will not be able to carry too many sizes.

Color, too, is an important consideration (see Figure 4–8). American Tobacco tried to evoke a surfing image when it introduced Malibu cigarettes in a package with a gold wave and shades of blue and green to suggest the sky and ocean.[11] From many studies, researchers have learned that certain colors have special meanings to consumers. General Foods, for example, changed the Sanka package when it learned that its yellow label suggested weakness.

The shape of a package may also offer special appeal. Containers of Janitor in a Drum and heart-shaped packages of Valentine's Day candy instantly tell what the product is and what it is used for.

Sometimes gift wrapping is used for special holidays. While often successful, it also increases the cost of packaging and poses problems if it doesn't sell out. Remaining items must be altered, offered at a discount, or held for the next holiday occasion.

The packaging of several items together may offer convenience as well as a discount price. Combination packaging also limits the waste that occurs with unit packaging.

If a package has a secondary use, that can also add appeal. For example, Kraft manufactures a cheese glass that, once emptied, can be used for serving fruit juice. Some tins and bottles even become collectibles. Liquor bottles can sometimes serve as decanters or vases. These packages are really premiums that give the buyer extra value for the dollars that have been spent.

Economy The manufacturer's use of a particular package depends on its cost. The costs of the features we have discussed—protection, identification, convenience, and consumer appeal—all add to the basic cost of materials and printing.

Some of the factors that affect packaging costs are:

1. Cost of packaging materials.
2. Cost of manufacturing the package.
3. Cost of storage and shipping.
4. Cost of equipment used to manufacture and fill packages.
5. Cost of associated labor.

Sometimes a small increase in production costs may be more than offset by increased customer appeal. Aluminum foil and waxed paper boxes now come with cutting edges. Kleenex tissues became a hit with the introduction of a package that dispensed one tissue at a time. And many

FIGURE   4–8

For a product like fruit juice, the color decision in packaging is critical. The company wants to communicate freshness, naturalness, and healthfulness. What sensations do the colors on these Welch's packages convey to you?

medicines are offered in "child-proof" plastic bottles. These benefits may make a considerable difference to the consumer and affect the way a product is advertised.

Product Positioning

In 1959, Avis, Inc., the car rental company, made advertising history by openly acknowledging that it was only number two. "Therefore," their ad said, "we try harder." The Avis campaign was immensely successful. Why? Was it because of packaging? Was it because they tried harder?

What was the real or perceived difference between Avis and the other car rental companies? The answer is one word: *positioning*.

Most products and services compete in a field of similar products and services. If the features or attributes of a particular product are distinct, the product will tend to occupy a particular product space, rank, or *position* in the consumer's mind. Part of the marketing effort, therefore, is to determine what desirable positions are open in the consumer's mind and to develop products to fill them.

Products may be positioned in many different ways. They may be ranked in the consumer's mind by the benefits they offer, by the way they are differentiated, or by the particular market segment to which they appeal. A product may even be positioned by the way it is classified (e.g., as a convenience good rather than a shopping good). As Avis demonstrated, though, the impact of positioning on a company's advertising and the rest of its marketing mix cannot be overstated.

How was Avis positioned? Avis had no product features that were significantly different from Hertz, National, or the other car rental companies. The product difference was, in effect, nonexistent. Hertz, on the other hand, was very distinct. It was the largest, and everyone knew it. Avis used this knowledge to position itself against Hertz as an alternative. By saying that it was number two, it separated itself from the pack and gained widespread recognition. Its claim of "trying harder," then, was just a logical conclusion to the fact that it was the underdog. The position Avis staked out is what gained it recognition and made its claim credible. (For more on positioning, see People in Advertising on pages 124–125.)

Product Life Cycle

Just as humans pass through stages in life from infancy to death, products also pass through a *product life cycle.*[12] Marketing and advertising people have identified four major stages in this cycle: introduction, growth, maturity, and decline. The advertising for a product depends to a great extent on where the product stands in its life cycle (see Figure 4–9).

For example, when a major new product is invented and *introduced,* nobody knows about it. So the company's objective may be to stimulate *primary demand*—that is, consumer demand for the whole product category (see Figure 4–10). To educate the consuming public about the new product, advertising will stress information about what the product does and how it works. Promotion to the trade will also be used to encourage distributors and retailers to carry the new product. During this introductory phase, losses are common as companies spend large amounts of money on product development and on advertising and promotion in order to build widespread distribution, awareness, and demand.

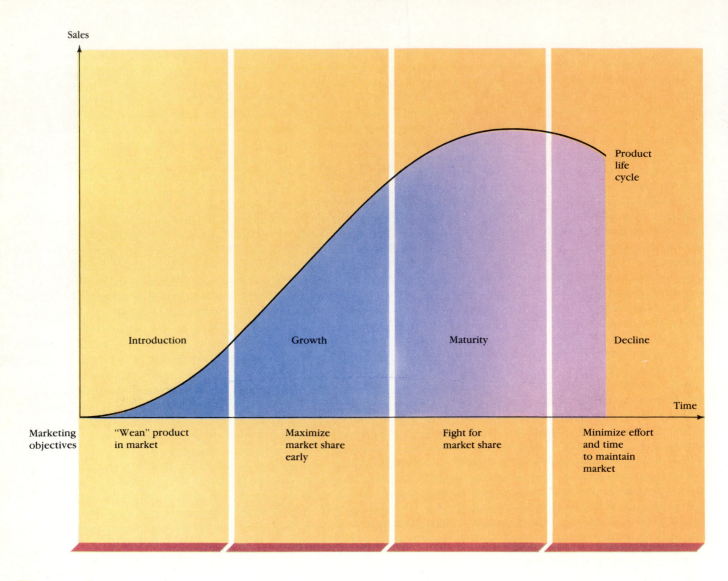

Sales

Introduction

Growth

Maturity

Decline

Product
life
cycle

Time

Marketing
objectives

"Wean" product
in market

Maximize
market share
early

Fight for
market share

Minimize effort
and time
to maintain
market

FIGURE   4–9

The product life cycle. Marketing objectives change as the product proceeds from one stage of the cycle to the next. So do marketing strategies. In the introductory and growth stages, promotional activities are aimed at creating product awareness and inducing trial. In later stages, efforts may be aimed at suggesting competitive comparison or maintaining brand loyalty.

As sales volume begins to rise rapidly, the product enters the *growth* stage. New customers make their first purchases while earlier customers are already repurchasing. As the demand for the product class expands, stimulated by mass advertising and word of mouth, competitive products emerge and create even more purchase pressure on the marketplace.

At this point, sheer momentum may carry the product's sales upward, so the ratio of advertising expenditures to total sales will begin to decrease, and the firm may begin to realize substantial profits. In 1978, for example, only half a million home videocassette recorders were sold—but that was four times the number sold in the previous year. By 1988, though, as many as 50 percent of all U.S. homes had VCRs, and many competitive brands with undifferentiated products had entered the scene to cash in on this growth.[13]

In the *maturity* stage, industry sales reach a plateau as the marketplace becomes saturated and the number of new customers dwindles. As competition intensifies, profits also diminish. Promotional efforts are in-

FIGURE   4–10

Diamonds are not a new product. But Diamond Information Centre traditionally uses a primary demand strategy to promote the whole product category.

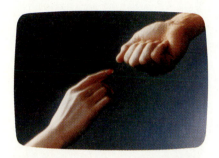

SFX: Music playing.

ANNCR: More profound than words. Diamonds.

creased, but the emphasis is on *selective demand* to impress customers with the subtle advantages of one brand over another. At this stage, companies increase sales only at the expense of competitors. Therefore, the strategies of product differentiation, market segmentation, and product positioning become more important as companies fight for even the smallest increases in market share.

During the maturity stage, as products approach the end of their life cycle, companies frequently take any of a variety of actions to try to extend their life. They may try to (1) add new users, (2) increase the frequency of use by existing customers, (3) develop new uses for the product, or (4) change the size of packages, design new labels, or improve quality. Arm & Hammer baking soda, for example, extended its life cycle by promoting new uses for the product. It started as a cooking aid but later was promoted successfully as a bath water treatment and even as a refrigerator deodorizer.

Finally, as products eventually enter or approach the *decline* stage due to obsolescence or changing consumer tastes, companies may choose to cease all promotion and phase them out quickly, as in the case of the Edsel automobile, or let them die slowly like old brands of cigarettes. They may also attempt to revitalize the product in order to prolong the mature stage. In the case of Crest toothpaste, Procter & Gamble created a new "great-tasting gel" formulation and designed it into the product as a perceptible difference. In addition, P&G developed its "advanced formula Fluoristat" and new "plaque fighters" and built these features into the product as imperceptible product differences (see Figure 4–11).

Now, before going on to the next section, consider how the product concept for Apple's Macintosh computer was developed. (See Ad Lab 4-C.)

Advertising and the Price Element

Price frequently has a great bearing on a product's advertising. Newspaper ads regularly announce that retail goods have been marked down for quick clearance. These ads communicate the low price and motivate people to enter the store. Conversely, many advertisements do not mention price at all but talk, instead, about other features of the product. And, finally, many premium-priced products are touted for the very fact that they do cost more. L'Oreal, for instance, excelled in promoting the expensive luxury of its hair-care products to the group called the "me" generation.

Key Factors Influencing Price

Since price plays such an important role in advertising, we must consider the factors that influence how a company determines the price for its products. Among the important considerations are market demand, the cost of production and distribution, competition, and corporate objectives. Based on these factors, companies may determine the appropriate pricing strategy. However, because of these factors, price is often the one element in the marketing mix over which the company has the least control.

Market Demand Most people are familiar with the law of supply and demand. If the supply of a product stays the same and the desire (or demand) for it

Crest shows three formulations of its product, all containing the Fluoristat cavity-fighting ingredient. While Crest has been a mature product for many years and has experienced tremendous competition from other brands, P&G has played an effective number-one positioning role, matching its competitors' moves with defensive moves of its own to constantly revitalize the product.

AD LAB 4-C   Marketing Mac: Understanding the Product

Steven Jobs, the former chairman of Apple Computer, has said: "The Macintosh is my vision of what a personal computer *should* be. If Mac's sales are just average, then our vision of the world is significantly wrong."

Laboratory Applications

1. What do you think is the product concept of the Macintosh?
2. How would this product be classified?
3. How is the Macintosh differentiated from other computers?
4. What competitive position does the Macintosh occupy?
5. What stage of the product life cycle is Macintosh in? How can you tell?

increases, the price tends to rise. If the demand decreases below the available supply, then the price tends to drop (see Figure 4–12).

In 1987, after receiving adverse media publicity about a safety defect in some of its cars, Audi was suddenly faced with a glut of unsold new cars and declining customer demand. The company offered a $5,000 factory rebate—in effect, a price cut—to current Audi owners to trade in their older cars for the new model. Audi immediately sold more cars because of the lower price. In this case, no amount of advertising or promoting would have had the same effect as simply cutting the price.

Production and Distribution Costs As pointed out in Chapter 1, the American mass-distribution system has enabled more manufacturers to produce and deliver more products to more consumers more inexpensively than in any other country. The price of goods depends largely on the cost of production and distribution. As these costs increase, they must be passed on to the consumer, or the company will eventually be unable to meet its overhead and be forced to close its doors. If too many companies were forced out of business, products would become scarce and prices would soar even higher.

Chrysler faced this same problem when Iacocca took the reins. Because the company sold fewer cars than either Ford or General Motors, it produced fewer. This meant that the production costs on each car were higher, making it that much more difficult to compete.

Competition Before the energy shortages of the 1970s, price wars between gasoline service stations were common. As far as the consumer was concerned, gasoline was gasoline, and the most important consideration was price. If one competing station lowered its prices, the consumer switched without hesitation. This all changed during the energy crisis. Suddenly, competition was not over price but availability. With the short supply, long lines formed and prices soared. But consumers didn't care as long as they could get a full tank of gas. Eventually, prices doubled and tripled, demand dwindled, fuel consumption dropped, the supply increased, and price competition among service stations returned.

FIGURE   4–12

If you plot the demand versus price and the supply versus price together, you get this graph. The demand curve is a schedule of the amounts demanded at various prices. The supply curve is a schedule of the amounts offered for sale at various prices. The point where the two curves cross is called the *market clearing price,* where demand and supply are in balance. It is the price that theoretically clears the market of supply.

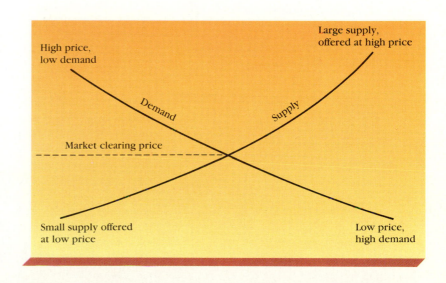

FIGURE   4–13

Hyundai compares itself to Mercedes in this humorous, price-oriented ad. They are not really comparing the products as much as the service features with the allusion to saving $30,000 on the phone call.

ANNCR VO: With a Mercedes, you get an 800# so you can phone for assistance day or night.

With a Hyundai, you get the same thing. But you save about $30,000 on the call.

Hyundai. Cars that make sense.

Corporate Objectives Prices are also influenced by the objectives of the company. When introducing a new product, a company may set a high price to recover its start-up costs as quickly as possible. Or it may position the product as a premium or luxury-priced item aimed at a smaller target market.

As a product enters the maturity stage of its life cycle, corporate objectives tend to aim at increased market share, and that tends to exert a downward pressure on prices.

Other Factors Also influencing the price of products and thus the advertising for those products are: consumer income and tastes, government regulations, and the supply of raw materials. Only after taking all these into consideration can marketing management determine the appropriate pricing strategy.

Pricing Strategies

The options a company has for determining its pricing strategy are numerous. Assume you are opening a retail store. You plan to sell stereo equipment, CD players, car stereos, and peripheral products. One of your first decisions is how to price your merchandise. Consider the following alternatives.

Competitive Pricing Strategy You could run ads declaring: "We won't be undersold!" Your ads could show or list a wide variety of products with a large, bold price next to each item. This would mean lower profit on each item and would require constant monitoring of competitive prices. It would also make you vulnerable to retaliatory actions by your competitors. Another approach to competitive pricing is to point out what a value your product is compared to high-priced brands (see Figure 4–13).

Comparative Pricing You could run ads for a new stereo system showing the regular list price and your special low price. By always comparing your low price with "normal" list prices, you might give the impression that your store offers discount prices on everything.

Skimming Strategy If yours is the only stereo store in the area, you might decide to start with relatively high prices to quickly recover all the money you had to spend furnishing, decorating, stocking, and promoting the store. Your ads would probably feature convenience and service. Later, you might lower your prices if a competitive store opens up.

Penetration Pricing Some stores open and immediately offer lower prices than they intend to have later on. Their hope is to penetrate the market quickly by creating immediate traffic and sales. As they develop regular customers, they gradually raise their prices to a more profitable level. Initial advertising might feature low prices, whereas later ads would promote store services, quality products, wide selection, or convenience.

Promotional Pricing To introduce a new line of equipment or to clear out old lines, you might use promotional pricing techniques. Two-for-one sales or end-of-month sales are typical of retail efforts to maintain traffic, stimulate demand, or make room for new merchandise.

Loss-Leader Pricing A special promotional strategy common to retail selling is the loss-leader strategy. You might select one stereo package and advertise it at $100 below your cost. The purpose is to create store traffic and sell other regularly priced merchandise. This presents the problem, though, of bait-and-switch advertising, which is illegal and unethical. If you offer loss leaders, you must have them in stock and be prepared to sell them without trying to talk customers out of them.

Prestige Pricing Rather than competing on the basis of price, you might prefer to offer the finest stereo equipment available, the best service, free delivery, and friendly clerks in plush surroundings. In this case, your ads might not mention prices at all. They would be aimed at a select clientele who could afford to pay your higher prices in exchange for convenience, service, and quality (see Figure 4–14).

Which of these strategies would you select for your stereo store? Why? What are the advantages and disadvantages of each? How would they affect your advertising?

Advertising and the Place Element

Every company must ask how and where their customers will buy their products. At the factory? From a door-to-door salesperson? In a store? Before the first advertisement can be created, this question of place—or distribution—must be answered. Companies may use two basic methods of distribution: direct or indirect.

Direct Marketing

The mail-order house that communicates directly with consumers through mail-order advertisements and catalogs is one of the many types of companies engaged in direct marketing because it does not use the traditional channels of distribution. It builds and maintains its own database of customers and uses a variety of media to communicate with those customers.

Today, the use of direct marketing is growing rapidly as companies discover its benefits of control, cost efficiency, and accountability. For example, many companies are using *telemarketing* programs to increase productivity through person-to-person telephone contact. By using the telephone in conjunction with direct-mail advertising, results have increased by 2.5 to 10 times over the response achieved by mail alone.[14]

Indirect Marketing

Most companies market their products through a distribution channel that includes a network of middlemen. A *middleman* is a business firm that operates between the producer and the consumer or industrial purchaser—someone who deals in trade rather than production.[15] The term includes both wholesalers and retailers, as well as manufacturers' representatives, brokers, jobbers, and distributors. A *distribution channel* is composed of all the firms and individuals that take title, or assist in taking title, to the product as it moves from the producer to the consumer.[16]

To help the massive flow of manufactured goods, various types of indirect distribution channels have developed to make products available to customers more economically than the manufacturers could accomplish through direct marketing. National appliance companies, for example, contract with exclusive regional distributors who buy the products from the factory and resell them to local dealers, who, in turn, resell them to consumers. Many industrial companies market their products through reps or distributors to original-equipment manufacturers (OEMs). These OEMs, in turn, may incorporate the product as a component in their own product, which is then sold to their customers.

Advertising and Distribution Strategy

The advertising a company uses depends on its method of distribution. Much of the advertising we see is not prepared or paid for by the manufacturer but rather by the distributor or the retailer. The amount of promotional support given to manufacturers over the years by members of the distribution channel cannot be overrated.

As part of their marketing strategy, manufacturers must determine what amount of market coverage is necessary for their products. Procter & Gamble, for example, defines adequate coverage for Crest toothpaste as almost every supermarket, discount store, drugstore, and variety store. Other products might need only one dealer for every 50,000 people. Consumer goods manufacturers traditionally use three types of distribution strategies: intensive, selective, and exclusive.

Intensive Distribution Soft drinks, candy, Bic pens, Timex watches, and many other convenience goods are available to purchasers at every possible location. This enables the consumer to buy with a minimum of effort. The profit on each unit is usually very low, but the volume of sales is high. For this reason, the sales burden is usually carried by the manufacturer's national advertising program. Ads appear in trade magazines to *push* the product into the retail "pipeline" and in mass media to stimulate consumers to *pull* the products through the pipeline. As a manufacturer modifies its strategy to either more push or more pull, special promotions may be directed at the trade or at consumers.

Selective Distribution By limiting the number of outlets, manufacturers can cut their costs of distribution and promotion. Many hardware tools, for example, are sold selectively through discount chains, home-improvement centers, and hardware stores. Manufacturers may use some national advertising, but the sales burden is normally carried by the retailer. In this case, the manufacturer may share part of the retailer's advertising costs through a *cooperative advertising* program, and the retailer agrees to display the manufacturer's products prominently.

Exclusive Distribution Some manufacturers grant exclusive rights to a wholesaler or retailer to sell in one geographic region. A town of 50,000 to 100,000 population will have only one Chrysler dealer and may not even have a Mercedes dealer. This is also common in the high-fashion business and in the marketing of some major appliance and furniture lines. What is lost in market coverage is often gained in the ability to maintain a prestige image and premium prices. Exclusive distribution agreements also force manufacturers and retailers to cooperate closely in advertising and promotion programs. For example, an Apple Computer retailer may receive substantial advertising allowances from the manufacturer for advertising the Macintosh in its local media. (See Ad Lab 4-D.)

AD LAB 4-D   Marketing Mac: Price and Distribution Strategies

When the Macintosh was introduced, the company had to determine the most appropriate price and distribution strategies. In setting price, market demand had to be considered as well as the cost of producing and distributing the product. Competitive prices had to be analyzed, and above all, Apple's corporate objectives for this product had to be weighed. Only then could price and distribution strategy be designed.

Laboratory Applications

1. Visit two or three stores where the Macintosh is sold. Can you determine what pricing strategy Apple is using?
2. Is Apple using intensive, selective, or exclusive distribution?

Vertical Marketing Systems

To be efficient, members of the distribution channel need to cooperate closely with one another. This need has given rise in recent years to the development of various types of vertical marketing systems. These include *corporate systems,* like Sears Roebuck, which own the manufacturers of many products sold in its stores; *administered systems,* like Magnavox, which gains strong retailer support because of the brand's reputation; and *contractual systems,* like I.G.A. Food Stores, which is a voluntary chain of independent members sponsored by a single wholesaler.

Other types of contractual systems include retail cooperatives, which set up their own wholesaling operations to better compete with chains, and *franchises,* like McDonald's, in which dealers (franchisees) operate under the guidelines and direction of the manufacturer (see Figure 4–15). Franchises in areas such as fast food (see Figure 4–16) have been so successful that now similar vertical marketing systems are even developing in the new do-it-yourself health-care business—retail dentistry, urgent/primary-care centers, and freestanding day surgery clinics.[17]

Vertical marketing systems offer both manufacturers and retailers numerous advantages: reduction of nonessential product offerings; streamlining of product and information flow; reduced duplication of efforts; standardization of record-keeping; centralized coordination of marketing efforts; and the realization of substantial savings as well as continuity in advertising.[18] A common store name and similar product inventories mean that a single newspaper ad can promote all of a chain's retailers in a particular trading area.

Advertising and the Promotion Element

After the other elements of the marketing mix are determined, the company can add, subtract, or modify its promotional activities. *Promotion* may be defined as the marketing-related communication between the seller and the buyer. Activities usually considered part of the *promotional mix* include personal selling, advertising, public relations, sales promotion, and collateral materials. Since most of these elements are so closely related to advertising, they will be treated in this text as they concern our discussions of advertising principles and techniques. That includes all the activities outlined below except personal selling.

Personal Selling

Selling is one of the oldest professions in the world; every product or service must be sold. However, the way in which personal selling is used may vary. Some products are sold by clerks in retail stores, others by salespeople who call on customers directly, and others by no salespeople, as in the case of mail order, where advertising carries the entire sales burden.

Advertising

Advertising has been called mass or nonpersonal selling. As we have discussed, advertising is used to inform, persuade, and remind customers about particular products and services. Some products, of course, lend

#1 BESTSELLER IN PRINT GETS RAVE REVIEWS.

If you're looking to make a wise investment, you should hear what the experts are saying about PIP, the world's largest business printer.

PIP is ranked one of "The 200 Best and Brightest Small Companies in America" by *Forbes* magazine (11/3/86), and is the first recipient of the International Franchise Association's Franchisor/Franchisee Relations Award.

The cash requirement is $32,500, which includes working capital. To find out how you can become a success story in the franchise field, call toll free: (800) 292-4747. In California call: (800) 638-8441 or (213) 653-8750. In Canada call: (800) 468-6747. Or write: PIP Printing Franchise Sales Dept., P.O. Box 48002, Los Angeles, CA 90048.

pip
PRINTING

This advertising is not an offering; an offering can only be made by a prospectus filed first with the state of New York. Such filing does not constitute approval by The Department of Law.

FIGURE   4–15

PIP Printing uses a clever headline to advertise its franchises to people looking for a "wise" investment.

themselves to advertising more than others. Typically, certain factors indicate an opportunity for advertising success, including:

1. High primary demand trend for the product.
2. Chance for significant product differentiation.
3. High relative importance to the consumer of hidden qualities as opposed to external qualities.
4. The opportunity to use strong emotional appeals.
5. Substantial sums to support advertising.

Where these conditions exist, as in the cosmetics industry, large advertising expenditures are favored, and the ratio of advertising to sales dollars is often quite high. For completely undifferentiated products, such as sugar, salt, and other raw materials or commodities, the importance of advertising is usually minimal, and price is usually the primary influence. An interesting exception to this is Sunkist, a farmer's cooperative that successfully branded a commodity (citrus) and markets it internationally.

These issues will be discussed further in Chapter 7, "Marketing and Advertising Planning." The role advertising should play depends on many factors and is a major decision in the marketing planning process.

Public Relations

Whereas advertising is paid-for communication, public relations usually has no clear or overt sponsorship. Many firms use public relations activities such as publicity as supplements to advertising to inform various audiences about the company and its products and to help build corporate credibility and image. Public relations, as we will discuss in Chapter 18, is an extremely powerful tool that should always be considered in the design of a company's promotional mix.

Sales Promotion

Sales promotion, the subject of Chapter 16, is a broad category covering nonmedia advertising activities such as free samples, displays, trading stamps, sweepstakes, cents-off coupons, and premiums. *Reader's Digest,*

FIGURE   4–16   The six largest restaurant chains, 1987

Rank	Company	Sales ($ millions)	Share of market as a percent of sales among top six chains
1	McDonald's	$14,110	45%
2	Burger King	5,590	18
3	Kentucky Fried Chicken	3,700	12
4	Hardee's	3,030	10
5	Wendy's	2,800	9
6	Pizza Hut	2,450	8

AD LAB 4-E   Marketing Mac: Deciding on Promotion

As mentioned in the text, some products lend themselves to promotion better than others.

Laboratory Applications

1. What about the Macintosh? What opportunities exist for advertising? What about other promotional tools?
2. If you were the brand manager for the Macintosh, would you try to use public relations? Sales promotion? Collateral materials? How would you do it?

for example, is famous for its annual sweepstakes designed to increase circulation. Manufacturers print and distribute over 200 billion coupons per year. Of these, only 7.3 billion are ever redeemed. But this 3.6 percent accounts for approximately $1.6 billion annually that manufacturers give their customers to try their products. Similarly, financial institutions spend untold millions on premiums to attract new accounts.

Collateral Materials

Collateral is a term used to refer to all the accessory advertising materials prepared by companies to help achieve marketing or public relations objectives. These may include booklets, catalogs, brochures, films, trade-show exhibits, sales kits, annual reports, or point-of-purchase displays.

The Marketing Mix in Perspective

When we look at the promotional mix outlined above, we see that advertising is just one of the elements companies have the option of using. (See Ad Lab 4-E.) And the promotional mix itself is just one element of the whole marketing mix. These relationships are important to understand in order to keep the highly visible (and often controversial) subject of advertising in perspective.

As we will discuss in Chapter 7, marketing and advertising planning is a continuous process of analysis, planning, execution, review, and replanning. In this process, the decision to use any or all of the elements of the promotional mix is based on experience and judgment. And companies constantly reevaluate their promotional mix.

Since most of the promotional elements are so closely related to advertising, they will enter our discussions of advertising principles and techniques.

Summary

The term *marketing* refers to all business activities aimed at facilitating the perceived equal-value exchange by: (1) finding out who customers are and what they want; (2) interpreting this information for management in order to improve old products or develop new ones; and (3) devising strategies aimed at executing the marketing exchange. In its simplest terms, marketing is the process companies use to satisfy their customers' needs and make a profit.

Advertising is concerned with the third step mentioned above. It is one tool marketers can use to inform, persuade, and remind customers about their products or services. To be effective, though, advertising depends on the adequate performance of the other marketing activities.

A market is a group of people who share a common need or desire for a product or service and who can afford it. There are several classifications of markets: consumer, reseller, industrial, government, and international.

To locate and measure potential markets, companies use market research and market segmentation. Based on common characteristics of customers, meaningful subgroups are built within larger markets. From these groups, companies can then select a target market at which they will aim all their marketing activities.

Every company can add, subtract, or modify four elements in its marketing program to achieve a desired marketing mix. The elements of the marketing mix are referred to as the four Ps: product, price, place, and promotion.

Product, as a marketing term, refers to the bundle of values offered to the customer. These values may encompass functional or symbolic consumer satisfactions. Marketing-oriented companies first try to determine what needs will be satisfied by their product. They then carry that concept into the product's design.

To satisfy the variety of customer tastes, marketers build differences into their products. Even the product's package is part of the product concept. The product concept may also be developed through unique positioning against competitive products in the consumer's mind.

Just as humans go through a life cycle, so do products. The location of a product in its life cycle determines to a great extent how it is advertised.

Price refers to what and how a customer pays for a product, and companies can use many common pricing strategies. Some products compete on the basis of price, but many do not.

The term *place* refers to how and where the product is distributed, bought, and sold. Companies may use either direct or indirect methods of distribution. Consumer goods manufacturers use several types of distribution strategies.

Promotion refers to the marketing-related communication between the seller and the buyer. Elements of the promotional mix include personal selling, advertising, public relations, sales promotion, and collateral.

Advertising is considered nonpersonal selling and is most effective when there is a high demand for the product, a chance for significant product differentiation, an importance to the consumer of hidden product qualities, the opportunity to use strong emotional appeals, and substantial sums to support an advertising program.

Questions for Review and Discussion

1. What effect, if any, has the evolution of the marketing concept had on the way advertising is created?
2. How does advertising relate to marketing?
3. What is the most important factor to consider when determining the elements of the marketing mix?
4. What examples of different kinds of markets can you give?
5. What are some other examples of product positioning not discussed in this chapter?
6. What effect does the product life cycle have on the advertising a company employs?
7. How do corporate objectives relate to the product life cycle?
8. What factors influence the price of a product?
9. How do the basic methods of distribution affect advertising?
10. What product characteristics encourage heavy advertising? Little advertising? Why?

5

CONSUMER BEHAVIOR AND MARKET SEGMENTATION

Do you know Joe Shields? Chances are you do, although you may know him by another name. He's 21 years old, bigger than average, good-looking, sports a well-trimmed moustache, and has medium-length sandy brown hair. Joe dresses casually but well, and he loves to have a good time. You have probably seen him cheering at football games or on the beach playing volleyball or at the local pub drinking beer and chatting with female friends.

He's not only big physically, but he has a strong personality, too. He hopes to be a lawyer one day, and he is already opinionated and has a way with words. He's not afraid to say what he wants, and he usually gets it. His friends look for his approval and tend to follow his lead. Joe's parents are definitely upper middle class. His dad is a building contractor and knows everybody in town.

With or without his parents, though, Joe does well. He's not at the top of his class, but his grades are well above average. He enjoys college and is conscientious about his work. But that doesn't stop him from having a good time. He's not a loner or a homebody. He likes to go out with both men and women. He likes parties where there are lots of music and talk, and women generally regard him as a bit of a swinger. But he's not at all rowdy. Actually, he can be very quiet at times.

Joe looks forward to going away to law school, although he hasn't decided where yet. And he doesn't seem too worried about it. Perhaps "casual" is the best way to describe Joe, because even his personal relationships seem to be light and easy rather than heavy and serious. Marriage and a family are a long way off, at least until after law school. And besides, Joe is having too much fun to be thinking seriously about that.

Do you recognize Joe? Do you know him well enough to describe what kind of car he'd like to buy? Do you think he eats a lot of fast foods, or does he prefer cooking for himself? What kind of beer does he drink? Does he smoke? If so, what brand? What stores does he frequent? Does he own a stereo? A CD player? A VCR? What makes?

In marketing and advertising, companies are constantly trying to match people and organizations (buyers) with products. To succeed, they need to understand what makes people, like Joe Shields, and organizations, like General Electric or Sam's Automotive, behave the way they do. That involves the study of *buyer behavior:* the activities, actions, and influencers of people and organizations that purchase and use goods and services.[1] There are basically two types of buying behavior: consumer behavior and industrial buying behavior. While the primary objective of this chapter is to understand the behavior of *consumers*—the people who buy and use products to satisfy their personal or household needs and wants—we will address the subject of industrial buying later, in the section on market segmentation.

CONSUMER BEHAVIOR: THE DIRECTIONAL FORCE IN ADVERTISING

Some people regard advertising as an art. Others consider it a science. Actually, it is a unique combination of the two. Advertising effectively blends the information and knowledge gained from the *behavioral sciences* (anthropology, sociology, psychology, etc.) with the craft and talent of the *communicating arts* (writing and printing, drama and theatrical production, graphic design, photography, etc.) to motivate, modify, or reinforce consumer perceptions, beliefs, attitudes, and behavior. To accomplish this, marketing and advertising people try to be conscious of people's attitudes, values, likes and dislikes, habits, fears, wants, and desires. And since these characteristics are always changing, steps must be taken to monitor them.

As societies alter their attitudes toward dress, recreation, morals, religion, education, economics, or even other people, advertising techniques change, too. Why? Because the behavioral characteristics of large groups of people give the directional force to any advertising aimed at those groups. Thus, consumer advertisers typically attempt to convert *trends* in mass consumer behavior to *fashion* in specific consumer behavior.

Look at the ad for the 1959 De Soto in Figure 5–1. What do you see? A young woman, white, affluent, dressed well and rather formally, concerned about stepping out of her new car "like a lady." Compare that with more recent automobile ads where we see young women, of various ethnic backgrounds, dressed according to modern styles, enjoying the many features of their high-tech vehicles (see Figure 5–2).

Not only does the tone of advertising reflect differences in accepted social behavior, but the customer herself has changed considerably over

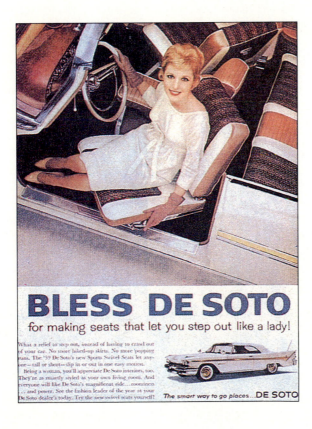

FIGURE   5–1

Automobile advertising then and now. In the 1950s, Chrysler's DeSoto developed product attributes like swivel seats to suit feminine tastes. Notice the way the model is dressed and the thrust of the ad copy.

FIGURE   5–2

As time passes, tastes change. And so do fashions, as evidenced by the chic but casual clothes worn by the model advertising the Jaguar XJ-SC. Similarly, the style of advertising has changed to reflect these newer values.

the last 30 years. The legendary middle-class world inhabited by the woman of the late 1950s and early 60s doesn't exist anymore. Today's woman thinks differently, acts and dresses differently, lives a very different lifestyle, and seeks completely different product benefits.[2]

There are two steps in understanding this relationship between consumer behavior and advertising. First, it is important to realize the complexity of human behavior—how extensive a variety of influences affect it. Second, we need to understand how marketers capitalize on these influences by clustering consumers who tend to behave in the same way. In so doing, we will see how the tendencies or characteristics of various behavioral groups become the foundation for market segmentation strategies and their associated advertising campaigns.

THE COMPLEXITY OF CONSUMER BUYING DECISIONS

When making even the simplest purchase, a consumer like Joe Shields goes through a complicated mental process. In Figure 5–3 we can view the typical anatomy of a purchase decision.

This model shows how external stimuli such as the company's marketing efforts as well as various noncommercial sources of information (family, friends, teachers, etc.) join to activate the decision-making process. At the same time, this process is also filtered by the many personal influences on consumer behavior such as motivation, personality, learned attitudes, and perception.[3] At any point, the decision process may be terminated if Joe loses interest or, after evaluating the product, decides not to buy. If he

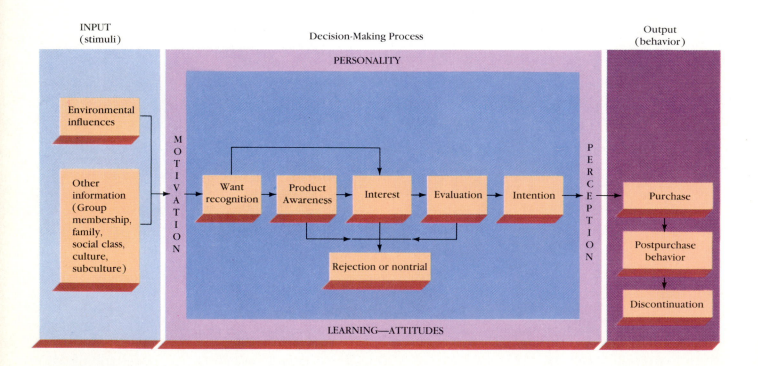

*FIGURE   5–3

Anatomy of a purchase decision.

does make a purchase, he has the opportunity to evaluate whether the product satisfies his needs. If it doesn't, then he will probably discontinue using that product.

For us to fully appreciate the complexity of the consumer's buying decisions, therefore, we need to be aware of the variety of *personal influences* on consumer behavior; recognize the impact of *environmental stimuli;* and examine how these components are integrated with commercial marketing efforts in the consumer's mind.

Personal Influences on Consumer Behavior: The Importance of Your Inner Self

The goal of all advertising is to influence people's attitudes and buying behavior, but it is difficult to predict the success of planned advertising programs because human beings are all individuals. Each behaves differently, thereby making mass consumer behavior essentially unpredictable. Consider some of the contrasts in individual behavior patterns we see every day:

People vary in their persuasibility. Some are easily persuaded to do something; others are skeptical and difficult to convince.

Some people have "cool" personalities, acting reserved, controlled, rational and analytical. Others have "hot" personalities—lively, responding emotionally, and laughing or angering easily.

Some people are loners; others like the security of people.

Some people love their work, and others dislike it.

Many people are driven by the craving for material possessions.

Some people are stirred by spiritual concerns.

Some people are frugal with their earnings. Others spend their money and use credit more freely.

People also vary in their sexual expressions, interests in sports and hobbies, religious preferences, self-worth, goal orientation, color preferences, musical expression, and fashion sense. All these affect consumer buying decisions (see Figure 5–4).

FIGURE   5–4

A few years ago, who would have thought that we would pay extra money for new clothes that look old and worn? Yet, this is the style today, as beautifully illustrated in this "urban renewal" ad for Levi's Street Jeans.

To further complicate the advertiser's goal of influencing consumer behavior, consider these observations. First, people's attitudes, beliefs, and preferences change. What we have liked for the last five years we may suddenly not like tomorrow or at some time in the future. That includes products, people, activities, and living conditions.

Second, individual behavior is inconsistent and difficult to predict from one day to the next. Joe Shields might react to an idea positively one day but negatively the next. He might enjoy going to a movie tonight, but he might prefer to stay home tomorrow.

Third, people are often unable to explain their behavior. A woman might say she bought a dress because she needed it and because it was marked down 30 percent. The real reason may be quite different.

Often, we may not understand why we behave as we do. And if we do understand our true motivations, we may fear expressing them. For example, an executive who buys a new Mercedes might be reluctant to admit that he bought it because he wanted to be accepted by his peers.

Needs and Motives

In the study of consumer behavior, *motivation* refers to the various underlying drives that contribute to the individual consumer's purchasing actions. These drives stem from the conscious or unconscious desire to reduce the *needs* and satisfy the *wants* of the consumer. Needs are the basic, human forces that motivate a person to do something. Wants are those needs that are learned during a person's life.[4]

Unfortunately, motivations cannot be directly observed. When we see Joe Shields eat, we assume he is hungry, but that may not be correct. People eat for a variety of reasons besides hunger—to be sociable, because it is time to eat, because they are bored, or because they are nervous.

Often a combination of motives underlies our decision-making process. The reasons (motives) a person stops shopping at Lucky and starts shopping at Safeway may be: (1) the Safeway store is closer to home, (2) Safeway has a wider selection of fresh produce, or (3) Safeway has an image of quality and status. These factors might be enough to make the shopper switch even if the prices on some items at Lucky are lower.

People have different needs and wants and, therefore, different motivations. Understanding needs is very complex. One need might be satisfied in many ways. Likewise, the same product might satisfy different needs for different people, and it is not always clear which need or want a product is satisfying.

Psychologists have tried to categorize needs to understand them better. Abraham Maslow developed the following *hierarchy of needs* on the theory that the lower biologic or survival needs are dominant in human behavior and must be satisfied before the higher, socially acquired needs (or wants) become meaningful.

1. Physiological needs—oxygen, food, drink, sex, and rest.
2. Safety needs—infantile dependency; avoidance of situations that are unfamiliar, threatening, or might lead to injury or illness; and economic security.
3. Social needs—friendship and affection and a sense of belonging.
4. Esteem needs—self-respect, recognition, status, prestige, and success.
5. Self-actualization—living up to one's potential (self-fulfillment).[5]

FIGURE 5–5		Promotional appeals and the hierarchy of needs
Product	**Need**	**Promotional appeal**
Small home	Physiological	Inexpensive housing for the family; small but well-built.
Smoke alarm	Safety	Could save your family's lives; think of your children and your spouse.
Gold chain	Social	Show your sweetheart you care on Valentine's Day.
Expensive luxury car	Esteem	Picture car in front of "gracious" home or club.
Graphite golf clubs	Self-actualization	For the three-day-a-week golfer; for the golfer who is looking for only two strokes.

The promise of satisfying the needs at each level establishes the basic promotional appeal for many advertisements (see Figure 5–5).

In affluent societies such as the United States, Canada, Western Europe, and Japan, most individuals pay little attention to such physiological needs as the availability of food or the safety of drinking water. They take the fulfillment of these needs for granted. As a result, marketing and advertising campaigns for many products stress fulfillment of social, esteem, and self-actualization needs, with some even offering the rewards of better love relationships. (See Ad Lab 5-A.)

Maslow's hierarchy is a very convenient way to classify human needs, but it would be a mistake to assume that needs occur one at a time. Usually people are motivated by some combination of two or more needs.

The analysis of motivations for marketing purposes is complicated by the fact that people are admittedly moved by both conscious and unconscious needs. To explore the depths of the unconscious, psychologists like Ernest Dichter have developed a discipline called *motivation research,* which, although limited to very small samples of consumers and hampered by analytical subjectivity, has offered some insights into the underlying reasons for unexpected consumer behavior. We will discuss this subject more thoroughly in Chapter 6, "Marketing and Advertising Research."

Individual Perception

While Joe Shields is motivated by his personal needs for self-esteem, love, or social recognition, his behavior is also affected by his particular perception of himself and of the world around him.

Perception is the personalized way of sensing the stimuli to which an

AD LAB 5-A   Using Needs to Stimulate Motivation

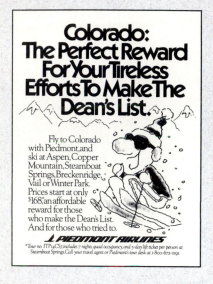

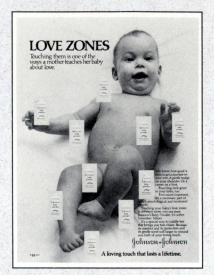

Laboratory Application

Human needs are the basis for many advertisements. By referring to Maslow's hierarchy of needs described in the text, can you determine what motivations these advertisers are attempting to stimulate?

individual is exposed—the act or process of comprehending the world in which the individual exists.[6] For example, when Joe looks at an automobile that he *needs* for transportation, he perceives more than a random collection of paint, tires, glass, and steel. He perceives an integrated entity designed to provide a variety of benefits—transportation, comfort, convenience, economy, and even status for the driver.

A person's perception of this integrated entity may be affected by the individual's self-concept, needs and motivations, knowledge, past experience, feelings, attitudes, and personality. As we suggested in our discussion of the product concept in Chapter 4, a person's perception or attitude might also be shaped by the messages in the advertising he or she has seen. A number of years ago, for example, research showed that the general public perceived some automobiles as highly masculine and others as very feminine.[7] As an exercise, consider the various models of cars available today. What "masculine" cars spring to mind? What "feminine" ones? What has created their gender in your mind? (See Ad Lab 5-B.)

Self-Concept and Roles We all carry images in our minds of who we are and who we want to be. (See Figure 5–6.) If Joe Shields wants to appear masculine and a bit racy, he may favor an automobile that supports that image.

AD LAB 5-B   Subliminal Manipulation: Fact or Fantasy?

Is it possible to manipulate people with subliminal advertising? This intriguing controversy started back in the 1950s when Vance Packard's best-seller *The Hidden Persuaders* described an experiment that appeared to show that if a message was perceived, perhaps unconsciously, at levels below the "limen," or perceptual threshold, it could motivate consumers.

The experiment involved showing movies while at the same time projecting the words *Eat Popcorn* and *Drink Coca-Cola* on the screen for 1/3,000 of a second. Sales figures jumped 57 percent for popcorn and 18 percent for Coca-Cola during the six-week term of the experiment. As expected, this finding caused quite a furor. Some states passed laws to prevent the practice. However, this study has never been replicated successfully. One reason perhaps was that a number of factors may have affected the results of the experiment. For example, the movie being shown during the experiment period was *Picnic,* which included many scenes of people eating and drinking in hot summer weather.

If subliminal advertising could persuade people "against their will," profound ethical questions would be raised. But there is general agreement that it is not possible. First, the threshold (or level) at which people perceive visual and aural stimuli varies greatly. Obviously, people with good eyesight perceive visual stimuli more easily than people who wear glasses. Furthermore, researchers are able to measure *galvanic skin response (GSR)*—changes in the electrical activity of the skin—when certain stimuli are introduced. But no GSR can be detected during supposed subliminal perception states. The conclusion, therefore, is that no message has been perceived. And even if a message were perceived, it could be easily distorted. "Drink Coke" might make a viewer "go smoke" or "think jokes."

The subliminal perception controversy has been rekindled with the publication of books that accused advertising people of planting hidden sexual messages in print ads—particularly in the ice cubes portrayed in liquor advertising.

Subliminal Seduction (subtitled "Here Are the Secret Ways Ad Men Arouse Your Desires to Sell Their Products") and *Media Sexploitation* include numerous examples of what the author (Wilson Bryan Keys) believes are sexual symbols, four-letter words, and pornographic pictures buried in the otherwise bland content of various ads. He concludes that such "hidden persuaders" were carefully contrived by major advertisers and their agencies to seduce consumers at a subliminal level.

The fact is that virtually all photographs used in national advertising are retouched, either by hand or by electronic means, in order to correct imperfections or add visual effects to the picture (see Chapter 10). At this point in the production process, it is entirely possible for some mischievous creativity to take place. A photo retoucher could, for example, add some carefully disguised sexual element into an ad which, when reduced down to final size, would not be noticeable and would only be known to him or her. However, this would be considered highly unprofessional and unethical in the business, and if discovered, it would be cause for immediate termination of the offender. It would also seriously endanger the agency's relationship with its client.

As far as Mr. Keys's idea of the insidious cunning of marketing decision makers goes, it is interesting to note that in more than 600 pages on the subject, he finds not a single individual who admits to, or even accuses others of, being involved in subliminal embedding.

Dr. Jack Haberstroh, professor in the School of Mass Communications at Virginia Commonwealth University, investigated Keys's charge that S-E-X is embedded on the face of Ritz crackers. His research even included a visit to a Ritz cracker factory. He concludes that the charges of S-E-X written on Ritz crackers in particular and of subliminal advertising in general are "preposterous, absurd, ludicrous, and laughable."

Laboratory Applications

1. Would words with sexual connotations hidden in an advertisement motivate you to purchase a product? Why or why not?
2. Do you feel that appeals to the consumer's prurient interests can help sell products? If so, what kind of products?

FIGURE   5–6

The role of women in business has changed profoundly in recent years as this ad for *The Wall Street Journal* demonstrates. As a result, the whole fabric of corporate America has changed, influencing the way women in the workplace are viewed and the way they view themselves. Twenty years ago, for example, how many people considered women to be prospective subscribers to the *Journal*?

The fabric of American business is changing.

It used to be that wearing a business suit meant being a businessman.
But in recent years, millions of women have entered the workplace. And their arrival has signaled a profound change. Not only in corporate dress, but in the very way of corporate life.

On March 24th, The Wall Street Journal will publish a special report on the increasingly important role of women in business.
Entitled "The Corporate Woman," the section will consider the nature of the new workforce, and the impact of

the growing female presence.
It will look at women's problems. Their progress. Their prospects for the future.
And it will measure their influence on some of the basic principles and assumptions of corporate America.
"The Corporate Woman"

will be included free of charge in your subscription or newsstand copy of The Wall Street Journal on Monday, March 24th. Be sure to read it.
Whether you're woman enough to or not.

The Wall Street Journal.
The daily diary of the American dream.

On the other hand, if he wants to be regarded as solid and respectable, he may choose a type of vehicle that represents good engineering, safety, and economy. According to John O'Toole, the former chairman of the Foote, Cone & Belding advertising agency, "If the information [in an automobile advertisement] is properly chosen and skillfully presented, it will point out [to the consumer] the relevance of the car to his needs and self-image sufficiently to get him into the showroom."[8]

Marketers are very concerned with the perceptions consumers have of their products because, to the consumer, the perception *is* the reality. As marketing consultant and psychophysicist Howard Moskowitz says, if the consumer wants a "natural taste" and if the consumer thinks lemonade with additives tastes natural, that's what she'll buy. "Lemon flavor is lemon flavor, whether you get it from a tree or from an artist flavorist. The constituents are different, but [to the consumer] what is perceived as lemon flavor *is* lemon flavor. That's reality."[9]

In one recent study, female consumers were asked how they perceived the Maidenform line of bras. Many described it as old-fashioned and conservative, a brand worn by housewives as opposed to young career women.[10] That was their reality. Maidenform's response was to use a bolder approach in its advertising to add more sex appeal to the product.

Obviously, each of us has his own reality. You may consider the tacos and burritos you buy at a fast-food outlet to be Mexican food. That perception is your reality, even though a man from Mexico might tell you that *in reality* that fast-food taco bears little resemblance to an "authentic" Mexican taco. His reality, based on his perception, is considerably different.

Selective Perception   One of the major problems advertisers face with this subject of perceptions is the fact that each of us exercises *selective perception*. As humans, we have the ability to unconsciously screen out or modify the many sensations bombarding our central processing unit and only choose those that relate to our previous experiences, needs, desires, attitudes, or beliefs.[11] The average adult is exposed to nearly 20,000 messages a day—twice as many as we received 10 years ago. Yet most people are hardly aware of most of these. We are limited not only by the physical capacity of our senses but also by our interests. We focus attention on some things and avoid others. A single newspaper may contain hundreds of advertisements, but the average reader recalls only a small number of these and is influenced by even fewer. Thus, advertisers may spend millions of dollars on national media advertising, sales promotion, and point-of-purchase displays only to discover in later research that consumers have little or no memory of the product or promotion.

This selectivity makes it important for marketers to obtain satisfied customers and build brand loyalty and for the product to fit the image created by advertising. If satisfied, customers are less likely to seek new information about competing products and may not even notice when it is put in front of them.

Theory of Cognitive Dissonance   Selective perception serves us in a variety of ways. Besides saving us time by filtering out irrelevant or uninteresting data, it protects us from facing unpleasant realities. In line with this, Leon Festinger developed the *theory of cognitive dissonance,* which states basically that people strive to justify their behavior by reducing the degree to which their impressions or beliefs are inconsistent with reality (dissonance).[12]

For example, you might purchase a Honda automobile because you believe it's the best automotive value on the market. However, if you see an ad or a consumer report that "proves" that the Mazda is an even better value, this exposure may create dissonance because of the gap between your previous thinking and the "new evidence." You may choose to ignore the Mazda information or subconsciously seek a reassuring Honda ad in order to reduce the dissonance. Research has shown, in fact, that new automobile buyers are more likely to read advertisements about the brands of cars they have already purchased than about competitive makes.[13] On the other hand, you may accept the new evidence and reduce the dissonance by changing your purchasing behavior—by either trading in your Honda or vowing to purchase a Mazda next time.

Naturally, advertisers hope their customers do not experience dissonance. But they also hope consumers of competitive products do, because those buyers might relieve that uncomfortable tension by switching to their product.

Consumer Learning and Habit Development

Another personal influence on consumer behavior is the way consumers learn new information and develop purchasing habits. A major objective of advertising is to inform (teach) people about products and where to buy them. So advertisers are extremely interested in how people learn. Many psychologists consider learning to be the most fundamental process in human behavior. The advanced, "higher-level" needs, for example, are learned. Learning produces our habits and skills. It also contributes to the development of attitudes, beliefs, preferences, prejudices, emotions, and standards of conduct—all of which contribute to our purchase decisions.

By definition, *learning is a relatively permanent change in behavior that occurs as a result of reinforced practices.* Theories of learning are numerous, but most can be classified into two broad categories: cognitive theory and stimulus-response theory. *Cognitive theory* views learning as a mental process of memory, thinking, and the rational application of knowledge to practical problem solving.[14] This theory may be an accurate description of the way we learn in school and the way we develop certain attitudes and beliefs. *Stimulus-response theory,* on the other hand, treats learning as a trial-and-error process. Some cue or *stimulus* triggers the consumer's need or want, which, in turn, creates the drive to *respond.* If the response reduces the drive, then satisfaction occurs, and the response is rewarded or reinforced. This produces repeat behavior the next time the drive is aroused, and learning will have taken place.[15] Figure 5–7 shows a simple schematic of these two theories.

Let's examine how the stimulus-response theory works in marketing. An advertisement is a stimulus, or *cue,* and a purchase is a positive response. If the product gives the consumer satisfaction, then there is reinforcement. Additional reinforcement may be given through superior product performance, good service, and reminder advertising.

Through *repetition* of the cues (advertisements), the learning process, including memory, may be reinforced and repeat behavior encouraged.

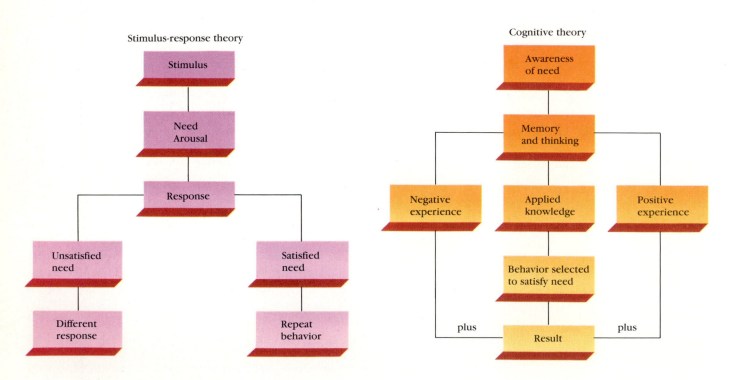

FIGURE   5–7

Two theories of learning.

Learning may be further enchanced by engaging the consumer's *participation* in the process through the use of free samples or free in-home trials of the product. Finally, if learning is reinforced enough and repeat behavior is produced, a purchasing *habit* may result.

Habit is the natural extension of learning. It is *an acquired or developed behavior pattern that has become nearly or completely involuntary.* The old cliché "People are the creatures of habit" is true.

What if the purchase turns out to be unsatisfactory? Learning still takes place, but then something else happens. As John O'Toole says:

> The mightiest weapon consumers have, and the one manufacturers fear most, is their refusal to repurchase. Advertising is powerful in that it can get them to buy a product once. But if it doesn't please them, the heaviest media budget in the world won't get them to buy again.[16]

Worse yet, unsatisfied customers will tell others of their experience faster than satisfied customers will. (Have you ever noticed how fast a bad movie dies at the box office?) Bad word of mouth creates negative attitudes and beliefs and thereby cancels the marketer's dream of creating a consumer purchasing habit.

Why Most Consumer Behavior Is Habitual Most consumer behavior is habitual for three reasons. First, we resort to habit when we select products because it is *easy.* Whenever we consider an alternative to our regular brand choice, we are forced to think, evaluate, compare, and then decide—and this is difficult for most of us, not to mention risky. We may be dissatisfied with a new choice or criticized by friends who disagree with our decision.

Second, we rely on habit because of *necessity.* Consider the person who purchases 50 items in a supermarket. To read all the labels of competitive brands would require hours of concentration, which almost no one has the time—or inclination—to do.

Third, we resort to habit because it is usually the *rational* thing to do. As we learn through trial and error which brands serve us well and which do not, we also learn which stores and service outlets satisfy us and which do not. When we find a product or a store to our liking, we continue to buy the product or patronize the store because it is the intelligent thing to do. Thus, as discussed in Chapter 4, we see again the added value that *branding* brings to a product. For the consumer, it delivers convenience and ease of mind; for the manufacturer, aid in habit development.

Interest of Advertisers in Habit Advertisers have three habit-related goals:

1. *Habit breaking*—To get consumers to break an existing purchase habit, that is, to stop buying their habitual brand and to try a new brand. Pepsi Cola, for example, aggressively raided habitual Coke drinkers with its Pepsi Challenge campaign. Many devices are used to induce consumers to try a different product or visit a new store. These include giving away free samples of the product, announcing something new about the product, giving limited-time price reductions, and holding grand openings.
2. *Habit acquisition*—To get consumers to acquire the habit of buying their brand or patronizing their establishment. To build a product preference habit, advertisers may use "reassurance" advertising to remind customers of an earlier, satisfactory purchase response. Examples of

advertising themes designed to encourage purchasing habits are: "Catch the Wave" (Coca-Cola), "Give me a Light . . . Bud Light!" and "Once in the morning does it" (Scope).

3. *Habit reinforcement*—To convince current users to remain habitual purchasers or patrons. Each time a consumer uses the product and is satisfied, the habit of buying the product is reinforced. Continued satisfaction may reinforce the purchase habit to such a degree that the purchase decision is virtually automatic (see Figure 5–8).

Much advertising is intended to remind consumers that a product they use satisfies their need. Some of the famous slogans used to help reinforce positive impressions in the minds of consumers are: "This Bud's for You"; "Coke is it"; and "I hate it . . . but I use it twice a day" (Listerine).

Of course, the overall objective is to produce the phenomenon in consumer behavior known as *brand loyalty.* Brand loyalty is the consumer's decision to repurchase a brand continually because he or she perceives that the brand has the right product features or quality at the right price.[17]

Measuring brand loyalty, or even defining its characteristics, is very difficult since so many aspects may be involved: consumer attitudes, perceptions, family pressure, friendship with the salesperson, and other factors. However, developing loyalty is the long-term objective of all marketers and a major reason for their continued study of consumer behavior.

Environmental Influences on Consumer Behavior: The Importance of What's Around You

In addition to the numerous internal, personal influences we have just discussed, many external, environmental factors—the family, social, and cultural environments of the consumer—influence consumer behavior.

Family

Our attitudes and beliefs about right and wrong, religion, work, male and female roles, political philosophy, sexual behavior, other races, ethical values, and economics receive their initial direction in the family setting. This influence is usually strong and long lasting. Few people who were brought up in one religion switch to another when they mature. Nor are people easily persuaded to accept a radically different political outlook or social philosophy. A person reared in a capitalist or socialist environment will probably die a capitalist or a socialist.

From an early age, family communication affects our socialization as consumers—our attitudes toward many products and our purchasing habits.[18] Food preferences in particular are shaped to a considerable extent by what people eat when growing up. If Joe Shields was raised on turnip greens and corn bread, he will probably continue to enjoy them as an adult. Many other product preferences are formed in the family environment. Being programmed at an early age to know that the "right" headache relief is St. Joseph and the "right" name for appliances is General Electric goes a long way toward shaping the purchasing behavior of adults.

In recent years, however, this family influence has diminished as working parents take a less active role in raising their children and as youngsters look outside the family for social values.[19]

FIGURE   5–8

This Canadian ad for Coca-Cola is a good example of habit reinforcement. Placed in the official Calgary Winter Olympics program, the ad promotes the Olympic theme with the headline "Universal symbol of friendship."

Society

We are all influenced by the social community in which we live. The social class to which we belong, the leaders whose opinions we value, and the groups with which we identify affect not only our views on life but also the products we buy. For instance, what social class do you believe Joe Shields falls into?

Social Class Most societies can be divided into social classes, and traditionally, people in the same social class have tended toward similar attitudes, status symbols, and spending patterns (see Figure 5–9). In recent years, though, this classification has been more difficult in the United States.

We are a socially mobile society; members of our society can move upward or downward. Many middle-aged Americans have moved up one or two classes. Few, however, have moved up three or more. Some people fall back a class or two, but not many. It is significant that, with the exception of the upper upper class and the lower lower class, people in the other four classes are motivated to move up. The "get ahead," "better than your peers," "move up," and "win greater admiration" philosophy is still a strong part of the American culture. Advertising people capitalize on the broad-based desire to "be the best you can."

But in recent times, due in great part to a 60 percent divorce rate, there has been a great muddling of the middle class. Defining it anymore is

FIGURE   5–9   American social classes

Upper upper class The upper upper class is the social elite. It consists of prominent people whose families have been wealthy for generations. Less than 1 percent of the population belongs to this privileged class. People in this class live graciously and quietly. They have great power but tend to use it inconspicuously.

Lower upper class This class is also small, consisting of less than 2 percent of the population. Sometimes referred to as the "Nouveau riche," members of this class include well-to-do industrialists, businesspeople, and professional people. People in the lower upper class are not yet fully accepted as the social peers of the people in the upper upper class.

Upper middle class The upper middle class consists of about 10 percent of the population. Its members are successful small businesspeople, middle- and upper-level managers in business and government, and professional people who are moderately successful. Many people who make up suburbia belong to this class. People in this class tend to be very success oriented and want to improve their status in life.

Lower middle class This class consists of approximately 30 to 35 percent of the population. Members work in nonmanagerial jobs, own small businesses, and occupy low-level positions in government. Those in the lower middle class are strongly motivated to win approval from their peers, have a strong family orientation, and tend to be very law-abiding.

Upper lower class This is the largest social class, consisting of an estimated 40 percent of the population. Its members are unskilled or semiskilled. Very few work in managerial positions or in the professions. When we think of the "working class," we think of people in this category. The upper lower class strives less to "get ahead," "succeed," and "make more money" than the four classes above it.

Lower lower class This group consists of an estimated 15 percent of the population. It is characterized by low-level motivation, despair, living day-to-day, lack of concern for education and "getting ahead," and a whatever-will-be-will-be attitude.

extremely difficult and presents marketers with new, and sometimes bewildering, challenges. The middle class is no longer tightly knit and no longer represents a definable set of values. This has also given greater importance to market segmentation strategies as single mothers, stockbrokers, and retired blue-collar workers all see themselves as part of the great middle class.[20]

Reference Groups Whenever we are concerned with how we will appear in the eyes of other people, or whenever we attempt to emulate members of some group, we are demonstrating the significance of *reference groups*. Reference groups are groups of people whom we try to emulate or whose approval concerns us. They can be personal (family, friends, fellow workers) or impersonal (movie stars, professional athletes, business executives). A special form of reference group—our peers—exerts a great influence on what we believe and on the way we behave. To win acceptance by his peers (fellow students, fellow workers, colleagues), Joe Shields may purchase a certain style of clothing, choose a particular place to live, and acquire habits that will earn him their approval.

Often an individual is influenced by two reference groups in opposite directions and has to choose between them. For example, to win peer

PEOPLE IN ADVERTISING

Jay Chiat

Chairman of the Board and
Chief Executive Officer
Chiat/Day, inc., Advertising

Jay Chiat is chairman of the board and chief executive officer of Chiat/Day, inc., Advertising, which has won more awards per client than any other advertising agency in the world. The 20-year-old agency commands annual billings of $350 million through its network of offices in Los Angeles, San Francisco, and New York City.

Chiat launched his advertising career as a copywriter at a small agency in Orange County, California. He soon rose to creative director of the firm's two-person creative department.

After serving two years in the Air Force, Chiat resumed his education. He graduated from Rutgers University, attended Columbia University's Graduate School of Broadcasting, and went on to graduate from the UCLA Executive Program. For three years, he taught advertising at the University of Southern California School of Journalism.

Chiat then launched his own agency. He attributes its success to these Chiat/Day rules for "How to Avoid Doing Bad Advertising":

1. Realize that your agency cannot work for everyone.
2. Recognize that there are no shortcuts. It's hard work to do great advertising.
3. Hire only those you believe can do the job better than you can. It makes the work brighter, and it makes you work brighter.

approval, some young people may engage in behavior that their family reference group considers wrong, such as taking drugs, smoking, or drinking.

Opinion Leaders An *opinion leader* is some person or organization whose beliefs or attitudes are considered right by people who share an interest in some specific activity. All fields (sports, religion, economics, fashion, finance, politics, and so on) have opinion leaders. Our minds reason, "If so-and-so believes Spalding is the right tennis racket then it must be so. She knows more about the game than I do." Or if *Vogue* says short skirts are in again, then the consumer may reason, "I'm going to buy a chic short skirt. After all, *Vogue* is the final word in fashion." Thus, the testimonials of opinion leaders are important to major marketers (see Figure 5–10).

Culture

Culture has an immeasurable influence on the consumer. Americans eat hot dogs, peanut butter, and apple pie. In Europe, you may find a few hamburger outlets, but hamburgers won't taste the same. And you probably won't get a chocolate milk shake, either.

4. Fire quickly those who do not measure up. They contaminate the agency by making good people question their judgment.

5. Recognize that all your people have creative capabilities and demand creativity from all departments.

6. Make sure your account-management people are smart marketers. It takes brilliant marketing support to quiet client nervousness.

7. Never stop at the first creative solution. Explore alternatives.

8. Dig for the facts. Interview relentlessly. Your research must be unquestioned.

9. Know your target better than you know yourself.

10. Make sure a clear, concise, creative brief is written for every ad. Yes, *every* ad.

11. Treat all advertising as equal. The trade is as important as the TV commercial. Perhaps more so.

12. Do not permit "closet" accounts. If the work is not good enough to show to new business prospects, the account is not good enough to keep.

13. Spend time training. Do not assume that people automatically understand what is expected of them.

14. Promote from within when possible. But do not hesitate to seek expertise elsewhere if it is lacking at the agency.

15. Treat everyone with the same level of dignity you expect yourself.

16. Have no expectations. You have the privilege of working on an account for as long as the client allows you to.

17. Perhaps most important, try to relax and have some fun.

Chiat, who has garnered gold and silver medals from the Los Angeles and New York Art Directors Shows, also has won several Andy Awards, numerous CLIOs, a shelf full of Belding Bowls, AAF "Best in the West" Awards, and CA Awards of Excellence. Named one of the "100 Top Creative People in the U.S." in *Ad Day* polls, Chiat has also had the distinction of being "Advertising Man of the Year" as designated by the WSAAA.

Similar top honors have gone to his agency. Chiat/Day was chosen "Advertising Agency of the Year" by *Advertising Age* in 1980 and, two years later, one of "the *Adweek* Eight" top creative agencies. In 1984, Chiat/Day won the Cannes "Grand Prix" Award.

Jay Chiat is past president of the Advertising Industry Emergency Fund and past president of the Greater New York Cystic Fibrosis Association.

LOOK, UP IN THE AIR.

FIGURE 5–10

Nike has used a variety of high-visibility professional athletes, like Michael Jordan here, to act as authoritative reference figures in the company's dramatically designed advertisements.

In the United States and Canada, our populations are made up of many subcultures. Some are based on race, national origin, religion, or simply geographic proximity. The advertiser must understand these subcultures because cultural differences may affect responses to products as well as to advertising.

According to the Population Reference Bureau, 29 million blacks, 17 million Hispanics, and 5 million Asians lived in the United States in 1985—plus an unknown number of illegal aliens. That accounts for over 21 percent of the American population; and by the year 2000, that figure should reach 25 percent or more.[21]

From generation to generation, these subcultures transfer their beliefs and values. Racial, religious, and ethnic groups all have backgrounds that affect their preference for styles of dress, food, beverages, transportation, personal-care products, and household furnishings, to name a few. Today, advertising agencies that specialize in minority markets are enjoying a boom in the industry as companies come to realize that a special appeal is often good business[22] (see Figure 5–11).

Similarly, the social environment in a foreign country is also based on that country's particular language, culture, literacy rate, religion, and lifestyle. (See Chapter 19.) These cultural customs, traditions, attitudes, and taboos cannot be ignored by advertisers.

FIGURE   5–11

The line "Brush often with Crest" is given new meaning in this ad aimed at the Hispanic market. The play is on the Spanish word *menudo,* which is also the name of the popular Latin singing group pictured in the ad.

Thus, we see that the many external influences on a consumer can be just as important as the internal influences. An awareness of all these factors helps marketers create the strategy behind much advertising. (See Ad Lab 5-C.)

Integrating the Components of Consumer Behavior

If Joe Shields needs a new shirt, we now know his decision will be affected by many internal and external factors. To better comprehend how Joe's purchase decision takes place, look back now at the purchase decision model in Figure 5–3 at the beginning of this chapter.

The shirt manufacturer may advertise or a local retail store may announce a sale on shirts. A friend of Joe's may have just bought a new shirt, or Joe's mother may have said she didn't like the shirt he was wearing. Any of these external influences might trigger the recognition by Joe that he needs or wants a new shirt. These external factors also influence the type or brand of shirt Joe selects.

At this point, however, Joe's decision to purchase a shirt is further influenced by internal forces. These include his needs and desires (which may be functional, psychological, or, most likely, a combination), his personality, his self-concept, his perception of the features or benefits of particular types of shirts, his attitude toward particular brands, and the education or experience he has had that has contributed to his normal purchasing habits.

As all these forces converge within Joe's mental computer, he realizes the need, becomes aware of shirts and ads for shirts, develops an interest, evaluates what he believes he should do, forms an intention to buy, and eventually selects a shirt. This process may take several days, or it may occur in a few seconds if Joe happens to be in a store or passing a window display. It stands to reason that if we knew all the forces influencing an individual and could weigh the effect of each force, we would be able to predict the individual's probable purchase behavior.

A simplified decision matrix whereby we can look at many of the factors influencing Joe Shields's decision to buy a new car and determine his probable course of action is shown in Ad Lab 5-D. Before testing your understanding of Joe's purchase behavior, though, reread the introduction to this chapter about Joe's personality and environment. Then see if you can figure out what car Joe would buy.

From the marketer's point of view, the more that is known about both the internal and external forces that influence Joe, the easier it is to create advertisements that will communicate with him and influence his purchasing decisions.

MARKET SEGMENTATION

As we mentioned in Chapter 4, *market segmentation* is a strategic process of aggregating subgroups within a total market to (1) locate and define target market segments, (2) identify the needs of those target markets, (3) design products to fill those needs, and (4) promote the products specifically to those target markets. One of the major responsibilities of the marketing manager, therefore, is to determine what segments within the total market offer the greatest potential for profit after considering the

AD LAB 5-C   How Understanding Consumer Behavior Helps Create Effective Advertising

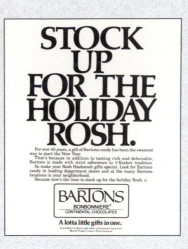

Laboratory Application

Study the advertisements pictured here. What principles of consumer behavior does each exemplify? Discuss each ad from the viewpoint of individual influences on consumer behavior—namely, needs and motives, individual perception, or learning and habit development. Then discuss them from the viewpoint of environmental influences—namely, family, society, and culture.

company's capabilities and objectives. The second major assignment is to find more effective means of communicating with each segment. An understanding of consumer behavior will assist in both tasks.

Segmenting Consumer Markets

When he plunked down $6,000 of his own money to start his first store 25 years ago, Leon Levine wanted to keep it small and simple—just like the ma-and-pa clothing store his mother managed in rural North Carolina. He came from hard-working, salt-of-the-earth stock, and those were the kind of people he knew best how to serve. He knew the value of a buck, and so did they. So he didn't have any "high-fallutin'" ideas about trying to be something he wasn't. He wanted his Family Dollar stores to offer traditional American values to traditional American consumers—mostly blue-collar, hard-working folks in the Southeast who earned considerably less than the national median.

To make a long story short, Leon Levine understood market segmentation intrinsically—and his success proved it. To this day, none of his stores is larger than 8,000 square feet; they are mostly located in small, rural

AD LAB 5-D   The Decision Matrix: Can You Predict Consumer Behavior?

Do you know Joe Shields well enough to predict what kind of car he would be inclined to buy?

Theoretically, if we knew consumers well enough, we could construct a model to help us determine what products they would be likely to purchase based on their personalities and the various forces that influence their decisions. For example, if we were to weigh each of those influences on Joe on a scale of 1 to 10, we could get a picture of how Joe might behave (1 = weakest influence; 10 = greatest influence).

	Decision forces	Considerations	Family sedan	Economy car	Sports car	Van or pick-up
Internal	**Needs or motives**	Maslow's hierarchy of needs: physiological; safety; social; esteem, self-fulfillment.				
	Perceptions	The way external stimuli are sensed when modified by needs, personality, experience, attitudes.				
	Learning and habits	How and what we learn in school and in life; experiences; habits in our lives.				
External	**Family**	Attitudes toward right and wrong, morality, ethics, religion; sex roles; politics; food.				
	Social	Social class and class mobility; importance of reference groups: family, neighbors, peers.				
	Cultural	Customs, tradition, attitudes; subcultural influences based on race, religion, and ethnicity.				
		Totals				

Laboratory Applications

1. What needs and wants does Joe have that would most influence his purchase of a vehicle: economy, status, transportation, sex appeal, self-esteem, other? How strong would each of these needs be in the consideration of different types of vehicles?
2. On the chart, assign a weight—on a scale of 1 to 10—to each of the decision forces Joe is subject to in the consideration of different vehicles (e.g., family influence might be strong for an economy car but very weak for a sports car; peer group influence might be exactly the opposite). Now total each column. Which car has the highest total? Is this result in line with the Joe Shields you know? Why?

communities; and they carry only about 5,000 items. Most of the merchandise is priced under $17, and the average sale is only about $6. He kept it simple, but it didn't stay small. Now he has over 1,000 stores; his company sells more than $375 million worth of merchandise a year; and Leon Levine himself is worth about $140 million.[23]

Levine obviously knew how to identify his market segment and how to cater to it. That's a major task in marketing today. Inasmuch as markets are heterogeneous and made up of many segments, a company may differentiate products and marketing for every segment, or it may concentrate its marketing activities on only one or a few segments.[24] Marketers use a variety of methods or variables to segment markets and identify behavioral groups. These variables generally fall into four categories: geographic, demographic, behavioristic, and psychographic (see Figure 5–12).

Geographic Segmentation

One of the simplest methods of segmenting markets is to classify them by their geographic location. People who live in one region of the country frequently have purchasing habits that differ from those in other regions. People in the Sunbelt states, for example, purchase more suntan lotion than people in the North or Midwest. On the other hand, those in the North purchase heavy winter clothing as well as special equipment for dealing with rain, snow, ice, sleet, and subzero temperatures.

When marketers analyze geographic data, they study sales by region, county size, city size, specific locations, and types of stores. Many products sell well in urban areas but poorly in suburban or rural areas. On the other hand, the market for a swimming pool contractor is very small in center-city areas but considerably larger in suburban areas.

Even in local markets, geographic segmentation is important. A retailer may attract people from only one part of town to his west-side store and therefore carry goods of special interest to people in that neighborhood. Or a local politician might send a mailer only to those precincts known to be supportive.

Demographic Segmentation

Demographics is the study of the numerical characteristics of the population. People can be grouped by sex, age, race, religion, education, occupation, income, and other quantifiable factors. For example, companies that sell products to middle-aged people may find it useful to know the size of that market segment along with where they live and how much they earn. Similarly, a company planning to distribute a new Mexican food product might consider an area's Latino population as a good primary target market and want to measure that group's size as well as distribution of income and age. How would you describe the demographic characteristics of the customers for Levine's Family Dollar stores?

As consumers grow older, their behavior changes, as expressed by their demand for goods and services. The kinds of products they buy, therefore, depend on what stage they are in in the human life cycle. Marketers have tried to chart this life cycle and have drawn some conclusions about product appeals for each stage. The chart in Figure 5–13 demonstrates that as people grow older and their responsibilities and incomes change, so do their interests in various product categories.

FIGURE   5–12   Methods used to segment consumer markets

Variables	Typical breakdowns	Variables	Typical breakdowns
Geographic			
Region	Pacific, Mountain, West North Central, West South Central, East North Central, East South Central, South Atlantic, Middle Atlantic, New England	City or SMSA size	Under 5,000, 5,000–19,999, 20,000–49,999, 50,000–99,999, 100,000–249,999, 250,000–499,999, 500,000–999,999, 1,000,000–3,999,999, 4,000,000 or over
County size	A, B, C, D		
Climate	Northern, southern	Density	Urban, suburban, rural
Demographic			
Age	Under 6, 6–11, 12–19, 20–34, 35–49, 50–64, 65+	Occupation	Professional and technical; managers, officials, and proprietors; clerical, sales; craftsmen, foremen; operatives; farmers; retired; students; homemakers; unemployed
Sex	Male, female		
Family size	1–2, 3–4, 5+		
Family life cycle	Young, single; young, married, no children; young, married, youngest child under six; young, married, youngest child six or over; older, married, with children; older, married, no children under 18; older, single; other	Education	Grade school or less; some high school; graduated high school; some college; graduated college
		Religion	Catholic, Protestant, Jewish, other
		Race	White, black, oriental
Income	Under $3,000, $3,000–$5,000, $5,000–$7,000, $7,000–$10,000, $10,000–$15,000, $15,000–$25,000, $25,000 and over	Nationality	American, British, French, German, Scandinavian, Italian, Latin American, Middle Eastern, Japanese
Behavioristic			
Purchase occasion	Regular occasion; special occasion	Loyalty status	None, medium, strong, absolute
Benefits sought	Economy, convenience, prestige	Readiness stage	Unaware, aware, informed, interested, desirous, intending to buy
User status	Nonuser, ex-user, potential user, first-time user, regular user		
Usage rate	Light user, medium user, heavy user	Marketing-factor sensitivity	Quality, price, service, advertising, sales promotion
Psychographic			
Social class	Lower lowers, upper lowers, lower middles, upper middles, lower uppers, upper uppers	Lifestyle	Straights, swingers, longhairs
		Personality	Compulsive, gregarious, authoritarian, ambitious

FIGURE 5–13		Heavy usage patterns of various age groups
Age	**Name of age group**	**Merchandise purchased**
0–5	Young children	Baby food, toys, nursery furniture, children's wear
6–19	Schoolchildren and teenagers	Clothing, sporting goods, records and tapes, school supplies, fast food, soft drinks, candy, cosmetics, movies
20–34	Young adults	Cars, furniture, housing, food and beer, clothing, diamonds, home entertainment equipment, recreational equipment, purchases for younger age segments
35–49	Younger middle-aged	Larger homes, better cars, second cars, new furniture, computers, recreational equipment, jewelry, clothing, food and wine
50–64	Older middle-aged	Recreational items, purchases for young marrieds and infants, travel
65 and over	Senior adults	Medical services, travel, pharmaceuticals, purchases for younger age groups

The study of demographics gives us useful statistical information about markets, but it fails to provide us with much information about the psychological makeup of the people who constitute markets. Not all people in one sex, one age group, or one income group have the same wants, attitudes, or beliefs. In fact, people in the same demographic segment may have widely differing product preferences.

Behavioristic Segmentation

Many marketers believe that the best starting point for determining market segments is to cluster consumers into patronage-related groups based on their attitude toward, use of, or response to actual products or product attributes. This is generally called *behavioristic segmentation*. Behavioristic segments are determined by any of a large number of variables that may be categorized as purchase occasion, benefits sought, user status, or usage rate.

Transportation for people who are already there.

FIGURE   5–14

The strategy here relates to the old question of what to give the person who has everything. On the surface the appeal seems to be fun, pure and simple. But it could be argued that the whole point of the headline is to make Riva the ultimate status symbol.

Purchase-Occasion Variables Buyers might be distinguished by *when* they buy or use a product or service. Air travelers, for example, might fly for business or for vacation. Thus, one airline ad might promote business travel while another promotes tourism. The purchase occasion might be affected by seasonality (water skis, snow skis, Christmas trees), by frequency of need (regular or occasional), or by some fad-and-fade cycle (candy, computer games). When some commonality in the purchase occasion can be discovered by the marketer, then there is a potential for creating a target segment. One consulting organization, Advertiming, was recently formed to recommend media scheduling based on a sophisticated system of correlating consumer purchase patterns with weather forecasts.[25]

Benefits-Sought Variables By determining the major benefits consumers seek in a product (high quality, low price, status, speed, sex appeal, good taste, and so forth), marketers may design products and advertising especially around those particular benefits. Gillette aims at one narrow segment of the hair-care market with its For Oily Hair Only product by offering a major benefit. Other hair-care companies may market "only natural ingredients" or "buy shampoo—get conditioner free" offers.[26] *Benefit segmentation,* as this is often called, is the objective of many consumer attitude studies today and is probably the foundation block for most successful advertising campaigns (see Figure 5–14).

User-Status Variables Many markets can be segmented by the types of users of the product—nonusers, ex-users, potential users, new users, and regular users. By targeting one or another of these groups, marketers might develop new products for nonusers or new uses for old products.

Usage-Rate Variables Also called *volume segmentation,* usage rates define consumers as light, medium, or heavy users of products. Marketers realize that it is usually easier to get a heavy user to increase usage than to get a light user to do the same.[27] In many product categories, 20 percent of the people consume 80 percent of the product. Marketers are usually interested in defining that 20 percent as closely as possible. For example, 67 percent of the population doesn't even drink beer. On the other hand, 17 percent drinks 88 percent of all the beer sold. Logically, a beer company would rather attract one heavy user to its brand than one light user (see Figure 5–15).

Marketers try to find common characteristics among heavy users of their products. In this way, product differences may be more easily defined and advertising strategies more simply drawn. For example, the traditional heavy beer drinkers have been primarily working-class men between the ages of 25 and 50 who watch more than three and one-half hours of television a day and prefer to watch sports programs. What implications can a beer advertiser draw from that in determining an advertising campaign?

Marketers of one product sometimes find that their customers are heavy users of other products, too. Therefore, they can define their target markets in terms of the usage rates of those other products. Bowling alleys, for example, can target their markets to heavy beer drinkers and their families. In one classic study, women who were heavy users of eye makeup were also found to be heavy users of face makeup, lipstick, hair spray, perfume, cigarettes, and gasoline.[28]

By discovering as many of the descriptive qualities of their markets as

FIGURE   5–15

Usage rates vary in many product categories. For example, of all households, 67 percent buy no dog food (nonusers), 16 percent buy 13 percent of the product (light users), and 17 percent buy 87 percent of the product (heavy users).

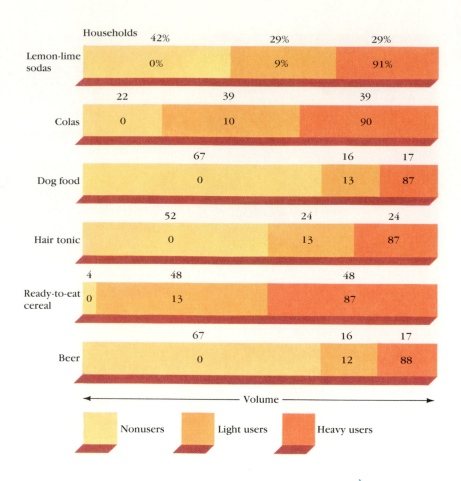

possible, marketers hope to end up with rich profiles that enable them to target all their marketing activities efficiently. Figure 5–16 presents an example of how users of different toothpaste brands were segmented by benefits sought, demographics, behavioristics, and psychographics. Try making a similar chart for the four vehicles that Joe Shields was considering in Ad Lab 5-D.

Psychographic Segmentation

Psychographics refers to the grouping of people into homogeneous segments on the basis of psychological makeup—namely, personality and lifestyle. Psychographics goes beyond standard demographics and behavioristics to indicate customers' dreams, hopes, fears and beliefs.[29] It classifies people according to their attitudes toward life (workers, achievers, traditionalists) and their purchasing habits (What newspapers do they read? Which magazines? Which brand of cigarettes do they buy? Which TV programs do they watch? What records do they buy?).

For years, marketers have attempted to categorize consumers by personality and lifestyle types in the hope of finding a common basis for making product appeals. Monitor, a service developed by Yankelovich, Skelly and White, was the first major syndicated study of changing U.S. values. Another classification system is VALS (Values and Lifestyles) which was originated by Arnold Mitchell at SRI International and was quickly adopted by marketers across the country.[30]

FIGURE 5–16   Segmenting the U.S. toothpaste market

Benefit segments	Demographics	Behavioristics	Psychographics	Favored brands
Economy (low price)	Men	Heavy users	High autonomy, value-oriented	Brands on sale
Medicinal (decay prevention)	Large families	Heavy users	Hypochondriac, conservative	Crest
Cosmetic (bright teeth)	Teens, young adults	Smokers	High sociability, active	Macleans, Ultra Brite
Taste (good tasting)	Children	Spearmint lovers	High self-involvement, hedonistic	Colgate, Aim

Values and Lifestyles (VALS™) VALS uses a hierarchical structure of four major lifestyle and personality divisions: need-driven, outer-directed, inner-directed, and integrated (see Figure 5–17). Each of these has various subgroups:

1. Need-driven—Composed of (a) Survivors and (b) Sustainers. These occasionally employed individuals include mostly the poor and the alienated and are not likely to be big spenders. They mainly need funds to support their day-to-day living.
2. Outer-directed—Includes traditional-minded individuals who are (a) Belongers: conservative and conforming members of the lower and middle classes, often blue-collar, often retired; (b) Emulators: intensely striving people who are often young and ambitious, have average educations and fairly good incomes, and are likely to be in debt; and (c) Achievers: leaders in business, professions, and government.
3. Inner-directed—Those individuals who tend to lead contemporary, innovative lifestyles and are categorized as (a) "I-Am-Me": young and individualistic people in transition, impulsive, often experimental; (b) Experientials: those who are active, artistic, well educated with good incomes, involved with experiencing life; and (c) Societally Conscious: those who are well educated with good incomes and are concerned with issues, trends, events, and personal growth; often professional people who prefer simple living.
4. Integrated—Those psychologically stable, self-actualized individuals who are middle aged, well educated, and financially comfortable; have a good sense of proportion; and probably give the most to charities.[31]

Which VALS group do you believe Levine's customers would fall into? Why? What does that indicate about the kind of advertising that should be directed to them or the type of media that would be best to reach them? Those are the kinds of questions marketers deal with daily.

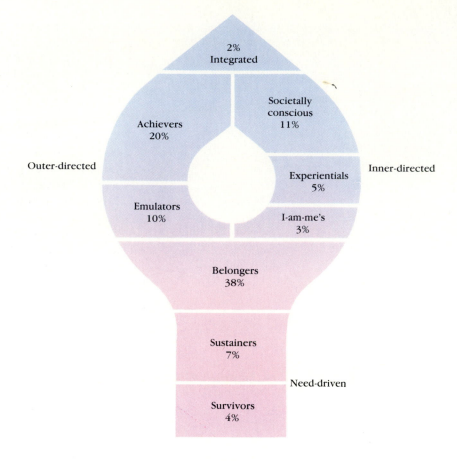

Arbitron, the company that measures radio station audiences for advertisers, has found that radio is an excellent device to reach the VALS lifestyle segments and demographic groups. Radio stations divide the population neatly by age and sex. For example, teens and women under 30, who often fall into the VALS Emulator category, typically listen to the "Contemporary Hits" station, while older, traditional, blue-collar people in the Belonger category often choose the "Country Music" station. Most radio markets have no more than 12 unique radio formats, so SRI's nine Values and Lifestyles typologies can fit radio listenership reasonably well.[32]

What other media do you think offer characteristics suitable for segmenting VALS groups? Magazines? Newspapers? Television? Why?

Numerous advertising agencies have jumped on the VALS bandwagon. Young & Rubicam, for example, has used VALS for a variety of its clients, including Mercury Capri, Dr Pepper, Kodak Instant Cameras, and Merrill Lynch. Most strong advertising campaigns today do not rest on facts alone but, rather, build on emotional appeals. By using VALS to understand their customers, advertisers can try to establish that emotional bond between the product and the consumer.[33]

For instance, Experientials make up the bulk of the market for health foods and self-improvement programs. They are targeted, with highly sensual ads, by a variety of manufacturers of exercise machines.[34]

Quasar has used a high-tech approach to sell its televisions to Achievers in its two-page, full-color magazine ads. Achievers are technology fans. They've earned such toys. They can afford them. So they buy them.[35]

Timex introduced a new brand of home health-care products under the Healthcheck name and targeted the Achiever and Societally Conscious categories. To do so, they used unique packaging with an abundance of reading material and showed models who were natural looking but also "statusy" enough for these well-educated, high-end segments.[36]

Limitations of VALS Advocates of VALS claim its greatest value is in developing creative strategies for advertising messages that directly address the factors that motivate consumers. However, the markets for many nationally advertised products comprise a cross section of the U.S. public far broader than one or two VALS segments. In these cases, VALS may offer little real value at all in developing persuasive sales messages.[37]

VALS and similar methods of classification are often criticized as oversimplifications of consumer personalities and purchase behavior. The many types of human personalities are influenced by a wide variety of factors (including cultural, social, or ethnic background), and describing them all within only nine categories seems simplistic at best, not to mention highly subjective.[38] While the VALS methodology defines personality on certain premises, there are also many other premises for defining personality.

Research into personality and lifestyles is also hampered by cost. It is very expensive, and that limits both the number of marketers who can use it and the number of times the research can be repeated for the same product.

Finally, the VALS research is difficult to administer, requiring highly trained field workers. This means it may be subject to bias inasmuch as responses from interviews may be reported out of context.[39] This has led consumer behaviorists to seek other segmenting systems and methods besides VALS.

Notwithstanding these problems, when marketers understand the attitudes, lifestyles, and personalities of the people who buy their products or services, the implications are considerable. Companies can better select potential target markets and match the attributes and the image of their products with the types of consumers using the products. This aids in the definition of specific advertising objectives, development of media plans, and the efficient budgeting of the marketer's dollars.[40] These potential benefits suggest that VALS and other psychographic segmentation systems will no doubt continue to flourish until something considerably better comes along.

Segmenting Business Markets

Business, or industrial, markets are composed of manufacturers, utilities, government agencies, contractors, wholesalers, retailers, banks, insurance companies, and institutions that buy goods and services to help them in their own business. These may be raw materials or parts that go into the product, or they might be desks, office equipment, vehicles, or a variety of business services used in conducting the business. The products sold to business markets are often intended for resale to the public, as in the case of retail goods.

In all these situations, identifying prospective business customer segments is just as important as identifying consumer market segments. In most cases, we can use many of the same variables that we discussed for

FIGURE   5–18

Illustrative breakdown of SIC codes for selected businesses (product categories) in the apparel industry.

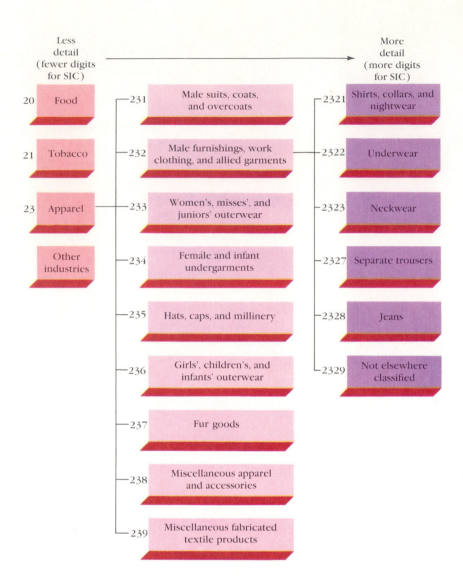

consumer markets. Most organizations may be segmented by geographic location and by several behavioristic variables, such as benefits sought, user status, usage rate, and purchase occasion. Business markets have several distinctive characteristics, however. They may be classified by SIC code; they may be concentrated geographically; they have a relatively small number of buyers; and they normally use a systematic procedure for making purchases.[41] These are important implications for those companies seeking ways to segment industrial markets.

Standard Industrial Classification

The U.S. Department of Commerce classifies all businesses—and collects and publishes data on them—by *Standard Industrial Classification (SIC) codes*. These codes are based on broad industry categories that are subdivided into major divisions, subgroups, and then detailed classifications of firms in similar lines of business. (See Figure 5–18.) In its reports, the federal government gives the number of establishments, sales volumes, and number of employees, broken down by geographic areas, for each SIC code. Many companies can relate their sales to their industrial customers' lines of business. These codes are a great help in segmenting those markets and performing research.

Market Concentration

The market for industrial goods is heavily concentrated in the Midwest, the mid-Atlantic states, and California. The stylized map in Figure 5–19 shows that for manufactured goods, more than 50 percent of U.S. industry is located east of the Mississippi and north of the Mason-Dixon line. This fact greatly reduces the number of geographic targets for the industrial marketing efforts of many companies.

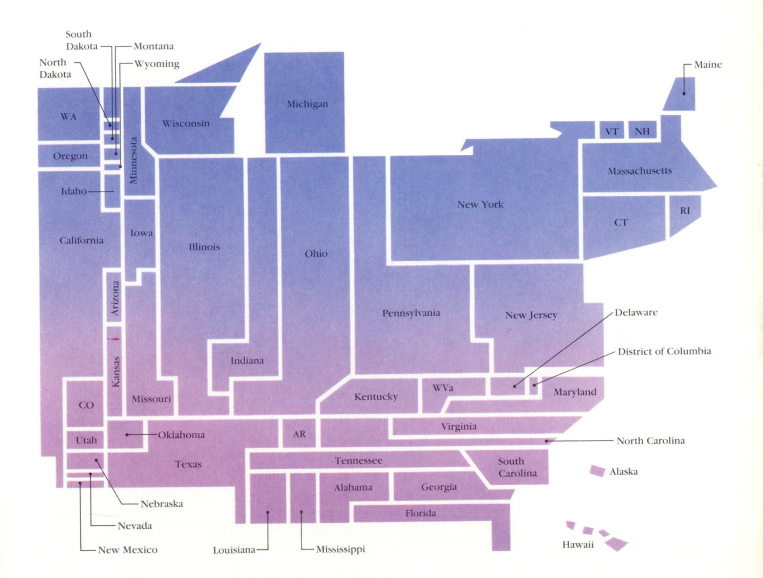

FIGURE   5–19

The United States in proportion to the value of manufactured products.

Moreover, industrial marketers deal with a very limited number of buyers. Less than 4 percent of all the companies in the United States account for nearly 60 percent of the production employees and over two-thirds of all the manufacturing dollars.[42] Thus, customer size is a critical basis for market segmentation. Companies may decide to concentrate all their marketing efforts on a few large customers or to target their products to the more numerous smaller customers. Steelcase, for example, manufactures office furniture and divides its marketing efforts between major accounts, on which its sales force calls directly, and dealer accounts, which resell their products to many small purchasers.

Business marketers can further break their markets down into who the end users are. For example, since computers are now used in virtually every kind of business, a firm that develops a new computer-related product may decide to design it for use in just one particular industry, such as banking.

Business Purchasing Procedures

The process businesses use to evaluate new products and make purchases is frequently far more complex and rigid than the consumer purchase process described at the beginning of this chapter. Marketers must design their communications programs with this in mind.

Large firms invariably have a purchasing department that acts as a professional buyer. Its job is to evaluate the need for products, analyze proposed purchases, seek approvals from those who will use the product and authorizations from managers who will pay for the product, make requisitions, place purchase orders, and generally supervise all the product purchasing in the firm. The purchase decision, therefore, may take weeks, months, or even years before a sale is finally consummated. This is especially true in government agencies. Frequently, purchase decisions also depend on factors besides product quality—delivery time, terms of sale, service requirements, certainty of continuing supply, and others.[43]

When analyzing market segments, many marketers consider the purchase decision process of various segments before determining the appropriate target market. Many new companies, for instance, target other small companies where the purchase decision can be made quickly and use commission-only representatives to call on larger firms that require more time to consummate the sale.

In general, the analysis of industrial markets and industrial buying behavior is as great a challenge as the analysis of consumer buying behavior and consumer market segments. Both are critical, though, to the formulation of effective marketing and advertising plans. To assist this task, marketers use marketing and advertising research—the subject of the next chapter.

Summary

In the effort to match people and organizations with products and services, marketers are keenly interested in the buying behavior of both consumers and industrial purchasers. The objectives of consumer advertising are to motivate, modify, or reinforce consumer attitudes, perceptions, beliefs, and behavior. This requires the effective blending of the behavioral sciences (anthropology, sociology, psychology) with the communicating arts (writing, drama, graphics, photography). Marketing and advertising people constantly monitor consumer attitudes, beliefs, likes and dislikes, habits, wants, and desires. The behavioral characteristics of large groups of people give the directional force to any advertising aimed at those groups. Thus, advertising uses trends in mass-consumer behavior to create fashion or habit in specific consumer behavior.

To be successful, advertising people must understand the complexity of human behavior and the variety of influences on behavior. As marketers become aware of group behavioral characteristics, they can use those characteristics to define new markets and develop advertising campaigns for those markets. Consumer behavior is affected by both internal, personal influences and external, environmental influences. Personal influences include the consumer's personal needs and motives, the consumer's perception of the world, the way the consumer learns, and habits the consumer has developed. External environmental influences include the consumer's family, social structure, and culture. The way these influencing factors are integrated within the consumer determines how that consumer behaves.

The interest in consumer behavior today stems from the desire of marketers to find more effective means of communicating with their customers and to use common purchase behavior patterns as the basis for market segmentation. Market segmentation is the process of aggregating subgroups within the company's total market to (1) locate target markets, (2) identify the needs of those target markets, (3) design products to fill those needs, and (4) promote products specifically to those target markets. Marketers use a variety of methods to segment markets and identify behavioral groups. The most common bases for segmenting markets are (1) geographic, (2) demographic, (3) behavioristic, and (4) psychographic.

Business markets are often segmented in the same way as consumer markets: by geographic location and by several behavioristic variables. In addition, they may be grouped by SIC code, by market concentration, or by business purchasing procedures.

Questions for Review and Discussion

1. Why is consumer behavior called the directional force in advertising?
2. Is advertising causative or reflective of mass-consumer trends?
3. How do personal influences affect your behavior as a consumer?
4. What is the significance of Maslow's theory of human behavior to advertisers?
5. What examples can you give to demonstrate that "the perception is the reality"?
6. What is the importance of the theory of cognitive dissonance to advertising?
7. How do environmental influences affect your family's consumer behavior?
8. What is the importance of market segmentation to advertisers?
9. How could you use VALS to develop the marketing strategy for a product of your choice?
10. How is the segmentation of business markets different from that of consumer markets?

6

MARKETING AND ADVERTISING RESEARCH: INPUTS TO THE PLANNING PROCESS

Now it was up to Agi—and to the several creative teams working under her. The agency that came up with the best campaign would win the account and the lucrative commissions that go along with placing millions of dollars worth of advertising.

In the advertising business, it was what they call a plum account—big and juicy—the kind every agency wants to get a crack at. In fact, just about every big agency in New York had tried to take a crack at it; but now the choice had been narrowed down to four finalists. Ayer was one of them— N. W. Ayer—the oldest agency in the United States. To win this $50 million plum, Agi (pronounced Ah-szhee) Clark and her people were going to have to win the client's confidence in Ayer and demonstrate that that confidence would not be misplaced. Their assignment was not a simple one— to come up with a new image for J. C. Penney that would be both honest and credible and would revolutionize the $200 billion-a-year department store industry.

The nation's third largest retailer, J. C. Penney had been struggling with image problems for a number of years. For decades, it had been a mass merchandiser of a wide range of household commodities. But in recent years, it seemed to have changed. So what was it now—in the eye of the consumer? Was it a nationwide discount retailer? Or was it a department store for fashionable apparel? Penney's customers said it wasn't the latter. But then they really couldn't say *what* it was, either. Agi Clark's creative assignment was to find a way to change that—to communicate that J. C. Penney was indeed changing, that now it really did offer quality, fashion, and style but at the same time the company had not forgotten its traditional promise of high value, fair prices, and honest dealing with customers (see Figure 6–1).

Clark's colleagues at Ayer provided her with reams of research information about retail industry trends and Penney's position in the market. The agency's research and account teams analyzed sales data, tested consumer attitudes, and studied Penney's strengths and liabilities—all in an effort to find the most effective way to change Penney's image and boost its sales. They knew that to get customers to consider Penney's for their fashion purchases, they had to convince them that Penney's had changed. Somehow they had to connect Penney's to the modern, active lifestyle of upscale American consumers: tie it to the way they work, the way they relax, the way they play; make "human contact" (Ayer's slogan and advertising philosophy).

It wasn't the first time Clark had played the high-stakes game. As a senior vice president and executive creative director, she had already directed campaigns for several of Ayer's well-known clients like DeBeers ("A diamond is forever"), AT&T ("Reach out and touch someone"), and others. While her years on the DeBeers account had given her invaluable experience working with outstanding photographers, directors, and hair and makeup people, she had never really worked on an honest-to-goodness fashion account. She hoped that very fact, along with her knowledge of the American consumer, would enable her to bring a fresh approach to this campaign.

In countless meetings with her teams of art directors and copywriters, the concepts began to evolve. As Penney's had changed, its advertising had to change, too. That meant a whole new look and feel. They came up with a design concept that was at once modern, fashionable, forward-looking, and simple. It could be used in magazine ads and newspaper ads and even on TV. OK. But what about the copy concept? What approach could they take that would be credible to the one-third of the women who make two-thirds of the fashion purchases?

The ideas and proposed layouts started to pile up. They could tie Penney's to all the new brand names they were carrying. They could tell customers that Penney's had "changed its looks but not its values." They could compare J. C. Penney with other well-known department stores. Agi consulted with Chuck Meding, Ayer's senior VP and the management supervisor who headed the Penney's account team. Finally, they settled on four basic concepts.

"All right," Agi said, "let's send these over to Research for testing." But instinctively she thought she knew which concept would test best—the one that played off of Penney's long history of responding to customers' needs. Tell them: "WE'VE CHANGED BECAUSE YOU'VE CHANGED."

THE NEED FOR RESEARCH IN MARKETING AND ADVERTISING

As we discussed in Chapter 5, advertising people are keenly interested in "what makes people tick." When companies like J. C. Penney plan to spend $30 or $40 or $50 million on advertising, they don't want to risk losing it on ads or commercials that you won't notice or respond to. They also don't want to waste time and money placing their messages on TV shows you don't watch or in magazines you don't read or on billboards if you don't drive a car.

Advertising is expensive. A single commercial on prime-time network TV might cost $100,000—or even a lot more. A single color-page ad in a national magazine might cost over $75,000. That is too much money to risk if people are not going to see the ad, don't pay attention to it, don't like it, don't believe it, or forget it two minutes after it's gone. That's why advertising decision makers need research. Without it, they use intuition or guesswork. In our fast-changing, competitive economy, this invites failure.[1]

Armed with the new concept from Ayer, a $22 million fall budget, and its own marketing and merchandising know-how, J. C. Penney launched an audacious assault on the department store industry in late 1984. The goal, stated simply, was to change the shopping habits of America.

FIGURE   6-1

J. C. Penney saw its challenge as a positioning problem—to position itself as a "regional comparison retailer in competition with department and specialty stores similarly oriented." It wanted to be perceived by consumers as having appealing selections and a variety of styles, colors, and brands of good quality, fashionable merchandise with recognizable value. Most of all, it wanted consumers to have an enjoyable experience—so that they would feel good shopping at Penney's.

Big bucks were at stake. Americans like clothes and fashionable merchandise. In fact, we spend more in department stores than many countries spend on food or national defense. And annually, for every man, woman, and child in this country, we consume an average of $1,000 worth of the type of merchandise sold in department stores. An increase of just 1 percent in share of this total market, therefore, means an added $2 billion in sales. A decrease of just 1 percent means a similar loss. These are high stakes; and the higher the stakes, the greater the marketer's need to know.

Marketing Research

Unfortunately, managers seldom have *all* the information they need to make the best decisions. That's where research comes in. The term *marketing research* refers to the systematic gathering, recording, and analyzing of information to help managers make marketing decisions.[2] For firms that operate under the marketing concept (discussed in Chapter 4), marketing research plays a key role in identifying consumer needs, developing new products and marketing strategies, and assessing the effectiveness of marketing programs and promotional activities.

As Kenneth Longman pointed out almost two decades ago:

To be of benefit to us, research must be designed to maximize the probability of uncovering the facts about the marketplace that will affect our judgment about what to do. We will want to know whether people are aware of the existence of our brand or, in some cases, aware of the product class in which we compete. We would like to know whether those who are aware of our brand have a favorable opinion of it and whether they think as favorably of our competitors. We will want to know how often our brand and competing brands are used and whether they are used regularly or erratically. We will want to know what kinds of people use our brand and what kinds of people use competing brands. We will want to know how different kinds of people characterize our brand and competing brands. And we will want to know which consumers buy the product in which channels of distribution, what different uses are made of the product, and on what different occasions the product is used.[3]

How important this information is depends on the amount of risk involved in the decisions to be made. In Chapter 1, we mentioned the colossal failure of the Edsel automobile. The mistake of ignoring research findings cost Ford Motor Company $350 million and earned them the dubious award for the greatest marketing failure in history.[4]

Naturally, major marketers like J. C. Penney have no desire to take the record away from Ford. So over the years, as the stakes in business have gotten larger, so has the dependence on sophisticated information. Today, over $4 billion per year is spent on marketing, advertising, and public opinion research. The 15 largest research organizations, led by the A. C. Nielsen Co.—now owned by Dun & Bradstreet Corp.—account for close to 50 percent of this amount.[5]

Actually, marketing research is useful in all stages of the management process. For instance, marketing research is used just as much in fields like financial planning and economic forecasting as in traditional marketing areas like advertising.

Advertising Research

Many of the decisions advertising people make cannot be made from intuition or knowledge of the product. Agi Clark would have had no guarantee—without research data—of what attitudes consumers had toward J. C. Penney or the other department stores. Before she could develop a campaign, Clark needed to know how consumers perceived Penney's, its strong points or liabilities, how that compared with competitive stores, and what image would be most credible.

For that information, she needed advertising research. *Advertising research* is the systematic gathering and analysis of information that is specifically intended to facilitate the development or evaluation of advertising strategies, advertisements and commercials, and media campaigns. It is, in effect, a subset of marketing research, as is *market research,* which is simply information gathering about the particular market. (See Ad Lab 6-A.)

AD LAB 6-A   Market Research versus Marketing Research: Xerox Knew the Difference

The difference between market research and marketing research is more than a semantic one. They can be distinguished on at least two substantive grounds. In the first place, they differ in scope. *Market research* is research about the market: its size, composition, structure, and so on. In contrast, *marketing research* is research about any problem in marketing: for example, pricing strategy, distribution, and advertising. Thus, the term *marketing research* is much broader in scope and is, therefore, preferable.

Another basis for distinction is that they differ in objective. Market research emphasizes measurement; it concentrates on *quantitative* dimensions. Marketing research, on the other hand, emphasizes creativity; it concentrates on *qualitative* aspects. It seeks to discover unsatisfied consumer needs and wants; it tries to ferret out unsolved problems in the marketplace, the so-called holes in the market that offer significant opportunities for innovation. The objective is to disrupt the parity between competitors in the marketplace—and to do this in the company's favor.

The resulting increase in market share flows to the innovator as a reward for detecting problems, frustrations, difficulties, or dissatisfactions and then for supplying solutions perceived by the market as providing true benefits. This is the heart of marketing research. It focuses on what could be rather than what is.

The dramatic and successful entry of Xerox into the copying market of the late 1950s is a classic example of the use of creative marketing research to discover and develop a huge, unexploited market opportunity. The two principal companies then in the market, Kodak (Verifax) and 3M (Thermofax), not only had inferior technology but required users to purchase their machines outright and to use only paper made exclusively by them. Defined this way, the market for copying machines (and copying) remained relatively small. If Xerox had used mere market research, it might have concluded, "The market is too small; why bother?"

However, its marketing research revealed the true potential for a company that could bring real innovation to the market, not only in technology (xerography) but in marketing strategy as well. It said, "We'll lend you our machine, and you can use any paper you wish!" The wedding of superior technology and superior marketing produced a striking synergistic effect; when copying was made easy, the market exploded! Xerox was not interested in what the market was but what it could be as a result of the constructive contribution Xerox could bring to it.

Laboratory Application

Explain how you could do market research for a fast-food chain in your area. Then explain how you could do marketing research.

Finally, to develop media strategies, choose media vehicles, and evaluate their results, advertisers use a subset of advertising research called *media research*. This particular type of research is usually performed by subscribing to any of a variety of well-known *syndicated research services* (e.g., A. C. Nielsen, Arbitron, Simmons, and Standard Rate and Data Service) that continuously monitor and publish information on the reach and effectiveness of the media vehicles available in every major geographic market in the United States.

In this chapter, our objective is to understand the basic procedures and techniques used in marketing and advertising research today, the importance of research to the development of marketing and advertising plans and strategies, and the various ways research can be used to test the effectiveness of ads and campaigns both before and after they have run.

BASIC STEPS IN THE RESEARCH PROCEDURE

The manager of marketing research and planning at J. C. Penney was Sid Stein. By 1980, he had been with the company for 15 years and, in that period, had seen significant management changes take place. But he was to play a key role in one of the largest repositioning efforts in corporate history. That was the year the chairman of the board, William Howell, selected a committee of four to assess Penney's competitive environment and to articulate a clear direction for the future of the company. Sid was named chairman of the committee, and over the next year, the research performed by his department would prove to be one of the most rewarding activities he had ever been involved in, for it was going to make a significant contribution to the positioning strategy they were charged with developing.

Problem Definition and Research Objectives

As Figure 6–2 shows, the first step in the marketing research process is to define the problem and set research objectives. This is often the most difficult and time-consuming task; but it's worthwhile if the objectives are well defined. Good research on the wrong problem is a total waste of effort. In Sid Stein's case, he was already well aware of the problem at J. C. Penney. His responsibility had been to conduct ongoing market research for the company and to develop a marketing information system. The company was not running blind, and he already had a good idea why Penney's position in the market seemed to be slipping.

During the 1960s and early 70s, Penney's merchandise mix had been very broad. Customers could expect to find everything they needed from automotive products to home furnishings and appliances. At Penney's, you could get paint, hardware, lawn and garden supplies, home entertainment products, and apparel. The strategy had been one-stop shopping, "from a spool of thread to a refrigerator." During this period, as regional shopping

FIGURE   6–2

Marketing research process.

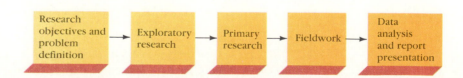

centers emerged and flourished, Penney's set its course and in time occupied more space in these regional malls than any other retailer in the country. The company experienced tremendous growth, and its sales doubled or tripled in most categories. But Penney's research also showed that, even though sales were increasing, it was steadily losing its share of the total market, particularly in the highly profitable women's apparel department.

Because of their own studies, Penney's researchers believed that the "contemporary" woman was shopping at Penney's for commodity merchandise but not spending many of her fashion apparel dollars there. Yet, that group—about one-third of the population—accounts for two-thirds of women's apparel sales. Moreover, they discovered a perceptual gap between J. C. Penney and the other department stores for fashionability and quality in women's apparel. It was becoming apparent that, in the process of trying to satisfy all consumers, Penney's had perhaps inadvertently neglected certain groups, especially the higher-spending segments. Since 1975, Penney's had tried to respond to these consumer attitudes by adopting a segmentation strategy and upgrading the merchandise, but they had not done so fast enough. The competition seemed to be moving faster in upgrading products and images, so the perceptual gap had remained unchanged.

As a result, Stein was confronted with several problem *symptoms*. His first objective therefore was to discover the *causes* of these symptoms so that the problem could be accurately defined and understood prior to designing any research studies.

At the beginning of any research project, a concise statement of the research problem and objectives should be written down. The statement should contain three basic elements:

1. The information to be gathered must be measurable.
2. It must be relevant to the problem.
3. The various pieces of information or knowledge to be gained must be related.[6]

In other words, before establishing research objectives, a company must decide what it is after, and then these objectives must be able to function side by side with the company's marketing and advertising plans.[7] For example, the statement of Penney's problem and research objectives might have been written as follows:

> J. C. Penney's sales, while still increasing, seem to have lost their momentum and are not producing the profit expected by our shareholders. In the last year, our share of the market has even slipped in several departments from X percent in the home furnishings department to Y percent in the ladies' apparel department. Is this slippage due to a decline in total sales in shopping malls? Is it due to increased competition from specialty stores, small boutiques, or mass merchandisers? Or are sales lost to another department store in the same mall? If sales are lost to other department stores, which ones and why?

This hypothetical statement of the problem is specific and measurable; the questions asked are relevant to the problem; and the information requested is directly related. Moreover, the answers to these questions would facilitate the development of practical marketing and advertising plans.

Exploratory Research

The second step in the research process is to investigate current knowledge through a number of information sources. The objective of exploratory research is simply to learn more about the market, the competition, and the business environment and to define the problem before undertaking any formal research.[8] This may consist of discussing the problem with informed sources inside the firm; with wholesalers, distributors, or retailers outside the firm; with customers; or even with competitors. These exploratory research interviews are not aimed at collecting a large number of respondents but, rather, at examining what is known by those few individuals who may have more information than the ordinary person.[9] Thus, the two main tasks of exploratory research are to analyze internal data and to examine external secondary data.[10]

Utilizing Internal Data

Company records are often a valuable source of information. Types of internal data useful to a marketing manager include product shipment figures, billings to customers, warranty card records, advertising expenditures, sales expenses, correspondence from customers, and records of meetings with sales staffs.

In the case of J. C. Penney, which has a well-developed marketing information system, an analysis of sales data, a review of past tracking studies, and an examination of previous marketing research data signaled the problem the company faced. In another situation, a marketing manager might discover from an analysis of marketing expense data that sales to certain customers or territories are unprofitable in relation to the cost incurred producing them.

Collecting Secondary Data

Information that has been previously collected or published, usually for some other purpose and by some other organization, is referred to as *secondary data.*[11] Much information is available—usually free—if the researcher just knows where to look for it. It might be government-issued materials, such as census data or publications from the Department of Commerce, published information from market research companies, trade associations, or various trade publications, or even computerized information databases. (See Ad Lab 6-B.)

Generally, collecting secondary data is less costly than collecting primary data and requires less time. However, there are problems with secondary data: (1) the information may be obsolete; (2) it may not be relevant to the problem at hand; (3) it may not be valid or reliable information, depending on the way it was collected; or (4) the very wealth of information available for review may be overpowering relative to the size of the problem being studied.[12]

Some of the most frequently used sources of secondary data are the following:

> Library reference materials (e.g., *Business Periodicals Index* for business magazines, *Reader's Guide to Periodical Literature* for consumer magazines, *Public Information Service Bulletin, The New York Times Index,* and the *World Almanac and Book of Facts*).

Government publications (e.g., the *Statistical Abstract of the United States*).

Trade association publications (e.g., annual fact books containing government data and information gathered by various industry groups listed in the *Directory of National Trade Associations*).

Research organizations publications (e.g., literature from university bureaus of business research, Nielsen retail store audits, MRCA consumer purchase diaries, and so forth, all available on a subscription basis).

Computer database services (e.g., Lockheed Corporation's DIALOG Information Service and Dow Jones News Retrieval Service, available by subscription to individuals and organizations that have access to a computer equipped with a modem).

When Sid Stein and his staff finished reviewing all the internal data and the outside secondary research on Penney's situation, they found that Penney's was *not* losing sales so much to the specialty shops and mass merchandisers as to other department stores. But the fact that Penney's itself had a long tradition of mass merchandising created confusion in the minds of its own management and, most important, in the minds of its customers. Penney's management personnel at the store, district, regional, and corporate levels were, themselves, not really clear about who the competition was. And consumers had difficulty describing just what kind of store J. C. Penney was.

This all meant one thing to Sid Stein and his committee. More than anything else, they had to chart an unequivocal course for the company and communicate it clearly. Everyone—their 170,000 employees, the

(continued on p. 188)

AD LAB 6-B   Using Marketing Research for New-Product Development

You are a marketing manager for a major manufacturer of prescription drug products, and management has indicated an interest in marketing a line of products to the proprietary market. After considerable brainstorming, you determine that your company has the research and development capability to produce a superior line of proprietary vitamin products that could be sold through your normal distribution channels.

The problem is to assess the opportunities to get into the over-the-counter vitamin business and to obtain volume share and profit levels consistent with corporate criteria.

The first step in obtaining the required information on the vitamin market is to consult available reference guides (see the chart on pages 186–187). These will lead you to most of the important sources specific to the normal market. Additional information can be obtained through direct contact with qualified persons at the sources. In most cases, they will lead you to less obvious data sources, which may turn up information of key significance to your overall findings. At this stage, you will also reach the "industry experts" who may confirm (or deny) your assessment of the opportunities to participate in the vitamin market. Having systematically gone through all these steps, your search is completed. With 50 pounds of data, however, your real job has just begun. *(continued)*

Laboratory Application

What are the implications of this kind of research for the advertising activities that the company might use for its new product line?

AD LAB 6-B   A guide to obtaining information on the vitamin market
(continued)

Topics	U.S. government	Trade and other organizations	Consumer/ business press	Publications
General reference guides	*U.S. Government Organizational Manual* *Federal Statistical Directory* Government reports and announcements	*Encyclopedia of Associations*	*Business Publications Rates & Data* *Consumer Magazine & Agri-Media Rates & Data*	*Business Periodicals Index* *Funk & Scott Index of Corporations & Industries* *Index Medicus* *Thomas Register of American Corporations* *Pharmaceutical News Index* *Reader's Guide to Periodical Literature*
Specific to the vitamin market Issues: Nature of the product Vitamins and how they are used New products and/or external issues influencing the market	National Technical Information Service (Department of Commerce) National Center for Health Statistics (HHS)	Vitamin Information Bureau American Dietetic Association National Science Foundation	*Consumer Reports* *Today's Health* *Drug Topics* *Prevention Magazine* *American Druggist* *Product Marketing*	*Journal of the AMA* *New England Journal of Medicine* *FDA Reports* (newsletter)
Role of government: Impact of existing and potential government rules and regulations	Food & Drug Administration (HHS) Reports of congressional committees	The Proprietary Association Pharmaceutical Manufacturing Association Consumer groups	Articles appearing in business and drug trade magazines and medical journals	*Pharmaceutical News Index* *FDA Reports*
Consumer behavior: Level of vitamin usage by consumers Consumers' perceptions and attitudes concerning vitamins	National Technical Information Service (Department of Commerce) National Center for Health Statistics (HHS)	Consumer groups	*Prevention Magazine* Readership studies of general consumer and trade magazines	*Findex-Directory of Market Research Reports, Studies & Surveys*

Topics	U.S. government	Trade and other organizations	Consumer/ business press	Publications
Competition: Nature of the competition and extent of leverage in the market	Form 10-K's (SEC)		Articles appearing in business and drug trade magazines	*Moody's Industrial Manual* Standard & Poor's corporation records *Value Line Investment Survey* *Dun & Bradstreet Reports* National Investment Library annual report Disclosure, Inc. annual report *Thomas Register of American Corporations*
Market trends and developments: Size of the market and growth rate Major vitamin categories and relative growth Traditional distribution channels and the major retail outlets Seasonal patterns or regional skews	Census of Manufacturers (Department of Commerce) Survey of Manufacturers (Department of Commerce) Current industrial reports (Department of Commerce)	The Proprietary Association Pharmaceutical Manufacturers Association	*Product Marketing* *Drug Topics* *Supermarket Business* Articles appearing in business and drug trade magazines	Standard & Poor's *Industry Surveys* *Pharmaceutical News Index*
Advertising: Kinds and levels of advertising support Creative strategies employed by advertisers			*Advertising Age* *Marketing Communications*	*Leading National Advertisers* *Publishers Information Bureau*

thousands of suppliers and vendors, the financial community, and the public—had to understand just what J. C. Penney stood for. Now the questions became: Who are our customers? Who are department store customers? What do they like and dislike about us and about our competitors? How are we currently perceived? And what do we have to do to clarify and improve that perception?

Performing Primary Research

The answers to these questions would become the foundation for Penney's evolving positioning strategy. That, in turn, would determine the kind of stores and merchandise the company would have and the kind of advertising and promotion the company could use. In short, it would set the company's course for years to come. Stein decided to do more primary research to get the answers.

Basic Methodology of Quantitative Research

Once the researcher has concluded the exploratory research phase, he or she may discover a need to gain additional information about the issue in question directly from the marketplace. There are basically three research methods used in collecting these primary data: observation, experiment, and survey.

PEOPLE IN ADVERTISING

Ruth Ziff

Executive Vice President,
Research & Marketing Services
DDB Needham Worldwide

After more than 30 years with two of the country's leading advertising agencies, Ruth Ziff is one of the industry's leading active practitioners and an acknowledged expert in the field of marketing and advertising research.

Dr. Ziff began her career in advertising at Benton & Bowles in 1950 where she became vice president and manager of research. In 1975, she joined Doyle Dane Bernbach as senior vice president, director of research and marketing services. In 1979, she was elected to the board of directors of DDB/New York and, two years later, was promoted to executive vice president. In that position, she is responsible for specific client and agency projects as well as publications of corporate interest. As the spokesperson for the agency in matters dealing with research, she has written numerous articles and has been a major speaker at industry and professional conferences.

Prognosticating on the decade of the 1990s, Dr. Ziff says research indicates that the 1990s will be an especially challenging period for marketers because of declining population growth. She believes the singles movement is likely to ease off in the years ahead, and more marrying will create a

FIGURE 6-3

The Universal Product Code on product packages reduces human error at the check-out counter. But more important, it provides a wealth of instantaneous market research information that is valuable to retailers and manufacturers alike.

Observation The *observation method* is used when researchers actually monitor the overt actions of the person being studied. It may take the form of a traffic count by outdoor billboard companies, a television audience count by means of an instrument hooked to TV sets, or a personal study of the way consumers react to products displayed in the supermarket.

A fairly recent development that has greatly assisted the observational method is the use of product labels with the *Universal Product Code*. This consists of a series of linear bars and a 10-digit number that identifies the product and the price (see Figure 6–3). With the aid of optical scanners, supermarkets now observe electronically which products are selling. This label not only facilitates timely inventory control but also permits the evaluation of alternative marketing plans, media vehicles, and promotional campaigns.[13]

In fact, the use of the UPC may be dramatically changing our understanding of certain consumer packaged goods markets. Whereas marketers have tended to assume that changes in market share and brand position usually appear slowly over time, the new ability to observe the actual incidence of sales has shown that, at least at the local level where sales occur, the packaged goods market is extremely complex and volatile. Moreover, the effects of advertising are invariably entangled and at cross-purposes with the effects of other advertising, both competitive and non-competitive.[14] Thus, at the local level, weekly sales and share figures may fluctuate considerably, and gauging the short-term effectiveness of advertising may be uncertain at best.

miniboom for businesses that cater to the concepts of courting and marriage.

At the same time, she says the concept of formal marriage may become obsolete. A major hidden market will be the growing number of informal families—transitory, semi-permanent, and permanent.

Finally, she believes, the health and fitness movement's growth will taper off.

During this period, Dr. Ziff predicts that several consumer segments will assume tremendous importance. These include:

Career Women—with potentially explosive growth in numbers, influence, and buying power.

Young Dynamics—the under-40s who will be the free spenders, the achievers, the do-it-alls and have-it-alls of the population, the trendsetters in the next decade.

The Established—the over-40 counterparts of the Young Dynamics and also the largest and most affluent of the consumer markets.

All in all, says Dr. Ziff, we will be marketing to an increasingly individualistic consumer—someone less disposed to follow the crowd; someone looking to satisfy his or her own personal needs with products and services that cater to those distinctive requirements.

Research, during this decade, will benefit from the new scanner technologies that offer immediate hard data to measure marketing results. However, she cautions, the risk of this is that marketers may tend to favor short-term strategies and tactics over longer, more profitable approaches.

Dr. Ziff is a Phi Beta Kappa and a *cum laude* graduate of Hunter College. She received her master's degree from Columbia and her doctorate from City University of New York. She is the former president of the Market Research Council and the New York chapter of the American Marketing Association. She has received the AAF Advertising Woman of the Year Award, the AAF Silver Medal, and the YWCA TWIN Award, and she has been inducted into the Hunter College Hall of Fame.

Experiment The *experimental method* is designed to measure actual cause-and-effect relationships. An experiment is a scientific investigation in which a researcher alters the stimulus received by a test group or groups and compares the results with that of a control group that did not receive the altered stimulus. This type of research is used primarily for test marketing new products in isolated geographic areas and in testing new advertising campaigns prior to national introduction. For example, a new campaign might be run in one geographic area but not in another. The sales results in the two areas are then compared to determine the effectiveness of the campaign. However, so that the variable that causes the effect can be accurately determined, strict controls must be used. And since it is so difficult to control all the marketing variables, this method is very expensive and not easy to use.

Survey This is the most common way to gather primary research data. By asking questions of current or prospective customers, the researcher hopes to obtain information on attitudes, opinions, or motivations. The political poll is one of the most common surveys with which we are all familiar. The three common ways of conducting surveys are by telephone, by mail, and by personal interview, and each of these has distinct advantages and disadvantages (see Figure 6–4).

Sid Stein's department ran a continuous stream of consumer surveys in locations around the country, asking shoppers to rate Penney's and competitive stores on a variety of issues: quality, integrity, fashionability, stylishness, newness and oldness, selection, store appeal, and so on.

In survey after survey, shoppers said they thought J. C. Penney stood for honesty, integrity, and value. That was the good news. But they also said that Penney's stores were unexciting. And across the board, they perceived that Penney's merchandise had less quality and was less stylish and contemporary than the merchandise carried by the department stores. That was the bad news. Moreover, the interviews convinced Sid and his committee that they *were* getting the same customers as the other department

FIGURE 6–4	Comparison of data collection methods		
	Personal	**Telephone**	**Mail**
Data collection costs	High	Medium	Low
Data collection time required	Medium	Low	High
Sample size for a given budget	Small	Medium	Large
Data quantity per respondent	High	Medium	Low
Reaches widely dispersed sample	No	Maybe	Yes
Reaches special locations	Yes	Maybe	No
Interaction with respondents	Yes	Yes	No
Degree of interviewer bias	High	Medium	None
Severity of nonresponse bias	Low	Low	High
Presentation of visual stimuli	Yes	No	Maybe
Field worker training required	Yes	Yes	No

stores but that these customers were buying a disproportionately smaller amount of "fashionable" merchandise at Penney's. The problem, therefore, ran much deeper than women's, or even men's, apparel. It affected every department where product characteristics such as style, appearance, and timeliness were considered important by their target customers.

Elements of Quantitative Research

These three methods of data collection are used by market researchers primarily to develop hard numbers so they can completely and accurately measure a particular market situation. These *quantitative,* or descriptive, methods require formal design and rigorous standards for collecting and tabulating information. Only in this way can inaccuracies be minimized and the data considered *valid* and *reliable* for future decision making.

Let's understand these two important terms. Assume a market contains 10,000 individuals, and you want to determine the attitude of that market toward a proposed new toy. You walk into a restaurant and show a prototype of the toy to five people, and four say they like it. If you then interpolate that to your entire market, you might predict an 80 percent favorable attitude. Is that test *valid?* Hardly. For a test to be valid, the results of your test must reflect the true status of the market.

In addition, if you were to repeat your test with five more people in the restaurant, you might come up with an entirely different response. And if you repeated it again, you might come up with a third result. If that happened, it would show that your test also lacks *reliability.* For a test to be reliable, it must be repeatable, producing the same result each time it is administered (see Figure 6–5).

FIGURE 6–5

The reliability/validity diagram. Using the analogy of a dart board, the bull's eye in this example represents the actual average of some value among a population of people (e.g., average age). The marks of the darts thrown at the target are analogous to the averages that might be obtained by polling various sets of people in the population. The first column shows high reliability because the results are all very similar. The second column shows low reliability because the darts are randomly scattered on the target. The top row shows the pattern for high validity—the marks are all centered on the bull's eye. The bottom row shows the effect of systematic bias and, therefore, low validity.

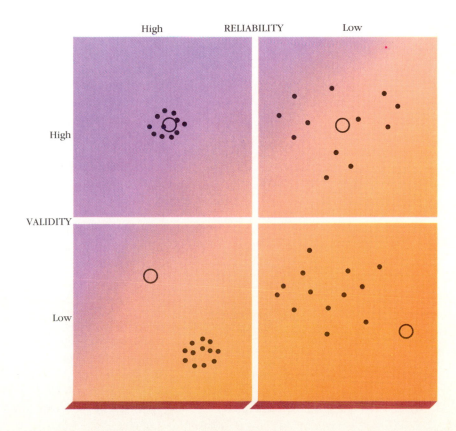

The validity and reliability of any research project, therefore, depends on several key elements. The most important of these are the sampling methods used, the way the survey questionnaire is designed, and the methods used for data collection and analysis. We will discuss these briefly.

Sampling Theories   When J. C. Penney wants to know what consumers think about its products or its image, it cannot possibly ask everybody in the country. That would be too expensive and time-consuming. However, it is important that the results of the research accurately reflect the *universe,* or the entire target population, of department store customers. Marketing researchers therefore select a *sample* of the population that they expect will give a representative minipicture of the true characteristics of the population.[15] To accomplish this, they must make several basic decisions. Who is to be surveyed? How many people should be surveyed? How should the respondents be chosen?

A sample can be representative only if it reflects the pertinent characteristics of the universe the researcher wants to measure. Naturally, if we survey people who normally do not vote in an election, we are not going to get a result representative of the voters. The *sample unit,* or whom we survey, therefore, is very important.

Theories of sampling are drawn from the mathematical theories of probability. For a sample to be considered adequate, it must be large enough to achieve satisfactory precision or stability. Naturally, the larger the *sample size,* the more reliable the results. (See Ad Lab 6-C.) However, adequate sample size has nothing to do with the size of the population. Good reliability can often be obtained with samples representing only a fraction of 1 percent of the population if the proper procedure is used. The two most commonly used *sampling procedures* are random probability samples and nonprobability samples.

Probability samples give every unit in the universe an equal and known probability of being selected for the research. If a researcher wishes to know the opinions of a community regarding a particular issue, all members of the community constitute the universe. Selecting various members of the community at random produces an unbiased sample and the most accurate results, but it also presents certain difficulties. It requires that every unit be known, listed, and numbered so that each has an equal chance of being selected. This is often prohibitively expensive and sometimes impossible, especially in the case of customers for nationally distributed products. J. C. Penney annually participates in a national probability study conducted by R. H. Bruskin Associates in order to identify the company's shopper base and to learn in what ways it resembles that of the targeted competiton, that is, department stores. These studies, when compared to earlier studies, provide an evaluation of how Penney's shopper base has changed over time.

Nonprobability samples do not provide every unit in the universe with an equal chance of being included. That means there is no guarantee the sample will be representative. Therefore, the researcher's level of confidence in the validity of the responses cannot be determined as it can when the statistical methods of probability sampling are used.[16] Nonetheless, nonprobability samples are used extensively because they are less expensive and less time-consuming and because random sampling is often not feasible. When only a general measure of the data is needed, nonprobability sampling can be extremely useful, and most advertising and marketing research studies use this method. For example, in the case of J. C. Penney, the nonprobability method of interviewing shoppers in malls was sufficient to determine shopping preferences and image attitudes of its customers.

Questionnaire Design   The construction of a good questionnaire requires considerable expertise. Much bias in research is blamed on poorly designed questionnaires. Typical problems include asking the wrong types of questions, asking too many questions, using the wrong form for a question, which makes it either too difficult to answer or too difficult to tabulate, and

---

AD LAB 6-C   How Reliable Is Sampling?

Most expert statisticians could give you some very comprehensive answers to that question. Probably too comprehensive, in fact, for anyone but another expert statistician. So let's explain sampling by using a photograph of a child.

The first picture is composed of several hundred thousand dots. Let's consider these dots as our total population and draw several samples.

The other three pictures represent samples of 2,000, 1,000, and 250 dots. These samples represent a specific kind of sample design called *area probability sampling* because the black and white dots in the samples are distributed in proportion to their distribution in the original picture (more black dots in the hair, more white dots in the face, etc.). Think of homes (which add up to our population) instead of dots (which add up to the pictures), and you have the sampling method used by companies involved in national polling and market research.

Now, if you put the book down and step back a few feet, you'll notice a very interesting thing as you look at these small pictures. Your eye will adjust to the overall image and stop trying to "read" the dots. See how the 250-dot sample provides a recognizable picture? Recognizable, yes, but

obviously not much detail. So, let's take a look at the 1,000-dot sample—again from a few feet away.

Now we find that the child is *very* recognizable; in fact, if all we wanted was a reliable idea of what she looked like, this sample would be quite adequate.

Another interesting thing about sampling: The 1,000-dot photograph is about twice as sharp as the 250-dot photograph because it has *four times* as many dots. And so it is with sampling. To double the accuracy, one must *quadruple* sample size.

These are some of the basic sampling laws followed in constructing a 1,200-home national sample. Just as the 1,000-dot photograph provides a reliable idea of what the child looks like, the advertising industry regards the 1,200-home sample as adequate in size to provide a reliable estimate of national consumer trends.

Laboratory Application

What types of consumer trends might advertisers try to measure using probability sampling?

using the wrong choice of words. The sample questionnaire in Figure 6–6 shows some of the various types of questions used in typical surveys.

Consider the simple question: "What kind of soap do you use?" The respondent doesn't know what the word *soap* means. Is it hand soap, shampoo, laundry detergent, dishwashing soap, cleansing cream, or dishwasher detergent? And take the word *kind.* Does that mean what brand, what size, or what use? Finally, what constitutes *use?* Does that mean what do you buy? You might buy one kind for yourself and another kind for your spouse. You probably use several different kinds. Answering the question accurately is impossible. Worse, if the question is answered, the researcher doesn't know what the answer signifies and will likely draw an incorrect conclusion. (See the Checklist for Developing an Effective Questionnaire.)

Effective survey questions have three important attributes: focus, brevity, and simplicity. They focus directly on the issue or topic of the survey. They are as brief as possible while still conveying the intended meaning. And they are expressed as simply and clearly as they can be.[17]

There are many ways to ask essentially the same question. Assume you are conducting a survey on J. C. Penney's advertising. Figure 6–7 lists four

FIGURE 6–6

J. C. Penney used a personal interview questionnaire similar to this (only much longer) to find out the feelings of shoppers toward the store, its merchandise, and its advertising.

1. Do you intend to shop at any J. C. Penney store between now and Sunday?
   Yes 1 No 2 (If no, skip question 5)

2. Do you intend to go into J. C. Penney to buy something in particular or just to browse?
   Buy 1 Browse 2

3. Have you seen any of the items you intend to buy advertised by J. C. Penney?
   Yes 1 (continue) No 2 (skip to question 5)

4. Where did you see these items advertised? Was it in a J. C. Penney advertising flyer included with your newspaper, a J. C. Penney flyer you received in the mail, on the pages of the newspaper itself, on TV, or somewhere else?

   Flyer in newspaper ____
   Flyer in mail ____
   Pages of newspaper ____
   On TV ____
   Somewhere else (specify) __________
   Don't recall ____

5. Now, I would like you to rate the J. C. Penney advertising insert on the attributes listed below. Please place an "X" in the box at the position that best reflects your opinion of how the insert rates on each attribute. Placing an "X" in the middle box usually means you are neutral. The closer you place the "X" to the left or right phrase or word, the more you believe it describes the J. C. Penney insert.

	1	2	3	4	5	6	7	
Looks expensive								Looks cheap
Cleverly done								Unskillful
Appealing								Unappealing
Shows clothing in an attractive manner								Does not show clothing in an attractive manner

6. Please indicate all of the different types of people listed below that you feel this J. C. Penney advertising insert is appealing to.

Young people	____	Quality-conscious people	__________
Bargain hunters	____	Low-income people	____
Conservative dressers	____	Budget watchers	____
Fashion-conscious people	____	Older people	____
Rich people	____	Middle-income people	____
Professionals	____	Blue-collar people	____
High-income people	____	Women	____
Men	____	Office workers	____
Someone like me	____	Smart dressers	____
Career-oriented women	____	Other (specify) __________	

FIGURE 6–7   Different ways to phrase research questions

Type	Questions
Open-ended	How would you describe J. C. Penney advertising?
Dichotomous	Do you think J. C. Penney advertising is too attractive? _____ Yes _____ No
Multiple choice	What description best fits your opinion of J. C. Penney advertising? _____ Modern _____ Well done _____ Believable _____ Unconvincing _____ Old-fashioned
Semantic differential (scale)	Please indicate on the scale how you rate the quality of J. C. Penney advertising. ___ ___ ___ ___ ___ ___ ___ 1 2 3 4 5 6 7 Excellent Inferior

Checklist for Developing an Effective Questionnaire

☐ List specific research objectives. Be sure the reason for the study is clear. Avoid the expense of collecting irrelevant data.

☐ Write short questionnaires. Don't tax the patience of the respondent, lest careless or flip answers result.

☐ State questions clearly so there is no chance for misunderstanding. Avoid generalities and ambiguous terms.

☐ Write a rough draft first. After all the information points have been covered, then polish it.

☐ Use a short opening statement. Include your name, the name of your organization, and the broad purpose of the questionnaire.

☐ Put the respondent at ease by opening with one or two inoffensive, easily answered questions.

☐ Ask general questions before the more detailed ones. Structure them so they flow logically.

☐ Avoid questions that suggest an answer or that could be considered "leading" questions. They tend to bias the results.

☐ Include a few questions that will serve to cross-check earlier answers. This aids in ensuring validity.

☐ Put the demographic questions (e.g., age, income, education) and any other personal questions at the end of the questionnaire.

☐ Pretest the questionnaire with 20–30 persons to be sure that the questions are being interpreted as intended and that all the information sought is included.

common types of questions that might elicit responses about the quality of Penney's ads. There are many ways to ask the questions even within these four types. For example, additional choices might be added to the multiple-choice format. Neutral responses might be removed from the scale format. And there is obvious bias in the dichotomous question.

What is important is that the questions elicit a response that is both accurate and useful to the researcher's needs. For this reason, it is advisable that all questionnaires be tested on a small subsample to detect any confusion, bias, or ambiguities.

Data Collection and Analysis   After all the data have been collected, they must be validated, edited, coded, and tabulated. Answers must be checked to eliminate errors or inconsistencies. For instance, one person might answer a question "two years" while another says "24 months." These must be changed to the same units for correct tabulation. Some questionnaires may be rejected because the answers are obviously the result of misunderstanding. Finally, the data must be counted and summarized. For small studies tabulation may be manual. But most research projects today use more sophisticated data processing equipment to count the answers and produce cross tabulations of the data.

For example, many researchers want a cross tabulation of product use by age group or other important demographic information. The researcher may take the raw data, apply advanced statistical techniques to them, and pass them through the computer again to seek additional findings. At this point, the cost of the research study can go through the ceiling if an unskilled marketer wants to see all the cross tabulations possible. The researcher must use skill and imagination to select only those cross tabulations that will show significant relationships.

Basic Methodology of Qualitative Research

At this point in the research, J. C. Penney wanted to understand its sales problem more clearly, especially since the company was rated so highly for honesty, integrity, and value. Penney's researchers initiated a series of focus-group sessions to probe customers' perceptions of who were Penney's most frequent shoppers, who weren't, and why. They also held interviews with over 400 of Penney's management personnel at the store, district, regional, and corporate levels to understand their views and solicit their suggestions.

Marketers use a variety of indirect research methods to understand the "why" of consumer behavior. No matter how skillfully posed, some questions are hard for the consumer to answer. As we discussed in Chapter 5, it is especially difficult for consumers to give the real reasons for their product choices. Thus, qualitative research is used more and more to enable marketers to get a general impression of the market, the consumer, or the product. Some marketers refer to it as *motivation research*.

Qualitative research seeks in-depth, open-ended responses aimed at getting people to share their thoughts and feelings on a subject in order to gain impressions rather than definitions.[18] The methods used in qualitative research are usually described as *intensive* or *projective*.

Projective Techniques   In order to get an understanding of people's underlying or subconscious feelings, attitudes, opinions, needs, and motives, researchers ask indirect questions or otherwise involve the consumer in a situation in which he or she can "project" feelings about the problem or product.

For example, when N. W. Ayer was vying for the J. C. Penney account, it conducted several studies of its own using a projective technique in a series of shopping center interviews. In one of them, Ayer personnel showed pictures of different types of shoppers to people in the mall and asked them where they thought these shoppers probably bought their clothes. This technique has long been used by psychologists for clinical diagnosis and is now being adapted to marketing use. All such techniques require highly experienced researchers to be used correctly.

Intensive Techniques Using this approach requires great care in administering the questions. One type, called the *in-depth interview,* uses carefully planned but loosely structured questions to enable the interviewer to probe respondents' deeper feelings. Although these interviews are very helpful at discovering individual motivations, they are also very expensive, extremely time-consuming, and limited because there is a lack of skilled interviewers.

The *focus-group method* is one of the most useful. Eight to 10 people, "typical" of the target market, are invited to a group session to discuss the product, the service, or the marketing situation. A trained moderator guides the often free-wheeling discussion for an hour or more, and the group interaction reveals the group's true feelings or behavior toward the product. These meetings are usually recorded and may even be viewed or videotaped from behind a one-way mirror (see Figure 6–8). These groups do not offer sampling validity. However, participants' thinking can often be used prior to a formal survey to assist in questionnaire design.[19] Or as in the case of Penney's, focus groups following a survey can put flesh on the skeleton created by raw data.

Chevrolet held a series of focus-group studies and learned that consumers were disappointed that the company had let Americans down by not building cars for modern America. In 1986, as a result of those studies, Chevrolet launched its "Heartbeat of America" campaign to impart a distinctive corporate identity and to unify the image of its cars and trucks.[20]

Interpreting the Findings

Marketing research is used to help solve management problems. If it doesn't do that, then it's not worth the cost (see Figure 6–9). The researcher, therefore, must prepare a complete analysis of the information gathered. Tables and graphs may be used, but it is important that these be explained in words management can understand. The use of technical jargon (such as "multivariate analysis of variance model") should be avoided or at least confined to an appendix. The report should state the problem and research objective, a summary of the findings, and the researcher's conclusions drawn from an unbiased analysis of the data. The researcher's recommendations for management action should also be described, and the whole report should be offered with an oral presentation to allow for management feedback and to highlight important points. A description of the methodology, statistical analysis, and raw data on which the report is based constitute the report's appendix.

FIGURE   6–8

Focus-group sessions are usually held in comfortable settings where participants can feel relaxed about discussing their attitudes and beliefs. The one-way mirror conceals recording or videotaping equipment and often agency or advertiser personnel viewing the proceedings.

Figure 6-9	How much does research cost using professional firms?
Telephone: 500 20-minute interviews, with report	$12,000–$15,000
Mail: 500 returns, with report—33 percent response rate	$7,000–$8,000
Intercept: 500 interviews, four or five questions, with report	$15,000
Executive interviews (talking to business administrators): 20 interviews, with report	$2,500–$7,500
Focus group: One group, 8 to 10 people, with report and videotape	$2,500–$3,800

APPLYING RESEARCH TO MARKETING AND ADVERTISING STRATEGY

Thus far, we have seen how Sid Stein and his department, in a step-by-step process, uncovered Penney's problem of declining market share, evaluated the company's competitive strengths and weaknesses, and measured consumer attitudes toward it. All this information was vital to the development of the company's positioning statement, marketing strategy, and subsequent advertising plans.

Developing Marketing Strategy

The pieces were all beginning to fit together. By the end of 1981, the J. C. Penney Stores Positioning Statement had the complete involvement and commitment of Penney's top management. The corporate direction for the decade was set. The nation's third-largest retailer was going to change from a mass merchandiser to a "fashion-oriented national department store."

To begin this evolution, the company announced two strategic moves in 1982. The first involved major changes in the stores' merchandise mix. In all stores, the automotive, paint and hardware, and lawn and garden departments would be discontinued. With the selling space thus made available, Penney's would make more dominant statements in its apparel lines by bringing in designer and higher taste level private labels (Halston III, Stafford, Lee Wright, and others). It would also bring in the brands customers wanted, which would help improve the perception of quality and fashionability (Levi, Nike, Jordache, Adolfo, etc.).

Second, Penney's began a five-year, $1.5 billion modernization program to inject fashion and excitement into all its stores. In 1983, 38 stores were completely modernized, and 138 were remerchandised. In 1984, 34 stores were modernized and 200 remerchandised. By the end of the decade, virtually all Penney's metropolitan stores would be modernized.

The program was finally underway. The target market had been selected and the marketing strategy determined. Now it was time to start letting the public know. That meant advertising—and more research.

FIGURE   6–10   Stages of research in advertising development

	Stage 1: Strategy determination	Stage 2: Concept development	Stage 3: Pre-testing	Stage 4: Post-testing
Timing	Before creative work begins	Before agency production begins	Before finished artwork and photography	After the campaign has run
Research problem	Product-class definition	Concept testing	Print pretesting	Advertising effectiveness
	Prospect-group selection	Name testing	Television storyboard pretesting	Consumer attitude change
	Message-element selection	Slogan testing	Radio commercial pretesting	Sales increases
Techniques	Consumer-attitude and usage studies	Free-association tests	Consumer jury Matched samples	Aided recall Unaided recall
		Qualitative interviews	Portfolio tests Storyboard test Mechanical devices	Sales tests Inquiry tests Attitude tests
		Statement-comparison tests	Psychological rating scales	

It is difficult to say where marketing research ends and advertising research begins since there is, admittedly, often quite an overlap. Some contemporary authors suggest there are three stages of advertising research:[21]

Stage 1. Advertising strategy research (which may be aimed at defining the product concept, target market selection, message-element determination, or media selection).

Stage 2. Concept development research (designed to measure acceptability of different creative concepts).

Stage 3. Pretesting of ads and commercials.

We would even add a fourth stage—posttesting (or campaign evaluation)—which is research designed to measure the effectiveness of a campaign after it has run (see Figure 6–10).

Developing Advertising Strategy

At this point, it is important to understand how advertisers apply the marketing research procedures we have discussed to basic advertising strategy and concept development (Stages 1 and 2).

We have already seen how J. C. Penney utilized its initial marketing research results to discover which consumers were currently shopping Penney's, which were not, and how the general market perceived Penney's position in the marketplace. Let's review for a moment the results of the Stage 1 research.

Product Concept Definition

Following its successful growth in the 1960s and 70s and its emergence as a major shopping mall tenant, J. C. Penney was positioned in the consumer's mind as a major mass merchandiser of basic apparel, housewares, hardware, and commodities like bedding and towels. The attributes applied to it were honesty, integrity, and good value. But the characteristics of fashion, style, and quality were not associated with the J. C. Penney name. From both its quantitative and qualitative studies, Penney's knew it was not the place where these same customers shopped for contemporary apparel, and it was not really perceived as a department store. In fact, in recent years, the consumer perception of the store's business had become unfocused.

Normally, it is easier to position a product in a manner consistent with consumer attitudes and perceptions than to reposition it by emphasizing other uses or attributes.[22] Trout and Ries, who wrote the book on positioning, would agree. However, the very fuzziness in the consumer perception of Penney's business could work to its advantage, and it is possible that Trout and Ries would agree with Penney's decision to change strategy. They believe it is virtually fruitless to try to dislodge a market leader unless the leader is making serious positioning mistakes. For many years, J. C. Penney's main competition had been with Sears, and Penney's was not really winning. It was still the number-three retailer.

By repositioning itself as a fashion-oriented national department store with its traditional attention to value, Penney's would remove itself from competing head-to-head with Sears. Then, instead of being in a number-three position it could jump to number one—the largest fashion department store chain in the country.

To accomplish this task, though, Penney's knew it had to not only upgrade its stores and merchandise lines but also gradually change and clarify the consumer perception of its stores. Repositioning any brand or product is an expensive and time-consuming process. To reposition a national chain of retail stores is an even more difficult and risky task. Just too many elements are involved for it to be accomplished overnight. And maintaining credibility with the consumer during the transition period is an absolute necessity. For this reason, Penney's was willing to and knew it had to commit several years, many millions of dollars, and a lot of fortitude to its new campaign.

Target Market Selection

Penney's qualitative studies had showed that, contrary to popular belief, the "traditional J. C. Penney customer" was the *same* as the "traditional department store customer." These consumers were attracted to regional centers where they could compare merchandise before buying. They were looking for fashionable apparel and home furnishings, and they wanted the opportunity to compare the offerings of several stores. Penney's heavy users, or "frequent" shoppers, were in the mall, but they were not shopping at Penney's as often as at the other department stores.

Quantitative studies showed that Penney's mix of male and female shoppers was about the same as the other department stores with a slight edge in men but a slight disadvantage in the high-spending, 18 to 34 female category. Yet this was the opportunity Penney's wanted—to appeal to this key, contemporary, fashion-buying segment with the offerings these customers wanted.

Message-Element Determination

It was at this point that N. W. Ayer came into the picture. Penney's had a very important message to communicate to its customers, and after seeing all the advertising agency presentations, Ayer was selected to help develop the message. And that meant more research.

Studies aimed at the selection of advertising message elements focus on particular themes and claims that may be promising and are "concerned with the likes and dislikes of consumers in relation to the brands and products being considered."[23]

In the qualitative attitude studies the agency had conducted and with the help of Agi Clark's creative group, Ayer discovered numerous themes that might be used: "Penney's looks different, but the value's the same"; "You're changing, so is Penney's"; and so on. The agency decided to immediately begin concept testing in order to discover which of these message-element options might prove most successful in the repositioning effort. This was the company's Stage 2 research aimed at advertising concept development.

Concept Testing

Ayer prepared four tentative advertising concepts, each with an illustration and a headline stressing a different Penney's appeal (see Figure 6–11). The agency then gathered numerous focus groups of volunteer consumers into their unique "developmental lab," which combines intensive qualitative interviews with certain quantitative techniques. While a discussion leader moderated the conversation, each group was shown the series of ads, and their reactions were measured as well as taped and observed by Ayer staff behind a one-way mirror.

The focus groups were nearly unanimous in their choice: the message that announced Penney's change but related it to the change in the customers themselves. The reason for their choice was clear: J. C. Penney was indeed changing. It did have more fashions than ever before. Why? Because *they,* the customers, had changed, and they needed more fashion than ever before. The message was logical and straightforward. The focus groups found it to be a believable position and a great promise. And that convinced Ayer to make it the backbone of the new campaign.

Once the concept of how to announce the change was accepted, Ayer had to develop a campaign that would express the results and show the benefits of that change to the consumer. Agi Clark and her creative teams developed a series of ads for magazines and TV using the campaign idea: "YOU'RE LOOKING SMARTER THAN EVER." They believed that theme complimented the customer for looking and being smarter than ever and simultaneously made the promise that J. C. Penney would also be smarter than ever before.

Bringing the two ideas together, the introductory ads read: "THERE'S A

Fashions for people. Not mannequins.

JC Penney.
Fashion, American Style.

We've changed our looks.
Not our values.

JC Penney.

We've changed
because you've changed.

JC Penney.

No, not Saks.
JC Penney's.

We're the best dressed Penney ever.

FIGURE   6–11

The four layouts used in concept testing each stressed a different appeal. In a series of intensive interviews, the reactions of shoppers to the various themes were monitored and measured.

CHANGE IN PENNEY'S BECAUSE THERE'S A CHANGE IN YOU. YOU'RE LOOKING SMARTER THAN EVER. J. C. PENNEY" (see Figure 6–12). Ayer liked it. Penney's liked it. Now it was time to pretest to be sure this campaign would get the attention and recognition Penney's hoped for.

Testing and Evaluation of Advertising

In some instances, advertising is the largest single cost in a company's marketing budget. According to *Advertising Age,* the nation's 100 leading advertisers spend $27 billion a year on advertising.[24] Its effectiveness, therefore, is naturally a major concern. Companies can't stop advertising, nor do they want to. But they *do* want to know what they are getting for their money—and if their advertising is working.

Testing is the primary instrument advertisers have to assure themselves that their advertising dollars are being spent wisely. It may prevent costly errors in judging which advertising strategy and what media will produce the greatest results. And it can give the advertiser some measure (besides sales results) of a campaign's effectiveness.

Objectives of Testing

Pretesting, the third stage of advertising research, is used to increase the likelihood of preparing the most effective advertising messages. Pretesting can help advertisers detect and eliminate communication gaps or flaws in message content that may ultimately result in consumer indifference or

There's a change in Penney's because there's a change   in you.

Today, you're both as comfortable on Wall Street as Sesame Street, and you want clothes that can take you there in style. So we're taking a new look at how you want to look. One of the most exciting changes at JCPenney is our exclusive Halston III™ Collection. Designed by Halston, it's a totally coordinated look for today's American woman. Men can look to the Lee Wright® Collection for contemporary designs. Or to the Stafford® Collection for more traditional styles. And for the career woman, we have the newest fall collections. Today there's more style in everything you do, and more style than ever at JCPenney.

You're looking smarter than ever. JCPenney.

FIGURE   6–12

The first ad in Penney's new campaign showed off the company's solid commitment to sophisticated style and fashion flair. It also demonstrated Penney's responsiveness to its customers. The campaign had two objectives. The first was to announce the change in Penney's from the perspective of the customer; the second was to explain the benefits these changes would bring to the customer.

negative audience response (such as changing the channel).[25] The fourth stage of advertising research, *posttesting,* is designed to determine the effectiveness of an advertisement or campaign *after* it has run. The findings obtained from posttesting can provide the advertiser with useful guidelines for future advertising.

Several areas of advertising that may be evaluated in pretesting include markets, motives, messages, media, budgeting, and scheduling. As we will see in Chapter 7, several of these variables are basic elements of the *creative mix,* and most are under the advertiser's control to add, subtract, or modify. Many of these same variables can be posttested. However, in posttesting, the objective is normally to evaluate rather than to diagnose. The intent is not to make changes but rather to understand what has already happened.

Markets Advertisers may pretest advertising strategy and commercials against various market segments or audience groups to measure their reactions. In this process, the advertiser may even decide to alter the strategy and target the campaign to a different market. In posttesting, advertisers are interested in determining the extent to which the campaign succeeded in reaching its target markets. Changes in awareness within the market segment or increases in market share, for instance, may indicate successful advertising exposure.

Motives While the consumer's motives are outside of the advertiser's control, the messages the advertiser uses to appeal to those motives are not. By pretesting advertisements, the advertiser can gauge various appeals that might influence a purchase decision based on the individual's needs and motives.

Messages Every advertising message has variables. Pretesting may be used to determine *what* a message says (from the customer's point of view) and to determine *how well* it says it. Some of the variables tested might be the headline, the text, the illustration, and the typography. Or the variables might be the message concept, the information presented, or the symbolism inherent in the ad.

On the other hand, through posttesting the advertiser can determine to what extent the advertising message was seen, remembered, and believed. Changes in consumer attitude or perception, for instance, indicate success in this area.[26] Similarly, success might be measured by the ability of consumers to accurately fill in the blanks in a campaign slogan or to identify the sponsor.

Media Today the cost of media is soaring while, at the same time, the size of media units is diminishing. As a result, advertisers are demanding ever-greater media accountability.[27] Pretesting can influence four types of media decisions: classes of media, media subclasses, specific media vehicles, and units of space and time.

Media classes refer to the broad media categories: print, electronic, outdoor, and direct mail. *Media subclasses* are radio or TV, news magazines or business publications, and so on. The specific *media vehicle* refers to, for example, the all-rock station in Dallas or the middle-of-the-road music station in Houston. And *media units* mean half-page ads or full-page ads, 30-second spots or 60-second commercials, and so forth.

After the campaign has run, posttesting can determine how effective the media mix was in reaching the target audience and communicating the desired message. (See the discussions of audience measurement in Chapters 12 and 14.)

Budgeting How large should a company's total advertising budget be? How much of this should be allocated to various markets and media? To specific products? Spending too little on advertising can be as hazardous as spending too much; but how much is "too little"—and how much is "too much"? Various pretesting techniques are used to determine the optimum levels of expenditure before introducing national campaigns. (Refer to Chapter 7, "Marketing and Advertising Planning," for further information on budgeting.)

Scheduling Advertisers can test consumer response to a product ad during different seasons of the year or days of the week. They can test whether frequent advertising is more effective than occasional or one-time insertions, or whether year-round advertising of, say, a gift product is more effective than advertising that is concentrated during the Christmas gift-buying season.

Overall Results Finally, advertisers want to measure overall results to evaluate the extent to which advertising accomplished its objectives. The results of posttests might be used to determine how to continue, what to change, and how much to spend in the future.

All these tests are designed with the hope of discovering to what extent advertising is the *stimulus* and changes in consumer behavior are *responses*. Perhaps the greatest problem for the researcher, though, is to determine which, and how many, of these advertiser-controlled variables to measure and which consumer responses to survey.

Methods Used to Pretest Print Ads

Although no infallible means of predicting advertising success or failure has been developed, certain popular pretesting methods can give the advertiser some useful insights if properly applied.

When J. C. Penney wanted to pretest Ayer's proposal for preprinted newspaper advertising inserts, for example, they interviewed 250 women in shopping malls around the country. Respondents were asked direct questions such as: What does the advertising say? What do you think the advertiser is trying to tell you about its merchandise? Does the advertising say anything new or different about the store? If so, what? Is the advertising well done? Is it believable? What effect, if any, does it have on your perception of the store?

As a method of pretesting, *direct questioning* is designed to elicit a full range of responses to the advertising. From customer responses, researchers can infer how well advertising messages convey key copy points. The researcher also takes note of verbatim comments made by the respondents, which often reveal more subtle but meaningful reactions to the advertisement. Direct questioning is especially effective for testing alternative advertisements in the early stages of development. Respondents are virtual participants in the creative process at a time when their reactions and input can best be acted on. During Penney's direct interviews, for example, the preprint format created by Ayer was compared to previous preprints created by Penney's own advertising department to evaluate the relative effect on shopper interest and Penney's image. Across the board, the proposed new format was determined to be more effective (see Figure 6–13).

In addition to direct questioning and focus groups, which we have

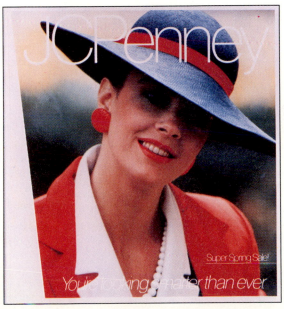

FIGURE   6–13

The preprint format proposed by Ayer (right) was compared to previous J. C. Penney newspaper inserts (left) in shopping center pretests. Across the board, shoppers preferred the newer, more contemporary design.

Checklist of Methods for Pretesting Advertisements

Print Advertising

☐ Direct questioning. Specific questions are asked about advertisements. Often used in testing alternative advertisements in the early stages of development.

☐ Focus groups. A free-wheeling discussion and interview is conducted with two or more people about a product, service, or marketing situation.

☐ Order-of-merit tests. Two or more advertisements are shown to respondents with instructions to arrange the advertisements in rank order.

☐ Paired comparison methods. Each advertisement is compared by respondents with every other advertisement in a group.

☐ Portfolio tests. Test ads are interspersed among other ads and editorial matter in an album-type portfolio. Consumers in an experimental group are shown this portfolio. At the same time, consumers in a control group are shown the same portfolio but without the test ads. Afterward, members of both groups are questioned to determine their recall of the portfolio contents and the advertisements being tested.

☐ Mock magazines. An actual magazine is used instead of a portfolio. Test ads are "stripped into" the magazine, and it is left with respondents for a specified time. Respondents are then questioned about the test ads. Also used as a post-testing technique.

☐ Perceptual meaning studies. Ads are shown to respondents in timed exposures on a specially designed electronic tachistoscopic presentation instrument. Questions are given about recall of the product, brand, illustration, copy, and main idea of the ad.

Broadcast Advertising

☐ Central location projection tests. Test commercials are run on a projector in a central location like a shopping center. Questions are asked before and after exposure to the commercials to determine brand awareness and to detect weaknesses in the commercials.

☐ Trailer tests. TV commercials are shown to people in trailers at shopping centers. Shoppers are then questioned about the commercials and are given packets of coupons that enable them to purchase products seen in the commercials at reduced prices. A matched sample of consumers who have not viewed the commercials are given identical packets of coupons. The impact of the commercials is measured in part by the difference in coupon redemption rates between the two groups.

☐ Theater tests. Electronic equipment enables respondents to indicate what they like and dislike as they view TV commercials in a theater setting.

☐ Live telecast tests. Test commercials are shown on closed-circuit or cable television. Respondents are interviewed by phone to test their reactions. Commercials may also be evaluated by sales audits at stores in the areas where the commercials were run.

☐ Sales experiments. Alternative advertisements are run in two or more different market areas to determine which ads are the most effective.

☐ Direct-mail tests. Two or more alternative advertisements are mailed to different prospects on a mailing list. By keying each ad, the source of the orders can be traced. The ad that generates the largest volume of orders is presumed to be the most effective.

Physiological Testing

☐ Pupilometric devices. Dilation of the pupil of the subject's eye is measured and presumed to indicate the subject's reaction to the illustration.

☐ Eye-movement camera. Route the subject's eye travels is superimposed over an advertisement to show the paths it takes and the areas that attracted and held attention. Used to obtain information on the placement of headlines, proper length of copy, and the most satisfactory ad layout.

☐ Galvanometer. A 25 milliampere current is passed through the subject, in at the palm and out at the elbow. When subject reacts to the advertisement, sweat gland activity increases, electric resistance decreases, and the current passes through faster. These changes are recorded on a revolving drum apparatus. It is assumed that the more tension an ad creates, the more effective it is likely to be.

☐ Voice-pitch analysis. A tape recording is made of a consumer's explanation of his or her reaction to an ad. A computer is then used to measure the changes in voice pitch caused by emotional responses to the ad. This technique presumes a direct link between voice pitch and advertising effectiveness.

☐ Brain-pattern analysis. A brain scanner monitors the reaction of the brain while ads are presented. Proponents of this approach believe that brain waves indicate whether people respond favorably or unfavorably to commercials.

already discussed, other techniques for pretesting print ads include order-of-merit tests, paired comparison methods, portfolio tests, mock magazines, and perceptual meaning studies. (See the Checklist of Methods for Pretesting Advertisements.)

Methods Used to Pretest Broadcast Ads

A number of methods are used specifically to pretest radio and television commercials. The most common of these are central location tests, trailer tests, theater tests, and live telecasts, as described in the checklist.

In *central location tests,* as the name suggests, videotapes of test commercials are shown to respondents on a one-to-one basis, usually in shopping center locations. Questions are asked before and after exposure to the commercials. J. C. Penney, for example, ran central location *clutter tests* of Ayer's television commercials in six dispersed markets before the campaign began. These tests had several objectives. By cluttering the Ayer commercials with other noncompetitive control commercials, Penney's could measure the effectiveness of the commercials in getting attention and increasing brand awareness; it could measure comprehension and resultant attitude shifts; and it could detect any weaknesses in the commercials. As expected, the commercials created by Agi Clark's team fared well in pretesting (see Figure 6–14).

Additional pretesting techniques in common use fall into the general categories of sales experiments, direct-mail tests, and physiological testing. (See the Checklist of Methods for Pretesting Advertisements.)

The Challenge of Pretesting

By now it should be obvious that there is no one best way to pretest advertising variables. Different methods have been devised to test for different aspects of effectiveness. But each of the methods devised has its own peculiar set of advantages and disadvantages, thus constituting a formidable challenge to the advertiser.

Certain techniques are referred to as *laboratory methods*—where consumers are brought individually or in groups into a studio or auditorium. Laboratory testing offers the advantages of speed, economy, and a high degree of control. The researcher knows for sure that the subject has seen the test advertisement and, in fact, can control the way respondents are exposed to it. Responses can be measured immediately. Laboratory testing often produces some information that would be unavailable in other settings. The validity of laboratory findings, though, may be highly questionable since forced exposure in a laboratory setting does not equate with real life.

Field testing, on the other hand, which may actually take place in the respondent's home or in a public place like a shopping center, still suffers from artificiality. Just as in the laboratory setting, the subject's response is actually a combined reaction to the test as well as to the advertisement.

Sales experiments, live telecasts, and direct-mail tests can actually approximate real-life conditions while still offering the necessary controls for experimentation. However, the depth of information available from these methods is usually more limited.

Trade-offs, therefore, are endless. Although pretesting is generally considered valuable in distinguishing very strong advertisements from very weak ones, much controversy still exists concerning the validity of other

FIGURE 6–14

TV commercials introduced Penney's new Wyndham collection of coordinated separates for the working woman. In one 30-second spot, a fashion executive and her assistant are portrayed dashing to a presentation. The successful meeting ends with the supervisor giving credit to her hard-working assistant. All the commercials and print ads emphasized attractive people in real-life situations.

research findings. Likewise, creative people question whether commercial testing stifles creativity.[28] Even so, most advertisers are still interested in finding out whether an advertisement is interesting, believable, comprehensible, and memorable to the consumer. Verbatim responses from test subjects can even provide some useful copy ideas, and contact with consumers can give the advertiser or agency beneficial information on consumer buying habits.

The limitations to pretesting, though, are numerous, and advertisers should be aware of them. Besides the fact that the test itself is an artificial situation, test respondents may cease being typical prospects—many of them will assume the role of expert or critic and give answers that may not reflect their real buying behavior. Consumers who do not have strong opinions about the test ad are likely to invent opinions on the spur of the moment to satisfy the interviewer. Some do not want to admit they could be influenced by the advertisement. Others may try to please the interviewer by voting for the advertisements they feel they *should* like rather than those they actually do like.

Research also shows that when multiple opinions are sought on alternative advertisements—based on such factors as interest, personal pertinence, credibility, and comprehensibility—consumers are likely to rank the one or two ads that make the best first impression as the highest in all categories. This is called the *halo effect*. Also, whereas the most relevant area of such tests may be questions about the respondent's ultimate buying behavior, responses in this area may be the least valid. Behavior intent, in other words, may not become behavior fact.

Posttesting Techniques

When Ayer launched its campaign for J. C. Penney in the fall of 1984, the client was anxious to know if customers saw it and paid attention to it

---

Checklist of Methods for Posttesting Advertisements

☐ Aided recall (recognition-readership). To jog their memories, respondents are shown certain advertisements. Questions are then asked to determine whether the respondents' previous exposure to the ad was through reading, viewing, or listening.

☐ Unaided recall. Questions are asked of respondents without prompting to determine whether they saw or heard advertising messages.

☐ Attitude tests. Direct questions, semantic differential tests, or unstructured questions are given to measure changes in respondents' attitudes after an advertising campaign.

☐ Inquiry tests. Additional product information, product samples, or premiums are offered to readers or viewers in an ad. Ads generating the most responses are presumed to be the most effective.

☐ Sales tests. Numerous types are used. Measures of past sales compare advertising efforts with sales. Controlled experiments may use, for example, radio advertising in one market and newspaper advertising in another, followed by an audit of the results. Consumer purchase tests measure the retail sales that result from a given campaign. And store inventory audits measure advertising effectiveness by determining the inventory of retailers' stocks before and after an advertising campaign.

BRC

Please look over these pictures and words from a TV commercial and answer the questions on the right.

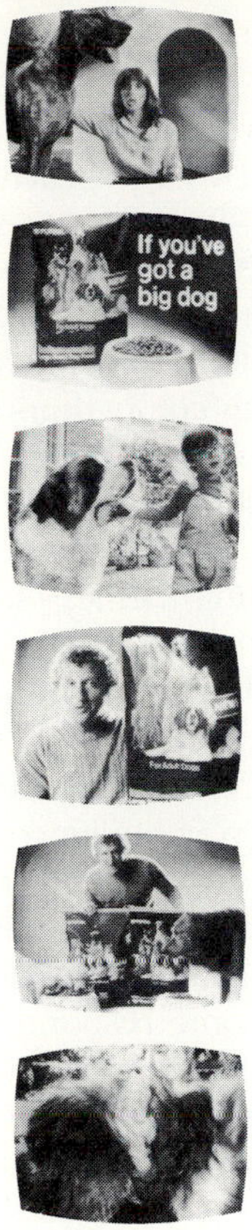

(Woman #1) My dog is so big ... we just built him a two-story dog house.

(Singing) brand name dog food, *
If you've got a big dog.

(Boy) My dog is so big ... we see eye to eye on everything.

(Singing) brand name dog food,
If you've got a big dog.

(Man) Introducing new brand name . The only dog food made for the special nutritional needs of big dogs. Growth food for large-breed puppies and adult food for large-breed adults.

(Woman with sheep dog) My dog is so big ... (rolls over and laughs)
(Singing) brand name dog food,
If you've got a big dog.

Do you remember seeing this commercial on TV?

7-1 ☐ Yes   -2 ☐ No   -3 ☐ Not sure-I may have

How interested are you in what this commercial is trying to tell you or show you about the product? Would you say you were:

Very   Somewhat   Not
8-1 ☐ interested   -2 ☐ interested   -3 ☐ interested

Please check any of the following if you feel they describe this commercial.

9-1 ☐ Amusing   10-1 ☐ Interesting
-2 ☐ Appealing   -2 ☐ Irritating
-3 ☐ Clever   -3 ☐ Lively
-4 ☐ Convincing   -4 ☐ Original
-5 ☐ Dull   -5 ☐ Phony
-6 ☐ Easy to forget   -6 ☐ Pointless
-7 ☐ Effective   -7 ☐ Silly
-8 ☐ Gentle   -8 ☐ Uninteresting
-9 ☐ Imaginative   -9 ☐ Well done
-0 ☐ Informative   -0 ☐ Worth remembering

* We have blocked out the name. Do you remember which brand was being advertised?

Do you have:

11-1 ☐ Hero   12-1 ☐ A large dog
-2 ☐ Mighty Dog   -2 ☐ A small dog
-3 ☐ Mainstay   -3 ☐ No dogs
-4 ☐ Don't know

13-

FIGURE 6–15

Bruzzone Research Company uses a direct-mail questionnaire to evaluate recall and attitude toward, in this example, a dog food commercial. Questionnaires are sent across the country to 1,000 households chosen at random from either auto registrations or telephone listings. Other users of this service include General Motors, Gillette, Holiday Inns, and Polaroid.

and what impression it made. So Ayer undertook a series of posttesting activities.

Posttesting is generally more costly and time-consuming than pretesting, but it permits advertisements to be tested under actual market conditions without the unnaturalness of pretest conditions. Advertisers can reap some of the benefits of both pretesting and posttesting by running advertisements in a few select markets before launching a major nationwide campaign.

A variety of quantitative and qualitative methods are used to determine what awareness or attitude changes have been achieved and what impact the advertising has had on sales. The most common posttesting techniques fall into five broad categories: aided recall, unaided recall, attitude tests, inquiry tests, and sales tests. Each of these has distinct advantages and limitations. (See the Checklist of Methods for Posttesting Advertisements.)

For example, *attitude tests* usually seek to measure the effectiveness of an advertising campaign in creating a favorable image for a company, its brand, or its products (see Figure 6–15). The standard presumption is that favorable changes in attitude predispose consumers to buy the company's product. On a regular basis, J. C. Penney uses lengthy questionnaires in shopping malls to determine shifts in attitudes as a result of its TV commercials and newspaper preprints. The tests also seek to measure the comparative ratings of the company and competitors with regard to products, services, and other attributes.

The Challenge of Posttesting

Each posttesting method offers unique opportunities for advertisers to study the impact of their advertising campaigns. However, each also has definite limitations.

Recall tests are designed to measure specific behavior, not opinions or attitudes. They test advertising under natural conditions of exposure, so they are very helpful in determining whether advertisements are being read, how well the ads are working compared with competitors' ads, and the extent to which the ads have implanted ideas in consumers' minds—whether consumers got the point of the advertiser's message. They can also yield useful data on the relative effectiveness of different advertising components, such as size, color, or attention-getting themes (see Figure 6–16). Aided recall tests are fairly simple to conduct and can be relatively inexpensive because, often, part of their cost is borne by the particular media vehicle being studied.

Recall tests do not measure advertising effect, however, but only what has been noticed, read, or watched. And readership or audience does not necessarily add up to product sales. Although more audience members than nonmembers may ultimately buy the product, it does not necessarily follow that the advertisement was the sole motivating force. Recall tests are subject to the variations of individual memory. Some respondents have better memories than others. Some are better able to express what they remember. Respondents are often confused. Some may say they saw an ad merely to impress the interviewer. The techniques used may also encourage guessing.

FIGURE 6–16

One of the leading firms in recall testing is Starch INRA Hooper. When it presents a readership report to its clients, the firm includes a copy of the magazine used in the test. In this Burger King advertisement from *Ebony,* for example, labels show readership of the ad as a whole and of component parts (headline, visuals, copy).

FIGURE   6–17

While advertisers continue to seek ways to measure advertising effectiveness, M. Wayne DeLozier has compiled a basic list of what does and doesn't work from his own research. While some may appear rather obvious (Number 15), any time is the right time to review the basics.

1. Unpleasant messages are learned as easily as pleasant messages.
2. Meaningful messages are learned more easily than unmeaningful messages.
3. Learning the conceptual idea is faster if massive advertising is followed by distributed advertising.
4. Products requiring mechanical skills are learned best if demonstrated in the ad as though the consumers were doing the task themselves.
5. Product benefits are learned best when presented at the beginning and end of a message.
6. Messages that are unique or unusual are better remembered than commonplace advertisements.
7. Rewarding the consumer who attends to a message enhances learning of the message.
8. Learning by consumers is enhanced when they are told the benefits they will receive from using the product.
9. Active participation in the message enhances learning.
10. Message learning is faster if previous or following messages do not interfere.
11. Repetition strengthens an older idea more than a newer idea.
12. Messages presented closer in time to an intense need are learned faster than those presented when the need is weaker.
13. The greater reward a consumer perceives from viewing (or listening to) an ad message, the faster his learning of the message.
14. The less effort required to respond to an ad, the faster learning occurs.
15. The more complex an ad message, the more difficult to learn.

Attitude tests, on the other hand, are often a better measure of sales effectiveness than recall tests. An attitude change relates more closely to the purchase of the product, and a measured change in attitude gives management the confidence to make informed, intelligent decisions about advertising plans.[29] Such tests are also fairly easy to conduct. They are low in cost because they can be made by phone or mail.

However, human attitudes represent a complex mix of feelings. Many people find it difficult to determine their attitudes and to express them. Deeply entrenched attitudes, like those shaped by religious or philosophical beliefs, are resistant to change even by highly aggressive advertising efforts. Finally, a favorable attitude does not necessarily promise ultimate purchase of the advertiser's product or service. As Figure 6–17 shows, though, years of research have shown certain advertising basics to be effective in stimulating memory and learning—both of which are critical to attitude change.

Inquiry tests are fairly easy to conduct. They enable the advertiser to test the attention-getting value of advertisements as well as their readability and understandability. They also permit fairly good control of the variables that motivate reader action, particularly if a split-run test is used (see Chapter 13). Unlike some methods, the inquiry test can be effective in testing small advertisements.

Unfortunately, inquiry tests are valid only when applied to advertisements that can logically make use of an offer to elicit inquiries. When applied to an ad with more indirect purposes, it is questionable whether inquiry tests actually measure the ad's effectiveness or merely its ability to attract inquiries. Such inquiries, in fact, may not even reflect a sincere interest in the product or its purchase. Finally, since responses to a magazine offer may take months to receive, inquiry tests can be time-consuming.

Since the principal objective of most advertisers is increased sales, *sales tests* are logically popular. Unquestionably, sales tests can be a useful measure of advertising effectiveness when advertising is the dominant element, or the only variable, in the company's marketing plan.

However, heavy reliance on sales tests has definite pitfalls. It is often difficult to gauge to what extent advertising has been responsible for sales since many other variables usually affect sales volume (e.g., competitors' activities, the season of the year, and even the weather). Sales response to advertising is usually long range rather than immediate. Sales tests, and particularly field studies, are often costly and time-consuming. And, finally, most of them are useful only for testing complete campaigns, not individual advertisements or the components of an advertisement.

Summary

Marketing research is defined as the systematic gathering, recording, and analyzing of data to help managers make decisions relating to the marketing of goods and services. Marketing research is useful in identifying consumer needs, developing new products and communication strategies, and assessing the effectiveness of marketing programs and promotional activities.

In conducting research, there are several steps: first, to define the problem and set research objectives; second, to conduct exploratory research by analyzing internal data and collecting secondary data; then, to collect primary data. Primary research projects may involve observation, experiment, or survey and may be either quantitative or qualitative.

Quantitative research is used to accurately measure a particular market situation. Its success depends on the sampling methods used and the design of the survey questionnaire. The two sampling procedures used are random probability and nonprobability samples. Survey questions should have the attributes of focus, brevity, and simplicity.

Marketers use qualitative research to get a general impression of the market. The methods used in qualitative research may be projective or intensive techniques.

Advertising research is used to develop strategies and test concepts. Research results help the advertiser define the product concept, select the target market, and develop the primary advertising message elements.

Advertisers use testing to ensure that their advertising dollars are spent wisely. Pretesting is used to detect and eliminate weaknesses in a campaign. Posttesting is used to evaluate the effectiveness of an advertisement or campaign after it has run. Testing helps evaluate several variables, including markets, motives, messages, media, budgets, and schedules.

Many techniques are used in pretesting, including order-of-merit tests, paired comparison tests, portfolio tests, mock magazine tests, direct questioning, and perceptual meaning studies. To test broadcast advertisements, the most common methods are central location tests, trailer tests, theater tests, and live telecasts.

The most commonly used posttesting techniques are aided recall, unaided recall, attitude tests, inquiry tests, and sales tests. Each has opportunities and limitations.

Questions for Review and Discussion

1. If marketing research is so important to advertisers, why do so many succeed without using it?
2. What example can you think of that demonstrates the difference between marketing research and market research?
3. Do most advertisers prefer secondary or primary data? Why?
4. Have you ever used observational research personally? How?
5. Do people use quantitative or qualitative research to evaluate movies? Explain.
6. Which of the major surveying methods is the most costly? Why?
7. What example can you give of research that offers validity but not reliability?
8. What specific example can you think of where research could help in the development of advertising strategy?
9. How would the halo effect bias an effort to pretest a soft drink ad?
10. How would you design a controlled experiment to test the advertising for a chain of men's stores?

7

MARKETING AND ADVERTISING PLANNING

It was 1979, and Paul Fireman was walking up and down the aisles of the sporting goods and camping trade show—one of those annual events that attract manufacturers and retailers from all over the country to show what's new in the industry and to consummate orders for merchandise for the next season. From 500 to 1,000 different manufacturer-exhibitors were all looking for that major retail buyer or some new retailer or distributor ready to make a big order.

Paul Fireman's family had been in the camping and sporting goods business for some time, so he was knowledgeable about what might sell. He was looking for something new—and that day he found it. But he had no idea that what he found would make him, at $13 million, the second highest paid man in America just seven years later.[1]

What he found was a small, but old and established, British shoe manufacturing company that had originally been known as Joseph W. Foster & Sons Athletic Shoes. It had developed the first spiked track shoe around the turn of the century and early on had become one of the premier running-shoe manufacturers for Olympic athletes. In fact, members of the 1924 British track team highlighted in the film *Chariots of Fire* all wore Foster running shoes. But in recent years, the company had renamed itself after the graceful, fleet African antelope—the reebok (see Figure 7–1).

Paul Fireman had found something he thought he could sell. The shoes were attractive, functional, well designed, and well made, and the company had a long and reliable history. Not only that, they were anxious to enter the North American market, so Fireman worked out an agreement with them—they would supply the shoes he requested, and from a small office in suburban Boston, he would be the exclusive North American distributor for Reebok.

All he had to do was figure out how to market and advertise this attractive new product against the formidable competition that already was established in the branded sports-shoe business. He would have to find a way to do war with the big boys—Nike, Converse, Adidas, and others. This was no small task, but one that proves the importance of marketing and advertising planning, the subject of this chapter.

Marketing is war and the marketplace is the battlefield. (See Ad Lab 7-A.) The athletic footwear business is no exception. As Reebok was seeking a foothold in the marketplace in the early 1980s, total U.S. industry sales were already reaching the $1 billion mark. Nike was the dominant leader with around a 35 percent share of the market, followed by Adidas and Converse with about 10 percent each.[2] And these leaders were already starting to spend massive sums on advertising. How was Fireman's fledgling company possibly going to compete against this kind of strength?

He found a way. By 1986, Reebok had not only significantly penetrated the U.S. market but led it. It had amassed close to a billion dollars in annual sales (up from $300 million just the year before) and had reached a 31.2 percent share of the total market.[3] Not only that, Reebok shoes were so popular they were backordered for several months. Reebok was almost drowning in the honey of its success.

For our purposes, the Reebok story demonstrates that marketing and advertising success usually depends less on creativity and more on strategy. Good advertising strategy depends on careful marketing planning. This process of marketing and advertising planning is the means by which we can bring together the topics of the last three chapters: marketing and advertising research, consumer behavior, market segmentation, and the various elements of the marketing mix—including advertising.

THE MARKETING PLAN

What did Reebok do to successfully appeal to the sports-shoe market and carve out such a large share in so short a time? It didn't have nearly as much money to spend as either the soap or the soft drink companies—or even its primary competitors selling shoes.

Was it because of great advertising? Perhaps. But where did the ideas for the advertising come from? How did its agency decide what to write the ads about, where to run them, and what to say?

The answer lies in one word: *planning*.

Yet, as Richard Stansfield, author of *The Advertising Manager's Handbook,* has emphasized for many years, "More money is poured down the drain—absolutely wasted—on advertising that doesn't have a ghost of a chance of doing its assigned job because of a dismal lack of adequate planning than for any other reason."[4]

What is a marketing plan? And what is an advertising plan? What is the difference, and what is their relationship? Let's deal with the first question first so we can better understand the overall success of Reebok's campaign.

What Is a Marketing Plan?

Stansfield believes the written marketing plan is like a road map to the tourist. "It helps him find the right route and, once found, helps him stay on it." Inasmuch as marketing is the *only* source of income for a company (except possibly for investments), the marketing plan may be the most important document a company can possess.

(continued on p. 218)

FIGURE   7–1

Early on in this century, Joseph W. Foster & Sons Athletic Shoes earned its stripes in Great Britain as a maker of premier running shoes. Its later name change to Reebok was a natural attempt to capture the image of the African antelope's grace and speed. The company's first offerings in the United States were also, logically, its running shoes. But under Paul Fireman's direction, this would soon change.

The 1980s: An Era of Marketing Warfare

In Chapter 4, we focused on Jack Trout and Al Ries's idea of positioning, which is primarily an advertising concept.

In this chapter, we share Trout and Ries's latest advice, which is to approach the marketplace as though it were a battlefield. What follows is taken from their latest book, *Marketing Warfare*.

Much of the language of marketing has been borrowed from the military.

We launch a marketing campaign. Hopefully, a breakthrough campaign.

We divide people into divisions, companies, units. We report gains and losses. Sometimes we issue uniforms.

From time to time, we go into the field to inspect those uniforms and review the progress of the troops. We have been known to pull rank.

In short, we have borrowed so many things from the military that we might as well adopt the strategic principles of warfare that have guided military thinking for centuries.

On War

Our "textbook" for marketing warfare is the classic book on military strategy, *On War*.

Written in 1831 by a Prussian general, Carl von Clausewitz, the book outlines the principles behind all successful wars.

Two simple ideas dominate Clausewitz's thinking.

First is the principle of force. Says Clausewitz, "The greatest possible number of troops should be brought into action at the decisive point."

Clausewitz studied all of the military battles of recorded history and found the vast majority of the time, the larger force prevailed. "God," said Napoleon, "is on the side of the big battalions."

The second principle is related to the first. It's superiority of the defense.

Take Napoleon at Waterloo. Napoleon actually had a slight superiority in numbers, 74,000 men versus Wellington's 67,000.

But Wellington had the advantage of being on the defense. And, of course, the defense prevailed.

So this year we predict that Crest will be the largest selling toothpaste and McDonald's the largest fast-food company—regardless of what the competition does.

A well-established defensive position is extremely strong and very difficult to overcome.

The Strategic Square

So how do the principles of warfare apply to marketing? It all comes down to what we call a "strategic square":

Out of every 100 companies

One should play defense	Two should play offense
Three should flank	And 94 should be guerrillas

Look at this strategic square from the point of view of the U.S. automotive industry.

General Motors	Ford
Chrysler	American Motors

General Motors is the leader and gets more than half the business. Its primary concern ought to be defense.

Ford, on the other hand, is a strong number. It's the only automobile company in a position to mount offensive attacks against GM.

Chrysler is a distant third and should avoid direct attacks. Rather, it should try flanking moves: smaller, bigger, cheaper, more expensive, and so on.

What can you say about American Motors? Head for the hills and become a guerrilla. The company should find a market segment small enough to defend. For AMC, the broad area of, say, "small cars" would be too much. But the Jeep business is distinctive and important enough to protect and make the most of. AMC's claim to that portion of the market should be further extended to include other four-wheel-drive vehicles. [Note: After this was written, AMC was sold to Chrysler, which has maintained the Jeep brand.]

Offensive Warfare

Let's look more closely at each of the four types of marketing warfare starting with offensive warfare.

Colgate had a strong number-one position in toothpaste. But rival Procter & Gamble knew a thing or two about Carl von Clausewitz.

"Many assume that half efforts can be effective," said Clausewitz. "A small jump is easier than a large one, but no one wishing to cross a wide ditch would cross half of it first."

P&G launched Crest toothpaste not only with a massive

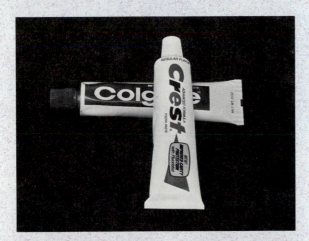

$20 million advertising budget but also with the American Dental Association "seal of approval."

Crest went over the top and is now the number one selling toothpaste in the country.

Overtaking the leader is not that common. Most companies are happy if they can establish a profitable number two position.

How can anybody topple Listerine, the king of halitosis hill?

With its "medicine breath" attacks on Listerine, Scope aimed straight for Listerine's weakest position. The campaign improved Scope's position and secured its long-term position.

But Listerine is still the leader, by a slim margin. A well-established defensive position is extremely strong and very difficult to overcome.

To sum up, here are the rules of the road in waging offensive marketing warfare:

1. The main consideration is the strength of the leader's position. No matter how strong a number two or three company is in a certain category or attribute, it cannot win if this also is where the leader is strong.
2. The attack should be launched on as narrow a front as possible. The "full line" of products is a luxury only for leaders. Offensive war should preferably be waged with single products.
3. The attack should be launched at the leader's weakest position.

Defensive Warfare

The battle of migraine mountain is an example of the advantages of quick response on the part of the leader.

Datril, as you might remember, opened up a war on Tylenol with a price attack.

Johnson & Johnson immediately cut Tylenol's price, even before Datril started its price advertising.

Result: It repelled the Datril attacks and inflicted heavy losses on the Bristol-Myers entry.

Here are the principles of defensive marketing warfare:

1. Defensive marketing warfare is a game only market leaders should play.
2. The best defense is a good offense. A leader should introduce new products and services before the competition does.
3. Strong competitive moves should always be "blocked." In a word, rapidly copy the competitive move. Too many companies "pooh-pooh" the competitor until it's too late.

Flanking Warfare

The third type of marketing warfare is where the action is for most companies.

Here's Clausewitz's suggestion: "Where absolute superiority is not attainable, you must produce a relative one at the decisive point by making skillful use of what you have."

In practice, this means attacking IBM where IBM is weak, not where it is strong—as Amadahl is doing successfully on the high end and Digital Equipment Corporation is doing successfully on the low end.

Orville Redenbacher is successfully flanking the popcorn market leader with a high-priced brand.

And who won the marketing battle between Cadillac and Lincoln Continental?

Answer: Mercedes.   *(continued)*

Here are the principles of flanking marketing warfare:

1. Good flanking moves must be made into uncontested areas. DEC introduced a small computer before IBM did.
2. Surprise ought to be an important element. Too much research will often snatch defeat from the jaws of victory by wasting time, the critical element in any successful flanking attack.
3. The pursuit is as critical as the attack itself. Too many companies quit after they're ahead.

Guerrilla Warfare

The fourth type of marketing warfare is guerrilla warfare. Most of America's companies should be waging guerrilla warfare.

The key attribute of successful guerrilla wars is flexibility. A guerrilla should not hesitate to abandon a given product or market if the tide of battle changes.

Here are the principles of guerrilla marketing warfare:

1. Find a market segment small enough to defend. It could be small geographically or in volume.
2. No matter how successful you become, never act like the leader.
3. Be prepared to "bug out" at a moment's notice. A company that runs away lives to fight another day.

Laboratory Applications

1. Think of a successful product and explain its success in terms of marketing warfare.
2. Select a product and explain how marketing warfare strategy might be used to gain greater success.

The marketing plan serves a number of very important functions. First, it assembles all the pertinent facts about the organization, the markets it serves, its products, services, customers, competition, and so on in one spot. It also brings all these facts up-to-date. Second, it forces all the functional managers within the company to work together—product development, production, selling, advertising, credit, transportation—to focus efficiently on the customer.[5] Third, it sets goals and objectives to be attained within specified periods of time and, finally, lays out the precise strategies and tactics that will be used to achieve them. Thus, it musters all the company's forces for the marketing battlefield (see Figure 7–2).

Effect of the Marketing Plan on Advertising

If it truly does all these things, the marketing plan should have a profound effect on the organization's advertising programs. For one thing, the marketing plan enables analysis, criticism, and improvement of all company operations including past marketing and advertising programs.

Second, it dictates the future role of advertising in the marketing mix. It determines those marketing activities that will require advertising support as well as those advertising programs that will need marketing support.

Finally, it provides focus and guidance to advertising creativity: it reduces the temptation to go off on tangents; it enables better implementation, control, and continuity of advertising programs; and it ensures the most efficient allocation of advertising dollars.[6]

In short, successful organizations do not separate advertising plans from marketing. They view each as a vital building block for success.[7]

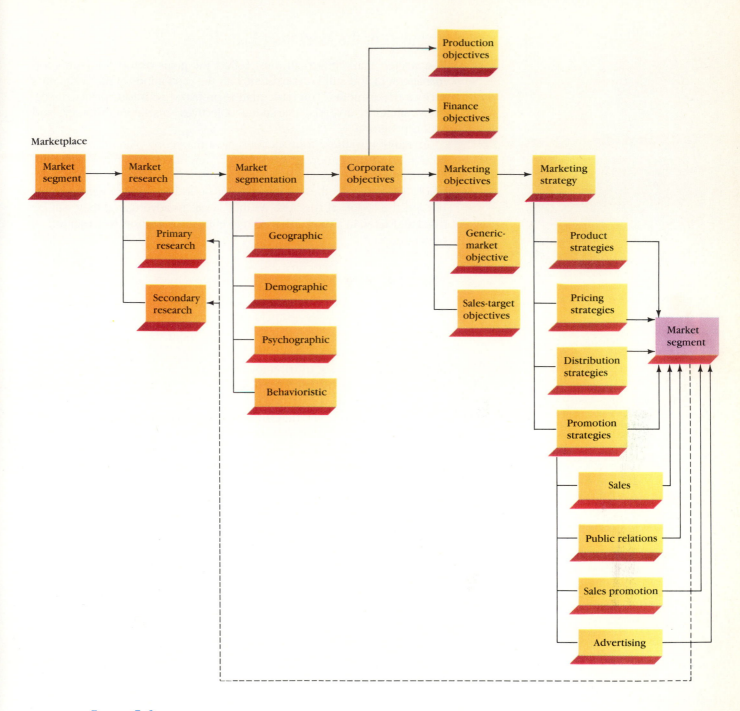

FIGURE   7–2

The marketing planning model. Marketing planning is a continuous process that begins and ends with the consumer. Research locates and measures the needs of various market groups. Potentially profitable segments are selected. Corporate objectives are set, and these lead to the determination of production, finance, and marketing objectives. To accomplish these objectives, various strategies are developed—all aimed at the targeted market segments. Finally, research evaluates the success or failure of the marketing plan and suggests modifications, and the process starts over again.

Elements of the Marketing Plan

The written marketing plan must reflect the goals of the company's top management and still be consistent with the capabilities of the company's various departments. The basic plan is prepared with four principal sections: situation analysis, marketing objectives, marketing strategy, and action programs.

In addition to these four sections, most marketing plans also include a section on measurement, control, and review, a section on resource allocation, and a summary at the beginning to briefly state the contents of the whole plan. Where these subjects relate purely to marketing, they are beyond the scope of this text. As they relate to advertising, they will be discussed later in the chapter. A marketing plan outline is presented in Appendix A.

Situation Analysis

The situation analysis section is usually the longest portion of the marketing plan. It is a statement of where the organization is today and how it got there. It should include all relevant facts about the company's history, growth, products or services, sales volume, share of market, competitive status, markets served, distribution system, past advertising programs, results of marketing research studies, company capabilities, strengths and weaknesses, and any other pertinent information.

The Checklist for Situation Analysis suggests some of the most important elements to be included. In addition, information should be gathered on key factors outside the company's immediate control. These might include the economic, political, social, technological, or commercial environment in which the company operates. Only when all this information is completely gathered, and its accuracy agreed upon, can management hope to plan for the future successfully.

What was Reebok's situation in 1980? The company was a new entry into the highly competitive and rapidly growing U.S. athletic shoe market. It had a quality product but no distribution, and nobody knew about it. Meanwhile, the American market was being dominated by Adidas, Nike, Converse, and others. These companies had capitalized on the running and tennis fads of the 1970s, and their development had been linked to technological innovations designed to improve functional performance and reduce the probability of injury. Reebok, too, had a good functional product for running and other sports. But it also offered something new— uniquely attractive styling with soft leather uppers and a variety of colors. As athletic footwear had become more comfortable, many consumers simultaneously felt the desire to "look" more athletic. This opened up the opportunity for manufacturers to focus on fashion trends. And that was the opening Paul Fireman would bank on.

Marketing Objectives

Once the situation analysis is completed, the company or organization can lay down specific marketing objectives to be attained within the time covered by the marketing plan. Even the U.S. Army, for example, determines specific marketing objectives for recruiting new soldiers every year.[8] These include numerical objectives for the regular army, the Army Reserve, and specific units within the army (such as the Nurse Corps), as well

Checklist for Situation Analysis

The Industry

☐ Companies in industry: dollar sales, strengths, and so forth.

☐ Growth patterns within industry: primary demand curve, per capita consumption, growth potential.

☐ History of industry: technological advances, trends, and so on.

☐ Characteristics of industry: distribution patterns, industry control, promotional activity, geographic characteristics, profit patterns, and so forth.

The Company

☐ The company story: history, size, growth, profitability, scope of business, competence in various areas, reputation, strengths, weaknesses, and so on.

The Product or Service

☐ The product story: development, quality, design, description, packaging, price structure, uses (primary, secondary, potential), reputation, strengths, and weaknesses.

☐ Product sales features: exclusive, nonexclusive differentiating qualities, product's competitive position in mind of consumer, and so forth.

☐ Product research: technological breakthroughs; improvements planned.

Sales History

☐ Sales and sales costs by product, model, sales districts, and so on.

☐ Profit history.

Share of Market

☐ Sales history industrywide: share of market in dollars and units.

☐ Market potential: industry trends, company trend, demand trends.

The Market

☐ Who and where is market, how has market been segmented in the past, how can it be segmented in future, what are consumer needs, attitudes, and characteristics? How, why, when, and where do consumers buy?

☐ Past advertising appeals that have proved successful or unsuccessful in speaking to consumer needs.

☐ Who are our customers, past customers, future customers? What characteristics do they have in common? What do they like about our product? What don't they like?

Distribution

☐ History and evaluation of how and where product is distributed, current trend.

☐ Company's relationship with members of the distribution channel and their attitudes toward product/company.

☐ Past policies regarding trade advertising, deals, co-op advertising programs, and so on.

☐ Status of trade literature, dealer promotions, point-of-purchase, displays, and so on.

Pricing Policies

☐ Price history: trends, relationship to needs of buyers, competitive price situation.

☐ Past price objectives: management attitudes, buyer attitudes, channel attitudes.

Competition

☐ Who is the competition? Primary, secondary, share of market, products, services, goals, attitudes. What is competition's growth history and size?

☐ Strengths of competition: sales features, product quality, size. Weaknesses of competition.

☐ Marketing activities of competition: advertising, promotion, distribution, sales force. Estimated budget.

Promotion

☐ Successes and failures of past promotion policy, sales force, advertising, publicity.

☐ Promotion expenditures: history, budget emphasis, relation to competition, trend.

☐ Advertising programs: review of strategies, themes, campaigns.

☐ Sales force: size, scope, ability, cost/sale.

as quality objectives based on the mental aptitude of enlistees (see Figure 7–3).

For a manufacturer or distributor introducing a new product like Reebok, though, marketing objectives might be expressed as follows:

1. Introduce the product to regional test markets and achieve a 10 percent share in those markets by the end of the first year.
2. Achieve national distribution to at least 40 states by the end of the second year.
3. Achieve a 10 percent share of the national market by the end of the third year.

Naturally, the marketing objectives that are set must take into consideration the amount of money the organization has to invest in marketing and production, its knowledge of the marketplace, and its analysis of the competitive environment.

Marketing objectives should be logical deductions from the review of the company's current situation, management's prediction of future trends, and its understanding of the hierarchy of company objectives.[9] For example, *corporate objectives* are usually stated in terms of profit or return on investment. Or they may be stated in terms of net worth, earnings ratios, growth, or corporate reputation. *Marketing objectives,* on the other hand, emanate from the corporate objectives but should relate (1) to the needs of specific target markets and (2) to specific sales objectives. These two types are referred to as, first, *generic-market objectives* and, second, *sales-target objectives.*[10]

The concept of a generic market is an attempt to shift management's view of the organization from a producer of products or services to a satisfier of market needs. For example, many people feel that one reason Penn Central Railroad went bankrupt was that it viewed itself as a railroad company rather than a provider of transportation. If it had adopted the latter view, it might have been able to diversify into other more profitable techniques for providing transportation for people or freight. The broader view allows management to consider additional options.

Today, many consumer product companies are good examples of this view. A soap company may now recognize that its basic product is cleaning, not soap. A cosmetic company's product is beauty, or hope, not lipstick. A publisher sells information, not just books.[11]

Sales-target objectives, on the other hand, should be specific, quantitative, and realistic. If Reebok simply stated that its marketing objective is to sell the most shoes possible, the objective would be nonspecific, unquantified, and unmeasurable. Rather, the objective should be stated in precise terms such as "attaining a 25.5 percent share of the market for men's basketball shoes and a 33.3 percent share of the women's casual sports-shoe market each year for the next three years." These objectives are specific as to product and market, quantified as to time and amount, and judging by the results, realistic.

Objectives may be expressed in a number of ways. For instance, many marketing organizations set objectives by the following criteria:

1. Total sales volume.
2. Sales volume by product, market segment, customer type.
3. Market share in total or by product line.
4. Growth rate of sales volume in total or by product line.
5. Gross profit in total or by product line.

FIGURE   7–3

The Army offers a wide range of job opportunities in a variety of fields to both men and women. This ad for the Nurse Corps was aimed at teachers as well as students and promoted the fact that nurses in the Army could go right into intensive care without the normal wait associated with civilian hospitals.

Other criteria for marketing objectives might relate to additions or deletions to the product line, creation of new distribution channels, development of new pricing policies, or retraining of field sales staff. Some firms today even include objectives relating to social responsibility, such as the preservation of natural resources, participation in community projects, and support of educational programs or institutions.[12]

As we will see in our discussion of the advertising plan later in this chapter, specific marketing objectives also have an important impact on the way advertising objectives are set. Only by setting specific objectives can management measure the degree of marketing and advertising success it is achieving.

Marketing Strategy

The third major section of the marketing plan is the statement of how the company is going to accomplish its marketing objectives. The *strategy* is the total directional thrust of the company, the "how to" of the marketing plan. For example, if you must travel from Boston to San Francisco, your objective is to get to San Francisco. Your strategy, then, might be to take the train, to take the plane, or to go around Cape Horn on a square-rigged schooner.

In marketing terms, the objectives are what you want to accomplish, while the strategy determines the methods.

People often confuse the terms *objectives* and *strategy*. This is understandable since, as Fred Posner, the director of marketing research for N. W. Ayer, points out, one person's strategy may be another person's objective: "The meaning will often depend on where you sit—whether you look at the marketing battlefield from a tank turret, a field command tent, or a computer console."[13]

The chairman of the board may have the objective of increasing the stock dividend. His strategies for accomplishing this may include increasing sales. To the marketing director, the chairman's strategy, increased sales, becomes an objective. He, in turn, may decide that to increase sales he will use advertising to persuade his current users to use the product more often. That then becomes the advertising agency's objective. The agency, in turn, concludes that its strategy is to make the product more appealing to its light users by defining more use occasions where the product is appropriate.

To be effective, a marketing strategy must stand the test of time. It must be an ingenious design for achieving a desired goal, and it must be result-oriented. The particular marketing strategy a company selects will have a dramatic impact on the advertising it uses. It will affect (1) the amount of advertising to be used, (2) the creative thrust of advertisements, and (3) the advertising media employed. In short, the marketing strategy will determine the objectives for advertising and provide the key to the advertising strategy.

Selecting the Target Market   The strategy a company chooses depends not only on the marketing objectives that have been set but also on the particular market being approached. The first step, therefore, is to select the *target market*. To some extent, this may already have been accomplished at the time corporate objectives were set. But through the process of market segmentation and research, management should define the target market very tightly within the scope of the broader market segment.

FIGURE 7-4

Nike targets a wide range of athletes but has been strongest with runners. The implied promise in this ad is very clever: the shoes will do the work if you just add the adrenalin.

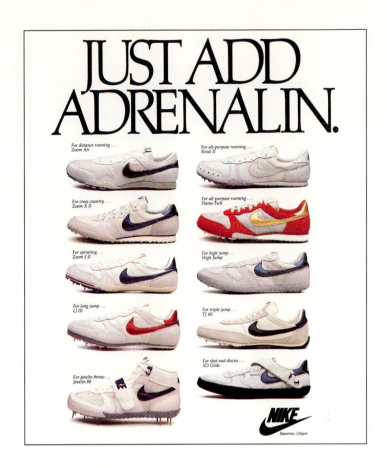

For instance, Paul Fireman knew that Reebok needed to market its products to the athletic footwear market. But within that segment were numerous other market segments: runners, tennis players, joggers, and so on. Converse, for example, was the strongest company targeting the basketball segment; Nike was strongest with runners (see Figure 7–4).

Reebok's first offerings were running shoes—its traditional business, but that is not where they achieved their great success. Fireman located an untapped segment—the aerobic fitness market. He also foresaw that there could be a dramatic shift toward fashion if one company offered something new and attractive in style and selection. Both of those segments were heavily female, and that's where Fireman saw the growth potential for Reebok shoes. He was right.

Determining the Marketing Mix. The second step in the development of the marketing strategy is to determine a cost-effective marketing mix for *each* target market the company pursues. The mix will consist of a blend of the four Ps: product, price, place, and promotion (see Chapter 4).

What was Reebok's marketing mix? First, they developed a line of attractive, new products to augment the company's traditional running-shoe line. These included comfortable but durable athletic shoes specifically designed for the rigors of aerobic exercise and a variety of fashionable, casual sport shoes with soft garment-leather uppers, available in a selection of pastel shades. Second, they decided on a premium pricing strategy that aimed at the higher end of the market. Next, they created a nationwide

distribution system, but only after several years of hard work and tenacity. Finally, they initiated a promotional program that included initial sampling to aerobics instructors, direct selling to dealers by Reebok's sales staff, and advertising in trade and consumer magazines (see Figure 7–5).

The variety of marketing strategies available leads to a wide variation in marketing mixes. For example, a company might decide to increase distribution, initiate new uses for a product, increase or change the product line, develop entirely new markets, or go into discount pricing. Each of these tends to emphasize one or more particular elements of the marketing mix, and their selection depends greatly on an understanding of the product's position in the market and its stage in the product life cycle.

Positioning Strategies / To determine the appropriate marketing mix, companies should first examine the wants of the market and the position of competitors and then decide on the competitive position they want to occupy in the target market.[14]

David Ogilvy has said the first decision in marketing and advertising is also the most important: *how to position your product*. To Ogilvy, positioning is defined as "what the product does and who it is for."[15] His agency (Ogilvy & Mather) developed the advertising for Lever Bros. product, Dove. As he points out, they could have positioned Dove as a detergent bar for men with dirty hands. But when Lever Bros. introduced Dove in 1957, they decided to position the new product as a complexion bar for women with dry skin, complete with a demonstration of the cleansing cream pouring into the bar. Dove maintained its position for 30 years, and the strategy never changed. Every commercial today still uses the same cleansing cream demonstration.

Companies usually have two choices in selecting a position. One is to pick a similar position next to a competitor and battle it out for the same customers ("Avis is only No. 2"). Another is to find a position not held by a competitor—a hole in the market—and quickly move to fill it, perhaps through product differentiation or market segmentation.

Or a company might elect to position itself through *price/quality differentiation*. It could offer a better-quality product at a higher price, like L'Oreal, and use the theme: "You deserve the best." Or it could advertise

FIGURE 7–5

Reebok targeted the aerobics market with both trade and consumer advertising. In fact, in this double-page consumer ad, the company even used an aerobics instructor as the model.

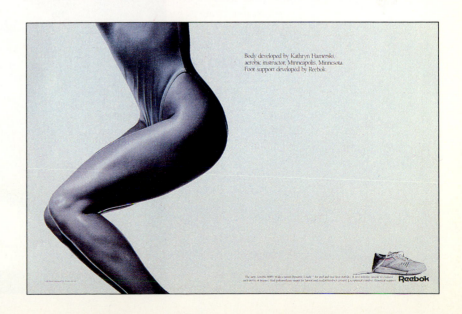

Body developed by Kathryn Hamerski, aerobic instructor, Minneapolis, Minnesota. Foot support developed by Reebok.

Reebok

the same quality at a lower price, like Suave, saying; "Why pay more for the same?"

What was Fireman's strategy for positioning Reebok? First, he positioned the company's existing, high-quality functional shoes as products designed specifically for the men and women committed to running, and he advertised them in the special-interest, runner magazines ("The Reebok tradition continues"). However, he believed that running shoes had already passed into the maturity stage of their product life cycle. And he wanted Reebok to be positioned in a growth stage. That's when he selected a new target market—active women interested in aerobics and in fashion—and developed new products to match their particular needs, promoting them first through aerobics instructors and only later through advertising. (See Figure 7–6.)

Since there are many variations of product differentiation strategies, price/quality strategies, positioning strategies, and segmentation strategies, finding the best strategy often requires exhaustive work. What is most important is for marketing and advertising managers to overcome the normal barriers to strategic thinking and to work together to generate a list of creative alternatives.[16] These must then be evaluated in terms of satisfying the needs of the marketplace, securing advantages over the competition, and creating company profits.

Action Programs

Once the overall marketing objectives and marketing strategy have been set, the company may determine what specific actions should be undertaken, by whom, and when regarding each element within the marketing mix. Some of these actions may be externally oriented, dealing with stan-

FIGURE   7–6

Reebok's trademarked slogan is a masterpiece of copywriting. What more needs to be said in this beautiful ad?

Because life is not a spectator sport. Reebok

dard marketing communication and distribution issues. Others, though, may be internally oriented, dealing with the effective use of technology, capital, and human resources.[17]

The *objectives* of a company indicate where it wants to go; the *strategy* indicates the general method and the intended route; and the *tactics* (or action programs) determine the details of those methods and routes.

In the case of a manufacturer of men's shirts, for example, a strategy might be to produce only the highest quality designer products, charge a premium price, sell only through better department stores, and rely heavily on advertising to promote the line. The action programs might then be to develop a fashionable shirt that will give two years of normal wear, be available at Bullocks and Macy's, sell for $33.95, and be supported by a $1.5 million advertising budget divided equally between retailer co-op newspaper ads and national men's magazines.[18]

It is in this world of action programs that advertising campaigns live. In the next section, therefore, we will discuss the process used for planning advertising.

THE ADVERTISING PLAN

Advertising is a natural outgrowth of the marketing plan. In fact, a company's communications or advertising plan is prepared in much the same way as the marketing plan. The company follows the same process of performing analysis, setting objectives, and determining strategy. From the strategy, specific tactics or advertising programs are conceived and created. An advertising plan outline is presented in Appendix B.

Review of the Marketing Plan

The advertising manager's first task is to review the marketing plan. It is important to understand where the company is going, how it intends to get there, and the role advertising will play in the marketing mix. Therefore, the first section of the advertising plan is a premises or situation analysis section. This briefly restates the company's current situation, target markets, long- and short-term marketing objectives, and decisions regarding market positioning and the marketing mix.

Setting Advertising Objectives

Once the organization's marketing objectives and strategies have been set, the advertising manager can determine the specific tasks assigned to advertising. Unfortunately, though, some corporate executives have little idea of the specific tasks or objectives of their advertising programs. They describe the purpose of advertising with vague expressions such as "keeping our name out in front" or "giving ammunition to the sales force."

This ignorance may be largely the fault of advertising managers themselves, who tend to state misty, generalized goals like "creating a favorable impression of the product in the marketplace in order to increase sales and maximize profits." Such wishy-washy gobbledygook serves the manager by protecting the program from ever being measured for effectiveness. However, it also reinforces the negative attitude shared by many executives about the large amount of money "wasted" on advertising.

FIGURE   7–7

Direct-action advertising is being used more and more to assist the fund-raising efforts of charities, political causes, and other nonprofit organizations. Here is an unusually effective appeal to get viewers to immediately pick up the telephone to pledge a donation to rebuild Casa Myrna Vasquez in Boston.

SFX: *Heavy footsteps coming upstairs/pounding/yelling (under—getting closer)*

MOTHER: C'mon—*hurry!* Where's your shirt?

SFX: *Footsteps/pounding/yelling*

VO: When you are tired of the beatings and fear.

CHILD: Momma?

MOTHER: Your shoes . . .

VO: When you have children . . . no job . . . and no money.

SFX: *(Footsteps/pounding at door)* Where do you go?

MOTHER: Hurry—get your coat, go on . . . there's not much time.

SFX: *Pounding—are coming through door*

VO: White, black, Hispanic, many battered women and their children lived at a place called Casa Myrna . . . *(fireman breaks through door)* until it burned down. Give to Casa Myrna—a home for battered women that's taken a beating of its own.

Understanding What Advertising Can Do

Advertising objectives should be defined specifically, but doing so requires a clear understanding of what advertising can do. Most advertising programs, of course, hope to eventually cause some action on the part of the prospective customers. *Direct-action advertising,* for example, attempts to induce the prospective customer to act immediately. This usually means mailing a coupon or dialing a phone number to order the product from the manufacturer (see Figure 7–7).

However, only a very small percentage of those exposed to particular advertisements are expected to act right away. Usually, a number of very important steps must be accomplished before customers can be persuaded to buy. *Delayed-action advertising,* therefore, seeks to inform, persuade, or remind its intended audience over an extended time about the company, product, service, or issue being advertised. This is the type of advertising generally used by retailers, manufacturers, banks, insurance companies, services, and associations.

The Advertising Pyramid

A simple way to understand the tasks advertising can perform is to think of advertising as building a pyramid. Before a new product is introduced, prospective customers live in a desert of unawareness, totally oblivious to the product's existence. The first task for advertising, therefore, is to lay the foundation of the pyramid by acquainting some portion of those unaware people with the product or service.

The next task, or level of the pyramid, is to increase comprehension—to communicate enough information so that some percentage of that foundation group is not only aware of the product but also recognizes its purpose and perhaps some of its features.

Next, advertising needs to communicate enough information about the product and its features to persuade a certain number of people to actually believe in its value. This is called the conviction block. Of those who become convinced, some can be moved to the next block of people who actually desire the product. And finally, after all the preceding steps have been accomplished, a certain percentage of those who desire the product will reach the top of the pyramid, the action block, and actually go out and purchase the product (see Figure 7–8).

At this point, it's important to understand that our pyramid is not static. The advertiser is actually working in three dimensions: time, dollars, and people. Advertising takes time to get up speed, especially for products that are not purchased regularly.[19] Over an extended time, as more and more dollars are spent on advertising, the number of people who become aware of the product increases. Likewise, more people comprehend the product, believe in it, desire it, and make the final action of purchasing it.

The objectives of delayed-action advertising, therefore, will change. At first, the greatest effort might be simply to create awareness of the product. Later, efforts might be focused on creating interest and desire or stimulating action.

Ideally, advertising objectives should be specified to time and degree in such a way that success can be measured by research studies and tests.[20] For example, a soap manufacturer might list the following advertising objective: "Among the 30 million housewives who own automatic washers, increase—from 10 percent to 40 percent in one year—the number who

FIGURE   7–8

The advertising pyramid.

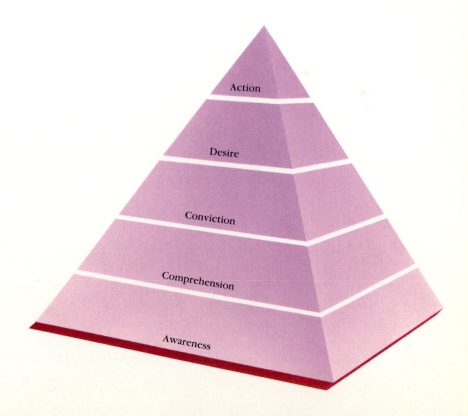

identify brand X as a low-sudsing detergent and the number who think it gets clothes cleaner.''

As we shall point out in a few moments, this theoretical approach has some problems. However, for our purposes in understanding the nature of advertising communication and the importance of trying to make advertising accountable, let's apply this principle to the development of objectives at each stage of the advertising pyramid for Reebok.

Specific advertising objectives for the first-year introduction of Reebok's new fitness shoe line might read as follows:

1. Communicate within the first year the existence and availability of Reebok's fashionable fitness shoes to 20 percent of the 20 million annual consumers of women's casual athletic footwear between the ages of 15 and 49 who spend an average of $45 on each pair of shoes.
2. Inform 50 percent of this "aware" group that Reebok footwear is a high-quality, premium-priced line, that it offers soft garment-leather uppers, comes in a variety of colors, and is available from select retailers.
3. Convince 50 percent of the "informed" group that Reeboks are very high quality, comfortable, stylish, and worth the price.
4. Stimulate the desire within 50 percent of the "convinced" group to try on a pair of Reebok fitness shoes.
5. Motivate 50 percent of the "desire" group to actually go to their local shoe retailer and test a pair of Reeboks.

PEOPLE IN ADVERTISING

Thomas J. Burrell

Chairman
Burrell Communications Group

McDonald's Corporation, Coca-Cola, Ford Motor Company, and Procter & Gamble are just a few of the many clients handled by Burrell Advertising, the largest American agency specializing in the growing black target market.

Beginning his career in 1960 in the mail room at Wade Advertising (now defunct), Burrell soon became a copy trainee and then a full copywriter on the Alka Seltzer account. He moved on to Leo Burnett/Chicago in 1964; worked in London for Foote, Cone & Belding; then returned to Needham Harper & Steers in 1968 as a copy supervisor. But as time went on, he became increasingly frustrated by what he viewed as the limitations of only being an employee.

In 1971, he left to open up his own shop, but he didn't get his first piece of business for six months. The breakthrough came in 1972 when he convinced McDonald's Corporation that his agency could help the company increase its share of the black market. Since that time, Burrell has created more than 100 commercials and ads for McDonald's which remains its biggest and oldest client. Many of those ads have also been major award winners.

In 1973, Coca-Cola came on board, and over the years, Burrell has created a string of highly memorable, award-winning commercials that have contributed to Coke's suc-

It's important to note here that these advertising objectives are both specific as to time and degree and quantified like marketing objectives. That means that, theoretically, at the end of the first year, a consumer attitude study could be performed to determine how many people are *aware* of the Reebok shoes; how many people *know* what Reebok makes; how many people *understand* the primary features of Reebok's new footwear; and so on. If these results can be measured statistically, so can the effectiveness of the advertising program.

If Reebok's hypothetical advertising objectives are all achieved, and if we assume that all those who try the shoes buy them, Reebok would gain approximately a 1.25 percent share of the targeted women's casual footwear market (or $11.25 million in sales) by the end of year one.

The second-year objectives might be to increase the percentage of women who are aware of the product, perhaps to 35 percent. Then greater emphasis could be placed on persuading more of them to believe in the product and eventually to try it.

In some cases, this process can be accelerated by using certain sales promotion devices, such as heavy sampling of a product, to convert people from being totally unaware one day to being users of the product the next. This is extremely expensive. Still, as we shall see in Chapter 16, many manufacturers use couponing and other sales promotion tools to speed up the results of their advertising.

cess with the black market. When the "Coke is it!" campaign was introduced, for example, Burrell created a high-energy production number featuring the Grambling College marching band. It not only tested well in recall measurements, it was also warmly received by Coke bottlers around the country and eventually ended up as a network commercial.

As Burrell's client roster filled out to include Johnson Products, Brown-Forman Distillers, L'eggs hosiery, the U.S. Navy, Procter & Gamble, Ford, and others, the agency grew in stature as well as billings. In 1987, Burrell Advertising billed over $60 million and was one of the 20 largest agencies based in Chicago.

The hallmark of Burrell's advertising has been the portrayal of black people in realistic settings—showing them as they really are. He calls it positive realism. Previously, he says, advertising portrayed blacks in stereotypical situations—the black maid on the one hand or, on the other, the successful businessman in a white world. "In the middle of those extremes," says Burrell, "are millions of black consumers—real people—dying to see themselves portrayed as they really are."

The other characteristic of Burrell's work, according to industry observers, is, simply, great advertising, especially in the sense of triggering human emotions and translating them into sales for his client's products. According to the chief marketing officer at McDonald's, "Burrell creates advertising that speaks directly to the black market but also can be enjoyed by everyone."

Representative of this is the famous "Double Dutch" ad for McDonald's featuring inner-city children playing jump rope. Another involves a matriarchal family reunion in which the mother's joy in the gathering is only dampened by occasional glances at a photograph of the son who is not there. When he arrives unexpectedly, the joy and the pathos of their tearful embrace concludes a highly emotional spot.

And as Burrell says, "The heartstring is attached to the purse string."

A past chairman of the Chicago Council of the American Association of Advertising Agencies, Tom Burrell has also served on the National Advertising Review Board and on the 4As committees on Agency Management and Government Relations. In 1985, he was honored by the Chicago advertising community as Advertising Person of the Year with their coveted Albert Lasker Award for lifetime achievement in advertising.

Repurchase

Repurchase

Repurchase

Action to
purchase

Desire

Conviction

Comprehension

Awareness

FIGURE   7–9

The advertising pyramids. As more
and more advertising impressions
are made, and as more and more
people purchase and repurchase the
product, new blocks of ever-expand-
ing numbers of customers may be
built on top of the original pyramid.

Satisfied Customers Invert the Pyramid

Once a certain percentage of people have actually made the purchase
decision, a new advertising objective may be introduced: to stimulate
reuse of the product. As more and more people make the purchase and
repurchase decision, our pyramid model will change. A new inverted pyramid will be built on top of the old one to represent the growing number of
people who have joined the action block and developed the repurchasing
habit (see Figure 7–9).

The inverted pyramid is actually built by customer satisfaction and good
word of mouth. The greater the satisfaction and the more people told
about the product, the faster the inverted pyramid will expand. At this
point, *reinforcement advertising* is often used to remind people of their
successful experience with the product and to suggest reuse.

The problem with these models and theories in real life is that they tend
to oversimplify the complex phenomena of consumer behavior: how communication takes place, how learning is achieved, how needs and desires
are stimulated, and how consumer purchasing actually happens. They pay
little or no attention to the dynamics of changing consumer tastes and
preferences, to the nature of different classes of products with different
life cycles, to the activities of competitors, or to the fact that people can
come into and leave the market continuously at various levels of the
pyramid due to any of innumerable internal and external stimuli besides
advertising.

The hypothetical pyramid model, though, does give us a simple way of
looking at the long-term building and reinforcing effects of media advertising. It also helps us realize that, as we find consumers at various levels of

the pyramid, our communication needs, the objectives we can achieve, and our strategies for achieving them all change. For new products, building awareness will probably be our primary objective. For well-known, established products, we will want to focus on building appeal. For well-known and well-liked products facing stiff competitive activity, we may want to promote additional use with ads that stress action. (See the Checklist for Developing Advertising Objectives.)

Advertising Strategy and the Creative Mix

In our discussion of marketing planning, we learned that the marketing objective is what the company wants to achieve, whereas the marketing strategy indicates how it is going to accomplish it. Similarly, the advertising or communications objective tells us where we want to be with respect to consumer awareness, attitude, and preference, whereas the advertising or creative strategy tells us how we are going to get there.

Marketing strategy refers to the way the marketing mix (product, price, place, promotion) is blended. Promotional strategy (see Chapter 4) refers to the way the promotional mix (personal selling, advertising, public relations, sales promotion, and collateral) is used. Similarly, advertising strategy is determined by the *creative mix*, which is composed of those advertising elements the company controls to achieve its advertising objectives. These elements include:

1. The target audience.
2. The product concept.
3. The communications media.
4. The advertising message.

The Target Audience

The *target audience* refers to the specific people the advertising is intended to address. In the marketing plan for Reebok, one of the target markets was described as young women 17 to 34 years old in the upper income categories involved in organized aerobics classes. In the advertising plan, however, the target audience differed slightly from the target market. The intended audience also included aerobics instructors, who, as opinion leaders, are important in the decision-making process. The company also targeted the women involved in running and that larger group of women who just wanted the "sports-shoe look" for casual or fashion purposes.

When determining the target audience, it is important to consider not only who the end user is but also who makes the purchasing decision and who influences the purchasing decision. Children, for example, may exert a strong influence on where the family decides to eat. So McDonald's includes children as a target audience and concentrates much of its advertising spending on campaigns directed to them.

The Product Concept

The "bundle of values" that the product represents to the consumer is the *product concept*. As we discussed in Chapter 4, the Dodge Daytona and the Honda Civic are medium-priced automobiles aimed at the American small-car market. However, the product concepts differ. One is conceived as a well-built, fast, fun, turbo sports car, whereas the other is conceived as sophisticated simplicity, practical, and easy to own.

When writing the advertising plan, the advertising manager should develop a simple statement to describe the product concept—that is, how the advertising will present the product. To create this statement, the advertiser must consider the company's marketing strategy as it relates to the product. How is the product positioned in the market? How is the product differentiated from the competition? Is price/quality differentiation used?

 ## Checklist for Developing Advertising Objectives

Does the advertising aim at closing an *immediate sale?* If so, the objectives might be to:

☐ Perform the complete selling function (take the product through all the necessary steps toward a sale).

☐ Close sales to prospects already partly sold through past advertising efforts ("Ask for the order" or "clincher" advertising).

☐ Announce a special reason for "buying now" (price, premium, and so forth).

☐ Remind people to buy.

☐ Tie in with some special buying event.

☐ Stimulate impulse sales.

Does the advertising aim at *near-term* sales by moving the prospect, step-by-step, closer to a sale (so that when confronted with a buying situation the customer will ask for, reach for, or accept the advertised brand)? If so, the objectives might be to:

☐ Create awareness of existence of product or brand.

☐ Create "brand image" or favorable emotional disposition toward the brand.

☐ Implant information or attitude regarding benefits and superior features of brand.

☐ Combat or offset competitive claims.

☐ Correct false impressions, misinformation, and other obstacles to sales.

☐ Build familiarity and easy recognition of package or trademark.

Does the advertising aim at building a "long-range consumer franchise"? If so, the objectives might be to:

☐ Build confidence in company and brand which is expected to pay off in years to come.

☐ Build customer demand, which places company in stronger position in relation to its distribution (not at the "mercy of the marketplace").

☐ Place advertiser in position to select preferred distributors and dealers.

☐ Secure universal distribution.

☐ Establish a "reputation platform" for launching new brands or product lines.

☐ Establish brand recognition and acceptance, which will enable the company to open up new markets (geographic, price, age, gender).

Specifically, how can advertising contribute toward increased sales? Among objectives would be to:

☐ Hold present customers against the inroads of competition.

☐ Convert competitive users to advertiser's brand.

☐ Cause people to specify advertiser's brand instead of asking for product by generic name.

☐ Convert nonusers of the product type to users of product and brand.

☐ Make steady customers out of occasional or sporadic customers.

☐ Advertise new uses of the product.

In what stage of the life cycle is the product? How is the product classified, packaged, branded? All these influence the product concept.

What was the product concept for Reebok? Functionally, the Reebok shoe boasted certain high-performance construction features such as its trademarked Foster Heel Cradle, its cooling mesh toe, and its water-repellent Gore-Tex inner liner. Conceptually, though, it was the modern representative of a tradition of excellence, a fashionable shoe for "men who know how to sweat" and serious women who believe "life is not a spectator sport."

☐ Persuade customers to buy larger sizes or multiple units.

☐ Remind users to buy.

☐ Encourage greater frequency or quantity of use.

Does the advertising aim at some specific step that leads to a sale? If so, objectives might be to:

☐ Persuade prospect to write for descriptive literature, return a coupon, enter a contest.

☐ Persuade prospect to visit a showroom, ask for a demonstration.

☐ Induce prospect to sample the product (trial offer).

How important are "supplementary benefits" of end-use advertising? Among objectives would be to:

☐ Aid salespeople in opening new accounts.

☐ Aid salespeople in getting larger orders from wholesalers and retailers.

☐ Aid salespeople in getting preferred display space.

☐ Give salespeople an entree.

☐ Build morale of company sales force.

☐ Impress the trade (causing recommendation to their customers and favorable treatment to salespeople).

Is it a task of advertising to impart information needed to consummate sales and build customer satisfaction? If so, objectives may be designed to use:

☐ "Where to buy it" advertising.

☐ "How to use it" advertising.

☐ New models, features, package.

☐ New prices.

☐ Special terms, trade-in offers, and so forth.

☐ New policies (such as guarantees).

To what extent does the advertising aim at building confidence and good will for the corporation among various groups? Targets may include:

☐ Customers and potential customers.

☐ The trade (distributors, dealers, retail people).

☐ Employees and potential employees.

☐ The financial community.

☐ The public at large.

Specifically, what kind of images does the company wish to build?

☐ Product quality, dependability.

☐ Service.

☐ Family resemblance of diversified products.

☐ Corporate citizenship.

☐ Growth, progressiveness, technical leadership.

The product concept can be developed in many ways. To assist its people in this process, Foote, Cone & Belding developed the FCB Grid (see Figure 7–10). This depicts the *degree* and the *kind* of *involvement* the consumer brings to the purchase decision for different products. Some purchases, like automobiles, require a great deal of involvement. Others, like soap, require little. The kind of involvement may range from very rational (thinking) at one extreme to very emotional or symbolic (feeling) at the other. By analyzing this information, the agency can hone its creative strategy and get to the idea stage more quickly.[21] (For more information on this subject, see the supplemental TextPLUS case study on Sunkist Growers associated with Chapter 7.)

The Communications Media

In the creative strategy, the *communications media* refer to the various methods or vehicles that will be used to transmit the advertiser's message. These may include traditional media such as radio, television, newspapers, magazines, or billboards. However, they may also include direct mail, publicity, and certain sales promotion techniques such as sample packs or coupons or events such as trade shows.

When Paul Fireman first started out, he didn't have the budget to compete with the big spenders in the traditional media. However, he knew he had to create awareness of his product. Because his target audience was so broad, Fireman had to design an artful mix of media vehicles with broad and narrow coverage. Placing small space ads (quarter pages) in the running magazines allowed a certain measure of consistency, while trade show exhibits and free samples to aerobics instructors zeroed in on the exercise market. Only later, after initial sales penetration, was he able to

FIGURE   7–10

The FCB grid. Foote, Cone & Belding uses the grid to classify products and brands based on (1) whether people tend to base their purchase decisions on reason or emotion, and (2) whether the item is a relatively important purchase or an unimportant one.

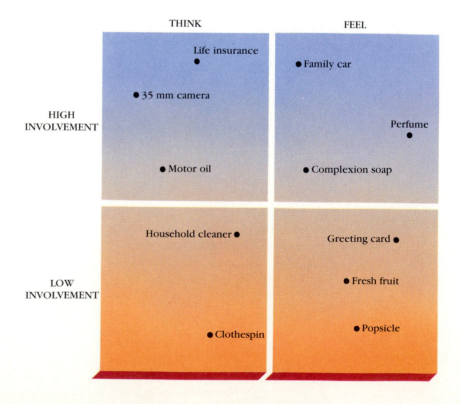

He made it up here in a pair of Reeboks.

It takes more than a chairlift to get to the top of La Clusaz.

You've got to run five miles a day. Do a few hundred leg lifts. And for good measure, spend a couple of hours sweating on the court of your choice.

Which means you need a pair of shoes that can carry you from a bench press to a hip sled. With a quick stop at the track in between.

A pair of shoes designed specifically for sports conditioning. A pair of Reebok Pro Workout shoes.

Their Lateral/Medial Support Straps keep your foot secure through three sets of lunges, four sets of calf raises, and five sets of wind sprints.

And when you find yourself standing under a squat rack with two hundred and fifty pounds balanced on your shoulders, you'll appreciate the support our dual density midsole offers.

So whether you're working on strength, flexibility, or endurance, our shoes let you be tougher on yourself when you're on your feet. And easier on yourself when you're not.

Reebok
Pro Workout

FIGURE   7–11

With success, Reebok has been able to step up from small, quarter-page ads to full-page and multiple-page ads for its rapidly expanding line of athletic shoes and, now, even apparel.

afford the full-page and multiple-page ads the company currently uses (see Figure 7–11).

Media considerations will be discussed more fully in Chapter 12. It's important to understand here, though, that the media to be used are determined by considering audience or readership statistics, potential communications effectiveness, relevance to the rest of the creative mix, and cost at the time the advertising plan is developed.

The Advertising Message

What the company plans to say in its advertisements and how it plans to say it—verbally and nonverbally—is the *advertising message.* Reebok wanted the message to center on technical superiority, safety, comfort, and looks. The copy in early ads focused on "performance" and the company's history of race winning. The Reebok logo was the British flag—again merchandising the company's proud heritage. And illustrations showed runners crossing the finish line, presumably first. Inset photos showed the shoes, large and in detail. Later ads placed more emphasis on style, mood, and feeling—the visuals of athletes were illustrations in muted tones rather than photos, and the shoes were shown in sharper detail through photography. The tag line was: "Because life is not a spectator sport."

In a nutshell, the combination of these copy, art, and production elements make up the message strategy in advertising. There is an infinite number of ways to combine these elements, and the most creative of these define the state of the art of contemporary advertising. (See Ad Lab 7-B.)

AD LAB 7-B   Creative Use of the Creative Mix

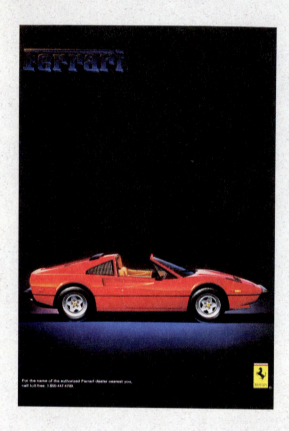

(John Cleese, dressed as a corporate exec, is struggling to carry his bulky computer home for the night.)

VO: You're taking your computer home.

CLEESE: Yes, Mr. Prince wants my report in the morning.

VO: You know, Compaq Plus is portable.

CLEESE: Portable? Yes, but Mr. Prince says big computers do more.

VO: Compaq Plus does everything yours does and more.

CLEESE: Yes, but Mr. Prince says big computers store more.

VO: Compaq Plus stores 30 times more than yours.

CLEESE: Does it have a handle?

VO: Yes.

(Cleese "accidently" drops his computer.)

CLEESE: Oh, drat!

VO: Compaq Plus. It simply works better.

CLEESE: Mr. Prince, something terrible has happened!

Laboratory Application

Describe which elements of the creative mix are being emphasized in these advertisements.

The advertising plan lays out the general direction of the campaign for the allotted time period. Then when it comes to creating the individual advertisements or commercials, a similar process is repeated. The same questions are asked: What is the overall objective of the campaign? What is the overall strategy? What is the specific objective of this ad? What is the best way to do it? Who are we talking to? What media are we going to use? What do we want to say? How do we want to say it? Answering those questions will be the objective of the next two units of this text: "Advertising Creativity" and "Advertising Media."

ALLOCATING FUNDS FOR ADVERTISING

In the late 1970s, the country experienced the first throes of the energy shortage. Motorists lined up for blocks, sometimes miles, to buy gasoline at the one open station in town. Plastics were in short supply. In fact, virtually everything made from petroleum or petrochemicals was back-ordered, and prices for energy-related items skyrocketed. Companies called their suppliers, begging for products.

With demand for their products outstripping inventory, many executives marched into their company advertising departments and ordered the immediate cancellation of all ads. Many cut advertising budgets to zero.

But as little as 12 months later, these same executives were behind their desks worrying about why sales were down. And the stockholders were wondering how their companies had just lost several percentage points in market share.

The fact is, money is the motor that drives every marketing and advertising plan. If you suddenly shut the motor off, it may coast for a while, but before long, it stops running. No advertising or marketing plan is complete, therefore, without a discussion of what the program is going to cost and how the money is going to be spent. The advertising department has to convince management that the suggested level of expenditure makes good business sense.

An Investment in Future Sales

Accountants and Internal Revenue Service agents consider advertising a current business expense. Consequently, many executives treat advertising as a budget item that can be trimmed or eliminated like other expense items when sales are either extremely high or extremely low. Although this is certainly understandable, it is also regrettable.

The cost of a new plant or distribution warehouse is considered an investment in the company's future ability to produce and distribute products. Similarly, advertising, as one element of the promotion mix, should be considered an investment in future sales. While advertising is often used to stimulate immediate sales, its greatest power is in its cumulative long-range effect.

Advertising builds a consumer preference and promotes goodwill. This, in turn, enhances the reputation and value of the company name. At first, advertising may move a person to buy a new kind of potato chip, but it also affects that person's next purchase of potato chips, and the one after that, and the one after that. This same advertising may also influence the consumer to try the firm's other snacks.

Thus, while advertising may be looked upon as a current expense for accounting purposes, it can also be considered a long-term capital investment. For management to consider advertising as an investment, however, it must have some understanding of the relationship between advertising and sales and profits.

Relationship of Advertising to Sales and Profits

As we have shown in the last four chapters, many internal and external variables influence a company's marketing and advertising efforts. Therefore, the research methodology that has been developed to measure the relationships between advertising and sales, as well as the relationships between sales and profit, is far from perfect and can give only rough estimates. However, enough data are available to verify certain facts:

1. Increases in market share are more directly related to increases in the marketing budget than to price reductions.[22]
2. Sales will increase if there is additional advertising. At some point, however, the rate of return will decline. (See Ad Lab 7-C.)

AD LAB 7-C   How Economists View the Effect of Advertising on Sales

Normally, the quantity sold will depend on the number of dollars the company spends advertising the product. And within reasonable limits (if its advertising program is not too repugnant), the more dollars spent on advertising, the more a company will sell—up to a point. Yet, even the most enthusiastic advertising agency will admit, reluctantly, that it is possible to spend too much on advertising.

To decide rationally how much to spend on this part of its marketing effort, management obviously should know just how quantity demanded is affected by advertising expenditure—how much more it will be able to sell per additional dollar of advertising and when additional advertising dollars cease being effective. It needs to have, not a fixed number representing potential demand, but a graph or a statistical equation describing the relationship between sales and advertising.

Notice that in our illustration most of the curve goes uphill as we move to the right (it has a positive slope). This means that additional advertising will continue to bring in business until (at a budget of x million dollars) people become so saturated by the message that it begins to repel them and turn them away from the product.

Even if the saturation level cannot be reached within the range of outlays the firm can afford, the curve is likely to level off, becoming flatter and flatter as the amount spent on advertising gets larger and larger and saturation is approached. The point at which the curve begins to flatten is the point at which returns from advertising begin to diminish. When the total advertising budget is small, even a

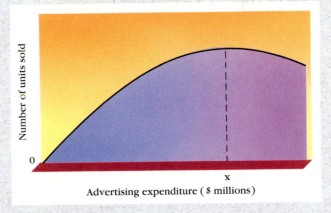

Advertising expenditure ($ millions)

$1 addition to the campaign may bring in as much as $10 in new sales and so be very much worthwhile to the firm. But when the market approaches saturation, each additional dollar may contribute only 30 cents in new sales, and that is not sound business.

Laboratory Applications

1. Can you give an example of when the advertising expenditure curve would have a negative slope?
2. Economists suggest that the quantity sold depends on the number of dollars the company spends on advertising. Is that a safe assumption? Discuss.

3. Sales response to advertising is spread out over a long period of time.
4. There are minimum levels below which advertising expenditures will have no effect on sales.
5. There will be some sales even if there is no advertising.
6. There are saturation limits imposed by culture and competition above which no amount of advertising can push sales.

To management, these facts, verified by numerous studies, might be interpreted into simple advice on how to allocate funds for advertising: spend more until it stops working. But in reality, the issue is not that simple. It is actually full of complexities. For instance, advertising is not the only marketing activity that affects sales. Increased sales may be due to the opening of more attractive outlets, to a better job of personal selling, or to seasonal changes in the general business cycle.

Furthermore, most companies do not have a clear-cut way to determine the relationship between sales and profit. What if the company sells many products? Then we have the problem of determining which advertising is contributing to which product.

One thing remains clear. Since the response to advertising is spread out over such an extended time, advertising should be viewed as a long-term investment in the company's future profits. Naturally, like all expenditures, advertising should be evaluated for wastefulness. But historically, companies that make advertising the scapegoat during periods of economic fluctuation invariably end up losing substantial market share when the economy returns to stable growth.

The Variable Environments of Business

Every business operates in several environments simultaneously, and the way the company relates to these environments may determine its success or failure. Before attempting to determine the advertising allocation, therefore, the advertising manager must consider the status of the economic, political, social, and legal environment. The level of general economic activity, social customs and attitudes, and the structure of tax rates all affect both total industry sales and corporate profits on sales.

The manager must consider the institutional and the competitive environment. What is the level of sales within the industry? The company can expect only a share of the total market demand. What activities of competitors might either help or hinder the company from making sales and achieving profits?

Finally, the manager should consider the internal environment. The activities of the company itself in relation to its competitors and its markets will have a bearing on the effectiveness of advertising expenditures.[23]

A thorough reappraisal of these factors at the time the advertising allocation is determined may have a profound effect on how much the company feels it can or should allocate and on what particular activities it should spend.

Methods of Allocating Funds

The typical attitude of business executives toward the advertising budget is relatively simple to understand. They will spend more money as long as they can be assured it will bring in a profit. If it takes a dollar in advertising to produce one more penny of profit, it is worth the expense. However,

Checklist of Ways to Set Advertising Budgets

☐ Percentage of sales. Advertising budget determined by allocating a percentage of last year's sales, anticipated sales for next year, or a combination of the two. The percentage is usually based on an industry average, on company experience, or else arbitrarily.

☐ Percentage of profit. Similar to percentage of sales except that percentage is applied to profit—either past years' or anticipated.

☐ Unit of sale. Also called the case-rate method, this is another variation of percentage of sales. Specific dollar amount is set for each box, case, barrel, or carton produced. Used primarily in assessing members of horizontal cooperatives or trade associations.

☐ Competitive parity. Allocates dollars according to the amounts spent by major competitors. Also called self-defense method.

☐ Share of market. Allocates advertising dollars by maintaining a percentage share of total industry advertising comparable to or somewhat ahead of its percentage share of market. Often used for new product introductions.

☐ Task method. Also referred to as the objective or budget buildup method, the task method has three steps: defining objectives, determining strategy, and estimating the cost to execute that strategy.

☐ Empirical research method. By running a series of experimental tests in different markets with different budgets, companies determine which is the most efficient level of expenditure.

☐ Quantitative mathematical models. Computer-based programs developed by certain major advertisers and agencies that rely on input of sophisticated data, history, and assumptions.

☐ All available funds method. Go-for-broke technique generally used by small firms with limited capital who are trying to introduce new products or services.

that is hard to predict in advance when advertising budgets are being developed.

Over the years, a number of methods have been developed to help companies determine how much to spend on advertising. The most common of these are the percentage-of-sales, percentage-of-profit, unit-of-sale, competitive-parity, share-of-market, and task methods. (See the Checklist of Ways to Set Advertising Budgets.)

Some organizations rely solely on one technique, while others use several in combination. Recently, the tendency has been to shy away from the simpler methods of the past, such as percentage of sales, and to use more sophisticated methods. However, no technique for allocating advertising funds is adequate for all situations. The three methods discussed in this section are those used primarily to arrive at national advertising budgets. Additional techniques used by retailers, who operate under a different set of variables, are discussed in Chapter 17, "Local Advertising."

Percentage-of-Sales Method

The *percentage-of-sales method* is one of the most popular techniques used to set the advertising appropriation. It may be based on a percentage of last year's sales, anticipated sales for next year, or a combination of the two. Businesspeople like this method because it is the simplest, it doesn't cost them anything, it is related to revenue, and it is considered safe. The problem is with the percentage to use. As Figure 7–12 shows, even among leaders within the same industry, percentages allocated to advertising vary widely.

Usually the percentage is based on an industry average or on company experience. Unfortunately it is too often determined arbitrarily. The problem of using an industry average is that it assumes that every company in the industry has similar objectives and faces the same marketing problems. When the percentage is based on company history, it assumes that the market is highly static, which is rarely the case.

However, this method does have some advantages. When applied against future sales, it often works well. It assumes that a certain number of dollars are needed to sell a certain number of units. If we know what that percentage is, the correlation between advertising and sales should remain constant if the market is stable and competitors' advertising remains relatively unchanged. Furthermore, management tends to think in terms of

FIGURE 7-12   Advertising expenditures by the top 25 leading advertisers, 1986 ($ in millions)

Category	Rank	Company	U.S. advertising expenditures	U.S. sales	Advertising as percent of U.S. sales
Automotive	20	Chrysler Corp.	$ 426.0	$20,489.0	2.1
	6	Ford Motor Company	648.5	50,034.0	1.3
	5	General Motors Corp.	839.0	91,343.0	0.9
Electronics	25	General Electric Co.	354.3	N/A	N/A
Food	13	BCI Holdings	535.9	5,809.0	9.2
	11	General Mills	551.6	N/A	N/A
	23	Kellogg Co.	374.1	2,269.0	16.5
	19	Kraft Inc.	438.0	6,278.3	7.0
	16	Pillsbury Co.	494.9	5,510.0	9.0
	17	Ralston Purina Co.	478.0	N/A	N/A
	4	RJR Nabisco	935.0	15,978.0	5.9
Pharmaceuticals	22	American Home Products Corp.	395.7	3,682.0	10.7
	21	Johnson & Johnson	410.7	3,970.0	10.3
	12	Warner Lambert	548.8	1,700.0	32.3
Retail	15	J.C. Penney Co.	496.2	14,117.0	3.5
	9	K mart Corp.	590.4	N/A	N/A
	3	Sears Roebuck & Co.	1,004.7	N/A	N/A
Restaurants	8	McDonald's Corp.	592.0	3,077.0	19.2
Soaps and cleaners	1	Procter & Gamble Co.	1,435.5	N/A	N/A
	14	Unilever N.V.	517.7	4,842.0	10.7
Soft drinks	24	Coca-Cola Co.	370.4	4.650.0	8.0
	10	PepsiCo Inc.	581.3	8,065.0	7.2
Telephone	18	American Telephone & Telegraph	439.9	N/A	N/A
Tobacco	2	Philip Morris Cos.	1,364.5	17,568.0	7.8
Wine, beer, and liquor	7	Anheuser-Busch Cos.	643.6	N/A	N/A

percentages, whether income or outgo. They think of advertising in the same way, so this method is simple. Also, because this method is common in the industry, it diminishes the likelihood of competitive warfare.

The greatest shortcoming of the percentage-of-sales method is that it violates a basic marketing principle. Marketing activities are supposed to stimulate demand and, thus, sales; they are not supposed to occur as a result of them. And if advertising automatically increases when sales increase and declines when sales decline, it ignores all the other environments of business that might be suggesting a totally opposite move.

Share-of-Market Method

In industries where products are very similar, there is usually a high correlation between a company's share of the market and its share of industry advertising. Knowing this, some firms set a goal for a certain portion of the market and then apply the same percentage of industry advertising dollars to their budget.

The *share-of-market method,* which was developed by J. O. Peckham, executive vice president of the A. C. Nielsen Company, has the advantage of being a bold attempt to achieve an objective. According to Peckham, a company's best chance of holding its share of the market is to keep a share of advertising somewhat ahead of its market share. For example, if you have a 30 percent share of the market, you should spend 35 percent of the industry's advertising dollars. One shortcoming is that there is no guarantee your competitors will not increase their advertising budgets.

For new products, share of market is a common method. According to Peckham's formula, when a new product brand is introduced, the advertising budget should be about one and a half times the brand's expected share of the market in two years. This means that if the company's two-year sales goal is 10 percent of the market, it should spend about 15 percent of the industry's advertising during the first two years.[24]

The share-of-market method assumes that to gain share of market, you must first gain share of mind. This is a logical approach to budgeting strategy. However, one hazard of this method is the tendency to become complacent. Companies compete on more than one basis, and advertising is just one tool of the marketing mix. Therefore, simply maintaining a higher percentage of media exposure may not be enough to accomplish the desired results. Companies must maintain an awareness of *all* the marketing activities of their competitors, not just advertising.

Task Method

The *task method* is also known as the objective or budget buildup method. In recent years, it has gained considerable popularity and is now used by about 80 percent of major national advertisers.[25] It is one of the few logical means of determining advertising allocations. It defines the objectives that are sought and how advertising is to be used to accomplish those objectives. It considers advertising a marketing tool to generate sales.

The task method has three steps: defining the objectives, determining strategy, and estimating the cost. After specific, quantitative marketing objectives have been set, the advertiser develops programs to be used in attaining them. If the objective is to increase the number of coffee cases sold by 10 percent, the advertiser will have to determine which advertising approach will work best, how often ads are to run, and which media will be used. The proposed cost of this program is determined, and this becomes the basis for the advertising budget. Naturally, it is necessary to consider this budget in light of the company's financial position. If the cost is too high, the objectives may have to be scaled down. Likewise, after the campaign has run, if the results are better or worse than anticipated, the next budget may require appropriate revisions.

The task method forces companies to think in terms of goals and whether they are being accomplished. The effectiveness of this method is most apparent when the results of particular ads or campaigns can be readily measured. Due to its nature, this method is adaptable to changing conditions in the market and is easily revised as dictated by past results.

Although it is easy to look back and determine whether money was spent wisely, it is often very difficult to determine in advance the amount of money that will be needed to reach a specific goal. This is the major drawback to the task method. Likewise, although techniques for measuring the effect of advertising are improving, they are still weak in many areas. As techniques become more exact, though, advertisers are using the task method more and more.

Additional Methods

There are several other methods for allocating funds that advertisers use to varying degrees. The *empirical research method* uses experimentation to determine the best level of advertising expenditure. By running a series of tests in different markets with different budgets, companies determine which is the most efficient level of expenditure.

Since the introduction of computers, there has been a great deal of interest in the use of *quantitative mathematical models* for budgeting. Foote, Cone & Belding, for example, developed a response-curve database from tracking studies on more than 40 clients' products and services. This program analyzes media programs and estimates customer response.[26] A number of other sophisticated techniques have also been developed. However, for the most part, these equations are not easily understood by line executives, and each relies on assumptions of data that are frequently unavailable or very expensive for the average business to obtain.

The Bottom Line

All these methods potentially assume one of two fallacies. The first fallacy is that advertising is a result of sales. We know this is not true, and yet the widespread use of the percentage-of-sales method indicates that many businesspeople think advertising should be a result of sales.

The second fallacy is that advertising creates sales. Only in rare circumstances (where direct-action advertising is used) can advertising be said to create sales. Advertising locates prospects and stimulates demand. It may even stimulate inquiries. Salespeople likewise may locate prospects and stimulate demand. They also close the sale. But, in reality, only customers create sales. It is the customer's choice to buy or not to buy the product, not the company's choice.

The job of advertising is to inform, persuade, and remind. In that way, advertising affects sales. However, advertising is just one part of the whole, and advertising managers must keep this in mind when preparing their plans and their budgets for management.

Summary

The marketing plan may be the most important document a company possesses. It assembles in one place all the pertinent facts about a company, the markets it serves, its products, and its competition and brings all these facts up-to-date. It sets specific goals and objectives to be attained and describes the precise strategies that will be used to achieve them. Thus, it musters all the company's forces for the marketing battlefield and, in so doing, dictates the role of advertising in the marketing mix.

The marketing plan should contain four principal sections: (1) situation analysis, (2) marketing objectives, (3) marketing strategy, and (4) action programs. A company's marketing objectives should be logical deductions from an analysis of its current situation, its prediction of future trends, and its understanding of corporate objectives. They should relate to the needs of specific target markets and sales objectives. The sales target objectives should be specific, quantitative, and realistic.

The first step in developing a marketing strategy is to select the target market. The second step is to determine a cost-effective marketing mix for each target market the company pursues. The marketing mix is determined by how the company uses the four Ps: product, price, place, and promotion. Advertising is one of the promotional tools companies may use.

Advertising is a natural outgrowth of the marketing plan, and the advertising plan is prepared in much the same way as the marketing plan. It includes a section on analysis, advertising objectives, and strategy.

Advertising objectives may be expressed in terms of moving prospective customers up through the advertising pyramid (awareness, comprehension, conviction, desire, action). Or they may be expressed in terms of generating inquiries, coupon response, or attitude change.

The advertising (or creative) strategy is determined by the advertiser's use of the creative mix. The creative mix is composed of the (1) target audience, (2) product concept, (3) communications media, and (4) advertising message. The target audience is the specific group of people the advertising will approach. It may or may not be the same as the target market. The product concept refers to the bundle of values the product is intended to represent to the customer. The communications media are the vehicles used to transmit the advertiser's message. The advertising message is what the company plans to say in its advertisements and how it plans to say it.

Several methods are commonly used for allocating funds to advertising. Historically, the most popular method has been the percentage-of-sales approach. Other approaches include the share-of-market method and the task method. The latter involves defining the advertising objective, determining the strategy, and estimating the cost to conduct that strategy.

Questions for Review and Discussion

1. Why should a marketing plan be created before any ads are designed?
2. What examples can you give to show the difference between generic-market objectives and sales-target objectives?
3. What are the elements of a marketing plan in outline form?
4. What is the most important consideration in developing any marketing strategy?
5. What are the elements of an advertising plan in outline form?
6. What examples can you give to show how one person's strategy might become another person's objective?
7. How might environmental factors affect an automobile company's expenditures for marketing and advertising?
8. What is the best method of allocating funds for advertising a real estate development? Why?
9. What types of companies would tend to use the percentage-of-sales method? Why?
10. How could a packaged foods manufacturer use the share-of-market method to determine its advertising budget?

PART III

ADVERTISING CREATIVITY

Enlightened Inspiration

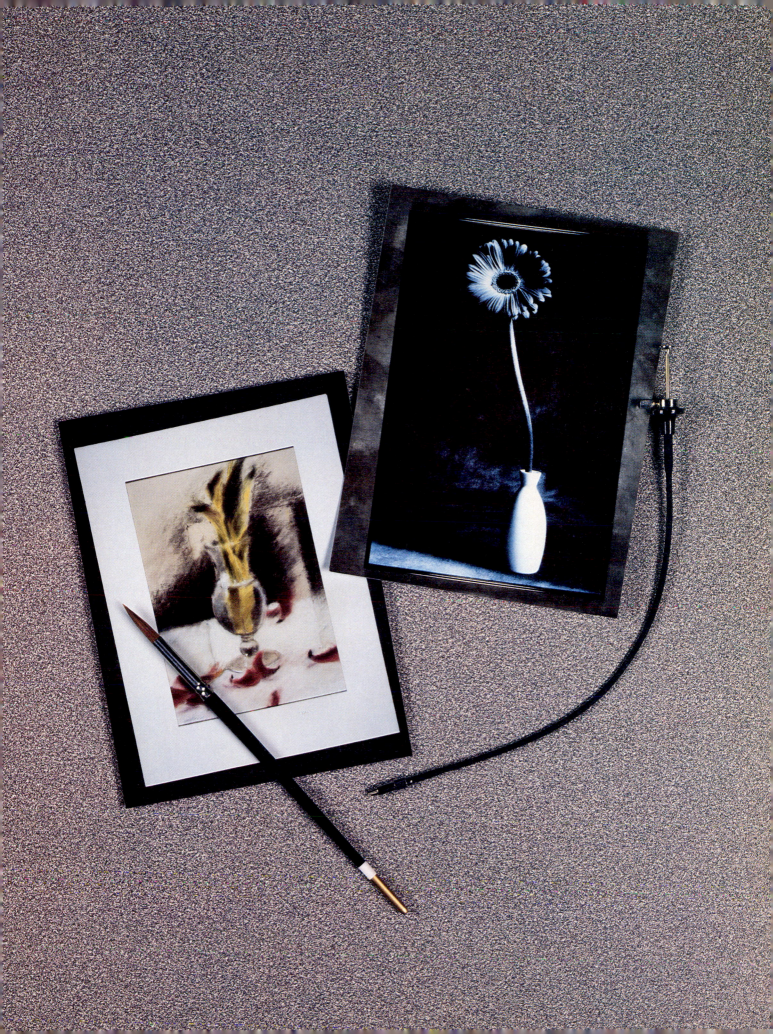

8

CREATIVE
COPYWRITING

uppose you are a manager in charge of advertising for *The Wall Street Journal,* the nation's daily newspaper for business. The *Journal* aims its advertising at two distinct markets: prospective subscribers and prospective advertisers. Your job is to plan the business-to-business campaign—the one aimed at the companies that are prospective advertisers.

After meetings with management and research, you determine that for this market there are actually two target audiences for your advertising: (1) those businesses that might advertise in the *Journal* and (2) the advertising agencies that prepare and place most of those companies' ads.

Your job is to develop a campaign that will support the efforts of the *Journal's* nationwide advertising sales force, will create awareness of the *Journal's* unique ability to speak to businesspeople around the country and around the world, and will convince national advertisers (and their agencies) of the logic of placing their corporate ads in *The Wall Street Journal.*

What will you do?

This, of course, is not a hypothetical situation. In fact, every advertising medium has the same marketing problem: attracting advertiser dollars. And to do so, many of them spend millions of dollars every year advertising their medium in the pages or on the airwaves of other media.

In 1987, *The Wall Street Journal* celebrated the 10th anniversary of its well-read and award-winning "Creative Leaders" campaign. The *Journal* had determined that its primary target should be the people who work in advertising agencies, since a fundamental responsibility of these people is to analyze and recommend media to their clients. Working with the head of its agency for business advertising, Jim Johnston Advertising, the *Journal* decided to feature full-page testimonials from key executives in target agencies who were responsible for creating some of the most outstanding advertising in the country. The ads would be informational and educational. They would express the advertising and business philosophies of these creative leaders, and they would aim to show how the brightest minds in the country value the pages of the *Journal*—not just for reading but also for advertising.

The ads, placed primarily in *Advertising Age,* featured a large, coarse-screened photograph (designed to look like a scratchboard illustration) of each creative leader, a short headline that cleverly played off the subject's first or last name (e.g., "Caples on Copy" for the famous copywriter John Caples; "O'Toole of the Trade" for John O'Toole), and a brief paragraph centered under the headline explaining who the subject was. Also, there were two to three columns of well-written copy wrapped around the illustration, summarizing the subject's wisdom and insights about advertising, creativity, excellence, and—in the last paragraph—*The Wall Street Journal* (see Figure 8–1).

Jim Johnston did everything he could to make people want to read the ads. The language was simple and direct. The headlines were short and fun. The ads were laid out in an easy-to-follow editorial style with short paragraphs and numerous subheadings in bold type.

The campaign was a smashing advertising and public relations success. Over the first 10 years that it ran, more than 30 well-known agency presidents, executives, and creative directors were highlighted. Thousands of reprints were ordered by the agencies themselves and by their clients.[1]

COPYWRITING AND ADVERTISING STRATEGY

The Wall Street Journal's primary advertising objective was to inform and convince business advertisers that the *Journal* was the national voice of business—that if they wanted their message read by business leaders, the *Journal* was the logical medium. In addition, the *Journal* hoped to stimulate desire and action on the part of advertisers and their agencies to put the *Journal* on their next media-placement list. The tremendous success of the paper's efforts was indicated by the number of requests it received for reprints of the ads and by the substantial increase in ad pages that followed. But what was the creative strategy that enabled *The Wall Street Journal* to achieve that success?

A review of Chapter 7 reminds us that advertising or creative strategy consists of four elements:

1. The target audience.
2. The product concept.
3. The communications media.
4. The message strategy.

Who was the target audience? In this case, it consisted of middle- and upper-management marketing and advertising people in agencies and corporations. The communications media included print media like *Advertising Age, Adweek,* and *The Wall Street Journal* itself. In the 10 years of the

FIGURE   8–1

Jay Chiat, profiled in Chapter 5, is the subject of this full-page ad for *The Wall Street Journal* in its Creative Leaders campaign. Chiat promotes the concept of print advertising, pointing out that his agency was started by two writers. And about the *Journal:* "in sales, or marketing, or advertising, there's no other way to stay current."

campaign, using these media, the campaign reached 10 million executives numerous times with its message.

What was the product concept? In this particular case, it was not just the *Journal's* primary functional product—newspapers. More than selling newspapers, the company was selling the product concept of a media vehicle—a national business paper—that could find the hard-to-reach corporate decision makers. It was promoting the *idea* that advertising in the *Journal* works.

What was the message strategy? Message strategy is determined by what the company wants to communicate and how it wants to express the message. *The Wall Street Journal* wanted to convey the message that since the top minds in business read the *Journal* on a daily basis, advertising in the *Journal* produces "the results that mean business success." How to communicate that thought involved developing a *verbal* and *nonverbal* presentation of the message that would be simple, interesting, informative, entertaining, enjoyable, and helpful.

In Chapter 9, "Creative Art Direction," we will discuss the nonverbal, graphic side of message strategy. The subject of this chapter, copywriting, concerns the verbal element of message strategy. The combined product of the art director and the copywriter is the creative nucleus, which is then translated through the production process into the final advertisement or commercial.

PEOPLE IN ADVERTISING

Hal Patrick Riney

Chairman/CEO
Hal Riney & Partners

Some people say Hal Riney writes the wittiest commercials on TV. Others admire how few words he needs to draw powerful emotions from 60 seconds of music and film. *Fortune* magazine has called him "America's Hottest Adman." And David Ogilvy calls Riney the best copywriter he has ever known.

These are just some of the many kudos offered to the chairman, chief executive officer, and namesake of Hal Riney & Partners, San Francisco. While Riney's career in advertising has been brilliant, it has also not been typical of the industry's stars.

For one thing, he has never worked in New York. His entire 30-year career has been in San Francisco. Starting as a mailroom clerk with BBDO, he rose through the ranks to the position of vice president/creative director. In 1972, he moved on to Botsford Ketchum where he was executive vice president/creative director. Then, in 1976, he founded the San Francisco office of Ogilvy & Mather with no accounts and, in 10 years, built the business to over $120 million in billings. In 1986, Ogilvy spun off the San Francisco office to avoid client conflicts, and Hal Riney & Partners was born. With offices now in Chicago, and more planned for New York and Los Angeles, the agency is rapidly expanding nationally.

While Riney is probably best known for creating the

Building the Message Strategy

Before the copywriter starts to think about writing an ad, he or she must understand the marketing and advertising strategies completely. This includes the *message strategy*. If the advertising plan has not spelled it out in detail (which is often the case), the copywriter should immediately build a message strategy, in collaboration with the art director if possible, and get it approved before going any further. The fastest way to have an advertisement rejected is to write a brilliant, creative piece of work that has nothing to do with the strategy set for the campaign.

The message strategy includes three specific elements:

1. Copy platform—what you're going to say and how you're going to say it.
2. Art direction—what you're going to show and how you're going to show it.
3. Production values—what you're going to create mechanically and how you're going to create it.

To develop these elements, the copywriter and the art director need to review the research, analyze the facts, and study the market, the product, and the competition. (See the Checklist of Product Marketing Facts for Copywriters.) How is the market segmented? How will the product be

mythical Frank Bartles and Ed Jaymes, his list of other credits and awards would fill pages. He has won, for example, 16 Clios, 13 Andy Awards, 15 Addys, and 14 gold medals, just to mention a few. He also won the grand prize at the Cannes Film Festival for the world's best commercial, and he has been nominated for an Academy Award. In all, he has won more than 300 major advertising industry awards for creative excellence and sales achievement.

Among his current accounts are Gallo Wines, Swanson Division of Campbell Soups, AMEX Life Assurance, California Prune Board, Dreyer's Ice Cream, MJB Coffee, See's Candies, Perrier and Calistoga Mineral Waters, and Anheuser-Busch Cos., Inc.

Riney's trademark is soft selling through understatement and wry, homespun humor. In fact, Riney often uses humor and visual tone to disguise the sales message in his commercials. As he says, "When everybody else is shouting, it is probably better to whisper." Consider, for example, the spot Riney wrote and produced for MJB coffee. The camera slowly pans a montage of old photographs of cowboys working in the depth of winter. A gentle, deep voice says: "There were plenty of times in a cowboy's life when he'd just about trade in his saddle for a cup of hot coffee. *(Pause)* Well, not really. But he might talk about it *(longer pause)* if it was MJB."

Riney is primarily a writer, but he is also an art director, film producer, cartoonist, and designer—in addition to his management responsibilities. Surprisingly, he is also a highly in demand voice actor who can be heard on dozens of TV commercials for agencies in addition to his own.

Philosophically, he also swims against the tide. He thinks an agency should have more creative people than any other group. (At most agencies, the creative department employs about 11 percent of the staff. At Hal Riney it's about 40 percent.) He doesn't believe the best way to reach the target audience is necessarily to portray them in one's advertising. He has had great success reaching young consumers by portraying old geezers on front porches. (For Henry Weinhard's Private Reserve as well as Bartles & Jaymes.)

Riney believes in research, but as information rather than as a means to test or measure creativity. And on information, Riney tries to deal less with distinctive product differences and more with distinctive product personalities.

Finally, he believes superior production values add substance to the message and help extend the life of the brand. While this certainly costs more, he feels it's worth it because sales are directly related to brand image.

positioned? Who are the best prospects for the product? Is the target audience different from the target market? What is the key consumer benefit? What is the product's image?

At this point, the results of research are important. Research identifies the best prospects; research identifies the best strategy; research can find the most important consumer appeals or product claims. *What* the advertising says is often more important than *how* it is said. But the reverse can be true. So the message strategy should be tested.

Writing the Copy Platform

In developing the message strategy, the copywriter's logical responsibility is to create the *copy platform,* a document that serves as the creative team's guide for writing and producing the ad. This should be a written statement

Checklist of Product Marketing Facts for Copywriters

Identity

☐ Trade name.

☐ Trademark.

☐ Product symbol.

☐ Other copyrighted or patented information.

Packaging

☐ Unit size or sizes offered.

☐ Package shape.

☐ Package design:
  Styling.
  Color.
  Special protection for product.
  A carrier for product.

☐ Package label.

Research

☐ What research about the product does the supplier have?

☐ Is research available?

Performance

☐ What does it do?

☐ What might it be expected to do that it does *not?*

☐ How does it work?

☐ How is it made or produced?

☐ What is in it?
  Raw materials.   Preservatives.
  Chemicals.   Special ingredients.
  Nutrients.

☐ What are its physical characteristics?
  Color.   Appearance.
  Smell.   Texture.
  Taste.   Others.

Effectiveness

☐ Is there proof it has been tested and works well?

☐ Are there any government or other regulations that need to be mentioned or observed?

Product Image

☐ How do people view the product?

☐ What do they like about it?

☐ What do they dislike about it?

☐ Is it a luxury?

☐ Is it a necessity?

☐ Is it a habit?

☐ Is it self-indulgent?

☐ Do people have to have it but wish they didn't?

about the most important issues to be considered in the advertisement or the campaign.

Who is the most likely prospect for the product? How tightly can he or she be defined and described in terms of demographic, psychographic, and behavioristic qualities? Finally, what would that prospect's personality be like?

What wants or needs does the consumer have that should be appealed to? In Chapter 5, we discussed the innumerable types of appeals or approaches used by advertisers. The two broadest categories are rational appeals and emotional appeals. The former is an appeal to the consumer's practical, functional need for the product or service. The latter relates to the consumer's psychological, social, or symbolic needs.

Other types of appeals used by advertisers, which may fall into one of these two broad categories, include positive and negative appeals, fear and

Life

☐ What is its life or use span?

Competitive Information

☐ Who are the competitors?

☐ Does it have any advantages over them?

☐ Does it have any disadvantages?

☐ Are they all about the same?

☐ Do rival products present problems that this one solves?

Manufacturing

☐ How is it made?

☐ How long does it take?

☐ How many steps in the process?

☐ How about the people involved in making it?

☐ Are there any special machines used?

☐ Where is it made?

History

☐ When was it created or invented?

☐ Who introduced it?

☐ Has it had other names?

☐ Have there been product changes?

☐ Is there any "romance" to it?

Market Position

☐ What is its share of the total market?

Consumer Use

☐ How is the product used?

☐ Are there other possible uses?

☐ How frequently is it bought?

☐ What type of person uses the product?

☐ Why is the product bought?
   Personal use.
   Gift.
   Work.

☐ What type of person uses the product most (heavy user)?

☐ What amount of the product is bought by the heavy user?

☐ Where does the best customer live?

☐ What kind of person is a heavy user or buyer?

Distribution

☐ How widely is the product distributed?

☐ Are there exclusive sellers?

☐ Is there a ready supply or limited amount?

☐ Is it available for a short season?

sex appeals, and humor appeals. Depending on the message strategy, any or all may be used to gain attention, create a personality for the product or service, and stimulate consumer interest, credibility, desire, and action (see Figure 8–2).

Next, it is important to identify those product features that satisfy the consumers' needs. What kinds of support are there for the product claim? What is the product's position? What personality or image can be or has been created?

The final question to address is, what style, approach, or tone will be used in the copy? And generally what will the copy say? The answers to all these questions make up the copy platform.

When the first ad is written, the copywriter should review the copy platform again to see whether the ad measures up. If it doesn't, the writer should reject it and start again.

Developing the Art Direction and Production Values

While the creative team is developing its understanding of what it wants to say and how it wants to say it, it will also consider the other elements of the message strategy—the nonverbal aspects. We shall examine both art direction and production in the ensuing chapters, but it is important to point out here that the process of developing the elements of message strategy is rarely accomplished step-by-step. Rather, because they are inexorably intertwined, all the elements normally evolve simultaneously. Most important, though, the completed strategy statement is the prerequisite for developing the creative idea around which the ad or campaign will be centered.

The strategy ensures that the advertising will be saying the right thing to the right person in the right context in the right tone and in the right manner. With that in place, we're ready for the next stage of development: getting the idea.[2]

FIGURE 8–2	Selected advertising appeals	
Appetite	Sympathy for others	Novelty
Taste	Devotion to others	Safety
Health	Guilt	Courtesy
Fear	Pride of personal appearance	Rest or sleep
Humor	Home comfort	Economy in use
Security	Pride in appearance of property	Economy in purchase
Cleanliness	Pleasure of recreation	Efficiency in operation or use
Sex attraction	Entertainment	Dependability in use
Romance	Opportunity for more leisure time	Dependability in quality
Social achievement	Avoidance of a laborious task	Durability
Ambition	Enhancement of earnings	Variety of selection
Personal comfort	Style (beauty)	Simplicity
Protection of others	Pride of possession	Sport/play/physical activity
Social approval/approval of others	Curiosity	Cooperation

Developing the Big Idea

For all creative people, the idea stage is always the toughest. But it can also be the most rewarding. It is the long, tedious, difficult task of assembling all the pertinent information, analyzing the problem, and searching for some verbal or visual concept of how to communicate what needs to be said. It means establishing a mental idea or picture of the advertisement, commercial, or campaign before any copy is written or artwork begun.

The process may be called *visualization* or *conceptualization,* and it is the most important step in planning the advertisement. It is the creative point where the search for the *big idea* takes place—that "flash of insight that synthesizes the purposes of the strategy, joins the product benefit with consumer desire in a fresh, involving way, brings the subject to life, and makes the reader or the audience stop, look, and listen."[3]

What's the difference between strategy and an idea? An idea adds meaning, interest, memorability, and drama to what is stated in a strategy document. As John O'Toole points out, it is the difference between "Convince suburban housewives and rural homeowners that Raid is the most effective bug killer available" and "Raid kills bugs dead!" One strategy was to communicate to prospective investors that Merrill Lynch is very optimistic about the stock market and business in general in the United States. The big idea was to use a bull in their commercials under the slogan "Merrill Lynch is bullish on America." While strategy requires deduction, an idea requires inspiration[4] (see Figure 8–3).

John Caples, dean of advertising copywriters, says that ideas are the most important thing in advertising. He believes there are 12 proven methods for discovering ideas for advertising: cash in on your personal experience;

FIGURE   8–3

Arrow, known for making high-quality formal dress shirts, developed a new strategy: to introduce a line of high-quality sport shirts. In its ads, the big idea was to announce boldly through the use of high-contrast color and clever copywriting that "after 75 years, we've loosened our collar."

After 75 years, we've loosened our collar.

That's why this fall you'll be able to wear our colorful new rugbys, sport shirts, and sweaters. And since you've always expected quality from an Arrow dress shirt, that's what you'll find in Arrow sportswear. We may have loosened our collar, but we'll never relax our standards.

Arrow

organize your experience; write from the heart; learn from the experience of others; talk with the manufacturer; study the product; review previous advertising for the product; study the ads of competitors; examine testimonials from customers; solve the prospect's problem; put your subconscious mind to work; and repeat a successful ad with variations.[5]

David Ogilvy suggests that recognizing a big idea is almost as difficult as coming up with one. He recommends that to evaluate ideas, we ask ourselves five questions:

1. Did it make me gasp when I first saw it?
2. Do I wish I had thought of it myself?
3. Is it unique?
4. Does it fit the strategy to perfection?
5. Could it be used for 30 years?[6]

As Ogilvy points out, you can count on your fingers those campaigns that have run five years or more. They are the superstars—the campaigns that keep on producing results and memorability through thick and thin.

OBJECTIVES OF GOOD COPY

By 1910, Henry Ford had spent five years and thousands of dollars perfecting his new Model T. Now the first models were ready; it was time to advertise. But what sort of ad should he run? Ads at that time were mostly art or photos with few if any words. But Ford believed art alone couldn't sell his Model T. It had to be described—in detail.

A few weeks later, readers of the *Saturday Evening Post* were startled to see a black-and-white ad, two pages long, that contained no pictures. Instead, it was all words! (See Figure 8–4.)

FIGURE   8–4

This 1910 advertisement, written by Henry Ford himself over the protests of all the "experts," contained 1,200 words—the longest copy of any advertisement of its time. It also sold more autos than any ad in previous history.

"When Ford speaks the world listens."

"Buy a Ford car because it is better—not because it is cheaper."

"The reason why can be given in a very few words . . . "

The "very few words" totaled about 1,200. They told how Henry Ford invented the Model T. They detailed the financial condition of the Ford Company. And they listed its 28 factories, assembly plants, and branches.

The ad was a first. It contained more words, or *copy,* than any ad of the day. It also caused some industry leaders to rebuke Ford. "Pictures sell cars," one said flatly, "not words." But Ford stood his ground and proved he was right. The ad soon produced more sales than any other auto ad in history. And it gave Henry Ford his first push toward what was to become, 10 years later, the largest and most profitable manufacturing company in the world.[7]

This example illustrates just one of many misconceptions about the creative function in advertising and the objectives of good copy.

The purpose of copywriting is usually to persuade or remind a group or groups of individuals to take some action in order to satisfy a need or want. But, first, people need to be made aware of the problem or, if the problem is obvious, of a solution. To create awareness, you have to get people's attention.

Attention

Gaining attention is the first objective of copywriting. The headline is usually the major attention-getting device. For example, an ad for Apple computers (see Figure 8–5) has a news/information headline that uses a large number to catch the eye and makes a simple, bold promise: "How to send mail at 670,000,000 mph." Many other devices—such as the illustration, layout, color, and size of the advertisement in print media as well as unusual sounds or visual techniques in electronic media—can also be used to gain attention.

However, the copywriter has little or no control over some factors. Obviously, the size of the advertisement influences whether it will be

FIGURE   8–5

The headline of this ad might have been "Now you can send mail fast" (which is informational) or "Now you can send mail at the speed of light" (which is provocative). This headline, though, with the large number and the "how to," is both informational and provocative, not to mention attention getting.

noticed, and the size is often determined before a copywriter is assigned to write the advertisement. Similarly, the ad's position in a publication may determine who will see it. The copywriter must take all these factors into account before deciding on an attention-getting device.

The device used should create drama for the product; but it must also be appropriate. It must relate to the product, to the rest of the advertisement, and to the intended audience.[8] This is especially true in business-to-business advertising. A manufacturer of laboratory ovens ran an ad with the headline: "The American work ethic is alive and well in Philadelphia." While that was probably good news to patriots and local politicians, not many patriots and politicians are known to be heavy users of laboratory ovens.[9]

Headlines that promise something but fail to deliver will not make a sale; in fact, the advertiser may alienate a potential customer. For example, ads that use racy headlines or nude figures unrelated to the product or sales ideas may attract attention but will often lose sales.

Interest

The second step in writing an advertisement is to create interest. We've gotten our customer's attention. She's looking at our advertisement. But if we can't keep her interest, we're going to lose her. So we have to talk to her, about her, and about her problems and needs. We may want to use the word *you* frequently.

Interest is the bridge between attention and credibility. It is an important step. There are several effective ways to build and maintain interest. We might use cartoon characters or other interior visuals, subheads, storyline copy, or charts and tables. We will discuss some of these later.

Credibility

The next step is to establish credibility. The legendary adman Howard Gossage believed that people read what interests them and ignore what doesn't. At the same time, they are more sophisticated, skeptical, and cynical today than in years past.[10] To them, the proofs in some advertisements are not only unbelievable but also insulting. In such cases, product sales suffer. If the advertiser offers test data, the data must give honest support to the product claim and not be the result of statistical manipulation.

Credibility is sometimes added to advertisements through the use of presenters. As a spokesman, comedian Bill Cosby has lent credibility to a variety of products, including Jell-O and Coke, because of his honest, personable, down-to-earth style.

Desire

To heighten desire, we need to inform the reader or viewer of the benefits of our product or service. This is why knowing the customer is so important. Each new benefit should heighten desire because it is matched with a real or perceived need of the customer. Even if there is only one benefit, it must be presented in such a way that customers believe it and understand its application to their own situations.

Figure 8–6

This all-copy ad directs the reader to "Ask for your personalized computer print-out telling exactly how the money would add up for you . . ."; "Just send us the coupon below, or see an Allstate agent . . ."; and "Yes! Tell me how Allstate Universal Life can give me insurance protection. . ."

Action

We want to motivate the reader to take some action, to do something, or at least to agree with us. The action might be immediate or future. Action may be directly requested: "Come to our sale May 15"; or it may be indirect or implied: "Fly the friendly skies." However, the request for action should be in the copy. We're asking for the order or at least that the reader agree with us. Too many advertisements forget that readers are generally preoccupied; they need a course of action spelled out for them. That's the job of good copy (see Figure 8–6).

UNDERSTANDING THE COPYWRITER'S TERMINOLOGY

All advertisements are made up of numerous elements or components. These elements may be moved, enlarged, reduced, reversed, changed, or eliminated until a new look or approach is achieved. To discuss copy, we must understand what these elements are and what they do.

The key elements in print advertising are the headline, the visual, subheads, body copy, captions, boxes and panels, slogans, logotypes (logos), seals, and signatures.

In broadcast advertising, the copy is normally spoken dialogue and is referred to as the *audio* portion of the commercial. The audio may be delivered as a *voice-over* by an announcer who is not seen but whose voice we hear. Or it may be *on-camera* dialogue by an announcer, a spokesperson, or actors playing out a scene. When copy is actually written on the screen, it may then be described by the same terms used in print advertising, which we shall discuss briefly here.

FIGURE 8–7

The headline in this ad flags the target audience. Although neither the headline nor the visual tells the reader anything about the subject, the ad is still effective. The soft-sell body copy is written in the same sophisticated tone as the headline. Also, the ad is beautifully designed and artfully produced in keeping with the institutional approach.

Headlines

Many consider the headline the most important element in a print advertisement. The term *headline* refers to the words in the leading position of the advertisement—that is, the words that will be read first or that are positioned to draw the most attention. As a result, headlines are usually set in larger type than other portions of the advertisement.

A headline has six functions. First, the headline must attract attention to the advertisement. The entire message is lost if no one reads the headline. To promote its "eternity ring" to husbands, DeBeers uses an effective headline: "You once said, 'I do.' Now you can say, 'I'm glad I did.'"

Second, the headline should select the reader; that is, it tells whether the subject matter of the ad interests the reader. Citibank's headline, "A word to the wealthy," means exactly what it says (see Figure 8–7).

Audiences may be qualified by demographic criteria (age, sex, income) or by psychographic criteria. However, care in advertising is essential. Psychographic qualification can backfire, and the results can be devastating. A noted copywriter, Stan Freeberg, developed a headline for an airline advertisement that used psychographic qualification. The headline read: "Hey, you with the sweaty palms!" The campaign was short-lived.

Third, the headline should lead the reader directly into the body copy. One good example is:

Headline: "What kind of man reads *Playboy?*"
Body copy: "He's a man who demands the best life has to offer."

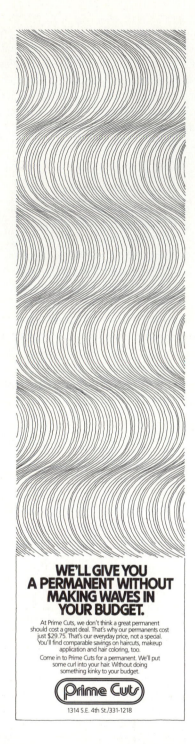

WE'LL GIVE YOU
A PERMANENT WITHOUT
MAKING WAVES IN
YOUR BUDGET.

At Prime Cuts, we don't think a great permanent
should cost a great deal. That's why our permanents cost
just $29.75. That's our everyday price, not a special.
You'll find comparable savings on haircuts, makeup
application and hair coloring, too.

Come in to Prime Cuts for a permanent. We'll put
some curl into your hair. Without doing
something kinky to your budget.

Prime Cuts

1314 S.E. 4th St./331-1218

FIGURE   8–8

A great example of how to do
award-winning creative advertising
on a small budget. The advertiser
had the intelligence not to destroy
the simplicity of the layout or to insert superfluous information.

Fourth, the headline must present the complete selling idea. It may be intended merely to carry through a campaign theme, but it should tell the whole story. Marlboro accomplishes this in beautiful magazine and out-door advertisements with nothing more than a western illustration, a cigarette pack, and the headline: "Come to where the flavor is. Marlboro Country." The headline creates the mood, suggests the image, asks for the sale, and states the brand name, all at once. Not only that, it is memorable and identifiable with the product. It, therefore, has the ability to trigger a recognition response in the consumer's mind.

David Ogilvy points out that on the average, five times as many people read the headline as read the body copy. Therefore, if you haven't done some selling in the headline, you've wasted 90 percent of your money.[11] Ogilvy also suggests that advertisers should not be afraid of long headlines; his best headline, he says, contained 18 words: "At 60 miles an hour the loudest noise in the new Rolls-Royce comes from the electric clock."[12]

Fifth, the headline should promise the customer a benefit. The benefit should be readily apparent to the reader and easy to get: "Picture Perfect Typing. Smith Corona."

Sixth, the headline should present product news of interest to the reader. Consumers look for new products, new uses of old products, or improvements on old products. Therefore, words that imply newness can increase readership and should be used whenever applicable. Some examples include *now, amazing, suddenly, announcing, introducing, it's here, improved, revolutionary, just arrived,* and *important development.*

Copywriters and advertising academicians have been trying to classify types of headlines and body copy for years. There are probably as many different classifications and types as there are authors on the subject. Richard Stansfield, for example, has come up with 23 "basic" types of headlines for which he has developed names that range from "teaser" to "so what?"[13]

The advertising practitioner would probably say "so what?" to the whole subject. However, for the student of advertising and the business-person with limited experience in the field, it may be helpful to briefly discuss certain common types of headlines and copy styles. This should facilitate understanding the role of copy and the skill required to write effective advertising.

Generally, we are able to classify effective advertising headlines into five basic categories: benefit, provocative, news/information, question, and command.

Benefit headlines make a direct promise to the reader. Two good examples are "Every time we race, you win" (Yamaha) and "We'll give you a permanent without making waves in your budget" (Prime Cuts haircutting salon) (see Figure 8–8).

Provocative headlines are written to provoke the reader's curiosity. To learn more, the reader must read the body copy. Of course, the danger is that the reader won't read on, and the headline won't have sold anything. For that reason, provocative headlines are usually coupled with visuals that offer clarification or some *story appeal.* For example: "Dear American Tourister: I fell flat on my attaché." The accompanying illustration shows the testimonial letter writer tumbling down a flight of stairs and landing on his American Tourister briefcase. To know the rest of the story, the reader must read on.

News/information headlines include many of the how-to headlines as well as headlines that seek to gain identification for their sponsors by announcing some news or providing some promise of information: "The

Perception.   Reality.

If you still think a Rolling Stone reader's idea of standard equipment is flowers on the door panels and incense in the ashtrays, consider this: Rolling Stone households own 5,199,000 automobiles. If you've got cars to sell, welcome to the fast lane. Source: Simmons 1984

FIGURE   8–9

The simple combination of words and pictures here makes a dramatic statement for *Rolling Stone* magazine: its audience is not what many people think it is.

Honda Civic. The car we designed around a shopping bag." Or Chivas Regal: "The most carefully poured Scotch in the world." This headline provides the reader with a considerable amount of information in a very short sentence. It tells the reader that Chivas Regal is precious and expensive. Neither of these headlines is necessarily "hot news," but both provide information and are memorable.

The agency for *Rolling Stone* magazine found that many upscale advertisers looked askance at the publication because they perceived its readers as radicals. Fallon McElligott developed a campaign using a series of two-page spreads with the simple news/information headline: "Perception . . . Reality." A photo on the left illustrates a preconceived notion of the *Rolling Stone* reader, while the right page shows another photograph that conveys the truth. For example, Perception—a flower-painted VW bus; Reality—a Ford Mustang. (See Figure 8–9.) Ad pages increased substantially the next year.[14]

Question headlines can be dangerous. If you ask a question the reader can answer quickly, or (even worse) negatively, the rest of the advertisement may not get read. Imagine a headline that reads: "Do you like food?" The reader answers "of course" and turns the page.

An American Airlines advertisement with the headline "If you don't show your kids where America began, who will?" did not fall into that trap.

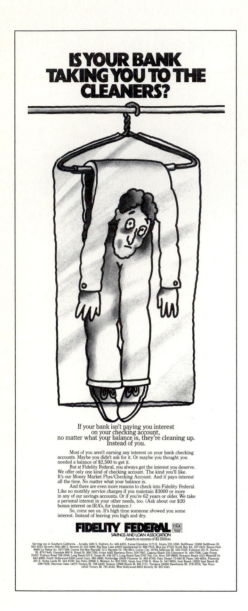

IS YOUR BANK TAKING YOU TO THE CLEANERS?

If your bank isn't paying you interest
on your checking account,
no matter what your balance is,
they're cleaning up.
Instead of you.

Most of you aren't earning any interest on your bank checking accounts. Maybe you didn't ask for it. Or maybe you thought you needed a balance of $2,500 to get it.

But at Fidelity Federal, you always get the interest you deserve. We offer only one kind of checking account. The kind you'll like. It's our Money Market Plus/Checking Account. And it pays interest all the time. No matter what your balance is.

And there are even more reasons to check into Fidelity Federal. Like no monthly service charges if you maintain $3000 or more in any of our savings accounts. Or if you're 62 years or older. We take a personal interest in your other needs, too. (Ask about our $20 bonus interest on IRA's, for instance.)

So, come see us. It's high time someone showed you some interest. Instead of leaving you high and dry.

FIDELITY FEDERAL
SAVINGS AND LOAN ASSOCIATION
Assets in excess of $2 Billion

FIGURE 8–10

This ad is a real attack on banks by the savings and loan. Its appeal goes straight to the customer's pocketbook, and chances are any bank customers reading it will feel they've been hung out to dry.

It was designed to motivate thoughtful parents about future travel plans. It accomplished the objective.

A *command headline* orders us to do something and, therefore, might seem negative. Yet we pay attention to such headlines. They motivate us through fear or emotion or because we understand the inherent correctness of the command. For example, "Drive safely. The life you save may be your own," is difficult to challenge. Other command headlines are more pleasant, such as "Listen to what you've been missing in cassette sound" (3M Company). And some may be couched in the form of a request: "If you smoke, please try Carlton." Perhaps the best command headline of all time was: "Promise her anything but give her Arpege."

We have touched on only a few types of headlines in this brief discussion. Trying to categorize all of them could take a lifetime and serves little purpose. Many headline types are easily combined, and some work better with visuals than others. Provocative headlines and question headlines, for example, usually require more support from definitive photos or illustrations. A good exercise for the beginning copywriter is to create a checklist of basic headline categories and then to write several different types for each new project. That is one way to find the best solution to the problem at hand.

Subheads

Subheads are misnamed because they can actually appear above or below the headline. They may also appear in the body copy or the text of the advertisement. A subhead that appears above the headline is called a *kicker*.

Subheads are like little headlines. While they usually appear in a smaller type size than the headline, they are almost invariably larger than the body copy or text type size. Subheads may appear in boldface (heavier) type or in a different ink color.

The purpose of the subhead is to transmit key sales points—fast! Most individuals read only the headline and subheads. Subheads should be reserved for important facts that may not be as dramatic or memorable as the headline information. Some may even require more space than a headline because they communicate more information and require more words.

The subheads should reinforce the headline and advertisement theme. Fidelity Federal's "Is your bank taking you to the cleaners?" is a headline well reinforced by the subhead: "If your bank isn't paying you interest on your checking account, no matter what your balance is, they're cleaning up. Instead of you." (See Figure 8–10.)

Body Copy

Body copy, or *text* as it is sometimes called, tells the complete sales story. It is a logical continuation of the headline and subheads. The body copy is set in smaller type than headlines or subheads. Body copy is also where the sale is closed.

The text should relate to the campaign appeal and to the reader's self-interest, and it must explain how the product or service being advertised satisfies the customer's need. The text may concentrate on a single benefit or several benefits as they relate specifically to the target audience. Copy should be written as if the writer were conversing with one person. In fact, to see how it sounds, copywriters often read their copy aloud—even if it's intended for print media. The ear is a powerful copywriting tool. (See Ad Lab 8-A.) Here are some pointers that experts have arrived at after years of copy research:[15]

1. Stress one major idea.
2. Position the product clearly.
3. Emphasize the consumer's ultimate benefit.
4. Keep the brand name up front and reinforce it.
5. Keep copy lean and tight. Tell the whole story and no more. When finished, stop.
6. Support audio with video.

In writing copy, we look for the techniques that provide the greatest sales appeal for the idea we are presenting. (See the Checklist for Writing Effective Copy.) Copy styles fall into many categories. The most common types include straight line, narrative, institutional, dialogue/monologue, picture caption, and gimmick.[16]

In *straight-line copy,* the text immediately explains or develops the headline and visual in a straightforward attempt to sell the product. Since the product's sales points are ticked off in order of their importance,

---

AD LAB 8-A   The Eye versus the Ear

Jack Trout and Al Ries, who pioneered the concepts of positioning and marketing warfare, here share their views on another controversial subject: the eye versus the ear.

It's a fact of life that we succeed or fail based on our preconceptions—preconceptions that we seldom think about, that we seldom debate. Today, there's an advertising preconception that is deeply rooted and fallacious.

Which Is More Powerful?

Which is more powerful, the eye or the ear? Has anybody ever asked you that question? Probably not, because the answer is obvious. Chances are that deep down inside you believe the eye is more powerful than the ear.

After all, 500 years before Christ, Confucius said, "A picture is worth a thousand words."

These seven words, not pictures mind you, have lived for 2,500 years. And the way things are going, these seven words will probably never die. What agency president, creative director, or art director hasn't quoted Confucius at least once in his or her career?

After analyzing hundreds of effective positioning campaigns, though, we ran into a surprising conclusion.

The programs were all verbal. There wasn't a single positioning concept that was exclusively visual. Could Confucius have been wrong?

In order to set the record straight, we went back to find out what Confucius actually said. We took the Chinese characters and had them translated.

Confucius said, "A picture is worth a thousand pieces of gold." Not words, but gold. Son of a gun! Here all these years we thought he was knocking words.

What Is a Picture Worth?

We all know television pictures are expensive. But what is a picture worth on television? That is, just the picture without the sound. Not much. As a matter of fact, without the words on the package or the graphics on the screen, pictures in a TV commercial have almost no communication value. But add sound, and the picture changes. If pictures alone make no sense, how about the sound alone? Strange as it may seem, the sound alone in a television commercial

(continued)

Ad Lab 8-A *(continued)*

usually carries an easy-to-understand message.

Most classic print advertisements illustrate the same principle. The visual alone makes no sense. Naturally, a print ad with both pictures and words is more effective than either alone. But individually, which is more powerful—the verbal or the visual?

Sound Alone Is Powerful

Evidence from controlled laboratory studies shows that when you present a list of words to people either auditorily, say on tape, or visually, say on slides, people remember more words if they hear the words than if they see them.

A recent study from Northwestern University shows that if you try to convince people about a product and you do it with just a verbal message, people are much more convinced about your product. They like it better; they want to buy it more than if you accompany those verbal messages with pictures. The verbal message alone seems to create in people's minds more of a positive feeling for the product.

Two Kinds of Words

There are two kinds of words: printed and spoken. We often confuse the two, but there's a big difference.

The ear is faster than the eye. Repeated tests have shown that the mind is able to understand a spoken word in 140 milliseconds. A printed word, on the other hand, can be understood in 180 milliseconds.

To account for this 40 millisecond delay, psychologists speculate that the brain translates visual information into aural sounds that the mind can comprehend.

Not only do you hear faster than you see, your hearing lasts longer than your seeing. A visual image—picture or words—fades in one second unless your mind does something to file away the essence of the idea. Hearing, on the other hand, lasts four or five times as long.

That's why it's easy to lose your train of thought when you read printed words. Often you have to backtrack to pick up the sense of the message. Because sound lasts much longer in the mind, the spoken word is easier to follow.

Thus, listening to a message is much more effective than reading it. First, the mind holds the spoken words in storage much longer, enabling you to follow the train of thought with greater clarity. And second, the tone of the human voice gives the words emotional impact that no picture can achieve.

But other things happen in your mind when you listen to the spoken word.

Auding and Reading

In newborn children, the process of listening occurs first, and then the process of auding, which is listening to the spoken language and comprehending the language. Only later do people actually learn to read.

Ordinarily, when children enter the school system, they learn to decode through the process of phonics training. So there is a very intimate relationship between written language and oral language, inasmuch as written language is ordinarily recoded into an internal form of the earlier-acquired oral language skill.

In other words, the mind apparently translates printed words into spoken equivalents before it can understand them. (The beginning reader often will move his lips when reading.)

Now we know why a deaf person has so much trouble learning to read—there are no sounds to translate the words into—and why a blind person has no trouble learning to read braille.

We also know the reason for the 40 millisecond difference between the printed and the spoken word. Printed words make a mental detour through the aural portion of the brain.

The ear drives the eye. There is much evidence that the mind works by ear, that thinking is a process of manipulating sounds, not images—even when pictures or photographs are involved.

Implications for Advertising

The implications of these findings for the advertising industry are staggering, to say the least. In many ways, they call for a complete reorientation from a visual to a verbal point of view.

We're not saying that the visual doesn't play an important role. Of course it does. But the verbal should be the driver, and the pictures should reinforce the words. All too often the opposite is the case.

Laboratory Applications

1. What are some of the possible implications of these findings for the way advertising is created? For the way copy is written? For the media used by advertisers?
2. Do you agree with the Trout and Ries findings? What do you think most consumers prefer for communication and entertainment, the eye or the ear? What do most advertisers prefer for communicating their messages?

Checklist for Writing Effective Copy

☐ Make it easy on your reader. Write short sentences. Use easy, familiar words.

☐ Don't waste words. Say what you have to say—nothing more, nothing less. Don't pad, but don't skimp.

☐ Stick to the present tense, active voice—it's crisper. Avoid the past tense and passive voice. Exceptions should be deliberate, for special effect.

☐ Don't hesitate to use personal pronouns. Remember, you're trying to talk to just *one* person, so talk as you would to a friend. Use "you" and "your."

☐ Clichés are crutches. Learn to get along without them. Bright, surprising words and phrases perk up readers, keep them reading.

☐ Don't overpunctuate. It kills copy flow. Excessive commas are the chief culprits. Don't give your readers any excuse to jump ship.

☐ Use contractions whenever possible. They're fast, personal, natural. People talk in contractions. (Listen to yourself.)

☐ Don't brag or boast. Write from the reader's point of view, not your own. Avoid "we," "us," "our."

☐ Be single-minded. Don't try to do too much. If you chase more than one rabbit at a time, you'll catch none.

☐ Write with flair. Drum up excitement. Make sure the enthusiasm you feel comes through in your copy.

straight-line copy is advantageous in industrial situations and for consumer products that may be difficult to use. Many camera advertisements, for example, use this straight, factual copy style to get the message across. The straight-line approach emphasizes the reason the consumer should buy something.

Narrative copy tells a story. It sets up a problem and then creates a solution using the particular sales features of the product or service. It may then suggest that you use the same solution if you have that problem.

Sometimes the advertiser will use *institutional copy* to sell an idea or the merits of the organization or service rather than sales features of a particular product. Often institutional copy is also narrative in style because it lends warmth to the organization. Banks, insurance companies, public utilities, and large manufacturing concerns are the most common users of institutional copy. However, beware of what David Ogilvy refers to as the "self-serving, flatulent pomposity" that characterizes the copy in most corporate advertisements.[17]

Dialogue/monologue copy can add the credibility that narrative copy sometimes lacks. The characters illustrated in the advertisement do the selling in their own words, either through a testimonial or quasi-testimonial technique, or through a comic-strip panel (see Figure 8–11). However, beginning copywriters often have trouble writing this kind of copy unless they have some playwriting experience. Not everything people say is interesting, so if it is not done well, dialogue copy can come off dull or, even worse, hokey.

Sometimes it is easier to tell the story through a series of illustrations and captions than through the use of a copy block alone. Then *picture-caption copy* is used. This is especially true when the product is shown in a number of different uses or when it is available in a variety of styles or designs.

FIGURE   8–11

The dialogue copy in this radio commercial for Kronenbourg beer is very funny and quite memorable. But to accomplish this commercial's desired effect, excellent writing, top-quality production, and professional acting are required. Otherwise, it will fall very flat.

ENGLISH ACCENT:	"Ah, look I've had a lot of rude letters about Kronenbourg's slogan 'Better not Bitter,' saying it isn't exactly literature. Well, look! Surely, what matters is whether it's true, and to further test this I have with me here an American beer-drinking person. Par excellence, welcome, Mr. Ivan Molomut."
BAD AMERICAN ACCENT:	"Gosh, what's cookin' pal?"
ENGLISH:	"Now, would you put this blindfold on, please."
AMERICAN:	"Sure thang. Thay're, ah done it."
ENGLISH:	"Now, Mr. Molomut, there are two imported beers here. Will you taste this one first."
AMERICAN:	"Yessiree. (Slurping noise) Yep. Well as we say in Arkansas, this first beer is jolly mediocre."
ENGLISH:	"I see. Now would you taste the second beer?"
AMERICAN:	(Slurping noise) "Gee, that's purty darn better."
ENGLISH:	"Better, Mr. Molomut? But not . . ."
AMERICAN:	"Well, it sure ain't acrid, or acerbic, or even slightly caustic."
ENGLISH:	"Is 'not bitter' the word you're looking for?"
AMERICAN:	"Shoot, yes Mac."
ENGLISH:	"And the second beer was . . . yes, Kronenbourg! And you've never even met me before."
AMERICAN:	"Well, I guess that proves Kronenbourg beer, imported by Kronenbourg, USA, Greenwich, Connecticut, really is 'Better not Bitter.'"
ENGLISH:	"So why don't you take the Kronenbourg taste test today."
AMERICAN:	"I just took it."
ENGLISH:	"I'm not talking to you, you yankee fathead."

Gimmick copy depends on wordplays, humor, poetry, rhymes, great exaggeration, gags, and other trick devices. Don't downgrade gimmick advertising. A gimmick carried out rationally is believable. An ad for WD-40 shows a close-up of the spray lubricant aimed directly at the reader. The copy says: "Take a shot at tools with moving parts, lawnmowers, sticky locks, and squeaky hinges. Anything that moves. WD-40. America's troubleshooter."

Humor is a popular form of gimmick copy, particularly in broadcast advertising. In fact, many creative directors look for humor in copy to serve as entertainment value in advertising.[18] One ad touched parental funny bones by featuring a cute little boy dipping into a bag of Kraft marshmallows, with the headline: "A marshmallow a day keeps your freckles on straight."

Humor can be effective when the advertiser needs high memorability in a short time, and it may be used to destroy an outmoded attitude or use pattern that affects a product. However, humor is also very subjective. It should always be used carefully and never in questionable taste. Some researchers believe humor can even be detrimental when used for financial services and insurance.[19]

The four basic elements to the construction of body copy are the lead-in paragraph, interior paragraphs, trial close, and close.

Lead-in Paragraph

The *lead-in paragraph* is a bridge between the headline, the subheads, and the sales ideas presented in the text. It transfers reading interest to product interest.

Headline: "It was easier to turn a Porsche into a luxury car than vice versa."
Lead-in paragraph: "Ever since the first 356 rolled off the assembly line and into automotive history, enthusiasts have associated the name Porsche with one thing. Performance."

The lead-in paragraph may perform other functions as well. In short-copy advertisements (an increasing trend) and outdoor advertising, the lead-in paragraph may be the only paragraph. It may include the promise, the claim-support information, and the close. A poster for the Minneapolis Planetarium, for instance, shows a large cartoon of Buck Rogers under the headline: "The Buck Stops Here." The single paragraph of body copy reads: "When you've had enough of science fiction, try some science fact at the Minneapolis Planetarium."

Interior Paragraphs

This is where we build interest and desire and provide proof for claims and promises. A good ad or commercial not only has to be truthful but also has to be believable to be effective. With increased consumer awareness and sophistication, claims must be made carefully. And proof should be offered. Proofs may fall into the following categories:

1. Research: government or private studies.
2. Testing: by case history, testing firm, consumers, or the advertiser.
3. Usage: product market rank, case history, testimonial, endorsements.
4. Guarantee: trial offers, demonstration offers, free samples, warranty information.

The keys to good copy are simplicity, order, credibility, and clarity. Or, as John O'Toole says, what's important is "that the prose be written clearly, informatively, interestingly, powerfully, persuasively, dramatically, memorably, and with effortless grace. That's all."[20] (See the Copywriter's Portfolio.)

Trial Close

Interspersed in the interior paragraphs should be requests for the order. Good copy asks for the order more than once. In mail-order advertisements particularly, it is necessary to ask for the order several times. Consumers may decide to buy without reading the entire body copy. The trial close gives them the option to make the buying decision early.

Close

An advertisement's close asks consumers to do something and tells them how to do it. This is the point in the advertisement when the sale, in its broadest sense, is made. Of course, not all advertisements sell products or services. We may be looking for a change in attitude, an understanding of our point of view, a vote, or a new preference for our product or service.

The close can be direct or indirect, a subtle suggestion or a direct command. English Leather's close is certainly indirect: "My men wear English Leather or they wear nothing at all." This headline is repeated in the last sentence of the body copy, suggesting indirectly that if you want to please a woman, you will wear English Leather or, conversely, if you want

(continued on p. 273)

COPYWRITER'S PORTFOLIO

A. The poignancy of this ad against drunk driving stems from the often-overlooked yet frightening truth of the headline and the visual. It's a sobering thought.

B. An all-copy ad that is, itself, so simple it needs no visual. The words tell the whole story.

C. Timberland promotes its product's quality and ruggedness with a simple innuendo. While you may have to replace the laces, you won't have to replace the shoes.

THIS YEAR IN SAN DIEGO, 38,000 KIDS WILL BE BORN.

AND ANOTHER 42,000 WILL WISH THEY WEREN'T.

We're all brought into this world kicking and screaming. For a lot of babies, it goes downhill from there.

They'll be unlucky enough to be born to an abusive parent. Last year, over 42,000 people called the County's hot line to report serious abuse and neglect. And who knows how many

people didn't even have the nerve to call.

We have long waiting lists of people who need help and counseling.

Try telling this baby he's on a waiting list.

So, this year, we have five separate agencies working on the problem.

And we're spending more money than ever to stop it. Call 260-6227. Make a pledge. And the next time a baby's brought into this world, let's make sure the baby doesn't regret the trip.

UNITED WAY/CHAD

Putting people first in San Diego County.

D. The use of an appalling statistic in a news/information headline for United Way shocks the reader into awareness of the problem and stimulates the very human desire to protect children from abuse.

E. A great example of radio copywriting. As you read the script, you can just hear what it would sound like on the radio.

SFX:	Chickens clucking
GUY:	I got two chickens here.
	One's a Five Star Chicken, from Eagle.
	The other isn't.
	Now you folks at home see if you can
	tell which is which.
	Give you a hint —— Five Star chickens are supposed
	to weigh at least two and a quarter pounds.
	Anything smaller just won't be meaty enough.
	Okay, So which is the Five Star . . .
	Chicken #1?
CHICKEN:	(Weakly) buck, buck, buck . . .
GUY:	Or chicken #2?
CHICKEN:	(Boldly) BUCK! BUCK! BUCK!
GUY:	Well, heck. Give it away, why dontcha.
ANNCR:	Five Star chicken from Eagle. You'll love it,
	or your money back.

to please a man, you will buy him English Leather. A direct close seeks immediate response either in the form of a purchase or a request for further details. The Levi's ad in Figure 8–12 directed to the trade closes with: "Ask your Levi's Representative for all the exciting details . . . And be sure to request a swatch of Premiere Corduroy."

The close should simplify the reader's response, making it as easy as possible for the reader to order the merchandise, send for information, or visit a showroom. The close tells the reader where to shop or what to send. A business reply card or a toll-free telephone number may be included. In fact, everything the reader needs in order to act should be in the close or near it.

Boxes and Panels

Boxes and panels are generally used in advertisements that contain coupons, special offers, contest rules, and order blanks to set these features apart from the rest of the advertisement.

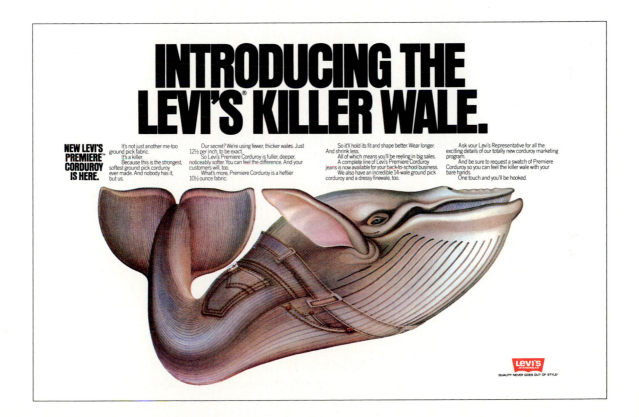

FIGURE   8–12

The dynamic graphics and the arresting headline make it easy to get hooked on this trade ad for Levi's. The tight technical copy reinforces the implied benefit in the headline with specific, objective information.

Specifically, a *box* is copy around which a line has been drawn. A *panel* is an elongated box that usually runs the whole length or width of an ad. Sometimes it may be shaded or completely black, with text or copy shown in reverse (white lettering).

Boxes and panels are used to draw greater attention to a specific element or message in an advertisement.

Slogans

Many *slogans* (also called themelines or tag lines) begin as successful headlines. Through continuous use, they become standard statements, not just in advertising but for salespeople and company employees. They become a battle cry for the company. In fact, the word *slogan* comes from the Gaelic term for "battle cry."

Slogans have two basic purposes: to provide continuity for a campaign and to reduce a key theme or idea the company wants associated with its product or itself to a brief, memorable positioning statement. DeBeers' ads, for example, still claim the famous premise in their slogan: "Diamonds are forever." On the other hand, Water Pik's promise, "You'll feel good about it," may be a good tag line but certainly lacks the endurance to become a full-fledged slogan (see Figure 8–13).

Slogans should be like old friends who stay the same year after year. You recognize them instantly, and you feel you understand them. Some slogans endure because they encapsulate a corporate philosophy: Hallmark's "When you care enough to send the very best." Another example of a corporate philosophy is Zenith's slogan: "At Zenith, the quality goes in before the name goes on."[21] Unfortunately, though, most slogans do not measure up to those lofty expectations. Rather, they fall into Ogilvy's category of "interchangeable fatuous bromides."[22]

Effective slogans are short, simple, memorable, easy to repeat, and, most important, helpful in differentiating the product or the company from its competitors: "When it rains, it pours" (Morton Salt). Rhyme, rhythm, and alliteration are valuable copy aids that can be used when writing slogans.

FIGURE   8–13

This Water Pik ad gets attention through the use of a highly recognizable celebrity smile. The tag line promise has a double meaning—you'll be happy you bought it and your mouth will feel better.

Seals, Logotypes, and Signatures

The term *seal* is the subject of much confusion among advertising students. For some, it indicates the seals of approval offered by such organizations as the Good Housekeeping Institute, Underwriters Laboratories, and Parents Institute. Seals are given only when a product meets standards established by these institutions. Since the organizations are all recognized authorities—and are trusted implicitly—it is beneficial to include the seals in an advertisement. The seals provide an independent, valued endorsement for the advertised product.

For others, the term *seal* refers to the company seal or trademark. These are actually called *logotypes*. Logotypes (logos) and signature cuts (sig cuts) are special designs of the advertiser's company name or product name. They appear in all the advertisements and are like trademarks because they give the product individuality and provide quick recognition at the point of purchase.

COMMON PITFALLS IN WRITING COPY

Today's consumer is intelligent, educated, and discriminating. Copy style, therefore, should reflect consumer tastes and values. Generalizations are not convincing—the consumer is looking for specific information to form judgments and make purchase decisions. Being specific means leaving out the trite advertising clichés like *amazing, wonderful,* and *finest.*

Words cost money. A print advertisement may cost $50 a word or $5,000 a word, depending on the medium. At those prices, every word counts. Words that do not sell cost more money than words that do, so use words that sell. Avoid the following pitfalls that plague beginning copywriters and annoy customers.

Obfuscation   The fundamental requirements of any advertisement are that it be readable and understandable. Avoid $10 words (like *obfuscation*) that nobody understands. Write simply in the everyday, colloquial English people use in conversation. (See Ad Lab 8-B.) Use small words. You will get your point across better if you use words and phrases that are familiar to your reader. Use short sentences. The longer the sentence, the harder it is to understand. Compare these paragraphs:

> The Armco vacuum cleaner not only cleans your rugs and drapes, it's invaluable on hard surfaces such as vinyl floors, wood floors, even cement. You won't believe how incredibly smooth and quiet the machine is as it travels across your sparkling floors.

AD LAB 8-B   Writing Readable Advertising Copy: A Self-Test

The Gunning Fog Index is a measure of your writing simplicity. Here's how it works:

1. Take 100-word samples from any given piece of writing—at least five or six samples if possible. Create a grid with three columns.
2. Count the number of words to the end of the sentence nearest the end of the 100-word sample (this could be more or less than 100) and enter in column 1.
3. Count the number of sentences in that sample and enter in column 2.
4. Count all of the words with three or more syllables in that sample. Do *not* count:

   Proper nouns—Chicago, Toronto, California, Jonathan.
   Compound words made of simple words—bookkeeper, furthermore, nevertheless.
   Words that become three syllables because of an added verb ending such as -ing or -ed—bargaining, donating, recanted, accounted.

5. Enter the total in column 3.
6. Total each column.
7. Find the average number of words per sentence; divide the total number of words (column 1) by the total number of sentences (column 2).
8. Find the average number of words with three syllables or more; divide the total of column 3 by the number of samples.
9. Add the two averages, then multiply by 0.4. The result is the reading grade level—the Fog Index—for that piece of writing.

Laboratory Application

Select five or six pieces of your writing. Compute the Fog Index.

The Armco vacuum cleaner cleans rugs . . . drapes. It cleans hard surfaces like woods and vinyl floors. Even cement! The Armco vacuum cleaner is smooth . . . quiet. Try it! Make your floors sparkle with new cleanliness.

Thousands of advertisements compete for your reader. The more understandable your advertisement, the more likely it will be read.

Filibustering We have discussed the importance of brevity. Look at this headline: "Winston tastes good like a cigarette should." Now imagine if it weren't concise: "Winston cigarettes taste exceedingly fine, the way every cigarette manufacturer wishes his cigarettes would taste."

Long-winded filibusters should be confined to the Senate. They are not allowed in advertising. Be complete, but be concise.

Clichés/Triteness/Superlatives Overused expressions do nothing for copy. Most superlatives (greatest, large economy) and clichés (tried and true, a penny saved is a penny earned) may once have been exciting statements, but time has worn their value into rags.

Certainly clichés can communicate, and not all stock expressions are clichés. But clichés erode consumer confidence. They contribute to an out-of-date image.

Abstract/Vagueness Abstract words, such as *fine, really, OK,* are words that do not provide specificity. Since they can't be measured, they are not easily understood or evaluated.

Superior copy is concrete and matched to the experience of the audience to which it appeals. Words should have tangible dollars-and-cents value. For example, in an ad for a new high-tech product, avoid vague, boastful generalities like: "Supporting the Nutech Spectra-flanstran are technological advances that give these instruments incredible capability." Be specific: "The Nutech Spectra-flanstran provides military specification tolerances to .005 inches."[23]

"Me-Me-Me" The advertisement must appeal to the reader's self-interest, not the advertiser's. If you want to get your message across and persuade the reader, use the "you" attitude. Talk about his or her needs, hopes, wishes, and preferences. In an industrial ad for Inter-Tel (see Figure 8–14), note the use of *you, your,* and *yourself.* Talk about the reader, and you are talking about the most interesting person in the world. For example:

Me	You
We are pleased to announce our new flight schedule from Cincinnati to Philadelphia which is any hour on the hour.	You can take a plane from Cincinnati to Philadelphia any hour on the hour.
We believe this vacuum cleaner to be technically superior to any other on the market.	Your house will be more beautiful because you'll be using the most powerful, easy-to-use vacuum we have ever offered.

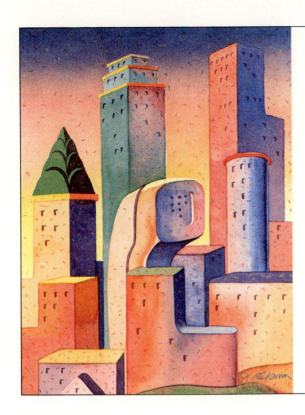

In your market there should be only one place to buy the one best phone system.

Your place.

Business is tough enough. Why make it even tougher by knocking heads with 20 other dealers selling the same product to the same prospects.

HAVE THE BEST, ALL TO YOURSELF.

When you become an authorized Inter-Tel dealer, your market is yours. No competition for product. Or delivery. Or support. Or price. Or customers. Because our new Phoenix communications system guarantees you'll have everything your customers need. 2 to 32 lines. 2 to 128 phones. And all the features they'd expect.

MORE HELP BEFORE THE SALE.

As an authorized Phoenix dealer, you'll enjoy the strongest sales support program in the industry. Instead of sending technical manuals, we send a top-notch training team. Our marketing support is just as strong. Liberal advertising allowances. Ad maker kits. Dealer display booths. And video tapes and special programs to help you make the sale.

...AND AFTER.

Your relationship with a client shouldn't end with the sale. With Inter-Tel, it won't. When your customers need to step up to a larger system, or simply expand the one they have, you'll be the one helping them do it. And your local service center will provide remote programming and diagnostics to meet their changing needs.

BE THE ONE AND ONLY.

Take the first step. Simply call or write our marketing department for full details on becoming an authorized Phoenix dealer. Inter-Tel, 6505 West Williams Field Road, Chandler, Arizona 85224. (602) 961-9000 or (800) 523-8180.

INTER-TEL
Better before the sale.
Better after the sale.

Better before the sale.
Better after the sale.

FIGURE   8–14

Inter-Tel uses a surrealistic John Kleber illustration to break out of the clutter of telephone equipment advertisers swamping the pages of telecommunications trade magazines. This particular ad was specifically designed for one such publication—*Teleconnect*—which is known and liked for its avant-garde use of graphics and satirical editorial content. Inter-Tel's agency, Phillips-Ramsey/Phoenix, hoped this unique approach would set its client apart from all the same-looking advertising for telephone push buttons, bells, and whistles. It did.

No, Not Negativity Think negatively, write negatively, and you may produce a negative response. Readers usually respond better to a positive viewpoint. Stress what things are or what they can be instead of what they are not. Remember, words often have connotations apart from their literal meanings. Also, be aware that different people react to the same word in different ways. Even *love,* that most beautiful word, may have a positive meaning for a single person and a negative implication for a divorced person.

Euphemisms To *euphemize* is to substitute an inoffensive, mild word for a word that is offensive, harsh, or blunt. When a copywriter euphemizes, he or she puts a good face on something. Calling toilet paper "bathroom tissue" doesn't change its appearance or function, but it may soften the mental impression for people. Other euphemisms are "resale cars" (for used cars), "package store" (for liquor store), "underarm wetness" (for sweaty armpits), "irregularity" (for constipation), and "midriff bulge" (for fat gut). But be careful in choosing euphemisms. They can be misleading, weaken your message, and, if considered fraudulent, invite investigation by the Federal Trade Commission.

Defamation Avoid portraying real people in a bad light. All advertising copy is governed by the laws of defamation. Making a false statement or allegation about a person or holding a person up to contempt is defamation. When defamation is done in print advertising it is called *libel.* In broadcast advertising or verbal statements, it is called *slander.* Defamation occurs when people's names are used or references are made to them in a libelous or slanderous manner. The size of audience is not a defense; a libelous statement, for example, need only be read by more than one person to be defamation.

CREATING NAMES FOR PRODUCTS

Copywriters are often asked to develop names for companies or products. Here are some ways in which names are chosen.

Personal Names One way to label a product is to name it after yourself: Gerber baby foods, Ford cars. Problems occur, however, because people have similar names. Names can be copied, and it is difficult to stop other people from using their names on their products. Using fictitious names, like Bartles & Jaymes, may avoid this problem.

Geographic Names If a geographic name is used in an arbitrary manner, like Newport cigarettes, it may function as a trademark. However, if it identifies a product's place of origin or suggests where the product may have come from, it cannot be protected as a trademark (e.g., Detroit Auto Works).

Coined or Invented Names The most distinctive names are often coined. Kodak was coined by George Eastman because he wanted a name beginning and ending with an infrequently used letter. Kleenex, Xerox, Betty Crocker, and Polaroid have an advantage because they are short, pronounceable, and arbitrary. It's unlikely others will use anything similar (see Figure 8–15). In recent years, the computer has been used to generate unique coined names for both companies and products.

Initials or Numbers Some common examples are IBM computers, RCA televisions, and A-1 steak sauce. In general, initials and numbers are not recommended as product names. How do you position your new RQS Company? What would the name Harris 5500 say about your product?

Company Name The company name is sometimes used also as a brand name—for example, Texaco, Gulf, Shell. More typically, though, companies choose to develop different names for their products so as to avoid confusion and create greater value for the brand itself.

Foreign Words Perfume companies often use French words to project an image of romance (Vol de Nuit). Auto manufacturers use foreign words to add mystery and intrigue: Cordova, Biarritz. Restaurants use them to identify the kind of food they serve: Del Taco, L'Auberge, La Scala.

Licensed Names Companies may license names for their marketability (Snoopy toothbrushes, Sunkist vitamins). The cost of using a licensed name is often steep, and the use of the name has tight restrictions.

Arbitrary Dictionary Words The most successful products often have dictionary names: Tide detergent, Whirlpool appliances, Arrow shirts.

Arbitrary marks are dictionary words that have nothing to do with product description. They are more easily protected than words that have some relationship to the product. Plus, they may give the product an image as well as an identity. Fragrance advertisers have used steamy advertising and shock-value names to pique consumer interest. Obsession, Poison, Decadence are just a few examples.[24]

No single chapter on the topic of copywriting can be complete since the study of advertising concerns the discipline of writing. For that reason, the issue of copywriting will be discussed in subsequent chapters on advertising production and media as it pertains to those subjects.

You Can't Drink Coffee From A STYROFOAM Cup.

There's No Such Thing.

We know. Because we make STYROFOAM® brand plastic foam. But we don't make it into cups, plates, coolers, egg cartons or fast food packages.

STYROFOAM is our trademark used to describe our top-quality line of plastic foam and construction products. Such as STYROFOAM brand insulation boards, easily recognized by their distinctive Blue® color. And STYROFOAM brand plastic foam blocks, which have a variety of uses in the marine, floral and hobby industries.

So, please use our trademark carefully. It should be used only to describe products that carry the STYROFOAM brand name. It shouldn't be used generically to describe other brands of plastic foam.

Remember, if it doesn't say STYROFOAM, it isn't.

For more detailed information, contact The Dow Chemical Company at 1-800-258-2436, extension 25/STYROFOAM Brand Products.

*Trademark of The Dow Chemical Company

Dow **Styrofoam**

FIGURE   8–15

Believe it or not, there's no such thing as a Styrofoam cup. Styrofoam is a coined name that suffers from its own success. People have a tendency to use the name as a generic substitute for other foam products, so now Dow Chemical has to invest considerable sums in an effort to protect its unique trademark from improper use.

Summary

Copy is the verbal presentation and art is the visual presentation of the message strategy. Before beginning to write, the copywriter must understand the intended marketing and advertising strategies. This usually requires a review of the marketing and advertising plans, an analysis of the facts, and an examination of the creative strategy. The copywriter should develop a brief written copy platform that tells what the copy will say and how it will support the message strategy.

To create an effective advertisement, the copywriter seeks to gain attention, create interest, achieve credibility, heighten desire, and stimulate action.

The key copy elements in print advertising are headlines, subheads, body copy, captions, boxes and panels, slogans, logotypes, seals, and signatures. In broadcast advertising, copy is normally spoken dialogue and is referred to as the audio portion of the commercial. The copy may be delivered as a voice-over by an unseen announcer or on camera by an announcer, spokesperson, or actor.

Many types of headlines and copy styles are used in print advertising. Good advertising headlines can generally be classified into five basic categories: (1) benefit, (2) provocative, (3) news/information, (4) question, and (5) command. Copy styles also fall into several categories: (1) straight line, (2) narrative, (3) institutional, (4) dialogue/monologue, (5) picture caption, and (6) gimmick.

The pitfalls for unsuspecting copywriters are many and varied. The most common ones are obfuscation, filibustering, clichés/triteness/superlatives, abstract/vagueness, "me-me-me," negative thinking, misleading euphemisms, and unintentional defamation.

Copywriters may develop names for products. Personal names, geographic names, coined or invented names, initials or numbers, foreign words, licensed names, and arbitrary dictionary words provide the basis for the selection of names of most products.

Questions for Review and Discussion

1. Based on an advertisement you have selected in this chapter, what is the advertiser's message strategy?
2. Based on an ad of your choice, how well has the advertiser achieved the five objectives of effective advertising copy? Explain.
3. Select a magazine advertisement you like. What functions are provided by the elements in the ad?
4. Choose an advertisement you don't like. How would you rewrite the headline using three different styles?
5. Find an advertisement with a tag line. What is its function, and what is your opinion of it?
6. Select an advertisement or commercial you like. What issues did the advertiser have to consider in writing the copy platform? Discuss.
7. What are the six basic functions of a headline?
8. What are some of the most effective methods for making copy interesting?
9. Find an advertisement you don't like. What is the message strategy? Which type of headline is used? What is the copy style? Do you think the copy and headline reflect the strategy? What don't you like about the ad? Why?
10. If you had just invented a new soft drink, what would you name it? Why?

9

CREATIVE ART DIRECTION

John Weiss still talks about that most risky and precious of opportunities he had—the chance to establish new standards in a fresh, uncharted market.

It all started just a few years ago when Godiva (the luxury chocolatier, not the mythical unclad equestrienne) came to him and John Margeotes of Margeotes/Fertitta & Weiss in search of promotional assistance. Unfortunately, the client was unable to give much help in formulating a campaign strategy because the luxury chocolate market was virtually nonexistent.

"It was really virgin territory," recalls Weiss. "We had no statistics as to who bought the chocolates or how much they were willing to pay."

With no established precedents to rely on, the Margeotes creative team journeyed to the source for inspiration—the Godiva plant. They toured the factory and saw people working with masks and gloves, discarding anything with a nick on it. These workers obviously had a love for the product.

The immediate challenge for Weiss, as the copywriter, and Margeotes, as the art director, was to translate this devotion into a viable strategy and then a commercially potent campaign.

In searching for the big idea for Godiva, Margeotes and Weiss worked through a wide variety of concepts. The stakes were high because, they believed, a lackluster effort would be completely obscured by the traditionally crowded field of upscale advertisers.

Weiss explains that, strategically, they wanted people to understand that Godivas are more than just ordinary chocolates. "They're exclusive, and they represent a chance for people to own something that's the best of its kind." The problem was how to translate that product concept into advertising.[1]

As we pointed out in Chapter 8, for all creative people, the first step in designing any advertisement or commercial is always the toughest. The same situation was true for Weiss and Margeotes. In this process, it is not unusual for 5, 10, 20, 50, or more ideas to come up, be considered, and then be rejected for any of a variety of reasons. Then it's back to the drawing board. Twenty more ideas are conceived. Some good, some not so good, some bad. No big ideas. And nothing clicks. That's when creative people recall the phrase: "Creativity is 10 percent inspiration, 90 percent perspiration."

Margeotes and Weiss finally hit on an idea they liked: to present the chocolates in an elegant, dreamlike, setting. As the dark of night bleeds off all sides of the page, a soft spot of light would fall upon the exquisitely sculptured chocolates. The delicate arrangement and moody photography would create a visual layout that was at once seductive and classy. Complementing this scene would be a brief, provocative headline and a short paragraph of elegant copy using classic Shakespearean allusions or subtle wordplays ("Mint Summer Night's Dream") to lend a poetic mood to the ads. The copy would be enticing, tasty, but never too sweet or syrupy (see Figure 9–1).

That was it. That was the big idea. That inspired creative nutshell, out of which grow all the verbal and visual details of every great advertisement—the creative concept. It was this creative concept that would give birth to what is now considered "the Godiva mystique." And that image would be responsible for swelling the company's sales eightfold over the next 10 years.[2]

In the case of Godiva, as in most cases, the nonverbal aspect of an advertisement or commercial carries fully half the burden of communicating the message. The way an advertisement *looks* will often determine to a great extent the way it *feels*. That, in turn, will flavor the message and determine the degree to which the advertiser's words are understood and believed. In this chapter, therefore, we will discuss advertising concepts from the standpoint of the visual details: the art in advertising—what it is, where it comes from, how it's done.

WHAT IS ART?

In advertising, *art* refers to more than what a cartoonist, a painter, or an illustrator does. The term refers to the whole visual presentation of the commercial or advertisement, including how the words in the ad are arranged, what size and style of type are used, whether photos or illustrations are used, and if so, how they should be organized. Art also refers to what style of photography or illustration is employed, how color is used, and how these elements are arranged in an ad and relate to one another in size and proportion.

In short, if copy is the spoken language of an ad, art is the body language. This is true for both print ads and television commercials. Art directors are as involved as copywriters in writing and producing the commercials we see on TV. Why? Because they are concerned with what the commercial *looks like*. In fact, many of the top agencies even have their art directors help write radio commercials. Their feeling is that effective radio advertising combines sounds and words to create visual *word pictures* in the mind of the listener. To help orchestrate this visual side of the radio commercial, the art director can be very instrumental. Thus, *every* advertisement employs *art*—even if that art is sometimes inappropriate to the advertiser or the market or the message.

FIGURE   9–1

The Godiva mystique was spawned by the campaign's elegant poster-style layouts and stunning photographic treatment of the company's sculpted sweets. A vast departure from typical candy advertising, the ad implies the price without ever mentioning it.

ROLE OF THE ADVERTISING ARTIST

Several different types of people are employed in advertising art, and all of them may be called artists, or commercial artists, as a general description even though they may perform entirely different tasks. What is often surprising to nonadvertising people is that some of these "artists" may not be able to draw particularly well—they have been trained for other artistic specialties.

Art Directors

Art directors are responsible for the visual presentation of the ad. They are, therefore, normally involved, along with a copywriter, in developing the initial concept of the ad—in the visualization process discussed in Chapter 8. They may do the initial sketches, or layouts, of what the ad might look like. From that point on, though, they may not touch the ad again themselves. Their primary responsibility, after conceptualization, is to supervise the ad's progress to completion.

The best art directors are strong conceptually in both words and pictures. They are usually highly trained in pure graphic design and experienced in various aspects of advertising and art. They must also have a strong understanding of consumer behavior and motivation since that is the very essence of developing their creative product.[3] Moreover, they should be good managers of people. They may have a large or small staff under them, depending on the organization. Or they may work *free-lance* (i.e., as an independent contractor), in which case they themselves probably do more of the work that would normally be handled by assistants in agency art departments.

Graphic Designers

The way advertising materials are initially designed establishes the artistic direction and eventually programs the result. Will the ad, for instance, be stunning, beautiful, a "work of art" as in the case of Godiva or Waterford Crystal? Or is the ad simply intended to make a standard commercial announcement? To achieve the former, graphic designers may be employed. Often the art director acts as the designer, too. Sometimes, however, a separate designer is used to offer a unique touch to a particular ad.

Graphic designers are precision specialists who are preoccupied with the shape and form of things. Their effort in advertising is to arrange the various graphic elements (type, illustrations, photos, white space) in the most attractive and effective way possible (see Figure 9–2). While they may work on ads, especially as free-lancers on special projects, they are more typically involved in the design and production of collateral materials such as posters, brochures, and annual reports.

Illustrators

The artists who paint or draw the pictures we see in ads are called *illustrators*. One of the greatest illustrators in this century was Norman Rockwell, whose pictures brought life in middle America to the cover of the *Saturday Evening Post* every week.

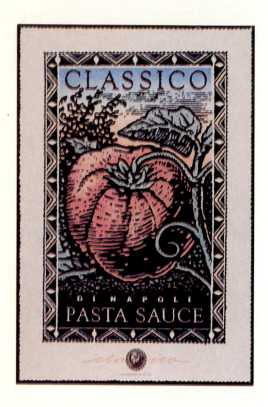

FIGURE 9–2

Italy is a land rich with unique regional cuisines, each a result of local culture and the fresh foods available. To capture the essence of each major region, Prince Foods created its Classico Pasta Sauce in a variety of sauce recipes. Then, to aim the product at the premium segment of the category, Duffy Design Group crafted distinctive product labels characterized by subdued tones and finely drawn, classic illustrations.

Illustrators are specialists. They are so specialized, in fact, that many frequently concentrate on just one type of illustrating. Fashion illustrators, for example, specialize in drawing clothing. Their training enables them to catch a particular look and communicate the unique feel of a garment. Furniture illustrators do the same thing with home furnishings. They might draw a manufacturer's sofa, for example, in pencil or with water-colors, paying great attention to the upholstery or wood veneer and showing it all off in a beautiful living room setting. The various types of illustration will be described later in this chapter.

Illustration is such a specialty that most advertising illustrators work free-lance. Very few agencies or advertisers retain full-time illustrators unless their work is of such a volume and so specialized that they require the continuous efforts of one type of illustrator. Rather, the agencies hire different illustrators for different jobs depending on the particular needs and the desired look and feel of the ad (see Figure 9–3).

Production Artists

Production or *pasteup* artists are responsible for assembling the various elements of an ad and mechanically putting them together the way the art director or designer has indicated. Good production artists are fast, precise, and knowledgeable about the whole production process (see Chapter 10). In addition, they have the tenacity to stand the tedious task of bending over a drawing board all day assembling little pieces of type, drawing perfectly straight, clean lines with a pen, or cutting delicate photographs with a sharp knife.

Most designers and art directors start their careers as production artists and work their way up. It's very difficult work, but it is also important since this is where the ads actually come together in their finished form.

FIGURE   9–3

Nocona boots uses a superb photo-realistic illustration to demonstrate the desirability of their product and create a supermacho image for the purchaser. Notice the detail of the stitching on the boots, the strands of hemp in the rein, the look of contempt in the horse's eye for the cowboy who is now upside down in midair, and even the subtle humor of the Let's Rodeo ring on the cowboy's fist. Note also the graphic design creating a gaze motion down through the ad ending right at the company logo.

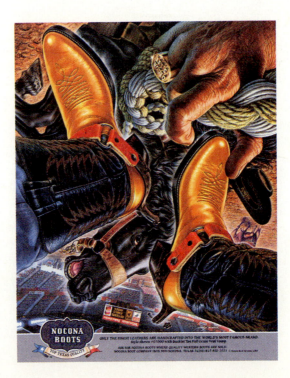

CREATING THE ADVERTISEMENT

The market for motorcycles in the United States and Canada is extremely large. It is also highly fragmented, with products from Germany, Italy, Sweden, England, and Japan successfully competing with American machines. To Americans, many of these bikes might look alike. However, the manufacturers of Yamaha motorcycles felt their Japanese bikes were superior to the rest in engineering, design, and performance. The question was how to communicate this.

Yamaha turned to its American agency at the time, Botsford-Ketchum (San Francisco), for help. The agency responded with a campaign that not only won numerous awards for its excellent copy, art, and design but, at the time, also set a new international standard for motorcycle advertising.[4]

The campaign combined beautiful photography, sophisticated technical illustrations, and straightforward, factual copy in a series of inviting, easy-to-read, full-color one-page ads and two-page spreads. Each ad supported the campaign theme: "When you know how they're built, you'll buy a Yamaha." The ads resembled the editorial format of slick specialty magazines. As such, they built great credibility with readers because readers were familiar with that editorial format in nonadvertising situations (see Figure 9–4).

Over several years, the ads grew in sophistication in both copy and illustration as readers became more familiar with the technical terminology associated with motorcycles. Unique features of Yamaha's superiority

PEOPLE IN ADVERTISING

George H. Lois

President
Lois Pitts Gershon

George H. Lois, hailed by *The New York Times* as "perhaps the most outstanding art director in America," has had an indelible influence on American advertising.

The son of Greek immigrant parents, born and raised in the upper Bronx, Lois attended P.S. 7, where his drawings were spotted by a teacher. She not only sent him to take the entrance exam for Manhattan's famed High School of Music and Art in 1945 but even gave him the dime for round-trip subway fare. Lois was accepted.

After high school, Lois entered Pratt Institute to study art. A professor there decided Lois's talents were too advanced for what Pratt could offer and sent him to see design studio owner Reba Sochis. She examined Lois's portfolio and promptly hired him.

At 21, Lois became an art director at CBS. He then joined Lennen & Newell. That same year, he created the first of the 92 brash, compelling covers he was to produce for *Esquire* magazine over the next 10 years. Lois was soon hired by Sudler & Hennessey. A year later, he went on to Doyle Dane Bernbach. There his work captured three gold medals in the New York Art Directors Club annual competition. After stints at several other agencies, he is today president of Lois Pitts Gershon.

Heralded by *ANNY* (an advertising trade publication) as

FIGURE   9–4

This is one of a series of award-winning ads for Yamaha motorcycles. Notice the lack of company signature at the bottom of the ad. This was intended to impart an editorial feeling in order to build credibility for the product's quality and the company's engineering skill. The volume and intricacy of work on the Yamaha campaign required the full-time efforts of three art directors, each of whom supervised a staff of other art specialists.

one of America's "most promising new agencies," Lois Pitts Gershon has already achieved $100 million in annual billings. Today, it occupies an entire floor of New York's prestigious Piaget building. Agency clients include *USA Today*, MTV, Nickelodeon, and Dreyfus Corporation. According to the LPG philosophy, "Great advertising not only conveys what has to be said about a product but does so with a sense of theater and style." These two qualities—theater and style—describe the maverick, often outrageous creative output of George H. Lois.

Explaining Lois's unorthodox style, Bill Pitts, executive vice president of Lois Pitts Gershon, wrote, "Headlines must sound like the words and cadences people use. Copy has to read like images, not abstractions. But above all else," Pitts emphasized, "coming up with the unexpected always matters most."

Lois confirmed this when he told an audience recently, "Advertising should aim to be seemingly outrageous." The reason? Advertising must be *visible* to be effective. It can be made visible, Lois said, by following these 10 rules:

1. Make advertising human.
2. Believe in advertising as though your life depended on it.
3. Talk in prose that everyone relates to.
4. Create concepts, not ads.
5. Never settle for *almost* perfect.
6. Never try to please the trade ahead of the consumer.
7. Never be defeated by government or industry regulations.
8. Relate to the *real* world.
9. Take risks.
10. Listen to your heart—and respect your instincts.

Today Lois continues to create uncommon, often audacious campaigns. He created the concept of Coca-Cola Clothes (a $250 million business in one year) and provided Purolator Courier with its engaging Road Runner campaign (1-800-BEEP-BEEP).

Arriving at his drawing table at 7:30 each morning, he works directly on every project, personally rendering each frame of his storyboards.

Lois's 92 *Esquire* covers and numerous other triumphs of his prolific 30-year career are featured in his book, *The Art of Advertising: George Lois on Mass Communication*. He has been inducted into both the Art Directors and the Creative Halls of Fame.

in engineering were shown with small *call-outs* or captions next to the photo illustrations. The illustrations became more intricate and diagrammatic as the agency introduced the design changes on new Yamaha models.

In test after test, the Yamaha ads consistently scored first or second in consumer memorability. Dealer feedback was excellent. And within two years, Yamaha's share of market rose three points, placing it behind only Honda in the American market.

What set Yamaha's advertising apart was, again, the "big idea"—the same thing that sets all good advertising apart. In this case, the big idea was the unique art direction, design, and execution in each ad in the campaign. Not only was the art concept unique and brilliantly executed, but most important, it was also relevant to the subject matter, the audience, the objectives of the company, and the verbal presentation in the headline and the copy.

Laying Out the Ad

One of the most impressive features about the Yamaha ads is the layout and design. Note how in Figure 9–4 the copy is set in neat, easy-to-read columns and yet works in and around the central, dynamic illustration. Note, also, the attractiveness of the style of type used in the headline and body copy and the effective use of rules and lines to structure the ad and organize the reading material. Finally, notice the total unity and balance in spite of the number of elements in the ad. The Yamaha campaign is a vivid demonstration of the importance of layout and design to advertising.

For print media, the first work from the art department is usually seen in the form of a *layout,* which is simply a pencil design of the advertisement within the specified dimensions. The term is used when referring to newspaper, magazine, and outdoor and transit advertisements. For direct-mail and point-of-purchase materials, which often require a three-dimensional presentation of the message, the layout is referred to as a *dummy.* For television, the script of a commercial is first seen as a layout in the form of a *storyboard,* which is a series of pictures or frames that correspond to the script.

In doing the layout or storyboard, the art director, in collaboration with the writer, draws upon all his expertise in graphic design, including photography, typography, and illustration, for the purpose of creating an effective ad or commercial.

The Use of Layouts

A layout is an orderly formation of all the parts of the advertisement. In print, that means the headline, subheads, illustration, copy, picture captions, trademarks, slogans, and signature (or logotype). In television, that means the placement of characters, props, scenery, and product elements, the location and angle of the camera, and the use of lighting.

The layout has two purposes. One is a mechanical function. The layout works as a blueprint. In print advertising, for example, it shows where the parts of the ad are to be placed, it guides the copywriter in determining the amount of copy to write, it helps the illustrator or photographer determine the size and style of pictures to be used, and it helps the art director plan

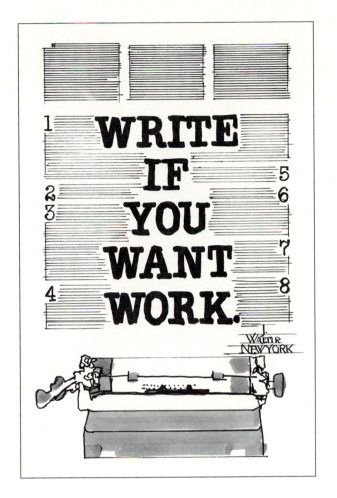

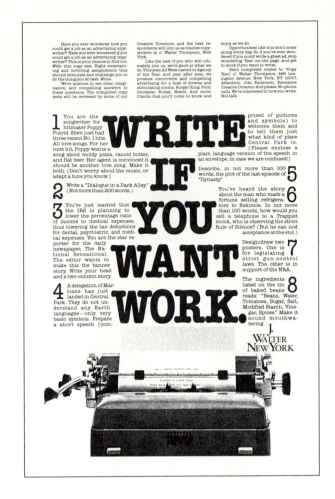

FIGURE   9–5

J. Walter Thompson used this approach to challenge would-be copywriters to complete a test of their skills and compete for a position at the agency. The ad, which ran in *The New York Times* and in college newspapers, was intended to allow job applicants to display their imagination. Note the interesting design with the bold headline and the wraparound type. The layout is on the left, the final copy on the right. As a fun exercise, try your hand at one or two of the test questions.

the size and style of type to be used (see Figure 9–5). And it is also helpful in determining costs.

The same is true in television advertising. However, the storyboard acts more as an approximation of how the commercial will look. (See Chapter 11, "Creative Production: Electronic Media.")

The second purpose of the layout is a psychological or symbolic function. As the Godiva story suggests, the ad's layout, as well as its execution, creates the feeling of the product. Depending on the way the layout is designed, it can be crucial in determining the image a business or product will present. For example, many grocery stores and drugstores lay their ads out in a cluttered, busy manner with rows and rows of items and bold, black prices. This is typical of bargain-basement advertising, and the purpose is to create the image of a store for price shoppers. On the other hand, stores that offer better-quality merchandise, service, and status at higher prices will tend to use large, beautiful illustrations, often in color, small blocks of copy, and ample white space.

Both types of layouts communicate store image and provide blueprint directions for the production artist. Therefore, when designing the initial layout, the art director must be very sensitive to the desired image of the product or business and use a format that projects that image. (See Ad Lab 9-A.) In the case of Yamaha, that was one of the primary reasons for the combination of editorial and picture-caption layout. The ad presented a highly credible image instantly.

AD LAB 9-A   Which Ad Would You Select?

1

2

3   4

Creating great advertising requires trust between the advertising manager and the creative team. Both must possess the courage to give the advertiser what is needed, rather than what he or she wants. The agency needs the courage to present it. The advertiser needs the vision to recognize its greatness and the courage to buy it. Mike Turner, the senior vice president of Ogilvy & Mather and managing director of OM's Houston office, offered this fictitious example of how a fearful agency account team systematically botched up a marvelous advertisement.

In this example, ad 1 is the famous Hathaway shirt ad as it originally was conceived in the mid-1950s. The ad created an outstanding image for Hathaway and made the agency, Ogilvy & Mather, famous. However, an account team terrified of taking risks nearly destroyed it at its birth.

When the ad was presented to an account executive at the agency, he added the ugly panel at the left (ad 2) and

changed the strong, simple statement to a lackluster headline. Next, in came a woman (ad 3) to add sex appeal. Then (ad 4), off went the "risky" eyepatch. Why? Because people might associate it with unpleasant eye diseases.

As Turner says, "This account team was so busy trying to outguess what the client wanted that they never gave one moment's thought to what was needed, and in the process a great advertisement was destroyed."

Laboratory Application

What would you have done if the agency had presented these four layouts? Would you have had the courage to buy the "risky" ad? Or would you have taken the "safe" route?

Steps in Advertising Layout

Each of the various steps in the layout process serves a particular purpose, and for a specific ad, some or all may be performed. Layouts are relied on as guides in the development of the advertisement by both those who are working on it and those who must approve it.

Thumbnail Sketches

Thumbnail sketches are drawings that are approximately one-fourth to one-eighth of the size of the finished ad (see Figure 9–6A), and they are used for trying out ideas. The best sketch can be chosen for further development.

A. Thumbnail sketch

B. Rough layout

C. Finished advertisement

FIGURE   9–6

Thumbnails are used to try out various layout ideas, while the rough layout is a larger sketch done to actual size.

Rough Layout

The next step in the layout process is the rough layout, which is drawn to the size of the actual advertisement. The headlines and subheads are lettered onto the layout, the intended illustrations and photographs are sketched in, and the body copy is simulated by using pencil lines (see Figure 9–6B).

If the advertisement is to be a television commercial, the proposed scenes in the commercial are drawn in storyboard form—in a series of boxes shaped like TV screens. The copy corresponding to each scene is indicated beneath each frame along with a description of sound effects and music.

Comprehensive Layout

The comprehensive layout, or "comp," is a facsimile of the finished advertisement and is prepared so the advertiser can gauge the final effect of the ad. Copy is set in type and pasted into position, and the illustrations are very carefully drawn. If a photograph will be included, it is pasted into position as well.

In national consumer advertising, the cost of producing layouts is usually covered by the commission the agency receives on the client's media billings. Comps, though, are normally created for the client's benefit rather than for the agency's, so it's not uncommon for a client to be charged for the expense of comps.

Mechanical

In print advertising, once the type has been set and the illustrations created or photographs taken, these elements of the ad are pasted into the exact position where they will appear in the final ad. This *mechanical* (or *pasteup*) is then used as a direct basis for the next step in the reproduction process.

Recently, the advent of desktop publishing and computer pagination systems has enabled the mechanical steps to be eliminated from some types of jobs. (See Chapter 10, "Creative Production: Print Media" for an in-depth discussion.)

Dummy

For layouts of brochures and other multipage materials used in advertising, a dummy is usually prepared. It is put together, page for page, to look exactly like the finished product. A dummy may go through the thumbnail, rough, comprehensive, and mechanical stages just as a regular print layout does.

Which Kind of Layout Design Works Best?

Readership studies over the years indicate that the highest scoring advertisements usually have a standard, poster-style layout with a single, dominant visual that occupies between 60 and 70 percent of the ad's total area.[5] In fact, some research has shown that ads scoring in the top third for stopping power devote an average of 82 percent of their space to the visual.[6] Next in ranking are ads that have one large picture and two more smaller ones. The visual is there to stop the reader and arouse the reader's attention. Therefore, the content of the picture or pictures must be interesting.

Headlines are also intended to stop the reader, and they may contribute more to long-term memory than the visual. (Refer to Ad Lab 8-A in Chapter 8.) Research shows that short headlines with one line are best but that a second line is acceptable. The total headline area needs to fill only 10 to 15 percent of the ad, so the type does not have to be particularly large. Headlines may appear above or below the photograph depending on the situation (see Figure 9–7). David Ogilvy believes that headlines below the illustration gain about 10 percent more readership.[7]

Research shows that readership drops considerably if ads have more than 50 words. Therefore, if the motive is to attract a large number of readers, copy blocks should be kept to less than 20 percent of the ad. However, with many products, the more you tell the more you sell.[8] So don't be afraid of long copy if it's appropriate. Long-copy ads can certainly be effective if they are laid out in a readable fashion.

Finally, company signatures do not have to be particularly large. Most people who read ads are also interested in who placed the ad. So company signatures or logos do not need to occupy more than 5 to 10 percent of the area. For best results, the signatures or logos should be placed in the lower right-hand corner or across the bottom of the ad. (See the Checklist of Design Principles.)

Maybe it's not a better body you need. Maybe it's better jeans.

All women are not created equal. But all women are created with curves.
The funny thing is, many jeans are cut on a straight line. Which may help explain why so many women blame their own bodies when they can't find jeans that fit.
At Lee, we don't think your body should have to fit your jeans. We think your jeans should fit you. When we make Relaxed Rider jeans, we cut them to conform to the natural contours of your body. So where you curve, your jeans curve along with you.
And since they're made of soft, stonewashed denim, they feel just as good as they fit.
Lee® Relaxed Rider® jeans.
Your body is fine. It's your jeans that need changing.

Relaxed Riders **Lee**
The brand that fits™

FIGURE   9–7

The five-line, two-sentence headline in this dynamic ad for Lee Relaxed Riders jeans fills fully 30 percent of the total ad space—a bit much by David Ogilvy's standards. Note also the position of the headline—next to the visual—rather than above or below it. Yet, from the standpoint of graphic design and message delivery, this layout seems to work exceedingly well.

THE ADVERTISING VISUAL

Most people who are unfamiliar with advertising think an artist is someone who paints or draws. As we discussed at the beginning of this chapter, many advertising artists have relatively little talent for drawing or painting. Their talent lies in the area of design or art direction or in the mechanical areas of pasteup and production.

The artists who paint, sketch, and draw in advertising are called *illustrators*. The artists who produce pictures with a camera are called *photographers*. Together they are responsible for all the *visuals,* or pictures, we see in advertising.

Purpose of the Visual

Most readers of advertisements (1) look at the picture, (2) read the headline, and (3) read the body copy, in that order.[9] If any one of these elements fails, the impact of the advertisement is decreased. Since the visual carries such a great deal of responsibility for the success of an

Checklist of Design Principles

Balance

The reference point that determines the balance of a layout is the optical center. The optical center is about one-eighth above the physical center, or five-eighths from the bottom of the page. Balance is the arrangement of the elements as they are positioned on the page—the left side of the optical center versus the right, and above the optical center versus below. There are two kinds of balance—formal and informal.

☐ Formal balance. Perfect symmetry is the key to formal balance: *matched elements* on either side of a line dissecting the ad have equal optical weight. This is used to strike a dignified, stable, conservative image.

☐ Informal balance. By placing elements of *different* size, shape, intensity of color, or darkness at different distances from the optical center, a visually balanced presentation can be achieved. Just like a teeter-totter, an object of greater optical weight near the center can be balanced by an object of less weight placed farther from the center. Most advertisements use informal balance because it makes the ad more interesting, imaginative, and exciting.

Movement

The principle of design that causes the reader of an advertisement to read the material in the sequence desired is called movement. This can be achieved through a variety of techniques.

☐ The placement of people or animals in the advertisement can cause their eyes to direct our eyes to the next important element to be read.

☐ Mechanical devices such as pointing fingers, rectangles, lines, or arrows (or, in television, moving the actors or the camera or changing scenes) direct attention from element to element.

☐ Comic-strip sequence and pictures with captions force the reader to start at the beginning and follow the sequence in order to grasp the message.

☐ Use of white space and color emphasizes a body of type or an illustration. Eyes will go from a dark element to a light, from color to noncolor.

☐ Design can take advantage of the natural tendency of readers to start at the top left corner of the page and proceed on a diagonal Z motion to the lower right corner.

☐ Using size itself attracts attention because readers are drawn to the biggest and most dominant element on the page and then to the smaller elements.

Proportion

☐ Elements in an advertisement should be accorded space based on their importance to the complete advertisement. For best appearance, elements are usually given varying amounts of space in some proportion to avoid the monotony of equal amounts of space for each element.

advertisement, it should always try to offer story appeal. Some advertisements have no visuals because someone made a conscious decision that a picture was not needed for effective communication to occur. If a visual is used, it should accomplish at least one, and preferably more, of the following tasks:

1. Capture the attention of the reader.
2. Identify the subject of the advertisement.
3. Qualify readers by stopping those who are legitimate prospects and letting others skip over the ad if they are so inclined.
4. Arouse the reader's interest in the headline.
5. Create a favorable impression of the product or the advertiser.
6. Clarify claims made by the copy.
7. Help convince the reader of the truth of claims made in the copy.
8. Emphasize unique features of the product.
9. Provide continuity for all advertisements in the campaign through the use of the same visual technique in each individual ad.[10]

Contrast

☐ An effective way of drawing attention to a particular element is to use contrast in color, size, or style. For example, a reverse ad (white letters on a dark background) or a black-and-white ad with a red border or an ad with an unusual type style creates contrast and draws attention.

Continuity

☐ Continuity refers to the relationship of one ad to the rest of the campaign. This is achieved by using the same design format, style, and tone for all advertisements, by using the same spokesperson in commercials, by incorporating an unusual and unique graphic element in all ads, or by the consistent use of other techniques such as a logo, a cartoon character, or a catchy slogan.

Unity

☐ Unity is the ad's bonding agent. It means that although the ad is made up of many different parts, these elements relate to one another in such a way that the ad gives a harmonious impression. Balance, movement, proportion, contrast, and color may all contribute to unity of design. In addition, many other techniques can be used:

☐ Type styles from the same family.

☐ Borders around ads to hold elements together.

☐ Overlapping one picture or element on another.

☐ Judicious use of white space.

☐ Graphic tools such as boxes, arrows, or tints.

Clarity and Simplicity

☐ Any elements that can be eliminated without damaging the effect the advertiser is trying to achieve should be cut. Too many different type styles, type that is too small, too many reverses, illustrations, or boxed items, and unnecessary copy make a layout complex and too busy. They make the advertisement hard to read and hurt the overall effect desired.

White Space (Isolation)

☐ White space is the part of the advertisement not occupied by other elements (even though the color of the background may be black or some color other than white). White space can be used to focus attention on an isolated element. Put a vast amount of white space around a block of copy and it almost appears as if it's in a spotlight. White space has a great deal to do with the image the artist desires to create.

Visualizing Techniques

Visuals are chosen on the basis of their need, cost, technical limitations of producing them, time required to obtain them, effect desired, printing process to be used, paper on which they are to be printed, and availability of the artist who can produce what is needed in the medium desired.

The two basic types of visuals used in advertising are photographs and drawn or painted illustrations.

Photography

A good photograph usually can make several important contributions to an advertisement.

Provides Realism   Photography adds the "real thing" to an ad. Good color photography can give an exciting, realistic look at all kinds of products, from up-close views of high-tech products to steaming-hot bowls of soup. Just look at some of the glorious food photography in any homemaker's magazine.

Photographs—especially news-type photos—put you right on the spot. You're on the goal line when the touchdown is scored. You're on the racetrack approaching the finish line, and you get the checkered flag. Photography gets you personally involved in the action.

Makes the "Cartoon Effect" Come Alive   Photographers have done some wonderful things in taking cartoon situations and giving them the added dimension of realism. Had the famous eye-patched Hathaway man, for instance, been shown as a drawing, it would have lacked the dynamic realism and story appeal expressed by the photograph of the actual man.

Adds Mood, Beauty, and Sensitivity   A photograph can carry a tremendous emotional wallop—like the picture of a battered wife or an abused child. In fact, children are superb attention grabbers when their pictures are used with warmth and sensitivity.[11] Photography may be used to create high sensuality and even shock value as in the case of some recent Calvin Klein underwear ads.[12] Some photographers, moreover, are able to achieve a high artistic level with their pictures—as in the case of Godiva chocolates or the Danskin poster in Figure 9–8.

Offers Speed, Flexibility, and Economy   A drawing or painting usually takes considerably longer to complete than a photograph. In fact, many photographs can be taken at one session and delivered almost overnight. If the advertiser doesn't want to pay to have custom photographs taken, *stock photos* of popular situations, people, and places can usually be purchased at reasonable cost.

It is typical for photographers to take hundreds of shots before being satisfied. The photographer may shoot a wide variety of poses at various angles and with various light settings. In the case of black-and-white photography, the negatives are then printed on a *contact sheet* in small size and in unretouched form. With the use of a magnifying glass, the art director finds the photo that is most suitable for use. In the case of color, photos are shot with slide film and the art director uses a light table or slide viewer to make selections.

Photography offers flexibility since photographs can be cropped to any

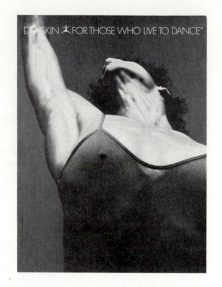

FIGURE   9–8

In this poster layout eye-stopper aimed at dancers, Danskin's agency, Grey Advertising, stretched its creative muscle and came up with an appealing photographic tribute to sinew and muscle.

size or shape and retouched with a paintbrush or airbrush to improve the image.

A word of caution about photography is appropriate here. When a photograph is bought by an advertiser or agency, whether it is a stock photo or a photograph taken by a commissioned photographer, a "legal release" is necessary. In the case of stock photos, the stock photo house will take care of legal releases. However, for photographs that are commissioned, any individuals who appear in the picture must sign a standard release (available from many stationery stores), which grants permission to the advertiser for the photo's use. For children, the release must be signed by the parent or guardian.

In addition, copyright laws restrict the rights of advertisers to use the work of photographers without compensating them equitably. The price a photographer charges, therefore, frequently depends on the intended use of the work. If the advertiser later decides to use the photograph in additional ways, the photographer usually has to be paid more money. These agreements are negotiable and should always be put in writing in advance.

Drawings

Often it is better to use drawn illustrations rather than photographs. The advertiser may want to show an unphotographed event that has already taken place or a future event. Or to accomplish the ad's objective, a drawing may be more appropriate or produce greater impact.

Illustrators are limited only by their own skill. Unlike photographers, they have no need to find just the right setting or the right models or the right lighting. The artist has the freedom to create, through personal style, the impression or effect desired. And drawings can exaggerate in some ways a photograph cannot.

The Yamaha campaign, for example, used *technical illustrators*. They have the ability to work from blueprints, if necessary, to create an extremely precise picture of a product and all its intricate components—and at the same time, to give the product a highly technical, editorial look.

Illustrators use a number of techniques (or media) to produce drawings, including (1) line drawings; (2) wash drawings; (3) scratchboard; (4) pencil, crayon, and charcoal; and (5) oil, acrylic, tempera, and watercolor.

FIGURE   9–9

Loose wash drawings, like this one from Lord & Taylor, enable readers to sense the look and feel of a garment while lending a classy image to the sponsor.

Line Drawings These are excellent for providing clear detail and sharpness. Everything is either black or white, with no shades of gray. Sometimes referred to as pen-and-ink drawings, line drawings are less costly to reproduce than drawings with tonal values. Cartoons are frequently done as line drawings. Line drawings are used quite often for small illustrations or in small ads.

Wash Drawings Sometimes it is too expensive or too time-consuming to photograph a situation. A wash drawing might then be used. As a painting done in various shades of one color, it can be almost as realistic as a black-and-white photograph. Moreover, it can overcome the limitations of a camera. There are two types of wash drawings: tight and loose. A tight drawing is quite detailed and is much more realistic than a loose drawing and comes closest to a photograph as an illustrative technique. A loose wash drawing is more impressionistic; this technique is used by fashion and furniture illustrators in newspaper advertising (see Figure 9–9).

Scratchboard On a special paper with a surface specifically made for this particular form of art, black ink is carefully applied to the area that will carry the illustration. Then, with the use of some type of scratching device (a stylus or other sharp instrument), the ink is removed and a white line is all that remains. The artwork is particularly distinctive and very different. In addition, it gives the impression of extremely fine workmanship. Unfortunately, the process is also quite expensive because the nature of the work requires many hours of meticulous craftsmanship.

Other Illustrative Techniques Numerous other media techniques are used in the drafting of different illustrations. These include, for example, pencil, crayon, airbrush, and charcoal illustrations as well as oil, tempera, and watercolor paintings. All of these media are used for the unique and individual effect that each creates. However, these techniques are less frequently used in advertising than either line drawings or wash drawings. These various techniques are ordinarily utilized when the artist is seeking to convey an impressionistic sensation or to create an image of quality that is both solid and dignified (see Figure 9–10).

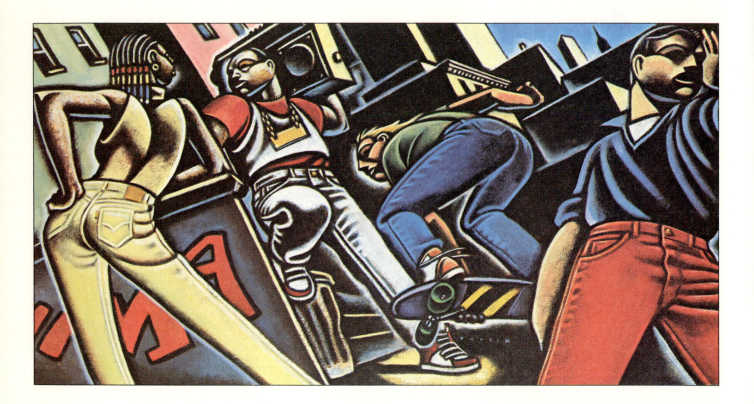

FIGURE   9–10

Levi's found that their 50 percent cotton/50 percent polyester, easy-care Streetlights jeans were quite popular with inner-city youth. So their agency, Foote, Cone & Belding, designed a Diego Rivera–style, mural-type ad to promote the line.

Using oil paint on board, the illustrator, Douglas Fraser, painted the graffiti-like, "urban heroic" visual to show the rainbow of colors Streetlights offered. The ad was then converted to in-store posters and even

was painted as a huge mural on the side of a building in Detroit. It was also cited as one of the best outdoor ads of the year by *Advertising Age*. The product sold out immediately.

Choosing the Visual

One dynamic aspect of advertising is the infinite number of pictures that can be used to communicate the benefits of a product or service. The kind of picture used is often determined during the visualization process. But frequently the desired visual is not determined until the art director or designer is actually laying out the ad. (For a list of the most common types of advertising pictures used, see the Checklist of Chief Focus for Visuals.) Advertising managers and art directors often keep similar checklists handy

Checklist of Chief Focus for Visuals

☐ The package containing the product. This is especially important for packaged goods because it helps the consumer identify the product on the grocery shelf.

☐ The product alone. Most advertising people discourage this approach because of the lower-than-average readership scores achieved by ads that show the product alone. However, the Godiva ad is an excellent example of how this technique can be used to advantage.

☐ The product in use. Automobile ads almost invariably show the car in use while talking about the ride, the luxury, the handling, or the economy. Cosmetic ads usually show the product in use with a close-up photograph of a beautiful woman wearing the mascara, the lipstick, or the eye shadow being advertised.

☐ How to use the product. For food products, recipe ads featuring a new way to use the product historically pull very high readership scores.

☐ Product features. The Yamaha campaign discussed at the beginning of this chapter is an excellent example of illustrating product features.

☐ Comparison of products. One mouthwash compares itself with another, or one electric razor claims a closer shave than competitors A, B, or C.

☐ User benefit. When Sylvania introduced its new 10-bulb flash cartridge, it illustrated user benefit through a series of 10 photographs of "Mona Lisa." The headline keyed the humor: "Now you have two more chances to get it right." It is often difficult to illustrate user benefits, especially intangible benefits. However, salespeople know that the best way to get a customer's attention is to show the customer a way to benefit from the product.

☐ Humor. There is no doubt that much advertising is entertainment. Humor in the right situations can make a positive, lasting impression. It can also destroy credibility if used incorrectly. Caution is always recommended when dealing with serious subjects. When appropriate, though, humor is like Pernod: "It grows on you."

☐ Testimonial. A common type of illustration is the photo of a star or of a real person such as a teenager touting the product.

☐ Before and after. This variation of the testimonial illustration has proved very effective for weight-loss products, skin-care lotions, and body-building courses.

☐ Negative appeal. Sometimes it is stronger to point out what happens if you don't use the product than if you do use it. Electricity, for example, is something we all take for granted, and illustrating it in use might be very difficult. Illustrating it not in use, however, is very simple—and compelling.

A Talon zipper doesn't slip.
Even on a banana peel.

FIGURE   9–11

Talon, Inc., used this humorous approach for years to advertise its various zipper models to consumers and to the trade. Other ads include a photograph of a football with a zipper on it and even one of a kangaroo with a zipper on the pocket.

(as well as an extensive file, or *morgue,* of noteworthy ads, photos, and illustrations) to serve as idea ticklers.

What if you're advertising a zipper? How exciting is a picture of a zipper? Do you show it on a man's pants or a lady's dress? Do you picture it opened or closed? Or do you picture something else? (See Figure 9–11.)

Selecting the appropriate photograph or visual for an advertisement is a difficult creative task and is often what separates the great from the not so great. (See the Art Director's Portfolio.)

Art directors have to deal with several basic issues in the selection of visuals:

1. Is a visual needed for effective communication to occur?
2. Should it be black-and-white or color, and is this a budgetary decision?
3. What should the subject of the picture be, and is that subject relevant to the advertiser's creative strategy?
4. Should an illustrator or a photographer be used?
5. What are the technical and budgetary requirements needed to accomplish the desired visual solution?

Although these questions are very basic, they are all too often overlooked. They should be asked and answered in the initial planning stages of the advertisement, and they should be asked again when the advertisement is being produced. This is where pretests, such as paired comparisons, come in (see Chapter 6).

Just as an exercise, thumb through any chapter in this book and study any one of the advertisements shown. Ask yourself the questions listed above as they apply to the ad you chose. On any day, in any given agency, top art directors perform this exercise routinely.

PACKAGING DESIGN

No discussion of advertising art direction can be complete without giving some attention to the way product packages are designed. Perhaps the best way to emphasize the importance of packaging design is by pointing out the amount of money spent on it: over $50 billion in 1987. In fact, business spends more money on packaging than it does on advertising. A major reason for the heavy emphasis on packaging is the trend toward self-service, which requires that the package play a major role in both advertising and selling.

Packaging encompasses the physical appearance of the container and includes design, color, shape, labeling, and materials. In designing a package, consideration should be given to three factors: (1) its stand-out appeal, (2) how it communicates verbally and nonverbally, and (3) the prestige desired.

Like advertising, packaging communicates both verbally and nonverbally. One bread manufacturer decided that a green wrapping would connote freshness. The only problem was that the customers associated it with fresh mold! Evidently the company chose the wrong shade—an easy mistake to make with green. (See Ad Lab 9-B.)

Even after consumers buy the product, they must continually be "sold" on it. A leading package designer, Walter P. Margulies, uses the cigarette package as a prime example. He stresses that it must be taken out 20 times and often placed in view of friends, intimates, co-workers, and strangers. Because of this, the design must "give consideration to what the user

AD LAB 9-B   The Psychological Impact of Color

Reaction to color, says Walter Margulies, is generally based on a person's national origin or culture. For example, "warm" colors are red, yellow, and orange; "these tend to stimulate, excite, and create an active response." Those from a warmer climate, apparently, are most responsive to those colors.

Violet and "leaf green" fall on the line between warm and cool. Each can be one or the other, depending on the shade used.

Here are some more Margulies observations:

Red Symbol of blood and fire. A runner-up to blue as people's "favorite color" but the most versatile; the hottest color with highest "action quotient." Appropriate for Campbell's soups, Stouffer's frozen foods, and meats. Conveys strong masculine appeal—shaving cream, Lucky Strike, Marlboro.

Brown Another masculine color, associated with earth, woods, mellowness, age, warmth, comfort—the essential male; used to sell anything (even cosmetics)—Revlon's Braggi.

Yellow High impact to catch consumer's eye, particularly when used with black; psychologically right for corn, lemon, or sun tan products.

Green The symbols of health and freshness; popular for tobacco products, especially mentholated—Salem, Pall Mall menthol.

Blue Coldest color, with most appeal; effective for frozen foods (ice impression); if used with lighter tints becomes "sweet"—Montclair cigarettes, Lowenbrau beer, Wondra flour.

Black Conveys sophistication, high-end merchandise and is used to simulate expensive products; good as background and foil for other colors.

Orange Most "edible" color, especially in brown-tinged shades; evokes autumn and good things to eat.

Laboratory Applications

1. Based on Margulies's observations, explain the moods or feelings that are stimulated by specific color advertisements or packages illustrated in this text.
2. Name products for which a redesign using different color combinations might make the product or package more attractive.

thinks others would regard as prestigious. Indeed, cigarettes are a classic example of these so-called irrational products in which fancy, whim, and mystique all operate in place of rational choice."[13]

The package must sell the product off the shelf. This can be done by using shape, color, size, or even texture to deliver a marketing message, give product information, and indicate in-use application.[14] A well-designed package is not only instantly recognizable, it can create product personality (see Figure 9–12 on page 304). Additionally, the package should continue promoting the product in the home, creating brand image and loyalty. Therefore, packages should be designed to open and close easily and not be awkward to handle.[15]

Packaging

Packages come in many forms including wrappers, cartons, boxes, crates, cans, bottles, jars, tubes, barrels, drums, and pallets. Packages are made of many substances, primarily paper, steel ("tin" cans), aluminum, plastic,

(continued on p. 304)

ART DIRECTOR'S PORTFOLIO

A. Channel 32 in Chicago wanted to
get attention for its Monday Night
Movie. An arresting art idea that
required simply a little bit of photographic retouching accomplished
the task.

B. Imaginative design and clever copywriting combine to give Masland Carpets the image of beauty, quality, and creativity.

C. A warm and human demonstration of the advertiser's photo-enlarging service commands immediate attention and produces a happy response—a very big idea that did not cost an arm and a leg.

D. The Minnesota Zoo promotes the idea of enjoyment and fun with a witty combination of art and copy.

You can drive the length of Inverlochlarig, Scotland, in less time than it takes to blink. But as local folk have known for centuries, "Ye canna do it at rush hour." The good things in life stay that way.

E. A magnificent photograph of Old Scotland drives home the idea that the good things in life don't change. While the art is beautiful, the copy tells the story.

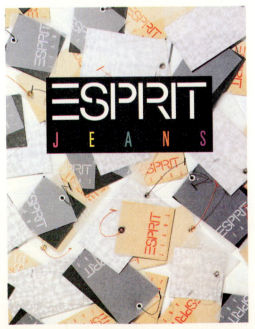

F. A potpourri of bright, colorful sales tags reinforces the contemporary, active image of Esprit's designer sportswear.

FIGURE   9–12

Newly designed packaging for Heinz salad dressings demonstrate both functional and aesthetic attributes. The packages are easy for the retailer to display and the user to handle. The design is pleasing to the eye and promotes the brand name conspicuously without being garish.

wood, glass, burlap, and other fibers. Newer packaging materials include plastic-coated papers, ceramics, and even straw.[16] Metal foils, which not only protect the contents but also add to the attractiveness of the package, have become common. Plastic provides a lightweight container as well as a safer one because it is unbreakable. Important improvements in packaging are occurring, such as amber-green glass wine bottles that protect the contents from damage by light and heavy-duty, gray computer diskette jackets that reflect heat and protect the diskette from damage.[17] The relatively new plastic film pouch for food products has become a substitute for tin cans and makes packages even more flexible, light, and compact.

Packaging Specialists

Management ultimately makes the final design decisions about packages and labels. However, because the right packages and labels have become increasingly important, numerous specialists have emerged to assist management in the decision-making process.

Because packaging is closely related to advertising, and because of the similar techniques used in advertising and packaging, the advertising department and the advertising agency usually play the most important role in package development. Many advertising agencies design labels and packages and prepare the copy that goes on them. Often their help is vital because they coordinate their work with the overall theme of the advertising campaign they have devised for the product. Also, packaging is now often considered part of the advertising and sales budgets of many manufacturers who previously viewed it as a facet of production.

However, packaging problems have become so complex in recent years that packaging specialists are being used increasingly by advertisers and their agencies. These specialists usually fall into one of three groups.

1. Consulting firms are used to provide package designs. These companies are staffed by designers and artists who are acutely aware of the effect of colors and shapes on consumer buying practices.
2. Design departments of larger corporations have their own personnel to work on packaging. In this case, the same people who design the package probably played a role in designing the product as well.
3. Container manufacturers often provide help with package design as a service to their present and potential customers. It is considered part of the service that goes along with the sale of the package manufacturer's products of metal, paper, plastic, or other packaging materials.

When Should a Package Be Changed?

Consider the old saying: "If you build a better mousetrap, the world will beat a path to your door." Unfortunately, this is not always true. A better Swedish mousetrap was introduced into the U.S. market several years ago and immediately encountered problems. Called The New Mousetrap, the product was packaged in a see-through polyurethane bag, but the graphics on the bag hid the product from view. In addition, the bag was difficult to handle and hard to open. The package was simply a poor marketing tool.

The manufacturer retained Selame Design Associates of Newton Lower Falls, Maine, to develop new packaging for the product. First, Selame

FIGURE   9–13

Compare the old to the new. Graphics and quality production can make the difference between success and failure.

wanted to create a catchy name (no pun intended). "Get'm!" was approved by the client, Wicander Enterprises.

Then, since minimizing costs was an important consideration, Selame created a highly practical and visible package using as little material as possible and incorporating the bright orange product itself into the design (see Figure 9–13).

The orange tent card matched the mousetrap color. A *die-cut* opening in the front panel served to show the product and also hold it in place with a single staple. The graphic design of the rear legs and tail of a mouse showed how the trap works. The card was made of coated material and printed in only two colors, orange and black (for economy). The name was reversed out in white.

When it was introduced, the product immediately sold well. The self-selling, easily usable package apparently outweighed the mousetrap's higher price tag.

There are many reasons why even successful packaging gets changed. If a product is altered or improved, repackaging may be required. New packaging may be necessitated by substitutions in materials, such as aluminum or plastic. Competitive pressure may also influence alterations in the existing package.

As the number of working women has increased and the role of television has declined as an advertising medium, package design is being used more often as a method of communicating product value. That has resulted in increased frequency of package redesigns over the last few years as companies strive to keep the brand image projected by the package current with constantly changing consumer perception.[18] Millions of dollars are spent in researching a new image and then promoting it. However, a decision to stay with the present form can be as crucial as a decision to change it. Margulies offers these caveats regarding making a packaging change:[19]

1. Don't change because of a new brand manager's desire to innovate.
2. Don't change to imitate your competition.
3. Don't change for physical packaging innovation only.
4. Don't change for design values alone.
5. Don't change when product identification is strong.
6. Don't change if it may hurt the branding.
7. Don't change if it will weaken the product's authenticity.
8. Don't change if it will critically raise the product's price.

When a decision to change has been made, designers often change the packaging very gradually so consumers will feel comfortable and not suspect that something has happened to the product they have known and believed in for so many years.[20]

Even the familiar appearance of Betty Crocker has changed numerous times to keep the company looking up-to-date, but tender loving care has always been exercised there, too. (See Ad Lab 9-C.)

To conclude our discussion of creative art direction and package design, it is important to understand that the many guidelines often offered as "rules" of good design are merely expressions of accumulated current thought and experience. They are merely guidelines. All the rules in the world will not make a great ad or design a great package. To do his or her job, the art director needs to push to bend and sometimes break rules—while still maintaining standards of good taste. That's a ticklish task. But then, art direction is not science. And that's why they call it art.

AD LAB 9-C   Bringing Up Betty

1936

1955

1972

1986

"She's an all-American girl with blue eyes. She's a good cook, a good administrator, a good mother, civic-minded, she's good at everything." So illustrator Jerome Ryan, the artist of a 1972 portrait of the world's most famous cake baker, describes Betty Crocker.

Thousands of visitors to the Betty Crocker Kitchens in Minneapolis have learned over the years that their favorite maker of frosting, super-moist cakes, muffins, and nearly 200 other products is fictional. "They react like children finding out about Santa Claus," says a General Mills food publicist.

Betty, as she is known to her publicists, was born in 1921. Gold Medal Flour had run an ad that featured a jigsaw puzzle of a flour delivery at a corner store. Readers pasted down the completed picture to win a cookbook. The response was so large "they decided not to use the name of some researcher to answer the letters," General Mills says.

Whence B.C.? William G. Crocker was a popular, recently retired director of the Washburn Crosby Company (a forerunner of General Mills). The first Minneapolis flour mill had been called Crocker. The name Betty was also popular and suggested warmth.

Home bakers heard Betty before they saw her. In 1924, the Betty Crocker "Cooking School of the Air" became the first daytime radio food-service program. It continued for 24 years, with over 1 million registrations from listeners who received recipes.

Betty's grandmotherly features did not grace cake boxes, however, until her 15th birthday in 1936, when Washburn commissioned a portrait from artist Neysa McMein. The features of several Home Service Department members served for the composite likeness that remained in use for almost 20 years.

But as the market changed, so did Betty. General Mills began selling more and more convenience foods, which were aimed at the younger women who would use them. In 1955, the company invited six artists to paint a new portrait and asked 1,600 women to pick their favorite. Illustrator Hilda Taylor's Betty was deemed the best.

In 1972, Jerome Ryan, who had painted all the U.S. presidents for the backs of General Mills cereal boxes, was asked to paint a new portrait. "I didn't think Betty should be too beautiful," Ryan says. Mercedes Bates, head of the Kitchens at that time, was given a hand in modeling the new Betty, since she had to live with large reproductions of the portrait all over her office. Betty's outfit had already been decided. She would wear a trademark red David Crystal suit and a Monet pin, both made by subsidiaries of General Mills.

Betty was changed again in 1986 so that her hairstyle and dress reflected the changing lifestyle of America's consumers. This, her sixth revamping, is a younger Betty, perhaps in her late 30s or early 40s. The newest Betty is intended to inspire trust in both male and female cooks.

Laboratory Applications

1. How would you compare the attributes of Betty Crocker with other trade characters currently used in the food field?
2. What do you feel are the benefits of using a trade character in food advertising?

Summary

Every advertisement uses art. In advertising, *art* refers to the whole visual presentation of the commercial or advertisement. This includes how the words in the ad are arranged, what size and style of type are used, whether photographs or illustrations are used, and how actors are placed in a television commercial.

The many types of artists involved in advertising include art directors, graphic designers, illustrators, and production artists, to name a few. Each has been trained to handle a particular specialty.

For print advertising, the first work from the art department is seen in the form of a layout, which is a design of the advertisement within specified dimensions. The layout has two purposes. One is a mechanical function to show where the parts of the ad are to be placed. The other is a psychological or symbolic function to demonstrate the visual image a business or product will present.

Several steps are used in laying out an ad: thumbnail sketch, rough layout, comprehensive layout, and mechanical. For brochures and other multipage materials, the layout is referred to as a dummy. For television, the layout is referred to as a storyboard.

A great deal of responsibility for the success of an advertisement is placed on the visual. The picture may be used to capture the attention of the reader, to identify the subject of the advertisement, to create a favorable impression, or for a host of other reasons.

The two basic devices for illustrating an advertisement are photography and drawings. Photography can make several important contributions to an advertisement, including realism; a feeling of immediacy; a feeling of live action; the special enhancement of mood, beauty, and sensitivity; and speed, flexibility, and economy.

Drawn illustrations can do many of these things, too, and may be used if the art director feels they can achieve greater impact than photographs. A number of techniques are used in producing drawings, including (1) line drawings; (2) wash drawings; (3) scratchboard; (4) pencil, crayon, and charcoal; and (5) oil, acrylic, tempera, and watercolor.

More money is spent on packaging than on advertising, primarily because of increased emphasis on self-service. This requires the package to play an important role in both advertising and selling.

Factors that should be considered in packaging design are (1) how the package communicates verbally and nonverbally, (2) the prestige desired, and (3) the stand-out appeal required.

Package design is often changed because of a desire to (1) align the package more closely with the product's marketing strategy, (2) emphasize the product's benefits, (3) emphasize the product's name, or (4) take advantage of new materials.

Questions for Review and Discussion

1. Choose any television commercial shown in this text. How would you describe the "art" in that commercial?
2. Select a print ad of your choice. What do you suppose the art director contributed to that advertisement?
3. What is a layout? What is its purpose?
4. What do you think is the best color to stimulate sales? Why?
5. What is a mechanical? How is it used?
6. What color is white space?
7. What is the purpose of a picture in an advertisement? When would you not use a visual?
8. Select an advertisement with a photograph in it. What are the advantages and disadvantages of using a photograph in that ad?
9. Select an advertisement with a drawing in it. What advantages and disadvantages does that illustration present?
10. What are five criteria for selecting visuals? Which do you think is the most important? Why?

10

CREATIVE PRODUCTION: PRINT MEDIA

Everyone is familiar with the efforts made by urban renewal groups in metropolitan areas to clean up their skid-row areas. If you gave a photograph of those slums to a retoucher like Emilio Paccione, he could perform a miracle of urban renewal—transforming run-down shacks into freshly painted, beautifully renovated historic landmarks replete with green lawns, flowering gardens, and majestic trees.

The role of the retoucher, whose accomplishments, style, and sensitivity help make the art director look good, is surprising to many. Most people don't realize that almost every photograph we see for a national advertiser, or on the covers of national magazines, has been altered or improved to some degree by a retoucher.

For example, recently *Esquire* magazine was preparing a full-page color shot of an actor costumed and made up to portray George Washington. On stage and at a distance away from the audience, he might have resembled the father of our country. But under the merciless scrutiny of the close-up camera, he just looked like a poor old actor with a terribly wilted wig, drooping eyelids, and a pitifully painted putty nose that was more than just a few shades darker than the rest of his face. *Esquire* immediately called for Paccione.

Working over the weekend, with a 102° temperature, Patch (as his friends call him) treated the photograph with various dyes and bleaches and then, with paintbrush and airbrush in hand, used his artist's skill to bring forth a finished product that looked uncannily like the famous portrait on the $1 bill (see Figure 10–1).

"I think I could have been a great plastic surgeon," Patch says with a modest smile.

Most of Paccione's business comes from advertising agencies preparing print campaigns for such big name advertisers as Clairol, Avon, Dr. Pepper, Volkswagen, and General Foods. In one case, Ron Travisano, the president of Della Femina, Travisano & Partners, called on Patch to assist him with a very special and sensitive ad for a public-action program called The Hunger Project. The professed aim of this project is to end world hunger by the year 2000.

The object was to show an undernourished skeletal child gradually progressing to become a smiling, healthy youngster (see Figure 10–2). Paccione worked in reverse. Taking four prints of a single 35 mm frame, Patch carefully bleached and shaded each print. What he created was a remarkable series showing the progressive stages of starvation, the child's eyes receding into the skull and skin stretching across protruding cheekbones and ribs.

"It was almost like animation," Paccione says, and the humanitarian point of The Hunger Project could not have been made clearer—or more striking.

Sometimes the retoucher's job is relatively simple—correcting blemishes on a model's face or straightening out the wrinkled crease in a pant leg. Other times, the task is far more complex, requiring the skill of an experienced painter or illustrator.

Says Paccione, "Our job is to correct the basic deficiencies in the original photograph." In truth, he adds an element to photography that photographers themselves often cannot provide—in effect, an improvement on the appearance of reality.[1]

THE PRODUCTION PROCESS

The average reader of advertisements has no notion of the intricate, detailed, technical stages those printed announcements go through from start to finish. Yet the entire advertising effort may be radically affected by the outcome of the production process. An otherwise beautiful ad can be destroyed by a poor selection of type, by a less-than-interesting photograph, by improper manufacture of printing material, or by the use of an incorrect procedure to reproduce photographs or artwork on a particular paper stock.

Any person connected with advertising, therefore, should have a fundamental grasp of basic production procedures. This knowledge and understanding will save a lot of money and disappointment in the long run.

In recent years, gaining a thorough knowledge of these mechanical production procedures has become more complex. An enormous technological progress has taken place in the graphic arts, due in particular to the revolutionary application of computers and electronics. Much of the work performed by Paccione, for example, can now be accomplished by a variety of computer graphics programs and *electronic pagination systems*. Through the use of computers, these systems enable the artist to treat printed pages, as well as photos and illustrations, as images that easily can be altered and corrected by the manipulation of the computer pixels on a monitor.

The new, sophisticated computer systems present numerous opportunities and benefits to major advertisers. They make the work of graphic designers and illustrators faster and easier. Offering a wide range of color options, they can produce high-quality images at the artist's direction, replacing traditional artwork and photographs. Possible for some time in the creation of television commercials, this approach is now becoming more practical for print advertising[2] (see Figure 10–3).

With the advent of the personal computer, graphics programs have now become available to the small businessperson. While these programs do

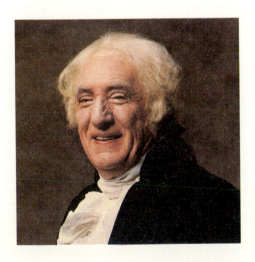 

FIGURE   10–1

These amazing "before" and "after" pictures show the portrait power of a great retoucher.

FIGURE   10–2

The power of this commercial for
The Hunger Project is delivered
through the heart-rending visual of
a poor, starving, emaciated child

gradually becoming healthy right
before your eyes—all in 30 seconds.
No words are necessary to tell or
sell the story.

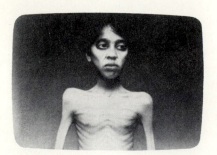
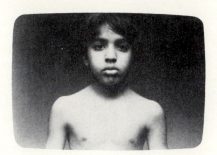

not offer the quality of big agency art, they do offer the small business both
flexibility and savings in printing, typesetting, and advertising costs. For the
first time, nonartists can render complex drawings with ease, and a choice
of basic type styles offers great variety at low cost.[3]

Notwithstanding the influence of these systems, though, the role of the
traditional advertising artist and illustrator will likely remain extremely
important to the company and to the agency wishing to retain quality and
individuality in their advertising.[4] As a result, knowledgeable professionals, experienced in the print production process, are vital to today's major
advertisers and advertising agencies.

PLANNING PRINT PRODUCTION

In Chapter 9, we looked at the award-winning ads Botsford-Ketchum created for Yamaha motorcycles. We discussed the editorial design of the ads,
the interesting combination of illustrations and photography, and the unity
of the art concept with Yamaha's campaign theme: "When you know how
they're built, you'll buy a Yamaha."

During the time Botsford-Ketchum handled the Yamaha motorcycle
account, Joe Sosa was the agency's production supervisor. He became
intimately involved in the campaign after the concept was developed. His
responsibility was to ensure that the final advertisement printed in the
magazine reflected exactly what the art director had intended.

This was no small task inasmuch as each advertisement presented numerous production complexities. These included the reproduction of fine
technical illustrations in full color, the precise specification and placement
of type around the illustrations, and the need to have all printing materials
checked, approved, duplicated, and shipped to the magazines in time for a
specific deadline. But these tasks are typical of the responsibilities faced by
every production manager.

Once an advertisement has been laid out and the artwork and copy
approved, the ad falls under the supervision of the print production manager and a staff of production artists and assistants. The print production
department specifies type and then physically creates the materials for
printing. It must also order printing materials and give any necessary technical instructions to outside production specialists.

FIGURE   10–3

The Apple Macintosh has been in the forefront of the desktop publishing movement. Through the use of computer graphics software and sophisticated laser printers, the artist can set type, design graphs and illustrations, and make up a whole page of print right on the computer.

The manager must decide at the earliest possible time what is most important for a particular project: speed, quality, or economy. The answer may determine which production methods are used; one will surely be sacrificed at the expense of another. In the Yamaha ads, what do you think was considered most important?

Working backward from the closing dates (deadlines) of the publications, the production manager schedules when each step of the work must be completed in order to meet the deadline. Deadlines can vary from months to hours.

The production manager acquaints the art director and copywriter with the opportunities and limitations of various production techniques and keeps them abreast of the progress of each job. In the case of Yamaha, this meant coordinating three teams of art directors and writers for just one account.

Finally, the production manager must check all proofs for errors, obtain all necessary approvals from agency and client executives, and release the approved advertisements to the publications.

For the production process to run smoothly, it is obviously important that everybody concerned understand the whole procedure. Consider the problem of correcting errors. After the advertisement has been delivered to the typographer, photoplatemaker, printer, or publication, it costs substantially more to make any changes than before the actual production begins. For example, the cost of changing a single comma after the copy has been typeset is well over $10.

Thus, the production process requires good planning, and the people involved need to develop a recognition and understanding of art, graphics, and type and learn all they can about typography, platemaking, printing, and color as well as the rather technical jargon of printing.

TYPOGRAPHY

Turn back to Chapter 9 and look carefully at the Yamaha ad in Figure 9–4. Now look at the Yamaha ad in Figure 10–4. It was created a year or two later by Yamaha's new agency, Chiat/Day Advertising in Los Angeles. What major differences do you notice between the two ads? Both use an illustrative technique to talk about the unique features of the bikes. Both use a somewhat similar design. Yet the ads look considerably different and create a very different feeling.

The major distinction, of course, is in the use of typography. The headline used in Figure 9–4 is set in a very attractive, traditional typeface called Goudy (pronounced gow-dee) Old Style. Notice the characteristics of this typeface: delicate curved *serifs* (tails) on each letter, variation in the thickness of the letter strokes, and the clear, easy-to-read roundness of style.

FIGURE   10–4

The Yamaha campaign, as executed by Chiat/Day, featured a continuation of the illustrative techniques already in use by Yamaha, with the addition of bold, newsy, action-oriented headlines. Many art directors feel this is more in tune with the intended audience of the ads—motorcycle enthusiasts.

The headline in Figure 10–4, on the other hand, is a larger, *sans serif* (no tails) typeface called Futura Bold. This typeface is characterized by no serifs on the letters; uniform thickness of strokes; wide, thick letters; and a bold, round, "newsy," announcement-style presentation.

Which of these type styles do you prefer? Do you find one easier to read? Is one more attractive than the other? Does one communicate news value better? Which attracts your attention more quickly? Do you get a different feeling, or a different impression, from the two type styles? Does one offer a greater feeling of credibility than the other? If you were the art director, which of these type styles would you prefer?

Consumers differ in the styles they prefer. Art directors, therefore, try to select type styles that suit the objectives and strategy of the campaign and that also communicate well with the target audience.

Classes of Type

Type is divided into two classes: display type and text type. *Display type* is larger and heavier than text type. It is used in headlines, subheads, logos, addresses, and when there is a need for emphasis in an advertisement. For body copy in an advertisement, the smaller *text type* is used.

Type Groups

Thousands of typefaces are available, and type designers are continually developing new ones. Typefaces are classified into various groups because of their similarity in design. There is no reason to learn the names of all the faces, because each typesetting house or printer has only a limited number of typefaces, depending on requirements and the kind of equipment it uses. Except for people who wish to become art directors or type specialists, an understanding of the five major type groups is sufficient (see Figure 10–5).

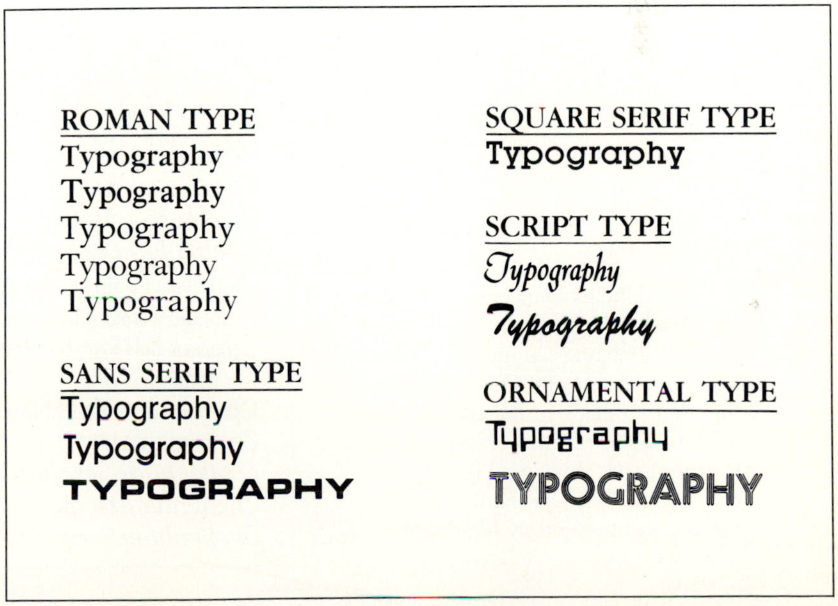

FIGURE 10–5

The five major type groups.

ROMAN TYPE
Typography
Typography
Typography
Typography
Typography

SANS SERIF TYPE
Typography
Typography
TYPOGRAPHY

SQUARE SERIF TYPE
Typography

SCRIPT TYPE
Typography

Typography

ORNAMENTAL TYPE
Typography

TYPOGRAPHY

Roman

Roman faces comprise the most popular type group. Roman offers the greatest number of designs, so contrast can be achieved without a basic design change. It is also considered the most readable. The two most distinguishing characteristics of roman type are (1) the small lines or tails, called serifs, that cross the ends of the main strokes and (2) variations in the thickness of the strokes. Roman type comes in a variety of sizes and has dozens of subclassifications that differ from one another on the basis of thickness of the strokes, the way the letters are designed (letterforms), and the size and regularity of the serifs.

Sans Serif

Sans serif is the second most popular type group. Also referred to as *block, contemporary,* or *gothic,* this large group of typefaces is characterized by (1) the lack of serifs (thus the name, sans serif) and (2) the relatively uniform thickness of the strokes.

Sans serif text typefaces are usually not as readable as roman faces. However, they are widely used because of the simple, clean lines, which give a modern appearance.

Square Serif

Combining sans serif and roman typefaces produces the square serif faces that have the same uniform thickness of strokes as sans serif faces have. Square serif is similar to roman typefaces in that it has serifs. However, the serifs have the same weight and thickness as the main strokes of each of the letters.

Cursive or Script

Cursive (or script) typefaces closely resemble handwriting. The letters are often connected and they may convey a feeling of femininity, formality, or beauty. Since they are rather difficult to read, they are used primarily in headlines or formal announcements. Also, they are used in cosmetic and fashion advertising.

FIGURE   10–6

Meet the Cheltenham family. Note the variety of looks that can be used without changing families. Art directors may use a boldface in the headline and lightface in the copy as well as different sizes or even italics for emphasis. Most art directors try to use only one type family in a single ad, and they rarely use more than two.

Cheltenham
Cheltenham Italic
Cheltenham Bold
Cheltenham Bold Italic
Cheltenham Bold Condensed
Cheltenham Bold Condensed Italic
Cheltenham Bold Extra Condensed
Cheltenham Nova
Cheltenham Bold Nova
Cheltenham Light
Cheltenham Light Italic
Cheltenham Book
Cheltenham Book Italic
Cheltenham Bold
Cheltenham Bold Italic
Cheltenham Ultra
Cheltenham Ultra Italic
Cheltenham Light Condensed
Cheltenham Light Condensed Italic
Cheltenham Book Condensed
Cheltenham Book Condensed Italic
Cheltenham Bold Condensed
Cheltenham Bold Condensed Italic
Cheltenham Ultra Condensed
Cheltenham Ultra Condensed Italic

Ornamental

Ornamental typefaces include designs that provide novelty and are highly embellished and decorative. They are used for special effects but are often difficult to read.

Type Families

Within each major type group are type families. A type family is made up of related faces identified by such names as Cheltenham, Futura, Goudy, Souvenir, Bodoni, and Caslon. The basic design remains the same within a family, but there are variations in the proportion, weight, and slant of the characters. The versions commonly available include light, medium, bold, extra bold, condensed, extended, and italic (see Figure 10–6). These variations enable the typographer to provide contrast and emphasis in an advertisement without changing type styles. For a particular typeface and size of type, a *font* consists of a complete assortment of capitals, small capitals, lowercase letters, numerals, and punctuation marks.

In an effort to control the exclusivity of how their advertising looks, some advertisers commission the design of a unique type style. The Volvo ad in Figure 10–7, for example, shows a bold, sans serif headline set in Volvo's own type style designed by John Danza, a creative director at Scali, McCabe, Sloves, Volvo's advertising agency.

Other advertisers might go in the opposite direction for uniformity. Oil of Olay, for example, tailored its advertisements to blend well with the typography and design elements of the different magazines in which they were placed. This gave the ads an editorial look and, the advertiser hoped, enhanced credibility (or at least interest).

Type Structure and Measurement

There are several terms used to describe the way that type is structured and measured.

FIGURE   10–7

Volvo has owned its own typeface for many years. Used in the headline and tag line of all ads, it guarantees an exclusive continuity to the company's advertising campaigns.

Points

Points measure the depth (or height) of the type. There are 72 points to the inch, so one point equals $\frac{1}{72}$ of an inch. The height of a line of type is measured from the bottom of the descenders (extensions downward from the body of the type) to the top of the ascenders (extensions upward from the body of the type).

The most common type sizes used in advertising have traditionally been 6, 8, 10, 11, 12, 13, 14, 18, 24, 36, 42, 60, 72, 84, 96, and 120 points (see Figure 10–8). However, with new, computerized phototypesetting equipment, any type size is possible. The smaller sizes, 6 through 14 points, are used for text type, and the larger sizes are normally used for display (headline) type.

Picas

The unit of measurement for the horizontal width of lines of type is the *pica.* There are exactly six picas to the inch and 12 points to the pica (see Figure 10–9).

The width of a single letter of type depends on the style of the typeface and whether it is regular or bold, extended or condensed. The width also depends on the proportions of the letter. But the averages for each type style and size have been established and are provided by the manufacturer of the type.

Uppercase and Lowercase

Capital letters are called *uppercase,* and small letters are called *lowercase.* The terms came about when type was set by hand and compositors stacked the two cases containing the capital and small letters one above the other.

Note from the material you are now reading how easy it is to read a combination of uppercase and lowercase. However, type can also be set using all caps (uppercase), commoncase (caps and small caps), or caps and lowercase. Advertising copy set in lowercase is more readable than copy set in all capitals, and that goes for headlines as well as body copy. Type set in solid capitals can be used for emphasis, but this should be done very sparingly.

FIGURE   10–8

Sample variations in type size.

text type		display type	
SIZE of type	6 POINT	SIZE of type	16 POINT
SIZE of type	8 POINT	SIZE of type	18 POINT
SIZE of type	9 POINT	SIZE of type	20 POINT
SIZE of type	10 POINT	SIZE of type	24 POINT
SIZE of type	12 POINT	SIZE of type	30 POINT
SIZE of type	14 POINT	SIZE of type	36 POINT

Type Selection

The art of selecting and setting type is known as *typography.* Because almost every advertisement has some reading matter, type has tremendous importance in advertising. The typeface chosen affects the advertisement's general appearance, design, and readability. Although good type selection cannot compensate for a weak headline, poorly written body copy, or a lack of appropriate illustrations, it can create interest and attract readers to the advertisement. (See Ad Lab 10-A.)

Knowledge of the effects and symbolism of typefaces requires great expertise. There may be fewer experts who can accurately interpret how a typeface will influence an ad than any other kind of expert connected with the advertising business. This art requires experience and skill and should not be left to the layperson. Among local advertisers, however, it is often the most overlooked aspect of advertising creativity.

Four important points should be considered in the selection of type: readability, appropriateness, harmony or appearance, and emphasis. We shall discuss each of these briefly.

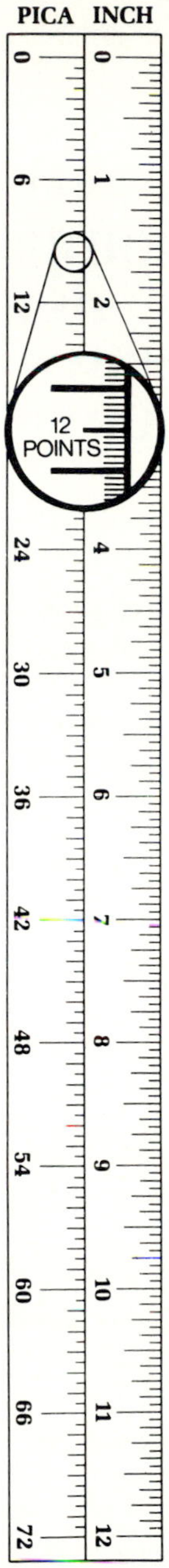

Readability

The most important consideration in selecting a typeface is readability. As David Ogilvy says, good typography helps people read while bad typography prevents them from doing so.[5] Some general factors that contribute to readability include the style of type, boldness, size, length of the line, and spacing between the words, lines, and paragraphs. An advertisement is printed so that it can be read, and reduced readability kills interest. Difficult-to-read typefaces should be used infrequently and only to create special effects.

Large, bold, and simply designed typefaces are, of course, the easiest to read. However, advertisers are limited by the amount of space in the advertisement and the amount of copy that must be written. Readability is also affected by the length of the line in which the copy is set. Newspaper columns are usually less than 2 inches wide; magazine columns, slightly wider. For advertisements, columns of copy less than 3 inches (18 picas) wide are usually recommended.

The way lines of type are spaced also influences readability of the advertisement. A small amount of space between lines of type is always allowed for descenders (j, g, p) and ascenders (b, d, k). When this is the only space between lines, type is "set solid." Sometimes an art director decides to add extra space between the lines to give a more "airy" feeling. In this case, *leading* (pronounced ledding) between lines is called for. The term dates back to the time when thin lead strips were actually inserted between lines of metal type.

A line of type set in 10-point type with 2 points of space (leading) between lines is specified as "10 on 12," or "10/12." This same terminology is used today in photocomposition.

Appropriateness

A typeface must be appropriate to the product being advertised. With many varieties of type available in terms of both style (typeface) and size, a host of moods and feelings can be conveyed quite apart from the meanings of

FIGURE 10-9

In the printing industry, picas and points are common units of measurement. One inch equals 6 picas or 72 points. Thus, type set at 36 points would be ½ inch tall, and an 18-pica column of type would be 3 inches wide.

AD LAB 10-A   How to Use Type as the Major Graphic Design Element

Type—and type directing—reaches its apex when the art director chooses it as the sole or major design element, as illustrated in these ads.

Type is used in many ways today, and nowhere is that more apparent than in headlines. Serifs, sans serifs, verticals, slants, condensed, expanded, across-the-gutter, loose, tight, all caps, uppercase and lowercase, small, huge, elegant, powerful, quiet, screaming, colored, dropped-out, plain, fancy—this is the type story today.

Art directors are not only using all possible headline styles, but they're also working *with* them—their directing reflects solid, effective judgment, with type matched to art to fulfill ad objectives.

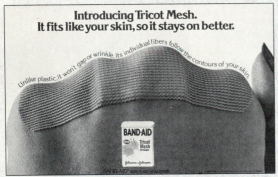

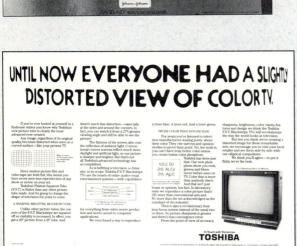

Laboratory Application

Discuss these ads with reference to the impact of type selection on the design concept and the execution.

the words themselves. (See Ad Lab 10-B.) Some typefaces suggest ruggedness and masculinity, while others give a feeling of delicateness and femininity. One typeface can whisper "luxury," while another can scream "bargain." A typeface that conveys the feeling of something old-fashioned obviously would be inappropriate in an advertisement for a space-age electronic watch.

Harmony/Appearance

A common mistake of advertising novices is the mixing of typefaces. This normally results in disharmony and a feeling of clutter. Type should harmonize with the other elements of an advertisement—including the illustration and the layout. Therefore, typefaces that belong to the same family or are closely related should be chosen.

Emphasis

Emphasis with type selection can be achieved by using contrast. Typical methods include using more than a single type style or using italic versus roman or upright type, lowercase versus uppercase, or small-size versus

AD LAB 10-B   The Most Unforgettable Characters You Will Ever Meet

Laboratory Application

Choose five of these type styles and discuss them from the standpoint of readability and appropriateness (give examples of products).

large-size type. Care must be taken because an effort to emphasize *all* of the elements in an advertisement will only result in emphasizing *none* of them.

Type Specification and Copy Casting

Type must fit into the space designated for it in the layout. So before the type can be selected, the number of characters in the copy has to be determined, or "cast off."

Two ways are used to fit copy to a particular space: the word-count method and the character-count method. With the word-count method, the words in the copy are counted and then divided by the number of words per square inch that can be set in a particular type style and size, as given in a standard table.

The character-count method gives greater accuracy. An actual count is made of the number of characters (letters, word spaces, and punctuation marks) in the copy. In a type specimen book or chart provided by the typographer, the average number of characters per pica is given for each typeface and type point size. From this information, it is relatively simple to determine how much space a given piece of copy set in a particular typeface will use.

PEOPLE IN ADVERTISING

Klaus F. Schmidt

Senior Vice President and
Manager, Production Services
Young & Rubicam Inc., New York

Klaus F. Schmidt is senior vice president and manager of production services at Young & Rubicam Inc., New York. In this capacity, he is responsible for the company's print production, art buying, audiovisual facilities, and art studio. Administratively, he also heads up the Television Production Department. Prior to his appointment in 1968, Schmidt served as type director and then as director of print operations for Young & Rubicam.

Born in Germany, where he received his graphic arts training, Schmidt came to the United States in 1951 as a union compositor and printer. He obtained a B.A. in advertising and marketing at Wayne State University in Detroit. Schmidt went on to become type director of Mogul, Williams & Saylor and then of Doyle Dane Bernbach Inc., both in New York, before joining Y&R in 1961.

Print production, says Schmidt, is the "vital step" that transforms an advertising concept into the final printed result. He notes that while account executives "need not become expert" in the technical complexities of typesetting, photoplatemaking, and printing, they "should understand at least the basics of graphic arts technology and print production procedures." Only with this working knowledge, Schmidt explains, can account executives expect to communicate successfully with their clients.

Schmidt stresses that print production people "are not merely technically knowledgeable purchasing agents as-

Copy sent to a typographer or publication should be marked with the type specifications written beside the copy. Usually the copy is accompanied by a layout. When specifying type, the art director or type director should provide the typographer with at least the following information: (1) the typeface by name, (2) the type size and the leading desired, and (3) the width of the line of type in picas.

The specification of type in advertising agencies is handled by art directors, type directors, or the print production staff. However, it is also important for copywriters and account executives to understand the basics of type specification and copycasting since copy must often be written to fit a particular space in an advertisement. Otherwise, the ad risks looking either overly crowded or too empty—thereby impairing its visual impact.

TYPESETTING METHODS

In recent decades, technology has rapidly revolutionized the printing industry in general and typesetting methods in particular. The old methods of metal type composition (letters were formed by pouring molten lead into brass molds) have become obsolete and have virtually disappeared. The "hot-type" era included a variety of composition processes with such names as Linotype, Monotype, and Ludlow. But it has yielded to a new "cold-type" era in which letters can be easily imprinted directly onto

signed to buying typesetting, printing image carriers, paper, and other graphic arts services and commodities." Schmidt points out that "they are, beyond that basic purchasing function, you and your client's graphic arts consultants, production planners, and production liaison people—internally, with the creative, traffic, media, and account management areas, and externally, with graphic arts vendors and with the print media."

Schmidt notes that at Young & Rubicam, New York, the print operations group includes the following:

1. *Art buyers,* who are versed in various forms of photographic/illustrative techniques. They know the available talent and make all business arrangements with photographers, model agencies, illustrators, retouchers (manual and electronic), photo labs, and others, in close cooperation with art directors.
2. *Type directors,* who are trained in the creative as well as the technical aspects of typography. Working with art directors, they select, specify, mark up, and purchase all typesetting.
3. *Print producers,* who coordinate all print production activities with the traffic, account management, and creative groups. They purchase image carriers for the various printed media from photoplatemaking houses and

provide the vital contact with publication production departments.
4. *Printing buyers,* who specialize in the production planning and buying of outdoor and transit advertising, newspaper and magazine inserts, and collateral printed material from brochures to elaborate die-cut direct-mail pieces. A printing buyer's knowledge reaches into properties of paper and ink and into the capabilities of printing, binding, and finishing equipment.

Schmidt, who has written numerous articles for both American and European graphic arts magazines, has been the recipient of the Typomundus Award of the International Center for the Typographic Arts and the International Book Exhibition Award.

Cofounder and former board chairman of the International Center for the Typographic Arts, Schmidt has also served as chairman of the American Association of Advertising Agencies' Subcommittee on Phototypography and of the Gravure Advertising Council of the Gravure Association of America. He was a member of the American Association of Advertising Agencies' Subcommittee on Newspaper Formats and is past president of the New York Advertising Production Club and the Type Directors Club and past vice president of the Art Directors Club.

photosensitized film or paper.[6] This new era, characterized by sophisticated, high-speed, electronic photocomposition equipment and operators schooled in computer technology, actually began in the 1960s and has brought tremendous changes in the tools available to art directors, designers, and writers. As a result, they can achieve more today in less time and at less cost.

Today's typesetting methods generally fall into two broad classifications: strike-on composition and photocomposition.

Strike-On Composition

Strike-on or *direct-impression composition* can be done on either a regular typewriter or on the new breed of intelligent electronic typewriters and word processors. These have microprocessors, can perform basic text-editing functions automatically, and also offer storage capabilities. This equipment is often used in typesetting direct-mail advertising, catalogs, and house organs.

Offering substantial savings over professional typesetting methods, this means of composition is primarily used when economy is the overriding consideration. Because the price of the equipment is relatively low, organizations can afford to have the equipment in-house, which offers the advantage of getting material set quickly when the need arises.

Previous drawbacks to this method were high cost and the limited range of typefaces available. Today, reasonably priced laser printers and "desktop publishing" software programs are replacing pure strike-on composition. These now permit digital data files to be output in low-resolution typographic quality, and they offer not only text but display type.

Photocomposition

A combination of computer technology, electronics, and photography, *photocomposition* is the most dominant method of producing advertising materials today. It offers an almost unlimited number of typefaces and sizes, faster reproduction at lower cost, and improved clarity and sharpness of image.

The basic function of all phototypesetting machines is to expose photosensitive paper, or film, to a projected image of the character being set. The most commonly used equipment operates photo-optically, by cathode-ray tube (CRT) technology or by laser scanning.

Photo-Optic Typesetters

Photo-optic typesetting equipment uses an electromechanical method of generating characters. Character fonts are stored on film grids, discs, drums, or a film strip matrix. The matrix is then rotated mechanically until the desired character is in the proper position. A xenon lamp flashes, and the light image of the character is projected through a lens, which magnifies it to the desired size. This image is then reflected off a mirror onto the photosensitive paper or film, thus setting the character. While photo-optic typesetters are no longer manufactured, they are still very common in the graphic arts field.

CRT Typesetters

In cathode-ray tube techniques, characters are stored digitally. They are retrieved from the computer's memory and passed to a print CRT (similar to a television receiver tube) where they are lined up and then exposed through a lens system onto the photosensitive paper or film. Since they are generated electronically, the characters can be modified (condensed, heavied, slanted, etc.) at the operator's command. These versatile machines can store hundreds of fonts and have extremely high speed capabilities. These digital typesetters are rapidly replacing photo-optic machines.

Laser Typesetters

With new computer-laser technology, type fonts and software programs can be stored digitally in a computer. As the computer turns the laser on and off, the laser beam "writes" onto (exposes) the output paper or film. No cathode-ray tube is necessary. Extremely high speeds are possible as well as great reliability and versatility. In addition, laser typesetters are usually able to put out graphics and halftones as well as type.

The Typesetting Process

Typesetting is actually a whole process encompassing a series of steps that include "inputting" (keyboarding), hyphenation and justification, setting the actual type by one of the methods explained above, developing the exposed photographic material, proofreading for errors and omissions, correcting and resetting, and makeup. Equipment available today ranges from machines that perform only one step in the process to complete *direct-entry systems,* which have the input and output capabilities all in one device (see Figure 10–10). Some of these devices, like the one illustrated, are able to make up entire pages of copy—just the way the art director laid

FIGURE   10–10

The on-screen layout of the Comp/Edit from AM Varityper gives a visual presentation of the typeset layout before the type is set. The final typeset output has all elements in position so there is little or no need for pasteup in straight-copy advertisements.

them out—with different typefaces, line rules, and exact spaces left for dropping in visuals. As noted earlier, this ability to "paginate" (make up pages) by computer has radically changed the standard typesetting and pasteup process that had been used for many years.

Direct-entry phototypesetters became affordable at the end of the 1970s. And in the 80s, desktop publishing via personal computers became a reality. Now, many advertising agencies, studios, and clients have one of these systems in-house, facilitating fast, cost-effective, do-it-yourself type-setting.

THE PRINTING PROCESS

The transfer of an image from one surface to another is the objective of all printing methods. Printed advertising materials are reproduced today by four major methods: letterpress, rotogravure, offset lithography, and screen printing.

We will discuss each of these methods shortly. But first, let's examine some basic principles of printing.

Preparing Materials for the Press

For all of today's modern, high-speed presses, whether the method is letterpress, rotogravure, or offset lithography, printing plates are required. A process called *photoplatemaking* is used to create the printing surface on the plates.

The photoplatemaking process can be compared to taking a picture with your own camera. When you take a picture, you produce a negative. The picture is then made by laying the negative on sensitized paper and exposing it to light. Photoplatemaking also begins with a picture. However, the negative of the image photographed is printed on a sensitized metal plate rather than on paper; this plate is then used for printing.

Before this plate can be made, though, the artwork has to be prepared properly.

Line Films

Unlike a piece of photographic paper, which prints its image in black, white, and any variety of shades of gray, a printing plate can only print or not print. That's fine if the artwork is simply typeset copy, pen-and-ink drawings, or charcoal illustrations. In that event, the artwork is simply photographed to create what is called a *line film*. From that, a *line plate* is produced for printing.

However, a photograph or other illustration requiring gradations in tone cannot be reproduced on a plate without using an additional process–namely, a halftone screen.

Halftones

Whereas line plates print lines and solid areas (like type), halftone plates print dots. The key element in making such a plate is the *halftone screen* that breaks up continuous-tone artwork into dots. The screen itself is glass or plastic, crisscrossed with fine black lines at right angles like a window screen. This screen is placed in the camera between the lens and the negative holder. When the artwork is photographed, this screen breaks up the picture into a series of tiny black dots of varying shapes and sizes.

In the dark areas of the (halftone) photograph, the dots are many and large; in the gray areas, they are fewer and smaller; and in the white areas, they almost disappear completely. The combination of big and little dots with a little or a lot of white space between them produces the illusion of shading in the photograph. The human eye, seeing minute dots of ink, mixes them and perceives them as gradations of tone. But in reality, the screened illustration is made up of only two tones, black and white.

The fineness of the halftone screen determines the quality of the illusion. A fine screen has more lines and thus more dots per square inch. Screens generally range from 50 to 150 lines to the inch each way, and the printed halftone may be described, for example, as a 65-line or a 110-line screen. Variation in the fineness of the screen is necessary because the quality of the paper on which the halftone is printed may be smooth and glossy or coarse and ink absorbent. Halftones printed on newsprint must be screened coarsely, whereas fine-quality magazine paper can take fine-screen halftones. Note that with a coarse screen the dots can be seen clearly with the naked eye (see Figure 10–11).

Different types of screens may also be used for artistic effect. Figure 10–12 demonstrates the result of using various screens to reproduce the same photograph.

Stripping

To make the printing plate, a single negative must be made of all the line and halftone artwork. First, separate photographs are made, one of the type and line art and one of each halftone illustration. Then, through a process known as *stripping,* the various negatives are carefully cut and taped together into one single negative that is used to make the combination plate.

Methods of Printing

Few advertisers maintain all the necessary capital equipment and personnel required for producing printed materials. As a result, they usually hire outside print production companies who work at their direction. These suppliers may include a typesetting house, a color separator, a photoplatemaker, a printer, or a duplicating house for newspaper material. All these sources are particularly important when media schedules include publications that print by different methods or when it is desirable to convert material from one printing process to another to save time and money.

Now that we understand some of the basics of printing, let's discuss the major printing methods used today.

Letterpress

For many years, letterpress was the major method of printing around the world. It was used in the reproduction of newspapers and many magazines that needed reasonable quality with sharp contrast. However, due to the advent of newer, higher-quality methods, very little letterpress printing is done in the United States anymore. Still, it may be helpful to understand

65-line screen.

100-line screen.

150-line screen.

FIGURE   10–11

These three examples of the same photograph show the effect of varying the fineness of halftone screens.

Two-color texture.

Random line.

Mezzo tint.

Wavy line (dry brush).

FIGURE   10–12

Many special effects are possible through the use of special line screens. All these processes use the same principle as the dot screen. They use lines, scratches, or some other technique and require much more careful photo work.

the basics of letterpress printing, not only for historical reasons but to have a well-rounded understanding of the printing process.

In letterpress, the printing is done from a metal or plastic printing plate on a large round drum or cylinder (see Figure 10–13). The process is similar to the way a rubber stamp works. Like a stamp, the image to be transferred is backward ("wrong reading") on the plate. The ink is applied to a raised (relief) surface on the plate and then transferred to the paper.

To produce the letterpress plate, the negative of the photographed image is laid on top of a sensitized plastic or copper plate and exposed to light. Since everything on a negative is in reverse, the image areas on the negative are transparent. This allows light to pass through the negative to the plate, which has been treated with a light-sensitive emulsion. The emulsion hardens in the areas exposed to the light and thereby forms an acid-resistant protective covering over the image area of the plate. The plate is then placed in an acid bath that etches away the nondesign areas—leaving the desired printing image raised on the surface of the plate.

The result is the line plate we discussed earlier. Sometimes a plastic plate may be used, in which case a photochemical process called *photopolymerization* followed by a simple washout is used to produce a relief plate.

Rotogravure

The process used in rotogravure differs from letterpress in several ways. First, two separate films are made—one for all type and line illustrations and the other for halftone illustrations. The negatives are combined into a single film "positive." In the gravure process, though, even type and line art are screened.

Then, instead of printing from a raised surface as in letterpress, the rotogravure process prints from a depressed surface. Like letterpress, the image to be transferred is backward ("wrong reading"). The design is etched or electromechanically engraved into a metal plate or cylinder, leaving depressions one or two thousandths of an inch deep. As the plate is inked and wiped clean with a metal blade, ink is left in the tiny depressions. It transfers this ink to the paper by pressure and suction (see Figure 10–13).

Preparing the printing plates or cylinders is time-consuming and costly, so rotogravure is practical and economical only for long press runs. Sunday newspaper supplements, mail-order catalogs, some major magazines, packaging, and other materials requiring a great number of photographs are well suited for this method. Rotogravure is noted for its good reproduction of color on both newsprint and quality paper stocks.

Offset Lithography

Today, offset lithography is the most popular printing process in the United States. The printing plates cost less than for other printing methods, the printing can be done on almost any paper quality, and the preparation time is short. Because the process is photographic, it meshes well with the most popular form of typesetting, photocomposition. Advertisers simply have to provide pasted-up art for the printer's camera (referred to as "camera-ready materials") or film for the platemaker.

Offset lithography employs the same line and halftone processes used to make letterpress plates. However, to the naked eye, the image on the

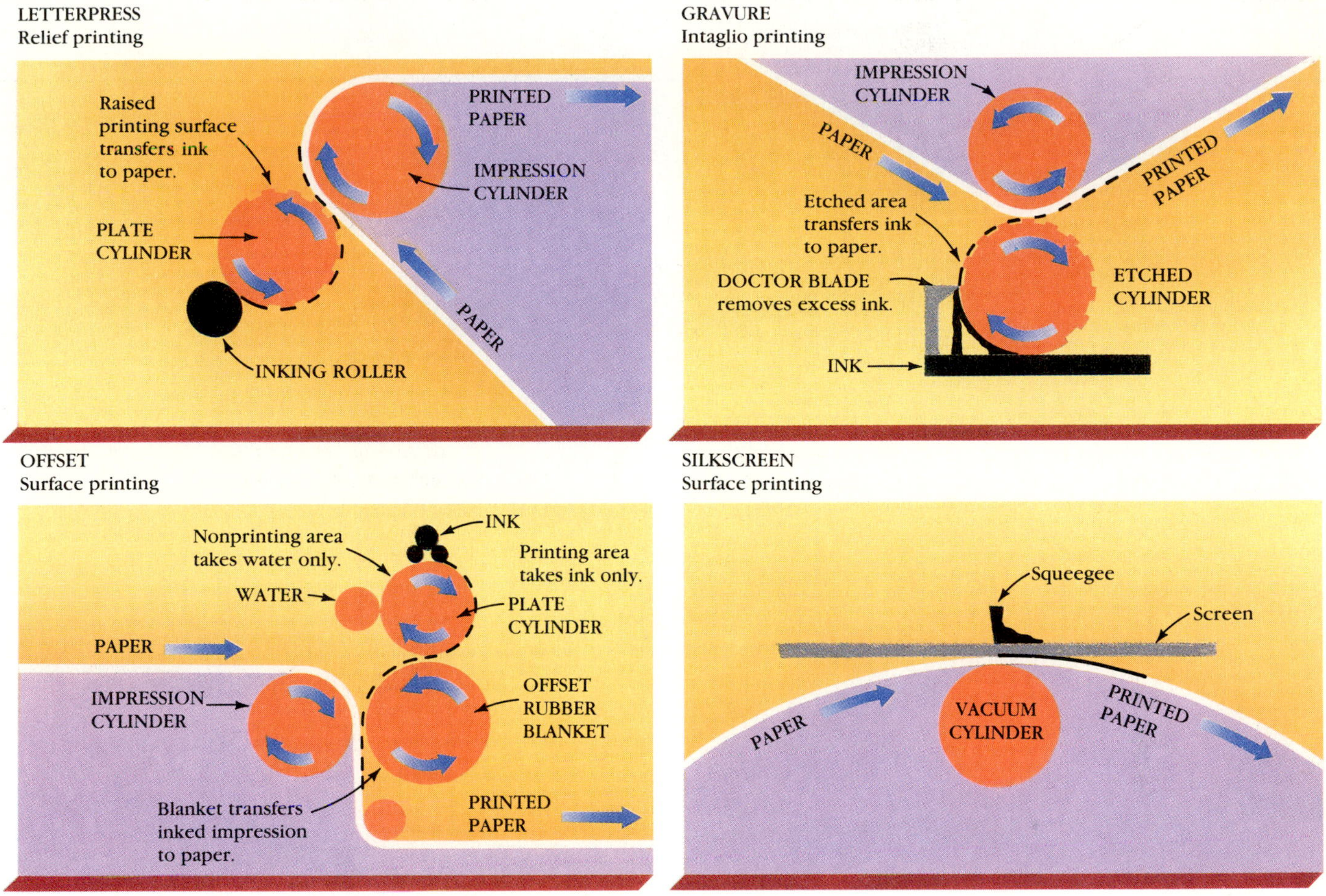

LETTERPRESS
Relief printing

Raised printing surface transfers ink to paper.

PRINTED PAPER

PLATE CYLINDER

IMPRESSION CYLINDER

PAPER

INKING ROLLER

GRAVURE
Intaglio printing

IMPRESSION CYLINDER

PAPER

PRINTED PAPER

Etched area transfers ink to paper.

DOCTOR BLADE removes excess ink.

ETCHED CYLINDER

INK

OFFSET
Surface printing

Nonprinting area takes water only.

INK

Printing area takes ink only.

WATER

PLATE CYLINDER

PAPER

IMPRESSION CYLINDER

OFFSET RUBBER BLANKET

Blanket transfers inked impression to paper.

PRINTED PAPER

SILKSCREEN
Surface printing

Squeegee

Screen

PAPER

VACUUM CYLINDER

PRINTED PAPER

FIGURE   10–13

Comparative illustrations of the major printing processes in use today. To complement your understanding of these processes, visit a local printer and ask to see the processes at work. It will be interesting and worthwhile.

lithographic printing plate appears to be flat instead of raised, as in letterpress, or depressed, as in rotogravure. Unlike letterpress and rotogravure, the image on the plate is "right reading."

The principle underlying lithography is that oil and water do not mix. To start, a photograph is made of the material to be printed. The negative from the photograph is laid on top of a zinc or aluminum printing plate and exposed to light. Chemicals are applied to the plate after the exposure, and the image takes the form of a greasy coating. The plate is then attached to a cylinder on a rotary printing press, and water is applied with a roller. The greasy-coated image repels the water, but the blank portions of the plate retain it. As the plate is covered with an oily ink, the moist, blank portions of the plate repel the ink. The greasy-coated image retains the ink for transfer to an intermediate rubber surface called a *blanket*, which comes in contact with the paper and enables the image to be printed (see Figure 10–13).

Lithography is used extensively for inexpensive advertising materials prepared at "instant" printing shops. Most newspapers and magazines are now printed by this process on high-speed offset presses (see Figure 10–14). Likewise, most books (including this one), direct-mail materials, and catalogs are printed by offset. And because it is suitable for printing on metal, most packaging materials, including beer and soft-drink cans, are also printed by lithography.

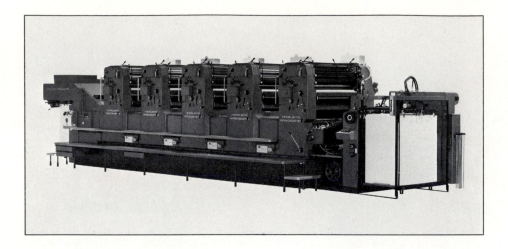

FIGURE   10–14

The high-speed Heidelberg five-color offset press is used for printing magazines. The first four units are used for four-color process printing, while the fifth may be used to varnish the printed page or to lay down a specific fifth color. Some art directors, for example, may want a "company blue," which is a specific colored ink rather than a combination of process colors.

Screen Printing (Serigraphy)

The signs and billboards we see along the highway often illustrate the use of screen printing. Billboards use sheets of paper that have historically been too large for many printing presses. Also, the quantities required for many outdoor advertising campaigns, especially local ones, are so small that it is often uneconomical to use other printing processes, like offset, that might be used for national campaigns.

Screen printing, an old process based on the stencil principle, requires no plates. A special screen is stretched tightly on a frame. The frame is placed on the surface on which the message or image is to be printed. A stencil, either hand cut from film or photographically prepared, is used to block out areas that are not part of the image to be printed. Ink is squeezed through the screen by a squeegee (rubber rollers) sliding across the surface, transferring the image onto the paper or other surface (see Figure 10–13). For printing in color, a separate stencil is made for each color.

Printing stencils are made of nylon or stainless steel mesh. Originally, silk was used, hence the old term *silk screen*. Today, automatic presses for screen printing are also available, making the process economical for even longer runs.

Printing in Color

If an advertiser wants to print an ad or a brochure in blue, green, and black, then three different plates are required, one for each color, and the job is referred to as a three-color job (see Figure 10–15). The method for printing full-color advertisements with tonal values, such as photographs and paintings, is called a *four-color process.* This process is based on the principle that all colors can be printed by combining the three primary colors—yellow, magenta (red), and cyan (blue)—plus black (which provides greater detail and density as well as shades of gray).

Each of the printing processes we have discussed can print color. However, a printing plate can print only one color at a time. Therefore, if a job is to be printed in full color, the printer must prepare four different printing plates, one for each color, including black.

The artwork to be reproduced is photographed through color filters

SELF RENEWAL.

Low interest loans to help you enjoy life after work. Call toll free 1-800-231-2130.
(Inside Washington State)

Weyerhaeuser
Credit Union

FIGURE   10–15

The Weyerhaeuser Credit Union in Longview, Washington used three colors to print this award-winning poster ad suggesting the subtle benefits of a low-interest loan. The headline and logo were printed in green, the copy was printed in black, and the photograph was printed in warm gray and black as a *duotone,* i.e., two colors printed together to add depth, texture, and feeling to the picture.

that eliminate all the colors except one. For example, one filter eliminates all colors except red and extracts every light ray of red to be blended into the final reproduced picture. An electronic scanning device may be used to make these color separations. Thus, four separate, continuous-tone negatives are produced to make a set of four-color plates: one for yellow, one for magenta, one for cyan, and one for black. The resulting negatives are in black and white and are called *color separation negatives.*

These color separations are photographed through a halftone screen to make a set of screened negatives from which the plates are made. In photographing the color separations, the halftone screen is rotated to a different angle for each separation. As a result, the dots do not completely overlap because the four plates superimpose the dots over one another during printing. On the printed page, tiny clusters of halftone dots of the four colors in various sizes and shapes give the eye the optical illusion of seeing the colors of the original photograph or painting. In printing, transparent inks are used, so people can see all colors through the four overlapping coatings of ink on the paper. For example, even though green ink is not used, green can be reproduced by a yellow and a cyan dot, each overlapping their respective colors on paper in the form of halftone dots. Dark green would have larger blue halftone dots than yellow. (See Creative Department: From Concept through Production of a Magazine Advertisement.)

(continued on p. 335)

CREATIVE DEPARTMENT

From Concept through Production of a Magazine Advertisement

Marketing Considerations

In September 1985, as a strategic defense against the recent introduction of a dry soup mix by Campbell Soup, the Thomas J. Lipton Company introduced a new product of its own, Lipton International Soup Classics. Designed to fit the contemporary consumer lifestyle, the product was a superior quality, single-serving convenience food. It could serve as an integral part of a light meal (e.g., salad, cheese, soup), as an appetizer for a formal dinner, or as a nutritious between-meal snack. Available in five delicious, creamy recipes, the product could satisfy a wide range of tastes. The Soup Classics were distinctively packaged in black cartons with dramatic product photos prominently positioned to display the soup's creamy texture and large, freeze-dried pieces. Distribution of the product was best developed in the East, followed by the central and western regions and, lastly, the South.

Creative Concepts

Lipton wanted to target upscale audiences in its primary market areas. Its advertising agency, Young & Rubicam, suggested showing both the distinctive packaging and the appetite appeal of the product in one shot. Since the package face displayed a picture of the product, the art director, Gary Goldstein, proposed a trompe l'oeil (optical illusion) layout where a beauty shot of a spoon in a steaming bowl of soup would replace the straight product shot. The idea even included having the spoon extend beyond the edge of the package—making the soup look ready-to-eat right off the front of the box (see A. Rough layout).

Shooting the Ad

To achieve the desired look, the concept required at least four photographs: one main visual of the package itself, one for the soup, one for the steam, and one for the row of other flavors. Working with a tight layout and acetates, the photographer carefully positioned the package shot and the soup shot so that the perspective and lighting would match. The hot soup shot was slightly overexposed to capture the steam, which was an important element both for the tromp l'oeil and the appetite appeal.

Preparing for Production

The creative department reviewed the film (shot in an 8 × 10 format) based on the original layout. Four chromes were selected, each having the color density needed for high-quality, four-color reproduction. Then a composite print was created to show the client for approval. Subsequently, a mechanical retouching and stripping guide was developed from stats of the photos and type and shown to the agency art buyer and print producer

A. Rough layout.

for their input. During a preproduction meeting, it was decided that it would be best to retouch this job on an electronic pagination system. Once client approval was obtained, the mechanical was given to the color separator, Potomac Color Industries, along with a timetable and the original transparencies. Reviewing the task with the separator, the following directions were developed:

1. Utilize the steam from chrome D (B.) and photocompose into main visual (C.). The steam should be transparent, allowing the background package to come through.
2. Photocompose the soup bowl (D.) into main visual. Create a shadow of the spoon in chrome A on the surface of the table.
3. Photocompose the package shots from chrome B (E.) into the main visual.
4. Color balance all packages and the background of the main visual.

A cost estimate was requested, and once approved, the job proceeded.

B. Chrome D, showing steam.

C. The main visual.

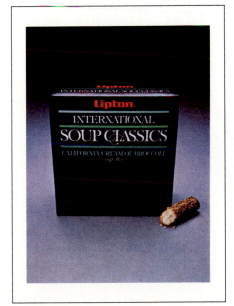

D. Chrome A, showing soup bowl.

E. Chrome B, showing package shots.

F. Marked copy for typesetter.

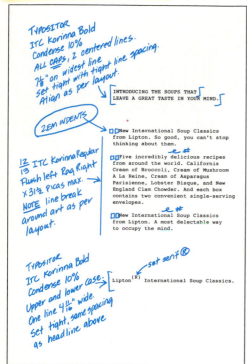

G. Photomechanical.

Production

First, each transparency was scanned into the electronic system, converting each of the images to digitized pixels. Next, at the computer workstation, the retoucher superimposed the bowl of soup on the main package shot and then added the steam to this composition. Behind the steam, the color had to be corrected very carefully to make the whole composition believable. Moreover, the steam itself was extended to break over the headline. A little soup was added to the spoon, and the drop shadow was created beneath the spoon.

From the computer's memory bank, the system was able to use a variety of selected applications as needed in the process, such as cloning, imaging, photocomposing, silhouetting, and vignetting.

When all adjustments had been made and the electronic retouching was finalized, Chromalins were sent to the agency for review and evaluation. After approval, the digitized film data with all corrections was stored in the computer for later disposition.

Typesetting

While this photo work was in process, type had to be set for the ad. The art director and the copywriter, Marvin Waldman, submitted the rough layout and the approved copy to the agency type director. Together they selected a suitable type style for the ad. The type director then determined the size of the headline and carefully marked up the copy for the style of typeface, spacing, and size (see F. Marked copy for typesetter).

The layout and copy were sent to the typographer, who set the headline and body copy with photodisplay equipment. From the film put out by this equipment, a photomechanical of the ad was created, according to the rough layout. The copywriter, art director, and type director then proofed the mechanical for errors and made whatever aesthetic or technical adjustments were required. The ad was then submitted to the client in this form for approval (see G. Photomechanical).

When all adjustments and corrections in copy and artwork had been determined, the mechanical was returned to the typographer. The corrections were made, and the new photomechanical was then used to make a negative line film for delivery to the photoplatemaker.

Photoplatemaking

Retrieving the corrected film data of the main visual from the computer, four-color screened film was manufactured. A line negative of the typographic elements was then incorporated with these screened separations. From these, four-color offset plates were made and placed on the press. A set of proofs and progressive proofs showing the single colors was pulled off the press and sent to the agency for approval (see H. Progressive proofs). Minor corrections were handled by sending the job back to the computer or by dot etching on the offset film masters.

H. Progressive proofs (color separations).

Yellow

Magenta

Yellow and magenta

Cyan

Yellow, magenta, and cyan

Black

After client and agency product group approval, the master films were duplicated by the platemaker, and the necessary quantity of films, proofs, and progressive proofs were sent to each of the publications involved. The proofs were then used by the publications as a guide for color at the press to be sure that a faithful reproduction would be achieved (see I. Completed ad).

I. Completed ad.

Recently developed electronic scanners can perform four-color separations and screening in one process, along with enlargement or reduction. In a single operation, an operator can achieve highlight/shadow density changes, contrast modification, color change, or removal of an area or a whole piece. All this can be accomplished in a period of several minutes instead of the hours or days that were previously needed for camera work and hand-etching. Lately, however, these scanners have grown into complete computerized color pagination systems that are capable of performing all positioning of illustrative and text elements as well as electronic retouching.[7]

Preparing Materials for Publications

Most local newspapers and magazines are willing and able to work with advertisers to help produce their advertisements. Frequently this service is free. The local dress shop or furniture store works with the newspaper's ad salesperson and provides the copy and illustrations, and the newspaper's production department takes care of the rest.

At some point in their growth, however, advertisers may decide to exercise more control over the production process to ensure consistency and quality. Major agencies always like to maintain complete control over the preparation of materials used for reproduction rather than giving the media that responsibility.

Media schedules frequently contain numerous publications that will run the advertisement at about the same time, requiring the advertiser to provide duplicate materials to each publication.

Production specifications can be obtained directly from the publication. It is often more convenient, however, to use the Standard Rate and Data Service *Print Media Production Data* directory. This directory contains critical information about the printing specifications and mechanical measurements (dimensions of advertising space acceptable) of every major publication.

For publications printed by rotogravure or offset lithography, duplicate materials consist of duplicate sets of color-separated film positives (for gravure) or photographic copies of the mechanical and screened art (for offset lithography). These photographic copies may be in the form of *photoprints* (a screened print or a Velox) or color-separated contact *film negatives,* depending on the requirements of the particular publication. From these materials, publications make their own printing plates.

Selecting Papers for Printing

When preparing materials for printing, it is important to know the kind of paper on which the advertisement will be printed. Some advertisers are so concerned about the appearance of their advertisements that they have them printed on a higher quality of paper stock than that used in the regular pages of a newspaper or magazine. They will then ship the printed material to the publication for insertion or binding.

Paper used in advertising can be broken down into three categories: writing, text, and cover stock.

Writing Paper This is commonly used in letters and other direct-mail pieces. Bond writing paper is the most durable and also the most frequently used.

Text Paper Many different types of text paper are available. Major classifications—news stock, antique finish, machine finish, English finish, and coated—range from less expensive, very porous, coarse papers (used for newspapers) to very smooth, expensive, heavier papers used for magazines, industrial brochures, and fine-quality annual reports.

Cover Paper Because of its tough, durable quality, cover paper is used for softcover book covers and sometimes for direct-mail pieces. Advertisers can choose from many finishes and textures.

While we have barely scratched the surface in our discussion of the print production process, it should be obvious that this field is very complex and, with expanding technology, becoming highly technical. That also means, though, that it is offering many new and exciting challenges and opportunities for those interested in specializing in the printing side of the advertising business.

Summary

The production process in print advertising is so critical that if it is not handled correctly, an otherwise beautiful ad can be destroyed. A fundamental understanding of production techniques, therefore, can save a lot of money and disappointment.

The print production manager's job is to ensure that the final advertisement reflects what the art director had in mind. That is often an impossible task, as the print production manager must work within the limited, specified confines of time requirements, quality objectives, and acceptable budgets.

The typeface chosen for an advertisement affects its appearance, design, and legibility. Type can generally be divided into two broad classes: display type and text type. In addition, typefaces can be classified by their similarity of design. The major type groups are roman, sans serif, square serif, cursive or script, and ornamental. Within each group are many type families, such as Bodoni, Futura, Goudy, and Caslon. In a type family, the basic design remains the same, but variations of weight, slant, and size are available.

Type is measured in terms of the number of points and picas. Points measure the vertical size of type. There are 72 points to an inch. Picas measure the horizontal width of a single line of type. There are six picas to an inch. Type may further be referred to as uppercase (capital letters) and lowercase (small letters).

Four important points should be considered when selecting type: readability, appropriateness, harmony or appearance, and emphasis. The process of determining how much type will fit a specified area in an advertisement is called copy casting. There are several methods used to cast copy today.

There are also several methods used to set type. The most important of these are the various photocomposition techniques, including photo-optical methods, cathode-ray tube (CRT) techniques, and laser exposure.

Printing processes have undergone great technological changes in recent decades. Today, the most common types of printing methods are offset lithography, rotogravure, and screen printing. Each method has its unique advantages and disadvantages.

Preparing plates for printing involves exposing an image to a sensitized metal plate. Two types of images are used for printing: line images and halftone images. Line images print only two tonal values—black and white. For gradations of tone, as in an illustration or photograph, halftone images are used. These print a series of black dots of various sizes, thus producing an optical illusion of tonal grades.

When full color is required, four halftone plates are used, one for each primary color and one for black. These print the colored dots in tiny clusters, creating the illusion of full color.

Questions for Review and Discussion

1. What are the characteristics of the five major type groups?
2. What does copy casting mean? Explain the ways in which it is done.
3. What is the importance of these terms: readability, appropriateness, harmony/appearance, emphasis?
4. What do these terms mean: point, pica, uppercase, lowercase?
5. The two broad classifications of display type and text type have basic differences. Explain what they are. Give some examples in which display type may be used.
6. What are the types of photocomposition, and what advantages does photocomposition offer?
7. What are the major differences between rotogravure and offset lithography?
8. What is a halftone? How is it produced?
9. How are color photographs printed? What are the potential problems with printing color?
10. What role is played by one of the typical production suppliers of advertising?

11
CREATIVE
PRODUCTION:
ELECTRONIC
MEDIA

In an era when a substantial percentage of the population is college educated, economically savvy, and generally cynical about extravagant advertising claims, what's an advertiser to do to break through this wall of skepticism? That's the job, today, of America's advertising creative directors.[1] And nowhere is their effort more evident than in the electronic media: television and radio.

In response to this dilemma of disbelief, there has recently been a startling appearance of rather unusual commercial presenters. "Hi, I'm Joe Isuzu," announces American Isuzu Motors' sleazy, slick car salesman who mouths outrageous lies while, at the bottom of the screen, the true story appears in subtitles. Then there's Bartles & Jaymes (whom we shall discuss further in Chapter 14)—two old codgers who act like a couple of hicks with their humorous, down-home naiveté. They were the brainchild of Hal Riney, the master of soft sell, and within just eight months of introduction, they captured the lead in wine coolers for their parent company, Ernest & Julio Gallo Winery.[2]

Another Riney client is Dreyer's Grand Ice Cream. In the Dreyer's ads, a cast of fundamentally unbelievable spokespeople (former Nixon aide John Ehrlichman, Howard Hughes's counterfeit heir Melvin Dummar, and others) help the sponsor capitalize on the seemingly inherent contradiction in the term *light ice cream*. The theory seems to be that the more outrageous the lie, the more believable the advertising claim. It's a new twist that turns the whole truth-in-advertising issue inside out by, in effect, showing the advertisers themselves laughing at the absurdity of extravagant claims.[3]

While all these characters are unusual, there is nothing new about the idea of using commercial presenters. Dick Wilson, for example, had been an actor for half a century, had appeared in over 300 television roles, and had played major parts in several series. But it wasn't until he started playing the finicky grocer Mr. Whipple that people began asking for his autograph. His role was simply to whine, "Please don't squeeze the Charmin," in a commercial for Procter & Gamble. For the next two decades, Charmin was the best-selling bathroom tissue in America.[4]

In recent years, comedian Bill Cosby has been the most highly touted commercial spokesman in the United States, and he has been sought out by a variety of the biggest advertisers—Ford, Coca-Cola, McDonald's, Texas Instruments, Kodak, and Jell-O, just to name a few. For Jell-O Pudding Pops, for example, he is highly identifiable. He comes across with great strength of character and memorability, and he seems to have an unequaled rapport with children.[5]

Continuing commercial presenters, according to most advertisers, produce tremendous goodwill and product identification. They attract attention, identify the brand immediately by their familiarity, act as friendly authority figures for the consuming public, and guarantee advertising continuity over the years to the brands they support. As such, they are an important consideration in the development of product advertising campaigns and in the production of commercials for electronic media (see Figure 11–1).

However, advertising creative directors must also contemplate many other considerations. For instance, how should the commercial concept be developed? What type of commercial should be used? What production techniques should be employed? And what is the most effective and cost-efficient production process to employ? In this chapter, we shall discuss a number of these considerations as they relate to the production of both radio and television commercials.

CREATING COMMERCIALS FOR TELEVISION

Advertisers produce more than 50,000 television commercials every year in an effort to sell their goods and services. No one knows exactly how much is spent in the production of all these commercials, but most estimates are in the many hundreds of millions of dollars.

Producing commercials for television is expensive. For a local advertiser, a simple spot might cost anywhere from $1,000 to $20,000. For national quality spots, though, the costs are considerably higher. The lowest figure is probably around $20,000, with the average now probably over $125,000.[6]

As the technology of electronic commercial production has soared, so have the costs and the complexity, resulting in greater specialization in the production process. Major agencies, for example, used to maintain complete production facilities in-house. Not anymore. The trend for several decades now has been toward the use of outside producers, directors, production companies, and other technical suppliers.

It is, therefore, more difficult today to gain an expert knowledge of electronic production. However, a general understanding of basic production concepts is still a must for anyone involved in advertising. This means recognizing how commercials are written, which types of commercials are most commonly used and which are most effective, what the basic terms and techniques are for producing a commercial, and how the production process is organized.

For the student of advertising, these concepts are important to understanding how commercials are made, why commercial production is so expensive, and what methods can be used to cut costs without sacrificing quality or effectiveness.

Developing the Concept for the Commercial

How did Dick Wilson get to be Mr. Whipple and David Leisure become Joe Isuzu? And where do these characters come from anyway? Put simply, they are born in the minds of the men and women who conceive of the original commercial—the art director, the copywriter, and the creative director.

Initially, if the concept is to create a dramatic scene, the script may call for an actor to play the part of a fictitious character. Or the creative team

FIGURE   11–1

As a commercial presenter for Charmin tissue, Dick Wilson has successfully played the finicky Mr. Whipple for many years, while Bill Cosby has been just as successful playing himself for a variety of sponsors.

may decide it wants to use a well-known celebrity to lend his or her credibility to presenting the product. In any case, casting these characters is a major area of deliberation at the time the commercial is written.

During the casting process, the most important consideration is relevance to the product. For example, it's considered unwise to use a comic to sell financial products—or mortuary services for that matter.[7] And in spite of Bill Cosby's success, David Ogilvy doesn't even believe in using celebrities. Viewers, he says, tend to remember the celebrity more than the product.[8]

As the concept for the commercial evolves, the creative team defines the personalities of the characters and usually writes a brief but detailed description of them. These descriptions are used in casting sessions as guides in the selection of prospective actors who are interviewed and auditioned for the roles. Sometimes a Mr. Whipple or a Frank Bartles and Ed Jaymes will be discovered—solid, believable characters who go beyond a simple role and actually create a personality or image for the product.

Basic Mechanics of Script Development

A television script is divided into two portions. The right side is labeled *audio* and lists the spoken copy, the sound effects, and the music. The left side is the *video*—for the camera action, scenes, and stage directions. (See the commercial script in the Creative Department: From Concept through Production of a Television Commercial, which is presented later in this chapter.)

After the basic script has been conceived, the writer and art director prepare a *storyboard*. The typical storyboard is a sheet preprinted with a series of 8 to 20 blank television screens (frames). The scenes from the video are sketched into the frames by the art director, and the audio, plus instructions for the video, are typed underneath. Due to space limitations, many abbreviations are used. See Figure 11–2 for some of the more common ones.

The visual value of television is such a powerful element that the role of the art director (relative to the copywriter) is particularly important today— more than ever before.[9] The art director designs each scene carefully in much the same way as in a print ad—arranging actors, scenery, props, lighting, and camera angles—to maximize impact, beauty, and emotionalism. The storyboard, then, helps both agency and client personnel visualize the complexities of the commercial, estimate the expense, discover any weaknesses in concept, present it to management for approval, and guide the actual shooting. However, at best, the storyboard is still just an approximation of what the final commercial will look like. Actual production sometimes results in many changes in lighting, camera angle, focal point, and emphasis. The camera sees many things the artist didn't consider, and vice versa.

During the last decade, the cost of both television production and media has soared, greatly increasing the pressure on agencies to pretest their commercial concepts prior to proceeding into final production. To supplement the storyboard or pretest the concept, therefore, a commercial may be taped in rough form using the writers and artists as actors.[10] Or an *animatic* may be shot—a film strip composed of the sketches in the storyboard accompanied by the audio portion of the commercial synchronized on tape.

FIGURE 11–2	Cut, zoom, and wipe, please! (Common abbreviations used in TV scripts)
CU:	Close-up. Very close shot of person or object.
ECU:	Extreme close-up. A more extreme version of the above. Sometimes designated as BCU (big close-up) or TCU (tight close-up).
MCU:	Medium close-up. Emphasizes the subject but includes other objects nearby.
MS:	Medium shot. Wide-angle shot of subject but not whole set.
FS:	Full shot. Entire set or object.
LS:	Long shot. Full view of scene to give effect of distance.
DOLLY:	Move camera toward or away from subject. Dolly in (DI), dolly out (DO), or dolly back (DB).
PAN:	Scan from one side to the other.
ZOOM:	Move rapidly in or out from the subject without blurring.
SUPER:	Superimpose one image on another—as showing lettering over a scene.
DISS:	Dissolve (also DSS). Fade out one scene while fading in another.
CUT:	Instant change of one picture to another.
WIPE:	Gradually erase picture from screen. (Many varied effects are possible.)
VO:	Voice-over. An off-screen voice, usually the announcer's.
SFX:	Sound effects.
DAU:	Down and under. Sound effects fade as voice comes on.
UAO:	Up and over. Voice fades as sound effects come on.

Effective Scriptwriting

In Chapter 8, we presented fundamentals of writing advertising copy. Television commercials demand that additional attention be given to credibility, believability, and relevance. That goes well beyond the use of words.

David Ogilvy points out that the millions of dollars spent on TV commercial research have resulted in the following principles:

The opening should be a short, compelling attention getter—a visual surprise, compelling in action, drama, humor, or human interest.

Demonstrations should be interesting and believable—authentic and true to life; they should never appear to be a camera trick.

The commercial should be ethical, be in good taste, and not offend local mores.

Commercials should be entertaining (to hold the viewers' attention), but the entertainment should be a means to an end and not interfere with the message.

The general structure of the commercial and the copy should be simple

Checklist for Creating Effective TV Commercials

☐ The opening should be pertinent, relevant, and not forced. It should permit a smooth transition to the balance of the commercial.

☐ The situation should lend itself naturally to the sales story—without the use of extraneous, distracting gimmicks.

☐ The situation should be high in human interest.

☐ The viewer should be able to identify with the situation.

☐ The number of elements should be held to a minimum.

☐ The sequence of ideas should be kept simple.

☐ The words should be short, realistic, and conversational, not "ad talk." Sentences should be short.

☐ Words should not be wasted describing what is being seen.

☐ The words should interpret the picture and prepare the viewer for the next scene.

☐ Audio and video should be synchronized.

☐ The audio copy should be concise—without wasted words. Fewer words are needed for TV than for radio. Fewer than two words per second is effective for demonstrations. Sixty-second commercials with 101 to 110 words are most effective. Those with more than 170 words are the least effective.

☐ Five or six seconds should be allowed for the average scene, with none less than three seconds.

☐ Enough movement should be provided to avoid static scenes.

☐ Scenes should offer variety without "jumping."

☐ The commercial should look fresh and new.

☐ Any presenters should be properly handled—identified, compatible, authoritative, pleasing, and nondistracting.

☐ The general video treatment should be interesting.

and easy to follow. The video should carry most of the weight, but the audio must support it.

Characters become the living symbol of your product—they should be appealing, believable, and most of all, relevant.[11]

These are a few of the principles research has shown to be true. For more, see the Checklist for Creating Effective TV Commercials.

To illustrate these principles, look at the award-winning, 30-second commercial for Jarman's "Manhole" illustrated in Figure 11–3. Created by The Bloom Agency in Dallas, this is a classic example of a well-written, simple, interesting, credible, and entertaining commercial. It was also relatively inexpensive to produce.

First, look at the commercial as a whole. It has one dominant mood and gives a single, unified impression. There are a minimum number of people. The situation is high in human interest. The structure is *simple* and easy to follow. The presenter is *appealing,* authoritative, and credible, and the whole commercial is a *close-up* of him. The entertainment value is high but perfectly *relevant.* In fact, everything not relevant to the commercial's objective has been deleted. The *sales points* are demonstrated smoothly, and the *product name* is mentioned frequently. Finally, there is a strong *closing identification* illustrating the name and the product.

Looking at some of the mechanics, note that there seems to be only one scene throughout. There are, in fact, four different camera setups. But the *unity* is so strong that the changes are hardly noticeable.

FIGURE   11–3

FIGURE   11–3

This commercial for Jarman shoes demonstrates the basic principles of creating an effective television ad.

Examine the opening scene. Before one word is spoken, we know who the man is and what he's doing. He looks the part and acts the part. In 12 words he has established the whole context of the commercial and is into the sell. By the second frame of the storyboard, he has already said the product name once and made a case for the popularity of the product. By the third frame, he's proving his first sales point and is into the second—style. Then he hits the name again. Two frames later, he hits it again, and then there is a third sales point—comfort. One more frame and he hits the fourth sales point—price. Then he hits the name again and the fifth point—for men only. Finally, the closing frame shows the shoes, the name, and the strong tag line: "Style to fit your style."

In all, the commercial contains only 76 words, yet it says so much. That's what makes a commercial memorable.

As an exercise, take a few moments to compare some of the other television spots illustrated in this text to that Jarman commercial. How many can you find that are as concise? As simple? As appealing? As credible? These are the qualities that make commercials effective.

Types of Television Commercials

The advertisements we have discussed have all been "presenter" commercials, where one person or character presents the product and carries the whole sales message. Sometimes these presenters are celebrities, like Bill Cosby for Jell-O and Ford Motor Company or Michael J. Fox for Pepsi-Cola. Other times they are corporate officers of the sponsor, like Frank Perdue for Perdue Chicken or Lee Iacocca, the chairman of Chrysler Corporation. In the case of Jarman, a professional actor plays the role of a fictitious underground worker and indirectly acts as a spokesman. Other sponsors,

FIGURE   11–4

Corning's demonstration of what happens to ordinary saucepans at 850° Centigrade (1,562° Fahrenheit) rapidly tells the story that there's a whole lot more to Corning than that little blue flower in their logo.

SFX: (MUSIC)

ANNCR: (VO) VISIONS rangetop cookware by Corning withstands heat that turns ordinary saucepans into sauce.

And unlike metal pans they're perfect for the microwave.

VISIONS by Corning. It's visibly superior.

like Bank of America, may use a noncelebrity actor who simply delivers a straight pitch rather than playing a particular role.

Of course, there are many types of commercials besides the presenter format. In fact, there may be almost as many ways to classify television ads as there are advertisers. The six basic categories, though, in addition to the presenter category, are the straight announcement, demonstration, testimonial, slice of life, lifestyle, and animation. These divisions often overlap and should not be considered ironclad.

We shall discuss each of these types briefly before considering the more practical subjects of production techniques and procedures.

Straight Announcement

The straight announcement is the oldest and simplest type of television commercial. An announcer delivers a sales message directly into the camera or off-screen while a slide or film is shown on-screen. It is a safe method and can be effective if the script is well written and the announcer convincing. The appeal may be either "hard sell" or relaxed. It is a relatively simple approach and needs no elaborate facilities, so the advertiser saves money. It may be combined with a demonstration.

By and large, the straight announcement has given way to more creative concepts. However, it is not uncommon to see this type of commercial still being used on late-night TV programs, by local advertisers, and by non-profit or political organizations.

Demonstration

Studies have shown that a demonstration convinces an audience better and faster than an oral message.[12] Memorable demonstrations have been used to show the product advantages of car tires, ballpoint pens, and paper towels, to mention just a few. Products may be demonstrated in three ways—in use, in competition, or before and after.

These techniques enable the viewer to project what the product's performance would be like if he or she owned it. Therefore, the theme of the demonstration should be as clear, simple, graphic, and *relevant* as possible. Most important, it should be interesting (see Figure 11–4).

Testimonial

People are often persuaded by the opinions of individuals they respect, and this holds true whether the "product" is a political candidate or a bar of soap. The true *testimonial* can make TV advertising highly effective.

Satisfied customers are the best sources for testimonials. While they may be camera shy, their natural sincerity is usually persuasive. Ogilvy suggests shooting candid testimonials when the subjects don't know they're being filmed.[13] But be sure to get their permission before use.

Using celebrities to endorse a product may gain attention, as we've discussed. But they must be believable and not distract attention from the product. Additionally, research has shown that those presenters who possess moderate to high physical attractiveness score greater credibility due to perceived trust, perceived expertise, and audience liking.[14]

Actually, people from all walks of life endorse products—from known personalities to unknowns and nonprofessionals. Which person to use depends on the product and the strategy.

Slice of Life (Problem Solution)

The *slice-of-life commercial* is a little play that portrays a real-life situation. It usually starts with just plain folks before they discover the solution to their problem. The situation is usually tense, often dealing with something of a personal nature—bad breath, loose dentures, dandruff, B.O., or yellow laundry. A relative or a co-worker drops the hint, the product is tried, and the next scene shows the result—a happier, cleaner, more fragrant person off with a new date or finally able to bite into an apple. Such commercials are often irritating to viewers and hated by copywriters, but their messages still break through and sell.[15]

The key to effective slice-of-life commercials is simplicity. The ad should concentrate on one product benefit and make it memorable. Often a *mnemonic device* is used to dramatize the product benefit. Users of Imperial Margarine suddenly discover a crown on their head, or the doorbell rings for the Avon representative.

Joe Sedelmaier (see People in Advertising) has developed a unique style of humor out of the slice-of-life form.[16] He turns Everyman's trials of daily life into caricatures. He builds sympathy for his beaten-down characters, and then he offers the solution (see Figure 11–5).

FIGURE   11–5

In a classic Sedelmaier commercial for Alaska Airlines, the exaggerated problem of reduced service with discounted airline fares is driven home with hilarity.

ANNCR: Many airlines offer reduced rate fares. Unfortunately, that's not all they've reduced.

It makes you wonder what's next.

MAN: I'd appreciate it, do you have four quarters for a dollar?

Anybody have two quarters for a dollar?

Yes, miss, do you have two quarters for two dollars? Two quarters for five dollars, Please? Oh boy I'd appreciate it.

ANNCR: On Alaska Airlines, we have low fares too. But you'd never know it by the way we treat you.

Recently, variations on the slice-of-life technique have been used that make the believability almost painful to watch. Anacin, for example, actually combined the slice-of-life and testimonial forms by showing highly believable, depressing headache complaints from a sooty coal miner, a weather-beaten farmer, and a plain-looking housewife—all actors, of course. Such ads, which approach the cinema verité art form with their natural lighting, subdued colors, erratic motion, extreme close-ups, and grainy film quality, have become a recent fad and been used for a variety of advertisers, including American Telephone & Telegraph, Home Savings, and Hospital Corporation of America.[17]

Believability is difficult to achieve in slice-of-life commercials. People don't really talk about "ring around the collar," so the actors must be highly credible to put the fantasy across. For that reason, most local advertisers don't, and shouldn't, use the slice-of-life technique. Creating that believability takes very professional talent and money.

Lifestyle

When they want to present the user rather than the product, advertisers will often use the lifestyle technique. Levi's targets its 501 Jeans messages to young, contemporary men working, walking, and playing in a variety of different occupations and pastimes with a bluesy, modern musical theme. Likewise, beer and soft drink advertisers frequently target their message to active, outdoorsy, young people, focusing on who drinks the brand rather than specific product advantages.

PEOPLE IN ADVERTISING

Joe Sedelmaier

Founder and President
Sedelmaier Film Productions, Inc.

Joe Sedelmaier, whose hilarious, offbeat TV commercials for Wendy's and numerous other companies have made him one of today's hottest—and most controversial—TV commercial directors, is the president of Sedelmaier Film Productions, Inc., in Chicago.

His TV spots are instantly recognizable—the fast-talking man for Federal Express, the Jartran commercial with the roomful of multiplying rabbits, and the GMAC ad in which the young couple try to get a car loan for their new Fiero from a cold group of bankers who know nothing about cars. "They are by far the strangest commercials on TV," writes an industry observer. "They may also be the best."

Sedelmaier, born John Josef Sedelmaier on May 31, 1933, in Orrville, Ohio, graduated from Chicago's Art Institute and the University of Chicago. He entered advertising in 1956 as an art director/producer for Young & Rubicam in Chicago, then served in the same capacity at Clinton Frank and J. Walter Thompson.

During these years, Sedelmaier directed and produced several short films. *Mrofnoc* ("conform" spelled backwards) and *Because That's Why* netted him top awards, including the Golden Lion at the Cannes Film Festival and the Mannheim Film Festival's Gold Ducat.

Animation

Cartoons, puppet characters, and animated demonstrations have traditionally been very effective in communicating difficult messages and in reaching specialized markets such as children. The way in which aspirin or other medications affect the human system is difficult to explain. Animated pictures of headaches and stomachs, however, can simplify the subject and make a demonstration understandable.

Today, computer-generated graphics are being used to animate television commercials for everything from high-technology products to bathroom cleaner. (See Figure 11–6.) Their use, though, has required a great deal of faith on the part of advertisers, since most of this very expensive work is done right in the computer and there is nothing to see until the animation is well developed.[18] TRW Inc., for instance, used state-of-the-art computerized animation to enhance the message that TRW is future-oriented.[19]

PRODUCTION TECHNIQUES

Animation is more than just a category of commercial. It is also a major production technique that has recently experienced startling technological progress. When Levi's spent a quarter of a million dollars to produce a single animated TV commercial back in 1977, it was called "a milestone in television advertising" by columnist Harry Wayne McMahan in *Advertising Age*.[20]

Launching his own production company in 1967, Sedelmaier soon became known for his comic TV commercials for clients such as Del Taco, Dunkin' Donuts, Alaska Airlines, PSA, and American Motors.

What do Sedelmaier's commercials have in common? They are funny. They are odd. They focus on everyday human anxieties. Most people have been victims of postal neglect, of awful fast-food chicken, of screwed-up cars. Sedelmaier sells through this human dread. Watching his commercials is oddly comforting, yet unsettling. You relate, you identify. And then you laugh.

Sedelmaier feels that casting is 50 percent of his job. He is famous for the group of mostly nonactors—former bricklayers, cabbies, CPAs, even former manicurist Clara Peller—who spark his commercials. If a face strikes him as evocative or funny, he'll use it. And he likes to let the people he chooses inspire his comic direction. "If an actor has some distinctive quality, I'll write him or her into the spot. Casting can change everything."

So can Joe Sedelmaier, as his clients attest. He takes total control over the commercials he directs, from idea to final print. Typically, he begins by dispensing with the client-approved storyboards for the commercial. Then he changes dialogue, alters sequence, adds characters. He revamps the entire commercial and leaves only the original idea intact. Sedelmaier likes things a certain way—his way—and his TV spots reflect this determination.

Sedelmaier is the only TV commercial director who works exclusively in comedy. While some in advertising claim that humor just doesn't sell, Sedelmaier's commercials suggest otherwise. They helped to shoot Federal Express from obscurity to number one in overnight delivery. And Wendy's sales reportedly climbed 15 percent after Sedelmaier's "Where's the beef?" spots first aired.

"The reason I've always held to comedy," explains Sedelmaier, "is that there's not much to be serious about. How can you be serious about toilet paper?"

The notion has paid off—for Joe Sedelmaier. He shoots 75 to 80 TV commercials a year, which reportedly earn him about a million dollars. His commercials have won over 50 Clio awards, the Golden Hugo award at the Chicago Film Festival, and top honors from The One Show, the Art Directors Club, and the Hollywood IBA.

FIGURE   11-6

Computer-generated animation characterizes the scrubbing bubbles from Dow Bathroom Cleaner. The entire commercial is animated, even the can and the logo; and nothing interrupts the bubbles' routine of cleaning to the music of the Sabre Dance except the narrator's voice at the end of the spot.

SFX: (MUSIC) "Sabre Dance"

VO: Dow Bathroom Cleaner with Scrubbing Bubbles™. We work hard so you don't have to.

The commercial did indeed make history—in more ways than one. It set a new record at the time for the production cost of just one commercial. It chalked up the highest test score up to that time in Burke's (a major advertising research company) experience—two to four times as high as "normal" commercials. It pioneered radically new and effective techniques in communication—especially with young people. And it continued to build the sales momentum of this 135-year-old firm, which uses more than 10 percent of all the cotton grown in this country.

The commercial—created by Levi's agency, Foote, Cone & Belding/Honig, San Francisco—was 60 seconds long and titled "Brand Name." It starred the red Levi's logo as an animated, fantasized puppy on a leash, barking and leading its owner down a lengthy street. Although the set was only 52 feet long, its unique design and perspective made it appear to stretch out to infinity (see Figure 11-7).

Animation was combined smoothly with live action in several scenes. For example, the logo was made to move and act by manipulating it with puppet strings. In one scene, when the "puppy" jumped through a window, the strings holding the logo would of course not go through the window frame, and several frames of animation were added to bridge the gap. In all, over 40 people took part in the production—in specialties ranging from choreography and costuming to optical design and puppeteering.

Apparently the commercial was worth it—considering all the word-of-mouth publicity and image building it gave to Levi's. After viewing the commercial during the Burke test, several people said: "Levi's must be better, the commercial is so well done." Interestingly, the cost of producing that commercial is almost standard fare today.

While this Levi's masterpiece opened the door to untold innovations in commercials, historically there have been relatively few basic types of executions. Possibly this is because the selling idea is generally considered more important than the way it is presented.

Animation Techniques

The Levi's commercial was an early example of the new style of modern, computerized, laser-light animation. Today, even more advanced animation techniques using computer-generated graphics and simulations produce scenes that appear to be filmed from live action (see Figure 11-8). However, the more traditional animation techniques involve the use of cartoons, puppets, photo animation, and stop-motion.

Cartoons

Commercials that feature cartoons often have the highest viewer interest, the longest life, and the lowest cost per showing, but many viewers consider them childlike. The several animation styles include Disney, contemporary, psychedelic, and others. Cartoons are sometimes supplemented by live action, especially when a serious purchase decision is to be made and the product benefits are described.

The technique is achieved by drawing illustrations of each step in the action and photographing them one frame at a time. Projecting the film at 24 frames per second gives the illusion of movement.

FIGURE   11–7

This animated Levi's commercial, produced by Robert Abel & Associates, has been credited with revolutionizing TV advertising.

MALE (VO): C'mon old Trademark, time for your walk. Where will you take me? Sure wish you could talk.

I know what you'd tell me. How your family began with

the same Levi's blue jeans worn by this man.

Hey, here come more Levi's; red, yellow and blue.

Free wheeling kiddos are wearing them, too!

And what a surprise! Look who's been window shopping for clothes.

Yeah, a gal in her Levi's instinctively knows of your special appeal. Enough of this kissing, little Register Mark.

Time that we meet some guys by the park. Dressed in your newest addition. Sums it up right there: Levi's Sportswear.

Hey, Trademark, this looks like the place where tomorrows begin.

Your family's future — sure looks like it should.

That's right, little Trademark —

Levi's don't have to be blue — just have to be good!

FIGURE   11–8

The use of special animation techniques inserted right in the middle of live action set the new Coors Light campaign apart from other lifestyle commercials. (For more on the way the Coors Light commercials were produced, see the TextPLUS Case Study supplement associated with Chapter 11.)

(MUSIC UP AND UNDER)

SUNG: It's the right place at the right time when the right day is a state of mind.

A way to shine in the pouring rain 'til the sun comes breaking thru again.

It's a feeling that's all around.

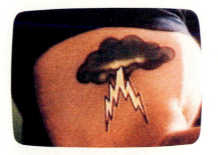

The Silver Bullet won't slow you down.

So come on into Coors Light . . . It's the right beer now.

It's a new plan on a new day.

Get a Coors Light comin' your way.

Set a fast pace, break some new ground.

Get a good taste 'cause the time is now to come on into Coors Light.

It's the right beer now.

To the good life, yeah . . .

G-G-G-Good Life, Yeah.

So come on into Coors Light . . .

It's the right beer now.

Puppets

Frequently, puppets or dolls are used instead of illustrations. Special kinds of action and effects can be accomplished, as witnessed by the Snuggles bear, the Pillsbury Doughboy, or the popular Muppets.

Photo Animation

This technique uses still photography instead of illustrations or puppets. Making slight movements of the photos from one frame to the next creates the animated illusion. This technique is especially effective for making titles move. However, it is considered a very low budget technique.

Stop-Motion

Stop-motion is an animation technique whereby objects and animals come to life—walk, run, dance, and do tricks—by means of stop-motion photography. One of the most famous recent examples of this special effect is the charming "claymation" campaign created for the California Raisin Advisory Board (see Figure 11–9). The raisin characters, fashioned from plasticene clay, dance in a conga line and perform on a construction worker's sandwich.[21] Created by Will Vinton Productions (Portland, Oregon), the raisins are flexible figures with movable joints. The arms and legs can be bent to simulate walking or dancing. Each frame of film is shot individually. An arm may be moved only $\frac{1}{32}$ of an inch on each frame, but when the frames are assembled, the effect is smooth and natural, combining the whimsy of

Figure   11–9

Through stop-motion animation techniques, the claymation California Raisins were made to sing and dance their way to advertising fame.

SFX: (LIQUID BEING POURED INTO A CONTAINER.)
(MUSIC IN.)

SFX: (LUNCH BOX TOP SLAMMING CLOSED.)
(MUSIC OUT.)

SFX: (SQUEAKY TOP OF LUNCH BOX OPENING.)
(MUSIC IN.)

LEAD RAISIN SINGER: Ooh, ooh, I heard it through the grapevine . . .
BACK-UP RAISIN SINGERS: Ooh.

LEAD RAISIN SINGER: . . . raised in the California sun . . . shine.
BACK-UP LEAD RAISIN (SPOKEN): California raisins . . . from the California vineyards.

LEAD RAISIN SINGER: Don'cha know that I . . .
BACK-UP RAISIN SINGERS: . . . heard it through the . . .
BACK-UP RAISIN SINGERS VO: . . . grapevine.
STEELWORKER: Sounds better'n what I got.
SFX: (Automobile Horn.)

animation with the substance of live action. Since film is projected at 24 frames per second, this means 1,440 frames must be shot for each minute of raisin dancing.[22]

Live Action

The basic production technique that portrays people in everyday situations is called *live action*. It gives the greatest realism but may lack the unique distinctiveness of animated commercials or commercials that use special effects.

Special Effects

Memorability is often achieved by using dramatic sound, music, or photographic effects. Coors Light, for example, uses striking, quick-cut shots of young adults at play, unusual colors, slow motion, new camera techniques, and even some animation, all mixed together to project the image of a fast-paced, youth-oriented drink. These visuals are reinforced by young actors and an upbeat, contemporary musical theme.

Special effects often entertain viewers and win awards. But if the sales message is complex or based on logic, another technique might be more successful. The obvious precaution is not to let your technique so enthrall the viewers that they pay more attention to it than to your product.

Most special effects should be limited to one fantasy or mnemonic device: a jolly green giant, the Imperial crown, or the water skier crashing through the lifelike photo of the yacht in the Fuji film commercials. In these cases, the fantasy is directly related to the product's claims, and heavy repetition makes strong impressions on the viewer.[23]

THE PRODUCTION PROCESS

The Tom Thumb Page stores in Dallas planned a promotion to sell Thanksgiving turkeys and talk about the store's money-back guarantee. Its advertising agency, KCBN, Inc., had developed a very simple concept for a television commercial. A live turkey would be shown in an extremely tight close-up. As the announcer spoke off-screen, the camera would slowly zoom back, showing the turkey bobbing his head and occasionally gobbling at the announcer's words. Finally, as the announcer promised to give any unsatisfied customers their money back—or another turkey—the turkey was supposed to run off the stage.

In concept, it was a very simple spot, but in the production process, it turned into a frustrating but hilarious farce reminiscent of the Keystone Kops. Many producers talk about the production problems of working with kids. They should try working with a turkey!

KCBN found a "trained" turkey in upstate New York. That was fine since they had already decided to go to New York to produce the commercial to ensure top-quality production.

On the day of shooting, everybody was at the studio. The agency account and creative people had flown in from Dallas, and the trained turkey had been trucked in from upstate. The agency had been assured the turkey would gobble on command and, with a simple hand signal, would run off-stage.

The lighting was painstakingly set up, tested, and checked. The announcer practiced his pitch in the sound booth. The audio and video levels were adjusted. Everything was just right, ready to go. The trainer picked up the turkey, carried him onto the set, and deposited him on the marked spot in front of the camera and stepped out of camera range.

The lights blazed, the film rolled, the red camera lights went on, the director called for action, and the announcer read the script. The trainer gave the turkey his cue to go. The turkey didn't move an inch.

"Cut!"

"OK. Let's try it again. Take two."

On the second try, the turkey again just sat there.

"I don't understand it," said the trainer. "He's never done this before."

Five takes later, the turkey was still sitting there. By this time, the trainer had abandoned his hand signals and was starting to shout at the bird, clapping his hands, screaming, stamping his foot. The pitch of his hysteria was rising rapidly. But the turkey just sat there. And the lights were getting hotter and hotter.

Finally, the trainer came on the set with a long broom handle.

"This'll do it," he said. There seemed to be a slight tone of hostility in his voice.

"Action," shouted the director.

Just as the announcer got to the cue in the script, the trainer lunged with the broom handle, stabbing the unsuspecting fowl in the belly. With a horrendous squawk, the turkey bolted from the set, crashed into one light stand and then another, toppling them over. He landed on top of one lamp, and as the searing heat scorched his wings, he squawked off in frenzied half-flight only to get tangled in more lights, cables, cameras, and props. All the while, the trainer and crew were chasing him around the set trying to capture him.

Finally, they subdued the poor bird and then spent an hour calming him down while the set was relit. But now the turkey knew what was out there. And of course, when they were finally ready to start up again, there was no way on earth he was going to move. He just sat absolutely still—terrified.

When all seemed lost, somebody got a bright idea. They decided to tie a cord to his ankles and string the line off-camera. When the cue came, they gently jerked the string, pulling the bird's feet out from under him. Frightened by this sudden turn of events, the turkey flapped his wings, squawked, and struggled to regain his footing. In the process, he moved sideways just enough to go off-camera, and the effect was finally achieved. The director and crew, the agency, the trainer, and, most of all, the turkey all heaved a hugh sigh of relief (see Figure 11–10).

The process of producing television commercials such as this one involves three stages or steps:

1. Preproduction—which includes all the work prior to the actual day of filming.
2. Production—the actual day (or days) that the commercial is filmed or videotaped.
3. Postproduction—all the work done after the day of shooting to finish the commercial.

Since all these steps have a dramatic impact on the cost and the eventual quality of the commercial, we shall discuss each briefly (see Figure 11–11).

FIGURE 11–10

Profits jumped 27 percent for Cullum Companies thanks, in part, to Tom Thumb TV spots.

Film commercial

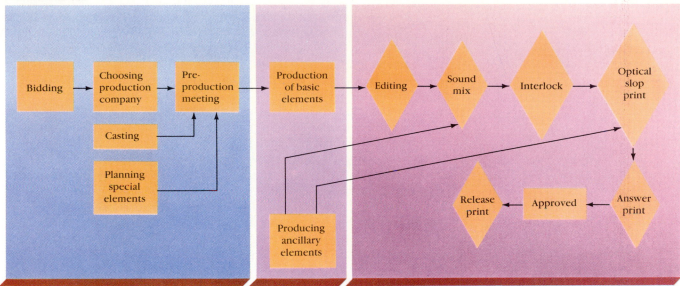

Videotape commercial

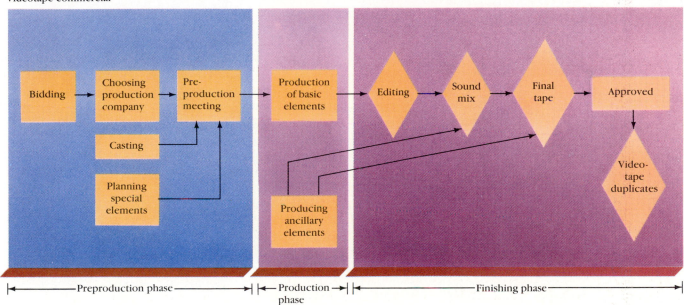

FIGURE 11–11

Production process for film and videotape commercials.

Preproduction

The greatest waste of money in commercial production inevitably occurs because of a lack of adequate preproduction planning. The converse is also true. The greatest savings can be effected by proper planning before the day of production.

Casting, for example, is a crucial decision and must be completely settled before the day of shooting. Children and animals, as we have just seen, are unpredictable and often cause production delays. Rehearsals before production, therefore, are a must.

After the advertiser approves a storyboard and budget, the production process begins. Few people have the background to handle the entire production from start to finish. For this reason, the commercial is a group effort. The team includes a writer, an art director, a producer, a director, and sometimes a musical composer and a choreographer. The person responsible for completion on schedule and within budget is the producer, who may be either in-house or free-lance.

The producer seeks competitive bids, usually sending copies of the storyboard to three studios. The bids include the services of a director, camera operators, electricians, and other technicians. The studio may do the film or tape editing, or it may be done elsewhere.

After the studio has been chosen, the cast is selected, and an announcer, if needed, is selected. Next, the set is built, and the crew and cast rehearse under the director's supervision.

Shooting days are expensive. The cost of studios, casts, crews, and equipment are normally figured on a full-day basis. Therefore, any unnecessary delays that could throw the production into an unexpected second shooting day must be avoided. This also suggests a problem for location shooting. Weather must be considered. Locations should be selected close to home whenever possible. Extra days on location are extremely expensive. Fortunately, it is no longer necessary to travel to the major cities like New York and Los Angeles to find quality production houses.[24]

All these factors should be taken into consideration during the preproduction phase, and every aspect of the commercial production discussed, decided, and approved by the client, agency, and production company prior to the shooting day.

During this preparatory period, preproduction meetings should be held and include the producer, the agency account representative, the writer, the art director, the studio director, possibly the advertiser, and anyone else deemed important to the production. At this time, any last-minute problems can be ironed out and final decisions made on the scenes, the actors, and the announcer. Music, sets, action, lighting, and camera angles are all reviewed. The more details settled at this time, the better. A finished 60-second commercial takes only 90 feet of film, but the shooting often requires several days and from 3,000 to 5,000 feet of film.

The soundtrack may be recorded before, during, or after the actual production of the film or videotape. Recording the sound in advance ensures that the commercial will be neither too long nor too short. This technique is used when the subject of the commercial has to move or dance to a specific rhythm. Sometimes, though, music or voice-over is recorded after the shooting.

Production

The actual shooting day (or days) of a commercial can be very long and tedious. Starting very early in the morning, the crew may take several hours just to light the set to the director's liking.

When the scenes are being shot, it may be necessary to try several "takes" to get them right. During this time, the lighting may be readjusted several times as unexpected shadows pop up. The director usually requires two or three good takes of every scene. In addition, each scene is probably shot from two or three different angles: one to establish the characters, one to show only the person speaking, and one to show the reaction of the person listening.

Scenes are not necessarily shot in order. For example, scenes with no synchronized sound are usually shot last since they don't require the full crew.

FIGURE 11–12

Location shooting for a TV commercial requires careful, time-consuming attention to the details of camera angle and changing light conditions. Even in broad daylight, additional lights must often be used to maintain the consistency of look and feel in the commercial.

Between the shootings of each scene, a long interval may be required to move the camera, reset the lights, reposition the actors, and pick up the action, sound, and look to match the other scenes (see Figure 11–12). This is extremely important since each piece of action must match what comes before and after. Otherwise, the commercial will contain disconcerting jumps that can potentially destroy the credibility of the message.

Postproduction

The postproduction phase is where the commercial is actually put together. It is also the stage that usually determines how good a commercial is. At this point, the responsibilities of the film editor, the sound mixer, and the director are enormous.

The visual portion of the filmed commercial is first assembled on one piece of celluloid without the extra effects of dissolves, titles, or *supers* (words superimposed on the picture). The sound portion of the film is assembled on another piece of celluloid. This is called the *work print* stage (also called *rough cut* or *interlock*). At this time, scenes may be substituted, music and sound effects added, or other last-minute changes made.

Next, the external sound is recorded. This includes the actors' voices, the announcer, the music track, the singers, and the sound effects. The announcer records the voice-over narrative. The music is recorded by musicians and singers, or prerecorded stock music may be bought and integrated into the commercial. Sound effects such as doorbells ringing or doors slamming are mixed.

The finished sound is put on one piece of celluloid which, combined with the almost-completed visual celluloid, is called the *mixed interlock*. When these two are joined, along with all the required optical effects and titles, a print called the *answer print* is made. This is the final commercial. If it receives all the necessary approvals, *dupes* (copies) are made and delivered to the networks or TV stations for airing.

Film versus Tape

Today, very few commercials are done live. Even those that look live are usually videotaped, and most commercials are made on color film. Film projects a soft texture that live broadcasts and videotape do not have. Because film is the oldest method of showing moving pictures, there is a large pool of skilled talent in this field. Also film is extremely flexible and versatile. It can be used for numerous optical effects, slow motion, distance shots, mood shots, fast action, and animation. The film size normally used for national commercials is 35 mm. If some rough-test commercials are to be run, 16 mm is sometimes used because it is much less expensive. Likewise, if a local commercial is filmed, it is usually shot on 16 mm for lower cost. Duplicate film prints are also cheaper than videotape dupes.

On the other hand, recording a commercial on 1 or 2 inch magnetic videotape offers a more brilliant picture and better fidelity than film. It certainly looks more realistic and appears to have a "live" quality. Tape is also more consistent in quality than film stock. The chief advantage of tape, though, is that it can provide an immediate playback to the take. This permits the work to be checked and redone while the props and actors are still assembled. Computerization has cut editing time by up to 90 percent of the time involved in film. Videotape can be replayed almost forever, but a film commercial can be run only about 25 times.

Some directors shoot their commercials on film to gain the advantages of texture and sensitive mood lighting. Then they dub their processed film onto videotape to do their editing. This is more costly, but it gives them the advantage of faster finishing and the opportunity to see the optical effects instantly as they are added. Most directors, however, still prefer to edit on film because of the wider range of effects possible, thereby achieving a higher level of "creative story telling." (See Creative Department: From Concept through Production of a Television Commercial.)

Costs

Many factors, some of which we've already mentioned in this chapter, contribute to the rising cost of commercial production. Roman and Maas list 14 of these factors.[25]

1. Children and animals (including turkeys).
2. Location shooting.
3. Large cast.
4. Superstar talent.
5. Night or weekend filming.
6. Animation.
7. Involved opticals, special effects, stop-motion.
8. Both location and studio shooting for one commercial.
9. Expensive set decoration.
10. Special photographic equipment.
11. A second day of shooting.
12. Legal requirements.
13. A single word or sentence of dialogue.
14. An extremely simple, close-up commercial.

About the last factor, they point out that the extremely simple close-up is the kind of commercial that frequently requires a whole day just to get lighting right. We might add: "or to get the turkey to move."

PRODUCING RADIO COMMERCIALS

Blue Nun was the best-selling imported wine in the United States in the mid-1980s. But it wasn't always that way. In fact, prior to 1980, sales of Blue Nun were fairly static at about 70,000 cases per year. The wine was positioned as a gourmet selection and advertised only in sophisticated gourmet magazines via small space ads.

Then Della Femina, Travisano & Partners got into the act. This agency was known for its highly creative approaches to marketing and advertising problems. In the case of Blue Nun, it lived up to its reputation.

The agency recommended repositioning the brand as an "all-purpose" wine that was perfectly suited to all meals and foods. It also suggested selling Blue Nun as a packaged goods item rather than a specialty good. This strategy put Blue Nun squarely against the leading all-purpose rosé wines such as Mateus and Lancers. The most interesting part of the strategy, though, was the suggestion to use radio exclusively to deliver Blue Nun's message. The agency felt that radio could be used best to target the intended market (men, high middle- to upper-class demographics) and simultaneously deliver the large audience numbers required for a packaged goods product.

Because of the uniqueness of the brand identification, it was decided to feature the Blue Nun name as the easiest way to order a premium wine for any meal.

The agency selected the husband/wife comedy team Stiller and Meara to deliver a series of humorous slice-of-life vignettes of the problems couples face while ordering and serving wine. The agency assigned an art director and copywriter, Mark Yusting and Kay Kavanagh, to develop the scripts.

Locking themselves in an office for several days, Yusting and Kavanagh hammered out the first series of radio commercials that would eventually catapult Blue Nun into market leadership. Simultaneously, these commercials repositioned radio as an action medium for advertisers.

The tone and manner of the commercials set a trend for the next decade of Blue Nun advertising by playing off the brand's name with sophisticated wit and humor (see Figure 11–13). (continued on p. 364)

STILLER: Excuse me, the cruise director assigned me this table for dinner.

MEARA: Say, weren't you the fella at the costume ball last night dressed as a giant tuna? With scales, the gills and the fins?

STILLER: Yeah—that was me.

MEARA: I recognized you right away.

STILLER: Were you there?

MEARA: I was dressed as a mermaid so I had to spend most of the night sitting down. Did you ever try dancing with both legs wrapped in aluminum foil?

STILLER: No, I can't say I have. Did you order dinner yet?

MEARA: I'm having the filet of sole.

STILLER: Hmmm. The filet mignon looks good. Would you like to share a bottle of wine?

MEARA: Terrific.

STILLER: I noticed a little Blue Nun at the Captain's table.

MEARA: Poor thing. Maybe she's seasick.

STILLER: No, Blue Nun is a wine. A delicious white wine.

MEARA: Oh, we can't have a white wine if you're having meat and I'm having fish.

STILLER: Sure we can. Blue Nun is a white wine that's correct with any dish. Your filet of sole. My filet mignon.

MEARA: Oh, it's so nice to meet a man who knows the finer things. You must be a gourmet?

STILLER: No, as a matter of fact, I'm an accountant. Small firm in the city. Do a lot of tax work . . . *[fade out]*

ANNOUNCER: Blue Nun. The delicious white wine that's correct with any dish. Another Sichel wine imported by Schieffelin & Company, New York.

FIGURE   11–13

This is one of the Blue Nun radio commercials that helped bring both the wine and radio advertising into greater prominence.

CREATIVE DEPARTMENT

From Concept through Production of a Television Commercial

Marketing Considerations

In a product category dominated by General Electric, North American Philips Lighting Corporation had a problem establishing a place for its Longer Life square-shaped light bulbs. This presented a distinct challenge to its advertising agency, Saatchi & Saatchi DFS Compton.

To understand the peculiarities of this category and to determine the best way to approach the consumer and trade markets, the agency conducted a variety of research efforts: store checks, interviews with key trade personnel, trips to housewares shows, a primary benefit/image study, and even a consumer psychological probe. These studies pointed up two consistent hurdles:

1. Lighting was a low-interest, low-involvement category. No one thought about light bulbs until they burned out.
2. GE's brand image was almost impenetrable, while Philips was virtually unknown or, perhaps worse, confused with screwdrivers or Milk of Magnesia.

Creative Strategy

At the same time, the agency's research uncovered two areas of opportunity:

1. Longer life is the primary product attribute that consumers desire when purchasing light bulbs.
2. Philips had a mnemonic device to set itself apart from other light bulbs—its square shape.

The goal of the creative strategy, therefore, was to increase consumer interest in light bulbs and to raise the level of involvement. Simultaneously, the agency wanted to point out the fact that GE was not meeting the universal consumer desire for a longer-life bulb at a reasonable price.

In addition, it was important to elevate the trade's recognition of Philips as a major lighting company. Many supermarkets carry only one high-quality light bulb brand. The agency hoped to persuade stores to stock Philips by building the company's reputation and, at the same time, by offering stores a competitively priced, long-life product sought by consumers.

To accomplish this, Philips was willing to try something different.

Creative Concept

Philips had come to S&S DFSC because of the agency's great success with the humorous, award-winning campaigns for Wendy's—"Where's the Beef?" and "Parts Is Parts." In the pursuit of consumer memorability, the company was looking for an advertising concept that would be slightly off-beat. It was willing to give the agency some creative license, and, as a result, the ideas flowed.

The tag line, "It's time to change your bulb," came first. Then the agency developed three creative concepts and presented the storyboards to the client. The first, titled "Elevator," showed a man in an elevator looking admiringly at a fellow passenger—a tall blonde (see A. Storyboard). He says hello to her but is rebuffed so he hides behind his newspaper. As a result, he fails to notice when she gets off and a big bruiser gets on the elevator. Suddenly the bulb blows out. Emboldened by the darkness, the first man declares, "I guess you know I think you're extremely attractive." "You want to run that by me one more time!" is the unexpected answer from his fellow passenger.

A. Storyboard.

In "Vacuum," a slightly frumpy housewife is vacuuming her living room carpet while her cat sleeps unperturbed in the center of the rug (see B. Storyboard). Suddenly, the light goes out with a "Pop!" The cat screeches, and we hear the sound of a large object being sucked into the vacuum.

The third commercial, "Cabin," opens on two men playing cards at night in a cabin in the woods. Suddenly, strange noises outside cause them to wonder if they're hearing the bogeyman. They reassure themselves that they are safe as long as the lights are on. "Zap!" goes the bulb, and we hear them scream, "Run for your life!" All three commercials end with a rotating Philips bulb and the tag line, "It's time to change your bulb."

Preproduction

With client approval secured, the next step was to cast the commercials. The auditions were taped and then reviewed by the director, agency, and client. The agency made casting recommendations, and these were approved by Philips. Next, a preproduction meeting was held to cover all the details of the shoot: casting and acting, set design, direction, lighting—in short, everything about the way in which the commercials would be shot.

At this point, some changes were made to the storyboards. For example, in "Elevator," the man was originally supposed to be a Bruce Willis type but became a timid businessman, while the muscle man became a blue-

B. Storyboard.

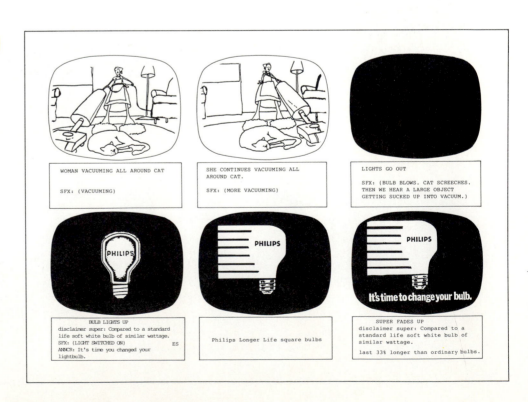

collar worker. During casting, it was realized that the spot would play better with a "sweeter" tone. The Bruce Willis type was thus changed to a nerdy businessman, and the muscle man became more amicable.

At the same time, it was decided to shoot a 30-second version of "Vacuum" as well as the 15-second edit originally planned. When the actual shooting was discussed with the director, it was decided that "Vacuum" would be shot from the floor to make it appear that the viewer was at eye-level with the cat and that the vacuum was aiming for the viewer. So as not to disturb the cat during shooting, the whirring sound of the vacuum would be added later off-set. To make it appear that the elevator changed floors, the elevator-bank walls would be repainted a different color after each successive take, and additional props would be used to complete the effect (see C. Picture board with script). All the spots were filmed on sets created by the production company's set designer and approved by the client.

C. Picture board with script.

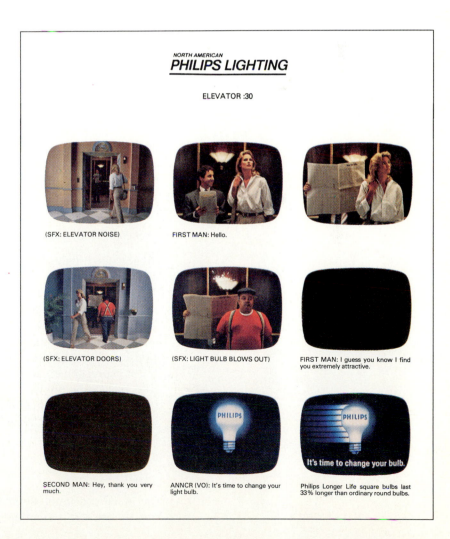

NORTH AMERICAN
PHILIPS LIGHTING

ELEVATOR :30

(SFX: ELEVATOR NOISE)

FIRST MAN: Hello.

(SFX: ELEVATOR DOORS)

(SFX: LIGHT BULB BLOWS OUT)

FIRST MAN: I guess you know I find you extremely attractive.

SECOND MAN: Hey, thank you very much.

ANNCR (VO): It's time to change your light bulb.

Philips Longer Life square bulbs last 33% longer than ordinary round bulbs.

It's time to change your bulb.

Shooting the Commercial

It took almost four days to shoot the first of the three commercials. After the shoot, the director and agency producer met to screen the film (known as "dailies") to select the best "takes." These were then edited into a rough cut, and special effects were added. These included the noises in "Vacuum" and the crickets and monster sounds in "Cabin," as well as the background music and the sound of the light bulb going out in all three commercials.

At the end of each commercial, they inserted a computer-graphics effect of the product logo. The light bulb clicked on and rotated until the Philips logo faced the viewer. Next, straight, white horizontal rays emerged from the side of the bulb to complete the image—a replica of the Philips package design. Finally, the tag line, "It's time to change your bulb," popped on. This graphic treatment was designed to enable customers to recognize the product in the store and associate it with the commercials (see D. Picture board with script).

The logo was created by Robert Able & Associates, which was the design firm most noted for computer graphics. This was the same firm that had designed the famous computer-graphic Levi's logo commercial discussed earlier in this chapter.

Finally, all the commercials were mixed with the sound tracks. The sound quality was perfected. Music was added to the logo, and a master tape was shown to the client for approval. Duplicate tapes (dubs) were then sent to the networks and television stations in spot TV markets for airing. Due to the unanimous positive feeling about the spots, testing was deemed unnecessary.

Promotion/Trade Program

To merchandise this high-visibility campaign, S&S DFSC created an extensive trade promotion program. A special sales video was created that showed the commercials, announced a variety of promotional events, and introduced the "It's Time to Change Your Bulb" campaign. This video was shown to dealers at the National Hardware Show, one of the most important trade shows of the year. The programs met with strong positive response from both the trade and the trade press covering the show.

Commercials were then aired on high-visibility television shows such as "The Bill Cosby Show," "Miami Vice," "Cheers," and "Family Ties." In addition, time was bought on major sporting events such as the World Series and the Super Bowl. The combined effort was aimed at making Philips highly visible, not just to consumers, but to the trade as well.

Campaign Results

The initial consumer campaign was budgeted at approximately $15 million—more than seven times the amount Philips had spent on advertising the year before. However, the results were immediately evident. In benchmark studies, when asked to identify a brand of light bulb, 48 percent more people named Philips than those polled prior to the start of the campaign. In addition, 72 percent said they would purchase Philips the next time they bought bulbs.

Finally, thanks to the effective trade announcement, major retail accounts that were responsible for large amounts of light bulb sales—such as Sears, Vons, Kroger, and Pathmark—began carrying the Philips brand.

D. Picture board with script.

(SFX: VACUUM)

(SFX: BULB BLOWS OUT)

(SFX: CAT HOWLS, VACUUM SUCKING NOISE)

ANNCR (VO): It's time to change your light bulb.

Philips Longer Life square bulbs last 33% longer than ordinary round bulbs.

Blue Nun no longer sells 70,000 cases per year. By the mid-1980s, the figure exceeded a million and a half cases per year and was still climbing. Blue Nun became this country's best-selling imported wine, beating out Lancers and Mateus, and its brand image equaled or exceeded those two previous leaders in all its advertised markets.

Schieffelin & Co., the U.S. distributor of Blue Nun, at one point tried taking the ads to TV but eventually returned to radio because of its ability to concentrate on markets where the product was the strongest.[26]

Producing radio commercials is similar to producing television commercials in several aspects. Radio uses the same basic techniques as television—namely, testimonials, slice of life, straight announcements, or music—and generally follows the same developmental patterns as television. Only the details differ.

Writing Radio Copy

Radio listeners usually decide within the first five to eight seconds whether they want to pay attention to a commercial. Research indicates that the primary determinant is the product category.[27] Therefore, to get and hold the attention of those not automatically attracted to a product category, radio copy must be intensive. To accomplish this, many techniques and devices can be used. Creativity knows no limits. (See the Checklist for Creating Effective Radio Commercials.)

Checklist for Creating Effective Radio Commercials

☐ Identify your sound effects. A sound effect is only effective when the listener knows what it means.

☐ Don't be afraid to use music as a sound effect. The commercial will work if the meaning of the music sounds is clearly explained.

☐ If you use a sound effect, build your commercial around it. It pays to make the message all about the relationship of the sound effect to your product.

☐ Give yourself time. You need time in radio to set a scene and establish a premise. A 30-second commercial that nobody remembers has zero efficiency. Fight for 60s.

☐ Consider not using sound effects. A distinctive voice or a powerful message straightforwardly spoken can be more effective than noises from the tape library.

☐ Beware of comedy. Professional funnymen devote their lives to their art. It's rare for anyone else to sit down at a typewriter and match the skill of the best comedians.

☐ If you insist on being funny, begin with an outrageous premise. The best comic radio commercials begin with a totally ridiculous premise from which all subsequent developments logically follow.

☐ Keep it simple. Radio is a good medium for building awareness of a brand. It's a rotten medium for registering long lists of copy points or making complex arguments.

☐ What one thing is most important about your product? That is what your commercial should spend 60 seconds talking about.

☐ Tailor commercials as to time, place, and specific audience. Radio is a local medium. You can adjust your commercials to talk in the language of the people who will hear them and to the time of day in which they'll be broadcast.

☐ Presentation counts a whole lot. Most radio scripts—even the greatest radio scripts—look boring on paper. Acting, timing, vocal quirks, and sound effects make them come alive.

The radio listener is often busy driving, washing dishes, or reading the paper. Therefore, the message has to be catchy, interesting, and unforgettable. In the effort to gain attention, though, care must be taken to avoid jarring the listener offensively. That can cause resentment. In most cases, a personal, relaxed, and cheerful style will be more effective.

Humor can be one of the best attention-getting devices and is being used with increasing success. But beware. It is difficult to master. Poorly done humor is worse than none at all.

Other guidelines for writing radio copy include:

Mention the advertiser's name early and mention it often—at least three times.

If the name is tricky, spell it—at least once.

Be conversational. Use easy-to-pronounce words and short sentences. Avoid tongue twisters.

Keep the message simple. Omit unneeded words. Concentrate on one main selling point. Make the *big idea* crystal clear.

Paint pictures with the words. Use descriptive language. Familiar sounds, such as a fire engine siren or a car engine, can help create a visual image.

Stress action words rather than passive words. Use verbs rather than adjectives.

Emphasize the product benefits repeatedly—with variations.

Make the script fit the available time.[28]

A good rule of thumb for the number of words in a commercial is as follows:[29]

10 seconds: 20–25 words.
20 seconds: 40–45 words.
30 seconds: 60–70 words.
60 seconds: 125–140 words.

And be sure to *ask for the order*. Try to get the listener to *do* something. The story is told that Martin Block, an early announcer on radio station WNEW, once made a bet. Figuring that many women drove from New Jersey to New York to shop, he bet he could persuade some of them by radio to turn around, go back through the tunnel, and buy their dresses from his New Jersey sponsor. He did, they did, and he won the bet.[30]

Types of Radio Commercials

Although not all radio commercials can be rigidly cataloged, the wide range of possibilities was considered by Wallace Ross and Bob Landers, who came up with 17 creative categories, including such types as customer interview, historical fantasy, comedian power, and hyperbole. (See Ad Lab 11-A.)[31] For our discussion here, we will consider four basic types: musical, slice of life, straight, and personality.

Musical

Jingles, or musical commercials, are among the best and the worst advertising messages produced. If done well, they can bring enormous success— well beyond that of the average nonmusical commercial. Likewise, when done poorly, they can waste the advertising budget.

AD LAB 11-A — Creative Ways to Sell on Radio

Product demo The commercial tells how a product is used or the purposes it serves.

Voice power The power of the commercial is in the casting of a unique voice.

Electronic sound Synthetic sound-making machines create a memorable product-sound association.

Customer interview A product spokesperson and customer discuss the product advantages—often spontaneously.

Humorous fake interview The customer interview is done in a lighter vein.

Hyperbole or exaggerated statement Overstatement arouses interest in legitimate product claims that might otherwise pass unnoticed; often a spoof.

Sixth dimension Time and events are compressed into a brief spot involving the listener in future projections.

Hot property Commercial adapts a current sensation—a hit show, performer, or song.

Comedian power Established comedians do commercials in their own unique style, implying celebrity endorsement.

Historical fantasy Situation with revived historical characters is used to convey product message.

Sound picture Recognizable sounds are used to involve listener by stimulating imagination.

Demographics Music or references appeal to a particular segment of the population, as an age or interest group.

Imagery transfer Musical logo or other sound reinforces the effects of a television campaign.

Celebrity interview Famous person endorses product in an informal manner.

Product song Music and words combine to create musical logo selling product in the style of popular music.

Editing genius Many different situations, voices, types of music, and sounds are combined in a series of quick cuts.

Improvisation Performers work out the dialogue extemporaneously for an assigned situation; may be postedited.

Laboratory Applications

1. Select three radio commercials with which you are familiar and discuss which creative techniques they use.
2. Select a radio commercial with which you are familiar and discuss how it could have been more effective by using a different creative technique.

Musical commercials have several variations. The entire message may be sung, jingles may be interspersed throughout the copy, or orchestras may play symphonic arrangements. Many producers use consistent musical themes for background color or as a close to the commercial. After numerous repetitions of the advertiser's theme, the listener begins to associate the jingle with the product being advertised. This is called a *musical logotype*.

Advertisers have three principal sources of music. They can buy the use of a tune from the copyright owner, which is usually expensive. They can use a melody in the public domain, which is free. Or they can hire a composer to write an original tune. Several of these original tunes, including the Coke song, "I'd like to teach the world to sing," discussed in Chapter 1, have turned into hits.

Slice of Life (Problem Solution)

As in television, the slice of life is a situation commercial in which professional actors discuss a problem and propose the product as its solution. Played with the proper drama, it can get attention and create interest. "Slice" commercials can be produced straight or for a humorous effect. In all cases, the story should be relevant to the product and simply told.

Straight Announcement

The straight commercial is probably the easiest to write. Delivered by one person, it can be designed as an *integrated commercial*—that is, woven into a show or tailored to a given program. The straight commercial has no special sound effects as a rule. The only music, if any, is played in the background. It is adaptable to almost any product or situation and is, therefore, used frequently. Getting and holding the listener's attention is its greatest problem, but once accomplished, the aural opportunity to educate the listener is almost unbeatable.

Personality

It is sometimes desirable to have a disc jockey or show host express the message in his or her own style. When such a commercial is done well, it is almost always better than anything the advertiser could supply.

The advertiser surrenders control of the commercial, however, and turns it over to the personality. The main risk, outside of occasional blunders, is that the personality may criticize the product. Even so, this sometimes lends a realism that is hard to achieve otherwise.

If the advertiser decides to use this technique, the personality is supplied with a sheet highlighting the product's or the company's features. This gives the main points to be stressed and the phrases or company slogans to be repeated. Most of the specific wording, though, and the mode of delivery are left up to the discretion of the announcer.

THE RADIO PRODUCTION PROCESS

A radio commercial is quicker, simpler, and less expensive to produce than a television commercial.

Live commercials require that the station be sent a script and a recording of music, or special effects, if any are to be used. Care must be taken to ensure that the material is accurately timed for length. A live commercial script should run about 100 to 120 words per minute, enabling the announcer to deliver the message at a normal conversational pace.

The disadvantage of live commercials is that announcers may not be consistent in their delivery. In addition, the use of sound effects is quite limited. Obviously, if uniformity in the delivery of the commercial is critical, a recorded commercial must be used. The process of producing a recorded commercial is diagrammed in Figure 11–14.

An agency may assign a radio producer from its staff or, as is often the case, hire a free-lance producer to develop the commercial. The radio producer first estimates the costs and then presents a budget to the advertiser for approval. Next, for recorded commercials, the producer selects a studio and a casting director.

The casting director casts professional actors for roles if it is a slice-of-

Radio commercial

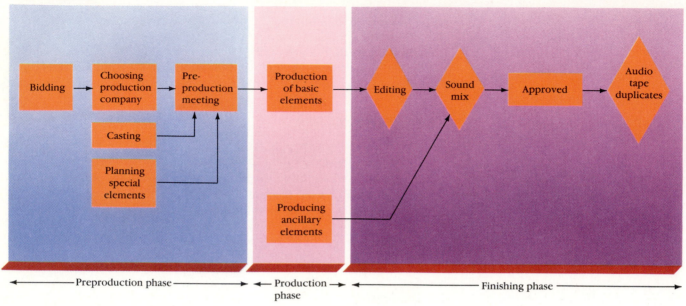

Preproduction phase ← Production → ← Finishing phase
phase

FIGURE 11–14

The process for producing a radio commercial.

life commercial or finds the right "voice" if there is only an announcer. If the script calls for music, the producer decides whether to use music already recorded or to hire a composer. The producer may also hire a music director, musicians, and singers. This is often done after hearing audition tapes of the recommended talent. Depending on the script, sound effects may be created or taken from prerecorded sources.

Next, a director supervises rehearsals until everything falls into place. Then the commercial is recorded several times, and the best take is selected. Music, sound, and vocal are usually recorded separately and mixed. In any case, the final recording is referred to as the *master tape.*

From the master tape, duplicates of the commercials, called *dubs,* are recorded onto ¼ inch magnetic tape and sent to radio stations for broadcast.

The question of which radio stations—and of which other communications vehicles to use in advertising—takes us to the next topic of our study: the advertising media.

Summary

Understanding broadcast production means knowing how commercials are written, the types of commercials that are most effective and most commonly used, the basic techniques for producing commercials, and the important steps in the production process.

A television script is divided into two portions. The right side is the audio for sound effects, spoken copy, and music, and the left side is the video for camera action, scenes, and instructions. On a sheet preprinted with a series of blank television screens, the writer and art director prepare a storyboard of the script. The video is sketched in by the art director, and the audio is typed underneath.

The six basic types of television commercials are straight announcement, demonstration, testimonial, slice of life, lifestyle, and animation. Animation techniques can be further categorized by whether they use cartoons, puppets, photo animation, or the new computerized laser-light methods.

Producing a television commercial involves three stages or steps: preproduction, production, and postproduction. The preproduction stage includes all the work prior to the actual day of filming—casting, arranging for locations, estimating costs, finding props and costumes, and other work. The production stage is the actual time that the commercial is filmed or videotaped. Postproduction refers to the work done after the day of shooting. This includes editing, processing film, recording sound effects, mixing, and duplicating final films or tapes.

Most commercials are shot on film. Film is extremely flexible and versatile, it can be used for numerous optical effects, and film prints are cheaper than videotape dubs. In recent years, though, many more commercials have been shot on tape. Videotape offers a more brilliant picture and better fidelity than film, it looks more realistic, and tape quality is more consistent than film stock. The chief advantage of tape, though, is that it can provide an immediate playback of the scene that was shot.

Producing radio commercials is similar to producing television commercials in several aspects. It uses the same basic techniques and generally follows the same development pattern. Only the details and the cost differ.

Radio offers a wide range of creative possibilities. The radio listener is often busy doing something else while the radio is on, so the message should be catchy, memorable, and simple. Radio commercials should be written to create a visual image in the mind of the listener. Action words should be used rather than passive words. The copy should fit the available time. The four basic types of radio commercials are musical, slice of life, straight announcement, and personality.

The radio production process is similar to the television production process, only simpler and less costly. The final commercial is dubbed onto ¼ inch tape for distribution.

Questions for Review and Discussion

1. What is the benefit of a continuing commercial presenter?
2. Why is an understanding of broadcast production techniques important for people involved in advertising today?
3. What is an animatic and how is it used?
4. What is the importance of unity to a television commercial?
5. What are the advantages and disadvantages of using animation in television advertising?
6. What leads to the greatest waste of money in broadcast commercial production? Explain.
7. Is it better to use film or tape in producing a television commercial?
8. Why is radio often described as theater of the mind? Explain.
9. What are the four basic types of radio commercials? Describe them. Which is most effective and why?
10. Select a radio commercial of your choice. Explain what, in your mind, makes it effective.

PART IV

ADVERTISING MEDIA

making Lasting Impressions

12

MEDIA PLANNING AND SELECTION

Just a decade ago, the market for cameras in the United States was neatly divided between amateur and serious photographers. The amateur market was the target for inexpensive, cartridge-loading Instamatic cameras or Polaroid "instant" cameras, which were advertised via mass media to the broad range of amateur snapshot consumers. The more expensive 35 mm cameras were advertised predominantly in photo-buff magazines to the smaller, more specialized market of serious and professional photographers.

In 1976, the Japanese optics maker Canon had just gone through some hard times but was on its way to becoming a billion-dollar, diversified, precision instrument concern. Its two major products were copiers and 35 mm cameras. However, it still lagged behind the other well-known 35 mm camera manufacturers (Minolta, Olympus, and Pentax) in U.S. sales. That year, Canon introduced its new, fully automatic, AE-1 single-lens reflex (SLR) camera and simultaneously made marketing history.

At that time, only about 6 percent of U.S. consumers owned 35 mm cameras. Canon believed the market was wide open for an aggressive marketing approach. Research showed that 80 percent of the people who bought SLR cameras were upscale, college-educated men between the ages of 18 and 45. Most were married, and about half had children. Canon felt this group would make an ideal market for its new automatic camera if they could just see how easy it was to operate.

Canon decided to use network television to introduce its new product to the masses. Hiring Grey Advertising in New York to create the campaign, Canon spent a modest $1.5 million in prime-time TV in the fourth quarter of 1976, just in time for Christmas. With tennis pro John Newcomb as the spokesman, Grey used the theme, "The Canon AE-1 is so advanced it's simple." Consumers could see the camera demonstrated, step-by-step, right on their TV screens in live-action sequences that no form of print advertising could parallel. The results were immediately successful.

In 1977, Canon increased its television spending to $3 million with heavy emphasis in the spring and fall months. Magazine advertising, handled by Dentsu Advertising, likewise rose to $1.7 million. The next year, the total budget shot up to $9.6 million with over $6 million of that in network and spot TV. The magazine lineup, which reflected the TV campaign, included regular insertions in leading consumer magazines with heavy male readership. These included *Time, Newsweek, Playboy, Sports Illustrated, Road and Track, Skiing, Golf, Tennis,* and *Esquire.*

The TV scheduling included heavy sports programming such as "Monday Night Football" and the World Series. Leading sports personalities were hired to show how simple the AE-1 was to operate, even for a novice photographer (see Figure 12–1).

To top it all off, Canon joined the host of other manufacturers sponsoring the Winter Olympics in 1980 and again in 1984 and 1988 by becoming the official camera of the games. The company used the Olympic logos in all advertisements and created a special series of corporate Olympic ads featuring the whole Canon line.

The success of Canon's media plan was evidenced by the fact that within a year, Canon came from behind and took over the 35 mm sales lead. Immediately, the other manufacturers jumped into the fray with new product introductions and hefty television buying. But they were too late. TV spending for all 35 mm cameras exploded to $50 million within two years In 1978, Minolta was the largest TV spender. But a year later, it was still

$50 million behind Canon in sales.[1] In three short years, Canon had captured a 32 percent share of the market. Quickly following with other product introductions aimed at particular niches within the market, Canon moved into the number-three spot in 1981 behind Kodak and Polaroid in camera and photo supply advertising expenditures. Today, Canon continues to lead the market in SLR sales, offering five other models besides the AE-1, and also dominates the non-SLR 35 mm (rangefinder camera) market, which has become the most popular type of amateur photography in the past few years.[2]

In short, Canon scored a huge marketing success, not so much because of what people usually call advertising creativity but because of extraordinary media planning and selection.

The decisions made in media planning frequently require as much creativity as the decisions made by senior art directors and copywriters. As we shall see in this chapter, media decisions, like good art and copy ideas, are made in the context of the larger marketing and advertising framework. They must be based on sound marketing principles and research as well as experience and intuition.

MEDIA PLANNING: AN OVERVIEW

Each of the major media—newspapers, magazines, radio, television, direct mail, outdoor, transit advertising, and others—has unique capabilities and unique audience characteristics. Each, therefore, appeals to the needs of advertisers seeking to reach specific target audiences. The advertiser and agency must *plan* which media to use to convey the message to those consumers identified as their target audience. Then the task of the media planner is to *select* from those media the particular radio stations, TV programs, newspapers, and so on that will reach the target audience most effectively. The media function, therefore, involves two basic processes: media planning and media selection.

Media planning today is much more complicated than it was even 5 or 10 years ago. One reason is that there are more media to choose from, and each medium offers an increasing number of choices. Television, for example, has fragmented into network television, syndicated television, local television, cable networks, and local cable. There are now magazines aimed at every possible population segment, and even generalized na-

FIGURE   12–1

The Canon AE-1 TV campaign emphasized how easy the camera was to use: "So advanced, it's simple." Well-known sports personalities were shown being photographed in action and then turning the tables on the photographer and capturing a few shots of their own.

tional magazines produce editions for particular regions of the country or specific demographic groups, offering advertisers literally hundreds of insertion choices. In addition, nontraditional media, from videotape and theater-screen advertising to blimps and balloons, widen the scope of choices.

Also complicating the media planner's job is the increasing fragmentation of the audience into demographic segments. As Valerie Zeithaml of Texas A&M University has put it, "The toughest job for today's media buyer may be figuring out how to reach market fragments without expending 10 times as much effort as was traditionally required."[3]

Another factor contributing to media planning difficulties is the increasing cost of almost all media. From 1981 to 1985, advertising costs in all major media outstripped inflation, with network television posting the greatest increases (see Figure 12–2).[4] The average media unit cost increase was about 6 percent in 1986, still outpacing inflation although lower than the percent increase in prior years.[5]

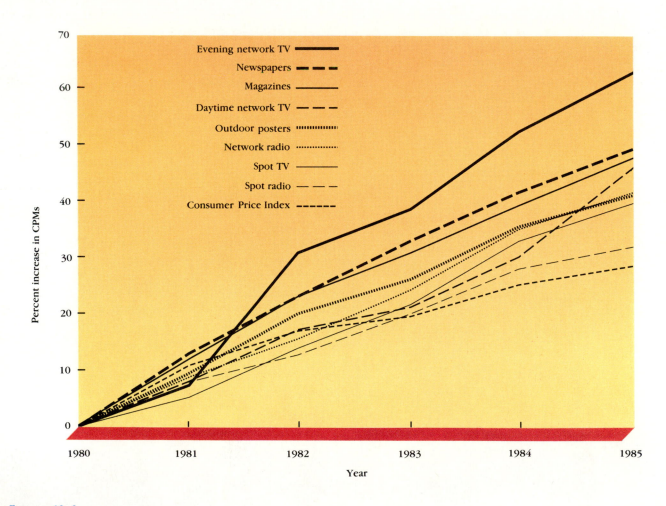

FIGURE   12–2

Yearly increases in ad costs for various media, compared to the Consumer Price Index (CPI), an indicator of the inflation rate.

Finally, the job of media planning has been made more difficult by changes in the way advertising is bought and sold. Prices on media rate cards are no longer carved in stone, and negotiation has become the norm. As choices widen and costs increase, shrewd media buying becomes a must, and services that specialize solely in media buying are taking over many of the tasks that used to be handled by agencies or in-house buyers. A similar centralization of selling is occurring in some types of media as well. Instead of having to contact each of dozens of independent cable stations or newspapers, for example, a media buyer can go to a sales representative who can put together multiple buys.

In this chapter, we will examine how media planners go about developing a basic plan, devising strategies to carry out the plan, and scheduling media buys. But first we need to see how media planning fits into the overall marketing plan.

THE ROLE OF MEDIA IN THE MARKETING FRAMEWORK

As we discussed in Chapters 4 and 7, advertising is a promotional activity, and promotion is just one of the four Ps that companies may use to achieve their marketing objectives. (The others are product, price, and place.)

When Canon made the decision to try television advertising, it was already exercising a new marketing plan with major changes in the product and price elements. The new, inexpensive Canon AE-1 automatic single-lens reflex camera was a great departure from the bigger, more complex, and more expensive 35 mm cameras of the past. In developing the marketing plan for this new product, Canon analyzed the marketing situation and determined realistic marketing objectives before developing a unique marketing strategy.

Marketing Objectives and Strategy

Before media planning can begin, the marketing objectives for the product, brand, or service must be precisely determined by the advertiser and the agency. These may include a decision to expand the market for the product—for example, by marketing 35 mm cameras not only to serious photographers but also to hobbyists. The marketer may seek to extend distribution into new geographic markets or income groups. Or the objectives may be to resell current users—by, for example, advertising a camera with "new, more advanced" capabilities to current camera owners.

Consider the risk that was involved for Canon. Only 6 percent of the people in the United States owned a 35 mm camera. To most marketers, that would indicate little interest in the product class and would discourage them from considering any mass-marketing techniques. Obviously, at some point, some optimistic person at Canon looked at those figures in reverse and said, "If only 6 percent of the people have a 35 mm camera, then there are still 94 percent we can sell to. What a wonderful opportunity!" That attitude turned out to be right. But in another situation, it might have been wrong.

Consider the other related risks. How much would it cost to develop and produce a new, untried camera for the small market that then existed? How would a lower-priced camera fare in a market that was used to paying high prices for high quality? How much would it cost to manufacture enough of these untried cameras to make it profitable even if they did sell well? How would camera retailers accept these new 35 mm cameras that sold for less and gave them less profit? Would the beginning photographer pay even that much for a first camera?

All these questions had to be answered satisfactorily before marketing objectives or a marketing strategy could be developed. Once that was accomplished, advertising objectives could be determined and advertising strategies considered.

Advertising Strategy

In Chapter 7, "Marketing and Advertising Planning," we defined the advertising strategy as the manner in which the advertiser blends the elements of the creative mix: (1) the product concept, (2) the target audience, (3) the communications media, and (4) the advertising message. How did Canon combine these elements?

Canon's plan targeted a whole new market—upscale men between the ages of 18 and 45 who were amateur photographers buying their first or second cameras. The men in this group were upper-income, active, educated, and family-oriented people for whom good photography would be a useful, enjoyable, recreational activity. This was definitely a large, mass market and a new target audience for 35 mm camera advertising.

This audience would be offered not just a new product but also a new product concept—a camera that offered ease and simplicity of operation, like the pocket cameras, along with the professional quality of 35 mm cameras. The price would be new, too—higher than that of the pocket cameras to be sure, but less than other 35 mm cameras and still affordable.

The message strategy was to be authoritative and positive, almost dogmatic, and as simple as the camera: "The Canon AE-1 is so advanced it's simple." And this message would be demonstrated by well-known, believable personalities who were not professional photographers.

By this time, the media choice appeared obvious. A mass market, the ability to demonstrate in live action, the audience desired, and the opportunity to tie in with relevant sporting events all dictated using television as the mainstay of the media plan with the support of special-interest magazines. How this media plan was developed depended, like a marketing or advertising plan, on two things: objectives and strategy.

DEFINING MEDIA OBJECTIVES

The media plan begins with a statement of objectives. These objectives are designed to help fulfill the marketing goals and strategies, as outlined in Figure 12–3. Objectives should be stated precisely so that once the plan is underway, the results can be measured against them.

A statement of general media objectives for marketing a new food product might be written as follows:

1. To reach large families with special emphasis on the homemaker, who is usually the chief purchasing agent.
2. To concentrate the greatest weight of advertising in urban areas where prepared foods traditionally have greater sales and where new ideas normally gain quicker acceptance.
3. To provide advertising continuity and a fairly consistent level of impressions throughout the year except for extra weight during the announcement period.

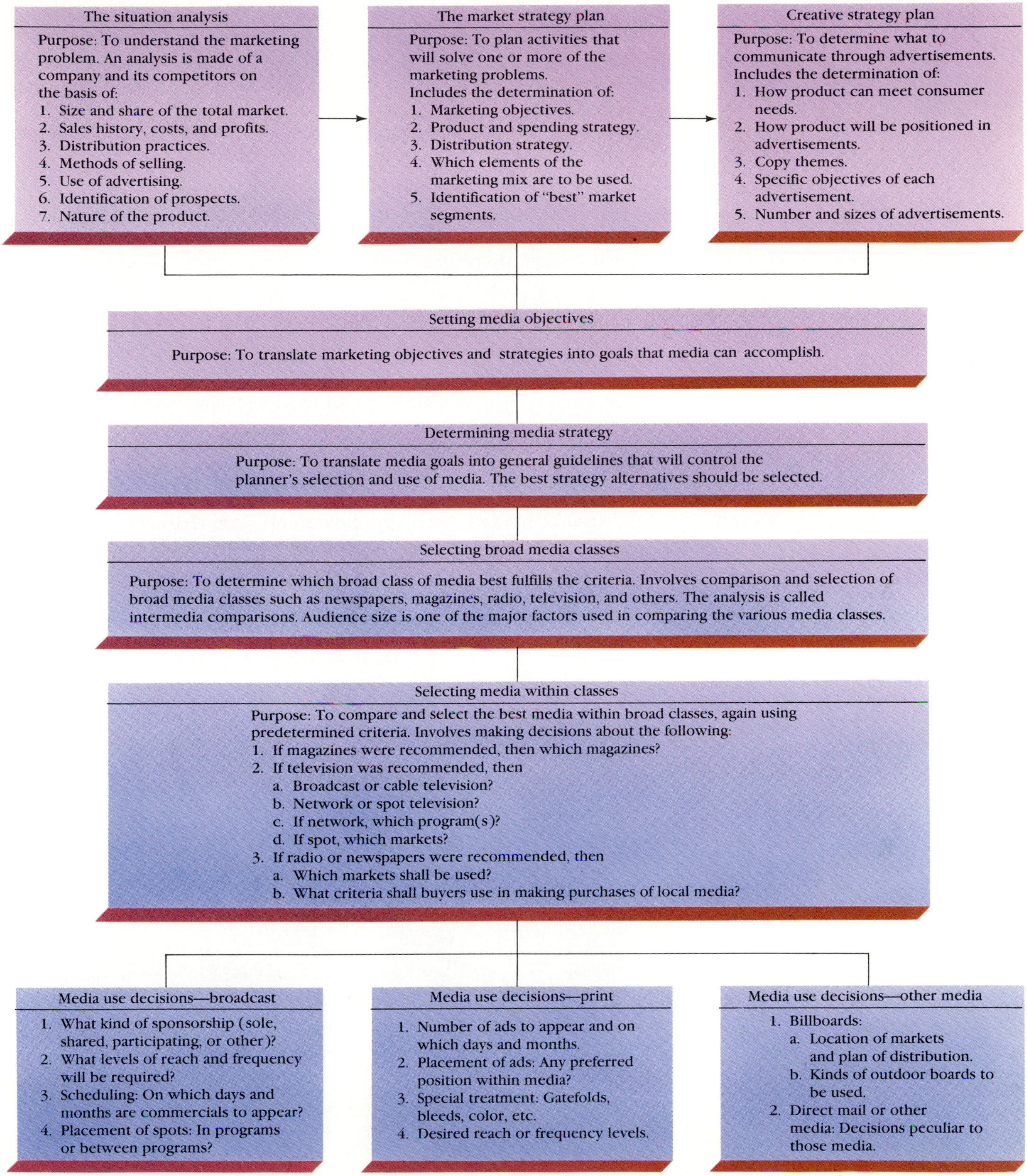

The situation analysis

Purpose: To understand the marketing problem. An analysis is made of a company and its competitors on the basis of:
1. Size and share of the total market.
2. Sales history, costs, and profits.
3. Distribution practices.
4. Methods of selling.
5. Use of advertising.
6. Identification of prospects.
7. Nature of the product.

The market strategy plan

Purpose: To plan activities that will solve one or more of the marketing problems.
Includes the determination of:
1. Marketing objectives.
2. Product and spending strategy.
3. Distribution strategy.
4. Which elements of the marketing mix are to be used.
5. Identification of "best" market segments.

Creative strategy plan

Purpose: To determine what to communicate through advertisements.
Includes the determination of:
1. How product can meet consumer needs.
2. How product will be positioned in advertisements.
3. Copy themes.
4. Specific objectives of each advertisement.
5. Number and sizes of advertisements.

Setting media objectives

Purpose: To translate marketing objectives and strategies into goals that media can accomplish.

Determining media strategy

Purpose: To translate media goals into general guidelines that will control the planner's selection and use of media. The best strategy alternatives should be selected.

Selecting broad media classes

Purpose: To determine which broad class of media best fulfills the criteria. Involves comparison and selection of broad media classes such as newspapers, magazines, radio, television, and others. The analysis is called intermedia comparisons. Audience size is one of the major factors used in comparing the various media classes.

Selecting media within classes

Purpose: To compare and select the best media within broad classes, again using predetermined criteria. Involves making decisions about the following:
1. If magazines were recommended, then which magazines?
2. If television was recommended, then
    a. Broadcast or cable television?
    b. Network or spot television?
    c. If network, which program(s)?
    d. If spot, which markets?
3. If radio or newspapers were recommended, then
    a. Which markets shall be used?
    b. What criteria shall buyers use in making purchases of local media?

Media use decisions—broadcast

1. What kind of sponsorship (sole, shared, participating, or other)?
2. What levels of reach and frequency will be required?
3. Scheduling: On which days and months are commercials to appear?
4. Placement of spots: In programs or between programs?

Media use decisions—print

1. Number of ads to appear and on which days and months.
2. Placement of ads: Any preferred position within media?
3. Special treatment: Gatefolds, bleeds, color, etc.
4. Desired reach or frequency levels.

Media use decisions—other media

1. Billboards:
    a. Location of markets and plan of distribution.
    b. Kinds of outdoor boards to be used.
2. Direct mail or other media: Decisions peculiar to those media.

FIGURE   12–3

The scope of media planning activities.

4. To deliver advertising impressions over the entire country in direct relation to food-store sales.
5. To use media that will help to strengthen the copy strategy and to put major emphasis on convenience, ease of preparation, taste, and economy.
6. To attain the greatest possible frequency of advertising impressions consistent with the need for broad coverage and the demands of the copy plan.[6]

Such objectives can be broken down into several component parts, but for convenience, we will focus on two main categories: audience objectives and message-distribution objectives.

Audience Objectives

Defining target audiences is an essential step in determining media objectives and strategy. The whole media effort will be wasted if the right people are not exposed to the ads in the campaign. In our sample objectives, the target audience is homemakers with large families who live in urban areas.

The target audience may consist of people in a specific income, educational, occupational, social, or ethnic group. Canon has one 35 mm rangefinder camera model, the Aqua Snappy, that is aimed primarily at young sports enthusiasts (see Figure 12–4). It has another, the Snappy 20, that comes in bright colors and is designed to appeal to young women. The media objectives for each of these two camera models are thus quite different from those for the AE-1.

FIGURE   12–4

Print ads for Canon's Aqua Snappy model are targeted at active young adults, who are encouraged to buy the camera and "take it anywhere."

As we will see in the section on media selection and scheduling, media vehicles are selected according to how well they "deliver" an audience that closely parallels the desired target audience. Advertisers like Canon are always concerned about wasting money on ads that reach consumers who are not likely to need or want the product or who are not important buying influences. Thus, for advertising the Aqua Snappy, Canon chose such magazines as *Boating, Skin Diver,* and *Outdoor Photography,* while ads for the Snappy 20 have appeared on early-morning and late-night network TV shows and in magazines such as *Glamour.*

Distribution Objectives

Whereas audience objectives answer the question of *whom* advertising will be aimed at, distribution objectives answer the questions of where, when, and how often advertising should appear. Should advertising be more heavily concentrated in particular geographic areas? Our sample food-product objectives specify urban areas all over the country but in relation to food sales. Should the level of advertising be continuous, or should it be greater at certain times of the year? Our example specifies greater emphasis during the announcement period. How much of the target market should the advertising be expected to reach, and how often? To answer these questions, a media planner must fully understand such concepts as reach, frequency, gross rating points, and continuity.

Reach

The term *reach* refers to the number of *different* people or households exposed to an advertising schedule during a given time, usually four weeks. For example, if 80 percent of a total of 10,000 people in the target market hear the Super Soap commercials on radio stations KKO and KXA at least once during a four-week period, the reach is 8,000 people. Reach, then, measures the unduplicated extent of audience exposure to a media vehicle and may be expressed either as a percentage of the total market (80) or as a raw number (8,000). However, as Figure 12–5 shows, the term *reach* may be used in a variety of different ways by media planners. Therefore, in setting reach objectives, clarity and specificity are important.

Frequency

Frequency refers to the number of times an advertising message reaches the same person or household. Across a total audience, frequency is calculated as the average number of times individuals or homes are exposed to the advertising. The figure is used to measure the *intensity* of a specific media schedule.

For example, suppose 4,000 of our radio listeners heard the Super Soap commercial three times during a four-week period and another 4,000 people heard it five times. To determine the *average frequency* the following formula would be used:

$$\text{Average frequency} = \text{Total exposures} \div \text{Audience reach}$$
$$= [(4,000 \times 3) + (4,000 \times 5)] \div 8,000$$
$$= 32,000 \div 8,000$$
$$= 4$$

FIGURE   12–5   Aspects of reach

Reach is . . .
1. A measurement of audience accumulation.
2. An unduplicated statistic.
3. Measured, although it can sometimes be estimated.
4. Measured for a single vehicle or a group of different vehicles.
5. Measured for subsequent issues of the same magazine, for example, the seven-issue reach of *TV Guide* is . . .
6. Reported for a four-week period of television watching.
7. Reported for almost any period of time in broadcast measurements.
8. Reported by the issue in print media.
9. Reported either as a raw number or as a percentage of some universe.
10. Reported for households or for individuals in a demographic category.
11. Another term for coverage in print media.
12. Measured on the basis of exposure to a vehicle or vehicles.
13. Not measured on the basis of exposure to ads in vehicles.
14. A measurement that tells the planner how many people had an opportunity to see ads in vehicles.

Thus, for the 8,000 listeners reached, the average frequency or number of exposures was four. Frequency, then, is an important planning tool because it offers a measure of the repetition that can be achieved by a specific media schedule. Repetition is important, of course, because the more times people are exposed to a message, the more likely they are to remember it.

What is the "right frequency" for a given message in a given medium? Although it is conventional wisdom in advertising that three to six contacts over a four-week period is the "effective frequency" for getting a message across, this rule of thumb has become a matter of some controversy. Critics point out that there are simply too many variables involved, from the nature of the product and the entertainment value of the ad to the characteristics of the medium and the audience, to be able to set such an ideal frequency level.[7] According to Stacey Lippman, senior vice president at the William Esty agency, "There will never be a 'right' answer to the question of how much frequency is required. But if we treat each product and each client as unique, we can make an intelligent judgment."[8]

Impressions

Impressions are the total of all the audiences delivered by a media plan. In the radio listener example, it would be the same as *total exposures*. It is calculated by multiplying the number of people who receive a message by the number of times they receive it—in this particular case, 32,000. If the same schedule was used for another four weeks, what do you think would be the total number of impressions? What do you think would be the average frequency?

Gross Rating Points

The total audience delivery or weight of a specific media schedule might be expressed by counting the total number of impressions. However, the more common method of expressing this information is in *gross rating points (GRPs)*. GRPs are computed by multiplying the reach, expressed as a percentage of the population, by the average frequency. In our example, 80 percent of the radio households heard the Super Soap commercial an average of four times during the four-week period. To determine the gross rating points of this radio schedule, we use the following formula:

$$\text{Reach} \times \text{Frequency} = \text{GRP}$$
$$80 \times 4 = 320 \text{ Gross rating points}$$

It is important to understand that gross rating points are used to describe the total message weight of a media schedule, without regard to audience duplication, over a given period of time. For broadcast media, gross rating points are often calculated for a week or a month. In print media, they are often calculated for the number of ad insertions in a campaign. And for outdoor advertising, they are calculated on the basis of daily exposure.

Continuity, Flighting, and Pulsing

Several terms are used to refer to the manner in which an advertising campaign is scheduled and sustained. For example, the Super Soap commercial might be scheduled on radio stations KKO and KXA for an initial four-week period. But then, to maintain *continuity* in the campaign, additional spots might be scheduled to run continuously every week throughout the year on station KXA.

On the other hand, the advertiser might decide to introduce the product with a four-week *flight* and then schedule three additional flights to run during seasonal periods later in the year.

A third alternative would be a mixture of the continuity and flighting strategies. Using these strategies, the advertiser could maintain a low level of advertising all year but use periodic *pulses* during peak selling periods. The differences between continuity, flighting, and pulsing are illustrated in Figure 12–6.

Naturally, the continuity of a campaign will affect how many people can be reached and how many times they can be reached. It will also affect how well the message is remembered over time. The ideal in most cases, of course, would be achieved if a company could simply advertise heavily all year long. However, the reach, frequency, and continuity of a media plan all depend on the advertiser's media budget. Because all budgets are limited, so are the media objectives that may be attained. In addition, these objectives have an inverse relationship to one another within the limits of the budget (see Figure 12–7). To achieve greater reach, some frequency may have to be sacrificed. Likewise, to gain greater continuity, short-term reach or frequency must be sacrificed. The goal of the media planner, therefore, is to optimize these objectives by getting enough reach, enough frequency, and the proper continuity to make the media plan work for the advertiser.

Once media objectives have been determined—that is, the best mix of reach, frequency, and continuity—the media strategy can be developed.

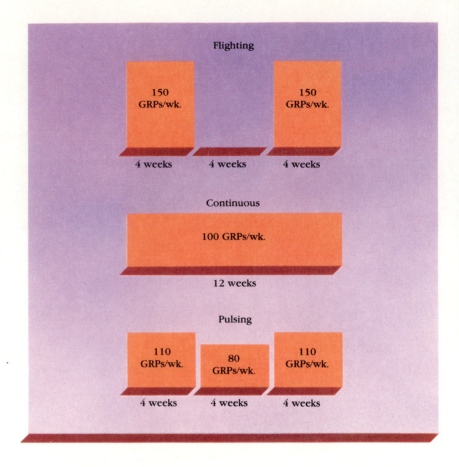

FIGURE   12–6

Comparison of flighting and pulsing schedules.

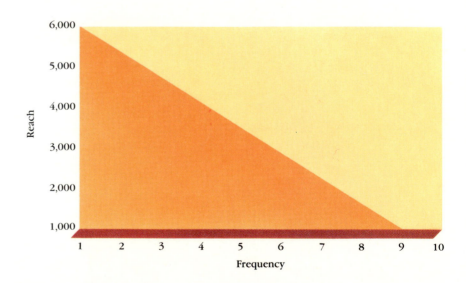

FIGURE   12–7

The inverse relationship between reach and frequency. For example, for the same budget, it might be possible to reach 6,000 people 1 time, 3,000 people 5.5 times, or 1,000 people 9 times.

DEVELOPING A MEDIA STRATEGY

The media strategy describes how the advertiser will achieve the stated media objectives. The strategy reflects the specific course of action to be taken with media: which media will be used, how often each will be used, how much of each will be used, and when they will be used.

Generally, media-strategy decisions fall into one of two broad areas: selection of media and choice of vehicles within each medium. Should the advertiser, for example, use television, radio, magazines, or some combi-

FIGURE   12–8

Because the Canon T-90 is a sophisticated camera designed for professionals and serious amateurs, the ads need to describe all the important features. Magazines were chosen as the primary ad medium not only because print ads can carry a great deal of information but also because vehicles can be selected that are aimed specifically at the target market.

nation? In 1986, Canon introduced another SLR camera, the T-90, aimed at the professional and the serious amateur. For this audience, Canon felt advertising would need to provide a great deal of information about the technical qualities of the product. Thus, the camera company chose magazines as the best medium to present this type of informative ad (see Figure 12–8). Within this print medium, Canon chose vehicles geared to upscale camera buyers, including *American Photographer, Modern Photography, Smithsonian,* and *Omni.*[9]

These types of strategy decisions must take into account a wide variety of factors, among them geographic scope, the nature of the medium and the message, consumer purchase patterns, mechanical considerations, and competitive strategy and budget considerations.

Geographic Scope

A key strategic decision relates to the breadth of the media plan, which is determined by the location and makeup of the target audience.

Normally, advertising should be limited to areas where the product is available. A *local* plan may be used, for example, if the product is available in only one city or if that market has been chosen to introduce or test-market a new product.

A *regional* plan, on the other hand, may cover several adjoining metropolitan areas, an entire state, or several neighboring states. Regional media objectives can be achieved by using local media, regional editions of national magazines, or spot television and radio. Regional plans are also used to accommodate sectional differences in taste or preference that affect product sales. For example, more instant coffee is sold in the Midwest than in New England.

Advertisers who want to reach consumers throughout the country generally use a *national* plan. The media used in a national plan are usually network television, network radio, full-circulation national magazines and newspapers, and nationally syndicated Sunday newspaper supplements. Figure 12–9 lists the media used by the 25 largest national advertisers. Figure 12–10 breaks down advertising expenditures devoted to each of the major media.

The scope of the media plan might also be based on other geographical considerations, such as urban versus rural areas, areas with predominantly wet versus dry regions or warm and humid versus very cold climates, and so on.

FIGURE 12–9

Media expenditures of 25 leading advertisers in 1986 (in measured media only, dollars in millions)

Advertiser	Total measured expenditures	Newspaper	Business publication	Magazine
Procter & Gamble Co.	$833,943	$ 4,030	$ 3,194	$ 86,506
Philip Morris Cos.	909,894	57,590	2,986	230,130
Sears Roebuck & Co.	276,398	0	741	42,934
RJR Nabisco	526,237	50,347	2,618	135,657
General Motors Corp.	646,904	146,430	10,256	129,409
Ford Motor Co.	497,324	76,136	5,251	125,071
Anheuser-Busch Cos.	400,427	11,744	843	18,335
McDonald's Corp.	333,808	0	0	609
K mart Corp.	83,022	0	0	20,462
PepsiCo Inc.	414,050	8,806	399	1,082
General Mills	304,927	705	1,109	23,306
Warner-Lambert Co.	189,745	850	3,405	14,499
BCI Holdings	146,771	3,652	2,717	15,682
Unilever N.V.	332,438	2,427	315	49,816
J.C. Penney Co.	74,924	0	3	8,487
Pillsbury Co.	260,150	1,346	323	7,011
Ralston Purina Co.	178,031	2,512	456	24,653
American Telephone & Telegraph	339,552	31,106	19,850	74,015
Kraft Inc.	200,592	2,017	774	33,823
Chrysler Corp.	317,565	42,203	1,257	78,906
Johnson & Johnson	205,959	1,339	620	22,471
American Home Products Corp.	226,351	87	1,400	14,802
Kellogg Co.	220,089	193	670	1,058
Coca-Cola Co.	222,135	5,227	668	5,712
General Electric Co.	163,317	26,987	13,737	50,777

Nature of the Medium and the Message

An important determinant in media strategy is the nature of the media themselves. Some media lend themselves better to certain types of messages or creative approaches than others. For an introduction to the creative advantages and disadvantages of each of the major media, turn to Ad Lab 12-A.

Often a combination of media will work together to get across the overall message. Ben Givauden, president of the Givauden Agency in New York, appreciates the media "synergy" between newspapers and magazines, for example: "Newspapers can be used to detonate an idea, with magazines following up for the harder sell." He points out that newspapers offer in-depth circulation, whereas magazines offer retentive value.[10]

Network TV	Spot TV	Cable TV networks	Network radio	Spot radio	Outdoor
$456,324	$233,932	$27,673	$13,879	$ 7,471	$ 293
$342,444	134,725	22,186	7,750	33,226	61,283
127,804	29,226	2,552	47,658	21,928	309
155,715	38,455	10,455	3,954	9,286	82,820
233,786	49,192	7,203	22,212	35,153	2,731
188,815	55,821	4,748	14,871	17,610	2,134
177,496	97,999	19,487	16,529	50,420	6,664
193,002	128,180	1,820	0	4,654	5,544
26,333	24,211	648	6,526	3,602	138
115,128	257,033	5,107	874	22,342	3,213
130,140	127,253	15,538	2,967	3,107	348
103,069	38,725	3,686	22,707	1,826	1
58,710	47,798	950	4,361	12,110	229
202,371	60,808	5,212	6,607	4,312	104
46,867	14,929	1,616	1,218	875	22
105,052	125,218	1,549	0	18,178	1,340
97,572	33,532	3,245	5,944	8,013	547
135,162	41,124	3,191	22,552	8,710	91
88,446	61,803	1,775	2,637	7,162	73
96,451	63,551	4,205	1,548	21,071	1,849
164,322	7,731	5,292	1,376	2,634	130
186,428	13,634	6,821	2,397	543	0
166,261	48,804	3,072	0	8	22
99,381	82,993	5,997	2,222	16,608	3,166
51,615	5,431	2,428	2,132	3,737	1,541

FIGURE 12–10

Advertising expenditures broken down by media, 1986.

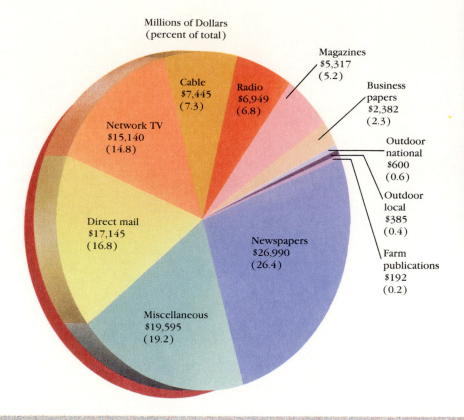

Millions of Dollars
(percent of total)

Magazines
$5,317
(5.2)

Business papers
$2,382
(2.3)

Cable
$7,445
(7.3)

Radio
$6,949
(6.8)

Network TV
$15,140
(14.8)

Outdoor national
$600
(0.6)

Outdoor local
$385
(0.4)

Farm publications
$192
(0.2)

Newspapers
$26,990
(26.4)

Direct mail
$17,145
(16.8)

Miscellaneous
$19,595
(19.2)

AD LAB 12-A   Media Selection: As the Creative Person Sees It

	Creative Disadvantages	Creative Advantages
Newspapers	Loss of fidelity, especially in reproduction of halftone illustrations. Too many ad-format variations among newspapers. Variance in column widths. Difficulty in controlling ad position on page.	Almost any ad size available. Impact of black against white (still one of the most powerful color combinations). Sense of immediacy. Quick response; easy accountability. Local emphasis. Changes possible at short notice.
Magazines	Size not as large as those of newspapers or posters. Long closing dates, limiting flexibility. Lack of immediacy. Tendency to cluster ads. Possible difficulties in securing favorable spot in an issue.	High-quality reproduction. Prestige factor. Accurate demographic information available. Graphic opportunities (use of white space, benday screen, reverse type). Color.
Television	No time to convey a lot of information. Air clutter (almost 25 percent of broadcasting is nonprogramming material). Intrusiveness (TV tops list of consumers' complaints in this respect). Capricious station censorship.	Combination of sight and sound. Movement. A single message at a time. Viewer's empathy. Opportunity to demonstrate the product. Believability: "What you see is what you get."
Radio	Lack of visual excitement. Wavering attention span (many listeners tune out commercials). Inadequate data on listening habits (when is the "listener" really listening?). Fleeting nature of message.	Opportunity to explore sound. Favorable to humor. Intimacy. Loyal following (the average person listens regularly to only about two stations). Ability to change message quickly.

Advertising messages differ in many ways. Some are simple, dogmatic messages: "AT&T: The right choice." Others are based on an emotional attitude, appealing to people's needs for safety, security, social approval, love, beauty, or fun: "You're in good hands with Allstate." Many advertisers use a reason-why approach to explain their product's advantages: "Lite. Everything you always wanted in a beer. And less." Some messages are complex, requiring considerable space or time for explanation. Others announce a new product or product concept and are, therefore, unfamiliar to the consuming public. In each of these circumstances, the media strategy will be considerably affected.

A message that is either new or highly complex, like the ad in Figure 12–11, may require greater frequency and exposure to be understood and remembered. A dogmatic message, like that for AT&T, for example, may require a surge at the beginning of the campaign to communicate the idea. But then it is usually advantageous to maintain low frequency and strive for greater reach.

Reason-why messages may be complex to understand at first, but once the explanation is understood, a pulsing of advertising exposures at irregular intervals is often sufficient to remind customers of the explanation. On the other hand, emotionally oriented messages are usually more effective if spaced at regular intervals to create a continuing feeling about the product.[11]

	Creative Disadvantages	Creative Advantages
Direct mail	Damper of state, federal, and postal regulations on creative experimentation. Censorship often unpredictable. Formula thinking encouraged by "proven" direct-mail track records.	Graphic and production flexibility, such as use of three-dimensional effect (folding, die-cuts, pop-ups). Measurable. As scientific as any other form of advertising. Highly personal.
Posters	Essentially a one-line medium with only a limited opportunity to expand on the advertising message. Inadequate audience research, especially in transit advertising.	Graphic opportunities. Color. Large size. High-fidelity reproduction. Simple, direct approach. Possibility of an entirely visual message.
Point of sale	Difficulty in pinpointing audience. Failure of retailers to make proper use of material submitted to them.	Opportunities for three-dimensional effects, movement, sound, and new production techniques.

Laboratory Applications

1. What creative disadvantages and advantages can you add to the list?
2. From the list of leading advertisers in Figure 12–9, select one, and explain why the primary medium it uses is specifically advantageous for its products from a creative point of view.

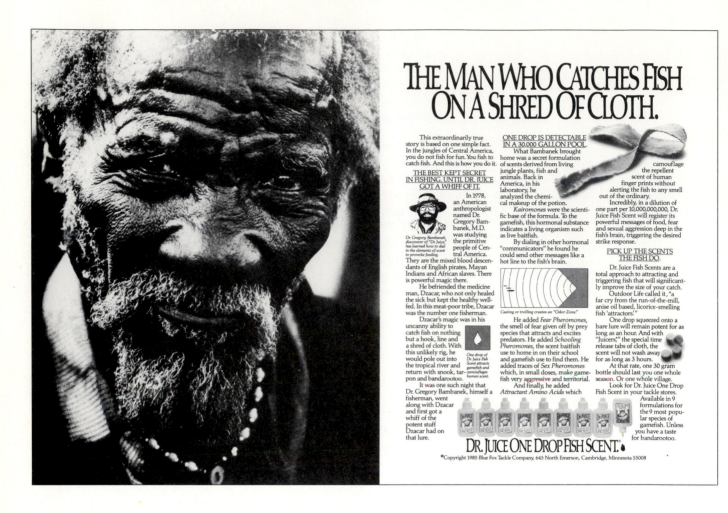

FIGURE   12–11

A complex message such as this one requires more than carefully prepared copy: it usually needs to be presented more frequently than less complex messages if it is to be understood and remembered.

Consumer Purchase Patterns

While the medium and the message are important considerations in developing media strategy, so are the normal purchasing habits of target customers for the product. Seasonal products such as snow tires or suntan lotion require concentrated exposures before peak buying periods.

Some products (such as convenience foods and paper towels) are purchased at regular intervals, and the advertising function is to influence the customer's brand choice. If this is the case, the goal is to reach prospects regularly and especially just before they make their next purchasing decision. Situations of this type call for relatively high frequency and high continuity, depending on the length of time of the purchasing cycle. As the purchasing cycle gets longer, the pulsing of messages becomes more appropriate.

In some cases (such as the buying of camera film), the purchase cycle is erratic but susceptible to influence by advertising. In these situations, advertising exposures should be spaced, alternating periods of high frequency with periods of low exposure. The purpose is to try to reduce the length of time between purchases.

Products that are bought on impulse require steady, high-frequency advertising, while those that are bought after great deliberation may require pulsing with alternately high and low frequencies depending on market conditions and competitive activity.

Products with a high degree of brand loyalty can usually be served with lower levels of frequency, allowing the advertiser to achieve greater reach and continuity.

Mechanical Considerations

Considerations of how to use the selected media may greatly affect the overall media strategy. For example, greater attention can usually be gained from a full-color ad than from a black-and-white ad (see Figure 12–12A). Likewise, a full-page ad attracts more attention than a quarter-page ad (see Figure 12–12B). With limited advertising budgets, though, larger units of space or time cost dearly in terms of such things as reach, frequency, and continuity.

Is it better for a small advertiser to run a full-page ad once a month or a quarter-page ad once a week? Should television advertisers use some

A.

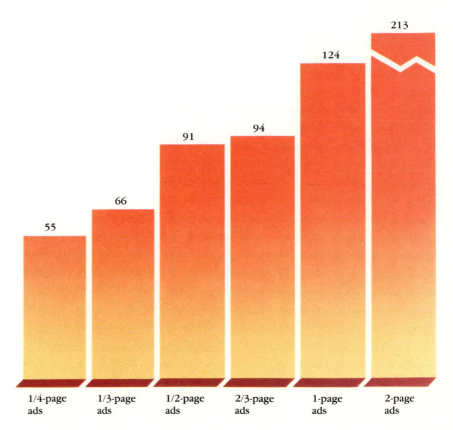

B.

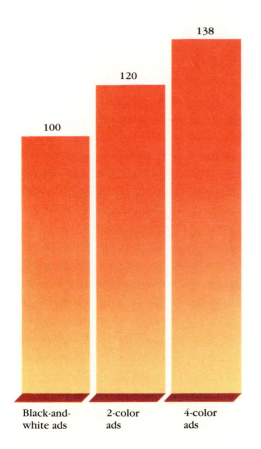

FIGURE   12–12

A. Readership scores for ads with various degrees of color. B. Readership scores for ads of various sizes. Although readership is the greatest for four-color, two-page ads, the increased readership may not

offset the additional cost in some publications.

occasional 60-second announcements or a lot of 15- and 30-second commercials? The answers to these questions are not simple. Some messages require more time and space to be explained. Competitive activity often dictates more message units. The nature of the product itself may demand the prestige of a full page or full color. On the other hand, the need for high frequency may demand smaller units. It is sometimes better to run several small ads consistently than to run one large ad occasionally.

Other mechanical considerations include using the preferred positions of magazine advertisements on front and back covers or sponsoring prime-time television shows. Special positions, sponsorships, and other mechanical opportunities are usually sold at a premium by the media. The media planner must, therefore, carefully weigh the benefits of these additional costs in terms of the potential sales impact against the loss of reach and frequency.

Competitive Strategy and Budget Considerations

Media strategy must consider what competitive advertisers are doing, particularly if their advertising budgets are larger. One general rule is to bypass media that competitors dominate and to choose, instead, those that offer a strong or dominant position. When Stresstabs vitamins were introduced, for example, the campaign was entirely in print. According to the agency handling the campaign, "We wanted to avoid what was then a large arena of TV advertising, and we reached our target audience more efficiently and effectively in print."[12]

As we've said before, the reach, frequency, and continuity of any media plan are greatly limited by the advertising budget. Of great importance to most small advertisers, therefore, is an understanding of how to use their budgets most effectively. Generally, the smaller the budget, the more pulsing is required. In this way, even with a low budget, the advertiser can sometimes attract as much attention as bigger competitors in the product class. As the budget grows larger and larger, advertisers can seek greater continuity by spreading their advertising messages more evenly. (See Figure 12–13) for a summary of guidelines for developing media objectives and strategies.)

Stating the Media Strategy

A written statement of the media strategy is an integral part of any media plan. Without one, it is difficult to analyze the logic and consistency of the overall media schedule that is recommended.

Generally, the strategy statement should tell what types of media will be used, how they will be used, and the rationale for the choices made. It should start with a brief definition of the target audiences and the priorities for weighting them, and it should outline specific reach, frequency, and continuity goals. The nature of the message should be explained. Then it should provide a breakdown of the various types of media to be used over the period of the campaign, the budget for each, and the cost of production and any collateral materials. Finally, the intended size of message units, along with any other mechanical or timing considerations, should be stated as well as the effect of budget restrictions.

FIGURE   12-13   Guidelines for developing media objectives and strategies

Considerations	Objectives			
	Reach	Frequency	Continuity	Pulsing
Needs				
New or highly complex message, strive for:		✔		
Dogmatic message, surge at beginning, then go for:	✔		✔	
Reason-why messages, high frequency at first, then use:				✔
With emotionally oriented messages, strive for:			✔	
When message is so creative or product so newsworthy that it forces attention, seek:	✔			
When message is dull or product indistinguishable, strive for:		✔		
Consumer purchase patterns				
To influence brand choice of regularly purchased products, use:		✔	✔	
As purchase cycle lengthens, use:		✔		✔
To influence erratic purchase cycles, strive for:				✔
To influence consumer attitudes toward impulse purchases, seek:		✔	✔	
For products requiring great deliberation, alternate between:	✔	✔		
To reinforce consumer loyalty, concentrate on:	✔		✔	
To influence seasonal purchases, anticipate peak periods with:	✔	✔		
Budget levels				
Low budget, use:				✔
Higher budgets, strive for:			✔	
Competitive activity				
Heavy competitive advertising, concentrate on:		✔		
When competitive budgets are larger, use:				✔
Marketing objectives				
For new product introductions to mass market, use:	✔			
To expand share of market with new uses for product, strive for:	✔			
To stimulate direct response from advertising, use:		✔	✔	✔
To create awareness and recognition of corporate status, use:	✔		✔	

MEDIA SELECTION AND SCHEDULING

After the media strategy has been developed, the task of selecting the specific media vehicles and scheduling their use falls to the media planner.

In developing its media strategy for the AE-1, Canon decided to use television sports programming to reach upscale young men. But which sports programs should be used? Boxing? Bowling? Golf? Baseball? Football? Basketball? And should advertising focus on network sports shows only or also include cable TV and localized sports programming? The choices seem endless. Which golf tournaments? Which football games? Should ads also be run in soccer programs or on baseball scorecards? How about an ad on the scoreboard at these events?

Obviously, the media planner must take many factors into consideration to make the most efficient media selection and then weigh a variety of other criteria to schedule these media appropriately.

Considerations in Selecting Individual Media

The media planner's job is to match the right media vehicles with the right audiences at the right time in the best environment and in the most logical place so that the advertising message will not only achieve the desired exposure but also attract attention and motivate customers to some action. And the planner must do this with cost efficiency so that the reach, frequency, and continuity goals can be met.

In considering specific media vehicles for use, the planner must first study several influencing factors: (1) overall campaign objectives and strategy; (2) size and characteristics of each medium's audience; (3) geographic coverage; (4) attention, exposure, and motivational value of the media being considered; (5) cost efficiency; and (6) the various approaches available for media selection. Several of these factors for major media are compared in Figure 12–14.

FIGURE　12–14　　　　　Comparative evaluation of advertising media

	Spot television	Network television	Spot radio	Network radio	Consumer magazines	Business publications	Farm publications	Sunday supplements	Daily newspapers	Weekly newspapers	Direct mail	Outdoor	Transit	Point of purchase
Audience considerations														
Attentiveness of audience	M	M	M	M	M	M	M	M	M	M	M	W	W	W
Interest of audience	M	S	M	M	S	S	S	S	S	S	W	W	W	W
Avoids excess selection by audience	M	M	M	M	W	W	W	W	W	W	W	W	W	W
Offers selectivity to advertiser	W	W	M	M	S	S	S	W	W	W	S	W	W	W
Avoids waste	W	W	W	W	S	S	S	M	W	W	S	W	W	W
Offers involvement	M	S	M	M	M	S	S	M	M	M	W	W	W	W
Avoids distraction	M	S	M	M	S	S	S	M	M	M	S	W	W	W
Avoids resistance	N	N	N	N	N	N	N	N	N	N	N	N	N	N
Provides impact	V	V	V	V	V	V	V	V	V	V	V	V	V	V
Offers prestige	M	S	W	M	S	S	M	S	M	W	W	W	W	W
Good quality of audience data	M	M	M	M	S	S	M	M	M	W	M	W	W	W
Timing factors														
Offers repetition	S	S	S	S	M	M	M	W	M	W	V	S	S	M
Avoids irritation	W	W	W	M	M	M	M	M	M	M	M	M	M	M
Offers frequency	S	S	S	M	M	M	M	W	M	W	M	S	S	M
Offers frequency of issuance	S	S	S	S	V	V	W	W	M	W	V	N	N	N
Offers flexibility in scheduling	S	S	S	S	V	V	W	W	M	W	V	N	N	N
Long life	W	W	W	W	S	S	S	M	W	M	W	W	W	W
Low mortality rate	W	W	W	W	S	S	S	M	W	M	W	W	W	W
Avoids perishability	W	W	W	W	S	S	S	M	W	M	W	W	W	W
Allows long message	M	M	M	M	S	S	S	S	S	S	S	W	W	W
Provides product protection	V	M	V	M	M	M	M	M	V	V	S	W	W	M

Note: W = Weak, M = Medium, S = Strong, N = Not a factor for this medium, V = Varies from one vehicle to another within the medium.

Overall Campaign Objectives and Strategy

When the selection process begins, the media planner's job is to review the nature of the product or service, the intended objectives and strategies that have been developed, and the primary and secondary target markets and audiences.

The nature of the product itself may suggest the type of media to be used. For example, when a product—such as a fine perfume—has a distinct personality or image, it might be advertised in media that have personality traits that reinforce this image. Some magazines are regarded as feminine or masculine, highbrow or lowbrow, serious or frivolous.

If one of the objectives of the marketing and advertising campaign is to gain greater product distribution, the media selected should be those that influence both consumers and potential dealers. For example, if the goal is to stimulate sales of a nationally distributed product in certain isolated

	Spot television	Network television	Spot radio	Network radio	Consumer magazines	Business publications	Farm publications	Sunday supplements	Daily newspapers	Weekly newspapers	Direct mail	Outdoor	Transit	Point of purchase
Geographic considerations														
Offers geographic selectivity	S	W	S	W	M	M	M	S	S	S	S	M	M	S
Offers proximity to point of sale	W	W	W	W	W	W	W	W	W	W	M	M	M	S
Provides for local dealer "tags"	M	W	M	W	M	M	M	M	S	S	S	M	M	S
Creative considerations														
Permits demonstration	S	S	W	W	M	M	M	M	M	M	S	W	W	S
Provides impact	S	S	M	M	M	M	M	M	M	M	S	W	W	M
Permits relation to editorial matter	M	M	W	M	S	S	S	M	M	M	S	N	N	N
Competitive factors														
Light use of medium by competitors	W	S	W	S	W	S	S	M	M	S	M	M	S	S
Low amount of total advertising	W	W	V	S	M	V	S	M	M	M	S	M	W	S
Control considerations														
Advertiser control of media content	W	M	W	M	W	W	W	W	W	W	S	N	N	N
Favorable environment	W	M	W	M	W	W	W	W	W	W	S	W	W	S
Advertiser control of location	N	S	N	S	M	M	M	W	W	W	S	W	W	M
Amount of government regulation	W	N	W	N	N	N	N	N	N	N	W	W	N	N
Number of other restrictions	W	W	W	W	V	V	V	V	V	V	W	W	W	W
Mechanical and production factors														
Ease of insertion	M	S	M	S	S	S	S	M	M	W	S	M	M	W
High reproduction quality	M	M	M	M	S	S	S	S	V	V	S	V	V	S
Flexibility of format	M	M	M	M	S	S	S	W	N	N	S	M	W	W
Avoids vandalism	N	N	N	N	N	N	N	N	N	N	N	W	W	W
Financial considerations														
Low total cost	M	W	M	W	W	W	W	M	S	S	W	M	M	M
High efficiency	M	S	S	M	M	M	M	M	M	W	S	S	S	W

markets, advertisements should be concentrated in the local and regional media that penetrate those markets rather than in national media. On the other hand, if the goal is to elevate product image or company reputation, the advertiser may be willing to sacrifice the sales potential of popular local programming in favor of the prestige of high-quality programs on network television.

The price of the product and the pricing strategy may influence media choices, too. Pricing is often a key consideration in product positioning. For example, a premium-priced product may require the use of prestigious or "class" media to support its market image.

Reviewing the product's target market and the campaign's target audience is another vital step in media selection. The more the media planner knows about the market, the better the media selections are likely to be. Data gathered on the target market should include its size, location, and demographic profile, such as age, sex, education, occupation, income, and religion. Psychographic characteristics, such as lifestyle, personality, and attitudinal traits, and behavioral characteristics, such as purchase cycles, benefits sought, and product use habits, should be studied.

The task of the media planner is then (1) to select from these data the characteristics most relevant to the acceptance, purchase, and use of the product and (2) to match these data to the characteristics of the audiences reached by the specific media vehicles under consideration.

This process may sometimes lead the media planner to go outside conventional advertising media and use nontraditional forms to reach the target audience for the particular product. For instance, Dr Pepper has become one of the major users of in-cinema advertising, placing 90-second spots in thousands of theaters throughout the United States (see

FIGURE   12–15

Advertisers wanting to reach the captive audience in movie theaters run the risk of alienating viewers if their commercials take a hard sell approach and aren't entertaining.

Dr Pepper's futuristic "Cola Wars" ad, inspired by the cult film *Mad Max,* is a 90-second "mini-movie" that film audiences have found appealing.

(SFX & MUSIC UNDER THROUGH-OUT)

OZY'S VOICE: I smell a rat.

WARRIOR #1: Give me two more colas and a little of your time sweetheart.

WAITRESS: Hello stranger . . . and stranger yet, what'll you have?

SPACE COWBOY: Something different.

WARRIOR #2: The Cola wars are over.

WARRIOR #1: There ain't nothing different.

WAITRESS: I have something different.

OZY'S VOICE: Jackpot!
Uh-oh.

WARRIOR #1: Trash it!

SPACE COWBOY: Freeze! It's better ice cold.

Figure 12–15). Although these spots cost considerably more than TV commercials in terms of cost per thousand (CPM) viewers, Dr Pepper's media director thinks they're worth it because the soft drink's target audience—teens and young adults—are found in high concentrations in movie audiences and because theater operators feel compelled to carry the advertised product. Furthermore, the audience is a captive one, the creative impact is greater on a large screen in a darkened theater with no competitive commercial clutter, and the spots can be run in the summer months—the peak season for soft drink sales, movie releases, and attendance levels.[13] Some of the other nontraditional media available to advertisers are described in Ad Lab 12-B.

AD LAB 12-B   Off-the-Wall Media That Pull Customers off the Fence

Advertising can be found everywhere these days, even places where we least expect it. Here are but a few of the unusual media being explored.

Videotapes

Advertisers are either sponsoring complete tapes, such as Mr. Boston's *Official Bartender's Guide* and Red Lobster Inns' *Eat to Win,* or are placing ads on the tapes for popular films, which help keep the price of the tapes down.

Aerial Banners and Lights

Banners carrying ad messages can be pulled by low-flying planes. After dark, traveling aerial lights can display messages of up to 90 characters. Slow-flying helicopters can also carry 40-by-80 signs lit by thousands of bulbs.

Blimps

Besides the familiar Goodyear blimp, you can now see blimps bearing messages for Citibank, Coca-Cola, and Fuji Film, among others. Computer-run lighting systems allow the blimps to advertise at night.

In-Flight Ads

Many airlines offer in-flight audio and video entertainment that is available for advertising. The travel industry and advertisers wanting to reach business fliers are the main purchasers of this type of ad.

Parking Meters

In Calgary, Alberta, or Baltimore, Maryland, you can't put money in a parking meter without seeing the signs on top advertising national products and local businesses. In development are solar-powered meters with liquid crystal displays for ad messages.

Electronic Billboards

Most modern sports stadiums and arenas have giant electronic displays on which ad space is sold.

Inflatables

Several companies are in the business of producing giant inflatable versions of beer cans, mascots, cereal boxes, and other items that can be used for advertising purposes.

Litter Receptacles

Some major cities offer ad space on concrete litter receptacles at major commercial intersections.

Taxicab Advertising

In addition to the familiar ads on the roofs and backs of taxis, some companies have taken to offering ad space inside, facing the riders. The most sophisticated system has an electronic message scrolling across a screen in the rider's view.

Milk Cartons

Government agencies and other noncommercial advertisers have used the sides of milk cartons to advertise issues deemed important to the public, such as missing children and immigration amnesty.

Laboratory Applications

1. What other off-the-wall media can you think of that are being used today?
2. How effective do you think off-the-wall media are for advertisers?

Characteristics of Media Audiences

When we speak of a medium's *audience,* we are referring to the total number of people reached by that medium. The media planner needs to know how many people are reached by a station or a publication to make a realistic judgment of that medium's potential effectiveness. Data on the size and characteristics of media audiences are readily available from a wide variety of media research organizations. Media vehicles often use these research findings about audience demographics to attract advertisers (see Figure 12–16).

In addition, the planner will want to know the degree of interest people have in the publication or program and how closely the characteristics of the medium's audience match the profile of the target market.

Readership and audience studies conducted by various media have yielded data that enable the media planner to determine how closely the audience characteristics match the profile of the target market prospects. For example, if the product is intended for tennis enthusiasts, it is essential that the medium selected be the one that reaches tennis players most efficiently. Such information is available from various media research organizations. Research data from the W. R. Simmons Company, for example, includes the age, income, occupational status, and other characteristics of a wide range of magazine readers. Simmons also publishes demographic and psychographic data on product usage among a varied group of consumers.

The *content* of a medium will also reflect the type of people in its audience. For instance, some radio stations emphasize in-depth news or sports; others, jazz or rock; and still others, symphonic music or operas. Each type of programming attracts a different audience, the character of which can be determined by analysis.

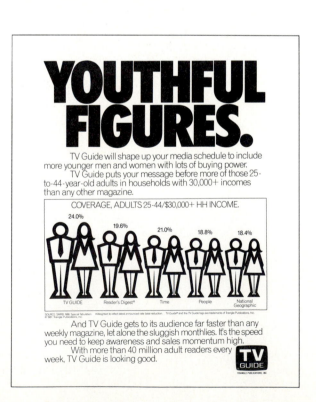

FIGURE   12–16

To attract advertisers, media vehicles promote favorable audience demographics. Here *TV Guide* touts the fact that it has a greater percentage of affluent consumers than several other big-circulation national magazines.

Geographic Coverage

The geographic coverage of a medium is often the determining factor in selection—there is no point in advertising to people who don't live in an area where the product or service is sold. Thus, airlines select media that cover the cities they serve and omit media that are circulated in other areas.

Since many national brands face tougher competition in certain regions than in others, extra advertising dollars are often concentrated in areas where competition is stiffer. Geographic considerations have also given rise to the popularity of regional editions of magazines, greater use of cable and spot TV instead of network TV, and the use of local media instead of national media for national advertisers.

Exposure, Attention, and Motivational Value

As we have already pointed out, the goal of the media planner is to match the right media with the target audience so that the advertisements not only achieve the desired *exposure* but also attract *attention* and *motivate* prospective customers to act. This task certainly is not easy, but it is made even more difficult by the fact that little reliable data have ever been developed to accurately measure the relative strength of one medium over another in terms of exposure, attention, or motivation values. However, these are still important issues that experienced media planners must consider every day.

Exposure To understand the concept of exposure, think in terms of how many people your ad "sees" rather than the other way around. If you place an advertisement in a magazine with 3 million readers, how many of those 3 million will your ad actually see? If a given television program has an audience of 10 million viewers, how many people will your commercial actually see?

The numbers are usually considerably less than the total audience or readership. Some people read only one article in a magazine, set it aside, and never pick it up again. Others thumb through every page with as much interest in the ads as in the articles. Many people watch television until the commercial, then change the channel or go to another room to get a snack. Thus, assessing the exposure value of one publication, radio station, or TV program over another is a very difficult task. And without statistics, it is up to the media planner to use his or her best judgment—based on experience.

The deputy director of media services at D'Arcy Massius Benton & Bowles has outlined five basic factors that can affect the probability of ad exposure:[14]

1. The senses required to perceive messages from the medium.
2. The amount and type of attention required by the medium.
3. Whether the medium is used as an information source or a diversion.
4. Whether the medium or program is aimed at a general audience or a targeted one.
5. The placement of the advertisement within the ad vehicle (within or between broadcast programs, adjacent to editorial material or other ads in print media).

Attention The degree of attention paid to ads by those exposed to them is another consideration. If you are not interested in motorcycles or cosmetics, you probably don't even notice ads for them when you do see them. On the other hand, if you are in the market for a new automobile, you probably notice every new-car ad you see.

Whereas exposure value relates only to the medium itself, attention value relates to the advertising message and copy just as much as to the medium. It is logical to assume that special-interest media, such as boating magazines, offer good attention value to a boating product. But what kind of attention value does the daily newspaper offer to a boating product? Will the boating enthusiast be thinking about a boat while reading the newspaper? These questions have no simple answers, and much research still needs to be done. But six factors have been found to positively affect the attention value of a medium:[15]

1. Audience involvement with editorial content or program material.
2. Specialization of audience interest or identification.
3. Number of competitive advertisers (the fewer, the better).
4. Audience familiarity with advertiser's campaign.
5. Quality of advertising reproduction.
6. Timeliness of advertising exposure.

Motivation These same factors affect a medium's motivation value. In some cases, though, they contribute more to motivation than to attention, and vice versa. For instance, familiarity with the advertiser's campaign may

---

PEOPLE IN ADVERTISING

Mark S. Oken

Senior Vice President and Media Director
The Bloom Agency

Media specialist Mark S. Oken is senior vice president and media director of The Bloom Agency in Dallas, Texas.

A graduate of Northwestern University, where he received a B.S. in business administration (accounting) in 1956, Oken went on to obtain an M.B.A. in marketing at the University of Michigan.

He launched his career in advertising as a media buyer for Kenyon & Eckhardt. Four years later, Oken joined Needham, Louis & Brorby as a time buyer. He moved to Foote, Cone & Belding in 1963 as manager of network facilities. Within four years, Oken became media supervisor at Needham Harper & Steers. In 1971, he was named senior vice president and media director of The Bloom Agency, whose clients include Nestlé Foods, Zales Jewelers, Frontier Airlines, and Alfa Romeo. The agency, which has more than doubled in size during the past five years, today has over 300 employees and annual billings of nearly $200 million.

The growing success of The Bloom Agency, according to Oken, is due in part to the fact that it performs media planning and selection for its clients not on the traditional 15 percent commission basis, as most agencies do, but on a fee basis. "This fee system," Oken reports, "has proven to

affect attention significantly but motivation very little. On the other hand, good-quality reproduction and timeliness can be very motivating to someone interested in the product (see Figure 12–17). Therefore, attention value and motivation value should be considered separately when assessing alternative media.

One method media planners use to analyze these values is to assign a specific numerical value to their subjective assessment of a medium's various strengths and weaknesses. Then, using either a simple or complex weighting formula, they basically just add them up. Similar weighting methods are used for evaluating other considerations, such as the relative importance of age demographics against income characteristics.

Cost Efficiency

The final step in determining what media to select is to analyze the cost efficiency of each medium available. A common term used in media buying is *CPM, or cost per thousand.* For example, if a daily newspaper has 300,000 subscribers and charges $5,000 for a full-page ad, then the cost per thousand is calculated as:

$$CPM = \$5,000 \div 300 = \$16.67$$

A weekly newspaper with a circulation of 250,000 that charges $3,000 for a full page would promote itself as less expensive because its cost per thousand would be considerably less:

$$CPM = \$3,000 \div 250 = \$12.00$$

make our media services for clients much more effective. It motivates better work," he explains, "and puts the emphasis in our work where the client wants it."

Oken also believes that the fee formula affords the agency greater flexibility in its approach to clients' media goals. For media people, he notes, the fee system "provides greater freedom to examine overall marketing objectives—and to offer useful suggestions for achieving them that might not otherwise be possible." These suggestions, says Oken, "might even recommend against media spending. We might urge heavier consumer or trade promotional activity instead." And where media use is indicated, Oken observes, "the fee system enables the agency to recommend certain unique types of media that might not be profitable for the agency were it compensated solely by media commissions."

Clients can help to make their agencies' media services even more effective, says Oken, by observing the following practices:

1. Formulate specific, realistic media objectives.
2. Share important data with your agency's media staff, and

include sales, budget, product development, and brand performance information.
3. Permit innovative media planning.
4. Be willing to look beyond "media numbers" to achieve more productive media plans.
5. Discuss and make media decisions with your agency rather than deviating from the plan or superseding it arbitrarily.
6. Avoid last-minute media buys or changes that can undermine the effectiveness of your media program.
7. Don't be drawn in by "bargain" buys that usually are not efficient.
8. Ask your agency to show you and your personnel how to understand and evaluate its media recommendations.

Oken is a frequent contributor to media trade publications and a member of the Newspaper Committee of the American Association of Advertising Agencies. He is active in numerous organizations and serves on the board of directors of the Advertisers Club, Chicago; the Association of Broadcast Executives of Texas; and the Dallas Advertising League.

FIGURE   12–17

This Yamaha guitar ad ran in *Rolling Stone*. The advertiser chose a medium that was not only likely to reach present or future guitar players but was able to give quality reproduction to attract readers in the market for an electric guitar.

However, media planners are normally more interested in the *cost efficiency* of reaching the target audience, not the cost of reaching the medium's total circulation. Thus, if the target audience is males ages 18–49 and 40 percent (100,000) of the weekly newspaper's readers fit in this category, the CPM will actually be $30 ($3,000 ÷ 100) to reach this target audience. The daily newspaper might turn out to be more cost-efficient if 60 percent of its readers (180,000) belong to the target audience: $5,000 ÷ 180 = $27.78 CPM.

The media planner must evaluate all the criteria to determine (1) how much of each medium's audience matches the target audience, (2) how each medium satisfies the needs of the campaign's objectives and strategy, and (3) how well each medium measures up in attention, exposure, and motivation value. After such an evaluation the planner can decide whether the daily or weekly newspaper is a better buy.

Selection Approaches

In our analysis of media efficiency, we may discover that several media are attractive to use because each contains a segment of prospects for our product. In other words, the best strategy is a *media mix*. The reasons for using a media mix include the following:

1. To reach people not reached with only one medium.
2. To provide additional repeat exposure in a less expensive secondary medium after optimum reach is obtained in the first medium.
3. To utilize some of the intrinsic values of a medium to extend the creative effectiveness of the advertising campaign (such as music on radio or long copy in print media).
4. To deliver coupons in print media when the primary vehicle in the media plan is broadcast.
5. To produce synergism, an effect achieved when the sum of the parts is greater than that expected by adding the individual parts.[16] An example of a synergistic media mix is presented in Figure 12–18.

When creating the media mix, the question arises: How do we reach the greatest number of prospects?

(SFX: CAR RADIO)

SONG: Whatever happened . . . to real food?

You know, the kind that just tastes real good.

Don't want a dinner I can't pronounce . . . I wanna order mine by the ounce.

Whatever happened . . . to real food?

You know, the kind that just tastes real good.

Give me a steak and I won't be blue.

I've got a taste for some real food.

VO ANNCR: Beef. Real food for real people. Sponsored by the Beef Industry Council and Beef Board.

FIGURE   12–18

The Beef Council developed separate campaigns for print and broadcast media, producing a synergistic media mix. The print campaign emphasizes the health aspects of beef, offering nutritional information to combat negative public conceptions about beef. The broadcast campaign has featured James Garner and Cybill Shepherd giving testimonials to the great taste of beef. Both campaigns are tied together with the "Real Food for Real People" slogan.

One consideration might be to use a *broadside approach,* sending an equal number of messages through each medium and hoping for the best. Another approach, called *profile matching,* might be to split up the media schedule so that the messages are delivered to each audience segment in proportion to that segment's importance among all prospects. This would probably result in greater reach than the broadside approach. The third method would be to work the various market segments as a gold miner works several claims—start with the richest claim first. This method, called the *high-assay principle,* suggests starting with the medium that produces the best return and then moving to other media only when the first becomes unavailable or loses its effectiveness. Unless prospects can be individually identified, this is the best method to maximize reach.[17] When the rate of return (added new reach) of the one medium falls below the potential rate of return from another, it is time to switch or add other media.

These principles are very important for the media planner to understand. However, they are also highly theoretical and based on extremely simple hypothetical cases. In the real world, many factors complicate the process. Cost factors must be considered. It is very difficult to weigh the actual sales potential of given market segments. And combination effects of media overlapping from the advertiser's media schedule produce distorted figures that make accurate measurement of results difficult. However, if the objective is to reach the most prospects, it is better to go with the media with the largest audiences and the greatest number of prospects for concentrated scheduling.[18] If the objective is higher frequency, it is better to select several media vehicles with smaller audiences.

Scheduling Criteria

After selecting the media vehicles to use, the media planner must decide how many of each media vehicle's space or time units should be bought and over what period of time these units should be used.

Types of Schedules

Many kinds of schedules are in use today. The following are the six basic types most commonly used:[19]

1. *Steady.* These are the easiest types of schedules to prepare: one ad per week for 52 weeks or one ad per month for 12 months.
2. *Seasonal pulse.* Seasonal buying patterns dictate heavy media use during peak selling periods (see Figure 12–19).
3. *Periodic pulse.* Media pulses are scheduled at regular intervals unrelated to the seasons of the year.
4. *Erratic pulse.* Spacing advertising at irregular intervals is used to try to effect changes in typical purchase cycles.
5. *Start-up pulse.* This pattern is designed to start off a campaign with a bang; it is commonly seen every fall when the new automobile models are introduced and almost always used to introduce a new product.
6. *Promotional pulse.* This schedule is designed to support some special promotion of the manufacturer so buying will be heavier during the time of the promotion than at other times.

As we can see, pulsing or flighting of some form characterizes all but

Change your view of winter.

Larger door. Less to saw. More to see. Heat fins. Radiating faster. Cast iron. Radiating longer. Masport. No other fire measures up.

Masport HEATING

FIGURE   12–19

Some products are given their great-est advertising thrust in particular seasons of the year, when consum-ers are most likely to buy. This ad for Masport Woodfires appeared in New Zealand publications as winter was approaching.

the simplest media schedules, and the degree of continuity (or pulsing) is a function of the media strategy. Therefore, at the time of preparing the actual schedule, the wise media planner will review the strategy section of the media plan to be sure the final schedule actually reflects what was originally intended.

Determining Reach, Frequency, and Continuity

It is up to the media planner to determine the right combination of reach, frequency, and continuity, keeping in mind these basic findings of re-search:

1. Continuity is important because advertising is often quickly forgotten when consumers are not continually exposed to it. In most cases, it is a waste of money for advertisers to run an ad one week, wait six weeks, and then run another ad. To achieve continuity requires committing dollars over some continuous period of time.
2. Repeated exposures are needed to impress a message on the memories of a large proportion of consumers. The advertiser who runs only four or five radio spots per week gives up so much frequency (usually for the sake of continuity) as to make the schedule almost worthless.
3. As the number of exposures increases, both the number of persons who remember it and the length of time they remember it increase. This is why so many media planners believe frequency is the most important media objective. It's the key to remembering.
4. An intensive "burst" of advertising is more likely to cause a very large

number of people to remember it, at least for a short time, than is spreading a schedule thinly over a 12-month period. This is the most common strategy for building frequency on a limited budget and the rationale behind pulsing advertising schedules.

5. Fewer exposures per prospect in a comparatively large group promote greater memory of the advertising than do more exposures per prospect in a smaller group. In other words, there's a point at which reach becomes more important than frequency in promoting memory.

6. As additional exposures per prospect are purchased, the dollar efficiency of advertising decreases. At some point, therefore, it is again more important to seek reach rather than additional frequency.

The Use of Computers in Media Selection and Scheduling

Computers have been an important part of media planning since the early 1970s. They can eliminate much of the drudgery of planning by performing the tedious "number crunching" needed to arrive at GRPs, CPMs, reach, frequency, and so on. They can also be used to construct media schedules, to evaluate various media vehicles geared to the target market, to cross-tabulate demographic data (such as the age and income of light, medium, and heavy users of a product), and to assess the cost efficiency of alternative media plans. Does this mean, then, that human media planners will soon be replaced by computers?

To answer that question, we need to know what computers can and can't do. What they *can* do is manipulate numbers. Fed data on the audience demographics of radio stations in Pittsburgh, for example, a computer can rank the stations in relation to how their audience profile most closely fits a product's target audience profile. Fed information on the Pittsburgh stations' ad rates, ratings, and so on, the computer can produce several alternate radio advertising schedules that fit within the ad budget. As each radio buy is made, the computer can keep track of how much of the budget has been spent, the percentage of the budget spent to reach the primary demographic group, the cost per ratings point, and the CPM by daypart. All these activities certainly make the media planner's job easier. And that's not all computers are used for.

Three main types of computer programs have been developed for use in media planning. One of the oldest types is the *linear programming model,* designed to create a complete media schedule that maximizes exposure within a given budget. Although this type of program would indeed replace many of the traditional functions of the media planner, a fully practical linear model has yet to be developed, simply because there are too many real-world variables that such programs are unable to take into account.[20] A second type of program is the *simulation model,* used to estimate the ability of already chosen media vehicles to reach target individuals within an audience. Simulation programs do not plan media schedules, but they are useful in evaluating individual vehicles in terms of target audience, cost efficiency, and so on. Specialized simulation models have also been developed for such purposes as calculating the optimum timing of an ad campaign. Finally, *formula models* calculate reach, frequency, and other statistics for alternative media vehicles and can rank the vehicles according to selected parameters: which offer the best reach, the best frequency, and so on. With any of these models, the computer instantly recalculates results whenever an assumption or factor is changed.

Since the advent of microcomputers in the early 1980s, software programs for media planning have proliferated, developed not only by software companies but also by ad agencies and by marketing or ad departments within companies. Some of these programs are highly customized, such as J. Walter Thompson U.S.A.'s special program for 20th Century Fox to help that movie company plan newspaper buys as it introduces films in various markets. Others are for general use in the advertising industry, such as Media Management Plus, a set of programs for planning, buying, and managing all forms of advertising media (see Figure 12–20).

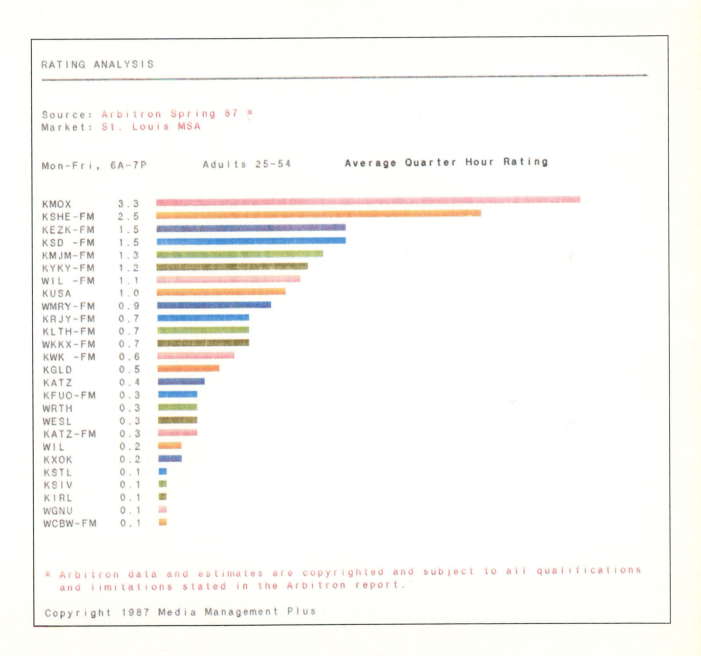

FIGURE   12–20

Example of the type of computer data (in this case, radio ratings) supplied by the Media Management Plus software system. This system can be used to analyze various media vehicles and then to plan media buys.

Another major change that has occurred with the increasing use of microcomputers (80 percent of ad agency media departments now have them) is the form in which media planners receive and keep data (audience demographics, broadcast ratings, readership statistics, etc.). In the past, ad agencies used computer terminals plugged into huge mainframe computers to gain access to such data provided by various research services. Now microcomputer users have a choice of going "on-line" and paying for access to giant databases or subscribing to services that provide data in the form of hard disks or floppy disks.

The problem for ad agencies is to make the best use of all this computerized data. Which brings us to the issue of what computers *cannot* do. They cannot decide which medium or which environment is best for the message. "Gray areas are a problem with the computer," notes William F. Bondlow, Jr., publisher of *House & Garden* magazine. "And to my knowledge, computers do not know how to evaluate the content of a magazine yet."[21] Computers can manipulate numbers, but they cannot judge whether the numbers they are fed are valid or reliable, and they cannot interpret the meaning of the numbers. Thus, computers can aid in the planning process, but they cannot take the place of human planners, at least as long as subjective judgment is an important part of the process.

Summary

The decisions made by media planners frequently involve as much creativity as the decisions made by art directors and copywriters. And like good art and copy ideas, media decisions should be based on sound marketing principles and research, not just on experience and intuition.

The media function involves two basic processes: media planning and media selection. Media planning begins by determining primary target audiences and then setting goals or objectives for communicating with those audiences. Media objectives may be expressed in terms of reach, frequency, impressions, gross rating points, and continuity.

In developing the appropriate media strategy, the planner must consider many variables, including the geographic scope, the nature of the medium and the message, consumer purchase patterns, mechanical limitations of the media, and competitive strategy.

After the media strategy is developed, the task of selecting specific media vehicles begins. Numerous factors influence the selection process: (1) campaign objectives and strategy; (2) the size and characteristics of each medium's audience; (3) geographic coverage; (4) the attention, exposure, and motivation value of each medium; (5) cost efficiency; and (6) the intended selection approach, including the media mix.

Once the particular media vehicles have been selected, the problem of how to schedule their use arises; that is, how many of each medium's space or time units should be bought over what period of time? There are many ways to schedule a media campaign, from steady, continuous advertising to erratic pulses of commercials. This decision is usually a function of the media strategy.

The final result must be a logical weighting of reach, frequency, and continuity to maximize the effectiveness of the campaign and the efficiency of dollars spent.

Questions for Review and Discussion

1. What are the major factors contributing to the increased complexity of media planning?
2. What must the media planner take into consideration before planning can begin?
3. How might the media objectives for the Canon AE-1 have been expressed?
4. What is the rule of thumb for determining the "right" frequency for a given message?
5. What is the difference between GRPs and CPMs? How is each calculated?
6. What major factors influence the choice of general advertising media?
7. What major factors influence the choice of individual media vehicles?
8. How might Canon have taken into account exposure, attention, and motivational value in choosing media for its AE-1 campaign? For its T-90 campaign?
9. What are the differences among the following media selection approaches: (a) broadside approach, (b) profile matching, and (c) high-assay principle?
10. What are the six basic types of media schedules? Give details on how each is used.

13

PRINT MEDIA

I f records were kept for creating the most successful newspaper campaign in the least time and for the least money, a campaign for a Minneapolis haircutting salon, 7 South 8th for Hair, might well hold the world title.

"This was a very easy campaign to create, really painless," says Jarl Olsen, the copywriter at Fallon McElligott. "The whole thing took less than a day to plan."

The campaign ran in local newspapers because of their ability to reach a large audience quickly at reasonable cost. Newspapers were also best for getting across the simple, straightforward message planned for the campaign.

"We wanted to generate some talk value, so we used something that everyone could laugh at." The instructions from the client were sparse; the only requirement was that the salon's name be on the ads. "We were all over the board," says Olsen, "and all of the ideas were weird."

Random scrawlings eventually led to the ad shown in Figure 13–1, featuring the snaked-haired Medusa. "We sat around trying to think of bad haircuts," Olsen recalls with a laugh. "We thought of several, but we could only think of a few copy lines that made any sense." The rest of the campaign was the result of spin-offs of that original idea.

The ads consisted of stock photos of famous bad haircuts, a witty line of copy, and the client's name and address. They appeared all over Minneapolis newspapers and later in local magazines and on posters. The campaign took the city by storm.

"These ads were everywhere," says Olsen, "and everyone was talking about them. Other shops were cutting the ads out and sticking their own logos on them. I called 7 South 8th to tell them about it. They laughed and said they knew. They thought it was funny."[1]

USING NEWSPAPERS IN THE CREATIVE MIX

Advertising people are constantly looking for *creative* solutions to their clients' marketing problems, as we pointed out in Chapter 7. However, many factors besides advertising creativity are involved in sales: the product, value offered, price, availability, competitive pressures, timing, and even the weather. Nevertheless, creative advertising can give the advertiser a chance to be heard, to present an offer. A fresh creative approach can do that superbly.

The printed page in general and the newspaper in particular provide a unique, flexible medium for the maker of advertising to express this creativity. Although in the mid-1980s, advertisers seemed to have been lured increasingly away from the print media in favor of the glamour of the electronic media, a disenchantment with TV advertising clutter and cost is bringing many advertisers back to the print fold.[2] And newspapers and magazines are encouraging this return by offering a number of new services, both in the production of quality ads and in the use of marketing techniques, to ensure that the ads will reach the targeted audience.

Advantages of Newspapers

Newspapers have inherent features that have traditionally set them apart from other media.[3] For example:

1. Newspapers are a *mass* medium, penetrating every segment of society. They are read by almost everybody who can reasonably be thought of as a consumer.
2. Newspapers are a *local* medium, covering a specific geographic area that comprises both a market and a community of people sharing common concerns and interests.
3. Newspapers are *comprehensive* in scope, covering an extraordinary variety of topics and interests.
4. Newspapers are read *selectively* as readers search for what is personally interesting and useful.
5. Newspapers are *timely* since they are primarily devoted to the news.
6. Newspaper readership is *concentrated* in time. Virtually all the reading of a particular day's paper is done that day.
7. Newspapers represent a *permanent* record that people use actively. The advertiser's printed message stands still for rereading and reconsideration, for clipping, and for sharing.

Newspaper advertising also has credibility. Studies have found that newspaper ads rank highest in believability over other kinds of ads; in fact, one survey showed that some 42 percent of respondents considered newspaper ads to be the most believable; TV ads came in a distant second, with only 26 percent ranking them as most believable.[4]

These features give rise to a number of special attributes of newspapers that offer clues to the ad maker who is seeking what will work best creatively:

FIGURE   13–1

Newspaper ads for 7 South 8th for Hair, a Minneapolis hair salon, consisted of stock photos of "bad haircuts" with a witty headline. This inexpensive-to-produce campaign was highly successful.

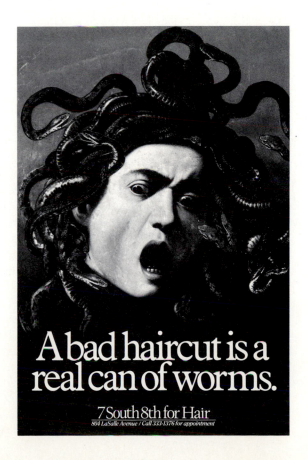

A bad haircut is a real can of worms.

7 South 8th for Hair
804 LaSalle Avenue / Call 333-1376 for appointment

FIGURE   13–2

FIGURE   13–2

A house-painting firm used the color capabilities of St. Paul, Minnesota, newspapers to add an eye-catching splash to its ads. The ads also cleverly played on the fact that people often use newspapers to catch stray drops when they paint.

1. Newspapers provide the opportunity for massive same-day exposure of an advertising message to a large cross section of any market. That means very broad *reach*.

2. Newspapers combine broad reach with highly *selective attention* from the very small number of active prospects who, on any given day, are interested in what the advertiser is trying to tell them or sell them.

3. Newspapers provide great creative flexibility to the advertiser. The ad's physical size and shape can be chosen and varied to give the degree of dominance or repetition that suits the advertiser's purpose. The advertiser can use black-and-white, color, Sunday magazines, or custom inserts (see Figure 13–2). The newspaper, therefore, is almost a media mix by itself.

4. With newspapers, the advertiser can go where the customers are. That may mean concentrating the messages in one market or spreading them out over a national schedule. It may mean running the ad in one part of the paper, in several sections, or just in certain demographic areas served by a single paper. The national advertiser can place ads on short notice, localize copy, and work with retailers by using co-op programs.

5. The newspaper is an active medium rather than a passive one. Readers turn the pages, clip and save, write in the margins, and sort through the contents, screening out what they don't want from those things they want to concentrate on. This reader-involving quality of newspapers offers unlimited creative opportunities to advertisers.

Some Drawbacks to Newspapers

While newspapers offer many advantages, like all media, they also have their drawbacks.

Newspapers enable advertisers to be *geographically selective,* but they do not isolate and cover specific socioeconomic groups. Instead, most newspapers reach broad, diverse groups of readers. The desires and needs of these broad groups may not be compatible with the marketing segmentation objectives of the advertiser. For example, a newspaper sports section may be a good place to advertise general sports products or services, such as surfboards or football tickets, but it would be highly inefficient for advertising sports products to retail sporting goods dealers because of the tremendous waste of circulation.

A second disadvantage is the short *life span* of a daily newspaper. Unless a reader clips and saves a newspaper ad or coupon, it may be lost forever.

In addition, newspapers lack *production quality;* there is no time to use high-quality reproduction techniques, and the coarse paper used for newspapers generally creates a finished product far less impressive than can be achieved with magazines that have slick, smooth paper stock. Moreover, many large metropolitan newspapers, including *The New York Times,* are not equipped for run-of-press color printing (color throughout the whole paper), and those that do have color capabilities have yet to match the quality of color printing readers are used to seeing in magazines.[5]

Another drawback is that each ad *competes for notice* with every other ad on the same page or spread. So many advertisements appear in a single issue of a newspaper (63 percent of the average daily paper) that the potential for any one ad to capture major attention is minimized. A related problem is that unless advertisers pay a premium rate for special placement, they have no control over where in the paper their ad will run.

Finally, many areas are served by newspapers that have *overlapping circulation;* that is, some residents read not one, but two or more different newspapers. Thus, advertisers may be paying for circulation that their ads have already reached in a different newspaper.

Newspapers are trying to overcome some of these shortcomings by providing special services to advertisers. For example, many papers offer "zoned" editions that go to specific neighborhoods or regions of the market area and are doing extensive market research to help link advertisers with their target audience. They are also attempting to broaden their own audience appeal by including material of interest to certain demographic segments of their market area and by changing their focus to adapt to changing lifestyles.

Who Uses Newspapers?

Newspapers are the nation's dominant medium in terms of advertising volume, receiving more than 26 percent of the dollars spent by the nation's advertisers. In 1986, newspapers derived an estimated $27 billion from advertising revenues.[6]

Consider these important facts:

1. Daily papers are read by more than 108 million American adults each weekday. Nearly two out of three Americans read a paper every day.

FIGURE 13-3		Top 10 newspaper advertisers
Rank	**Advertiser**	**Newspaper ad expenditures 1986**
1	General Motors Corp.	$146,430*
2	Ford Motor Co.	76,136
3	Texas Air Corp.	63,417
4	Philip Morris Cos.	57,590
5	RJR Nabisco	50,347
6	Chrysler Corp.	42,203
7	American Telephone & Telegraph	31,106
8	Trans World Airlines	29,329
9	General Electric Co.	26,987
10	Allegis Corp.	26,900

*Dollars are in thousands.

2. The typical daily newspaper reader spends an average of 44 minutes a day reading one or more newspapers. One-fifth of all newspaper readers read more than one newspaper every day.
3. An average of 2.2 persons read each of the 63 million daily papers circulated in the United States each day.
4. In 1986, there were 1,657 daily newspapers in the United States with a total circulation of 62.7 million. The nation's 7,419 weekly newspapers have a combined circulation of nearly 77 million.
5. U.S. advertising volume in newspapers increased by more than 7 percent in 1986, with total sales of nearly $27 billion—$4.4 billion more than its nearest competitor.[7]

Although the newspaper is the major community-serving medium for both news and advertising, the huge growth of radio and television over the past 20 years has caused more and more national advertising to be shifted to these electronic media. The result is that radio and television today carry most of the national advertising, while 87 percent of newspaper advertising revenue comes from local advertising. The major national advertisers in newspapers are automobile manufacturers, tobacco companies, and airlines (see Figure 13–3).

How Newspapers Are Categorized

Newspapers may be classified by their frequency of delivery, by their physical size, or by the type of audience they reach.

Frequency of Delivery

The two basic types of newspapers are *dailies* and *weeklies*. Dailies are published at least five times a week, Monday through Friday.

Dailies are produced as either morning or evening editions. Of the 1,676 dailies in the United States, 1,194 are evening papers, 456 are morning papers, and 26 are "all-day" newspapers.[8] Morning editions tend to have a broader geographic circulation and a larger male readership, while evening editions are read more by women. Despite these broad characteristics, each daily newspaper has its own circulation traits, determined chiefly by the geographic region it serves and the demographic makeup of its readers.

Weekly newspapers characteristically serve readers in small urban or suburban areas or farm communities. Recently, this has become the fastest-growing class of newspapers, due in part to its exclusive emphasis on local news and advertising. Weekly newspapers offer their readers relief from unsettling national and international crises in the form of familiar names, news of local personalities, and hometown sports, entertainment, and social coverage.

The weekly newspaper usually offers advertisers a high degree of readership but at a cost per thousand that is often higher than that of the daily paper. This higher rate may be justified, however, as the weekly has a longer life than the daily and is often exposed to more readers per copy.

Physical Size

The two basic newspaper formats are standard and tabloid. The *standard-size newspaper* is about 22 inches deep and 13 inches wide and is divided into six 2 1/16 inch columns. The *tabloid newspaper* is generally about half the size of a standard-size newspaper, about 14 inches deep and 11 inches wide. Three national tabloid newspapers, all fighting with sensational news stories for single-copy sales through grocery supermarkets across the country, are the *National Enquirer, The Star,* and the *Globe.* In contrast, other national tabloids, such as the *New York Daily News,* emphasize "straight" news and features.

Prior to 1984, placing ads in papers across the country was a complex task because papers varied greatly in their widths, number of columns, and methods of calculating ad space. But 1984 saw the initiation of a new *standard advertising unit (SAU) system* that has changed all that. This system uses inches, not the old system of lines or "agate lines," as the main unit of measure, and standardizes both page sizes and ad sizes (see Figure 13–4). There are now 56 standard ad sizes for standard papers and 32 sizes for tabloids, instead of the 400 or so different sizes used previously. Estimates are that 99 percent of all dailies have already converted to the SAU system (some at great expense), with the remaining 1 percent planning to convert as well.[9] Only about half of the weekly papers have adopted the SAUs, however.

Specialized Audience

Some dailies and weeklies are aimed at particular special-interest audiences. Their specialized news and features enable them to achieve high readership. They generally contain advertising oriented to their special audiences, and they may have unique advertising regulations.

Among these newspapers, for example, are those that specifically serve black readers. Today, more than 200 dailies and weeklies, such as the Ft. Worth, Texas, *Times* and the New York *Amsterdam News,* are oriented to blacks. Still other specialized papers serve foreign-language ethnic groups,

Figure   13–4

Standard Advertising Units (SAUs).

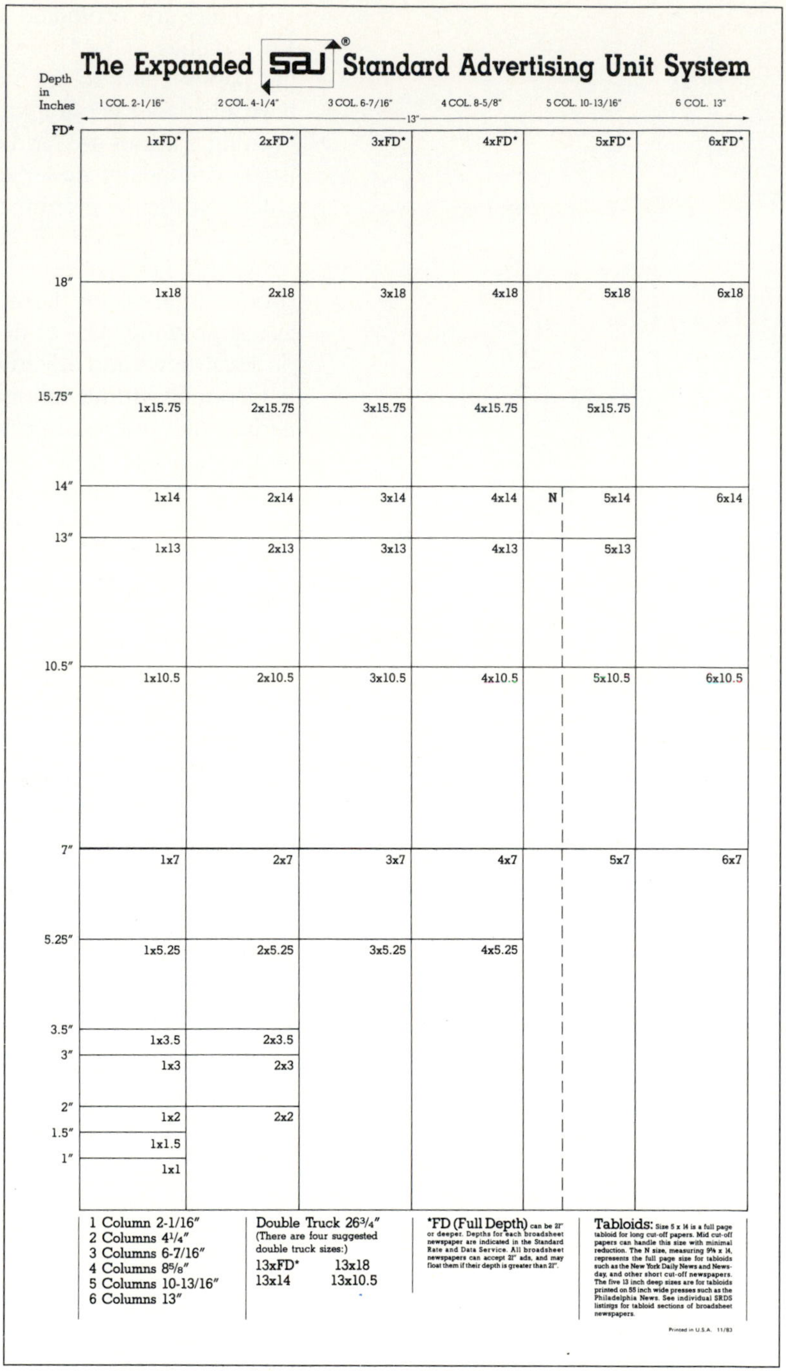

The Expanded SAU® Standard Advertising Unit System

Depth in Inches

Depth	1 COL. 2-1/16"	2 COL. 4-1/4"	3 COL. 6-7/16"	4 COL. 8-5/8"	5 COL. 10-13/16"	6 COL. 13"
FD*	1xFD*	2xFD*	3xFD*	4xFD*	5xFD*	6xFD*
18"	1x18	2x18	3x18	4x18	5x18	6x18
15.75"	1x15.75	2x15.75	3x15.75	4x15.75	5x15.75	
14"	1x14	2x14	3x14	4x14 N	5x14	6x14
13"	1x13	2x13	3x13	4x13	5x13	
10.5"	1x10.5	2x10.5	3x10.5	4x10.5	5x10.5	6x10.5
7"	1x7	2x7	3x7	4x7	5x7	6x7
5.25"	1x5.25	2x5.25	3x5.25	4x5.25		
3.5"	1x3.5	2x3.5				
3"	1x3	2x3				
2"	1x2	2x2				
1.5"	1x1.5					
1"	1x1					

1 Column 2-1/16"
2 Columns 4-1/4"
3 Columns 6-7/16"
4 Columns 8⅝"
5 Columns 10-13/16"
6 Columns 13"

Double Truck 26¾" (There are four suggested double truck sizes:)
13xFD*   13x18
13x14   13x10.5

*FD (Full Depth) can be 21" or deeper. Depths for each broadsheet newspaper are indicated in the Standard Rate and Data Service. All broadsheet newspapers can accept 21" ads, and may float them if their depth is greater than 21".

Tabloids: Size 5 x 14 is a full page tabloid for long cut-off papers. Mid cut-off papers can handle this size with minimal reduction. The N size, measuring 9¾ x 14, represents the full page size for tabloids such as the New York Daily News and News-day, and other short cut-off newspapers. The five 13 inch deep sizes are for tabloids printed on 55 inch wide presses such as the Philadelphia News. See individual SRDS listings for tabloid sections of broadsheet newspapers.

Printed in U.S.A. 11/82

such as Spanish, German, Polish, Chinese, or Armenian readers. The United States has ethnic newspapers published in 43 languages other than English.

Specialized newspapers are also produced for business and financial audiences. *The Wall Street Journal* is the leading national business and financial daily, with a circulation of nearly 2 million. Other papers are published for fraternal, labor union, or professional organizations, religious groups, or hobbyists. Some weekly newspapers are put out just for stamp and coin collectors, for example.

Daily and Sunday European and Pacific editions of the leading U.S. military newspaper, *Stars and Stripes,* are read by more than 1 million overseas armed services personnel.

Other Types of Newspapers

There are nearly 800 Sunday newspapers, mostly Sunday editions of daily papers, with a combined circulation of 58.8 million.[10] Sunday newspapers generally combine standard news coverage with their own special functions, which include the following:

1. Much greater classified advertising volume.
2. Much greater advertising and news volume.
3. In-depth coverage of developments in the arts, business, sports, housing, entertainment, and travel.
4. Review and analysis of the past week's events.

Most Sunday newspapers also feature a newspaper-distributed magazine, or *Sunday supplement.* Some publish their own supplement, such as the *Los Angeles Times*'s "Home" magazine. The remaining newspapers subscribe to syndicated magazine supplements, which are compiled, edited, and printed by a central organization and then shipped to individual newspapers for insertion in their Sunday editions.

Sunday supplements are distinct from other sections of the newspaper since they are printed by rotogravure on smoother paper stock. This heavier, higher-quality paper is more conducive to quality color printing, enabling Sunday supplements to attract and feature higher-quality national advertising.

Another type of newspaper is the independent shopping guide or free community newspaper. Sometimes called pennysavers or shoppers, most newspapers of this type carry little news and practically no features. Instead, they are distributed free and are filled with advertising aimed at essentially the same audience as the weekly newspapers—urban and suburban community readers. Shoppers may be published weekly, biweekly, or monthly. Readership is generally high, and the publisher strives to achieve maximum saturation of the circulation area. A study of one chain of shoppers in the Long Island, New York, area found, for example, that 83 percent of those receiving the papers read them regularly, and 91 percent said these papers give them information they couldn't get from other newspapers.[11]

There are also a handful of national newspapers, including *USA Today* and the *Christian Science Monitor.* Since its debut in September 1982, *USA Today* has achieved a circulation of more than 1.3 million, making it second only to *The Wall Street Journal* in national distribution and first among general interest dailies, surpassing the *New York Daily News.* In mid-1986, *USA Today* became the number-one print vehicle for automotive ads.[12] The newspaper also has a distinctive look that savvy advertisers take advantage of (see Figure 13–5).

Types of Newspaper Advertising

The major classifications of newspaper advertising are display, classified, public notices, and preprinted inserts.

FIGURE   13–5

Procter & Gamble's special insert to *USA Today* demonstrates how an ad message can be created to fit a specific media vehicle. The design of the ad insert is based on the distinctive *USA Today* look but is not a direct copy.

Display Advertising

The size of display advertising varies. Display ads are featured in all areas of the newspaper except on page one, the editorial page, the obituary page, the first page of major sections, and the classified section.

The two principal types of display advertising are *local* and *general* (national). About 87 percent of all newspaper display advertising is local, and the largest source of newspaper display revenue is local retail merchants (see Figure 13–6).

Most newspapers charge the local advertiser and the national advertiser different rates. The national rate averages 60 percent higher than the local rate, with some papers charging as much as 160–180 percent more for national ads.[13] Newspapers attribute these higher national rates to the added costs they incur in serving national advertisers. For instance, they point out that this advertising is usually placed by an advertising agency to which the newspaper gives a 15 percent commission. Some newspapers serve these agencies through media representatives, to whom they must

FIGURE   13–6

Local retail ads make up the lion's share of newspaper display advertising. This appealing ad is one of a series done for Country Cottage by the Fallon McElligott agency, which also did the 7 South 8th for Hair campaign described at the opening of this chapter.

also pay a commission. If the advertising comes from another city or state, still other costs are involved. Therefore, publishers feel the higher national rates are justified.

This dual rate system has been controversial among advertisers, particularly since the rate differential is at an all-time high. In fact, national advertisers appear to be actively rebelling against the high rates and are taking their business elsewhere—only about 6 percent of national ad dollars are going to newspapers, and that proportion may shrink even further.[14] In response to declining national ads, newspapers began experimenting with national discount rates in the summer of 1987. At that time, a group of 258 papers banded together to offer packaged goods advertisers an average 30 percent discount on orders of a quarter page or larger size that are run 13 times. This special rate was still 25 percent above local rates but lower than the usual 60 percent differential.[15] Smaller groups of papers have also joined forces to test other types of discount plans to see whether they can lure back national accounts.

Display ads can be black-and-white, multicolored, or full colored, with or without pictures. Most local display advertising is either black-and-white or some basic colors printed directly on the newspaper. In contrast, much national advertising is preprinted on magazine-supplement–type paper and fills an entire page. The opposite side of the page may then be left for the newspaper to use.

One common variation of the display ad, the *reading notice,* looks like editorial matter and is sometimes charged for at a higher space rate than normal display advertising. To prevent readers from mistaking it for editorial matter, the law requires that the word *advertisement* appear at the top of the reading notice. Many, but not all, newspapers accept reading notices.

Classified Advertising

Classified advertisements are a unique and important feature of newspapers. They provide a community marketplace for goods, services, and opportunities of every type, from real estate and new-car sales to employment openings and business proposals of major magnitude. They are also a significant source of ad revenues for papers. Such ads are usually arranged under subheads that describe the class of goods or the need the ads seek to satisfy. For example, you would look for a job under the classification "Help Wanted" and for an employee in the listings headed "Situations Wanted." Classified rates are based on the amount of space purchased and how long the ad is to run. Most employment, housing, and automotive advertising run today is in the form of classified advertising.

Some newspapers also accept classified display advertising. Such ads are run in the classified section of the newspaper and are generally characterized by larger-size type, photos, art borders, abundant white space, and sometimes even color.

Public Notices

For a nominal fee, newspapers will carry legal notices of changes in business and personal relationships, public governmental reports, notices by private citizens and organizations, and financial reports. These ads follow a preset format and thus require little creativity.

Preprinted Inserts

Preprinted inserts are inserted into the fold of the newspaper and look like a separate, smaller section of the paper. Printed by the advertiser, these inserts are delivered to the newspaper plant to be inserted into a specific edition either by machine or by the newscarriers. Sizes range from a typical newspaper page to a piece no larger than a double postcard, and formats include catalogs, brochures, mail-back devices, and perforated coupons.

A number of large metropolitan dailies allow advertisers to distribute their inserts to specific circulation zones only. A store that wants to reach shoppers in its immediate area only can place an insert in the local-zone editions. Retail stores, auto dealers, large national advertisers, and others have found it less costly to distribute their circulars in this manner than by mailing them or delivering them door-to-door.

HOW TO BUY NEWSPAPER SPACE

It is important that the media buyer and advertiser know the characteristics of a newspaper's readership—the median age, sex, occupation, income, educational level, and buying habits of the typical reader. Some of this readership information is available in standardized form from the

Simmons Market Research Bureau and Scarborough Research Corporation for 50 major markets, covering more than 150 dailies. In addition, most large papers can provide extensive readership data, including data on various geographic editions.

In single-newspaper cities, the demographic characteristics of readers are likely to reflect some cross section of the population as a whole. In cities with two or more newspapers, however, these characteristics may vary widely. Los Angeles, for example, is served by the *Los Angeles Times,* noted for its moderate political outlook, and the *Herald-Examiner,* considered politically conservative. Each newspaper has a different readership.

Readership is also determined by the time of day a newspaper is published. An advertiser, for example, may have to decide between advertising a bedding sale in a morning newspaper that has a 70 percent male readership or an evening newspaper read by equal numbers of men and women. Each alternative has its advantage. The morning paper can advertise the sale that day and attract immediate shoppers, and the evening paper can be read by husband and wife together and motivate them to come to the sale the following day. The advertiser must decide about these and other factors to determine the optimum timing and placement for the ad.

PEOPLE IN ADVERTISING

Rance Crain

President and Editorial Director
Crain Communications, Inc.

Publishers should stay "alert and aggressive—and not become smug or complacent," cautioned G. D. Crain, Jr., founder of Crain Communications, Inc. His son Rance listened. At 34, Rance Crain became president and editorial director of the Chicago-based firm that has produced some of the nation's leading trade publications for over half a century. One of them is the prestigious *Advertising Age,* which Rance Crain heads today as editor-in-chief.

Crain, whose college-boy appearance belies his 49 years, pursued an early interest in publishing by attending Northwestern University's Medill School of Journalism, from which he graduated in 1960. He soon became a reporter for the Washington bureau of *Advertising Age* and later went on to its New York and Chicago offices. In 1965, he was named senior editor of *Advertising Age* and the first editor of *Business Insurance.* Crain advanced to editorial director of *Advertising Age* in 1971. Two years later, after the death of his father, he became president and editorial director of Crain Communications, Inc.

Under Rance Crain's leadership, the company quickly embarked on an aggressive program of expansion. Within four years, *Advertising Age* had nearly doubled its circulation. The firm started *Pensions & Investments* and acquired *Rubber & Plastics News* and *Modern Healthcare.* It expanded into the consumer market with *AutoWeek* and

Reading Rate Cards

Newspapers provide potential advertisers with a printed information form called a *rate card* that lists the advertising rates, mechanical and copy requirements, advertising deadlines, and other information the advertiser needs to know. Because rates vary greatly from paper to paper, advertisers need to be able to calculate which papers are delivering the most readers for their money.

Flat Rates and Discount Rates

National advertisers, as noted earlier, are usually charged a higher rate than local advertisers. Local advertisers can sometimes earn even lower rates by buying large or repeated amounts of space at *volume discounts.* Such incentives are not offered by all newspapers, however. Many national papers charge *flat rates,* which means they allow no discounts for large or repeated space buys. And a few newspapers offer a single flat rate to both national and local advertisers.

Newspapers that offer the advertiser volume discounts have an *open*

---

other titles. In 1978, the company launched *Crain's Chicago Business* with Rance Crain as editor-in-chief and, two years later, *Crain's Cleveland Business.* Today, the firm publishes 26 titles, including *Automotive News* and *Business Marketing,* with editorial offices in nine U.S. cities, in Frankfurt, in Tokyo, and in London, where four publications are based. The family-owned company is run by Crain, his brother Keith, as vice chairman and the publisher of *Automotive News* and *AutoWeek,* and their mother, Gertrude Crain, as chairman of the board.

Rance Crain continues to be the idea man of the organization while dividing most of his time between his New York and Chicago offices. Despite administrative demands, Crain spends more than half his time as editor-in-chief of *Advertising Age,* personally overseeing myriad editorial and production details.

Advertising Age is the leading trade publication of the nation's advertising and marketing industries, a $25 million enterprise with 70 full-time reporters. Its international coverage is constantly expanding, and it now has 50 correspondents worldwide. It is widely read by persons in publishing and other allied fields. It's a slick, attractively illustrated weekly tabloid that reports the latest advertising and business news, including information on government actions that affect advertisers, agencies, media, and suppliers. Also covered are advertising campaigns for new and established products, as well as agency appointments and personnel changes.

Explaining his success, Crain says, "Change and growth have become a way of life in our company. My brother and I pride ourselves on our ability and willingness to constantly build on that philosophy, avoid stagnation, and keep pace with a world which is changing faster than ever before. We intend to keep up with it, and—if possible—to even anticipate it."

That anticipation, he notes, has resulted in *Electronic Media,* a publication for the broadcast industry started in 1982, and the 1984 acquisition of *Detroit Monthly,* a city magazine. The start-up of *Crain's New York Business* began in 1984, and *Crain's Detroit Business* began in 1985. *City & State,* Crain's newspaper of public business and finance, also began in 1985.

Crain is a past president of the Chicago Business Publications Association. He is on the business committee of the Metropolitan Museum of Art in New York, is a trustee of Emerson College in Boston, and is on the board of directors of the Museum of Broadcast Communications, Chicago.

The Boston Globe
135 Morrissey Blvd., Boston, MA 02107.
Phone 617-929-2000, TWX, 710-333-0294.

AD SAU
SAU
newsplan
DISCOUNTS FOR CONTINUITY
ABC Coupon Distribution Verification Service

Media Code 1 122 1125 5.00   Mid 016696-000
MORNING, SATURDAY AND SUNDAY MORNING.
Member: INAME; NAB, Inc; ABC Coupon Distribution Verification Service; ACB, Inc.

1. PERSONNEL
Publisher—Wm. O. Taylor.
V.P./Mktg. & Sales—Millard G. Owen.
Adv. Dir—John F. Reid, Jr.
Display Adv. Mgr.—Oliver H.P. Rodman.

2. REPRESENTATIVES and/or BRANCH OFFICES
Million Market Newspapers/Times Mirror National Marketing.
Canada—American Publishers' Representatives Ltd.
Europe—Colin Turner Group, LTD.

3. COMMISSION AND CASH DISCOUNT
15% agency discount: 2%—20th of following month.

4. POLICY-ALL CLASSIFICATIONS
30-day notice given of any rate revision.
Alcoholic beverage and cigarette advertising accepted.

ADVERTISING RATES
Effective July 1, 1987.
Received May 11, 1987.

5. BLACK/WHITE RATES

	Morn.	Sun.
SAU open, per inch	170.50	200.00

Saturday and/or Holidays will be billed at 90% of ads morning rate. Sunday as may repeat once within 6 days at 80.00 per col. inch, (same copy). Morning full rate ad may repeat once in the Daily paper within 6 days at 80.00 per col. inch, (same copy). Combination ad will count toward bulk contract.
Inches charged full depth: col. 21; pg. 126.

BULK CONTRACT RATES

	Morn.	Sun.
31"	168.25	198.00
63"	166.00	195.00
126"	162.00	189.50
250"	159.75	187.25
500"	157.50	186.25
750"	156.50	185.00
1,200"	155.50	184.00
1,600"	153.25	183.00
3,200"	150.00	182.00
6,500"	147.00	178.00
9,000"	145.00	175.00
12,500"	143.00	170.00
18,000"	141.00	166.00
25,000"	138.00	161.00
31,000"	135.00	157.00
38,000"	132.00	155.00
44,000"	129.00	153.00
50,000"	127.50	150.75
57,000"	125.50	148.75
66,000"	124.00	146.50
76,000"	122.50	144.50
85,000"	120.50	142.25

APPLICATION OF DISCOUNTS
Must be signed in advance to qualify for volume or frequency discounts. All advertising will be accumulated against the contract. Contracts not fulfilled will receive a short rate billing. A refund will be available if lower rate is earned. Ads will be rated at the contract level in each type or class of advertising.

NEWSPLAN—SAU

Pages	% Disc.	Morn.	Sun.	Inches
6	8.21	156.50	185.00	756
13	10.11	153.25	183.00	1,638
26	12.02	150.00	182.00	3,276
52	13.78	147.00	178.00	6,552
65	13.78	147.00	178.00	8,190
78	14.95	145.00	175.00	9,828

See Newsplan Contract and Copy Regulations—items 4, 5, 6, 7, 9, 10, 11, 13, 14, 18, 19, 21, 22, 23, 24, 29.

7. COLOR RATES AND DATA

	Daily b/w 1 c	b/w 4 c		Daily b/w 1 c	b/w 4 c
1 ti.	2,340.00	2,890.00	18 ti.	1,755.00	2,165.00
6 ti.	2,105.00	2,600.00	24 ti.	1,695.00	2,095.00
12 ti.	1,870.00	2,310.00	30 ti.	1,640.00	2,020.00

	Sunday b/w 1 c	b/w 4 c		Sunday b/w 1 c	b/w 4 c
1 ti.	2,580.00	3,175.00	18 ti.	1,935.00	2,380.00
6 ti.	2,325.00	2,860.00	24 ti.	1,870.00	2,300.00
12 ti.	2,065.00	2,540.00	30 ti.	1,805.00	2,225.00

Reservations, 7 days in advance of insertion date.
Closing dates: Reservations 10 days in advance. Complete material or cancellation 7 days in advance.

9. SPLIT RUN
50/50 only—Minimum size 45 col. inches. Both ads must be same dimensions and same products.
STRIPS ADS: Min. 6 cols. x 1" deep. 41.50 per col. inch extra Morning or Sunday. Chargeable on any Strip Ad measuring less than 6 cols. x 7".

11. SPECIAL DAYS/PAGES/FEATURES
Best Food Day: Wednesday.
Sci-Tech, Monday; Business Extra, Tuesday; Calendar Section, Money-A Guide to Personal Finance, Thursday; At Home, Sports Plus, Friday.
Books, Home & Garden, Living, Arts, Travel, Learning, Theatre, Hobby pages Business: Sunday.

12. R.O.P. DEPTH REQUIREMENTS
Ads over 18 inches deep charged full col.

13. CONTRACT AND COPY REGULATIONS
See Contents page for location of regulations—items 1, 2, 3, 7, 10, 11, 12, 13, 16, 18, 19, 23, 24, 25, 26, 31, 32, 33, 34, 35.

14. CLOSING TIMES
B/w reservation and copy daily; 4 p.m. 2 days preceding publication. Sunday reservation 10 a.m. Wednesday preceding; copy due 3:00 p.m. Thursday preceding; except Sunday Amusements,Books, Hobbies, Home & Garden, Living, Travel Resort & Special Sections reservation by noon Wednesday with released copy 5:00 p.m., Wednesday preceding.

15. MECHANICAL MEASUREMENTS
For complete, detailed production information, see SRDS Print Media Production Data.
PRINTING PROCESS: Offset/Direct Lithography.
6 col; ea 2-1/16"; 1/8" betw col.
Inches charged full depth: col. 21; pg. 126.

17. CLASSIFIED RATES
For complete data refer to classified rate section.

18. COMICS
POLICY—ALL CLASSIFICATIONS
When orders are placed through Metro Sunday Comics Network Group—see that listing.
Effective July 1, 1987.
Received May 11, 1987.

COLOR RATES AND DATA
Black and 3 colors:

1 page	14,535.00
2/3 page	11,195.00
1/2 page (h)	7,270.00
1/3 page	5,600.00
1/6 page	3,925.00

DISCOUNTS

2- 5 insertions	2%
6-12 insertions	4%
13-25 insertions	8%
26-38 insertions	12%
39-51 insertions	15%
52 or more insertions	20%

Sunday Comic and Roto may combine to earn discounts.

CLOSING TIMES
42 days before publication.

MECHANICAL MEASUREMENTS
PRINTING PROCESS: Flexography.
Standard page size: 13" wide x 20" deep.
Colors available: ANPA/AAAA: Four.

19. MAGAZINES
Rotogravure Section
SUNDAY.
POLICY—ALL CLASSIFICATIONS
When orders are placed through Metropolitan Sunday Magazine Group—see that listing.
Effective January 1, 1987.
Received December 4, 1986.

BLACK/WHITE RATES

MONOTONE		MONOTONE	
Full page	7,350.00	3/10 page	2,204.00
7/10 page	5,144.00	1/5 page	1,471.00
3/5 page	4,410.00	1/10 page	735.00
1/2 page	3,675.00	1/20 page	368.00
9/20 page	3,308.00	1/40 page	185.00
2/5 page	2,939.00		

COLOR RATES AND DATA

	b/w 1 c	b/w 2 c	4 color
Full page	8,634.00	8,934.00	9,703.00
7/10 page	6,429.00	6,729.00	7,497.00
3/5 page	5,694.00	5,994.00	6,763.00
1/2 page	4,960.00	5,260.00	6,028.00
9/20 page	4,592.00	4,892.00	5,661.00
2/5 page	4,224.00	4,524.00	5,292.00
3/10 page	3,489.00	3,789.00	4,557.00

DISCOUNTS
Within 1 year:

4-7 pages, 1 issue	5%
8-11 pages, 1 issue	10%
12 or more pages, 1 issue	15%

Roto advertisers may combine with Sunday Comics to earn discounts.

ROP DEPTH REQUIREMENTS
Min. space monotone 1/40th pg. (1/8 col.) color 3/10 pg.

CONTRACT AND COPY REGULATIONS
Less than 6 pages, premium charge for back to back 4 color pages.

CLOSING TIMES
Color and Monotone reservations, copy due 6th Wednesday prior to publication. Final Color Release 5th Wednesday prior to publication. Final Monotone Release 4th Wednesday prior to publication.

MECHANICAL MEASUREMENTS
PRINTING PROCESS: Rotogravure.
Trim size 10-3/4" wide x 12-3/8" deep. 5 cols. to page.
Colors available: GTA Standard; 4 Color.
1 col., 12-1/8" deep, page 10" w x 12-1/8" D.

FIGURE 13-7

Example of newspaper advertising rates.

rate, which is their highest rate for one-time insertions, and *contract* or *earned rates*. Local advertisers can obtain discounts of up to 70 percent by signing a contract for frequent or bulk space purchases. Bulk discounts offer the advertiser decreasing line rates as the number of inches used increases, and frequency discounts may be earned when a given ad is run repeatedly during a specific period of time. More than 1,000 newspapers are also participants in NEWSPLAN, a program of the Newspaper Advertising Bureau that offers discounts to national and regional advertisers who purchase six or more pages per year. Figure 13-7 shows a newspaper rate card, listing various contract rates.

Short Rate

An advertiser who contracts to buy a specific amount of space during a one-year period at a discount rate and then fails to buy this amount of space is charged a *short rate*. This is computed by determining the difference between the standard rate for the lines run and the discount rate contracted. Conversely, an advertiser who buys more lines than the number contracted may be entitled to a rebate because of the additional advertising.

Combination Rates

Combination rates are offered for placing a given ad in (1) morning and evening editions of the same newspaper; (2) two or more newspapers owned by the same publisher; and (3) in some cases, two or more newspapers affiliated in a syndicate or newspaper group. Combination rates are sometimes also offered for placing a given ad in consecutive Saturday and Sunday editions of the same newspaper. At one time, some newspapers required advertisers to buy combinations, but courts declared this practice illegal, and combinations are now optional.

Run of Paper (ROP)

ROP advertising rates entitle a newspaper to place a given ad on any newspaper page or in any position it desires—in other words, where space permits. Most newspapers, however, make an effort to place an ad in the position requested by the advertiser.

Preferred Position

An advertiser can assure a choice position for an ad by paying a higher *preferred position rate.* For example, a dictating machine manufacturer must pay this rate if it wants to ensure that its ad will be on the business or financial page. And a tire manufacturer may do the same to ensure a position in the sports section.

There also are preferred positions on the newspaper page itself. The preferred position near the top of a page or on the top of a column next to reading matter is called *full position.* It is usually surrounded by reading matter and costs the advertiser 25 to 50 percent more in many newspapers. Slightly less desirable, but also a preferred position, is placement "next to reading matter" (NR), which generally costs the advertiser 10 to 20 percent more.

Color Advertising

Color advertising is available in many newspapers on an ROP basis. Since newspapers are not noted for their high-quality color printing because of high-speed presses and porous paper stock, advertisers frequently preprint ads using processes known as HiFi color and Spectacolor. The advertisement is printed on a roll, and the roll is fed into the press by the newspaper, which prints its own material on the blank side. The cost of color ads is usually based on black-and-white rates; the rate card will list additional color costs to add to the basic rate. An example of the creative use of the newspaper's color capabilities is provided in Figure 13–8.

Split Runs

Many newspapers (as well as magazines) offer *split runs.* The advertiser runs two different ads of identical size for the same product or service in the same or different press runs on the same day. In this way, the advertiser can test the pulling power of one ad against the other. Newspapers set a minimum space requirement and charge extra for this service.

FIGURE 13–8

Creative use of color makes this Schick ad jump out from the newspaper page.

Co-op Insertions

As an aid to national advertisers wanting to place ads in several markets and several papers, the Newspaper Advertising Bureau (NAB) has instituted the Newspaper Co-op Network (NCN). With this system, advertisers are able to use salespeople from the respective newspapers to line up retailers for dealer listing ads, for example. The system also helps manufacturers control local advertising tie-ins to national campaigns and themes. Before the development of NCN, national advertisers had to place ads individually and sign up local dealers on an individual basis—a process that could require hundreds of phone calls and a great deal of paperwork. Now an insertion in up to 1,745 papers need only entail a few phone calls and a much shorter time period.[16]

Another type of group insertion program, pioneered by *The New York Times,* places a particular ad in a comparable position in multiple major dailies on the same day. For example, the *Times* was able to arrange for a Merrill Lynch ad to appear on the New York Stock Exchange quotes page in 26 major metropolitan newspapers every other Tuesday for a year.[17]

Insertion Orders and Tear Sheets

An advertiser who is ready to run an advertisement submits an *insertion order* to the newspaper. This form states the date(s) on which the ad is to run, its size, the position, and the rate. It also states whether finished art, mechanicals, Velox prints, or mats will be furnished with the ad.

When the newspaper creates advertising copy and art, it provides the advertiser a *proof copy* for checking purposes before running the ad. In contrast, most national advertising is submitted with the art, copy, and layout in final form. It is important that the agency or advertiser receive verification that the ad has run. Therefore, the newspaper tears out the page on which the ad appeared and sends it to the agency or advertiser. Today most *tear sheets* for national advertisers are forwarded through a private central office, the Advertising Checking Bureau.

When a tear sheet arrives, it is examined to make certain that the advertisement ran according to the instructions of the agency or advertiser—particularly with regard to the section of the paper in which it ran, its page position, and its reproduction. If the advertisement did *not* run as instructed, the agency or advertiser may be entitled to an adjustment. This may be a percentage discount or even a free rerun of the ad.

USING MAGAZINES IN THE CREATIVE MIX

How do you make carpets interesting? That was the challenge facing the Ally and Gargano agency when they needed to develop a print campaign for Karastan Carpets. Copywriter Helayne Spivak and art director Tom Wolsey knew that the market for the high-quality carpets was affluent suburban couples and that the ads would appear in up-scale home magazines. The idea of the home as a place of family nurture led Wolsey to think of "nesting instincts," which, in turn, led to the ad theme "Some of us have more finely developed nesting instincts than others."

The images Wolsey came up with to illustrate this theme were definitely out of the ordinary: seemingly giant birds "nesting" in rooms decorated with Karastan carpets (see Figure 13–9). The ads were created by inserting

Some of us have more finely developed nesting instincts than others.

Karastan Rug Mills, a Division of Fieldcrest Mills, Inc

INVEST IN *Karastan*

Figure 13–9

Surrealism, effective use of color, and high-quality reproduction add to the appeal of Karastan's "nesting instincts" magazine campaign.

stock photos of birds into miniature rooms. "Only the carpet is real," says Wolsey. "We wanted to create a look that would be Karastan's own. Karastan has always had a mystique, but we wanted to enforce that."[18]

The ads have obviously had more than novelty appeal—since they began appearing in 1984, Karastan's sales have grown substantially, outpacing sales in the carpet industry as a whole. For Karastan Carpets, magazine ads geared to the target market have had the desired results.

Advantages of Magazines

The Karastan campaign illustrates many of the advantages of magazines as an element of the creative mix: flexible design, availability of color, excellent reproduction quality, permanence, prestige, and most of all, excellent audience selectivity.

Magazines offer *flexibility* in both readership and advertising. They cover the full range of prospects—with a wide choice of regional editions as well as national coverage. Each magazine lends itself to a variety of lengths, approaches, and editorial tones. The advertiser therefore has the choice of using long copy, black-and-white, editorial ads; short copy, colorful poster ads; humorous cartoons; or any of an infinite variety of approaches. (See the Portfolio of Award-Winning Magazine Advertisements.)

Magazine *color* spreads a spectrum of exciting visual pleasure before the reader. Nowhere can better color reproduction be seen than in the slick

(continued on p. 429)

PORTFOLIO OF AWARD-WINNING MAGAZINE ADVERTISEMENTS

A. Each year, the Magazine Publishers Association gives the Kelly Award to honor creative excellence in magazine advertising. This North Carolina Travel and Tourism ad won the Kelly Award in 1986. The striking, symmetrical photo, grabber headline, and inviting copy all work together to make a quintessential magazine ad.

B. When the manufacturers of Hush Puppies shoes wanted to shed their dull image, they enlisted Fallon McElligott, Minneapolis to produce a print ad campaign that would emphasize the wide variety of fashionable styles offered by the footwear line. The result was a series of clever magazine ads featuring the brand's familiar basset hound. The ads make their point with minimal copy and plenty of humor.

C. Sometimes a great photograph is all that is needed to make a great print ad. Chiat/Day, the agency for Nike, Inc., enlisted the services of photographer Mark Coppos to produce a series of moody photos of active individuals, all caught at a moment of repose, all wearing Nike sports clothing.

D. The immediate response to this ad is, "Gee, this isn't a typical car ad"—which gets across the message that a Jeep isn't a typical car. The whimsical ad imbues the Jeep with a personality that target buyers (urbanites who share the Jeep's wistfulness for backroads) find appealing.

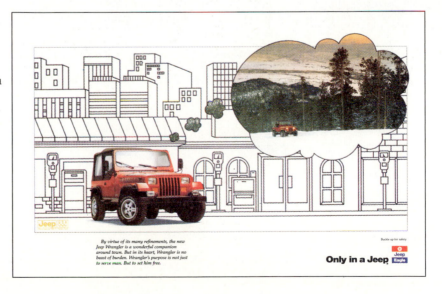

Original.   Chunky.

When we make Prince Spaghetti Sauce, we give you a choice. Because no two people have quite the same taste.

E. Fallon McElligott scored another winner with this nutty ad for spaghetti sauce. Magazine ads for food products usually emphasize the look and taste of the food item, tempting the reader with realistic photos of the prepared product. The ad agency broke all the rules here (won't some readers think this product will make them fat?) and got away with it.

magazines. Color in such publications as *National Geographic* enhances image and identifies the package. Would the Karastan ads have been as effective in black-and-white? It's doubtful. In short, color sells.

If the advertiser wants to speak with *authority* and *believability,* magazines can enhance the message. People believe what magazines say. Their influence affects people's ideas, opinions, and desires. Stephen Martin, a marketing expert, quotes John Naisbett as having said, "We are drowning in information but starving for knowledge and meaning." Martin points out that TV, radio, and newspapers offer lots of information but little knowledge or meaning, while "magazines are one place we can often find all three."[19]

Magazines offer *permanence.* For the advertiser who wants to communicate lasting information and enjoyment, magazines give the reader more opportunity to appraise ads in considerable detail. Advertisements can deliver a more complete educational/sales message and can effectively communicate the total corporate personality. As Judith Ranzer, vice president for advertising and sales promotion at MCI has emphasized, "It really does pay off to tell your story comprehensively. . . . The ad is not just a teaser to a product but a complete description of everything you need to know about it."[20] Magazines also enable advertisers to generate reprints and materials that further promote their advertising campaigns.

Advertising a product in certain magazines can also provide the advertiser with *prestige* for the product. That's one reason why Karastan Carpets chose such "class" publications as *Metropolitan Home* and *Connoisseur* for its ads.

Perhaps most important, magazines are the most *selective* of all media except for direct mail. The predictable editorial environment selects the audience and enables advertisers to pinpoint their sales campaign. Most mgazines are written for special-interest groups. *Golf Digest* helps a golf club manufacturer reach golfers; *Business Week* reaches businesspeople; *Seventeen* reaches teenage girls; *Ebony,* a black-oriented magazine, helps advertisers reach upscale members of the black community; and *American Photographer* is aimed at professional and semiprofessional photographers (see Figure 13–10). According to Steve Kurtzer, media supervisor at

FIGURE   13–10

This is one of an award-winning series of ads featuring works of well-known photographers. The ads ran in such photography magazines as *American Photographer* and *Popular Photography.*

Rank	Advertiser	Magazine ad expenditures 1986
1	Philip Morris Cos.	$230,130*
2	RJR Nabisco	135,657
3	General Motors Corp.	129,408
4	Ford Motor Co.	125,071
5	Procter & Gamble Co.	86,506
6	Chrysler Corp.	78,905
7	American Telephone & Telegraph	74,014
8	CBS Inc.	58,871
9	Time Inc.	51,166
10	General Electric Co.	50,776

FIGURE 13–11   Top 10 magazine advertisers

*Dollars are in thousands.

BBDO, the proliferation of specialized magazines has been a real boon to advertisers: "Such specialized vehicles enable marketers to target their messages to a well-defined segment of consumers in what can be a highly compatible (depending on the category of product) editorial environment."[21]

Finally, magazines can be very *cost-efficient*. By selecting the specific magazines and editions that reach prospects, the advertiser can keep wasted circulation to a minimum. The selling power of magazines has been proven and results are measurable, so they are the growing choice of many leading advertisers (see Figure 13–11).

Magazines also have some other advantages. They have extensive "pass-along" or secondary readership; they generate loyalty among readers that sometimes borders on fanaticism; and they may reach prospects that salespeople can't because of geographic or other reasons. Hard-to-reach occupational groups, such as doctors and entertainment personalities, are nearly all reached readily by magazines. (See the Checklist of What Works Best in Print.)

Some Drawbacks to Magazines

Although magazines offer excellent creative capabilities for advertisers in a print medium, they do have drawbacks. The immediacy of newspapers, for example, is lost in magazines. Likewise, magazines don't offer the depth of geographic coverage or the local reach of newspapers. Nor do they offer the national reach of the broadcast media. They also suffer from the inability to deliver high-frequency figures or mass audiences at a low price. The disadvantages of magazines, therefore, are several.

1. Advertising in magazines requires long *lead time*. Space must be purchased and the advertisement prepared well in advance of the date of publication—sometimes as long as three months. Weekly magazines, par-

Checklist of What Works Best in Print

☐ Use simple layouts. One big picture works better than several small pictures. Avoid cluttered pages. (Layouts that resemble the magazine's editorial format are well read.)

☐ Always put a caption under a photograph. Readership of picture captions is generally twice as great as of body copy. The picture caption can be an advertisement by itself.

☐ Don't be afraid of long copy. The people who read beyond the headline are *prospects for your product or your service*. If your product is expensive—like a car, a vacation, or an industrial product—prospects are hungry for the information long copy gives them. Consider long copy if you have a complex story to tell, many different product points to make, or an expensive product or service to sell.

☐ Avoid negative headlines. People are literal minded and may remember only the negatives. Sell the positive benefits in your product—not that it won't harm or that some defect has been solved. Look for emotional words that attract and motivate, like *free* and *new* and *love*.

☐ Don't be afraid of long headlines. Research shows that, on the average, long headlines sell more merchandise than short ones.

☐ Look for *story appeal*. After the headline, a striking visual is the most effective way to get a reader's attention. Try for story appeal—the kind of visual that makes the reader ask: "What's going on here?"

☐ Photographs are better than drawings. Research says that photography increases recall an average of 26 percent over artwork.

☐ Look at your advertisement in its editorial environment. Ask to see your advertisement pasted into the magazine in which it will appear—or, for newspapers, photostated in the same tone as the newspaper page. Beautifully mounted layouts are deceptive. The reader will never see your advertisement printed on high-gloss paper, with a big white border, mounted on a board. It is *misleading* for you to look at it this way.

☐ Develop a single advertising format. An overall format for all print advertising can double recognition. This rule holds special meaning for industrial advertisers. One format will help readers see your advertisements as coming from one large corporation, rather than several small companies.

☐ Before-and-after photographs make a point better than words. If you can, show a visual contrast—a change in the consumer or a demonstration of product superiority.

☐ Do not print copy in reverse type. It may look attractive, but it reduces readability. For the same reason, don't surprint copy on the illustration of your advertisement.

☐ Make each advertisement a complete sale. Your message must be contained in the headline. React to the overall impression as the reader will. Only the advertiser reads all his advertisements. Any advertisement in a series must stand on its own. *Every one* must make a complete sale. Assume it will be the only advertisement for your product a reader will ever see.

---

ticularly those that run color advertisements, often require that advertising materials be in their hands weeks in advance of the publication date. And once the closing date has been reached, no changes in copy or art can be allowed. Some magazines are trying to overcome this drawback by offering a "fast-close" service at no extra cost to the advertiser.

2. Magazines have problems offering *reach* and *frequency*. Where selectivity is not a major marketing consideration, using selective magazines is very costly for reaching broad masses of people. Frequency can actually be built faster than reach by adding numerous smaller-audience magazines to the schedule. However, most magazines are issued only monthly, or at best weekly, so building frequency in one publication is very difficult.

3. Magazines that are popular have the problem of heavy *advertising competition*. This can deter other advertisers. In the 50 or so magazines that account for the majority of total magazine circulation, the average

relationship of advertising to editorial linage is 51.4 percent advertising to 48.6 percent editorial matter.[22]

4.   The *cost* of advertising in magazines can be very high. While national consumer magazines offer an average black-and-white cost per thousand that ranges from $3 to $12 or more, some trade publications with highly selective audiences have a cost per thousand of over $20 for a black-and-white page.

Magazines are also having to contend with the problem of declining circulations. In particular, newsstand sales have dropped 10 percent over the past five years.[23] The loss of single-copy sales has been attributed to a number of things, including increased subscription sales, the ever-increasing number of magazines on the stands, changing consumer buying patterns, and competition from VCRs. Magazine publishers are quick to point out, however, that what they may be losing in quantity of readers is made up for in quality of readers. Through the use of sophisticated research techniques, they can often back this claim with extensive demographic and psychographic data on their readers. Magazines are also courting advertisers by offering a number of creative methods for getting ad messages across, as we will see in the next section.

Special Possibilities with Magazines

Magazines offer advertisers a wide variety of creative possibilities through various technical or mechanical elements. These include bleed pages, cover positions, inserts and gatefolds, and special-size ads such as junior pages and island halfs.

When the dark or colored background of the advertisement extends to the edge of the page, it is said to "bleed" off the page. Most magazines offer *bleed pages,* but advertisers usually have to pay a 10 to 15 percent premium for them. The advantages of bleeds include greater flexibility in expressing the advertising idea, a slightly larger printing space, and a more dramatic impact than might be achieved with a white border.

The front cover of American magazines is commonly referred to as the "first cover." It is almost never sold. The inside front, inside back, and outside back covers are almost always sold at a premium. They are called the second, third, and fourth covers, respectively.

Pages that extend and fold over to fit into the magazine are called *gatefolds.* A gatefold may be a fraction of a page or two or more pages. It may occupy the cover position or the centerfold. Gatefolds, also called *dutch doors,* are useful in making spectacular and impressive announcements. Not all magazines provide gatefolds, and they are always sold at a premium.

Often an advertiser will have an ad printed on a special paper stock to add weight and drama to the message. This can then be inserted into the magazine at a special price. Another option is multiple-page inserts. Such inserts may be exclusively devoted to the product being advertised, or they may have editorial content that is consonant with the content of the particular magazine, accompanied by ads. For example, Chevrolet produced a series of eight-page inserts for *Cosmopolitan* that took the form of a "mini-magazine" titled "Women in Motion." The campaign was highly successful in selling cars to the magazine's readers, and many other advertisers are choosing the multiple-page insert route as a result.[24] Other advertising inserts may be geared to a particular editorial theme, such as winter sports or Hawaii travel, with all ads, from a variety of advertisers, related to that theme. Some of the many innovative approaches being tried in magazine advertising are discussed in Ad Lab 13-A.

Another way to make creative use of magazine ad space is to place the ad in very unusual places on the page or dramatically across spreads (see

AD LAB 13-A   Innovations in Magazine Advertising

In the past few years, magazines have been working closely with advertisers to develop new technologies for creative presentations of ideas and products. Out of these efforts have come such innovations as fragrance strips, color strips, and pop-ups.

Since fragrance strips first came on the scene in 1981, they have become a great favorite with perfume advertisers. Through a unique method called the Scentstrip, perfume samples can be tucked into magazines, yielding their scents to readers upon opening of a sealed insert. Despite some consumer complaints about not wanting to smell like perfume after reading a magazine, Scentstrips have become incredibly popular as they offer perfume makers a direct means of providing consumers with samples of their product. Odors have been used for other products as well— a Rolls Royce ad in *Architectural Digest* carried a Scentstrip bearing the essence of leather.

Following on the heels of fragrance samples has been the development of a method for including cosmetic samples with magazine ads. Now cosmetics manufacturers can insert strips containing color samples of eyeshadow, blusher, lipstick, and makeup that readers can immediately try. Production of the color strips doesn't come cheap, but many advertisers think the expense is well worth it.

Another costly production innovation that is appealing to certain advertisers is the pop-up ad. Corporate advertisers such as Honeywell and TransAmerica were among the first to experiment with this eye-catching approach, but product ads, such as a pop-up Dodge Dakota, were not far behind.

Other intriguing approaches explored recently include 3-D ads (complete with 3-D glasses), other forms of product samples (such as facial tissues and paper towels), and unusual shapes and sizes for inserts. An ad for Sarah Lee cheesecake, for example, took the form of a single heavy-stock page with what appeared to be a bite taken out of the large-as-life cheesecake slice. A half-page insert for Gleem toothpaste featured a mylar mirror with the slogan "Check

Your Mirror," asking readers to check whether their teeth were white enough.

Additional research is probing the possibilities of holographic ads and of ads that "talk" through the assistance of a device that is passed across the page. There are already ads that "sing"—two liquor companies included microchips that played Christmas carols in their December 1987 magazine ads, and Camel cigarette ads played "Happy Birthday" on the occasion of the brand's 75th anniversary in 1988.

All these innovative approaches are designed not only to attract readers' attention but to *involve* them in the ad experience by appealing to more than just the visual sense.

Laboratory Application

Do you think these special gimmicks are worth the extra expense of producing them and paying premium ad rates? Why or why not?

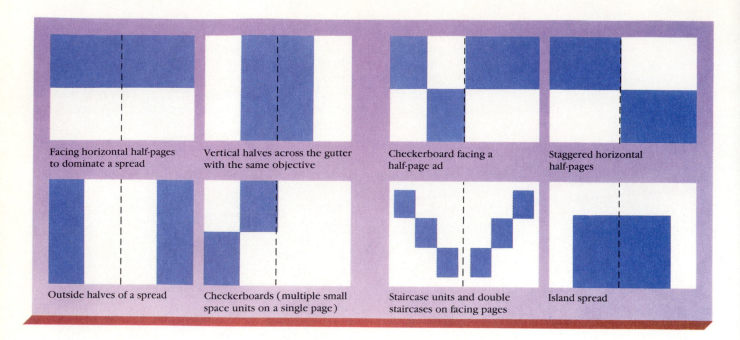

Facing horizontal half-pages to dominate a spread

Vertical halves across the gutter with the same objective

Checkerboard facing a half-page ad

Staggered horizontal half-pages

Outside halves of a spread

Checkerboards (multiple small space units on a single page)

Staircase units and double staircases on facing pages

Island spread

FIGURE 13–12

Magazine space combinations that can create big impact.

Figure 13–12). For example, a *junior unit* is a large ad (60 percent of the page) placed in the middle of a page and surrounded with editorial material. Similar to junior units are *island half-pages,* except there is more editorial matter surrounding them. The island sometimes costs more than a regular half-page, but since it dominates the page, many advertisers consider the premium a small price to pay.

How Magazines Are Categorized

Although magazines may be classified in many ways, the most common methods are by content, geography, and size.

Content

One of the most dramatic developments in publishing during the last three decades has been the emergence of magazines with specialized appeal and content. Although specialization has been no guarantee of success in the field, it has given many publications good prospects for long-term growth.

The broadest classifications of content are consumer magazines, farm magazines, and business magazines. Each of these, though, may be broken down into hundreds of categories. *Consumer magazines* are purchased for entertainment, information, or both and are edited for people who buy products for their own consumption. The *farm publications* are magazines directed to farmers and their families or to companies that manufacture or sell agricultural equipment, supplies, and services. The most widely circulated farm publications are the *Farm Journal, Progressive Farmer, Prairie Farmer,* and *Successful Farming* (see Figure 13–13). Finally, *business magazines,* by far the largest category, are directed to business readers. They include (1) trade publications (aimed at retailers, wholesalers, and other

FOR 4 MONTHS OUT OF THE YEAR, THE WEATHER MAKES FARMING IMPOSSIBLE. DURING THE OTHER 8, THE GOVERNMENT DOES.

Imagine what it would be like if the weather kept you from buying media for four months out of every year.

Then imagine that during the other eight, your hands were tied. Tied while trade deficits, tight money, and foreign policy dictated how you'd buy your media. Essentially, that's what running a farm is like these days.

Given all that, wouldn't you look for the best advice you could find? Sure you would.

That's why so many farmers read Successful Farming® every month. Successful Farming ties together the total farm operation. Not with long-winded feature articles, but with concise, informative how-to articles on contemporary management practices.

They also read the ads as proved by the high Chilton readership scores. Which is great for our advertisers, considering that our magazine reaches the high-income farmers responsible for 85% of all production expenses in America.

Which is why if you have a product that can help today's farmers make a better living off the land, there's no better place to tell them about it than Successful Farming.

For more information, contact your nearest Successful Farming sales executive. Or call Gil Spears, collect, at 515-284-3118. Successful Farming. Meredith Corporation, Locust at Seventeenth. Des Moines, Iowa 50336.

FIGURE   13–13

Drinking Buddies Advertising, an agency based in Richmond, Virginia, created this award-winning ad that informs potential advertisers about the benefits of buying space in *Successful Farming,* one of the top-selling farm publications.

distributors); (2) industrial magazines (aimed at businesspeople involved in manufacturing); and (3) professional magazines (aimed at lawyers, physicians, dentists, architects, teachers, and other groups of professional people).

Magazines may also be classified as local, regional, or national. *Local magazines* have become popular, and now most major American cities have magazines named after them: *San Diego Magazine, New York, Los Angeles, Chicago, Philadelphia, Palm Springs Life,* and *Crain's Chicago Business,* to name a few. Their readership is usually upscale, professional people interested in the arts, fashion, culture, and business. *Regional publications* are targeted to a specific area of the country, such as the West or the South, and examples include *Sunset, Southern Living,* and *Pacific Northwest.* In addition, national magazines sometimes offer advertisers special market runs that allow the selection of specific geographic regions. *Time, U.S. News & World Report, Newsweek, Woman's Day,* and *Sports Illustrated* have developed their coverage to such an extent that an advertiser wishing to buy a single major market can easily do so (see Figure 13–14).

There are thousands of *national magazines* as well. They range from those with enormous circulations, such as *TV Guide,* which in 1987 had a circulation of over 16.8 million, and *Reader's Digest,* with a national circulation of 17.3 million, to lesser-known national magazines with circulations well under 100,000, such as *Modern Drummer* and *Volleyball Monthly.*

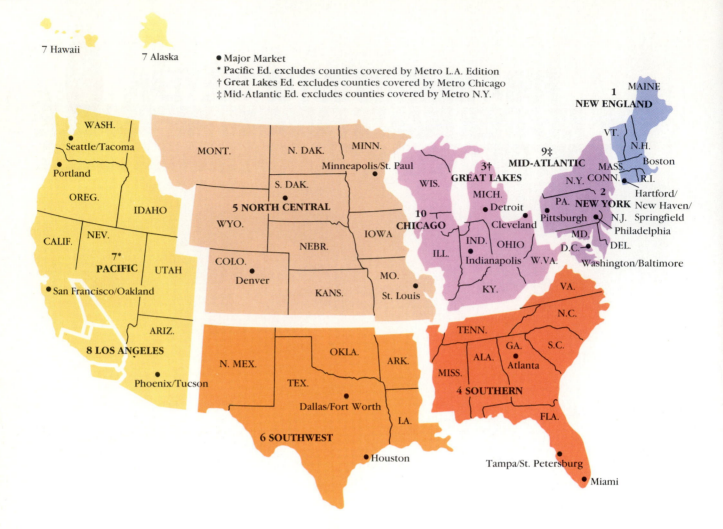

7 Hawaii   7 Alaska

● Major Market
* Pacific Ed. excludes counties covered by Metro L.A. Edition
† Great Lakes Ed. excludes counties covered by Metro Chicago
‡ Mid-Atlantic Ed. excludes counties covered by Metro N.Y.

FIGURE   13–14

The 10 major geographic editions of *Reader's Digest.*

Size

It doesn't take a genius to figure out that magazines come in different shapes and sizes, but sometimes it takes one to figure out how to get the same advertisement to run in different-sized magazines and still look the same. Magazine sizes run the gamut from very large to very small, which makes efforts at production standardization an occasional nightmare. The most common magazine sizes might be grouped as follows:

Classification	Magazine	Approximate size of full-page ad
Large	*Life*	4 col. × 170 lines (9⅜ × 12⅛ inches)
Flat	*Time, Newsweek*	3 col. × 140 lines (7 × 10 inches)
Standard	*National Geographic*	2 col. × 119 lines (6 × 8½ inches)
Small or pocket	*Reader's Digest, TV Guide*	2 col. × 91 lines (4½ × 6½ inches)

At one time, most magazines appeared in the standard format, but today few use it. Most magazines now are in the flat format size.

HOW TO BUY MAGAZINE SPACE

The effective media buyer considers the selection of magazines on the basis of circulation, readership, and cost and mechanical requirements. The buyer must understand the magazine's circulation statistics and rate card information.

Understanding Magazine Circulation

A magazine's audience may be determined by several factors: its primary and secondary readership, the number of subscription and vendor sales, and the number of copies that are guaranteed versus those that are actually delivered.

Primary and Secondary Readership

The Audit Bureau of Circulations or other verified reports tell the media buyer what the magazine's total circulation is. This is *primary circulation, and it* represents the number of people who receive the publication. They may purchase it on newsstands or through a regular subscription. *Secondary* (or pass-along) readership is exactly what the name suggests. After the first reader is finished, he or she may give it to others to read. Pass-along readership can be very important to some magazines since some publications may be read by more than six different people. Multiply that by a million subscribers, and the magazine can boast substantial readership.

Vertical and Horizontal Publications

The two classifications of business publications are vertical and horizontal. A choice of one or the other depends on how deeply an advertiser wishes to penetrate a particular industry or how widely the advertiser wishes to spread the message.

Vertical publications cover a specific industry; for example, *Retail Baking Today* is aimed only at those people interested in selling baked goods on the retail level. *Horizontal publications,* such as *Electronic Design* and *Purchasing,* deal with a particular job function that cuts across industry lines (see Figure 13–15).

Subscription and Vendor Sales

Since World War II, the ratio of subscriptions to newsstand sales has increased, and today subscriptions account for the majority of sales for most magazines. Newsstands (which also encompass magazine sales in bookstore chains) are still a major outlet for sales of single copies, but no newsstand can handle more than a fraction of the magazines available. Display space is limited, and vendors sometimes complain that distributors make them take publications they do not want to get others they do.

From the advertiser's point of view, newsstand sales are impressive because they indicate that the purchaser really wants the magazine and is

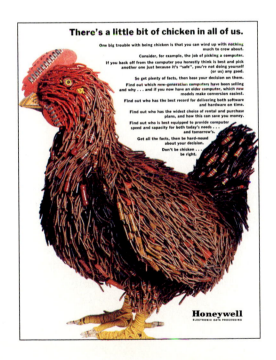

FIGURE   13–15

Business advertisers with products that appeal to a wide variety of industries, such as computer equipment, make use of horizontal business publications.

not merely taking a subscription out of habit. Single-copy sales account for an average of 26 percent of all sales, according to the Magazine Publishers Association. Some publications are sold entirely through newsstand sales. Others, such as most trade publications, are sold entirely through subscription.

Paid and Controlled Circulation

Business publications are published on a *paid* basis or a *controlled* basis. If the publication is available on a paid basis, the recipient must pay the subscription price in order to receive it. Circulation that is free (controlled) means it is mailed to a selected list of individuals who the publisher feels are in a unique position to influence the purchase of advertised products. To get the publication, these people must indicate in writing a desire to receive it and must give their professional designation or occupation. Ordinarily, to qualify for the subscription list, they must also include information about their job title, function, and purchasing responsibilities.

Since advertising rates are based principally on circulation, controlled circulation magazines can characterize their readers as good prospects for the goods and services advertised in the publication's pages. Advertisers are not paying for subscribers who have little or no interest in what they are offering. Publishers of paid circulation magazines say that subscribers who pay are more likely to read the publication than are those who get controlled or free copies. On the other hand, publishers of controlled circulation publications state that giving the publication away without charge is the only way to get good coverage of the market and that there is little or no effect on readership.

In order to avoid confusing these terms, it should be pointed out that some paid circulation publications "control their circulation" in a sense by allowing persons to subscribe only if they represent the kind of circulation they want to build, even though they require the subscriber to pay for the subscription.

Guaranteed versus Delivered Circulation

A magazine's rate structure is based on its circulation. The advertiser who purchases space is assured of reaching a certain number of people. The *guaranteed* circulation figure is the number of copies of the magazine the publisher expects will be sold. Since some of these copies are usually sold on newsstands, it is possible that the guaranteed circulation figure may not be reached. If this *delivered* figure is not reached, the publisher will have to give a refund. For that reason, most guaranteed circulation figures (on which advertising rates are based) are stated safely below the average actual delivered circulation.

Reading Rate Cards

Magazine rate cards, like newspaper rate cards, follow a standard format (see Figure 13–16). This enables advertisers to readily determine the cost of advertising, any discount opportunities, the mechanical requirements of the publication, the issue and closing dates, special editions, and the additional amount required for features like color, inserts, bleed pages, or split runs.

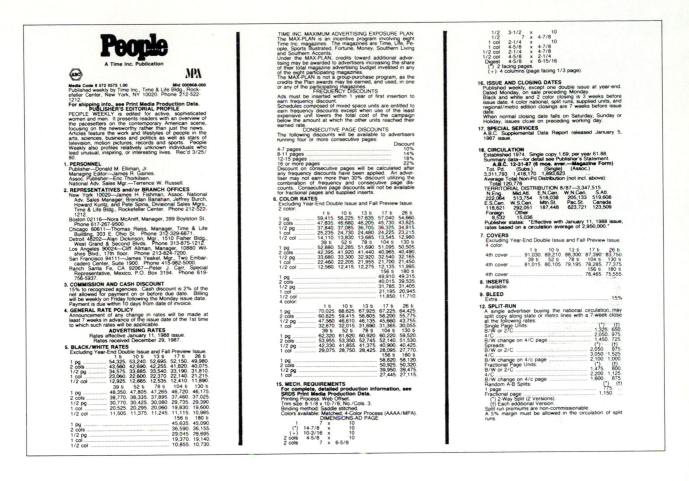

FIGURE   13–16

Example of magazine advertising rates.

Rates

One means of comparing magazines is to look at the one-time cost for a full-page black-and-white ad, multiplied by 1,000, and divided by the publication's total circulation:

$$\frac{\text{Page rate} \times 1,000}{\text{Circulation}} = \text{Cost per page per thousand (CPM)}$$

For example, in 1987, the page rate for a one-time, black-and-white ad in *Flying* magazine was $12,560 on a rate base (guaranteed circulation) of 330,000. At the same time, *Plane and Pilot* magazine offered a full-page, black-and-white ad for $2,935 on a rate base of 70,000. Can you tell which was the better buy from the standpoint of cost per thousand? Figure 13–17 lists the circulations, readership, and page rates for 18 leading consumer magazines. Using these data, you can calculate which national buys offer the best CPMs.

Each of these publications, by the way, claimed substantial pass-along readership, thereby giving *Flying* a total audience of 1,082,400 and *Plane and Pilot* a total of 273,000 readers. If you believed these readership figures, which magazine would then have the better cost per thousand?

As with newspapers, discounts are given based on frequency and volume. Frequency discounts are generally based on the number of insertions, while volume discounts are offered on the total space used during a specific period. Almost all magazines offer cash discounts—usually 2 percent, and some offer discounts on the purchase of four or more consecu-

FIGURE 13–17   Selected consumer magazines: Circulation, readership, and cost

Magazine	Total paid circulation	Readers per copy			Page cost (one time)	
		Men	Women	Total	Black-and-white	Four-color
TV Guide	16,400,000	1.29	1.59	2.88	$ 84,600	$ 99,750
Reader's Digest	16,250,000	1.27	1.72	2.99	95,900	115,300
Modern Maturity	13,600,000	.62	1.03	1.65	143,500	159,000
National Geographic	8,375,000	1.93	1.76	3.69	100,240	130,315
Better Homes and Gardens	8,000,000	3.12	1.04	4.16	85,550	103,480
Family Circle	5,800,000	.67	3.82	4.49	61,310	72,960
Woman's Day	5,400,000	.44	4.04	4.48	53,465	64,000
Good Housekeeping	5,000,000	.96	5.08	6.04	66,965	84,025
Ladies Home Journal	5,000,000	.49	3.31	3.80	52,300	64,300
Time	4,600,000	2.12	1.83	3.95	77,010	120,130
National Enquirer	4,500,000	1.90	2.96	4.86	32,180	40,570
Redbook	3,800,000	.49	2.90	3.39	46,160	61,040
Star	3,500,000	1.02	1.99	3.01	24,680	30,450
Playboy	3,400,000	3.02	.87	3.89	41,680	58,370
Newsweek	3,050,000	3.94	2.89	6.83	54,095	86,500
People Weekly	3,311,793	4.28	6.99	11.28	54,325	70,025
Sports Illustrated	2,875,000	4.64	1.43	6.07	57,350	89,470
Cosmopolitan	2,500,000	.89	4.26	5.15	36,215	48,735

tive pages in a single issue. Recent declines in the amount of magazine advertising have led many publications to offer other forms of discounts as well. An estimated 30 to 35 percent of consumer magazines and 50 percent of trade magazines are willing to negotiate their rates, and this rate-cutting trend is expected to continue.[25]

Color, if it is available, normally costs 25 to 60 percent more than black-and-white. Some publications, such as *Money,* even offer metallic and aluminum-based inks and the use of five colors by special arrangement.

Bleed pages add as much as 20 percent to regular rates, although the typical increase is about 15 percent.

Typically, second and third cover rates (the inside covers) are less than the rate for the fourth (back) cover. The cover rates usually include color, whether the ad is to be run in color or not. *Newsweek* charges $86,500 for the second and third covers and $110,895 for the fourth cover.

Magazines offer different rates for advertisements in issues that go to a particular market, either geographic or demographic. *Time* offers one-page four-color ads (one-time insertion) in Boston for $9,120 (177,000 circulation); in Texas for $11,319 (239,000 circulation); to college students for $26,920 (550,000 circulation); and to the 50 largest metropolitan markets for $93,020 (3,425,000 circulation).

Issue and Closing Dates

In buying magazine advertising, there are three important dates:

Cover date—the date appearing on the cover.
On-sale date—the date the magazine is actually issued.
Closing date—the date when all ad material must be in the hands of the publisher for inclusion in a specific issue.

The closing date is sometimes the first thing the advertiser looks at. After determining whether the advertising materials can be ready by a certain date and which issue would be best, the space can be bought according to the factors we have discussed.

Merchandising Services

Like newspapers, magazines often provide special services to advertisers. These include mailings prepared for the advertiser to notify dealers of the impending advertisement. Also, countercards for use in stores stating "As advertised in" are sometimes forwarded to retailers. Other services provided by magazines include special promotions to stores; marketing services that help readers find local outlets through a single phone number; response cards that allow readers to send for brochures and catalogs from a variety of advertisers; aid in handling sales force, broker, wholesaler, and retailer meetings; advance editions for the trade; and research into brand preference, consumer attitudes, and market conditions.

SOURCES OF PRINT MEDIA INFORMATION

There are many general sources of information about newspapers and magazines; more specific, detailed information about the publication itself may be obtained through direct contact. Here are some of the principal sources of information commonly analyzed by media planners.

Audit Bureau of Circulations (ABC) The ABC was formed in 1914 to verify circulation and other marketing data on magazines and newspapers. Each publication submits a semiannual statement that is checked by specially trained ABC field auditors. They examine all records necessary to verify the figures the publisher reports.

The information the publisher supplies includes paid circulation for the period covered broken down by subscription, single-copy sales, and average paid circulation—by regional, metropolitan, and demographic editions. The ABC also analyzes new and renewal subscriptions by price, duration, channel of sales, and type of promotion.

Because the ad revenues of many publications depend on ABC circulation figures, the bureau's auditing practices have at times come under fire. One 1984 lawsuit charged the ABC with aiding a New Jersey newspaper in falsifying its circulation figures. The suit was brought by a rival newspaper, whose publisher also charged the ABC with training its auditors poorly and not providing adequate standards for judging whether a publication's circulation figures are accurately reported.[26] The suit was subsequently dropped. Defenders of the ABC point out that it is not the ABC's job to act as policeman; it can only work with the data that publications provide.

Newspaper Advertising Bureau Several industry organizations and publications offer helpful aids for planning newspaper advertising. One of them is the Newspaper Advertising Bureau of the American Newspaper Publishers Association, the promotional arm of the nation's newspaper industry. The bureau also provides its newspaper members with market information by conducting field research and collecting case histories. And as mentioned earlier, it has created such programs as NEWSPLAN and the Newspaper Co-op Network to aid national advertisers in obtaining better rates and reaching multiple markets in a timely fashion.

Magazine Publishers Association (MPA) The MPA has a total membership of more than 200 publishers who represent 800 magazines. This trade group makes available the combined circulation of all ABC member magazines (general and farm) from 1914 to date, with yearly figures related to population. It estimates the number of consumer magazine copies sold by year from 1943, and it lists the 100 leading ABC magazines according to circulation.

The association provides the industry with a sales, research, and promotion arm that attempts to stimulate greater and more effective use of magazine advertising.

Standard Rate and Data Service (SRDS) SRDS publishes *Newspaper Rates and Data, Consumer Magazine and Agri-Media Rates and Data,* and *Business Publication Rates and Data,* as well as other monthly directories that eliminate the necessity for advertisers and their agencies to obtain rate cards for every publication.

Audience Studies Provided by Publications Circulation figures are not enough. Newspapers and magazines also offer media planners many other types of statistical reports. The information contained in these reports details reader income, demographic profiles, percentages of different kinds of advertising carried, and much more. Figure 13–18 is an example of this type of audience information.

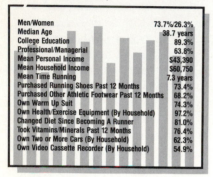

THE LONGEST RUNNING SUCCESS STORY

Since 1966 RUNNER'S WORLD has been America's most widely read running publication, chronicling the impressive growth of this highly visible and popular sport.

Today's runners are young, upscale men and women deeply concerned with health and fitness; ambitious achievers who demand the best in themselves and the products they buy.

Our Subscriber Study tells the story.

Men/Women	73.7%/26.3%
Median Age	38.7 years
College Education	89.3%
Professional/Managerial	63.8%
Mean Personal Income	$43,390
Mean Household Income	$60,750
Mean Time Running	7.3 years
Purchased Running Shoes Past 12 Months	73.4%
Purchased Other Athletic Footwear Past 12 Months	68.2%
Own Warm Up Suit	74.3%
Own Health/Exercise Equipment (By Household)	97.2%
Changed Diet Since Becoming A Runner	81.0%
Took Vitamins/Minerals Past 12 Months	76.4%
Own Two or More Cars (By Household)	62.3%
Own Video Cassette Recorder (By Household)	54.9%

This quality market depends on RUNNER'S WORLD for informed and intelligent advice and encouragement. And we've delivered the goods for over 20 years, becoming a trusted partner in nearly 2 million busy, successful lives.*

Running has grown up, and we've grown up with it.

Runner's World®
The life guide of the serious runner.

Source: RUNNER'S WORLD Subscriber Study—1986
*MRI—Spring, 1986

FIGURE   13–18

Many magazines try to attract advertising by conducting studies to show that the publication's readers fit advertisers' target demographics.

Summary

The printed page in general and the newspaper in particular provide a unique, flexible medium for advertisers to express their creativity. The newspaper is a mass medium that is read by almost everybody. It offers great flexibility, which assists creativity, and its printed message lasts. However, newspapers also have their disadvantages. These include lack of audience selectivity, short life span, poor production quality, heavy advertising competition, potentially poor ad placement, and overlapping circulation. Still, the newspaper is the major community-serving medium today for both news and advertising.

The newspaper's rates, mechanical requirements, and other pertinent information are printed on its rate card. The rates listed vary for local and national advertisers. Also listed are the newspaper's short-rate policy, combination rates, frequency discounts, run-of-paper rates, and other data.

Magazines offer different advantages. They are the most selective of all media. They are flexible in both readership and advertising. They offer unsurpassed availability of color, excellent reproduction quality, believability and authority, permanence, and prestige at an efficient cost. However, they often require long lead times, they have problems offering reach and frequency, and they are subject to heavy advertising competition. And the cost of advertising in some magazines is very high.

In selecting magazines for advertising, the media buyer must consider a publication's circulation, its readership, and its cost and mechanical requirements. A magazine's rates may be determined by several factors: its primary and secondary readership, the number of subscription and vendor sales, and the number of copies guaranteed versus those actually delivered.

Magazine rate cards, like newspaper rate cards, follow a standard format so advertisers can readily determine the cost of advertising. The rate card lists black-and-white rates, discounts, color rates, issue and closing dates, and mechanical requirements.

Questions for Review and Discussion

1. If you were working for a retailer, would you recommend the use of newspaper advertising? Why or why not?
2. In what ways can advertisers improve the selectivity of their newspaper ads?
3. What factors should advertisers consider in deciding which of several local papers (including dailies and weeklies) to use for advertising?
4. Do you agree with newspaper publishers that national advertisers should be charged a higher rate than local advertisers? Support your position.
5. How do advertisers benefit from split runs?
6. If you worked in the advertising department of a bank, would you recommend magazine advertising? Support your answer.
7. If you were the advertising manager for a magazine aimed at senior citizens, what advantages would you cite to potential advertisers?
8. What is the advantage of magazine advertising to businesses that sell to other businesses?
9. If you were buying magazine space for a blue-jeans manufacturer, what factors would you take into account in choosing the magazines?
10. What is the importance of the Audit Bureau of Circulations?

14

ELECTRONIC MEDIA

 n 1980, if you had wanted a wine cooler, you would have been out of luck—the product didn't exist yet. Today, you can choose from over 100 different brands of wine cooler, including top sellers California Cooler, Sun Country, White Mountain cooler, and Bartles & Jaymes.

California Cooler started it all in 1981 when its first bottles hit the stores. The tremendous success of this light alcoholic beverage soon had dozens of other companies rushing to enter the wine cooler market with their own version of the drink. In early 1985, California Cooler still had 58 percent of the market, but that all changed with the appearance on the scene of two folksy entrepreneurs, Frank Bartles and Ed Jaymes. These down-home fellows entered our homes via TV to tell us how they had come to the conclusion that "Between Ed's fruit orchard and my vineyard, we could make a truly superior premium-grade wine cooler. So Ed took out a second on his house and wrote to Harvard for an M.B.A., and now we're preparing to enter the wine cooler business." (Actually, Frank is the one who told us all this—Ed just sat behind him on the company's rustic front porch, nodding at appropriate moments throughout Frank's monologue.)

In the ensuing series of commercials, Frank told us how they had acquired the snazzy label for their product (Ed had ordered it by mail from France), how they needed to sell more wine cooler to be able to make the balloon payment on Frank's second mortgage, and how Bartles & Jaymes complements all foods except for kohlrabi and candy corn (see Figure 14–1).

Viewers were instantly captivated by Frank and Ed, and sales of the product skyrocketed. After only three months, B&J had captured 7 percent of the wine cooler market, and by early 1986, it had become the leader, with 27 percent.

Why was this ad campaign so successful? One reason is that Americans love entrepreneurs. As A. Craig Copitas put it in *Inc.* magazine, "You have to admire these two old men willing to take on the American vintners for a slug of the $700 million-a-year wine cooler market."[1] Of course, Copitas also noted that Frank and Ed actually have little to do with entrepreneurship, since they are in reality a California contractor and an Oregon farmer who were hired by Ernest and Julio Gallo to portray the fictitious Bartles and Jaymes.

The commercials were created by Hal Riney of Hal Riney and Partners, Inc., San Francisco. His task was to establish an identity for Gallo's wine cooler. He also needed to design a campaign that would appeal to two main market segments: young upscale consumers and hard-core beer drinkers. The ads succeeded on both fronts because their humor appealed to young sophisticates and the good-ole-boy image appealed to beer drinkers. And though most consumers are now aware that Frank and Ed are clever inventions and that Bartles & Jaymes is a Gallo product, they are continuing to make B&J a market leader.

The Bartles & Jaymes campaign is a stunning example of how commercials on broadcast television can be used to establish product identity and to reach a large proportion of the population. In this chapter, we will explore some of the other advantages of broadcast TV, as well as the various drawbacks of this medium. We will also see how other electronic media, including cable television and radio, are providing competition to broadcast television and can also be used as important parts of the creative mix.

USING BROADCAST TELEVISION IN THE CREATIVE MIX

Although advertising on television seems to come under severe attack on a somewhat regular basis, no one ever denies the creative potential of the television medium. In fact, it is television's very potential for creativity and impact that has fueled so much criticism. As a means of reaching a mass audience, no other medium today has the unique creative abilities of television: the combination of sight, sound, and movement; the opportunity to demonstrate the product; the potential to use special effects; the believability of seeing it happen right before your eyes; and the empathy of the viewer.

Advantages of Broadcast Television

Broadcast television has grown faster than any other advertising medium in history. From its beginnings after World War II, TV has emerged as the medium that attracts the largest volume of national advertising—totaling over $15 billion in 1986. Why? Because contemporary television offers advertisers unique advantages over competing media.

Mass Coverage and Low Cost

A substantial portion of broadcast television's national advertising revenue comes from the packaged goods industry (foods and drugs). Procter & Gamble, for instance, has led all other advertisers in spending since 1951. Its broadcast TV expenditures in 1986 were nearly $800 million, of which more than $450 million went to network programs. In Procter & Gamble's nationwide distribution of high-volume, low-profit products in supermarkets, it uses television to reach a mass audience and presell its brand names at a very low cost per thousand (see Figure 14–2).

A full 98 percent of all American homes have a TV set, and most have more than one. Of the households that own TV sets, 88 percent view TV at least once during the average day. More than 94 percent of television

FIGURE   14–1

As a result of a series of clever TV commercials, Frank Bartles and Ed Jaymes have become popular "folk heroes" of the 80s.

FIGURE   14–2

National broadcast television is the ideal medium for advertisers that produce mass market household products, such as Procter & Gamble.

(MUSIC UNDER)

WOMAN: When towels feel this soft . . .

CHORUS: *Jump in . . .*

WOMAN: Sheets feel this fresh.

CHORUS: *Jump.*

WOMAN: And there's no cling to most anything.

CHORUS: *Jump, jump, jump, jump.*

WOMAN: You've got Bounce clothes.

(SINGS): *Clothes you can't wait to jump into.*

CHORUS: *Jump.*

WOMAN SINGS: *Feel the touch.*

CHORUS: *Jump in.*

WOMAN SINGS: *You are the one, you feel so good around me.*

CHORUS: *Jump, jump, jump, jump.*

WOMAN: You could use this or even this, but Bounce is the softener more people use.

And they feel like this about their clothes.

So soft sweaters, sweet smelling linens, no cling things.

CHORUS: *Jump.*

WOMAN SINGS: *Feel the touch.*

CHORUS: *Jump in.*

WOMAN: Bounce . . .

(SINGS): *For clothes you can't wait to jump into.*

CHORUS: *Jump, jump, jump.*

households tune in during an average week. The amount of viewing time for the average household has increased over the past few decades, from five hours six minutes per day in 1960 to more than seven hours per day today.[2]

Typical network nighttime programs reach 15 percent of all television households. The more popular shows and special attractions reach 25 percent and more. For example, over 40 percent are usually reached by a Super Bowl game.

Broadcast television, therefore, has historically been a mass medium for mass-consumption products. Despite the often huge initial outlays for commercial production and advertising time, television's equally huge audiences bring the per-exposure cost for each commercial down to a comparatively low level.

Selectivity

In spite of the fact that television audiences are mass audiences, they can vary a great deal depending on the time of day, the day of the week, and the nature of the programming. This permits the advertiser to present the message when the potential audience is best. Furthermore, advertisers can reach geographically selective audiences by buying local and regional markets.

Impact

The ability to bring a moving picture with sound into the living rooms of America is tantamount to having an army of door-to-door sellers. Television offers an immediacy that other forms of advertising are unable to achieve, with the product being demonstrated in full color right before the customer's eyes. Seeing a hamburger being cooked and eaten on the living room screen has sent many a viewer off to the fast-food outlet for a similar meal.

Creativity

Television's creative potential is limited only by the commercial creator's talents. The various facets of the television commercial—sight, sound, motion, and color—permit an infinite number of original and imaginative appeals. For some interesting facts on how to create effective TV commercials, see the Checklist of What Works Best in Television.

Prestige

Hallmark, Xerox, Mobil, Exxon, and IBM have all experienced an increase in prestige and corporate awareness by sponsoring dramatic presentations and other cultural programs. Potential distributors, the company's sales force, and customers are impressed by a product's association with quality programming.

Social Dominance

Television has exhibited a power that goes beyond impact and prestige. The entire nation has been emotionally stirred by TV screenings of the Olympic Games, space travel, assassinations, wars, and political scandals. Most Americans under age 35 don't know what life is like without television—they have grown up with it as an important part of their environment.

The real relationship between the power of television and the sale of an advertiser's product is difficult to gauge. However, we can safely assume that the magnetic attraction of television events gives this medium a potential for advertising unlike any other.

Drawbacks of Broadcast Television

Although television's power as a creative tool may be unmatched, broadcast television still has many drawbacks that keep it from being used by most advertisers. In many instances, television just doesn't "fit" in the creative mix. This may be because of cost, lack of audience selectivity, inherent brevity, or the clutter of competitive messages.

Cost

Broadcast television suffers its greatest handicap from the high cost of producing commercials and buying airtime. The production costs for a TV spot vary with how the advertiser chooses to present the product. Most

Checklist of What Works Best in Television

☐ The picture must tell the story. Forget every other rule in this chapter, and you will still be ahead of the game. Television is a *visual* medium. That's why the people in front of a set are called *viewers*. Try this trick for looking at a storyboard. *Cover the words.* What is the message of the commercial with the sound turned off? Is there a message at all?

☐ Look for a "key visual." Here's another test to apply to the storyboard. Can you pick out *one* frame that visually sums up the whole message? Most good commercials can be reduced to this single "key visual." A commercial with many different scenes may look interesting in storyboard form but can turn out to be an overcomplicated piece of film.

☐ Grab the viewer's attention. The *first five seconds* of a commercial are crucial. Analysis of audience reaction shows either a sharp drop or a sharp rise in interest during this time. *Commercial attention does not build.* Your audience can only become less interested, never more. The level you reach in the first five seconds is the highest you will get, so don't save your punches. Offer the viewer something right off the bat. *News.* A *problem* to which you have the solution. A *conflict* that is involving.

☐ Be single-minded. A good commercial is uncomplicated. Direct. It never makes the viewer do a lot of mental work. The basic commercial length in U.S. television is 30 seconds. The content possible in that time is outlined in the phrase: "name-claim-demonstration." The name of your product, your consumer benefit, and the reason the consumer should believe it. Longer commercials *should not add copy points.* A 60-second commercial tells the same story as the 30-second one, with more leisure and detail. Or—best of all—*repetition.* The 60-second allows

time for a mood to be created; the 30-second generally does not. The 10-second and 15-second commercials are one-point messages. The 10-second registers the brand name and promise. The 15-second makes the promise more explicit.

☐ Register the name of your product. Too often, a viewer will remember the commercial but not the name of your brand. This is a problem particularly troublesome with new products. Showing the package on screen and mouthing the name is not enough. Take extra pains to implant your product name in the viewer's mind.

☐ The tone of your advertising must reflect your product personality. If you are fortunate enough to have a product with an established brand image, your advertising *must* reflect that image. It takes dedication on the part of advertiser and agency to build a brand personality. Discipline yourself to reject advertising that conflicts with it. (It helps to have a written "personality statement" of your product; if it were a person, what sort of person would it be?) When you launch a new product, the very *tone* of your announcement commercial tells viewers what to expect. From that moment on, it is hard to change their minds. Once you have decided on a personality for your product, sustain it in every commercial. Change campaigns when you must but retain the same tone of voice.

☐ Avoid "talky" commercials. Look for the simplest, and most memorable, set of words to get across your consumer benefit. Every word must work hard. A 30-second commercial usually allows you *no more* than 65 words, a 60-second commercial twice that amount. Be specific. Pounce on clichés, flabbiness, and superlatives. Try this discipline. When you ask for 10 words to be added to a commercial, decide which 10 you would *delete* to make room for them.

national advertisers film their commercials and usually pay $50,000 or more for each. The second major area of expense is network time (see Figure 14–3). A single 30-second commercial during prime time may cost as much as $400,000 for the top-rated shows; the average cost is about $120,000.[3] Special attractions can cost much more. A half-minute of commercial time during the 1988 Super Bowl cost $675,000, for example.

For the large advertiser, television can be relatively efficient, with the cost per thousand viewers running from $2 to $10. But the cost of large coverage, even at relatively low rates, usually prices the small and medium-sized advertisers out of the market.

FIGURE   14–3   Network advertising rates

	Average rating		Cost of :30 commercial		:30 CPM/HH	
	Low	High	Low	High	Low	High
Daytime						
Early morning (7–9 A.M.)	3.0	5.0	$ 5,000	$ 13,000	$2.00	$ 3.00
Weekday (10 A.M.–4:30 P.M.)	3.0	8.5	5,400	28,000	2.10	3.85
Weekend (children)	3.0	8.0	5,000	28,000	2.00	4.00
Prime time	8.0	20.0	41,000	172,000	6.00	10.00
Late night	3.0	7.5	9,000	35,000	3.50	5.50

Lack of Selectivity

Many advertisers are seeking a very specific, small audience. In these cases, broadcast television is not cost-effective and is therefore at a disadvantage. In other cases, broadcast television is losing some of the selectivity that advertisers have historically found appealing. For example, daytime network TV used to deliver a large female audience, but now fewer women are tuning in to network shows during the day, either because they are working or because they are watching programs on cable or independent stations.[4] This is frustrating to advertisers who have traditionally promoted their products on soap operas to reach the target audience of women under age 50.

Brevity

An advertising message on broadcast television is brief, usually lasting only 30 seconds. The objective is to grab viewers' attention and leave them with a favorable attitude toward the product (or at least make them remember it). But in 30 seconds, that's a tall task.

Studies have shown that most TV viewers can't remember the product or company promoted in the most recent TV ad they watched—even if it was within the last five minutes.[5] Recall is improved with the length of the commercial—60-second spots are remembered better than 30-second spots.

Despite this fact, the trend is actually toward shorter and shorter commercials. In 1984, all three major networks began offering *split-30s,* which are 30-second spots in which the advertiser promotes two separate products with separate messages. Then, in the fall of 1985, CBS started accepting 15-second spots. It was another year before ABC and NBC followed suit. Now an estimated 30 percent of commercials aired are :15s, and that proportion is predicted to be half of all ads by 1990.[6] Currently, networks

FIGURE 14-4

The challenge of producing 15-second TV spots is to catch the viewer's attention and make a memorable impression in a very brief time. Polaroid's ads for its Spectra system have been among the best at meeting this challenge.

SPORT ANNCR.: That's left tackle Jim Daniels' first league score. A big touchdown.

V.O.: There's only one camera system you can buy that lets you hold the picture in your hand while you

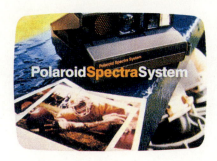

still hold the feeling in your heart. The Polaroid Spectra System.

are making about a third of their commercial time open for :15s, with the majority of that in the daytime periods. Only two :15s are allowed in a network commercial break.

The reason for the popularity of 15-second spots among advertisers is that they cost half as much as :30s yet are 70 to 80 percent as effective. Although the lower cost makes network advertising more feasible for some of the smaller advertisers, it is apparently the big companies, such as Nabisco, General Mills, Burger King, and Polaroid that are committing large parts of their TV ad budgets to :15s (see Figure 14–4).

Clutter

One major drawback to television advertising is that a commercial is seldom seen in an isolated position. It is usually surrounded by station-break announcements, credits, public-service announcements, and "billboards" (just the name or slogan of a product), not to mention six or seven other commercials. With all these messages competing for attention, the viewer often comes away annoyed and confused and with a high rate of product misidentification. And now with more and more 15-second commercials, the clutter is expected to increase.

Zipping and Zapping

With the advent of videocassette recorders (VCRs) and other home electronic gadgets, television advertisers are faced with the additional challenges of zipping and zapping. *Zipping* refers to the ability of VCR users to skip through the commercials when replaying programs they have taped; *zapping* refers to the tendency of remote-control users to change channels at the beginning of a commercial break.

To counteract the problems of zipping, zapping, clutter, and brevity, the creators of TV commercials will need to concentrate their efforts on devising messages that immediately capture viewer attention, present a single message in an entertaining way, and avoid irritating or insulting the intelligence of their audience. However, what is an advertiser to do when its brilliantly created, captivating message is sandwiched in with four or five other ads during a commercial break? The viewer may already be gone and the advertiser's dollars wasted.

OVERVIEW OF THE BROADCAST TELEVISION MEDIUM

In 1947, five television stations began broadcasting. By 1986, the number had grown to more than 900 commercial stations. Of these, more than 500 were VHF (very high frequency—channels 2 through 13), and more than 400 were UHF (ultrahigh frequency—channels 14 through 83).

Until 1952, all stations were VHF. Then the Federal Communications Commission (FCC) authorized 70 more channels (14 through 83) and referred to them as UHF. To equalize coverage, a law was passed in 1965 requiring all new TV sets to be designed to receive UHF broadcasts. This, along with the tremendous growth of cable networks in the late 70s, brought many more UHF stations into existence. Between 1984 and 1986 alone, 150 new UHF stations were born.

All commercial broadcast television stations, whether VHF or UHF, are either affiliated with one of the four national networks (ABC, NBC, CBS, Fox) or are independent stations. Both network affiliates and independent stations may subscribe to nationally syndicated programs as well as originate their own programming.

Audience Trends

Middle-income, high school–educated viewers and their families are the heaviest viewers of broadcast television. There are two possible reasons for this. First, most television programming is directed at this group. Second, people with considerably higher income and education usually have a more diversified range of interests and entertainment options.

The average number of television viewing hours has steadily increased since the medium was introduced. Children under 12 view an average of 27 hours per week; middle-aged men, nearly 29 hours; and middle-aged women, 34. By age 18, the average child has watched more than 22,000 hours (two and one-half years) of TV. Older women watch TV the most (42 hours a week); teenage females, the least (23 hours).

Individual program audiences vary a great deal. A sporting event, for example, attracts proportionately more men in the 18–34 age category than any other group. Look at the audience composition statistics in Figure 14–5. How would you describe the primary viewers of network movies?

The audience for broadcast TV may be changing as more households acquire cable and VCRs. Already households with cable watch less network TV than noncable households do, and predictions are that home video will have a 25 percent share of overall TV viewing by 1995.[7]

Growth of Television Advertising

As television viewing has increased over the years, so have the number of advertisers and the amounts they spend. In 1950, only 3 percent of total advertising volume was placed on television. That amounted to $171 million. By 1986, that figure had grown to over $20 billion and accounted for

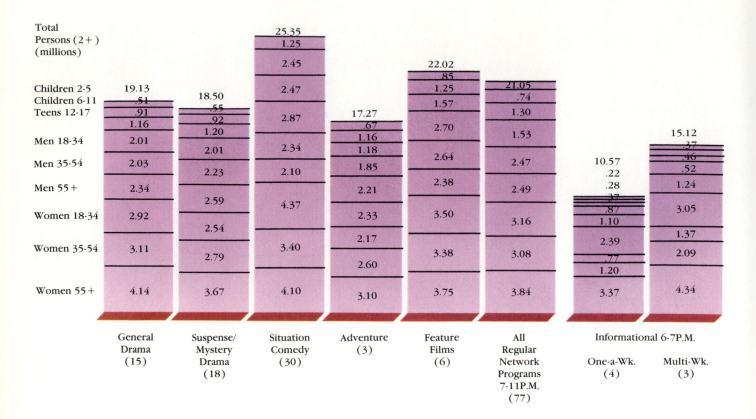

FIGURE 14–5

Audience composition by selected program type, regularly scheduled programs, 7–11 P.M. (average minute audience).

more than 29 percent of all ad spending. The major broadcast television advertisers and their expenditures are listed in Figure 14–6.

Types of Broadcast Advertising

Advertisers can buy advertising time on broadcast television several ways: they may sponsor an entire program, participate in a program, purchase spots from syndicators, or use spot announcements between programs.

Network Advertising

One way to advertise is to purchase airtime from one of the national networks: Columbia Broadcasting Company (CBS), National Broadcasting Company (NBC), American Broadcasting Company (ABC), or the new Fox Broadcasting Company (FBC). Networks offer the large advertiser convenience and efficiency because the message can be broadcast simultaneously throughout the country.

When an advertiser undertakes to present a program alone, it is called a *sponsorship*. The advertiser is responsible for the program content and the cost of production as well as the advertising. This is generally so costly that single sponsorships are usually limited to specials.

For companies that decide on this method (AT&T, Xerox, and Hallmark, for example), there are two important advantages. First, the public more readily identifies with the product(s), and the company gains from the prestige attached to sponsoring first-rate entertainment. Second, the sponsor has control over the placement and content of the commercials. The commercials can be fit to the program and run any length desired as long as they are within network or station regulations.

Figure 14–6		Top 10 network TV advertisers
Rank	**Advertiser**	**Network TV ad expenditures 1986**
1	Procter & Gamble Co.	$456,324*
2	Philip Morris Cos.	342,444
3	General Motors Corp.	233,786
4	Unilever NV	202,371
5	McDonald's Corp.	193,002
6	Ford Motor Co.	188,815
7	American Home Products Corp.	186,428
8	Anheuser-Busch Cos.	177,496
9	Kellogg Co.	166,261
10	Johnson & Johnson	164,322

*Dollars are in thousands.

The centralization offered by networks also simplifies bookkeeping, as the advertiser gets only one bill. The total cost per thousand is low—lower even than time purchased on a spot basis, which we will discuss later.

The high cost of sponsoring a program has encouraged many advertisers to *cosponsor* programs, permitting them to realize some of the advantages of sponsorship but at lower cost and risk. They often sponsor on alternate weeks or divide the program into segments. Most sporting events, for instance, are sold as multiple sponsorships.

Most network television advertising is sold on the *participating* basis, with several advertisers buying 30- or 60-second segments within the program. Advertisers can participate in a program once or several times on a regular or irregular basis. This allows the advertiser to spread out the budget and makes it easier to get in and out of a program without a long-term commitment. It also enables smaller advertisers to buy a limited amount of time and still have nationwide coverage.

Network advertising has its disadvantages. An advertiser who desires to buy fewer stations than the full network lineup often finds that preference is given to those willing to buy more. The advertiser who seeks to advertise to a limited market usually finds that the network lineup does not coincide with that need. Furthermore, placing network ads requires a long lead time, which reduces flexibility. Finally, all ads accepted by networks must go through their standards and practices departments and must meet a number of strict rules and guidelines.

Spot Announcements

National spot advertising offers the advertiser greater flexibility since commercials can be concentrated in the desired markets. In addition, spot ads are less expensive than participations because they are run in clusters between programs. Spots may also be used to introduce a new product into one area at a time, which advertisers with limited distribution and budgets find advantageous.

Spots may be sold either nationally or locally and can be purchased in segments of 10, 15, 30, or 60 seconds. Spot advertising is more difficult to purchase than network advertising because it involves contacting each station directly. However, the station rep system, in which individuals act as sales and service representatives for a number of stations, has helped reduce this problem.

The mid-1980s saw a shift toward greater national spot advertising as a means of regional marketing. According to Roger Rice, president of the Television Bureau of Advertising, "Regional marketing is an emerging trend. Advertisers no longer look at the total United States as one pie but as pieces of varying size."[8] Campbell's Soup Co., for example, has increased its local spot TV ad budget to address regional differences in eating habits.

A major drawback to spot advertising is that during network programming, it is available only at station breaks and when network advertisers have purchased less than the full lineup. Thus, spot ads are likely to be lost in the clutter and tend to have lower viewership.

Syndication

An increasingly popular alternative to network advertising is advertising on syndicated programs. Television syndication comes in three forms: off-network, first-run, and barter. Off-network programs are those that originally appeared on the networks and are now available to individual

PEOPLE IN ADVERTISING

Jerry Della Femina

Chairman of the Board
Della Femina, Travisano & Partners, Inc.

It was Jerry Della Femina's first day on the job at Ted Bates & Company. With him in the conference room were six account, art, and copy supervisors. They were engaged in a life-and-death struggle to dream up a campaign for Panasonic, a Japanese electronics firm. During the silent meditation, it hit him. "I've got it! I've got it! How about this headline: From those wonderful folks who gave you Pearl Harbor."

At first there was only stupefied silence. The account executive dropped his pipe, and an art director started to laugh hysterically. The line was never used in the campaign, and the horrified reaction of the agency was one of the things that compelled Della Femina to eventually start his own agency.

Jerry Della Femina, who made his mark in American advertising before he was 30 with some of the most provocative and effective ad copy ever written, is founder and chairman of the board of Della Femina, Travisano & Partners, Inc., a Madison Avenue agency.

Della Femina was born in Brooklyn, the son of Italian-speaking immigrant parents. When he entered school at age six, he was unable to speak English.

stations for rebroadcast. First-run programs are original shows produced specifically for the syndication market. Finally, bartered shows are first-run programs that are offered free or for a reduced rate to stations but come with some of the ad space presold to national advertisers. The most popular barter programs, including "Wheel of Fortune," "Entertainment Tonight," and "The Oprah Winfrey Show," can be found on stations in nearly every U.S. city. Barter syndication is one of the fastest-growing trends in television, with advertising revenues tripling between 1981 and 1985.[9] Figure 14–7 diagrams how barter syndication works.

Local

Retailers, often in cooperation with nationally known manufacturers, may buy time from local stations. As a rule, local airtime is sold as spot announcements, but sometimes programs are developed and sponsored by local advertisers. Local firms may also buy the rights to a syndicated film series and sponsor it in their own market.

TELEVISION AUDIENCE MEASUREMENT

Assume you are the director of corporate advertising for a major international corporation whose stock is traded on the New York Stock Exchange. A study you have commissioned reveals that your company, as large as it is, is suffering from an "identity void"; that is, nobody hates you, nobody loves you, nobody knows you. Furthermore, because of this identity void, your company's stock is rarely recommended by financial analysts, and

After graduating from high school, he went to work as an advertising messenger for *The New York Times.* He recalls, "I used to deliver proofs of ads to department stores on Fifth Avenue. Wherever I went . . . I used to see guys sitting around with their feet propped up on their desks. That's when I made up my mind that copywriting was for me." He enrolled in Brooklyn College and took night courses in advertising, but it took seven years of working at odd jobs before he finally landed a job in the field.

In 1961, Della Femina joined Daniel & Charles, writing ads for Kaiser-Roth, and over the next six years, he worked for four other agencies, turning out award-winning print and broadcast campaigns. One of his best-known print ads was a spread for Talon zippers in which a Little League catcher informed his pitcher on the mound, "Your fly is open." While creative supervisor at Ted Bates & Company in 1966, he persuaded Yogi Berra to appear in Ozone Hair Spray TV commercials alongside copy that read, "Yogi Berra is one of those sissies who uses his wife's hairspray."

In 1967, with Ron Travisano and two other Bates associates, Della Femina launched his own agency. Three years later, he gained acclaim by writing the book *From Those Wonderful Folks Who Gave You Pearl Harbor: Front-Line Dispatches from the Advertising War,* an industry classic.

Today, Della Femina, Travisano & Partners, Inc., is owned by London-based Wight Collins Rutherford Scott PLC, and Della Femina remains as chairman of the board. The agency has offices in Los Angeles, Atlanta, and Tokyo and annual billings of over $250 million. Its clients include Blue Nun, Gillette, Isuzu, Lipton, and Ralston Purina (for which Della Femina and partner Ron Travisano created the memorable "singing" cat for Meow Mix). The majority of the agency's media dollars are spent on television advertising, including the highly acclaimed Joe Isuzu commercials ("Hi, I'm Joe Isuzu. [He's lying.]")

Now in his early 50s, Della Femina says, "I guess I'm still the enfant terrible, the world's oldest enfant terrible. I'm still saying we've got to take chances and try something different." He urges young people coming into the advertising business to do as he did—try new things rather than sticking with the tried and true.

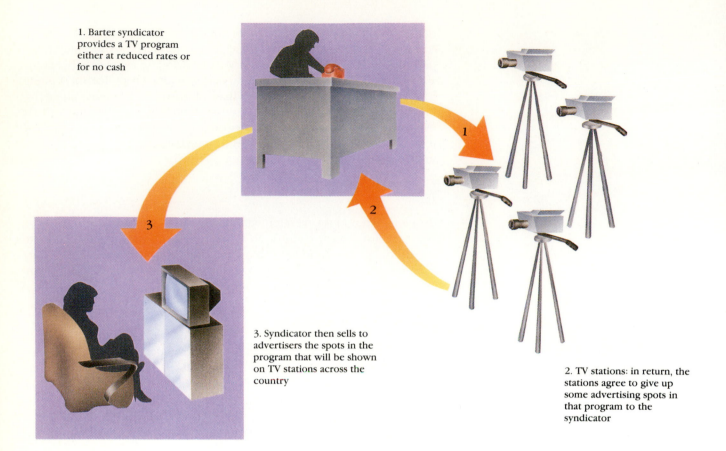

1. Barter syndicator provides a TV program either at reduced rates or for no cash

3. Syndicator then sells to advertisers the spots in the program that will be shown on TV stations across the country

2. TV stations: in return, the stations agree to give up some advertising spots in that program to the syndicator

FIGURE 14–7

How barter syndication works.

even your current shareholders are dissatisfied with your stock's performance.

You decide you need to advertise—to inform financial decision makers (analysts, pension fund managers, bank portfolio managers, investment bankers, stockbrokers, and corporate executives) about your company, its activities, its growth, and its future. Would you use television as the mainstay in your creative mix?

A company called TRW did. But first they had to be sure they could reach their target audience efficiently with that medium. That meant studying the audiences of various programs and analyzing the programs' impact and cost effectiveness against those of other media vehicles. To do that, of course, required an understanding of audience measurement techniques and the terminology used for television advertising.

Rating Services: "The Book"

A number of rating services measure the program audiences of TV and radio stations for advertisers and broadcasters. They pick a representative sample of the market and, through various techniques, furnish data on the size and characteristics of the audiences that view or listen to the programs.

Several of these research organizations gather the data at their own expense and publish it. Companies interested in their findings subscribe to the service and use it as a basis in making media plans for advertising.

The most commonly used services for TV are provided by A. C. Nielsen, Arbitron, and AGB. For demographic studies of TV audiences, advertisers also commonly use the *Simmons Reports*. These services publish their findings two or more times per year, depending on the size of the market, in a publication generally referred to as "The Book." The book reports a wide array of statistics on how many people, in what age groups, and of what sex are watching TV at various times of the day within a specific market area. Ad Lab 14-A describes how methods such as the "people meter" are used to arrive at the TV ratings provided by Nielsen and AGB.

Television Markets

Television rating services use a more precise definition of their markets to minimize the problem of overlapping TV signals.

Areas of Dominant Influence (ADI)

Arbitron introduced the concept of calling TV markets *areas of dominant influence (ADI)*. An ADI is defined as "an exclusive geographic area consisting of all counties in which the home market stations receive a preponderance of total viewing hours." Thus, the Charlotte ADI is all counties in which the Charlotte TV stations are the most watched.

Designated Market Areas (DMA)

The Nielsen station index uses a similar method known as *designated market areas (DMA)*. When TRW decided to try television advertising as a means to fill up its identity void, the company discovered that approximately half of all its shareholders were in the top 10 DMAs, which include the nation's largest cities from New York to Pittsburgh. Therefore, the company's first ads were scheduled in these top 10 markets with one exception: Houston was substituted for Pittsburgh because of the number of TRW customers in that area.

Dayparts

The next questions for TRW were when to air its commercials and on which programs. Unlike radio, there is little or no station loyalty in television. Viewer loyalty is to programs, and programs continue to run or are canceled depending on the size of their ratings (percentage of the population watching). Ratings also depend on what time of day a program runs. Television time is divided into *dayparts* as follows:

	Daytime:	9 A.M.–4 P.M. (EST)
Combine as early fringe	Early fringe:	4–5:30 P.M. (EST)
	Early news:	5 or 5:30–7:30 P.M. (EST)
	Prime access:	7:30–8 P.M. (EST)
	Prime:	8–11 P.M. (EST)
Combine as late fringe	Late news:	11–11:30 P.M. (EST)
	Late fringe:	11:30 P.M.–1 A.M. (EST)

AD LAB 14-A   Where Do Those Infamous TV Ratings Come From?

For three and a half decades, the life and death of network TV programs was in the hands of the "Nielsen families"—the randomly chosen households used by A. C. Nielsen Company to measure audience viewing patterns. There were actually two types of such families: those who kept diaries and those who simply had a "black box" attached to their TV sets. Someone in each of 2,400 diary homes kept a written record of which shows were watched by each member of the household during the week. Those in the 1,700 black-box households had an audimeter device attached to their TV sets that kept track of when the set was on and what channel it was tuned to. It was on the basis of data from these 4,100 households that Nielsen computed its Nielsen Television Index (NTI), the sole source of national TV ratings.

But that method of determining national ratings is now gone forever. It has been replaced by the *people meter,* an electronic device that automatically records a household's TV viewing, including the channels watched, the number of minutes of viewing, and who in the household is watching. This last requires that each person "punch in" and "punch out" on a keypad whenever beginning or ending a viewing session. The microwave-based people meter keeps track of second-by-second viewing choices of up to eight household members and relays the data to a central computer, which tabulates all the data overnight.

The original people meter was developed by AGB Research, a British company, and was first tested in the United States in 1984. It proved to eliminate a lot of problems that had plagued the diary system. The diary approach had been criticized on several counts: The diarist would often record several days' viewing at one time, trying to recall what had been watched by the family in the previous week; one person usually kept track of the diary for the whole family; and the diarist often had difficulty keeping track of the burgeoning number of channels available for viewing and of time spent recording and playing back shows with a VCR. All these factors tended to bias the NTI toward major network shows, which were easier for diarists to remember. In addition, the black boxes were unreliable in that they could not indicate who was watching—only that the set was on. The people meter eliminated all these problems.

AGB immediately found clients in ad agencies, cable networks, and syndicators—all of whom felt that broadcast network shows were overreported and other types of shows underreported. The biggest blow to the NTIs came when CBS signed on for the AGB people meter system for the fall 1986 season. Nielsen, which had its own people meter system in development, made the decision to abandon its old methods entirely and go solely with the people meter in fall 1987.

The people meter is not without its critics. Some worry that requiring viewers to punch in and out will affect demographic findings, since some types of people are more likely to cooperate than others. And NBC and ABC were slow to come around to the system because early tests of the meters had yielded lower ratings for network shows than the NTI had, which would mean a loss of ad revenues if the trend were consistent.

For better or for worse, the people meter appears to be around for a while. AGB planned to have meters in 5,000 households by the fall of 1988, while Nielsen was scheduled to have them in 4,000 homes. Meanwhile, even more sophisticated methods of audience measurement are in the works, and the people meters themselves may be replaced much sooner than they replaced their predecessors.

Those who are fond of TV diaries may be happy to learn that this method of audience measurement has not been abandoned completely. Arbitron, which provides ratings of local television programming, uses the diary method during the four "sweeps" periods of each year. Both Arbitron and Nielsen conduct surveys of major market areas during these special ratings periods and publish "sweeps books" that provide the basis for local stations' ad rates.

Laboratory Applications

1. What are the advantages and disadvantages of the various television audience measurement methods?
2. Which audience rating method do you consider to be the best? Why?

FIGURE   14–8

When TRW aired its M. C. Escher–inspired commercials, it sought time slots when potential investors would be more likely to be watching, such as during the late evening news.

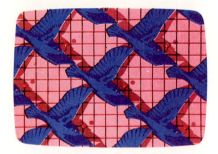

ANNCR VO: Did you ever notice that just when you think you see the whole picture, the picture changes?

Technology from a company called TRW lets us look at our world in fresh ways.

Because there's more to everything than meets the eye.

Tomorrow is taking shape at a company called TRW.

There are different levels of viewing during each daypart. The highest viewing level, of course, is in prime time (8–11 P.M.). Late fringe time also ranks fairly high in most markets among adults. Daytime and early fringe tend to be viewed most heavily by women.

To reach the greatest percentage of the advertiser's target audience with maximum frequency, all within budget, the media planner determines a *daypart mix* based on the TV usage levels reported by the rating services.

In TRW's initial studies of its target group, it learned its target audience watched television for entertainment and information, principally during prime time and late evening news; they listened to the radio on the way to work; and they read trade publications related to their work. When TRW scheduled its first TV ads, then, it bought enough late evening news from the two top-rated stations in each market to achieve a balance of good reach and frequency totaling a minimum of 50 gross rating points per week (see Figure 14–8). This TV schedule was then supported with additional ads on morning radio and in major business publications.

Audience Measures

Rating services and media planners use numerous other terms to define a television station's audience, penetration, and efficiency.

TV households (TVHH) refers to the number of households that own television sets. In the United States, approximately 87.4 million households (over 98 percent of all households) own television sets. By looking at the number of households that own TVs in a particular market, we can gain a sense of the size of that market. Likewise, by looking at the number of TV households tuned in to a particular program, we can get a sense of how popular the program is and how many people a commercial is likely to reach.

The percentage of homes in a given area that have one or more TV sets turned on at any particular time is expressed as *households using TV (HUT)*. If there are 1,000 TV sets in the survey area and 500 are turned on, the HUT figure is 50 percent.

We're all familiar with TV shows that have been canceled because their ratings slipped. What does that really mean? The percentage of TV households in an area tuned in to a specific program is called the *program rating*.

$$\text{Rating} = \frac{\text{Number tuned to specific station}}{\text{TVHH}}$$

Networks are interested in high ratings because they are a measure of a show's popularity. If a show is not popular, advertisers will not want to advertise on it, and a network's revenue will fall. Similarly, local stations often make changes in their programming in order to increase their popularity and, thereby, their ratings.

The percentage of homes that have sets in use (HUT) tuned in to a specific program is called the program's *share of audience*. A program with only five viewers could have a 50 share if only 10 sets are turned on. For that reason, the program rating figures are important because they measure the audience as a percentage of all TV households in the area, regardless of whether the TV sets are on or off.

The total number of homes reached by some portion of a program is referred to as *total audience*. This figure is normally broken down to determine *audience composition* (the distribution of audience into demographic categories).

Gross Rating Points

In television, *gross rating points (GRPs)* represent the total rating points achieved by a particular media schedule over a specific period, such as a week or a month. Thus, a weekly schedule of five commercials on programs with an average household rating of 20 would yield 100 GRPs.

TRW determined that a schedule of 50 GRPs per week would be sufficient at the beginning of its television campaign. This might have been accomplished by buying 10 spots with an average rating of 5 or only 2 spots with an average rating of 25. The latter might have been feasible by using a highly rated prime-time program, but then the frequency would have been very low. So TRW opted to use the late evening newscasts, which had lower ratings against total TV households but higher shares of those adults watching; it also afforded the company the ability to gain frequency.

The results of TRW's decision demonstrated the wisdom of its choice. In key markets where the commercials ran, surveys were taken, and the number of respondents who looked on TRW as an attractive investment alternative had increased 20 percent—to more than 60 percent total. In control markets where the TRW commercials did not air, the company's image remained virtually unchanged.

BUYING TELEVISION TIME

The process of buying TV time can be rather lengthy as advertisers determine which programs are available to them at what cost, analyze the various programs for efficiency, negotiate with stations or reps on price, determine what reach and frequency they are achieving, eventually sign the broadcast contracts, and, finally, review the affidavits of performance to be sure the commercials ran as agreed. The buying procedures for television are so complex that most large advertisers seek the assistance of advertising agencies or media-buying services. Buying services are gaining in popularity because they charge less than ad agencies and are proving successful in saving advertisers money by negotiating for desirable time slots at reduced rates.[10] For the local advertiser, the assistance of station reps also proves invaluable in determining the best buys for the money.

Requesting Avails

To find out which programs are available to them, media buyers contact the sales representatives for the stations they are considering. These may be local station salespeople, national media rep organizations that sell for one station in each market, or network reps. The media buyer gives the rep information about the advertiser's media objectives and target audiences and asks the rep to supply a list of available time slots along with their prices and estimated ratings (see Figure 14–9).

The *avails* submitted by the rep should include all the data requested

WALB-TV
(Airdate April 15, 1954)
ALBANY

GRAY COMMUNICATIONS SYSTEMS INC.

NBC Television Network

nab   TvB

Gray Communications Systems, Inc.
Media Code 6 211 0050 2.00   Mid 007346-000
WALB-TV
1709 Stuart Ave., Albany, GA 31707. Phone 912-883-0154, TWX, 810-781-5104.
Mailing Address: Box 3130, Albany, GA 31708.

6. TIME RATES
No. A5 Ann rates eff 10/1/84—Rec'd 10/29/84.
No. P2 Prog. rates eff 7/20/84—Rec'd 8/14/84.

7. SPOT ANNOUNCEMENTS
30 SECONDS-DAYTIME & FRINGE

	F	I1	I2	I3
MON THRU FRI, AM:				
6-6:30, Sunrise	60	55	45	35
6:30-7, Today In Georgia	80	70	60	55
7-9, Today Show	100	85	75	70
9-10, Hour Magazine	85	70	55	45
10-noon, NBC Rotation	110	90	70	60
PM:				
Noon-12:30, Town & Country	100	85	80	70
12:30-4, NBC Afternoon Rotation	140	130	120	110
4-4:30, Heathcliff	120	100	85	75
4:30-5, happy Days	120	100	95	90
5-5:30, People's Court	140	120	110	100
5:30-6, Three's Company	160	140	120	110
6-7, NewsCenter 10	350	300	275	250
7:30-8, Barney Miller	400	350	275	250
11-11:30 Mon thru Sun, NewsCenter 10	300	250	225	200
11:30-12:30 am, Tonight Show	80	65	55	50
12:30-1:30 am Mon thru Thurs, Late Night w/Letterman	65	50	35	30
12:30 am-concl, Friday Night Videos	65	50	35	25
WEEKEND				
SAT, AM:				
7-7:30, Georgia Farm Monitor	100	85	70	40
7:30 am-1 pm, Kid's Rotation	120	100	95	85
PM:				
1-7, Various	120	100	95	85
6-6:30, NewsCenter 10	300	250	225	200
7-8, Hee Haw	350	300	275	250
11:30 pm-12:30 am, Solid Gold	130	110	90	75
12:30 am-concl, Saturday Night Live	90	75	60	50
SUN, AM:				
7-8, Gospel Singing Jubilee	75	60	50	40
8-noon, Religious/Various	70	55	45	40
PM:				
Noon-7, Various	120	100	85	75
6-6:30, NewsCenter 10	300	250	225	200
11:30-concl, Barnaby Jones/Love Boat	65	50	45	40

PRIME TIME

	F	I1	I2	I3	I4
8-11 Mon thru Sat; 7-11 Sun	900	800	700	600	500

60 sec: double the 30 sec.
10 sec: 50% of 30 sec rounded to next dollar.
No 10 seconds within NewsCenter 10.
F—Fixed.
I—Immediately preemptible.

10. PROGRAM TIME RATES

Daily:	1 hr	1/2 hr	1/4 hr	10 min	5 min
8-11 pm	2500	1800	1500	1400	1200
6-8 pm	1500	1200	1100	1050	1000
Noon-6 pm & 11-11:30 pm	1000	600	500	450	400
Sign-on-noon & 11:30 pm-sign-off	600	400	300	250	225

11. SPECIAL FEATURES
COLOR
Schedules network color, film, slides, tape and live.
Equipped with high and low band VTR.

13. CLOSING TIME
48 hours prior telecast; Sat & Sun material closes at 5 pm Thurs.

FIGURE   14–9

The *Spot Television Rates and Data* listing for WALB–TV in Albany, Georgia, shows the rate charged on its grid plan for various time slots during the week. The grid used will depend on program audience estimates at the time.

based on the most recent Nielsen, Arbitron, or AGB book. Many media buyers ask for the information based on the last two or three books to see whether a show's ratings are consistent or have an upward or downward trend.

Selecting Programs for Buys

To determine which shows to buy, the media buyer must select the most efficient ones in relation to the target audience. To do this, a simple computation is made of the cost per rating point (CPP) and the cost per thousand (CPM) for each program, as follows:

$$\frac{\text{Cost}}{\text{Rating}} = \text{CPP} \qquad \frac{\text{Cost}}{\text{Thousands of people}} = \text{CPM}$$

For example, assume "Wheel of Fortune" has a rating of 25, reaches 200,000 people in the primary target audience, and costs $2,000 for a 30-second spot on station WXYZ in Everittown, U.S.A. Then,

$$\frac{\$2,000}{25} = \$80 \text{ CPP} \qquad \frac{\$2,000}{200} = \$10 \text{ CPM}$$

Obviously, the lower the cost per thousand, the more efficient the show is against the target audience. The media buyer's task, therefore, is to compare the packages of each station, substituting stronger programs for less efficient ones.

Negotiating Prices and Contracts

While print media normally adhere to rate cards because of their guaranteed circulation, broadcast stations are willing to negotiate prices since their audiences are, at best, estimated.

The purpose of price negotiation from the advertiser's standpoint is to get the best schedule possible within the budget. The media buyer contacts the rep and explains what efficiency the advertiser needs in terms of delivery and CPM to make the buy. The buyer may negotiate lower rates by working out a package deal, may take advantage of *preemption rates*, which allow the station to sell the spot for a higher price to another advertiser if such an offer is made, or can receive a lower rate by accepting run-of-schedule positioning, which means the station chooses when to run the commercial.

Each station contract is a legal document. As such, it is imperative that the media buyer catch any discrepancies before signing it. The contract indicates the dates, times, and programs on which the advertiser's commercials will run, the length of the spots, the rate per spot, and the total amount. The reverse side of the contract defines in small print the various obligations and responsibilities of the advertiser, the agency, and the station and the terms of payment.

After the spots run, the station returns a form to the advertiser or agency, signed and notarized, indicating when spots aired and what *make-goods* are available to compensate for spots the station missed or ran incorrectly. This *affidavit of performance* is the station's legal proof that the advertiser got what was paid for.

USING CABLE TELEVISION IN THE CREATIVE MIX

For over 30 years, broadcast TV, especially network TV, was the dominant entertainment medium in the lives of most Americans. But today, other electronic media are threatening to change that dominance forever. Chief among the challengers is cable television.

Cable TV has been around since the late 1940s. For most of its existence, its main purpose was to carry TV signals by wire to areas that had poor reception. But in the 1970s, several developments occurred that suddenly made cable more attractive to people who otherwise had perfectly good TV reception. The major innovations that contributed to cable's popularity were the advent of satellite TV signals, the capacity of cable to carry dozens of channels, and the introduction of uncut first-run movies in the home via pay-cable channels such as Home Box Office and Showtime.

At first, many subscribers felt cable was worthwhile simply to receive a full array of regional channels and to have access to the premium services such as HBO. But once the novelty wore off, subscribers started to want more for their money. The need for more cable programming was soon filled by a variety of advertiser-supported cable networks, more diversified pay services, and increased local cable programming, all of which drew more and more subscribers.

Cable's growth in the last decade has been extraordinary. In 1975, only 13.2 percent of TV households had cable. In 1980, that proportion had grown to 22.6 percent, and only six years later, it had leaped to 48 percent, with the 50 percent mark reached in late 1987. There are now over 44 million cable subscribers, and cable reaches 98 percent of all U.S. counties.[11]

The presence of cable in American homes has significantly altered both TV viewing patterns and use of other media. Households with cable spend less time watching broadcast TV, even though they watch more television overall than noncable TV households. Whereas noncable households tune into networks and their affiliates 79 percent of the time, cable households tune them in only 56 percent of the time and instead watch cable programming. People in cable households also tend to spend less time listening to the radio, reading, or going out for drives or to the movies. These statistics seem to indicate that, in many cases, cable is reaching an audience that is difficult to get to in any other way.

Advantages of Cable

The primary advantages of cable TV are its selectivity, low cost, and great flexibility.

Selectivity

According to cable's supporters, this medium reaches the kind of households advertisers like best. Cable subscribers are younger, are better educated, are more affluent, have higher-level jobs, and live in larger households than nonsubscribers. Those in cable households are also more likely to try new products and buy more high-ticket items, such as cars, appliances, and high-tech equipment.[12]

In addition to delivering this highly desirable audience, cable offers specialized programming aimed at particular types of viewers. There are cable networks devoted solely to sports, news, business, children's programming, and music, for example. Furthermore, specific cable shows may deliver desirable demographics. Among the highest-rated shows on the Cable News Network (CNN) are the financial programs "Your Money" and "Inside Business," which appeal to an affluent audience. According to July 1987 people meter findings, the viewers of "Your Money" are 92 percent more likely to have a household income over $40,000, while viewers of "Inside Business" are 85 percent more likely.[13] Such *narrowcasting* allows advertisers to choose programming with the viewer demographics that best match their target customers.

Low Cost

The costs of advertising on cable are much lower than the costs for broadcast television and, in many cases, are comparable to radio ad costs. Thus, many small companies that can't afford to advertise on broadcast TV can benefit from TV's immediacy and impact without the enormous expenditures of network TV. One award-winning spot for a video store cost only $200 to produce (see Figure 14–10). In fact, cable costs are low enough that advertisers are able to run longer commercials and even to sponsor entire programs inexpensively. Many national advertisers are finding sponsorship particularly attractive, since an entire cable series can cost less to produce than a single broadcast TV commercial.[14]

Flexibility

One of the most appealing things about cable advertising is the great flexibility it offers. Commercials can be of just about any length, they can be tailored to fit the programming environment, and they can be used for experimentation and test marketing.

FIGURE   14–10

This slapstick spot for a video store, featuring a Groucho Marx imitator, was produced by Comcast Cablevision in Willow Grove, Pennsylvania. The spot cost only $200 to produce.

The costs of the wacky award-winning commercial were kept down by borrowing the props and shooting the whole 30-second commercial in one take.

Welcome, welcome, welcome to West Coast Video where the secret word is *movies*. Say the secret word, the West Coast Video duck will drop down with thousands of movies for you to choose from. Or adventures, comedies, dramas, horror films,

kids' films, and more copies of the hits. I could go on forever but I'm about to hit a wall. And of course every movie rents for just $1.98 overnight. Come to think of it, renting a movie anywhere but West

Coast Video is the most ridiculous thing I've ever heard!

West Coast Video—in the Leo Mall, Krewstown Shopping Center, and Welsh and the Boulevard.

You bet your life!

Whereas broadcast TV commercials need to be short because of the high costs of producing and airing them, cable ads can run up to two minutes and longer. Such long spots are desirable when a minute or less is just not enough time to tell a product's story. One highly praised cable commercial was a two-minute ad for the State of Alaska Division of Tourism. This minitravelogue revealing Alaska's wonders might have been much less effective at 30 seconds.

One long form of ad popular on cable TV is the *infomercial*. The purpose of this longer format (usually three to eight minutes) is to give consumers detailed information about the product or service. It may take the form of demonstrating how to use the product, showing how the product is made, or highlighting special features of the product. Another type of longer ad is the 90-second segment that devotes 60 seconds to a brief feature and 30 seconds to the actual product pitch, such as Noxema's "Another Close Shave" series of ads on ESPN or Crest's "Phillip Molar, Private Tooth" ads on Nickelodeon.

Cable also allows advertisers to produce commercials that will fit a specific programming environment. Thus, different ads for the same product could be developed to fit well on MTV, the Nashville Network, and the Arts and Entertainment Network.

Finally, cable is a good place to experiment, testing both new products and various advertising approaches. Major marketers such as Campbell Soup Co., Bristol-Myers, Colgate-Palmolive, and Johnson & Johnson are using cable to experiment with such variables as ad frequency, copy impact, and media mix.[15] Many of the larger cable systems are working on technical innovations to help in test-marketing efforts, taking advantage of the fact that cable lines reach into individual households.

Drawbacks of Cable

While cable's greatest strength is selectivity, its main weakness is limited reach. Some areas of the country are still without cable, and even in markets with the greatest cable penetration, the proportion of cable homes is only 50 percent, leaving another half of the population without coverage. However, cable subscriptions are growing at a rate of some 400,000 households a day, so the percentage of TV homes without cable should continue to shrink with each passing year.

Another drawback is cable's audience fragmentation. With 40 or more channels at their disposal, cable viewers do not watch any one show in enormous numbers. Thus, reaching the majority of the cable audience in a particular market requires advertising on a great many stations.

Cable, particularly local cable, also has a bit of an image problem to overcome. Poorer production quality and less desirable programming than can be found on broadcast TV have led many to think of cable as less than glamorous. This image appears to be improving, however, as cable network programming becomes stronger and as local cable systems become more sophisticated in their use of a great variety of production techniques.

Cable TV is also subject to some of the same drawbacks as broadcast TV, including zipping and zapping. Well-produced longer-form commercials and infomercials that integrate programming with subtle promotion may be helping to combat these electronic enemies.

Overview of the Cable Medium

Subscribers to cable TV pay a monthly fee to receive TV signals over wires that are laid into the home. The basic price covers as many as 40 or more advertiser-supported stations, including not only the local network affiliates and independents but also cable networks, superstations, and local cable system channels. Subscribers can also pay additional fees to receive premium services, such as HBO, the Disney Channel, and Cinemax, and to see special events such as first-run films, boxing matches, and baseball games (pay-per-view service).

There are now more than 20 national cable networks and a number of regional networks. Figure 14–11 provides a rundown of the most widely carried networks. There are also a handful of *superstations,* which are local television stations that broadcast to the rest of the country via satellite and carry national advertising. The best-known superstation is Ted Turner's WTBS-Atlanta, for which the term was coined.

Most advertising on cable is done through the networks, although local cable advertising is starting to come into its own. Cable systems derive their main income from subscribers and from the premium and pay-per-view services; however, they are finding they need other forms of revenue as well and are starting to actively woo advertisers. According to Paul Kagan Associates, a media consulting company, local cable is by far the fastest-growing segment in advertising, with ad revenues

FIGURE   14–11   The major cable networks

Network	First air date	Subscribers (million)	Cost range*	Program type
Arts & Entertainment	2/84	31.5	$800–2,000	Cultural, family
Black Entertainment Television	1/80	17.5	100–600	Music, sports, family, ethnic
CBN Cable Network	4/77	38.0	600–1,650	Family, Christian
CNN	6/80	41.4	470–5,900	News, finance, weather
The Discovery Channel	6/85	25.6	300–3,000	Science, nature, adventure documentaries
ESPN	9/79	44.3	1,500–6,000	Sports
Financial News Network	11/81	28.5	500–1,000	Business and financial
Headline News	12/81	31.4	500–5,900	News
Lifetime	2/84	35.4	200–2,000	Health and fitness, parenting, relationships, fashion, beauty
MTV	8/81	37.0	2,000–8,000	Rock music
Nashville Network	3/83	37.0	250–5,000	Country music
Nickelodeon	4/79	36.3	1,000–2,250	Children, young adult
USA Network	9/77	40.1	500–5,500	Entertainment, sports
The Weather Channel	5/82	32.0	200–650	Regional and local weather

*Average prime time costs for 30-second spots.

more than doubling between 1984 and 1986.[16] We may also see advertising on the pay channels in the near future, most likely in the form of infomercials at intermissions between programs.

Audience Trends

Information on who watches cable has been hard to come by because traditional audience measurement techniques rely on too small a sample for findings on cable to be statistically significant. Nevertheless, it appears that cable households do watch TV more than noncable TV households, and they seem to watch cable at all times of the day. They spend 34 percent of their daily TV viewing time watching cable programs, and they tend to watch cable more often in the late fringe period and less often in the early fringe period. In all, they watch about 8½ hours of cable per week.[17]

Who Uses Cable?

Cable advertising revenues have grown steadily since 1980, exceeding the $1 billion level in 1987 (see Figure 14–12). The lion's share of these revenues has gone to the cable networks.

National advertisers have been actively using cable since the late 1970s, and by the end of 1981, the top 50 nationally advertised brands could all be seen on cable. One of the companies that has gone into cable advertising in a big way is Anheuser-Busch, which advertises regularly on several cable networks, with special emphasis on sports programming. As Charles B. Fruit, media director at Anheuser-Busch explained, the broadcast networks can program only a limited amount of sports, and "we felt that the hard-core sports fan wanted more and would search it out. . . . Cable TV

FIGURE   14–12

Cable ad revenues, 1980–1987.

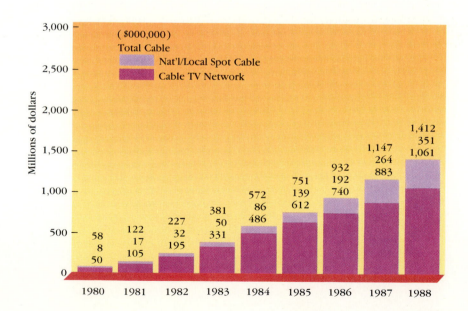

offered us another way to reach this important segment of our target audience. Cable TV also allowed us program and team associations prohibitively costly on network television."[18]

Local retailers are also finding that cable is a good place to advertise. Fisher Big Wheel, a discount department store in Midvale, Ohio, decided to run a series of special promotions only on cable after their first cable promotion brought an extra 15,000 customers into the store. Even tiny businesses have found cable advertising affordable and effective: A luncheonette on Main Street in Beacon, New York, placed a single spot on the local cable newscast and was deluged with hungry customers the next day.[19]

Buying Cable Time

Cable can be bought on three main levels: national, regional, and local. As with broadcast TV, national advertising is divided into network and local spots. Cable network advertising operates much like broadcast network advertising—the media buyer can sponsor network shows or purchase spot ads on network shows. Sponsorships are much more common on cable networks than on broadcast networks, however, because of the lower costs. Thus, we have, for example, Mazda's daily "Sports Look" on USA Network and Tandy's "Technology Today" on the Financial News Network. In 1987, 14 major cable networks banded together to offer package deals on advertising time. Called Cable One, the alliance makes available commercial time on several networks during the same time slot.

Purchasing national spot advertising on local cable systems has been time-consuming for media buyers, as there are over 1,000 cable systems to deal with. However, the larger local systems are becoming more sophisticated in their ad sales and are getting more assistance from the networks in filling local spots on network shows.

Regional cable advertising is facilitated by the use of *interconnects,* groups of cable systems joined together for advertising purposes. An advertiser can use an interconnect to buy the same ad time on all systems in a particular area. The largest interconnect, Cable Television Network of New Jersey, serves 1.3 million subscribers of 36 separate cable systems in 21 New Jersey counties.

Ad spots and sponsorships on local cable stations are purchased in much the same way as ad time on local broadcast TV stations. Local advertisers are particularly attracted to community-oriented local programs, such as newscasts and sports events, that reach customers in their immediate area.

Other Forms of Television

Cable is not alone as an electronic challenger to traditional broadcast television. It has its own competitors, although they are all in minor usage at present. The various electronic systems go by the initials of DBS, MDS, STV, and SMATV.

DBS refers to *direct broadcast satellite,* which involves beaming programs from satellites to special satellite dishes mounted in the home or yard. Because DBS is expected to carry only four or five channels, it is not considered to be a major competitor to cable.

MDS, or *multipoint distribution systems,* is a microwave delivery system that can carry up to a dozen channels. It is offered in some areas where cable is not available.

STV, *subscription television,* is over-the-air pay TV. Subscribers pay for a descrambler that allows them to watch programs that are carried over a regular TV channel.

SMATV is *satellite master antenna television.* It makes use of a satellite dish to capture signals for TV sets in apartment buildings and other complexes, acting as a sort of mini–cable system.

So far, none of these systems has managed to capture the public's imagination the way cable has, and since most are more expensive and carry fewer channels, they have yet to pose much of a threat to either broadcast or cable TV.

USING RADIO IN THE CREATIVE MIX

How do you go about marketing a product when just saying its name causes people to laugh? That was the challenge for BBDO/Minneapolis four years ago when their client, George A. Hormel & Co., asked them to create a campaign for Spam luncheon meat that would draw a younger group of consumers to their product.

The ad agency decided to place the major thrust of its campaign in radio advertising. It chose radio for two main reasons: its frequency, offering a constant reminder of the product to listeners, and its reach to a younger audience. BBDO also felt that people are well enough aware of the appearance of Spam's familiar blue and yellow can that visuals were not necessary to their main message.

The main problem to overcome, of course, was Spam's image as a joke food—something that Johnny Carson and David Letterman love to make fun of and that Monty Python created a memorable sketch around. The agency chose to go with the humor and capitalize on it. The ads recorded conversations with consumers who had just sampled crepes, quiche, and other foods containing Spam. When they were told the main ingredient, their spontaneous laughter was infectious. The interviewer then unobtrusively cleared up some common misconceptions about the product, pointing out that it contains no fillers, just pork shoulder and ham (see Figure 14–13).

As Jerry Figenskau, director of marketing and advertising for Hormel's grocery product division, explained, "By taking that kind of lighthearted look at the product, we can kind of contemporize it and put it in a position where we might be able to attract some of the new, young users."[20]

Hormel placed a high priority on the advertising of Spam, giving it a $1.6 million budget. Of that, $1.1 million was committed to radio, "for the acknowledged benefits of the medium."

Advantages of Radio

Radio is an integral part of our daily lives. We rely on clock radios to wake us in the morning. At breakfast, we tune in the morning news. Radio informs and entertains us while we drive to work or school or do household

FIGURE   14–13

This script for BBDO's SPAM radio campaign will give you some idea of the approach taken, but its appeal becomes more obvious when you can hear the voices and the infectious laughter.

SFX:	(PARTY CONVERSATION, LAUGHTER UNDER THROUGHOUT)
DICK:	We've just served up an elegant brunch with recipes made from SPAM luncheon meat, but our guests don't know it's SPAM.
	Hi. What have you tried so far?
JAY:	The crepe thing.
DICK:	What else?
JAY:	And, uh, it was like the crepe thing, only it was a different shaped thing.
DICK:	(LAUGHING) That's called quiche. Did you enjoy it?
JAY:	(LAUGHS) I went back twice.
DICK:	You enjoyed it. Is there anything you won't eat?
JAY:	Zucchini.
DICK:	All right. And how about you? Did you like it?
BARB:	I loved it.
DICK:	Do you pride yourself as a cook. I mean, do you know food?
BARB:	Well, I'm Italian. So food is my life.
DICK:	So you know food. What was the meat in the crepes and quiche and so on then?
BARB:	It tasted like ham to me.
DICK:	You're sure it's ham.
BARB:	I think I'm sure ... should I not be sure?
DICK:	No, no. What would you say if I told you it was SPAM!
MICHAEL:	SPAM?
THERESA:	(LAUGHS) It was very good!
BARB:	I'd be shocked. And it was delicious.
DICK:	O.K., What is SPAM? Do you know, Jay?
JAY:	Zucchini ...
DICK:	No, no. SPAM is pork shoulder and ham. No fillers. Just very good meat. So what do you think?
JAY:	Uh, it was good.
DICK:	And, would you have SPAM again?
JAY:	I certainly would, as long as I didn't have to make it with zucchini.
DICK:	O.K. Come on, America, discover the great taste of SPAM. It just might surprise you.
JAY:	Can I go back for thirds? (Laughter)

chores. And chances are good that if you work in an office or plant, you enjoy background music supplied by a local radio station. With its unique ability to relax, inform, and entertain, radio has become the daily companion of millions at work, at play, and on the highway.

In an average week, 95.2 percent of all the people in the United States listen to the radio—over 80 percent on an average day. The average adult spends 3 hours and 21 minutes per day listening to the radio.[21] In fact, radio leads all other media in both daily and weekly reach (see Figure 14–14). This has tremendous implications for advertisers, and as a result, radio's advertising revenues have grown steadily.

The largest national advertisers are beer and wine producers, automotive companies, travel companies, retail stores, clothing manufacturers, food producers, consumer services, and makers of drug and health-care

FIGURE 14–14

Daily and weekly reach of major media.

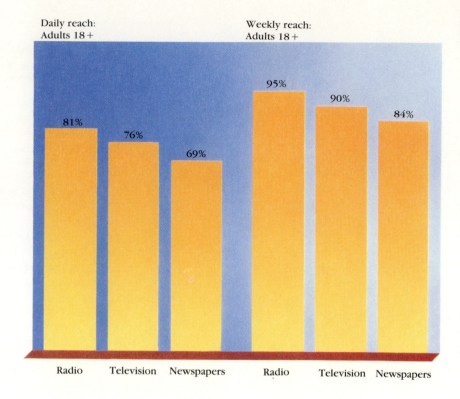

Daily reach			Weekly reach		
Radio	Television	Newspapers	Radio	Television	Newspapers
81%	76%	69%	95%	90%	84%

products (see Figure 14–15). But radio's biggest source of revenue is composed of the many thousands of local businesses that use the medium to reach out and talk to their local customers. Of the $6.9 billion spent in radio in 1986, over $5 billion came from local advertisers.[22] Among the features of radio that both national advertisers like Hormel and local advertisers like banks and car dealers find appealing are its reach and frequency, its selectivity, and its cost efficiency.

Reach and Frequency

Radio offers an excellent combination of reach and frequency. With the average adult listening more than three hours a day, radio builds a large audience quickly, and a normal advertising schedule easily allows repeated impact on the listener. This ability to quickly expose people a sufficient number of times to motivate them to buy makes radio particularly attractive to local merchants.

Selectivity

The wide variety of specialized radio formats available, with their prescribed audiences and coverage areas, enables advertisers to select just the market they want to reach. Commercials can be aimed at listeners of a specific sex, age group, ethnic or religious background, income group, employment category, educational level, or special interest. General Electric, for example, has been working to increase its product recognition among Hispanics and blacks by placing commercials on stations aimed at those groups.

FIGURE 14–15		Top national radio advertisers
Rank	**Advertiser**	**Ad expenditures 1986**
Network radio		
1	Sears Roebuck & Co.	$47,658[*]
2	Warner-Lambert Co.	22,707
3	American Telephone & Telegraph	22,552
4	General Motors Corp.	22,212
5	Anheuser-Busch Cos.	16,529
6	Bayer AG	16,206
7	Greyhound Corp.	15,545
8	Ford Motor Co.	14,871
9	Procter & Gamble Co.	13,879
10	Schering-Plough Corp.	11,442
Spot radio		
1	Anheuser-Busch Cos.	$50,420[*]
2	General Motors Corp.	35,153
3	Philip Morris Cos.	33,226
4	PepsiCo Inc.	22,342
5	Sears Roebuck & Co.	21,928
6	Delta Air Lines	21,708
7	Chrysler Corp.	21,071
8	Southland Corp.	19,962
9	Van Munching	18,670
10	Pillsbury Co.	18,178

[*]Dollars are in thousands.

Cost Efficiency

Radio's strong appeal to advertisers is largely its economy. Radio has the ability to offer its reach, frequency, and selectivity at one of the lowest costs per thousand. Thus, the budget needed for an effective radio schedule is often less than that needed for newspapers, magazines, or television. Business advertisers who want to reach upscale professional men, for example, are finding that twenty 60-second spots a week on the 50 news-oriented stations (in the top 25 markets) of the CBS Radio Network can be bought for the same price as one 30-second spot on CBS's "60 Minutes" TV show.[23] Both the radio and TV audiences reach the targeted audience, but radio offers a much greater frequency for the money spent on the advertising message.

Radio production is also relatively inexpensive. National spots can usually be produced for one-tenth the cost of a TV commercial. And in some cases, there are no production costs at all since local radio stations frequently produce commercials free for their local advertisers.

FIGURE   14–16

Local advertisers can build a personality and identity as part of the community through their radio ads.

3 BROS.:	Hi, we're the Sisters brothers!
SID:	Sid ——
SAM:	Sam ——
SY:	and SY.
SID:	We're here to tell you about the grand opening of the newest Sisters Restaurant.
SAM:	A grand opening so big ——
SY:	It takes all three of us to tell you about it.
SID:	First, there's our famous Sisters chicken!
SAM:	Light, flakey and made from scratch every day.
SY:	Those are the biscuits.
SID:	He's on the wrong page.
SFX:	PAGE TURN
SAM:	Sorry.
SY:	The chicken comes either spicy or mild.
SID:	And it's always fresh, never frozen.
SY:	And what goes better with chicken than ——
SAM:	Acres of free parking!
SID:	You're on the wrong page.
SAM:	Sorry.
SFX:	PAGE TURN
SY:	Than side-dishes, like baked beans, mashed potatoes and gravy, Sisters rice ——
SID:	But we've got more than that!
SY:	Sisters has a full menu of sandwiches!
SID:	Our "More Than A Salad Bar" salad bar!
SY:	A full breakfast menu!
SAM:	Batteries not included!
SID:	Hey, what page is that, anyway?
SFX:	PAGE TURN
SAM:	Sorry.
SY:	So come visit the friendly Sisters brothers!
SID:	At the grand opening of the new Sisters Restaurant!
SY:	Where our motto is:
SAM:	"If you can't stop, honk as you go by."
SY:	What?
SID:	OK, let me see that script!
SY:	Sisters! You've never had it this good!
SFX:	PAGE TURN /SID & SAM ARGUE UNDER
SY:	See, that's our motto.
SAM:	I like mine better ... (CONTINUE ARGUING AD LIB & FADE OUT)

Radio has a number of other advantages as well. It has a timeliness and immediacy that few other media can match; the low cost adds to its creative flexibility (the commercial message can be changed for each market segment, for example); and it has a local flavor that helps build an identity for the advertiser in the community (see Figure 14–16).

Drawbacks to Radio

In spite of its great advantages, radio has traditionally suffered from certain limitations: it is only an aural medium; its audience is highly segmented; the advertiser's commercials are short-lived, and often they are only half heard; and each ad must compete with the clutter of other ads.

Checklist of What Works Best in Radio

☐ Stretch the listener's imagination. Voices and sounds can evoke pictures.

☐ Listen for a memorable sound. What will make your commercial stand out from the clutter? Offer a distinctive voice, a memorable jingle, a solution to the listener's problem.

☐ Present one idea. It is difficult to communicate more than one idea in a television commercial. In radio, which is subject to more distractions, it is nearly impossible. Be direct and clear.

☐ Select your audience quickly. It pays to flag your segment of the audience at the beginning of the commercial— before they can switch to another station.

☐ Mention your brand name and your promise early. Commercials that do so get higher awareness. It heightens awareness if you mention the brand name and promise *more than once.*

☐ Capitalize on events. Exploit the flexibility of radio to tie in with fads, fashions, news events, or the weather.

☐ Use radio to reach teenagers. Teenagers don't watch much television. They do listen to a lot of radio. Media experts say it's the best way to reach teens. Some say it's the *only* way.

☐ Music can help. It is particularly effective in reaching teenagers who prefer the "now sounds" offered by music stations. You can give your campaign infinite variety with the same lyrics arranged in different ways and sung by different people.

☐ Ask listeners to take action. People respond to radio requests for action. They call the station to exchange views with the disc jockey or ask for certain music. Don't be afraid to ask listeners to call now, or write in, or send money.

☐ Make use of radio's merchandising services. Associate your business with a popular on-air personality; sponsor promotions such as contests and give-aways.

Limitations of Sound

Radio is heard but not seen. This fact can limit the effectiveness of commercials for products that need to be seen to be understood. Advertising agencies often prefer the freedom of creating with sight, sound, color, and motion, as in television. Some see radio as restricting their creative options.

Notwithstanding, many brilliant creative efforts have been achieved with radio through the use of "theater-of-the-mind" techniques. Pittsburgh Paints, for example, used a campaign that actually capitalized on radio's aural limitation. "Imagine yellow . . ." the announcer said, and soft music swelled in the background. The campaign, which used the same concept to describe other colors with music, proved to be highly effective. (See the Checklist of What Works Best in Radio.)

Segmented Audiences

Radio's ability to deliver highly selective audiences can also be a handicap to some advertisers. The large number of radio stations competing for the same audience may make the purchase of effective airtime difficult for the advertiser. For example, while one city may have only three television stations, it may have 20 radio stations competing for a market of, say,

1.5 million people. Clearly, the advertiser who is seeking to blanket this market will have to buy multiple stations, which may not be cost-effective.

Short-Lived and Half-Heard Commercials

A radio commercial is brief and fleeting. You can't keep it like a newspaper or a magazine ad. It lasts only moments, and then it's gone.

For many listeners, radio provides only a pleasant background sound while they are driving to work, reading, studying, or entertaining. Thus, radio must compete with other activities for their attention, and it does not always succeed.

Clutter

The more successful a radio station is, the more commercials it carries. Therefore, stations that have the greatest appeal for advertisers also offer the most competition from other commercials. The challenge is to produce a commercial that will stand out from the rest.

OVERVIEW OF THE RADIO MEDIUM

Unlike watching TV or reading a newspaper, radio listening is usually done by one person alone. It is a personal, one-on-one medium. And it is mobile. Radio can entertain a person while driving, while walking, and while at home or away from home. Where commuting is done by automobile, radio is a particularly strong medium.

Radio is also adaptable to moods. In the morning, some people may want to hear the news, upbeat music, or interesting chatter from a disc jockey to help them wake up. In the afternoon, the same people may want to unwind with classical or easy-listening music. As a result, most people consistently listen to two or three different radio stations representing different types of programming, although they tend to be quite loyal to their chosen stations.

Who Uses Radio?

In increasing numbers, national advertisers are discovering the reach and frequency potential of radio. In 1983, Miles Laboratories wanted to promote Bactine first-aid spray to a target audience of young mothers. The budget was too small to make much of an impact with TV advertising, so Miles chose to spend its entire ad budget on radio spots in an effort to reach young mothers either at home or on their way to or from work. The radio campaign was so successful that Miles Laboratories now allots 15 percent of its total advertising budget to network radio, promoting such products as Alka-Seltzer and Flintstones vitamins.[24]

Although many big-budget national companies, such as AT&T, Anheuser-Busch, PepsiCo, General Motors, and Chrysler, spend a lot of money on radio advertising, smaller national companies are also choosing radio to try to gain on the competition. Dial Corporation, which makes Purex laundry products and has nowhere near the ad budget of giants such as Procter & Gamble, calls radio its giant killer.

Local retailers also like the medium because they can tailor it to their immediate needs, because it offers defined audiences, and because they can create an identity for themselves by doing their own ads. In recent years, many types of local businesses have significantly increased their radio advertising expenditures. Banks and savings and loans spent 223 percent more on radio advertising in 1985 than they did in 1980; major spending increases have also been posted by jewelry stores, lumber and home improvement centers, grocery stores and supermarkets, and real estate brokers.[25]

Radio Programming and Audiences

Radio stations plan their programming carefully to reach specific markets and to capture as many listeners as possible. The larger its audience, the more a station can charge for commercial time. Therefore, extensive planning and research go into radio programming and program changes.

Stations have a number of options available to them in program planning. They can make use of tried-and-true formats, they can subscribe to network or syndicated programming, or they can devise their own unique approaches (one successful station in Sante Fe, New Mexico, for example, plays sets of classical, jazz, and light rock music back-to-back). However, programming choices are greatly influenced by whether a station is on the AM or FM band.

For most of the history of radio, AM dominated the airwaves. But in the 1960s, with the advent of stereo and the growth of underground programming on FM, things began to change. Today, FM has more than 70 percent of the radio audience, and AM stations are scrambling for listeners.[26] It's not surprising that FM is so popular: it has much better sound fidelity (AM is more subject to interference), there are fewer commercial interruptions, and the programming is more varied. These features have attracted the younger listeners away from AM.

To counteract the inroads made by FM, many AM stations have switched to programs that do not rely heavily on sound quality, such as talk, news, and sports. Some AM stations are also experimenting with new formats, such as all-comedy, midday game shows with audience participation, children's programming, and formats geared to unique regions, such as KHJ's "car radio" in Los Angeles, which provides traffic reports every 10 minutes, tips on driving, and features on cars and travel.[27] AM stations are also trying to win back music listeners by improving their sound quality and by offering AM stereo broadcasting.

The great majority of stations, whether AM or FM, tend to adopt one of the dozen or so standard programming formats: contemporary hit radio (CHR), adult contemporary, country, album-oriented rock, easy listening, news/talk, black/urban, middle of the road (MOR), nostalgia (big band), classical, religious, and so on. Each of these formats tends to appeal to specific demographic groups (see Figure 14–17). The most popular format, contemporary hit radio, appeals primarily to teenagers and to women under age 30. This format, always found on FM stations, emphasizes a constant flow of "Top 40" hits, usually with minimal intrusion by disc jockeys (although the talky, zany "zoo" approach to CHR has caught on in several markets). Another popular format, adult contemporary (or "easy oldies"), is often advertised as "light rock, less talk." This format is said to appeal to the desirable target group of working women age 25 to 44.[28] The news/talk, easy-listening, and nostalgia formats all tend to have high listenership among men and women over age 50.

Advertisers can take advantage of listenership studies to determine which radio formats in a particular market deliver the greatest share of the target audience for a product. A company selling denture cream would want to place spots on a nostalgia or talk-oriented station, for example, while a manufacturer of acne cream would go for CHR stations.

A major trend in radio today has been a resurgence by the radio networks. Unlike TV networks, which supply affiliates with the bulk of their programming, radio networks offer services and programs that stations can subscribe to, in order to complement their local programming. Thus, a single station might subscribe to ABC's hourly newscasts, to CBS's weekly "Entertainment Coast-to-Coast," and to Mutual Broadcasting System's nightly "Larry King Show."

There are now some 18 national radio networks, including the multiple "mininetworks" of ABC, NBC, and CBS. In addition, numerous syndicators offer a variety of programs, from live rock concerts and sporting events to public-affairs programs and talk shows. To stand out in an increasingly competitive radio environment, more and more stations are opting to avail themselves of the syndicated and network offerings.[29] And as more stations carry these programs and more listeners tune in, national advertisers are finding them increasingly attractive as a means for reaching target audiences.

FIGURE   14–17   Demographics for various radio formats*

Age format	U.S. population (millions)	Adult contemporary	AOR progressive	Beautiful music	Black	Classical	CHR
18–24	16.5	107	255	69	138	50	219
25–34	23.7	123	164	73	141	103	134
35–49	24.4	111	56	130	105	144	92
50–64	19.8	80	22	134	70	106	35
65 +	15.6	65	7	83	28	72	18
Education							
Attended/graduated college	32.9	124	131	137	66	227	118
High school graduate	39.3	98	106	99	123	53	108
Less than high school	27.8	74	55	58	108	17	68
Household Income							
$40,000	25.9	118	151	137	62	188	122
$30,000–$40,000	18.3	116	110	105	93	119	118
$20,000–$30,000	21.8	100	93	106	91	68	103
$10,000–$20,000	20.7	85	68	82	140	47	80
Under $10,000	13.3	68	48	38	135	37	57

*Data reflect cumes for the average day for the format shown.
†Data reflect the average Monday–Sunday 6 A.M.–12 P.M. half-hour audience.

BUYING RADIO TIME

As in television buying, advertisers need to have a basic knowledge of the medium to buy radio effectively. First, it's important to be aware of the types of radio advertising available for commercial use. Second, a basic understanding of radio terminology is necessary. And finally, the advertiser needs to know the steps in preparing a radio schedule.

Types of Radio Advertising

Radio time may be purchased by an advertiser in one of three forms: network, spot, or local. Local purchases account for 75 percent of all radio time sold; spot radio, another 20 percent; and networks, 5 percent.

Networks

Advertisers may use one of the national radio networks (ABC, CBS, NBC, Mutual, United Stations) to carry their messages to the entire national market simultaneously via the networks' affiliated stations. In addition, more than 100 regional radio networks in the United States operate as news, sports, and farm networks with information oriented toward specific geographic markets.

Country	Jazz	News	Oldies	Religious and gospel	Talk	Variety	Total usage†
82	118	25	90	70	30	101	148
103	180	65	149	139	59	109	112
130	100	120	141	118	103	113	97
102	52	156	47	81	154	71	77
64	20	130	40	67	164	101	66
83	196	147	113	123	127	136	108
108	61	87	120	99	91	69	105
109	41	63	56	74	80	101	83
89	145	163	110	100	125	112	109
102	80	109	124	100	105	96	107
113	91	71	107	120	94	88	100
96	107	70	80	91	83	73	91
105	44	59	67	80	82	144	86

The use of networks provides national and regional advertisers with simple administration and low effective net cost per station. The amount of paperwork and clerical time is greatly reduced, and the cost per station is usually lower than if comparable times were bought on individual stations. The costs of advertising on various national networks are listed in Figure 14–18. However, the disadvantage lies in the lack of flexibility in choosing the affiliated stations, the limitation of the number of stations on the network's roster, and the long lead time required to book time.

Spot Radio

Buying spot radio affords national advertisers great flexibility in their choice of markets, stations, airtime, and copy. The advertiser can choose as long or as short a flight as is required. In addition, spot advertising enables the message to be presented to listeners at the most favorable times.

By purchasing radio time in this way, commercials can be tailored to the local market, and they can be put on the air quickly—some stations are willing to run a commercial with as little as 20 minutes' lead time.

FIGURE   14–18   Network radio costs

Network	Number of stations	Monday–Friday				Saturday–Sunday		
		6–10 A.M.	10 A.M.–3 P.M.	3–7 P.M.	7 P.M.–12 A.M.	12–6 A.M.	6 A.M.–7 P.M.	7 P.M.–12 A.M.
ABC								
Contemporary	252	$2,300	$2,300	$2,300	$2,300	$2,300	$2,300	$2,300
Direction	428	1,000	1,000	1,000	1,000	*	*	*
Entertainment	590	2,000	2,000	2,000	2,000	2,000	2,000	2,000
FM	136	2,000	2,000	2,000	2,000	2,000	2,000	2,000
Information	614	3,000	3,000	3,000	3,000	3,000	3,000	3,000
Rock	96	2,000	2,000	2,000	2,000	2,000	2,000	2,000
Talk	128	*	500	*	*	500	500	500
CBS								
Radio Network	400	4,000	2,000	2,000	500	300	1,200	500
Radio-Radio	155	2,100	2,100	2,100	2,100	2,100	2,100	2,100
NBC								
Adult	379	2,264	1,371	1,371	621	250	1,200	621
Source	118	3,721	3,721	3,721	1,775	250	3,721	3,721
Talk Net	284	*	*	*	757	757	*	757
MBS								
Mutual	800	3,461	2,632	2,370	251	100	800	225
US 1	154	2,729	1,957	2,657	1,871	1,000	2,300	1,100
US 2	246	1,814	1,371	1,532	971	500	1,200	800
Sheridan	129	1,200	850	850	650	*	850	850

Note: Costs based on 30-second spots, 12 times per week equal rotation schedule.
*No network clearance during this time.

Spot advertising also enables advertisers to build local listener acceptance of their product or service by using local personalities or by purchasing airtime on locally produced programs.

Local Radio

Local time denotes radio spots purchased by a local advertiser. It involves the same procedure as national spots. The sole difference is the location of the advertiser.

Radio advertising can also be classified as live, taped, or transcribed (a form of record). In recent years, there has been a trend toward recorded shows with live news in between. Nearly all radio commercials today are recorded to reduce costs and maintain broadcast quality.

Radio Terminology

Buying radio time requires a basic understanding of radio terminology. Naturally, much of the language used for radio advertising is the same as that used for other media. But radio also has numerous terms that are either peculiar to it or have a special meaning when applied to radio advertising. The most common of these are the concepts of dayparts, average quarter-hour audiences, and cumes (cumulative audiences).

Dayparts

The radio day is divided into five basic dayparts:

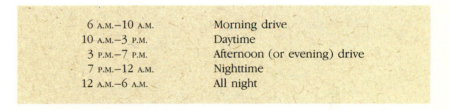

6 A.M.–10 A.M.	Morning drive
10 A.M.–3 P.M.	Daytime
3 P.M.–7 P.M.	Afternoon (or evening) drive
7 P.M.–12 A.M.	Nighttime
12 A.M.–6 A.M.	All night

The rating services measure the audiences for only the first four of these dayparts, because all-night listening is very limited and not highly competitive. (See Ad Lab 14-B.) The heaviest radio use occurs during drive times (6–10 A.M. and 3–7 P.M.) during the week (Monday–Friday).

This information is important to advertisers because usage and consumption vary for different products. For example, radio's morning drive time coincides perfectly with most people's desire for a steaming, fresh cup of coffee, so it is a great time for advertising coffee brands. Late evening, on the other hand, is a poor time to advertise coffee.

Radio stations base their rates on the time of day the advertiser wants commercials aired (see Figure 14–19). To achieve the lowest rate, an advertiser can order spots on a *run-of-station (ROS)* basis, similar to ROP in newspaper advertising. However, this leaves total control of spot placement up to the station. Most stations, therefore, offer a *total audience plan (TAP)* package rate, which guarantees a certain percentage of spots in the better dayparts if the advertiser buys the total package of time.

FIGURE   14–19

The *Spot Radio Rates and Data* listing for WNEW–FM radio in New York City shows that spot announcement rates vary from a high a $350 to a low of $40 per minute, depending on the number bought and the dayparts used.

AD LAB 14-B   The Reports that Make or Break Radio Stations

Three major audience rating services are offered to radio broadcasters and advertisers. Media buyers use the data obtained from these services to determine which programs and stations will deliver the greatest number of target listeners.

Arbitron

The Arbitron rating service chooses a group of representative listeners in each of 257 cities and provides them with a diary for keeping track of all the time they spend listening to radio. Listeners return the diaries to Arbitron at the end of each week for tabulation, and Arbitron compiles the results into a quarterly report.

The Arbitron "book" reports not only the number of listeners to particular stations and shows but also their age, sex, and preferred listening times. The service is available to clients on a subscription basis. The major clients are radio stations, but some ad agencies and radio sales representatives also subscribe.

Birch Research

Birch uses telephone surveys rather than diaries to obtain listener data. Interviewers talk to representative listeners in 130 major radio markets. Results are published on a monthly basis, with quarterly summaries. Birch also offers Birchscan, a monthly computerized report.

RADAR

Ratings of network radio programs are determined by RADAR (Radio's All-Dimension Audience Research). RADAR audience estimates are based on telephone interviews. Each listener is called daily for a week and asked about listening habits from the day before until that moment. The research is conducted year-round and is published annually in *Radio Usage* and *Network Radio Audiences*. A number of specialized reports are also available.

Laboratory Applications

1. What do you think might be the advantages and disadvantages of these radio audience measurement methods?
2. Which audience measurement method, diary or phone interview, would you consider better? Why?

Average Quarter-Hour

The term *average quarter-hour* is used to identify the average number of people who are listening to a specific station during any 15-minute period of any given daypart. For example, station KAKZ in Figure 14–20 has an average quarter-hour listenership of 4,200, meaning that any day, during any 15-minute period between 6 A.M. and midnight, it is probable that 4,200 persons over age 12 are tuned in to the station.

This same idea can be expressed in terms of "share" if the station's audience is shown as a percentage of the total listening audience in the area. For example, in our illustration, the total average quarter-hour listening audience for all stations is 48,900. Therefore, the average quarter-hour audience of radio station KAKZ could be expressed as an average quarter-hour "share" of 8.6:

$$\frac{42}{489} = .086 \text{ or } 8.6 \text{ percent}$$

Rating Points

By extending our computations a little further, this same audience could be expressed in terms of rating points if we show it as a percentage of the population. For example, if radio station KAKZ were located in a city of

MONDAY–SUNDAY
6 00AM–MIDNIGHT

STATION CALL LETTERS	AVERAGE PERSONS--METRO SURVEY AREA, IN HUNDREDS												STATION CALL LETTERS	SHARES--METRO SURVEY AREA											
	TOT. PERS. 12+	MEN					WOMEN					TNS. 12-17		TOT. PERS. 12+ %	MEN					WOMEN					TNS. 12-17 %
		18-24	25-34	35-44	45-54	55-64	18-24	25-34	35-44	45-54	55-64				18-24 %	25-34 %	35-44 %	45-54 %	55-64 %	18-24 %	25-34 %	35-44 %	45-54 %	55-64 %	
KAKZ	42	2	6	6	2	1	2	6	6	1	3	2	KAKZ	8.6	3.8	12.2	18.2	7.4	6.3	4.4	11.1	15.4	2.7	10.0	3.9
KARD	35	1	6	1	4		6	7	3	3	2	2	KARD	7.2	1.9	12.2	3.0	14.8		13.3	13.0	7.7	8.1	6.7	3.9
														7.4				14.8							
KOEZ	7									5	1		KOEZ	1.4									13.5	3.3	
KSKU	3	1					1					1	KSKU	.6	1.9							2.2			2.0
	489	53	49	33	27	16	45	54	39	37	30	51													

TOTAL LISTENING IN METRO SURVEY AREA

FIGURE 14-20

Average quarter-hour listening estimates.

100,000 people, its average quarter-hour audience could be expressed as an average quarter-hour "rating" of 4.2:

$$\frac{4,200}{100,000} = .042 \text{ or } 4.2 \text{ percent}$$

Determining the gross rating points of a radio schedule simply requires multiplying the average quarter-hour rating by the number of spots. For example,

4.2 (Rating points) × 12 (Number of spots) = 50.4 GRPs

The GRPs could also be determined by multiplying the average quarter-hour audience by the number of spots and dividing by the population. For example,

4,200	× 12	= 50,400
(Average quarter-hour audience)	(Number of spots)	(Gross impressions)

Therefore:

$$\frac{50,400}{100,000} = .504 \text{ or } 50.4 \text{ GRPs}$$

Cume Audience

The *cume audience,* a capsule term for "cumulative audience," is the total number of *different* people listening to a radio station for at least one 15-minute segment over the course of a given week, day, or daypart (see Figure 14–21).

In our example, we generated 50,400 gross impressions with our schedule on station KAKZ. But that does *not* mean that 50,400 *different* people heard our commercials. Many people might have heard our commercials three, four, or five times.

By measuring the cumulative number of different people listening to KAKZ, the rating services give us an idea of the reach *potential* of our radio schedule.

Thus, cume and average quarter-hour are important concepts. A high cume figure means a lot of different people are tuning in to the station for

WICHITA, KS
OCT/NOV 1980

MONDAY-SATURDAY 6:00 AM–10:00 AM

STATION CALL LETTERS	TOTAL PERS. 12+	MEN 18-24	25-34	35-44	45-54	55-64	WOMEN 18-24	25-34	35-44	45-54	55-64	TNS. 12-17
KAKZ	569	28	96	65	28	27	38	79	67	19	25	44
KARD	354	10	78	11	20	9	78	52	38	14	14	25
KBRA	313		36	16	25	31	8	23	33	49	39	6
KOEZ	57				11	4			21	7		
KSKU	35	18					5			6		6
METRO TOTALS	2867	257	323	218	174	141	224	309	230	183	161	353

MONDAY-SATURDAY 10:00 AM-3:00 PM

STATION CALL LETTERS	TOT. PERS. 12+	MEN 18-24	25-34	35-44	45-54	55-64	WOMEN 18-24	25-34	35-44	45-54	55-64	TNS. 12-17
KAKZ	361	9	65	21	14	13	23	56	58	8	14	18
KARD	200		36	5	16		31	52	28	6	7	19
KBRA	300		24	11	19	22	15	14	14	40	47	
KOEZ	85				14	4	8		5	29	11	
KSKU	47	9	12				15	5				6
METRO TOTALS	2407	210	246	152	137	115	232	277	206	137	136	284

FIGURE   14–21

Cume listening estimates.

at least 15 minutes. A high average quarter-hour figure usually means that people are listening and staying tuned in.

Preparing a Radio Schedule

A procedure similar to that discussed in the television section is used by advertisers to prepare their radio schedules. The steps are as follows:

1. Identify those stations with the greatest concentration (cume) of the advertiser's target audience by demographics (e.g., men 25 to 34).
2. Identify those stations by format type that typically offer the highest concentration of potential buyers. You may know, for instance, that while many men and women between the ages of 35 and 49 listen to beautiful music stations, the best format for potential tire purchasers in that age group is an all-news or sports format.
3. Determine which time periods (dayparts) on those stations offer the greatest number (average quarter-hour) of potential buyers. Here again, it is more likely that prospective tire buyers will be concentrated in drive time rather than midday.
4. Using the stations' rate cards for guidance, construct a schedule with a strong mix of these best time periods. An average weekly spot load per station may be anywhere from 12 to 30 announcements depending on the advertiser's budget. At this point, it is often wise to contact the station reps, give them a breakdown of your media objectives, suggest a possible budget for their station, and ask what they can provide for that budget. This gives the media buyer a starting point for analyzing costs and negotiating the buy.
5. Determine the cost for each 1,000 target people each station delivers. The operational word here is *target*. You are not interested in the station's total audience.
6. Negotiate and place the buy.
7. Assess the buy (with the help of the agency's or radio station's computer) in terms of reach and frequency.

While these steps are far from all-inclusive, they demonstrate some of the complexity media planners and buyers deal with daily in their efforts to match an advertiser's message with a target audience on radio.

Summary

As a means of reaching the masses, no other medium today has the unique creative ability of television. Broadcast television has grown faster than any other advertising medium in history because of the unique advantages it offers advertisers: mass coverage at low cost, audience selectivity, impact, prestige, and social dominance.

While television's power as a creative tool may be unmatched, the medium still has many drawbacks. These include high cost, lack of selectivity, brevity, clutter, and susceptibility to zipping and zapping.

The four forms of television advertising are: network, spot, syndication, and local. Within these classifications are many commercial opportunities for advertisers.

To determine which shows to buy, the media buyer must select the most efficient ones against the target audience. The task, therefore, is to compare the packages of each station, substituting stronger programs for less efficient ones, and negotiating prices to get the best buy.

Broadcast television's dominance is being challenged by new electronic media, particularly cable. Cable offers the visual and aural appeal of television at a much lower cost and with greater flexibility. The cable audience is highly fragmented, which helps advertisers target specific markets but is a drawback for those wanting to reach the mass audience. Cable advertising can be done at the national, regional, or local level and can take the form of program sponsorships, segment sponsorships, and spots of varying lengths, including the longer infomercials.

Like television, radio is recognized as a highly creative medium. However, its greatest attribute is probably its ability to offer excellent reach and frequency to selective audiences at a very efficient price. Its drawbacks relate to the limitations of sound, the fact that radio audiences are very segmented, and the nature of short-lived and half-heard commercials.

Radio stations are normally classified by the programming they offer and the audiences they serve. Radio stations may be AM or FM, may make use of network or syndicated programs, and may follow one of a dozen or more popular formats.

Radio time may be purchased by an advertiser in one of three forms: local, spot, or network.

Buying radio time requires a basic understanding of radio terminology. The most common terms are *dayparts, average quarter-hour,* and *cumulative audiences*.

Questions for Review and Discussion

1. What are the advantages of broadcast television advertising for a product such as Bartles & Jaymes wine cooler?
2. What are the advantages of 15-second commercials? What are the drawbacks?
3. How can advertisers overcome the problems of zipping and zapping?
4. Why has advertising on network TV come to be seen as less desirable in recent years?
5. What would you do to purchase time from a local television station? Outline the procedure you would follow.
6. In what ways is cable TV's selectivity a strength? In what ways is it a drawback?
7. Why do you suppose some advertisers don't believe in the effectiveness of radio advertising?
8. What is the format of the radio station you listen to most? How would you describe the demographics of its target audience?
9. What is the difference between average quarter-hour and cume audiences? Which is the better measure for media planners?
10. What is the importance of dayparts to advertisers?

15

DIRECT MAIL AND OUTDOOR MEDIA

ecause its publications are not sold on newsstands or in bookstores, the National Geographic Society has learned how to use direct mail effectively to market to its membership its monthly magazine and many special books. *Journey into China,* a recently published 518-page book with 400 full-color illustrations, was the beneficiary of this long experience.

The society had set aside $1.8 million to sell 380,000 copies of the new book to its members and subscribers. The offer included a separate wall map of China.

Before putting all $1.8 million into a mass mailing, the society conducted a test mailing. One thing it wanted to find out was which of three prices to sell the book for: $19.95, $22.95, or $24.95. In addition, for the first time it offered the option of buying a more expensive deluxe edition for an extra $10.

The test also sought to determine which of two brochure covers would work best. One displayed a photograph of a person carrying two baskets through a deep-green rice paddy, bannered with the caption "Take a spectacular tour of today's China." The other cover was red with a small color photograph of a pagoda and a waterfall; its caption read "Take a family tour of China for only [book's price]."

The brochure was accompanied by a perforated order card and a blue-and-black two-tone photograph of the Forbidden City in Beijing. A four-page sales letter on National Geographic Society letterhead used the blue and black inks for alternating paragraphs. The package was completed by enclosing a half-page letter from the publisher that was folded inside a small map of China. Portions of this direct-mail package are shown in Figure 15–1.

The version with the photograph of the rice paddy achieved the best response in the test, so it was chosen for the mass mailing. And the most profitable price turned out to be $19.95.

The results were stunning. It was the second most successful direct-mail campaign for a single book in the society's history. The original mailing to society members produced sales of more than 410,000 (a 4.28 percent response), well above the goal of 380,000. Moreover, 30 percent requested the deluxe edition. Since only 420,000 copies were printed in the first run, two additional press runs of 50,000 were required that year to fill later orders resulting from an insert card sent out with bills and from the society's Christmas catalog.[1]

DIRECT MAIL ADVERTISING

Direct-mail advertising is the term given to all forms of advertising that are sent directly to prospects through the United States Postal Service or through private delivery services. In dollars spent, direct mail is the third-ranked advertising medium today, surpassed only by newspapers and television.

No matter how large or small a company may be, direct mail is nearly always used in its advertising program. When a firm starts in business, its first medium of advertising is generally direct mail, and as it grows, it usually continues to use direct mail. The reason is clear. The shortest distance between two points is a straight line. And of all the media, direct mail offers the "straightest" line to reach the desired prospective customer.

Direct Mail versus Direct Marketing

Several other terms are frequently confused with direct mail. These include *direct marketing, direct response advertising, direct advertising,* and *mail-order advertising.* How are these concepts similar, and how do they differ?

Direct marketing is a marketing system in which the advertiser uses the media to build a database of customers. The choice of media can be direct mail, newspapers, magazines, radio, or television used alone or in combination. The objective of direct marketing is to get inquiries, to sell merchandise or services direct, to provide support to salespeople and distributors, to encourage feedback, to get contributions, or to get people to visit stores.[2] Underlying all direct marketing success is the ability to trigger a direct, measurable action that is cost-effective. This can be achieved by using any of these selling methods: (*a*) buyer seeks out seller through a retailer or exhibit, (*b*) seller seeks out buyer through personal selling, or (*c*) buyer seeks out seller by mail or phone in order to obtain a mail order.[3]

Direct response advertising is a message that asks the reader, listener, or viewer for an immediate response. A newspaper or magazine ad, for example, may ask the reader to fill in and mail a featured coupon to obtain

National Geographic's direct-mail package included a four-page sales letter, a brochure, a duotone photograph of the Forbidden City, a half-page letter from the publisher folded inside a map of China, and a perforated order card, all to promote its book *Journey into China.*

FIGURE 15–2

This direct-response ad, written by Don Hauptman, has run virtually unchanged since 1976. Sales resulting from the ad (and others in this language-training series) have hit the $5 million mark.

information or to actually order the advertised product (see Figure 15–2). Direct response advertising can take the form of direct mail, or it can use a wide range of other media, from matchbook covers or magazines to radio or TV. With the advent of toll-free phone numbers, television ads that urge viewers to "Call now! Operators are standing by!" have become much more common (see Figure 15–3). Another burgeoning area of direct response advertising is *telemarketing,* in which prospective customers are called directly on the phone and given an oral sales presentation. A recent Gallup Poll indicated that about 1 in 10 adults who had made a direct-marketing purchase within the prior two weeks had done so because of a promotional telephone call.[4] However, this is a form of advertising that consumers find particularly displeasing—the Gallup Poll also discovered that nearly 90 percent of respondents were annoyed to some extent when salespeople called them at home to sell products.[5]

Mail-order advertising is both a form of direct response advertising and a method of selling in which the product or service is promoted through advertising and the prospect orders it *through the mail.* It involves no intermediate salespeople. As it is practiced today, mail-order advertising may be received in any of three distinct forms: mail-order catalogs (like Sears or Spiegel); advertisements in a wide variety of print and electronic media; and direct-mail advertising.

Direct advertising is any form of advertising issued directly to the prospect through the use of the mails, salespeople, dealers, or other means as opposed to through the traditional mass media. Such advertising may take the form of door-to-door circulars, telephone solicitations, handbills, or direct mail.

Direct mail is any form of direct advertising that is sent through the mail. It is perhaps the most popular form of direct advertising today. A brochure sent to a prospect by mail is direct-mail advertising. But if the same brochure is distributed door-to-door, it is not direct mail. (It is still direct advertising.) The difference, then, is the method of distribution.

FIGURE 15–3

Direct-response TV ads, which ask viewers to use an 800 number to order, are now used for everything from kitchen appliances to magazine and newspaper subscriptions. Although in the past direct-response TV ads were known for their low production values, many are now

high quality, such as this commercial for the *Boston Globe,* which featured an impersonator who imitated celebrities such as Woody Allen and Julia Child to highlight features of the paper. As a result of the one-month campaign, circulation increased by nearly 40,000.

JEFF BERGMAN: Here's a terrific offer from the *Boston Globe.*

Subscribe now, and get 13 weeks of the *Globe* for only $1.50 a week. (SUPER) 1-800-543-1500

WOODY ALLEN: That's very encouraging for a social flop like me. Now at parties, I can talk about news . . . entertainment . . . what's on sale . . . whatever.

BERGMAN: You get the *Globe* 7 days a week, delivered right to your door, for $1.35 off the regular home delivery price. (SUPER): 45% off regular home delivery price 1-800-543-1500

ROD SERLING: That's like getting Monday through Friday free. It's a whole new dimension in savings.

BERGMAN: 13 free Mondays with Sci-Tech. 13 free Tuesdays with Business Extra. (SUPER) 1-800-543-1500

JULIA CHILD: 13 free Wednesday food sections with lovely coupons.

BERGMAN: 13 free Thursday Calendars. 13 free Fridays with At Home. (SUPER) 1-800-543-1500

JOHNNY MOST: All right, don't fiddle and diddle. How about Sports Plus?

BERGMAN: And Sports Plus on Friday too. All free.

So call 1-800-543-1500 to subscribe today. Because without the *Globe* . . . (SUPER) 1-800-543-1500

MAXWELL SMART: My life would be chaos. Hello, *Globe?* (SUPER) 13 weeks $1.50 a week. Call 1-800-543-1500. Offer available to new subscribers in the *Globe* home delivery area only.

Growth of Direct Mail

In 1986, 55.5 billion pieces of direct mail found their way into American homes and offices, and that figure does not include the 10 billion catalogs mailed each year. Sales of consumer goods as a result of direct-mail advertising hit $50 billion that year, up $4 billion from the previous year.[6]

Direct mail is successful because it uniquely meets the needs of today's changing lifestyles. With more and more women in the work force, families are finding they have more discretionary income but less time to shop. Shopping at home through the mail takes much less time than going out to stores, and consumers can often get more detailed information about products from catalogs and sales brochures than they can from harried or unknowledgeable salespeople in retail shops.

Direct-mail advertising also has boomed as a result of the consumer credit card explosion. Credit-based mass marketers have expanded their profits by stuffing monthly customer statements with tempting mail-order

FIGURE 15–4	Top 10 mail-order product categories	
Rank	**Category**	**Sales (millions)**
1	Insurance/financial	$6,940
2	General merchandise/housewares/gifts	4,318
3	Magazine subscriptions	3,125
4	Ready-to-wear	2,473
5	Books	1,691
6	Sporting goods	1,490
7	Collectibles	1,428
8	Auto club memberships	1,220
9	Crafts	843
10	Electronic goods	783

product offers from small personal items to major appliances. And the increased availability of credit has enabled them to sell high-priced items to consumers. Products that are innovative, can be shipped fairly easily, and are not readily available through other distribution channels are the most likely candidates for direct-mail selling. Among the top consumer products bought through the mail are books, housewares, clothing, and electronic gadgets (see Figure 15–4).

With more and more major companies entering into the direct-mail field, its image is improving daily. Consumers are becoming more comfortable ordering by mail, knowing that when they deal with reputable companies, they can get quality merchandise, often at a reduced price. Many mail-order companies have highly sophisticated systems for ordering, fulfillment, and after-sale follow-up designed to make shopping easy and satisfying.

Among the biggest users of direct-mail advertising are insurance companies, financial institutions, and other types of financial services. American Express is one of the strongest believers in direct mail—it is the largest single customer of the New York City Post Office. Charles Schwab & Company, one of the country's leading discount brokerage houses, originally achieved its status exclusively through the use of direct marketing, primarily direct-mail advertising.[7]

USING DIRECT MAIL IN THE CREATIVE MIX

Direct mail is an efficient, effective, and economical medium for sales and business promotion. Thus, it is used by a wide variety of retail, commercial, and industrial companies, charity and service organizations, and individuals. Direct mail can also increase the effectiveness of advertising in other media if carefully coordinated. Publishers Clearinghouse, for example, uses TV spots in conjunction with its direct-mail campaigns. These advertisements alert viewers to the coming arrival of direct-mail sweepstakes promotions from Publishers Clearinghouse.

AD LAB 15-A   College Grad Gets Job through Mail

A 21-year-old college graduate of Glassboro State College (B.A. in communications/liberal arts) skillfully used his education in direct response marketing to get a job.

He sought to test a direct-mail package and personal sales presentation in the Philadelphia area before proceeding to New York to meet industry leaders, to secure at least 10 interviews at direct response marketing agencies in New York City, and to obtain two job offers.

His marketing plan included a direct-mail package, a mailing envelope, a letter to get interest, a folder to explain the product, and a reply card to make responding easier.

Chief executive officers or presidents of direct response marketing agencies or of direct response divisions of advertising agencies were contacted. The test market was composed of medium-sized to large advertising agencies in the Philadelphia area who listed direct-mail or direct response advertising as part of their media breakdown. The Philadelphia list was compiled from an area business publication, *Focus Magazine,* which annually devotes one issue to Philadelphia's advertising agencies.

The initial mailing consisted of 43 pieces to Philadelphia, mailed the first week of June, and later, 24 pieces to New York, mailed the first week of July. Two weeks following the mail drop, he initiated a telephone call to each nonrespondent. The purpose was to confirm receipt of the direct-mail package and to ask for a personal interview. The total allocated budget for this program was $723.

The result of this campaign was that the graduate secured nine interviews in New York City and received two job offers in New York City.

Attention Advertising Executives! When You're Ready To Make A Sound Investment . . .

Here Are Five Profitable Reasons Why You Should Hire This Adman

Direct Marketing Honors!

1. EXPERIENCE: The main reason.

2. ADVERTISING SKILLS: The tools.

3. EDUCATION: Laying the groundwork.

4. LEADERSHIP QUALITIES: How to recognize a leader.

5. SELF MOTIVATION: The deciding factor.

ADVERTISING PHILOSOPHY:

WHAT OTHERS SAY ABOUT KARL DENTINO

KARL G. DENTINO
3330 Hollywood Circle
Pennsauken, New Jersey 08109
(609) 662-0387

Laboratory Application

If you were to prepare a job-hunting direct-mail advertising campaign for yourself, what reader benefits would you include? (See Chapter 8 on copywriting.)

Advantages of Direct Mail

Next to the personal sales call, direct mail is the most effective medium an advertiser can use to put a message in front of a prospect (see Ad Lab 15-A). However, it is also the most expensive on a cost-per-exposure basis.

As a medium competing for advertisers' dollars, direct mail traditionally offers several key advantages over its competition.

Selectivity

Direct mail enables the advertiser to select the prospects he or she wants to reach. By mailing only to these prime prospects—the ones most likely to buy the product or service—the advertiser can reduce sales costs and increase profits.

For example, if you wanted to advertise a 10-gallon paint compressor to professional painters, you wouldn't want to use TV. TV's reach is too broad, and you would have to pay for the total audience. But by acquiring a list of professional painters and mailing your message directly to them, you could reach your desired audience more efficiently, at a lower cost, and with greater results. Today, the availability of computerized mailing lists enables advertisers to obtain names of people in a variety of occupational groups, in specific regions or states, in given age groups, in particular income categories, and in other demographic classifications.

Manufacturers of baby food, diapers, and toys wanting to advertise their products to new mothers can, for example, obtain mailing lists compiled by *American Baby* magazine or by companies that buy names from diaper services, maternity shops, or childbirth training instructors. In fact, each year more than 3 million women with new babies receive at least a dozen direct-mail pitches targeted specifically at them.[8]

Intensive Coverage and Extensive Reach

Most of the mass media are limited in the number of readers, viewers, or listeners they can reach. Not all viewers, for example, have their TV sets tuned to the same channel at the same time to see a given commercial. Not everyone in a community subscribes to and reads the local newspaper on the day a given ad is run. But virtually everyone has a mailbox, and by using direct mail, an advertiser can achieve 100 percent coverage of the homes in a given area. Direct mail literally reaches out and touches everyone you select.

Flexibility

Few limitations exist on direct-mail format, style, or capacity (see Figure 15–5). In addition, the wide variety of materials and processes available enable direct-mail advertising to be uniquely creative and novel, limited

FIGURE 15–5

The great ingenuity that can be used in creating direct-mail packages is demonstrated by this clever piece produced by the Health and Tennis Corporation of America. These size 60 boxer shorts, bearing information on how corporate fitness programs can help reduce employee absenteeism, were sent to corporate executives.

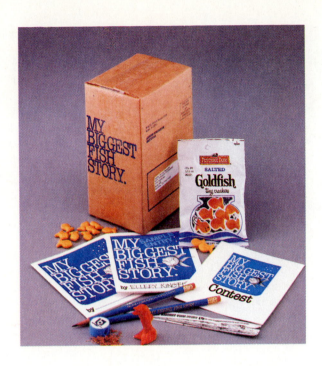

FIGURE 15-6

Direct-mail campaigns can be quite elaborate. For example, when Beam Communications wanted to interest media buyers in purchasing time on its TV stations, it developed a campaign that took a series of 15 mailings over the course of a year. The first mailing consisted of an apothecary jar and a box—labeled "Why be a little fish in a big pond?"—containing Pepperidge Farm Goldfish crackers. The next 13 mailings, over nine months, were refill packages of crackers for the jar, accompanied by an ad for Beam's TV stations. The final piece was a cardboard box containing items to help the recipients compete in a contest called "My Biggest Fish Story": a sample story, a booklet for the contestant's entry, whimsical contest rules, a tape measure to measure the fish with, and more crackers. The campaign was highly successful, resulting in 36 percent higher sales and increased recognition of Beam Communications in the broadcast and advertising industries.

only by the ingenuity of the advertiser, the size of the advertising budget, and the regulations of the U.S. Postal Service.

The direct-mail piece may be a simple postcard or letter, or it may be a large folded broadside, multipage brochure, or even a box containing several elements (see Figure 15–6). The advertiser can tell the prospect a little bit or include all the details necessary to understand a complex product. Moreover, the advertiser can usually produce a direct-mail piece and distribute it in considerably less time than it would take with most other mass media. So when speed is important, direct mail is usually considered.

Control

Direct-mail advertisers have a high degree of control over the circulation and the quality of the message. They can choose the exact audience they want as well as the number of recipients and their locations, ages, gender, and other factors.

Preprinted direct-mail pieces enable a large advertiser, such as a department store chain, to control the quality of advertising reproduction for all its outlets. In contrast, a retail organization conducting a chainwide advertising campaign in 16 different newspapers is likely to encounter significant differences in their quality of printing, page placement, position, and reader responses.

Personal Impact

Direct mail can be conceived and personalized to the needs, wants, and whims of specific audiences (see Figure 15–7). The privacy of direct mail also allows the advertiser to make special offers to a specific group without offending other prospects or customers. And a customer acquired by mail often remains a mail-oriented customer and can be sold again and again,

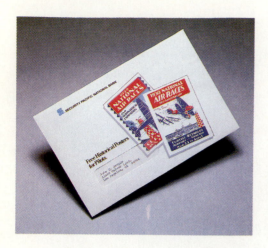

FIGURE 15-7

Direct mail can be aimed at extremely narrow market segments. When Security Pacific National Bank wanted to promote its aircraft loan program among pilots and aircraft owners, Krupp/Taylor put together a direct-mail piece that included a premium of two historical aviation posters, reproduced full size. The test mailing alone (14,000 pieces) resulted in booked loans of more than $4 million.

often without expensive sales calls, by using highly targeted direct-mail promotions.

These factors, however, can also cause occasional problems for unwary advertisers. One major airline invited company executives to bring their wives along on their next flight and then sent a cordial thank you note to each "wife." Unfortunately, some of the wives who received these notes hadn't gone on the flights after all. The airline's gracious effort not only unsettled a number of households but also lost at least a few executive customers—perhaps permanently. The personal nature of direct mail requires more caution—and discretion—by the advertiser than most other media. (See the Checklist of What Works Best in Direct Mail.)

Exclusivity

When the prospect opens the mailbox and takes out a piece of direct-mail advertising, competitive distractions are at a minimum. In contrast, a magazine contains many eye-catching ads as well as articles, stories, and illustrations. These distractions reduce the attention the reader is likely to give to a single ad.

Response

Direct mail normally achieves a higher percentage of response per thousand people reached than any other advertising medium. And with direct mail, it's easy to measure the results. In addition, direct mail is unique in its ability to measure the performance of a campaign strategy. As a rule of thumb, the direct-mail advertiser receives 15 percent of the responses within the first week of a mailing and therefore knows almost immediately whether the campaign is going to be successful.

This relatively short-term measurement affords the advertiser still another advantage. The early stages of a campaign can be used to test product acceptability, pricing, audiences, offers, copy approaches, sales literature, and so on to analyze prospect reactions. Like the National Geographic Society, direct-mail advertisers often test two or more different approaches to a campaign before deciding on the final format and contents. In fact, each element of the mailing can be tested individually, including the offer (thought to account for about 40 percent of the package's success), the mailing list (40 percent), and the writing and graphics of the package itself (20 percent).[9]

Drawbacks to Direct Mail

Although direct mail's advantages are many and unique, it also has disadvantages in relation to other media forms.

High Cost per Exposure

Direct mail has the highest cost per thousand prospects of any of the major media—about 14 times as much per thousand readers as most magazine and newspaper advertising. The reasons for this are apparent. Postal rates have soared in recent years and continue to climb. Paper costs also have risen sharply. Production and printing costs, particularly for full-color

Checklist of What Works Best in Direct Mail

☐ Make sure your offer is right. More than any other element, what you offer the consumer—in terms of product, price, or premium—will make the difference. Consider combinations instead of single units, optional extras, different opening offers, and commitment periods. *Free* is the most powerful offer you can make, but beware of its attracting lookers instead of buyers.

☐ Demonstrate your product. Offer a free sample, or enclose a sample if you can. Sampling is the most expensive promotion in absolute cost but is often so effective that the investment is quickly paid back with a larger business base. If you measure response on a profit per piece mailed, it sometimes pays to spend a few more cents.

☐ Use the envelope to telegraph your message. Direct mail must work fast. Your envelope has only seconds to interest the prospect, or go unopened into the wastebasket.

☐ Have a copy strategy. Like any other advertising medium, direct mail will be more productive if you decide *in advance* the important issues of target audience, consumer benefit, and support, tone, and personality. While your promise should relate specifically to your product, experts say the most potent appeals in direct mail are how to make money, save money, save time, or avoid effort.

☐ Grab the reader's attention. Every beginning copywriter in direct mail learns the AIDA formula. The letters stand for the ideal structure of a sales letter: Attention, Interest, Desire, Action. Look for a dramatic opening, one that speaks to the reader in a very *personal* way.

☐ Don't be afraid of long copy. The more you tell, the more you sell—particularly if you're asking the reader to spend a great deal of money or invest time. A Mercedes-Benz Diesel car letter was five pages long. A Cunard Line letter for ocean cruises was eight pages long. The key to long copy is *facts*. Be specific, not general. Make the letter visually appealing. Break up the copy into smaller paragraphs and emphasize important points with underlines or handwritten notes. Including several pieces in a direct-mail package often improves response.

☐ Don't let the reader off the hook. Leave your readers with something to do, so that they won't procrastinate. It's too easy to put off a decision. Use action devices like a yes/no token to be stuck on a reply card. *Involvement* is important. Prod them to act *now*. Set a fixed period of time, like 10 days. Or make only a limited supply available. Make it extremely easy for the reader to respond to your offer. But always ask for the order.

☐ Pretest your promises and headlines. Don't guess at what will appeal to the reader. There are many ways to sell your product benefits and as many inexpensive testing methods. Avoid humor, tricks, or gimmicks. It pays to be serious and helpful.

mailers, are at an all-time high. Even a one-page sales letter cannot be produced and printed and prepared for mailing for much less than $85 per thousand, and that doesn't include postage. Figure 15–8 provides a worksheet that is useful for estimating costs and profits for a direct-mail campaign.

Delivery Delays

A newspaper offers subscribers precise delivery times. The Sunday morning paper, for example, is home-delivered on Sunday mornings. Similarly, radio and TV shows are nearly always aired at the exact time scheduled. However, the U.S. Postal Service makes no delivery commitments on third-class mail. This may pose problems, particularly for "dated" mailers. Large retail stores generally allow 48 to 72 hours for the mail delivery of special sale announcements. In some cases, however, sale mailers have arrived four to six days after a sale ended.

FIGURE 15–8

Worksheet for projecting costs and profits of a direct-mail campaign.

WORKSHEET FOR PLANNING PROFITABLE MAILINGS

Date: June 27, 1985

PROPOSITION _____ Underwater Watch _____   KEY _____ 64 _____

1 Price of Merchandise or Service	$25.00	
2 Cost of Filling the Order		
a) Merchandise or Service	5.00	
b) Royalty		
c) Handling Expense	.75	
d) Postage and Shipping Expense	.60	
e) Premium Including Handling and Postage	.30	
f) Use Tax, if any (1 × 15%)	.75	
TOTAL COST OF FILLING THE ORDER		7.40
3 Administrative Overhead		
a) Rent, Light, Heat, Maintenance, Credit Checking, Collections, etc. (10% of #1)	2.50	
TOTAL ADMINISTRATION COST		2.50
4 Estimated Percentage of Returns, Refunds, or Cancellations	10%	
5 Expense of Handling Returns		
a) Return Postage and Handling (#2c plus #2d)	1.35	
b) Refurbishing Returned Merchandise (10% of #2a)	.50	
TOTAL COST OF HANDLING RETURNS	1.85	
6 Chargeable Cost of Returns (10% of $1.85)		.19
7 Estimated Bad Debt Percentage	10%	
8 Chargeable Cost of Bad Debts (#1 × #7)		2.50
9 Total Variable Costs (#2 plus #3, #6, and #8)		12.59
10 Unit Profit after Deducting Variable Costs (#1 less #9)		12.41
11 Return Factor (100% less #4)	90%	
12 Unit Profit Per Order (#10 × #11)		11.17
13 Loss Per Unit Profit Due to Returned Merchandise (10% of #2a)		.50
14 Net Profit Per Order (#12 less #13)		10.67
15 Cost of Mailing per 1,000	96.03	
16 NUMBER OF ORDERS PER 1,000 NEEDED TO BREAK EVEN		9.0

Lack of Content Support

Magazine advertising usually owes its readership to the articles, stories, and illustrations that surround it. Direct mail, on the other hand, has to stand alone; it must capture and hold the reader's attention without assistance. It must also stand out in some way from the handful of other direct-mail appeals that may arrive the same day. For these reasons, direct-mail advertising must be conceived, written, and produced very carefully. To be successful, it must combine strong verbal and nonverbal appeals in an attractively laid out and well-produced format.

Selectivity Problems

If the advertiser incorrectly identifies the prime audience for the mailing or does not obtain a good list of prospects, the mailing may fail.

Some groups of prospects have been saturated by volumes of mail and are therefore less responsive than others to direct-mail advertising. Physicians, for example, are the target of many financial, real estate, and insurance advertisers because of their favorable income image. The result is that the response rate among physicians is lower than that among most other professional groups.

To avoid sending mail to people who do not want it, advertisers can take advantage of the name-removal service offered by the Direct Marketing Association. This unique service is described in Figure 15–9.

Negative Attitudes

Many consumers have negative attitudes toward what they perceive as "junk mail" and as a consequence, automatically throw it away or are at least suspicious of mail solicitations. Some of the more common attitudes toward direct-mail advertising are outlined in Figure 15–10. These attitudes must be responded to if consumers are to be reached through this advertising medium.

Types of Direct Mail

Direct-mail advertising has many forms. These include sales letters, brochures, and even handwritten postcards. The message can be as short as one sentence or as long as dozens of pages. And within each format—from tiny coupon to giant 100-page catalog—an almost infinite variety is possible.

Sales letters are the most common form of direct mail. They can be typewritten, typeset and printed, printed with a computer insert (such as your name), or fully computer-typed. They are often mailed with brochures, price lists, or reply cards and envelopes.

Postcards are generally used to announce sales, offer discounts, or otherwise generate customer traffic. Postcards may travel by first- or third-class mail. The first-class postcard may feature a handwritten message. Third-class postcards, however, must be printed and may not contain any handwritten material.

Some advertisers use a double postcard, enabling them to send both an advertising message and a perforated reply card. A recipient who wants the product or service advertised simply tears off the reply card and mails it back to the advertiser. To encourage this, some advertisers use a postpaid reply card. This requires having a first-class postal permit, which is available for a nominal fee from the local postmaster.

Leaflets or *flyers* are generally single, standard-size (8½ by 11 inch) pages printed on one or both sides and folded one or more times. They usually accompany a sales letter and are used to supplement or expand the information it contains.

Folders, larger than leaflets in most cases, are printed on heavier paper stock. Their weight and size enable them to "take" a printed visual image well. They are often designed with photos or other illustrations, usually in full color. Folders can accommodate a longer, more detailed sales message than most leaflets. Often they are folded and sent as self-mailers, without envelopes, for increased economy.

Broadsides are larger than folders. Though sometimes used as window displays or wall posters in stores, they can be folded to a compact size that will fit into a mail bag.

Self-mailers are any form of direct mail (postcards, leaflets, folders, broadsides, brochures, catalogs, house organs, magazines) that can travel by mail without an envelope. Such mailers are usually folded and secured by a staple or seal. They have a special blank space on which the prospect's name and address can be written, stenciled, or labeled.

Reprints are direct-mail enclosures that are frequently sent by public

MAIL PREFERENCE SERVICE

Most people enjoy receiving information in the mail about subjects that interest them or products and services they may need or want. Millions of people spend billions of dollars annually shopping through the mail.

If you like to shop at home and enjoy getting interesting mail, ask for DMA's pamphlet, *The World in Your Mailbox.* Just send a note or postcard to the address below, asking for the pamphlet by name.

On the other hand, some people don't like to receive advertising mail and, since 1971, the Direct Marketing Association's Mail Preference Service (MPS) has been offering to help them. Computers have made it possible for many national advertisers to remove specific names from their lists, and the many companies that participate in Mail Preference Service are eager to do so upon request.

So, if you would like to receive less national advertising mail, just use this coupon to let us know. We'll try to stop as much of this mail as possible by advising mailers of your wishes.

After a few months MPS should significantly reduce the amount of direct mail you receive, although most local businesses and community organizations as well as some charitable and political groups do not participate in the program.

Name ___
Street ___ Apt. ___
City ___
State ___ ZIP ___
Variations of my name ___

MAIL PREFERENCE SERVICE
Direct Marketing Association
6 East 43rd Street
P.O. Box 3861 Grand Central Station
New York, NY 10163

FIGURE 15–9

Direct mail is just too expensive to waste on people who don't want it. For those who want to reduce the amount of direct mail they receive, the Direct Marketing Association offers a unique service: removal of their names from many national lists. The DMA also offers consumers a chance to receive *more* direct mail if they want.

　　　Consumer attitudes toward direct response advertising

I would buy more via direct response if:	Percent of all adults	I would buy more via direct response if:	Percent of all adults
I could be sure I would get what I expected.	79	It were easier to get problems straightened out.	69
Offers were from companies I could trust.	78	Offers were from well-known companies.	64
They offered things I couldn't buy near me.	77	I were offered a free-trial period to examine order.	61
It were easier to return merchandise.	77	I were billed after order is received.	59
They gave me a money-back guarantee.	75	I could pay over a period of time.	43
Prices were lower.	74	I could use my credit card.	40
They offered things that interest me.	71	They gave me a charge account.	28
They sent me a receipt or confirmation of order.	70		

PEOPLE IN ADVERTISING

Don Hauptman

Free-Lance Copywriter/Consultant

Don Hauptman is a New York–based direct-response copywriter and creative consultant who specializes in the marketing of information.

Newsletters, magazines, books, conferences, seminars, computer software, instructional tapes—these are the kinds of products for which he writes promotions. He may be best known for his Audio-Forum ads, "Speak Spanish [or French, German, and so on] Like a Diplomat!" This long-running series has sold $10 million worth of language lessons on cassette tapes. Subscription-generating packages Hauptman created won the *Newsletter of Newsletters* promotion award for six straight years, a feat unduplicated by any other writer.

While most successful free lancers got their training in an advertising agency or other corporate position, Hauptman's story is different. He recalls with obvious relish that he went directly "from unemployment to self-employment" following his discharge from the Navy in 1974. He credits a Washington publisher of financial newsletters with giving him his start; from that first client, his career as an independent writer took off.

Though he attended a few advertising courses as an undergraduate English major at New York University and,

relations agencies or departments. They are duplications of publication articles that show the company or its products in a favorable light.

Statement stuffers are advertisements enclosed in the monthly customer statements mailed by department stores, banks, or oil companies. A wide variety of products—from camping equipment to stereo systems—are sold in this way. To order, all the customer needs to do is write the credit card number on the reply card.

House organs are publications produced by business organizations. They take many forms, including stockholder reports, newsletters, consumer magazines, and dealer publications. Most are produced by the company's advertising or public relations department or by its agency. Today, an estimated 10,000 different house organ publications are mailed in the United States each year and read by more than 3.5 million people.

Catalogs are reference books that list, describe, and often picture the products sold by a manufacturer, wholesaler, jobber, or retailer. Nearly everyone is familiar with the Sears Roebuck and J. C. Penney catalogs, but similar catalogs are mailed by the millions each year by industrial, mail-order, and retail firms. With more people shopping at home, specialized catalogs have become big business in recent years. In 1986, there were 6,279 mail-order catalogs of all types, up from 4,000 in 1981. Sears, logging catalog sales of nearly $4 billion a year, now has 50 different "specialogs" that focus on specific types of merchandise, such as power tools. Other

later, at the School of Visual Arts, Hauptman says he learned most of what he knows about copywriting by writing copy. The books of such masters as David Ogilvy, Claude Hopkins, John Caples, and Eugene Schwartz were also a strong influence.

From his 13 years of copywriting experience, Hauptman offers these five principles and techniques for writing direct-mail materials:

1. *Start with the prospect instead of the product.* Avoid superlatives and brag-and-boast language. Wherever possible, incorporate anecdotes, testimonials, success stories, and other believable elements of human interest.
2. *Do research.* Interview customers, ask questions, listen carefully. Hauptman's favorite question is, "What are your [the prospect's] greatest problems, needs, and concerns right now?" At least half the time he spends on an assignment is pure research—before attacking the blank page or computer screen.
3. *Use specifics to add power and credibility.* Use precise, documented figures and facts in advertising. Cite data or opinions from outside, impartial sources. A lot of copy is anemic and ineffective because it's superficial, vague,

and unspecific. Concrete statements and detail supply the ring of truth. But to find this kind of material, you've often got to dig for it.
4. *Don't try to change behavior.* It's time-consuming, expensive, and often futile. It's usually wise to capitalize on existing motivations. In other words, preach to the converted. Unless you have an unlimited budget, avoid products and services that require the buyer to be educated or radically transformed.
5. *Be a "creative plagiarist."* You can learn by studying the work of others. But don't imitate; emulate or re-create. When you see an idea you admire, try to identify the principles behind it, then apply those principles in a fresh, original way to your own work.

The people Hauptman and his clients target are "information seekers." In his words, these people "need and want specialized data, and they are willing to pay well for it—often hundreds or thousands of dollars a year for a subscription to a single publication. It's a fertile, lucrative market—but it's essential to understand this special breed, how to reach them, and what motivates them."

FIGURE 15–11

Now that the well-known mail order company Banana Republic has opened a chain of retail stores, will its distinctive catalogs fall by the wayside? Not a chance. The company, through careful testing, has learned that catalog mailings in store locales actually boost store sales—in some cases by as much as 50 percent.

mail-order companies that are prospering with specialized approaches are those offering outdoor clothing and equipment (L. L. Bean, Campmor), electronic gadgets (Sharper Image), gourmet foods (Balducci's), and children's items (Childcraft, Just for Kids).[10] The downside of the catalog boom is that with so many choices available, consumer response per catalog is down, while the costs of preparing and mailing catalogs are increasing. As a result, some companies, including Montgomery Ward, have gone out of the mail-order business, and many firms that were exclusively mail order have begun to open retail stores to market their goods, including Banana Republic (see Figure 15–11).[11]

BUYING DIRECT MAIL

Direct-mail advertising entails three basic costs: (1) list rental or purchase; (2) conception, production, and handling of the direct mailer; and (3) distribution.

Direct-Mail Lists

Bob Stone, author of *Successful Direct Marketing Methods,* speaks of mailing lists as being the "heart" of every direct-mail operation. Each list, he points out, actually defines a market segment. These may be grouped as house lists, mail-response lists, and compiled lists.[12]

1. *House lists.* A company's customers are its most important asset. It stands to reason, therefore, that the list of names of customers and prospects compiled by the company over a long time is also its most important and valuable direct-mail list. This list may contain current customers, recent customers, and long-past customers or future prospects. William Morrisey, general manager of Ogilvy & Mather Direct, suggests six ways a store can build its own house list: (1) offer a credit plan; (2) offer to send useful booklets or other service information; (3) exchange names with other retailers with similar customer profiles; (4) capture the names of customers who ask for home delivery; (5) offer warranties or service plans; and (6) ask current customers to provide names of friends and neighbors.[13]

2. *Mail-response* lists. Second in importance are those who have responded to the direct-mail solicitations of other companies, especially those whose efforts are complementary to the advertiser's. For example, if you plan to advertise wool scarves and sports car caps, you might find the most attractive response list to be held by a company that markets driving gloves. Thousands of such response lists are available from an array of firms. They are simply the house lists of other direct-mail advertisers, and they are usually available for rental with a wide variety of demographic breakdowns.

3. *Compiled lists.* The third kind of list is the most readily available in volume but offers the lowest expectation. It is simply a list compiled for one reason or another by a source. These may include lists of automobile owners, new-house purchasers, city business owners, Chamber of Commerce presidents, union members, or what have you. Compiled lists are often computer merged with mail-response and house lists. This *merge and purge* process involves merging all names and purging all duplicates so that no more than one piece of mail is sent to one name.

Direct-mail lists can be purchased or rented. They can be brokered or exchanged with list houses or other noncompetitive companies. The variety of lists available today is virtually unlimited. The SRDS *Direct Mail List Rates and Data* comes in two volumes: Volume I, *Consumer Lists,* and Volume II, *Business Lists.* They contain over 50,000 list selections in hundreds of different classifications. An example of an SRDS listing is provided in Figure 15–12.

The quality of mailing lists can vary enormously. One owner of a wine store in San Francisco found this out firsthand when he purchased a mailing list that turned out to include hundreds of out-of-date addresses, not to mention names of people who lived too far away to patronize his store, who were not wine drinkers, or who could not afford his fine, expensive wines. After learning from his experience and obtaining the services of a mailing list broker, he purchased a second list that produced much better results. This second list included the names of people who lived near his wine shop, who subscribed to an expensive wine journal, and who were owners of moderately expensive homes.[14]

The prices of mailing lists vary according to their quality. Rental rates

---

Doubleday Book Clubs Merchandise Buyers

DOUBLEDAY MAILING LISTS

(This is a paid duplicate of the listing under classification No. 553.)

Media Code 3 520 9365 2.00　　　**Mid 035614-000**
Member: D.M.A.
Doubleday Mailing Lists.
501 Franklin Ave., Garden City, NY 11530. Phone 516-873-4065, QWIP, 516-873-4774.

1. PERSONNEL
Manager, List Marketing—Diane Silverman.
Assistant Manager, List Marketing—Liz Maletta.
List Mktg. Coordinator—Linda Jackson.
Broker and/or Authorized Agent
All recognized brokers.

2. DESCRIPTION
Members of Doubleday book clubs who have purchased items from the Doubleday merchandise catalog.
ZIP Coded in numerical sequence 100%.

3. LIST SOURCE
Direct mail and space ads.

4. QUANTITY AND RENTAL RATES
Rec'd Nov. 30, 1987.

	Total Number	Price per/M
Total list	750,000	70.00
Hotline (last 3 months)	100,000	80.00

Selections: enroll/compl. date, 5.00/M extra; Mr., Mrs., Miss, Ms., sex, demographics, 3.00/M extra; state, SCF, ZIP Code (tape), 4.00/M extra; book club payments to date, 6.00/M extra; number of purchases, 2+, 3.00/M extra; 3+, 4.00/M extra.

5. COMMISSION, CREDIT POLICY
20% commission to all recognized brokers. Payment due 30 days after billing.

6. METHOD OF ADDRESSING
4/5-up Cheshire labels. Pressure sensitive labels, 5.00/M extra. Magnetic tape (9T 1600/6250 BPI).

7. DELIVERY SCHEDULE
Ten working days from date order received.

8. RESTRICTIONS
Sample mailing piece required.

9. TEST ARRANGEMENT
Minimum 10,000; on hotline, 5,000.

11. MAINTENANCE
Cleaned and updated quarterly.

FIGURE 15–12

A typical listing from *Direct Mail List Rates and Data (Consumer Lists),* published by Standard Rate and Data Service.

average about $28 per thousand, but lists can be secured for as little as $15 per thousand or as much as $300 per thousand. The more stringent the advertiser's selection criteria, the more expensive the list. As the San Francisco wine store owner discovered, spending an extra $10 per thousand is often well worth the savings in wasted mailers and postage that result from using a less precise list.

The average mailing list changes more than 40 percent a year. One reason for this is that some 20 percent of the nation's population relocate to a new address each year. Large numbers of people also make job changes, get married, or die. Therefore, mailing lists must be continually updated. This cleaning, as it is called, ensures that the list is current and correct.

Use of computers is also allowing mailing lists to be enhanced in a number of ways, making the lists into valuable databases of information. In the process of *overlaying,* for example, information from several different sources is combined, producing an in-depth profile of each customer or company on the list. Such information may include the customer's purchasing history as well as demographic information. Such detailed databases allow marketers to pinpoint customers and narrowly target mailings to those who are most likely to be interested in the product or service. Robert Perlstein, president of a list-compiling service in Atlanta, has predicted that direct mail will eventually be so specific that "there won't be any more 'junk mail.' Everything will be of value to its audience."[15]

With the computer, an advertiser can also test the validity and accuracy of a given list. This is done by renting or buying every nth name and sending a mailer to that person. If the results are favorable, additional names can be purchased, usually in lots of 1,000.

Mailing lists are usually rented for one use only—the advertiser agrees to use the list for a single mailing. Most list owners require the advertiser to submit a sample mailer in advance. This enables them to be sure the advertiser will not mail anything that reflects poorly on them or that conflicts with their own products or services.

Many lists are handled by *list brokers.* A list owner who does not want to be bothered with the details of renting it can retain a broker to handle it. For this service, brokers are paid a commission (usually 20 percent) by the list owner. The advertiser also gains by getting the broker's direct-mail knowledge and expertise without paying more than the rental cost of the list.

Production and Handling

The advertiser can create a direct-mail package or retain the services of an advertising agency or free-lance designer and writer. Some agencies specialize in direct mail.

Once the mailing package is conceived and designed, it is ready for printing. The size and shape of the mailing pieces as well as the specified type, illustrations, and colors all influence the printing cost. Special features such as simulated blue-ink signatures, cardboard pop-ups, and die cutting (the cutting of paper stock into an unusual shape) add to the cost. The larger the printing volume, or "run," however, the lower the printing cost per unit.

The remaining production tasks can be handled by a local *letter shop* unless the advertiser prefers to do them internally. On a cost-per-thousand basis, such firms stuff and seal envelopes, affix labels, calculate postage, and sort, tie, and stack the mailers. Some also offer creative services. If the advertiser plans to use third-class bulk mail, the mailers must be separated by ZIP Code and tied into bundles to qualify for low bulk rates. When these tasks are finished, the lettershop delivers the mailers to the post office.

Distribution

Distribution costs are chiefly based on the weight of the mailer and the method of delivery. The advertiser can choose among several such methods, including the U.S. Postal Service, United Parcel, air freight, and private delivery services.

Direct mail has been found to be most effective when it arrives on Tuesdays, Wednesdays, and Thursdays. This may be because some people are affected by Monday back-to-work blues and Friday can't-wait-for-the-weekend elation or because the growing acceptance of the four-day workweek and expanded weekends means fewer people are "in town" from Friday through Monday.

The most common means of delivery is the U.S. Postal Service. It offers the advertiser a choice of several types of mail delivery.

1. *First-class mail.* Contrary to popular belief, a large amount of direct-mail advertising is sent first class. The reasons are that first class ensures fast delivery, returns any mail that is undeliverable, and forwards mail (without additional charge) if the addressee has moved and filed a forwarding address.
2. *Business reply mail.* This type of mail enables the recipient to respond without paying postage. The advertiser must first obtain a special permit number, which is available from the local postmaster. This number must be printed on the face of the return card or envelope. On receiving a response, the advertiser must pay postage plus a few cents handling fee. This "postage-free" incentive tends to increase the rate of response.
3. *Third-class mail.* The four types of third-class mail are: single piece, bulk, bound books or catalogs, and nonprofit organization mail. Most direct-mail advertising travels by third-class mail, which represents a significant savings over first-class rates.
4. *Fourth-class mail.* This class applies only to mail that weighs over 16 ounces.

OUTDOOR ADVERTISING

In late 1984, Sharlene Wells was crowned Miss America for 1985 on a network television show with an audience of over 50 million viewers. In fact, it was one of the highest rated television specials of the year. Shortly thereafter, Sharlene appeared on five more network television shows as well as dozens of local television and radio programs. The Sharlene Wells name and picture were also shown in hundreds of newspapers and a considerable number of national magazines.

In December 1984, a study sponsored by the Institute of Outdoor Advertising was conducted in two test markets by an independent research organization, Lee Cobb & Associates. One simple question was asked: "What is the name of Miss America for 1985?" In spite of all the national

publicity, all the network TV shows, and all the newspaper and magazine
photos, only 1.5 percent of the respondents could give the correct answer.

On January 15, the institute sponsored a one-month coast-to-coast billboard campaign. Some 2,500 poster panels (billboards) carried a photograph of Miss Wells and the simple statement: "Sharlene Wells, Miss America 1985" (see Figure 15–13). When the institute conducted a second wave
of interviews in March and April, 11.9 percent of those questioned knew
who Miss America was—an eightfold increase in awareness. If those results could be projected nationally, it would mean that outdoor advertising
had communicated a new and unusual name to more than 15 million adult
Americans, about 1 in every 10.

Advantages of Outdoor Advertising

The advantages of outdoor advertising are numerous and distinct. They
relate to the medium's reach, frequency, flexibility, and cost as well as to
its impact.

Reach

Often an advertiser requires saturation of a market to accomplish objectives such as the introduction of a new product or feature or a change in
package design. Outdoor advertising is a mass medium that makes broad
coverage possible overnight.

The term describing the basic unit of sale for posters is "100 gross
ratings points daily" or a 100 *showing*. One rating point is equal to 1
percent of a particular market's population. Buying 100 gross rating points
does not mean, however, that the message will appear on 100 posters
within a market. It means the message will appear on as many panels as are
needed to provide a daily exposure theoretically equal to 100 percent of
the market's population. In actuality, however, an advertiser who buys a
showing of 100 gross rating points will reach about 88.1 percent of adults
in a market per day over the 30-day period during which the posters are
"bought."[16] An advertiser desiring less saturation can decrease the number
of posters, and the units of sale would be expressed as fractions of the
basic unit, such as 75, 50, or 25 gross rating points. An advertiser desiring
more saturation can increase the number of posters to reach as high as 200
or 300 GRPs per day (see Figure 15–14).

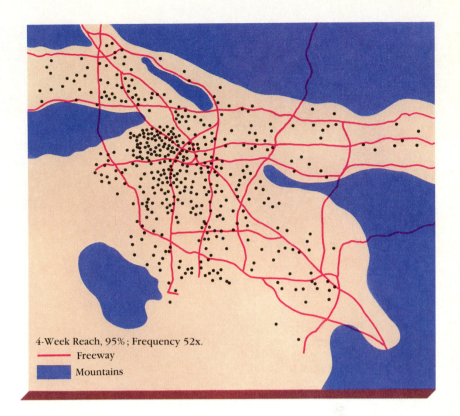

FIGURE 15–14

A map of billboard locations throughout Los Angeles and Orange counties that would achieve at least 100 GRPs each day for four weeks. The cost of such a showing would be about $250,000.

4-Week Reach, 95%; Frequency 52x.
— Freeway
■ Mountains

Even more important to most advertisers is the audience reached by outdoor advertising. For the most part, its audience is a young, educated, affluent, and mobile population—very attractive to most national advertisers.

Frequency

Outdoor offers frequency of impressions. According to the Institute for Outdoor Advertising, the 9 out of 10 people reached with a 100 GRP showing receive an average of 29 impressions each over a 30-day period. This frequency increases for groups that are better educated and have higher incomes—again, very attractive.

Data on frequency and reach for more than 8,000 markets are available from Audience Market by Market for Outdoor (AMMO), one of the services of the Institute for Outdoor Advertising.

Flexibility

In addition, outdoor offers advertisers great flexibility. They can place their advertising geographically where they want it—in any of 9,000 markets across the country—nationally, regionally, or locally. An outdoor advertiser can buy just one city or even a small section of that city.

The flexibility can be demographic. Messages can be concentrated in areas frequented or traversed by young people, upper-income people, or people of specific ethnic backgrounds (see Figure 15–15). One outdoor company, Winston Network, has even developed a computerized method for characterizing outdoor audiences by age, sex, income, and lifestyle down to the block level.[17]

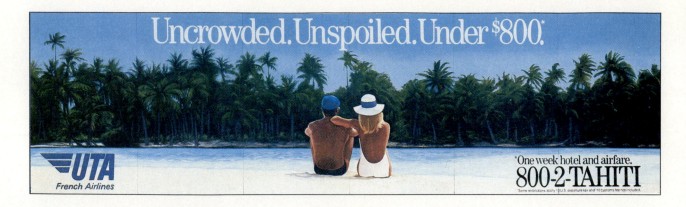

FIGURE 15–15

An important advantage of bill-boards is that they can be targeted to a desired audience by careful placement. This billboard for UTA French Airlines was placed in rotating locations in Los Angeles and San Francisco targeted to high-income households. Studies have shown that outdoor advertising delivers a more affluent audience than television because younger, wealthier consumers tend to be on the go—eating out, attending the theater and concerts—rather than staying home watching TV.

Outdoor can even be targeted by activity—shoppers on their way to the store, businesspeople on their way to and from work, travelers on their way to the airport.

Cost

Outdoor advertising offers the lowest cost per message delivered of any major advertising medium. Rates vary depending on the size of the particular market and the intensity desired.

The industry uses the term *showing* to indicate the relative number of outdoor posters used during a contract period. If a showing provides 750,000 total impression opportunities daily in a market with a population of 1 million, it is said to deliver 75 gross rating points (GRPs) daily. Over a period of 30 days, this showing would earn 2,250 gross rating points (30 × 75). The GRP system makes cost comparison possible from market to market.

Local and national advertisers are charged the same rates. These are quoted on a monthly basis for various GRP levels, and they vary considerably from market to market. Differences are due to variations in property rentals, labor costs, and market size. Higher rates are found in larger markets where traffic volume is high (see Figure 15–16).

Detailed rate information may be found in the *Buyers Guide to Outdoor Advertising,* which is published twice a year by the Institute of Outdoor Advertising.

Impact

All this adds up to economical intensity of impressions for the advertiser. With relatively low cost, the advertiser can build up GRPs very fast by hitting a large percentage of the market many times over a short period. This, of course, is ideal for advertisers who have a short, simple, dogmatic message.

The inherent features of outdoor add impact to the advertiser's message. Outdoor offers the largest display of any medium. Plus, it offers the spectacular features of lights, animation, and brilliant color (see Figure 15–17).

Finally, whereas other media carry the message to the prospect, outdoor catches people on their way to shop, work, or play, selling continuously day and night. This gives it additional impact for impulse products as

FIGURE 15–16	Monthly rates for standard posters (12′ by 25′) in some major metropolitan markets						
	25 daily GRPs		**50 daily GRPs**		**100 daily GRPs**		
Market	Number	Cost	Number	Cost	Number	Cost	Average/ poster
Atlanta	30	$12,250	60	$ 24,500	120	$ 49,000	$408
Boston	90	40,500	170	76,500	340	153,000	450
Denver	21	9,050	39	16,800	78	33,600	430
Detroit	46	25,760	92	51,520	184	103,040	560
Los Angeles	125	63,250	250	126,500	500	253,000	506
New Orleans	25	10,250	50	20,500	100	41,000	410
Philadelphia	70	32,900	140	65,800	280	131,600	470
Phoenix	22	11,220	44	22,440	88	44,880	510
Seattle	40	18,325	80	36,795	160	72,865	455
St. Louis	40	18,905	80	37,810	160	75,635	473

Note: Costs are for space only; they do not include production. Discounts are available.

FIGURE 15–17

Motorists in California and Florida were treated to this high-impact painted bulletin. The cleaning woman is a 500-pound sculpture.

well as hotels, motels, restaurants, tourist attractions, and auto-related services. (See Portfolio of Outdoor Advertising: A 20th-Century Art Form.)

Drawbacks to Outdoor Advertising

Just as outdoor has numerous advantages, it also has numerous disadvantages. Posters are passed very quickly. To be effective, therefore, outdoor advertising must intrude. The design and legend must tell a story briefly and crisply, and they must sell. (See the Checklist of What Works Best in Outdoor.) .

Although outdoor advertising is fine for reaching a wide audience, it has limitations for reaching a narrow demographic group. Furthermore, the demographics of outdoor audiences are difficult to measure.

Printing and posting outdoor messages are very time-consuming, so outdoor campaigns must be planned far in advance. Usually a six- to eight-week lead time is required.

The high initial preparation cost may sometimes discourage local use, although printing methods such as silk screening offer lower preparation costs. For national advertisers, buying outdoor can be a major headache because sales are highly fragmented among a number of outdoor companies serving different markets. And even in a single market, as many as 30 companies may be selling ad space.

Another disadvantage is the difficulty of physically inspecting each outdoor poster panel (as opposed to checking tear sheets of space advertising or monitoring commercials).

Outdoor advertising is also hampered by its past history. Countrysides dotted with advertising messages gave rise to complaints about billboards despoiling the landscape and "polluting" the scenery. Governments responded to such complaints with laws banning outdoor advertising in

Checklist of What Works Best in Outdoor

☐ Look for a big idea. This is no place for subtleties. Outdoor is a bold medium. You need a poster that registers the idea quickly and memorably—"visual scandal" that shocks the viewer into awareness.

☐ Keep it simple. Cut out all extraneous words and pictures and concentrate on the essentials. Outdoor is the art of brevity. Use only one picture and no more than seven words of copy—preferably less.

☐ Personalize when you can. Personalized posters are practical, even for short runs. Mention a specific geographic area ("New in Chicago"), or the name of a local dealer.

☐ Look for human, emotional content for memorability. It can be an entertainment medium for travelers who are hungry or bored.

☐ Use color for readability. The most readable combination is black on yellow. Other combinations may gain more attention, but stay with primary colors—and *stay away from reverse*.

☐ Use the location to your advantage. Many new housing developments capitalize on their convenient locations with a poster saying: "If you lived here, you'd be home now." Use outdoor to tell drivers that your restaurant is down the road, your department store is across the street. Don't ignore the ability of outdoor to reach ethnic neighborhoods. Tailor the language and the models to your consumer.

certain areas and limiting it in others. Although the reputation of outdoor advertising has improved in recent years, because of innovative and entertaining uses of this "art form," the supply of space available for such ads is now far less than the demand.

And finally, the outdoor message is influenced somewhat by its environment. A billboard in a generally run-down area will certainly detract from the medium's ability to lend prestige to the product being advertised.

Standardization of the Outdoor Advertising Business

Most advertising that appears out of doors is not *standardized* outdoor advertising but rather on-premise signs that identify a place of business. This type of sign, though certainly helpful to a business, does not provide coverage of a market. Conversely, standardized outdoor advertising locates its structures scientifically to deliver an advertiser's message to an entire market. Standardized outdoor advertising is a highly organized medium available to advertisers in more than 15,000 communities across the country. The structures on which the advertising appears are owned and maintained by individual outdoor advertising companies known as plants. The structures are built on private land that the outdoor plant operators own or lease and are concentrated in commercial and business areas where they conform to all local building code requirements.

The industry consists of about 600 local and regional plant operators. They find suitable locations, lease or buy the property, erect the outdoor structures, contract with advertisers for poster rentals, and post the panels or paint the bulletins (see Figure 15–18). They also have to maintain the outdoor structures so lights are working and torn sheets are replaced and keep the areas surrounding the structures clean and attractive.

(continued on p. 511)

FIGURE 15–18

A. Printed poster sheets are collated, prepasted, and vacuum-sealed in plastic bags. The glued sheets will remain moist for weeks. Erecting the poster begins with pasting on "blanking paper" to form a border. Next, beginning at the bottom, the prepasted sheets are applied to the first section of the panel.

B. By starting at the bottom and working upward, each sheet can overlap the previous section. This forms a "rain-lap" and helps prevent flagging or tearing of the poster. Because the sheets have been prepasted, a dry brush can be used to make the paper adhere to the panel. Prepasting also eliminates glue streaks from dark backgrounds.

C. Sheet by sheet, the giant paper mosaic is assembled to build the advertiser's message into a clean, colorful 12′ by 25′ display. Since a poster is a series of sheets, some sections of the poster can be varied for specific locations. Thus, some posters may have a different dealer's name or a change in package.

PORTFOLIO OF OUTDOOR ADVERTISING: A 20TH-CENTURY ART FORM

A. Motorists in San Diego were grabbed by this series of striking billboards along one of the city's major freeways.

B. This imaginative billboard graphically demonstrates its point without an illustration and with a message that just fits into the maximum seven words.

C. A billboard this unique is hard to ignore. Visual interest is enhanced by the ever-changing landscape as one drives by the structure.

D. The in-house agency for Robinson's Department Stores has produced an award-winning series of outdoor boards featuring products that expand beyond the confines of the traditional billboard. Most of these are co-op ads depicting products not normally seen in the outdoor medium.

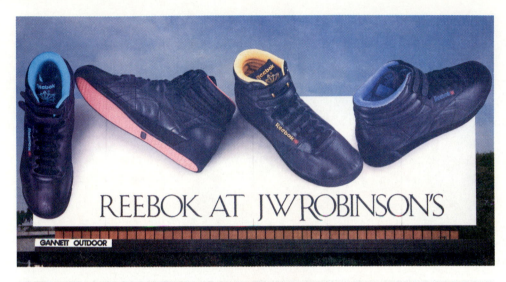

E. The best billboards are often those specifically targeted at the people most likely to see them—motorists. No one expects drivers to read all these signs, but they should still get the message that taking the bus could reduce some of the stresses they are no doubt currently experiencing.

F. If this startling outdoor ad doesn't catch your attention, nothing will. It demonstrates that the medium has no limits for those who approach it imaginatively.

Although national advertising makes up the bulk of outdoor business, about one-fourth of the business of a typical outdoor plant is from local advertisers. Usually, the smaller the market, the larger the percentage of local advertisers. The outdoor firm may employ an art staff to perform creative services for local advertisers, but the creative work for national advertisers is usually handled by advertising agencies. By far the biggest national advertisers are makers of cigarettes and alcoholic beverages, which together accounted for about 34 percent of all outdoor expenditures in 1986.[18]

Types of Outdoor Structures

Standardized outdoor advertising structures have three basic forms: the poster panel, the bulletin, and the spectacular.

Posters

Posters ("billboards") are the basic form of outdoor advertising and the least costly per unit. A poster is a structure of blank panel with a standardized size and border. It is usually anchored in the ground, but it may be affixed to a wall or roof. Its advertising message is first printed at a lithography or silk screen plant on large sheets of paper. These are then mounted by hand on the panel.

Poster sizes are referred to in terms of sheets. At one time, covering a structure 12' by 25' required 24 of the largest sheets a printing press could hold. The designation "24-sheet" is still used even though press sizes have changed and most poster sizes are larger. The poster is still mounted on a board with a total surface of 12' by 25', but today there are two basic sizes of posters:

1. 30-sheet poster—with a 9'7" by 21'7" printed area surrounded by a margin of blank paper. The 30-sheet provides 25 percent more copy area than the old 24-sheet size of 8'8" by 19'6".
2. Bleed poster—with a 10'5" by 22'8" printed area extending all the way to the frame. The bleed poster is about 40 percent larger than the old 24-sheet poster.

One way some local advertisers get high-quality outdoor advertising at lower than usual cost is to use ready-made 30-sheet posters. These stock posters are available in any quantity, and they often feature the work of first-class artists and lithographers. Local advertisers simply order as many as they need and have their name placed in the appropriate spot. These ready-made posters are particularly suitable for such local firms as florists, dairies, banks, and bakeries.

Advertisers of grocery products and many local advertisers like to use smaller poster sizes, such as "junior panels." These are also referred to as 8-sheet posters and offer a 5' by 11' printing area on a panel surface 6' wide by 12' deep.

Painted Bulletins

Painted bulletins or displays are meant for long use and are usually placed in only the best locations where traffic is heavy and visibility is good. Painted bulletins are usually painted in sections in the plant's shop and then transported to the site, where they are assembled and hung on the billboard structure.

Although usually standardized in width and height, actual sizes depend on the available location, the advertiser's budget, and the character of the message. Bulletins are more custom-made than posters, are generally larger, and are usually longer. Typical bulletins are 14′ by 48′; however, some even extend to 18′ by 62′10″.

Painted displays are normally illuminated and are repainted several times each year to keep them looking fresh. Some are three-dimensional or embellished by cutouts that extend beyond the frames (see Figure 15–19). Variations include the use of cutout letters, plastic facing, backlighting,

FIGURE 15–19

Three-dimensionality has come to outdoor ads in the form of inflatables. This Honda Accord inflates every 30 seconds, demonstrating how Custom Auto Body gets out the dents.

moving messages, clocks, thermometers, electric time and temperature units called jump clocks, and novel treatment of light and color. (See Ad Lab 15-B.)

Some advertisers overcome the higher expense of painted bulletins by using a *rotary plan.* The bulletins are rotated to different choice locations in the market every 30, 60, or 90 days, giving the impression of wide coverage over time.

AD LAB 15-B   How to Use Color in Outdoor Advertising

Color Contrast and Value

The availability of a full range of colors, vividly and faithfully reproduced, is one of the outstanding advantages of outdoor advertising. A huge poster or bulletin alive with brilliant reds and greens and yellows and blues can produce an effect approached by no other medium.

In choosing colors for outdoor, the designer should seek out those with high contrast in both hue (the identity of the color, such as red, green, yellow) and value (the measure of the color's lightness or darkness). Contrasting colors work well at outdoor-viewing distances, while colors without contrast blend together and obscure the message.

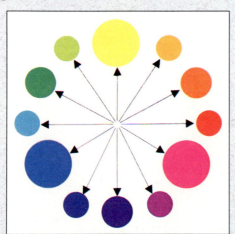

The color wheel illustrates the need for contrast in both hue and value. For example, green and red are opposite each other on the wheel and are therefore complementary colors. They represent a good contrast in *hues,* but in *values* they are very similar. As a result, they set up an annoying vibration. The same is true of blue and orange.

Blue and green and orange and red are especially poor combinations because they are similar in both hue *and* value.

On the other hand, yellow and purple—*dis*similar in both hue and value—provide a strong and effective contrast for outdoor. Of course, white goes well with any dark-value color, while black is good with colors of light value.

Color Impact

Among the color combinations shown, legibility ranges from best in combination 1 to poorest in combination 18.

Color Combinations

Color combinations illustrate need for contrast in hue and value. Blue and green do *not* work well together; yellow and purple *do* work well.

Laboratory Applications

1. Which outdoor advertisements in this chapter use color the most effectively?
2. What examples of outdoor advertising have you seen that use color effectively?

FIGURE 15–20

Spectaculars are expensive, elaborate animated signs found primarily in the heart of large cities such as New York and Tokyo.

Spectaculars

Spectaculars are giant electronic signs that usually incorporate movement, color, and flashy graphics to grab the attention of viewers in high-traffic areas. Spectaculars are very expensive to produce and are found primarily in the largest cities, such as the Times Square area of New York City (see Figure 15–20).

TRANSIT ADVERTISING

In 1910, Wrigley's Gum decided to undertake a new test campaign in Buffalo, New York, because gum had been so difficult to sell there. Wrigley's contacted the Collier Service Company in New York City, which had been established to provide copy and illustration service as well as to sell transit (bus) advertising. At the time, Collier employed some of the best writers in America, including F. Scott Fitzgerald and Ogden Nash. Collier's organization developed the famed "spear man."

Wrigley's spear man was then printed on cards and carried on buses throughout Buffalo. The Buffalo program was so successful it was repeated in city after city across the nation.

It was around the same time that the Campbell Soup company began to think of using advertising to sell its products. Spending its first $5,000 on car card advertising, Campbell contracted to place its advertisements on one-third of the surface buses in New York City for one year. After only six months, the campaign was so obviously successful that the contract was enlarged to include all surface vehicles in New York City. This produced a

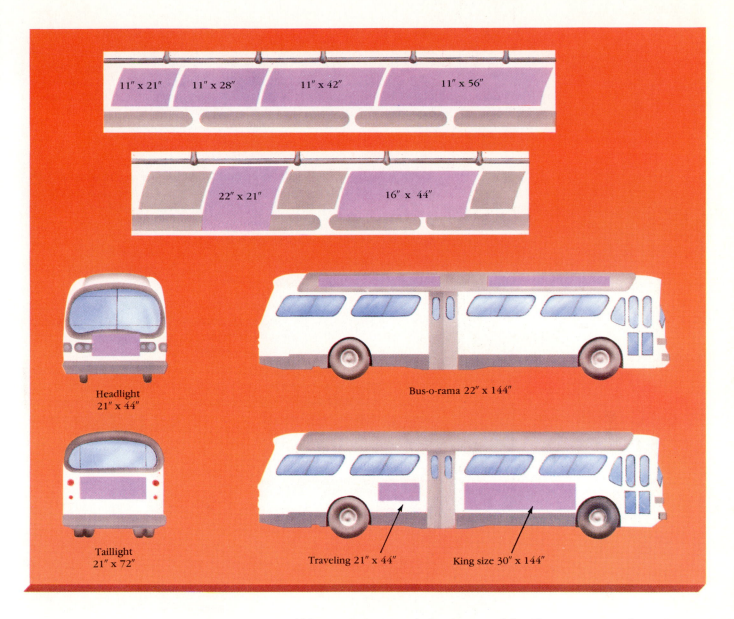

11" x 21"   11" x 28"   11" x 42"   11" x 56"

22" x 21"   16" x 44"

Headlight
21" x 44"

Bus-o-rama 22" x 144"

Taillight
21" x 72"

Traveling 21" x 44"   King size 30" x 144"

FIGURE 15–21

The common sizes for inside cards and outside posters available in transit advertising.

100 percent increase in business, and for 12 years transit advertising was the sole medium used by the company.

Types of Transit Advertising

Transit advertising depends on the millions of people who use commercial transportation facilities (buses, subways, elevated trains, commuter trains, trolleys, and airlines) plus pedestrians and auto passengers.

Transit advertising actually includes three separate media forms: inside cards; outside posters; and station, platform, and terminal posters.

Inside Cards

The standard size of the inside card, placed in a wall rack above the windows, is 11" by 28" (see Figure 15–21). Four other widths are available (11" by 21", 11" by 42", 11" by 56", and 11" by 84"). Cost-conscious advertisers print both sides of the card so it can simply be reversed to change the message, thus saving on paper and shipping charges.

Inside car-end posters (in "bulkhead" positions) are usually larger and of varying sizes. One common size is 22″ by 21″. Some top-end or over-door cards are 16″ by 39″ or 16″ by 44″. The end and side positions carry a premium rate.

Outside Posters

Printed on high-grade cardboard and often varnished to be weather resistant, the most widely used exterior units are (1) side of bus—king size (30″ by 144″), queen size (30″ by 88″), and traveling display (21″ by 44″); (2) rear of bus—taillight spectacular (21″ by 72″); and (3) front of bus—headlight (17″ by 21″ and 21″ by 44″).

Station, Platform, and Terminal Posters

In many bus, subway, and commuter train stations, space is sold for one-sheet, two-sheet, and three-sheet posters. Also, major train and airline terminals offer a variety of special advertising forms that might be compared to outdoor spectaculars. These are usually custom designed and include such attention getters as floor displays, island showcases, illuminated signs, dioramas (three-dimensional scenes), and clocks with special lighting and moving messages. In large cities with major mass-transit systems, advertising at bus shelters and on the backs of bus-stop seats is also popular.

Advantages of Transit Advertising

Why was Campbell's campaign on bus cards so successful? What was it about transit that helped Wrigley become a household name? The answers to these questions are numerous, and they define the many advantages of transit advertising: high reach, frequency, exposure, and attention values at very low cost.

Transit advertising gives long exposure to the advertiser's message because the average ride is about 25 minutes. It has repetitive value; many people take the same routes day after day. The messages are eagerly read by riders attempting to escape from boredom, and surveys show that readership is high. For ads in the New York subway trains, which have a captive audience with no outside scenery to attract their attention, readership is not only high but ad recall averages 55 percent.[19]

The cost of transit advertising is low. This is partly because capital costs are paid for by the fares, with no huge capital investment needed for equipment. The dollar outlay is generally less than for any other medium.

Transit advertising also reaches mass audiences. It offers geographic flexibility and can reach various ethnic or neighborhood groups. New York Subway Advertising uses census tracts and city population reports to develop a complete picture of subway riders. It claims that 89 percent of all blacks and 90 percent of Hispanic adults in New York are reachable through the subways. As a result, many advertisers have placed subway ads that are specifically targeted to the black and Hispanic markets (see Figure 15–22).[20]

Flexibility is another advantage of transit advertising. It permits special

FIGURE 15–22

This subway poster ("Take a clean break from the IRT . . . with basic natural Ivory") was targeted at the large Hispanic ridership on many New York City trains (the IRT is one of the subway lines).

constructions and color effects at relatively low cost, and ads can be specifically targeted to the needs and desires of riders. In the summer, for example, ads for cool drinks are a natural. Food advertising also does well, as riders on their way home from work contemplate what to do about dinner.

While outdoor advertising has been a target of the environmental movement, transit advertising has been one of its beneficiaries. Environmental considerations have increased social pressure to use public transportation instead of private autos. At the same time, federal subsidies for the transit industry have resulted in larger and better transit systems as well as some new ones.

As the industry has progressed, it has developed more efficient standardization, better research, additional statistical data, and measured circulation, thus making it easier for national advertisers to include transit advertising in their schedules.

National advertisers who have used the medium in recent years have included tobacco companies, oil companies, financial institutions, proprietary medicines, and food and beverage producers (see Figure 15–23). The medium is especially suitable for reaching middle- to lower-income urban consumers, providing supplemental coverage to these groups.

Transit advertising is equally popular with local advertisers. Such advertisers as theaters, restaurants, and retailers find it a productive medium for reminders and special announcements.

Drawbacks to Transit Advertising

Among the weaknesses of transit advertising, especially inside cards, are its general lack of coverage of some segments of society, such as suburbanites who drive their own cars, rural dwellers, and business and professional people who seldom use mass transportation. Other disadvantages include:

It lacks the status of an important advertising medium.
Its rush-hour crowds limit the opportunity and ease of reading.

FIGURE 15–23

Nabisco sought Canadian consumers for its cookies with a series of striking transit ads.

It reaches a nonselective audience, which may not meet the needs of some advertisers.

Cards are so numerous and look so similar that they may be confusing.

The transit vehicle environment, which may be crowded and dirty, may not lend prestige to the product.

The trend to outlying shopping centers means fewer shoppers make trips downtown.

Although transit cards may carry longer messages than billboards, copy is still somewhat limited.

Buying Transit Advertising

One of the most often cited advantages of transit advertising is the cost per exposure: approximately 13.7 cents per thousand in the nation's "A" markets (the 22 largest metropolitan areas in the United States). In fact, outside transit ad costs can be as low as 6 cents per thousand exposures.

The unit of purchase is a showing, also known as a run or service. In transit advertising, a full showing (or No. 100 showing) means that one card will appear in each vehicle in the system. Space may also be purchased as a one-half (or No. 50) showing or a one-quarter (or No. 25) showing. Exterior displays are purchased on a showing basis.

Rates are usually quoted for 30-day showings—with discounts for 3-, 6-, 9-, and 12-month contracts. The advertisers must supply the cards at their own expense.

Cost depends on (1) the length of the showing, (2) the saturation of the showing, and (3) the size of the space. Rates vary extensively, depending primarily on the size of the system.

Rates for specific markets may be obtained from the local transit company and from Transit Advertising Association's *TAA Rate Directory of Transit Advertising* (the industry's rate book).

Special Inside Buys

In some cities, advertisers may buy all the inside space on a group of buses, thereby gaining complete domination. This buy is called the *basic bus*. In addition, pads of business reply cards or coupons (called *take ones*) may be affixed to interior advertisements for an extra charge. This allows passengers to request more detailed information, send in application blanks, or receive some other advertised product benefit.

Special Outside Buys

Some transit companies offer *bus-o-rama signs*. This is a jumbo roof sign, which is actually a full-color transparency backlighted by fluorescent tubes, running the length of the bus. Two bus-o-rama positions are on each side of the bus. A single advertiser may also buy a *total bus*—all the exterior space on a bus including the front, rear, sides, and top. This gives the product message powerful exclusivity.

Some transit companies offer other unique capabilities. With the introduction of new advance-design buses, for instance, the Winston Network (transit advertising company) offers advertisers up to 20 feet of sign space along the street side of the bus. The new, futuristic buses provide a smooth outer surface to which WN is able to directly apply pressure-sensitive vinyl. Available in several reflective colors and textures, the 30″ by 240″ vinyl signs offer a versatile alternative to advertisers. In addition, they can be die-cut to any shape within the sign area, so anything from soft drink bottles to carpenter's pencils can travel the streets daily (see Figure 15–24).

To keep advertisers informed of opportunities in transit advertising, the industry has two organizations—the Transit Advertising Association and the American Public Transit Association. The TAA is the main source of

FIGURE 15–24

Among recent innovations in transit advertising is the use of pressure-sensitive vinyl to place a variety of die-cut shapes on smooth bus sides.

FIGURE 15–25

Mobile billboards—ads on the sides of tractor-trailers or on specially designed flatbed trucks—are starting to appear in some areas of the country, to mixed reaction.

information—it performs research and supplies industry data on the number of vehicles, trends, and rider demographics. The TAA is the national trade organization and promotion arm of the industry. Its members represent 80 percent of the transit advertising volume in the United States and Canada.

One variation on out-of-home advertising being experimented with is the "mobile billboard," which is something of a cross between traditional billboards and transit advertising (see Figure 15–25). The mobile billboards were first conceived of as ads on the sides of tractor-trailer trucks. After seeing an American Trucking Association's survey showing that 10.1 million people see the average tractor-trailer in a year and that 91 percent notice trucks displaying words and pictures, the president of a ready-made salad company came up with the idea. He had his fleet of 50 trucks outfitted with 9′ high by 48′ long billboards touting his "Salad Singles." The company, Orval Kent Food Company, also leases space to other advertisers on its 250 other trucks.[21]

Although the idea of advertising on trucks has yet to catch on, a variation on this theme has appeared in some large cities, where specially designed flatbed trucks carry 10′ high by 22′ long billboards up and down busy thoroughfares. Unlike the tractor-trailers, which display their advertising on long hauls, the flatbeds can be limited to a specific local area, reaching a particular target audience. Local routes for mobile ads are also being offered on delivery trucks in San Francisco, Los Angeles, and Seattle. *Entrepreneur* magazine predicts that rolling advertising will proliferate over the next 10 years and become a common sight on our streets and freeways.[22]

Summary

Direct-mail advertising includes all forms of advertising sent directly to prospects through the mail. As an advertising medium, it ranks third in dollars spent, surpassed only by newspapers and television.

Next to the personal sales call, direct mail is the most effective way an advertiser can put a message in front of a prospect. It is also the most expensive on a cost-per-exposure basis. As an advertising medium, it offers several advantages. These include selectivity, intensive coverage, flexibility, control, personal impact, exclusivity, and response performance.

The drawbacks to direct mail include the high cost per exposure, the delays often experienced in delivery, the lack of other content support for the advertising message, certain problems with selectivity, and negative attitudes toward the medium.

Direct-mail advertising comes in many forms. Sales letters, brochures, and even handwritten postcards all qualify as direct-mail advertising. The message can be as short as one sentence or as long as dozens of pages.

The direct-mail list is the heart of the medium because each list actually defines a market segment. There are three types of direct-mail lists: house lists, mail-response lists, and compiled lists. Their prices vary according to their quality.

Of the major advertising media, outdoor advertising offers the lowest cost per message delivered. In addition, the medium offers other attractive features. These include instant broad coverage (reach), very high frequency, great flexibility, and high impact. Drawbacks include the necessity for brief messages, the limitations for reaching narrow demographic groups, the lead time required, and the medium's past reputation. In addition, the high initial preparation costs and difficulty of physically inspecting each billboard discourage some advertisers.

The standardized outdoor advertising industry consists of about 600 local and regional plant operators. National advertising makes up the bulk of outdoor business.

The two most common forms of standard outdoor advertising structures are the poster panel and the bulletin. The poster panel is the basic form, is the least costly per unit, and is available in a variety of sizes. Painted bulletins are meant for long use and are usually placed in the best locations where traffic is heavy and visibility is good. Some advertisers overcome the relatively higher expense of painted bulletins by using a rotary plan. An additional form of outdoor available in some cities is the spectacular, an expensive electronic display.

Transit advertising offers the features of high reach, frequency, exposure, and attention values at very low cost. Furthermore, it gives long exposure to the advertiser's message and offers repetitive value and good geographic flexibility. In addition, advertisers have a wide choice in the size of space used.

Its disadvantages, of course, are numerous. It does not cover some segments of society, it reaches a nonselective audience, it lacks prestige, and copy is still somewhat limited.

Questions for Review and Discussion

1. What advantages does direct mail offer the National Geographic Society as compared to other forms of advertising it might use?
2. What is the difference between direct-mail and direct response advertising?
3. Although direct mail offers the advantage of selectivity, what are the associated problems?
4. What are the three types of mailing lists? Which is the best? Why?
5. What costs are advertisers likely to incur in a direct-mail campaign?
6. Which advertising objectives are the outdoor media mostly suitable for?
7. Do you feel outdoor is an effective advertising medium for a politician? Why?
8. What is the difference between a poster panel and a painted bulletin?
9. Why is transit advertising considered three separate media forms?
10. Which characteristics of transit advertising benefit advertisers the most?

16

SALES PROMOTION AND SUPPLEMENTARY MEDIA

The competition for breakfast cereal sales is fierce, especially among the presweetened cereals designed primarily for children ages 6 to 12. The folks at Quaker Oats, makers of Cap'n Crunch and Life cereals, know this fact all too well. At the beginning of 1985, Cap'n Crunch, which had been around for nearly 25 years, was the number-two cereal in this market, but its market share had been steadily dropping. To revive interest in this well-established brand, Quaker devised a promotion that revolved around the "disappearance" of the character Cap'n Crunch.

The promotion had two objectives: to regain awareness and interest in the cereal among children and to introduce a more modern image for the Cap'n. (The revamped image was introduced when it was eventually revealed that the Cap'n was in outer space in the Milky Way.)

The foundation of the promotion was a "Where's the Cap'n?" game, in which consumers had to buy three boxes of the cereal to get each of the clues to the Cap'n's whereabouts (each box was clearly marked as having clue 1, 2, or 3). The prize was $100 each to 10,000 children whose names were drawn from the pool of correct answers. The game was promoted in Saturday morning TV commercials, print ads in children's magazines, and free-standing newspaper coupons that offered either cents off or free boxes of cereal with purchases. A unique aspect of the campaign was that Cap'n Crunch's image was removed from the cereal package and replaced by a question mark, so the package itself played an important role in the promotion (see Figure 16–1).

The result was a 50 percent increase in sales during the six-month promotion. In addition, the campaign raised interest among college students (who had grown up with the cereal), leading to the development of "The Crunch Chronicle," a newsletter distributed on college campuses. It contained puzzles for students to solve and mail in to Quaker, which awarded $1,000 to each of 100 winners. The promotion also drew a lot of free publicity, including jibes on NBC's "Saturday Night Live."

In 1986, Quaker Oats received the Promotion Marketing Association of America's Super Reggie and Gold Reggie awards for the "Where's the Cap'n?" campaign.[1]

ROLE OF SALES PROMOTION

What would the sales of Cap'n Crunch have been without the promotion—if Quaker had simply placed all its efforts into advertising? The answer to this question is the key to understanding what sales promotion is and how it works.

The purpose of all marketing tools such as advertising, public relations, and sales promotion is to help the company achieve its marketing objectives (see Chapter 4). Types of marketing objectives may include the following:

1. To introduce new products.
2. To induce present customers to buy more.
3. To attract new customers.
4. To combat competition.
5. To maintain sales in off-seasons.
6. To increase retail inventories so more goods may be sold.

As we know, the marketing strategy the company uses to achieve these objectives may include a high degree of personal selling. It may also include nonpersonal selling activities such as advertising the company's products in the national media or in trade journals read by its dealers. It may include public relations activities such as feature stories and magazine interviews. Or it may include a major sales promotion campaign like Quaker's.

Sales promotion is used to help produce and increase sales. It is sometimes referred to as *supplementary* to advertising and personal selling because it binds the two together, making both more effective. In reality, however, it is far more than supplementary since it may now represent as much as 65 percent of the typical marketing budget versus 35 percent for advertising.[2]

By definition, *sales promotion is a direct inducement offering extra incentives all along the marketing route—from manufacturers through distribution channels to consumers—to enhance the movement of the product from the producer to the consumer.* Therefore, three important things should be remembered about sales promotion:

1. It is an *acceleration tool* designed to speed up the selling process.
2. It normally involves a *direct inducement* (such as money, prizes, extra products, gifts, or specialized information) that provides *extra incentives* to buy, visit the store, request literature, or take some other action.
3. It may be used *anywhere along the marketing route:* from manufacturer to dealer, from dealer to consumer, or from manufacturer to consumer.

FIGURE   16-1

As part of its "Where's the Cap'n?" promotion, Quaker Oats had Cap'n Crunch "disappear" from cereal boxes and asked children to play detective and figure out where the Cap'n had gone.

Sales promotion is used to *maximize* sales volume. It does so, in some cases, by motivating consumers who have been unmoved by other advertising efforts, or in other cases, by motivating particular brand selection when all brands are considered more or less equal. In short, sales promotion ideally generates sales that would not otherwise be achieved.

SALES PROMOTION: THE SALES ACCELERATOR

S. C. Johnson & Son, manufacturers of Johnson's Wax, has been a leader in the car, floor, and furniture wax business since its beginning many years ago. When that market appeared to level off, Johnson decided to turn to the health and beauty aids market for additional business. It successfully introduced Edge Shaving Creme in the late 1960s, but that was followed by a number of dismal failures over the succeeding years.

Finally, the company developed a hair creme rinse, Agree, with an extra benefit that "helps stop the greasies" (see Figure 16–2). It was priced competitively against the market leader, Revlon's Flex, Balsam & Protein.

However, the company was aware that its Johnson's Wax sales force had little experience with this highly competitive, fast-turning, dog-eat-dog product category. And retailers, who had witnessed Johnson's other product failures, would not be inclined to give much shelf space to a new Johnson entry.

Johnson's introductory objectives for Agree, therefore, were rather ambitious: to rapidly promote enough sales of the new product to (1) achieve and maintain market leadership and (2) create a positive image for Johnson as a marketer of personal-care products with its trade customers as well as with consumers. To succeed, Johnson had to develop a sales promotion strategy for Agree that would *push* the product into the dealer pipeline and also induce consumers to try the product, thereby *pulling* it through the pipe. After testing the product's acceptance with consumers and testing possible sampling techniques, Johnson prepared to launch Agree.

Prepacked floor displays that together would hold over 7 million 29-cent, 2-ounce, trial-size bottles were constructed and shipped to retailers. The dealers were offered introductory price allowances, distribution allowances, and advertising dollar allowances just to stock the product and set up the prepacked displays.

Then samples were distributed to consumers—31 million samples—along with 41 million coupons allowing 15 cents off on the purchase of the product. This alone catapulted Agree into a leadership position by generating rapid awareness and trial among its target group of women 14 to 30. And to top it all off, the company ran 300 prime-time network TV commercials, ads in 26 leading magazines, and the heaviest creme rinse radio campaign in history.

In all, the company spent over $17 million to introduce Agree. Within five months, the product had grabbed a 20 percent share of market and was running neck and neck against Revlon's Flex. A consumer attitude study revealed that awareness of Agree was at a whopping 77 percent, with trial of the product at 38 percent and repurchase intent estimated at 78 percent.

As a result, Johnson not only achieved its leadership position with Agree, but it also earned its spurs with the trade, which should make its next product entry infinitely easier.[3]

How does a company go from 0 to a 20 percent share of market in

FIGURE   16–2

S. C. Johnson & Son put $17 million into marketing its new Agree creme rinse and conditioner. This effort catapulted the product into a leadership position.

creme rinse conditioners in only five months? Simply by spending lots of money? Hardly.

Johnson started with a superior product. Then they tested it along with the levels of advertising and sales promotion that would make it go. They developed a national strategy based on their test results. This strategy would ensure that consumers who sought the product would be able to find it in the stores. And it ensured that dealers who bought the product would have customers wanting to try it.

Then, and only then, did Johnson commit the very big dollars— $6 million in advertising, over $6 million in sampling, and another $5 million in trade promotion—to its assault on the market.

What do you suppose would have been the result if Johnson had not spent money on the trade promotion? On the sampling? On the advertising? How vital was each of these individual elements to accomplishing Agree's success? Do you think any of them could have been left out?

PUSH STRATEGY TECHNIQUES

The success of Agree was dependent to a great extent on the cooperation of retail dealers. To get this cooperation, though, S. C. Johnson had to offer substantial inducements in the form of introductory price allowances, other dollar-saving devices, and usable product displays.

Any manufacturer who markets through normal channels must secure the cooperation of retailers. This sometimes is easier said than done because the retailers, in turn, have specific problems of their own. In today's crowded supermarkets, shelf space and floor space are hard to come by. Department stores, in order to maintain their own images, have been forced to set standards for manufacturers' displays. This means that retailers are often unable to use the special racks, sales aids, and promotional literature supplied by the manufacturers. As a consequence, substantial waste occurs as material is thrown away or left unused in a stockroom. Many retailers are pressed for time and lack the personnel to effectively use the flood of manufacturers' sales promotion material. So packages of promotion literature remain unopened, and displays remain unassembled.

Despite these problems, many manufacturers do an excellent job of implementing push strategy in sales promotion. They do so by using a wide range of promotional programs closely keyed to retailer needs. One example is the dealer plan book used in the automotive industry. Its many color pages present a well-organized and complete selection of advertising and promotion tools—from window and showroom display materials, to catalogs, ad kits, wall plaques, and color charts—all designed to make the dealer's job easier (see Figure 16–3).

Another example of a far-sighted program was that of an appliance manufacturer. Dealers and distributors complained to the manufacturer that they were under a constant barrage of separate and unrelated bulletins and letters from different factory departments concerning new products, display material, promotion booklets, service problems, policy, ad mats, and countless other topics. The manufacturer solved this problem by incorporating all such necessary information into one compact monthly newsletter, a newsy publication that the dealers and distributors actually looked forward to receiving each month.

Manufacturers use many sales promotion techniques to offer dealers extra incentives to purchase, stock, and display their products. Among the

BMW provides dealers with hand-some collateral materials that not only provide data on BMW cars but also inform dealers about BMW con-sumer demographics, ad campaigns, and so on.

more common are trade deals, display allowances, dealer premiums, co-operative advertising, advertising materials, push money, collateral materi-als, and company conventions and dealer meetings.

Trade Deals

Trade deals offer short-term discounts on the cost of the product or other dollar inducements to sell the product. Trade deals must comply with the Robinson-Patman Act by being offered on an equal basis to all dealers. Dealers pass the savings on to customers through short-term sales on the products.

Overreliance on trade deals to boost short-term sales has become a controversial issue in marketing. As summarized in *Advertising Age,* "The main bone of contention for marketers is whether trade promotions bring about incremental profits through increased use of products, or whether the products eventually would have been sold anyway, regardless of pro-motions."[4]

Trade deals are also seen as a threat to brand loyalty, since they encour-age consumers to buy whatever brand happens to be "on special" this week. Furthermore, those marketers who make extensive use of trade discounts find themselves in a trap—if they cut back on such trade promo-tions, they face the prospect of losing their market share.

The issue is further complicated by the fact that many retailers abuse trade discounts by engaging in the practices of forward buying and divert-ing. With *forward buying,* a retailer will stock up on a product when it is on discount and buy smaller amounts when it is at list price. *Diverting* is purchasing large quantities of an item offered on a regional promotion discount and shipping portions of the buy to areas of the country where the discount is not being offered. The result is not only large fluctuations in a manufacturer's sales coinciding with promotions but also fluctuations in work-force and other production needs in response to sales.[5]

Display Allowances

In-store displays, counter stands, and special racks are designed to provide the retailer with ready-made, professionally designed vehicles for selling more of the featured products. A well-designed dealer display can induce dealers to stock more of the product than they normally would. Manufacturers often encourage the use of their displays by offering additional discounts to the retailer or by actually paying for display space.

Dealer Premiums and Contests

Prizes and gifts are often used to get retail dealers and salespeople to reach specific sales goals or to stock or display a certain product. Hanes Hosiery, for example, encouraged salesclerks to become more knowledgeable about the Hanes line by offering them free pairs of panty hose and the chance to win larger prizes such as a hot tub. In another type of promotion, KLM Dutch Airlines ran a sweepstakes for travel agency employees to help increase U.S. air travel to Amsterdam. Two grand prizes of dinner/ dance parties were awarded in each of five U.S. regions (see Figure 16–4).

Cooperative Advertising and Advertising Materials

Local advertising expenses are often shared by the retailer, distributor, and manufacturer through cooperative advertising plans. The manufacturer may repay 50 to 100 percent of the dealer's advertising costs or some other

FIGURE   16–4

To increase awareness of KLM Royal Dutch Airlines among travel agency employees, the airline staged a sweepstakes: "It All Begins in Amsterdam." Two grand prizes were awarded in each of five regions of the United States. The prize was a dinner and dance party at a hotel in the winner's hometown, with all the winner's co-workers invited.

amount based on sales. Sometimes special cooperative allowances are made to introduce new lines, advertise certain products, or combat competitive activity.

In addition to sharing the cost of advertising, many manufacturers provide extensive prepared advertising materials: ads, glossy photos, sample radio commercials, preprinted inserts, and other advertising components. Most appliance manufacturers, for instance, supply the material and insist that it be used in order for their dealers to qualify for co-op advertising money.

Push Money

Retail salespeople are encouraged in many ways to push the sale of particular products. One of these inducements is *push money (PM)*, also called *spiffs*. For example, when you buy a pair of shoes, frequently the salesperson will push special cushioned insoles or shoe polish or some other high-profit "extra." For each item sold, the salesperson may receive a 25- to 50-cent spiff, depending on the product.

PEOPLE IN ADVERTISING

William A. Robinson

President
William A. Robinson, Inc.

Marketing and sales promotion specialist William A. Robinson is founder and president of William A. Robinson, Inc., Chicago, one of the nation's leading market service agencies. Since its inception in 1961, the Robinson agency has developed successful promotional programs for clients such as Amtrak, Apple Computer, AT&T, Borden, Colgate-Palmolive, Federal Express, Frito-Lay, McDonald's, Stroh Brewery, United Airlines, and Zenith.

"Our goal is to move products and purchasers closer together," says Robinson. "We begin by examining the client's brand—its marketing strategy, selling proposition, and promotional stance. Next, we look at the brand's objectives—its sales and share projections, distribution, and communications goals." Armed with this, he says, "We determine how to sell *more* of the product."

Yet sales promotion doesn't always work, Robinson warns. "If a product is unacceptable to consumers," he notes, "promotion won't change that. If an established product is experiencing declining sales, promotion won't turn it around. Promotion can't create an 'image' for a brand. And a single promotion won't motivate consumers to buy a product over a long period of time."

What promotion *can* do, Robinson explains, is offer consumers an immediate inducement to buy. It can also prompt a consumer who knows nothing about a product to try it—and to buy it. Promotion can make current users buy more of a brand or buy larger sizes. And it can moti-

Collateral Material

In industrial sales and high-ticket consumer product sales, it is usually difficult to get a purchase decision from the buyer without giving considerable data on every aspect of the product. For this reason, dealers request catalogs, manuals, technical specification sheets, brochures, presentation charts, films, audiovisual materials, or other sales aids available from the manufacturer. As a category, these are all referred to as collateral sales material.

Company Conventions and Dealer Meetings

To introduce new products, sales promotion programs, or advertising campaigns, most major manufacturers hold dealer meetings. These are also opportune times to conduct sales and service training sessions. Meetings are frequently promoted as opportunities to learn and also share experiences with other company salespeople and executives. As such, they may be used as a dynamic sales promotion tool by the manufacturer.

vate salespeople, wholesalers, and retailers to get squarely behind a product.

"Consumers today are exposed to more advertising than ever before," Robinson says. "Thus, it takes more impact to get their attention in the marketplace."

To determine what type of sales promotion works best for a product, the Robinson agency tests the value of various promotion techniques from their inception, using focus groups, interviews, and field surveys. "We set measurable goals and assign specific responsibilities for their accomplishment," Robinson states.

He has the following comments on the 10 promotion techniques most often used: "*Samplings* and *coupons* are best for generating trial. *Value packs* (bonus packs, price-offs) can load present users and convert triers to users. *Refund offers* reinforce brand loyalty. *Trade allowances* in combination with trade communications programs are valuable in gaining distribution and building trade inventories. *Contests and sweepstakes* can extend brand image and increase advertising readership. Premium offers frequently increase purchases by present users and reinforce brand loyalty. On or near the product, *premium packs* help attract new triers. *Mail-in premiums,* free or self-liquidated, often result in obtaining store displays at low cost to the brand. *Continuity programs* can create differences among parity products and build loyal users. *Special events* can enhance brand image."

"Every promotion technique has well-defined strengths and weaknesses," Robinson observes. "By maneuvering these techniques, alone or in combination, we determine the most effective strategy."

In 1973, Robinson originated the popular Best Promotions of the Year, now known as the Robbie Awards. His Best Promotions program has been featured in *Advertising Age* and presented around the world since then. Six volumes of his annual review of the outstanding work in the field, *Best Sales Promotion,* are now in print. He is the coauthor, with Don E. Schultz, of two definitive texts on the industry, *Sales Promotion Essentials* and *Sales Promotion Management,* and he is a major contributor to *Professional Development Program on Sales Promotion,* published by Crain Books.

Robinson has participated in creativity and promotion workshops sponsored by *Advertising Age,* the American Marketing Association Spring Seminar, the APAA Annual Show, and the national conferences of the American Academy of Advertising, the Boston Ad Club, and the International Foodservice Manufacturers' Association. Robinson has also lectured and presented numerous seminars on sales promotion throughout America, Europe, and Japan for a host of corporations and agencies.

Robinson has taught sales promotion courses at the undergraduate and graduate levels at several leading universities, including the University of Florida, Michigan State University, and Northwestern University.

Much of the advertising created and placed by companies today is invisible to the consumer because it appears only in trade journals read by particular businesspeople. Also usually invisible are the push techniques of sales promotion used to help accelerate sales by offering inducements to dealers, retailers, and salespeople. If the inducements are successful, the product will be given more shelf space, special display, or extra interest and enthusiasm by salespeople. The difference between no interest and extra interest can spell the difference between product failure and success in today's competitive marketplace.

PULL STRATEGY TECHNIQUES

Many types of trade promotion are seen primarily as defensive tactics, designed to protect shelf space against competitors. Today, many marketers are shifting their promotion focus away from defense and more toward offense: attracting customers first to try their brands and inducing them to stay with the brands.[6] In fact, there has been a definite trend toward reduced spending on push strategies and greater spending on pull strategies, or *consumer promotion*. Whereas allocations for trade promotions dropped from 41 percent to 37 percent of overall promotion budgets between 1982 and 1986, consumer promotion allocations increased from 26 percent to 29 percent in that four-year period.[7]

One reason for the increased focus on consumer promotions may be the proliferation of cable TV channels and the use of VCRs, which have altered TV viewing habits and reduced the proportion of the audience seeing any one program. With advertising audiences becoming increasingly fragmented, major manufacturers are turning to methods that will reach mass numbers of consumers, such as coupons, sweepstakes, and in-store displays.

The list of consumer promotion techniques used to accelerate the sales of products is long and constantly growing as new ones are always being devised. Some of the most common and successful include sampling, cents-off promotions, coupons, refunds/rebates, combination offers, premiums, contests and sweepstakes, and point-of-purchase advertising. A successful promotional campaign, such as Quaker's "Where's the Cap'n?" makes use of a combination of these techniques to achieve its objectives. Some basic "commandments" for consumer promotion campaigns are outlined in Ad Lab 16-A.

Sampling

Sampling is the most costly of all sales promotions. It offers consumers a free trial, hoping to convert them to habitual use. To be successful, sampling must deal with a product that is available in small sizes and purchased frequently. And as was the case with Agree, the success of a sampling campaign depends heavily on the merits of the product. Also, the sampling effort should be supported by advertising.

Samples may be distributed by mail, door-to-door, in stores, or via coupon advertising. They may be given free or for a small charge. Among products that have lent themselves to direct-mail sampling are cigarettes, cold remedies, candy, teabags, disposable shavers, and laundry products. Sometimes samples are distributed with related items, but then their distribution is restricted to those who buy the other product.

AD LAB 16-A   The 10 Commandments of Creative Promotion

Creativity is not limited to the advertising sphere—sales promotion calls for some creative effort as well. You should find these 10 commandments handy for both developing and reviewing promotions.

1. *Thou shalt set specific objectives.* Undisciplined or undirected creative work is a frivolous waste. The first step in developing a promotion is to exercise your creativity by setting meaningful goals. Lack of creativity at this stage results in vague and useless directions—and wasted time. You need to determine at this point whether your goal is to increase brand awareness, build up trade inventories, bring in triers, or whatever.

2. *Thou shalt know how basic promotion techniques work.* Knowing what a promotion technique can and cannot do is an important part of the creative challenge. A sweepstakes shouldn't be used to encourage multiple purchases or a refund used to get new customers. A price-off deal cannot reverse a brand's downward sales trend.

3. *Thou shalt have simple, attention-getting copy.* Although there are times when promotional concepts become so complex that it seems impossible to write a simple or even understandable headline, most promotions are built around a simple idea such as "Save 75 cents." The trick is to emphasize this idea and not get bogged down trying to be cute.

4. *Thou shalt lay out contemporary, easy-to-track graphics.* This task usually falls to the art director, but design considerations must be taken into account when developing a promotion. For example, a designer shouldn't be expected to fit 500 words of text and illustrations of 20 items into a quarter-page, free-standing insert.

5. *Thou shalt clearly communicate your concept.* Words and graphics must work together to get the message across.

6. *Thou shalt reinforce your brand's advertising message.* When a brand has a big-budget, long-term ad campaign, promotions should be tied to it. For example, Smirnoff vodka had an ad campaign showing unusual party situations, such as a cookout in the snow with the tag line "Cookout—Smirnoff Style." Originally, Smirnoff ran a $25,000 contest called "Contest—Smirnoff Style" that re-

quired entries to have a snapshot of an unusual party and a title for it. It takes an extra shot of creativity on everyone's part to tie in a prize or premium with advertising, but it does make the marketing effort easier in the long run.

7. *Thou shalt support the brand's positioning and image.* What would you think if Kraft offered a recipe book of potent drink recipes or if Marlboro offered panty hose free in the mail? Especially for image-sensitive brands and categories—the family-oriented Kraft, the macho Marlboro—it is important to be creative about supporting positioning and image.

8. *Thou shalt coordinate your promotional efforts with other marketing plans.* In other words, let the right hand know what the left hand is doing when it comes to scheduling and planning. A promotion that requires a lengthy sales pitch to the trade should not be scheduled when salespeople are slated to go to a national sales convention for a week. Creative scheduling would time a consumer promotion to break simultaneously with a big trade promotion or set up a free sample promotion in conjunction with the introduction of a new line.

9. *Thou shalt know the media you work through.* This means determining which media will work best for achieving a particular promotion's goals. If you plan to distribute samples, would it be best to use in-store, door-to-door, or direct-mail distribution? Should you provide newspaper or magazine support? These are creative decisions that require expert knowledge of the media.

10. *Thou shalt know when to break the other nine commandments.* This is the ultimate creative exercise. It takes a confidently creative person to know when breaking any of these rules is really the smartest way to go.

Laboratory Application

Choose a currently running promotion for a product and determine whether the creators of the campaign have followed these commandments.

In-store sampling has experienced a recent surge in popularity, with demonstrators on hand to dispense samples of foods, beverages, and other products to passing shoppers. Campbell Soup Co., for example, had men in tuxedos dishing out samples of its new entrees in Washington, D.C., supermarkets. Most such sampling programs hinge on the products being appealing enough for samplers to want to buy more, and they are usually tied to a coupon campaign: "If you liked that taste of the new Cherry 7UP, here's a coupon to get 50 cents off the purchase of a six-pack." Among sampling flops have been samples of instant baby food, a line of micro- wave pasta that shoppers said tasted overcooked, and a gourmet mustard dip that the Price Choppers supermarket chain mistakenly served with hot dogs.[8]

Many times samples are distributed to target markets, such as cosmetics to college coeds (pull), new drugs to physicians (push), or shampoo to beauty shop operators (push). Several firms provide specialized sample distribution services, including Welcome Wagon, Gift Pax, and Reuben H. Donnelley Corporation.

Cents-Off Promotions and Refunds/Rebates

Cents-off promotions are short-term reductions in the price of a product. They take various forms, including basic cents-off packages, one-cent sales, free offers, and box-top refunds. One common method is for a package to bear a special sticker indicating "25 cents off on this package" or some- thing similar. The sticker is removed by the clerk at the checkout counter.

Another common approach is to offer a refund in the form of either cash or coupons that can be applied to future purchases of the product; to obtain the refund, the consumer must supply proof of purchase of the product, such as three box tops. The coupon method is gaining in popular- ity among manufacturers, since it has been found that 9 out of 10 coupons sent to consumers as refunds are redeemed. With cash refunds, manufac- turers have no way of knowing whether any of the money is actually spent to buy more of their product. Rebates are generally refunds on large-ticket items, such as a $700 rebate on the purchase of a car.

Cents-off and refund promotions are often offered in combination with other promotional techniques, such as sweepstakes and contests. Peter Paul, for example, sponsored an "Exotic Island Game" in which purchas- ers of Almond Joy and Mounds candy bars could be instant winners of various prizes and could also collect inner wrappers that in the right com- bination would win them a $6,000 island vacation. Accompanying the con- test was an offer of a $1 refund for six Peter Paul wrappers. Not only did sales of the candy bars increase 50 percent over the period of the promo- tion, but more than 400,000 consumers sent in the requisite proofs of purchase for the $1 refund.[9]

Coupons

A coupon is a certificate with a stated value that is presented to the retail store for a price reduction on a specified item (see Figure 16–5). A record 202.6 billion coupons were distributed in 1986, but only about 7.3 billion were actually presented at the checkout counter.[10] Coupons may be dis- tributed in newspapers, in magazines, door-to-door, on packages, in stores, and by direct mail. By far, the greatest number of coupons are distributed through free-standing inserts (FSIs) in newspapers—a full 68 percent reach consumers by this means.[11] Quaker Oats used FSI cou- pons extensively in its "Where's the Cap'n?" promotion. One reason for the growing reliance on FSIs is that they have a higher redemption rate than regular newspaper and magazine coupons—4.2 percent as compared

New Pillsbury Crusty French Loaf.
Ooooh la la.

MmmmAhhhOhhh Pillsbury
Poppin' Fresh dough

© 1985 The Pillsbury Company

MANUFACTURER COUPON   NO EXPIRATION DATE

Pillsbury

Save 15¢
on new Pillsbury Crusty French Loaf.
In the Dairy Case.

15¢

Coupon good only on purchase of product indicated. Not valid if transferred or reproduced. ANY OTHER USE CONSTITUTES FRAUD. RETAILER: We will reimburse you the full value of this coupon plus 8¢ handling provided it is redeemed by a consumer at the time of purchase on the brand specified. Proof of purchase may be requested. Coupons not properly redeemed will be void and held. Mail to Pillsbury, Box 802, Minneapolis, MN 55460. Cash value .001¢. Void where taxed or restricted. LIMIT ONE COUPON PER ITEM PURCHASED.

SAMPLE

FIGURE   16–5

Coupons are distributed in a multitude of ways, from newspaper ads to direct mail to in-store handouts. Pillsbury made use of magazine ads to distribute coupons for its refrigerator bread sticks, rolls, and French Loaf.

to about 2.3 percent. The coupons with the highest redemption levels are those in or on the package (15.4 and 12.2 percent, respectively).[12]

After consumers redeem coupons, the retailer sorts the coupons, submits them to the manufacturer or a coupon clearinghouse, and is then reimbursed for the coupons' face value plus a handling charge. In 1986, handling charges amounted to $586 million for retailers.

Fraudulent submission of coupons is now costing the industry some $250 million annually. Coupon fraud comes in a variety of forms, including counterfeiting and submitting coupons for products that were never purchased. Quaker Oats has been in the forefront of manufacturers battling coupon fraud, or "misredemption." Unlike other companies, which generally randomly check 5 percent of coupons, Quaker employees examine 100 percent of submitted coupons and enter pertinent data about each into their computerized system. With this system, Quaker is not only able to spot fraud but can gather useful data about how the coupons have been used for particular products in various areas of the country. According to Quaker officials, the computerized process has allowed the company to cut costs and increase efficiency as well as gather marketing data.[13]

Combination Offers

Food and drug marketers have successfully used combination offers, such as a razor and a package of blades or a toothbrush with a tube of toothpaste, at a reduced price for the two. For best results, the items should be related. Sometimes a combination offer may be used to introduce a new product by tying its purchase to an established product at a special price.

Premiums

A *premium* is an item that is offered free or at a bargain price to encourage the consumer to buy an advertised product. Premiums are intended to improve the product's image, gain good will, broaden the customer base, and produce quick sales. Procter & Gamble was able to accomplish all these objectives with a campaign for Spic and Span in which a gem (garnet, emerald, sapphire, or diamond) was inserted in each package. Lots of new customers bought the product, and it gained a higher quality image through its association with the precious stones.[14] In a similar campaign,

Figure   16–6

Kraft Inc. offered premiums galore to teenagers with this ad that ran in teen magazines and as a direct-mail insert. With this promotion, teens could get famous brand-name products at reduced prices with proof of purchase of Kraft products.

bags of Ken-L Ration dog food were a literal gold mine in the spring of 1986: some $5 million in gold and silver coins were tucked into random bags.

A good premium should have strong appeal and value and should be useful or unusual. Besides being included in the product's package, it may be mailed free, or for a certain amount of money, on receipt of proof of purchase (box top or label) (see Figure 16–6). Or it may be given with the product at the time of purchase; cosmetics companies, for example, often have department-store promotions in which scarves, purses, and cosmetic samplers are given with a purchase or are purchased (for a low price) with a purchase.

The purchased cosmetics sampler is an example of a *self-liquidating premium*—the consumer pays the cost of the premium. The seller does not attempt to make a profit on such a premium but only tries to break even. A variation of the self-liquidating premium is the continuity premium. This type of premium is given weekly to customers who return to the store to complete their sets of dinnerware or encyclopedias, for example.

In-pack premiums, such as the Spic and Span diamonds or the prizes in Cracker Jack, are particularly popular in the food field, especially cereals. *On-pack premiums* (those attached to the outside of the package) have good impulse value, but they may encourage pilferage. Another drawback to these types of premiums is that they sometimes are difficult for the retailer to stack on the shelves. As a result, the product causes problems for the retailer.

Coupon premiums, which require customers to save and collect in-pack coupons for later redemption of valuable premiums, can create great consumer loyalty. For instance, one long-time user of this device, Brown & Williamson Tobacco Corporation, consistently receives as many as 2 million Raleigh coupons daily from repeat cigarette customers who send for more than $10 million worth of premiums annually.

Related to coupon premiums are trading stamps. This promotion device was introduced by the Sperry & Hutchinson Company in 1896. For years, the popularity of S&H Green Stamps in department stores, supermarkets, and service stations fluctuated. Finally, as discount stores and suburban shopping centers grew and the energy crisis affected service stations, interest in trading stamps began to wane. Today, the several brands of trading stamps have largely given way to other forms of retail promotion such as games.

Contests and Sweepstakes

A *contest* offers prizes based on the skill of the entrants. A *sweepstakes* offers prizes based on a chance drawing of entrants' names. A *game* has the chance element of a sweepstakes but is conducted over a longer time. Games include local bingo-type games designed to build store traffic. Their big marketing advantage is that customers must make repeat visits to the dealer to continue playing.

Both contests and sweepstakes have the common purpose of encouraging consumption of the product by creating consumer involvement. These devices are highly popular and pull millions of entries. Usually contest entrants are required to send in some proof of purchase, such as a box top or label. For more expensive products, the contestant may only have to visit the dealer to pick up an entry blank.

Contests range from puzzle solving (such as "Where's the Cap'n?"), to cooking competitions (Pepto-Bismol's chili cook-offs, Pillsbury's bake-offs), to photo contests (Johnson & Johnson's annual "Adorable Babies Photo Contest," Mazda's family photo contest) (see Figure 16–7).

In recent years, sweepstakes and games have become more popular than contests. They are much easier to enter and take less time than contests and, therefore, have greater appeal for the average person. Sweepstakes require careful planning. No purchase can be required as a condition for entry, or else the sweepstakes becomes a lottery and therefore illegal. All postal laws must be obeyed in planning contests and sweepstakes.

To encourage a large number of entries, sponsors try to keep their contests as simple as possible. The prize structure must be clearly stated and rules clearly defined. National contests and sweepstakes are handled and judged by independent, professional contest firms.

Contests and sweepstakes must be promoted and advertised to be successful. This can be expensive. An important element of this promotion is dealer support, and to ensure dealer cooperation, many contests and sweepstakes require the entrant to give the name of the particular product's local dealer. In these cases, prizes may also be awarded to the dealer who made the sale.

FIGURE   16–7

One of the best-known national contests is the Pillsbury Bake-Off, now called the Bake-Off Plus. All recipes submitted for the contest must use either a Pillsbury product (flour, cake mix, pie crust, etc.) or Green Giant canned or frozen vegetables.

Point-of-Purchase (P-O-P) Advertising

As a push technique, good dealer displays may induce a retailer to carry a certain line or promote a new product. However, *point-of-purchase (P-O-P)* advertising is primarily a pull technique consisting of advertising or display materials at the retail location to build traffic, advertise the product, and promote impulse buying.

This type of promotion has become increasingly important in light of the fact that more than 80 percent of purchase decisions are not made until the customer is in the store. Spurred by this startling finding (reported by the Point of Purchase Advertising Institute), manufacturers have greatly increased their P-O-P budgets, spending a record $9 billion in 1986 on in-store materials.[15]

These materials may include window displays, counter displays, floor and wall racks to hold the merchandise, streamers, and posters. Often the product's shipping cartons are designed to double as display units. At times, a complete "information center" provides literature, samples, and product photos.

In-store materials have increased in importance with the trend toward self-service retailing. With fewer and less knowledgeable salespeople available to help them, customers are on their own to make purchasing decisions. Eye-catching and informative displays can give them the push they need to make a choice (see Figure 16–8). Even in stores that have clerks, display material can offer extra selling information and make the product stand out from the competition.

FIGURE   16–8

This inviting P-O-P display was used in AT&T stores to attract college students. Customers were invited to help themselves to a color pamphlet, "The AT&T Spring Break Survival Guide." The booklet offered tips on everything from tanning to automobile emergencies. The purpose was to get students to sign up for an AT&T Card.

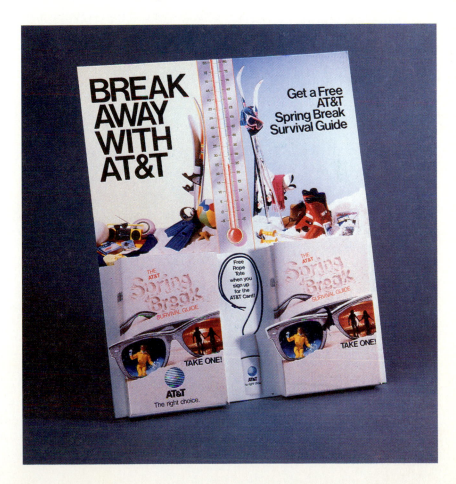

The proliferation of P-O-P displays has led many retailers to be more discriminating in what they actually use. Most are beginning to insist on well-designed, attractive materials that will fit in harmoniously with their store atmosphere. Some retailers are actively working with manufacturers to develop appropriate P-O-P displays; a few are even designing their own P-O-P materials to create an in-store identity. One supermarket chain in New Jersey has gone so far as to refuse almost all outside P-O-P materials.[16]

The current emphasis on P-O-P has led to the development of a variety of new approaches, including ads on shopping carts, "talking" antacid boxes, beer jingles activated by opening refrigerator doors, and interactive computer systems for selecting everything from shoe styles to floor coverings. One innovation gaining attention is the Product Information Center (PIC), a video-display terminal located primarily in supermarkets, that carries a series of 15-second "commercials" in a five-minute rotation, interspersed with community-interest items. Use of PIC spots is currently being done in conjunction with overall promotional campaigns. Johnson & Johnson found that a promotion for Band-Aid Medicated 20's resulted in sales increases of 24 to 38 percent in cities without PIC supplementation but saw a 75 percent sales increase in Ft. Worth, Texas, where the PIC spots were used.[17]

In this section, we have discussed only a few of the wide variety of sales promotion tools available today. The choice of which methods to use in any given instance depends on a combination of factors. Timing is important. Fads and fashions come and go in sales promotion as in anything else. (See Ad Lab 16-B.) To be successful, sales promotions must take advantage of current consumer preferences.

A promotion needs to be unique to attract attention yet time tested to ensure probable success. For instance, certain types of sales promotion are

AD LAB 16-B   Smell: Powerful Armament in the Retailer's Arsenal

You are strolling past the bakery in your local shopping mall. Isn't that the irresistible aroma of fresh-baked chocolate chip cookies wafting your way?

Maybe not.

International Flavors & Fragrances, Inc., has succeeded in synthesizing the mouth-watering aroma of not only chocolate chip cookies but also hot apple pie, fresh pizza, baking ham, and even nongreasy french fries.

IF&F packages the artificial odors in aerosol cans and markets them along with time-released devices that periodically fire a burst of scent into the shopping mall to tempt customers. The sprays are reportedly selling briskly and cost retailers just pennies a day.

Ledan Inc., a New York promotion firm, is developing scented materials that stick to in-store displays. The company is already marketing chocolate scents for candy racks and piña colada aromas for the liquor department, and it hopes to have the smell of bacon available before long.

The purpose of these smells is, of course, to make people feel hungry or thirsty. What has some people concerned, however, is the possibility of a store full of competing odors. With that kind of result, the idea of using smells as a promotional gimmick could turn out to be a real stinker.

Laboratory Application

Do you think that using artificial odors is a legitimate sales promotion technique?

known to work well for new products—namely, sampling, couponing, and refund offers. Other types have proved helpful in increasing the use of established products, such as premiums, price-off promotions, and contests and sweepstakes. Often it is a well-orchestrated mix of methods, such as Quaker used in its Cap'n Crunch campaign, that achieves promotion objectives.

SUPPLEMENTARY MEDIA

Many miscellaneous promotional media are difficult to classify because they are tailored to individual needs and do not necessarily fall into any major category. They include specialty advertising, trade shows and exhibits, and yellow pages and directories to mention just a few.

Specialty Advertising

Today, nearly every business uses advertising specialties to some degree, including everything from key chains, ballpoint pens, and calendars to matchbooks, thermometers, and billfolds (see Figure 16–9). They are used by national advertisers, local merchants, banks and insurance companies, industrial firms, and service stations, to name just a few. There are said to be as many as 15,000 different items sold, representing an annual volume of more than $3 billion.

While companies often spend substantial sums for these goodwill items, they must also exercise care. It is the one business in the advertising field where industry practice dictates that the advertiser pay for any production overage incurred, up to an agreed-on limit.

An advertising specialty is different from a premium. The recipient of a premium must give some consideration to the advertiser—buy a product, send in a coupon, witness a demonstration, or perform some other action of advantage to the advertiser. A premium may be an expensive item; therefore, it frequently bears no advertising message. An advertising specialty, on the other hand, is given free. It is a goodwill item—a reminder that carries the company or product name or logo. It may feature a new product, a new plant, or some special event or promotion. Some specialty

FIGURE   16–9

Among the many items used for specialty advertising are office supplies such as staplers. Office and business items are popular because they serve as a daily reminder of the advertiser's name in the place where the customers do their ordering.

items, especially if they are useful, may be kept for years and thereby serve as continuous, friendly reminders of the advertiser's business.

Because people tend to associate the quality of a specialty item with the quality of the company providing it, there has been a definite trend toward more expensive gifts. According to the Specialty Advertising Association International, items costing $3 to $5 are becoming the norm, as opposed to cheap key rings and pencils, for example.[18] Even more expensive items, such as silk jackets, Pierre Cardin leather goods, and the like, are being used as specialty items.

There has also been a trend toward structured promotions, in which target customers receive a series of specialties. Beckman Instruments, for example, wanted to increase its number of clients in a four-state area before assigning sales personnel to that region. To gain the attention of clinical lab supervisors and purchasing agents in 250 hospitals and clinics, Beckman sent them a series of specialty gifts, including coffee mugs, calendars, paper-clip dispensers, and a jigsaw puzzle, over a 12-month period.[19]

Trade Shows and Exhibits

Every major industry sponsors annual trade shows and exhibitions where manufacturers, dealers, and buyers of the industry's products can get together for demonstrations and discussion. Exhibitors have the opportunity of exposing their new products, literature, and samples to new customers as well as old. At the same time, they can meet potential new dealers for their products (see Figure 16–10).

More than 9,000 industrial, scientific, and medical shows are now held in the United States each year, and many companies exhibit at more than one show. As a result, the construction of booths and exhibits has become a major factor in sales promotion plans for many manufacturers. To stop traffic, booths must be simple in design and attractive, with good lighting. The exhibit should also provide a comfortable atmosphere to promote conversation between salespeople and prospects.

FIGURE   16–10

Companies that promote their products at trade shows must carefully plan their booths, sales materials, and special trade show promotions.

Many regular trade-show exhibitors are turning toward state-of-the-art technology, such as holograms, fiber optics, and interactive computer systems, to communicate product features quickly and dramatically. Pratt & Whitney, for example, uses holograms to present quarter-scale cutaway images of its aircraft engines. The company has found that holograms are easier to transport, less expensive to make, and more dramatic than traditional engine models.[20]

In planning exhibits or trade-show booths, advertisers need to consider the following factors:

1. Size and location of space.
2. Desired image or impression of the exhibit.
3. Complexities of shipping, installation, and dismantling.
4. The number of products to be displayed.
5. The need for storage and distribution of literature.
6. The use of preshow advertising and promotion.
7. The cost of all of these factors.

Trade-show costs have increased substantially in the last decade. Space rental costs rose 70 percent between 1976 and 1985, and other costs more than doubled.[21] Despite the high costs involved, many companies find exhibiting at trade shows to be a cost-effective means of reaching sales prospects.

Directories and Yellow Pages

Thousands of directories are published each year not only by phone companies but by trade associations, industrial groups, and others. While serving mainly as locators, buying guides, and mailing lists, they may also carry advertising aimed at specialized fields.

In the United States there are approximately 6,000 local telephone directories with a combined circulation of 286 million. Since deregulation of the phone industry and the 1984 breakup of AT&T, the yellow pages business has been booming, with hundreds of independent publishers now competing with phone company directories for advertising dollars (see Figure 16–11). *Forbes* calls yellow pages directories the fastest-growing major advertising medium in the country, with revenues reaching an estimated $11 billion in 1987.[22]

Ralph Rose, vice president of Ketchum Yellow Pages in New York, attributes the popularity of this medium to the fact that "nothing else beats the reach and frequency of this everywhere and year-round buyer's guide—not only among adult consumers but also among business and industrial buyers."[23] Yellow pages are often the sole advertising medium for local businesses, but they are also heavily utilized by national companies. U-Haul, for example, spends more than $10 million a year on yellow pages ads. National advertisers may seek help from the National Yellow Pages Service Association for rates, data, creative aid, and one-order placement.

Because of competition, phone and directory companies have been coming up with ways to make their particular yellow pages more distinctive. Some are beefing up the contents, offering emergency medical guides, color street maps, and other useful information. Others contain discount coupons. Also, highly specialized directories are aimed at particular audiences, such as the Silver Pages for senior citizens, Chinese-language Yellow Pages in San Francisco, a directory for students at the

FIGURE   16–11

The Yellow Pages directory business has become highly competitive, especially in large metropolitan markets such as New York City.

University of Massachusetts, and national yellow pages targeted for the industrial security industry.

With all these directories available, advertisers are becoming somewhat overwhelmed, having to decide which will offer them the best coverage for their advertising dollar. It will probably be a few years, however, before solid information can be obtained on who actually uses the various directories and whether directory ads are actually being seen.

Summary

Sales promotion supplements advertising and personal selling for the purpose of stimulating or accelerating sales. It includes widely varied types of promotional activities with unlimited applications aimed at salespeople, distributors, retailers, and consumers. By offering direct inducements, such as money, prizes, gifts, or other opportunities, it provides extra incentives to buy a product, to visit a store, to request literature, or to take other action.

Sales promotion techniques are used in the trade to *push* products through the distribution channels or, with the ultimate customer, to *pull* them through the channel.

Manufacturers use a variety of sales promotion techniques to offer dealers extra incentives to purchase, stock, and display their products. These include trade deals, display allowances, dealer premiums, cooperative advertising, advertising materials, push money, collateral material, and company conventions and dealer meetings.

The most visible forms of sales promotion are those aimed at the ultimate purchaser of the product. They include sampling, cents-off promotions, coupons, combination offers, premiums, contests and sweepstakes, and point-of-purchase advertising.

Supplementary media are quite diverse. They include specialty advertising, trade shows and exhibits, and yellow-pages directories to mention just a few.

Questions for Review and Discussion

1. How does the definition of sales promotion differ from the definition of advertising?
2. What are the main purposes of sales promotion?
3. Why have trade deals become controversial?
4. What are the most commonly used push strategies? Which would you use if you were a major cosmetics manufacturer?
5. What are the most common pull strategies? Which would you use if you wanted to launch a new soft drink?
6. Why is there a trend away from push strategies and toward pull strategies?
7. Why are FSIs the most popular means for distributing coupons?
8. What is the difference between an advertising specialty and a premium?
9. What is the importance of trade shows to marketers?
10. Should advertisers be interested in using directories and the yellow pages? Why?

PART V

SPECIAL TYPES OF
ADVERTISING

from **Local** *to* **Global**

17
LOCAL ADVERTISING

A few years ago, Ray Lemke was a barber in the little town of Papillion, Nebraska. His young wife, Gwen, stayed at home caring for their three small children. But she was bored doing the same thing every day.

Following a survey predicting that by the mid-1980s Papillion would be in the center of the growing metropolitan area around Omaha, the Lemkes decided to go into real estate. They rented a little store-front office next to the barber shop and started listing homes and selling insurance. Gwen jumped in with both feet, answering the phone, helping with the contracts, and getting involved in the advertising and the sales. Soon Ray was forced to make a choice. With some trepidation, he sold the barber shop and moved into the real estate business full-time.

They called this business Action Realty—it signified movement and gave them the first position in the phone book. They designed a dynamic "Action" logo to use on signs and in their newspaper ads, and they created a standard ad layout that very quickly became recognizable as the Action format: large space, heavy borders, dominant logo, numerous listings of property, and bold type (see Figure 17–1). They ran their ads in the local newspaper every week without fail.

They both got involved in local community activities—service clubs, charities, trade associations. They affiliated with a nationwide realty network, Homes for Living, and participated in the programs that organization sponsored. They concentrated on developing training programs for their staff and offered exciting incentives, like vacation trips, for their top producers.

They encouraged their employees to be active in community affairs, and they publicized their successful employees with news releases and ads in the local press. They constantly tested new ideas.

Action Real Estate rapidly became the fastest-growing real estate firm in Sarpy County. Within 10 years, the company was operating six offices, had a sales staff of over 75 people, 20 secretaries, and an annual gross sales volume of over $40 million.

By this time, Gwen had become president of the firm and Ray had retired from active participation so he could pursue his ambition of becoming a personal counselor and motivational speaker. They had both witnessed the potential of consistent, strong local advertising. And they had kept the promise made by their advertising—Action.

LOCAL ADVERTISING: WHERE THE ACTION IS

Local advertising, as opposed to regional or national advertising, refers to advertising by businesses within a particular city or county to customers within the same geographic area. In 1986, 44 percent of all dollars spent on advertising were for local advertising as opposed to national advertising.

Quite often, local advertising is referred to as retail advertising because it is commonly performed by retail stores. However, retail advertising is not necessarily local—it can be regional or national as well, as witnessed by the volume of commercials run by national retail firms such as Sears and J. C. Penney. Moreover, many businesses not usually thought of as retail stores use local advertising—real estate brokers, banks, movie theaters, auto mechanics, plumbers, radio and TV stations, restaurants, museums, and even dance studios (see Figure 17–2).

Local advertisers can be thought of as belonging in one of three categories: (1) dealerships or local franchises of regional or national companies that specialize in one main product or product line (such as Toyota, McDonald's, or H & R Block); (2) stores that sell a variety of branded merchandise, usually on a nonexclusive basis (such as department stores); and (3) specialty businesses and services (such as music stores, shoe repair shops, florists, hair salons, travel agencies). Businesses in each of these categories will obviously have different advertising goals and approaches.

Local advertising is important because of the arena in which it is performed. Most sales are made or lost locally. A national auto manufacturer may spend millions advertising new cars, but local auto dealers as a group spend just as much or more to bring customers into their showrooms to buy the cars. In fact, if they don't make a strong effort on the local level, the efforts of the national advertisers may be wasted. So when it comes to consummating the sale, local advertising is where the action is.

While the basic principles used by national advertisers are applicable to local advertising, local advertisers have special problems that stem from the simple, practical realities of marketing in a local area. There are many differences between local and national advertisers, not only in basic objectives and strategies but also in perceived needs of the marketplace, amount of money available to spend on advertising, greater emphasis by local advertisers on newspaper advertising, use of price as a buying inducement, and the use of specialized help in preparing advertisements.

FIGURE   17–1

The Action Real Estate ad format may not be pretty, with its extensive use of heavy type and bold reverses. Nevertheless, it has been highly effective in creating a consistent presence for the realty firm and has lent credence to the promise inherent in the Action name.

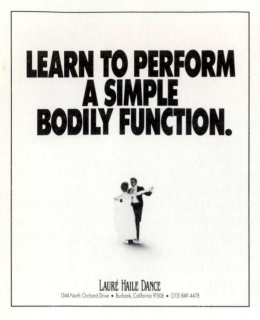

LEARN TO PERFORM A SIMPLE BODILY FUNCTION.

LAURÉ HAILE DANCE
1344 North Orchard Drive • Burbank, California 91506 • (213) 849-4478

FIGURE 17–2

Not all local advertising is for retail stores. This local ad cleverly draws attention to the services offered by a dance studio.

Types of Local Advertising

The two major types of local advertising are product and institutional. *Product advertising* is designed to sell a specific product or service. It also hopes to get immediate action. *Institutional advertising,* on the other hand, attempts to obtain favorable attention for the business as a whole, not for a specific product or service that the store or business sells. The effects of institutional advertising are intended to be long term rather than short range.

Product Advertising

For most local advertisers, product advertising constitutes the greatest portion of their advertising efforts. Product advertising can be further subdivided into three major types:

Regular Price-Line Advertising The purpose of this type of advertising is to inform consumers about the services available or the wide selection and quality of merchandise offered at regular prices (see Figure 17–3).

Sale Advertising To stimulate the movement of particular merchandise or generally increase store traffic, local merchants advertise items on sale. This type of advertising places the emphasis on special reduced prices.

Clearance Advertising Local advertisers may do clearance advertising to make room for new product lines or new models or to rid themselves of slow-moving product lines, floor samples, broken or distressed merchandise, or items that are no longer in season.

Institutional Advertising

Institutional advertising, which involves selling an idea about the company, is usually designed to make the public aware of the company and to build a solid reputation or image. An advertisement might stress longer hours of operation, a new credit policy, or store expansion. This type of advertising is expected to reap long-term rather than short-term benefits.

Readership of institutional advertising may sometimes be lower than that of product advertising. But, if done effectively, institutional ads can be very helpful in building a favorable image and identity for the business, in attracting new patronage, and in developing loyalty from existing customers (see Figure 17–4).

Objectives of Local Advertising

The objectives of local advertising differ from the objectives of national advertising in both emphasis and time. National manufacturers tend to emphasize long-term objectives of awareness, image, and credibility. On the local, retail level, the advertiser's needs tend to be more immediate. The emphasis is on keeping the cash register ringing—increasing traffic, turning over inventory, and bringing in new customers. (See the Checklist of Local Advertising Objectives.)

As a result, on the local level there are constant promotions, sales, and clearances, all designed to create immediate activity. The trade-off, of

If you love this ad, you must have holes in your head.

Zell Bros has hundreds of ways to fill those tiny holes. At hundreds of different ✔ prices, from $20 to $25,000. Now, if you don't happen to have holes in your head, don't despair. We also have a rather ✔ impressive collection of clasp-type earrings.

Open Sunday. Downtown Store 12-5 pm / 227-8471, Clackamas Town Center 10am-9pm / 654-6504, Washington Square 10am-10pm / 620-3610. Items enlarged individually to show detail. Subject to prior sale.

FIGURE   17–3

Zell Bros. jewelers found a unique way to advertise its wide selection of pierced earrings at regular prices.

course, is that the day after the promotion or sale the traffic may stop. So to increase traffic again, the merchant may plan another sale or another promotion. Then another and another. What can result is a cycle of sporadic bursts of activity followed by inactivity, sharp peaks and valleys in sales, and the image of a business that should be visited only during a sale.

Long-term and short-term objectives work against each other when one is sought at the expense of the other. Successful local advertisers must therefore think of long-term objectives first and then develop short-term goals in keeping with their long-term objectives. This usually increases the emphasis on institutional and regular price-line advertising and reduces the reliance on sales and clearances for creating traffic.

PLANNING THE ADVERTISING EFFORT

The key to success in any advertising program, local or national, is adequate planning. Planning is not a one-time occurrence, however, but a continuous process of research, evaluation, decision, execution, and review. On the local level, more advertising dollars are no doubt wasted because of inadequate planning than for any other reason. Action Realty's success was due to the fact that Gwen and Ray Lemke made planning a

FIGURE 17–4

Institutional advertising, such as this handsome newspaper ad with subtle use of color, doesn't promote a specific product. Rather, it helps create an image for the advertiser and builds public awareness.

Checklist of Local Advertising Objectives

☐ To introduce new customers. Ever year, many old customers are lost due to relocation, death, inconvenience, or dissatisfaction. To thrive, a business must continually seek new customers, primarily through advertising.

☐ To build awareness and image. Because many local businesses provide essentially the same services, stores can use advertising techniques to distinguish themselves from each other.

☐ To help retain old customers and increase their frequency of visits. More customers are lost because of inattention than any other single reason. In addition, a barrage of advertising from competitors may lure customers away. A steady, consistent program of advertising can keep present customers informed and reinforce their desire to remain customers and visit your business more often.

☐ To reduce sales expense. By preselling many customers, advertising lightens the load on sales personnel. By increasing traffic, it allows salespeople to make more sales in a shorter time. Both contribute to reducing the cost of sales.

☐ To curtail seasonal peaks. Each year there are dips and swings in the business cycle. One way to level off the peaks and valleys is to advertise consistently.

☐ To accelerate inventory turnover. Some businesses sell all the merchandise in a store four or five times a year. Others turn over the inventory 15 to 20 times. The more times inventory is turned, the more profit can be made. Rapid inventory turnover also keeps prices down. In this way, advertising contributes to lower customer prices.

continuous, flexible process, which allowed for change, improvement, new facts, and new ideas.

Several steps are involved in planning the local advertising effort: analyzing the local market, analyzing the competition, conducting adequate research, determining objectives and strategy, establishing a realistic budget, and planning media strategy.

Analyzing the Local Market and Competition

Careful research must be used to identify the type of local market in which the business is located. Whenever possible, local advertising should reflect the needs of the immediate area. Items to consider, therefore, are whether the area is rural or urban, conservative or progressive, high or low income, white-collar or blue-collar. A thorough knowledge of the local market and potential customers influences the goods and services the business offers, the prices established, and the design and style of advertising. Accurate analysis at this point prevents advertising misfires later on.

Similarly, a careful study should be made of all the competitors in the local area. What merchandise and services do they offer? What is their pricing strategy? Where are they located? How large are they? What is their advertising strategy? What media do they use? How much do they spend on advertising? Do their places of business invite customers to shop there or do they repel customers?

Constant competitive research alerts the advertiser to new ideas, comparative advantages and disadvantages, new merchandising techniques, and new material for advertising campaigns.

Conducting Adequate Research

The local advertiser usually cannot afford to hire a specialized firm to conduct formal market research programs. However, because of its proximity to the marketplace, a local store or business should be well attuned to the attitudes of customers and should be able to conduct informal research to measure customer reaction to merchandise and advertising campaigns. A good local advertising agency might assist in this regard.

Chapter 6 contained a thorough discussion of the field of advertising and marketing research. In this chapter, we want only to examine those aspects of research that are unique to the local advertiser. As discussed in Chapter 6, there are two types of research: primary research, which is data collected firsthand, and secondary research, which is data accumulated by others that can be adapted to the needs of the advertiser.

Primary Research

To be successful, a local advertiser must have the answers to many important questions. Who are our present customers? Who are our potential customers? How many are there? Where are they located? How can our company best appeal to them? Where do they now buy the merchandise or services that we want to sell to them? Can we offer them anything they are not getting at the present time? If so, what? How can we convince them they should do business with us? To answer these questions, local advertisers should conduct primary research in the following areas.

Customer and Sales Analysis It is important to keep track of customers—both charge and cash customers—so that their addresses can be correlated to census tract information. Census information includes such data as average income, family size, education, vehicle and home ownership, and age.

In retail stores, sales should be tabulated by merchandise classification. Careful analysis of this information helps identify changes in consumer buying patterns, which, in turn, affect the merchandise or services that will be bought and advertised in the future.

A comparison should be made of a company's sales by merchandise lines in relation to those of other companies in the area. Information about other companies' market share can be obtained from several sources mentioned later in this section.

Customer Attitudes and Satisfaction Feedback from sales personnel can provide valuable information about customers. In addition, having salespeople solicit information about customers can forestall problems by locating areas of customer satisfaction and dissatisfaction at an early stage. Customers will also feel that the store cares if it actively seeks information from them. One method for soliciting information is to provide response forms that allow customers to offer comments about the business's products and services and to make suggestions for improvement, such as carrying certain merchandise not currently stocked. Such response forms are particularly common in restaurants, where customers have time before and after meals to fill them out.

PEOPLE IN ADVERTISING

Jane Trahey

President
Trahey Advertising, Inc.

Popular author, screenwriter, columnist, playwright, and talk-show guest Jane Trahey has made her major mark in the advertising world as founder and president of Trahey Advertising, Inc., New York and Chicago, an agency widely known for its retail campaigns.

Born in Chicago, Trahey received a B.A. from Mundelein College. After graduate studies at the University of Wisconsin, she went to work for the *Chicago Tribune.* Her interest in retail advertising led her to join Carson Pirie Scott, a Chicago department store. She went on to Neiman-Marcus, Dallas, where she became advertising and sales promotion director. Trahey was then named advertising director of a New York manufacturing firm, where she founded and led an in-house advertising agency. Two years later, she decided to launch her own agency, and Trahey Advertising, Inc., was born.

Since then, Jane Trahey has become a leading name in fashion advertising, serving clients ranging from Elizabeth Arden, Bill Blass, Pauline Trigere, and Adele Simpson to

Advertising Testing Because of the vast number of ads prepared by most local advertisers, it's unusual to test advertisements in advance of their placement. However, posttesting should be conducted to determine the advertising campaign's effect on sales, if any. One method for posttesting is to provide a discount coupon with an ad and to tabulate the number of customers who take advantage of the coupon offer. A similar way to test the effectiveness of broadcast ads is to tell customers they will receive a special discount or premium if they mention some slogan or line from the commercial. Some businesses also make a point of having employees ask customers where they heard about the business or the particular promotion being staged.

Secondary Research

Local advertisers should be aware of the many secondary sources of information that are available and can be adapted to their particular needs. These sources include manufacturers and suppliers, trade publications and associations, local advertising media, and various government organizations.

Manufacturers and Suppliers Manufacturers and suppliers want their dealers to succeed. Their dealer-aid programs usually include valuable research on the retail market for their products, and many manufacturers conduct dealer seminars to explain these research results.

---

major retailers like B. Altman, Neiman-Marcus, Bergdorf's, and Harzfeld's.

Year after year, her agency's campaigns for retail clients have scored impressive successes. To achieve this, Jane Trahey first focuses on learning what is unique about the store. "Try to find a uniqueness," she urges "or help to create one. If a retail account lets you create such a uniqueness," adds Trahey, "chances are it has one."

The next step, says Trahey, is to convey this uniqueness in advertising. "Ads should reflect the heart of the store," she emphasizes. "Ads should tell me what these institutions are—what they mean in their communities—what contributions they make to my life." Do most retail ads do this? No, says Trahey. "I can count on one hand the stores that have that extra readability in their ads that holds me for more than the flip of the page." Defining this "extra readability," Trahey makes clear, "doesn't matter a lot about the art. It's what the ad *says* that sells the store—and sells the merchandise."

Trahey believes an ad should communicate directly to the store's target customers: "Anyone who reads the ad should feel it is specifically addressed to him or her." She feels that most retail advertising lacks this personalized touch.

To be able to talk directly to customers, an advertiser needs to have a good idea of who those customers are. That means careful research not only on those who currently shop in the store but on those whom the store would like to have as customers. A principal target for many of Trahey's clients is the professional working woman. She cites studies indicating that such women want to get into a store, find what they want, and get out. Thus, advertising aimed at those women must emphasize not only quality merchandise but also ease of shopping.

In creating ads for retailers, Trahey feels she must serve both the client and the customer if an ad campaign is to be successful. She reflects: "You should do the *best* you can for the client. The client trusts you. You want to be worthy of that trust."

Retail Trade Publications and Associations Trade publications are excellent sources of information for a local advertiser's business. These publications contain important articles about trends in the business, new technology, and research studies that apply to the particular category of business to which the publication is directed. Just a few of the hundreds of such publications are *Stores, The Merchandiser, Progressive Grocer, Automotive News, Farm Supplier, Hotel & Motel Management, Modern Jeweler,* and *Shopping Center World.* A complete list of publications is available in *The Standard Periodical Directory* or *Ulrich's International Periodicals Directory.*

Advertising is a common topic in other publications as well. A glance under "Advertising" in the *Business Periodicals Index* will give a local businessperson an idea of some of the publications that cover aspects of advertising he or she may be concerned with.

The National Retail Merchants Association (100 W. 31st Street, New York, NY 10001) publishes an extensive list of materials on research topics of interest to retailers. It also publishes *Ad/Pro,* a monthly news magazine that explores advertising issues of interest primarily to department and specialty stores. Another helpful publication is the Mass Retailing Institute's study of shoppers' behavior, available at reasonable cost (579 7th Avenue, New York, NY 10018).

Typical of the many associations that are good sources of research information are the National Office Products Association, National Association of Drug Stores, Menswear Retailers of America, United States Savings and Loan League, National Sporting Goods Association, and American Society of Travel Agents. The *Encyclopedia of Associations,* available at most libraries, indicates the associations pertinent to a particular area of interest. A short letter will bring the desired research data.

Advertising Media and Media Associations The amount of research data that will be provided by local media depends on the size of the community. In large cities, the major newspapers and broadcast stations provide in-depth market data about the communities they serve.

Even if a local advertiser lives in a community so small that the media are unable to provide any research data, the newspaper and broadcasters probably belong to national associations that conduct extensive research. Organizations of particular interest are the Direct-Mail Advertising Association, Newspaper Advertising Bureau, Radio Advertising Bureau, Magazine Publishers Association, Television Bureau of Advertising, and Institute of Outdoor Advertising.

Government Organizations Various government bureaus can provide information to the local advertiser, including data on population projections, birth and death information, marriage license statistics, and so on. In every state government, departments in charge of commerce, taxation, labor, highways, and justice provide reports and data. These materials can be useful in measuring local markets and making projections.

Of particular interest to most local advertisers is the Small Business Administration (SBA). It publishes a wealth of information on a wide variety of topics, most of it free or available for only a nominal charge.

The U.S. Department of Commerce also offers pertinent materials, including: *Retail Data Sources for Market Analysis, Business Service Checklist* (a weekly guide to Department of Commerce reports, books, and news releases); *Bureau of Census Catalog, Census Track Studies;* the annual edition of the *U.S. Industrial Outlook; Current Retail Trade; Survey of*

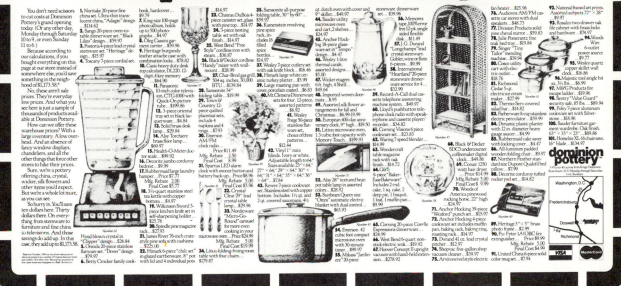

FIGURE 17–5

One of the decisions a local business must make is its product/service concept. From this ad, it is obvious that Dominion Pottery has chosen to carry a broad line of household items at discount prices.

Current Business; Monthly Department Store Sales; County Business Patterns; the annual edition of the *Statistical Abstract of the United States;* and the *County and City Data Book.*

Determining Objectives and Strategy

The stated objectives of any marketing and advertising program determine the particular marketing mix or strategy to be used. A local advertiser has the same options as a national advertiser when it comes to developing its local marketing strategy: product, price, place, and promotion.

Product

What merchandise should be sold? What services should be offered? Should some lines be expanded or dropped? How wide a selection should be offered? If a store intends to be a discount house, it may want to carry a broad line. If it wants to be a specialty shop, it may opt to carry only selected lines. In short, what is the business's product/service concept? (See Figure 17–5.) For the existing business, these questions are answered by experience. For the new business, research is a must in order to avoid the substantial losses that can result from carrying the wrong lines of merchandise or providing the wrong service.

Price

What will the local market support? Should prices be high, low, or moderate? What should be included in the price? What about terms and warranties? What about the use of charge cards? What policy should be established on refunds? Are all these policies in keeping with the desired image of the business? Local advertisers have the tendency to cut prices first rather than seek other ways to compete. That is often self-defeating in the long run.

Place

Where should the business be located? What is the trading area? For a bank, how many branches can be established? What kinds of areas should be served? What is the cost of doing business in different areas? How large should the facilities be? Additional branches or locations can create great economies in advertising costs, but these economies may be offset by greater problems and costs in the management and administration of the business.

Promotion

Should the business be highly promotional, semipromotional, or nonpromotional? Should advertising concentrate on the regular price line, special sales, or clearances? What percentage of advertising should be institutional? What is the impact of advertising activities on this type of business? How much advertising should be done, and in what media? A business that has few regular customers and has to rely on discount prices, sales, and other promotions to bring customers in will have to do a great deal of advertising (*highly promotional strategy*). A business that has regular customers but uses periodic sales and promotions to increase store traffic will need to use a *semipromotional strategy*. Finally, a business that relies on a clientele that returns and shops regularly at the business may have little need for advertising and related types of promotion (*nonpromotional strategy*).

Determining the objectives and strategies of any business—local, regional, or national—is the most important policy decision management ever makes. The chosen objectives and strategies determine the whole complexion of the business in the years that follow. They give direction to the enterprise, continuity to its various promotional efforts, and an understanding of the company in the marketplace. For that reason, the decisions regarding objectives and strategies should be highly specific and should be written down. Then these objectives and strategies should be reviewed frequently and updated or revised on a regular basis as the business situation warrants. (For more on this subject, see the TextPLUS Case Study Program on Great American First Savings Bank associated with this chapter.)

Perhaps the biggest mistake a local advertiser can make is to put too little thought or effort into ensuring that advertising is well integrated with overall business objectives. This lack of integration can lead to a number of advertising difficulties—see Ad Lab 17-A.

AD LAB 17-A — Mistakes Commonly Made by Local Advertisers

Even the best-laid plans for local advertisers may go awry. However, chances of success are much greater if certain potential pitfalls are avoided.

Inattention to the advertising effort Advertising is sometimes not given the attention it deserves, whether because of distractions, lack of time on the part of the local advertiser, or lack of skill or interest in this aspect of the business.

Ego involvement Local advertisers sometimes succumb to the temptation to become celebrities by appearing in their own television commercials or placing photographs of themselves (or their family) in ads. This practice is dangerous. Most local advertisers are not effective spokespersons.

Inadequate supply of merchandise If the business has an insufficient supply of merchandise to meet the demand generated by the advertising, the advertiser loses more than the potential sales revenue—the money spent on the advertising is wasted, and harm is done to customer goodwill.

Unqualified individuals handling the advertising Successful advertising requires competent individuals to plan, produce, and implement it. The smaller the establishment, the greater the chance that the person who handles the advertising will be unqualified to do so. Large stores have the advantage of being able to afford an advertising manager.

Compensating for mistakes by advertising Even the best advertising efforts cannot compensate for a bad location, poor selection of merchandise, untrained personnel, unreasonable high prices, or a host of other difficulties. A good advertising campaign only speeds up the failure of a poorly run business.

Lack of knowledge about what to advertise One of the most important decisions involves what to advertise. If an advertisement is to be successful, it must contain merchandise or services in which people have some interest. A good rule of thumb is to advertise items that are selling well already. Promote items that build traffic and feature items in advertisements that are nationally advertised brands. These get attention because of the identifiable name, they take less explanation because of national promotion by manufacturers, and they help the local advertiser build a good reputation by association with a well-known brand.

Wasting money on charity advertising A host of charitable causes are always waiting for contributors. Particularly difficult to turn down are requests for advertising in high school yearbooks, church bulletins, athletic programs, and publications of fraternal organizations. Rarely do these ads prove cost-effective, however. If contributions are made by placing advertisements, the expense should be charged to "contributions to charitable organizations" rather than calling it an advertising expense.

Lack of coordination Advertising must be coordinated with buying of merchandise. Employees should be informed about the advertising so they can answer customers' questions. Merchandise must be properly priced and marked. Displays need to be in position. And local advertising should be coordinated with national advertising by manufacturers so that the advertising efforts reinforce each other.

Laboratory Applications

1. As an observer of local advertisers, identify and describe mistakes you feel they make in addition to those given above.
2. What should they do to correct their mistakes?

Establishing the Budget

How much should a local business invest in advertising? New businesses usually require greater advertising expenditures than established ones. After the public becomes familiar with a company's goods or services, advertising costs should settle at a natural profitable level. But an advertising budget must be precisely designed for a particular business.

FIGURE 17–6   Average advertising investments of retail businesses

Commodity or class of business	Average percent of sales	Commodity or class of business	Average percent of sales
Appliance, radio, TV dealers	2.3	Insurance agents, brokers	1.8
Auto accessory and parts stores	0.9	Jewelry stores	4.4
Auto dealers	0.8	Laundromats (under $35,000 in sales)	1.3
Bakeries	0.7	Liquor stores (under $50,000 in sales)	0.7
Banks	1.3	Lumber and building materials dealers	0.5
Beauty shops	2.0	Meat markets	0.6
Book stores	1.7	Men's wear stores (under $300,000)	2.4
Camera stores (under $100,000 in sales)	0.8	Motels	3.7
Children's and infants' wear stores	1.4	Motion picture theaters	5.5
Cocktail lounges	0.9	Music stores ($25,000 to $50,000)	1.8
Credit agencies (personal)	2.4	Office supplies dealers (under $100,000)	1.0
Department stores ($1 million–$2 million)	2.5	Paint, glass, and wallpaper stores	1.3
Discount stores	2.4	Photographic studios and supply shops	2.4
Drugstores (independent, under $70,000 in sales)	1.1	Real estate (except lessors of buildings)	0.6
Dry cleaning shops (under $50,000 in sales)	1.7	Restaurants (under $50,000)	0.6
Florists	2.1	Savings and loan associations	1.5
Food chains	1.1	Shoe stores	1.9
Furniture stores	5.0	Specialty stores ($1 million and over)	3.0
Gift and novelty stores	1.4	Sporting goods stores	3.5
Hardware stores	1.6	Taverns (under $50,000)	0.7
Home centers	1.3	Tire dealers	2.2
Hotels (under 300 rooms)	6.7	Travel agents	5.0
		Variety stores	1.5

Figure 17–6 lists, by type of establishment, the average percentage of sales invested in advertising. Since these figures are national averages, it is important to remember that they do not reflect the tremendous variety of factors that can affect the budget. The most important of these factors is the policies established when the company's objectives and strategies are determined. Other influences include:

1. Location of the business.
2. Age and character of the firm.
3. Size of the business.
4. Type of product or service offered.
5. Size of the trading area.
6. Amount and kind of advertising done by competitors.
7. Media available for advertising, their degree of coverage of the trading area of the business, and the costs of these media.
8. Results obtained from previous advertising.

The goal of the local advertiser is to set a budget in which the optimum amount of advertising money will be spent. If more is spent on advertising than necessary, the advertiser is wasting money. On the other hand, if the advertiser doesn't spend enough to generate the necessary sales, even

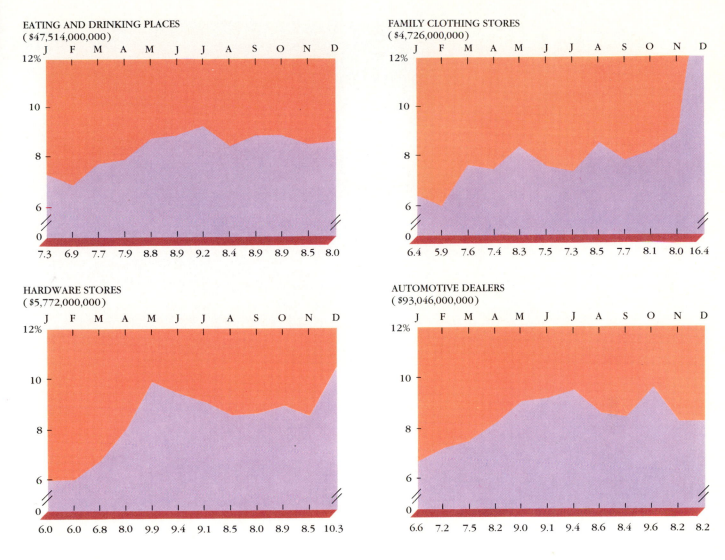

EATING AND DRINKING PLACES
($47,514,000,000)

7.3 6.9 7.7 7.9 8.8 8.9 9.2 8.4 8.9 8.9 8.5 8.0

FAMILY CLOTHING STORES
($4,726,000,000)

6.4 5.9 7.6 7.4 8.3 7.5 7.3 8.5 7.7 8.1 8.0 16.4

HARDWARE STORES
($5,772,000,000)

6.0 6.0 6.8 8.0 9.9 9.4 9.1 8.5 8.0 8.9 8.5 10.3

AUTOMOTIVE DEALERS
($93,046,000,000)

6.6 7.2 7.5 8.2 9.0 9.1 9.4 8.6 8.4 9.6 8.2 8.2

FIGURE   17–7

Total retail sales by types of stores. Percentage of the year's total sales is indicated for each month. Note how important each month is to the sale of certain types of products and services: Clothing sales are highest in December; hardware sales are highest in May and December. Advertising budgets should be geared to these fluctuations.

more money is wasted. Therefore, it is easier to waste money by not spending enough than by spending too much.

Budgeting Strategy

Advertising programs should be continuous. One-shot ads are almost invariably ineffective. Also, advertising money should be spent when prospects are most receptive to buying a local advertiser's goods or services. In practice, this requires that advertising dollars be allocated in relation to sales volume.

Local advertisers have several strategies or methods they can use to budget their advertising expenditures. Some of these were discussed in Chapter 7. However, most advertisers still use the percent-of-sales method, since it is the simplest to calculate and the easiest to defend with company bookkeepers and accountants.

To achieve the objective of selling more merchandise at lower unit cost, well-timed advertising should be run to create month-by-month sales and advertising patterns like those illustrated in Figures 17–7 and 17–8.

For Action Realty, discussed at the beginning of this chapter, advertising has become such a large and complicated activity that Gwen Lemke now

FIGURE 17–8

Advertising expenditure curves.

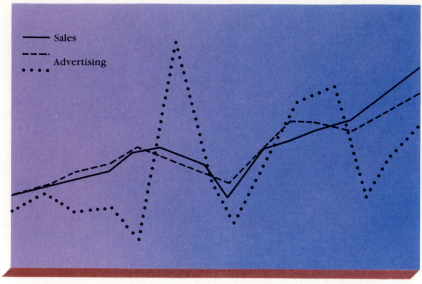

If you want well-timed advertising to sell more merchandise at lower unit costs, you want a sales advertising pattern that month by month looks like this – – – – not this • • • • •

FIGURE 17–8

Advertising expenditure curves.

uses a computer to determine the advertising budget. The computer analyzes last year's sales along with various influencing factors to determine a budget based on anticipated sales this year. What results is an advertising expenditure curve that month by month slightly precedes the sales curve, as illustrated by the dashed line in Figure 17–8.

Developing the Annual Sales and Advertising Plan

Not all local advertisers have a computer to use to forecast sales for the coming year. However, by doing some research, a businessperson can make a fairly accurate sales forecast. Some basic questions a local merchant needs to have answered might be: (1) What is the anticipated increase in population for the local area during the next year? (2) What is the anticipated increase or decrease in overall retail sales? (3) What is the outlook for local employment? (4) How are similar businesses doing?

Local accountants, bankers, trade associations, Chambers of Commerce, and media representatives can be helpful in answering these questions. After all the factors that affect finance, production, and marketing have been considered, a realistic sales plan for the year, month by month and even week by week, should be developed. From that sales plan an advertising expense plan can be formulated.

Advertising should precede sales. The most advertising dollars should be spent just before the time when customers are most likely to respond. For a retailer to determine the appropriate ad expenditures, he or she must first compute the percentage of yearly sales anticipated for each month (or, better yet, each week) of the year and plot this information on a graph. Next, he or she must plot an advertising curve that slightly precedes the sales curve, as shown with the dashed lines in Figure 17–8. (Note that advertising peaks are slightly lower than sales peaks, but the valleys are slightly higher.) The advertising curve indicates what percentage of the annual advertising expenditure should be spent each month.

This concept of plotting anticipated sales patterns enables business owners to allot a percentage of the total yearly advertising to each month.

Checklist for Setting Local Advertising Budgets

Set a Sales Goal

☐ Write down the sales figures for each month last year—for the whole store and for each department. Then in view of this performance and your own knowledge and judgment of this year's picture, rough in sales goals for next year. Use these profit pointers as a reminder of the factors to be considered in making your sales goal realistic but challenging:

Your sales last year.
Population, income, employment levels.
New and expanded departments.
Tie-ins with merchandising events.
What competitors are doing, getting.
More aggressive selling and advertising.

Decide How Much Advertising

☐ Write down how much advertising you used each month last year. Then, considering your planned sales goal and what your competition is likely to do, write in your planned advertising budget for the coming year. Your budget as a percent of sales can be checked against the expenditure of other stores in your classification. The following profit pointers can be used to double-check your own thinking on the advertising budget you can afford and need to do the job:

Stores in less favorable locations advertise more.
So do those that are new and expanding.
Strong competition raises the size of the budget needed.
Stores stressing price appeal usually promote more.
Special dates and events offer additional sales opportunities.

Added sales produced by increased expenditure are more profitable—more money can be spent to get them.
Taking advantage of co-op support can stretch ad dollars and increase ad frequency.

Decide What to Promote

☐ Let your business experience guide you in weighing the advertising you will invest in each of your departments each month. For instance, if the sales goal of department A is 9 percent of the total store sales objective this month, then earmark for it something like 9 percent of the month's planned advertising space. Your list shouldn't be a straitjacket but a basic outline.

Check the month's heavy traffic pullers.
Look for departments whose seasonal curve drops next month and should be cleared now.
Dig for "sleepers," currently hot, but that don't show up in last year's figures.
Promote newly expanded departments harder.
Calculate co-op support available for each line of merchandise.

Make a Schedule

☐ For each month, fill in a day-by-day schedule to take full advantage of:

Payroll days of important firms.
Days of the week traffic is heaviest.
National and local merchandising events offering tie-in possibilities.
New or expanded departments.
Current prices and your stock on hand—jot down items, prices, and ad sizes for each day.

By plotting actual sales as the year progresses, the advertiser can compare weekly and monthly expenses to weekly and monthly sales goals.

A simple device commonly used by local advertisers is a monthly promotional calendar. It should be large enough to accommodate information about media schedules, costs, in-house promotions, sales, and special events. The calendar then enables the advertiser to tell at a glance the shape and direction of the advertising program.

To establish such a calendar, the advertiser should enter all the holidays as well as traditional community events like "Washington's Birthday Specials." The local media, trade associations, and trade publications can be especially helpful in supplying this information. (See the Checklist for Setting Local Advertising Budgets.)

Planning Media Strategy

Choosing the right local advertising media is important for two reasons: (1) most local advertisers have advertising budgets so limited they can't use all media that might be appropriate, and (2) certain media are more effective for some businesses than others because the business is restricted either geographically or by type of customer.

Just like national advertisers, local advertisers select media depending on the types of customers the business is attempting to reach; the type of store or business doing the advertising; its location, trading area, competition, and size of budget; and the nature of the message to be delivered.

Newspapers

For local advertisers, newspapers receive the greatest emphasis—for a number of reasons (see Figure 17–9). The local newspaper is the shopper's most trusted source of local information, and recognizing this fact, retailers look to the medium for informing the community about their stores, merchandise, and services.[1] Newspapers offer other advantages as well:

1. Most newspapers are oriented to the local community. This makes it possible for the local advertiser to reach the desired audience with a minimum of wasted circulation.
2. The cost is low considering the large number of prospects reached—so low, in fact, that it is affordable for most businesses. Also, most newspapers have a special rate for local or retail advertisers that is considerably lower than their national rates.
3. Advertising can be placed in the newspaper on very short notice.
4. Some selectivity is possible by advertising in special-interest sections of the newspaper, such as sports or business news.
5. Consumers read newspapers at their leisure, and when they see ads of interest, they may clip and save them for future reference.

Drawbacks to newspapers include their limited selectivity, their sometimes poor reproduction, and potential ad clutter. Nevertheless, newspapers remain by far the number-one medium for local advertising. More than 50 percent of local advertising expenditures go to newspapers, with television and radio far behind at 13 and 11 percent, respectively.

To compete with such increasingly popular ad media as free papers, direct mail, and "shoppers" (to be discussed shortly), most daily newspapers have also instituted a service called *total market coverage* (*TMC*). A TMC is a free advertising vehicle sent out weekly to 100 percent of the residents in the newspaper's market area. It may be in tabloid or similar format and may contain varying amounts of editorial matter as well as ads. However, the primary function of the TMC is advertising. Some newspapers prefer to call the TMC "alternative distribution," particularly since the publication may be either sent through the mail or hand delivered by newspaper employees.[2] Since the ads in TMCs are the same as those run in the paper, no ad production costs are involved, making it handy for the local advertiser who wants to reach everyone in the local market area. The biggest drawback to TMCs is uncertainty of readership. Just because people receive something doesn't mean they'll read it. So readership must always be analyzed carefully.

FIGURE 17–9

Many local retail businesses, like this florist shop, find newspapers to be the best medium for reaching potential customers.

Newspapers have both display and classified advertising departments. These departments are usually equipped to help advertisers prepare the complete advertisement including copy, art, typesetting, and layout/design. Often the service is given without charge. Large papers even have personnel who will visit an advertiser's place of business to do artwork (clothing is a good example) for advertisements.

For more details on newspaper advertising, review Chapter 13.

Shoppers and Free Papers

A growing number of cities have all-ad publications, called *shoppers,* that are published as a forum for local advertisers. Some use the mail to distribute their publications and offer total circulation of a given area. This can be ideal for a local advertiser seeking distribution to the immediate trading area. Unlike newspaper TMCs, shoppers can be segmented into highly selected market areas, and the advertiser chooses just those areas of the market that his or her business serves.

Some shopper publications are responding to competition from TMCs by adding editorial content. On Long Island in New York, for example, the *Center Island Pennysavers* used to be 100 percent ads, but with competition from *Newsday Extra,* a weekly TMC of the giant daily paper, the shopper switched to a format with 70 percent ads and 30 percent local news. The shopper's publisher explained the decision to add editorial content: "We went to local news because our advertisers wanted it and because *Newsday* couldn't really cover the local news."[3]

In addition to shoppers, many cities have free newspapers, usually geared toward carrying entertainment information. These papers are usually distributed in establishments that advertise in them and at other key locations throughout the city. The advantage of these papers is that people tend to like them and read them, often because the papers provide information they can't get elsewhere. The disadvantage is that distribution can be erratic.

Magazines

The growth of local, slick, special-interest magazines has given local advertisers the opportunity to communicate with upper-income prospects through a prestigious medium. Publications such as *Palm Springs Life, Dallas Home and Garden,* and *Los Angeles Magazine* offer excellent photographic reproduction as well (see Figure 17–10). Local advertisers who seek even greater prestige and selectivity can also use special city or regional editions of major national publications such as *Time, Newsweek,* and *Sports Illustrated.*

The attractiveness of magazine advertising may be limited because of cost or because a store's trading area may be much smaller than the market reached by the magazine. In addition, magazines require that advertising be submitted long before the publication date.

Review Chapter 13 for further information about magazine advertising.

Broadcast Media

Advertising on local radio and TV stations is used increasingly by local advertisers because it usually reaches a strictly local audience, offers high

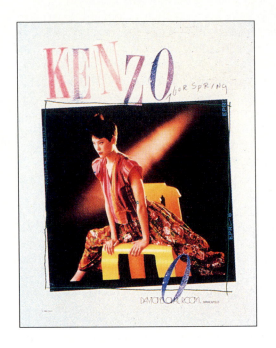

FIGURE   17–10

This award-winning ad for the Oval Room, a boutique in Dayton's department store, ran in Minneapolis/ St. Paul–area magazines. The high production values of the magazines allowed the art director to use unconventional design elements, such as hand-drawn rules and handstamped type.

FIGURE   17–11

Local television advertising doesn't need to cost an arm and a leg. This witty commercial for the Denver Museum was done on a low budget.

Is it going to be de tube or Degas?

Monotony or Monet?

Pinball or Picasso? Would you rather mow the lawn or Modigliani?

Hang around a pool hall or a Warhol?

Next time you're looking to entertain yourself, entertain your brain.

At the Denver Art Museum.

impact, and has a relatively low cost per thousand (see Figure 17–11). Because broadcast advertising requires multiple exposures to be effective, however, the total cost may be considered high by some advertisers.

Broadcast commercial time is highly selective since time slots can be purchased next to the most suitable programs for the product or service being offered. Top-40 radio stations, for example, are ideal advertising media for record dealers.

Immediacy and believability are additional benefits of broadcast media, since local personalities, or the advertisers themselves, can present the commercial message personally. In Chicago, for example, one men's clothing store used well-known baseball and football players and a college president, among others, in a popular radio campaign. In a typical commercial, a man reminisces about a key life event that at some point involved wearing a suit from Bigsby & Kruthers men's clothiers. A narrator then humorously identifies the speaker and his suit size, such as "Chicago Cub Rick Sutcliffe wears the Cy Young Award from the National Baseball League and a 46 extra-long from Bigsby & Kruthers. They both fit." Interestingly enough, none of the spokesmen is paid to do the ads—they are all volunteers who happen to like the store.[4]

Most radio and television stations gladly offer assistance in the writing and production of commercials for local advertisers. Normally this assistance is provided at a nominal charge for studio time plus additional fees for talent, special set designs, and tape dubbing.

For additional information on broadcast advertising, review Chapters 11 and 14.

Signs

The most direct method for businesses to invite customers into their stores or to use their services is through the use of signs. Three types of signs are used by local advertisers: store signs, outdoor advertising, and transit advertising. Signs offer mass exposure with color, potentially large size, and very low cost per viewer (see Figure 17–12). A disadvantage is the inability to make frequent changes, which limits their use for promotion of many types of merchandise. When signs are used for specific products, it is usually for items that have continuous appeal such as automobiles or fast-food restaurant items.

Sign companies offer copy and art services, frequently without charge. However, producing signs is usually quite expensive and should be investigated thoroughly.

Chapter 15 gives more complete information on the use of outdoor and transit advertising.

Classified Directories

Because the telephone book stays in the home or office as a ready source of information, it is widely used by local advertisers. For some businesses, it is their sole means of advertising. Every business that has a telephone qualifies for a one-line listing without charge. Additional advertising must be paid for.

Local communities in large urban areas and military bases usually have privately published classified telephone directories, which are less expensive than the large telephone company directories. These private directories cater to the special interests of the immediate locale and therefore

FIGURE   17–12

This "retro" billboard for Chicago radio station WLUP was part of an overall local campaign that also included imaginative TV spots.

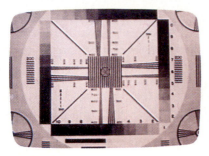

SFX: COUNTDOWN

SFX: STATIC

STEVE: Hello? . . . Hello . . .

SFX: STATIC

STEVE: Hello? Are you out there?

(STATIC STOPS)

GARRY: Hey, if you get through, tell them we're on AM 1000, the LOOP.

SFX: TAPE REWIND

GARRY: AM 1000, the LOOP.

SFX: TAPE REWIND

GARRY: AM 1000, the LOOP.

SFX: TONE; WOWS AND FLUTTERS BEFORE SETTLING

SFX: TONE CONTINUES; STATIC CONTINUES

SFX: "EL" TRAIN WITH STATIC

GARRY: Steve, its the wave of the future. And we're on it.

STEVE: Hello . . . Hello.

offer excellent support to the small retail merchant or local professional service.

Yellow pages directories published by both telephone and private companies are a vital advertising medium for most local businesses. The main problem faced by small businesses now is that the proliferation of directories makes it difficult to decide which ones to choose. If businesses

appear in all directories, their ad budget will be shot, but staying out of key directories might be a mistake as well. Adding to the problem is the sky-rocketing costs of yellow pages ads. A quarter-page ad in Bell Atlantic's 1987 Baltimore directory, for example, was $4,956.[5]

Handbills

Handbills may be single sheets (flyers) or multiple-page ads (circulars) and can be distributed on the street, in parking lots, or door-to-door. The main advantages of handbills are low cost, high speed of production, flexibility, and direct distribution to the target audience. Disadvantages include a high level of throwaways, potential poor production quality, and clutter.[6] Handbills are especially useful for making grand opening announcements, advertising sales, and periodically reminding people of the merchandise or service offered.

Handbills should be carefully planned to create a good appearance, and attention should also be given to the message so that effective appeals are built into the headline and body copy. Although the printer should not be relied on for advice about the copy, a good printer can provide sound advice about the quality of paper to use, colors, size, cost, and general appearance.

Direct Mail

Although it can be used to reach mass markets, the superior advantage of direct-mail advertising is its ability to reach specific market segments. Perhaps the greatest use of direct mail is envelope stuffers that accompany monthly bills mailed to charge-account customers. Direct mail may also take the form of catalogs, flyers, postcards, letters, or coupon packets.

One type of direct-mail vehicle that has been increasing in popularity is *shared mail,* in which two or more advertisements are wrapped around each other and then mailed as a single piece. Introduced by Advo-Systems of Hartford, Connecticut, in 1980, this method accounted for more than 12 billion ad pieces mailed in 1985 for that company alone.[7] Two-thirds of Advo-Systems' client list of more than 26,000 advertisers consists of small, local businesses. The majority fall into four distinct groups: retail, food, do-it-yourself, and chain drugstores. One of the major appeals of shared mail is that a particular piece can be sent to selected ZIP codes, thereby reaching only those households in the advertiser's targeted area.

Whatever the vehicle for delivery, direct mail is likely to get the reader's undivided attention because it has no competition from other advertisers at the same time. Local advertisers with limited budgets can use direct mail to great advantage—the number of pieces mailed and the printing costs are simply adjusted to the budget, and unlimited graphic possibilities can be used to meet the requirements for most any product or service. Most local direct-mail houses can offer copy, art, and printing as well as mailing services.

For more on direct-mail advertising, see Chapter 15.

Sales Promotion

Many sales promotion methods discussed in Chapter 16 can be uniquely effective for local advertisers.

Sampling Mrs. Fields Cookies has discovered that giving the customer a small sample of the product is highly effective. Among businesses that lend themselves to this approach are ice cream stores, delicatessens, bakeries, and fabric stores.

Specialties Specialty items, including calendars, rulers, shoehorns, and pens, are inexpensive for the store but can be valuable to the customer. These items generally contain the store name, address, telephone number, and often a brief sales message.

Coupons Coupons provide a special inducement to the customer to make a purchase. Usually a price reduction is given when the customer presents the coupon, which has been clipped from a newspaper ad or handbill or received in the mail. Coupons can be used to build store traffic, to encourage the use of a product for the first time, and to test the effectiveness of a particular advertisement (see Figure 17–13).

Telephone Selling Businesspeople can use telemarketing to reach both customers and potential customers—calling charge-account customers about a sale, reviving inactive accounts by asking the individuals to return to the

FIGURE   17–13

A Boston ad agency came up with a new twist on using coupons in this ad for Paine Furniture.

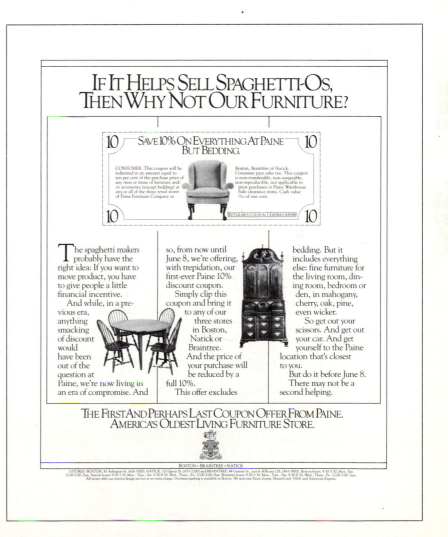

store once again, and developing new accounts. Photography studios, for example, may phone prospects with offers of free portraits.

Special Events Local advertisers can schedule a variety of special events, ranging from product demonstrations to lectures and films, to get customers into the store. Many retailers develop their own demonstrations according to their product line and their market. Bridal shops can give sessions on how to plan for a wedding, and sporting goods stores can hire a golf pro to give lessons. Other retailers rely on manufacturers to present demonstrations. Thus, a camera store might have a demonstration of video equipment conducted by a representative from a video company. Other types of special promotions might include a travel film sponsored by a travel agency or a talk on vitamins presented by a health foods store.

Another type of special event a business can sponsor is a show. Probably the most common type of local show is the fashion show given by a clothing retailer. Other types include building and home shows staged by hardware stores and new-car shows staged by local car dealers.

Free Publicity The media are always on the lookout for unusual items that may be of interest to their readers or listeners. Stores that hold major grand openings, have important personnel changes, or have new and unusual lines of merchandise are often newsworthy and might be covered by the local media. Moreover, publicity is often more cost-effective than advertising and offers greater credibility. Examples of newsworthy events might include an autograph signing by a celebrity, an unusual display (such as a runner jogging on a treadmill for hours at a time to demonstrate a sport shoe), or a tie-in with a local sports event (such as giving away free baseball caps to everyone who attends a particular major league baseball game).

One of the masters of free publicity is Aaron Hull, founder of Office Furniture Warehouse, a 10-store chain in Chicago. For example, when construction work was being done outside one of his stores, he decided to have a "sidewalk sale" and, in fact, donned hardhat and jackhammer and distributed chopped-up slabs of cement sidewalk as souvenirs of Chicago. On another occasion, Hull acquired a batch of canvas bags bearing a logo for the "Six Million Dollar Man" TV series. He advertised them as "bionic bags" carrying a list price of $6 million but on sale for 99.5 percent off list price: $3. These promotions and others like them received plenty of attention from the local media. Hull believes that once people stop laughing at his outrageous promotions, "they discover that our company offers the best savings on office furniture and supplies."[8]

Community Involvement Making contributions to the community can be an effective method of enhancing the image of a business. It can involve sponsoring a local activity such as a baseball team, a summer camp for needy youngsters, or a scholarship. Another way of becoming involved with the community is allowing store facilities to be used for social or civic organizations for fund raisers or meetings. Many businesses such as banks and savings associations have rooms specifically designed for community use.

The Media Mix As with a national advertising plan, the local plan will necessarily involve a mixture of kinds of advertising. Take the example of Younkers department stores in Des Moines, Iowa. Although the primary advertising effort is made in the Des Moines *Register,* the store also uses smaller newspapers, radio, TV, telemarketing, and direct mail to reach customers.

For the *Register,* Younkers runs "hard-sell" ads every Thursday, Friday, and Saturday and then runs an "idea" ad on Sundays, focusing on prestige goods that promote the store's image. Radio stations are carefully selected for specific ads: country and western for jeans, rock for teenage outerwear, easy listening for ladies' fashions. Television ads are used only for major promotions, such as spring and fall sales. Finally, major emphasis is placed on telemarketing and direct mail. According to Carl Ziltz, marketing vice president, "Even though direct mail is the most expensive medium we have, it's the most dollar-effective. We're mailing primarily to our own list of charge customers, but this is so effective we keep going further and further back into our files . . . and have turned many stale and random-purchase accounts into steady actives."[9]

The great majority of Younkers' direct-mail pieces take the form of tabloids or catalogs. Customers can order through the mail or by phone in addition to purchasing the items in the store. Younkers makes double use of the direct-mail pieces by transforming them into inserts for the *Register* and other papers. Although this leads to a lot of duplication with charge customers, Ziltz says the results justify the practice.

This media mix works well for a department store in the Midwest. Obviously, the particular mix that is best for any one type of business in a specific location will vary with a number of factors, and as we pointed out in Chapter 12, choosing an appropriate media mix for a business can be an art in itself.

CREATING THE LOCAL ADVERTISEMENT

One of the most competitive businesses in any local market is the grocery business. Characterized by high overhead, low profit, heavy discounting, constant promotion, and massive doses of advertising, food retailing is a difficult and highly competitive business at best.

The Tom Thumb Page stores in Dallas had an additional problem. They had elected to avoid price competition whenever possible and, instead, to compete on the basis of quality and service. This policy made it potentially difficult to attract new customers and create store traffic since grocery customers tend to be very price-oriented.

The Tom Thumb chain had been doing what might best be described as "maintenance advertising" in routine food-day newspaper sections for about four years. When they hired a new advertising agency, KCBN, Inc., the chain's owners, Bob and Charles Cullum, explained their situation and their objectives. They asked the agency to develop a campaign that would show that Tom Thumb was, in fact, very competitive in giving top value even though the prices might be slightly higher.

Barbara Harwell and Chuck Bua, the agency's creative directors, responded by developing a local institutional campaign that made grocery advertising history. They suggested opening the campaign with a television promotion for Thanksgiving turkeys. They convinced the Cullums and Tom Hairston, the chain's president, that to present a truly quality image they would have to create an absolutely outstanding commercial in terms of production quality. Furthermore, to communicate that Tom Thumb's policies truly warranted higher prices, they persuaded them to make such a bold, risky statement that it would actually impress the viewing public.

Hairston and the Cullums agreed. Two weeks before Thanksgiving the campaign began.

The commercial opened with a tight closeup of a live turkey. As the off-camera announcer spoke, the camera pulled slowly back, and the turkey reacted to the copy with an occasional "gobble."

The announcer said:

> At Tom Thumb we stand behind everything we sell . . . and that's a promise. It's always been that way. Even when we started, Mr. Cullum said, "We want our customers to be happy with everything they buy in this store. If a woman buys a turkey from us and comes back the day after Thanksgiving with a bag of bones and says she didn't like it, we'll give her her money back . . . or give her another turkey."

The moment he said that, the turkey reacted with a big "gobble" and ran off-camera. (The production hassles involved in working with this turkey are detailed in Chapter 11.) The commercial closed on the company logo with the announcer saying, "That's the way we do business at Tom Thumb . . . we stand behind everything we sell, and that's a promise" (see Figure 17–14).

The company merchandised the campaign by printing the slogan "We stand behind everything we sell . . . and that's a promise" on grocery sacks, on red lapel buttons for employees, and on outdoor billboards. The audio portions of the commercials were aired as radio spots. Most important, employee-orientation meetings were held to explain the concepts to the company's personnel and to make absolutely sure that any customers returning merchandise received a friendly, cordial smile from the employee handling the transaction.

The reaction to the campaign was astounding. First, it became the topic of local conversation. Then people began to wonder how many turkeys might be returned for the money. Local newspeople began talking about the campaign and showing the commercial in their newscasts. Finally, the top disc jockey in Dallas started a contest inviting listeners to guess how many turkeys would be returned to Tom Thumb. The day after Thanksgiving, the local television film crews were waiting at the stores to count and interview people carrying bags of bones.

One woman said she returned a turkey and got her money back with no questions asked. Another said she was given her money immediately but that she then gave the money back. She had just wanted to test them to see whether they were telling the truth.

The final score was 30,000 turkeys sold and only 18 returned, a fantastic marketing, advertising, and publicity success. Since that time, the story has been reported in numerous grocery and advertising trade journals, and Tom Thumb Page has successfully continued the "We stand behind everything we sell" advertising campaign theme.

This "talking turkey" example shows that creativity in developing an ad campaign is just as important at the local level as it is on the national level. Many local advertisers fail to realize that their print and broadcast messages are competing for attention with national messages in the same media. And with the budgetary constraints of local businesses, creativity becomes even more important in grabbing the consumer's attention. In this final section of the chapter, we will look at a few of the elements that go into creating local ads, and we will discuss the kinds of creative assistance available to local advertisers.

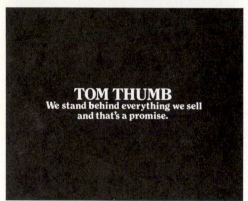

FIGURE   17–14

Tom Thumb stores talked turkey with customers by promising to stand behind everything they sell.

Creating the Message

It was 1951 when Cal Worthington first started appearing on Los Angeles television stations to pitch his car dealership. Sponsoring third-rate movies on late-night and Saturday afternoon TV, Worthington appeared in a western outfit and cowboy hat and introduced a variety of hillbilly singers who were on hand all weekend to entertain the customers who were looking at cars.

Thirty-eight years later he was still at it, only the zaniness had increased. He is noted for appearing in his TV ads with any of a variety of domesticated wild animals (all of whom are introduced as "my dog Spot") and crooning a tune promising to "stand upon my head" to make a deal on a new or used car (see Figure 17–15).

Worthington has achieved far more than just sales success. He is ribbed by talk show host Johnny Carson in his monologues, and people stop him in airports to get his autograph. His fame, therefore, has spread well beyond the local market he serves.

The same thing has happened to local advertisers in St. Louis, New York, Des Moines, and around the country. *Dun's Review* refers to these pitchmen as the "Kings of the Tacky Commercials," calling them a "jarring, growing phenomenon on local TV."[10] Some of these low-budget, do-it-yourself advertisers have been so successful they have engendered a near-cult following of viewers and imitators.

On the other hand, many who have tried the same approach of producing an assortment of low-budget, in-house commercials for viewing on late-night TV have failed miserably and eventually quit trying to utilize such commercials.

In print advertising, many local advertisers have achieved remarkable success using what some professional advertising agency artists might refer to as a "schlock" approach. Heavy bold type, items crowded into advertising space, loud headlines, and unsophisticated graphic design contribute to the "schlock" look.

As in the case of Action Realty, one has to ask: What are they selling? Is the creative message honest, consistent, and effective? If the answer is yes, then many people say that's all that matters. Invariably, the question comes down to whether the objectives of the company are being met. To direct and control the creative aspects of advertisements and commercials, the local advertiser should develop a checklist of creative dos and don'ts for his or her particular business and follow it. This will at least ensure consistency. (See the Checklist for Creating Local Advertising.)

Coming up with ideas for local ad campaigns can be extremely difficult. When NRMA's *Ad/Pro* magazine asked various sales promotion and advertising executives, "Where do your ideas come from?" the answers were wide ranging. Some looked to the merchandise for ideas, while others looked to the customer. Magazines, scrapbooks, photography exhibits, and recent movies were also mentioned as idea sources.[11]

An important goal of local advertising is to have a consistent, distinctive look to one's ads that makes them both appealing and immediately identifiable. Bullock's department store in Los Angeles provides a good example. Since 1985, readers of the *Los Angeles Times* have been accustomed to seeing a Bullock's ad on the back page of every Sunday edition. The ad is always in the same place on the same day, and the layout is always the same: a dramatic four-color photograph (usually a fashion shot), a script

FIGURE   17–15

Cal Worthington and his "dog" Spot prove that advertisers who do their own commercials can be highly successful.

Checklist for Creating Local Advertising

☑ Make your ads easily recognizable. Studies have shown that advertisements that are distinctive in their use of art, layout techniques, and typefaces usually enjoy a higher readership than run-of-the-mill advertising. Try to make your ads distinctively different in appearance from the advertising of your competitors—and then keep your ads' appearance consistent. This way, readers will recognize your ads even before they read them.

☑ Use a simple layout. Ads should not be crossword puzzles. The layout should carry the reader's eye through the message easily and in proper sequence: from headline to illustration to explanatory copy to price to your store's name. Avoid the use of too many different typefaces, overly decorative borders, and reverse plates.

☑ Use a dominant element—a large picture or headline—to ensure quick visibility. Photographs and realistic drawings have about equal attention-getting value, but photographs of real people and action pictures win more readership. Photographs of local people or places also have high attention value. Color increases the number of readers.

☑ Use a prominent benefit headline. The first question a reader asks of an ad is: "What's in it for me?" Select the main benefit that your merchandise offers and feature it in a compelling headline. Amplify this message in subheads. Avoid generalized quality claims. Your headline will be easier to read if it is black on white and is not surprinted on part of the illustration.

☑ Let your white space work for you. Don't overcrowd your ad. White space is an important layout element in newspaper advertising because the average page is so heavy with small type. White space focuses the reader's attention on your ad and will make your headline and illustration stand out. When a "crowded" ad is necessary, such as for a sale, departmentalize your items so that the reader can find his or her way through them easily.

☑ Make your copy complete. Know all there is to know about the merchandise you sell and select the benefits most appealing to your customers. These benefits might have to do with fashion, design, performance, or the construction of your merchandise. Sizes and colors available are important, pertinent information.

☑ State price or range of prices. Dollar figures have good attention value. Don't be afraid to quote your price, even if it's high. Readers often will overestimate omitted prices. If the advertised price is high, explain why the item represents a good value—perhaps because of superior materials or workmanship or extra luxury features. Point out the ac-

tual saving to the reader and spell out your credit and layaway plans.

☑ Specify branded merchandise. If the item is a known brand, say so in your advertising. Manufacturers spend large sums to sell their goods, and you can capitalize on their advertising while enhancing the reputation of your store by featuring branded items.

☑ Include related items. Make two sales instead of one by offering related items along with a featured one. For instance, when a dishwasher is advertised, also show a garbage disposal.

☑ Urge your readers to buy now. Ask for the sale. You can stimulate prompt action by using such phrases as "limited supply" or "this week only." If mail-order coupons are included in your ads, provide spaces large enough for customers to fill them in easily.

☑ Don't forget your store name and address. Check every ad to be certain you have included your store name, address, telephone number, and store hours. Even if yours is a long-established store, this is important. Don't overemphasize your signature, but make it plain. In a large ad, mention the store name several times in the copy.

☑ Don't be too clever. Many people distrust cleverness in advertising, just as they distrust salespeople who are too glib. Headlines and copy generally are far more effective when they are straightforward than when they are tricky. Clever or tricky headlines and copy often are misunderstood.

☑ Don't use unusual or difficult words. Many of your customers may not understand words familiar to you. Words like *couturier, gourmet, coiffure,* as well as trade and technical terms, may be confusing and misunderstood. Everyone understands simple language. Nobody resents it. Use it.

☑ Don't generalize. Be specific at all times. Shoppers want all the facts before they buy. Facts sell more.

☑ Don't make excessive claims. The surest way to lose customers is to make claims in your advertising that you can't back up in your store. Go easy with superlatives and unbelievable values. Remember: if you claim your prices are unbelievable, your readers are likely to agree.

☑ Ad attention increases with the size of the ad.

☑ People note more ads directed at their own sex.

☑ Tie-ins with local or special news events are effective in attracting readers.

Figure   17–16

Bullock's uses the same format and placement for its *Los Angeles Times* ads to build identity and continuity.

letter *B* at the top, and the Bullock's logo at the bottom (see Figure 17–16). In speaking of the award-winning newspaper campaign, Judy Farris, vice president for sales and promotion, noted, "The ad's position is important. It is a consistent statement. Repetition in advertising is important. You can establish an image over time. It has a cumulative effect."[12]

Of course, not all local businesses are as large as Bullock's with a separate advertising department that can devise such a major campaign. Fortunately, smaller businesses with smaller budgets have a number of creative options to choose from.

Seeking Creative Assistance

Local businesses have a number of sources to which they can turn for creative help, including (1) advertising agencies, (2) the local media, (3) free-lancers and consultants, (4) creative boutiques, (5) syndicated art services, and (6) wholesalers and manufacturers.

Advertising Agencies

Because they are usually not equipped to do their own advertising work, local advertisers increasingly turn to agencies for help. One misconception is that all agencies are large and handle only sizable accounts. In many communities there are small agencies that assist local advertisers (see Figure 17–17). Local advertisers find they need help in locating markets, determining media mixes, developing better ads, and following up their advertising with effective evaluation. Of course, the quality of agencies

FIGURE 17–17

Northlich Stolley, a Cincinnati ad agency, came up with this novel approach to attracting local clients.

When was the last time you ran into an ad you simply had to read? Chances are, it was, as we say in the trade, a "stopper." An ad with an idea so strong that it literally stops you in your tracks. An ad that not only invites readership, but demands it.

Ads like that have certain things in common. They're creative. Unusually persuasive. Maybe even a little outrageous. And, more often than not, they employ the unexpected to great advantage. But all the creativity in the world is only as good as its aim. Without it, advertising becomes nothing more than target practice. And, although practice may ultimately make perfect, what does one do in the meantime?

In your business, like ours, time is money. And the longer it takes to develop the kind of advertising that finds its mark and moves your business forward, the further you fall behind your competition. Which is something neither of us can allow to happen.

At Northlich, Stolley, we offer the talent it takes to develop highly creative advertising. And, equally important, we offer the skill it takes to keep it on target.

Call 421-8840 for the kind of advertising there's just no getting around.

NORTHLICH, STOLLEY, INC.
200 West Fourth Street, Cincinnati, Ohio 45202

varies tremendously, and only the competent agency can be a real aid to an advertiser. Specifically, an agency can help a local advertiser in the following ways:

1. Analyzing the local advertiser's business and the product or service being sold; evaluating the markets for the business including channels of distribution.
2. Evaluating the advertiser's competitive position in the marketplace.
3. Determining the best advertising media and providing advice on the costs and effectiveness of each.
4. Devising an advertising plan and, once approved, implementing it by preparing the advertisements and placing them.
5. Simplifying the advertiser's administrative work load by taking over media interviewing, analysis, checking, and bookkeeping.
6. Assisting in other aspects of the advertising and promotion effort by helping with sales contests, publicity, grand openings, and other activities.

Advertising agencies tend to be used less extensively with local advertisers than with national advertisers. A major reason is that most media, including newspapers, have two sets of advertising rates—one for national advertisers and another for retail or local advertisers. The local rate is lower and is not commissionable. Because the vast majority of local advertising is placed directly by the local advertiser rather than through an advertising agency, the advantage is a lower cost to the retailer for advertising media. Also offered are frequency and quantity discounts that give additional savings to the local advertiser.

Many advertisers simply don't spend enough money on advertising to warrant the hiring of an advertising agency. And many advertising agencies do not accept local advertisers as clients because of low budgets.

For a complete discussion of advertising agencies, review Chapter 3.

Local Media

The advertising media, in addition to selling space or time, offer a multitude of advertising services to local advertisers. These services range from planning advertising campaigns to actually preparing the advertisement.

Free-Lancers and Consultants

Because some advertising people like to be their own bosses, they act as free agents who often work out of their homes preparing copy, art and layout, photography, or other services. Free-lancers often specialize not only in the type of service they perform but also in the type of advertisers, such as car dealerships, clothing stores, or travel agencies.

Creative Boutiques

A boutique performs only the creative work. Employees of such shops specialize as copywriters, graphic designers, and illustrators. They charge a negotiated fee or a percentage of the media expenditure. Local advertisers who want the best creative work but are not interested in any other services provided by a full-service agency frequently turn to this source for help (see Figure 17–18).

FIGURE   17–18

This series of ads for a shopping complex in Santa Barbara was produced by a local creative group called Mark Oliver, Inc.

Syndicated Art Services

Syndicated art services can be useful to local advertisers by offering them a large book of artwork, called *clip art,* ready to be clipped and used in an advertisement. Clip art is available for various types of businesses and is often tied in to seasons, holidays, and other promotional angles. Clip art is available by direct subscription or through the advertising department of a local newspaper.

Wholesalers, Manufacturers, and Associations

As a service to their distributors and dealers, wholesalers and manufacturers as well as some trade associations often provide ready-made advertising (see Figure 17–19).

The most common type of help from manufacturers that local advertisers receive is called *vertical cooperative advertising.* The manufacturer normally provides the ad and a percentage of the cost of the advertising time or space. Some typical allowances for co-op advertising in various businesses are listed in Figure 17–20. The local advertiser only has to have the local newspaper drop in the name and address of the business or have the radio and TV station add a tag line with the name, address, and telephone number of the firm. Co-op advertising has both advantages and disadvantages—see Ad Lab 17-B.

FIGURE   17–19

Volkswagen of America is one of many manufacturers that provide high-quality cooperative ads to their dealers.

FIGURE 17–20	Typical allowances for co-op advertising		
Store	Co-op dollars as a percentage of total ad budget	Store	Co-op dollars as a percentage of total ad budget
Appliance dealers	80	Food stores	75
Clothing stores	35	Furniture stores	30
Department stores	50	Household goods	30
Discount stores	20	Jewelers	30
Drugstores	70	Shoe stores	50

AD LAB 17-B   The Co-op Battleground

On the surface, co-op advertising seems like a great arrangement for retailers. A manufacturer will supply advertising materials (saving the retailer production costs) and will also pay a percentage of the cost of running the ad. All the retailer needs to do is drop in the store's logo, arrange for the ad to run, and collect the co-op dollars from the manufacturer.

By using co-op advertising, the retailer not only is able to stretch an always too-small ad budget but is able to associate his or her business with a nationally advertised product. Furthermore, the retailer can be proud of professionally prepared ads and acquires greater leverage with the local media that carry the co-op ads.

There are, however, a few significant drawbacks to the co-op system. For one thing, a retailer has to sell a lot of merchandise to qualify for significant co-op funds. And some retailers who do qualify for co-op funds do not take advantage of them because they feel the supplied ads will not fit with their store's image. However, the major problem is that the retailer and manufacturer often have different advertising objectives and, thus, different ideas of how the ads should actually be executed.

Often the manufacturer wants to exert total control, specifying when, where, and in what form the ad will run. As a national advertiser, the manufacturer expects co-op ads to tie in with national advertising promotions. It wants the right product to be advertised at the right time. Retailers, on the other hand, have their own ideas of which products they want to advertise at a particular time. They are more concerned with daily volume and with projecting an image of value and variety. Thus, an appliance store might prefer to advertise the most inexpensive models of a refrigerator line, even though the appliance manufacturer wants to emphasize the top-of-the-line models.

Manufacturers also worry that retailers will place a picture of their product in the midst of a cluttered, ugly ad, that their up-scale product will be featured next to inferior products, that the ad will run in inappropriate publications, and that it will not come out at optimal times. Retailers counter with the argument that they know the local market better than the manufacturer does and should be trusted to advertise appropriately. In short, manufacturers feel they do not have enough control over co-op ads, while retailers think the manufacturers have too much control.

A retailer who is contemplating using co-op funds should consider the following questions:

What advertising qualifies, in terms of products and special requirements?
What percentage is paid by each party?
When can advertisements be run?
What media can be used?
Are there special provisions regarding message content?
What documentation is required for reimbursement?
How does each party benefit?
Do cooperative advertisements obscure the image of the individual retailer?

Laboratory Application

Look through today's edition of a daily paper in your city. Try to determine which ads qualify as co-op. Do the ads fit the particular store's image? What effect do the ads have on the images of the national products being featured?

Horizontal cooperative advertising is a joint effort on the part of real estate agents, insurance agents, pharmacies, car dealers, or travel agents to pay for an ad to create traffic for their type of business rather than for one particular business. Auto dealers in a central area of town often attempt to build traffic for all their businesses by pooling their advertising dollars and advertising the central area as the place to shop for cars. Shopping centers often do the same thing.

Summary

Local advertising is placed by businesses within a particular city or county and aimed at customers in the same geographic area. Local advertising is important because it is in the local arena that most sales are made or lost. While the basic principles used by national advertisers are applicable to local advertisers, local advertisers have special problems they must address. Local advertising appears as either product advertising or institutional advertising. Product advertising can be further subdivided into regular price-line advertising, sale advertising, and clearance advertising.

The objectives of local advertising differ from those of national advertising in terms of emphasis and time. The needs of local advertisers tend to be more immediate. Therefore, advertising is usually intended to increase traffic, turn over inventory, or bring in new customers right away.

Successful local advertisers realize the importance of marketing and advertising planning. This includes analyzing the local market, analyzing the competition, conducting adequate research, determining objectives and strategy, establishing a realistic budget, and planning media strategy.

Local businesses are often highly seasonal. By plotting anticipated sales patterns throughout the year, business owners can allot a percentage of their total yearly advertising to each month. In general, the most advertising dollars should be spent just before the time when customers are most likely to respond.

There are many media normally available to local advertisers. These include newspapers, individual shopping guides, local magazines, local radio and television, and outdoor advertising. In addition, many local advertisers use direct mail, classified directories, sales promotion, and free publicity.

Perhaps the biggest problem for local advertisers is determining creative direction. Fortunately, there are a number of sources to whom they can turn for help. These sources include local advertising agencies, the local media, free lancers and consultants, creative boutiques, syndicated art services, and wholesalers, manufacturers, and distributors.

Questions for Review and Discussion

1. What are the objectives of the various types of local advertising?
2. What does a local advertiser expect to learn by analyzing the local market?
3. How can analyzing the competition give local advertisers the competitive edge?
4. What kind of primary research could you conduct to find out what customers think of your retail business?
5. What sources of secondary research data could inform local advertisers about future retail trends?
6. What are the most important factors influencing the advertising budget of a shopping-mall tenant?
7. What basic questions would a local merchant need to answer to formulate an annual advertising plan?
8. Which media usually receive the most emphasis by local advertisers? Explain why.
9. Which sales promotional tools would be uniquely useful for local advertisers? Why?
10. If you were a local advertiser, which sources would you turn to for creative assistance? Why?

18

CORPORATE ADVERTISING, PUBLIC RELATIONS, AND NONCOMMERCIAL ADVERTISING

Jim Murray, the assistant public relations director at Johnson & Johnson, was performing a rather mundane task at the company's corporate headquarters in New Jersey when the call came in. He had been preparing a speech for one of the company's directors. But then at 9:30 A.M., the phone rang, and a reporter from the Chicago *Sun-Times* started asking for background data on the company's leading pain-reliever product. At first the call seemed innocuous enough, but then Murray became suspicious. "What's going on?" he thought. "Why's he asking all these questions?"

Murray decided he'd better call Elsie Behmer at Fort Washington, Pennsylvania. She was the director of communications for McNeil Consumer Products Company, the Johnson & Johnson subsidiary that manufactured and marketed the product, so she might know if something was afoot. In fact, she herself had just picked up a scanty report from an assistant to McNeil's medical director, Thomas Gates. Gates had just finished talking with the chief toxicologist of Cook County, Illinois, and he wanted her to meet with him in the company president's office immediately. She was just leaving when Murray's call came in. "Is this about that terrible thing in Chicago?" she asked. They compared the sparse details they both had, and then she headed for the meeting with Gates and McNeil's president, Joseph Chiesa.

Murray meanwhile ran two doors down the hall and told his boss, J&J's public relations director Robert Kniffin. Kniffin immediately called Gates, who confirmed that his office had just received press inquiries about the first three Chicago deaths. Kniffin quickly alerted the vice president of public relations, Lawrence G. Foster, and an emergency strategy session of J&J's top management was hastily assembled in the president's office. Within an hour, Kniffin and a group of J&J staffers were in a helicopter on their way to McNeil to help Behmer and Gates field the flood of calls and official inquiries they knew would start pouring in from all over the country.

At noon, the Cook County coroner held a press conference in Chicago and officially confirmed the rumors that had been flying around the country. The headlines the next day would scream about an unprecedented disaster—the Tylenol terrorism.

Three people had already succumbed, and another was ill and dying. A madman had tampered with some bottles of Extra-Strength Tylenol capsules and laced them with cyanide (see Figure 18–1).[1]

THE ROLE OF PUBLIC RELATIONS

Public relations is a term that is widely misunderstood and misused to describe anything from sales to hostessing, when in fact it is a very specific communications process. Every company, organization, association, and government body has groups of people who are affected by what that organization does or says. These groups might be employees, customers, stockholders, competitors, or just the general population of consumers. Each of these groups may be referred to as one of the organization's publics. To manage the organization's relationship with these publics, the process called public relations (PR) is used.

As soon as Tylenol was linked to the Chicago deaths, the small PR staffs at Johnson & Johnson and McNeil suddenly became responsible for handling the deluge of phone calls from the press and the public and for managing all of the companies' communications with the media. Simultaneously, other company departments had to deal with the police and numerous local, state, and federal government agencies, distributors and trade customers, and the community at large—not just in Chicago or New Brunswick, New Jersey, but anywhere in the world someone was touched by this horrible disaster. In addition, a myriad other publics suddenly popped into the spotlight demanding special attention and care: the Proprietary Association of other drug manufacturers, the Food and Drug Administration, both houses of Congress, local politicians, police groups, the financial community, stockholders, employees, the local press, national networks, and the families, friends, and acquaintances of the victims, to mention just a few.

Companies and organizations have learned that they must consider the

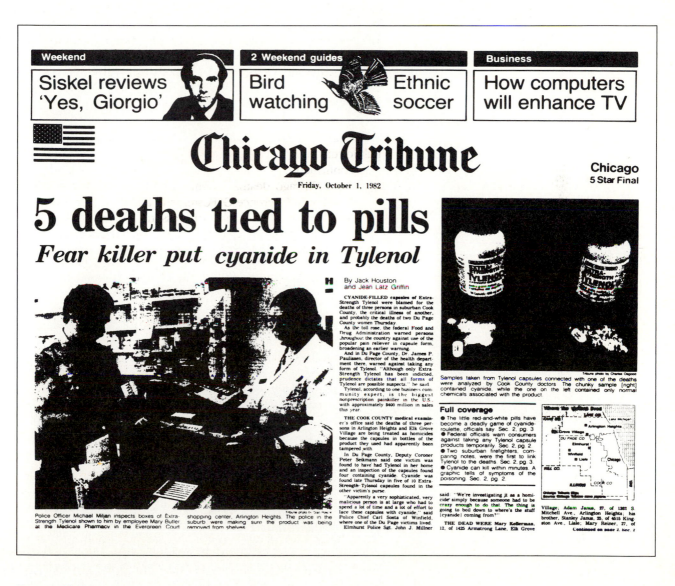

FIGURE   18–1

The front page of the *Chicago Tribune* announced the Tylenol poisonings.

public impact of their actions and decisions because of the powerful effect of public opinion. This is especially true in times of crisis, emergency, or disaster. But it is just as true for major policy decisions concerning changes in business management, pricing policies, labor negotiations, introduction of new products, or changes in distribution methods. Each of these affects different groups in different ways. Conversely, effective administrators can use the power of these groups' opinions to effect positive changes.

In short, the purpose of everything labeled *public relations* is to influence public opinion. In one instance, the effort might be to rally public support; in another, to obtain public understanding or neutrality; or in still another, simply to respond to inquiries.

Put yourself in the position of Lawrence G. Foster. As J&J's public relations vice president, he was in charge of overall corporate communications. Therefore, he also had the primary communications responsibility for McNeil. What do you suppose was the major purpose of his staff's efforts in the days immediately following the discovery of the Tylenol terrorism? What are some things they might have been called on to do?

We will discuss these and other questions in this chapter. But first it is important to understand the relationship between public relations and advertising since they are so closely related but so often misunderstood.

Advertising versus Public Relations

Advertising is generally described as openly sponsored and paid for media communications between sellers and buyers. Certainly, like public relations, the purpose of advertising is to affect public opinion. However, this purpose is normally accomplished through the open attempt to sell the company's products or services.

Public relations activities, like product advertising, may also involve media communications, but these communications are not normally openly sponsored or paid for. Usually they take the form of news articles, editorial interviews, or feature stories. One means of relaying a public relations message, though, is through corporate advertising, as we shall see later in this chapter.

As public relations expert Amelia Lobsenz has pointed out, public relations is less precise than advertising. Whereas advertising can be strictly controlled so that its reach and impact can be charted in advance, public relations communications are not so easily quantifiable: "PR's results depend more on the experience, ingenuity, and tenacity of the people engaged in its day-to-day execution."[2] Although PR communications may be less controlled than advertising, such communications often have greater credibility.

Advertising versus Public Relations Practitioners

Another interesting difference between public relations and advertising is the orientation or perspective of professional practitioners in the fields. Advertising professionals tend to be sales- or marketing-oriented (the perspective of this text, for example). They view marketing as the umbrella process used by companies to determine what products the market needs and what means will be required to distribute and sell the products to the market. To advertising professionals, advertising and public relations are

primarily tools of marketing used to promo
ucts and services. As a rule, therefore, t'
public relations as "good news" vehicles

Public relations professionals, on the o.
tions as the umbrella process that companies s.
continuing relationship with their various publics. Fi
marketing and advertising are simply tools of public rela..
be used in the company's sales relationship with customers and ,

Very few companies are structured with a public relations orienta.
but the "news" perspective and open information orientation of the professional public relations person is important and interesting to understand. In times of crisis or emergency, it is normally considered the better
perspective to adopt.

To achieve the greatest effectiveness, advertising and public relations
efforts should be closely coordinated. As a result, many advertising agencies have public relations departments or perform public relations services. Many company advertising departments also supervise company
public relations activities. And students of advertising are frequently interested in the public relations field. It is for these reasons that the topic of
public relations is presented in this textbook.

CORPORATE ADVERTISING

To help manage their reputation in the marketplace, companies use public
relations. As mentioned earlier, one of the basic tools of public relations is
corporate advertising. However, there are several types of corporate advertising, including public relations advertising, institutional advertising,
corporate identity advertising, and recruitment advertising. Their use depends on the needs of the particular situation, the audience or public
being addressed, and the message that needs to be communicated.

Public Relations Advertising

Immediately following the discovery of the Tylenol tamperings, J&J made a
major effort through the national press to inform the American public of
the danger and to get people to stop using the product. In fact, in Chicago,
police used bullhorns on the streets to warn residents of the problem. As a
result, many customers threw their bottles of Tylenol capsules away instead of returning them to the store and exchanging them for unaffected
Tylenol tablets. Others turned their bottles in to authorities for testing.

To many it looked like the end of the Tylenol brand. Stock analysts
predicted a long and lingering effect on Johnson & Johnson stock, and
adman Jerry Della Femina predicted the product would never make a
comeback. But in the days and weeks following the poisonings, there was a
huge outpouring of support not only for the families of victims but for the
company itself. J&J was gratified to learn through its public opinion surveys that people also viewed the company as a victim of the terrorist.
Buoyed by this reaction, J&J felt it could indeed reintroduce the product,
and the company moved to express its gratitude to its loyal customers.
Throughout the country, in over 180 newspapers, Johnson & Johnson
placed an unusual *public relations advertisement*. The ad expressed thanks
to the American public for its confidence and offered product coupons
good for a free replacement bottle of Tylenol (see Figure 18–2).

This unusual public relations ad from Johnson & Johnson offered coupons to customers to replace their bottles of Extra-Strength Tylenol.

The makers of TYLENOL® want to say "Thank You America" for your continuing confidence and support.

Since the recent tragic criminal tampering incident in Chicago involving Extra-Strength TYLENOL Capsules, we've talked with many people all over the country.

The attitude toward TYLENOL is overwhelmingly positive. People tell us they have trusted the TYLENOL name for many, many years, that they still have the highest regard for TYLENOL, and that they will continue to use TYLENOL. We are delighted by this response, because for over 20 years we have worked hard to earn your trust. We are now working even harder to keep it.

Following the Chicago tragedy, we know that many of you disposed of your TYLENOL product. We want to help you replace that product—*at our expense*. Just tear out the attached $2.50 certificate and redeem it at your local store.

You have made TYLENOL a trusted part of your health care program for over 20 years. This offer is a token of our appreciation for your loyalty, understanding, and continued trust.

Free!

A $2.50 certificate to purchase a free bottle of Regular Strength or Extra-Strength TYLENOL (24's/30's size) or to apply against the purchase of any other TYLENOL product. Just tear it out and take it to your local store.

Free REGULAR OR EXTRA-STRENGTH **TYLENOL®** acetaminophen 24's or 30's Size

Take this coupon to your local store for ONE free package of either Regular Strength tablet/capsule 24's or Extra-Strength TYLENOL® tablet 30's/capsule 24's size up to a retail price of $2.50. If your store does not carry this size, you may redeem this coupon for credit up to $2.50 toward the purchase of a larger size of Regular or Extra-Strength TYLENOL® tablets or capsules. You may also redeem this coupon for up to $2.50 toward the purchase of any Children's TYLENOL®, Children's or Adult COTYLENOL®, or Maximum-Strength TYLENOL® sinus medication product. You must pay any applicable sales tax.
Dealer: See reverse side for redemption

Public relations advertising is a type of corporate advertising often used when a company wishes to communicate directly with one of its important publics to express its feelings or enhance its point of view to that particular audience. Other public relations ads might be used for improving the company's relations with labor, government, customers, or suppliers.

Similarly, when companies sponsor programs on public television, arts events, or charitable activities, they frequently place public relations ads in other media to promote the programs and their sponsorship. These ads are designed to enhance the company's general community citizenship and to create public goodwill (see Figure 18–3).

Corporate/Institutional Advertising

In recent years, the term *corporate advertising* has come to denote that broad area of nonproduct advertising used specifically to enhance a company's image and increase lagging awareness. The traditional or historic term for this is *institutional advertising*.

Institutional or corporate ad campaigns may be used for a variety of

FIGURE   18–3

Many corporations provide funding for cultural events and activities, and it's good public relations to advertise such corporate sponsorship.

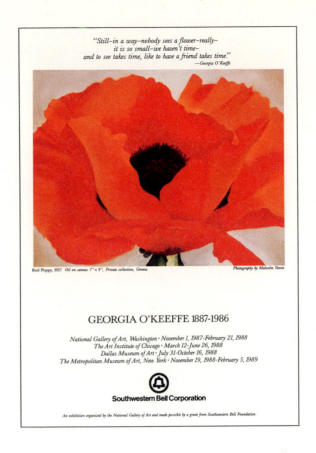

purposes—to report the company's accomplishments, to position the company competitively in the market, to reflect a change in corporate personality, to shore up stock prices, to improve employee morale, or to avoid a communications problem with agents, dealers, or customers.

Companies and even professional advertising people have historically questioned, or simply misunderstood, the effectiveness of corporate advertising. Retailers, in particular, have clung to the idea that institutional advertising may be pretty or nice but that it "doesn't make the cash register ring." However, a series of market research studies sponsored by *Time* magazine and conducted by the Yankelovich, Skelly & White research firm offered dramatic evidence to the contrary.

In the first of these studies, 700 middle- and upper-management executives were interviewed in the top 25 U.S. markets. The researchers evaluated five companies that were currently doing corporate advertising and five that were not. They found that the companies that used corporate advertising registered significantly better awareness, familiarity, and overall impression than those that used only product advertising. In fact, the five corporate advertisers in the study drew higher ratings in every one of 16 characteristics measured, including being known for quality products, having competent management, and paying higher dividends.[3] Perhaps the most interesting aspect of the research was the fact that the five companies with no corporate advertising spent far more for total advertising than did the firms engaged in corporate advertising.

David Ogilvy, the founder and creative head of Ogilvy & Mather, has been an outspoken advocate of corporate advertising. However, he is appalled by most corporate advertising, characterizing it as filled with "pomposity, vague generalizations, and fatuous platitudes." (For more on his views, see Ad Lab 18-A.) Corporate advertising has also been criticized for being beautiful but bland, self-serving, and oblivious to the needs of the audience.

Responding to such criticisms and to other forces in the marketplace, corporations have been making major changes in their corporate advertis-

AD LAB 18-A   David Ogilvy Talks about Corporate Advertising

I have had some experience with corporate advertising—for Shell, Sears, IBM, International Paper, Merrill Lynch, General Dynamics, Standard Oil of New Jersey, and other great corporations.

Big corporations are increasingly under attack—from consumer groups, from environmentalists, from governments, from antitrust prosecutors who try their cases in the newspapers. If a big corporation does not take the initiative in cultivating its reputation, its case goes by default.

If it were possible, it would be better for corporations to rely on public relations (i.e., favorable news stories and editorials) rather than paid advertising. But the media are too niggardly about disseminating favorable information about corporations. That is why an increasing number of public relations directors have come to use paid advertising as their main channel of communication. It is the only one they can control with respect to *content,* with respect to *timing,* and with respect to *noise level.* And it is the only one which enables them to *select their own battleground.*

So I guess that corporate advertising is here to stay. Why is most of it a *flop?*

First, because corporations fail to define the *purpose* of their corporate campaigns.

Second, because they don't *measure the results.* In a recent survey conducted by *The Gallagher Report,* only one in four of U.S. corporate advertisers said that it measured changes in attitude brought about by its corporate campaigns. The majority fly blind.

Third, because so little is known about what works and what doesn't work in corporate advertising. The marketing departments and their agencies know a good deal about what works in *brand* advertising, but when it comes to *corporate* advertising they are amateurs. It isn't their bag.

Fourth, very few advertising agencies know much about corporate advertising. It is only a marginal part of their business. Their creative people know how to talk to housewives about toilet paper, and how to write chewing-gum jingles for kids, and how to sell beer to blue-collar workers. But corporate advertising requires copywriters who are at home in the world of big business. There aren't many of them.

I am appalled by the *humbug* in corporate advertising.

The *pomposity.* The *vague generalities* and the *fatuous platitudes.*

Corporate advertising should not insult the intelligence of the public.

Unlike product advertising, a corporate campaign is the voice of the chief executive and his board of directors. It should not be delegated.

What can good corporate advertising hope to achieve? In my experience, one or more of four objectives:

1. It can build *awareness* of the company. Opinion Research Corporation states, "The invisibility and remoteness of most companies is the main handicap. People who feel they know a company well are five times more likely to have a highly favorable opinion of the company than those who have little familiarity."

2. Corporate advertising can make a good impression on the financial community, thus enabling you to raise capital at lower cost—and make more acquisitions.

3. It can motivate your present employees and attract better recruits. Good public relations begins at home. If your employees understand your policies and feel proud of your company, they will be your best ambassadors.

4. Corporate advertising can influence public opinion on specific issues.

Abraham Lincoln said, "With public opinion against it, nothing can succeed. With public opinion on its side, nothing can fail."

Stop and Go—that is the typical pattern of corporate advertising. What a waste of money. It takes time, it takes *years,* for corporate advertising to do a job. It doesn't work overnight—even if you use television.

A few companies—a *very* few—have kept it going long enough to achieve measurable results.

Laboratory Application

Discuss a corporate advertisement with which you are familiar that demonstrates what David Ogilvy refers to as the humbug in corporate advertising, the pomposity, the vague generalities, and the fatuous platitudes.

ing policies and campaigns. Expenditures for this type of advertising have increased dramatically since the early 1980s, jumping from $403.2 million in 1982 to $776 million in 1986.[4] The primary medium used for corporate advertising is consumer (primarily business) magazines ($343.7 million spent in 1986), followed by network television ($246 million).[5]

This increase in corporate ad spending has been accompanied by a change in message strategy. In the past, most corporate ads were designed primarily to create "goodwill" for the company. Today, with "merger madness," increasing diversification within companies, and competition from foreign advertisers, companies are finding that their corporate ads must do much more—they must help accomplish specific objectives. These might include: (1) to develop awareness of the company and its activities, (2) to attract investors, (3) to improve a tarnished image, (4) to attract quality employees, (5) to tie together a diverse product line, and (6) to take a stand on important public issues (advocacy advertising). Look at the examples in the Portfolio of Corporate Advertising. What do you feel are the objectives of these campaigns? How well are those objectives addressed?

Corporate advertising is also increasingly being used to set the company up for future sales. Although this is traditionally the realm of product advertising, many advertisers have instituted "umbrella" campaigns that simultaneously communicate messages about the products and the company. This has been termed *market prep corporate advertising*. For example, the "Gee . . . No, GTE" series of ads has emphasized GTE products or services in a way that points up the company's technological sophistication. As Philip Stevens, GTE's director of corporate advertising, explained, "Our global objective is to get in touch with business customers and derive the most money for our telecommunications products."[6] Similarly, AT&T's "right choice" campaign emphasizes both its dependable image and its products and services (see Figure 18–4).

(continued on p. 594)

FIGURE   18–4

Today's corporate advertising strives to do more than simply create a positive image for the company. As this AT&T ad demonstrates, modern corporate ads communicate messages about the company's products or services as well.

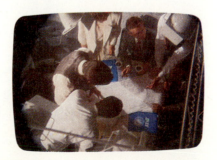

SINGERS: *We can help put people together . . . "*

AT&T can help your business grow . . .

VO: For us at American Express, building one worldwide nerve center was a dream come true.

Finding the communications and information systems that could grow with us might have been a nightmare.

We chose AT&T.

You don't trust your dream to just anyone.

ANNCR VO: Whether it's telephones, information systems, long distance services or computers . . .

SINGERS: *The Right Choice, AT&T.*

PORTFOLIO OF CORPORATE ADVERTISING

A. Alluring photographs by award-winning photographer Jay Maisel set this and other ads in a series for United Technologies one cut above the others.

B. The Japanese electronics firm Mitsubishi uses handsome ads such as this to tell Americans that it is a good corporate neighbor.

C. Looking almost like a magazine editorial spread, this ad for 3M emphasizes a lesser-known aspect of the company—its health technology expertise.

Like Nature, We Custom Design The Product For Its Environment.

D. John Hancock's "Real life, real answers" campaign revolutionized TV advertising for financial services and helped blur the line between product and corporate advertising.

BRO: Ah gee, I don't know. You remember . . . Maggie . . . I certainly remember. When he could pick up the both of us in one hand. One hand.

SIS: I know. I remember.

BRO: Oh man. Now . . . it's like it's our turn. You know what I mean?

SIS: I know. I know.

BRO: He can't drive at night anymore. Did you know that? Mom told me that.

SIS: I know. I know.

BRO: But that's really nothing. I mean 5 years or 7 years from now, what happens then? He won't ask us. Even if he needs our help he won't ask us. The thing is . . . we've got to do something. We're the ones . . . you know. Michael isn't even working.

E. The high-tech look and sophistication of this ad contribute to the image Rockwell International wants to establish.

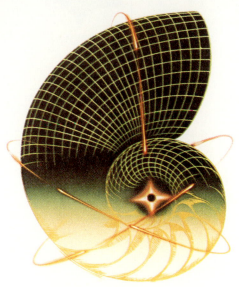

'ek·sə·ləns

Excellence
• *Distinguished by superiority; e.g., 123,000 committed, dedicated employees—highly skilled in complementary technologies.*
• *A standard, like the quality of products being developed in our five core business areas.*
• *A surpassing achievement, such as '85 sales exceeding $11 billion.*

$$F = FR_1 / \frac{d}{dz} \left[\log \left(T - T_{pv} - T_{os} \right) \right]$$

The Nautilus Configuration: It is nature's inspiration for excellence in science and engineering. It is also a symbol of the commitment of Rockwell employees.

The quest for excellence by our 25,000 engineers, scientists and supporting technical personnel shapes the work of Rockwell's 123,000 employees worldwide. And results in the elegant solutions to customer needs that make Rockwell a leader in five diverse areas of commercial and government business.

Excellence is also a major reason for the ongoing record of financial growth that brought us more than $11 billion in sales and record earnings in 1985.

To learn more about us, write: Rockwell International, Department 815B-3, 600 Grant Street, Pittsburgh, PA 15219.

Rockwell International

...where science gets down to business

**Aerospace / Electronics / Automotive
General Industries / A-B Industrial Automation**

F. Unlike the Rockwell ad, this one for McDonnell Douglas shows a product and talks specifics. It still qualifies as a corporate ad, however, because rather than trying to convince readers to purchase a specific product it presents the company as innovative, skillful, and reliable.

Satchel Paige didn't pitch in the World Series until he was 42. Or, was it 52?

Hall of Fame Plaque.

Or, was it 62? The older the better, right Satch? Fact is, your age took on mythical proportions.

And that sure was fine with you. It was fine when you made the jump from the Old Negro Leagues to the majors. When you made the American League All Star Team. Even when you made the Hall of Fame at Age 65. Or, was it 75?

You got the nickname "Satchel" when you carried baggage as a kid at the railroad station in Mobile. You hustled so many satchels that your buddies said you "looked like a walking satchel tree."

And you never stopped hustling, did you? You pitched over 2,500 games and barnstormed more than a million miles in old black leagues before the shameful color barrier of the major leagues was broken.

You had, as Cleveland owner Bill Veeck said, "Charisma. Same as Babe Ruth and Dizzy Dean."

You befuddled would-be hitters and dazzled fans. You pitched a Long Tom ball, a bee ball, a hummer, and the unhittable hesitation pitch.

You were billed as "Satchel Paige, World's Greatest Pitcher." And you pitched and pitched and pitched until you were 48. Or, was it 58?

Your plaque at the National Baseball Hall of Fame and Museum in Cooperstown, N.Y., reads that your "pitching was a legend among major league hitters."

And your legend will endure as long as men and women are willing to throw a high, hard one past the ignoble whims of fate.

The people at Denny's think that people like you, Satchel, are an inspiration. Because people like you show us how to celebrate the pure joy of living.

You once told us, "Don't look back, something may be gaining on you." We hear you, Satchel. We're looking nowhere but ahead.

The ball shaped end was thought to work as a counterbalance. It didn't.

One of the many outfits in Satchel's wardrobe.

People have 5 fingers. Mitts had 4.

Denny's

For a free reprint of this ad, visit your nearest Denny's. Photography courtesy of National Baseball Hall of Fame & Museum, Inc.

G. Long, interesting copy and a zingy layout make this corporate ad for Denny's Restaurants inviting and different.

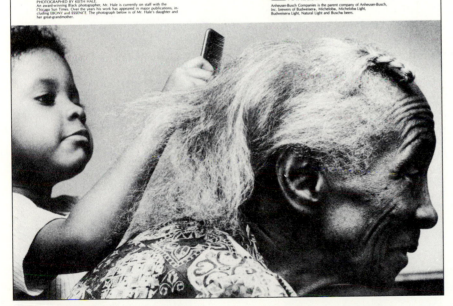

Being Black in America: A Real Picture

Remember your first real history lesson?

When Grandma used to sit you down and talk about her life she wasn't just telling tales. She was following a long line of Black historians who passed their precious knowledge from generation to generation using the most expressive instrument created. The human voice.

This knowledge is power. Because when you know where you come from you know who you are. Our grandparents knew this. So did W.E.B. Dubois, Sojourner Truth, Carter G. Woodson and Martin Luther King.

They also knew how important it was that this knowledge continue to be handed down. Black History Month is a reminder for us to learn from the past, because it positively affects the quality of our future.

Anheuser-Busch appreciates this fact. We have an ongoing commitment to forging partnerships with Black organizations across the country which are involved in preserving the Black cultural heritage.

And we've brought Black history into the community through our Great Kings and Queens of Africa art collection.

A real picture of being Black in America includes all of us. The future rests on people of all races working together to make our common reality one we can all be proud of.

Building a future in partnership with the community.

 ANHEUSER-BUSCH COMPANIES

Anheuser-Busch Companies is the parent company of Anheuser-Busch, Inc. brewers of Budweiser, Michelob, Michelob Light, Budweisers Light, Natural Light and Busche beers.

PHOTOGRAPHED BY KEITH HALE.
An award-winning Black photographer, Mr. Hale is currently on staff with the Chicago Sun Times. Over the years his work has appeared in major publications, including EBONY and ESSENCE. The photograph below is of Mr. Hale's daughter and her great-grandmother.

H. Anheuser-Busch surprised a lot of people when it came out with a series of "articles" titled "Being Black in America: A Real Picture." The campaign, which focused on unsung heroes and their histories, set a new trend in corporate advertising.

Another tack is being used by Raytheon, whose corporate name is not nearly as well known as those of such subsidiaries as Beech Aircraft and Amana Refrigeration. The goal of the Raytheon corporate campaign is to "provide a tighter focus on the whole company" and "create stronger ties between the subsidiary companies," according to Raytheon's director of advertising.[7]

Of course, no amount of image advertising is going to accomplish desired goals if the image does not match the corporation. As noted image consultant Clive Chajet put it, "You can't get away with a dissonance between the image and the reality—at least not for long."[8] If, for example, a sophisticated high-tech corporation like IBM were to try to project a homey, small-town family image, it would lose credibility very quickly.

Corporate Identity Advertising

Companies take pride in their logos and corporate signatures. In fact, the graphic designs that identify corporate names and products are considered valuable assets of the company, and great effort is expended to protect their individuality and ownership. What does a company do, though, when it decides to change its name, logos, trademarks, or corporate signa-

A company can only be as great as the people it employs. For people are a company's source of innovation and ideas.

Sperry and Burroughs are two companies built by people with bold ideas, willing to make bold moves.

Dedicated people who have led both companies to the forefront of engineering achievement in aerospace, defense and business applications.

Skillful people who have earned a reputation for excellence and reliability. Savvy people who understand they're in the business of service. And people of vision who can transform your problems into solutions.

Now, the people of Sperry and Burroughs join forces as Unisys. And the power of their talents is not merely doubled, but elevated to a new level.

They form a new association. One that understands how to put the power of its extraordinary people to work for you.

PeoplePower²

UNISYS
The power of ²

FIGURE   18–5

When the giant Burroughs and Sperry corporations merged to become Unisys, ads such as this one appeared in newspapers and magazines to inform the public about the new name and to create an identity for the new corporation.

How would you solve this problem?

☐ A. Deductive reasoning.
☐ B. Perseverance and dedication.
☐ C. A sword.

Mobil
We like people with fresh ideas.

FIGURE   18–6

Although most corporate recruitment advertising is found in the classified sections of newspapers and business publications, some national corporate magazine ads are used for recruitment purposes.

tures, as when it merges with another big company? How does it communicate that change to the market it serves and to its other influential publics? This is the job of corporate identity advertising.

Take the situation when two giant corporations, Burroughs and Sperry, merged in 1986. The name chosen for the new company was Unisys, and the task of corporate advertising was to convey the company's new identity to employees, existing customers, and potential customers. The ad campaign began with three-page all-type newspaper ads and a series of five two-page ads in business magazines emphasizing that Unisys represented the merger of two equals into something greater than the sum of the parts (see Figure 18–5). The print campaign was buoyed by TV ads on public affairs and sports programs and by direct-mail pieces. The campaign is estimated to have cost some $20 million.[9] Interestingly, Burroughs Corporation was one of the five companies in the Yankelovich study mentioned earlier that had *not* been doing corporate advertising.

Among other major name changes that have received large amounts of corporate advertising dollars in recent years are the switch from American Harvester to Navistar International, the renaming of Western Bankcorporation to First Interstate Bankcorp, and the change of Consolidated Foods to Sara Lee Corporation.

Recruitment Advertising

When the prime objective of corporate advertising is to attract employment applications, companies use recruitment advertising (see Figure 18–6). Recruitment advertising is most frequently found in the classified sections of daily newspapers and is typically the responsibility of the personnel department rather than the advertising department. Recruitment advertising has become such a large field, though, that many advertising agencies now have recruitment specialists on their staffs. In fact, some agencies specialize completely in recruitment advertising, and their clients are corporate personnel managers rather than advertising department managers. These agencies create, write, and place classified advertisements in newspapers around the country and prepare recruitment display ads for specialized trade publications.

PUBLIC RELATIONS ACTIVITIES AND TOOLS

Prior to the Tylenol tragedy, the public relations plan for that product had been rather low-key. Originally introduced in the 1950s as a prescription-only children's elixir, the company promoted Tylenol through educational conferences for health care professionals. After the mid-1970s, Tylenol was repositioned as an over-the-counter adult product, and the promotion burden was carried exclusively by consumer advertising. With that history, the product had no ongoing public relations program, and the firm had no emergency public information plan. That was the first thing that Johnson & Johnson and McNeil's management strategists had to prepare. Together, they formulated three stages of action to be taken:

1. Identify the problem and take immediate corrective action. This meant getting information from the press, police, FDA, and FBI; identifying the geographic dimensions of the problem; correcting rumors; and withdrawing all affected products from the marketplace.

2. Cooperate with the authorities in the investigation to find the killer. (Rather than simply reacting to situations as they developed, Johnson & Johnson decided to get actively involved by helping the FBI and other law enforcement agencies in their efforts to generate leads and investigate security at the McNeil plants. The firm even offered a $100,000 reward for information leading to the arrest and conviction of the murderer.)

3. Rebuild the Tylenol name and capsule line including the Regular Strength capsules, which had been recalled along with the Extra-Strength.

The first job was to ensure that the tampering had not occurred at McNeil. The company's two capsule production lines had to be shut down and dog teams brought in to search for evidence of cyanide. While everyone believed the problem was probably confined to the retail end of the chain, they had to be sure.

Simultaneously, the enormous appetite of the news media for background information and updates on the crisis, along with a flood of inquiries from anxious consumers, put the firms' public relations people under enormous pressure. Faced with a crisis of such severe proportions, a firm has little choice but to be open in handling inquiries. However, all communications between the media and the company had to be channeled through Foster's department. In addition, all customer communications, all trade communications, and all government communications had to be coordinated within the company. Only in this way could open, clear, consistent, *legal,* and credible communications be maintained. And only in this way could the potentially disastrous effects of rumormongering, political backbiting, and corporate defensiveness be minimized.

In the first 48 hours after the coroner's press conference, calls to Johnson & Johnson and McNeil were incessant. The moment one caller hung up, the telephone rang again. In the basement at McNeil, a bank of 800 phones, usually used for sales, was pressed into service and staffed by employees. But employees had to know what to say, what they were not allowed to say, and to whom unanswerable questions should be referred. That, of course, depended on who was calling and what they were asking.

At the same time, management and employees had to be notified, various authorities had to be contacted, and many others who were involved had to be reached. And all this had to be planned, coordinated, and supervised efficiently. That was suddenly the job of Lawrence Foster and his staff.

As unusual as disasters might be, they are the most important activities of PR professionals and public information officers in such highly sensitive organizations as airlines, police departments, military organizations, chemical and oil companies, and public utilities. These people are all employed in industries characterized by a high demand for news and information. As a result, their press relations activities are performed in a variety of pressure-cooker situations.

Since the Tylenol incident, many other companies in nonsensitive areas have directed their public relations departments to develop crisis-management plans. As noted by PR expert Art Stevens, "How a corporation handles news during crises determines in large measure the impact that news has on the public. When corporations have no plans for coping with crisis news, the resulting press coverage can be disastrous."[10] The crisis may range from a small noninjury fire in an office to a run on a bank to criminal behavior on the part of an employee (see Figure 18–7). The main advice

TOSHIBA CORPORATION EXTENDS ITS DEEPEST REGRETS TO THE AMERICAN PEOPLE.

Toshiba Corporation shares the shock and anger of the American people, the Administration and Congress at the recent conduct of one of our 50 major subsidiaries, Toshiba Machine Company. We are equally concerned about the serious impact of TMC's diversion on the security of the United States, Japan, and other countries of the Free World.

Toshiba Corporation had no knowledge of this unauthorized action by TMC. And the United States and Japanese Governments have not claimed that Toshiba Corporation itself had any knowledge or involvement.

Nevertheless, Toshiba Corporation, as a majority shareholder of TMC, profoundly apologizes for these past actions by a subsidiary of Toshiba.
- As a measure of *personal* recognition of the grievous nature of TMC's action, both the Chairman and the President of Toshiba Corporation have resigned. *For the Japanese business world, this is the highest form of apology.*
- In TMC, the subsidiary where the diversion occurred, wrongdoers are now being prosecuted.

For the future, Toshiba Corporation takes full responsibility to insure that never again will such activity take place within the Toshiba Group of companies.
- We are working with the Governments of the United States and Japan in this endeavor.

The relationship of Toshiba Corporation, its subsidiaries and their American employees with the American people, one marked by mutual trust and cooperation, has developed over many years of doing business together. We pledge to do whatever it takes to repair, preserve, and enhance this relationship.

Toshiba Corporation already has begun to take corrective measures throughout its hundreds of subsidiaries and affiliate companies:
- We immediately directed all our companies to institute stringent measures guarding more securely against this kind of misconduct.
- We obtained the resignation of the President of TMC and the three other Board members who had corporate responsibility for the conduct of those TMC employees actually involved.

- We also obtained TMC's commitment to stop exports to the Soviet Bloc countries for an unlimited time.
- We have authorized an extensive investigation to find all the facts concerning TMC's actions and to design safeguards to prevent repetition of such conduct. This investigation is being directed by American counsel, assisted by a major independent accounting firm.
- We will discharge all officers and employees found to have knowingly participated in this wrongful export sale.
- We have appointed the former senior auditing official of Toshiba Corporation to TMC's Board with direct responsibility for Toshiba's policy of full observance of the law and of Japan's security arrangements with its allies.
- We are going to develop a rigid compliance program in cooperation with the Governments of Japan and the United States.
- We intend to establish Toshiba's new compliance program as a model for all future export controls throughout Japanese industry.

In its 22 years of doing business with the United States, Toshiba Corporation has been a leader in introducing American products to the Japanese market, and also has significantly shifted the manufacture of Toshiba products to the United States. At a time when many of the U.S.-based corporations competing with Toshiba are moving production facilities and jobs abroad, Toshiba's American companies are steadily expanding the extent to which their products are manufactured in the United States. Today, Toshiba employs thousands of Americans in 21 states from New York to Texas to California. It is these Americans who have played a large and crucial part in earning Toshiba its reputation for producing top quality products, reliable service, and ongoing innovation that millions of American consumers and industrial customers know they can trust.

These bonds of cooperation are signs of our commitment to America. We earnestly wish to continue our efforts to develop our relationship with America.

We ask our American friends to work with us and help us to do so.

Joichi Aoi
Joichi Aoi
President/CEO
Toshiba Corporation

Mudge Rose Guthrie Alexander & Ferdon, 2121 K Street, N.W., Suite 700, Washington, D.C. 20037, is registered under the Foreign Agents Registration Act as an agent of Toshiba Corporation for the research, writing, publication and dissemination of this document. The material is filed with the Department of Justice, Washington, D.C., where the registration statement is available for public inspection. Registration does not indicate approval of the contents of this document by the United States Government.

FIGURE   18–7

This apology by the president of Toshiba Corporation ran in 60 American publications following the revelation that one of Toshiba's subsidiaries had sold submarine technology to the Soviets. This public apology was made on the assumption that the American people hate coverups and are more forgiving if parties admit guilt and offer reparation.

all experts on crisis management give is to follow J&J's example by being open and candid. Says Stevens, "Withholding information or evading questions is almost certain to backfire."[11]

Public Relations Activities

Fortunately, most public relations professionals are not occupied in handling crisis communications. Rather, they are employed to *generate* news from basically low-news-demand organizations, and the activities they are concerned with reflect that fact. These activities range from publicity and press agentry to special events management and speech writing.

One of the most important functions of a practitioner is to plan and execute the overall public relations program. To do so, the practitioner has to analyze the relationships between the organization and its publics; evaluate public attitudes and opinions toward the organization; assess the organization's policies and actions as they relate to the organization's publics; and finally, plan and execute the various PR activities.

Publicity and Press Agentry

Publicity is the generation of news about a person, product, or service that appears in broadcast or print media. Publicity is usually thought of as being "free" because the media do not bill anyone for the publicity they run, and the media cannot be "bought" to run the publicity. The organiza-

PEOPLE IN ADVERTISING

Herb Schmertz

Vice President of Public Affairs
Mobil Oil

Herb Schmertz has been called the most powerful and successful corporate public relations man in the world. He is "the Man from Mobil," overseeing Mobil's more than 90-member public relations staff, managing Mobil's public affairs, and representing the corporation in TV interviews, and at cultural events and political dinners.

Before joining Mobil in 1966, Schmertz, who has a law degree from Columbia, did intelligence work for the Army, was a private labor arbitrator, and served as a labor law professor. His first job with Mobil was manager of corporate labor relations, but it wasn't long before he moved into the public relations area.

In his tenure at Mobil, Schmertz has been responsible for the text-only advocacy ads that run every week in *The New York Times* and other publications (the first one appeared in 1970) and for Mobil's involvement in sponsoring prestige PBS series.

The advocacy ads have tackled such topics as the oil crisis, America's economic system, and mass transit. According to Schmertz, these ads follow in the tradition of the ancient and honorable art of pamphleteering. "I am, in

tion that seeks the publicity may go to considerable expense in an effort to get it, but there's no bill for the space or time received. Of course, for publicity to be effective, it must be newsworthy. Opportunities for publicity include the introduction of a new product, awards, company sales and earnings, mergers, retirements, parades, and speeches by company executives.

Press agentry refers to the planning of activities and the staging of events to attract attention and generate publicity that will be of interest to the media. Although celebrities, circuses, sports events, politicians, motion pictures, and rock stars come to mind as requiring press agentry, many public relations people use it to bring attention to new products or services or to put their company or organization in a favorable light. For example, if a company makes a major donation to a charitable cause, press agentry can be used to bring the donation to the attention of the public.

For print media, the publicity person deals with editors and feature writers. For broadcast media, he or she deals with a program director, assignment editor, or news editor. One of the most important functions of public relations is to develop and maintain ties with such editorial contacts.

Public Affairs and Lobbying

Frequently, companies and organizations need to deal with public officials, regulatory and legislative bodies, and various community groups. This is the task of *public affairs* people. Sometimes this work is handled by

effect," he says, "the manager of an ongoing political campaign. My job is a lot closer to the confrontational style of politics than it is to the conventional niceties of corporate public relations. We're constantly out there trying to win more votes for our positions."

Schmertz is well known for his run-ins with the media, and he sees his role as highly confrontational. As he puts it, "There are situations that pose immediate threats to a company, such as inaccurate or distorted reporting, that leave no alternative but to respond by confrontations." He has put this philosophy in the form of a book, *Good-Bye to the Low Profile: The Art of Creative Confrontation,* coauthored with William Novak.

His advice to other PR practitioners who deal regularly with the media includes: Be unpredictable (so that people will spend time trying to figure out what you're likely to do), go first (so that the other person is forced to react), avoid saying "no comment," and don't let the press intimidate or seduce you by flattery or friendliness (never assume a conversation is off-the-record).

In addition to its regular issue advertising, Mobil adds to its image by sponsoring quality TV programming ("made possible by a grant from Mobil" was first heard in 1971 when Schmertz brought "Masterpiece Theater" to PBS), funding cultural events such as free concerts, and contributing to museums. As Schmertz points out, "Cultural excellence generally suggests corporate excellence. These are image enhancers."

Schmertz feels that both the issue ads and the corporate sponsorships he has initiated and maintained for Mobil have created a positive, distinctive personality for the corporation. "And that contributes to the sale of our product, something never anticipated."

In addition to his many responsibilities at Mobil, Schmertz writes a weekly syndicated column in which he engages in his favorite pastime, "media baiting." The column, as he puts it, "tries to cover the press the way the press covers politics—to talk about its process, its foibles, and all the rest."

the public relations office; other times, by specialists in public affairs. For example, Johnson & Johnson's director of federal affairs was Bertram Levine. During the crisis, his office contacted all members of Congress on Capitol Hill to offer aid in answering constituents' questions. Then his office worked with various congressional committees to rapidly push through emergency legislation regarding tamper-resistant packaging.

Because every organization is affected by the government, companies are doing an increasing amount of lobbying. Lobbying involves trying to inform and persuade government officials in the interests of the client to promote or thwart administrative action or legislation.

Community Involvement

The goal of community involvement is "to have the company officers, management, and employees contribute to the community's social and economic development."[12] Such contributions may take the form of providing leadership for civic and youth groups, participating in fund-raising drives for local charities, sponsoring medical programs, providing educational programs for schools, and sponsoring cultural or recreational activities. One of the roles of the company public relations department is to help set up such programs and to publicize their existence to the community.

Promotion and Special Events Management

For profit-making organizations, promotion means using advertising and public relations techniques as a means of selling a product or service as well as enhancing the reputation of the organization. Promotion can be achieved through press parties, open houses, celebrations, sponsoring of contests, or a variety of other activities.

There are two kinds of public relations events: (1) those designed to create publicity and (2) those designed to improve public relations through personal contact. Often these two purposes overlap. For example, Macy's Thanksgiving Day parade in New York creates tremendous publicity as well as a great deal of community goodwill because of personal contact. Also, an event designed to improve public relations among members of an association—such as the annual convention of the American Bar Association—can generate vast amounts of publicity.

Another type of event used as a public relations tool is the company-sponsored cultural or sports event (see Figure 18–8). Some companies associate their names with existing events. For example, Mercedes-Benz, Perrier, and Seiko have been among the sponsors of the New York Marathon, while Miller Brewing and Playboy have helped sponsor major jazz festivals. Other companies devise their own events to sponsor: Virginia Slims has a women's tennis tournament, Kentucky Colonel sponsors gospel music concerts, and McDonald's has its All-American High School Band and its All-American High School Basketball Game. American corporations spend about $1 billion a year on such event marketing.[13]

Sponsorship of charity events is another tried-and-true public relations activity. A number of large corporations, including Chevrolet, AT&T, American Airlines, PepsiCo, and Eastman Kodak, helped enhance their identities by cosponsoring the Live Aid concert in 1985. "Helping the less fortunate is good business," says one of the organizers of Live Aid.[14]

FIGURE   18–8

Among companies that have used sports event sponsorship as a means of promotion is Beatrice, which sponsors America's Marathon in Chicago.

Publications

Materials for which public relations persons are responsible often include company publications; news releases and media kits; booklets, leaflets, pamphlets, brochures, manuals, and books; letters, inserts, and enclosures; annual reports; posters, bulletin boards, and exhibits; audiovisual materials; and speeches and position papers. We will discuss these tools of communication in more detail later in this chapter.

Research

Because the purpose of all public relations activities is to influence public opinion, it is vital that the public relations person be concerned with measuring and analyzing changes in public attitude and sentiment. One common form of public relations research is opinion sampling. During the Tylenol crisis, for instance, Johnson & Johnson performed continuous public opinion surveys so they could monitor the potential for reintroducing the product. Another method is to provide communications channels for feedback from consumers. Johnson & Johnson continues to use its 800 phone number to learn about public concerns. Other research techniques include focus groups, analysis of incoming mail, field reports, and panel studies.

Fund Raising and Membership Drives

A public relations person may be responsible for soliciting money for the organization or for a cause the organization deems worthwhile, such as the United Way or a political action committee (PAC).

Charitable organizations, labor unions, professional societies, trade associations, and other groups rely on membership fees or contributions as a primary means of support. Often considered the chief communicator of an organization, the public relations specialist must communicate to potential contributors or members the purposes and goals of the organization.

Public Speaking

Because public relations practitioners frequently have to represent their employers at special events, it's essential that they be able to speak well. They must be able to prepare speeches for company officials who may have to talk at stockholders meetings, conferences or conventions, and other such functions. Preparation for public speaking includes not only constructing speeches but arranging for speaking opportunities and developing answers for the most common questions a representative from the company might be asked. Similar preparations must be made for press conferences and interviews.

Public Relations Tools

The tools of communication at the PR person's disposal are many and varied—from news releases and photographs to audiovisual materials and even advertising.

News Releases and Media Kits

A *news release* is one or more typewritten sheets of information (usually 8½ by 11 inches) issued to generate publicity or shed light on a subject of interest (see Figure 18–9). Subjects may include the announcement of a new product, promotion of an executive, an unusual contest, landing of a major contract, or establishment of a scholarship fund, to name a few. For pointers to help in preparing news releases, see the Checklist for Writing News Releases.

A *media kit* is used to gain publicity at staged events such as press conferences or open houses. Such a kit includes a basic fact sheet detailing the event, a program for the event or a schedule of the activities, and a list of the participants including biographical data. In addition, the kit contains brochures prepared for the event, appropriate photos, a news story for the broadcast media, and news and feature stories for use by the print media.

FIGURE   18–9

Note in this example of a news release that the style follows that of a regular news story, complete with headline. Note also that information is provided on whom to contact at Johnson Wax for additional information.

Glade
Litter fresh

FOR IMMEDIATE RELEASE   CONTACT: Jamie Diamond
                                         -or-
                                         Julie O'Rourke
                                         Golin/Harris Communications
                                         312/836-7279

NEW BROCHURE IS THE CAT'S MEOW

Pet lovers can now get firsthand information on living compatibly with their pets in a free booklet from Glade® LitterFresh. "Coexisting With Your Two-Footed Friend," a brochure written from a cat's perspective, is full of tongue-in-cheek tips on "domesticating humans" and includes helpful hints for cat owners as well.

This delightful brochure gives "hints for humans" on topics such as preventing household "cat-astrophe," plants that may be poisonous to cats, and keeping the litter box smelling fresh. The "author" describes his first experience at the veterinarian, his favorite pastimes and the important bonds that are formed between pet and owner.

To obtain a free copy of "Coexisting With Your Two-Footed Friend," send a self-addressed, stamped business-size envelope to: Glade Litter Fresh, P.O. Box 11172, Chicago, IL 60610.

# # #

Johnson Wax 1525 Howe Street • Racine, WI 53403

Checklist for Writing News Releases

For a news release to be effective, it must be read and accepted by a busy editor who may have only a moment or two to glance at it. Here are some guidelines for producing successful press releases.

☐ Identify yourself. Include not only the name and address of the company (preferably on a letterhead) but also the name and number of whom to contact for further information.

☐ Provide a release date. Even if the item is marked "for immediate release," it is helpful to the editor to know when the item was sent.

☐ Use wide margins. Copy should be double-spaced for print media and triple-spaced for broadcast media.

☐ Keep it short. One page is the preferred length. If the release needs to be longer, don't break in the middle of a paragraph.

☐ Proof your copy. Typos and other mistakes will detract from your message.

☐ Update your mailing list. Editors change, offices move. Make sure you have the most recent information on the media you are informing.

☐ Don't call to see whether the editor has received your release. Editors don't like to be pressured into using PR materials; calling won't help your case.

☐ Don't ask for tear sheets. If the item gets published, don't expect the editor to take time out to send you a copy.

☐ Don't promise you'll advertise if the item is published. You will only offend the editor, who usually has nothing to do with the advertising department of the publication.

☐ Send a thank you. If an article is run, send the editor a note saying you appreciated the write-up.

Photography

Photographs of events, products in use, new equipment, or newly promoted executives can lend credence or interest to an otherwise dull news story. The photos must, however, be of good quality and are most effective if they need a minimum of explanation. Captions describing the subject of the photo and accurately identifying the people in the picture should be typed on plain white paper and attached to the back of the photo with a piece of tape.

Feature Articles

Many publications, particularly trade publications, will run feature articles about companies, products, or services. Such articles may be written by someone on the public relations staff, someone at the publication, or a third party (such as a free-lance business writer). Feature articles can be invaluable, since the company or product is given credibility by the publication.

Possible formats for features include case histories, illustrated how-to's (such as how to use the company's product), problem-solving scenarios (how the company's product was used by a customer to increase production, for example), and state-of-the-art updates. In addition, possible formats might include roundups of what's happening in a specific industry and editorials (such as a speech or essay by a company executive on a current issue).[15]

FIGURE   18–10

Rather than being dry summaries of financial data, many annual reports are elaborate, full-color booklets with photos, illustrations, and sophisticated designs.

Printed Materials

Printed materials are used extensively in public relations. They may take the form of brochures or pamphlets about the company, letters to customers, inserts or enclosures that accompany bills, the annual report to stockholders (see Figure 18–10), other types of reports, or house organs.

A *house organ* (or house publication) is a company publication. Internal house publications are for employees only. External house publications may go to company-connected persons (customers, stockholders, and dealers) or to the public. They may take the form of a newsletter, a tabloid newspaper, or a magazine (see Figure 18–11). Their purpose is to promote goodwill, increase sales, or mold public opinion. A well-produced house organ can do a great deal to get employees or customers to feel they know the people who make up a company. However, writing, printing, and distributing a house organ can be expensive.

Posters, Exhibits, and Bulletin Boards

Posters can be used internally to stress safety, security, reduction of waste, and courtesy. Externally, they can be used to impart product information or other news of interest to the consumer.

Exhibits can give a history of the organization, present new products,

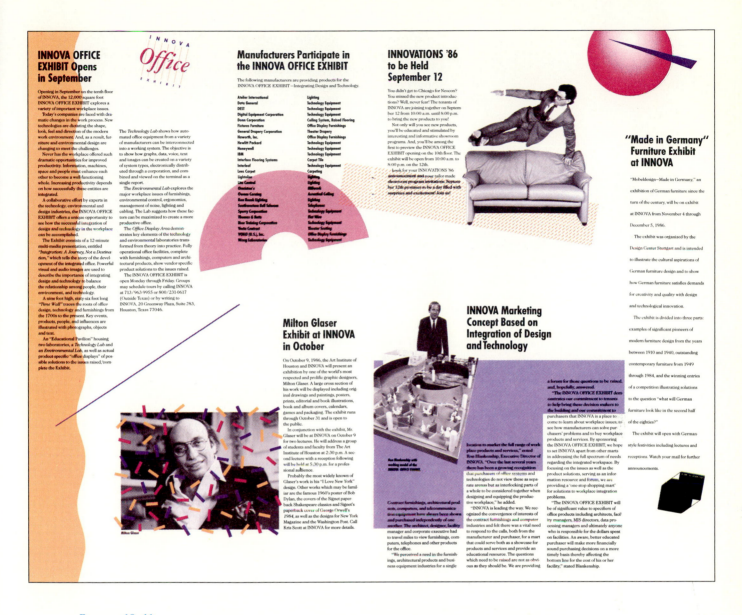

Figure   18–11

House organs circulated outside the company can be an important public relations tool, worth the extra expense for strong editorial content, glitzy design, and high production values.

show how products are made, or tell about future plans of the organization. Exhibits are often prepared for local fairs, colleges and universities, and trade shows.

Bulletin boards can announce new equipment, meetings, promotions, new products, construction plans, and recreation news.

Audiovisual Materials

Audiovisual materials can take many forms, including slides, films, filmstrips, and videocassettes used for training, sales, or public relations. Considered a form of corporate advertising, "nontheatrical" or "sponsored" films (developed for public relations reasons) are furnished without charge to movie theaters, organizations, and special groups, particularly schools and colleges. Examples of these films are "Why Man Creates," produced for Kaiser Aluminum, and Mobil Oil Corporation's "A Fable," starring the famous French mime Marcel Marceau.

Among the newer audiovisual media being used by public relations departments are "video press releases"—news or feature stories prepared by a company and offered free to TV stations. The TV stations may use the whole video story or just parts. Electronic press releases are the subject of some controversy, since critics see them as subtle commercials or even as propaganda. Particularly at issue is stations running the stories without disclosing that they came from a public relations firm and were not developed by the station's news staff.[16]

NONCOMMERCIAL ADVERTISING

In 1987, a coalition of more than 200 ad agencies plus other companies in the communications business launched an all-out attack on drug abuse. Calling itself the Media-Advertising Partnership for a Drug-Free America, the coalition set as its goal a "fundamental reshaping of social attitudes about illegal drug usage." The three-year, $1.5 billion program entails the efforts of ad agencies across the country, each developing components of the campaign at their own cost.

The antidrug program includes hundreds of newspaper and magazine ads as well as more than 50 different TV and radio commercials. The space and time allotted for the ads have all been donated by the media, amounting to an estimated $500 million value per year. Similarly, most of the creative and production personnel have donated their services.

The wide variety of ads have been created to reach specific target groups. Some are aimed at cocaine users, some at marijuana smokers; some are aimed at parents, some at children. Most present hard-hitting messages about the dangers of drug abuse, depicting drug use as a sure route to the hospital or the cemetery. In a TV ad targeted toward teenagers who smoke marijuana, for example, the N. W. Ayer agency suggests that pot smokers are subjecting themselves to risk of physical and mental health problems (see Figure 18–12). Other TV ads compare the brain on drugs to

FIGURE   18–12

One in a series of TV commercials produced by the Partnership for a Drug-Free America, this particular ad is aimed at teens who smoke marijuana. The ad was created by the N. W. Ayer agency, one of 200 agencies participating in the public service campaign.

(MUSIC UP AND UNDER)

ANNCR: (VO) Young people from all walks of life have volunteered to take part in a frightening experiment.

They are allowing their brains to be altered.

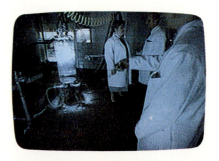

Altered to induce paranoia, heart malfunction, memory loss, even early senility.

(MUSIC)

Unfortunately, this is not an experiment.

It's what slowly happens to you when you keep smoking pot.

No one has to alter your brain.

You've already volunteered to do it to yourself.

an egg in a frying pan or show dead rats that have succumbed to cocaine abuse. Print ads have also emphasized the dangers of cocaine abuse, including a series of ads developed by DDB/Needham Worldwide that enumerate cocaine's effects (see Figure 18–13). In addition, ads have been developed that speak to parents who use drugs ("If parents stop, kids won't start"), to women tempted to use cocaine ("What to do if he hands you a line"), and to parents who have put off talking to their children about drugs ("If everybody says it can't happen to their kids, then whose kids is it happening to?").

The effort is being billed as the "largest and most ambitious private-sector, voluntary peacetime effort ever undertaken." Believing that America cannot succeed as a drug culture and that advertising can "denormalize" drug use, the organization wants nothing less than a drug-free America.

Of course, not all public service advertising is done on such a massive scale. We see advertisements daily for intangible humanitarian social

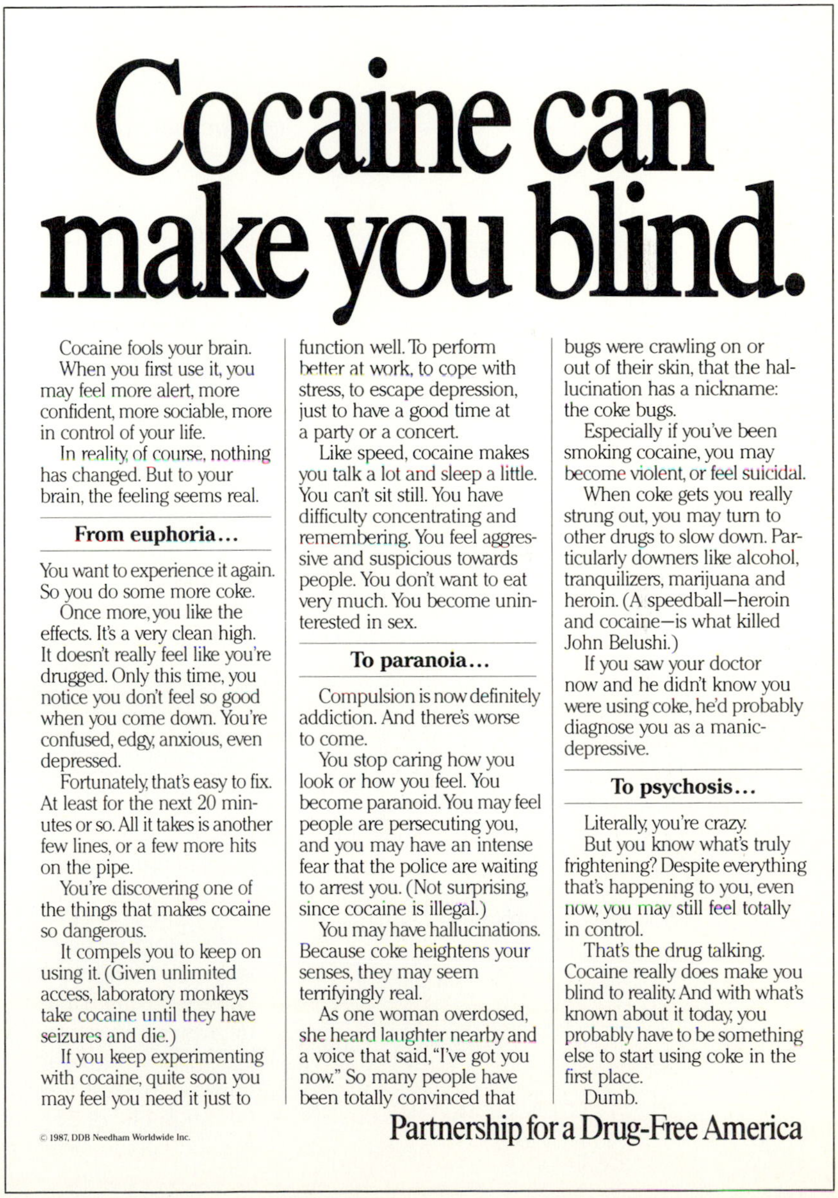

FIGURE 18–13

Many of the print ads produced by the Partnership for a Drug-Free America have focused on the drugs that adults are most likely to abuse, especially cocaine and crack. This is one in a series of magazine ads created by DDB Needham Worldwide.

Cocaine can make you blind.

Cocaine fools your brain.

When you first use it, you may feel more alert, more confident, more sociable, more in control of your life.

In reality, of course, nothing has changed. But to your brain, the feeling seems real.

From euphoria...

You want to experience it again. So you do some more coke.

Once more, you like the effects. It's a very clean high. It doesn't really feel like you're drugged. Only this time, you notice you don't feel so good when you come down. You're confused, edgy, anxious, even depressed.

Fortunately, that's easy to fix. At least for the next 20 minutes or so. All it takes is another few lines, or a few more hits on the pipe.

You're discovering one of the things that makes cocaine so dangerous.

It compels you to keep on using it. (Given unlimited access, laboratory monkeys take cocaine until they have seizures and die.)

If you keep experimenting with cocaine, quite soon you may feel you need it just to

function well. To perform better at work, to cope with stress, to escape depression, just to have a good time at a party or a concert.

Like speed, cocaine makes you talk a lot and sleep a little. You can't sit still. You have difficulty concentrating and remembering. You feel aggressive and suspicious towards people. You don't want to eat very much. You become uninterested in sex.

To paranoia...

Compulsion is now definitely addiction. And there's worse to come.

You stop caring how you look or how you feel. You become paranoid. You may feel people are persecuting you, and you may have an intense fear that the police are waiting to arrest you. (Not surprising, since cocaine is illegal.)

You may have hallucinations. Because coke heightens your senses, they may seem terrifyingly real.

As one woman overdosed, she heard laughter nearby and a voice that said, "I've got you now." So many people have been totally convinced that

bugs were crawling on or out of their skin, that the hallucination has a nickname: the coke bugs.

Especially if you've been smoking cocaine, you may become violent, or feel suicidal.

When coke gets you really strung out, you may turn to other drugs to slow down. Particularly downers like alcohol, tranquilizers, marijuana and heroin. (A speedball—heroin and cocaine—is what killed John Belushi.)

If you saw your doctor now and he didn't know you were using coke, he'd probably diagnose you as a manic-depressive.

To psychosis...

Literally, you're crazy.

But you know what's truly frightening? Despite everything that's happening to you, even now, you may still feel totally in control.

That's the drug talking. Cocaine really does make you blind to reality. And with what's known about it today, you probably have to be something else to start using coke in the first place.

Dumb.

Partnership for a Drug-Free America

causes (Red Cross), political ideas or issues (Sierra Club), philosophical or religious positions (Church of Latter Day Saints), or particular attitudes and viewpoints (labor unions). In most cases, these advertisements are created and placed by nonprofit organizations, and the product they are advertising is their particular mission in life, be it politics, welfare, religion, conservation, health, art, happiness, or love. Such advertising in general is called *noncommercial advertising*. Commercial firms use advertising to stimulate sales by persuading people to buy. In noncommercial advertising, the most similar objective would be to stimulate donations or persuade people to vote one way or another.

Objectives of Noncommercial Advertising

Whereas commercial advertisers may want to stimulate brand loyalty, the noncommercial objective might be to bring attention to a social cause. If a specific commercial objective for a new shampoo is to change people's *buying* habits, the related noncommercial objective for an energy conservation program might be to change people's *activity* habits, such as turning off the lights. Figure 18–14 lists a variety of related specific objectives for commercial and noncommercial advertisers.

Types of Noncommercial Advertising

One way to categorize the various types of noncommercial advertising is by the organizations that use them. For instance, advertising is used by churches, schools, universities, hospitals, charitable organizations, and many other *nonbusiness institutions*. We also see advertising by *associations,* such as labor groups, professional organizations, and trade and civic associations. In addition, we witness millions of dollars worth of advertising placed by *government organizations:* the Army, Navy, Marine Corps, Postal Service, Social Security Administration, Internal Revenue Service, and various state chambers of commerce. In addition, in election years we are bombarded with all sorts of political advertising that qualifies as noncommercial.

FIGURE 18–14	Comparison of advertising objectives
Product advertising	**Noncommercial advertising**
Create store traffic.	Stimulate inquiries for information.
Stimulate brand loyalty.	Popularize social cause.
Change buying habits.	Change activity habits.
Increase product use.	Decrease waste of resources.
Communicate product features.	Communicate political viewpoint.
Improve product image.	Improve public attitude.
Inform public of new product.	Inform public of new cure.
Remind people to buy again.	Remind people to give again.

It's like being grounded for eighteen years.

Having a baby when you're a teenager can do more than just take away your freedom, it can take away your dreams.

The Children's Defense Fund.

Among organizations that use public service advertising are those wanting to prevent child abuse, diseases such as AIDS, drunk driving, and unwanted teenage pregnancy.

Advertising by Nonbusiness Institutions

"It's a matter of life and breath" is a familiar line to anyone who watches television. Every year the American Lung Association places an estimated $10 million worth of advertising on television and radio, in newspapers and magazines, and on outdoor and transit media. All this space and time are donated as a public service by the media involved. Such donated ads are termed *public service announcements (PSAs)* (see Figure 18–15). In its effort to educate the public about the damaging effects of smoking or the early warning signs of emphysema, lung cancer, and tuberculosis, the Lung Association joins a long list of nonbusiness institutions that use noncommercial advertising to achieve their objectives.

The objectives of nonbusiness institution advertising are varied. The Foster Parents Plan uses massive doses of advertising to ask readers to adopt children from the country of their choice by spending $22 per month for their care and support. The Church of the Nazarene advertises "Our church can be your home" to build an image of a church in which members can be personally involved. The National Council on Alcoholism wants children and teenagers to say no to drinking "And say yes to life."

Not all nonbusiness institution advertising is donated. If you live in a large metropolitan area and want to place an ad for your favorite charitable organization, you will probably be charged a special nonprofit institution rate by your local city newspaper. Newspaper, radio, and TV advertising departments are besieged by requests from local churches, charity groups, hospital guilds, and other do-good social organizations to donate advertising space and time to these "favorite causes." Out of self-defense, they are forced to charge for most local nonbusiness institution advertising (see Figure 18–16).

On the national level, the number of organizations seeking to place free public service ads on the three major networks grew 45 percent between 1979 and 1987. CBS, for example received 6,000 ideas, storyboards, and finished PSAs in 1987 and ran about 24,000 spots.[17] In light of this tough competition, sponsors of PSAs are having to become more sophisticated in their campaigns, supplying ads that are more likely to be aired.

Many nonprofit organizations and religious groups are turning to paid advertising to get their message to the public.

We know Someone whose Sunday morning priority never involved an all-you-can-eat brunch.

We invite you to sit down with Him next Sunday morning and get to know Him better.

Morgan Park Presbyterian Church
11056 S. Longwood Drive
Chicago, IL 60643   779-3355

FIGURE   18–17

The California Almond Growers Association has been highly successful with its series of TV commercials

featuring real almond growers up to their waists in nuts: "Just one can a week, that's all we ask."

GROWER #1: Hi, we're almond growers. Now is the perfect time of the year to have, or attend, an almond roast.

We've put everything you'll need right here in this handy almond roast kit. This kit is so complete, the almonds are already roasted.

GROWER #2: The forks are not included.

ANNCR (VO): Blue Diamond Almonds. Roasted and six other great tastes.

GROWER #1: Don't you wish you had some right now?

GROUP: We wish you had some right now.

GROWER #1: A can a week, that's all we ask.

Advertising by Nonprofit Business Associations

Business, professional, trade, labor, farm, and civic associations all use advertising to achieve their individual objectives. Frequently, the purpose of advertising by nonprofit business associations is simply to create goodwill and a positive impression of the association's members by spotlighting the good works of individuals within the organization. Labor unions, for example, use advertising to inform the public how important union workers are to the nation's economy. By stimulating goodwill in this way, they are potentially able to enlist more public support during labor disputes.

Other business association ads plug the product that all members produce: dairy products, California raisins, Florida grapefruit, and so on (see Figure 18–17). The Beef Industry Council, for example, has been running TV commercials featuring James Garner and Cybill Shepherd talking about how they like "real food for real people." The objective of these associations' advertising is sometimes indirectly, and often directly, commercial.

Finally, some business association ads are devoted to specific causes that are in some way linked to their business. Thus, the Magazine Publishers' Association has sponsored a $26 million campaign against adult illiteracy.

Advertising by Government Organizations

Government bureaus and departments have been highly effective advertising and propaganda practitioners for years. In its effort to communicate with the voters, the government employs advertising agencies and public relations firms and maintains well-staffed, in-house graphics, communications, and press-relations departments.

Much government advertising announces the availability of such valu-

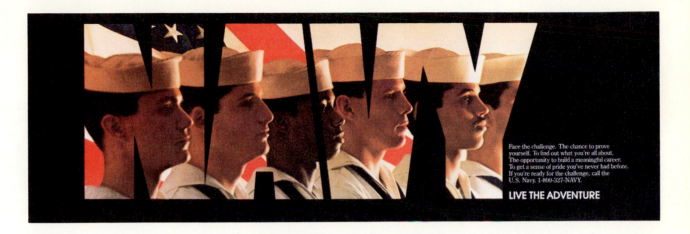

Face the challenge. The chance to prove
yourself. To find out what you're all about.
The opportunity to build a meaningful career.
To get a sense of pride you've never had before.
If you're ready for the challenge, call the
U.S. Navy. 1-800-327-NAVY.

LIVE THE ADVENTURE

FIGURE   18–18

Each branch of the armed services has its own recruitment campaign.

able government services as consumer assistance, welfare aid, or career guidance. Similarly, great effort is given to instructing people on how to use government services correctly. The U.S. Postal Service, for example, has maintained a strong campaign for years to persuade and remind citizens to use ZIP codes and also to mail early for Christmas.

The 1970s also saw the Army, Navy, Air Force, and Marine Corps enter the paid advertising arena. With the end of the Selective Service draft came the need to recruit for the all-volunteer force, so the military pursued aggressive advertising techniques to draw young men and women to its ranks.

The Army, which has the biggest advertising budget, relies heavily on paid television commercials. The Navy, with its "Live the Adventure" and, more recently, "You are tomorrow, You are the Navy" campaign themes, also utilizes paid spots when their budget, which is less than one-fifth the size of the Army's, permits. The Navy also spends about $300,000 a year on producing PSAs and receives some $3 million worth of free media placement (see Figure 18–18).

Advertising by the individual armed services is supplemented by the Defense Department's joint military ad program, which has a $20 million annual budget channeled primarily into paid TV commercials that mention all services together.[18]

Beyond the national level, many state governments use advertising to attract new businesses, tourists, or workers to aid their economy. Ohio advertises the availability of skilled workers and placement services for industrial concerns; North Carolina beckons with a rural, homey image; and California offers a wide variety of attractions.

The Advertising Council

Most of the national PSAs you see on television have been placed there by the Advertising Council, a private, nonprofit organization that links non-commercial campaign sponsors with ad agencies. The sponsors pay for production costs, while the ad agencies donate their creative services.

The Ad Council's policy today is basically the same as when it began during World War II: "Accept no subsidy from government and remain independent of it. Conduct campaigns of service to the nation at large,

FIGURE   18–19

The Ad Council has produced many
memorable campaigns, including
this one.

avoiding regional, sectarian, or special-interest drives of all kinds. Remain
nonpartisan and nonpolitical. Conduct the Council on a voluntary basis.
Accept no project that does not lend itself to the advertising method. Accept no campaign with a commercial interest unless the public interest is
obviously overriding."

Among familiar campaigns created by the Ad Council are those for the
United Negro College Fund ("A mind is a terrible thing to waste"), child
abuse prevention ("Help destroy a family tradition"), the United Way ("It
works for all of us"), crime prevention ("Take a bite out of crime"), and
the U.S. Department of Transportation ("Drinking and driving can kill a
friendship") (see Figure 18–19). The Ad Council's two longest-running
campaigns are those for the American Red Cross and forest fire prevention. According to the Ad Council's research, the number of forest fires has
been cut in half over the life of the Smoky the Bear campaign.[19] The
council is currently playing a role in overseeing the Media-Advertising
Partnership for a Drug-Free America effort.

Summary

Public relations is a process used to manage an organization's relationships with its various publics. These publics include the organization's employees, customers, stockholders, and competitors as well as the general populace. Many public relations activities involve media communications. However, unlike product advertising, these are not normally openly sponsored or paid for.

To help create a favorable reputation in the marketplace, companies use various types of corporate advertising, including public relations advertising, corporate (or institutional) advertising, corporate identity advertising, and recruitment advertising.

The many types of public relations activities include publicity and press agentry, public affairs and lobbying, promotion and special-events management, publication prepara- tion, research, fund-raising and membership drives, and public speaking.

The tools used in public relations are many and varied. They include news releases and media kits, photography, feature articles, all sorts of printed materials, posters and exhibits, and audiovisual materials. Noncommercial advertising includes advertising by nonbusiness institutions (churches, schools, charitable organizations), associations (labor groups, business and professional organizations), and governments.

To assist with important causes, members of the advertising profession formed the Advertising Council during World War II. During its more than four decades of operation, the Ad Council has conducted memorable campaigns for such projects as U.S. Savings Bonds and the United Way.

Questions for Review and Discussion

1. How does the definition of public relations differ from the definition of advertising?
2. How is the perspective of advertising practitioners different from that of PR professionals?
3. What are the various types of corporate advertising? Describe them.
4. In what ways is the line between product and corporate advertising beginning to blur?
5. What is the purpose of recruitment advertising? Why is it under the domain of corporate advertising and public relations?
6. If you handled the public relations for a utility company, what activities do you think would be the most useful?
7. What is the importance of establishing a crisis management plan? What types of companies are most likely to need such a plan?
8. What do you think are the most important public relations tools for a major corporation? Why?
9. What is the difference between commercial and noncommercial advertising?
10. What are the major types of noncommercial advertising? Which are more likely to receive free media space?

19

INTERNATIONAL ADVERTISING

In this text, we have discussed marketing and advertising planning, advertising creativity, and the advertising media. We have also offered some overall advertising perspectives and focused on certain special types of advertising. However, most of this discussion has been centered on advertising as it is practiced in the United States and Canada. The question arises, therefore, as to how applicable this discussion is to advertising in the rest of the world.

Companies advertising abroad face a variety of difficulties, as we will see in this chapter. To gain an understanding of these difficulties, consider the problems of advertising in the People's Republic of China. Although advertising was banned prior to 1978 as a "capitalist tool," the Chinese government has since then begun to welcome advertising both internally and by foreign companies. The vastness of the Chinese market—a quarter of the world's population—may seem like a gold mine to many U.S. companies, but there are some problems. For one thing, the discretionary income of most Chinese is minute. Major purchases of any product in China are made by "work units" who use foreign exchange credits to buy necessary goods. In many cases, the purchasing decisions by work groups can take up to a year. However, the purchasing power of individual Chinese consumers is increasing, and they are now able to buy some foreign products with local currency.

Another problem is lack of media time or space. China has an estimated 80 million television sets (most of them black-and-white), and 200 million to 600 million Chinese supposedly tune in regularly to CCTV, China's national television network.[1] The main vehicles for U.S. advertisers on CCTV are a weekly documentary program called "One World" and occasional CBS programs (CBS has an agreement to supply 64 hours of programming a year in exchange for five minutes of advertising per program). Foreign companies have found that sponsoring televised sports events is a good form of advertising, since signs and logos on display in the stadium get plenty of screen time.

The Chinese are voracious readers, which makes print advertising an attractive medium. But placing an ad in the 6 million circulation *People's Daily* may require a six-month wait, since only 10 percent of the paper is devoted to advertising. (Advertisers can speed up the process a bit if they're willing to pay even more than the staggeringly high standard rates.) Fortunately, a number of other publications take advertising, including an English-language daily newspaper, several business publications, and numerous magazines, including Chinese editions of *Scientific American, Discover,* and other American scientific and technical periodicals. Billboards are a popular alternative to broadcast and print media for reaching a mass audience.

In addition to difficulties with reaching buyers and with the media, American advertisers in China have problems with producing an appropriate message. Much of current foreign advertising in China is corporate, simply trying to create an image of the company among the Chinese people in anticipation of greater spending power in the future. However, specific product advertising is also being done for such items as soft drinks, coffee, cigarettes, laundry detergents, and razor blades. Gillette, affectionately known as the "Old Man" blade because of the picture of the Company's founder, King C. Gillette, on its Blue Blade package, has resumed advertising in China for the first time since before World War II (see Figure 19–1).

Creating messages for the Chinese audiences requires a great deal of care, since even the slightest detail can potentially damage the ad campaign. For example, when Coca-Cola first went into the Chinese market, the brand name was translated into Chinese characters that sounded like "Coca-Cola" but read as "Bite the wax tadpole." To remedy the problem, the company chose new characters that mean "Tasty, evoking happiness"—the Chinese equivalent of "Have a Coke and Smile."[2] As another example, Procter & Gamble had to change a TV spot for Tide in which a mother was shown folding bath towels when it was discovered that the Chinese don't use big bath towels and don't know what they are.

Foreign advertisers must also be careful that written translations be in the appropriate Chinese characters (the characters used in Taiwan, for example, are not the same as those used in the People's Republic) and that spoken ads be in the appropriate dialect (speakers from Hong Kong use a dialect that most Chinese will not understand).

In general, foreign advertisers wanting to reach the Chinese audience are advised to emphasize facts and figures in their ads and to forget about gimmicks. The Chinese want to know how a particular product will help them achieve the Four Modernizations (industry, agriculture, science, and technology), not whether the product has sex appeal.

The example of advertising in the People's Republic of China illustrates the potential problems faced by all advertisers who contemplate entering a foreign market with a different culture, language, tastes, and system of values. In this chapter, we look at the growing appeal of selling products and services to an international market and the challenges this type of advertising faces.

FIGURE   19–1

Gillette promotes its razors and blades in Chinese TV ads by emphasizing the company's "lead in shaving products technology" around the world and the fact that Gillette is "continuously innovating their products." This type of approach is designed to appeal to the Chinese interest in technology; a commercial showing a woman fondling a man's freshly shaved face would not go over with this audience.

MUSIC: (Space, with appropriate high-lighting sound effects.)

VO: In 1901, American Gillette Company invented the world's first safety razor; then it introduced the Gillette Blue Blade . . . which was widely welcomed by the world!

Since then, Gillette always takes the lead in shaving products technology, continuously innovating and improving their products, and invented this . . . pivoting-head . . .

SFX: Lightning

twin-blade razor . . .

SFX: Mnemonic sound emphasis.

that follows the contour of the face, gives smoother, and more comfortable shaves!

Gillette shaving products—leading the technological way!

FIGURE   19–2

This Italian TV commercial demonstrates some of the style and wit that characterize many European ads. In it, a beautiful woman and her handsome companion are enjoying a lavish meal. She smiles at him seductively, not knowing about the pieces of food stuck between her teeth. The solution? "Samurai. The world-famous toothpick."

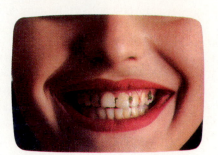

GROWTH AND STATUS OF INTERNATIONAL ADVERTISING

As U.S. companies entered world markets after World War II, consumption of American products grew tremendously. Today, U.S. advertising expenditures account for over 50 percent of the world total. However, in the last 15 years, expenditures by other countries have increased even more rapidly than American expenditures due to improved economic conditions and a desire to grow outward. As national economies have expanded and personal incomes have increased, the use of advertising has also increased (see Figure 19–2).

Advertising in one form or another is practiced in every country of the world. Actual figures are not available, but recent estimates of worldwide advertising expenditures outside the United States exceed $40 billion per year. The emphasis placed on advertising in individual countries, though, depends on the country's level of development and the national attitude toward promotion. Generally, advertising expenditures are higher in countries where personal income is higher.

Today, advertising is used worldwide to sell ideas, policies, and attitudes as well as products. The Communist countries, including China, once condemned advertising as an evil of capitalism and still frequently express their theory of advertising as economic waste. But now even the Soviet Union is beginning to admit the benefits of advertising in developing planned economies. (See Ad Lab 19-A.)

Certainly, as a communication form, international advertising is contributing to the shrinking of the world. And one benefit is increased understanding among people as foreign products, values, and ideas are introduced to new markets. As technology progresses, international advertising will continue to flourish. As a creative director for Ogilvy & Mather in Paris has said, "Nous n'avons pas mal de budgets," which can be loosely translated as "We're not hurting for business."

MANAGING INTERNATIONAL ADVERTISING

Imagine you are the advertising manager of an American company planning to market its products abroad. You are aware that in the foreign market you may have to use a different creative strategy. You will be speaking to a new audience with a different system of values, a different environment, and probably a different language. Your foreign customers will

AD LAB 19-A   Advertising in the Soviet Union

Whoever would have thought that more than 100 advertising agencies would be plying their trade today in the Soviet Union? Certainly not Marx! According to traditional Marxist-Leninist doctrine, advertising is a tool of capitalistic exploitation. It siphons off the surplus value belonging to underpaid workers and puts it in the hands of overpaid white-collar workers who are nonproductively employed writing jingles.

Yet there has been an impressive growth of advertising agencies in the Soviet Union. The initial argument was that these agencies exist to develop advertising to support Soviet goods in export markets where it is necessary to compete against Western and other nations. But many advertisements also appear in print and broadcast media reaching Russian consumers. Another rationale was established at the 1957 Prague Conference of Advertising Workers of Socialist Countries, which made three points as to how advertising was to be used: (1) to educate people's tastes, develop their requirements, and thus actively form demand; (2) to help the consumer by providing information about the most rational means of consumption; and (3) to help to raise the culture of trade. Furthermore, Soviet advertising is to be ideological, truthful, concrete, and functional. The Soviets claim that their advertising does not indulge in devices used in the West. Their ads will not use celebrities—only experts will be used to promote a product. They will not use mood advertising. They will not create brand differentiation when none exists.

Experts think that the main use of Soviet advertising is to help industry move products that come into excess supply when the Soviets do not want to do the logical thing, cut prices.

Laboratory Application

How does the Pepsi-Cola advertisement illustrated succeed in satisfying Soviet policies on the use of advertising?

---

probably have different purchasing abilities, different purchasing habits, and different motivations than the average American. The media you generally use may be unavailable or ineffective in a foreign market. As a result of these and other factors, your advertising may have to be different, too.

You also face another problem. How will the advertising be managed and physically produced? Will your in-house advertising department do it? Will your domestic advertising agency do it? Or will you have to set up a foreign advertising department or hire a foreign advertising agency?

To answer these questions, we need to ask two more: How does the company structure its foreign marketing operations? Within that structure, what are the most economical and effective means to conduct advertising activities?

Foreign Marketing Structures

Just as in domestic situations, managing advertising in foreign markets depends to a great extent on the company's foreign marketing structure. Does the company intend to market its products internationally, multinationally, or globally? What is the difference?

Marketers frequently use the terms *international* and *multinational* interchangeably, especially since the introduction of the newest term, *global*. However, the difference between all these terms relates to the degree of involvement in foreign markets.

International Structure

Many firms get into international marketing simply by exporting the products they already produce. As companies get more involved, though, they may contract for manufacture, enter into joint ventures, or invest in some other foreign operations, such as sales offices, warehouses, and plants or manufacturing subsidiaries. However, these operations tend to be operated and viewed from headquarters as "foreign marketing divisions."

At first, foreign marketing activities are controlled and operated from the home office, but as the complexities of foreign operations expand, the pressure to decentralize grows. For years, the 3M Company has operated internationally with autonomous units in various countries. Similarly, the foreign operations of many large retailers are structured internationally, with local management responsible for its own product lines, its own marketing operations, and its own profits and losses.

Multinational Structure

As companies grow and prosper, they may become true multinational corporations with direct investment in several countries and a view toward business based on choices available anywhere in the world.[3] Their essence is full and integrated participation in world markets. Foreign sales, a large part of the multinational's activities, usually grow faster than domestic sales.[4] Well-known American multinationals today include Warner-Lambert, 3M, Ford, IBM, ITT, H. J. Heinz, Gillette, and Eastman Kodak (see Figure 19–3), all of whom earn over a third of their total sales abroad. The top 25 U.S. multinational corporations derive 43 percent of their revenues and 53 percent of their profits from overseas. There are also many well-known foreign-based multinationals such as Nestlé, Royal Dutch Shell, Nissan, Philips, Unilever (Lever Bros.), and Mitsubishi.

A multinational's marketing activities are typically characterized by strong centralized control and coordination. Companies like Coca-Cola are called multinational organizations because they sell in many countries, they have strong direction and coordination from one central headquarters, and they have a standardized product line and a uniform marketing structure. The chairman of Coca-Cola called this strategy, "One sight, one sound, one sell" (see Figure 19–4).

The Global Marketing Debate

According to Harvard marketing professor Theodore Levitt, Coca-Cola is actually the perfect example of a *global* brand. Levitt envisions total worldwide product, marketing, and advertising standardization. In his book *The*

FIGURE   19–3

Eastman-Kodak is a multinational corporation whose distinctively packaged films can be found in just about every country in the world. This is one of a series of arresting ads that appeared in Swiss magazines. The headline reads "It sees color better."

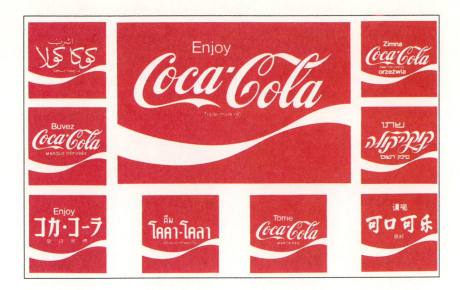

1.		8.
2.		7.
3.	4.	5.	6.

1. Arabic   5. Spanish
2. French   6. Chinese
3. Japanese 7. Hebrew
4. Thai   8. Polish

FIGURE   19–4

Coca-Cola's trademark varies from country to country, but the overall look is retained through use of similar letterforms and style, even with different alphabets.

Marketing Imagination, Levitt theorizes that companies that do not become true global marketers, with world brands like Coca-Cola, will surely perish on the rough seas of what he calls the new global realities.

He argues that, thanks to cheap air travel and new telecommunications technology, the world is becoming a common marketplace in which people have the same tastes and desires and want the same products and lifestyles no matter where they live. This, he believes, allows for world-standardized products at low prices sold the same way around the world.[5]

Levitt's admittedly exaggerated theory has stirred up a lot of dust on Madison Avenue. In fact, several large multinationals have dumped their multiple agency relationships in favor of one worldwide agency. Meanwhile, the large international agencies have raced to prove they are each best equipped to handle global brands.

Nevertheless, many feel that Levitt's approach is all wet. Tony Brignull, vice chairman of Collett Dickenson Pearce & Partners, has stated, "Great advertising and global advertising are a contradiction in terms." He says, "Global advertising can only succeed if there is a global consumer. There isn't."[6] Concurring is Bill Tragos, chairman of Ted Bates Worldwide: "I believe advertising is a mirror of the country. The most effective ads communicate the gestures, nuances, and idiosyncracies of that place. The case for advertising uniformity is thus rarely justifiable."[7]

Philip Geier, chairman and chief executive officer of the Interpublic Group of Companies, Inc., points out that a separation must be made between global products and global advertising. He notes that globalization is a reality, that we are seeing more and more global companies and brands each year, and that many media are becoming global as well. But whereas products and services can be standardized on a worldwide basis, advertising executions cannot. "Advertising, to be effective, is in and of a culture," Geier says. "While consumers and companies and brands and communications technologies and ad agencies are becoming global, advertising itself must be local."[8] To underscore his case, he points out that the archetypal global product, Coca-Cola, is indeed advertised differently in different countries. Its "General Assembly" commercial, featuring a thousand children from around the world singing a song of hope at St. George's Hall in Liverpool, is available in 21 languages. For each of the 16

FIGURE   19–5

Coca-Cola's commercial "General Assembly" shows 1,000 teenagers from around the world joining together in a song of hope for tomorrow. There are actually 16 different versions, each beginning with a teen from the target country singing in his or her own language "I am the future of the world, I am the hope of my nation. . . . " Coke's ad agency in each country has the freedom to edit the commercial for its market so that more can be shown of the teens from that country.

GIRL SOLO: *I am the future of the world.*

I am the hope of my nation.

I am tomorrow's people.

I am the new inspiration and we've got a song to sing to you.

GROUP: (Under solo) *Ooh.*

GIRL SOLO: *We've got a message to bring to you.*

Please let there be for you and for me a tomorrow . . .

ALL TOGETHER: *Tomorrow.*

If we all can agree, there'll be sweet harmony tomorrow, tomorrow . . .

GROUP: (Under solo) *Aah.*

GIRL SOLO: *And we all will be there, Coca-Cola to share . . .*

GROUP: *Coca-Cola to share . . .*

GIRL SOLO: *Feelings so real and so true.*

GROUP: *Feelings so real and so . . .*

ALL TOGETHER: *True.*

GIRL SOLO: *Promise us tomorrow and we'll build a better world for you.*

GROUP: *Build a better world for you.*

countries in which the ad is run, the commercial has been edited to focus on children from that country (see Figure 19–5).

Grey Advertising has suggested three questions companies should ask themselves before attempting a global strategy:

1. Has the market developed in the same way from country to country? (The continued popularity of clotheslines in Europe has discouraged the demand for fabric softening products used in dryers.)
2. Are the consumer targets similar in different nations? (Canon found that while Japanese consumers like sophisticated, high-tech products, many consumers in the United States are fearful of complex technological products.)
3. Do consumers share the same wants and needs around the world? (Tang was successfully positioned as an orange juice substitute in the United States. But in France, where people never drink orange juice at breakfast, Tang had to be repositioned as a daytime refreshment, as shown in Figure 19–6.)

Grey suggests that a negative answer to any one of these questions indicates that a global marketing attempt will probably fail.[9]

In reality, the direction a company takes depends on many variables, among them the breadth of its product line, the availability of qualified management, the ability to use similar marketing techniques, and the

GOÛT FRAMBOISE SUR
FRÉQUENCE TANG.

TANG TOUT PRÊT.
TOUT NOUVEAU. TOUT BON.

FIGURE   19–6

This French ad for Tang positions it as a refreshing beverage rather than a breakfast drink. The youngster is floating along listening to his Tang "radio," which plays "raspberry taste on the Tang frequency." The copy below says Tang is "All ready. All new. All good."

economic impact of particular marketing strategies. It goes without saying, though, that the decision to operate internationally, multinationally, or even globally has a strong influence on the advertising decisions that follow.

Agency Selection

To conduct foreign advertising activities, several types of agencies are available to advertisers. For example, when Mexico's oldest bank, Banamex (Banco Nacional de Mexico), wanted to promote an awareness of its bank to Americans, it selected a local California agency to handle its advertising in the border areas from California to Texas. Banamex already had an agency in Mexico City and another for its worldwide banking services in New York. But it knew that most of its potential American customers lived within several hundred miles of the border. So Banamex selected an agency that understood the local market and local media and could give local service.

Similarly, American companies have a wide choice available based on their needs. They might use an international or global agency, a local foreign agency, an export agency, their normal domestic agency, or their house agency.

International and Global Agencies

Even though Banco Nacional de Mexico selected a local foreign agency (from their perspective), many international advertisers find that only a large agency with offices or affiliates in many markets can do the job adequately.

As advertising has grown around the world, many of the larger American general agencies have established themselves in major foreign mar-

FIGURE 19–7	Top 10 agencies by worldwide billings	
Rank	**Agency**	**Worldwide billings 1987***
1	Young & Rubicam	4,905.71
2	Saatchi & Saatchi Advertising	4,609.44
3	Backer Spielvogel Bates	4,068.70
4	BBDO Worldwide	3,664.50
5	Ogilvy & Mather Worldwide	3,663.80
6	McCann-Erickson Worldwide	3,418.50
7	J. Walter Thompson Co.	3,221.80
8	Lintas: Worldwide	2,787.20
9	DDB Needham Worldwide	2,581.55
10	D'Arcy Masius Benton & Bowles	2,494.28

*In millions of dollars.

kets and shifted their focus from domestic advertising to international and even global marketing. Figure 19–7 lists the 10 largest American agencies in terms of worldwide billings.

Companies planning large multinational campaigns often deal with a large international agency. The agency's overseas offices are usually staffed with multilingual, multinational personnel in both creative and administrative positions. Each country in which they operate can be treated as a distinct market, or the campaign can be coordinated and controlled under one roof for a series of countries or markets. Another strategy used by some companies is to use different international agencies for different regions of the world. For example, Rolex uses J. Walter Thompson in 25 countries, Pimo in the Middle East, Ogilvy and Mather for Southeast Asia, and Intercom in South Africa.

People in other lands have distinct attitudes, buying habits, business systems, and laws. Therefore, it is seldom practical to translate American advertising into the other languages. A foreign-based staff of advertising specialists can transform and adapt basic concepts and strategies and add the verbal and visual elements that appeal to local consumers.

Local Foreign Agencies

As Banamex did, American companies may also select local foreign agencies to coordinate their activities in particular markets. The foreign agencies, of course, boast local talent who understand local attitudes and customers as well as the local media (see Figure 19–8).

For many consumer products, a local agency in key markets might work out best. However, using a variety of local agencies in different markets can make it hard to coordinate a multinational advertising program.

Companies planning a multinational campaign with all activities centralized and coordinated from one location usually benefit by using one international advertising agency. But if a company plans a program that must

FIGURE   19–8

Welch Foods used Tokyo agency
Nihon Keizaisha Advertising to develop a Japanese print campaign for
Welch's fruit juices. The ad stresses
the high quality of the juices and
their health advantages. In the ad
copy, a mother describes her child's
active life and tells how drinking
Welch's juices is good for his health.

promote differently to various markets, it may be better off appointing
local agencies that understand the needs of those particular markets. Companies normally choose those agencies that correspond in size to their
service needs. In this way, clients don't pay for unnecessary services.

Export Agencies

Some agencies specialize in creating ads for American companies engaged
in international advertising. These *export agencies* may work in association
with domestic agencies on particular accounts in addition to having clients
of their own for whom they perform this same specialty.

   Export agencies usually specialize in preparing ads for particular language groups or geographic areas and employ native-born writers in those
languages and specialists familiar with foreign media opportunities.

Domestic and House Agencies

Many small companies exporting their products abroad simply ask their
existing domestic agency to prepare their first ads for them. And in fact,
many domestic agencies handle the job quite adequately. Some domestic
agencies are affiliated with foreign shops where they may receive media
counsel, translation services, or production assistance. Other domestic
agencies join international *agency networks* to receive similar services in
foreign markets as well as specialized services such as arranging local
press conferences or trade fairs. However, one of the problems with using
a domestic agency is that it may not have experience in international

advertising; and advertising abroad, as we will see in the next section, can offer many unique and difficult challenges.

Some companies, especially industrial firms, choose to use their company advertising departments or house agencies for their foreign advertising. While these may lack the creativity and objectivity of outside agencies, in-house services have to please only one master and can involve themselves completely in the company's projects. Moreover, house agencies may possess greater technical knowledge of the subtle differences between certain industrial products and may offer certain economies over outside professional help. Again, though, they may lack expertise in the pitfalls of foreign advertising, and that can prove far more costly in the long run.

CREATIVE STRATEGIES IN INTERNATIONAL ADVERTISING

As we have discussed throughout this text, creative strategy is determined by the mix of product concept, target audience, communications media, and advertising message. The same is true in international advertising, except that very often the creative strategy used in foreign markets is different from the strategy used in the United States. There are several reasons for this:

1. Influenced by their own particular environment, foreign markets reflect their local economy, social system, political structure, and degree of technological advancement. Therefore the *target audiences* for advertising messages may be different, too.

PEOPLE IN ADVERTISING

Keith Reinhard

Chairman and Chief Executive Officer
DDB Needham Harper Worldwide

"You deserve a break today." "Like a good neighbor, State Farm is there." These are but a few of the memorable ad campaigns created by Keith Reinhard in his years with Needham, Harper & Steers. He originally joined the agency as a writer in 1964 and worked his way up to creative director in 1969, executive vice president in 1976, president of the Chicago office in 1980, and chairman and chief executive officer in 1984.

The agency was renamed DDB Needham Harper Worldwide when Reinhard took the helm, reflecting his commitment to global advertising. Among the agency's international clients are McDonald's, Xerox, Sara Lee, and Wrigley.

Reinhard has definite opinions on what is global and what's not. He points out, for example, that while everyone's basic needs are global, the products and services that meet those needs are not. Similarly, human emotions are global, but the degree to which they are publicly

2. The media used in domestic markets may not be available, or as effective, in foreign markets. Or they may simply be uneconomical. Therefore, the *media strategy* may also have to be different.
3. Consumers may not want to buy, or be able to buy, the same products (or product concepts) as here. Their motivations may be different, and there may be considerable differences in the way they buy. Therefore, the advertising *message,* and possibly even the product concept, may have to be altered.

In this section we will discuss these three Ms of advertising strategy—markets (audiences), media, and messages—to understand their relationship to international advertising and the products marketed abroad.

Market Considerations

What is the difference between the foreign market for a product and an American market for the same product? The answer is simply environment. Any market is influenced by, and reflects, the market in which it exists. The environment in France is different from the environment in Japan. The environment in Brazil is different from the environment in Saudi Arabia. And sometimes, as in the case of Canada, environments vary widely within a single country.

Many countries have more than one official language. Canada and Norway have two; Belgium, three; and Switzerland, four. Canadians may be

expressed is not; and basic thought processes are global, but value systems are not.

"Creative people, given an understanding of what's global and what's not, can create powerful advertising that cuts across all lines," he emphasizes.

Reinhard is critical of much American advertising, particularly the "slice-of-life" or lifestyle commercial that doesn't really ring true. He feels that ads that place the product into people's lives and show how those consumers use the product won't translate well to other cultures. "We are going to have to get back to the product" if we want to produce truly global messages, he notes.

In Reinhard's view, the only thing holding back the growth of global advertising is the lack of global media: "Once the media are in place, the need will be there." He sees three basic scenarios emerging when global marketing hits its full stride: (1) global products and global brands—products that are identical in formula and appearance everywhere in the world; (2) local products and local brands—products sold only in particular countries or regions ("The global brands will create the opportunity for more local brands"); and (3) local products and global brands—local products marketed under a global brand name. According to Reinhard, all three scenarios "are compatible and they show signs of taking shape."

In addition to his work with Needham Harper Worldwide, Reinhard is active in the advertising industry, serving on the board of the American Association of Advertising Agencies and as chairman of the AAAA's Committee on the Image of Advertising. He is also on the board of the New York City Ballet and on the business committee of the Museum of Modern Art. Among the many awards he has received are the Advertising Person of the Year (Chicago Advertising Club, 1983) and Outstanding Advertising Agency Executive of 1983 (*The Gallagher Report*).

FIGURE   19–9

What is the difference between these two Canadian ads for Toyota? Both use the same creative concept and say approximately the same thing. But one is not a literal translation of the other. The French headline translates "The Toyota Corolla is renowned for surpassing requirements." In French that headline works, but in English it's not good copy. The reworded English headline, "A well-earned reputation for exceeding expectations," conveys the same meaning and is effective copy. Note the additional space required for the French copy. The layout of Canadian ads has to be flexible to accommodate these linguistic differences.

used to this situation (see Figure 19–9), but this presents an immediate problem to the American advertiser.

To communicate with the foreign consumer, the environment that affects that consumer must be considered. And language is only one consideration. In fact, several environments influence people's attitudes, tastes, and the way in which they think, speak, and feel. In addition to the social environments, of which language is a part, are the economic environments, the technological environments, and the political environments. We will consider each of these briefly.

Social Environments

In the United States and Canada, we live in a particular social environment based on our family background, our language, our education, our religion, the friends with whom we associate, and the style of life we enjoy. Similarly, the social environments in Italy, Indonesia, and Upper Volta are based on language, culture, literacy rate, religion, and lifestyle.

In the United States, which is basically a Protestant culture, we are encouraged and coaxed (through advertising) to keep our mouths clean, our breath fresh, and our teeth healthy by brushing after every meal. Part of the Protestant ethic is that "cleanliness is next to godliness." On the other hand, in many southern European countries, interfering with one's body by overindulging in toiletries and bathing has the opposite meaning. That type of behavior is considered vain, immoral, and improper.[10] So only one of three people brushes his or her teeth. If you are marketing a toothpaste brand, you might find it more acceptable to advertise your product as something modern and chic rather than as a cavity preventer.

Gillette International discovered that fact in the effort to market deodorants and ladies' shavers in Europe. In the first case, it found an inherited cultural resistance toward anything that impedes perspiration. People thought it unhealthy.[11] In the second case, Gillette learned that it didn't have to advertise women's razors because it could "personally give razors to all four Austrian women who wanted them."[12] The great majority of European women do not shave their legs or under their arms.

Economic Environments

The economic environment of a country refers to several things: the standard of living, the country's wealth and its distribution, the amount of business transacted, the principal occupations, and people's possessions. In countries where people earn less money, the demand for expensive products is lower. In some countries, the creative strategy for automobiles might be a target market approach to the small group of wealthy, upper-class people. In a country with a large middle class, it might be a mass-market approach positioning the car as a middle-class product.

In the early 1960s, Ernest Dichter divided the world into six groups of countries based on their attitudes toward automobile ownership.[13] In Figure 19–10 we have adapted his chart to reflect those foreign attitudes characteristic of the 1980s.

FIGURE   19–10   World attitudes toward automobile ownership

Group number	Title	Characteristics/attitudes
Group I	The almost classless society, contented countries	Primarily the Scandinavian countries. The middle class takes up the whole scale with very few rich or very few poor people. Automobiles are strictly utilitarian. Reliability and economy most important. No special status value.
Group II	The affluent countries	Includes the United States, West Germany, Switzerland, Holland, Canada, Japan. Large middle class, but still room at the top for financial aristocracy. People want individuality in their products. However, they seek quiet elegance and reliability rather than cars for show-off.
Group III	Countries in transition	Spain, Portugal, Argentina, Brazil, South Africa. Working class still exists, but they are struggling to join the comfortable middle class. Upper classes still exist with maids and Rolls-Royces but diminishing in size. Living standards are lower, but prestige still important. Cars are pampered extensions of one's personality. They represent major investments and for many people are living examples of their "success." Fluid, unstable markets. People hold onto their cars for 6 to 10 years. Style is important, though, and a desire for product adventure exists.
Group IV	Developing countries	Latin America, Middle East, India, China, Philippines, and so forth. Large groups of people emerging from extreme poverty. Large number of extremely rich people. Very small emerging middle class. Automobiles available to relatively small group. Expensive and considered a luxury. Taxed very highly. American cars considered the ideal. People show off with their cars. Small cars are a way to get started.
Group V	Primitive countries	Newly liberated countries of Africa and few remaining colonies. Very small group of wealthy businessmen, political leaders, and foreign advisors. Few cars sold are to government bureaucrats. No real car market yet.
Group VI	The new class society	Russia and satellite countries. Emerging class of bureaucrats who represent a new form of aristocracy. Everybody else in slow-moving, low middle class. Auto represents symbol of a new industrial society. Interest increasing in prestige cars. All the bourgeois symbols of capitalist countries are being copied—especially those of United States.

The country groups are based on the degree of social and economic development of a large middle class, which is the clue, Dichter believed, to appraising different cultures. Cultures range from the almost classless, contented Scandinavian countries to the primitive, underdeveloped countries. In the former, the automobile is viewed strictly as a functional vehicle, and luxury values are dismissed. In the latter, the automobile is a sign of wealth and position, and the few cars sold are usually driven by officials and bureaucrats.

Technological Environments

The degree to which a country has developed its technology will, of course, have a bearing on that country's economic and social conditions. But it will also affect the market for certain products and services within that country. For example, countries that don't manufacture computers might not be good markets for certain peripheral products like disk drives and microprocessors. On the other hand, they might be very good markets for low-priced, imported computers.

Political Environments

Some foreign governments exert far greater control over their citizens and businesses than the U.S. government does. For example, until fairly recently, there was virtually no market for American-made products in many of the Soviet bloc countries and China. They simply weren't allowed. The political environment, therefore, has a great effect on the potential market for certain products. Political control also extends to what products may or may not be advertised, what media may or may not be used, and what may or may not be said in commercials. In Scandinavia, for example, promoting a product as a sign of wealth and luxury is very risky. Due to the political environment of these socialist states, it is simply considered very bad taste.

The Importance of Marketing Research

In the domestic market, one of the reasons we conduct marketing research is to help us understand our domestic environments so we can make better advertising decisions. The same is true in international markets. Unfortunately, the research skills available in some developing countries are not comparable to those found in, say, the United States, Canada, Western Europe, Australia, Japan, Mexico, and Brazil.[14] For example, while some secondary research statistics may be available, they may be out-of-date or invalid and therefore unreliable. When studying secondary data developed outside of the firm, managers should ask the following questions:

1. Who collected these data and why?
2. What research techniques were employed?
3. Would the source of the data have any reason to bias the data?
4. When were the data collected? How old are the data?

The answers to all these questions are not always readily available, but the international advertising manager needs to exercise caution when presented with ''facts'' about foreign markets.[15]

Primary research conducted overseas is often more expensive than domestic research. But if a company is planning a worldwide or even just a Pan-European campaign, it is important to understand if the message will be viable in each of the individual markets. Companies that ignore an individual society's particular "design for living" risk the failure of their entire international marketing effort.[16]

Examples of mistakes made because of inadequate (or no) research abound. Pepsodent failed in Southeast Asia because it promised white teeth to people who considered black or yellow teeth to be symbols of prestige. Maxwell House was advertised as the "great American coffee" in Germany until General Foods discovered that Germans have little respect for American coffee. Germans were also unresponsive to ads for Imperial margarine in which crowns miraculously appeared on consumers' heads, since Germans pride themselves on their democracy and are offended by references to monarchy.

Marketers need more than just factual information about a particular country's culture. They need to develop an understanding and appreciation of the special nuances of different cultural traits and habits. This is difficult to achieve without living in a country and speaking its language. So the international marketer must depend on consultation with and cooperation of experienced, bilingual nationals with marketing backgrounds. And the marketer must be prepared to conduct primary research when necessary.

Mattel Toys International learned the lesson of conducting primary research the hard way. For years, Mattel tried to market the Barbie Doll in Japan and met with little success. The company finally granted the manufacturing license to a Japanese company, Takara. Takara did its own research and found that most Japanese girls and their parents considered Barbie's breasts to be too big and her legs too long. Takara modified the doll accordingly, including changing the blue eyes to brown, and proceeded to sell 2 million dolls in two years.

Performing original research, though, can be fraught with problems. First, it must be conducted in the language of the country being studied. But translating questionnaires can be very tricky. Second, customer information depends on people's willingness and ability to give researchers accurate information about their lives, opinions, and attitudes. This willingness is not always present. In many cultures, people view strangers with much greater suspicion and, correspondingly, have a greater desire to keep their personal life private. In Japan, for example, American companies have learned that mail surveys and telephone interviews simply don't work the way they do in the United States and that in many cases the personal interview (an expensive and time-consuming technique) is the most fruitful research method.[17] One of the major pitfalls in the interview method, however, is that Japanese respondents will invariably answer all yes or no questions with *hai* (meaning yes), which often simply indicates "Yes, I heard the question." When asked to amplify, the person may then go on to give a negative answer to the question.

Local conditions may further interfere with data collection. Tax evasion, for example, is common and tolerated in many Latin American countries. Under these conditions, an interviewer is not likely to get accurate information about income or even major appliance ownership. In fact, some interviewers have been suspected of being tax collectors in disguise and treated somewhat rudely.[18]

Regardless of all these problems, marketers should realize the importance of continuous research to the success of their efforts. Competent research personnel are available in all the developed countries; and in most of the developing nations, research assistance is available through local offices of major international research firms.

Media Considerations

It has been said that American advertising people can get used to the foreign styles of advertising faster than they can get used to foreign media. In the United States, if you want to promote a popular soft drink as a youthful, fun refresher, you use television. In several European countries, you are unable to. The same is true in many countries of Asia, South America, and Africa. Around the world, most broadcast media are owned and controlled by the government, and many governments do not allow commercials on radio or television.

In countries that do allow television advertising, you may have another problem. How many people own television sets, and who are they? In Europe, the vast majority of the population now own TVs. But in less-developed nations, TVs are found only among the upper-income groups. The result may be a different media mix in foreign markets than in the United States.

FIGURE   19–11

Countries vary in the types of advertising media available. A familiar sight in Paris, for example, is the advertising kiosk.

Types of Media Available

The same media we find here exist around the world. Virtually every country has radio, television, newspapers, magazines, outdoor, and direct mail. However, as we have pointed out, it may not always be legal to use all these media for advertising. In addition, cinema advertising is a very popular medium in many countries, as are some other selective specialty media that either do not exist here or are not widely used (see Figure 19–11).

Generally, the media available to the international advertiser can be categorized as either international media or local media, depending on the audience the particular medium serves.

International/Global Media Several large American publishers, including Time, Inc., McGraw-Hill, and Scientific American, circulate international editions of their magazines abroad. Likewise the *International Herald Tribune, The Wall Street Journal,* and London's *Financial Times* are circulated widely throughout Europe, the Middle East, and Asia. Usually written in English, these publications tend to be read by well-educated, upper-income consumers and are, therefore, the closest things to global media for reaching this audience. The *Reader's Digest,* which is no doubt the oldest global mass-audience medium, is distributed to 170 foreign countries. However, it is printed in the local language and tailored to each country and, therefore, is sometimes viewed more as a local medium.

Recently, the number of international trade or specialty publications has increased. *European Business* is published in Switzerland in English but is distributed throughout Europe. *Electronic Product News,* published in Belgium, is likewise printed in English and distributed throughout Europe.

In the past, international media have been limited primarily to newspapers and magazines. However, in 1985, Sky Channel, a satellite-to-cable Pan-European TV channel, was the first to offer advertisers an opportunity to reach over 2 million viewers throughout Europe. With English language programming and advertising, it is being eyed as an experiment to see whether global or pan-regional TV is a realistic possibility. As of 1987, the channel was still losing money (to the tune of $8.5 million in 1986) but was joined in the Pan-European marketplace by London-based Superchannel.

For decades, the Voice of America (VOA) and Radio Luxembourg have also served as examples of international broadcast media. In recent years, in an effort to correct the American trade deficit, the VOA has carried spots for American products on its broadcasts.

Local Media Due to the scarcity of effective international media, international advertisers are usually obliged to use the local media of the countries in which they are marketing. Foreign media cater to their own local national audience. This, of course, requires advertisers to produce advertisements in the language or languages of each country. In countries where there is more than one official language, some magazines produce two separate versions.

Overspill Media In addition to international and local media, a recent phenomenon is overspill media. These are actually local media that are inadvertently received by a substantial portion of the population of a neighboring country. For example, French media may spill over into Belgium and Switzerland. Media also overspill into countries that are short on publications, particularly specialized ones, in their own native languages. English and German media have a large circulation in Scandinavian countries. French and English media are popular in Spain, Italy, North Africa, and various Middle Eastern countries. And a wide variety of foreign language media are spilling into the Eastern bloc countries.

According to a study by the Foote, Cone & Belding advertising agency, multinational advertisers are now faced with the danger that these media may carry both international and local campaigns for the same product or service. This may confuse potential buyers. As this media area develops, local subsidiaries or distributors must coordinate their programs to avoid confusion. However, overspill media offer the potential to save money by regionalizing campaigns.

Within the broad categories of international, foreign, and overspill media are the various types of media we are familiar with in the United States—namely, radio, magazines, television, newspapers, and so on. The difference lies not so much in the availability of the media as in the coverage offered and the economics of using one medium over another.

Media Coverage

Whereas in the United States the broad middle class may be reached by any of innumerable media, this is not necessarily true in many foreign markets. For one thing, in some countries lower literacy rates and general education levels may restrict the coverage of mass press media. Furthermore, where income levels are low, ownership of televisions is similarly low. What occurs, therefore, is a natural segmentation of the market by the selective coverage of the various media.

In countries dominated by national newspapers, circulation may be primarily to upper-class, well-educated people. On the other hand, both Pepsi and Coca-Cola have reached the lower-income markets successfully through the use of radio, which enjoys almost universal ownership. Moreover, in some developing countries, many stores and bars allow their radios to blare into the street, making the sound available to any passersby. Auto manufacturers use television and magazines successfully to reach the upper class. And cinema advertising is used to reach whole urban populations where television ownership is low, since motion picture attendance there is still very high. However, there may be some selectivity by simply restricting the showing of commercials to upper-income areas or to lower-class theaters, depending on a particular product's market. (See the Checklist for International Media Planning.)

Checklist for International Media Planning

Basic Considerations (Who Does What?)

☐ What is the client's policy regarding supervision and placement of advertising? Make sure you know when, where, and to what degree client and/or client branch offices abroad want to get involved.

☐ Which client office is in charge of the campaign? North American headquarters or local office or both? Who else has to be consulted? In what areas (creative or media selection and so forth)?

☐ Is there a predetermined media mix to be used? Are there any "must" media? Can international as well as foreign media be used?

☐ Who arranges for translation of copy if foreign media are to be used?

☐ Client headquarters in North America.

☐ Client office in foreign country.

☐ Agency headquarters in North America.

☐ Foreign media rep in North America.

☐ Foreign media advertising department.

☐ Other.

☐ Who approves translated copy?

☐ Who checks on acceptability of ad copy in foreign country? Certain ads, especially those of financial character, sometimes need special approval by foreign government authorities.

☐ What is the advertising placement procedure?

☐ From agency branch office in foreign country, after consultation with agency headquarters, directly to foreign media.

☐ From North American agency to American-based foreign media rep to foreign media.

☐ From North American agency to American-based international media.

☐ From North American agency to affiliated agency abroad to foreign media.

☐ Other.

☐ What are the pros and cons of each of these approaches? Is a commission split with foreign agency branch or affiliate office necessary or can campaign be equally well placed directly from North America? Does the client save money by placing from North America to save certain ad taxes (in Belgium and the Netherlands, for instance)? Some publications quote local rates and higher U.S. dollar rates. In those instances, local ad placement results in a lower rate. Therefore, in what currency does client want to pay?

☐ Who receives checking copies?

☐ Will advance payment be made to avoid currency fluctuation possibilities? What will the finance folks in the back room have to say about your choice?

☐ Who bills whom? What currency is used? Who approves payment?

Budget Considerations

☐ Is budget predetermined by client?

☐ Is budget based on local branch or distributor recommendation?

☐ Is budget based on recommended media schedule of agency?

☐ Is budget based on relationship to sales in the foreign markets?

☐ What is the budget period?

☐ What is the budget breakdown for media, including ad taxes, sales promotion, translation, production and research costs?

Economics of Foreign Media

As pointed out in Chapter 1, a major purpose of advertising is to communicate with customers less expensively than through the use of personal selling. In many underdeveloped countries, however, this is not necessarily true. Colgate-Palmolive found that in countries where labor is extremely cheap, it could send people around with baskets of samples twice a year.[19] This kind of personal contact is impossible in the United States,

---

☐ What are the tie-ins with local distributors, if any?

Market Considerations

☐ What is your geographical target area?

  ☐ Africa and Middle East.

  ☐ Asia, including Australasia.

  ☐ Europe, including U.S.S.R.

  ☐ Latin America.

  ☐ North America.

☐ What are the major market factors in these areas?

  ☐ Local competition.

  ☐ GNP growth over past four years and expected future growth.

  ☐ Relationship of country's imports to total GNP in percent.

  ☐ Membership of country in a common market or free trade association.

  ☐ Literacy rate.

  ☐ Attitude toward North American products or services.

  ☐ Social and religious customs.

☐ What is your basic target audience?

  ☐ Management executives across the board in business and industry.

  ☐ Managers and buyers in certain businesses.

  ☐ Military and government officials.

  ☐ Consumers; potential buyers of foreign market goods.

Media Considerations

☐ Availability of media to cover market: Are the desired media available in the particular area (e.g., business magazines, news magazines, trade and professional magazines, women's magazines, business and financial newspapers, TV, radio)?

☐ Foreign media and/or international media: Should the campaign be in the press and language of a particular country, or should it be a combination of the two types?

☐ What media does the competition use?

☐ Does medium fit?

  ☐ Optimum audience quality and quantity.

  ☐ Desired image, editorial content, and design.

  ☐ Suitable paper and color availability.

  ☐ Justifiable rates and CPM (do not forget taxes on advertising, which can vary by medium).

  ☐ Discount availability.

  ☐ Type of circulation audit.

  ☐ Availability of special issues or editorial tie-ins.

☐ What are the closing dates at North American rep and at the publication headquarters abroad?

☐ What is the agency commission (when placed locally abroad at the agency, commission is sometimes less than when placed in North America)?

☐ For how long are contracted rates protected?

☐ Does the publication have a North American representative to help with media evaluation and actual advertising placement?

ENROLE SUA NAMORADA. DÊ TOALHAS ARTEX.

Figure   19–12

Outdoor advertising is very popular in Brazil. This billboard tells viewers, "Wrap your loved one in Artex towels."

where Colgate uses advertising to do the entire consumer selling job.

In North America, legislation and the cost of labor have inhibited the growth of outdoor advertising. In most foreign markets, though, outdoor enjoys far greater coverage, since it costs less to have people paint the signs, and there is often less government restriction about placement of billboards (see Figure 19–12). In Mexico, for example, almost every street seems to have a "Disfrute Coca-Cola" sign. In Nigeria, billboards with the slogan "Guiness gives you power" next to the bulging biceps of an African arm kept Guiness stout ale the best seller for many years—despite an 80 percent illiteracy rate.

Of course, just as economics determines which medium is used, economics also determines the availability of media. We have just seen this in the case of outdoor advertising. Likewise, one factor that inhibits the growth of TV is its cost. This same factor, however, causes some countries to consider opening TV to commercial use to help pay for it. We may expect, therefore, that as more countries allow commercial broadcasts, and as international satellite channels begin to gain a foothold, TV will proliferate. On the other hand, as labor rates increase, we may see reductions in the number of press and outdoor media available in foreign markets. Likewise, the use of personal selling and sales promotion may similarly become more restricted due to the costs involved.

Message Considerations

Developing the message strategy for foreign markets calls for numerous considerations. Advertising appeals must be based on the consumer's purchasing abilities, habits, and motivations. The whole question of language must be decided. And the issue of what can be legally advertised in each region will have to be resolved. We will consider each of these here.

Purchasing Characteristics in Foreign Markets

Advertising messages must be geared to the characteristics of the market that can afford to buy the product. In low-income countries where only the wealthy can afford to purchase automobiles, ads that stress a car's luxury qualities would logically find an interested audience. Where middle-class consumers exist in large numbers, though, a message stressing the functional or economical aspects of the car will probably be more effective. Just as in the domestic market, many of these middle-class consumers are hard pressed financially, and they welcome economy choices.

How purchases are made and *when* they are normally made are also important considerations. Most important, though, is the question of *who* makes the buying decision. In North America and Europe, for instance, the balance of power between marriage partners is fairly equal. In Latin American countries, though, the wife often has a clearly subordinate role in major decision making. In the United States, children may even have a strong influencing voice (especially in the selection of breakfast cereals, snacks, toothpastes, and fast-food chains), but this is much less common in foreign markets.

These differences, though, vary from country to country and product to product, and the advertiser must consider the issues carefully before creating ads or buying media. One company introduced a new detergent in Holland by advertising solely in one magazine read by children under 10. A miniature sports car was offered as an in-pack premium. The success of the introduction indicated that, in this case at least, the children did have a strong influencing voice in the buying decision.

Consumer Motives and Appeals

In some countries, certain appeals are logically more significant than others, and care must be taken to understand the particular personal motivations inherent to each market. Swiss women, for example, live under a social code that stresses hard work in the home. Advertising American dishwashers as labor- and time-saving devices only created guilt feelings. What proved more successful to the spic-and-span Swiss housewife was to communicate the sanitizing qualities of automatic dishwashers.[20]

Selling a deodorant in Japan is difficult because most Japanese don't think they have body odor—and they don't, due to their low-protein diets. A commercial for Feel Free deodorant, therefore, positioned the product as youthful, chic, and convenient rather than as a solution to odor problems. This was accomplished by simply showing a young girl, on her way out for a date, who suddenly remembers her deodorant and uses it quickly before leaving.

National pride is also an important consideration for foreign advertisers. Many lower-income, less-developed nations envy American wealth and technology at the same time they fear and profess disdain for it. Thus, a strange paradox exists. On one hand, they respect and desire American products. On the other hand, they may harbor hidden inferiority feelings and resent what they perceive as American influence and power. Many American advertisers, therefore, toe a careful line to avoid aggravating this understandable national sensitivity in certain foreign markets.

Another important consideration to keep in mind is social roles in particular cultures. In Saudi Arabia, for example, husbands traditionally make decisions concerning the purchase of durable goods such as cameras and cars (women are not allowed to drive), whereas women decide on nondurable items such as food, toiletries, clothing, and household furnishings. Shopping is a social affair, and Saudi Arabians almost always shop in groups. Thus, an ad campaign that stresses peer approval might be more appropriate than one emphasizing individual growth or self-indulgence.[21]

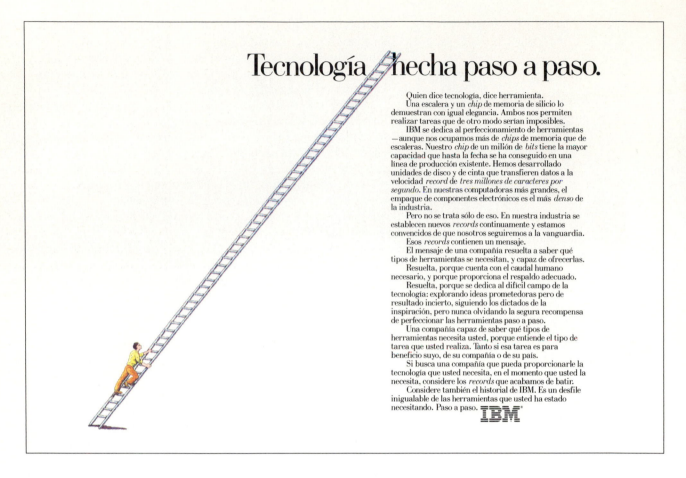

FIGURE   19–13

IBM's ads for business publications vary little from country to country.

In business and industrial advertising, differences in taste and attitude may not be so apparent or important as in the marketing of consumer products. The businessperson's problems are fairly universal, as are the appeals (see Figure 19–13). The difference in approach comes down to the economics of the area. Professor Levitt's global marketing disciples would probably echo this sentiment.

On the other hand, Paul Aass, the president of MarkCom, a Belgian advertising agency, says, "The only thing the European countries and Europe's submarkets have in common is the fact that they are different." This is certainly true when it comes to language.

The Question of Language and Campaign Transfer

In Western Europe, at least 15 different languages and more than twice as many different dialects are spoken today. This presents a problem of potentially enormous magnitude to the American marketer entering Europe for the first time. A similar problem exists in Asia, to a lesser extent in South America, and to an even greater extent in Africa.

For years, a controversy has raged in international advertising circles over the transferability of campaigns. On one hand are those who feel it is too expensive to create a unique campaign for each national group. They believe it is acceptable to take one campaign and simply translate it into the necessary languages (see Figure 19–14). This group has now been aided and abetted by the globalists who believe consumers have become

FIGURE   19–14

In global advertising, a single basic ad is used and is translated into the languages of the various countries where it will be run. This global campaign for BankAmerica Travelers Cheques, with the slogan "Known the World Over," ran simultaneously in 27 countries.

so homogeneous that product and advertising standardization is possible around the world.

On the other hand, some feel this approach never works out right and that the only way to ensure success is to create a special campaign for each market. In addition, a few feel that both these solutions are uneconomical and unnecessary. They simply run their ads in English and don't concern themselves with the problems of local markets.

Obviously, no one of these solutions is always correct, and the problem of transferability of campaigns remains unsolved. Marketers probably don't have to create different campaigns for every country of the world. Moreover, the hard facts of life are that the economics of various promotional strategies must be weighed against the anticipated promotional objectives. Thus, each situation must be looked at individually. Identifying the target audience and knowing the cultural preferences in that market are basic. However, even if we are talking to similar audiences and detailing similar product characteristics so that we could use the same basic campaign, we still have the translation problem.

One well-known story concerns Exxon Corporation's attempts to market gasoline in Japan under its old brand name, Enco. Exxon couldn't understand why sales were so low. It sent a team of executives to Japan to investigate the situation. After an exhaustive study of Japanese driving habits, gasoline consumption figures, and service station sites, the executives decided to interview Japanese consumers. The first person they could find who spoke English gave them a very simple answer to their question. He told them that in Japanese *Enco* means "stalled car."

A similar event occurred when General Motors introduced their new Chevrolet Nova to Puerto Rico. In Spanish, *no va* means "it doesn't go." Parker Pen attempted to translate its American billboard campaign in Latin America: "You'll never be embarrassed with a Parker Pen." Unfortunately, Parker was embarrassed when it discovered too late that in Spanish *embarazada* means "pregnant."

English is spoken in the United States, Canada, England, Australia, and South Africa, but among these five countries are wide variances of vocabulary, word usage, and syntax. Similarly, the difference in the French spoken in France, Canada, Vietnam, and even Belgium may be as great as the difference in English spoken by a high-brow Britisher and a sharecropper from Tennessee. Even within single countries there is wide variation in the language used. In the Japanese language, five "gears" are used, from haughty and condescending to fawning and servile, depending on the speaker's and the listener's respective stations in life. The Japanese translator must know when to change gears.

Suffice it to say certain basic rules must be followed when translating advertisements:

1. The translator must also be an effective copywriter. Just because the translator speaks a foreign language doesn't mean he or she can write advertising copy effectively. The logic of this should be clear. All of us can speak English, yet relatively few of us are good writers, and even fewer are good copywriters. Still, advertisers too often fall into the trap

FIGURE 19–15   Advertising regulations in selected countries of Western Europe

Country	General regulations		Limitations on
	Comparative advertising	Advertising to children	Alcoholic beverages
Austria	Banned if denigrating.	Direct appeal forbidden.	None.
Belgium	Banned if denigrating.	Banned by law in all media.	Ads for absinthe drinks banned.
Denmark	Minor restrictions.	None.	None.
Finland	None.	None.	Banned on TV.
France	Banned.	Prebroadcast screening of commercials.	Hard liquor banned on all media, others on radio and TV.
Germany	Banned.	Voluntary for TV and radio.	Voluntary limits by industry.
Italy	Direct comparisons banned; indirect OK if substantiated.	Cannot show children eating.	Some restrictions on TV ads.
Netherlands	OK if comparison is fair, detailed.	Voluntary restraints.	Voluntary restraints on TV and radio.
Sweden	Banned if denigrating.	Ban on showing children in danger.	Voluntary control on ads for wine and hard liquor.
Switzerland	None.	None.	Banned in all media.
United Kingdom	Banned if denigrating.	Voluntary rules designed to protect children.	No commercials before 9 P.M.

of simply having a translation service rewrite their advertisements in the foreign language—rarely a good solution.

2. The translator must have an understanding of the product, its features, and its market. It is always better to use a translator who is a specialist rather than a generalist for particular products or markets.

3. The translator should translate into his or her native tongue and should be a native resident of the country where the ad will appear. Only in this way can the advertiser be certain the translator has a current understanding of the country's social attitudes, culture, and idiomatic use of the language.

4. The English copy submitted to the translator should be easily translatable. Double meanings and idiomatic expressions, which make English

specific products		Media regulations	
Tobacco	**Drugs and medicine**	**Restricted or banned media**	**Limitations on commercials**
Voluntary ban on TV ads.	Ads need approval of government.	None.	Maximum length of 30 seconds.
Cigarette ads banned in cinema, TV, and radio.	Banned by law in all general media.	No commercial TV or radio.	Not applicable.
Voluntary control over cigarette ads.	Banned in all general media.	No commercial TV or radio.	Not applicable.
Banned on TV and media directed at youth.	Voluntary control over copy.	No domestic radio.	No television commercials on certain days.
Cigarettes banned on TV and radio.	Copy clearance needed.	Total receipts from one advertiser limited to 8 percent of total TV.	Blocks, or groups, of commercials only (no spots).
Banned on TV and radio.	Banned in all media.	None.	TV commercials between 6 and 8 P.M., none on Sunday.
All tobacco banned in all media.	Copy clearance needed.	None.	Sold in broadcast packages.
Voluntary restraints on TV and radio.	None.	None.	No more than two TV commercials per week per product.
Banned in all media.	Prescription drug ads banned.	No commercial TV or radio.	Not applicable.
Banned in all media.	Banned in all media.	No commercial radio.	No more than two TV commercials per week per product.
Cigarette ads banned on TV and radio.	Voluntary control.	None on major media.	None.

such an interesting language for advertising, are usually not translatable. They only make the translator's job more difficult.

Finally, remember the Italian proverb, "Tradutori, traditori" (Translators are traitors). There is perhaps no greater insult to a national market than to misuse its language. The translation must be accurate, but it must also be good copy.

English is rapidly becoming the universal language used for corporate advertising campaigns directed to international businesspeople. However, some industrial firms, completely baffled by the translation problem, have printed their technical literature and brochures in English. This kind of poor solution may incite nationalistic feelings against the company. Worse yet, this approach automatically limits a product's use to those people who can read and understand technical English. It also greatly increases the probability of misunderstanding and thus additional ill will toward the company.

Legal Restraints on International Advertisers

No discussion of the creative message in international advertising is complete without some consideration of the problem of restrictions imposed by foreign cultures and governments on what may or may not be said, shown, or done in an ad. Some restrictions are legal ones; others are moral and ethical ones that determine the boundaries of good taste. A sampling of the regulations on advertising in Western European countries is offered in Figure 19–15.

Advertising claims are strongly regulated in many countries, and superlatives of any kind are frequently outlawed. In Germany, for example, superlatives may be used only if they are scientifically provable, and no reference may be made to a competitive product. In the United States, the seller is often in a more favorable position than the buyer. In many European countries, just the reverse is true. Many countries bar practices such as two-for-the-price-of-one offers, coupons, premiums, one-cent sales, box-top gimmicks, and free tie-in offers.

These restrictions can cause problems in international advertising. McCann-Erickson once tried to translate the old Coca-Cola slogan, "Refreshes you best," into foreign languages. In the United States, this slogan would merely be considered harmless exaggeration. In Germany, however, it was outside the boundaries of the law. The agency, therefore, substituted "Das erfrischt richtig," or "Refreshes you right."

In Europe, "official sales periods" are the only times price cuts may be advertised. These periods vary from country to country, but control is very strict and fines are extremely high. And before a sale ad may be published, it frequently must be approved by a government-controlled agency.

In Saudi Arabia, alcohol and pork are forbidden and therefore cannot be advertised. The ban on pork advertising even extends to images of pigs, such as stuffed toys and piggy banks. Saudi Arabia also bans pictures of anything sacred, such as photos of Mecca or cross symbols. Ads in this country must also show only people with Arabic appearance, and no women's faces can be shown. Furthermore, all TV and radio advertising is banned.[22]

The only solution to these and the myriad other legal problems encountered by international advertisers is to have a good local lawyer on retainer who is familiar with advertising laws.

Summary

Since the end of World War II, advertising has grown worldwide. As economic conditions and the standard of living have improved in foreign lands, the use of advertising has also increased. However, the status of advertising varies from country to country depending on local attitudes toward promotional activities in general.

The way advertising activities are managed in foreign markets depends on the marketing structure and strategy of the firm and on the availability of qualified talent. Some companies are organized to market internationally; others, multinationally; and some, globally. Depending on the needs of their international advertising program, these companies may elect to use large American or foreign-based international agencies, local foreign agencies, export agencies, their normal domestic agencies, or even an in-house agency.

In overseas markets, companies often find it necessary to use different creative strategies than they use in their domestic campaigns. For one thing, foreign markets are characterized by different social, economic, technological, and political environments. And in some developing countries, market research may not be as reliable as it is in North America, thereby making it more difficult to understand local customs, culture, and attitudes.

Second, the media in foreign markets are different. Some media may not be available, others may not be as effective, and still others may not be economical.

Third, advertising messages often must be different. They must be based on the purchasing ability, habits, and motivations of the consumer in the particular foreign market being approached. And of course, they usually must be communicated in the consumer's language.

Finally, advertisers must be ever mindful of foreign cultural and governmental restrictions on what may or may not be said, shown, or done in an ad. Some restrictions are legal ones; others are moral and ethical ones that determine the boundaries of good taste.

Questions for Review and Discussion

1. Why do companies advertise in China if the Chinese people are unable to purchase the advertised products?
2. What is the difference between an international firm and a multinational firm? How does this affect the way their advertising is managed?
3. What are the pros and cons of the global advertising debate? How would you evaluate each side's position?
4. What kinds of products lend themselves best to global advertising? What kinds are more likely to require individual variations?
5. What factors differentiate American markets from foreign markets?
6. How would a country's political environment affect the local market for television sets or other major appliances? How would that affect advertising used for these products?
7. What do you suppose is the primary advertising medium in most foreign countries? Why?
8. What major factors influence the creation of advertising messages in foreign markets?
9. What are "official sales periods," and why are they important?
10. Overall, what is the basic difference between advertising in the United States or Canada and advertising in overseas markets?

APPENDIX A

MARKETING PLAN OUTLINE

DATE:

COMPANY NAME:

TITLE OR PRODUCT:

Encapsulation, for executive review, of entire marketing plan in no more than two or three pages.

I. Executive Summary

    A. Summary of situation analysis
    B. Summary of marketing objectives
    C. Summary of marketing strategies
    D. Budget summary

Complete statement of where the organization is today and how it got there.

What business the organization is in and characteristics of the industry as a whole. Information available from industry trade publications, trade association newsletters, consumer business press, Department of Commerce publications.

II. Situation Analysis

    A. The industry
        1. Definition of industry and company business
        2. History of industry
            a. Technological advances
            b. Trends
        3. Growth patterns within industry
            a. Demand curve
            b. Per capita consumption
            c. Growth potential
        4. Characteristics of industry
            a. Distribution patterns and traditional channels
            b. Regulation and control within industry
            c. Typical promotional activity
            d. Geographical characteristics
            e. Profit patterns

All relevant information on the company and its capabilities, opportunities, and/or problems. Information may be found in annual reports, sales records, warranty card records, customer correspondence, sales staff reports.

    B. The company
        1. Brief history
        2. Scope of business
        3. Current size, growth, profitability
        4. Reputation
        5. Competence in various areas
            a. Strengths
            b. Weaknesses

Complete description and all relevant information on the product/service mix, sales, and the strengths and weaknesses therein. See sales literature, sales reports, dealer correspondence, and so forth.

    C. The product/service
        1. The product story
            a. Development and history
            b. Stage of product life cycle
                (1) Introduction
                (2) Growth
                (3) Maturity
                (4) Decline
            c. Quality factors
            d. Design considerations
            e. Goods classification

       (1) Consumer or industrial good
       (2) Durable, nondurable good or service
       (3) Convenience, shopping, or specialty good
       (4) Package good, hard good, soft good, service
   f. Packaging
   g. Price structure
   h. Uses
       (1) Primary
       (2) Secondary
       (3) Potential
   i. Image and reputation
   j. Product/service strengths
   k. Product/service weaknesses
2. Product sales features
   a. Differentiating factors
       (1) Perceptible, imperceptible, or induced
       (2) Exclusive or nonexclusive
   b. Position in mind of customer
   c. Advantages and disadvantages (customer perception)
3. Product research and development
   a. Technological breakthroughs
   b. Improvements planned
   c. Technical or service problems
4. Sales history
   a. Sales and cost of sales
       (1) By product/service
       (2) By model
       (3) By territory
       (4) By market
   b. Profit history for same factors
5. Share of market
   a. Industry sales by market
   b. Market share in dollars and units
   c. Market potential and trends
D. The market
1. Definition and location of market
   a. Identified market segments
       (1) Past
       (2) Potential
   b. Market needs, desires
   c. Characteristics of market
       (1) Geographic
       (2) Demographic
       (3) Psychographic
       (4) Behavioristic
   d. Typical buying patterns
       (1) Purchase patterns
       (2) Heavy users/light users
       (3) Frequency of purchase
   e. Buying influences on market
2. Definition of our customers
   a. Present, past, and future
   b. Characteristics
       (1) Shared characteristics with rest of market

All relevant information about the people or organizations that comprise the current and prospective market for the firm's offerings. See market research reports, consumer/business press, trade publications, Census of Manufacturers, trade association reports.

Complete information about the competition, the competitive environment, and the opportunities or challenges presented by current or prospective competitors. See SEC Form 10-Ks, consumer/business press articles, *Moody's Industrial Manual,* Standard & Poor's reports, Dun & Bradstreet reports, *Thomas Register of American Corporations.*

Complete discussion of how the firm's products/services are distributed and sold, what channels are available, and characteristics of channel members. See dealer and distributor correspondence, sales staff reports, advertising reports, trade publication articles.

Background and rationale for firm's pricing policies and strategies, discussion of alternative options. Study sales reports, channel-member correspondence, customer correspondence, competitive information.

(2) Characteristics unique to our customers
c. What they like about us or our product
d. What they don't like
3. Consumer appeals
   a. Past advertising appeals
      (1) What has worked
      (2) What has not worked, why
   b. Possible future appeals
4. Results of research studies about market and customers
E. The competition
   1. Identification of competitors
      a. Primary competitors
      b. Secondary competitors
      c. Product/service descriptions
      d. Growth and size of competitors
      e. Share of market held by competitors
   2. Strengths of competition
      a. Product quality
      b. Sales features
      c. Price, distribution, promotion
   3. Weaknesses of competition
      a. Product features
      b. Consumer attitude
      c. Price, distribution, promotion
   4. Marketing activities of competition
      a. Product positioning
      b. Pricing strategies
      c. Distribution
      d. Sales force
      e. Advertising, publicity
      f. Estimated budgets
F. Distribution strategies
   1. Type of distribution network used
      a. History of development
      b. Trends
   2. Evaluation of how distribution is accomplished
   3. Description and evaluation of channel members
   4. Promotional relationship with channel members
      a. Trade advertising and allowances
      b. Co-op advertising
      c. Use of promotion by dealer or middlemen
      d. Point-of-purchase displays, literature
      e. Dealer incentive programs
G. Pricing policies
   1. Price history
      a. Trends
      b. Affordability
      c. Competition
   2. Price objectives and strategies in past
      a. Management attitudes
      b. Buyer attitudes
      c. Channel attitudes

All relevant data concerning the firm's personal sales efforts and effectiveness as well as complete discussion of the firm's use of advertising, public relations, and sales promotion programs. Examine sales reports, advertising reports, articles in *Advertising Age, Marketing Communications,* etc., in-house data on advertising, sales, and training.

H. Promotion strategies
   1. Past promotion policy
      a. Personal versus nonpersonal selling
         (1) Use of sales force
         (2) Use of advertising, public relations, sales promotion
      b. Successes and failures of past policy
   2. Sales force
      a. Size
      b. Scope
      c. Ability/training
      d. Cost per sale
   3. Advertising programs
      a. Successes and failures
      b. Strategies, themes, campaigns
      c. Appeals, positionings, and so on
      d. Expenditures
         (1) Past budgets
         (2) Method of allocation
         (3) Competitor budgets
         (4) Trend

Enumeration of those environmental factors that may be beyond the firm's immediate control but impact on the firm's business efforts. See government reports and announcements, consumer/business press, trade association articles.

I. Environmental factors
   1. Economy
      a. Current economic status
      b. Business outlook and economic forecasts
   2. Political situation
   3. Societal concerns
   4. Technological influences

Recitation of relevant attitudes and directives of management as they pertain to the firm's marketing and advertising efforts. Information available from corporate business plan, management interviews, internal memos and directives.

J. Corporate objectives and strategies
   1. Profitability
      a. Sales revenue
      b. Cost reductions
   2. Return on investment
   3. Stock price
   4. Shareholder equity
   5. Community image
   6. New product development
   7. Technological leadership
   8. Mergers and/or acquisitions

Enumeration or summary of those problems considered most serious to the firm's marketing success.

K. Potential marketing problems

Summary of those opportunities which offer the greatest potential for the firm's success.

L. Potential marketing opportunities

What general and specific needs the firm seeks to satisfy. Determine through study of Situation Analysis factors and management discussions and interviews.

III. Marketing Objectives

A. Generic market objectives
   1. Market need–satisfying objectives
   2. Community need–satisfying objectives
   3. Corporate need–satisfying objectives

Organization sales goals defined for whole company or for individual products by target market, by geographic territory, by department, or by some other category. Must be specific and realistic based on study of company capabilities, funding, and objectives.

B. Sales target objectives
1. Sales volume
   a. Dollars
   b. Units
   c. Territories
   d. Markets
2. Share of market
3. Distribution expansion
4. Other

The method(s) by which the organization plans to achieve the objectives enumerated above.

IV. Marketing Strategy

A. General marketing strategy
   A general description of the type of marketing strategy the organization intends to employ.
   1. Positioning strategy
   2. Product differentiation strategy
   3. Price/quality differentiation strategy

A detailed description of the marketing mix(es) the firm intends to use to achieve its objectives.

B. Specific market strategies
   1. Target market A
      a. Product
      b. Price
      c. Place
      d. Promotion
         (1) Personal selling
         (2) Advertising
         (3) Sales promotion
         (4) Public relations
   2. Target market B
      a. Product
      b. Price
      c. Place
      d. Promotion
         (1) Personal selling
         (2) Advertising
         (3) Sales promotion
         (4) Public relations

The detailed tactical plans for implementing each of the elements of the firm's marketing mix.

V. Action Programs (Tactics)

A. Product plans
B. Pricing plans
C. Distribution plans
D. Promotional plan
   1. Sales plan
   2. Advertising plan
   3. Sales promotion plan
   4. Public relations plan

Description of the methods the firm will use to review, evaluate, and control its progress toward the achievement of its marketing objectives.

VI. Measurement, Review, and Control

A. Organizational structure
B. Methodology for review and evaluation

Determination of the amount of money needed to conduct the marketing effort, the rationale for that budget, and the allocation to various functions.

VII. Marketing Budget

    A. Method of allocation
    B. Enumeration of marketing costs by division
       1. New product research
       2. Marketing research
       3. Sales expenses
       4. Advertising, sales promotion, public relations

Details of information, secondary data, or research conducted to develop information discussed in the marketing plan.

VIII. Appendixes

    A. Sales reports
    B. Reports of market research studies
    C. Reprints of journal or magazine articles
    D. Other supporting documents

ADVERTISING PLAN OUTLINE

DATE:

COMPANY (PRODUCT) NAME:

Brief encapsulation, for executive review, of entire advertising plan in no more than two or three pages.

I. Executive Summary

  A. Premises—summary of information presented in marketing plan
  B. Summary of advertising objectives
  C. Summary of advertising strategy
  D. Budget summary

Condensed review of pertinent elements presented in the marketing plan.

II. Situation Analysis

  A. Company's (product's) current marketing situation
    1. Business or industry information
    2. Description of company, product, or service
      a. Stage of product life cycle
      b. Goods classification
      c. Competitive or market positioning
    3. General description of market(s) served
    4. Sales history and share of market
    5. Description of consumer purchase process
    6. Methods of distribution
    7. Pricing strategies employed
    8. Implications of any marketing research
    9. Promotional history
  B. Target market description
    1. Market segments identified
    2. Primary market
    3. Secondary markets
    4. Market characteristics
      a. Geographic
      b. Demographic
      c. Psychographic
      d. Behavioristic
  C. Marketing objectives
    1. Generic market objectives
    2. Long- and short-term sales target objectives
  D. Marketing mix for each target market—summarized from marketing plan
    1. Product
    2. Price
    3. Place
    4. Promotion
  E. Intended role of advertising in the promotional mix
  F. Miscellaneous information not included above

Analysis and statement of what the advertising is expected to accomplish—See Checklist for Developing Advertising Objectives (Chapter 7).

III. Advertising Objectives

  A. Primary or selective demand
  B. Direct action or indirect action
  C. Objectives stated in terms of advertising pyramid
    1. Awareness
    2. Comprehension
    3. Conviction
    4. Desire
    5. Action
    6. Repurchase reinforcement
  D. Quantified expression of objectives
    1. Specific quantities or percentages
    2. Length of time for achievement of objectives
    3. Other possible measurements
      a. Inquiries
      b. Increased order size
      c. Morale building
      d. Other

Intended blend of the creative mix for the company as a whole, for each product, or for each target market.

IV. Advertising (Creative) Strategy

  A. Product concept—how the advertising will present the product in terms of:
    1. Product or market positioning
    2. Product differentiation
    3. Life cycle
    4. Classification, packaging, branding
    5. FCB Grid purchase-decision position
      a. High/low involvement
      b. Rational/emotional involvement
  B. Target audience—the specific people the advertising will address
    1. Detailed description of target audiences
      a. Relationship of target audience to target market
      b. Prospective buying influences
      c. Benefits sought/advertising appeals
      d. Demographics
      e. Psychographics
      f. Behavioristics
    2. Prioritization of target audiences
      a. Primary
      b. Secondary
      c. Supplementary
  C. Communications media

The strategy for selecting the various media vehicles that will communicate the advertising message to the target audience—see Chapters 12–16.

    1. Definition of media objectives
      a. Reach
      b. Frequency
      c. Gross rating points
      d. Continuity/flighting/pulsing
    2. Determination of which media reach the target audience best
      a. Traditional mass media
        (1) Radio
        (2) Television
        (3) Newspapers
        (4) Magazines

(5) Outdoor
    b. Other media
        (1) Direct mail
        (2) Publicity
    c. Supplemental media
        (1) Trade shows
        (2) Sales promotion devices
        (3) Off-the-wall media
3. Availability relative to purchase patterns
4. Potential for communication effectiveness
5. Cost considerations
    a. Size/mechanical considerations of message units
    b. Cost efficiency of media plan against target audiences
    c. Production costs
6. Relevance to other elements of creative mix
7. Scope of media plan
8. Exposure/attention/motivation values of intended media vehicles

What the company wants to say and how it wants to say it, verbally and nonverbally—see Chapters 8–11.

D. Advertising message
    1. Copy elements
        a. Advertising appeals
        b. Copy platform
        c. Key consumer benefits
        d. Benefit supports or reinforcements
        e. Product personality or image
    2. Art elements
        a. Visual appeals
            (1) In ads and commercials
            (2) In packaging
            (3) In point-of-purchase and sales materials
        b. Art platform
            (1) Layout
            (2) Design
            (3) Illustration style
    3. Production elements
        a. Mechanical considerations in producing ads
            (1) Color
            (2) Size
            (3) Style
        b. Production values sought
            (1) Typography
            (2) Printing
            (3) Color reproduction
            (4) Photography/illustration
            (5) Paper
            (6) Electronic effects
            (7) Animation
            (8) Film or videotape
            (9) Sound effects
            (10) Music

The amount of money to be allocated to advertising and the intended method of allocation.

V. The Advertising Budget

    A. Impact of marketing situation on method of allocation
       1. New or old product
       2. Primary demand curve for product class
       3. Competitive situation
       4. Marketing objectives and strategy
       5. Profit or growth considerations
       6. Relationship of advertising to sales and profits
       7. Empirical experience
    B. Method of allocation
       1. Percentage of sales or profit
       2. Share of market
       3. Task method
       4. Unit of sale
       5. Competitive parity

The research techniques that will be used to create the advertising and evaluate its effectiveness—see Chapter 6.

VI. Testing and Evaluation

    A. Advertising research conducted
       1. Strategy determination
       2. Concept development
    B. Pretesting and posttesting
       1. Elements tested
          a. Markets
          b. Motives
          c. Messages
          d. Media
          e. Budgeting
          f. Scheduling
       2. Methodology
          a. Central location tests
          b. Sales experiments
          c. Physiological testing
          d. Aided recall tests
          e. Unaided recall tests
          f. Attitude tests
          g. Inquiry tests
          h. Sales tests
          i. Other
       3. Cost of testing

APPENDIX C

CAREER PLANNING IN ADVERTISING

GETTING A JOB IN ADVERTISING

The cliché is old but true: The process of looking for a job is a full-time job in itself. It should not be approached haphazardly. With careful research and planning (and lots of patience), an individual aspiring to work in advertising can obtain not only a job but one that fits with his or her abilities, interests, and career goals.

The job-hunting process, in advertising or any other field, can be broken down into five main steps:

1. Self-assessment and goal setting.
2. Conducting the job search.
3. Preparing a résumé, cover letter, and portfolio.
4. Interviewing.
5. Following up.

Self-Assessment and Goal Setting

The first (and some would argue the most important) step in the job search process is to determine exactly what you have to offer potential employers and what you really want out of a career. You have a variety of ways to go about assessing your interests, marketable skills, strengths and weaknesses, and other characteristics that will influence the kind of job you will do best in and enjoy the most. There are many books on career planning that provide inventories and questionnaires to help you in such a self-assessment.

Through self-evaluation you can determine not only your interests and job qualifications but also your career goals and objectives. What type of work would you like to do? What do you expect to get out of your work—Money? Power? Fame? Personal fulfillment? What kind of work environment do you prefer? You should be able to make a list of musts and preferences regarding size of company, location, salary, benefits, training programs, and other employer characteristics. Again, career planning books provide guidelines that can help you set goals and objectives.

After completing your self-assessment, you may find you are simply unprepared to enter the career of your choice. At this point, you have the opportunity to undertake any additional schooling you might need, to get some job experience (even if summer or part-time) in a related field, or to serve as an intern (unpaid worker) at an advertising agency, in a company advertising department, with the media, or with a supplier. Your object should be to improve your marketability so you can get the job you really want.

Conducting the Job Search

Before looking into specific jobs that might be available, you will need to investigate the advertising field to determine what types of jobs will fit your career goals. Advertising jobs can be broken down into six main areas: creative (art direction, copywriting), account services, media (planning, scheduling), production (print, broadcast), research, and public relations. (See Figure C–1 for specific jobs and their salaries.) Most advertising jobs are found in agencies, but they are also available in the advertising departments of large companies, in media, and in allied services (such as media-planning agencies or production companies). To find out about jobs in the advertising field, you can read books on the topic, write to organizations that have career information, and keep up with the most popular trade periodicals, especially *Advertising Age* and *Adweek*. See the listings at the end of this appendix.

In addition to exploring the types of jobs available in advertising, you will want to find out more about what the industry is really like and what is actually involved in doing the work. One way is to obtain interviews with people in the business. Find out the names of people who are highly regarded in their advertising jobs in your community and ask for a few moments of their time for an informative interview. Many will be flattered to be sought out as experts in their field. Be sure to be prepared with specific questions, not take up too much of the person's time, and thank him or her in person and in a follow-up note.

When the time comes to begin conducting your actual job search, you can draw on a number of sources. The most obvious source is want ads in your local paper or in the city where you would like to work. However, it has been estimated that some 80 percent of jobs are filled without an ad ever appearing. How do you hear about these job openings? Cracking this hidden job market will require a great deal of time and effort on your part because you will need to create a network of people who can help you get a job. That will entail telling everyone you know that you are looking for a job and asking everyone you encounter whether he or she knows of any job openings in your field or of anyone who works in that field. You can begin with relatives, friends, and teachers. You should follow up on every lead they give you and ask each new person for additional leads. Networking should eventually land you some interviews for the kind of job you want.

While you are setting up your network, you should also be preparing a list of target employers. These are the companies you most want to work for. That will entail doing some research, such as checking the *Standard Directory of Advertisers* and *Standard Directory of Advertising Agencies*. Also helpful are publications such as the *Advertising Career Directory*. (See the listings at the end of this appendix.) You should make a file card for each company, including information on who is in charge of the specific department where you would like to work.

Other leads for potential employers include college placement offices, employment sections of industry trade papers, and employment agencies (some specialize in jobs in the advertising field).

FIGURE C–1   Careers in advertising

Job title	Job description	Requirements	Salary range	Entry level
Art director	Responsible for visual elements in print and broadcast ads: supervises or creates layouts, hires photographers, illustrators.	B.A. desirable but not required; art school degree helpful; portfolio a must.	$24,000–$61,000 (senior art director)	Assistant art director ($18,000)
Copywriter	Writes copy for print and broadcast advertisements; works with art director to develop ad concept; can work for ad agency or advertiser.	B.A. with courses in advertising, marketing, liberal arts, social sciences; portfolio a must.	$25,000–$61,000 (senior copywriter)	Junior copywriter ($18,000)
Account executive	Serves as link between client and ad agency; acts as business manager for account; does market planning; coordinates advertising planning process.	B.A. in business; M.B.A. often preferred; marketing background desirable.	$34,000–$82,000	Junior account executive (B.A.: $18,000–$23,000; M.B.A.: $26,000–$34,000)
Media planner	Decides media to advertise in and plans media mix; chooses media vehicles; conducts media tests.	B.A. with emphasis in marketing, merchandising, or psychology.	$26,000–$150,000 (media director)	Trainee ($11,000–$14,000)
Media buyer	Buys space in print media and time in broadcast media; negotiates price and position of ads; may work for ad agency or media-buying firm.	B.A. with emphasis in marketing, economics, mathematics, or statistics; M.B.A. preferred.	$26,000–$150,000 (media director)	Trainee ($11,000–$14,000)
Traffic manager	Schedules, supervises, and controls an ad agency's work flow.	B.A. not required but highly desirable; good general education helpful.	$20,000–$38,000	Traffic assistant ($13,500)
Print production manager	Prepares ads for printing; works with typesetters, color separators, printers, and other suppliers.	B.A. helpful but not essential; background in graphic arts, printing useful.	$22,000–$56,000	Production assistant ($13,000–$15,000)
Broadcast producer	Supervises all aspects of production for radio and TV commercials, including hiring the director and production company and controlling budget.	B.A. preferred; background in some area of broadcasting helpful.	$27,000–$89,000	Production assistant ($13,000–$15,000)

Job title	Job description	Requirements	Salary range	Entry level
Market researcher	Conducts studies of consumers and their buying habits; conducts tests of consumer reactions to products and ads; may work in ad agency or with research firm.	Degree a must; M.B.A. or Ph.D. desirable; background in statistics useful; computer literacy an advantage.	$37,000–$92,000 (market research manager)	Trainee ($13,500)
Public relations manager	Obtains publicity for clients; serves as intermediary between client and public; handles contacts with press; may work for ad agency, client company, or public relations firm.	College degree with emphasis on liberal arts; journalism or marketing background helpful.	$26,000–$84,000	PR assistant or trainee ($15,000–$17,000)
Advertising director/manager	Runs advertising department at company, managing all advertising and coordinating with any outside agencies used.	B.A. in marketing or M.B.A.	$32,000–$46,000	Advertising assistant ($17,000–$20,000)
Brand/product manager	Is responsible for the marketing of a specific product or brand at a company, including sales and advertising.	B.A. in marketing or M.B.A.	$35,000–$46,000	Advertising assistant ($17,000–$20,000)
Copywriter for retail ad department	Writes copy for newspaper ads, catalogs, direct-mail pieces for retail business.	B.A. preferred, with courses in advertising, English, sociology, psychology; portfolio helpful.	$27,000–$32,000	($15,000–$22,000)
Artist for retail ad department	Illustrates print ads, catalogs, and direct-mail pieces for retail business.	B.A. desirable; commercial art courses useful; portfolio a must.	$28,000–$32,000	($15,000–$23,000)
Photographer	Photographs products, other setup shots for ad agency or in-house ad department.	B.A. from professional art school; portfolio a must.	$22,000–$33,000	Usually free-lance
Sales representative	Handles advertising sales for a particular newspaper, magazine, radio or TV station, or other medium.	B.A. preferred, with emphasis on business courses; sales experience valuable.	Commission	—
Jingle creator	Writes the music and lyrics for jingles used in radio and TV commercials, usually on a contract or free-lance basis.	B.A. preferred (but not required), with emphasis on music and business.	$35,000–$600,000	$25,000

Preparing a Résumé, a Cover Letter, and a Portfolio

Armed with your list of potential employers, including those obtained through networking and your own research, you are ready to begin contacting them to apply for a job. In most cases, your initial contact will be through a résumé and cover letter. Because these items are tools for marketing your product—you—they must be carefully prepared to create a good first impression.

Your résumé should be attractive, well written, and professional. There's no need to do anything fancy—colored paper, professional typesetting, slick design—as most employers will ignore the trappings (unless they're particularly sloppy or amateurish) and focus on the content. For an impressive-looking résumé, stick with clean black type and white bond paper. Leave generous margins to enhance readability. And keep it short—two pages at the most. Always proofread your résumé (even better—have someone else proof it for you) to make sure there are no errors in grammar, punctuation, and spelling.

An example of a résumé is shown in Figure C–2. Here are specific tips for preparing your résumé:

FIGURE   C–2

Résumé.

```
                     SHARON LEE ANDERSON

        4150 Prairie Avenue    Elgin, Illinois  60120    Phone (312) 888-7043

        Career Objective:  Copywriter in a medium-sized Chicago agency.
                           Advancement to creative supervisor within five
                           years.

                          Education for Advertising

        Bachelor of Arts (1989), University of Illinois, Chicago, Illinois.
        Major:  Advertising and Journalism.  Minor:  Marketing.

        Honors:  Dean's list, six semesters.  Graduated in upper 10 percent of
        class.

                           Advertising Experience

        Junior Copywriter (part-time)        Advertising Salesperson
        Goldblatt's Department Store         Campus newspaper
        Skokie, Illinois                     University of Illinois
        (May 1987-September 1988)            (October 1986-March 1987)

        Responsible for creative copy        Serviced existing accounts and
        for direct-mail brochures            contracted with 22 new accounts

                       Awards, Activities, Affiliations

        First-place winner.  Copywriting category.  National Student Adver-
        tising Campaign Competition, 1989.  Sponsored by the Federation of
        Advertising Agencies.

        Program Chairman, 1988-89.  University of Illinois Advertising Club.

        Recipient.  Summer 1988 scholarship from Advertising Institute.

                        Other Relevant Information

        Write and speak Spanish.  Type 70 wpm.  Proficient with WordPerfect and
        Microsoft Word programs for IBM PC and PageMaker for Macintosh.

                              Personal Data

        Hobbies include reading (science fiction, history, behavioral
        sciences), flute playing, dancing, racquetball.

                               References

        Dr. Harold G. Simpson, Professor of Advertising, School of Journalism,
        University of Illinois, Chicago, Illinois  60680

        Dr. Barbara Wasserman, Professor of Marketing, School of Business,
        University of Illinois, Chicago, Illinois  60680

        Linda Dolan, Director of Advertising, Goldblatt's Department Store,
        Skokie, Illinois  60076
```

Heading This should include a title (such as "Résumé") and basic information about you (name, address, phone number). It should also include your career objective. The objective should be stated as specifically as possible (e.g., "an entry-level position in the media department of a large ad agency with a long-term goal of media planning for major accounts"), as opposed to something vague ("a challenging position in the advertising industry" or "a job where I can put my enthusiasm and interpersonal skills to good use").

Education Include any degrees you have already earned and any outstanding honors or scholarships. If you have little work experience, this section should emphasize courses you have taken that might prepare you for your chosen career.

Work Experience Emphasize jobs that are relevant to your target field. Include any part-time or volunteer work that shows an interest in the type of job you are seeking. For all relevant work experience, be sure to include a brief description of your duties and any worthy accomplishments. Briefly list other jobs held to show that you have the ability to get and hold a job and have at least contributed to your support.

Activities and Achievements This is a good spot to include any other information that might be of interest to an employer, such as language skills, relevant hobbies, and community activities.

References If you wish to include names of past employers who can be contacted about your skills and experience, be sure to get their permission first before listing them. If you have good references, it's best to list them. It's acceptable to state "References available upon request."

Accompanying the résumé should be a cover letter that catches the reader's attention, provides evidence of your qualifications, and requests an interview (see Figure C–3). Like the résumé, the letter should be professionally presented (not handwritten, for instance) and businesslike. It should answer the employer's question, "What's in it for me?" A number of books provide help with writing good résumés and cover letters. Several are listed at the end of this appendix.

If you are looking for a job as an art director or a copywriter, you will also need to prepare a portfolio, or "book," to show potential employers. This portfolio can include published pieces, pieces done for school courses, or self-projects. What it should *not* include is bad work. The fact that something you did was published does not automatically qualify it for your portfolio, especially if it is not among your best work. A portfolio should be carefully thought out and prepared, as it may be the sole basis on which some employers do their hiring. It should contain a small number of items that represent the kinds and quality of work you can do.

Interviewing

The purpose of the résumé and cover letter is to land you a job interview. It is usually on the basis of the interview (and your portfolio, if you have one) that employers will make their decision. You should therefore work on developing your interviewing skills. Learn the most commonly asked

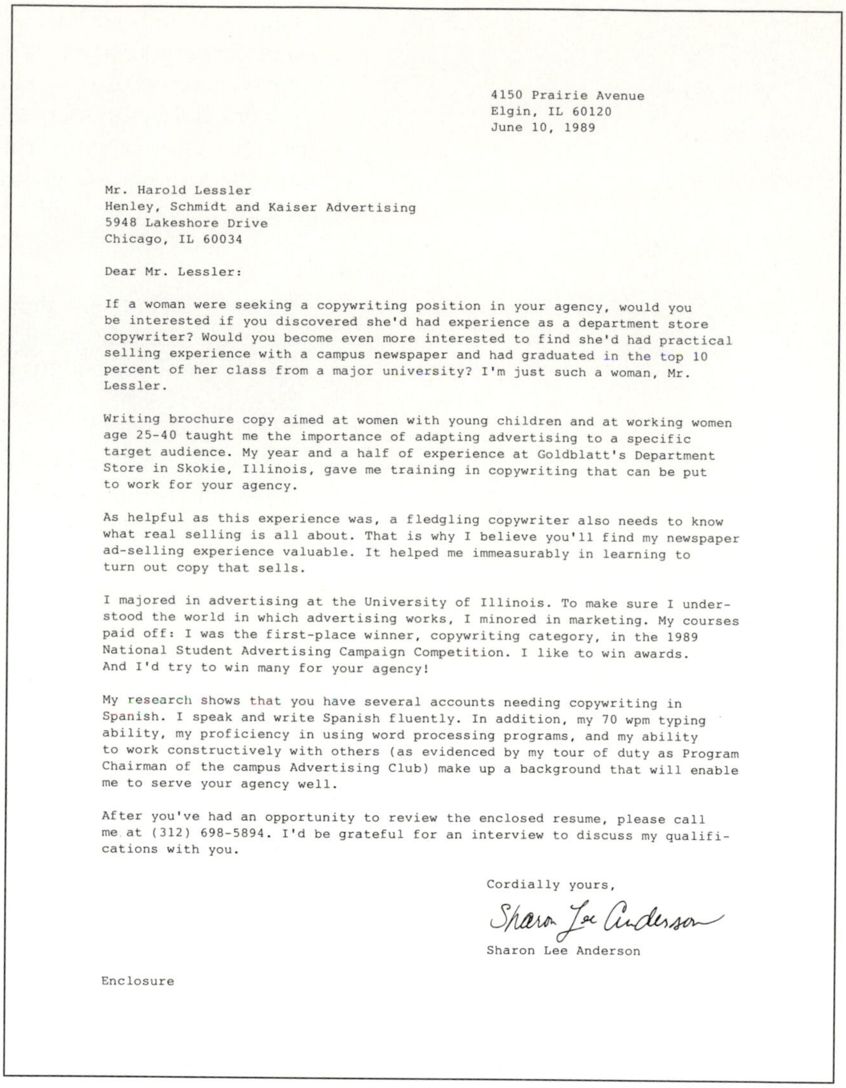

FIGURE   C–3

Letter of application.

4150 Prairie Avenue
Elgin, IL 60120
June 10, 1989

Mr. Harold Lessler
Henley, Schmidt and Kaiser Advertising
5948 Lakeshore Drive
Chicago, IL 60034

Dear Mr. Lessler:

If a woman were seeking a copywriting position in your agency, would you
be interested if you discovered she'd had experience as a department store
copywriter? Would you become even more interested to find she'd had practical
selling experience with a campus newspaper and had graduated in the top 10
percent of her class from a major university? I'm just such a woman, Mr.
Lessler.

Writing brochure copy aimed at women with young children and at working women
age 25-40 taught me the importance of adapting advertising to a specific
target audience. My year and a half of experience at Goldblatt's Department
Store in Skokie, Illinois, gave me training in copywriting that can be put
to work for your agency.

As helpful as this experience was, a fledgling copywriter also needs to know
what real selling is all about. That is why I believe you'll find my newspaper
ad-selling experience valuable. It helped me immeasurably in learning to
turn out copy that sells.

I majored in advertising at the University of Illinois. To make sure I understood the world in which advertising works, I minored in marketing. My courses
paid off: I was the first-place winner, copywriting category, in the 1989
National Student Advertising Campaign Competition. I like to win awards.
And I'd try to win many for your agency!

My research shows that you have several accounts needing copywriting in
Spanish. I speak and write Spanish fluently. In addition, my 70 wpm typing
ability, my proficiency in using word processing programs, and my ability
to work constructively with others (as evidenced by my tour of duty as Program
Chairman of the campus Advertising Club) make up a background that will enable
me to serve your agency well.

After you've had an opportunity to review the enclosed resume, please call
me at (312) 698-5894. I'd be grateful for an interview to discuss my qualifications with you.

Cordially yours,

Sharon Lee Anderson

Sharon Lee Anderson

Enclosure

interview questions and rehearse your answers. Read about preparing for interviews and follow suggestions for scheduling, attire, and appropriate interview behavior.

Before an interview, you should find out about the company. If it is an advertising agency, how big is it? How is it structured? What are its major accounts? Who are the major figures? Who will you be talking to, and what is the correct pronunciation of his or her name?

At the close of the interview, be sure to thank the interviewer and to politely inquire about what will happen next. Should you expect additional interviews? Will someone from the company be in touch? Show that you are interested—but not desperate.

Following Up

Record keeping is a must when you are conducting a job search. You should have files or cards for recording letters and résumés sent, dates of interviews, and so forth. If, within a reasonable time, you have not had responses to your letters to certain target employers, write follow-up letters. After an interview, it is always a good idea to write a brief thank-you note, reiterating your interest in the job. Such notes should always be typed.

Eventually, as the result of your employment-seeking efforts, you will receive one or more job offers. Accept the job that best fits your objectives, and you will at last be on your way to a career in advertising.

CAREER PLANNING PUBLICATIONS

Books

Advertising Career Directory. 2nd ed. Hawthorne, N.J.: The Career Press, Inc., 1987.

Bolles, Richard N. *What Color Is Your Parachute? A Practical Manual for Job Hunters and Career Changes.* Berkeley, Calif.: Ten Speed Press, 1987.

Chorba, Thomas, and Alex York. *Winning Moves: Career Strategies for the Eighties.* New York: Anchor Books, 1986.

College Placement Manual. Bethlehem Pa.: College Placement Council, Inc., 1985.

Corwen, Leonard. *There's a Job for You in Advertising, Commercial Art, Fashion, Films, Public Relations and Publicity, Publishing, Television and Radio, Travel and Tourism.* New York: New Century, 1983.

Craig, James. *Graphic Design Career Guide.* New York: Watson-Guptill Publications, 1983.

Deckinger, E. L., and Jules B. Singer. *Exploring Careers in Advertising.* New York: Rosen Publishing Group, 1985.

Greenberg, Jan. *How Advertising Works and the People Who Make It Happen.* New York: Henry Holt and Company, 1987.

Haas, Ken. *How to Get a Job in Advertising.* New York: Art Direction Book Company, 1979.

Holtz, Herman. *Beyond the Résumé.* New York: McGraw-Hill, 1984.

Katz, Judith A. *The Ad Game.* New York: Harper & Row, 1984.

Lareau, William. *The Inside Track: A Successful Job Search Method.* New York: New Century Publishers, 1986.

Laskin, David. *Getting into Advertising: A Career Guide.* New York: Ballantine Books, 1986.

Mogel, Leonard. *Making It in the Media Professions: A Realistic Guide to Career Opportunities in Newspapers, Magazines, Books, Television, Radio, the Movies, and Advertising.* Chester, Conn.: Globe Pequot, 1987.

Paetro, Maxine. *How to Put Your Book Together and Get a Job in Advertising.* New York: Executive Communications, 1980.

Public Relations Career Directory. 2nd ed. Hawthorne, N.J.: The Career Press, 1987.

Schmidt, Peggy J. *Making It on Your First Job: When Your're Young, Inexperienced, and Ambitious.* New York: Avon Books, 1981.

Shelling, Robert O. *Jobs: What They Are . . . Where They Are . . .* New York: Simon & Schuster, 1986.

Wasserman, Dick. *How to Get Your First Copywriting Job.* New York: Center for Advancement of Advertising, 1985.

West, Jonathan P. *Career Planning Development and Management: An Annotated Bibliography.* New York: Garland Publishing, 1983.

Wilson, Robert F., and Adele Lewis. *Better Résumés for Executives and Professionals.* Woodbury, N.Y.: Barron's Educational Series, 1983.

Periodicals

Business Week's Guide to Careers, 1221 Avenue of the Americas, New York, NY 10010.

Career Opportunity News, Garrett Park Press, Garrett Park, MD 20896.

Journal of Career Planning and Employment, College Placement Council, 62 Highland Avenue, Bethlehem, PA 18017.

Occupational Outlook Quarterly, Superintendent of Documents, U.S. Government Printing Office, Washington, DC 20402.

Pamphlets

Advertising: A Guide to Careers in Advertising, American Association of Advertising Agencies, 200 Park Avenue, New York, NY 10017.

Where Shall I Go to Study Advertising, Advertising Education Publications, 3429 Fifty-Fifth Street, Lubbock, TX 79413.

SELECTED PERIODICALS

Advertising Age, 740 N. Rush Street, Chicago, IL 60611.

Advertising Techniques, 10 East 39th Street, New York, NY 10016.

Adweek, 49 E. 21st Street, New York, NY 10010.

Adweek's Marketing Week, 49 E. 21st Street, New York, NY 10010.

Archive, P.O. Box 6338, Syracuse, NY 13217.

Art Direction, 10 E. 39th Street, New York, NY 10016.

Broadcasting, 1735 DeSales Street N.W., Washington, DC 20036.

Business Marketing, 740 Rush Street, Chicago, IL 60611.

Canadian Journal of Communication, St. Thomas More College, 1437 College Drive, Saskatoon, Saskatchewan, Canada S7N 0W6.

Communication Arts, P.O. Box 10300, Palo Alto, CA 94303.

Direct Marketing, 224 Seventh Street, Garden City, NY 11530.

Editor & Publisher, 575 Lexington Avenue, New York, NY 10022.

Incentive Marketing, 633 Third Avenue, New York, NY 10017.

Inside Print, Six River Bend, Box 4949, Stamford, CT 06907.

Journal of Advertising, American Academy of Advertising, c/o Ron Lane, School of Journalism, The University of Georgia, Athens, GA 30602.

Journal of Advertising Research, Advertising Research Foundation, 3 E. 54th Street, New York, NY 10022.

Journal of Broadcasting, Broadcast Education Association, 1771 N Street N.W., Washington, DC 20036.

Journal of Marketing, American Marketing Association, 250 S. Wacker Drive, Suite 200, Chicago, IL 60606.

Madison Avenue, 369 Lexington Avenue, New York, NY 10017.

Marketing, Maclean-Hunter Ltd., 777 Bay Street, Toronto, Ontario, Canada M5W 1A7.

Marketing & Media Decisions, 342 Madison Avenue, New York, NY 10017.

Marketing Communications, 475 Park Avenue S., New York, NY 10016.

Marketing News, American Marketing Association, 250 S. Wacker Drive, Suite 200, Chicago, IL 60606.

MIN/Media Industry Newsletter, 145 East 49th Street, New York, NY 10017.

Modern Packaging, 205 East 42nd Street, New York, NY 10017.

Print, 355 Lexington Avenue, New York, NY 10017.

Public Relations Journal, 845 Third Avenue, New York, NY 10020.

Sales and Marketing Management, 633 Third Avenue, New York, NY 10164.

Stores, National Retail Merchants Association, 100 W. 31st Street, New York, NY 10001.

Television/Radio Age, 1270 Avenue of the Americas, New York, NY 10020.

Winners, 49 East 21st Street, New York, NY 10010.

Zip, 401 North Broad Street, Philadelphia, PA 19108.

REFERENCE BOOKS AND DIRECTORIES

Standard Directory of Advertisers. Wilmette, Ill.: National Register Publishing Company, 1989.

Standard Directory of Advertising Agencies. Wilmette, Ill.: National Register Publishing Company, 1989.

RESEARCH AND INFORMATION SERVICES

A. C. Nielsen Company, Nielsen Plaza, Northbrook, IL 60062.

Advertising Checking Bureau, 165 North Canal Street, Chicago, IL 60606.

Audit Bureau of Circulations, 900 North Meacham Road, Schaumburg, IL 60195.

Broadcast Advertisers Report (BAR), 500 Fifth Avenue, New York, NY 10036.

Gallup & Robinson, Research Park, Princeton, NJ 08540.

Leading National Advertisers, (LNA), 515 Madison Avenue, New York, NY 10022.

Mediamark Research, 341 Madison Avenue, New York, NY 10017.

Simmons Marketing Research Bureau, 219 East 42nd Street, New York, NY 10017.

Starch INRA Hooper, 566 E. Boston Post Road, Mamaroneck, NY 10543.

The Arbitron Company, 1350 Avenue of the Americas, New York, NY 10019.

PROFESSIONAL AND TRADE ASSOCIATIONS

The Advertising Council, 825 Third Avenue, New York, NY 10022.

Advertising Research Foundation (ARF), 3 East 54th Street, New York, NY 10022.

American Advertising Federation, 1400 K Street N.W., Suite 1000, Washington, DC 20005.

American Association of Advertising Agencies, 666 Third Avenue, 13th Floor, New York, NY 10017.

American Business Press, 205 East 42nd Street, New York, NY 10017.

American Marketing Association, 250 S. Wacker Drive, Chicago, IL 60606.

Association of National Advertisers, 155 E. 44th Street, New York, NY 10017.

Business/Professional Advertising Association, 205 E. 42nd Street, New York, NY 10017.

Council of Better Business Bureaus, 1515 Wilson Boulevard, Arlington, VA 22209.

Direct Marketing Association, 6 E. 43rd Street, New York, NY 10017.

International Advertising Association, 475 Fifth Avenue, New York, NY 10017.

Magazine Publishers Association, 575 Lexington Avenue, New York, NY 10022.

Marketing Communications Executives International, 2602 McKinney Avenue, Dallas, TX 75204.

Marketing Research Association, 111 E. Wacker Drive, Suite 600, Chicago, IL 60601.

National Advertising Review Board (NARB), 845 Third Avenue, New York, NY 10022.

National Association of Broadcasters, 1771 N Street N.W., Washington, DC 20036.

National Council of Affiliated Advertising Agencies, 6 East 45th Street, New York, NY 10017.

National Retail Merchants Association, 100 West 31st Street, New York, NY 10001.

National Yellow Pages Service, 999 W. Big Beaver Road, Troy, MI 48084.

Newspaper Advertising Bureau, 1180 Avenue of the Americas, New York, NY 10036.

Outdoor Advertising Association of America, 1899 L Street N.W., Suite 403, Washington, DC 20036.

Point-of-Purchase Advertising Institute, 2 Executive Drive, Ft. Lee, NJ 07024.

Public Relations Society of America, 845 Third Avenue, New York, NY 10022.

Radio Advertising Bureau, 304 Park Avenue S., New York, NY 10010.

Sales and Marketing Executives International, 6151 Wilson Mills Road, Suite 200, Cleveland, OH 44143.

Specialty Advertising Association International, 1404 Walnut Hill Lane, Irving, TX 75062.

Television Bureau of Advertising, 477 Madison Avenue, New York, NY 10022.

Transit Advertising Association, 1025 Thomas Jefferson Avenue, Suite 502E, Washington, DC 20007.

ENDNOTES

Chapter 1

1. "A New Look for Coca-Cola: A Synopsis of the 70s," Coca-Cola Company, 1970.
2. McGraw-Hill Laboratory/Laboratory of Advertising Performance, 1985 study.
3. Isaac Ehrlich and Lawrence Fischer, "The Derived Demand for Advertising: A Theoretical and Empirical Investigation," *American Economic Review,* June 1982, pp. 366–88.
4. Stanley M. Ulanoff, *Advertising in America* (New York: Hastings House, 1977), p. 27.
5. *Advertising Age,* September 21, 1987.
6. Jack Trout and Al Ries, "The Positioning Era Cometh," *The Wall Street Journal,* November 2, 1972.
7. Daniel Yankelovich, "New Rules: Some Implications for Advertising," *Journal of Advertising Research,* October–November 1982; pp. 9–14.
8. Daniel Thomas Seymour, "Demarketing: New Segmenting Tool," *United States Banker,* August 1983, pp. 71–72, 74.
9. Richard Schmalensee, "Product Differentiation Advantages of Pioneering Brands," *American Economic Review,* June 1982, pp. 349–65.
10. David A. Aaker and John G. Meyers, *Advertising Management* (Englewood Cliffs, N.J.: Prentice-Hall, 1975), pp. 559–60.
11. Joseph M. Winski, "Once-Holdout Hershey Becomes Big Advertiser," *Advertising Age,* September 7, 1981, pp. 3, 67–68.
12. Ernest Dichter, *Handbook of Consumer Motivations* (New York: McGraw-Hill, 1964), pp. 6, 422–31.
13. Richard E. Kihlstrom and Michael H. Riordan, "Advertising as a Signal," *Journal of Political Economy,* June 1984, pp. 427–50.
14. *The Borden Co.* v. *FTC,* 381F.2d 175, 5th Cir., 1967.
15. Walter Taplin, *Advertising: A New Approach* (Boston: Little, Brown, 1963), p. 106.
16. Louis F. DeMarco, "How Advertising Helps Promote the Good Life," *Advertising Age,* April 30, 1980, p. 46.
17. Richard H. Holton, "How Advertising Achieved Respectability among Economists (or Anyhow, They've Heard of It)," *Advertising Age,* April 30, 1980, pp. 56–64.
18. Charles Yang, "Variations in the Cyclical Behavior of Advertising," *Journal of Marketing,* April 1964, pp. 25–30.
19. Vincent W. Makin, "Sell Management—Me—On Advertising," *Industrial Marketing,* February 1977, pp. 69–72.

Chapter 2

1. John O'Toole, "Afterword," *Madison Avenue,* May 1980, p. 98.
2. Abraham Maslow, *Motivation and Personality,* 2nd ed. (New York: Harper & Row, 1970), pp. 39–51.
3. Michael Shudson, *Advertising, the Uneasy Persuasion* (New York: Basic Books, 1985).

4. "Importance of Image," *The Wall Street Journal,* August 12, 1985, p. 19.
5. Robert J. Samuelson, "The Sovereign Consumer," *Newsweek,* July 29, 1985, p. 54.
6. "Ads That Shatter an Old Taboo," *Time,* February 2, 1987, p. 63.
7. Jeffrey A. Trachtenberg, "It's Become Part of Our Culture," *Forbes,* May 5, 1986, p. 134.
8. "Sex Roles Modified in Changing of Ads," *The New York Times,* May 13, 1985, p. 21.
9. "TV Ads Show Struggle to Replace Bygone Images of Today's Mothers," *The Wall Street Journal,* October 5, 1984, p. 29.
10. Trachtenberg, "It's Become Part of Our Culture," p. 135.
11. Ibid.
12. Jane Bryant Quinn, "New Handcuffs on the Cops," *Newsweek,* September 3, 1984, p. 62.
13. Dorothy Cohen, "Legal Interpretations of Deception Are Deceiving," *Marketing News,* September 26, 1986, p. 12.
14. Robert J. Watkins, "Government Controls of Advertising," in *Legal and Business Aspects of the Advertising Industry,* ed. Felix H. Kent and Elhanan C. Stone (New York: Practising Law Institute, 1986), p. 83.
15. Robert Garfield, "Advertisers: All's Fair in Commercials," *USA Today,* April 19, 1985, p. 83.
16. Watkins, "Government Controls," p. 88.
17. Steven A. Meyerowitz, "Endorsements: What You Can and Cannot Do," *Business Marketing,* March 1986, p. 8.
18. Janet Meyers, "Health Claims Clear Hurdle," *Advertising Age,* August 10, 1987, p. 3.
19. Steven A. Meyerowitz, "Don't 'Xerox' This Article! How to Defend Your Trademarks," *Business Marketing,* December 1984, p. 64.
20. Steven A. Meyerowitz, "The New Threat to Advertising Freedom," *Business Marketing,* October 1986, p. 20.
21. Michael Brody, "The Supreme Court Shakes the Ad Biz," *Fortune,* August 4, 1986, p. 152.
22. Linda Johnson Blake, "FTC Chairman Donald Oliver Denounces Government Censorship of Ads," *The 4A's Washington Newsletter,* April 1987, p. 7.
23. "Lawyers Learn the Hard Sell—And Companies Shudder," *Business Week,* June 10, 1985, p. 70.
24. Mary C. Wagner, "Physicians Write Advertising Prescription," *Advertising Age,* October 24, 1985, p. 33.
25. Steven A. Meyerowitz, "When Privacy Goes Public in Advertising," *Business Marketing,* March 1987, p. 104.
26. Steven A. Meyerowitz, "The Developing Law of Comparative Advertising," *Business Marketing,* August 1985, p. 81.
27. Ibid.
28. "Deceptive Ads: The FTC's Laissez-Faire Approach Is Backfiring," *Business Week,* December 2, 1985, pp. 136–37.

29. Steven A. Meyerowitz, "The Marketing Downside to States' Rights," *Business Marketing,* November 1986, p. 64.

30. David Shaw, "Newspapers Draw Foggy Lines on Ads," *Los Angeles Times,* February 15, 1987, p. 1.

31. Ibid.

32. Paul Farhi, "Agencies, Networks Battle over Censors' Role," *Adweek,* November 14, 1983, p. 50.

33. Felix H. Kent, "Control of Ads by Private Sector," *New York Law Journal,* December 27, 1985; reprinted in Kent and Stone, eds., *Legal and Business Aspects of the Advertising Industry,* 1986, pp. 207–9.

34. *"Dear ***, Your Advertising Has Recently Come to the Attention of the National Advertising Division . . . "* (New York: Council of Better Business Bureaus, 1983), p. 1.

35. Ronald H. Smithies, "Industry Self-Policing," in Kent and Stone, eds., *Legal and Business Aspects of the Advertising Industry,* 1986, p. 171.

Chapter 3

1. "Is Frank Perdue Chicken?" *Forbes,* November 5, 1984, pp. 223–24.

2. "Successful Farming 400," *Successful Farming Magazine,* January 20, 1987.

3. Christian McAdams, "Frank Perdue Is Chicken!" *Esquire,* April 1973, pp. 113–17. Copyright 1973 by Esquire Publishing, Inc.; and "Frank Perdue," *Inc.,* February 1984, pp. 21–23.

4. *PR Newswire,* January 10, 1986, p. 19.

5. R. Craig Endicott, "Where Those Ad Dollars Go," *Advertising Age,* August 20, 1987, pp. 134–36, 210–12.

6. Laurie Freeman, "The House That Ivory Built," *Advertising Age,* August 20, 1987, pp. 4–14, 162–200.

7. Joseph M. Winski, "One Brand, One Manager," *Advertising Age,* August 20, 1987, pp. 86–90, 204–5.

8. Jolie Solomon and Carol Hymowitz, "Team Strategy: P&G Makes Changes in the Way It Develops Its Products," *The Wall Street Journal,* August 11, 1987, pp. 1, 10.

9. Ibid; see also: Lenore Skenazy, "Brand Managers Shelved? Professors Offer Alternative for Changing Market," *Advertising Age,* July 13, 1987, p. 81.

10. Robert Selwitz, "Media Buying Moves In-House," *Marketing Communications,* September 1986, pp. 19–23, 79, 86.

11. Ibid.

12. M. E. Ziegenhagen, "Advertising: Which Is Best . . . In-House or Outside Agency?" *Sales & Marketing Management in Canada,* August 1986, pp. 10–11.

13. Sam Sparrow, "Design: In-House or Agency?" *Industrial Marketing Digest (U.K.),* 2nd Quarter 1987, pp. 35–39.

14. Frederic R. Gamble, *What Advertising Agencies Are—What They Do and How They Do It,* 7th ed. (New York: American Association of Advertising Agencies, 1970), p. 4.

15. Ibid.

16. Joanne Lipman, "Colgate Drops Ted Bates as Its Agency; Move Seen as Blow to Ad-Firm Mergers," *The Wall Street Journal,* June 2, 1986.

17. John K. Smalley, "Creative Ad Ventures/Automatic Returns/ Great Moments in Advertising/Zapping Viewer Apathy," *World,* January–February 1986, pp. 8–20.

18. "The Mice That Roar," *Venture,* June 1985, pp. 110–14.

19. Dianne Lynn Kastiel, "Are You Using Your Agency Enough?" *Business Marketing,* January 1987, pp. 85–89.

20. Gamble, *What Advertising Agencies Are,* p. 4.

21. *Communication Arts,* April 1973, pages unnumbered.

22. George A. Hathaway III, "Account Execs—Choosing the Right Path," *Advertising Age,* September 2, 1985, p. 30.

23. "Current Advertiser Practices in Compensating Their Advertising Agencies," pamphlet (New York: Association of National Advertisers, 1983), pp. 1–2.

24. Franchellie Cadwell and Herman Davis, "Why Is It That Ad Agencies Don't Advertise?" *Advertising Age,* November 19, 1979, p. 51.

25. Pradeep K. Korgaonkar and Danny N. Bellenger, "Correlates of Successful Advertising Campaigns: The Manager's Perspective," *Journal of Advertising Research;* December 1986– January 1987, pp. 29–41. See also: Korgaonkar, Bellenger, and Smith, "Successful Industrial Advertising Campaigns," *Industrial Marketing Management,* May 1986, pp. 123–28.

26. Daniel B. Wackman, Charles T. Salmon, and Caryn C. Salmon, "Developing an Advertising Agency–Client Relationship," *Journal of Advertising Research,* December 1986–January 1987, pp. 21–28.

27. Paul C. Katz, "Getting the Most of Your Advertising Dollars: How to Select and Evaluate an Ad Agency," *Bottomline,* March 1987, pp. 35–38.

28. Christy Marshall, "In Spite of Image, Agency-Client Links Do Often Endure," *Advertising Age,* July 1982, pp. 33–34, 41.

29. Paul C. N. Mitchell, "Auditing of Agency-Client Relations," *Journal of Advertising Research,* December 1986–January 1987, pp. 29–41.

Chapter 4

1. "Lee Iacocca of Chrysler: Crisis Plans Paying Off," *Advertising Age,* January 2, 1984, pp. 1, 30–31.

2. "Dealer Ads Featuring Iacocca Fail to Amuse AMC," *The Wall Street Journal,* April 23, 1987.

3. Theodore Levitt, "Marketing Myopia," *Harvard Business Review,* July–August 1960.

4. Richard P. Bagozzi, "Marketing as Exchange," *Journal of Marketing,* October 1975, pp. 32–39.

5. Philip Kotler, "A Generic Concept of Marketing," *Journal of Marketing,* April 1972, pp. 46–54.

6. The now widely popularized conceptual model of the four Ps was originally developed by E. J. McCarthy, *Basic Marketing* (Homewood, Ill.: Richard D. Irwin, 1960); and the usage of the "marketing mix" derived from Neil H. Borden, "The Concept of the Marketing Mix," *Journal of Advertising Research,* June 1964, pp. 2–7.

7. The classic article on this subject was first written by Wendell R. Smith, "Product Differentiation and Market Segmentation as Alternative Marketing Strategies," *Journal of Marketing,* July 1956, pp. 3–8.

8. E. Jerome McCarthy and William D. Perreault, Jr., *Basic Marketing,* 9th ed. (Homewood, Ill.: Richard D. Irwin, 1987), pp. 62–92.

9. Stanley Stasch, "1980s Marketing to Require Wisely Chosen Strategies," *Marketing News,* May 30, 1980, p. 16.

10. Cass Bettinger, "Developing Marketing Strategy," *Banker's Magazine,* January–February 1987, pp. 64–71.

11. "Cigarette Packs Get Flashier to Attract Younger Smokers," *The Wall Street Journal,* April 30, 1987.

12. McCarthy and Perreault, *Basic Marketing,* 9th ed., pp. 250–63.

13. Meg Cox, "More Work Leaves Less Time for Arts, Harris Survey Says," *The Wall Street Journal,* March 16, 1988.

14. Murray Roman, "What Telemarketing Can Do," *Banker's Magazine,* March–April 1984, pp. 55–58.

15. McCarthy and Perreault, *Basic Marketing,* 9th ed., p. 15.

16. Philip Kotler, *Principles of Marketing* (Englewood Cliffs, N.J.: Prentice-Hall, 1980), p. 48. Copyright 1980 Prentice-Hall, Inc. Adapted by permission.

17. Terry Paul and John Wong, "The Retailing of Health Care," *Journal of Health Care Marketing,* Fall 1984, pp. 23–34.

18. Michael Etgar, "Effects of Administrative Control on Efficiency of Vertical Marketing Systems," *Journal of Marketing Research,* 4 February 1976, pp. 12–24.

Chapter 5

1. David Cravens, Gerald E. Hills, and Robert B. Woodruff, *Marketing Management* (Homewood, Ill.: Richard D. Irwin, 1987), p. 124.

2. John Koten, "The Shattered Middle Class," *The Wall Street Journal,* March 9, 1987, p. 19.

3. J. Paul Peter and Jerry C. Olson, *Consumer Behavior: Marketing Strategy Perspectives* (Homewood, Ill.: Richard D. Irwin, 1987), pp. 231–73.

4. E. Jerome McCarthy and William D. Perreault, Jr., *Basic Marketing,* 9th ed. (Homewood, Ill.: Richard D. Irwin, 1987), p. 172.

5. Abraham H. Maslow, *Motivation and Personality,* 2nd ed. (New York: Harper & Row, 1970), pp. 39–51. Copyright 1970 by Abraham H. Maslow. By permission of Harper & Row, Publishers, Inc.

6. Robert B. Settle and Pamela L. Alreck, *Why They Buy* (New York: John Wiley & Sons, 1986), pp. 71–73.

7. Edward L. Grubb and Gregg Hupp, "Perception of Self-Generalized Stereotypes and Brand Selection," *Journal of Marketing Research,* February 1968, pp. 58–63.

8. John O'Toole, *The Trouble with Advertising,* 2nd ed. (New York: Random House, 1985), p. 13.

9. Bibi Wein, "Psychographics," *Omni,* July 1980, p. 97.

10. "Maidenform Tries New Approach in Latest Lingerie Ad Campaign," *The Wall Street Journal,* April 23, 1987.

11. McCarthy and Perreault, *Basic Marketing,* p. 175.

12. Leon Festinger, *A Theory of Cognitive Dissonance* (Evanston, Ill.: Row, Peterson, 1957), p. 83.

13. Edmund Faison, *Advertising: A Behavioral Approach for Managers* (New York: John Wiley & Sons, 1980), p. 132.

14. Burton Marcus et al., *Modern Marketing Management* (New York: Random House, 1980), p. 83.

15. Harold W. Berkman and Christopher C. Gilson, *Consumer Behavior* (Encino, Calif.: Dickenson Publishing, 1978), pp. 226–27.

16. O'Toole, *The Trouble with Advertising,* p. 21.

17. Burton Marcus et al., *Modern Marketing Management,* p. 86.

18. George P. Moschis, "The Role of Family Communication in Consumer Socialization of Children and Adolescents," *Journal of Consumer Research,* March 1985, pp. 898–913.

19. Jeffrey Zaslow, "Children's Search for Values Leading to Shopping Malls," *The Wall Street Journal,* March 13, 1987.

20. Koten, "The Shattered Middle Class," p. 19.

21. John Wall, "Minorities Slice the Advertising Pie," *Insight,* March 9, 1987, pp. 46–47.

22. Ibid.

23. Settle and Alreck, *Why They Buy,* pp. 279–80.

24. Laszlo Unger, "Better Knowledge of the Consumer through Market Segmentation," *European Research,* April 1982, pp. 81–87.

25. "Forecasters Can Tell Weather to Advertise," *Advertising Age,* January 31, 1985, p. 38.

26. Joanne Cleaver, "Awash in a New Wave of Haircare," *Advertising Age,* February 28, 1983, pp. M-22, M-24.

27. "Strategies: Put Your Money on Your Market," *Marketing Communications,* March 1984, pp. 29–32.

28. Philip Kotler, *Principles of Marketing* (Englewood Cliffs, N.J.: Prentice-Hall, 1980), p. 32. Copyright 1980 Prentice-Hall, Inc. Adapted by permission.

29. Bickley Townsend, "Psychographic Glitter and Gold," *American Demographics,* November 1985, pp. 22–29.

30. Daniel F. Hansler, "VALS: Perspective in Support of Value-Based Giving," *Fund Raising Management,* May 1985, pp. 104–5.

31. Ibid.; and Settle and Alreck, *Why They Buy,* pp. 276–85.

32. Michael Hedges, "Radio's Lifestyles," *American Demographics,* February 1986, pp. 32–35.

33. "Emotions Important for Successful Selling," *Marketing News,* April 12, 1985, p. 18.

34. Settle and Alreck, *Why They Buy,* p. 282.

35. Ibid., pp. 283–84.

36. "Timex and VALS Engineer a Psychographic Product Launch," *Ad Forum,* September 1984, pp. 12–15.

37. Frank P. McDonald, 'Whither the New Segmentation Systems," *Marketing & Media Decisions,* May 1985, pp. 94, 96.

38. Ed Zotti, "Thinking Psychographically," *Public Relations Journal,* May 1985, pp. 26–30.

39. Ibid.

40. John H. Mather, "No Reason to Fear Frightening Reality of VALS," *Marketing News,* September 13, 1985, p. 15.

41. McCarthy and Perreault, *Basic Marketing,* pp. 195–206.

42. Ibid., p. 195.

43. Cravens, Hills, and Woodruff, *Marketing Management,* pp. 156–78.

Chapter 6

1. E. Jerome McCarthy and William D. Perreault, Jr., *Basic Marketing,* 9th ed. (Homewood, Ill.: Richard D. Irwin, 1987), p. 124.

2. Ibid., p. 127.

3. Kenneth Longman, *Advertising* (New York: Harcourt Brace Jovanovich, 1971), pp. 177–78.

4. "Volks Called Biggest Success: Edsel Gets Booby Prize," *Advertising Age,* April 30, 1980, pp. 130–32.

5. Jack H. Honomichl, "Marketing/Advertising Research: Ranking Top Players in Growing Global Arena," *Advertising Age,* November 24, 1986, pp. S1–S17.

6. Don E. Schultz and Dennis G. Martin, *Strategic Advertising Campaigns* (Chicago: Crain Books, 1979), p. 108.

7. "Researcher Says Test First, Then Advertise," *Bank Advertising News* 11, no. 17 (April 20, 1987), p. 7.

8. David W. Cravens, Gerald E. Hills, and Robert B. Woodruff, *Marketing Management* (Homewood, Ill.: Richard D. Irwin, 1987), p. 635.

9. Chester R. Wasson and Richard R. Shreve, "Research on Consumer Products and Services," in *Marketing Manager's Handbook,* 2nd rev. ed., ed. Steuart Henderson Britt and Norman F. Guess (Chicago: Dartnell Corporation, 1984), p. 393.

10. Robert M. Smith, "Knowledge Is Power. Research Can Help Your Marketing Program Succeed," *CASE Currents,* May–June 1982, pp. 8–12, 14.

11. Definition adapted from McCarthy and Perreault, *Basic Marketing,* p. 132; and Martin Zober and Herbert J. Schulte, "Gathering Marketing Information," in *Marketing Manager's Handbook,* ed. Britt and Guess, p. 315.

12. Zober and Schulte, "Gathering Marketing Information," p. 318.

13. Gerald J. Eskin, "Applications of Electronic Single-Source Measurement Systems," *European Research* 15, no. 1 (1987), pp. 12–20.

14. Leo Bogart, "What the Scanners Show," *Advertising Age,* June 8, 1987, pp. 18, 20.

15. Cravens, Hills, and Woodruff, *Marketing Management,* pp. 639–41.

16. Ibid.

17. Pamela L. Alreck and Robert B. Settle, *The Survey Research Handbook* (Homewood, Ill.: Richard D. Irwin, 1984), p. 98.

18. McCarthy and Perreault, *Basic Marketing,* p. 135.

19. Ibid.

20. "Heartbeat," *Advertising Age,* January 12, 1987, pp. 3, 44.

21. Edward Faison, *Advertising: A Behavioral Approach for Managers* (New York: John Wiley & Sons, 1980), pp. 664–65.

22. Ibid., p. 665.

23. Ibid.

24. "100 Leading National Advertisers—1987," *Advertising Age,* September 24, 1987.

25. Van Wallach, "Pretesting—A Necessary Evil or a Creative Tool?" *Advertising Age,* February 13, 1986, pp. 18–19.

26. William R. Dillon, Teresa Domzal, and Thomas J. Madden, "Evaluating Alternative Product Positioning Strategies," *Journal of Advertising Research,* August–September 1986, pp. 29–35.

27. Mary McCabe English, "Test Marketing: Higher Costs Boost Test Commercials," *Advertising Age,* February 13, 1986, pp. 14–15.

28. Ibid.

29. Robert Judson, "Marketing Mature Brands Requires Ad Analysis," *Marketing News,* January 2, 1987, pp. 20–21.

Chapter 7

1. John A. Byrne, "Executive Pay: Who Got What in '86," *Forbes,* May 4, 1987, pp. 50–58.

2. *Sports Management News,* November 25, 1985.

3. Marcy Magiera, "Avia Buy Puts Reebok on Nike Turf," *Advertising Age,* March 16, 1987, pp. 12, 87.

4. Richard Stansfield, *Advertising Manager's Handbook* (Chicago: Dartnell Corporation, 1969), p. 84.

5. William Giles, "Marketing Planning and Customer Policy," *Management Decision (U.K.)* 24, no. 3 (1986), pp. 19–27.

6. Margaret L. Friedman, "How to Write a Marketing Plan for Your Service Organization," *Agency Sales Magazine,* February 1987, pp. 42–46.

7. G. A. Marken, "Success Is No Accident; You Need a Plan," *Marketing News,* May 23, 1986, p. 28.

8. Courtland L. Bovée and William F. Arens, *Contemporary Advertising,* 2nd ed. (Homewood, Ill.: Richard D. Irwin, 1986), p. 223.

9. David W. Cravens, Gerald E. Hills, and Robert B. Woodruff, *Marketing Management* (Homewood, Ill.: Richard D. Irwin, 1987), pp. 245–46.

10. Philip Kotler, *Marketing Management: Analysis, Planning, and Control* (Englewood Cliffs, N.J.: Prentice-Hall, 1973), p. 369.

11. Philip Kotler and Sidney J. Levy, "Broadening the Concept of Marketing," *Journal of Marketing,* January 1969, pp. 10–15.

12. Burton Marcus et al., *Modern Marketing Management* (New York: Random House, 1980), p. 556.

13. Fred Posner, "Smart Strategy + Superb Execution = Great Advertising" (Speech before American Marketing Association, Marketing Management Conference, New York, March 31, 1982).

14. Kotler, *Marketing Management,* p. 89.

15. David Ogilvy, *Ogilvy on Advertising* (New York: Random House, 1985), p. 12.

16. "Barricades to Strategic Marketing Thinking," *Planning Review,* February 1987, pp. 8–15.

17. Richard L. Erickson, "Marketing Planning: There Is No Magic," *Journal of Business & Industrial Marketing,* Fall 1986, pp. 61–67.

18. Kotler, *Marketing Management,* pp. 360–70.

19. John O'Toole, *The Trouble with Advertising,* 2nd ed. (New York: Random House, 1985), p. 103.

20. Russell H. Colley, *Defining Advertising Goals for Measured Advertising Results* (New York: Association of National Advertisers, 1961), p. 1.

21. David Clark Scott, "Finding Out What Makes Us Tick," *The Christian Science Monitor,* January 27, 1987, pp. 1, 16; and O'Toole, *Trouble with Advertising,* pp. 128–30.

22. Robert D. Buzzell and Frederick D. Wiersema, "Successful Share-Building Strategies," *Harvard Business Review,* January–February 1981, p. 135.

23. Leo Bogart, *Strategy in Advertising* (New York: Harcourt Brace Jovanovich, 1967), p. 28.

24. Ibid., pp. 19–23.

25. Kent M. Lancaster and Judith A. Stern, "Computer-Based Advertising Budgeting Practices of Leading U.S. Consumer Advertisers," *Journal of Advertising* 12, no. 4 (1983), pp. 4–9.

26. Richard Vaughn, "How Advertising Works: A Planning Model Revisited," *Journal of Advertising Research,* February–March 1986, pp. 57–66.

Chapter 8

1. "Stars in Your Eyes: *The Wall Street Journal* Creative Leaders, 1977–1987," Supplement to *Advertising Age,* March 26, 1987.

2. John O'Toole, *The Trouble with Advertising,* 2nd ed. (New York: Random House, 1985), p. 131.
3. Ibid., p. 132.
4. Ibid., pp. 132–33.
5. John Caples, "A Dozen Ways to Develop Advertising Ideas," *Advertising Age,* November 14, 1983, pp. M4–M5, M46.
6. David Ogilvy, *Ogilvy on Advertising* (New York: Random House, 1985), pp. 17–18.
7. F. Allen Foster, *Advertising: Ancient Market Place to Television* (New York: Criterion Books, 1967), pp. 166–67.
8. O'Toole, *Trouble with Advertising,* p. 143.
9. Herbert L. Kahn, "Your Own Brand of Advertising for Non-consumer Products," *Harvard Business Review,* January–February 1986, p. 24.
10. Kim B. Rotzoll, "Gossage Revisited: Reflections of Advertising's Legendary Iconoclast," *Journal of Advertising* 9, no. 4 (1980), pp. 6–14; and Richard Rapaport, "The San Francisco Creative Heritage," *Madison Avenue,* October 1985, pp. 50–54, 117.
11. Ogilvy, *Ogilvy on Advertising,* p. 71.
12. Ibid., pp. 10–11.
13. Richard Stansfield, *The Advertising Manager's Handbook* (Chicago, Dartnell Corporation, 1969).
14. Marie Spadoni, "Fallon McElligott Rolls Stone into the '80s: Trade Advertising," *Advertising Age,* August 18, 1986, pp. S3, S9–S10.
15. Harold M. Spielman, "In Copy Research, Practice Makes Almost Perfect," *Advertising Age,* November 1, 1984, pp. 16–22.
16. Philip Ward Burton, *Advertising Copywriting* (Columbus, Ohio: Grid, 1974), p. 73. Reprinted with permission from Grid Publishing, Inc.
17. Ogilvy, *Ogilvy on Advertising,* p. 119.
18. Laurie Freeman, "Lou Centlivre Has One Thing in Mind: FUN," *Advertising Age,* July 25, 1985, pp. 3, 63.
19. Spielman, "Practice Makes Almost Perfect," pp. 16–22.
20. O'Toole, *Trouble with Advertising,* p. 149.
21. Ibid., p. 148.
22. Ogilvy, *Ogilvy on Advertising,* pp. 118–20.
23. Kahn, "Your Own Brand of Advertising," p. 24.
24. Pat Sloan, "Obsession Leads to Poison, Decadence: Fragrance Marketers Aim for Shock," *Advertising Age,* July 29, 1985, p. 33.

Chapter 9

1. Mark Lawrence, "The Sweet Taste of Success," *Advertising Techniques,* January 1984, pp. 8–10, 12, 13.
2. Debra Kent, "Savoring the Sense of Success," *Advertising Age,* July 6, 1987, pp. C8–C19.
3. Ken Gofton, "Design: Heading for the Shelf," *Marketing (U.K.),* February 12, 1987, pp. 43–44.
4. Joel G. Kahn, *Print Casebooks 3: 1978–79 Edition, The Best in Advertising* (Washington, D.C.: R. C. Publications, 1978), pp. 78–84.
5. J. Douglas Johnson, *Advertising Today* (Chicago: Science Research Associates, 1978), pp. 91–92.
6. John O'Toole, *The Trouble with Advertising,* 2nd ed. (New York: Random House, 1985), p. 144.
7. David Ogilvy, *Ogilvy on Advertising* (New York: Random House, 1985), pp. 88–89.

8. Ibid.
9. Ibid.
10. Richard H. Stansfield, *Advertising Manager's Handbook* (Chicago: Dartnell Corporation, 1969), pp. 640–41.
11. Carol Moog, "Youth Marketing—Cashing In on Children's Smiles," *Advertising Age,* February 14, 1985, pp. 18, 20.
12. Ann Cooper, "Making Ads That Sizzle: Rochelle Udell Takes the Sensual and Striking Approach," *Advertising Age,* July 18, 1985, pp. 9, 45–56.
13. Walter P. Margulies, *Packaging Power* (New York: World Publishing, 1970), p. 62.
14. Michael Gershman, "Packaging's Role in Remarketing," *Management Review,* May 1987, pp. 41–45.
15. Sheila Clark, "Packaging—Not Just a Pretty Design," *Chief Executive (U.K.),* November 1986, pp. 80–81.
16. Teresa Reese, *Print Casebooks 7, 1987/1988: The Best in Packaging* (Bethesda, Md.: R. C. Publications, 1986), pp. 88–90.
17. Ibid., pp. 46–49.
18. Phyllis Furman, "Grocery Marketing: Redesign Puts Old Packages in a New Light," *Advertising Age,* May 4, 1987, pp. S20–S21.
19. Margulies, *Packaging Power,* pp. 62–67.
20. Ibid.

Chapter 10

1. Peter Gambaccini, "The Amazing Paccione," *American Photographer* 4, no. 5 (May 1980), pp. 34–39.
2. Winnie O'Kelley, "Computers Create Graphic Palette," *Advertising Age,* April 28, 1986, p. 54.
3. Jeffrey Young, "Computer Graphics: Toys or Tools?" *Personal Computing,* February 1985, pp. 53–59.
4. Roger Hill and Jeff Macharyas, "Talking with the Illustration Man," *Publishing Trade,* July–August 1986, pp. 20–23.
5. David Ogilvy, *Ogilvy on Advertising* (New York: Random House, 1985), pp. 96–97.
6. "In-House Photocomposition Gets Better, Less Costly" *Office,* June 1986, pp. 84–86, 111.
7. Stephanie Cook, "The Electronic Palette Has Retouchers on the Run," *Business Week,* Industrial/Technology Edition, January 12, 1987, pp. 122H–122I.

Chapter 11

1. Aimee Stern and David Kiley, "Advertising: Reality Makes a Comeback," *Business Month,* May 1987, pp. 48–50.
2. Pamela Ellis-Simons, "Bartles & Jaymes Wine Coolers: There's Gold in Them Thar Hicks," *Marketing & Media Decisions,* March 1987, pp. 69–76.
3. Ed Fitch, "Truth Be Told, Deception Is In," *Advertising Age,* April 20, 1987, p. 56.
4. "TV's Mr. Whipple, Dick Wilson, Wraps His 20th Year," *People,* December 12, 1984, p. 151.
5. "Ten Newsmakers of 1986," *Advertising Age,* December 29, 1986, pp. 3, 9, 13, 20, 25; and Barbara Milbauer, "GF Puts Jell-O on Ice with Pudding Pops," *Madison Avenue,* May 1983, p. 104.
6. "Cost of TV Spot Production Escalates to Nearly $125,000," *Marketing News,* September 26, 1986, p. 6.

7. Harold M. Spielman, "In Copy Research, Practice Makes Almost Perfect," *Advertising Age,* November 1, 1984, pp. 16–22.

8. David Ogilvy, *Ogilvy on Advertising* (New York: Random House, 1985), p. 109.

9. Hooper White, "TV Commercial Production: Creatives Redirect a Complex Scene," *Advertising Age,* March 31, 1986, pp. S1–S2.

10. Mary McCabe English, "Test Marketing: Higher Costs Boost Test Commercials," *Advertising Age,* February 13, 1986, pp. 14–15.

11. Ogilvy, *Ogilvy on Advertising,* pp. 103–13.

12. Ibid., p. 107–8.

13. Ibid., p. 105.

14. Gordon L. Patzer, "Source Credibility as a Function of Communicator Physical Attractiveness," *Journal of Business Research,* June 1983, pp. 229–41.

15. Ogilvy, *Ogilvy on Advertising,* p. 105.

16. Dylan Landis, "Sedelmaier Spots Have Alaska Airlines Roaring," *Adweek,* July 29, 1985, p. 10.

17. "Forget Jingles and Jokes in These Cinema Verité Ads," *The Wall Street Journal,* April 16, 1987.

18. Judith Reitman, "Cutting the Clutter with Computer Graphics," *Marketing & Media Decisions,* May 1985, pp. 52–58, 168.

19. Ed Fitch, "TRW Image Campaign Frees Wyse Ideas," *Advertising Age,* November 29, 1984, p. 50.

20. Harry Wayne McMahan, "Levi's," *Advertising Age,* October 31, 1977, p. 58.

21. Albert R. Karr, "Lively Raisins on TV Are Grapes of Wrath to One Distributor," *The Wall Street Journal,* January 21, 1987.

22. Joan Hamilton, "You've Come a Long Way, Gumby: 'Claymation' Is the Hottest Thing in Commercials, and Will Vinton's Ad for California Raisins Is the Reason," *Business Week,* December 8, 1986, p. 74.

23. Ogilvy, *Ogilvy on Advertising,* p. 112.

24. Alan Radding, "TV Commercial Production: Secondary Markets Step into the Spotlight," *Advertising Age,* March 31, 1986, p. S–18.

25. Kenneth Roman and Jane Maas, *How to Advertise* (New York: St. Martin's Press, 1976), pp. 79–81.

26. James Suckling, "Choosing the Right Medium: It's No Mean Feat/Making a Habit of Radio," *Advertising Age,* January 16, 1984, pp. M–34, M–36.

27. Murphy A. Sewall and Dan Sarel, "Characteristics of Radio Commercials and Their Recall Effectiveness," *Journal of Marketing,* January 1986, pp. 52–60.

28. Ogilvy, *Ogilvy on Advertising,* pp. 113–16; Bob Weinstein, "Radio Is a Riot," *Madison Avenue,* June 1985, pp. 70–74.

29. Albert C. Book and Norman D. Cary, *The Radio and Television Commercial* (Chicago: Crain Books, 1978), p. 18.

30. Milton H. Biow, *Butting In—An Adman Speaks Out* (Garden City, N.Y.: Doubleday, 1964), p. 136.

31. Wallace A. Ross and Bob Landers, "Commercial Categories," *Radio Plays the Plaza* (New York: Radio Advertising Bureau, 1969).

Chapter 12

1. "Canon Clicks with AE-1 Camera Campaign," *Marketing Communications,* May 1980, pp. 73–74.

2. Carol Hall, "Sharp Shooters," *Marketing and Media Decisions,* May 1986, p. 128.

3. Valarie A. Zeithaml, "Piecing Together a Fragmented Market," *Marketing and Media Decisions,* April 1986, p. 160.

4. "Bates Rates CPM Performance," *Marketing and Media Decisions,* August 1986, p. 46.

5. "Watch Your Step!" *Marketing and Media Decisions,* August 1986, p. 34.

6. Jack Z. Sissors and Jim Surmanek, *Advertising Media Planning,* 2nd ed. (Lincolnwood, Ill.: NTC Business Books, 1982), p. 220.

7. Ed Papazian, "The Frequency Fracas," *Marketing and Media Decisions,* June 1986, p. 85.

8. Stacey Lippman, "How Much Frequency?" *Marketing and Media Decisions,* May 1986, p. 117.

9. Hall, "Sharp Shooters," p. 139.

10. "Effective Use of Print: The Current Thinking," *Inside Print,* January 1987, p. 119.

11. Kenneth Longman, *Advertising* (New York: Harcourt Brace Jovanovich, 1971), pp. 211–12.

12. "Effective Use of Print," p. 119.

13. David Kalish, "The Cinema Sell," *Marketing and Media Decisions,* August 1986, p. 24.

14. Stephen P. Phelps, "Media Planning: The Measurement . . . Gap," *Marketing and Media Decisions,* July 1986, p. 151.

15. Longman, *Advertising,* p. 351.

16. Jim Surmanek, *Media Planning* (Lincolnwood, Ill.: NTC Business Books, 1985), p. 24.

17. Longman, *Advertising,* p. 351.

18. Ibid., pp. 207–10.

19. Ibid., pp. 371–72.

20. Sissors and Surmanek, *Advertising Media Planning,* p. 358.

21. Rich Zahradnik, "Media's Micro Age," *Marketing and Media Decisions,* April 1986, p. 50.

Chapter 13

1. Tom Goss, *Print Casebooks 6: 1984–85 Edition, The Best in Advertising* (Washington, D.C.: R. C. Publications, 1984), pp. 25–26.

2. Aimee Stern, "Resurgence in Print Advertising," *Dun's Business Month,* January 1986, p. 46.

3. Leo Bogart, "Newspapers Fight Off Broadcast Challenge, Survive, and Prosper," *Advertising Age,* April 30, 1980, p. 176.

4. Opinion Research Corporation, reported in *Key Facts about Newspapers and Advertising, 1982* (New York: Newspaper Advertising Bureau, 1982), p. 1.

5. Russell Shaw, "Papers Losing Ground in National Advertising," *Advertising Age,* July 25, 1985, p. 52.

6. *'86 Facts about Newspapers* (Washington, D.C.: American Newspaper Publishers Association, 1986).

7. "U.S. Advertising Volume," *Advertising Age,* May 18, 1987.

8. *'86 Facts about Newspapers.*

9. Chris Woodward, "SAUs Meet Nearly Uniform Acceptance," *Advertising Age,* July 25, 1985, p. 46.

10. *'86 Facts about Newspapers.*

11. Eileen Norris, "Ad Vehicles Bombard Consumers," *Advertising Age,* November 7, 1985, p. 16.

12. Margaret Rosser, "*USA Today,* Yesterday and Tomorrow," *Marketing and Media Decisions,* December 1986, p. 108.

13. Shaw, "Papers Losing Ground," p. 50.

14. Ibid.

15. William F. Gloede, "Newspapers Cut National Ad Rate," *Advertising Age,* June 8, 1987, p. 1.

16. "A Network of Co-op Power," *Marketing Communication,* June 1986, p. 80.

17. "Effective Uses of Print: The Current Thinking," *Inside Print,* January 1987, p. 119.

18. Tom Goss, *Print Casebooks 7* (Bethesda, Md.: R. C. Publications, 1986), p. 72.

19. Stephen H. Martin, "Magazines: A Medium to Watch," *Marketing and Media Decisions,* August 1985, p. 79.

20. "Reader's Choice: Ads with Impact," *Inside Print,* January 1987, p. 35.

21. Steve Kurtzer, "Magazines: The Next Decade," *Marketing and Media Decisions,* June 1985, p. 142.

22. Magazine Publishers Association, February 1987.

23. Belinda Halin-Salkin, "Viewing the Future in a New Light," *Advertising Age,* October 3, 1985, p. 16.

24. "Effective Uses of Print," p. 118.

25. Joanne Lipman, "Magazines Escalate Rate-Cutting for Ads," *The Wall Street Journal,* September 8, 1986, p. 6.

26. Robert Reed, "Audit Bureau Makes Numbers Count," *Advertising Age,* January 9, 1984, p. M4.

Chapter 14

1. A. Craig Copetas, "The Selling of the Entrepreneur," *Inc.,* March 1986, p. 34.

2. *TV Basics 1986–87* (New York: Television Bureau of Advertising, 1986), p. 2.

3. *Adweek's Marketer's Guide to Media,* October–December 1987, p. 12.

4. Ronald Alsop, "Advertisers Go Beyond Soaps to Reach Daytime Audience," *The Wall Street Journal,* September 19, 1985, p. 33.

5. "Terminal Television," *American Demographics,* January 1987, p. 15.

6. Verne Gay, "Pressure on TV Nets as 15s Usage Grows," *Advertising Age,* April 14, 1986, p. 1.

7. Joe Mandese, "Is Home Video the Real Fourth Network?" *Adweek,* March 18, 1986, p. 4.

8. Marianne Paskowski, "See Spot Jump," *Marketing and Media Decisions,* April 1986, p. 66.

9. Richard W. Stevenson, "Bartering for TV Ad Time," *The New York Times,* August 3, 1985, p. 19.

10. Aimee Stern, "New Power in Buying TV Time," *Dun's Business Month,* June 1985, p. 59.

11. *1987 Cable TV Facts* (New York: Cabletelevision Advertising Bureau, Inc., 1987), p. 4.

12. Ibid., p. 10.

13. Len Strazewski, "Advertisers Wired about Cable's Reach," *Advertising Age,* October 19, 1987.

14. David Samuel Barr, *Advertising on Cable: A Practical Guide for Users* (Englewood Cliffs, N.J.: Prentice-Hall, 1985), p. 71.

15. Judann Dagnoli, "Cable Tests Hot-Wired to Consumer Preferences," *Advertising Age,* December 1, 1986, p. S-10.

16. Alan Breznick, "Local Cable Catches onto Ad Sales," *Adweek,* March 18, 1986, p. 34.

17. *1987 Cable TV Facts,* p. 5.

18. Barr, *Advertising on Cable,* p. 34.

19. Ibid., p. 43.

20. Marianne Miller, "SPAM's Media Plan: It Might Surprise You," *Marketing and Media Decisions,* October 1985, p. 69.

21. *Radio Facts, 1987–1988* (New York: Radio Advertising Bureau, Inc., 1987).

22. Ibid.

23. William H. Dunlap, "Staying Tuned to Business/Industrial Radio Advertising," *Business Marketing,* October 1985, p. 108.

24. Ronald Alsop, "More Firms Tune into Radio to Stretch Their Ad Budgets," *The Wall Street Journal,* July 17, 1986, p. 25.

25. *Radio Facts, 1986–1987* (New York: Radio Advertising Bureau, Inc., 1986), pp. 28–31.

26. Helen Rogan, "AM Radio Fights to Win Listeners with Stereo and Format Changes," *The Wall Street Journal,* October 21, 1985, p. 25.

27. Janice Steinberg, "New Formats Gain Frequency on AM Band," *Advertising Age,* August 29, 1985, p. 18.

28. Michael Hedges, "Radio's Life Styles," *American Demographics,* February 1986, p. 3.

29. Julie Liesse Erickson, "Networks Sharing Airwaves with Syndicators," *Advertising Age,* August 29, 1985, p. 28.

Chapter 15

1. "National Geographic Sells 380M Journey to China Books," *Direct Marketing,* November 1983, p. 76.

2. "Direct Marketing: A Useful Advertising Medium and a Valuable Sales Tool," *Small Business Report,* September 1985, p. 71.

3. "Direct Marketing: What Is It?" *Direct Marketing,* September 1983, p. 20.

4. "Ringing Up Annoyance," *Target Marketing,* February 1987, p. 30.

5. Ibid.

6. Christine Adamec, "Niche Marketing by Mail," *In Business,* November–December 1986, p. 32.

7. Albert Haas, Jr., "How to Sell Almost Anything by Direct Mail," *Across the Board,* November 1986, p. 49.

8. Bob Davis, "Baby Goods Firms See Direct Mail as the Perfect Pitch for New Moms," *The Wall Street Journal,* January 29, 1986, p. 33.

9. Haas, "How to Sell Almost Anything," p. 50.

10. Louise Tutelian, "Catalogs Turn a Page in Marketing," *USA Today,* October 17, 1986, p. 1B.

11. Edmund L. Andrews, "A Catalog of Woes," *Venture,* May 1986, p. 54.

12. Bob Stone, *Successful Direct Marketing Methods* (Chicago: Crain Books, 1979), p. 79.

13. William R. Morrisey, "Gain Competitive Edge with Data-Based Direct Marketing," *Marketing News,* March 15, 1985, p. 22.

14. Diane C. Donovan, "Marketing," *Nation's Business,* July 1986, p. 35.

15. Peter Finch, "The Direct Marketing Data Base Revolution," *Business Marketing,* August 1985, p. 46.

16. Institute of Outdoor Advertising.
17. Robert Levy, "Breakout in Billboards," *Dun's Business Month,* May 1985, p. 44.
18. Ronald Alsop, "Billboard Firms Lure New Ads as Tobacco, Liquor Sales Slide," *The Wall Street Journal,* May 7, 1987, p. 29.
19. Barbara Walton, "How to Reach a Very Specific Market Target Rather Efficiently," *Madison Avenue,* November 1985, p. 98.
20. Ibid.
21. Nancy L. Croft, "Spiels on Wheels," *Nation's Business,* February 1987, p. 14.
22. "Grandesigns Turns Truck Space into Sales," *Entrepreneur,* October 1985, p. 9.

Chapter 16

1. Julie Franz, "Quaker Oats Finds Cap'n Crunch Lost with Hide-and-Seek," *Advertising Age,* May 26, 1986, p. 53.
2. "Seventh Annual Advertising and Sales Promotion Report, *Marketing Communications,* August 1986, p. 8.
3. William A. Robinson, *Best Sales Promotions* (Chicago, Crain Books, 1979), pp. 40–41.
4. Richard Edel, "Trade Wars Threaten Future Peace of Marketers," *Advertising Age,* August 15, 1985, p. 18.
5. Ronald Alsop, "Retailers Buying Far in Advance to Exploit Trade Promotions," *The Wall Street Journal,* October 9, 1986, p. 35.
6. "Seventh Annual Advertising and Sales Promotion Report," p. 8.
7. Donnelly Marketing, *9th Annual Survey of Promotional Practices.*
8. Alix M. Freedman, "Use of Free Product Samples Wins New Favor as Sales Tool," *The Wall Street Journal,* August 28, 1986, p. 19.
9. William A. Robinson, *Best Sales Promotions,* 6th ed. (Lincolnwood, Ill.: NTC Business Books, 1987), p. 261.
10. Steven R. Martin, "Consumers' Use of Coupons Rose 13% to 7.32 Billion in 1986," Manufacturers Coupon Control Center, special release.
11. Ibid.
12. "Seventh Annual Advertising and Sales Promotion Report," p. 10.
13. "Computers Help Foil Coupon Fraud," *Marketing News,* August 15, 1986, p. 1.
14. Edward D. Meyer, "Promotion Magic," *Boardroom Reports,* January 1, 1987, p. 6.
15. Point of Purchase Advertising Institute, New York. 1987.
16. J. Max Robins, "Making Point-of-Purchase More Pointed," *Adweek,* November 10, 1986, p. 9.
17. Mark Paul, "The Electronic Salesman," *Marketing Communications,* December 1986, p. 32.
18. Kevin T. Higgins, "Specialty Advertising Thrives," *Marketing News,* October 11, 1985, p. 20.
19. Richard G. Edel, "Specialties: Gifts of Motivation," *Marketing Communications,* April 1986, p. 75.
20. Kate Bertrand, "Attention-Grabbing Trade Show Gadgetry," *Business Marketing,* November 1986, p. 106.
21. A. J. Faria and J. R. Dickinson, "Behind the Push to Exhibit at Trade Shows," *Business Marketing,* August 8, 1985, p. 100.

22. "The Rush to Mine Gold from Yellow Pages," *Forbes,* September 29, 1986, p. 133.
23. Ralph D. Rose, "Yellow Pages: Vital Marketing Tool Is Changing Rapidly," *Marketing News,* May 24, 1985, p. 39.

Chapter 17

1. Irving Burstiner, *Basic Retailing* (Homewood, Ill.: Richard D. Irwin, 1986), p. 577.
2. Mary McCabe English, "Total Market Coverage: Shared Mail Digging In," *Advertising Age,* June 14, 1984, p. 17.
3. Eileen Norris, "Total Market Coverage: Ad Vehicles Bombard Consumers," *Advertising Age,* November 7, 1985, p. 16.
4. "Bigsby & Kruthers Puts 'Suitbook' on Radio," *Ad/Pro,* March 1987, p. 5.
5. "Mining for Gold in Yellow Pages," *U.S. News & World Report,* October 13, 1986, p. 53.
6. Barry Berman and Joel R. Evans, *Retail Management: A Strategic Approach* (New York: Macmillan, 1986), p. 401.
7. Norris, "Total Market Coverage," p. 16.
8. Susan Sachs, "The P. T. Barnum of the Office Furniture Trade," *Entrepreneur,* December 1985, p. 74.
9. "Younkers' Carl Zitz, Marketing VP, Tells How Store Is Changing," *Ad/Pro,* October 1986, p. 4.
10. "Kings of the Tacky Commercials," *Dun's Review,* May 1979, pp. 60–64.
11. "Creativity in Ads: How Ideas Flow," *Ad/Pro,* February 1987, p. 1.
12. "At Bullock's: Always on Sunday, in Four Color," *Ad/Pro,* March 1987, p. 1.

Chapter 18

1. "Product Survival: Lessons of the Tylenol Terrorism" (Washington, D.C.: Washington Business Information, 1982), pp. 11–17.
2. Amelia Lobsenz, "How to Blend PR into Your Marketing Mix," *Marketing News,* March 15, 1985, p. 37.
3. *Corporate Advertising/Phase II,* an Expanded Study of Corporate Advertising Effectiveness, conducted for *Time* magazine by Yankelovich, Skelly & White, Inc. No date.
4. Meryl Davids, "16th Annual Review of Corporate Advertising Expenditures," *Public Relations Journal,* September 1987, p. 29.
5. Ibid.
6. Maureen F. Hartigan and Peter Finch, "The New Emphasis on Strategy in Corporate Advertising," *Business Marketing,* February 1986, p. 48.
7. Ibid., p. 49.
8. Anne B. Fisher, "Spiffing Up the Corporate Image," *Fortune,* July 21, 1986, p. 72.
9. Kate Bertrand, "When Silence Isn't Golden," *Business Marketing,* February 1987, p. 64.
10. Art Stevens, "How to Handle Bad News," *Industry Week,* October 14, 1985, p. 63.
11. Ibid., p. 64.
12. "Public Relations: Creating a Company Image," *Small Business Report,* February 1987, p. 49.
13. Michael Hiestand and Laurie Petersen, "High-Brow Tie-Ins Gain Ground," *Marketing Week,* February 23, 1987, p. 1.

14. A. Craig Copetas, "Make Profits, Not War," *Inc.,* January 1986, p. 21.
15. John A. Platta, "Energizing Sales with Public Relations," *Business Marketing,* June 1986, p. 133.
16. Jeanne Saddler, "Public Relations Firms Offer 'News' to TV," *The Wall Street Journal,* April 2, 1985, p. 6.
17. Data supplied by ABC, NBC, and CBS.
18. John Moes, "Military Asks What It Can Do for Recruits," *Advertising Age,* July 19, 1984, p. 36.
19. "Peddling a Social Cause," p. 58.

Chapter 19

1. Marian Katz, "The Appeal of China TV," *International Advertiser,* June 1986, p. 37.
2. "Advertisers Take On China," *Newsweek,* December 1, 1986, p. 65.
3. E. Jerome McCarthy, *Basic Marketing* (Homewood, Ill.: Richard D. Irwin, 1984), p. 693.
4. John Fayerweather, *International Marketing* (Englewood Cliffs, N.J.: Prentice-Hall, 1970), p. 2.
5. "The Ad Biz Gloms onto 'Global,'" *Fortune,* November 12, 1984, p. 77.
6. Christy Marshall, "As Ad Boundaries Blur, Creatives Seek Global Solutions," *Adweek,* November 11, 1985, p. 34.

7. Ibid.
8. Philip Geier, "Global Products, Localized Messages," *Marketing Communications,* December 1986, pp. 24–26.
9. "Efficacy of Global Ad Projects Is Questioned in Firm's Survey," *The Wall Street Journal,* September 13, 1984, p. 29.
10. Ernest Dichter, "The World Customer," *Harvard Business Review,* July–August 1961, p. 116.
11. "Yankee Goods—and Know-How—Go Abroad," *Advertising Age,* May 17, 1982, pp. M-14, M-16.
12. "The Ad Biz Gloms onto 'Global,'" p. 80.
13. Dichter, "World Customer," p. 80.
14. Dean M. Peebles and John K. Ryans, *Management of International Advertising* (Boston: Allyn & Bacon, 1984), p. 145.
15. Ibid., p. 149.
16. Philip R. Cateora, *International Marketing* (Homewood, Ill.: Richard D. Irwin, 1983), pp. 85–87.
17. Michael Brizz, "How to Learn What Japanese Buyers Really Want," *Business Marketing,* January 1987, p. 72.
18. Fayerweather, *International Marketing,* pp. 92–93.
19. Ibid., p. 90.
20. Ibid., p. 84.
21. Maria Katz, "No Women, No Alcohol; Learn Saudis Taboos before Placing Ads," *International Advertiser,* February 1986, p. 11.
22. Ibid.

CREDITS AND ACKNOWLEDGMENTS

Chapter 1

Figures 1–1, 1–2, 1–3, 1–4, and Ad Lab 1-A   Courtesy The Coca-Cola Company.

Figure 1–5   Dick Sutpen, *The Mad Old Ads* (New York: McGraw-Hill, 1966).

Figure 1–6   Courtesy Fallon McElligott.

Figure 1–7   Courtesy Henkel Corporation.

Figure 1–8   Courtesy Stanley Hardware.

Figure 1–9   Courtesy BBDO International, Inc.

Figure 1–10   Courtesy J. Walter Thompson USA.

Figure 1–11   Courtesy Great American First Savings Bank and Palmer/Sharrit & Co.

Figure 1–12   Courtesy McCann-Erickson/Toronto.

Figure 1–13   Adapted from Frank Presbey, *History and Development of Advertising* (Garden City, N.Y.: Doubleday, 1929), p. 361. Copyright 1929 by Frank Presbey. Reprinted by permission of Doubleday & Company, Inc.

Figure 1–14   Reprinted with permission from September 24, 1987, issue of *Advertising Age.* Copyright 1987 by Crain Communications, Inc.

Figure 1–15   Dick Sutpen, *The Mad Old Ads* (New York: McGraw-Hill, 1966).

Figure 1–16   Reprinted with permission from April 30, 1980, issue of *Advertising Age.* Copyright 1980 by Crain Communications, Inc.

Figure 1–17   Henry Ford Museum/ Edison Institute.

Figure 1–18   Courtesy Philip Morris U.S.A.

Figure 1–19   Courtesy Volkswagen of America.

Figure 1–20   Courtesy The American Lung Association of Los Angeles County and Ketchum Advertising/Los Angeles.

Coca-Cola Portfolio   Coke and Coca-Cola are registered trademarks of the Coca-Cola Company and permission for use granted by the Company. Permission for use of ads granted by The Coca-Cola Company.

Figure 1–22   Courtesy Union Oil of California.

Figure 1–23   The Hershey Kisses chocolate advertisement is reprinted by permission of the copyright owner, Hershey Foods Corporation, Hershey, Pennsylvania, U.S.A. The conical configuration, the attached plume device and the words HERSHEY'S KISSES are registered trademarks of Hershey Foods Corporation.

Figure 1–24   Photograph by Gordon Wagner/Bookworks.

Figure 1–25   Concialdi Design.

Figure 1–26   Historical Pictures Service, Chicago.

Chapter 2

Figure 2–1   Courtesy Sunkist Growers Inc.

Figure 2–2   Courtesy Harry Kerker-HCM.

Figure 2–3   Courtesy Fallon McElligott.

Figure 2–4   Courtesy Walt Disney World Co.

Figure 2–5   Courtesy Northwestern Bell.

Figure 2–7   Courtesy Martin Scorsese; Mitsubishi Electric Sales.

Figure 2–8   Courtesy Foote, Cone & Belding.

Figure 2–9   Courtesy Xerox Corporation.

Figure 2–10   Courtesy The Coca-Cola Company; courtesy The Quaker Oats Company; courtesy Nabisco Brands, Inc.; courtesy The Prudential Insurance Company of America; courtesy The Pillsbury Company; courtesy The DuPont Company; courtesy Federal Deposit Insurance Corporation.

Figure 2–11   Courtesy HLS Management Company.

Figure 2–12   Courtesy Pagano Schenck & Kay.

Figure 2–13   Courtesy BBDO.

Ad Lab 2-C   Courtesy The Procter & Gamble Company.

Ad Lab 2-D   Courtesy W. R. Grace & Co.

Figure 2–14   Courtesy NARB.

Chapter 3

Figure 3–1   Courtesy Scali, McCabe, Sloves, Inc.

Figure 3–3   *Printer's Ink,* December 16, 1960, p. 27.

Figure 3–5   Courtesy Benton & Bowles, Inc. and the Procter & Gamble Company.

Figure 3–8   Courtesy Bloomingdale's.

Ad Lab 3-A   Reprinted with permission from the March 14, 1988, issue of *Advertising Age.* Copyright 1988 by Crain Communications, Inc.

Figure 3–9   Courtesy J. Walter Thompson U.S.A.

Figure 3–10   Courtesy Young & Rubicam, Inc.

Figure 3–11   Courtesy The van Bronkhorst Group, Inc.

Figure 3–12   Courtesy Scali, McCabe, Sloves, Inc.

Figure 3–13   Courtesy Kerlick, Switzer & Johnson Advertising, Inc.

Figure 3–14   Courtesy Martin/Williams.

Figure 3–18   Adapted from American Association of Advertising Agencies data.

Figure 3–20   Courtesy Justamere Advertising Agency.

Figure 3–21   Courtesy Chiat/Day.

Chapter 4

Figure 4–1   Courtesy Kenyon & Eckhardt, Inc.

Ad Labs 4A–4E   Adapted from "Apple Computer, Inc.," *Business Marketing,* November 1983, p. 50; "Apple Launches a Mac Attack," *Time,* January 30, 1984, p. 68; "Desktop Wars: Will Apple's Mac Trip the Dancing Elephant?" *Industry Week,* January 23, 1984, pp. 16–17; "IBM and Apple Battle for the Business Market," *Dun's Business Month,* April 1984, pp. 123–24; "Reviewing the Mac," *Newsweek,* January 30, 1984, p. 56. Photograph Courtesy Apple Computer, Inc.

Figure 4–3   Courtesy Clearwater Federal.

Figure 4–4   Courtesy Comtal/3M.

People in Advertising   From Al Ries and Jack Trout, *Positioning: The Battle for Your Mind* (New York: McGraw-Hill, 1981). Used with permission.

Figure 4–6   Courtesy Rubin Postaer and Associates. Courtesy Chrysler Corporation.

Figure 4–7   Courtesy Sunkist Growers, Inc.

Figure 4–8   Courtesy Sidjakov Berman & Gomez Design Communications.

Figure 4–9   Adapted from Ben M. Enis, *Marketing Principles* (Santa Monica, Calif.: Goodyear Publishing, 1980), p. 351.

Figure 4–10   Courtesy Diamond Information Centre, Art Director: Yoshiko Koike, Photographer: Masamitsu Yokosuka, Writer: Naoki Watanabe, Client: Diamond Information Centre, Editor: Soichi Kimura, Director: Soichi Kimura, Producer: Seiichi Takahashi, Agency: J. Walter Thompson Company Japan.

Figure 4–11   Courtesy Benton & Bowles, Inc. and The Procter & Gamble Company.

Figure 4–12 Adapted from Elwood S. Buffa and Barbara A. Pletcher, *Understanding Business Today* (Homewood, Ill.: Richard D. Irwin, 1980), p. 37.

Figure 4–13 Courtesy Backer Spielvogel Bates.

Figure 4–14 Courtesy BMW of North America, Inc.

Figure 4–15 Courtesy PIP Printing.

Figure 4–16 *Nation's Restaurant News,* August 3, 1987, p. F10.

Chapter 5

Figure 5–2 Courtesy Jaguar Cars Inc.

Figure 5–3 Adapted from Burton Marcus et al., *Modern Marketing Management* (New York: Random House, 1980), p. 66.

Figure 5–4 Courtesy Foote, Cone & Belding.

Figure 5–5 Adapted from William H. and Isabella C. M. Cunningham, *Marketing: A Managerial Approach* (Cincinnati: South-Western Publishing, 1981), p. 121; and data based on hierarchy of needs in "A Theory of Human Motivation," in *Motivation and Personality,* 2nd edition, by Abraham H. Maslow. Copyright 1970 by Abraham H. Maslow. By permission of Harper & Row Publishers, Inc.

Ad Lab 5-A Left, Courtesy McKinney, Silver & Rockett. Middle, Courtesy Young and Rubicam, Chicago. Right, Courtesy Young & Rubicam, New York.

Ad Lab 5-B Adapted from Harold W. Berkman and Christopher C. Gilson, *Consumer Behavior: Concepts and Strategies,* 2nd ed. (Boston: Kent Publishing Co., 1981), p. 249. Reprinted by permission of Kent Publishing, a Division of Wadsworth Inc.; and Jack Haberstroh, "Can't Ignore Subliminal Ad Charges," *Advertising Age,* pp. 3, 42, 44.

Figure 5–6 Courtesy Fallon McElligott.

Figure 5–8 Coke and Coca-Cola are registered trademarks of the Coca-Cola Company and permission for use granted by the Company.

Figure 5–9 Adapted from W. Lloyd Warner, Marchia Meeker, and Kenneth Eels, *Social Class in America* (New York: Harper & Row, 1960), pp. 6–32.

Figure 5–10 Courtesy Nike, Inc.

Figure 5–11 Courtesy Badillo/Compton, Inc.

Ad Lab 5-C Courtesy California Prune Board; courtesy Laurence, Charles & Free, Inc.; courtesy Young & Rubicam.

Figure 5–12 Philip Kotler, *Principles of Marketing* (Englewood Cliffs, N.J.: Prentice-Hall, 1980), p. 297. Copyright Prentice-Hall, Inc. Adapted by permission.

Figure 5–13 Adapted from David L. Kurtz and Louis E. Boone, *Marketing* (New York: Dryden Press, 1981), p. 146.

Figure 5–14 Courtesy Chiat/Day, Inc.

Figure 5–15 Adapted from Dik Warren Twedt, "How Important to Marketing Strategy Is the 'Heavy User'?" *Journal of Marketing,* January 1964, p. 72.

Figure 5–16 Adapted from Russell I. Haley, "Benefit Segmentation: A Decision-Oriented Research Tool," *Journal of Marketing* 32 (July 1968), p. 33.

Figure 5–17 Adapted from Arnold Mitchell, *The Nine American Lifestyles: Who We Are and Where We Are Going* (New York: Macmillan, 1983) and the Values and Lifestyles (VALS™) Program, SRI International, Menlo Park, California.

Figure 5–18 Adapted from E. Jerome McCarthy and William D. Perreault, Jr., *Basic Marketing,* 9th edition (Homewood, Ill.: Richard D. Irwin, 1987), p. 197.

Figure 5–19 Adapted from U.S. Department of Commerce, Bureau of the Census, Census of Manufacturers, Area Statistics (Washington, D.C.: U.S. Government Printing Office, 1977) p. 749.

Chapter 6

Figure 6–1 Courtesy NW Ayer Incorporated.

Ad Lab 6-A Adapted from Steuart Henderson Britt, *Marketing Managers Handbook* (Chicago: The Dartnell Corporation, 1973), pp. 286–87.

Figure 6–2 Adapted from Philip Kotler, *Principles of Marketing* (Englewood Cliffs, N.J.: Prentice-Hall, 1980). Copyright 1980 Prentice-Hall, Inc. Adapted by permission.

Ad Lab 6-B Adapted from Natalie Goldberg, "How to Use External Data in Marketing Research," *Marketing Communication,* March 1980, pp. 76–82.

Figures 6–4 and 6–5 Pamela L. Alreck and Robert B. Settle, *The Survey Research Handbook* (Homewood, Ill.: Richard D. Irwin, 1985), pp. 41, 65.

Ad Lab 6-C Adapted from *Everything You've Always Wanted to Know about TV Ratings,* A.C. Nielsen Company, 1978.

Figure 6–6 Courtesy NW Ayer Incorporated.

Checklist for Developing an Effective Questionnaire From Don E. Schultz and Dennis G. Martin, *Strategic Advertising Campaigns* (Chicago: Crain Books, 1979).

Figure 6–8 Photograph courtesy of Kenneth Hollander Associates, Inc.

Figure 6–10 Adapted from Edmund W. J. Faison, *Advertising: A Behavioral Approach for Managers* (New York: John Wiley & Sons, 1980), p. 664.

Figures 6–11, 6–12, 6–13, and 6–14 Courtesy NW Ayer Incorporated.

Figure 6–15 Courtesy Bruzzone Research Company.

Figure 6–16 Courtesy J. Walter Thompson USA and Starch INRA Hooper.

Figure 6–17 M. Wayne DeLozier, *The Marketing Communication Process.* Copyright 1976 by M. Wayne DeLozier. Used with permission of McGraw-Hill Book Company.

Chapter 7

Figure 7–1 Reprinted by permission of Reebok International Ltd.

Ad Lab 7-A Jack Trout and Al Ries, "Marketing Warfare," *Southern Advertising,* July 1978. Photographs by Wayne Bladholm.

Checklist for Situation Analysis Adapted from Russell H. Colley, *Defining Advertising Goals for Measured Advertising Results* (New York: Association of National Advertisers, 1961), pp. 62–68.

Figure 7–3 Courtesy NW Ayer Incorporated.

Figure 7–4 Courtesy Nike, Inc.

Figures 7–5 and 7–6 Reprinted by permission of Reebok International Ltd.

Figure 7–7 Courtesy Casa Myrna, Boston.

Figure 7–10 David Clark Scott, "Modern Advertising, 'The Subtle Persuasion,'" *The Christian Science Monitor,* January 27, 1987, pp. 1, 16.

Figure 7–11 Reprinted by permission of Reebok International Ltd.

Ad Lab 7–B Courtesy Hank Forssberg Advertising; advertisement and photograph reproduced with the permission of General Foods Corporation; courtesy Chiat/Day, Inc.; courtesy Scali, McCabe, Sloves, Inc.; courtesy Ogilvy & Mather/Houston; and courtesy Bozell & Jacobs, Inc.

Figure 7–12 Reprinted with permission from March 24, 1987, issue of *Advertising Age.* Copyright 1987 by Crain Communications, Inc.

Chapter 8

Figure 8–1 Courtesy *The Wall Street Journal.*

Figure 8–3 Courtesy Chiat/Day Inc. Advertising, New York.

Figure 8–4 Courtesy Henry Ford Museum/Edison Institute.

Figure 8–5 Courtesy Apple Computer, Inc.

Figure 8–6 Courtesy Allstate Insurance.

Figure 8–7 Courtesy Citibank.

Figure 8–8 Courtesy Advertising au Gratin/Minneapolis.

Figure 8–9 Courtesy Fallon McElligott.

Figure 8–10   Courtesy Kresser/Craig.

Ad Lab 8-A   Reprinted with permission from *Advertising Age,* March 14, 1983. Copyright Crain Communications, Inc.

Figure 8–11   Courtesy Levine, Huntley, Schmidt & Beaver.

Copywriters Portfolio   Courtesy Chiat/Day Inc. Advertising, New York; courtesy Levine, Huntley, Schmidt & Beaver; courtesy Timberland; courtesy Phillips-Ramsey; courtesy Ogilvy & Mather.

Figure 8–12   Courtesy Foote, Cone & Belding; Jozef Sumichrast, illustrator.

Figure 8–13   Courtesy Doyle Dane Bernbach Inc. Advertising.

Ad Lab 8-B   Adapted from Robert Gunning, *The Technique of Clear Writing,* rev. ed. (New York: McGraw-Hill, 1968), p. 38.

Figure 8–14   Courtesy Phillips-Ramsey.

Figure 8–15   *Trademark of The Dow Chemical Company.

Chapter 9

Figure 9–1   Courtesy Margeotes/Fertitta & Weiss.

Figure 9–2   Courtesy Prince Foods; Charles Spencer Anderson, Designer.

Figure 9–3   Courtesy Ackerman & McQueen.

Figure 9–4   Courtesy Yamaha Motor Corporation, U.S.A.

Figure 9–5   Courtesy J. Walter Thompson USA.

Ad Lab 9-A   Adapted from Mike Turner, "What Makes a Good Account Executive?" *Viewpoint* I (1980), pp. 27–28.

Figure 9–6   Courtesy Leo Burnett Company, Inc.

Figure 9–7   Courtesy Fallon McElligott.

Figure 9–8   Courtesy GreyCom Public Relations.

Figure 9–9   Courtesy Lord & Taylor.

Figure 9–10   Courtesy Foote, Cone & Belding.

Figure 9–11   Courtesy Talon.

Ad Lab 9-B   Adapted from Walter Margulies, "What Colors Should You Use?" *Media Decisions* (New York: Decision Publications).

Checklist for Choosing Illustrations   Left: Courtesy Austin Nichols & Co., Inc. Right: Courtesy The Martin Agency, Inc.

Art Director's Portfolio   Courtesy Fallon McElligott; courtesy Cole Henderson Drake; courtesy Marc Deschenes; courtesy Leo Burnett U.S.A.; Courtesy Esprit.

Figure 9–12   Courtesy Heinz U.S.A.

Figure 9–13   Courtesy Selame Design.

Ad Lab 9-C   Used with permission of General Mills, Inc.

Chapter 10

Figure 10–1   Courtesy Emilio Paccione, retoucher; Carl Fischer, photographer.

Figure 10–2   Courtesy Della Femina, Travisano & Partners, Inc.

Figure 10–3   Courtesy of Apple Computers, Inc.

Figure 10–4   Courtesy Chiat/Day.

Figure 10–7   Courtesy Scali, McCabe, Sloves, Inc.

Ad Lab 10-A   Courtesy Young & Rubicam, Inc.; courtesy Bozell & Jacobs, Inc.; courtesy Stimpson Associates; courtesy Calet, Hirsch & Spector, Inc.; courtesy Doyle Dane Bernbach Inc.

Figure 10–10   Courtesy AM Verityper, division of AM International.

Figure 10–14   Courtesy Heidelberg Eastern, Inc.

Figure 10–15   Courtesy Weyerhaeuser Credit Union.

Creative Department   Courtesy Young & Rubicam, Inc.

Chapter 11

Figure 11–1   Courtesy Benton & Bowles and Shooting Star.

Figure 11–3   Courtesy Genesco Inc.

Figure 11–4   Courtesy Corning Glass Works.

Figure 11–5   Courtesy Livingston & Company.

Figure 11–6   Courtesy Dow Consumer Products, Inc.

Figure 11–7   Courtesy Foote, Cone & Belding.

Figure 11–8   Courtesy Adolph Coors Company.

Figure 11–9   Courtesy Foote, Cone & Belding.

Figure 11–10   Courtesy KCBN, Inc.

Figure 11–11   Adapted with permission of Macmillan Publishing Co., Inc., from *Advertising,* by William M. Weilbacher, p. 273. Copyright 1962 by The Free Press.

Figure 11–12   Courtesy Commonwealth Edison Company.

Figure 11–13   Courtesy Della Femina, Travisano & Partners, Inc.

Creative Department   Courtesy Saatchi & Saatchi DFS Compton.

Ad Lab 11-A   Adapted from Wallace A. Ross and Bob Landers, "Commercial Categories," in *Radio Plays the Plaza* (New York: Radio Advertising Bureau, 1969).

Figure 11–14   Adapted with permission of Macmillan Publishing Co., Inc., from *Advertising,* by William M. Weilbacher, p. 273. Copyright 1962 by The Free Press.

Chapter 12

Figure 12–1   Courtesy GreyCom Inc.

Figure 12–2   Adapted from "Bates Rates CPM Performance," *Marketing and Media Decisions,* August 1986, p. 46. Data from Ted Bates Advertising.

Figure 12–3   Adapted from Jack Z. Sissors and E. Reynold Petray, *Advertising Media Planning* (Chicago: Crain Books, 1976).

Figure 12–4   Courtesy Canon U.S.A. Inc.

Figure 12–5   Jack Scissors and Jim Surmanek, *Advertising Media Planning,* 2nd ed. (Lincolnwood, Ill.: NTC Business Books, 1982), p. 64.

Figure 12–6   From Jim Surmanek, *Media Planning* (Lincolnwood, Ill.: NTC Business Books, 1988), p. 125.

Figure 12–8   Courtesy Canon U.S.A. Inc.

Figure 12–9   Reprinted with permission from *Advertising Age,* September 24, 1987, pp. 10, 12. Copyright Crain Communications, Inc.

Figure 12–10   Reprinted with permission from *Advertising Age,* June 8, 1987. Copyright Crain Communications, Inc.

Ad Lab 12-A   Adapted from Stephen Baker, *Systematic Advertising Research Report* (New York: McGraw-Hill, 1979), p. 154.

Figure 12–11   Courtesy Carmichael Lynch.

Figure 12–12   Adapted from *Cahners Advertising Research Report.*

Figure 12–14   From Donald W. Jugenheimer and Peter B. Turk, *Advertising Media* (Columbus, Ohio: Grid Publishing, 1980), p. 90.

Figure 12–15   Courtesy Young & Rubicam.

Ad Lab 12-B   Adapted from Stephen Baker, *Systematic Approach to Advertising Creativity* (New York: McGraw-Hill, 1979), pp. 176–83.

Figure 12–16   Courtesy *TV Guide.*

Figure 12–17   Courtesy Yamaha Music Corporation.

Figure 12–18   Courtesy Beef Industry Council.

Figure 12–19   Courtesy Saatchi & Saatchi Compton (NZ) Ltd.

Figure 12–20   Copyright 1987 Media Management Plus.

Chapter 13

Figure 13–1   Courtesy Fallon McElligott.

Figure 13–2   Courtesy Bob Brihn.

Figure 13–3   Reprinted with permission from *Advertising Age,* September 24, 1987, p. 36. Copyright Crain Communications, Inc.

Figure 13–4   Courtesy Standard Rate & Data Service.

Figure 13–5   Courtesy of The Procter & Gamble Company.

Figure 13–6   Courtesy Fallon McElligott.

Figure 13–7   Courtesy Standard Rate & Data Service.

Figure 13–8   Courtesy Warner Lambert Company.

Figure 17–5   Courtesy Dominion Pottery.

Figures 17–6, 17–7, and 17–8   Data from Newspaper Advertising Bureau, Inc.

Figure 17–9   Courtesy Ben Vergati.

Figure 17–10   Courtesy Dayton Hudson Department Store.

Figure 17–11   Courtesy Evans/Barthalemew Pollack Norman, Inc.

Figure 17–12   Courtesy Eisaman, Johns & Laws.

Figure 17–13   Courtesy Paine Furniture Company.

Figure 17–14   Courtesy KCBN, Inc.

Figure 17–15   Courtesy Cal Worthington Ford.

Checklist for Creating Local Advertising   Data from Newspaper Advertising Bureau, Inc.

Figure 17–16   Courtesy Bullock's.

Figure 17–17   Courtesy Northlich, Stolley, Inc.

Figure 17–18   Courtesy Mark Oliver, Inc.

Figure 17–19   Reprinted with the permission of Volkswagen United States, Inc. Copyright Volkswagen United States, Inc.

Ad Lab 17-B   Adapted from "A Network of Co-op Power," *Marketing Communications,* June 1986, pp. 65–68+; and Barry Berman and Joel R. Evans, *Retail Management: A Strategic Approach* (New York: Macmillan, 1986), p. 402.

Chapter 18

Figure 18–1   Historical Pictures Service, Chicago.

Figure 18–2   Courtesy McNeil Consumer Products Company.

Figure 18–3   Courtesy Southwestern Bell Corporation.

Ad Lab 18-A   Adapted from David Ogilvy, "Corporate Advertising," *Viewpoint* 1 (1979).

Figure 18–4   Courtesy AT&T.

Portfolio of Corporate Advertising   Courtesy United Technologies; courtesy David Nathanson; courtesy 3M; courtesy John Hancock Mutual Life Insurance Company; reprinted with permission of copyright holder, Rockwell International Corporation, All Rights Reserved; courtesy McDonnell Douglas; courtesy Denny's Inc.; courtesy Anheuser-Busch Companies, Inc.

Figure 18–5   Courtesy Unisys Corporation.

Figure 18–6   Reprinted with permission of Mobil Corporation. Copyright 1987 Mobil Corporation.

Figure 18–7   Courtesy Calet, Hirsch & Spector, Inc.

Figure 18–8   William Meyer: Click/Chicago.

Figure 18–9   Courtesy Golin/Harris Communications, Inc.

Figure 18–10   Courtesy Samata Associates.

Figure 18–11   Courtesy Creel Morrell, Inc.—Atlanta, Austin, Newport Beach, Washington, D.C.; Design Principle: Eric G. Morrell; Executive Vice President/Design: Cinda K. Debbink; Project Description: A Quarterly publication produced for an International Audience and Sponsored by Innova.

Figure 18–12   Courtesy N. W. Ayer for the partnership for a Drug-Free America.

Figure 18–13   Courtesy DDB Needham Worldwide.

Figure 18–15   Courtesy Fallon McElligott.

Figure 18–16   Courtesy Smith, Badofsky & Raffel, Inc.

Figure 18–17   Courtesy Blue Diamond.

Figure 18–18   Courtesy Department of the Navy.

Figure 18–19   Courtesy The Advertising Council Inc.

Chapter 19

Figure 19–1   Courtesy Gillette International.

Figure 19–2   Courtesy STZ S.r.l.

Ad Lab 19-A   Adapted from June 2, 1980, issue of *Television/Radio Age.*

Figure 19–3   Reprinted courtesy of Eastman Kodak Company.

Figure 19–4   Coke and Coca-Cola are Registered Trademarks of the Coca-Cola Company and permission for use granted by The Company.

Figure 19–5   Coke and Coca-Cola are Registered Trademarks of the Coca-Cola Company and permission for use granted by The Company.

Figure 19–6   Courtesy GreyCom, Inc.

Figure 19–7   Reprinted with permission from *Advertising Age,* March 30, 1988, p. 1. Copyright Crain Communications, Inc.

Figure 19–8   Courtesy Welch Foods.

Figure 19–9   Courtesy Dancer Fitzgerald Sample, Inc.

Figure 19–10   Reprinted by permission of the Harvard Business Review. An exhibit from "The World Customer" by Ernest Dichter (July/August 1962). Copyright 1962 by the President and Fellows of Harvard College; all rights reserved.

Figure 19–11   Stephen Dunn.

Checklist for International Media Planning   Courtesy Directories International, Inc.

Figure 19–12   Courtesy MPM Propaganda.

Figure 19–13   Courtesy IBM.

Figure 19–14   Courtesy Grey Advertising, Inc.

Figure 19–15   Adapted from *Advertising: Its Role in Modern Marketing,* Fifth Edition, by S. Watson Dunn and Arnold M. Barban. Copyright 1982 by The Dryden Press, a division of Holt, Rinehart and Winston, Publishers. Reprinted by permission of Holt, Rinehart and Winston.

Glossary*

AAAA (2)(3) The American Association of Advertising Agencies, the national organization of the advertising business. It has members throughout the United States and controls agency practices by denying membership to any agency judged unethical.

AAF (2) The American Advertising Federation, a nationwide association of advertising people. The AAF helped to establish the Federal Trade Commission, and its early "vigilance" committees were the forerunners of the Better Business Bureaus.

ABC (13) See *Audit Bureau of Circulations.*

Abundance principle (1) The idea that in an economy that produces more goods and services than can be consumed, advertising serves two purposes: keeping consumers informed of selection alternatives and allowing companies to compete more effectively for consumer dollars.

Account executive (3) The liaison between the agency and the client. The account executive is responsible, on the one hand, for mustering all the agency's services for the benefit of the client and, on the other hand, for representing the agency's point of view to the client.

Action programs (7) The precise details of a company's marketing strategy that spell out the specific tactics it will use to achieve its marketing objectives.

ADI (14) See *Area of dominant influence.*

Advertising (1) Nonpersonal communication of information, usually paid for and usually persuasive, about products, services, or ideas. The information is communicated through the various media and paid for by identified sponsors.

Advertising Age (2) The industry's leading trade publication. It continually champions the cause of more ethical and responsible advertising.

Advertising agency (3) An independent organization of creative people and businesspeople that specializes in the development and preparation of advertising plans, advertisements, and other promotional tools for advertisers.

Advertising appeal (8) The motive to which an ad is directed and that is intended to get a person to comply with the goal the advertiser has established.

Advertising Council (18) A nonpartisan, nonpolitical volunteer organization supported by the American Association of Advertising Agencies. It conducts public service ad campaigns to the nation at large, avoiding regional, sectarian, or special-interest drives of all kinds.

Advertising manager (3) Person in the advertiser's employ who is responsible for the administration, planning, and budgeting of advertising activities; supervision of outside advertising services; and coordination with other company departments.

Advertising message (7) An element of the creative mix comprising what the company plans to say in its advertisements and how it plans to say it—verbally or nonverbally.

Advertising objectives (7) The goals of the company's advertising campaign and a logical deduction from the firm's marketing plan. Objectives may include building awareness and appeal or promoting additional use.

Advertising plan (7) An overall statement of the company's advertising objectives and strategy. The plan tells the intended role of advertising in the marketing mix, defines target audiences, and describes how the elements of the creative mix will be used.

Advertising pyramid (7) A simple graphic model for understanding the tasks advertising can accomplish in preparing customers to act.

Advertising research (6) Types of research designed for advertising strategy determination, concept development, pretesting of ads and commercials, and campaign evaluation.

Advertising specialty (16) An inexpensive, but useful, goodwill gift—a reminder that carries the company or product name or logo, such as a pen, key chain, coffee mug, or cap. (Also called *specialty advertising.*)

Advertising strategy (7) The methodology the advertiser will employ to achieve its stated advertising objectives. The strategy (also called *creative strategy*) is determined by the advertiser's use of the creative mix.

Affidavit of performance (14) A signed and notarized form sent by a television station to an advertiser or agency indicating what spots ran and when. It is the station's legal proof that the advertiser got what was paid for.

Agency commission (3) Compensation paid by a medium to recognized advertising agencies, usually 15 percent (16⅔ percent for outdoor), for advertising placed with it.

Agency network (20) An affiliation of domestic and/or foreign advertising agencies organized to give and receive media counsel, translation services, production assistance, or other specialized services in unfamiliar markets.

Aided recall (6) A research technique of verifying readership, viewership, or listenership in which respondents are given the advertisement or other aids to help them remember.

A la carte services (3) Specialized advertising businesses that are offshoots of the agency business, such as creative boutiques and media buying services.

Alcohol and Tobacco Tax Division (2) Federal agency that has almost absolute authority over liquor advertising through its powers to suspend, revoke, or deny renewal of manufacturing and sales permits for distillers, vintners, and brewers found to be in violation of regulations.

ANA (2) The Association of National Advertisers, composed of 400 major manufacturing and service companies that are clients of member agencies of the AAAA. These companies, which are pledged to uphold the ANA code of advertising ethics, work with the ANA through a joint Committee for Improvement of Advertising Content.

Animatic (11) A rough television commercial produced by photographing storyboard sketches on a film strip with the audio portion synchronized on tape. It is used primarily for testing purposes.

Animation (11) The use of cartoons, puppet characters, or photo animation in television commercials to create a live effect in inanimate objects. Often used to communicate especially difficult messages or whimsical ideas.

Annual report (18) A formal document issued yearly by a corporation to its stockholders to reflect the corporation's condition at the close of the business year.

Answer print (11) The final print of a filmed commercial, along with all the required optical effects and titles, used for review and approval before duplicating.

Arbitrary marks (8) Dictionary words used as product names that have nothing to do with the product description other than to give the product image or identity.

Arbitron (14) A commonly used rating service that regularly publishes statistics on how many people, in what age groups, and of what sex are watching TV or listening to radio at various times of the day within a specific market area.

Area of dominant influence (ADI) (14) Arbitron's term for a television market—defined as "an exclusive geographic area consisting of all counties in which the home market stations receive a preponderance of total viewing hours."

Art (9) The whole visual presentation of a commercial or advertisement, including how the words in the ad are arranged, what size and style of type are used, whether photos or illustrations are used, and how they are organized. Art also refers to what style of photography or illustration is employed, how color is used, and how these elements are arranged in an ad and related to one another in size and proportion.

Art director (9) The individual responsible for the visual presentation of the ad.

Ascender (10) In typography, any letter that rises above the x height; for example, d, t, l.

Attention value (12) A consideration in selecting media based on the degree of attention paid to ads in a particular medium by those exposed to them. Attention value relates to the advertising message and copy just as much as to the medium.

Attitude test (6) Type of posttest that usually seeks to measure the effectiveness of an advertising campaign in creating a favorable image for a company, its brand, or its products.

Audience (12) The total number of people who are reached by a particular medium.

Audience composition (14) The distribution of an audience into demographic categories.

Audio (8) (11) The right side of a script for a television commercial, indicating sound effects, spoken copy, and music. Also, the spoken dialogue or copy in broadcast advertising. The audio may be delivered as a *voice-over* by an announcer who is not seen but whose voice is heard, or it may be delivered *on-camera* by an announcer, a spokesperson, or actors playing out a scene.

Audit Bureau of Circulations (13) An organization supported by advertising agencies, advertisers, and publishers that verifies circulation and other marketing data on newspapers and magazines for the benefit of its members.

Avails (14) An abbreviated term referring to the TV programs that are *available* to an advertiser. Media buyers contact the sales reps for the stations they are considering and ask them to supply a list of available time slots along with prices and estimated ratings.

Average quarter-hour (14) A radio term referring to the average number of people who are listening to a specific station during any 15-minute period of any given daypart. A high average quarter-hour figure usually means that people are listening and staying tuned in.

Bait-and-switch advertising (2) The illegal practice of baiting customers with an unusually low advertised price on a product that they are then unable to buy or are discouraged from buying.

Barter syndication (14) Marketing of first-run television programs to local stations free or for a reduced rate because some of the ad space has been presold to national advertisers.

Basic bus (15) In transit advertising, all the inside space on a group of buses, which thereby gives the advertiser complete domination.

BBB (2) The Better Business Bureau, a volunteer group of over 100,000 member companies. It monitors business and advertising practices to protect consumers against fraud and deception.

Behavioristic segmentation (5) Method of determining market segments by aggregating consumers into product-related groups based on their knowledge, attitude, use, or response to actual products or product attributes.

Benefit headline (8) Type of headline that makes a direct promise to the reader.

Benefits (4) The functional or symbolic satisfactions the consumer receives from a product or service.

Benefit segmentation (5) Method of segmenting markets by determining the major benefits consumers seek in a product (high quality, low price, status, speed, sex appeal, good taste, etc.).

Billboards (15) See *Poster panels.*

Birch Research (14) A radio research service that relies on telephone surveys to obtain listener data.

Bleed page (13) A magazine advertisement in which the dark or colored background of the ad extends to the edge of the page. Most magazines offer bleed pages, but they normally charge advertisers a 10 to 15 percent premium for them.

Body copy (8) The text of an advertisement that tells the complete story and attempts to close the sale. It is a logical continuation of the headline and subheads and is usually set in a smaller type size than headlines or subheads.

Boxes and panels (8) A *box* is copy around which a line has been drawn, while a *panel* is an elongated box that usually runs the whole length or width of an ad. Boxes and panels are generally used in advertisements to set apart coupons, special offers, contest rules, and order blanks.

Brain-pattern analysis (6) A research method in which a brain scanner monitors the reactions of the brain while ads are being presented.

Brand (2)(4) Name that identifies one particular product or line of products and its source.

Brand loyalty (5) The consumer's decision to repurchase a brand continually because the consumer perceives that the brand has the right product features or quality at the right price.

Brand manager (3) The advertiser's employee responsible for the success of a particular brand. The brand manager works with the division's advertising department to coordinate sales promotion and merchandising programs and has the support of the corporate advertising department's media and research supervisors for statistical information and guidance. In addition, each brand manager normally has an advertising agency that creates and places the brand's media advertising.

Broadcast television (14) Television sent over airwaves as opposed to over cables.

Broadside (15) A form of direct mail advertisement, larger than a folder and sometimes used as a window display or wall poster in stores. It can be folded to a compact size and fitted into a mailer.

Broadside approach (12) A media scheduling theory or method in which an equal number of messages are sent to each target audience group without regard to priority.

Business advertising (1) Advertising directed at people in business who buy or specify products for business use.

Business magazines (13) Periodicals directed to a particular industry, trade, profession, or occupation.

Business markets (5) Markets composed of manufacturers, utilities, government agencies, contractors, wholesalers, retailers, banks, insurance companies, and institutions that buy goods and services to help them in their own business.

Business reply mail (15) A type of mail that enables the recipient of direct-mail advertising to respond without paying postage and thereby tends to increase the rate of response.

Bus-o-rama (15) In transit advertising, a jumbo roof sign, which is actually a full-color transparency backlighted by fluorescent tubes, running the length of the bus, with space for two advertisers on each side of the bus.

Buyer behavior (5) The actvities, actions, and influences of people and organizations that purchase and use goods and services.

Cable TV (CATV)(14) Television signals carried to households by cable and paid for by subscription.

Call-outs (9) Small captions placed next to and describing particular elements in a photo or illustration.

Caption (8) The words under a picture that describe the illustration.

Casting off (10) See *Copy casting.*

Catalogs (15) Reference books mailed to prospective customers that list, describe, and often picture the products sold by a manufacturer, wholesaler, jobber, or retailer.

Central location test (6) Type of pretest in which videotapes of test commercials are shown to respondents on a one-to-one basis, usually in shopping center locations.

Centralized advertising department (3) A staff of employees, usually located at corporate headquarters, responsible for all the organization's advertising. The department is often structured by product, advertising subfunction, end user, media, or geography.

Cents-off coupon (16) A certificate with a stated value that is presented to a retail store for a price reduction on a specified item. Coupons may be distributed in newspapers, in magazines, door-to-door, on packages, and by direct mail.

Cents-off promotion (16) A common sales promotion device designed to induce trial and usage. Cents-off promotions take different forms, including basic cents-off packages, one-cent sales, free offers, and box-top refunds.

Certification mark (2) A symbol or label that guarantees the origin, trade, or quality of a product; for example, Teflon II.

Channels of distribution (4) See *Distribution channels.*

Civil Aeronautics Board (CAB)(2) Federal agency that regulates air traffic and advertising of all air carriers engaged in interstate commerce.

Classified advertising (13) Newspaper and magazine advertisements usually arranged under subheads that describe the class of goods or the need the ads seek to satisfy. Rates are based on the amount of space purchased and on how long the ad is run. Most employment, housing, and automotive advertising run today is in the form of classified advertising.

Clearance advertising (17) A type of local advertising designed to make room for new product lines or new models or to get rid of slow-moving product lines, floor samples, broken or distressed merchandise, or items that are no longer in season.

Clients (3) The different businesses advertising agencies work for in an effort to find customers for their goods and services.

Clip art (17) Stock drawings available for clipping and reproduction.

Close (8)   In ad copy, the point at which the consumer is asked to do something and is told how to do it.

Close-up (11)   A television or film shot in which one object or face fills the screen.

Closing date (13)   The final date for supplying printing material for an advertisement to a medium.

Cognitive dissonance (5)   Theory that people try to justify their behavior by reducing the degree to which their impressions or beliefs are inconsistent with reality.

Cognitive theory (5)   Approach that views learning as a mental process of memory, thinking, and the rational application of knowledge to practical problem solving.

Coined names (8)   Distinctive product or company names that have been coined or invented, such as Kodak, Exxon.

Cold type (10)   Modern method of typesetting characterized by high-speed electronic photocomposition equipment and operators schooled in computer technology.

Collateral materials (4)(16)   All the accessory nonmedia advertising materials prepared by companies to help achieve marketing or public relations objectives.

Collective mark (2)   A mark used to indicate membership in an organization.

Color separation negatives (10)   Four separate continuous-tone negatives produced by photographing artwork through color filters that eliminate all the colors but one. The negatives are used to make four printing plates for reproducing the color artwork.

Column inch (13)   In newspaper advertising, a measurement of depth one inch deep by one column wide. Most newspapers now sell advertising space by the column inch.

Combination offers (16)   A sales promotion device in which two related products are packaged together at a special price; for example, a razor and a package of blades. Sometimes a combination offer may be used to introduce a new product by tying its purchase to an established product at a special price.

Combination rate (13)   A special newspaper advertising rate offered for placing a given ad in (1) morning and evening editions of the same newspaper; (2) two or more newspapers owned by the same publisher; and (3) in some cases, two or more newspapers affiliated in a syndicate or newspaper group.

Command headline (8)   A type of headline that orders the reader to do something. Command headlines attempt to motivate action through fear or emotion or because the reader understands the inherent correctness of the command.

Commercial advertising (1)   Advertising that promotes goods, services, or ideas for a business with the expectation of making a profit.

Communications media (7)   An element of the creative mix, comprising the various methods or vehicles that will be used to transmit the advertiser's message. May include the traditional media as well as vehicles such as publicity, sales promotion, trade shows, and so on.

Commission (3)   See *Agency commission*.

Comparative advertising (2)   Advertising that claims superiority to competitors in some respect.

Comparative pricing (4)   Pricing strategy that involves comparing the advertised low price with "normal" list price to give the impression of overall discount prices.

Competitive pricing (4)   Pricing strategy aimed at meeting or beating the prices of all competitors.

Compiled list (15)   A kind of direct-mail list that has been compiled for one reason or another by another source; for example, lists of automobile owners, new-house purchasers, business owners, and so forth. It is the most readily available in volume but offers the lowest expectation.

Comprehensive layout (9)   A facsimile of a finished ad with copy set in type and pasted into position along with proposed illustrations. The "comp" is prepared so the advertiser can gauge the effect of the final ad.

Concept testing (6)   A type of advertising research used to develop thematic concepts for ads or campaigns.

Consumer advertising (1)   Advertising directed at the ultimate consumer of the product or at the person who will buy the product for someone else's use.

Consumer magazine (13)   A periodical directed toward individuals or ultimate consumers who buy products for personal or nonbusiness use.

Consumer market (4)   People who buy products and services for their own personal use.

Consumer Product Safety Commission (2)   Federal agency that develops and enforces standards for potentially hazardous consumer products.

Consumer promotion (16)   See *Pull strategy*.

Consumerism (2)   Social action designed to dramatize the rights of the buying public.

Contact sheet (9)   All of the images from a roll of film printed on one sheet of paper, produced by placing the negatives directly on the photographic paper.

Contest (16)   A sales promotion device for creating consumer involvement in which prizes are offered based on the skill of the entrants.

Continuity (9)(12)   The length of an advertising campaign and the manner in which it is scheduled and sustained over an extended period of time. Also, the consistent use of a graphic theme in all ads in a campaign.

Contract rate (13)   A special rate for newspaper advertising usually offered to local advertisers who sign an annual contract for frequent or bulk space purchases. As the number of inches contracted for increases, the rate decreases.

Contrast (9)   The degree of difference between the lightest and darkest tones in photographs or on television. Contrast in an ad can also be created with the use of color, size of type or elements, or style.

Controlled circulation (13) Free subscriptions to business publications given to individuals the publisher feels are in a position to influence buying decisions.

Cooperative advertising (4)(16) The sharing of advertising costs by the manufacturer and the distributor or retailer. The manufacturer may repay 50 or 100 percent of the dealer's advertising costs or some other amount based on sales. Under the Robinson-Patman Act, the same terms must be extended to all distributors and dealers. See also *Horizontal cooperative advertising; Vertical cooperative advertising.*

Copy (3)(8) The words that make up the headline and message of an advertisement or commercial.

Copy casting (10) The act of fitting type into the space designated for it in the layout by determining the number of characters in the copy. The two methods used for this are the word-count method and the character-count method.

Copy platform (8) A document that serves as a guide for writing an ad. It describes the most important issues that should be considered in writing the copy, including a definition and description of the target audience in terms of demographic, psychographic, and behavioristic qualities; the rational and emotional appeals to be used; the product features that will satisfy the customer's needs; the support for the product claim; the product's position; the product's personality or image; the style, approach, or tone that will be used in the copy; and, generally, what the copy will say either verbally or nonverbally.

Copyright (2) Exclusive right granted by the Copyright Act to authors and artists to protect their original work from being plagiarized, sold, or used by another without their express consent.

Copywriters (3) People who create the words and concepts for ads and commercials.

Copywriting (8) Creating the verbal element of the advertising message.

Corporate advertising (1)(18) The broad area of nonproduct advertising aimed specifically at enhancing company reputation, familiarity, and overall impression and improving lagging awareness.

Corporate identity advertising (18) Type of corporate advertising used to communicate a change in corporate name, logos, trademarks, or corporate signatures. Also used when companies need to communicate an ownership change or a change in corporate personality or when the company is suffering from generally lagging awareness.

Corporate objectives (7) Goals of the company stated in terms of profit or return on investment. Goals may also be stated in terms of net worth, earnings ratios, growth, or corporate reputation.

Cost efficiency (12) The cost of reaching the target audience through a particular medium as opposed to the cost of reaching the medium's total circulation.

Cost per rating point (CPP)(14) A simple computation used by media buyers to determine which broadcast programs are the most efficient ones in relation to the target audience. The CPP is determined by dividing the cost of the show by the show's expected rating against the target audience.

Cost per thousand (CPM)(12) A common term describing the cost of reaching 1,000 people in a medium's audience. It is used by media planners to compare the cost of various media vehicles.

Coupon (16) A certificate with a stated value that is presented to retail stores for a price reduction on a specified item.

Cover position (13) A special magazine advertising position on the inside front, inside back, and outside back covers (called the second, third, and fourth covers, respectively), which is almost always sold at a premium.

CPM (12) See *Cost per thousand.*

Creative boutique (3)(17) Organization of creative specialists (such as art directors, designers, and copywriters) who work for advertisers and occasionally advertising agencies to develop creative concepts, advertising messages, and specialized art. A boutique performs only the creative work.

Creative department (3) The department in an advertising agency that provides creative services such as copy and art.

Creative mix (7) Those advertising elements the company controls to achieve its advertising objectives, including the product concept, the target audience, the communications media, and the advertising message.

Credibility (8) The believability of an advertisement, an advertiser, or a spokesperson.

Crisis management (18) A company's plan for handling news and public relations during crises.

CRT typesetter (10) A modern type of typesetting equipment, based on cathode-ray tube technology, in which characters are stored digitally, retrieved from the computer's memory, and passed to a print CRT (similar to a television receiver tube) where they are lined up and then exposed through a lens system onto photosensitive paper or film.

Cue (5) The stimulus that triggers a consumer's need or want, which in turn creates a drive to respond. An advertisement might be a cue.

Cume audience (14) The capsule term for cumulative audience, which describes the total number of different people listening to a radio station for at least one 15-minute segment over the course of a given week, day, or daypart. The number gives an indication of the reach potential of a radio schedule, since a high cume figure means a lot of different people are tuning in to the station for at least 15 minutes.

Cursive type (10) A type style that resembles handwriting. Also called *script.*

Dailies (13) Newspapers published at least five times a week, Monday through Friday, in either morning or evening editions. Some are published on Saturday and Sunday as well.

Dayparts (14) See *Radio dayparts; Television dayparts.*

Dealer displays (16) In-store displays, counter stands, and special racks designed to provide the retailer with ready-made, professionally designed vehicles for selling more of the featured products. Also called *point-of-purchase advertising*.

Dealer premiums (16) Prizes and gifts used to get retail dealers and salespeople to reach specific sales goals or to stock or display a certain product.

Decentralized advertising department (3) The establishment of advertising departments by products or brands or in various divisions, subsidiaries, countries, regions, or whatever other categories most suit the firm's needs.

Deceptive advertising (2) According to the FTC, any ad in which "there is a misrepresentation, omission, or other practice that is likely to mislead the consumer acting reasonably in the circumstances, to the consumer's detriment."

Defamation (8) Making a false statement or allegation about a person or holding a person up to contempt.

Delayed-action advertising (7) Advertising that seeks to inform, persuade, or remind its intended audience over an extended time about the company, product, service, or issue being advertised.

Demarketing (1) The marketing and advertising techniques used by some companies and organizations to discourage the purchase or use of certain products.

Demographics (5) The study of the numerical characteristics of the population.

Demonstration (11) A type of TV commercial in which the product's performance is shown.

Department of Agriculture (2) Federal department that works closely with the FTC to enforce regulations governing certain products. It has regulatory authority over false and deceptive advertising for seeds and grain products.

Department of Justice (2) U.S. department that enforces federal laws governing advertising.

Descenders (10) In typography, a letter that drops below the base line; for example, p, g, y.

Designated market areas (DMA) (14) The concept of a television market area, according to the Nielsen Station Index; similar to Arbitron's ADI method.

Dialogue/monologue copy (8) A type of body·copy in which the characters illustrated in the advertisement do the selling in their own words either through a testimonial technique or through a comic strip panel.

Direct-action advertising (1) (7) Advertising intended to bring about immediate action on the part of the reader or viewer.

Direct advertising (15) Any form of advertising issued directly to the prospect through the use of mails, salespeople, dealers, or other means. It does not involve the traditional mass media.

Direct broadcast satellite (DBS) (14) A television delivery system that involves beaming programs from satellites to special satellite dishes mounted in the home or yard.

Direct-entry typesetting (10) A modern typesetting system that has all the input and output capabilities in one device.

Direct mail (15) All forms of advertising sent directly to prospects through U.S. or private postal services. In dollars spent, direct mail is the third-ranked advertising medium today, surpassed only by newspapers and television.

Direct-mail test (6) Method of pretesting advertisements through the use of direct mail. For example, two or more alternative ads can be tested by mailing each ad to different prospects on mailing lists. By keying (coding) each ad, the sources of the responses can be determined. The ad that generates the largest volume of orders is presumed to be the most effective.

Direct marketing (4) (15) A marketing system in which the seller does not rely on the traditional channels of distribution but rather builds and maintains its own database of customers and uses a variety of media to communicate directly with those customers.

Direct questioning (6) A method of pretesting designed to elicit a full range of responses to the advertising. Direct questioning is especially effective for testing alternative advertisements in the early stages of development.

Direct-response advertising (15) An advertising message that asks the reader, listener, or viewer for an immediate response. Direct-response advertising can take the form of direct mail, or it can use a wide range of other media, from matchbook covers or magazines to radio or TV.

Directories (16) Locators, buying guides, and mailing lists published by telephone companies, trade associations, state and city agencies, chambers of commerce, newspapers, industrial groups, advertising services, and others that also carry advertising aimed at the publishers' specialized fields.

Display advertising (13) Newspaper and magazine ads that normally use illustrations as well as type. They may range in size from small boxes to one- and two-page ads.

Display allowances (16) Encouraging the use of a manufacturer's display by offering additional discounts to the retailer or actually paying for display space.

Display type (10) Large, bold type, heavier than text type, used in headlines, subheads, logos, addresses, or wherever there is a need for emphasis in an advertisement.

Distribution channel (4) Network of all the firms and individuals that take title to the product or assist in taking title to the product as it moves from the producer to the consumer.

Diverting (16) Purchasing large quantities of an item offered on a regional promotional discount and shipping portions to areas of the country where the discount isn't being offered.

DMA (14) See *Designated market areas*.

Dogmatic message (12) A simple, easy-to-understand statement presented in an advertising headline as an indisputable fact; for example, "AT&T: The right choice."

Dubs (11) Duplicates of radio commercials made from the master tape and sent to stations for broadcast.

Dummy (9) A layout of a brochure or other multipage advertising piece. It is put together, page for page, just like the finished product will eventually appear.

Dupes (11) Copies of a finished television commercial that are delivered to the networks or TV stations for airing.

Dutch doors (13) See *Gatefold*.

Earned rate (13) A special newspaper advertising rate offered to local advertisers (1) as a frequency discount earned when a given ad is run repeatedly during a specific period of time or (2) as a volume discount earned as the number of inches used within one year increases.

Electronic pagination systems (10) Computerized systems that enable the graphic artist to alter and correct photos, illustrations, and complete pages by manipulating the pixels on the computer screen.

Empirical research method (7) A method of allocating funds for advertising that uses experimentation to determine the best level of advertising expenditure. By running a series of tests in different markets with different budgets, companies determine the most efficient level of expenditure.

Entrepreneurial agency (3) Any of the thousands of small agencies, usually owned by 1 or 2 people and employing fewer than 100 people, that inhabit every major city in the country.

Environmental influences (5) The various external factors that influence the behavior of consumers, such as family, society, and culture.

Erratic pulse (12) Spacing advertising at irregular intervals to try to effect changes in typical purchase cycles.

Euphemism (8) The substitution of an inoffensive, mild word for a word that is offensive, harsh, or blunt.

Exclusive distribution (4) Distribution strategy used to maintain prestige image and premium prices by granting exclusive rights to a wholesaler or retailer to sell in one geographic region.

Experimental method (6) A method of research designed to measure actual cause-and-effect relationships.

Exploratory research (6) A type of initial research used to learn more about the market, the competition, the business environment, and the problem before any formal research is undertaken.

Export agency (19) Agency that specializes in creating ads for American companies engaged in international advertising.

Exposure (12) A consideration in selecting media based on the number of people who actually see an advertisement in a given medium as opposed to the total audience of that medium. (Or, from another perspective, how many people an ad sees in a given medium.)

Eye-movement camera (6) Instrument used chiefly to track the subject's eye movement over the layout and copy of advertisements to obtain information on the placement of headlines, the proper length of copy, and the most satisfactory layout.

Farm advertising (1) Advertising directed to farmers as businesspeople and to others in the agricultural business.

Farm publications (13) Magazines directed to farmers and their families or to companies that manufacture or sell agricultural equipment, supplies, and services.

FCC (Federal Communications Commission) (2) Federal regulatory body with jurisdiction over radio, television, telephone, and telegraph industries. Through its authority to license broadcasting stations and to remove a license or deny license renewal, the FCC has indirect control over broadcast advertising.

FDA (Food and Drug Administration) (2) Federal agency that has authority over the advertising, labeling, packaging, and branding of packaged foods and therapeutic devices.

Fee-commission method (3) Compensation method whereby the agency establishes a fixed monthly fee for all its services to the client and retains any commissions earned for space or time purchased on behalf of the client.

Field testing (6) Type of testing technique that takes place in a respondent's home or in a public place as opposed to a laboratory setting.

First-class mail (15) A U.S. Postal Service classification of mail delivery used by direct-mail advertisers to ensure fast delivery, mail forwarding (at no additional charge), and return of undeliverable mail.

Flat rate (13) A standard newspaper advertising rate with no discount allowance for large or repeated space buys.

Flight (12) A media scheduling term that describes a period of advertising activity scheduled between periods of inactivity.

Flyer (15) A form of direct-mail advertising that is usually a single, standard-size (8½ by 11 inches) page printed on one or both sides and folded one or more times. It often accompanies a sales letter to supplement or expand the information it contains.

Focus groups (6) A qualitative method of research in which 8 to 10 people, "typical" of the target market, are invited to discuss the product, the service, or the marketing situation with a trained moderator in a free-wheeling discussion lasting an hour or more.

Folders (15) Large, heavy-stock flyers, often folded and sent out as self-mailers.

Font (10) For any typeface and size of type, the complete assortment of capitals, small caps, lowercase letters, numerals, and punctuation marks.

Formal balance (9) Perfect graphic symmetry with matched elements on either side of an ad to achieve equal optical weight. This is often used to create a dignified, stable, conservative image.

Formula model (12) A type of computer program used to calculate the reach, frequency, and other statistics for various media vehicles and to rank the vehicles according to selected parameters.

Forward buying (16) A retailers' stocking up on a product when it is discounted and buying smaller amounts when it is at list price.

Four-color plates (10) Printing plates used in the four-color process. Since a printing plate can print only one color at a time, the printer must prepare four different printing plates, one for each color: one for yellow, one for magenta, one for cyan, and one for black.

Four-color process (10) The method for printing color advertisements with tonal values, such as photographs and paintings. This process is based on the principle that all colors can be printed by combining the three primary colors—yellow, magenta (red), and cyan (blue)—plus black (which provides greater detail and density as well as shades of gray).

Four Ps (4) See *Marketing mix*.

Frames (11) The blank television screens on a typical pre-printed storyboard sheet that are sketched in by the art director to represent the video. Also, any single image of motion picture film. Since film is projected at 24 frames per second, this means 1,440 frames must be shot for each minute of activity.

Franchises (4) A type of vertical marketing system in which dealers operate under the guidelines and direction of the manufacturer.

Free lancers (9) (17) Advertising specialists who act as free agents, often working out of their homes preparing copy, art and layout, photography, or other services.

Free-standing inserts (FSIs) (16) Coupons distributed through inserts in newspapers.

Frequency (12) The number of times an advertising message reaches the same person or household. Across a total audience, frequency is calculated as the *average* number of times individuals or homes are exposed to the advertising.

Fringe (14) Television dayparts immediately before and after prime time. Early fringe runs from 4 to 8 P.M. EST, and late fringe covers the 11 P.M. to 1 A.M. time.

FTC (Federal Trade Commission) (2) The major federal regulator of advertising used to promote products sold in interstate commerce.

Full position (13) In newspaper advertising, the preferred position near the top of a page or on the top of a column next to reading matter. It is usually surrounded by editorial text and may cost the advertiser 25 to 50 percent more.

Full-service agency (3) An agency equipped to serve its clients in all areas of communication and promotion. Its advertising services include planning, creating, and producing advertisements as well as performing research and media selection services. Nonadvertising functions include producing sales promotion materials, publicity articles, annual reports, trade show exhibits, and sales training materials.

Galvanometer (6) A device used to measure changes in sweat gland activity as a subject looks at an advertisement. Best used for testing advertisements for products people have strong feelings about.

Game (16) A sales promotion activity in which prizes are offered based on chance. Games include local bingo-type games designed to build store traffic. Their big marketing advantage is that customers must make repeat visits to the dealer to continue playing.

Gatefold (13) A magazine cover or page extended and folded over to fit into the magazine. The gatefold may be a fraction of a page or two or more pages, and it is always sold at a premium.

General agency (3) An agency that is willing to represent the widest variety of accounts but that concentrates on companies that make goods purchased chiefly by consumers.

Generic-market objectives (7) Type of marketing objectives that view the organization as a satisfier of market needs rather than a producer of products.

Geographic segmentation (5) Method of dividing a market along geographic lines.

Gimmick copy (8) A type of body copy that depends on wordplay, humor, poetry, rhyming, great exaggeration, gags, and other trick devices.

Global advertising (19) Using the exact same ad, with translation, in all international markets.

Global marketing (19) The theory that, thanks to cheap air travel and new telecommunications technology, the world is becoming a common marketplace in which people have the same tastes and desires and want the same products and lifestyles no matter where they live—thus allowing for world-standardized products at low prices sold the same way around the world.

Gothic (10) See *Sans serif*.

Government advertising (1) (18) Advertising placed by government organizations such as the Army, Navy, Marine Corps, Postal Service, Social Security Administration, Internal Revenue Service, and various state chambers of commerce.

Government markets (4) Governmental bodies that buy products for the successful coordination of municipal, state, federal, or other government agencies.

Graphic designer (9) Designer responsible for the shape, dimension, and placement of the elements in an ad. The initial design of the ad will dictate its artistic direction and eventually determine whether that ad is to be stunning, beautiful, a "work of art," or just another ad.

Gross rating points (12) (14) (15) The total audience delivery or weight of a specific media schedule computed by multiplying the reach, expressed as a percentage, by the average frequency. In television, gross rating points are the total weight of a media schedule against TV households. For example, a weekly schedule of five commercials with an average household rating of 20 would yield 100 GRPs, or a total audience equivalent to the total number of TV households in the area. In outdoor advertising, a 100 gross rating point showing (also called a number 100 showing) covers a market fully by reaching 9 out of 10 adults daily over a 30-day period.

Group system (3) System in which the agency is divided into a number of little agencies or groups, each composed of an account executive, a copywriter, an artist, a media buyer, and any other specialists needed for the particular clients being served by the group.

GRP (12) (14) (15) See *Gross rating points*.

Guaranteed circulation (13) The number of copies of a magazine that the publisher guarantees to advertisers will be delivered. If this figure is not reached, the publisher must give a refund.

Gunning Fog Index (8) A technique for evaluating the ease of reading of a text.

Habit (5) An acquired or developed behavior pattern that has become nearly or completely involuntary.

Halftone screen (10) A glass or plastic screen, criss-crossed with fine black lines at right angles like a window screen, which breaks continuous-tone artwork into dots. The key element in making halftone plates, this screen is placed in the camera between the lens and the negative holder and, in effect, converts the artwork being photographed into a series of black dots. In the dark areas of the (halftone) photograph, the dots are large; in the gray areas, they are small; and in the white areas, they almost disappear. The combination of big and little dots with a little or a lot of white space between them produces the illusion of shading in the photograph.

Halo effect (6) In ad pretesting, the fact that consumers are likely to rate the one or two ads that make the best impression as the highest in all categories.

Handbills (17) Low-cost flyers or other simple brochures distributed by hand to offices, local residences, people on the street, or cars in parking lots.

Headline (8) The words in the leading position of the advertisement—that is, the words that will be read first or that are positioned to draw the most attention.

Hierarchy of needs (5) Maslow's theory that the lower biologic or survival needs are dominant in human behavior and must be satisfied before higher, socially acquired needs become meaningful.

High-assay principle (12) A method or theory of media scheduling based on the mining principle of working the richest claim first. This method suggests that to maximize reach, the advertiser should start with the medium that produces the best return and then move to other media only when the first becomes unavailable or loses its effectiveness.

Horizontal cooperative advertising (17) Joint advertising effort of related businesses (car dealers, realtors, etc.) to create traffic for their kind of business.

Horizontal publications (13) Business publications targeted at people with particular job functions that cut across industry lines, such as *Purchasing* magazine.

Hot type (10) An obsolete method of metal type composition that formed letters by pouring molten lead into brass molds.

House list (15) A company's most important and valuable direct-mail list, which may contain current customers, recent customers, and long-past customers or future prospects.

House mark (2) A trademark used on most or all of the products of a particular company.

House organs (15)(18) Internal and external publications produced by business organizations, including stockholder reports, newsletters, consumer magazines, and dealer publications. Most are produced by a company's advertising or public relations department or by its agency.

Households using TV (HUT)(14) The percentage of homes in a given area that have one or more TV sets turned on at any particular time. If 1,000 TV sets are in the survey area and 500 are turned on, the HUT figure is 50 percent.

Illustrator (9) The artist who paints, sketches, or draws the pictures we see in advertising.

Image (1) The personality of a product or company, created by advertising or consumer experience.

Imperceptible differences (4) Distinguishing characteristics of products that are not readily apparent without close inspection or use.

Impressions (12) The total of all the audiences delivered by a media plan. Also called *total exposures,* it is calculated by multiplying the number of people who receive a message by the number of times they receive it.

In-depth interview (6) An intensive interview technique that uses carefully planned but loosely structured questions to probe respondents' deep feelings.

In-house advertising agency (3) Agency wholly owned by the company and set up and staffed to do all the work of an independent full-service agency.

In-pack premiums (16) Sales promotion device, popular in the food field, in which inexpensive gifts are placed inside the package for the buyer; for example, plastic toys for children.

Indirect-action advertising (1) Advertising that attempts to build the image of a product or familiarity with the name and package in order to influence the audience to purchase a specific brand at some future time when they are in the market for that product.

Indirect marketing (4) Distribution strategy involving use of a network of middlemen.

Induced differences (4) Distinguishing characteristics of products effected through unique branding, packaging, distribution, merchandising, and advertising.

Industrial advertising (1) Advertising aimed at individuals in business who buy or influence the purchase of industrial goods.

Industrial agency (3) An agency representing client companies that make goods to be sold to other businesses.

Industrial goods (1) Products and services that are used in the manufacture of other goods or that become a physical part of another product. Industrial goods also include products that are used to conduct business and that do not become part of another product, like capital goods (office machines, desks, operating supplies) and business services for which the user contracts.

Industrial markets (4) Individuals or companies that buy products needed for the production of other products or services such as plant equipment and telephone systems.

Infomercial (14) A long (3 to 8 minutes) TV commercial that gives consumers detailed information about a product or service.

Informal balance (9) A type of visually balanced presentation achieved by placing elements of different size, shape, intensity of color, or darkness at different distances from the optical center.

Inquiry test (6) A test of advertising based on responses such as inquiries or returns of coupons.

Insertion order (13) A form submitted to a newspaper or magazine when an advertiser wants to run an advertisement. This form states the date(s) on which the ad is to run, its size, the requested position, and the rate. It also states whether finished art, mechanicals, Velox prints, or mats will be furnished with the ad.

Inside cards (15) A transit advertisement normally 11 by 28 inches placed in a wall rack above the windows.

Institutional advertising (17) (18) A type of advertising that attempts to obtain favorable attention for the business as a whole, not for a specific product or service the store or business sells. The effects of institutional advertising are intended to be long rather than short range.

Institutional copy (8) A type of body copy in which the advertiser tries to sell an idea or the merits of the organization or service rather than the sales features of a particular product.

Integrated commercial (11) A straight television or radio commercial, usually delivered by one person, woven into a show or tailored to a given program to avoid any perceptible interruption.

Intensive distribution (4) Distribution strategy for heavily advertised, high-volume, low-profit items like convenience goods to make them available for purchase at every possible location with a minimum of effort.

Intensive techniques (6) An extension of the interview method of research designed to probe the deeper feelings of the respondent.

Interconnects (14) Groups of cable systems joined together for advertising purposes.

International advertising (1) Advertising directed at foreign markets.

International agency (19) A large advertising agency with overseas offices usually staffed with multilingual, multinational personnel in both creative and administrative positions.

International marketing structure (19) Organization of companies with foreign marketing divisions, typically decentralized with autonomous units in various foreign countries.

International media (19) Media that offer substantial audiences in a variety of foreign countries.

Interview (6) See *In-depth interview.*

Island half (13) A half-page of magazine space that is surrounded on two or more sides by editorial matter. This type of ad is designed to dominate a page and is therefore sold at a premium price.

Issue advertising (2) A type of corporate advertising that advocates a particular point of view on a public issue.

Jingle (11) Musical commercial, usually sung with the sales message in the verse.

Junior unit (13) A magazine advertisement produced in a single size, whose dimensions are a full page in some publications and a partial page in larger-sized publications, with editorial matter on two or more sides.

Laboratory methods (6) A research methodology in which consumers are brought into a studio or auditorium to view ads and commercials in a controlled environment.

Laser typesetting (10) A modern computer-laser method of setting type in which type fonts and software programs can be stored digitally in a computer that also controls the on/off action of the laser beam as it "writes" onto (exposes) the output paper on film. No CRT is used. Extremely high speeds are possible as well as great reliability and versatility. Laser typesetters are usually able to output graphics and halftones besides type.

Layout (3) (9) A pencil design and orderly formation of the parts of the advertisement within the specified dimensions. The layout will include the headline, subheads, illustrations, copy, picture captions, trademarks, slogans, and signature (or logotype). The layout serves a mechanical function, working as a blueprint to show where the parts of the ad are to be placed. It also serves a psychological or symbolic function, creating a feeling for the product or company.

Lead-in paragraph (8) In print ads, a bridge between the headlines, the subheads, and the sales ideas presented in the text. It transfers reader interest to product interest.

Lead time (13) The length of time between the closing date for the purchase of advertising space or time and the publication or broadcast of the ad. Advertising in magazines requires a long lead time—sometimes as long as three months. And once the closing date has been reached, no changes in copy or art can be allowed.

Leading (10) The space between lines of type. Art directors may vary this space to give a slightly more airy or condensed feeling.

Leaflet (15) See *Flyer.*

Learning (5) A relatively permanent change in behavior that occurs as a result of reinforced practice.

Letter shop (15) A firm that stuffs envelopes, affixes labels and postage, sorts pieces into bundles, and otherwise prepares items for mailing.

Letterpress (10) The old process of printing in which the ink is applied to a raised (relief) surface on a metal or plastic printing plate and transferred to the paper similar to the way a rubber stamp works. Like a stamp, the image to be transferred is backward ("wrong reading").

Libel (8) A printed false statement or allegation about a person; holding a person up to contempt in print.

Library of Congress (2) Federal body that registers and protects all copyrighted material, including advertising.

Licensed name (8) The paid use of another company's trademark for marketing products, such as Mickey Mouse watches, Sunkist vitamins.

Lifestyle technique (11) A type of TV commercial that focuses on the lifestyle of the target user rather than the specific product advantages.

Line drawings (9) Sometimes referred to as pen-and-ink drawings because everything is either black or white with no shades of gray. Line drawings provide clear detail and sharpness. They are also less costly than drawings with tonal values.

Line film (10) Film made from photographs, straight text, and line art. From the line film, a line plate is produced for printing.

Line plates (10) The plates used to print solid black-and-white images (not tonal values) such as typeset copy, pen-and-ink drawings, or charcoal illustrations.

Linear programming model (12) A type of computer program designed to create a complete media schedule that maximizes exposure within a given budget.

List broker (15) A middleman who handles rental of mailing lists for list owners on a commission basis.

Live action (11) The basic production technique in television that portrays people in everyday situations.

Live telecast test (6) Type of test conducted on closed-circuit television, CATV stations, or nonnetwork UHF stations in which commercials being studied are substituted for regular commercials on established TV programs.

Local advertising (1) (17) Advertising directed to customers and prospects in only one city or local trading area.

Local rates (13) The lower rate charged by newspapers for local display advertising. The largest source of newspaper display revenue is local retail merchants.

Logotype (8) Special design of the advertiser's name (or product name) that appears as a *signature* in all advertisements. It is like a trademark because it gives the advertiser individuality and provides quick recognition at the point of purchase.

Loss-leader pricing (4) Pricing strategy involving use of items advertised below cost in order to create store traffic and sell regularly priced merchandise.

Lowercase (10) See *Uppercase and lowercase.*

Macroeconomics (1) The large world of national and international economics.

Magazine Publishers Association (MPA) (13) A trade group made up of more than 200 publishers who represent 800 magazines. It compiles data on ABC member magazines and promotes greater and more effective use of magazine advertising.

Mail-order advertising (15) A form of direct response advertising and a method of selling in which the product or service is promoted through advertising and the prospect orders it. Mail-order advertising is usually received in three distinct forms: catalogs, advertisements in magazines and newspapers, and direct-mail advertising.

Mail response lists (15) Type of direct-mail list, composed of people who have responded to the direct-mail solicitations of other companies, especially those whose efforts are complementary to the advertiser's.

Mailing lists (15) Computerized lists of potential customers. They may be house lists, mail responses lists, or compiled lists.

Majority fallacy (4) A common marketing misconception that, to be successful, a product or service must appeal to the majority of people.

Makegoods (14) TV spots that are aired to compensate for spots that were missed or run incorrectly.

Market (4) A group of potential customers who share a common interest, need, or desire. The group must be able to use the product or service offered to some advantage and must be able to afford the purchase price.

Market concentration (5) The reduced geographic target and the limited number of buyers for most industrial marketing efforts.

Market research (4) (6) The systematic gathering of information about the market: its size, composition, structure, and so forth.

Market segmentation (4) (5) The strategic process of (1) aggregating subgroups of customers into meaningful segments to determine which groups are potentially profitable markets, (2) designing products specifically for these segments, and (3) aiming all marketing activities at these groups.

Marketing (4) An umbrella business process that includes all activities aimed at: (1) finding out who customers are and what they want, (2) developing products to satisfy those customers' needs and desires, and (3) getting the products into the customers' possession.

Marketing mix (4) (7) Four elements, called the four Ps (product, price, place, and promotion), that every company has the option of adding, subtracting, or changing in order to create a desired marketing strategy.

Marketing objectives (7) Goals of the marketing effort that may be expressed in terms of (1) the needs of specific target markets and (2) specific sales objectives.

Marketing-oriented period (4) The modern marketing era in which companies determine in advance what customers want and then make products that will satisfy those needs or desires.

Marketing plan (7) The plan that directs the company's marketing effort. It assembles and brings up-to-date all the pertinent facts about the organization, the markets it serves, and its products, services, customers, and competition. It sets goals and objectives to be attained within specified periods of time and lays out the precise strategies that will be used to achieve them.

Marketing research (6) The systematic gathering, recording, and analyzing of data about the size, composition, and structure of markets for particular goods and services.

Marketing strategy (1) (7) The statement of how the company is going to accomplish its marketing objectives. The strategy is the total directional thrust of the company, that is, the "how-to" of the marketing plan. It identifies the company's target markets and presents a marketing mix for each of those targets.

Markup (3)   Traditionally, the 17.65 percent that agencies add to the net cost of outside purchases to obtain a commission of 15 percent of the new gross amount.

Mass-distribution system (1)   The huge network of warehouses, transportation facilities, wholesalers, distributors, dealers, packing plants, advertising media, salespeople, clerks, and stores organized to deliver low-priced, mass-produced goods from the manufacturer to the consumer.

Master tape (11)   The final recording of a radio commercial, with all the music, sound, and vocals mixed, from which dubs (duplicates) are recorded and sent to radio stations for broadcast.

Mechanical (9)   A large piece of white cardboard with the set type and the illustrations or photographs pasted into the exact position in which they will appear in the final ad. Also called a *pasteup,* this is then used as a direct basis for the next step in the reproduction process.

Media (1)   Plural of *medium,* referring to communications vehicles paid to present an advertisement to its target audience.

Media-buying service (3)   Organization that specializes in purchasing and packaging radio and television time.

Media commission (3)   See *Agency commission.*

Media director (3)   The person who evaluates media according to efficiency and cost and then recommends the best medium or media combination to use.

Media kit (18)   A package of material used to gain publicity at staged events such as press conferences or open houses. It includes a basic fact sheet detailing the event, a program for the event or a schedule of the activities, a list of the participants with biographical data, brochures prepared for the event, a news story for the broadcast media, and news and feature stories for print media.

Media objectives (12)   Audience and message distribution objectives designed to help fulfill marketing goals and strategies. The statement of media objectives leads off the media plan.

Media planning (12)   The process of (1) determining which media to use to convey a message and (2) choosing specific vehicles that will reach the desired target audience.

Media strategy (12)   A statement of the course of action to be taken to achieve media objectives: which media will be used, how often, and when.

Medium (1)   See *Media.*

Merge and purge (15)   In compiling mailing lists, the process of merging mail response and house lists and purging all duplicates.

Message element testing (6)   Research aimed at the selection of potential advertising themes and claims based on the likes and dislikes of consumers.

Message strategy (8)   The specific determination of what an ad or campaign will say and how it will say it. The elements of the message strategy include: copy (what you're going to say and how

you're going to say it), art (what you're going to show and how you're going to show it), and production (what you're going to create mechanically and how you're going to create it).

Microeconomics (1)   Issues dealing with particular aspects of economics such as the costs and revenues of individual enterprises.

Middleman (4)   A business firm that operates between the producer and the consumer or industrial purchaser.

Mixed interlock (11)   The earliest edited version of a filmed television commercial mixed with the finished sound track. Used for initial review and approval prior to finishing the editing process.

Mnemonic device (11)   Literally, a device used to assist the memory. Often a gimmick is used to dramatize the product benefit and make it memorable; for example, the Imperial Margarine crown or the Avon doorbell.

Mock magazine test (6)   Type of test in which ads being studied are "stripped into" an actual magazine and left with the respondents for a time. They are told to read the magazine, including the ads that interest them. Afterward the respondents are questioned about the test ads.

Motivation (5)   The underlying drives that stem from the conscious or unconscious needs of the consumer and contribute to the individual consumer's purchasing actions.

Motivation research (5) (6)   The scientific analysis of consumer motivations for marketing purposes.

Motivation value (12)   A consideration in selecting media based on the characteristics of a particular medium that might enhance that medium's ability to motivate its audience to action; for example, good quality reproduction or timeliness.

Movement (9)   The principle of graphic design that causes the reader of an advertisement to read the material in the sequence desired.

MPA (13)   See *Magazine Publishers Association.*

Multinational marketing structure (19)   Approach to international marketing in which a corporation has full and integrated participation in world markets and a view toward business based on choices available anywhere in the world. The multinational's marketing activities are typically characterized by strong centralized control and coordination. See also *International marketing structure.*

Multipoint distribution system (MDS) (14)   A microwave TV delivery system that can carry up to a dozen channels.

Musical logotype (11)   A jingle that becomes associated with a product or company.

NAB (13)   See *Newspaper Advertising Bureau.*

NAD (2)   The National Advertising Division of the National Advertising Review Council, a self-regulatory body. It investigates and monitors advertising industry practices.

NARB (2)   The National Advertising Review Board, a five-member panel, composed of three advertisers, one agency representative, and one layperson, selected to review decisions of the NAD.

NARC (2) The National Advertising Review Council, an organization founded by the Council of Better Business Bureaus and various advertising industry groups to promote and enforce standards of truth, accuracy, taste, morality, and social responsibility in advertising.

Narrative copy (8) A type of body copy that tells a story. It sets up a problem and then creates a solution using the particular sales features of the product or service as the key to the solution.

National advertising (1) Advertising aimed at customers in various parts of the country.

Needs (5) The basic human forces that motivate a person to do something.

Networks (3) (14) Any of the national television or radio broadcasting chains or companies such as Columbia Broadcasting System (CBS), National Broadcasting Company (NBC), or American Broadcasting Company (ABC). Networks offer the large advertiser convenience and efficiency because the message can be broadcast simultaneously throughout the country.

News/information headline (8) A type of headline that includes many of the "how-to" headlines as well as headlines that seek to gain identification for their sponsors by announcing some news or providing some promise of information.

News release (18) A typewritten sheet of information (usually 8½ by 11 inches) issued to print and broadcast outlets to generate publicity or shed light on a subject of interest.

Newspaper Advertising Bureau (NAB) (13) A bureau of the American Newspaper Publishers Association. It provides newspapers with marketing information by conducting field research and offers advertisers help with placing newspaper ads.

Newspaper Co-op Network (NCN) (13) The NAB's system by which advertisers are able to line up local dealers for ads through a central clearinghouse.

Nielsen Station Index (14) One of the most commonly used rating services for TV, providing a wide array of statistics on how many people, in what age groups, and of what sex are watching TV at various times of the day within a specific market area.

Nonbusiness institutions (18) Nonprofit organizations whose primary objective is noncommercial: churches, schools, universities, hospitals, charitable organizations, and so forth.

Noncommercial advertising (1) (18) Advertising sponsored by or for a charitable institution, civic group, religious order, political organization, or some other nonprofit group to promote an idea, a philosophy, an attitude, a social cause, or a political issue.

Nonprobability samples (6) Research samples that do not provide every unit in the population with an equal chance of being included. As a result, there is no guarantee that the sample will be representative; however, nonprobability samples are less expensive to conduct.

Nonproduct advertising (1) Advertising designed to sell ideas or a philosophy rather than products or services.

Objectives (7) See *Advertising objectives; Marketing objectives.*

Observational method (6) A method of research used when researchers actually monitor the overt actions of the person being studied.

Office of Consumer Affairs (2) The chief consumer protection agency of the federal government.

Offset lithography (10) A modern printing process in which the image is transferred from the printing plate to an intermediate rubber surface, called a blanket, which comes in contact with the paper and enables the image to be printed.

On-camera (11) Actually seen by the camera, as an announcer, a spokesperson, or actors playing out a scene.

On-pack premium (16) Premium designed to have a good impulse value attached to the outside of a package.

Open rate (13) The highest newspaper advertising rate for one-time insertions.

Opinion leader (5) Someone whose beliefs or attitudes are considered right by people who share an interest in some specific activity.

Order-of-merit test (6) Type of test in which two or more advertisements are shown to potential prospects with instructions to arrange the ads in order of preference.

Ornamental type (10) A group of typefaces comprising designs that provide novelty and are ornamental or decorative.

Out-of-home media (15) Media like outdoor advertising (billboards) and transit advertising (bus and car cards) that reach prospects outside their homes.

Outside posters (15) The variety of transit advertisements appearing on the outside of buses, including king size, queen size, traveling display, taillight spectacular, and headlights.

Overlaying (15) In developing mailing lists, the process of combining information from several sources to produce an in-depth profile of each customer or company.

Overspill media (19) Foreign media aimed at a national population that is inadvertently received by a substantial portion of the population of a neighboring country.

Packaging (4) (9) Method of containing and protecting a product and identifying it to consumers. The package should offer convenience, consumer appeal, and economy.

Paid circulation (12) The total number of copies of an average issue of a newspaper or magazine that are distributed through subscriptions and newsstand sales.

Painted displays (15) Large outdoor painted bulletins and walls, normally 14' by 48' or larger, meant for long use and usually placed in only the best locations where traffic is heavy and visibility is good.

Paired-comparison method (6) Type of test in which each advertisement is compared with every other advertisement in the group. Only two ads are evaluated at any one time.

Participation (14)   The basis on which most network television advertising is sold. Advertisers can participate in a program once or several times on a regular or irregular basis by buying 30- or 60-second segments within the program. This allows the advertiser to spread out the budget and makes it easier to get in and out of a program without a long-term commitment.

Pass-along readership (13)   Readers of a publication in addition to the purchaser or subscriber.

Pasteup (9)   See *Mechanical* and *Production artist*.

Patent and Trademark Office (2)   Federal office that registers and protects all patents and trademarks.

Penetration pricing (4)   Pricing strategy often used by new businesses in which low prices are offered initially to penetrate the market quickly by creating immediate traffic and sales.

People meter (14)   An electronic device that automatically records a household's TV viewing, including channels watched, number of minutes of viewing, and who is watching.

Perceived equal value exchange (4)   The economic transaction between an organization and its customers, in which the organization provides customers with products or services that meet their utilitarian or symbolic objectives, in places that are convenient, and at prices they can afford.

Percentage-of-sales method (7)   A method of advertising budget allocation based on a percentage of sales—either the previous year's sales, the anticipated sales for the next year, or a combination of the two.

Perceptible differences (4)   Distinguishing characteristics of products by means that are visibly apparent to the consumer.

Perception (5)   The sensing of stimuli to which an individual is exposed—the act or process of comprehending the world in which the individual exists.

Perceptual meaning studies (6)   Type of test in which ads are shown at controlled exposures using a tachistoscope. Respondents are questioned on recall of product, brand, illustrations, copy, and the main idea of the ad.

Periodic pulse (12)   Scheduling media placement at regular intervals unrelated to the season of the year.

Personal influences (5)   The various characteristics of individual human beings that make each behave differently, such as their particular needs and motives, individual perception, self-concept, and way they learn and develop habits.

Personal selling (4)   Sales method based on person-to-person contact, such as by a salesperson at a retail establishment or by a telephone solicitor.

Photo animation (11)   An animation technique that uses still photography instead of illustrations or puppets. By making slight movements of the photos from one frame to the next, the animated illusion is created.

Photocomposition (10)   A method of typesetting that combines computer technology and electronics. It offers an almost unlimited number of typefaces and sizes, faster reproduction at lower cost, and improved clarity and sharpness of image.

Photo-optic typesetters (10)   Type of typesetting equipment that uses an electromechanical method of projecting characters through a lens, which magnifies the characters to the desired size. This image is then reflected off a mirror onto photosensitive paper or film, thus setting the characters.

Photoplatemaking (10)   A process for making printing plates, similar to taking a picture, in which an image is photographed and the negative is printed in reverse on a sensitized metal plate rather than on paper. This plate is then used for printing.

Physiological testing (6)   The use of pupilometric devices, eye-movement cameras, galvanometers, tachistoscopes, and electroencephalographs to measure unconscious responses to advertisements.

Pica (10)   The unit of measurement for the horizontal width of lines of type. There are six picas to the inch and 12 points to the pica.

Picture-caption copy (8)   A type of body copy in which the story is told through a series of illustrations and captions rather than through the use of a copy block alone.

Place element (4)   In the marketing mix, how and where customers purchase a product or service.

Point (10)   The unit of measurement for the depth (or height) of type. There are 72 points to the inch, so 1 point equals $\frac{1}{72}$ of an inch.

Point-of-purchase advertising (P-O-P) (16)   Advertising or display materials set up at the retail location to build traffic, advertise the product, and promote impulse buying. Includes window displays, counter displays, floor and wall displays, streamers, and posters.

Portfolio test (6)   A method of testing in which ads being studied are interspersed with other ads and editorial matter in an album-type portfolio. Consumers in an experimental group are shown this portfolio, while consumers in a closely matched control group are shown the portfolio without the test ads. Afterward, members of both groups are questioned to determine their recall of the portfolio contents and the advertisements being tested.

Positioning (1) (4) (7)   The way in which a product is ranked in the consumer's mind in relation to the benefits it offers, to the competition, or to certain target markets.

Postcards (15)   Cards sent by advertisers to announce sales, offer discounts, or otherwise generate consumer traffic.

Poster panel (15)   The basic form of outdoor advertising and the least costly per unit. It is a structure of blank panel with a standardized size and border, usually anchored in the ground, with its advertising message printed by lithography or silkscreen and mounted by hand on the panel.

Postproduction (11)   All the work done after the day of shooting to finish a television commercial. Includes editing, processing film, recording sound effects, mixing audio and video, and duplicating final films or tapes.

Posttesting (6)   The fourth stage of advertising research, designed to determine the effectiveness of an advertisement or campaign *after* it runs.

Preemption rate (14)   Lower TV advertising rate for spots that may be sold for a higher price to another advertiser if such an offer is made.

Preferred position (13)   A choice position for a newspaper or magazine ad for which a higher rate is charged.

Premium (16)   An item offered free or at a bargain price to encourage the consumer to buy an advertised product.

Preprinted inserts (13)   Newspaper advertisements printed in advance by the advertiser and then delivered to the newspaper plant to be inserted into a specific edition. Preprints are inserted into the fold of the newspaper and look like a separate, smaller section of the paper. Sizes range from a typical newspaper page to a piece no larger than a double postcard.

Preproduction (11)   All the work done prior to the actual day of filming a television commercial, including casting, arranging for locations, estimating costs, obtaining necessary permissions, selecting technical suppliers and production companies, and finding props and costumes.

Presentation (3)   See *Speculative presentation*.

Press agentry (18)   The planning of activities and the staging of events to attract attention to new products or services and to generate publicity about the company or organization that will be of interest to the media.

Prestige pricing (4)   Pricing strategy that aims at a select clientele who can afford to pay higher prices in exchange for convenience, service, and quality.

Pretesting (6)   The third stage of advertising research, used to increase the likelihood of preparing the most effective advertising messages.

Price element (4)   In the marketing mix, the amount charged for the product or service. The factors affecting price are market demand, cost of production and distribution, competition, and corporate objectives.

Price/quality differentiation (7)   A type of product differentiation strategy based on differences in price and quality. For example, a company could offer a better-quality product at a higher price, or it could advertise the same quality at a lower price.

Primary circulation (13)   The number of people who receive a publication, whether through direct purchase or subscription.

Primary data (6)   Research information gained directly from the marketplace. The three basic alternatives in collecting primary data are observation, experiment, and survey.

Primary demand (4)   Consumer demand for the whole product category.

Prime time (14)   The highest TV viewing time of the day, namely 8 to 11 P.M.

Probability sample (6)   A sampling procedure in which every unit in the population has an equal and known probability of being selected for the research.

Product (4) (6) (7)   See *Product concept*.

Product advertising (1)   Advertising intended to promote products and services.

Product concept (4) (6) (7)   The "bundle" of values built into a product that are aimed at satisfying various functional, social, psychological, economic, and other consumer needs.

Product differentiation (4)   The idea of building unique differences into products to satisfy consumer demand.

Product element (4)   The most important element of the marketing mix: the product or service being offered and the values associated with it.

Product life cycle (4)   Progressive stages in the life of a product—including introduction, growth, maturity, and decline—that affect the way a product is marketed and advertised.

Production (10) (11)   The process of converting ideas, scripts, sketches, copy, and so forth, into finished advertisements, brochures, films, and commercials. Also, the actual day (or days) that a television commercial is filmed or videotaped.

Production artist (9)   The person responsible for assembling the various elements of an ad and mechanically putting them together the way the art director or designer has indicated. Also called *pasteup artist*.

Production-oriented period (4)   An era when there were few products and many consumers and companies only had to worry about creating and producing enough products to satisfy the huge demand.

Production values (8)   One of the elements of message strategy. Production values determine what is to be created mechanically and how it is to be created.

Professional advertising (1)   Advertising directed at individuals who are normally licensed and operate under a code of ethics or professional set of standards.

Profile matching (12)   A method or theory of media scheduling in which the schedule is split so that messages are delivered to each segment of the target audience in proportion to that segment's importance among all prospects.

Program rating (14)   The percentage of TV households in an area that are tuned in to a specific program.

Programming (14)   Carefully planning a radio station format to reach a specific market and capture as many listeners as possible. The larger its audience, the more a station can charge advertisers for commercial time.

Projective techniques (6)   Research methods designed to involve the consumer in a situation in which he or she can "project" feelings about the problem or product.

Promotion (4) (18)   The marketing-related communication between the seller and the buyer. For profit-making organizations, promotion means using advertising and public relations techniques as a means of selling a product or service as well as enhancing the reputation of an organization.

Promotion element (4)   The aspect of the marketing mix that consists of personal selling, advertising, public relations, sales promotion, and collateral materials.

Promotional mix (4)   See *Promotion element.*

Promotional pricing (4)   Using strategies such as two-for-one sales or end-of-month sales in order to maintain traffic, stimulate demand, or make room for new merchandise.

Promotional pulse (12)   A method of media scheduling designed to support some special promotion of the advertiser or manufacturer so that buying will be heavier during the time of the promotion than at other times.

Proof copy (13)   A copy of a newspaper-created ad provided to the advertiser for checking purposes before the ad runs.

Proportion (9)   The space accorded the elements in an advertisement. For best appearance, designers frequently use varying amounts of space to avoid the monotony of equal amounts of space for each element.

Provocative headline (8)   A type of headline written to provoke the reader's curiosity so that, to learn more, the reader will read the body copy.

Psychographic segmentation (5)   The grouping of consumers into market segments on the basis of psychological makeup—namely, personality and lifestyle.

Public affairs (18)   All activities related to the community citizenship of an organization, including dealing with community officials and working with regulatory bodies and legislative groups.

Public relations (4)(18)   Communications activities usually not overtly sponsored that act as supplements to advertising to inform various publics about the company and its products and to help build corporate credibility and image.

Public relations advertising (18)   A type of advertising used to communicate directly with a company's important publics in order to express its feelings, enhance its point of view, promote a program sponsorship, or improve relations with labor, government, customers, or suppliers. This kind of advertising is designed to enhance the company's general community citizenship and create public goodwill.

Publicity (18)   The generation of news about a person, product, or service that appears in broadcast or print media and is usually thought of as being "free" because the medium has no publicity rate card.

Pull strategy (4)(16)   Marketing, advertising, and sales promotion activities aimed at inducing trial, purchase, and repurchase by consumers.

Pulse (12)   An increased schedule of advertising above normal levels, usually during peak selling periods.

Pupilometric device (6)   A device that measures the dilation of the pupil of a subject's eye in an effort to gauge the subject's reaction to ads, graphic designs, and packages.

Purchase occasion (5)   Method of segmenting markets on the basis of *when* consumers buy and use a product or service.

Push money (16)   An inducement for retail salespeople to push the sale of particular products. Also called *spiffs.*

Push strategy (4)(16)   Marketing, advertising, and sales promotion activities aimed at getting products into the dealer pipeline and accelerating sales by offering inducements to dealers, retailers, and salespeople. Inducements might include introductory price allowances, distribution allowances, and advertising dollar allowances to stock the product and set up displays.

Qualitative research (6)   A type of research, usually exploratory or diagnostic in nature, involving small numbers of people surveyed on a nonprobability basis to gain impressions rather than definitions.

Quantitative research (6)   A type of data collection method used by market researchers to develop hard numbers so they can completely and accurately measure a particular market situation.

Question headline (8)   A type of headline that asks the reader a question.

RADAR Report (14)   Radio's All-Dimension Audience Research audience estimates (ratings), based on daily telephone interviews that cover seven days of radio listening behavior.

Radio dayparts (14)   The five basic parts into which the radio day is divided: morning drive, daytime, afternoon drive, nighttime, all night. The rating services measure the audiences for only the first four of these dayparts, as all-night listening is very limited and not highly competitive.

Rate card (13)   A printed information form listing a publication's advertising rates, mechanical and copy requirements, advertising deadlines, and other information the advertiser needs to know before placing an order.

Rating services (14)   The research organizations that, through various techniques, furnish data on the size and characteristics of the audiences that view or listen to TV and radio programs. Companies interested in their findings subscribe to a service and use it as a basis in making media plans for advertising.

Ratings (14)   See *Program rating.*

Reach (12)   The number of different people or households exposed to an advertising schedule during a given time, usually four weeks. Reach measures the *unduplicated extent* of audience exposure to a media vehicle and may be expressed either as a percentage or as a raw number.

Reading notice (13)   A variation of a display ad designed to look like editorial matter. It is sometimes charged at a higher space rate than normal display advertising, and the law requires that the word *advertisement* appear at the top.

Recall tests (6)   Posttesting methods used to determine the extent to which an advertisement and its message have registered with consumers.

Recruitment advertising (18)   A special type of advertising, most frequently found in the classified sections of daily newspapers and typically the responsibility of a personnel department, aimed at attracting employment applications.

Reference groups (5) Groups of people we try to emulate or with whom we identify.

Refund promotion (16) The offer of either cash back or discount coupons on future purchases with proof of purchase of a product.

Regional advertising (1) Advertising for products sold in only one area or region of the country. The region might cover several states but not the entire nation.

Regular price-line advertising (17) A type of retail advertising designed to inform consumers about the services available or the wide selection and quality of merchandise offered at regular prices.

Reinforcement advertising (7) Advertising designed to remind people of their successful experience with a product and to suggest using it again.

Reliability (6) An important characteristic of research test results. For a test to be reliable, it must be repeatable, producing the same result each time it is administered.

Reprints (15) Duplications of published articles that show the company or its products in a favorable light, used as direct-mail enclosures and frequently sent by public relations agencies or departments.

Reseller markets (4) Individuals or companies that buy products for the purpose of reselling them.

Retainer (3) See *Straight-fee method*.

Retoucher (10) The artist who alters photographs used in advertising and on magazine covers to add desired elements or subtract undesired elements.

Roman type (10) The most popular type group, considered to be the most readable and offering the greatest number of designs. It is characterized by the serifs (or tails) that cross the ends of the main strokes and by variations in the thickness of the strokes.

ROP (13) Run of paper. A term referring to a newspaper's normal discretionary right to place a given ad on any page or in any position it desires—in other words, where space permits. Most newspapers make an effort to place an ad in the position requested by the advertiser.

Rotary plan (15) In outdoor advertising, the rotation of painted bulletins to different choice locations in the market every 30, 60, or 90 days, giving the impression of wide coverage over time.

Rotogravure (10) A printing process that works in the reverse of letterpress. Instead of the printing design being raised above the printing plate as in letterpress, the rotogravure process prints from a depressed surface. Ink in the tiny depressions is transferred to the paper by pressure and suction.

Rough layout (9) A pencil drawing of the proposed ad drawn to actual size. The headlines and subheads are lettered onto the layout, the artwork and intended photographs are drawn, and the body copy is simulated with pencil lines.

Run of paper (13) See *ROP*.

Run of station (14) Leaving placement of radio spots up to the station in order to achieve a lower ad rate.

Sale advertising (17) A type of retail advertising designed to stimulate the movement of particular merchandise or generally increase store traffic by placing the emphasis on special reduced prices.

Sales letters (15) The most common form of direct mail. Sales letters may be typewritten, typeset and printed, printed with a computer insert (such as your name), or fully computer typed.

Sales-oriented period (4) An era when the marketplace was glutted with products and the selling function was characterized by business's use of extravagant advertising claims and an attitude of *caveat emptor* (let the buyer beware).

Sales promotion (4) (16) A direct inducement offering extra incentives all along the marketing route—from manufacturers through distribution channels to consumers—to accelerate the movement of the product from the producer to the consumer. A broad promotional category that covers nonmedia advertising activities like sweepstakes, contests, premiums, and so on.

Sales-target objectives (7) Marketing objectives that relate to a company's sales. They should be specific as to product and market, quantified as to time and amount, and realistic. They may be expressed in terms of total sales volume; sales by product, market segment, or customer type; market share; growth rate in total or by product line; or even gross profit.

Sales tests (6) Methods used to obtain information on the sales-producing value of specific ads or whole campaigns. These include six types: measures of past sales, controlled experiments, matched samples of consumers, mail-order selling, consumer purchase tests, and store inventory audits.

Sample (6) A portion of the population selected by marketing researchers to represent the appropriate targeted population. Theories of sampling are drawn from the mathematical theories of probability. If a sample is to be considered adequate, it must be large enough to achieve satisfactory precision or stability.

Sampling (16) Offering consumers a free trial of the product, hoping to convert them to habitual use.

Sans serif (10) A large group of typefaces characterized by (1) the lack of serifs (thus the name, sans serif) and (2) a relatively uniform thickness of the strokes. Also referred to as *block, contemporary,* or *gothic*.

Satellite master antenna television (SMATV) (14) A method for TV signal delivery that makes use of a satellite dish to capture signals for TV sets in apartment buildings and other complexes.

Scratchboard (9) A distinctive and different type of illustration that gives the impression of fine workmanship. On a special paper with a surface specifically made for this art form, black ink is applied to the area of the illustration. With the use of a scratching device (a stylus or other sharp instrument), the ink is removed, leaving a white line.

Screen printing (10) An old printing process that requires no plates and is based on the stencil principle. As ink is squeezed through a special stencil screen stretched tightly on a frame, the desired image is reproduced. For printing in color, a separate stencil is made for each color.

Script (10) See *Cursive type*.

Seal (8) A type of certification mark offered by such organizations as the Good Housekeeping Institute and Underwriters' Laboratories when a product meets standards established by these institutions. Seals provide an independent, valued endorsement for the advertised product.

Seasonal pulse (12) A media scheduling method based on seasonal buying patterns that dictate heavy media use during peak selling periods.

Secondary data (6) Data that already exist somewhere, having been collected for some other purpose.

Secondary readership (13) The number of people who read a publication in addition to the primary purchasers.

Selective demand (4) Consumer demand for the particular advantages of one brand over another.

Selective distribution (4) Distribution strategy in which manufacturers can cut their costs of distribution and promotion by selling through only a limited number of outlets.

Selective perception (5) The ability of humans to select from the many sensations bombarding their central processing unit those sensations that relate to their previous experiences, needs, or desires.

Self-concept (5) The images we carry in our minds of who we are and who we want to be.

Self-liquidating premium (16) A special offer in which the consumer pays the cost of the premium plus handling charges. The seller does not attempt to make a profit on such a premium but only tries to break even.

Self-mailer (15) Any form of direct mail that can travel by mail without an envelope. Usually folded and secured by a staple or a seal, self-mailers have a special blank space for the prospect's name and address.

Serifs (10) Delicate curved tails that cross the end of each letter stroke of roman type.

Serigraphy (10) See *Screen printing*.

Service mark (2) The name or symbol that identifies a service rather than a product.

Share of audience (14) The percentage of homes that have sets in use (HUT) tuned in to a specific program. A program with only five viewers could have a 50 share if only 10 sets are turned on.

Share-of-market method (7) A method of allocating advertising funds based on determining the firm's goals for a certain share of the market and then applying the same percentage of industry advertising dollars to the firm's budget.

Shared mail (17) A direct-mail vehicle in which two or more ads are wrapped around each other and mailed as a single piece.

Shoppers (17) Weekly local ad vehicles that may or may not contain editorial matter. They can be segmented into highly selected market areas.

Short rate (13) The rate charged to advertisers who, during the year, fail to fulfill the amount of space for which they have contracted. This is computed by determining the difference between the standard rate for the lines run and the discount rate contracted.

Showing (15) A traditional term referring to the relative number of outdoor posters used during a contract period, indicating the intensity of market coverage. For example, a 100 showing provides an even and thorough coverage of the entire market.

Signature (8) See *Logotype*.

Silk screen (10) See *Screen printing*.

Simulation model (12) A type of computer program used to estimate the ability of specific media vehicles to reach target individuals.

Situation analysis (7) A statement in the marketing plan telling where the organization is and how it got there. It includes relevant facts about the company's history, growth, products or services, sales volume, share of market, competitive status, market served, distribution system, past advertising programs, results of market research programs, company capabilities, and strengths and weaknesses.

Skimming pricing (4) Pricing strategy that employs high prices to quickly recover the money invested by manufacturers in developing a new product or by retailers in furnishing, decorating, stocking, and promoting their stores.

Slander (8) Defamation of a person in broadcast advertising or verbal statements.

Slice of life (11) A type of commercial consisting of a short play that portrays a real-life situation in which the product is tried and becomes the solution to a problem.

Slogan (8) A standard company statement or tag line for advertisements, salespeople, and company employees. Slogans have two basic purposes: to provide continuity for a campaign and to reduce a key theme or idea the company wants associated with its product or itself to a brief, memorable positioning statement.

Special-events management (18) The planning, staging, and supervision of activities such as the grand opening of a store, an autograph party for an author, the announcement of a new product, or the groundbreaking for a new facility.

Specialty advertising (16) See *Advertising specialty*.

Spectaculars (15) Giant electronic signs that usually incorporate movement, color, or flashy graphics to grab viewers in high-traffic areas.

Speculative presentation (3) An agency's presentation of the advertisement it proposes using in the event it is hired. These presentations are usually made at the request of a prospective client but are not paid for by the client and are therefore generally considered unethical and unprofessional.

Split run (13)   A feature of many newspapers (as well as magazines) that allows advertisers to test the comparative effectiveness of two different advertising approaches by running two different ads of identical size, promoting the same product or service, in the same or different press runs on the same day.

Sponsorships (14)   The presentation of a radio or TV program by a sole advertiser. The advertiser is responsible for the program content and the cost of production as well as the advertising. This is generally so costly that single sponsorships are usually limited to specials.

Spot announcement (14)   An individual commercial message run between programs but having no relationship to either.

Spot radio (14)   National advertisers' purchase of airtime on individual stations. Buying spot radio affords advertisers great flexibility in their choice of markets, stations, airtime, and copy. In addition, spot advertising enables the message to be tailored to the local market and presented to listeners at the most favorable times.

Spot television (14)   Individual television commercials sold either nationally or locally in segments of 10, 15, 30, or 60 seconds. National spot advertising offers the advertiser greater flexibility since commercials can be concentrated on the markets most likely to pay off, and they are less expensive than participations because they are run in clusters between programs. Most advertising time of network affiliates is sold in this way.

Square serif (10)   A kind of typeface that combines sans serif and roman. The serifs have the same weight and thickness as the main strokes of the letters.

SRDS (13)   See *Standard Rate and Data Service*.

Standard advertising units (SAUs) (13)   A system of standardized newspaper advertisement sizes that can be accepted by all standard-sized newspapers without consideration of their precise format or page size. This system allows advertisers to prepare one advertisement in a particular size or SAU and place it in various newspapers regardless of the format.

Standard Industrial Classification (SIC) codes (5)   Method used by the U.S. Department of Commerce to classify all businesses. The SIC codes are based on broad industry groups, which are then subdivided into major groups, subgroups, and detailed groups of firms in similar lines of business.

Standard Rate and Data Service (13)(14)(15)   A publisher of media information directories that eliminate the necessity for advertisers and their agencies to obtain rate cards for every publication.

Standard size (13)   A newspaper size generally 22 inches deep and 14 inches wide. This type of newspaper has usually been eight columns wide, although the recent trend has been toward a six-column layout and a slightly reduced page size.

Start-up pulse (12)   A media scheduling method designed to start off a campaign with a bang. Used to introduce new products, it is also seen every year when the new automobile models are introduced.

Statement stuffers (15)   Advertisements enclosed in the monthly customer statements mailed by department stores, banks, or oil companies.

Stimulus-response theory (5)   Theory that treats learning as a trial-and-error process whereby needs, motives, or drives are triggered by some cue to cause the individual to respond in an effort to satisfy the need.

Stock photos (9)   Existing photos that can be purchased for advertising purposes, usually from photo agencies.

Stop-motion (11)   An animation technique whereby objects and animals come to life—walk, run, dance, and do tricks—by means of stop-motion photography. Each frame of film is shot individually. An arm may be moved only 1/32 of an inch on each frame, but when the frames are assembled, the effect is smooth and natural.

Storyboard (3)(9)(11)   A layout in a comic-strip series of sequential frames to indicate the conception of a television commercial. A storyboard helps in estimating the expense, visualizing the message, revealing any weakness in concept, presenting for client approval, and guiding the actual shooting.

Straight announcement (11)   The oldest type of television commercial, in which an announcer delivers a sales message directly into the camera or off-screen while a slide or film is shown on-screen.

Straight-fee method (3)   The straight fee, or retainer, is based on a cost-plus-fixed-fees formula. Under this system, the agency estimates the amount of personnel time required by the client, determines the cost of that personnel, and multiplies by some factor.

Straight-line copy (8)   A type of body copy in which the text immediately begins to explain or develop the headline and illustration and the product's sales points are ticked off in the order of their importance, all in a clear attempt to sell the product.

Strategy (7)   See *Advertising strategy; Marketing strategy*.

Strike-on composition (10)   A simple method of setting cold type, also called *direct-impression composition*, which can be done on a regular typewriter, an electronic typewriter, or a word processor.

Stripping (10)   The assembly of the various line and halftone negatives into one single negative, which is then used to produce the combination plate.

Subheads (8)   Secondary headlines in advertisements that may appear above or below the headline or in the text of the ad. Subheads are usually set in a type size smaller than the headline but larger than the body copy or text type size. They may also appear in boldface type or in a different ink color.

Subscription television (STV) (14)   Over-the-air pay TV. Subscribers pay for a descrambler that allows them to watch programs carried over a regular television channel.

Sunday supplement (13)   A newspaper-distributed Sunday magazine. Sunday supplements are distinct from other sections of the newspaper since they are printed by rotogravure on smoother paper stock. This heavier, higher-quality paper is more conducive to quality color printing. Therefore, it enables Sunday supplements to attract and feature higher-quality national advertising.

Supers (11) Words superimposed on the picture in a television commercial.

Superstation (14) A local TV station that relays programs to a satellite, which then broadcasts them nationally. The best-known superstation is Ted Turner's WTBS out of Atlanta.

Suppliers (3) People and organizations that specialize in some ancillary aspect of the advertising business such as photography, illustration, printing, and production.

Supply and demand (4) Law of economics stating that, in a free market, if the supply of a product stays the same and the desire (or demand) for it increases, the price will tend to rise. If the demand decreases below the available supply, the price will tend to drop.

Survey method (6) The most common way to gather primary research data. By asking questions of current or prospective customers, the researcher hopes to obtain information on attitudes, opinions, or motivations.

Sweepstakes (16) A sales promotion activity in which prizes are offered based on a chance drawing of entrants' names. The purpose is to encourage consumption of the product by creating consumer involvement.

Syndicated art services (17) Low-cost artwork (also called *clip art*) available by subscription to local media and advertisers. Clip art is available for various types of businesses and is often tied in to seasons, holidays, and other promotional angles.

Syndicated research services (6) Companies that continuously monitor and publish information on the media as well as other marketing and advertising information.

Syndication (14) The marketing of television programs to local stations on an individual basis.

Synergism (12) An effect achieved when the sum of the parts is greater than that expected from simply adding together the individual components.

Tabloid (13) A newspaper size generally about half as deep as a standard-sized newspaper and usually about 14 inches deep and 10 inches wide. It is sold flat, without folding, and looks like an unbound magazine. Most tabloid pages have five columns, each about two inches wide.

Tactics (7) See *Action programs*.

Take-ones (15) In transit advertising, pads of business reply cards or coupons affixed to interior advertisements for an extra charge that allow passengers to request more detailed information, send in application blanks, or receive some other product benefit.

Target audience (1) (7) The specific group of individuals to whom the advertising message is directed.

Target market (4) (6) (7) The market segment or group within the market segment toward which all marketing activities will be directed.

Task method (7) Method of allocating advertising funds that defines the objectives sought and how advertising will be used to accomplish those objectives. The task method occurs in three steps: defining the objectives, determining the strategy, and estimating the cost.

Tear sheet (13) The page of a newspaper or magazine where the advertiser's ad appears; it is torn out and sent to the advertiser or forwarded through the Advertising Checking Bureau for verification purposes.

Technical illustrators (9) Illustrators who specialize in drawing, from blueprints if necessary, extremely precise pictures of products with all their intricate components.

Telemarketing (4) (15) Selling products and services by using the telephone to contact prospective customers.

Television dayparts (14) The various parts of the day into which TV programming and viewing is divided. These include: daytime, early fringe, early news, prime access, prime time, late news, and late fringe.

Terminal posters (15) One-sheet, two-sheet, and three-sheet posters in many bus, subway, and commuter train stations as well as in major train and airline terminals. These are usually custom designed and include such attention getters as floor displays, island showcases, illuminated signs, dioramas (three-dimensional scenes), and clocks with special lighting and moving messages.

Testimonial (11) The use of satisfied customers and celebrities to endorse a product in advertising.

Testing (6) See *Posttesting; Pretesting*.

Text type (10) The smaller type used in the body copy of an advertisement.

Theater tests (6) A captive audience technique for pretesting television commercials in which a variety of methods may be used. For example, respondents may be asked to press a button to indicate what they like and don't like as they view a commercial.

Third-class mail (15) The inexpensive classification of mail usually used for direct-mail advertising. The four types of third-class mail are single piece, bulk, bound books or catalogs, and nonprofit organization mail.

Thumbnail sketch (9) Miniature pencil sketches, approximately one-fourth to one-eighth the size of the finished ad, that are used for trying out ideas.

Total audience (14) The total number of homes reached by some portion of a TV program. This figure is normally broken down to determine the distribution of audience into demographic categories.

Total audience plan (TAP) (14) A radio package rate that guarantees a certain percentage of spots in the better dayparts.

Total bus (15) In transit advertising, all the exterior space on a bus, including the front, rear, sides, and top, giving the product message powerful exclusivity.

Total market coverage (17) A free advertising vehicle delivered weekly to 100 percent of residents in a newspaper's market area.

Trade advertising (1) The advertising of goods and services to middlemen to stimulate wholesalers and retailers to buy goods for resale to their customers or for use in their own businesses.

Trade characters (2) People, birds, animals, or other objects used to advertise a product. May also be applied to the goods as a trademark.

Trade deals (16) Short-term dealer discounts on a product or other dealer incentives to sell a product.

Trade name (2) The name under which a company does business.

Trade shows (16) Exhibitions where manufacturers, dealers, and buyers of an industry's products can get together for demonstrations and discussion; expose new products, literature, and samples to customers; and meet potential new dealers for their products.

Trademark (1) (2) Any word, name, symbol, device, or any combination thereof adopted and used by manufacturers or merchants to identify their goods and distinguish them from those manufactured or sold by others.

Trading stamps (16) A once-popular sales promotion device for department stores, supermarkets, and service stations in which customers making purchases received stamps that can be redeemed for valuable products.

Traffic department (3) Department responsible for coordinating all phases of production and seeing that everything is completed on time and that all ads and commercials are received by the media before the deadline.

Trailer test (6) A type of test in which trailers are situated in shopping center parking lots and shoppers are invited in to be shown TV commercials. The impact of the commercials is measured in part by the difference in coupon redemption rates between shoppers exposed to the commercials and those who are not.

Transit advertising (15) An out-of-home medium that actually includes three separate media forms: inside cards; outside posters; and station, platform, and terminal posters.

Trial close (8) In ad copy, an early request for the order. It gives consumers the option to make the buying decision early.

TVHH (TV households) (14) The number of households in a market area that own television sets.

Type families (10) Related typefaces in which the basic design remains the same but that have variations in the proportion, weight, and slant of the characters. Variations also commonly include light, medium, bold, extra bold, condensed, extended, and italic.

Type groups (10) Typefaces classified into various groups because of their similarity in design. The five major type groups are roman, sans serif (or gothic), square serif, cursive (or script), and ornamental.

Typography (10) The art of selecting and setting type.

UHF (14) The more than 250 ultra-high frequency (channels 14 through 83) television stations.

Unaided recall (6) Method of posttesting in which respondents are questioned about advertisements they have seen or read without any assistance from the interviewer about the brand or the advertising.

Unfair advertising (2) According to the FTC, advertising that causes a consumer to be "unjustifiably injured" or that violates public policy.

Unit-of-sale method (7) A method of allocating advertising funds, also called the case-rate method, in which a specific dollar figure is set for each case, box, barrel, or carton produced or for each unit anticipated to be produced.

Unity (9) The appearance or impression created when all the elements in an ad (such as balance, movement, proportion, contrast, and color) relate to one another in a harmonious way.

Universal Product Code (6) Labels consisting of a series of linear bars and a 10-digit number that identify a product and its price.

Universe (6) The entire target population of a research study.

Uppercase and lowercase (10) Capital letters are called *uppercase,* and small letters are called *lowercase.* Type directions may call for type to be set in all upper, all lower, or upper and lower.

User status (5) Method of segmenting markets by types of product users, including nonusers, ex-users, potential users, new users, and regular users.

USP (1) The *unique selling proposition,* or differentiating features, of every product advertised; a concept developed by Rosser Reeves of the Ted Bates advertising agency.

U.S. Postal Service (2) Federal corporation that maintains control over false and deceptive advertising, pornography, and lottery offers sent through the mails.

Validity (6) An important characteristic of a research test. For a test to be valid, it must reflect the true status of the market.

VALS (5) Acronym meaning Values and Lifestyles—refers to a method of segmenting consumer markets based on certain psychographic attributes. These categories may also be used to govern aspects of a product's marketing strategy.

Vertical cooperative advertising (17) Co-op advertising in which the manufacturer provides the ad and pays a percentage of the cost of placement.

Vertical marketing system (4) A system of marketing in which members of the distribution channel cooperate closely with one another in selling, pricing, promotion, and advertising.

Vertical publications (13) Business publications aimed at people in various job functions within a specific industry; for example, *Retail Baking Today.*

VHF (14) The more than 500 very high frequency (channels 2 through 13) television stations. Until 1952, all stations were VHF.

Video (11) The left side of a television script, indicating camera action, scenes, and instructions. Also, the visual part of a television commercial.

Videotape (11)   Magnetic tape used to record television programs and commercials. Videotape offers a brilliant picture, better fidelity, and more consistent quality than film stock. It also provides an immediate playback.

Visual (9)   The picture in an advertisement. It may be an illustration or a photograph.

Visualization (8)(9)   The task of analyzing the problem, assembling any and all pertinent information, and developing some verbal or visual concept of how to communicate what needs to be said. It is the creative point where the search for the "big idea" takes place.

Voice-over (8)(11)   In television advertising, the spoken copy or dialogue delivered by an announcer who is not seen but whose voice is heard.

Voice-pitch analysis (6)   A research method in which a tape recording is made of a consumer's explanation of his or her reaction to an ad. A computer is then used to measure the changes in voice pitch caused by emotional responses to the ad.

Volume discounts (13)   Reduced newspaper ad rates earned by purchasing large or repeated amounts of space.

Volume segmentation (5)   Defining consumers as light, medium, or heavy users of products.

Wants (5)   Needs learned during a person's life.

Wash drawings (9)   The closest illustrative technique to a black-and-white photograph. A tight wash drawing is quite detailed and is much more realistic than a loose drawing. A loose wash drawing is more impressionistic and is used extensively by fashion illustrators.

Weeklies (13)   Newspapers that are published once a week and characteristically serve readers in small urban or suburban areas or farm communities with exclusive emphasis on local news and advertising.

White space (9)   The space in an advertisement unoccupied by text or illustration.

Work print (11)   The first visual portion of a filmed commercial assembled without the extra effects of dissolves, titles, or supers. At this time, scenes may be substituted, music and sound effects added, or other changes made.

Yellow pages directories (16)   Business phone directories in which advertising is sold.

Zapping (14)   The tendency of TV users to change channels during commercials.

Zipping (14)   The ability of VCR users to skip through commercials when replaying taped programs.

INDEX

Aaker, David A., 36
Aass, Paul, 636
ABC (American Broadcasting Company), 449, 452, 477–78
Robert Abel & Associates, 349
Abundance principle, 41
Acne-Statin, 59
Action Realty, 546, **547,** 549, 571, 559
Active versus passive media, 410
Adams Tutti Frutti Gum, 18
Adidas, 214
Ad/Pro, 554, 571
Advertiming, 169
Advertisers
  agency relationship to, 112
  agency review by, 110
  budgets of, 82, **83**
  defined, 79
  information sources on, 91
  with in-house agencies, 89–90
  large, 82–87
  local, 546–47
  media expenditures by, 384–85, 412, 430, 471
  nature of, 80–81
  program organization, **80,** 81–82
  small, 87–89
Advertising
  budget determination methods, 240–46; see also
    Local advertising
    empirical research, 246
    percent-of-sales, 243–45
    quantitative mathematical, 246
    share-of-market, 245
    task or buildup, 245–46
  classification of, 12–19
  cost effectiveness of, 9
  costs of, 179, 202
  credibility of, 48
  defined, 4–5
  economic effects of, 10, 19, 27–42
  educational value of, 10
  evolution of, 19–27
  and the GNP, 40
  illustrations in, 21; see also Art
  information value of, 10
  language choice in, 47
  and materialism, 47
  media, 16–17, 23
  me-too, 25–27
  nature of, 5, 17–19, 118
  nonmedia, 143
  nonproduct, 17; see also Corporate advertising
    and Noncommercial advertising
  offensive, 49, **50,** 51–53, 61
  persuasiveness of, 48
  positioning era of, 25
  and prices, 38–39
  product, 6–8, 17; see also Product advertising
  versus public relations, 6, 502; see also Public
    relations
  public service, 5, **11;** see also Noncommercial
    advertising
  purposes of, 5–8
  relationship to marketing, 118
  of services, 6, 17
  social criticisms of, 45–55
  social effects of, 11–12
  success factors, 143, 211, 285
  volume, 49
Advertising Age, **50,** 73, 116, 187, 420–21, 645, 653
Advertising agencies
  a la carte, 92, 96–97

Advertising agencies—Cont.
  cash handling by, 101–2
  client relations, 92–93, 95, 109–12
  consumer, 92, 94
  creative services, 96, 99
  entrepreneurial, 95
  ethnic specialty, 95
  evolution of, 22
  export agencies, 623
  fees and retainers, 104–7
  full-service, 92–94
  general, 94
  global, 621–22
  industrial, 93, 96
  information sources on, 91
  in-house versus autonomous, 89–90
  international, 621–22
  liability of, 72
  and local advertisers, 574–75
  local foreign, 622–23
  markup commissions, 105
  media commissions, 91, 94, 104
  media interface, 90–91, 94, 96
  merger trend in, 92–93, 104
  networks of, 623
  nonadvertising services by, 93–94, 102, 106
  organization of, 102–3
  public relations for, 107–9
  role of, 79, 90–92, 97–98
  rules for success, 160–61
  switching, 92, 110
  types of, 92–97
  U.S. top ten, 91
Advertising campaigns
  Canon, 372–73, 375–76, 378–79, 383, 391, 620
  Cap'n Crunch, 522, **523,** 530
  Coca-Cola, 4, 6–7, **8–9, 30–33,** 131, 158
  continuity in, 381
  flighting, 381
  Godiva chocolates, 280, **281,** 282, 287, 297
  international transferability of, 636–40
  J. C. Penney, 178, **179,** 182–84, 190–91, 194–95
  Perdue Chicken, 78, **79,** 80, 98
  pulsing, 381
  Reebok, 214, **215,** 220, 224–25, **226,** 230, 233, 235–37
  test marketing of, 190
  The Wall Street Journal, **154,** 250–52
Advertising Career Directory, 653
Advertising Checking Bureau, 424
Advertising Council, 611, **612**
Advertising departments
  administration of, **80,** 81, 85
  budgeting for, 82, **83**
  centralized, 83–85
  decentralized, 85–87
  and outside services, 82
  planning by, 82
Advertising objectives checklist, 234–35
Advertising plan
  and the advertising strategy, 233
  creative mix in, 233–40
  creative services in, 99
  and the marketing plan, 227
  need for, 99
  objectives for, 227, 234–35
  outline for, 648–51
  success factors, 143
Advertising Principles of American Business, 72
Advertising production, 87, **88**
Advertising pyramid
  inversion of, 232–33

Advertising pyramid—Cont.
  nature of, 228–29
Advertising research; see also Marketing research
  concept development, 199–201
  costs of, 180
  defined, 181
  importance of, 22–23, 98–99, 179
  versus marketing research, 181
  posttesting in, 199, 203
  pretesting in, 199, 202–8
  stages in, 199
  strategy determination, 199–200
Advertising specialties, 539–40
Advertising strategy
  copywriting for, 251
  elements of, 233–37, 251
  idea stage in, 257–58
  media planning in, 376
  and message strategy, 353–56
  and the unexpected, 285
Advo-Systems, 566
Adweek, 653
Aerial banners, 395
Africa, 627, 631, 634
Agate lines, 413
AGB Research, 457
Agency review checklist, 110
Agree shampoo, **524,** 525
Aim toothpaste, 171
Alaska Airlines, **345,** 347
Alcohol and Tobacco Tax Division, 56
Alfa Romeo, 398
Alka Seltzer, 230
Allegheny Airlines, 125
Allegis Corporation, 412
Allstate Insurance, **260**
Ally and Gargano agency, 424
Almond Growers Association, **610**
B. Altman, 553
Amadahl, 217
Amana Refrigeration, 594
American Advertising Federation (AAF), 72
American Airlines, 263, 600
American Association of Advertising Agencies
  (AAAA), 20, 44, **48**
  Creative Code, 72
  regulatory role of, 72
  Standards of Practice, 72, 97–98
American Baby, 490
American Express Company, 18, 488
American Home Products Corp., 19, 244, 384, 453
American Isuzu Motors, 338, 455
American Lung Association, **27**
American Motors, 216, 347
American Photographer, 429
American Public Transit Association, 519
American Red Cross, 612
American Society of Travel Agents, 554
American Tobacco Company, 132
American Tourister, 262
American Trucking Association, 520
American Vegetable Grower, 14
AMEX Life Assurance, 253
AMTRAK, 528
AM Varityper, 323
Anacin, 346
Anheuser-Busch Cos., Inc., 19, 125, 244, 253, 384, 453, 466, 471, **593**
Animatic, 340
Animation
  cartoons, 348
  claymation, **350,** 351

Animation—Cont.
  computer-generated, 347
  photo, 350
  puppets, 350
  stop-motion, 350–51
Answer print, 355
A-1 steak sauce, 278
Apple Computer Co., **111**, 118, 120, 126, **136**, 141, **259**, 528
Arbitron, 172, 182, 457–58, 480
Architectural Digest, 433
Archives of Ophthalmology, 14
Areas of dominant influence (ADI), 457
Argentina, 627
Arm & Hammer Baking Soda, 38, 135
Armour Beef Extract, 18
Arpege perfume, 264
Arrow shirts, **257**, 278
Art
  buyers, 321
  clip, 576
  defined, 281
  departments, 99
  directors, 282, 654
  for local advertising, 563, 576
  for newspaper ads, 563
  syndicated services, 576
  types of, 295–96
Arts and Entertainment Network, 464–65
Association of National Advertisers (ANA), 72
AT&T, 528, **537, 587**, 600
  advertising expenditures, 19, 384, 412, 430, 471
  sales, 244
  slogan for, 178
Atlas, Charles, **127**
Attitude tests, 208–9, 211
Audi, 137
Audience Market by Market for Outdoor (AMMO), 503
Audience share, 459
Audio-Forum, **486**
Audit Bureau of Circulation (ABC), 437, 441
Australia, 628, 637
Austria, 638
Automotive News, 421
Autoweek, 420–21
Avis, Inc., 25, 133
N. W. Ayer & Son, **606**
  advertising philosophy of, 178
  history of, 22, 95
  J. C. Penney campaign of, 178–79, 181, 197, 201, 205, 207–9
  methods of, 201, 223

Backer Spielvogel Bates Worldwide, 91, 622
Bactine, 474
Baker's Cocoa, 18
Banamex (Banco Nacional de Mexico), 621–22
Banana Republic, 498
Band-Aid brand adhesive bandages, 62, **318**
BankAmerica traveler's cheques, **637**
Bank of America, 94, 344, **637**
Barter syndication, 455–56
Bartles & Jaymes, 253, 278, 338, 340, 444, **445**
Bartons Bonbonniere Continental Chocolates, **164**
Ted Bates advertising agency, 24, 92–93, 454, 619
Batten, Barton, Durstine & Osborn, Inc.; *see* BBDO Worldwide
Bayer AG, 471
Bayer aspirin, **37**
BBDO Worldwide, 91, 93, 252, 430, 468, **469**, 622
BCI Holdings, 19, 244, 384
Beam Communications, **491**
Beatrice Companies, **599**, 600
Beckman Instruments, 540
Beech Aircraft, 594

Beef Industry Council, **401, 610**
  deceptive ads by, 66
Beeman's Pepsin Gum, 18
Behmer, Elsie, 580
Belgium, 625, 630–31, 637–39
Bergdorf's, 552
Bermudez Associates, 96
Better Business Bureau
  children's ad guidelines, 68
  investigations by, 68–69
Better Homes and Gardens, 440
Betty Crocker, 278, 305, **306**
Biarritz automobile, 278
Bic pens, 140
Bigsby & Kruthers, 564
Billboards, 49, 395, 504, **507–10**, 511, **520**, 614, 634; *see also* Outdoor advertising
Billiard-ball principle, 27, **28**
Birch Research, 480
Black boxes, 458
Black Entertainment Television, 465
Bill Blass, 552
Bleed pages, 432
Blimps, 395
Block, Martin, 364
Bloom, Robert, 93
The Bloom Agency, 342, 398–99
Bloom Companies, 93
Bloomingdale's department store, **89**
Blue Diamond Almonds, **610**
Blue Nun, 356, **357**, 364, 455
BMW automobiles, **139, 526**
Body copy, 264–65, 267–69, 273
Bondlow, William F., Jr., 406
Boone, Pat, 59
Borden Company, 37–38, 528
Boston Globe, 70, **487**
Boston Newsletter, 21
Botsford-Ketchum, 252, 284, 310
Bounce, **446**
Boxes in print ads, 274–75
Bozell & Jacobs, 93
Brain-pattern analysis, 206
Brand loyalty
  creation of, 29, 158
  and design changes, 305
  maintenance of, 134
  and message frequency, 389
  and trade deals, 526
Brand names
  and positioning strategy, 125
  and product value, 37–38, 157
  regulation of, 56
Brazil, 627–28, 634
Brignull, Tony, 619
Bristol-Meyers Co., 217, 464
Broadcast advertising; *see also* Radio advertising *and* Television advertising
  copy for, 261; *see also* Scripts
  evolution of, 23
  intrusiveness of, 49
  local, 563–64
  logs of, 61
  overseas, 630–34
  pretests in, 206–7
  production for, 99
  regulation of, 56, 61
Broadsides, 495
Brown & Williamson Tobacco Corp., 535
Brown-Forman Distillers, 231
R. H. Bruskin Associates, 192
Bruzzone Research Company, 209
Bua, Chuck, 569
Bud Light, 158
Bullock's department store, 571, **573**
Bureau of Census Catalog, 554
Burger King
  agency for, 94
  chain size, 143

Burger King—Cont.
  print ads for, **210**
  television ads for, **16**
Burke Research Corporation, 348
Leo Burnett Co., 91
Burrell, Thomas J., **230**, 231
Burrell Advertising, 96, 230–31
Burroughs, **594**, 595
Business advertising
  agencies for, 96
  market segmentation for, 173–76
  in mass media, 12
  nature of, 12
  periodicals for, 13
  types of, 12–14
Business Insurance, 420
Business Periodicals Index, 184, 186, 554
Business Publications Rates and Data, 186, 442
Business Service Checklist, 554
Business Week, 13, 429
Bus-o-rama signs, 519
Buyer behavior; *see also* Consumers
  of businesses, 176
  and buyer perceptions, 152
  decision-making process in, 148–49, 163, 165
  defined, 146
  environmental influences in, 158–63
  gleaned through pretests, 208
  habits in, 155–58
  motivation in, 150
  and opinion leaders, 161
  and peers, 160–61
  personal influences in, 149–58
  by reference groups, 160–61
  self-concept in, 152, 154
  by social class, 159
Buyers Guide to Outdoor Advertising, 504

Cable News Network (CNN), 463, 465
Cable One, 467
Cable television
  advantages of, 462–64
  audience demographics, 464–63, 466
  buying time on, 467
  costs of, 463, 465–66
  disadvantages of, 464
  evolution of, 462
  interconnects, 467
  local ads on, 467
  local systems, 467
  major networks, 465
  national ads on, 466
  nature of, 465–57
  sponsorships on, 467
Cable Television Network, 467
Cadillac, 24, 217
California Cooler, 444
California Farmer, 14
California Milk Advisory Board, **61**
California Prune Board, **164**, 253
California Raisin Advisory Board, **350**
Call-outs, 286
Camel cigarettes, **433**
Camera-ready materials, 326
Campbell Soup Co., 253, 454, 464, **514**, 516, 531
  deceptive ads by, 66–67
Canada, 625–28, 637
Candler, Asa G., 8
Canon, 372–73, 375–76, 378–79, 383, 391, 620
Caples, John, 257–58
Cap'n Crunch, 522, **523**, 530
Pierre Cardin, **15**
Careers in advertising, 84, 86, 88, 102
  account managers, 95, 100, **654**
  artistic, 99, 282–83, 654
  brand managers, 85–86, 655
  copywriters, 99, 654

Careers in advertising—Cont.
  information sources for, 659–62
  interviewing for, 657–59
  job search, 652–59
  media directors, 100, 654
  new business representatives, 101, 655
  portfolio preparation, 656–57
  in print operations, 321, 654
  production supervisors, 310, 654
  production supervisors, 310, 654
  résumé writing for, 656–57
  types of, 654–55
Carlton cigarettes, 264
Carson Pirie Scott & Co., 552
Cartoons, 348
Casa Myrna Vasquez, **228**
Castor Spanish International, 96
Catalogs
  copy for, 269
  offset for, 327
  rotogravure for, 326
  use of, 497–98
CBN Cable Network, 465
CBS Inc., 284, 430, 449, 452, 471, 477–78
Celebrities
  as commercial presenters, 340, **401**
  and consent laws, 65
  endorsements by, 260
  look-alikes for, 65
Census of Manufacturers, 643
Census Track Studies, 554
Central location projection tests, 206–7
Certification mark, **63**
Chajet, Clive, 594
Charmin, 338, **339**
Chesebrough-Pond's Inc., 66
Chevrolet, 197, 432, 600, 637
Chiat, Jay, **160,** 161, **251**
Chiat/Day Advertising, 111, 160–61, 312, **427**
Chicago Tribune, 70, 552, **581**
Chiesa, Joseph, 580
Children
  in commercials, 353, 356
  marketing toward, 67, 233
    Better Business Bureau guidelines on, 68
    network guidelines, 68
    overseas, 638
  as models, 295
Children Protection Act of 1966, 57
Children's Defense Fund, **609**
China, 614–16, 627–28
Chivas Regal, 263
Christian Dior, 65
Christian Science Monitor, 415
Chrysler Corp., 19, 116, **117,** 118, 121–22, 137, **147,** 216, 245, 343, 384, 412, 430, 471
Church of the Nazarene, 609
Cigarettes
  advertising regulation of, 61, 64, 639
  demarketing, **27**
  image of, **25**
Cinema advertising, 394–95, 632
Cinemax, 465
Circulars, 495, 566
Citibank, **261**
City & State, 421
Civil Aeronautics Board, 57
Clancy Shulman, 93
Clark, Agi, 178–79, 181, 201, 207
Clausewitz, Carl von, 216–17
Clearwater Federal Savings and Loan Association, 119, **121,** 123, 125–26
Client's success checklist, 112
Clinton Frank, 346
Clip art, 576
Clutter tests, 207
Lee Cobb & Associates, 501
The Coca-Cola Company, **30–33,** 124, **158,** 230
  advertising expenditures, 19, 384

The Coca-Cola Company—Cont.
  advertising philosophy, 4, **32–33,** 260
  bottling, 7–8, **9,** 34, 131
  clothing, 285
  early promotion of, 7–9, 29
  international ads, 615, 618, **619, 620,** 640
  jingle, 366
  sales, 245
  slogans, 4, **6–7,** 29, 158
  trademarks of, 7–8
Cognitive dissonance, 155
Cognitive theory of learning, 156
Colgate-Palmolive Co., **23,** 92–93, 171, 216, **217,** 464, 528, 633
Collateral materials, 102, 144
Collective mark, **63**
Collett Dickenson Pearce & Partners, 619
Collier Service Company, **514**
Color
  versus black and white ads, 389
  in magazine ads, 425, 440
  in newspaper ads, 423
  for outdoor advertising, 506, 513
  in packaging, 131–32, 298
  printing in, 328–29
  psychological impact of, 299
  wheel, **513**
Color separation negatives, 329, 333
Comcast Cablevision, **463**
Commercials
  foreign regulation of, 638–39
  in-house facilities for, 339
  local advertising production, 564
  presenters of, 338, 340, 343–44, 367
  prevalence of, 49
  radio, 356–57
    casting of, 368
    costs of, 171
    effectiveness in, 364–66
    humor in, 365–67
    length of, 365, 367, 390
    live, 367
    musical, 365–66
    personality, 367
    presenters of, 367
    production of, 367
    recorded, 367–68
    scheduling of, 482
    scripts for, 364–65, 473
    slice of life, 367
    straight announcement, 367
    types of, 365–67
  skepticism regarding, 338
  television
    animated, 347–51
    casting of, 340, 353
    cinema verité, 346
    concept development, 339
    contracts for, 461
    costs of, 179, 339, 356, 447–49
    demonstration, 344
    editing of, 355–56
    effective, 342, 448
    film versus tape for, 355–56
    humor in, 345–47
    key visuals in, 448
    length of, 390, 448–50
    live action, 351
    location shooting of, 354–56
    mnemonic devices for, 345
    positioning strategy, 390
    presenters for, 338, 340, 343–44
    pretesting, 206
    production stages, 352–55
    rehearsals for, 353
    script development, 340–43, 448
    slice of life, 345
    special effects in, 351
    straight announcement, 344

Commercials—Cont.
    testimonial, 344
    using animals, 351–53, 356
    using children, 353, 356
Commercial speech, 63–64
Commoncase type, 316
Communications Act of 1934, 56, 61
Compaq computers, **239**
Comparative advertising
  court rulings on, 65–66
  objective measurement in, 66
  overseas regulations on, 638
  sample of, **66**
Comp/Edit, 323
Competition through advertising, 35–37
Compton Advertising, 93
Computers
  database services, 185, 406
  graphics program, 309–10, 335
  for interactive displays, 538, 541
  limitations of, 406
  for media planning, 404–6
  in print production, 291, 309, 322–23, 332, 335
  product names generated by, 278
  for typesetting, 322–32
Comtal/3M, **122**
Concept testing, 201
Conceptualization process, 257–58
Cone, Fairfax, 20
Connoisseur, 429
Consent laws, 65, 295
Consolidated Foods, 595
Consumer advertising
  agencies for, 96
  early, **22**
  defined, 12
  regulation of, 22, 66
  segmentation, 121–22
Consumer Federation of America (CFA), 75
Consumer Magazine and Agri-Media Rates and Data, 186, 442
Consumer Products Safety Commission, 57
Consumer purchases; *see also* Buyer behavior
  diaries of, 185
  patterns in, 388
Consumer Reports, 186
Consumers
  advocate groups, 76
  attitude changes in, 199
  defined, 146
  information networks of, 75–76
  manipulation of, 48, 153
  movements, 22, 26, 75
  preference research, 23, 299; *see also* Buyer behavior
Consumers' Research, 76
Consumers Union, 76
Contact sheets, 294
Contests
  legal considerations in, 536
  in sales promotion, 527, 529, 535–36
  structures for, 536
Continental Airlines, **50**
Converse, 214
Cook's Tours, 18
Cooperative advertising
  advantages of, 578
  disadvantages of, 578
  horizontal, 578
  nature of, 141, 527–28
  in the total budget, 577
  vertical, 576
Coors Light, **349,** 351
Copitas, A. Craig, 444
Coppos, Mark, 427
Copy
  asking for the order in, 269, 273
  attention gaining through, 259–60
  body, 264–65, 267–69, 273

Copy—Cont.
brevity in 276
casting, 320–21
checklist for effectiveness in, 267
clarity in, 275–76
creating interest through, 260
defamation through, 277
dialogue/monologue, 267–68
direct requests in, 261
establishing credibility in, 260
euphemisms in, 277
for foreign ads, 636–40
gimmick, 268
heightening desire through, 260
humor in, 268
institutional, 267
interior paragraphs of, 269
lead-in paragraphs for, 268
marking of, 321, **332**
motivating action through, 261
narrative, 267
objectives of, 258–61
picture-caption, 267
point of view in, 265, 276
punctuation for, 267
readability of, 431
straight line, 265, 267
superlatives in, 276
trial close, 269
truthfulness in, 269, 277
writing of, 267, 269, 275–77
Copy platform, 254–56
Copyright
eligible material, 62
infringement of, 62, 295
international, 62
registration, 56, 62
Copywriters
product checklist for, 254–55
role of, 99, 654
terminology for, 261–74
Cordova automobile, 278
Corning, **343**
Corporate advertising; *see also* Institutional advertising
expenditures on, 586–87
guidelines for, 586
identity emphasis with, 594–95
market preparation, 587
nature of, 17–18, 584
objectives of, 587, 594
and product ads, 587
for recruitment, 595
and social accountability, 26
types of, **583**
Corrective advertising, 60
Cosby, Bill, 338–40, 343
Cosmopolitan, 432, 440
Council of Better Business Bureaus, Inc., 68–69
Countercards, 441
County and City Data Book, 555
County Business Patterns, 555
Coupons
ad copy containing, 273
clearinghouses for, 533
in direct response advertising, 485
foreign regulations on, 640
fraud with, 533
for local advertisers, 567
marketing data from, 533
purpose of, 8–9, 18
in sales promotion, 143–44, 529–33
in transit ads, 518
Cover stock, 336
Crain, G. D., Jr., 420
Crain, Gertrude, 421
Crain, Keith, 421
Crain, Rance, **420,** 421
Crain Communications, Inc., 420–21

Crain's Chicago Business, 421, 435
Crain's Cleveland Business, 421
Crain's Detroit Business, 421
Crain's New York Business, 421
Creative boutiques
and local advertisers, 575
nature of, 96
Creative mix
and the advertising message, 237
and the advertising strategy, 233
communications media in, 236
elements in, 203, 233, 408
and the product concept, 233–36
and the target audience, 233
Creative people, 95
Credibility, 260, 269, 409, 429
Crest toothpaste, **69, 85,** 135, **136,** 140, **163,** 171, 216, **217,** 464
international ads for, 15, **163**
Cullum, Bob, 569
Cullum, Charles, 569
Cullum Companies, **352**
Current Retail Trade, 554
Custom Auto Body, **512**
Cuticura Soap, 18

Dallas Home and Garden, 563
Dancer Fitzgerald Sample, 93
Daniel & Charles, 455
Danskin, **294**
Danza, John, 315
D'Arcy Masius Benton & Bowles, 91, 397, 622
Datril, 38, 217
Dayparts, 457, 459, 479
Dayton's department store, 563
DDB Needham Worldwide, 91, 188, 607, 622, 624
Deadlines, 100
Dealer ads, 102
Dealer contest materials, 102
DeBeers, 178, 261, 274
Deceptive advertising
correction of, 60
defined, 53, 56–57
FTC standards for, 55
investigation of, 60
penalties for, 60
postal service regulations of, 56
practices included in, 53
and "reasonable" consumers, 58
state regulation of, 66–67
unintentional, 53
Decision matrix, 163, 165
Delayed-action advertising, 228–29
Della Femina, Jerry, 454–55, 583
Della Femina, Travisano & Partners, 357, 454–55
Del Monte Corporation, **18**
DeLozier, M. Wayne, 211
Delta Air Lines, 471
Del Taco, 347
Demarketing, 26–27
Demographics, 166
Denmark, 638–39
Denny's Restaurants, 592
Dentino, Karl, **489**
Dentsu Advertising, 372
Denver Art Museum, **564**
Designated market areas (DMA), 457
Desktop publishing, 291, 309, 322, 324
DeSoto, **147**
Detroit Free Press, 70
Detroit Monthly, 421
Dewar's Scotch, **303**
Dial Corporation, 474
DIALOG Indormation Service, 185
Diamond Information Centre, **135**
Dichter, Ernest, 37, 151, 627–28
Digital Equipment Corporation, 124, 217–18

Direct-action advertising
disadvantages of, 19
good uses for, 228
nature of, 18
Direct broadcast satellite television, 467–68
Direct mail advertising
advantages of, 387, 392–93, 484, 487–92, 566
consumer attitudes toward, 495–96
coordination with other media, 488
copywriting, 492–94
cost projections for, 494, 498–501
defined, 484, 486
disadvantages of, 387, 392–93, 492–95
effectiveness, 492–93
evolution of, 22
free-lancing in, 496–97, 500
graphics, 492–93
guidelines for, 493, 497
innovations in, 490, **491**
local, 566
mailing lists for, 490, 499–500
personalizing of, 5
pretests, 206–7, 492
prevalence of, 484, 487
production of, 500–501
products for, 488
reach of, 490
schedules for, 501
shared mail, 566
signatures on, 5, 500
and telemarketing, 140
typesetting of, 322
types of, 495, 497–98, 566
Direct-Mail Advertising Association, 554
Direct Mail List Rates and Data, **499**
Direct Marketing, 55
Direct Marketing Association, 495
Direct questioning, 205–6
Direct response advertising, 485
Discover, 614
Discovery Channel, 465
Disney Channel, 465
Display allowances, 527
Distribution
channels, 140
levels of, 140–41
and vertical marketing, 142
Diverting, 526
Dodge Dakota, 433
Dodge Daytona, 127, **128**
Dog and pony shows, 108
Dominion Pottery, **555**
Reuben H. Donnelly Corporation, 532
Doubleday & Company, Inc., 54–55
Dove soap, 225
Dow Bathroom Cleaner, **348**
Dow Chemical, **278**
Dow Jones News Retrieval Service, 185
Downtown Flowers, **562**
Doyle Dane Bernbach, Inc., 93, 320; *see also* DDB Needham Worldwide
Dreyer's Grand Ice Cream, 253, 338
Dreyfus Corporation, 285
Drinking Buddies Advertising, 435
Dr. Juice One Drop Fish Scent, **388**
Dr. Lyon's Toothpowder, 18
Dr Pepper, 172, **394,** 395
Duffy Design Group, 282
Dummy, 286, 290
Dun & Bradstreet Reports, 187, 644
Dunkin' Donuts Incorporated, 347
Duotone printing, **329**
Du Pont Orlon, **13**
Dutch doors, 432

Eagle supermarkets, 272
Eastman Kodak, 18, 172, 278, 505, 600, **618**

Ebony, 429
Edison Mimeograph, 18
Edison Phonograph, 18
Edsel, **24,** 135, 180
Electronic Media, 421
Electronic pagination systems, 291, 309, 324, 331–32, 335
Electronic Product News, 630
Electronics, 13
Elgin Watches, 18
Elizabeth Arden, 552
Encyclopedia of Associations, 186, 554
Endorsements; *see* Testimonial advertising
English Leather, 269, 273
ESPN, 464–65
Esquire, 284, **309**
Esprit sportswear, **303**
William Esty agency, **380**
Ethnic-specialty agencies, 95–96
Euphemisms in copy, 277
European Business, 630
Export agencies, 623
Exposure, 380, 397, 403–4
Exxon Corporation, 637
Eye-movement cameras, 206

Fallon McElligott agency, **11,** 263, 408, **418, 426, 428**
Falstaff Brewing Company, 67
Family Circle, 440
Farm advertising, 14
Farris, Judy, 573
FBC (Fox Broadcasting Company), 452
FCB Grid, 236
Federal Communications Commission, 55–56, 61
Federal Express, 346, 528
Federal Hazardous Substances Act of 1960, 57
Federal Statistical Directory, 186
Federal Trade Commission
    on advertising by the professions, 38
    advertising standards of, 54–55
    and affirmative disclosure, 60
    on claims substantiation, 58–59
    investigation by, 60
    on price differentials for branded products, 37–38
    publications of, 60
    reasonable man standard of, 58
    role of, 56–60
    standards for false advertising, 55, 58
    and testimonial ads, 58–60
Federal Trade Commission Act of 1914, 56–57
Feel Free deodorant, 635
Ferrari, **238**
Ferry's Seeds, 18
Festinger, Leon, 155
Fidelity Federal Savings & Loan Association, **264**
Figenskau, Jerry, 468
Financial News Network, 465, 467
Financial Times, 630
Finland, 638–39
Fireman, Paul, 214, 224, 226, 236
Fisher Big Wheel, 467
Flags in advertisements, 67
Flammability of Children's Sleepwear standard, 57
Flammable Fabrics Act of 1954, 57
Flighting strategies, 381–82, 390, 402–3
Flyers, 495, 566
Focus groups, 197, 206, 601
Focus Magazine, **489**
Fog index, 275
Folders, 495
Foote, Cone & Belding Communications, Inc., 20, 44, 94–95, 110, 230, 236, 246, 296, 348, 398, 631
Ford Motor Co., 19, **24,** 180, 216, 230, 245, **258,** 259, 278, 343, 384, 412, 430, 453, 471, 618

Forward buying, 526
Foster, Lawrence G., 580, 582, 596
Joseph W. Foster & Sons Athletic Shoes, 214, **215**
Foster Parents Plan, 609
Four-color process, 328
Fox, Michael J., 343
Fragrance
    in-store promotion through, 538
    strips, 433
France, 620, **621,** 625, 630–31, 637–39
Franchises, 142, 547
Franco American Soup, 18
Franklin, Benjamin, 21
Fraser, Douglas, 296
Frederick Rauh & Company, 509
Free-association tests, 199
Freeburg, Stan, 261
Free-lance services; *see also* Creative boutiques
    for art, 99, 102, 282–83, 655
    for local advertising, 575
    for media buying, 96–97
    for public relations, 603
Free-standing inserts, 532
Frito-Lay, 528
Frontier Airlines, 398
Fruit, Charles B., 466
Funk & Scott Index of Corporations & Industries, 186

The Gallagher Report, 586
Gallo Wineries, 253, 444
Gallup, George, 23
Galvanic skin response, 153
Galvanometer, 206
Gatefolds, 432
Gates, Thomas, 580
GE, 19, 158, 245, 358, 384, 412, 430, 470
Geier, Philip, 619
General Dynamics Corp., 586
General Foods, 93, 132, **238,** 629
General Mills, Inc., 19, 83–84, 245, 306, 384
General Motors Acceptance Corp., 346
Gerber baby foods, 278
Germany, 627, 629, 631, 638–40
Get'm!, **305**
Gift Pax, 532
Gillette, 169, 455, 614, **615,** 618, 626
Gimmick copy, 268
Givauden, Ben, 385
Gleem toothpaste, 433
Global marketing
    future of, 618–19
    nature of, 618, 624–25
    need for, 619–20
GM, 19, 216, 245, 384, 412, 430, 453, 637
Godiva Chocolates, 280–82, 287, 297
Goldstein, Gary, 330
Golf Digest, 429
Good Housekeeping, 70, 440
    seal of approval, 70, 274
Goodis-Wolf, 95
Goodyear, 395
Gossage, Howard, 260
Government markets, 122
Government publications, 185–87
W. R. Grace & Co., **71**
Graphic designers, 282
Gravure Advertising Council, 321
Great American First Savings Bank, **17**
Green Giant, **289, 536**
Grey Advertising, 94, 294, 372, 620
Greyhound Corp., 471
Gross rating points (GRP)
    billboard, 504
    nature of, 381, 404
    radio, 480–81
    television, 459–60

GTE, 587
Guiness Stout Ale, 634
Gulf Oil, 278
Gunning Fog Index, 275

Haberstroh, Jack, 153
Habits, 156–58; *see also* Brand loyalty
Halftones
    fineness of, **325**
    for offset, 326
    preparation of, 324
    for rotogravure, 326
    stripping of, 325
Halo effect, 208
John Hancock, **589**
Handbills, 566
Hanes Hosiery, 527
Hardee's, 143
Harwell, Barbara, 569
Harzfeld's, 553
Hathaway shirts, **288,** 294
Hauptman, Don, 496–97
HCM/New York, 96
Headline News, 465
Headlines
    cadence of, 285
    effectiveness of, 261, 285, 290–91
    functions of, 261–64
    length for, 262
    provocative, 262
    and subheads, 264
    types of, 262–63
Health and Tennis Corporation of America, **490**
Healthcheck, 173
Health Jolting Chair, **22**
H. J. Heinz, 18, 131, **304,** 618
Helicoptors, 395
Hershey Foods, **36**
Hertz, 94, 133
Hierarchy of needs (Maslow), 150–51
Hires' Root Beer, 18
Home Box Office, 462, 465
Honda, 94, 127, **128,** 263
Honeywell, 433, **437**
George A. Hormel & Co., 468
Hot shops, 100
Households using television (HUT), 459
House marks, **63**
House organs, 497, 604, **605**
Hoyt Development, 509
Hull, Aaron, 568
Humor
    in commercials, 345–47, 357, 365–67
    in copy, 268
    in visuals, 297
The Hunger Project, 308, **310**
Hush Puppies shoes, **426**
Hyatt Legal Services, **64**
Hyundai, **138**

Iacocca, Lee, 116, **117,** 137, 343
IBM, 94, 217–18, 278, **318,** 586, 618, 636
Ideas, 258, 298
I.G.A. Food Stores, 142
Illustrators
    role of, 282–83, 292, 295
    technical, 295
Image
    in commercial messages, 448
    corporate, 587, 594, 599
    importance of, 37–38
    and package design, 305
    in sales promotions, 531
    through specialty gifts, 540

Image advertising
  for corporations, 587, 594; *see also* Corporate
      advertising
  in electronic media, 18–19
  evolution of, 24
  nature of, 17–18
Impulse buying, 388
India, 627
Indirect-action advertising
  on electronic media, 18
  nature of, 18, 228
Industrial advertising
  agencies for, 96
  market segmentation, 122, 173–76
  nature of, 12–13
Inflatables, 395
In-flight ads, 395, 519
Infomercial, 464
INNOVA, **605**
Inquiry tests, 208, 211–12
Institute of Outdoor Advertising, 501, 503, 554
Institutional advertising; *see also* Corporate adver-
    tising
  market research on, 585
  nature of, 17–18, 583–84
Intercom, 622
Interlock, 355
International advertising
  agency selection for, 621–25
  creative strategies in, 624–25
  and cultural differences, 615–16, 622, 624, 629,
      634–36
  department organization for, 85
  expenditures on, 616
  language problems in, **15,** 615, 622, 625, 636–40
  legal considerations in, 638–40
  management of, 616–21
  market considerations in, 123, 624–30
  marketing research for, 628–30
  and market segmentation, 123, 631–32
  media available for, 630–31, 634
  media planning checklist, 632–33
  media strategy for, 625
  message considerations, 634–36
  nature of, 15, 618
  through personal selling, 633
  regionalized campaigns in, 631
  television sponsorship, 614
International Center for the Typographic Arts, 321
International Flavors & Fragrances, Inc., 538
International Harvester, 58
International Herald-Tribune, 630
International Paper Company, 586
Interpublic Group of Companies, Inc., 619
Inter-Tel, **277**
Iron Age, 13
Island half-pages, 434
Issue advertising
  controversial, 71
  and demarketing, 27
  during the energy crisis, **35**
Italy, **616,** 631, 638–39
ITT, 618
Ivory Soap, 18

Jaguar, **147**
Janitor in a Drum, 132
Japan, 620, **623,** 625, 627–29, 635, 637–38
Jarman shoes, 342, **343**
Jartran, 66, 346
Jeep, **427**
Jell-O, 62, 260, 338, 343
Jingles, 365, 655
Jobs, Steven, 136
Johnson & Johnson, 19, 217, 244, 384, 453, 464,
    538, 580–83, **584,** 595–96, 598, 600–601
S. C. Johnson & Son, 524–25

Johnson Products, 231
Johnson Wax, **602**
Jim Johnston Advertising, 250
Jones, Larry R., **94,** 95
Junior units, 434
Justamere Agency, **107**

Kaiser Aluminum, 605
Kansas City Star and Times, 70
Karastan Carpets, 424, **425,** 429
Kavanagh, Kay, 357
KCBN, Inc., 351, 569
Kellogg Co., 19, 244, 384, 453
Kelly Award, 426
Ken-L-Ration, 535
Kent cigarettes, **50**
Kentucky Colonel, 600
Kentucky Fried Chicken, 143
Kenyon & Eckhardt, 93, 398
Kerlick, Switzer & Johnson Advertising, Inc., **99**
Ketchum Advertising, 27
Keys, Wilson Bryan, 153
Kickers, 264
Kiosks, 630
Kleber, John, **277**
Kleenex tissues, 62, 132, 278
Calvin Klein, 294
KLM Royal Dutch Airlines, **527**
K mart Corp., 19, 244, 384
Kniffin, Robert, 580
Kraft, Inc., 19, 132, 244, 268, 384, **534**
Kronenbourg Beer, 268
Krupp/Taylor, 492
Kurtzer, Steve, 429
Kvamme, E. Floyd, 120

Labels, 56, 61
Ladies Home Journal, 49, 440
Landers, Bob, 365
Language
  clarity of, 44, 275
  in food ads, 61
  in international advertising, **15,** 615, 622, 625,
      636–40
  on labels, 61
  offensive, **50**
  on packaging, 61
  usage of, 46–47
Lanham Trade-Mark Act of 1947, 56, 62, 66
Lasker, Albert, 4
Laure Haile Dance studio, **548**
Layout
  balance in, 292
  in broadcast ads, 286–87
  copy block size in, 291
  design principles for, 292–93
  headlines in, 290–91
  and image projection, 287
  importance of, 286
  movement through, 292
  on-screen, 323
  optical illusions in, 330
  poster-style, 290–91
  in print ads, 286
  proportion in, 292
  purposes of, 286–87
  responsibility for, 99
  steps in, 288–90
Leading National Advertisers, 187
Leaflets, 495
Ledan Inc., 538
Lee jeans, **291**
Legal releases, 295
L'eggs, 130, 231
Leisure, David, 339

Lennan & Newell, 284
Letterpress, 325–26
Letter shops, 500
Lever Bros., 225
Levine, Bertram, 600
Levi's, 15, **149, 273, 296,** 346–48, **349**
Levitt, Theodore, 618–19
Libel, 277
Library materials for research, 184–87
Library of Congress, 56, 62–63
Life, 436
Lifetime, 465
Lincoln Continental, 217
Line drawings, 295
Line films, 324
Line plates
  for offset, 326
  production of, 324
  stripping of, 325
  use of, **326**
Linotype, 321
Lintas: Worldwide, 91, 622
Lippman, Stacey, 380
Lipton soup, **330–34,** 455
Lipton's Teas, 18
Liquor ads, 56, 67
Listerine, 60, 158, **217**
Litter receptacles, 395
Live Aid concert, 600
Lobsenz, Amelia, 582
Local advertising
  through advertising agencies, 574
  through broadcast media, 563–64
  budgets for, 557–61, 577
  charitable, 557
  choosing media for, 562–69
  commercial approaches for, 346
  through community involvement, 568
  consultants for, 575
  coupons in, 567
  creation of, 571–73
  creative assistance for, 563–64, 566, 574–76
  customer analysis for, 552
  differences from national advertisers, 547
  direct mail for, 566
  expenditures on, 546
  feedback from, 552–53
  fluctuations in, 560–61
  free, 568
  guidelines for, 572
  handbills for, 566
  importance of, 547
  information sources for, 551–55
  institutional, 548, **550**
  in magazines, 563
  market analysis for, 551
  marketing strategy for, 555–56
  nature of, 16, 546
  in newspapers, 412, 416–18, 421–22, 547, 562
  objectives of, 548–50, 556, 571
  pitfalls in, 557
  planning of, 549, 551, 571
  primary research for, 551–53
  product, 548
  promotional calendars for, 561
  publicity events as, 568
  samples as, 567
  schlock approach to, 571
  secondary research for, 553–55
  with signs, 564
  special events as, 568
  specialty items for, 567
  telemarketing in, 567
  in telephone directories, 564–66
Logotypes
  defined, 274
  musical, 366
  size of, 291
Lois, George H., **284,** 285

Lois Pitts Gershon, 284
Longman, Kenneth, 180
Lord & Taylor, **295**
L'Oreal, 26, 135, 225
Los Angeles Magazine, 563
Los Angeles Times, 70
Loss-leader pricing, 139

Maas, Jane, 356
McCabe, Ed, 78–79
McCann-Erickson Worldwide, 4, **18,** 91, 622, 640
McDonald's Corporation, 19, 142–43, 230, 233, 245, 384, 453, 528, 600, 624
McDonnell Douglas, **591**
Macintosh computers, 118, 120, 126, 135, **136,** 141, **311**
Macleans toothpaste, 171
McMahan, Harry Wayne, 347
McMein, Neysa, 306
McNeil Consumer Products Company, 580, 582, 595–96
Macy's department store, 600
Magazine Publishers Association, 426, 442, 554, 610
Magazines
    ads accepted by, 70
    advantages of, 385–86, 392–93, 425, 429–30
    bleed pages, 432, 440
    business, 420–21, 434–35, 437–38
    circulation terminology, 437–38
    closing dates for, 440–41
    consumer, 434
    cost efficiency of, 430, 432
    disadvantages of, 386, 392–93, 430–32
    discounts from, 439–40
    dutch doors, 432
    early ads in, 21
    farm, 434
    gatefolds, 432
    horizontal publications, 437
    island half-pages, 434
    junior units, 434
    layouts for, 431
    lead time for, 430–31, 440–41
    local, 435
    local advertising in, 563
    merchandising services by, 441
    mock, 206
    national, 435
    paper stock for, 432–33
    personalities of, 393
    pop-up ads in, 433
    preferred positions in, 390, 432, 440
    pretests in, 206
    product samples in, 433
    rate cards for, 438–40
    rates, 179, 432, 439–40
    reach of, 431
    readership of, 429–30, 434–35, 437–38, 442
    regional, 435
    vertical publications, 437
Magnavox, 142
Maidenform, **154**
Mailing lists
    brokers for, 500
    compiled, 499
    by demographic classifications, 490
    house, 499
    mail-response, 499
    merge and purge process of, 499
    obtaining, 499
    overlaying, 500
    pretesting of, 500
    quality of, 499–500
Mail order advertising
    copy for, 269
    defined, 486

Mail order advertising—Cont.
    offset for, 327
    rotogravure for, 326
Maisel, Jay, **588**
Majority fallacy, 120–21
Make-goods, 461
Malibu cigarettes, 132
Margeotes, John, 280
Margeotes/Fertita & Weiss, 280
Margulies, Walter P., 298–99, 305
Mark, Reuben, 93
MarkCom, 636
Market clearing price, 137
Marketing
    careers in, 655
    direct, 140, 485
    and distribution, 140–42
    evolution of, 117
    exchange cycle, 118–19
    indirect, 140
    nature of, 117–18
    purpose of, 118, 123
    strategies, 216–18; *see also* Marketing plan
    support services, 87–88
    vertical, 142
    as warfare, 216–18
Marketing Communications, 187, 645
Marketing mix
    elements in, 8–9, 126–27
    focus for, 127
    and the marketing plan, 218, 224–25
Marketing plan
    action program, 226–27
    and the advertising plan, 227
    marketing objectives in, 220, 222, 522
    model, 219
    nature of, 215, 218
    outline for, 642–47
    situation analysis for, 220–21
    strategy, 223–26
Marketing research
    costs of, 180
    importance of, 180
    nature of, 123, 180–81
    for new-product development, 185, 190
    overseas, 628–30
    process, 182
Marketing strategies
    for local advertisers, 555–56
    and marketing mix determination, 224–25, 218
    media planning in, 375–76
    nature of, 8, 223
    nonpromotional, 556
    positioning in, 225
    semipromotional, 556
    short-term versus long-term, 189
    stages in, 199
    target market selection in, 223–24
Markets
    future trends in, 188–89
    generic, 222
    nature of, 121
    research in, 123, 181
    target, 125–26; *see also* Target audience
    types of, 121–23
Market segmentation
    behavioristic, 167–71
    benefit, 169
    of business markets, 173–76
    demographic, 166–67, 171
    geographic, 164, 166–67, 175
    and media planning, 374
    nature of, 123–25, 163
    psychographic, 167, 170–73
    strategies, 226
    variables in, 169
Mark Oliver, Inc., **576**
Marlboro cigarettes, **25,** 262
Martin, Stephen, 429

The Martin Agency, 95
Martin/Williams, **101**
Masland Carpets, **301**
Maslow, Abraham, 150
Masport Woodfires, **403**
Mass Retailing Institute, 554
Mattel Toys International, 629
Maxwell House coffee, 629
Mazda, 467
Media-Advertising Partnership for a Drug-Free America, **606–7,** 612
Media associations, 554
Media-buying
    as a career, 654
    effectiveness in, 399
    and fee formulas, 398–99
    services for, 96–97
Media kits, 602
Media Management Plus software, 405
Media placement
    cost saving in, 89, 91, 398–99
    elements of, 87–88
    specialists in, 96–97
Media planning; *see also* Media selection *and* Media strategy
    in the advertising strategy, 376
    audience reach in, 379, 391, 403–4
    with computers, 404–5
    costs, 179, 339, 356, 374
    exposures in, 380, 397, 403–4
    with formula models, 404
    with linear programming, 404
    and market segmentation, 374
    in the marketing strategy, 375–76
    message frequency in, 379–81, 391, 403–4
    nature of, 373–75, 377
    objectives for, 376–78
    of schedules, 381, 402–6
    with simulation models, 404
Media research
    on audience characteristics, 396
    need for, 182
    syndicated services for, 182, 396
Media scheduling
    with computers, 404
    continuity in, 381, 391, 402–3
    flighting in, 381–82, 391, 402
    and gross rating points, 381
    pulsing in, 381–82, 391, 402
    types of, 402
    and weather forecasts, 169
Media selection
    broadside approach to, 402
    with computers, 404
    for consumer motivation, 398–99
    for cost efficiency, 389–91, 398–99
    creative factors in, 286–87
    for desired exposure, 397
    for geographic coverage, 397
    with high-assay principle, 402
    mechanical considerations in, 389–90
    nontraditional vehicles, 395
    through profile matching, 402, 404
    and target market, 394–99
Media strategy
    budget considerations in, 390–91
    and the competition, 390–91, 395
    and consumer purchase patterns, 388–90
    development, 382, 390
    geographic scope in, 383–84
    and message complexity, 385–88
    for seasonal products, 388
Media units
    defined, 204
    frequency considerations, 379–81, 389
    size considerations, 389
Mennen's Talcum Powder, 18
Menswear Retailers of America, 554
Meow Mix, 455

Mercedes-Benz, 217, 600
Merck, 124
Mercury Capri, 172
Merrill Lynch, Pierce, Fenner & Smith, Inc., 172, 257, 586
Message elements
    consumer absorption of, 211
    and the creative mix, 237
    determination of, 201
Message strategy
    art direction in, 256
    copy platform in, 254–56
    elements of, 253
    in foreign markets, 634–36
    and message complexity, 385–88
    and message frequency, 379–81
    production values for, 256
    types of appeals in, 255–56
Me-too era, 25–27
Metro, **510**
Metropolitan Home, 429
Mexico, 628, 634
Michelob, 125
Middle East, 631, 635, 640
Middleman, 140
Miles Laboratories, 474
Milk cartons, 395
Miller, James C., III, 58
Miller Brewing, 600
Minneapolis Planetarium, 269
Minneapolis Star Tribune, **510**
Minnesota Federal, **50**
Minnesota Zoo, **302**
Minolta, 372
Minorities
    advertising to, 162–63
    stereotyping of, 51
Mitchell, Arnold, 170
Mitsubishi, **59, 588,** 618
MJB Coffee, 253
Mobil Oil Corporation, **595,** 598–99, 605
Modern Healthcare, 420
Modern Maturity, 440
Mogul, Williams & Saylor, 320
Money, 440
Monitor (service), 170
Monotype, 321
Monsanto, 124
Monthly Department Store Sales, 555
Moody's Industrial Manual, 187, 644
Morgan Park Presbyterian Church, 609
Morrisey, William, 499
Morton Salt, 274
Moskowitz, Howard, 154
Motivation
    and the advertising pyramid, 228–29
    and behavioristic market segmentation, 167–70
    nature of, 150–51
    and social class, 159
Mrs. Fields Cookies, 567
MTV, 285, 464–65
Multinational marketing, 618
Multipoint distribution systems, 468
Munsing Underwear, 18
Muppets, 350
Murray, Jim, 580
Music Educators Journal, 14
Mutual Broadcasting Co., 477–78
Myers, John G., 36

Nabisco, Inc., 19, 244, 384, 412, 430, **518**
Naisbett, John, 429
Names
    creation of, 278
    computer-generated, 278
    licensing of, 278
    in positioning, 125, 200
    testing of, 199

Nashville Network, 464–65
National advertising
    leaders in 1890s, 18
    leaders in 1986, 19
    nature of, 15, 21–23
National Advertising Review Council (NARC)
    composition of, 69, 73–75
    regulatory divisions of, 73
    reports by, 75
    review process, 74
National Association of Broadcasters Television Code, 70, 72
National Association of Drug Stores, 554
National Consumer League, 75
National Council of Senior Citizens, 75
National Council on Alcoholism, 609
National Enquirer, 440
National Geographic, 429, 436, 440, 484, **485**
National Office Products Association, 554
National Retail Merchants Association, 554
National Sporting Goods Association, 554
National Technical Information Service (NTIS), 186
National Yellow Pages Service Association, 541
NBC, 449, 452, 477–78
Needham Harper & Steers, 230, 398, 624
Needham Harper Worldwide, 93
Needham, Louis & Brorby, 398
Neiman-Marcus Co., 552–53
Nestlé Foods, 398, 618
The Netherlands, 627, 635, 638–39
Network Radio Audiences, 480
Newcomb, John, 372
New product marketing, 185, 190
Newsday Extra, 563
Newspaper Advertising Bureau, 422, 424, 441–42, 554
Newspaper Co-op Network, 424, 442
Newspaper Rates and Data, 70, 442
Newspapers
    ads accepted by, 70
    advantages of, 385–86, 392–93, 408–10, 562
    advertising departments of, 563
    alternative distribution of, 562
    categories of, 412–15
    classified ads in, 419
    cost efficiency of, 399
    disadvantages of, 386, 392–93, 411, 562
    display ads in, 416–19
    free, 563
    group insertion programs, 424
    local advertising in, 412, 416–18, 421–22, 547, 562–63
    major advertisers in, 412
    morning versus evening editions, 413, 420
    national, 415
    nature of, 20–23
    preferred positions, 423, 562
    preprinted inserts for, 419, 424
    production quality, 411
    public notices in, 419
    rates, 417–19, 421–23
    reach of, 410
    readership of, 411–15, 419–20, 442
    shoppers, 415, 563
    specialized, 413–15
    standard advertising units for, 413–14
    submitting ads to, 424
    Sunday, 415
    tabloid, 413
    tear sheets from, 424
    total market coverage, 562
    volume discounts from, 418, 421–22
    weekly, 413
    zoned editions of, 411
NEWSPLAN, 422, 442
News releases, 602–3, 606
Newsweek, 70, 435–36, 440, 563
New York Air, **270**
The New Yorker, 70

The New York Times, 49, 184, 411, 424, 455
Nickelodeon, 285, 464–65
A. C. Nielsen Company, 23, 180, 182, 245, 457
    black boxes, 458
    retail store audits, 185
    Television Index (NTI), 457–58
Nigeria, 634
Nihon Keizaisha Advertising, 623
Nike, Inc., **162, 214, 224, 427**
Nikon, **239**
Nissan Motor Corporation, 618
Nocona Boots, **283**
Noncommercial advertising
    and the Advertising Council, 611–12
    donated, 609
    by government organizations, 610–11
    nature of, 18, 606–8
    by nonbusiness institutions, 609
    by nonprofit business associations, 610
    public service, 5, **11, 17,** 609
    by state governments, 611
    types of, 608
North Carolina Travel and Tourism, **426**
Northlich, Stolley, Inc., **574**
Norway, 625, 627
Novak, William, 599
Noxema, 464

Obfuscation, 275–76
Obsession perfume, 52–53
Ocean Spray Cranberry Juice, 60
Office Furniture Warehouse, 568
Offset lithography, 326–27
Ogilvy, David, 78, 225, 252, 258, 262, 267, 274, 290–91, 317, 340–41, 344, 585–86
Ogilvy & Mather Worldwide, 91, 95, 225, 252, 288, 616, 622
Oil companies, **35**
Oken, Mark S., **398,** 399
Oliver, Daniel, 64
Olsen, Jarl, 408
Onassis, Jacqueline Kennedy, 65
Oneita Knitted Goods, 18
One World program, 614
Opinion Research Corporation, 586
Optical scanners, 189
Order-of-merit tests, 206
Orlando Sentinel, 70
Orville Kent Food Company, 520
O'Toole, John, **20,** 21, 44–46, 154, 157, 257, 269
Outdoor advertising; *see also* Billboards
    advantages of, 502–6
    cost of, 504–5
    demographic considerations, 503, 506
    disadvantages of, 506–7
    effectiveness of, 502, 504
    erection of, 507
    guidelines for, 506
    innovative, 504–5, 510, 512–14
    local, 511, 564
    nature of, 381, 392–93
    overseas, 634
    placement of, 507
    reach of, 502
    standardized, 507
    types of, 511–14
Overspill media, 631
Ozone Hair Spray, 455

Paccione, Emilio S., 308–9
Packaged goods market, 189
Packaging
    arbitrary changes in, 305
    color in, 131–32, 299

Packaging—Cont.
  combination, 132
  communication through, 298
  costs, 132
  design, 298–99, 304–5
  die-cuts in, 305
  functions of, 130–33, 297
  image in, 299, 305
  materials, 299, 304
  printing methods for, 327
  regulation of, 56, 61
  sales promotion through, 522
  secondary uses for, 132
  specialists in, 304
  stand-out appeal of, 298–99
  type sizes for, 131
  unit, 132
Packard, Vance, 153
Paine Furniture, **567**
Painted bulletins, 511–13
Paired comparison methods, 206
Palmer, Volney B., 22
Palmolive shampoo, **23**
Palm Springs Life, 563
Panels in print ads, 273–74
Paper
  cover stock, 336
  die cut, 500
  test, 336
  writing, 335
Parents Magazine, 70, 274
Parker Pen, 637
Parking meters, 395
Partnership for a Drug-Free America, **606–7,** 612
Pasteup, 283, 290
Patent and Trademark Office, 55–56, 62
Patents, 56, 62
Peat Marwick, **239**
Peckham, J. O., 245
Peller, Clara, 347
Pemberton, John S., 4, 7, **8,** 29, 34
Penetration pricing, 138
J. C. Penney Company, Inc.
  advertising expenditures, 19, 384
  advertising research, 182–84, 190–91, 194–95, 199
  advertising volume, 546
  catalogs, 497
  concept testing by, 202
  image of, 178, 179
  positioning strategy, 179, 198, 200
  sales, 245
  segmentation strategy of, 183
  target market of, 200
Pensions & Investments, 420
People meters, 458
People's Daily, 614
People Weekly, 440
Pepperidge Farm Goldfish, **491**
PepsiCo, Inc., 343, 384, 471, 600, 631
  advertising expenditures, 19
  challenge campaign, 157
  international ads for, 15, **617**
  sales, 244
Perceived equal-value exchange, 118, 126, 130
Perception
  selective, 155
  of subliminal messages, 153
Perceptual meaning studies, 206
Perdue, Frank, 78–80, 98, 343
Perdue Farms, 79
Performance affidavits, 461
Perlstein, Robert, 500
Pernod, **297**
Perrier, 253, 600
Peter Paul, 532
Philip Morris Incorporated, 19, 244, 384, 412, 430, 453, 471
Philippines, 627

Philips light bulbs, 358–63
Philips, 618
Phillips-Ramsey/Phoenix, 277
Photography
  advantages of, 294
  careers in, 655
  copyright laws regarding, 295
  disadvantages of, 295
  invention of, 20
  printing of, 324–29
  in public relations, 603
  retouching of, 153, **300,** 308–9, **310,** 332
Photoplatemaking
  halftones, 324–25
  line films, 324
  nature of, 324–26, 332
  stripping in, 325
Photopolymerization, 326
Photoprints, 335
Physiological testing, 206
Picas, 316
Pillsbury Co., 19, 244, 350, 384, 471, **533, 536**
Pimo, 622
PIP Printing, **142**
Pittsburgh Paints, 473
Pizza Hut, 143
Playboy, 261, 440, 600
Point of Purchase Advertising Institute, 537
Point-of-purchase displays
  innovations in, 538
  and self-service retailing, 537
  use of, 102, 144, 387, 392–93, 537–39
Polaroid, 278, **450**
Popular Photography, 429
Porsche, 269
Portfolio preparation, 656–5
Portugal, 627
Posch, Robert J., Jr., **54,** 55
Positioning
  adjustments, 200
  names as an element in, 125
  nature of, 124, 133, **179**
  as a strategy, 25, 125, 225
Positive realism, 231
Posner, Fred, 223
Post cards, 495
Posters, 387, 511, 516, 604; *see also* Outdoor advertising
Post-testing
  advantages of, 210
  disadvantages of, 209
  messages in, 204
  nature of, 199, 203
  techniques, 208–10
Postum Cereal, 18
Potomac Color Industries, 331
Pounce, **46**
Prague Conference of Advertising Workers of Socialist Countries, 617
Pratt & Whitney, 541
Premiums
  versus advertising specialties, 539
  continuity, 535
  foreign regulations on, 640
  self-liquidating, 535
  types of, 535
  use of, 529, 534–35
Prestige pricing, 139
Pretesting
  advantages of, 207–8
  of broadcast ads, 206–7
  budgeting for, 204
  customer questioning in, 205
  disadvantages of, 207–8
  markets, 203
  methods for, 206–7
  nature of, 199, 202–3
  of print ads, 205
  results from, 204

Price
  and costs, 137
  market clearing, 137
  and market demand, 135, 137
  strategies, 138–39, 225–26, 394
Price-line advertising, 548–49
Prime Cuts, **262**
Prince Foods, **282, 428**
Print advertising; *see also* Magazines *and* Newspapers
  boxes and panels in, 273
  copywriting for, 261–74
  and desktop publishing, 291
  guidelines for, 431
  information sources for, 441–42
  offensive, 49–50
  overseas, 614, 630
  pretesting in, 205–6
  prevalence of, 49
  production for, 99
  terminology used by, 261–74
Printer's Ink, 66
Print Media Production Data, 335
Print production
  careers in, 310, 321, 654
  computers in, 309
  copymarking, 321, **332**
  paper stock, 335–36
  printing process in, 324–35
  for publications, 335
  steps in, 311, 330
  type in, 312–21
  typesetting in, 321–24
  typography, 317–20
Privacy
  advertising infringement on, 63, 65
  and celebrity look-alikes, 65
Procter & Gamble, 66, **85,** 135, 136, 216, 231, 338, **339, 416,** 430, 445, **446,** 471, 534, 615
  advertising expenditures, 19, 384, 453
  agency for, 92–93
  brand manager system of, 85–87
  marketing strategy, 140
Product advertising
  agency responsibility in, 72
  importance of research to, 98–99
  nature of, 6–8, 17
  positioning in, 25
  and product image, 37
Product classification checklist, 129
Product differentiation
  and the FCB grid, 236
  nature of, 39, 48, 130, 226
  and packaging design, 305
Product Information Centers, 538
Production artists, 283
Product Marketing, 186
Products
  combination offers on, 533–34
  concepts, 129, 200
  demonstrations, 211
  foreign advertising restrictions on, 638–39
  life cycle, 133–34, 168
  seasonal, 388
  types of, 129
  usage patterns, 168–69
Product testing organizations, 76
Professional advertising, 13–14
Professions
  advertising by, 38, 64–65
  types of advertising for, 127
Profile bread, 60
Program ratings, 459; *see also* Rating services
Progressive Grocer, 13
Promotional Marketing Association of America, 522
Promotional strategy
  through advertising, 142
  and collateral materials, 102, 144
  through personal selling, 142

Promotional strategy—Cont.
  through pricing, 138
  through public relations, 143
  sales, 143–44
Prudential Insurance Co., 18
PSA, 347
Psychological rating scales, 199
Public Affairs Information Service Bulletin (PAIS),
  184
Public Health Cigarette Smoking Act of 1970, 61
Public relations
  versus advertising, 6, 582–84
  audiovisual materials for, 605
  careers in, 655
  and community involvement, 600
  defined, 580–82
  during disasters, 595–98
  events, 600, 603–4
  and fund raising, 601
  media relations in, 599
  and press agentry, 599
  and public affairs, 599–600
  through publications, 601–3
  through publicity, 598–99
  through public speaking, 601
  research techniques for, 601
Public service advertising, 5, **11, 17,** 609
Publishers Clearinghouse, 488
Publishers Information Bureau, 187
Puerto Rico, 637
Pulsing strategies, 381–82, 390, 402–3
Pupilometric devices, 206
Purolator Courier, 285
Push money, 528

Quaker Oats, 18, 522–23, 530, 532–33, 539
Quasar, 172
Questionnaires
  design of, 194–96
  personal interview, 194–95
  in post-testing, 209
  pretesting of, 195

RADAR (Radio's All-Dimension Audience Research),
  480
Radio advertising; *see also* Commercials, radio
  advantages of, 386, 392, 468–72
  AM versus FM, 475
  audience characteristics, 396, 473–77
  commercial pretesting, 199
  costs of, 471, 474, 478–79
  disadvantages of, 386, 392, 472
  indirect action, 18
  local, 470, 479
  national, 469
  nature of, 474–75
  networks, 476–78
  programming formats, 470, 475–77
  program sponsors, 23
  reach of, 470
  regulation of, 56, 61
  scheduling of, 482
  spot, 478–79
  theater-of-the-mind techniques for, 473
Radio Advertising Bureau, 554
Radio audiences
  average quarter-hour, 481
  characteristics of, 396, 473–77
  cume, 481–82
Radio Luxembourg, 631
Radio time
  dayparts for, 479
  run-of-station basis, 479
  selection of, 482
  total audience plan, 479
Radio Usage, 480

Raid, 257
Ralston Purina Co., 19, 244, 384, 455
Ranger, Judith, 429
Rating services
  radio, 480–81
  television, 457–60
Raytheon, 594
RCA Corporation, 278
Reach
  aspects of, 380–81
  defined, 379
  maximizing, 402
  and media strategy, 390, 403
Reader's Digest, 435, **436,** 440, 630
  advertisements accepted by, 70
  sweepstakes, 143–44
Reader's Guide to Periodical Literature, 184, 186
Readership scores, 389
Reading notices, 419
Recall tests, 199, 208, 210
Recruitment advertising, 595
Red Book, 91
Redbook, 440
Redenbacher, Orville, 217
Red Lobster, 395
Reebok, 214–15, 220, 224–25, **226,** 230, 233, 235–
  36, **237, 510**
Reeves, Rosser, 24, 78
Reference groups, 160–61
Refund offers, 529, 532
Reggie awards, 522
Regional advertising
  nature of, 15
  overseas, 631
  publications for, 16
Regulation of advertising
  by consumer groups, 75–76
  through the courts, 63–66
  early, 22
  federal agencies for, 55–63
  international, 638–40
  local, 67
  by the media, 69–72
  self, 67–69, 72–75
  by the states, 66–67
Reinforcement advertising, 232
Reinhard, Keith, **624,** 625
Reliability/validity diagram, 191
Reprints, 495
Research; *see also* Advertising research *and* Mar-
    keting research
  advertising, 22–23, 98–99, 179–81
  costs of, 198
  data analysis in, 196–97
  direct mail surveys, 190
  experiment method, 190
  exploratory, 184–88
  focus group method, 197
  intensive techniques, 197
  market, 123, 181
  media, 182
  and new product development, 185
  observation method, 189
  personal interviews in, 190, 194–97, 205
  primary, 188–98
  problem statement for, 183
  projective techniques, 196–97
  qualitative, 181, 196–97, 199
  quantitative, 181, 188–96
  questionnaire design in, 193–96
  reliability in, 191–93
  sampling theory in, 192–93
  scanner technologies for, 189
  secondary data sources, 184–87
  services, 182, 661
  survey method, 190
  telephone interviews in, 190
  validity in, 191–92
Reseller markets, 122
Response cards, 441, 485–86, 493, 518

Retail advertising; *see also* Local advertising
  careers in, 655
  fluctuations in, 559
  of food, 569
  information sources for, 554–55
  nature of, 16, 546
  in newspapers, 562
  personalizing of, 553
Retail Data Sources for Market Analysis, 554
Retainers, 107
R. J. Reynolds Tobacco Co., 46
Rhode Island Hospital, **65**
Rice, Roger, 454
Ries, Al, 25–26, **124,** 125, 200, 216, 265
Riney, Hal Patrick, **252,** 253, 338, 444
Hal Riney & Partners, 252–53, 444
Riva, **169**
Robinson, Frank M., 7, **8**
Robinson, William A., **528,** 529
Robinson-Patman Act, 526
Robinson's Department Stores, **510**
Robbie awards, 529
Rockwell, Norman, 282
Rockwell International, **590**
Rolex, 622
Rolling advertising, 520
Rolling Stone, **263, 400**
Rolls-Royce, 25, 262, 433
Roman, Charles, 127
Roman, Kenneth, 356
Rose, Ralph, 541
Ross, Wallace, 365
Rotogravure, 326
Rough cut, 355
Rubber & Plastics News, 420
Rubin/Postaer, 95
Ruhr/Paragon, 95
Runner's World, **442**
Run-of-paper advertising, 423
Run-of-station radio spots, 479
Ryan, Jerome, 306

Saatchi & Saatchi DFS Compton, 91–93, 358–63,
  622
St. Joseph aspirin, 158
Sales experiments, 206–7
Sales letters, 495
Sales materials, 102
Sales promotions
  collateral material for, 529
  consumer, 530–36
  copy for, 531
  creativity in, 531, 538, 541
  and marketing objectives, 522–23
  method mixing in, 539
  pull strategies in, 530–39
  push strategies in, 525–30, 537
  retailer cooperation in, 525–30
  role of, 522–23, 528
  for sales acceleration, 523–25
  scheduling of, 531
  and specialized directories, 541–42
  techniques, 529–36
  using fragrances, 538
Sales targets, 222
Sales tests, 208, 212
Sampling (product)
  distribution services, 532
  in-store, 531
  in local advertising, 567
  for sales promotion, 529–32
Sampling (statistical), 192–93, 199
Samuelson, Robert, 48
Samurai toothpicks, **616**
San Diego Zoo, **508**
Sanka, 132
Sara Lee Corporation, 433, 595, 624
Satellite master antenna television, 468
Savin, 125

Scali, McCabe, Sloves, 78, **98, 100**–102, 315
Scandinavia, 627–28, 631, 638–39
Scanner technologies, 189
Scarborough Research Corporation, 420
Schering-Plough Corp., 471
Schick, **423**
Schmerz, Herb, **598,** 599
Schmidt, Klaus F., **320,** 321
Schultz, Don E., 529
Charles Schwab & Company, 488
Scientific American, 614
Scope, 158, **217**
Scorsese, Martin, **59**
Scotch brand tape, 62
Scratchboard illustrations, 250, 296
Screen printing, 328
Scripts
  radio
    guidelines for, 364–65, 473
    humor in, 365–67
    length of, 365, 367
  television
    abbreviations used in, 340–41
    basic principles of, 341–42, 448
    development of, 340
    humor in, 345–47, 357
    length for, 342, 448
Scully, John, 120
Seals, 274
Sears Roebuck & Co., 19, 142, 244, 384, 471, 497,
  546, 586
Seasonal products, 388
Securities and Exchange Commission, 57
Security Pacific National Bank, 492
Sedelmaier, Joe, 345–47
Sedelmaier Film Productions, Inc., 346
See's Candies, 253
Seiko, 600
Selame Design Associates, 304–5
Self-mailers, 495
Self-service retailing, 537
Sensationalism, 50
Sentiment in ads, 231, 256
Serifs, 312
Service mark, **63**
7 South 8th for Hair, 408, **409**
Seventeen, 429
7UP, 25
Sex in advertising, 52, 67, 253, 256, 260, 278
Shared mail, 566
Shell Oil, 278, 586, 618
Sheridan network, 478
Shoppers, 415, 563
Showtime, 462
Shudson, Michael, 48
Signature cuts, 274, 291
Signs, 564; *see also* Outdoor advertising *and* Tran-
  sit advertising
W. R. Simmons Company, 396
Simmons Market Research Company, 420
Simmons Reports, 457
Simpson, Adele, 552
Singer Company, 125
Sisters Restaurant, **472**
Situation analysis, 221
Skimming, 138
Sky Channel, 630
Slander, 277
Slice, **92**
Slice of life commercials, 345, 367, 625
Slogans, 199, 274
Small Business Administration, 554
Smith Corona, 262
Smoky the Bear, 612
Snuggles bear, 350
Sochis, Reba, 284
Social classes, 159–61
Sosa, Joe, 310
Sosa & Associates, 96
South Africa, 627, 637

Southeast Asia, 629, 637
Southeast Bank, **550**
Southern Messenger, 21
Southland Corp., 471
Southwestern Bell Corporation, **585**
Soviet Union, 617, 627–28
Spain, 627, 631
Spam, 468, **469**
Specialty Advertising Association International, **540**
Specialty items, 539, 567
Spectaculars, 514
Sperry and Hutchinson Company, 535
Sperry Rand Corp., **594,** 595
Speculative presentations, 108
Spic and Span, 534–35
Spiffs, 528
Spivak, Helayne, 424
Sports Illustrated, 435, 440, 563
Spot Television Rates and Data, 461, 479
SRI International, 170
Standard advertising unit system, 413–14
Standard & Poor's Industry Surveys, 187, 644
Standard Directory of Advertisers, 91, 653
Standard Directory of Advertising Agencies, 91, 653
Standard Industrial Classification (SIC) codes, 174–
  75
Standard Oil of New Jersey, 586
The Standard Periodical Directory, 554
Standard Rate and Data Service, 182, 335, 442, 499
Stanley Hardware, **14**
Stansfield, Richard, 215, 262
Star, 440
Starch, Daniel, 23
Starch INRA Hooper, 210
Stars and Stripes, 415
State laws regarding advertising, 66–67
Statement stuffers, 497
Statistical Abstract of the United States, 185, 555
Stein, Sid, 182, 185
Steinem, Gloria, 52
Stevens, Art, 596, 598
Stevens, Philip, 587
Stiller and Meara, 357
Stimulus-response theory of learning, 156
Stock photos, 294
Stone, Bob, 499
Storyboards
  abbreviations for, 340–41
  for layout, 286–87, 289
  pretesting of, 199
  television, 99, 340–41
Stresstabs vitamins, 390
Stroh Brewery, 528
Studebaker, **42**
Styrofoam, **278**
Suave, 226
Subheads, 264
Subliminal advertising, 153
Subscription television, 468
Subway posters, 100, 515–16; *see also* Transit ad-
  vertising
Successful Farming, **435**
Sudler & Hennessey, 284
Suisse Mocha, **164**
Sunkist, **45,** 109, **131,** 143, 278
Superstations, 465
Suppliers, 79
Survey of Current Business, 554–55
Sweden, 638–39
Sweeps books, 458
Switzerland, 618, 625, 627, 630–31, 635, 638–39
Sylvania, 297
Syndicated programs
  radio, 476
  television, 454–46

TAA Rate Directory of Transit Advertising, 518
Taco Bell, 94–95
Takara, 629
Take-ones, 518

Talon, Inc., **298,** 455
Tandy, 467
Tang, **621**
Taplin, Walter, 40
Tappan, James, 93
Target audiences; *see also* Television audiences
  and audience trends, 451
  children as, 67–68, 233
  classification of, 12–14
  defined, 9, 12
  in international advertising, 624
  and media selection, 394–99
  minorities as, 413–14
  profile matching, 402, 404
  selection of, 378
  studies of, 396
  versus target market, 233
  women as, 52
Target markets; *see also* Market segmentation
  children in, 67–68, 233
  classifications of, 167, 171
  defined, 8–9, 12, 124
  and marketing objectives, 222
  and media selection, 394
  minorities as, 162–63
  selection of, 200, 223
  versus target audience, 233
  women as, 52, 147–48
Taxicab ads, 395
Taylor, Hilda, 306
Telecast tests, 206–7
Telemarketing
  effectiveness of, 486
  in foreign markets, 629
  for local advertisers, 567–68
  nature of, 140
Television advertising; *see also* Cable television
  and Commercials, television
  acceptable, 70–72
  advantages of, 386, 392–93, 445–47
  and audience trends, 451
  contracts for, 461
  costs of, 179, 445, 447–49
  daypart mix for, 457, 459
  daytime, 449
  disadvantages of, 386, 392–93, 447–50
  evolution of, 451
  indirect action, 18
  late night, 449
  local, 455
  national, 15, 23, 339, 453
  network, 452–53
  prime time, 15, 179, 390, 448–49
  regional, 16, 339
  regulation of, 56, 61
  sponsorship versus cosponsorship, 452–53
  spot announcements, 453–54
  on syndicated programs, 454–55
  and zapping, 450
  and zipping, 450
Television audiences
  composition of, 460
  measurement of, 455, 457–60
  and program selection, 461
  and rating services, 456–58
  trends in, 451
  in various dayparts, 459
Television Bureau of Advertising, 454, 554
Television households (TVHH), 459
Television time
  dayparts of, 457, 459
  make-goods, 461
  preemption rates for, 461
  price negotiations with, 461
  program selection, 461
  requesting avails, 460–61
Testimonial advertising, **31**
  candids, 344
  copy for, 267
  and credibility, 260

INDEX

Testimonial advertising—Cont.
  early, 22
  false, 53
  FTC regulations regarding, 58–60
  visuals in, 297
Texaco, 278
Texas Air Corp., 412
Theater of the mind, 473
Theater tests, 206
Thermos, **50,** 62
Thomas Register of American Corporations, 186, 644
J. Walter Thompson Company, 91, **92, 287,** 346, 405, 622
3M Company, 264, **589,** 618
Thumbnail sketches, 288–89
Tide detergent, 278, 615
Timberland shoes, **271**
Time, 436, 440, 585
  ad reviewing by, 70
  national ads in, 16
  media expenditures by, 430
  regional ads in, 16, 435, 563
Timex watches, 38, 140, 173
Tom Thumb Page stores, 351, **352,** 569–70
Toshiba Corporation, **318, 597**
Total market coverage, 562
Toyota Corolla, **626**
Trade advertising, 13–14
Trade associations, 185–87
Trade deals, 526–27
Trademarks
  versus generic names, 62
  global, **619**
  registration of, 56
  types of, **63**
Trade show exhibits, 540–41
Trading stamps, 535
Traffic, 100, 654
Tragos, Bill, 619
Trahey, Jane, **552,** 553
Trahey Advertising, Inc., 552
Trailer tests, 206
TransAmerica, 433
Transit advertising
  advantages of, 516–17
  costs, 516, 518
  custom designed, 516, 519
  demographics of, 516
  disadvantages of, 517–18
  effectiveness of, 517
  local, 564
  and mobile billboards, 520
  nature of, 514
  sizes of, 515–16
  total bus, 518–19
  units of purchase, 518
  use of, 100, 392–93
Transit Advertising Association, 518–20
Travisano, Ron, 308–9
Trigere, Pauline, 552
Trout, Jack, 25–26, **124,** 125, 200, 216, 265
Trout & Ries, Inc., 124
Truth-in-advertising model statute, 66
TRW Inc., 347, 456–57, **459,** 460
Turner, Mike, 288
Turner, Ted, 465
TV Guide, **396,** 435–36, 440
TWA, 412
Twentieth Century-Fox Film Corporation, 405
Tylenol, 38, 217, 580, **581,** 583, **584,** 595, 601
Type
  and copy casting, 320–21
  display, 313
  families, 315, 319
  fonts, 315
  groups, 313–15
  measurement of, 315–16
  sans serif, 312–13
  selection of, 317–20

Typesetting
  cold-type, 321–22
  CRT, 323
  digital, 323
  direct-entry systems, 323
  direct-impression composition, 322
  hot-type, 321
  in-house, 324
  laser, 323
  photocomposition, 322, 332
  photo-optic, 322
  strike-on composition, 322
Typography
  and copy casting, 320–21
  defined, 317
  design principles with, 317, 319–20
  leading in, 317
  readability of, 317

U-Haul, 66
Ulrich's International Periodicals Directory, 554
Ultra Brite toothpaste, 171
Underwriters Laboratories, 76, 274
Unfair advertising, 58; *see also* Deceptive advertising
Unilever N.V., 19, 244, 384, 453, 618
Union Oil, **35**
Unique selling proposition, 24
Unisys, **594**
United Airlines, 528
United Kingdom, 638–39
United Negro College Fund, 612
United Savings and Loan League, 554
U.S. Army, 220, **222,** 611
U.S. Department of Agriculture (USDA), 56–57
U.S. Department of Commerce, 554
U.S. Department of Justice, 57
U.S. Department of Transportation, 612
U.S. Food and Drug Administration, 55–56, 61, 186–87
U.S. Government Organization Manual, 186
U.S. Industrial Outlook, 554
U.S. Navy, 231, **611**
U.S. Office of Consumer Affairs, 56
U.S. Postal Service, 56, 611
United Stations network, 477–78
United technologies, **588**
United Way, **272,** 612
Unit packaging, 132
Universal Product Codes, 189
USAir, 125
USA Network, 465, 467
USA Today, 49, 285, 415, **416**
UTA French Airlines, **504**

VALS (Values and Lifestyles) system, 171–73
Value Line Investment Survey, 187
Value packs, 529
van Bronkhorst Group, Inc., **97**
Van Munching, 471
Vepco, **297**
Vertical marketing systems, 142, 576
Victoria Court, **576**
Videotapes, 395, 606
Will Vinton Productions, 350
Virginia Slims, 600
Visa, **66**
VisionLab II, **122**
Visualization
  process, 257–58
  techniques, 294
Visuals
  focus for, 297
  pretests of, 298
  role of, 293
  size of, 291

Visuals—Cont.
  story appeal of, 262
  types of, 294–96
  versus verbal messages, 265–66
Visual scandal, 506
Vogue, 161
Voice of America, 631
Voice-overs, 261
Voice-pitch analysis, 206
Volkswagen, 25, **26, 577**
Volvo typeface, **315**

Wade Advertising, 230
Waldman, Marvin, 332
The Wall Street Journal, 16, 21, **154,** 250–52, 414–15, 630
Walt Disney World, **51**
Warner-Lambert Co., 19, 60, 244, 384, 471, 618
Wash drawings, 295
Water Pik, **274**
WD-40, 268
Weather Channel, 465
Weiss, John, 280
Welch Foods, **132, 623**
Welcome Wagon, 532
Wells, Sharlene, 501–2
Wendy's, 143, 346
Western International Media, 96
Weyerhaeuser Credit Union, **329**
WFLD-TV, **300**
Whirlpool, 278
Wicander Enterprises, 305
Wight Collins Rutherford Scott PLC, 455
Wilson, Dick, 338–39
Window posters, 102
Winston cigarettes, 46, 276
Winston Network, 503, 519
WLUP-AM, **565**
Wolsey, Tom, 424–25
Woman's Day, 435, 440, **520**
Women
  stereotyping of, 51–52
  as a target audience, 52, 147–48, 305
Work print, 355
World Almanac and Book of Facts, 184
Worthington, Cal, 571
Wrigley's Gum, **514,** 516, 624
Wrong reading plates, 326
WTBS-Atlanta, 465

Xerox Corporation, **62,** 181, 124–25, 278, 624

Yamaha guitars, **400**
Yamaha motorcycles, **238,** 262, 284–87, 297, 310–11, **312**
Yang, Charles Y., 40
Yankelovich, Skelly and White, 93, 170, 585, 595
Yellow Pages, 541–42, 564–66
Young & Rubicam, 91, 93, 95, **96,** 172, 320, 330, 346, 622
Younkers department stores, 568–69
Yusting, Mark, 357

Zales Jewelers, 398
Zapping, 450, 464
Zeithaml, Valerie, 374
Zell Bros. jewelers, **549**
Zenith, 274, 528
Ziff, Ruth, **188,** 189
Ziltz, Carl, 569
Zipping, 450, 464